A REGIONAL GEOGRAPHY OF
THE UNITED STATES
AND CANADA

A REGIONAL GEOGRAPHY OF
THE UNITED STATES
AND CANADA

Toward a Sustainable Future

CHRIS MAYDA

Rowman & Littlefield Publishers, Inc.

Lanham • Boulder • New York • Toronto • Plymouth, UK

Published by Rowman & Littlefield Publishers, Inc.
A wholly owned subsidiary of The Rowman & Littlefield Publishing
    Group, Inc.
4501 Forbes Boulevard, Suite 200, Lanham, Maryland 20706
www.rowman.com

10 Thornbury Road, Plymouth PL6 7PP, United Kingdom

British Library Cataloguing in Publication Information Available

Library of Congress Cataloging-in-Publication Data
Mayda, Chris, 1948–
    A regional geography of the United States and Canada : toward a
sustainable future / Chris Mayda.
        p. cm.
    Includes bibliographical references and index.
    ISBN 978-0-7425-5689-8 (cloth : alk. paper) —
    ISBN 978-0-7425-5730-7 (ebook)
    1. United States—Geography. 2. Canada—Geography. 3. Human
geography—United States. 4. Human geography—Canada.
5. Sustainable development—United States. 6. Sustainable
development—Canada. 7. United States—Environmental conditions.
8. Canada—Environmental conditions. 9. United States—Economic
conditions. 10. Canada—Economic conditions. I. Title.
E161.3.M343 2013
917.3—dc22   2008018423

∞™ The paper used in this publication meets the minimum
requirements of American National Standard for Information
Sciences—Permanence of Paper for Printed Library Materials,
ANSI/NISO Z39.48-1992.

Printed in the United States of America

Brief Contents

Part One
MOVING TOWARD SUSTAINABILITY: Themes

Part Two
MOVING TOWARD ECOREGIONS: Places

Detailed Contents

Illustrations

Photos

Tables

Preface

This book is about the United States of America and Canada, two countries I truly love. And it is about what has happened and what *can* happen in leading the world—leading in a new way, of course. Leading does not have to be a pounding-on-the-chest scream for monetary power alone. We can re-create the word *leadership* in our vocabulary and adopt and move into an ecological age. We need to stop turning our back on nature, conquering nature, and begin working with and respecting nature. Beginning our education in what has happened to our countries and how we are beginning to change our zeitgeist is the goal of this book.

It is my belief that the United States along with Canada can lead the world from the modern age into the ecological age, However, we both lag behind in understanding the changing zeitgeist and climate of the world. The United States still hangs onto its belief that it is the one superpower, but it has failed to understand that the kind of power exemplified is no longer appropriate. Canada, ahead of the United States in its acceptance of climate change (because it must be, as a far north country), still lags behind in relation to the more forward-looking countries of the EU and is tempted mightily by the last bastions of oil production.

The United States has been resting on past laurels and, in so doing, has stopped leading and become a country that is afraid of change, because change means something different. As the last man standing in the twentieth-century superpower race, why change? Ask Britain. Ask China, a country that continues to build coal power plants even as they corner the renewable energy market. The U.S. powers that be are afraid of what change might bring and want to keep what they have, but nothing is static. The laws of thermodynamics continue, and entropy reigns supreme when the energy of power dissipates.

A leader does not cower in fear, but leads, even into the future. Instead, the United States has separated into polarized groups—none of which are dealing with the issue at hand. Instead of partisan political battles, we need leaders who have in mind the common good of the state, its people, and its environment; we need leaders, statesmen and stateswomen, not politicians. We need to begin educating our future leaders about the state of the economy, the environment, and social issues in the United States and Canada. We live in a global economy and environment where everything is connected. So we can begin at home, local if you will, and set a positive example that leads the world in a healthy balance of cooperation and competition ("coop-etition").

We are at a radical break with history, equal to the last great break of industrialization, as we harnessed nonrenewable energy sources. We have seven billion people living in the world, seven times the number of people who lived on the planet during the period of industrialization, seven times as many people living and polluting as at the beginning of the nineteenth century. The developed world controls the heavy majority of world resources and wealth. The affluence has been at the cost of future generations, consumers, resources, and caused pollution. While there are seven times the number of people, there is still but one planet.

The gung-ho, "progress at any cost" mind-set of America is much of what made the nation great, but this has been at the cost of short-term thinking. Humans are the only species to create waste. We are the poor immigrants who won the lottery and have been spending the winnings (our resources) foolishly. We have not provided for our children or the long-term future. But that is only the half of it. This is an age that does not promise you the same old jobs that we had in the past. These jobs are indeed gone, but there will be new jobs based on working with nature (biomimicry, for example) and on a sustainable industry that creates no waste. Ecoindustry that is circular, where the "waste" of one industry provides the resource for another, are some long-term answers to a sustainable economy. We are far from this goal, true. In fact, many people will only shake their head in wonder, but so we have done in the past when cars replaced the horse, when the Internet replaced the mail, and when technology replaced human body parts for a healthier life. But do not be fooled into thinking that technology is the one and only answer.

The many great technological advantages we have experienced have had a cost that we have not yet recognized fully. While profit and living standards have risen for a billion, it has been at the cost of billions of others who have paid the indirect cost, environmentally and socially. Everything is connected.

We only look at everything as problems, but these are our opportunities.

Acknowledgments

This book was made possible with the help of all the students, friends, and people I met along the way. Since everything is connected, then everyone I have ever met has helped me along, as did many I have met only through literature.

But there are some people who deserve personal thanks because of their support. First there were the technical aspects: the maps, the graphs, the charts. Certainly two former students, Don Lafreniere and Doug Rivet, who stand out as supportive as well as GIS experts, which they now are refining as they complete their PhDs in geography and GIS. Others who have contributed maps include Jennifer Mapes, Miriam Hill, and Reed Hall. I also discovered the talents of my colleague Professor Hugh Semple, who provided beautiful and clean maps. My son, Zachary Napier, helped in graphics and readings, and my husband, Jay, with his advice and tireless work on keeping my computer up to snuff. Special thanks also to two mentors who believed in me and made any of my work possible: Robert Newcomb and John Fraser Hart. All are part of the team that made this book possible.

I also owe thanks to Gerald McNeill, who enlightened me about Louisiana and offered a box about what happened to public housing in New Orleans after Hurricane Katrina. I thank Artimus Keiffer, who believed in the project and was there at this project's inception but did not live long enough to see the project through.

Thanks to my dear friend Laura Fisher, who spent a week in the Caribbean working on my bibliographic details, even while her husband, Ken, wanted to go play in the sun. She has always been a detail person and I love that she worked so diligently to see that tiresome task through. I also thank all my friends who guided me, read proofs, and gave me shelter as I roamed across the United States and Canada. They include the Burgesses of Big Beaver, Saskatchewan; Candia Fisher (New York, Massachusetts, and Florida), Judy Goodspeed (Oklahoma), Laura Carr (Arizona), John and Joeanne Yednock (California), Marti Walker (Washington), Jim O'Donnell (Washington), Andrea Pinhey (California), and Donna Lasseter (Georgia). My family has also always supported my efforts. They include George and Diane Mayda, Rik Mayda, Zosia Kilbourn, and of course my mom, Lola Mayda, and her husband, Curly Czaban, who helped many times and offered "my bedroom" whenever I arrived.

When the going got rough and I needed a boost, I relied on Bob and Bobbe Christopherson, who were there for me several times and offered me author advice and help as needed. Bobbe also took a photo for me when my camera was not working. (I now carry at least two cameras!) I also thank the readers of chapters, who gave excellent advice and ideas.

Finally, I am indebted to Susan McEachern, my editor at Rowman & Littlefield. Patience and Faith must be her middle names. I appreciate the hard work of Grace Baumgartner and Jehanne Schweitzer, who guided me through the process. Without their collective support this book might not have been published.

Part One

Moving toward Sustainability

THEMES

PHOTO 1.1. Lower Colorado River Valley in Arizona and California (33.998°, −114.458°). Transitions in nature are usually gradual, but along this valley they have been dramatic. In this dry hot desert area the few natural plant and animal habitats are threatened. Water management of the river basin has been contested between the riparian vegetation and agriculture.

1

REGIONS AND ECOREGIONS

An Approach to Sustainable Geography

Chapter Highlights

After reading this chapter, you should be able to:

- Recognize regions, ecoregions, and sustainable geography
- Describe an ecological approach to the study of geography
- Explain a holistic systems approach
- Discuss the importance of an ecological point of view
- Define ecoregional transitions
- Compare the regions and ecoregions of the United States and Canada

Terms

anthropocentric
bioregion
cultural adaptation

ecology
ecoregion
ecosystem (or ecological system)
ecotone

external costs
holistic systems
reductionist
region
site and situation

subregion
sustainability
sustainable geography
unintended consequences
watershed

Introduction

Reductionism still holds sway in science. . . . As noted by Ian McHarg (1997), integration requires bridging between separate sciences, an attitude resisted by universities and government institutions. . . . Holistic studies require a scientist to examine systems as more than the sum of its parts, as opposed to the narrow focus of one piece of the system.

—Robert G. Bailey, USDA Forest Service[1]

What hooked me on geography was its depth. Geography answered my search for interdisciplinary study. The beauty of seeing and understanding the multifaceted and interconnected world reached right out and grabbed me, as it might you, if you are lucky! Maybe you will find an appreciation for geography, a subject that is so much more than reciting the capitals, demographics, land area, and rivers of a country. Geography, to me, is a bridging discipline between the humanities, the arts, and the sciences. All I had to do was reach beyond geography's study of the relation of humans to the environment and

extend its purview to studying the **holistic systems** relationship between the human, biologic, and physical environments—**sustainable geography**. These relationships express how changes in one component will affect all systems from micro to macro scales. Everything is connected.

Studying **ecological system** change is important because humans are a part of and dependent on both biotic and abiotic natural systems. If all ecological systems are linked, then humans and what they create are also part of ecological systems. But humans have created systems that result in the only part of nature to create waste and pollution—the by-products of unsustainable values and actions. The creation of waste that is thrown "away" is a linear model, unlike the rest of nature. Working within interrelated holistic systems is circular, where resources are not wasted but used multiple times in multiple ways.

The systems approach is the path to **sustainability** or what I call the ecological age, when humans adopt the sustainable mind-set—when people stop trying to conquer nature (themselves) and decide to live more in alignment with the natural world. Now, this will require change—not changing a light bulb or recycling but changing the design of our thinking. To live in the ecological age is to think about our actions and then act accordingly—it is simple and complex all at once; the changes will create the road to leadership and jobs in the ecological world. We have to stop looking for the old energy-intensive jobs that pollute and destroy, and begin the path to the ecological world. In this book, we will examine the path of the United States and Canada in relation to sustainability and how people are adjusting their vision and have started to work within a sustainable mind-set that recognizes and works within the limits of world resources.

Geography has a strong foundation of studying physical and human relationships but has not yet centered on how exceeding sustainable limits has resulted in pollution, waste, and climate change. Geography's next step is to address the connections between all aspects of the biotic and abiotic world, moving from the isolated vertical silo approach (unable to exchange information) to a more horizontal sharing based on cross-fertilization and teamwork across boundaries, one that is cooperative while still competitive.

Every discipline has a specific focus, but the threat of competition over cooperation creates fear and has caused few to willingly cooperate and recognize the contributions of others, contributions that complement their own. When geography and all disciplines reach across disciplinary boundaries to share information, all will be enriched in the process. The place humans find themselves in today is not about any one person winning or about "saving the Earth"; it is about finding a healthy way for humans to continue living on Earth. Working in a sustainable mind-set requires expanding horizons to recognize the underlying structures of actions and then move toward a dynamic and ever-changing equilibrium. Equilibrium does not mean the system is static; nature is not static but stable. Moving toward equilibrium is complex and very different from the path of the current dominant society, but this shift in values and actions will propel society toward a more sustainable and less polluted future.

Holistic systems are interrelated from micro to macro scales within ecosystem communities. At the micro scale are patches and small ecosystem communities; at the macro are biomes of multiple ecosystems that share biotic characteristics. Working at multiple scales is a way of seeing the world in which everything has a place and a purpose, resulting in a whole that is greater than the sum of the parts.

Ecology is the interdisciplinary science that studies the interactions of living organisms (including humans) with each other and with the surrounding physical world.[2] Ecology studies whole ecosystem components and has been applied to the study of human interactions with the rest of the natural world, including human cultural ecologies such as the ecology of commerce.[3] Ecological systems are the foundation for studying sustainable geography. Studying geography ecologically has not been the standard, but it is not without precedent.[4] The fragmentation that has broken geographic study for years[5] comes

together when studying holistically. Sustainable geography has room for all geographic studies and all other disciplines that add to understanding the workings of the world. It gives a new and much-needed focus to the goals for a healthy quality of life for all life.

The first level of studying ecosystems, both biologically and in human constructs, is to recognize the relationship and interactions between different structural elements. In nature, this includes studying the interactions in a small ecosystem; in human constructs, it would be the local level of politics or economics. Ecosystems are not limited to their own scale but interact with the surrounding areas at multiple scales, both in nature and in human constructs as political systems. Any change in one level affects the surrounding levels in a nested ecoregional system, a natural region with ecological cohesion. A systematic ecoregional economy respects the limitations of ecosystems, honors past cultural influences, and emphasizes meeting needs as locally as possible. Each level of the system operates as a whole but is interconnected to the surrounding levels. Changes at one level will affect the surrounding levels, as has always been the case, but now **unintended consequences** of actions will be limited. Holism works within the natural ecosystem world, of course, but it also works for humans, who are part of the natural ecosystem structure.

Systems

The geography of the United States and Canada is a complex subject. Many books and thousands of articles have examined singular and independent geographic subjects. These studies provide the facts and components for a systematic study of interconnected relationships. A systems approach requires building on nested social and natural ecosystems that study relationships within biological ecosystems, which include human constructs, rather than studying individual species, resources, or human-produced designs. The mantra of systems study is that everything is connected.

Human-produced designs are a part of the natural ecosystem; however, many Americans and Canadians live an **anthropocentric** (human-centered) life, as though they were separate from the rest of nature. This has led to a population that consumes unsustainably. For example, Americans are the most consuming nation; they live well beyond their resource supply and do not respect limits.[6] Nature is our model and mentor. There is but one Earth. Choosing to live as though the Earth offered limitless resources for a growing and consuming population has damaged ecosystems and cannot go on forever, or even for our lifetimes. Even now, the quality of life of the developed world has become the goal for developing countries. China, India, and Brazil are all growing based on the old Industrial Revolution model of waste and pollution. The question is whether Earth, a limited resource, can continue to provide the same quality of life—one that is energy intensive, wasteful, and polluting—for billions more people. Is the problem not the opportunity?

The way the developed world lives, and especially the United States and Canada, has created an unstable environment ripe for change, a change that will bring our developed countries to the brink of a new kind of leadership, to move beyond the old fossil fuel–based Industrial Revolution and build a new revolution based on using energy efficiently. To correct past faults and move sustainably into the future requires a new way of viewing the world and transforming values, ideas, and scientific and social institutions. A systems approach works at multiple levels, nesting ecosystems to understand how they work and affect each other.

In the modern world, most decisions are made to satisfy a single intended positive consequence. Any action has both positive and negative effects, depending on the interpretation or agenda, but the positive effects have usually been limited to economics. Choosing to operate for profit alone has resulted in unintended consequences, sometimes for the better, but usually negatively affecting the environment and social equity. These effects are called **external costs**. The current method of measuring profit does not reflect these externalities—the full costs or benefits of production or consumption. The external costs are passed on to the community and to environmental degradation.

Measuring the external costs and unintended consequences of our actions has not been the standard. To consider the entire cost of actions requires a holistic systems approach.[7] The costs and consequences of not thinking systematically are evident at many scales. As an introduction to these ideas, let us look at a couple of examples: one on a national/global scale and another regional.

The United States and Canada: Climate Change

The developed world was the first to adopt the Industrial Revolution and become dependent on fossil fuel energy. Europeans settled the United States and Canada as capitalism began its reign. The zeitgeist of capitalism has been attaining profit by reaping natural resources. The New World offered these opportunities when resources seemed scarce in Europe. Both countries built their economies based on their abundant resources without much heed to long-term consequences. The United States became for a time the undisputed leader in the industrial age, using cheap and nonrenewable fossil fuel energy to create a thriving consumer economy.

Unintended Consequences

The results of the consumer economy have been a standard of living that many in the less developed world yearn for and many are now attaining, but not without consequences. The unintended consequences of the fossil fuel–powered industrialized economy are multiple, but for now, we will focus on anthropogenic (human-induced) climate change caused by a reliance on fossil fuel–based electricity, deforestation, and automobile use, all of which are instrumental in raising the level of atmospheric carbon dioxide (CO_2). The level of CO_2 in the atmosphere was 280 parts per million (ppm) at the beginning of the Industrial Revolution, when the developed world began to rely on fossil fuel energy. In 2011, the CO_2 level is about 393 ppm, when it has been argued that any more than 350 ppm will be disastrous for humanity.[8] In truth, no one is sure exactly what will happen as CO_2 levels continue to rise or where the tipping point is. At what level will it completely alter how we live? But scientists do know that the rise in CO_2 has created the greenhouse effect, which holds in heat and has begun what could be a dramatic change for all habitats. Carbon dioxide is the most important measurement of greenhouse gas emissions, although not the most potent. With 5 percent of the total world population, the United States and Canada produce a quarter of greenhouse gas emissions and are responsible for many of the unintended consequences, which include:

- Warming of land and sea temperatures
- Sea level rise
- Erratic and extreme weather events (hurricanes, flooding)
- Drought
- Altered ecosystems

There are positive unintended consequences, such as increased agricultural output in cold-weather areas (and concomitant decrease of agricultural output in warm-weather areas) and reduced heating costs, but the positives as well as the negatives need to be examined within the full scope of how climate change will affect the way society has been operating and what effects the changes will bring.

Local and Ecoregional Impacts

Ecosystems range in size from the molecular level to Gaia (whole earth) systems. Each is related to the surrounding **regions** and levels. Every biotic being has a specific range where it can live. Exceeding the range results in habitat shifts or alters land configurations, causing the loss of a species because of deforestation, the loss of coastal zones because of rising sea levels. We hear about this shift when favored animals, such as the polar bear, are threatened—but every plant and animal lives within the dynamic equilibrium of its ecosystem, and altering the system alters the complex relationships between ecosystem components. Recently, some of these complex relations have been calculated.[9] The loss of species and land use changes result in deforestation, altered water supplies, and loss of agricultural output. With human-constructed shifts, the interactions have seldom been cross-charted with each other and with the rest of the natural world.

For example, the Great Plains and Midwest have conditions that are best for growing specific crops; the semiarid Great Plains specialize in wheat, which grows well with little rain, and the Midwest has the ideal humid and wet conditions for corn. But the crop cycle has changed. Fossil fuel–powered irrigation now grows water-intensive crops such as corn in the Great Plains, and that has created a catch-22. Irrigation methods have become more efficient, and therefore more water-intensive crops have been grown, which has led to escalating the depletion rate of an aquifer that has little recharge. In order for the

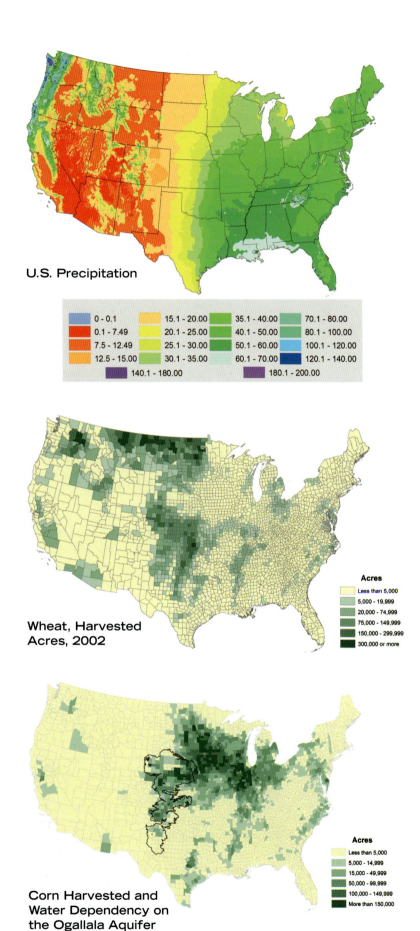

U.S. Precipitation

0 - 0.1	15.1 - 20.00	35.1 - 40.00	70.1 - 80.00
0.1 - 7.49	20.1 - 25.00	40.1 - 50.00	80.1 - 100.00
7.5 - 12.49	25.1 - 30.00	50.1 - 60.00	100.1 - 120.00
12.5 - 15.00	30.1 - 35.00	60.1 - 70.00	120.1 - 140.00
	140.1 - 180.00		180.1 - 200.00

Wheat, Harvested
Acres, 2002

Acres
Less than 5,000
5,000 - 19,999
20,000 - 74,999
75,000 - 149,999
150,000 - 299,999
300,000 or more

Corn Harvested and
Water Dependency on
the Ogallala Aquifer

Acres
Less than 5,000
5,000 - 14,999
15,000 - 49,999
50,000 - 99,999
100,000 - 149,999
More than 150,000

MAP 1.1. The relationship of regions, water, and crops. Crops grow best in ideal conditions. Corn requires 30 inches of precipitation and a humid climatic regime, whereas wheat requires less precipitation and less humidity. The corn and wheat belts share common climatic characteristics, which are related to precipitation patterns. However, since the 1960s technology has allowed the drier Great Plains to be irrigated from the underlying Ogallala aquifer. Water used to irrigate humid weather crops far exceeds sustainable standards. Water withdrawals lower the water table and may be economically infeasible in another 20 to 30 years.

agricultural area to remain profitable, more water must be used on more crops, but the more water is used, the less is available (Map 1.1). While growing corn has been a profitable venture for Great Plains producers, it is short-term and does not take the external cost of environmental degradation into account. The aquifer is being depleted much faster than it is recharging, and therefore the current irrigation regime will not provide for our children.

Depletion of Ogallala water will have regional, national, and global impact. As climate change continues to alter agricultural production, it is difficult to determine its impact on regions and the country. There are multiple ways to approach this subject, all of which need to be addressed in a systematic way. Regional warming would decrease soil moisture and precipitation, which could require shifting production or using more aquifer water. On the other hand, if climate change does shift the water regime and if fossil fuels used to pump the water to the surface continue to increase in price, is it not in our best interest to pump now? Many of the new jobs of the ecological age, jobs that will replace the jobs lost in the modern age, will be based on answering tough questions such as the above.

External Costs

The external costs of climate change are the multiple environmental issues (deforestation, loss of habitat, loss of biodiversity, soil erosion, etc.) and the social issues that will arise (health, immunity, education, homelessness, violence, war, etc.) as climate change changes how we make decisions.

For example, an external cost of climate change is climate-altering pollutants emitted into the air, water, land, and into our food. The pollutants deteriorate human health and are being linked to respiratory diseases and cancers that proliferate in the polluted environment. Pollutants also affect the physical environment, causing species to decline, injuring or killing plants, and causing the sterilizing effects of acid rain. The overall nonlinear nature of the changes will upset biodiversity, agricultural production, human health, and the economy.

Nonlinear? The modern age—the Age of Reason, the Enlightenment—was based on linear thinking: The quickest path from A to B is a straight line. The results of only looking in a single direction are that many of the consequences produced instabilities such as war, famine, and social unrest. The linear path ignored the environmental and social consequences of the action. But the natural world does not work linearly. The path is not direct but connected to many other paths. The jobs of the future are to find the most effective, the most energy efficient, but least polluting path to continue a good quality of life. Not easy, not simple, not quick, not direct. But therein lie plenty of jobs, plenty of opportunity.

In the United States and Canada, climate change has already affected some people disproportionately. The Inuit in the far north are farthest from chemical industry but most affected by it, because the food they eat—seals, whales, and mollusks—are high on the food chain, and toxic chemicals, such as PCBs (polychlorinated biphenyls) and mercury, are highly concentrated. Mercury poisoning suppresses immune functions, increases respiratory infections, and alters brain development in babies. Those who are first being affected by climate change are those who did not create the problems.

Regional: Tennessee River Coal Slurry Spill

Coal plants are the source for almost half of all electricity in America and are a major source of pollution. Coal has remained the primary source of electric energy because it is cheapest, but only when the environmental and social costs are not calculated in its expense.

PHOTO 1.2. Coal Fly Ash Slurry Spill, Kingston, Tennessee, December 2008. Coal ash, a toxic by-product of burning coal in a power plant, is mixed with water to create a slurry that is stored in unlined ponds. An unintended consequence of these ponds is regular leaching into the groundwater, which affects the ecoregional watershed of the Tennessee River and its tributaries.

Fly ash is the residue of scrubbers placed on coal plant stacks to reduce sulfur emissions. In the United States, about 131 million tons of fly ash are produced annually by 460 coal plants and stored in 1,300 locations. On December 22, 2008, a Tennessee Valley Authority coal plant impoundment burst, sending 500 million gallons of toxic coal ash into the Tennessee River and its tributaries.[10] The spill was more than forty times larger than the *Exxon Valdez* oil spill. That spill was followed a few weeks later by another ash pond leak. The spill was part of the environmental and social costs of using coal. The Tennessee spill was large enough to call attention to the numerous smaller spills over the past few decades that have been overlooked.

Unintended Consequences

Scrubbers have been placed on coal-burning-plant stacks to reduce air pollution caused by combustion of coal; however, as pollution standards increase so does the residue called fly ash. Typically, fly ash contains any number of concentrated toxic compounds and carcinogens that have been removed from the coal. A few of the toxic elements and substances are arsenic, cadmium, chromium, mercury, and dioxins. A portion of the ash is used in beneficial ways such as in Portland cement, but more than half are stored as slurry in unlined earthen dams near the plant. The resulting unintended consequences are that the ash leaches into drinking water supplies above accepted levels and can spill into rivers and lakes (Photo 1.2). There are no federal regulations to control fly ash.

Local and Ecoregional Impacts

The coal ash spill of December 2008 was a wake-up call for U.S. coal ash containment areas. The direct impact was devastating for local residents, some of whom lost their homes. The spill also directly impacted the drinking water supply and contaminated water downstream. On a macro level, the spill created an awareness of coal-burning plants and their waste across the United States and into Canada, where coal-fired power plants also contaminate soil with fly ash. In August 2010, twenty-one states were found to have contaminated water from coal combustion.[11]

External Costs

The Environmental Protection Agency had not declared fly ash hazardous at the time of the spill, and it remains exempt from federal hazardous waste regulations. The December 2008 spill cleanup costs have been more than $1.2 billion and are paid for by the American taxpayer. Might a better way to spend tax dollars be treating waste instead of treating lobbyists, or better yet to change the mind-set from one of producing waste to one of eliminating or never producing waste—living as the rest of nature, without waste?

Environmental degradation immediately after the spill included a huge fish kill in the rivers. Coal-fired plants are also responsible for 40 percent of CO_2 emissions, making the plants a large part of the climate change problem. The plants also emit two-thirds of all sulfur dioxide and almost one-quarter of

nitrogen dioxide, both air pollutants creating smog and acid rain. The social costs of using coal are the thousands of people who die annually from respiratory diseases linked to coal and the strip-mined areas of Appalachia.

The preceding examples are just two of many U.S. and Canadian examples within this book. This chapter will lay a foundation for understanding the following chapters. Keeping within the systems and ecological approach to the geography of the United States and Canada will require examining our notions of regions, ecoregions, and borders.

Regions and Ecoregions

Regional geography is one of the cores of geographical study,[12] but geographical fragmentation has left many questioning geography's place in the disciplines. Geography has always been concerned about patterns and place. Regions are specified areas with distinct qualities that differ from the surrounding areas. North America's regions (Mexico is also part of North America but is not covered in this book) have been identified in numerous ways over the years.[13]

Land divisions have been overwhelmingly political or geometric, but over the past century, the regional geography of the United States and Canada has been mapped following more natural divisions. In 1917 and 1928, Nevin Fenneman defined regional physical division maps of the United States (Map 1.2).[14] Physical landforms are an important element of landscape classification, which lead to understanding how a place works. However, landforms are only one element of ecoregions, an interrelated system of components. In 1995, Robert G. Bailey created an ecoregion map of the United States (Map 1.3).[15] In Canada, the Department of Agriculture and Agri-Food Canada and the Nature Conservancy have created maps of Canadian ecoregions (Map 1.4).[16]

Ecoregions define more than physical landform patterns. An ecoregion is similar to a **bioregion**, the latter term being more concerned with living matter while an ecoregion is an interrelated and hierarchal system with characteristic climate, soil, and landforms Ecoregions and **watersheds** (the region draining into a river), while not synonymous, share geographic similarities. Both terms are used to help define systems of regional difference. The ecoregional concept has nineteenth-century roots in the latitudinal zones described by Alexander von Humboldt and has continued to form as others studied relationships of climate, earth, and water.[17] Ecoregional study reveals how a place evolves and why problems, such as erosion, happen when they do. Understanding ecoregions is essential as climate change progresses, as climate is an underlying control of all earthly systems. As the climate changes, every level of an ecosystem also changes. No ecosystem exists in isolation but is connected to its surrounds. For example, warming temperatures have affected the lifecycle of pine beetles in western America's conifer forests, resulting in the loss of millions of forested acres. The result is a changed ecosystem. The dead trees increase fire

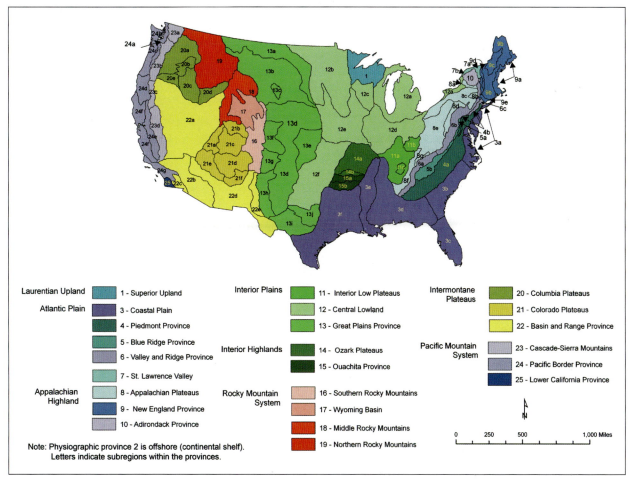

MAP 1.2. Map after Fenneman, "Physiographic Divisions of the United States."

Source: Nevin M. Fenneman, "Physiographic Divisions of the United States," *Annals of the Association of American Geographers* 18, no. 4 (December 1928): 261–353

Legend:

Laurentian Upland
1 - Superior Upland

Atlantic Plain
3 - Coastal Plain
4 - Piedmont Province
5 - Blue Ridge Province
6 - Valley and Ridge Province
7 - St. Lawrence Valley

Appalachian Highland
8 - Appalachian Plateaus
9 - New England Province
10 - Adirondack Province

Interior Plains
11 - Interior Low Plateaus
12 - Central Lowland
13 - Great Plains Province

Interior Highlands
14 - Ozark Plateaus
15 - Ouachita Province

Rocky Mountain System
16 - Southern Rocky Mountains
17 - Wyoming Basin
18 - Middle Rocky Mountains
19 - Northern Rocky Mountains

Intermontane Plateaus
20 - Columbia Plateaus
21 - Colorado Plateaus
22 - Basin and Range Province

Pacific Mountain System
23 - Cascade-Sierra Mountains
24 - Pacific Border Province
25 - Lower California Province

Note: Physiographic province 2 is offshore (continental shelf).
Letters indicate subregions within the provinces.

0   250   500   1,000 Miles

threats, which lead to mudslides, erosion, and sediment buildup in waterways, while shifting and destroying habitats.

Ecoregions can be read at different scales each nested within a larger system. The smaller scales in this book are called **subregions**, which have distinctive characteristics of the larger region but have unique features that differentiate them from the controlling behavior of the overall ecoregion. For example, in the Great Plains region low precipitation and grasslands are common, but several subregions characterize the variety in the Great Plains landscape. Most of the Great Plains has an almost overwhelming expanse of level topography, yet western South Dakota's Dissected Missouri Plateau subregion has uplifted topography, the Black Hills, where the climate and vegetation differ from the surrounding plains. The uplift has caused a microclimate of increased precipitation that has also shifted the vegetation from one of grasslands to pine-covered hills.

Ecoregions and their subregions do not have definitive and absolute borders. Ecosystems do not fit snugly within all ecoregional divisions. They all share interrelated systems and components but often at different scales. Our current political divisions of land fragment ecosystems and cause many of the environmental problems plaguing the world today.

Borders

The current worldview has fragmented the study of subjects and resources rather than finding the interconnections between them. We have chosen to concretize and polarize nature's reality into distinct and polar opposites: humans and nature; cause and effect; present and future. So it is with borders. On one side of the 49th parallel is the United States; on the other side is Canada. The division is arbitrary, unless you are living by the laws of the land on either side, where borderland farmers of each country use their land based on national policy. Ecoregional patterns have seldom been considered when borders are made. Thinking ecoregionally endorses a dynamic system rather than static snapshots of permanent borders. As climate change progresses, the present independent and politically created borders will be stressed, as ecosystems change without regard to those borders.

Current borders are overwhelmingly shaped by politics, but they may also be defined naturally or culturally. Most

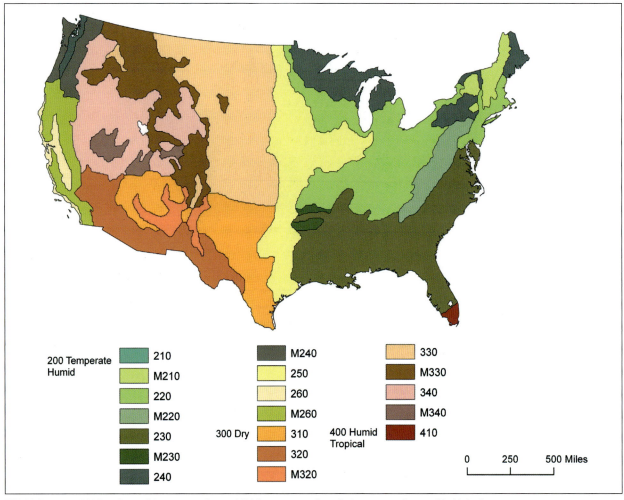

MAP 1.3. Ecosystem Divisions. Some of the more prominent subdivisions are generally equivalent to ecoregions used in this book:

200 Temperate Humid
- 210
- M210
- 220
- M220
- 230
- M230
- 240

300 Dry
- M240
- 250
- 260
- M260
- 310
- 320
- M320

400 Humid Tropical
- 330
- M330
- 340
- M340
- 410

0   250   500 Miles

230: Subtropical division (Atlantic and Gulf coastal plain)
220, 250: Prairie, including the prairie peninsula (Central Lowlands)
260: Mediterranean (California)

310, 330: Temperate steppe division (Great Plains)
320, 340: Temperate desert division (Basin and Range)

Source: Robert G. Bailey, *Description of the Ecoregions of the United States.* 2nd ed. (map). Miscellaneous Publication No. 1391. Washington, D.C.: U.S. Department of Agriculture, U.S. Forest Service, 1995, at http://www.fs.fed.us/land/ecosysmgmt/colorimagemap/ecoreg1_divisions.html

recognized political borders—such as the geometric outline of Colorado—bear no relationship to the surrounding ecological systems or watersheds.[18] They are the result of nation-state conformity and are part of a zeitgeist that fragments everything and makes "thinking outside the box," seemingly outrageous—until you realize how outrageous it is to be thinking inside a box. Imagine no lines. Imagine borders that are defined by natural rhythms, the ecoregion.

Borders between natural systems are not usually abrupt (Photo 1.1) but transitional. While some natural borders are decisive, most borders may be better served by frontier zones, transitional areas between regions as recognized by Islamic and political geographers.[19] A frontier zone border can be equated to an **ecotone**, a transition between ecological communities. However, the patterns of nature are not easily boxed.

Ecosystems may be dominant in a specific physical region but do not necessarily follow the same natural borders. Working within the laws of nature is complex, and it is best understood by working within related systems.

Sometimes physical features, especially rivers, define state or national borders—the Red River between Oklahoma and Texas, the Colorado River dividing Arizona and California, the Rio Grande separating the United States and Mexico—but these borders do not reflect watersheds or ecological boundaries (Photo 1.3). Rivers are the core of a watershed. A river's watershed boundaries extend to the headwaters of its tributaries and are encompassed by drainage basins. A few state and county boundaries along the East Coast are watershed based, and the border of Labrador is defined by the Atlantic watershed; the Rocky Mountain Continental Divide defines the Pacific and Atlantic

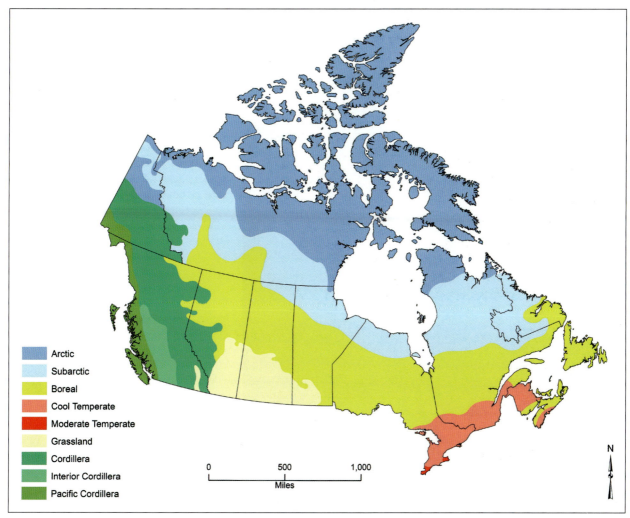

MAP 1.4. Ecoregions of Canada.

Source: Agriculture and Agri-Food Canada, at http://www.agr.gc.ca/index_e.php

Legend:
- Arctic
- Subarctic
- Boreal
- Cool Temperate
- Moderate Temperate
- Grassland
- Cordillera
- Interior Cordillera
- Pacific Cordillera

0   500   1,000
Miles

N

watersheds, as well as portions of Idaho, Montana, Alberta, and British Columbia; but most borders are along the core of a watershed and therefore create more problems than solutions.

Disregarding natural transitions, as artificial political borders do, results in dividing ecosystems and watersheds between two or more states or provinces. Few states or provinces as they exist today are contained within one region, which leaves the political entities trying to satisfy needs based on political rather than more natural boundaries. Multiple governmental bodies usually act autonomously and competitively and rarely practice interjurisdictional cooperation, which exacerbates regional and ecosystem needs.[20] The overall health of the ecosystem or watershed is neglected for the short-term betterment of the political unit. This happens at every political level.

For example, national water policies vary east and west of the Mississippi River. In Canada and east of the Mississippi in the United States, riparian rights are connected to land ownership and cannot be sold outside the watershed, but the western

United States is under the principle of prior appropriation, where water is unconnected to land ownership and is considered a commodity. These are two very different ways to allocate water use. As we shall learn, these artificial water policies and the fragmented political entities that decipher them have wrenched the United States without regard to dependent watersheds and the ecological communities. In the Basin and Range subregion, cities grow beyond their carrying capacity and claim as much water as possible without regard for the surrounding areas. There has been talk of shipping water from the Great Lakes to water-starved areas as if it were as simple as just moving water, ignoring the multiple ecosystems that would be affected, perhaps even destroyed, and how it would then affect the environment, the economy, and humans.

Although many ecologically based nongovernmental organizations (NGOs) recognize border problems, it is difficult to overcome barriers when political units are mutually uncommunicative. The lack of U.S. and Canadian ecological integration of

PHOTO 1.3. The Colorado River, along the California-Arizona border, is the largest river in the driest part of America (35.026°, −114.637°). The border divides the states and the watershed. Therefore, the states fight for water rights. Rather than working with the river, they work against it, and they have overallocated the river's water.

the physical landscape and the human element underlies unsustainable policies.

Learning to live with nature rather than exploit nature will not be easy. It goes against the founding mind-set of the United States and Canada, but the time has come to move to the next level. Humans, the only part of the ecological world that wantonly creates waste and pollution, need to align with the rest of the natural world. To make the connections work requires addressing the unintended consequences of actions.

So where does that leave us with borders? We need to recognize the interrelated natural patterns that our geography offers us to have a complete, healthy, and whole world that is best for humans and for the ecological world. And it is at this point that the amorphous divisions of the ecoworld require a reorganization of human logic and attention to the advantages of technology used in a sustainably appropriate manner. Humans live by the grace of the entire biosphere, but that life is not in competition alone, out to conquer the world, but also cooperation—the lost art of community interaction—seeking what is best for the common good of humans and

the world they live in. It is about competition and also cooperation—coop-etition?

Working within these complex relationships will not be easy, and perhaps this is why prior **reductionist** policies have prevailed, but the stresses placed on humans and the environment no longer allow unilateral or fragmented solutions that only satisfy short-term goals. Working ecologically and with systems allows long-term solutions that reach down to the core problems created by the reductionist modern approach. "Away" no longer exists. It is here and now.

Regions of Canada and the United States

In this book, physical, human, and ecoregional components have been considered in creating each of the chapters. In some cases, physiographic characteristics were paramount (as in the Intermontane), in others ecological (as in the Gulf Coast or Florida), and in others human culture (as in Megalopolis). The book follows many traditional geographic

BOX 1.1   HOW REGIONS INFLUENCE CULTURE

Ecoregions influence cultural development and affect how people adapt to their land. The Plains Native Americans lived nomadically following the buffalo; the European settler farmed the Midwest and Great Plains ecoregions in relation to their cultural past and the landscape of the regions. In doing so, they changed the cultures and settlement patterns that had existed in those regions. The Appalachian small-farm culture developed in relative isolation, largely because of the rugged and mountainous area. In each case, the physical landscape and ecological life melded and helped shape the people, as the people shaped the region for their use. Cultural development is not random but partially shaped by the land.

Few people were attracted to settle in places without water or a reliable food supply or agriculturally friendly soil. Newfoundland settlement was not agriculturally based; it was settled because of the abundance of fish, a reliable food source, which became the effective Newfoundland currency. While Newfoundland had abundant water and timber resources, it was the fishery that supported the hundreds of small coastal villages that were so economically dependent on the Grand Banks fishery.

The relationship of humans to the landscape shaped cultural characteristics. Native Americans varied in relation to their landscape: the Sioux roamed the Plains following buffalo; the Inuit or Dene chased whales in the ocean or caribou across the tundra; the Iroquois grew corn in upstate New York. When a people moved away from their homeland, their culture would ostensibly also change in relation to their new home; however, the ease of modern transportation allows many cultural groups to migrate to regions with dissimilar characteristics from their homeland. Since the culture was formed in relation to the physical landscape, the shift in location should also cause a shift in the culture. As part of the ecosystem, humans and their cultures are not static but constantly changing in relation to their surroundings. However, many cultures relocate to new landscapes and environments and are unable or unwilling to adapt to the new landscape, but instead force their culture on a landscape that is unrelated to their culture.

The arrival of Europeans redefined North America according to European-based cultures, but it also redefined their European cultural roots. Europeans usually re-created what they could of their past culture with the land and its available natural resources, using the offerings of the new physical landscape and slowly changing their culture to reflect the new land (**cultural adaptation**).* French peasants from the Normandy region of France settled New France. They brought with them their culture, housing styles, religion, language, and technology, but while the basic culture continues to influence eastern Canada, change occurred over time in relation to the new land. Linguistically, Québécois French varies from Old World French for several reasons, including New World influences and settlers accepting the new environment into their language and life.

At other times, a cultural group is overrun by another culture that changes the cultural region to satisfy the new group's desires, leaving the native culture bereft. For example, the Inuit were seminomadic, following the seasons and animals, but since the mid-twentieth century they have been permanently located to satisfy governmental schooling and health-care requirements. These changes in their traditional culture have created problems that are only now being addressed. The Inuit of the Alaskan and the Canadian tundra still depend on hunted meat–based "country food" for their sustenance, because of the lack of vegetation in the Arctic. The hunted animals provided food, clothes, home goods, and artistic mediums for the culture. But permanent housing and modern transportation have altered the traditional Inuit life, causing a cultural breakdown. The formation of Nunavut in Canada had its roots in the cultural meltdown and is meant to provide transitional support. Losing a way of life on the land disrupts culture. The way of life developed by a culture is intimately related to the land that helped form that culture.

Shifts in culture began as organic changes in response to the new landscape. People settled in areas because of the land's agricultural worth or for its hunting potential. Agriculture changed the landscape, as it changed the people who grew to intimately know their land. Most U.S. and Canadian settlers until the twentieth century arrived for the opportunity to own and work land, an opportunity denied in their homelands. In 1790, the United States was more than 90 percent farmers, but today few know their soil, few work the land. The tie to the land has been replaced with aesthetic ideals of the land and climate, both of which are skewed by inappropriate technology to fit an unstable and unsustainable existence. For example, the most popular region to move to in the twenty-first century is the dry Basin and Range subregion, which has been historically unsuccessful in supporting large human communities over long periods. Past residents disappeared for reasons still unknown, but their disappearance may hint at what issues are being pushed into the future in this desert land.

Humans are part of Earth's ecological systems and therefore need to rethink how humans work with their landscape, their region, and their community. The ideas in this book are not the commonly held ideas of consumption, growth, and progress. Instead, this book hopes to instill ideas of how the United States and Canada can continue to lead the world with new definitions of consumption (sustainable), growth (ecological), and progress (cooperative).

---

* "Nature is seen by men through a screen composed of beliefs, knowledge, and purposes, and it is in terms of their cultural images of nature, rather than in terms of the actual structure of nature, that men act. Therefore . . . if we are to understand the environmental relations of men [it is necessary] to take into account their knowledge and beliefs concerning the world around them, and their culturally defined motives for acting as they do. But . . . although it is in terms of their conceptions and wishes that men act in nature it is upon nature herself that they do act, and it is nature herself that acts upon men, nurturing or destroying them." Roy A. Rappaport, "Nature, Culture, and Ecological Anthropology," in *Man, Culture and Society*, ed. H. L. Shapiro, 2nd ed., 237–67 (Oxford, UK: Oxford University Press, 1971).

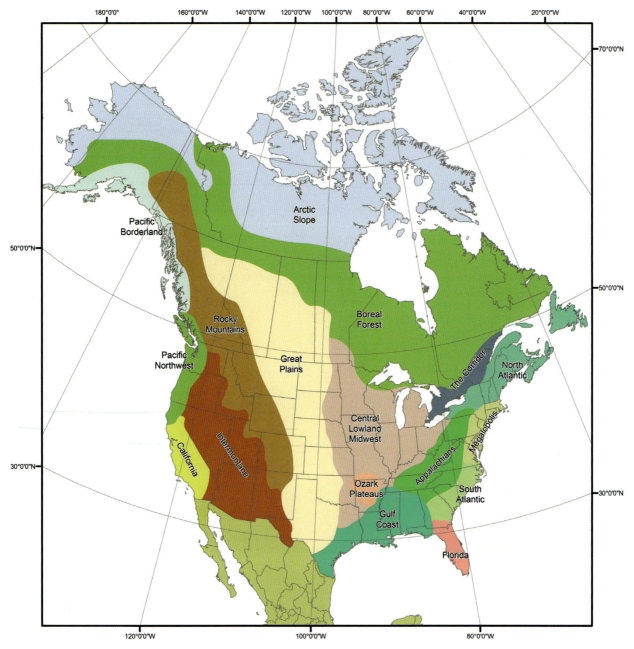

MAP 1.5. The Ecoregional Divisions of the United States and Canada as Used in This Book.

patterns of regional boundaries but places more emphasis on sustainable relationships within ecoregions and their surroundings.

The regions as defined in the book are shown in Map 1.5 and are discussed in Part II, one per chapter, in the following order:

- Canadian Corridor
- North Atlantic
- Megalopolis
- Appalachia and the Interior Plateau
- South Atlantic
- Florida
- Gulf Coast
- Ozarks
- Midwest
- Great Plains and Canadian Prairie
- Rocky Mountains
- Intermontane
- Pacific Northwest
- Alaska, Pacific Borderlands, and Arctic Boreal Canada
- California
- Hawai`i

BOX 1.2. URBAN DEVELOPMENT

Regions have cores and peripheries. The core is the nucleus for industry, population, and commerce and is often represented by cities. The periphery is outside the core and provides many of the resources used by cities.

Cities have a center, which is usually the founding site, and a peripheral area that the city services, the situation. The **site and situation** are the internal and external factors for a city's success or decline.

Historically, the sites of cities have been located near water (the most valuable attribute); near soil suitable for agriculture; or at sites that were more easily defended by natural barriers, such as hilltops, islands, or along rivers. A city prospered or failed in direct correlation to its situation, the relationship with its natural and cultural environment. For example, a city far from water sources had limited growth. Traditionally, the largest cities grew where the natural environment was conducive: fertile land, fresh water, and good transportation links. Cities with natural endowments thrive. The following cities were founded because of traditional natural endowments, but in addition they grew because of exemplary situations, their relationship to external factors.

- Philadelphia: agriculture
- Baltimore: trade
- Quebec City: defense
- Chicago: transportation (Photo 1.4)

In the late twentieth century, however, many of the fastest-growing American cities lack a natural source of fresh water or have grown beyond their water supply source; therefore they lack long-term sustainability. The importance of water supply of each of these cities will be discussed in the following chapters.

- Phoenix, Arizona
- Las Vegas, Nevada (Photo 1.5)
- Atlanta, Georgia

To create sustainable urban centers will require assessments of long-term water supplies.

While site and situation have been seen as less important because of technologic innovations, many of these innovations are inappropriate for the overall relationship of the city to its environs, and therefore they are not sustainable.

PHOTO 1.4. Chicago, Illinois, was in its initial growth stage when transportation technology changed from waterways to railroads. Commodities could now be easily transported overland. While Chicago was located on a major waterway, Chicago chose to become a railroad hub, allowing it to grow much faster than cities that continued to rely only on water transport.

PHOTO 1.5. Las Vegas, Nevada, is one of the fastest-growing cities in America, despite droughts that leave it with an unsustainable water footprint. However, the city has worked to reduce its water usage. For example, the green grass at its famous welcome sign is actually artificial turf. Most "lawns" in Vegas are now drought resistant.

The Importance of Ecoregions in a Sustainable World

This book shows humans as active participants in building sustainable ecosystems and ecoregions, and it shows that they are not the only ones affected. To be a steward requires taking the whole into consideration. The ecological point of view connects biological and physical elements within ecosystems.

Recognizing humans as part of nature instead of apart from nature is the basis for an ecologically based paradigm of holistic systems. The ecoregional and ecosystems study of geography holistically addresses environmental issues. The interrelationships between features—landform, biota, climate, soil, location—provide logical though complex interrelated patterns from the micro to the macro scale. Instead of living within blank and interchangeable political landscapes, we may choose to work and live within ecoregions, which may inculcate a sense of place and, I daresay, love, rather than the constant struggle to overcome natural limitations.

Physical and ecological regions do not follow political borders. The political boundaries of the United States and Canada are artificial boundaries that straddle ecosystems and set up the constant competition for resources between the political entities. Humans and their constructs are in need of a retooling to a more ecologically based holistic system, where unintended consequences are addressed and external costs are included in decisions.

Humans as agents of change are an important part of the ecoregion pattern. In the twentieth century, humans multiplied fourfold, devoured nonrenewable resources, and damaged the environment, resulting in the unintended consequence of climate change. Humans need to understand their role within the world, take responsibility for their past errors, and have the courage to change and enter the ecological age of a sustainable, healthy global environment. One way to do this is to understand ecological, human, and physical regions. Studying geography ecoregionally establishes a foundation to live sustainably.

Geography is a bridging discipline, an interdisciplinary subject, and it incorporates not only its fragmented nature but its ability to connect information about a place across many disciplines. The ability to cross disciplines to gather interconnected information about a place is complex, stimulating, and the definition of an ecoregional sustainable geography.

Questions for Discussion

1. How do ecoregional boundaries differ from political boundaries?

2. What is the difference between studying geography anthropocentrically and ecologically? Explain the advantages and disadvantages of each.

3. The modern world chose to conquer the landscape. How would a sustainable world differ from the modern approach?

4. Who and what will benefit from living in a more sustainable world?

5. How much of the landscape has changed as technology has allowed massive cultural shifts to flow freely across landscapes that are alien to the new cultures? What have the interactions garnered in the world?

6. How do nation-state borders differ from ecoregional borders? Which is more sustainable? Explain.

Suggested Readings

Anderson, J. R. "Major Land Uses" [map]. *The National Atlas of the United States of America*. Reston, Va.: U.S. Geological Survey, 1970.

Ayers, Edward L., ed. *All over the Map: Rethinking American Regions*. Baltimore: Johns Hopkins University Press, 1996.

Bailey, Robert. G. *Description of the Ecoregions of the United States*. 2nd ed. (map). Miscellaneous Publication No. 1391. Washington, D.C.: U.S. Department of Agriculture, U.S. Forest Service, 1995, at http://www.fs.fed.us/land/ecosysmgmt/colorimagemap/ecoreg1_divisions.html.

——. *Ecoregion-Based Design for Sustainability*. New York: Springer, 2002.

——. *Ecosystem Geography*. New York: Springer, 2009.

Botkin, Daniel. *Discordant Harmonies: A New Ecology for the Twenty-First Century*. New York: Oxford University Press, 1992.

Bradshaw, Michael. *Regions and Regionalism in the United States*. Jackson: University Press of Mississippi, 1988.

Brown, Lester. *State of the World*. New York: Norton, annual since 1984.

Commission for Environmental Cooperation (CEC). *Ecological Regions of North America: Toward a Common Perspective*. Montreal: Commission for Environmental Cooperation, 1997.

Fenneman, Nevin M. "The Circumference of Geography." *Annals of the Association of American Geographers* 9 (1919): 3–11.

——. "Physiographic Divisions of the United States." *Annals of the Association of American Geographers* 18, no. 4 (December 1928): 261–353.

Garreau, Joel. *The Nine Nations of North America*. Boston: Houghton Mifflin, 1981.

Hart, John Fraser. "The Highest Form of the Geographer's Art." *Annals of the Association of American Geographers* 72, no. 1 (March 1982): 1–29.

McDonnell, Mark J., and Steward T. A. Pickett, eds. *Humans as Components of Ecosystems: The Ecology of Subtle Human Effects on Populated Areas*. New York: Springer-Verlag, 1997.

McGinnis, Michael Vincent, ed. *Bioregionalism*. London: Routledge, 1999.

McHarg, Ian. *Design with Nature*. Garden City, N.Y.: Natural History Press, 1969.

——. "Natural Factors in Planning." *Journal of Soil and Water Conservation* 52, no. 1 (1997): 15–17.

Omernik, James M. "Map Supplement: Ecoregions of the Conterminous United States." *Annals of the Association of American Geographers* 77, no. 1 (March 1987): 118–25.

Sale, Kirkpatrick. *Dwellers in the Land: The Bioregional Vision*. Athens: University of Georgia Press, 2000.

Van Andruss, Christopher Plant, Judith Plant, and Eleanor Wright, eds. *Home! A Bioregional Reader*. Gabriola Island, B.C.: New Society Publishers, 1990.

Warkentin, John. "Canada and Its Major Regions: Bouchette, Parkin, Rogers, Innis, Hutchinson." *Canadian Geographer* 43, no. 3 (Fall 1999): 244–48.

Zelinsky, Wilbur. "North America's Vernacular Regions." *Annals of the Association of American Geographers* 70, no. 1 (March 1980): 1–16.

Zimmerer, Karl S. "Human Geography and the 'New Ecology': The Prospect and Promise of Integration." *Annals of the Association of American Geographers* 84, no. 1 (March 1994): 108–25.

Internet Sources

Atlas of Canada, at http://atlas.nrcan.gc.ca/site/english/index.html.

Parks Canada. Terrestrial Ecozones of Canada, at http://www.pc.gc.ca/apprendre-learn/prof/itm2-crp-trc/htm/ecozone_e.asp.

Reliable Prosperity: A Project of Ecotrust, at http://www.reliable prosperity.net/.

Systems Thinking, at http://www.thinking.net/Systems_Thinking/systems_thinking.html.

U.S. Department of Agriculture. 2007 Census of Agriculture: Maps and Cartographic Resources, at http://www.agcensus.usda.gov/Publications/2007/Online_Highlights/Ag_Atlas_Maps/index.asp.

———. 2007 Agricultural Census of the United States, at http://www.agcensus.usda.gov/index.asp.

U.S. Environmental Protection Agency, Western Ecology Division, Corvallis, Ore. Ecoregion Maps and GIS Resources, at 2006. http://www.epa.gov/wed/pages/ecoregions.htm.

PHOTO 2.1. Arches National Park, Utah. More than two thousand natural sandstone arches, spires, and pinnacles highlight the dramatic setting. The formations are the result of salt, erosion, and uplift exposed to wind and water.

2

THE NONHUMAN WORLD
Understanding the Limits

Chapter Highlights

After reading this chapter, you should be able to:

- Describe the relationship between physical systems
- Outline the creation of U.S. and Canadian landforms
- Describe basic shared physical features of the United States and Canada
- Discuss characteristics and interconnections between mountain types, water, climate, soil, ecology, and natural hazards

Terms

alpine glaciation	continental glaciation	glacier	Pleistocene
aquifer	continental shelf	global warming	pocosin
basalt	continental slope	greenhouse gas (GHG)	Precambrian
biome	craton	groundwater	precipitation
bog	dome mountain	ice age	rain shadow
boreal forest	drainage basin	karst	shield
caldera	erosion	marsh	subduction
carbon cycle	fault	Mediterranean climate	swamp
carbon sequestration	fault-block mountain	moraine	taiga
carbon sink	feedback loop	orographic precipitation	tundra
climate change	fjord	pedalfer	volcanic mountain
continental climate	folded mountain	pedocal	wetland
	glacial drift	platform	xerophytic

Introduction

I don't believe in magic. I believe in the sun and the stars, the water, the tides, the floods, the owls, the hawks flying, the river running, the wind talking. They're measurements. They tell us how healthy things are. How healthy we are. Because we and they are the same thing.

—Billy Frank, Nisqually[1]

I am I plus my surroundings; and if I do not preserve the latter, I do not preserve myself.

—José Ortega y Gasset (1883–1955)

Humans live in this world and are a product of its beneficence. Our being is a mirror of our surroundings. The healthier the world is, the healthier we are. We are connected with everything around us. It only makes sense that to know the world is to know ourselves; our health is an indication of world health. While humans of many different times, places, and educations have stated similar views, this has not been the practiced ethic of most Americans and Canadians.

In Canada and especially in the United States, the population has been trained to separate themselves from the rest of the natural world. Many residents no longer relate to or understand the landforms, climate, and ecological communities they live in. The general tone of the two countries has been a short-term "conquering" of nature, rather than the long-term being part of nature and nurturing the community of life. While many have realized this folly and recognized that conquering "nature" was the equivalent to conquering ourselves, the general consensus and educational model has been one that defines progress as more conquest, more domination, more technology, more short-term solutions to the problems created by such an ideology.

Defining success by economics alone has resulted in a consumer-based lifestyle. Resources are used in an unaccountable manner in relation to ecosystems and the land. The results—pollution and waste—require that we rethink how we use our economic and technological prowess. Right now, the conquest and power ideology continues to dominate the mind-set, but many people have shifted toward a more sustainable human interaction with the rest of the physical and biophysical world.

One of the shifts away from the traditional modern and linear approach is a systems approach that studies interactions between the living and nonliving worlds. Knowing and understanding the physical environment and its connections with the living community is a first step toward living sustainably. Sustainable science and geography is not about conquering, but about humans living peaceably and comfortably with Earth and maybe even with each other.

The human urge to conquer has been long-standing, beginning perhaps with the first agricultural revolution about ten thousand years ago, but human impact has been most extreme since fossil fuel dependence and the resulting change in quantity and quality of life. Since the Industrial Revolution, the exponential growth of human population has resulted in unheard-of luxury for developed countries but has also spawned multiple unintended consequences, from the exploitation of other humans to reliance on nonrenewable resources. For example, dependence on fossil fuels resulted in the unintended consequences of increased toxins, pollutants, and carbon dioxide levels. The sustainable mind-set requires moving toward being a part of the ecological world. Instead of treating Earth as the giver of all, we need to reconsider our relationship.

Understanding how unique physical regions and distinct landforms may be affected by human intervention requires a basic knowledge of the complex physical and ecological landscape and an appreciation of its natural beauty (Photo 2.1). That would result in reconciling the natural landscape with human demands so that minimal harm is done. Minimal harm? Every action has both positive and negative consequences, depending on perspective, and that is a challenge for living sustainably. Humans need to think about how their actions impact Earth while still seeking a quality of life across the physical and biophysical spectrum. The world population has grown and now consumes at an unsustainable level. Globally, lifestyles now require 1.5 Earths to support human activities.[2] For all humans to live as the average American would require 5 Earths. Humans can grow beyond current understandings and live within the limits of Earth, but that will require a new way of thinking.

The study of our environment has evolved from studying fragments to the holistic systems approach, which studies the interaction of systems components and external factors over time scales that vary from seconds to millennia. This chapter will introduce the physical and ecological environment so that we begin once again to live as part of Earth's systems, instead of apart from them.

Physical Geography

The climate and landforms of the United States and Canada range from the tropics to **tundra**; they have shaped the land, soil, vegetation, and life, and have been the foundation for every ecosystem, culture, and for the built environment. The physical landscape is not for humans to scrape clean for their purposes alone (Photo 2.2). The physical and ecological world provides the essential ingredients for all life. Our actions need to respect and maintain what we can, while still providing for a healthy quality of life. To do this, we need to understand the ground beneath our feet and how it got to be that way.

On a broad scale, the United States and Canada have different physical landscapes and ecological systems, although a physiographic map reveals some shared patterns (Map 2.1, Table 2.1). **Boreal forest** occupies almost half of Canada, and another quarter is tundra. Most of the United States outside of Alaska has a temperate climate. Only 1 percent of Canada is urban, whereas urban settlement in the United States occupies 6 percent of the land. Latitude accounts for some of the reasons the land cover and settlement patterns differ, but knowing the geologic history of the two countries reveals a more complete tale.

A Brief Geologic History of the United States and Canada

The physical and ecological landscapes have evolved over billions of years. The continental landforms emerged from the sea, and tectonic forces folded and faulted the Earth's crust and shaped masses within the Earth (endogenic); weathering and erosion on the Earth (exogenic) shaped the landforms.

Each continental mass has a **shield,** which is the oldest and most stable rock on that continent. The oldest of all continental cores is the North American shield (Map 2.2). The core, centered on Hudson Bay, emerged from the seas in fits and starts as small pieces of land collided, causing them to accrete (fuse) to the core margins.

Coastal landforms reflect their age and climatic history. The older east coast margin, the **continental shelf,** extends many miles to the **continental slope,** where it drops miles into the abyss. The more recent, tectonically active west coast shelf plummets near the shore to the slope. The eastern continental shelf extends far beyond the tectonic margin, a passive

PHOTO 2.2. Housing Tract near Atlanta, Georgia (33.607°, 84.311°), built after the heavily forested area was completely scraped clean of vegetation, obliterating the natural landscape.

boundary. In North America the Atlantic, Gulf, and Arctic coasts are passive margins with extensive shelves far from tectonic plate boundaries. The east coast shelf is up to 200 miles (320 km) wide and covers about 140,000 square miles at a relatively shallow maximum depth of 600 feet (180 m).[3]

An active plate is closer to tectonic plate boundaries and has a narrow shelf before the plate plunges into the abyss. The active Pacific margin, where the North American Plate meets the Pacific Plate, averages only 20 miles wide (30 km) and covers only 25,000 square miles (64,750 km²).

The continental shelves were exposed as land when **ice age** glaciations locked ocean water in miles-thick ice sheets. When the glacial water melted, the water covered much of the shelves and created the current shoreline. The ice and water have shaped, moved, and sculpted the continents over billions of years.

How the United States and Canada Formed

Studying continental formation reveals why landforms and natural resources appear where they do. The story begins more than four billion years ago along the edge of Hudson Bay, where small drifting landmasses collided and formed the Canadian or Laurentian Shield. At that time, the continental crust was about 25 percent of the continent's current size. The shield formed when volcanic magma (liquid rock) cooled, solidified, and rose above sea level. Sedimentary deposits covered and extended the shield to form the **platform**. Together the shield and platform form the tectonically stable **craton**.

The Canadian Shield is the exposed North American craton, which extends from the edges of the Rocky Mountains to the Appalachian Uplands. The platform overlies much of the shield. Glaciated and eroded multiple times, the once mountainous shield is now a low-lying, rocky, bare, and gouged landscape, littered with **wetlands** and millions of lakes. The **Precambrian** volcanic action was during the oldest geologic period, during which volcanic magma heated and pressurized metals, forming mineral resources. Canadian Shield ores are important twenty-first-century resources.

By 1.5 billion years ago, the continental crust had grown to about 80 percent of its current size. During the next 600 million years, the North American landmass was part of Rodinia, one of the first supercontinents formed by continental drift (Map 2.3). New land accreted to today's east coast, forming the roots of the Appalachian Mountains. However, at this time the continent straddled the equator. The warm climate produced the first forms of life. This period was followed by a significant "snowball Earth" (there have been several) about 650 million years ago.

North America then spawned a vast inland sea; oceans widened and then closed as Gondwana and Laurasia formed supercontinents. About 500 million years ago, new life forms were established on the equator-centered continent. As the tropical plants of this period died, they were buried and pressurized, forming some of America's many coal basins. Small skeletal organisms deposited on the oceanic floor became limestone.

BOX 2.1. DID YOU KNOW . . . THE GROUND WE STAND ON

- In Boston, two-thirds of the city is built on landfill, at such a low elevation that sea level rise affects these areas first.
- The Atlantic coastline was one continuous marsh that had to be reclaimed in order to realize the agricultural potential.
- Malarial epidemics were once common in New Jersey and Philadelphia because of the wetlands.
- Some of the longest-running water wars are in the moist, humid South.
- The artificial levees on the Mississippi River make it more likely to have a major flood event.
- Much of the land in the Great Lake states is drained and tiled, so it can be used for agriculture.

- The settlers on the Great Plains believed that if they plowed the fields, rain would come.
- Most water used along the Front Range of Colorado is transported across the Rocky Mountains.
- Lake Mead is at 49 percent capacity and may be dry by 2021.
- Southern California has more than half the state's population but only 2 percent of its water.
- The Pacific Northwest has recently been told to conserve water because of drought.
- In Alaska, 183 of 213 indigenous villages will require funds for flooding and erosion problems due to climate change.

Portions of Africa attached to the east coast, forming Massachusetts and Atlantic Canada.

During the geologic Mesozoic era (250 to 65 million years ago), Pangaea formed and an interior seaway across the Great Plains region divided North America. Another period of heat and pressure transformed more tropical plants to coal. Then about 250 million years ago, the Pacific Plate on the west coast began to subduct beneath the North American Plate, and much of the coastal states accreted to the continent. California remained an offshore island, and a submerged Florida broke off from Africa and attached to the continent.

About 200 million years ago, Pangaea broke up and the east coast of the continent attained a more recognizable shape (Map 2.4). As South America moved south, the empty space evolved into the Gulf of Mexico; North America drifted away from Africa, opening up the Atlantic Ocean. Along the Atlantic coast the Appalachians, as tall as today's Rockies, began to erode. Their soil built up the Atlantic Coastal Plain. Inland, the Keweenaw Rift helped form Lake Superior and left a volcanic mineralized belt of copper ore.

The next step in the continental formation was the rise of the Rocky Mountains, the shaping of volcanoes and mountains in the far west and the accretion of land to form the Alaskan peninsula. The Great Plains and the Atlantic and Gulf coasts were still submerged, but the United States was beginning to take a recognizable shape about 100 million years ago.

In the next 30 million years, the Atlantic and Gulf coastal plains emerged from the seas as sediment washed down from the inland. After another 30 million years, the Pacific Plate isle of California accreted to the North American Plate, becoming part of the mainland. The plate margins are defined by the San Andreas Fault.

From 5 to 15 million years ago, the Columbia River Plateau was flooded with magma that hardened into **basalt**, which was then ravaged many years later by the Missoula Floods, leaving the Channeled Scablands. Northern Florida emerged from the

sea. Most of the continent was recognizable when the most recent ice ages arrived 2 million years ago and scoured the northern continent, until about twelve thousand years ago. The continental shelf emerged and then was submerged once again as the **glaciers** retreated, leaving behind islands and capes: Martha's Vineyard, Nantucket, Long Island, and Cape Cod.

The ice age retreat left the two countries' landscapes close to what they are today. The Great Lakes Basin and the millions of glacial lakes left Canada and the United States with plentiful supplies of freshwater. The continental margin took shape as sediments were deposited along the Atlantic coast. Along the Pacific coast, uplift occurred. Glaciers shrank.

The human age began to alter the physical world when agriculture developed about ten thousand years ago. Humans made their way to the Americas. Another minor ice age occurred between 1400 and 1800 CE. And then the climate began to warm about 150 years ago, when fossil fuels that had been trapped in the Earth's lithosphere began heating the atmosphere as carbon dioxide was released.

Landforms and Processes

Earth's landforms have been shaped by processes involving physical, chemical, and biological actions. Most of the shaping is related to climate and location.

Location influences the physical, chemical, and biological features of the United States and Canada. Canada at higher latitudes and closer to the Arctic has far more boreal forest and tundra, while the United States has a more temperate latitudinal range.

- In the United States, lowlands constitute about half the land area, occupying the east coast and interior prairie from the Appalachians to the Rocky Mountains.
- The most recent continental ice sheets covered most of Canada and the northern U.S. lowlands until about

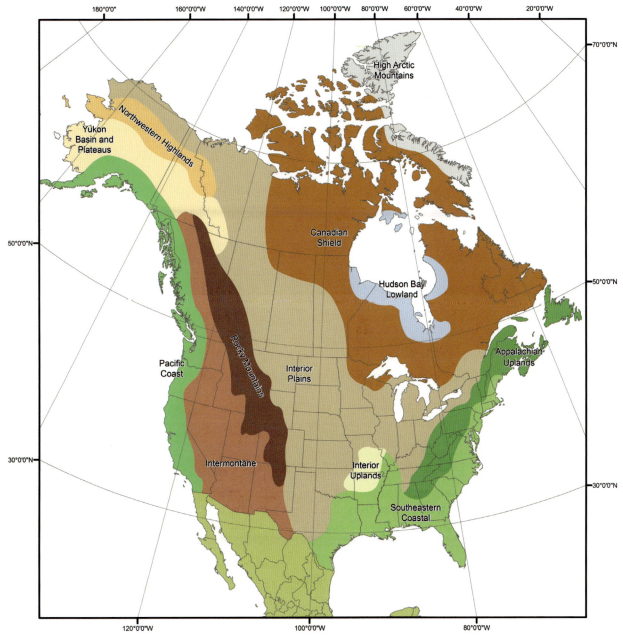

MAP 2.1. The Basic Physical Landforms of the United States and Canada.

twelve thousand years ago. The glacial retreat left a prime agricultural landscape of flat land and fertile soil.
- Plateaus are uplifted, flat-topped tablelands and comprise about one-quarter of the U.S. land area. The premier plateaus are in the Appalachian, Ozark, and Intermontane regions. The Cumberland and Ozark Plateaus are often called mountains, but their geology reveals plateaus dissected by waterways. In Canada,

the major plateau region is in interior British Columbia.
- Mountains occupy about one-quarter of the land area in both countries.

To better understand the nonhuman geography of Canada and the United States, the rest of the chapter will discuss characteristics such as mountain types, water, climate, soil, ecology, and natural hazards.

TABLE 2.1. Physical Makeup of Canadian and American Geographic Extent

	Forest (%)	Arctic tundra (%)	Open land (%)	Cropland (%)	Urban land (%)
Canada	43.7	27.4	14.0	6.6	0.3
United States	23.0	2.6	27.0[a]	20.0	5.0

Note: Forests and grasslands physical ecosystems have been converted to range, crop, and urban land.
[a] Range land 21%, pasture 6%.

Mountains

The oldest mountains in North America and perhaps the oldest in the world are the Appalachians, formed almost 500 million years ago. The Rocky Mountains and the Cascade–Sierra Nevada mountain systems formed at the western margins of the continent about 65 million years ago. Active mountain building continues today in Hawai`i and the Cascades.

Mountain systems are composed of many ranges. The Rocky Mountain system contains about thirty ranges, such as the Wasatch, Teton, and Bitterroot ranges. The west coast linear backbone—from the Brooks Range to Tierra del Fuego—includes the Sierra-Cascade ranges (Table 2.2).

Geologic processes build the four mountain types—folded, dome, volcanic, and fault-block, Examples of each are found in the United States and Canada, although in various states of erosional development. Erosion wears down mountains, changing their original shape and exposing core rocks.

Folded mountains are the most common; they are formed when two plates collide, compress the rock, and having

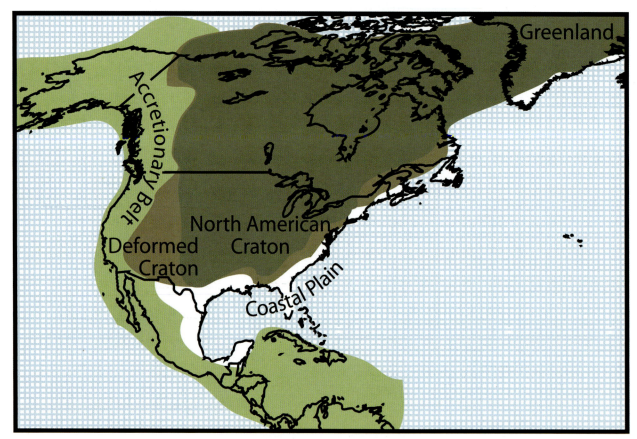

MAP 2.2. The North American Craton. This is the oldest in the world and the nucleus of the continent. The craton is made up of the stable platform and the shield. The North American craton extends from the Rocky Mountains to the Appalachians.

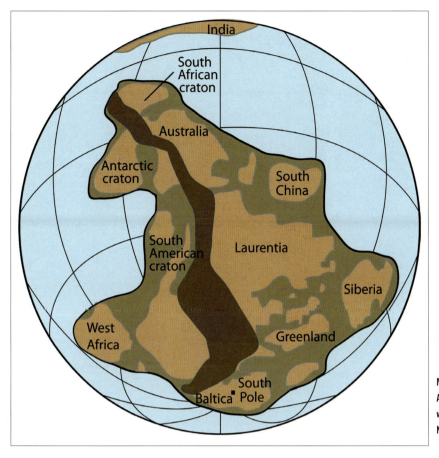

MAP 2.3. Rodinia, Formed about 1.2 Billion Years Ago. The core of the supercontinent was Laurentia, which was composed of the ancestral rocks of the North American continent.

nowhere to go but up, elevate the mountains in folds like a rug pushed against a wall. The Appalachian Ridge and Valley subregion and the White Mountains of New Hampshire (Photo 2.3) are folded mountains, as is the Rocky Mountains' Bighorn Range.

Stress can fracture rock and result in crustal movement called faulting. Displaced rock layers structure **fault-block mountains**—Wyoming's Tetons, Basin and Range, and California's Sierra Nevada—with one gently sloping side and one steep side.

When plates collide, one plate thrusts upward while the other plate plunges into the mantle, where heat and pressure melt the plate and form magma. A **dome mountain** develops when the magma rises from the mantle, creating pressure that warps or folds the crust but does not reach the surface. The rounded magma "dome" is only revealed when the crust cracks, splits, and erodes. The Black Hills of South Dakota are characteristic dome mountains.

When magma rises to the surface and erupts (at which point it becomes lava), the mountain is a volcano, which is formed separately and is usually much higher than surrounding mountains (Photo 2.4).

Volcanic mountains consist of stratovolcanoes (such as those in the Cascades) and shield volcanoes (such as those in the Hawaiian Islands). Stratovolcanoes are steep-sided, symmetrical cones formed by explosive ejections of lava, which can tear mountains down or build them up. For example, Washington's Mount St. Helens exploded in 1980, causing the stratovolcano to lose 1,300 feet of elevation. The Hawaiian Islands are an example of gently sloping shield volcanoes. As the Pacific Plate moved over the mid-Pacific hot spot, the successive accumulation of fluid lava flows created the islands.

Water—Hydrography

The United States and Canada are endowed with freshwater, especially in formerly glaciated areas; however, freshwater remains a precious resource. Ninety-seven percent of all water is found in oceans and is therefore saline; freshwater is either locked in glaciers (2 percent) or in surface or **groundwater** systems (1 percent). Of the 1 percent of accessible water, only one-quarter is located on the surface in rivers, lakes, and streams, which are all divided into watersheds.

A watershed defines the total geographical area of numerous individual **drainage basins,** which drain a river to a single termination point, usually from mountains to lowlands and out to sea. Dams, levees, and roads have altered drainage basins and increased their vulnerability to hazards. Watershed divides are typically perceived as located along high mountain ridges, but other divides are found along slight increases of elevation, such as the Great Lakes Basin and the Mississippi

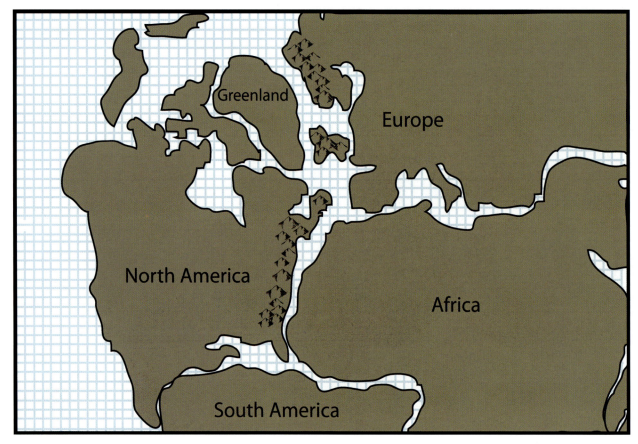

MAP 2.4. Pangaea as It Broke Apart. Note the Appalachian Mountains extending into Scandinavia.

drainage. Political borders, however, seldom follow or respect watersheds, resulting in fragmented policies regarding the use and sharing of water resources. Managing water requires a wide-ranging ecological understanding of the landscape, including watersheds, erosion, deposition, and the effects of water use and pollution.

Water follows the path of least resistance, usually to the ocean. Along its path, water erodes or deposits sediment, causing beneficial or adverse effects. Sediment deposited on floodplains leaves behind fertile soils, provides natural flood and erosion control, and recharges groundwater. Rivers build natural levees in relation to the river flow, but often human intervention with artificial levees meant to facilitate economic growth has caused environmental degradation that has worsened flooding. For example, areas that are prone to flooding should not be built upon. The massive 1993 flood of the Mississippi and Missouri river confluence was due to artificial levees that did not allow the floodplains to accept the water and caused more flooding than if the artificial levees had not been built. The costs for the flooding were the loss of about a hundred thousand homes, millions of acres of farmland, and $15 billion to $20 billion in damages. Flooding in 2011 resulted in additional damages to the same area, when levees were intentionally ruptured in one less-populated area

in order to save more-populated areas. Damages again were in the billions.

Water shortages and pollution plague all countries. While the United States and Canada contain about 25 percent of the world's freshwater, competition for water is fierce among agricultural, residential, and industrial users. Stressed freshwater and groundwater sources require a sustainable systems approach to mitigate the effects of human-induced channeling or pumping. To achieve sustainable water systems requires knowledge about the relationships between surface water, groundwater, drainage basins, wetlands, and glacial landforms.

Surface Water

Watersheds and Rivers

Water on continents is classified as surface water (lakes, rivers, and streams) or groundwater; it is divided between drainage basins, wetlands, and glacial landforms. The United States and Canada have seven major watershed drainage areas, along with major rivers (Map 2.5):

- Atlantic (Hudson River, Delaware River)
- St. Lawrence/Great Lakes (St. Lawrence River)
- Pacific (Columbia, Snake, Sacramento, Yukon, and Fraser rivers)

TABLE 2.2. Major Mountain Systems in the United States and Canada

	Location	Highest peak	Extent
Eastern mountains			
Torngat	Labrador, Quebec, Nunavut	5,420 ft.	182 miles north–south 125 miles east–west
Laurentians	Quebec	3,825 ft.	267 miles north–south 459 miles east–west
Appalachians	U.S. and Canada, from Newfoundland to Mississippi	Mt. Mitchell 6,684 ft.	1,896 miles north–south 2,114 miles east–west
Western mountains			
Rocky Mountains	Along British Columbia/Alberta border at Yukon south to New Mexico (including Idaho, Montana, Wyoming, Colorado, Utah)	Mt. Elbert 14,433 ft.	1,709 miles north–south 1,097 miles east–west
Sierra Nevada	California, Nevada	Mt. Whitney 14,491 ft.	389 miles north–south 231 miles east–west
Cascade Mountains	Washington, Oregon, California, British Columbia	Mt. Rainier 14,411 ft.	725 miles north–south 194 miles east–west
Coastal Mountains	British Columbia, Washington, Oregon, California	Mt. Eddy 9,025 ft.	1,455 miles north–south 752 miles east–west
Alaska and Canadian coastal ranges	Alaska, British Columbia, and Yukon	Mt. McKinley 20,320 ft.	1,393 miles north–south 11,901 miles east–west
Brooks (northern extension of Rocky Mountain system)	Alaska/Yukon	Mt. Chamberlin 9,020 ft.	336 miles north–south 740 miles east–west

- Gulf of Mexico (Mississippi, Ohio, and Missouri rivers, and the Rio Grande)
- Gulf of California (Colorado River)
- Arctic (Mackenzie River)
- Hudson Bay (Nelson River, La Grande Rivière)
- Great Basin (Humboldt River, interior drainage)

Major American rivers are the Mississippi along with its primary tributaries, the Ohio and Missouri; the Colorado; the Columbia and its major tributary, the Snake River; and the Yukon. Both the Columbia and Yukon rivers have their headwaters in Canada. Canada's major rivers are the Mackenzie, the Fraser, and the St. Lawrence (Table 2.3). Rivers and streams are often connected to lakes and human-made reservoirs.

Lakes

Glacial, structural, and artificial processes form lakes. Glacial lakes are the most numerous. They are remnants of the last ice age, and they span Canada and the northern tier of the United States. The Great Lakes, linking the borders of both countries, are the largest glacial lakes; they contain the largest single lake within the United States, Lake Michigan, and the largest lake, which is shared by both countries, Lake Superior. The Canadian Shield lakes include more than a million lakes in Quebec alone, while Minnesota, Wisconsin, and Michigan each contain thousands of glacial lakes. Kettle or pothole lakes are formed when ice calves from a glacier and sets in the land, while other lakes are the result of glacial scour, such as the Finger Lakes of upstate New York or the Mission Bay district of Michigan.

In the Intermontane, former ice age lakes have either dried up or are ephemeral, adjusting their size annually according to weather conditions—smaller in the spring and summer when water flow declines, and larger during the cooler autumn when water flow exceeds evaporation. In the Great Basin, evaporation exceeds **precipitation**, resulting in high-salt-content lakes with no exterior drainage.

Structural lakes may be formed by any one of several geologic processes. Oregon's Crater Lake **caldera** was formed

PHOTO 2.3. Mount Washington, in the Appalachian White Mountains of New Hampshire, is the highest point in the Northeast at 6,288 feet. It has been a popular tourist destination and hiking area since the mid-nineteenth century, despite a reputation for erratic weather.

when ancient Mount Mazama collapsed after a volcanic eruption emptied the magma chamber. Other structural lakes include **fault** valleys (e.g., Lake Tahoe) and cut-off meander oxbow lakes, which form during flood events. Sinkholes form in **karst** areas, when chemical and mechanical weathering dissolves limestone. Sinkhole lake levels rise and fall periodically in response to subsurface water levels. Karst lakes are found in humid environments, such as the Ozarks and Florida.

Artificial lakes and reservoirs store river and stream runoff for urban, recreational, hydroelectric, and irrigational uses. Some of the largest artificial lakes are Lake Mead on the Nevada-Arizona border, Lake Powell in Utah and Arizona, and Lake Eufaula in Oklahoma. Most artificial lakes and reservoirs were built without considering the ecological consequences, and they have caused massive aquatic imbalances.

As ecosystem interactions are understood, the focus has changed to maintaining healthy ecosystems and creating compatible water-release programs for spawning fish and shellfish. Since 2002, the Nature Conservancy and the Army Corps of Engineers have formed the Sustainable Rivers Project to protect river ecology while maintaining human services. For example, when dams create more problems than they solve, they are being removed. In Oregon, two dams have been removed to facilitate salmon spawning, and more are scheduled to be removed in the near future.[4]

Groundwater

Groundwater is stored in the cavities and spaces between subsoil layers beneath plant root zones. Most soil has moisture within it, but groundwater soil is saturated. The upper level of the saturated ground, the water table, can occur at any depth, fluctuating in relation to use and climatic conditions. About 50 percent of Americans and 25 percent of Canadians rely on groundwater for drinking, and 65 percent of groundwater is used for irrigated crop production.

Groundwater has traditionally been a source of uncontaminated water. The soil filtered out contaminants and pollutants before they reached the water table. However, the amount of contaminants now entering the soil often far outweighs the soil's filtering capability. The major contaminants include gasoline, oil, road salts, chemical fertilizers, and sewage from ill-maintained septic systems. Concern over groundwater pollution caused by unregulated water quality in septic systems has caused recent legislation and action in Washington, Texas, and California.[5] Groundwater pollution due to extensive agricultural and residential runoff has affected supplies in Wichita, Miami, Los Alamos, San Antonio, and Spokane, as well the Ogallala Aquifer, the largest aquifer in the nation.

An **aquifer** is an underground, water-soaked layer of rock and sand, which can be accessed by pumping or pressure. Across the Great Plains, thousands of windmills pump water from shallow aquifers, but the Ogallala is more than two hundred feet below the surface. Groundwater in deep aquifers is accessed with a well and a gasoline pump. Aquifers recharge (replenish) when rainwater seeps down through the soil, but sometimes more water is withdrawn than replenished. For example, the Ogallala Aquifer fossil water (water sealed in the aquifer for millions of years) has a low recharge rate, and overpumping and low precipitation have caused the water table to

PHOTO 2.4. Volcanic Mount Hood is the highest mountain in Oregon at 11,240 ft., rising above the clouds and the Cascade Mountains. Volcano formation is separate from and usually higher than the surrounding mountains.

decline. Groundwater and aquifer abuse has reduced available water and lowered water tables.

Wetlands

Wetlands—**swamps**, **bogs**, and **marshes**—are ecotones, or transitional zones between dry land and permanent water bodies. Wetlands filter impurities before surface water reaches the groundwater. However, many wetlands have been destroyed or impaired, which has increased groundwater pollution.

Throughout American history, wetlands were disparaged and drained for conversion to agricultural or residential use. But in the 1950s, a semantic shift began to redefine "smelly" swamps and marshes as "useful" wetlands. Still, although the importance of wetlands ecology was noted throughout the twentieth century, only since the 1980s has wetland removal been regularly challenged and the ecological benefits of wetlands—flood buffers, erosion control, water filtration, recreation, and wildlife habitation—been promoted.[6]

Removing wetlands increased water pollution and destroyed coastal buffer zones that protected inland areas. For example, the Louisiana coastal wetlands buffered the mainland against storm surges; therefore, wetland loss increased the destruction caused by Hurricane Katrina. Most states have lost a majority of their wetlands (Map 2.6). California has lost 91 percent of its limited wetlands; in the wetland-rich Great Lakes states, 50 to 90 percent are drained.

Glaciers

A glacier is a large ice mass that slowly flows downhill. There have been many geologic glacial events, but the North American event most referred to is the **Pleistocene** advances, ending about twelve thousand years ago. Glaciers are classified as alpine (mountain) or continental (from a central mass over a continent).

Alpine Glaciation

Alpine glaciation, dependent on seasonal temperatures and changes in precipitation, is restricted to mountainous areas. Stream channels incise V-shaped mountain valleys; the passage of glaciers makes the valleys U-shaped. Alpine glaciers are found in high-elevation mountains. Mount Rainier has twenty-six glaciers, while more than a hundred thousand North American glaciers line the British Columbia and Alaska Panhandle coastline, fed by abundant precipitation at high latitudes. Most alpine glaciers today are receding due to **climate change**.

Continental Glaciation

For the past two billion years, Earth's climate has cycled between glacial and interglacial periods. Over the past 70 million years, three major ice age periods flattened vast portions of Earth with massive miles-deep ice sheets (**continental glaciation**). The recent glacial period, commonly called the "Ice Ages," began about eight hundred thousand years ago. The most recent glaciations ended about twelve thousand years ago (Table 2.4). The past twelve thousand years, the Holocene, has been an interglacial warm period and the ice has receded, although there have been at least twenty occurrences of minor recessions and advances. The most recent advance was the Little Ice Age, which ended in the nineteenth century.

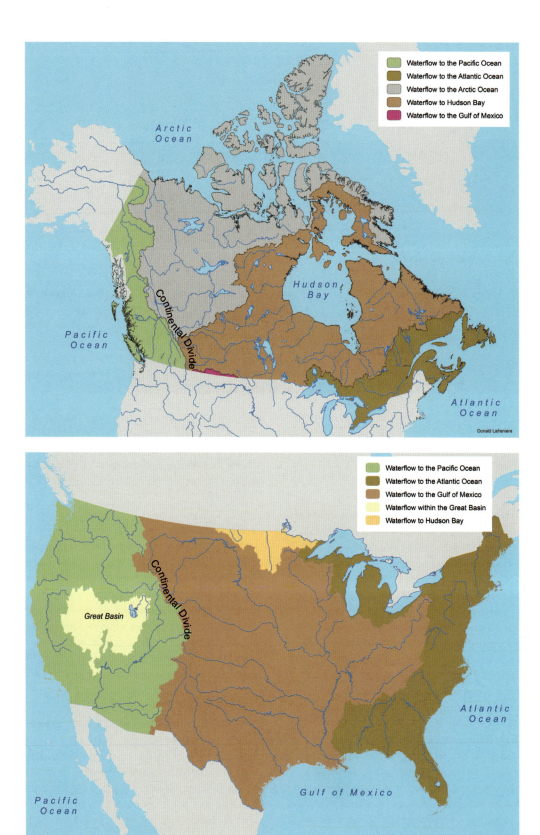

MAP 2.5. Major Canadian and U.S. Watershed Drainage Areas.

Waterflow to the Pacific Ocean
Waterflow to the Atlantic Ocean
Waterflow to the Arctic Ocean
Waterflow to Hudson Bay
Waterflow to the Gulf of Mexico

Waterflow to the Pacific Ocean
Waterflow to the Atlantic Ocean
Waterflow to the Gulf of Mexico
Waterflow within the Great Basin
Waterflow to Hudson Bay

BOX 2.2 SWAMPS, BOGS, POCOSINS, MARSHES, BAYOUS, AND FENS

The numerous wetland types in the world are often simply called swamps. But swamps are only one type of wetland; there are bogs, **pocosins**, marshes, bayous, and fens. A swamp specifically is a wetland with saturated soils and standing water during the growing season. Swamps proliferate because of low elevation, numerous floodplains, and tidal surges. Typical vegetation is shrubs and trees, but swamps do not contain cattails and other nonwoody plants. Many swamps are found in formerly glaciated lands. For example, there are 219 named swamps in Michigan. About one-third of Michigan's swamps have been drained.

Bogs are wet and spongy waterlogged ground, covered usually by a sphagnum moss and characteristic shrubs. Bogs are usually found in formerly glaciated areas and in former lake bottoms, as in Michigan, Minnesota, Ontario, and Quebec. Bogs do not take well to draining and therefore tend to be sparsely populated. A few examples are:

- Minnesota's Big Bog, found at the southern end of former Lake Agassiz.
- Eastern Ontario's Mer Bleue sphagnum bog, near the Ottawa River.
- Pennsylvania's Tannersville Cranberry Bog, a sphagnum bog. Although this bog is not known for its cranberries, many bogs are.

Pocosins are found along the mid-Atlantic Coastal Plain, especially in North Carolina. Pocosins are usually saturated, though they can be dry during prolonged droughts. They are deficient of nutrients, especially phosphorus, and are often pine flatwoods or what is known as shrub bogs. They are often drained, and this has led to their loss and the loss of the ecosystems aligned with them.

Marshes are shallow water, wet most of the year, and contain grasses and nonwoody water-loving plants such as cattails and water lilies. They may be either freshwater or salt marshes. Many former pothole lakes have naturally drained and evolved into marshes. When an area has more open water, it is then called a swamp. Marshes are important reproductive areas for aquatics. Some marsh areas include estuaries and waterways along the barrier island of the Atlantic South. In the Canadian Shield and along the Great Lakes are many freshwater marshes.

Bayous are found in the Gulf Coastal region, a flat region that has slow-moving, almost stagnant secondary watercourses of rivers. A bayou is similar to a swamp, except it is slowly moving. A bayou has both trees and nonwoody vegetation.

Fens are similar to bogs, except that fens are neutral or alkaline and fed by groundwater. Vegetation favors alkaline-loving plants that are more diverse than bogs, such as grasses, sedges, and wildflowers. The major fen in the United States is the Geneva Creek Iron Fen in Colorado; it is rich in iron oxide deposited by the groundwater.

TABLE 2.3. Major U.S. and Canadian Rivers

World rank by drainage	River	Drainage area (000 sq. mi.)	Length (miles)
5	Mississippi-Missouri	2,001	3,740
12	Mackenzie	1,144	2,635
14	St. Lawrence	909	2,485
19	Nelson	666	1,600
23	Columbia	415	1,249
24	Rio Grande	336	1,900

Source: Environment Canada, at http://www.ec.gc.ca/eau-water/default.asp?lang=En&n=45BBB7B8-1#canada; U.S. Geological Survey, at http://pubs.usgs.gov/of/1987/ofr87-242/

North American Pleistocene glaciations covered and reshaped the landscape from Canada south through the Central Lowlands. For example, the Ohio and Missouri river systems were formed as the glaciers melted. Today their channels roughly mark the southern extent of the ice sheets (Map 2.7). Fertile **glacial drift** was deposited over the scoured surface, and the physical landscape was pockmarked with millions of glacially formed kettle lakes. Along coastal areas, such as in Newfoundland, retreating glaciers carved the long steep **fjords** that finger out to the sea.

Characteristic glacial landscapes over Canada and the northern United States include:

- Bare rock that is scoured of soil (e.g., the Canadian Shield).
- Drained glacial lakes, leaving behind deposits of fertile sediment. Lake Agassiz, straddling the U.S.-Canadian border, became the fertile Red River Valley.
- Boggy soils, such as those found throughout the Great Lakes region.

- **Moraines** found throughout the Great Lakes and Northern Atlantic coastal regions, including Cape Cod, Long Island, Nantucket, and Martha's Vineyard.
- The scoured Puget Sound mainland and islands.

Climate

The changing climate has become a focus that has led many to endorse sustainable living. Changing climatic patterns need to be accounted for when discussing sustainable practices, but they are not the only reason to adopt a more sustainable way of life.

The overall climatic effect in the early twenty-first century has been most noticed in Arctic warming and glacial melting, but all regions are experiencing unusual patterns. Since the 1970s, weather anomalies have increased. Indicators of climate change can include sea level rise, increased numbers of tornadoes, floods, rising wind velocities, and record heat and snows; however, their existence alone is not a sure sign of climate change. Climate is a complex system with multiple natural and human-induced variables.

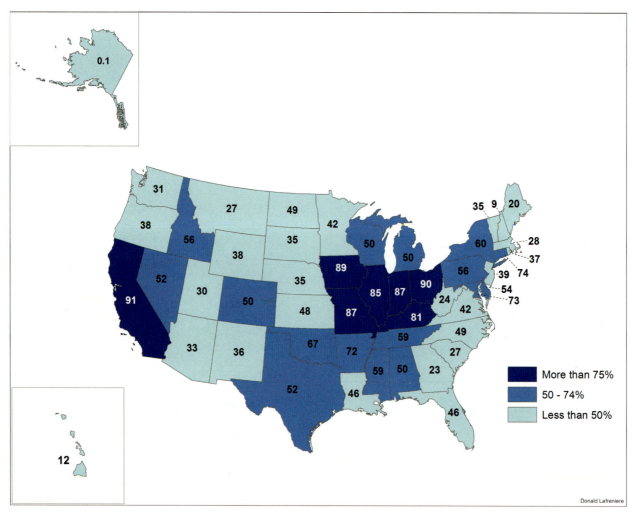

MAP 2.6. Percentage of Wetlands Acreage Lost, 1780s–1980s. Twenty-two states have lost at least 50 percent of their original wetlands. Seven states—Indiana, Illinois, Missouri, Kentucky, Iowa, California, and Ohio—have lost more than 80 percent of their original wetlands. Since the 1970s, the most extensive losses of wetlands have been in Louisiana, Mississippi, Arkansas, Florida, South Carolina, and North Carolina.

BOX 2.3 DID YOU KNOW . . . GLACIERS

- There are two kinds of glaciers: continental and alpine.
- Continental glaciers spread from a central mass of ice over continents.
- Continental glaciers comprise over 90 percent of all glacial ice.
- Alpine glaciers are found in mountains ranges and descend from high valleys.
- Alaska has more than a hundred thousand glaciers.
- Seventy-seven percent of all freshwater is in the form of ice, mostly locked in glaciers.
- When the last ice age peaked about eighteen thousand years ago, glaciers covered 30 percent of the land. Today they cover about 10 percent.

- During the most severe ice age (about eight hundred million years ago), glaciers were present in tropical latitudes and may have reached within degrees of the equator.

While glacial activity has been a natural part of the physical cycle, the current melting may be the result of human activity. However, regardless of fault, the current melting of glaciers has affected river flows, decreased hydropower generation, and caused species migration, as well as affected forestry and agriculture-based livelihoods. These effects are causing and will continue to cause interruptions in human activities and may be a factor in redefining progress.

While no absolute statement can be made about the causes of the current climate change, the scientific community believes that human activities—the burning of fossil fuels and clearing of land—have increased **greenhouse gas (GHG)** concentrations, a primary driver of climate change. Climate change has been a subject of intense discussion for more than a decade. The results point to increased levels of CO_2, the major greenhouse gas that was stable at around 280 parts per million (ppm) in 1850 but had risen to 393.69 ppm by June 2011.[7] There has been a lot of talk, but CO_2 continues to rise: 1.89 ppm in 2009; 2.42 ppm in 2010. Other variables that determine climatic patterns include wind circulation, topography, and land-water relationships, while locational factors influence specific areas.

The Canadian and U.S. climatic range varies from the tropics of Hawai`i and Florida's southern tip to the Arctic tundra. Climate regions are not the same as ecoregions, but there are many relationships. The differences are because of changes in latitude and elevation, as well as specific idiosyncrasies that create microclimates and can happen at any scale from subregional to a few feet. Microclimates are formed from a variety of variables, including bodies of water, slope and aspect of land, wind, and the amount of natural flora.

Most U.S. inhabitants live in the temperate zone of the lower forty-eight states. North of the 38th parallel, residents generally enjoy a four-season climate, while those to the south have less seasonal variation. Most of Canada is north of the 49th parallel (about the latitude of Frankfurt, Germany), but Canadian weather is usually colder than European cities at equivalent latitudes for two reasons:

1. Canada's high western mountains block the oceanic warmth of the westerly winds.
2. Canada lacks the warm North Atlantic Drift that moderates the western European climate.

Living sustainably requires understanding basic climatic patterns (wind and precipitation). Climatic conditions affect settlement and distribution for humans and other life forms.

Wind patterns across the United States and Canada blow from the west and carry weather systems from the West Coast to the east. The Pacific Northwest has a wet climate, because westerly winds are subject to pressure systems bringing sunshine in summer and rain the rest of the year. The leeward (eastern) side of the West Coast spine of mountains is in the **rain shadow** and therefore drier.

TABLE 2.4. Most Recent Pleistocene North American Glaciations

Glaciation name	Time spanned (years ago)
Wisconsin	75,000–12,000
Illinoian	186,000–120,000
Kansan	480,000–230,000
Nebraskan	800,000–600,000

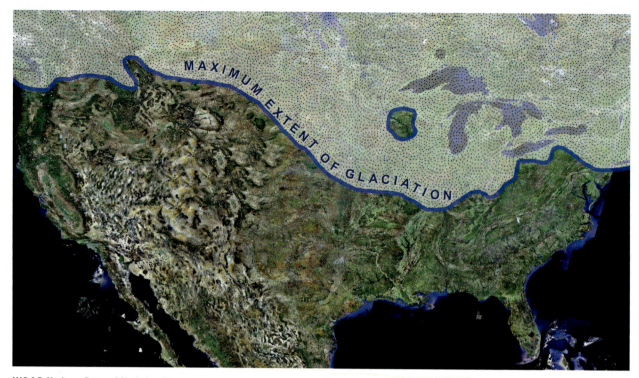

MAP 2.7. Maximum Extent of Glaciation. The southern extent of glaciation from the last round of Pleistocene ice was roughly the Ohio and Missouri rivers.

The Arctic jet stream and the warm, humid Gulf weather influence weather east of the Rocky Mountains. The jet stream is a narrow band of high-speed winds moving from west to east five to ten miles above the surface, and fluctuating north or south depending on air pressure. The jet stream brings more cold weather in the winter when it moves south; in the summer the jet stream tends to retreat north into Canada. The jet stream has commercial value and energy possibilities. Pilots seek out the time- and fuel-saving west-to-east stream to decrease fuel consumption and shorten flying times. Scientists have been studying how to harness the power of the jet stream wind to meet world electricity needs.[8]

The Gulf of Mexico transports moisture-laden winds into the central and southeastern United States and generates climatic events. Fronts occur when cold, heavy polar air collides with the Gulf's tropical air. When warm, moist air collides with a polar air mass, powerful thunderstorms and tornadoes can develop. The cold air stays close to the surface, while the warmer air is pushed upward, cools, and forms clouds and precipitation. Hurricanes often enter into the belly of North America by way of the Gulf.

Precipitation is scattered over the physical landscape. The southeastern low relief allows rainstorms to spread over wide areas, whereas along the western coast the narrow rain bands are forced up mountains, producing **orographic precipitation**. Moisture condenses as the ascending air cools, delivering rain and snow in higher elevations. Upon reaching the mountains' summit, the air descends and warms, and the rains cease, leaving the leeward slopes in the rain shadow found in the Intermontane and east of the Rockies.

Climate Regions

The 100th meridian is a general divide between the wet and humid eastern half of the continent and the drier steppe to the west (Map 2.8). The 38th parallel (just north of San Francisco on the West Coast and just south of Washington, D.C., on the East Coast) separates the southern mild winters from northern "real" winters with snow even at low elevations. The Southwest is very dry, even desert, whereas the Gulf of Mexico influences the much more humid and wet Southeast, although it lies at the same latitude as the Southwest.

The Northeast has four distinct seasons. The interior areas of the Northeast experience a **continental climate** with its more seasonal variation in temperatures, the result of land losing heat more rapidly than water. The Northeast is generally colder, with an annual temperature below 65°F (18°C), although it is often divided between a warmer region to the south with long summers, and a colder region at the 42nd parallel north into Canada along the St. Lawrence lowlands. Annual precipitation averages 30 to 60 inches (75–150 cm) distributed throughout the year (Map 2.9).

The humid, subtropical Southeast has a long growing season enhanced by more than 30 inches (75cm) of annual rain, mostly during the summer months. The average annual temperature is above 67°F (19°C), and frost is infrequent. In the southernmost region, trade winds influence the subtropical to tropical weather.

BOX 2.4 GLOBAL WARMING AND CLIMATE CHANGE

Warming of the climate system is unequivocal, as is now evident from observations of increases in global average air and ocean temperatures, widespread melting of snow and ice and rising global average sea level. Eleven of the last twelve years (1995–2006) rank among the twelve warmest years in the instrumental record of global surface temperature (since 1850).

—International Panel on Climate Change, 2007 *

Temperatures vary, usually within a relatively static range. However, temperatures began to rise during the Industrial Revolution and have increased significantly over the late twentieth century. By 2007, the scientific community agreed that human activities have been the sole or an important cause of climate change.

Global warming and climate change are terms used interchangeably, but climate change is becoming the preferred term because it "helps convey that there are other changes in addition to rising temperatures."† Some of these changes are the position of the sun in relation to Earth, shifts in ocean circulation, and human activities.

Increased carbon dioxide (CO_2) and methane (CH_4) levels are the result. The ensuing climate change has been most noticed in the Arctic, where permafrost is melting and seawater temperatures are increasing. In the past, permafrost areas and tundra were considered **carbon sinks**, places that held more carbon than they released, but climate change indicates these areas are now releasing carbon. This is serious because 14 percent of the world's carbon has been held in the Arctic.‡

Greenhouse gas (GHG) emissions are predominately water vapor (H_2O), carbon dioxide (CO_2), methane (CH_4), and nitrous oxide (N_2O); however, CO_2 has the most global warming potential. In 2008, CO_2 accounted for 80 percent of all human-produced GHGs in the United States.§ The transportation sector is the largest source of CO_2, producing more than 30 percent of the nation's total. CO_2 concentrations have risen from approximately 280 ppm in 1850 to 393.69 ppm (June 2011) and are rising approximately 2 ppm annually. To limit global warming to less than 2°C (approximately 3.5°F), the atmospheric CO_2 concentration must not exceed 450–500 ppm. Current models show this threshold may be surpassed by 2050, even with a large reduction in the use of fossil fuels. It took many years to create the problem and will take many years to alleviate it.

Climate change affects different regions in different ways, depending on a variety of variables measured as indirect effects and parts of complex systems. Reinforcing and balancing **feedback loops** are signs of nonlinear instabilities that can surpass sustainable thresholds and cause irreversible change.

A reinforcing feedback loop in a global warming scenario would be variables that amplify global warming, such as increased methane production from defrosted peat and bogs. Balancing feedback loops stabilize, basically acting as a thermostat, such as dust reflecting from desertification dust storms. The dust reflects light and warmth and therefore decreases warming. Thus reinforcing feedback loops tend to be destabilizing (warming the earth), and balancing feedback loops tend to be stabilizing (opposing warming and maintaining stability). The multiple variable feedback loops that occur have yet to be fully analyzed, but most identified climate change feedback loops are reinforcing. Their amplification may accelerate the phenomena beyond predictions, especially if they do not incorporate complex system loops.

The effects of warming are global, and not solely related to the United States and Canada. Some of the effects are rising global temperatures, extreme weather events, glacier melting, rising sea levels, and loss of biodiversity. Though the effects are now being felt worldwide, those who will be most adversely impacted are the poor, and those living along coastal shores.

The source of the warming has instigated a long controversy and political debate: Did Earth's natural cycle or human action cause the warming cycle? Current theories find human activity raising the levels of multiple greenhouse gases and carbon into the atmosphere from carbon sinks (fossil fuels, coal, hydrocarbons, deforestation).** Cutting down forests and increasing use of fossil fuels together have increased CO_2 levels, trapped the reradiated heat of the sun, and raised temperatures. During the past century, global temperatures have risen more than 1.1°F and are continuing to increase, resulting in shifting weather patterns, chaotic weather events, and changing biodiversity in reaction to the weather conditions.

---

* International Panel on Climate Change (IPCC), *Climate Change 2007: Synthesis Report*, at http://www.ipcc.ch/publications_and_data/publications_ipcc_fourth_assessment_report_synthesis_report.htm

† Environmental Protection Agency (EPA), *Climate Change*, at http://www.epa.gov/climatechange/basicinfo.html

‡ Underlying the tundra, peat stabilizes and regulates the flow of CO_2. When the air warms, peat releases both CH_4 and CO_2, which thaws and destabilizes the regional ecology. The increase in hydrocarbons and carbon oxides raises the surface temperatures and creates a feedback, generating additional CO_2 that affects the global ecosystem. Intergovernmental Panel on Climate Change, 2007, at http://www.ipcc.ch/pdf/assessment-report/ar4/syr/ar4_syr.pdf.

§ National Aeronautics and Space Administration (NASA), "NASA Study Illustrates How Global Peak Oil Could Impact Climate," at http://www.giss.nasa.gov/research/news/20080910/

** International Panel on Climate Change, at http://www.ipcc.ch/

BOX 2.5 THE CARBON CYCLE

Carbon is the basis of all life as we know it. It connects all organic substances, from humans to fossil fuels. Carbon distribution on Earth causes the balances or imbalances in life processes, but it is extremely difficult to measure because of the range of scales from individual plants to continents. Carbon distribution operates at two scales, geologic (long-term) and biologic (short-term).

The geologic **carbon cycle** takes place over millennia. Carbon molecules from space have been hitting Earth over billions of years and are studied as a basic building block of life. Since arriving on Earth, carbon has basically stabilized and been recycled within a closed system. Carbon formed carbonic acid, interacted with water and other minerals and formed insoluble carbonates, which eroded into the ocean, settled, and were drawn into the atmosphere by **subduction** and then reemitted into the atmosphere via volcanic eruption.

The biologic cycle involves photosynthesis and respiration. Solar energy and CO_2 are absorbed by plants and then converted into chemical form as sucrose (carbohydrates), providing the energy that all life forms depend on. Plants use some of the CO_2 as energy, which is returned to the atmosphere. Some plants are crops and their carbon is removed during harvest, but much of the carbon remains in the soil, a carbon sink (repository for CO_2 removed from the atmosphere), and slowly decomposes. Carbon dioxide also results from chemical reactions, such as manufacturing cement, creating pig iron, and fermentation of sugar for alcohol.

This system, locked within the closed system of Earth, has maintained a delicate balance. The amount of carbon in the atmosphere has varied widely though, from 100 times the present CO_2 content billions of years ago to about half the current level during the last ice age. Currently, climate change has become important because it upsets the delicate balance achieved during the era that human occupation has multiplied. Humans have created societies based on a stable environment, and instability in the climate is cause for concern. Climate change for billions is far more complex than for millions, and an overshot economy and political grandstanding in developed countries, such as the United States and Canada, will make them unable to protect their citizenry.

Increased CO_2 levels are at least partially due to the release of carbon into the atmosphere from carbon sinks (such as coal, oil, and gas). Two main causes in the world today are automobiles (a pound of CO_2 is released into the atmosphere with every mile we drive) and deforestation (20 percent of the CO_2 is from burning forests, releasing all the stored carbon sequestered in the trees, plants, and soil). **Carbon sequestration** is removing carbon from the atmosphere and storing it in a reservoir. At this time sequestration is regularly done in agricultural and forest soils in the United States and Canada, while larger sequestering is being attempted, though at great cost and controversy.[*] In Saskatchewan, the world's largest carbon sequestration plant has been operating since 2000 in conjunction with oil recovery.[†] The ocean has also been proposed as a possible site for sequestering, but not without consequences.[‡]

Understanding how humans interact with ecosystems is an important part of finding how humans can live sustainably with nature. As humans study the effect of human intervention on ecosystems, they find that there is either amplification or dampening in an ecosystem's response in relation to what humans have done. This response is what is known as a feedback loop.

If the response increases the ecosystem's action, it is a reinforcing feedback loop; if it reduces or remains stable, it is a balancing feedback loop. Over most of human history, the feedback has been balanced; however, current models of climate change with increased CO_2 levels in the atmosphere indicate a reinforcing feedback loop. The more it amplifies, the more it has the ability to amplify—it continues to further climate change in the direction of warming.

Climate change may alter the traditional feedback loops and create additional problems, rather than solutions. The Earth interacts with all parts of the ecosystems and additional change can happen despite the original intention.[§] Such is the world of unintended consequences, when actions are taken without thinking through complex interactions. While the complexity may seem daunting, systems thinking can begin to avoid many actions and address others. Jobs of the future are waiting on this doorstep.

[*] F. Montagnini and P. K. R. Nair, "Carbon Sequestration: An Underexploited Environmental Benefit of Agroforestry Systems," *Agroforestry Systems* 61–62, nos. 1–3 (July 2004).

[†] Cenovus, at http://www.cenovus.com/operations/technology/co2-enhanced-oil-recovery.html.

[‡] Jessica Marshall, "Ocean Geoengineering Scheme May Prove Lethal," at http://news.discovery.com/earth/geoengineering-carbon-sequestration-phytoplankton.html.

[§] "Climate Change Will Affect Carbon Sequestration in Oceans, Model Shows," *Science News,* September 8, 2005, *at* http://www.sciencedaily.com/releases/2005/09/050908082414.htm.

The Northwest can be wet or dry, depending on its location in relation to the Cascades. The westerly winds of the marine west coast bring moisture from the Pacific Ocean, making this small region from the coast to the Cascades the wettest in the two nations. Most precipitation falls between October and March. The greatest precipitation in the continental United States occurs on the Olympic Mountains, which receives over 150 inches (380 cm) annually. British Columbia's Vancouver Island is the wettest in Canada, receiving 80 to 100 inches (200–250 cm) annually. Most of the region, though, receives around 38 inches (95 cm) of annual rainfall, enough to keep the evergreen forests green, but not enough to deter population growth.

Moving beyond the Cascades, the northern Intermontane and interior prairie of Canada are a climatic world apart from the western shore. Most moisture falls on the windward side of the Cascades. The leeward, drier side of the mountains falls within the rain shadow. Warmer summers and colder winters characterize the Intermontane continental climate.

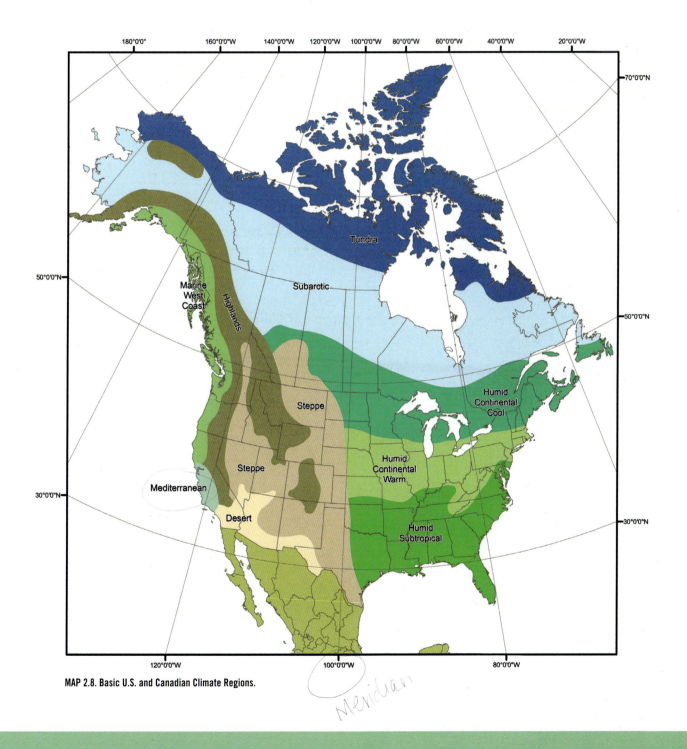

MAP 2.8. Basic U.S. and Canadian Climate Regions.

The Southwest's desert and steppe are the nation's driest and warmest. Seasons vary subtly, with few days below freezing. Most of the region receives less than twenty inches (51 cm) of rain annually; desert areas receive less than five inches (13 cm). The **Mediterranean climate** of the southern Pacific Coast differs from the rest of the United States. Mild but moist winter months average a semiarid fifteen inches (38 cm) of rain annually, but summers are hot and dry. The year-round growing season was a prime attractor for initial settlement.

Extending from the Atlantic to the Pacific and roughly from the 52nd parallel to the 60th parallel, the subarctic region boreal forest continues to the Arctic tree line. A long, dark, cold winter and brief, dry summer dominate the subarctic seasons. The region has little precipitation, as the cool air's tenuous hold on moisture forms less rain or snow. Mountains block warmer Pacific air, and the region is too far north to be influenced by the Gulf of Mexico's warm, moist air.

North of the 60th parallel, the tundra region supports fewer trees, lichen, and plant life. Temperatures rarely exceed 50°F (10°C) at any time during the year, and winter temperatures average –30°F (–34°C). The tundra region receives little precipitation and is often referred to as a polar desert. The ground is covered with mosses, peat, and permafrost.

Soils

Soil is a fundamental element for building a sustainable world. A healthy soil grows food, sequesters carbon, maintains biodiversity, holds moisture, and fights off wildfires. Healthy food production depends on maintaining a healthy soil rich in organic material that both feeds crops and builds soil structure. Synthetic fertilizers may feed plants short-term but will break down soil structure and biotic activity.

Soils are composed of organic matter, living organisms, and weathered layers of rock transported over time by water, wind,

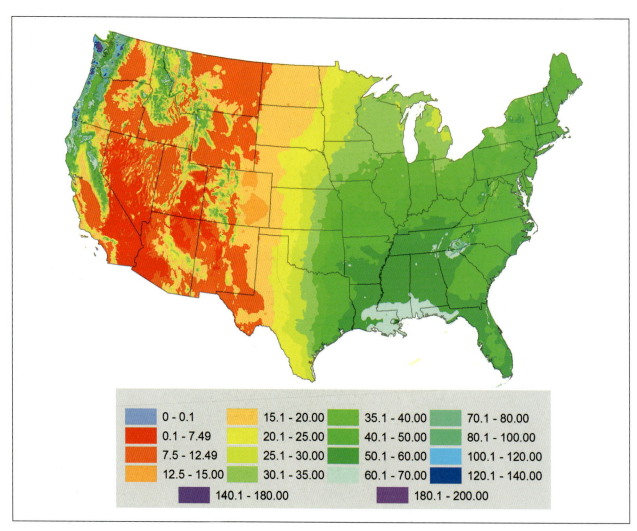

0 - 0.1	15.1 - 20.00	35.1 - 40.00	70.1 - 80.00
0.1 - 7.49	20.1 - 25.00	40.1 - 50.00	80.1 - 100.00
7.5 - 12.49	25.1 - 30.00	50.1 - 60.00	100.1 - 120.00
12.5 - 15.00	30.1 - 35.00	60.1 - 70.00	120.1 - 140.00
	140.1 - 180.00		180.1 - 200.00

MAP 2.9. U.S. Precipitation. Notice how the twenty-inch line falls at about the 100th meridian (the eastern edge of the Oklahoma Panhandle).

BOX 2.6 GEO-TALES: STRANDED IN THE SNOW IN RALEIGH, NORTH CAROLINA

It was January 25, 2000. The conference in Raleigh, North Carolina, was over, and I was returning to Michigan to teach that evening. It was snowing lightly, but this is normal in Michigan, so I didn't give it a second thought—until I realized that none of the airplanes were moving. The few inches of snow had the airport crews in overdrive and falling behind (Photo 2.5).

Runways need to be completely free of snow and ice so that planes can stop quickly and not slide off. Raleigh does not regularly receive measurable snowfall and therefore lacks the snow removal equipment essential in northern cities. Matters were made worse because of a long (for Raleigh) "nor'easter" cold spell. The electronic board began listing cancelled flights. I made the phone call: "Hi, I am snowed in at Raleigh, North Carolina." The storm eventually dumped 20 inches of snow, an airport record at the time. Annual snowfall averages 4.5 inches.

The news that day validated my tardy arrival:

A near-blizzard clobbered North Carolina Tuesday, burying Raleigh's airport under a foot and a half of snow and leaving hundreds of thousands without power. Gov. Jim Hunt declared a

PHOTO 2.5. Snowstorm in Raleigh, North Carolina, January 25, 2000.

state of emergency. . . . The airports in Richmond, Virginia, and Raleigh were closed until further notice.*

The blizzard conditions in Raleigh were repeated in 2009 and 2010.

* CNN, at http://www4.ncsu.edu/~nwsfo/storage/cases/20000125/CNN_news_article.htm

---

or glaciers. A fertile, porous, and structurally sound soil includes stable minerals and organic compounds. Although more than twenty thousand soil types are found in the United States, for the purpose of this book we will only look at the basic soils of the eastern and western United States and the basic soils of Canada and Alaska.

The 100th meridian also divides eastern and western North American soils and vegetation types. Eastern soils are aluminum- and iron-rich and called **pedalfer** (Greek *ped* [soil] + *al* [aluminum] + *fer* [ferrous oxide, which is iron]); western soils are calcium- and lime-rich and called **pedocals** (*pedo* [soil] + *cal* [calcium]) (Map 2.10).

Pedalfer soils receive more precipitation and can be productive soils because the clay content holds water near the surface. But the precipitation may also leach nutrients and diminish soil fertility. Pedocal soils are quite fertile because precipitation rarely reaches the water table and soil nutrients are recycled, but the lack of water limits agricultural productivity.

Many Canadian boreal soils are acidic due to the lack of leaf litter. In the grasslands, soils tend to be black and rich in calcium carbonate. In the north, peat forms in poorly drained, waterlogged permafrost ground.

Organic material and soil organisms make up the nutrient-rich topsoil, which forms slowly—about 1 inch every five hundred to one thousand years. In the United States, topsoil erosion is about eighteen times faster than formation. Protecting the topsoil from erosion is the first step toward sustainable soil and agricultural production. Topsoil erosion during the 1930s Dust Bowl was caused by tilling, drought, and ill-managed land. Subsequent soil management programs introduced conservation tillage, contour plowing, and terracing.

Natural processes form soil types specific to place. A pedologist (one who studies soil) can tell a great deal about a place by an integrated reading of the parent material rock, climate, precipitation, and vegetation. For example, prior to European settlement, the Great Plains grasslands had the necessary tillage (soil organisms and bison hooves) and fertilizer (bison manure and decomposed grasses) for maintaining healthy soils. Soil erosion accelerated when the dense Plains grasslands were replaced by cultivation and the livestock shifted from bison, whose diet is based on perennial grasses, to cattle, whose diet requires more forbs and processed feed. In addition, bison hooves break up the ground and allow water penetration, while cattle hooves pack soil and cause more soil erosion.

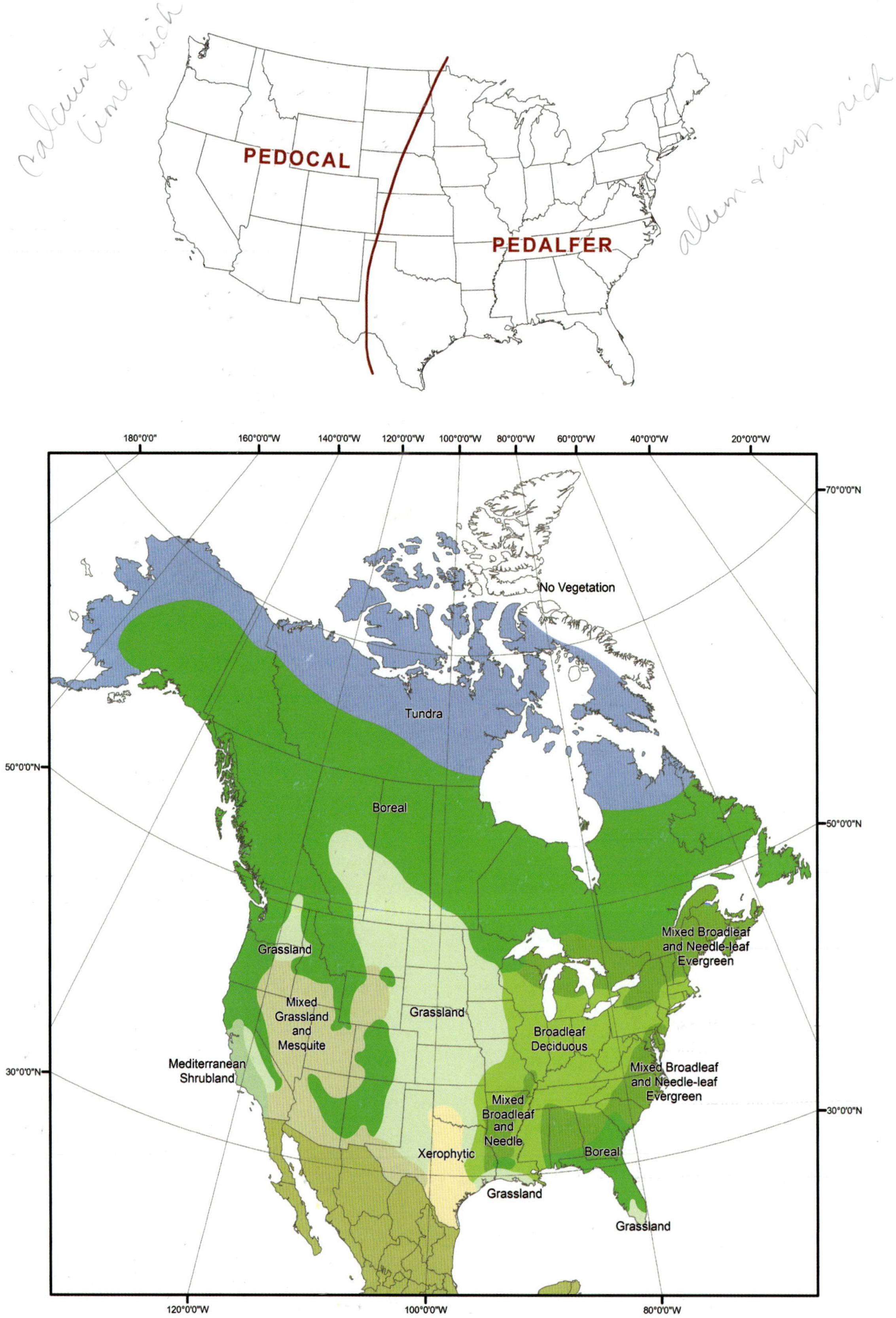
calcium & lime rich
PEDOCAL
PEDALFER
alum & iron rich
180°0'0"
160°0'0"W
140°0'0"W
120°0'0"W
100°0'0"W
80°0'0"W
60°0'0"W
40°0'0"W
20°0'0"W
70°0'0"N
50°0'0"N
30°0'0"N
No Vegetation
Tundra
Boreal
Grassland
Mixed Broadleaf and Needle-leaf Evergreen
Mixed Grassland and Mesquite
Grassland
Broadleaf Deciduous
Mediterranean Shrubland
Mixed Broadleaf and Needle-leaf Evergreen
Mixed Broadleaf and Needle
Xerophytic
Boreal
Grassland
Grassland
120°0'0"W
100°0'0"W
80°0'0"W

MAP 2.10. Soil Type (top) and Major Vegetation Regions (bottom). Vegetation type is related to climate, precipitation, altitude, and latitude. The soil type is also related to each of these variables and helps determine what grows where. Pedocal soils are drier and have a layer of calcium carbonate that lessens leaching, whereas pedalfer soils receive more precipitation and many nutrients are leached from the soil.

Anything done to change soil, such as changing fauna, draining wetlands, or irrigating crops, disturbs existing ecosystems. A sustainable soil maintains its natural profile and reflects its ecological community.

Ecological Communities

Interactions between the living and nonliving environments range in scale from small patches to a dynamic interacting global system. Within ecosystems are diverse ecological communities that function as wholes. Ecosystems are nested within larger ecosystems, all related. An ecosystem is not merely a group of organisms that share space, but a community of organisms that cooperate and compete for resources, resulting in a whole that is more than the sum of the parts. Each ecosystem member has some functions in common with the others, such as recycling nutrients, using the sun's energy, creating soil, and maintaining a healthy environment. As part of the ecosystem structure, humans depend on ecosystem health. A healthy system benefits humans, a sick ecosystem degrades the quality of life.

Ecological communities influence one another and are never static. Energy flows continually between the producer, consumer, and decomposer levels. Most ecosystem energy flows produce little if any waste. Only humans produce voluminous waste. Human consumers produce hazardous and intrusive waste in ecosystems. Although many early cultural groups lived symbiotically with ecological communities, modern humans have often lost this dynamic equilibrium, causing waste, pollution, and species loss.

Re-creating a healthy landscape necessitates establishing a point of reference that describes the landscape before significant human intrusion. Since ecological communities are living, dynamic systems, it is difficult to establish a "natural" reference. Pre-European settlement is usually chosen as the baseline, but studies have revealed that the landscape was not pristine before European arrival: Native American tribes had altered the landscape to fit their needs and cultures.

What follows is a basic division of ecological communities on a semicontinental scale that includes vegetation and wildlife in relation to landforms, climate, and soil. The three major divisions are eastern (wet, forest), western (dry, grassland), and boreal (cool, coniferous forest).

Eastern Community

European settlers encountered the eastern ecological community upon arrival from Europe. The physical and climatic makeup of the Atlantic coast, especially the northern coast, was similar to the English homeland and was called New England. Farther south, the English favored the climate and vegetation for the variety of crops unable to be grown in England.

Eastern ecological communities' ample precipitation patterns support broadleaf deciduous hardwoods in the lowlands and conifers at higher elevations and latitudes or on poor soils. In the northern regions, deciduous hardwood forests have

added organic leaf litter that enriched agricultural soil. The midwestern deciduous forests do best in rich loamy soils. Pines grow best in nutrient-deficient sandy soils, as in the Pine Barrens of New Jersey or the Atlantic and Gulf coastal plains.

From the coast to the Midwest, the presettlement landscape was forested, but few native forests survived agricultural settlement. However, some land was abandoned and new forests emerged or were planted. In New England, the cutover forests were often abandoned because of the stony soil remnants of ice age drift. The settlers either turned away from agriculture and toward the sea or moved west as the land opened for settlement. In the Tidewater South, lands were cut over but often abandoned later because of poor soil management. Forests, often tree plantations, now occupy much of the land again.

Large carnivores such as bison retreated from the eastern community after European settlement. Deer, raccoons, and squirrels remain and even thrive despite dense human settlement.

Western Community

The drier western grasslands have the potential to evaporate more moisture than they gain from precipitation. Seasonal rains support grasses but inadequately support forests. Most native grasslands have been converted to abundant agricultural production, which benefits for a limited time from recycled nutrients and irrigation. However, the loss of the long, rooted grasses that maintained moisture and held the soil in place has caused erosion. Crops forced to yield beyond natural limits have become unsustainable due to fossil fuel–based inputs.

The Intermontane is the driest region. In the Basin and Range desert, **xerophytic** plants (cactus, yucca, and creosote) have adapted to the dry conditions by limiting water loss and storing moisture in their stems.

Since the 1960s, the Great Plains and Intermontane have depended on irrigation to increase agricultural production. However, irrigation has caused land degradation, which alters vegetation, soils, and water distribution. Irrigation has encouraged farmers to grow crops that are inappropriate for this arid region, such as corn or cotton. Irrigation may be sustainable if the land grows appropriate crops for the region.

Presettlement grasslands supported bison and antelope. Most native wildlife has been killed. Only a few species—coyotes, rattlesnakes, and a variety of lizards and other reptiles—survive today in what has become the overgrazed cattle and sheep ranches that require land management systems to maintain pasture health.

Boreal Forest

The continent-wide boreal forest, or **taiga**, ranges from Labrador to the Bering Sea and extends in latitude from the northern Prairie to the tundra. The boreal forest also extends across Asia and Europe and is the world's largest **biome**—a geographic area defined by its climate, soil, plants, and animals. Boreal trees include coniferous needle-leaf evergreens, including firs, spruces, and pines, and small-leaved deciduous trees such as birches and willows.

The boreal ecosystem receives little precipitation but is inundated with wetlands due to low evaporation rates and underlying discontinuous permafrost. The appearance of continuous permafrost marks the transition to tundra.

Some of the denizens of the boreal region are black bears, gray wolves, moose, and beavers. Black bears are found throughout North America but especially in the boreal forest. Gray wolves have occupied the entire boreal forest area. Moose live in the boreal forest of Canada and the Atlantic Northeast. The beaver is an environment-influencing animal that builds systems of dams and canals, resulting in ponds where they live. Most are found in the boreal forest today, although during the early nineteenth century they were hunted almost to extinction across the United States and Canada.

North of the boreal forest, mosses, lichens, and the shallow-rooted black spruce constitute the permafrost tundra vegetation.

Vegetation and Climate Change

Climate change has affected the forested vegetation in the United States and Canada, although often in unpredictable, nonlinear patterns far more complex than science has been able to unravel. Vegetation shifts between 1990 and 2010 show that gardening hardiness zones may have shifted in a warming direction, although the evidence is as yet inconclusive.

Biota in ecosystems react to climate change unevenly. Additionally, extreme weather may also affect forest productivity, causing storm damage, fires, and increased pest populations.

While it might seem that the northern regions will benefit most as species migrate from the southern regions, each biota has its own climatic tolerances. The tolerances of each plant and animal in an ecosystem vary; as climatic patterns shift, ecosystems will change. The South may lose the most because of the drying effects of warmer weather and pests on its current large forest stock.[9] Vegetation shifts may be seemingly chaotic until the science of complexity understands the movement and stable patterns are reestablished.

Natural Hazards

Natural disasters, such as earthquakes, hurricanes, tornadoes, and volcanic eruptions, are radical disruptions in systems and may be growing in magnitude due to climate change. But understanding the interrelations of the multiple variables is a complex science still in its infancy. Adding to the complexity is population increase and the concomitant surpassing of the human carrying capacity, which makes each natural disaster more economically devastating.

An additional problem is understanding humans' place in the ecological world. The current worldview of controlling or conquering nature places humans outside the natural system. While levees, human-made lakes, dams, and numerous other human contrivances have temporarily contributed to economic

success, they have also added to desertification, erosion, deforestation, depletion of the fisheries, loss of biodiversity, excessive energy consumption, and destruction of coastal environments. Ameliorating these effects will require learning to live more in tune with nature. Many of these subjects will be the focus of regional environmental topics in the coming chapters.

Many disturbances in the natural environment have been indirectly caused or exacerbated by human intervention or the stresses placed on the environment by continued population growth. Some of these "natural" disasters include:

- Drought: Abnormally dry weather in regions that depend on precipitation to provide food and water for the entire biotic community. Major drought conditions throughout the Great Plains in the 1930s created the Dust Bowl, caused by farmers leaving the dry topsoil exposed to the wind. While lessons were learned from the Dust Bowl, continued droughts are still a problem. In 2006, a continued drought throughout the Southeast hindered growing populations, fisheries, and energy usage. In 2008, California vegetation left dry due to long-term drought was susceptible to lightning strikes and erupted into fires during the early summer months.
- Aerosols: Airborne particles, such as smoke and dust, irritate eyes and lungs and sometimes cause serious medical problems. Smoke and smog can also decrease visibility for drivers. Aerosols are still not held accountable for the damage they do. During a five-year dry spell beginning in 2006, Texas had a spate of fires that sent aerosols into the atmosphere. The aerosol effects of these fires were similar to the devastating 1930s Dust Bowl storms.
- Fire: Lightning and volcanic eruptions are fires caused by other than human intervention. Organisms have adapted to fire as part of their lifecycle. In the Great Plains' grasslands or California's sequoia forests, the effect of wildfire on native vegetation has been positive, clearing invasive species, adding nutrients to soil, and germinating seeds. Fire is a natural part of many cycles of plant life, but human intervention has caused major fires and interrupted these cycles. Western culture has traditionally viewed wildfire as negative and attempted to prevent wildfires and extinguish them when they occur. The U.S. policy toward fires has changed since the 1960s from total suppression to controlled burns, such as in Yellowstone National Park in 1988. Within months of the burn, the vegetation began to regrow and the forest became healthier.
- Severe storms: Massive storms such as tornadoes, flash floods, and hurricanes have been a subject of inquiry on the North American continent. Tornadoes, which occur when massive fronts collide, are most common in the United States, especially in Tornado Alley, where they are now watched closely. Early warning systems have

BOX 2.7 SEA LEVEL RISE

Climate change leading to global warming has taken center stage in the twenty-first century. Scientific evidence and on-the-ground analysis reveal physical changes that will continue to affect both the United States and Canada. One of the most serious, sea level rise, will have increasing environmental and human costs. Sea level rise will affect wetland resources, recreational opportunities, coastal development, and coastal habitats for all forms of life. While all coastal areas will be affected, the Atlantic and Gulf coasts are the most threatened because their wide and low coastal plains have emerged and been submerged throughout history, as climatic conditions warrant.

Global climate weather models have consistently predicted increased sea levels of 0.6 and 2 feet (0.18 to 0.59 meters) by 2100, more than double the sea level change in the twentieth century, which will therefore have a disastrous impact on coastal communities, especially where the coastal plain is widest and lowest, such as along the Chesapeake Basin to the barrier islands off the South Atlantic coast and the Louisiana coastline.* These regions are especially vulnerable because of low-lying topography and the possibility of intense and frequent storms, and they are one of the most populated and built-up areas within the nation.

Along the Atlantic and Gulf coastal areas, sea level rise could inundate up to 22,000 square miles (35,000 km^2) of land and force cities such as New York, Washington, D.C., Miami, and New Orleans to upgrade their flood defenses and drainage systems or face adverse consequences.

The Pacific coast is not as vulnerable, except for the heavily populated and low-lying areas in San Francisco Bay and Puget Sound.

* Environmental Protection Agency (EPA), at http://epa.gov/climatechange/effects/coastal/index.html.

---

saved lives and reduced property losses. However, severe tornadoes in the spring of 2011 and 2012 killed hundreds despite early warning systems. The increased intensity of tornadoes, flash floods, and hurricanes may be linked to climate change, but this is still a subject of scientific debate.

- Earthquakes formed by the grinding of plate boundaries release energy measured on the Richter scale. Most earthquakes occur along the Pacific Ocean Ring of Fire. Major earthquakes have struck Alaska and California in the past century. In 1964, Alaska had one of the largest earthquakes ever recorded (9.2). California has had several major quakes: the San Francisco earthquakes of 1906 (6.9 estimate) and 1989 (7.1) and the Northridge earthquake of 1994 (6.7). The fact that few lives have been lost has been attributed to higher building standards in the United States. But building standards aside, the cost of a "big one" in California, where one in eight Americans resides, may be more than the United States can afford.

- Earthquakes, meteorite impacts, landslides, or volcanic eruptions cause the massive displacement of water that creates tsunamis. Tsunamis caught the world's attention in late 2004, when an offshore earthquake in Indonesia generated a devastating wave that destroyed shoreline communities across the Indian Ocean basin, killing hundreds of thousands and reducing entire villages to rubble. Tsunamis were once again destructive in 2011, when Japan was struck by major earthquakes and resulting tsunamis. The United States has also been the recipient of tsunamis on the Atlantic and Pacific coasts, as well as Hawai'i and Alaska. Tsunami prediction can now occur after a wave is generated, but it gives little time to protect life and property.

Sustainability

A growing human population, industry, and consumption have resulted in the extinction of other species and exceeded a sustainable human carrying capacity. Developed countries have prospered, while diminishing the quality of life for millions of people around the globe. Examples of natural resource overexploitation are legion: collapsing fish stocks, deforestation, fossil fuel consumption, decreased water quantity and quality, depleted soils, erosion, desertification, and air-water-land pollution. All are tied to an economic system that does not hold the polluter accountable for environmental degradation. The result has placed the cost for pollution and waste on the consumer.

Preventing, adapting, and mitigating the many human and natural impacts on the physical environment requires a long-term sustainable relationship. For example, cut forests are replanted, and many cities are now seeking ways to use renewable energy and encouraging water and fuel conservation.

Canada and the United States have taken different paths toward sustainability and climate change. The average Canadian conserves more than Americans and is less dependent on fossil fuels for electricity, but Canada is also one of the major producers of oil sand fossil fuels, which are among the most polluting and intense greenhouse gas emitters in the world.

Climate change affected the northern physical landscape of Canada before it affected more temperate areas to the south. Because of this, Canada has been at the forefront with many energy-efficient initiatives. In 2009, the United States began to shift its focus toward more sustainable energy and business practices; however, a long-term recession has left the country in an economic crisis that stymies many sustainable investments.

The potential consequences of climate change may be the reason that many people adapt to more sustainable practices, but living sustainably reaches beyond climate change. The sustainable life is a long-term acceptance of living in an ecological dynamic equilibrium and therefore leaving future generations with a healthy, bountiful Earth. The first step to living sustainably, though, is to move beyond thinking we can control nature and to choose to know and work with the land.

Questions for Discussion

1. Are humans a part of nature or apart from nature? Justify your answer.

2. Do most Americans live as though they are a part of or apart from nature? Justify.

3. Give an example of increased severe weather patterns in the past decade and how they might be tied to climate change.

4. Where are the most active physical landforms on the North American continent and why is it so?

5. How are soil and other ecological communities interconnected?

6. Where has climate change been most evident? What are some of the signs?

Suggested Readings

Ahrens, C. Donald. *Meteorology Today.* 6th ed. St. Paul, Minn.: Brooks/Cole, 1999.

Atwood, Wallace W. *The Physiographic Provinces of North America.* Boston: Ginn, 1940.

Briggs, David, et al., eds. *Fundamentals of the Physical Environment.* London: Routledge, 1997.

The Canadian System of Soil Classification. Agriculture and Agri-Food Canada Publication 1646. 3rd ed. Ottawa: NRC Research Press M-55, Soil Classification Working Group, 1998.

Chase, Alston. *Playing God in Yellowstone.* Fort Washington, Pa.: Harvest Books, 1987.

Christopherson, Robert. *Geosystems.* Upper Saddle River, N.J.: Prentice Hall, 2005.

Condie, Kent C. *Plate Tectonics and Crustal Evolution.* 4th ed. Burlington, Mass.: Butterworth-Heinemann, 1997.

Gersmehl, Philip J. "Soil Taxonomy and Mapping." *Annals of Association of American Geographers* 67, no. 3 (1977): 419–28.

Grossman, D. H., et al. *International Classification of Ecological Communities: Terrestrial Vegetation of the United States.* Vol. 1, *The National Vegetation Classification System: Development, Status, and Applications.* Arlington, Va.: The Nature Conservancy, 1998.

Hunt, Charles B. *Natural Regions of the United States and Canada.* San Francisco: Freeman, 1973.

Jones, Alan G., et al. "Electric Lithosphere of the Slave Craton." *Geology* 29 no. 5 (May 2001): 423–26.

Mackenzie, F. T., and J. A. Mackenzie. *Our Changing Earth: An Introduction to Earth System Science and Global Environmental Change.* Upper Saddle River, N.J.: Prentice Hall, 1995.

Rogers, John J. *A History of the Earth.* New York: Cambridge University Press, 1993.

Sedjo, Roger A. *The Forest Sector: Important Innovations.* Discussion Paper 97-42. Washington D.C.: Resources for the Future, 1997.

Thornbury, William D. *Regional Geomorphology of the United States.* New York: Wiley, 1965.

Trenhaile, Alan S. *Geomorphology: A Canadian Perspective.* Toronto: Oxford University Press. 1997.

Wilson, E. O. *The Diversity of Life.* New York: Norton, 1992.

Internet Sources

The Nature Conservancy: Rivers and Lakes, at http://www.nature.org/initiatives/freshwater/.

Geological History of Jamestown, Rhode Island, at http://www.jamestown-ri.info/prelude.htm.

Intergovernmental Panel on Climate Change, at http://www.ipcc.ch/.

National Aeronautics and Space Administration (NASA), Natural Hazards, at http://earthobservatory.nasa.gov/NaturalHazards/.

Peakbagger.com, at http://www.peakbagger.com/.

U.S. Geological Survey, History of Wetlands in the Conterminous United States, at http://water.usgs.gov/nwsum/WSP2425/history.html.

U.S. National Atlas, at http://www.nationalatlas.gov/.

The Atlas of Canada, at http://atlas.nrcan.gc.ca/site/english/index.html.

PHOTO 3.1. Wind Turbines near Rock Springs, Wyoming. Wind power provides only 1 percent of America's energy. Ninety-two percent of energy in the United States is nonrenewable and polluting.

3
SUSTAINABILITY
Redefining Progress

Chapter Highlights

After reading this chapter, you should be able to:

- Explain the triple bottom line
- Describe cradle-to-cradle production
- Distinguish between nonrenewable and renewable energy resources
- Define the ecological footprint
- Discuss the differences between sprawl and smart growth

Terms

biofuel	ecological footprint	natural capital	sprawl
biomimicry	Kyoto Protocol	nonpoint source pollution	sustainable development
cradle to cradle (C2C)	Leadership in Energy and	nonrenewable resource	transit-oriented
cradle to grave (C2G)	Environmental Design	point source pollution	developments (TODs)
downcycle	(LEED)	renewable resource	triple bottom line
	life cycle assessment	smart growth	wind turbine

Introduction

I am not an advocate for frequent changes in laws and constitutions, but laws and institutions must go hand in hand with the progress of the human mind. As that becomes more developed, more enlightened, as new discoveries are made, new truths discovered and manners and opinions change, with the change of circumstances, institutions must advance also to keep pace with the times. We might as well require a man to wear still the coat which fitted him when a boy as civilized society to remain ever under the regimen of their barbarous ancestors.

—Thomas Jefferson, 1810[1]

Geography is the study of humans and their interactions with the environment, and as such, championing a sustainable biosphere is a natural part of the discipline. Throughout history, humans have interacted with and affected the places they inhabit, resulting in cultures and landscapes being imposed on ecosystems. All life forms and Earth movements impact ecosystems, but humans have hyperactively altered ecosystems.

Human impact in the past has worked within the larger global ecological balance, but since the Industrial Revolution the reliance on **nonrenewable resources**, those that cannot be renewed as quickly as they are consumed, has had the unintended consequence of population growth and consumerism based on unlimited resources in a limited world.

The modern age worked on only an economic, profit-based model, while the ecological age recognizes limits and the external costs of environment and social equity, such as waste, pollution, and social injustice. Including environmental and social equity within the cost of goods reflects the full cost to the consumer. Including environmental and social equity costs with the economic is called the **triple bottom line**, "planet, people, and profit."

The ecological age will reduce many impacts of the original Industrial Revolution, such as climate change and greenhouse gases, but it will not be easy, simple, or completely green. It will reduce the human impact, not eliminate it. Many of the suggested

BOX 3.1 TRIPLE BOTTOM LINE

changes will still have toxic elements, still be consumptive, and still cause pollution, but the impact can be reduced and brought to sustainable levels.

In the two hundred years since the Industrial Revolution, the actions of humans and the growing population have had measurable effects on the dynamic equilibrium of Earth's ecosystems. Humans have used water and resources, and they have built an infrastructure that has traumatized the biosphere. This chapter will examine the importance of water and resource use in a sustainable world, renewable and nonrenewable energy sources, and the environmental impact of the human-built world.

Water

There is no life without water, and yet freshwater is in short supply. While it would behoove us to make water systems an integral part of ecosystems, allocating water to satisfy economic or political interests has been the practice. For example, political borders divide watersheds arbitrarily. As population and water use have increased, serious disputes have arisen over allocations, causing people to fight over the divisions in the watersheds. Each political entity fights to gain water in relation to themselves, and not for the benefit of the watersheds, ecosystems, and the common good, not for the benefit of the community, the society. Water wars occur in expected regions, such as the deserts of Arizona and Nevada, but also in unexpected regions, such as the humid Southeastern states, where population growth and a lack of conserving water have depleted supplies. Adding to the water worries is the decline in freshwater quantity and quality.

Water pollution has been a long-standing problem in both countries. Approximately 40 percent of U.S. freshwater is polluted, and Canada continues to dump raw sewage into the open sea.[2] Water may be affected by either **point source pollution** or **nonpoint source pollution**. Point sources are identified in specific locations, such as industrial plants or agricultural feedlots. Government regulations have mitigated many point sources. However, diffuse nonpoint sources, such as crops and urban runoff, are difficult to control and remain the largest source of water-quality issues. The most common pollutants are nutrients and sediment.

Nutrients usually have agricultural origins; excess nitrogen and phosphorus are the most egregious, the result of overfertilization by inorganic or synthetic fertilizers dependent on nonrenewable fossil fuels. Sediment picked up by flowing water is deposited in streams and groundwater. Pesticides, salts, oil, and heavy metals are also common nonpoint pollutants.

The amount of water on Earth is finite, and water is continually reused. Climate change and environmental degradation have limited clean water. Virtually all freshwater requires some form of purification process for human consumption. Even water from high-elevation mountain streams requires water filtration to eliminate giardia or other organisms.

Government agencies manage water use. In the United States, the federal Bureau of Reclamation manages water; Environment Canada manages Canadian water. Navigable waterways were the government's first responsibility, but later federally subsidized water development projects increased water supplies. As the countries industrialized, water quality degraded and water issues became a subject of public concern. In 1970, the Canada Water Act addressed water-quality standards, while in 1972 the United States passed the Clean Water Act to restore integrity to the nation's waters. Although there were some environmentally important aspects to the change, water usage was still defined for human use alone and not for ecosystems and the common good. Dumping pollutants in waterways has also continued, by those who choose to ignore laws or find loopholes to evade clean water standards.

The result has been an uneven and ill-managed water system that was meant to support economic development alone and not the more inclusive triple bottom line. The response to environmental degradation has been a more holistic water-quality-management system that includes biodiversity, ecosystem integrity, and public health. However, a truly sustainable water use program will require managing water ecologically within watershed boundaries while respecting social equity and economics.[3]

As the demand for water grows, more attention is diverted to Canada's 7 percent of global renewable freshwater. Canadians have been happy to sell their oil and gas, but they have drawn the line at selling water to the United States. Canadians have abundant freshwater and do not have the water shortages of the

United States, but Canadian water pollution and water rights *Riparian rights* are issues. For example, in 2000 *E. coli* from agricultural runoff contaminated the water of Walkerton, Ontario, resulting in illness in 2,500 and seven deaths. Turning water into a private commodity rather than a public resource has threatened some Canadian towns, as have bottled water issues. Several Canadian municipalities, including Toronto, have restricted bottled water sales to halt commodification of water and to decrease the amount of plastic in landfills.

Both the United States and Canada are in need of leadership and policies to conserve and protect their water.

Resource Use

The old American dream was built on a vision of economic growth. For generations, immigrants have poured into the United States seeking to reap the wealth of geographic expansion and booming industry. Now that the United States and the rest of humanity have begun to confront the natural limits to our resources, however, we are in need of a new vision—a vision of a sustainable economy.

—Herman Daly, 2003[4]

Exploiting natural resources has provided a comfortable life for people in the industrialized nations, including Canadians and Americans, but at the cost of pollution, waste, and the exploitation of people. Recycling has been an incomplete answer to resource extraction, because recycling goods for new uses is often impossible because of the product's original construction. Recycling has often been little more than a "feel good" action.

Recycling rates have varied across the globe. Sweden, where renewable energy has been emphasized, is one of the most efficient recyclers. Sweden recycles more than 42 percent of all aluminum and plastic containers (2008). The United States creates more waste per person than any other country, nearly a ton per person annually (1642 pounds), but only 33 percent is recycled (2008), excluding hazardous waste (Table 3.1). Canada's per-person waste produced was 921 pounds annually, and Canada's recycling rate has been about 27 percent (2004).[5] Clearly there is

room for improving the rate and methods of reusing resources; in fact, there is room to improve what recycling is.

Twentieth-century recycling revolved around reducing wastes via street-side bins or recycling centers. Recycling produced **downcycled** goods. Each time a good is downcycled its quality and value is degraded, until it is disposed of as waste. Examples of downcycled goods are recycling plastics to a lesser quality, office paper to toilet paper, reusing towels or old clothes for cleaning, or breaking apart computers to retrieve valuable metals.

Recycling or downcycling goods has been hampered by the toxicity or contaminants within the original engineering, collection costs, or landfill costs, which lead to a lack of market demand. Without demand, the curbside "recycled" materials may go directly to a landfill because they are too expensive to recycle. Goods that are recycled are often downcycled, considered disposable, and may soon end up as waste. Downcycling to lower quality and eventual disposal is termed **cradle to grave (C2G)**, and it increases waste. Everything in nature has a purpose and therefore produces no waste, but humans have a propensity for creating waste. Goods have been engineered for short-term use, for being thrown "away," rather than seeking long-term reuse of limited natural resources.

C2G is a term used in **life cycle assessment**—the impact of a good through all stages of its useful life. A product's life cycle follows it from the raw materials used to produce it, through manufacturing, use, and ultimate disposal. Along the way, the product's environmental and social costs are factored in. A good life cycle assessment includes transportation, waste, emissions, energy and water use, and labor costs. In C2G, the good ends up disposed in a landfill.

An item that is taken back at the end of its useful life and its components or materials then used in a new product of equal or higher value is termed **cradle to cradle (C2C)**, a process that more closely mimics nature. C2C production minimizes environmental impact and aims for more sustainable production as well as social responsibility.[6]

TABLE 3.1. U.S. Recycling Activity, 1960–2008

Activity	1960	1970	1980	1990	2000	2007	2008
Generation (million tons)	88.1	121.1	151.6	205.2	239.1	254.6	249.6
Recovery for recycling	6.4	6.6	9.6	14.2	22.1	24.9	33.0
Recovery for composting	Neg.	Neg.	Neg.	2.0	6.9	8.5	8.8
Total materials recovery	6.4	6.6	9.6	16.2	29.0	33.4	33.2
Discards to landfills	93.6	93.1	88.6	69.3	56.9	54.0	54.0

Source: Environmental Protection Agency, at http://www.epa.gov/epawaste/nonhaz/municipal/pubs/msw2008rpt.pdf
Note: %, unless otherwise noted

The twenty-first century is about moving toward the C2C, closed-loop recirculation of materials, reducing waste, stopping pollution, acting responsibly, and using resources and their by-products many times and in many forms. C2C limits extracting primary resources and is more energy efficient. However, C2C will be difficult to achieve. While C2C brings us closer to how nature operates, this has not been the chosen path of the developed countries. The production of goods has emphasized short-term use for profit alone. The common mind-set in developed countries is geared toward the short-term and cheap product, rather than the more efficient and reusable product over a longer time span. The development of a C2C economy is a path to the jobs of the future. These jobs do not yet exist and offer tremendous opportunities.

Biomimicry is one path to C2C; it aims to minimize human problems by mimicking nature's creations. Biomimicry studies designs in nature to find solutions to human problems through advanced technologies. Biomimicry thrives on low-energy and high-efficiency sources, is often toxin-free, and uses closed-loop feedback processes. By using nature as a model to solve human problems, we are living closer to how the natural world works and therefore more sustainably. Biomimicry has already been changing how people study the natural world. One of the first products that used biomimicry was Velcro. Velcro originated in 1941 when an engineer in the Swiss Alps was removing burrs from his dog and became curious about how the burrs worked. He pursued how to implement his idea for several years before finding the solution after working with textile manufacturers. Another example of biomimicry is sonar technology, which was developed after studying how bats and whales use echolocation (sound waves) for navigation. Biomimicry combined with C2C production has the ability to alter the manufacturing environment in the developed world.

During the latter twentieth century, both the United States and Canada outsourced their manufacturing economy. The reasons are multiple: lower labor costs and evading pollution laws, but also because the existing manufacturing economy is based on unsustainable resource use. At first, manufacturing locations moved within the United States; for example, the textile industry moved from the Northeast to the Piedmont of the Atlantic South. Later, foreign auto manufacturers chose right-to-work states over union states where auto manufacturing had flourished. When profits dropped, manufacturing left the country without considering the environmental impact and social costs of the move for America and Canada as well as the new manufacturing centers. Outsourcing was a short-term fix for a long-term problem—operating in a cradle-to-grave economy. C2C, studying life cycle assessment, and biomimicry are the paths to the next Industrial Revolution, a sustainable revolution. The new manufacturing model requires innovating and studying how nature works, but ultimately it will create more jobs in a healthier and sustainable economy that will help to lead the world.

By working with nature instead of exploiting and trying to overcome nature, the new manufacturing process allows more recyclable products, rather than the ineffective recycling of the twentieth century. The cradle-to-cradle manufacturing model offers long-term sustainability by improving efficiency and reducing waste.

Universities and companies are beginning to use nature as a model. At MIT, scientists are creating innovations such as storage of solar power and energy production by learning and imitating the paths of photosynthesis.[7] In San Rafael, California, Pax Scientific is using the swirling patterns (not in a straight line) of natural fluid flow to emulate nature to increase energy efficiency.[8] There are unlimited opportunities for innovation open to those willing to work in the new paradigm.

Energy

The human impact on Earth has become increasingly pronounced since the Industrial Revolution. Since 1850 the human population has grown sevenfold and become dependent on fossil fuels to accommodate the consumption and technology of the developed countries. As humans relied on fossil fuel energy, their relationship with the environment and resources veered from a sustainable "working with" nature to an unsustainable "conquering" of nature.

Prior to the Industrial Revolution, humans used renewable resources: sun, wind, water, wood, and human and animal energy. When humans began to depend on nonrenewable sources—resources that cannot be replaced on a human time scale—the quality of life for developed countries improved over the short-term (geologically speaking). However, local resources were exploited beyond replacement, and developed countries began importing resources from less developed countries—for example, the developed world came to depend on oil from the Middle East.

The availability of fossil fuels enabled technological advances that transformed the quality of life. While this has been a huge advantage for some humans, it was balanced by losses for other humans and the rest of the natural world. The fossil fuel–dependent paradigm was based on the idea of Earth's being for humans' exclusive use.[9] For a short period of geologic time, humans have multiplied, consumed resources, and created and dumped waste. While the natural world creates little if any waste, humans, a part of the natural world, have been littering the planet with their waste. The oceans are filled with discarded plastic debris that is not biodegradable, indicating that a fossil fuel–dependent life is a life out of balance with the rest of nature. As a result, climate is changing and ecosystems are compromised due to human intervention. In the oceans, marine organisms are ingesting plastic bits thinking they are food, and becoming sick and dying. To return to a healthy planet will require that humans accept responsibility for their actions by reducing waste and pollution and breaking the addiction to nonrenewable resources.

Fossil fuel is a short-term proposition that is nearing its end as a cheap and sustainable energy source. The developed world grew wealthy on the "progress" of releasing carbon-based

BOX 3.2 DID YOU KNOW . . . ENERGY USE

- The United States and Canada, with about 5 percent of the world's population, consume about one-third of world energy.
- On a per capita basis, Canada uses more energy than the United States (9.53 [Canada], 7.82 [U.S.], 1.58 [world] metric tonnes of oil equivalent).
- The average person in the United States uses twenty-five times more resources than a person in developing countries such as those in sub-Sahara Africa (excluding South Africa).
- Five Earths would be necessary if everyone in the world were to live like an average American.

- Ninety-two percent of the energy used in the United States is nonrenewable.
- Eight percent of current energy consumption in the United States is renewable.* Hydropower and biomass provide 84 percent of renewable energy. Wind and solar power create less than 3 percent of total energy production.
- Nuclear energy produces 9 percent of consumed electricity.
- The United States and China were the top oil consumers in 2009. Chinese oil consumption is increasing seven times faster than U.S. consumption.

* Renewable as used here does not include nuclear power.

---

energy, but there was little thought given to how the release of carbon from fossil fuels impacted the environment.

The 1960s environmental movement began to raise the public consciousness about the relationship of humans and Earth.[10] There has been a polarization between those who want to save trees for aesthetics and to protect habitat, and those who see trees as jobs and resources alone. The polarization is based on either living with the environment and saving resources, or building an economy by using or harvesting resources. The polarization is false, though, because adopting a sustainable mind-set will allow both saving the environmental balance and providing jobs. Progress can be defined as using nature for human benefit alone, or it can be redefined as the efficient use of resources while maintaining a quality of life. The redefined progress will be based on both nonrenewable and renewable resources and will benefit all—and it will leave a healthier and sustainable environment for our descendants.

Living within a renewable framework requires a major mind-set shift: exchanging exploitation for conservation and recognizing and working with (not conquering) **natural capital** (the natural environment and living systems). Up until recently, the definition of capital was limited to economics alone, whereas the concept of natural capital honors the value of all environmental assets (air, minerals, water, etc.) that provide the raw material for human production. During the modern age (since the Renaissance), humans have consumed resources as a right, with little thought to conservation or efficiency. Consumption has intensified since the Industrial Revolution. The results have been waste and pollution. Humans have been living beyond their means, spending the principal (using resources) in a limited bank account rather than living on the interest (reusing resources).

For the past few decades, many countries have adopted **sustainable development** long-term goals, and the United States and Canada have haltingly followed suit. A sustainable approach to consumption requires a new paradigm that addresses energy, water, the built environment, and resource use, all of which will be discussed throughout this book.

The latter modern age Industrial Revolution was powered by resources that will require aeons of geological time to replace. These nonrenewable resources (oil, gas, and coal) stored in the Earth are the energy-rich carbon remains of living matter. The stored energy of the carbon is released when burned, creating carbon dioxide, a greenhouse gas that retains heat in the atmosphere. Human-induced climate change is the result of emitting multiple environmental pollutants and greenhouse gases (GHG), such as CO_2 (carbon dioxide), NO_x (nitrogen oxide), SO_2 (sulfur dioxide), VOCs (volatile organic compounds), and CH_4 (methane), which reflect solar radiation back to Earth and contribute to rising temperatures. Human-made devices that burn carbon-based energy are a major factor in producing climate change. For example, coal-burning power plants produce about half of U.S. electricity and are responsible for 40 percent of emitted CO_2, two-thirds of SO_2, and almost a quarter of NO_x emissions. These power plants have contributed to climate change.

Renewable energy resources were the standard prior to the nineteenth century. The only fossil fuel used was coal, and that was minimal compared to today's levels of consumption. In the past, most power from renewable energy included:

- Wood and biomass
- Solar power
- Wind, used for pumping water and grinding grains
- Water, used in the first textile mills

Nuclear power has been called a renewable resource, although that is controversial, because of the fear of accident and problems of waste storage where leakage from storage units could contaminate groundwater.

Solar energy has been slow to develop, largely because of a lack of consistent government support. However, there are now several types of solar energy systems, including photovoltaic (which converts sunlight directly), parabolic troughs (which concentrate energy to drive a generator), and solar water heaters. The largest solar generators are in California and Nevada. Solar power is still a small part of total energy, but estimates are that 10 percent of all energy will be solar by 2025.

While Europe leads the world in using wind energy, both the United States and Canada have been actively investing in wind farms (Photo 3.1). The wind power capacity has been growing rapidly since the millennium. In the first quarter of 2010, there were 44,400 megawatts of installed U.S. wind power, equaling about 2.3 percent of electricity generated. Texas, Iowa, and California were the wind power leaders. Most states had begun to add wind power to their energy portfolio, except the southeastern states and Nevada. The goal is 20 percent wind power generating capacity by 2030.

Canada's wind power generation of 4,588 megawatts equals about 2 percent of generating capacity (2011); Canada has a goal of 20 percent by 2025. Ontario has the most wind farm capacity, followed by Quebec and Alberta (Map 3.1).

Many claim that renewable energy is not the answer because of its cost, inefficiency, and insufficiency. At the present time, they are right. Until the first decade of the twenty-first century, investments in fossil fuels received most of the time and money. From 2008 to 2009, U.S. energy consumption began to shift away from coal (23 to 21 percent) and toward renewable energy (7 to 8 percent) and natural gas (24 to 25 percent) (Chart 3.1). Natural gas use, though, is dependent on a polluting technology.

In the 1990s, the price of natural gas elevated as traditional sources were exhausted. The price hike allowed new and more expensive experimental methods to be practiced, resulting in hydraulic fracturing, or fracking, which has come under attack as being environmentally damaging—polluting groundwater and air, as well as creating seismic events. While natural gas produces less GHG than other fossil fuels, it is still a nonrenewable source. Hydraulic fracturing is a short-term use of resources and uses highly toxic techniques that pollute both land and water.

Renewable energy may not be as inexpensive or as plentiful as current fossil fuel energy sources, but fossil fuels are more expensive when external costs are considered. Renewable energy is, along with conserving resources, a more efficient and nonpolluting source if given the same time and money that is invested in fossil fuels. As more money is invested in renewable energy sources, they can develop to best serve future populations and reduce overall GHG emissions.

Advantages and Disadvantages of Alternative Energy Sources

Every energy source has positive and negative effects. All alternative sources mentioned herein have the advantage of not creating GHG emissions and being renewable, but each—biofuels, geothermal, solar, and wind—has disadvantages in relation to nonrenewable fossil fuels.

Biofuels include fuels made from solid, liquid, or gas biomass derived from living matter. In the United States, the most touted biofuel is corn-based ethanol; however, the energy produced by ethanol has been questioned. It may cost more to produce and use more fossil fuels to produce than it returns as renewable energy. Using corn for energy production has also been responsible for a large carbon footprint, increased food prices, and inefficient use of prime agricultural land. Seeking a nonfood crop that can be grown on marginal land (so agricultural lands can be used more efficiently) may be a more responsible approach to increase available biomass energy. Of course, farmers are very happy with the boost that ethanol has given to corn prices, but is it the best way to help the farmers, the economy, and the people?

Geothermal power, while efficient and inexhaustible, is expensive and awkward to install in existing facilities. Some geothermal systems require access to abundant clean water, which limits it to coastal or nearby water sources. Geothermal energy is most accessible in volcanic regions such as Iceland, and while Iceland is a cold-weather climate, geothermal energy is generally less accessible and more expensive in cold-weather climates where its benefits would be most effective.

Solar and wind energy are limited by weather and storage capacity. Solar power is processed actively by photovoltaic cells or solar thermal collectors and passively by architectural orientation.

Wind farms are clusters of wind turbines located in areas with average wind speeds of more than ten miles per hour. Solar and wind production present energy transmission problems. Batteries have been underresearched and lack the efficiency needed for storing power. Elements used in batteries are toxic and pollute. Mismanaged wind energy may disrupt pathways of movement for birds and bats. Distribution of solar and wind energy is hampered by the grid needed to transmit power over large areas. On the other hand, wind and solar energy are pollution free, require no fossil fuel, are free of greenhouse gases, and produce no radioactive waste.

Water was the first power source for the Industrial Revolution. It remains important in some areas, such as Canada and the Pacific Northwest, and offers cheap and reliable power to additional areas, such as Alaska. Hydropower generates 80 percent of the nation's renewable energy. Hydropower has the advantage of being a mature industry able to tap into the existing power grid. Water power reduces the production of GHG while securing energy independence. However, dam building in the United States and Canada has come under increasing criticism because of the effects to rivers' ecosystems and habitats.

Renewable energy has been chronically underfunded. However, even well-funded renewables may be insufficient to replace all fossil fuel uses, heightening worry that switching to renewable energy will lower the quality of life because of insufficient power. However, fossil fuels have been affordable in part because they have been subsidized for decades. The current efficiency or use of renewable energy sources lacks political and economic support, which has curtailed development. Energy has been affordable and abundant because it serves financial interests only, and not environmental and social equity issues. Leveling the supportive playing field will make multiple energy sources more competitive.

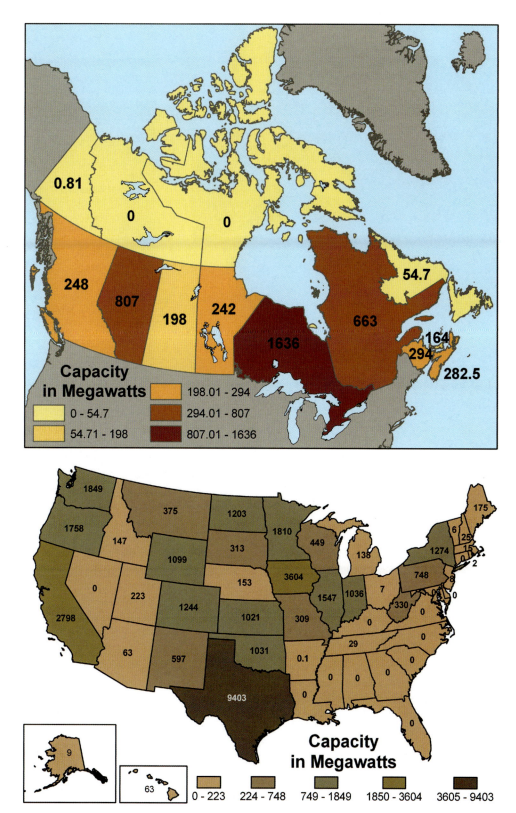

MAP 3.1. Wind Power Capacity in Canada and the United States. Wind capacity in both nations is expected to double by 2015. Many more projects are being planned in both countries.

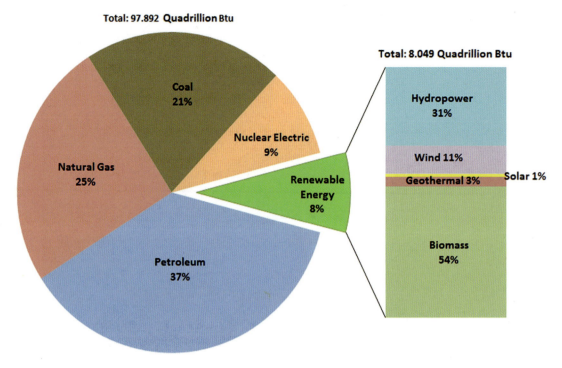

Total: 97.892 Quadrillion Btu

Coal 21%

Nuclear Electric 9%

Natural Gas 25%

Renewable Energy 8%

Petroleum 37%

Total: 8.049 Quadrillion Btu

Hydropower 31%

Wind 11%

Geothermal 3%   Solar 1%

Biomass 54%

CHART 3.1. U.S. Energy Consumption, 2010. Nonrenewable and renewable energy in the United States.

Source: U.S. Energy Information Administration

Nuclear power, while free of polluting carbon and toxic emissions, is dependent on the use of radioactive uranium. No long-term storage facility in the United States has been accepted, despite more than thirty years of stockpiling spent fuel rods. Nuclear accidents in the United States, Russia, and Japan have resulted in limited enthusiasm for nuclear power production. Nuclear facilities in the United States are all at least thirty years old; the few facilities currently under construction will benefit from technological advances.

Alternative energy sources are not a panacea in the energy crisis, but they can offer some cleaner and long-term solutions as the economy begins to adjust to a more flexible energy environment. There are no silver bullets, no magic. (In fact, the metaphors we choose to describe success or progress, often about killing and military might, shape our worldview and need to be rethought in order to move toward a more sustainable worldview.[11]) The solutions to a healthy and ecological environment are within reach, if we decide we want to clean up our act.

Built Environment

Concerns about sustainability and energy use extend beyond energy sources and into where people live. The built environment includes human-made structures and infrastructure. Transportation and industry use the majority of energy

(Chart 3.2). The past sixty years of U.S. urban planning theory was based on land-use regulations that permitted only single-use zoning (residential, commercial, or industrial). Policies endorsing single-use zoning and **sprawl** (the low-density process of land development) have been responsible for dependence on automobile transportation. Mass transit requires higher-density living areas.

The current U.S. sprawl footprint wastes energy and has sapped community vitality. Sprawl has become endemic across the landscape and is often cited as part of the American Dream—but partially because public policies have favored highways over public transit. Atlanta, Georgia; Raleigh and Greensboro, North Carolina; and several Southern California metropolises are ideal examples of sprawl, while cities such as San Francisco, Boston (both limited by peninsulas), and Portland, Oregon, are examples of higher-density development.

Smart growth originated in the 1970s but became a force during the 1990s. It was created to reverse urban sprawl, decrease auto dependence, and improve energy efficiency, while reducing traffic congestion and transportation costs. Smart growth favors quality of life, emphasizing conservation over sprawl, and encourages urban villages built in relation to convenient public transportation links. A range of medium- to high-density housing choices and mixed land uses encourages working and living within walking or easy commuting dis-

tances. Many smart growth communities now incorporate ecologically and resource-efficient green building design.

Planning initiatives within the United States, such as those adopted in the early 1990s by Oregon, New Jersey, and Florida, favor smart growth, features of which include:

- Conservation of natural resources
- A balance of business and housing, mixed-use development
- Transit-oriented development that maximizes access to public transportation
- Walkable and compact neighborhoods
- Green building design

Transit-oriented developments (TODs) are mixed-use developments with networks of sidewalks, street lighting, and pedestrian-friendly neighborhood retail establishments. TODs discourage car use and encourage pedestrians, bicyclists, and mass transit. TODs are found in walkable and compact neighborhoods that often contain mixed-use development.

While new planning sometimes addresses energy-efficient growth, the bulk of American housing is already built. Subsidies and incentives will be required to encourage conservation and efficiency.

Green building was standardized in 1998 when the U.S. Green Building Council created **Leadership in Energy and Environmental Design (LEED)** certification. By 2008 there were more than fourteen thousand LEED-certified projects around the world. The LEED rating system addresses six sustainable issues:

- Sustainable site development
- Water savings
- Energy efficiency
- Materials selection (favoring recycled materials)
- Indoor air quality
- Design innovation

Green buildings maximize efficient ventilation, use recycled and sustainable building materials, landscape with native species, collect rainwater, and often have vegetation-covered green roofs. The buildings maximize sunlight and wind, and endorse alternative transportation—walking, mass transit, and bicycles.

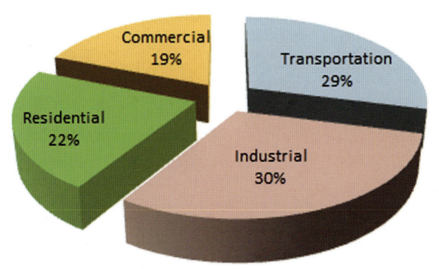

CHART 3.2. Share of Energy Consumed by Major Sectors of the Economy, 2009.

Source: U.S. Energy Information Administration

While LEED certification is worthwhile, it adds cost to buildings. LEED is advantageous for architects and from a business perspective, because of tax credits, the ability to attract high-quality tenants and charge premium rents, and projecting an environmentally sensitive image. But LEED construction costs exceed those of traditional construction (despite materials that are only marginally more expensive); there is additional cost because of LEED's required forms; and LEED does not endorse the social benefits of the triple bottom line. LEED certification is not a necessity for sustainable buildings, but it is a standard.

Reducing Dependencies

In the twenty-first century, the world is changing rapidly. Population continues to soar; another nine hundred million people were added during the first decade of the twenty-first century—the equivalent of adding the population of the North American continent to the world population every decade. This larger population requires far more energy production than ever before. China and India, whose populations alone are one-third the total world population, are expanding their middle class and require more energy to maintain them and grow.

Energy consumption accelerated in the 1990s as new Chinese and Indian manufacturing centers added five hundred million people to the consumer-based modern world, all seeking the comforts of technology, all seeking cars, and all using fossil fuels. The world demand for resources has many people questioning the carrying capacity of Earth with so many people at a high standard of living. The **ecological footprint** offers a measurement of human demand on Earth's ecosystems and natural resources. We face the question of how we choose to live—by uncontrolled consumption of resources or by conserving and becoming more efficient.

The United States and Canada both have rising consumption levels, but their energy supplies differ. Canada is one of the world's largest producers and exporters of fossil fuel energy, and since the 1950s, the United States has increased dependence on imported energy. As both population and energy consumption increase, this imbalance will continue and become more serious. The United States depends on imported oil for almost 60 percent of its petroleum, while doing little to provide incentives to conserve or to subsidize energy production from renewable sources.

Germany is the world leader in renewable energies. Wind farms, solar cells, and biofuel plants are government subsidized and common, as they are in most European Union (EU) countries. The twenty-seven EU countries have agreed to adopt energy targets that will boost renewable energy sources and cut 1990 carbon dioxide emissions 20 percent by 2020. While maintaining a high standard of living, Western Europe emits less than half the per capita CO_2 emissions of the United States and Canada (Table 3.2).

The U.S. federal government has been lax in its commitment to renewable energy and to accepting and arresting global climate change. The investment in renewable energy needs "coordinated, sustained federal and state policies that expand renewable energy markets, promote and deploy new technology, and encourage renewable energy use in all critical market sectors."[12] The switch, though, must be on an objective level and not make subjective decisions that will be peppered with exorbitant profits for renewables because they are now profitable. The renewable investment requires clear thinking that is not in crisis mode.

The paramount importance of increasing energy demands and the emerging energy crisis has been internationally recognized since the 1992 Earth Summit in Rio de Janeiro. Many countries agreed on the need to stabilize GHG emissions and to make the shift to a more sustainable lifestyle. Participating countries signed the U.N. Framework Convention on Climate Change, setting a voluntary goal for reduction to 1990 levels by 2000. Few countries were able to realize these goals, but they recognized the need for stronger action.

In 1997 the **Kyoto Protocol** was negotiated. Its main goal was for industrialized countries to arrest and reverse GHG emissions to 1990 levels by 2012. The Kyoto Protocol was originally adopted by 169 countries including the EU countries, Canada, and the United States. However, the protocol was never placed before the U.S. Senate, and when a new administration entered in 2000, the protocol was opposed because of a perceived harm to the economy.[13] In 1997 India and China were exempt because of their fledgling industrial status; however, their participation will be expected on future protocols. While Canada did sign the protocol, it reneged in 2007, when the liberals were dethroned and the conservatives came into power. Instead of meeting 2012 Kyoto goals, Canada intends to reduce 2006 emissions 20 percent by 2020.

The U.S. federal government's lack of political will to reduce emissions was countermanded by many cities in 2005. Seattle's mayor urged other cities to join Seattle and achieve the protocol's climate protection goals.[14] More than five hundred mayors responded and accepted the protocol's goals. The action pressured the federal government to reconsider its stance on climate change.

Developed countries are targeted for reducing their 1990 emissions of greenhouse gases by at least 5 percent by 2012. Emissions in Canada and the United States are far beyond what other countries emit; in fact, each state and province produces the equivalent of emissions of entire countries (Map 3.2). With the expiration of the Kyoto Protocol in 2012, a new compact is needed. The touted meeting of 2009 in Copenhagen did not achieve the aims necessary to bring the global community to consensus; perhaps the next meeting will.

Sustainability

The term "sustainability" has become clichéd and difficult to precisely define. The Brundtland Commission (1987) most famously defined sustainable development: "Humanity has the ability to make development sustainable to ensure that it meets the needs

BOX 3.4 ECOLOGICAL FOOTPRINT

A sustainable life requires living within the limits of global resources. Population experts do not consider the size or consumption levels of the current population sustainable.

The populations of the United States and Canada live well beyond their available land, which is measured by an equation called the ecological footprint—measuring human consumption of resources in relation to Earth's renewable capacity. The ecological footprint approximates how much productive land and water are needed to provide for a population. The ecological footprint can be measured at any scale, from individuals to global. The land used is then compared to the land occupied. In the United States and Canada, the ecological footprint is much larger than the land it occupies and therefore unsustainable on a global scale.

On average, there are 4.5 acres of productive land per person in the world. The average productive land needed for developed countries is 15.8 acres, for middle-income countries 5 acres, for low-income countries 2 acres, but Americans require 24 acres, and Canadians require 22 acres. Calculating the number of acres times the population gives the number of Earths necessary (as if we had more than one) to live in that fashion. For example, if everyone on Earth were to consume at the American rate, there would need to be 5.3 Earths; to consume as the average Canadian would require 4 Earths.*

The footprint quiz generates numbers that equate to the standard of living in America in relation to world averages. The quiz does not propose that all people live exactly the same, but it does allow people to see where they are in relation to the rest of the world population. For example, if everyone (seven billion people) lived at the same level, dividing up all resources equally, the standard of living on Earth would be something like the following:

- Strict vegetarian, eggs a few times a week
- No processed food
- 2 people living in 500 square feet
- No running water
- No electricity
- Public transportation or bicycle
- No flying

While the footprint equation has been criticized because of some of its assumptions, it is a rough measure of the demands on nature caused by a large population consuming resources. The human consumption of natural resources by the current world population is approximately 140 percent more than the Earth can sustain. The current ecological footprint of world population is unsustainable. Another way to say this is: The Earth is spending its principal rather than only its interest. If the principal is continuously spent there will be no interest, no principal, and Earth will soon be bankrupt to maintain a healthy quality of life standard of living for the human population.

Earth's ecological footprint can be reduced by limiting population and consumption. The countries that can conserve most are the developed countries, where population growth is small but consumption continues to grow. The countries where population growth rates are high are usually the less developed countries, where consumption is stagnant or dropping.

This divide is at the root of being unsustainable. Developed countries are unwilling to give up on their consumption rates; less developed countries are unwilling to decrease population growth. Neither side wants to give in, feeling that the way they live or how many children they have is their birthright, yet both are living unsustainably. Humans are burning the candle at both ends.

---

* The footprint calculator is available online at http://www.footprintnetwork.org/en/index.php/GFN/page/calculators/. It should be noted that the ecological footprint does not represent all environmental impacts, but it is a representative measure.

---

of the present without compromising the ability of future generations to meet their own needs."[15] Sustainability, though, is not only prescribed actions but a way to think—holistically. To have the sustainable mind-set is to see that everything is connected and that there are limits to our world, and then to act accordingly. Living within the limits, recognizing impact, and understanding the complexity and unintended consequences of our actions will bring humans closer to a sustainable existence and into the interconnections necessary for an ecological age.

Sustainability aims for an ecological dynamic equilibrium of Earth's interconnected ecosystems that maximizes efficiency, minimizes waste, and spends interest but not principal. Sustainable study and practices are being adopted globally, especially in Europe. North America has been slow to recognize the need. However, no country is operating sustainably yet.

Sustainability is allied with renewable sources of energy; recycling of natural resources; decreasing the pollution on land, air, and water; and living with a mind-set that seeks to live in an alliance with Earth (rather than conquering and exploiting its assets) and to slow down if not halt climate change.

Achieving a sustainable lifestyle will be unlike anything achieved by citizens of the developed world. It will not be easy. The ecological age is a radical break from the modern age, equivalent to the radical break between the Middle Ages and the Renaissance at the beginning of the modern age. Moving into the ecological age will require equivalent changes in the way we live and think. Achieving a sustainable lifestyle will require changing agricultural methods and environmental, energy, and urban planning practices. It will require changing a mind-set that has dominated the developed world for the past several hundred years.

TABLE 3.2. Carbon Dioxide Emissions per Capita

Region	Metric tons per capita 2006	Metric tons per capita 2008
United States	5.18	4.71
Canada	4.55	4.46
Western Europe	2.14	2.08
China	1.32	1.43
World	1.25	1.30

Source: Carbon Dioxide Information Analysis Center (CDIAC), at http://cdiac.ornl.gov/

Sustainable practices will be covered from a variety of angles in this text within the context of historical precedents, systems thinking, the values of cultures, ecological balance, industry, housing, transportation, food, and commodities. Sustainable goals will be discussed in numerous ways, including adopting economies of scale and density, reducing automobile dependence, and reducing per capita use of resources and waste while improving livability.

A Sustainable World

A sustainable world includes the following elements:

- Minimizing nonrenewable resource consumption
- Maximizing resource and energy efficiency
- Minimizing polluting toxins
- Respecting and working with the natural environment rather than against it
- Cradle-to-cradle industry
- Ecological balance and integrating ecosystems
- Including humans aligned with nature as part of the many ecosystems
- Living with sustainable agricultural practices
- Controlling population growth
- Reducing material consumption
- Taxing environmental pollution through shifting the tax burden or cap and trade.
- Reducing poverty
- Educating holistically

Most of these issues have been discussed in the press, with the exception of population growth, which is the gorilla in the room that few want to discuss. It is estimated that by 2042 the population will increase to nine billion.[16] Sustainability at nine billion people will be more difficult to achieve than sustainability at seven billion. Limited resources will need to be shared by more people. Adopting sound population policies will be required to leave a sustainable world for future generations, as well as our own. We will require new ideas that will create new economies and opportunities. Population issues will be discussed in the next chapter.

Sustainable living requires adjusting every scale from micro to macro—from the individual to global, from urban to agricultural, and within ecosystems from the smallest patch to watersheds, continents, and the globe. The complex interactive global biosystem has become more stressed as human impact on Earth has grown. The political and economic structures and policies that supported nonrenewable systems require change. Environmental issues and the social inequities of the triple bottom line will no longer be externalities but equally important in the economy.[17]

The change that needs to happen, change that can be accepted by the developed world public who wish to maintain their way of life, can be accomplished, but it requires a shift in mind-set from the past Industrial Revolution, which provided simple linear solutions to problems, to a new Industrial Revolution that works with and understands the complexity of natural systems. Humans are a part of nature and have the ability to live within the world ecosystem, but we have chosen the easy way out—growth without developing a balancing sense of our limitations and the opportunities that living within limits provides.

In order for humans to work within the complexity of nature, people with expertise in specific areas of the complexity will need to see how they fit within the larger holistic systems they work within. Human teams of experts will need to address issues objectively and cooperatively so that the complexity of nature can be realized as part of the human challenge to live within the bounds of an ecological age.

Accepting the limits to our resources and reducing waste and pollution are the biggest challenge for public policy, business, and industry. The shift to sustainability is not about giving up what we have, but about answering the same type of innovative challenges met by the first Industrial Revolution. The shift is about bringing us closer to establishing a healthier relationship with nature. It is a change radical enough to recast our nations back into leadership rather than partisan politics.

Donald Lafreniere

Donald Lafreniere

MAP 3.2. Greenhouse Gas Emissions from Energy National Equivalents. Data based on U.S. Department of Energy statistics for 2001 to 2003.

Source: Sightline Institute

Becoming sustainable is not a choice but a pragmatic necessity. It requires change, and change does not come easily, even when one is committed to the process and the outcome. A sustainable life demands a change in how we choose to define success and progress. Living sustainably will have both negative and positive effects, as does any action. It will require a shift of mind-set from short-term gain to long-term benefit. Some of the positive effects of long-term change will be a shift to collaboration and cooperation among peoples and countries; it will build healthier social communities and a unified effort to develop new sustainable energy sources and technologies. In building new ways to live our lives, new business models will form and new jobs will revitalize economies. Sustainability offers hope rather than despair for the future, as the world is transformed and progress is defined anew.

Questions for Discussion

1. Should there be caps on wealth? What should they be?

2. Can we have economic success and still fail as a country?

3. How would business change if the triple bottom line were adopted?

4. How would your world change if sustainability became the norm? How long would it take?

5. What, in your opinion, will happen to the United States and Canada in the next twenty-five years if sustainability does not become the norm?

6. What is the impact on the world of the dependence on fossil fuel energy?

7. How would your life change if there were extensive and adequate transportation options beyond the car?

8. How would your life change if you could not have a car?

9. How have Canada and the United States differed in their stance toward the Kyoto Protocol?

10. How would the waste and pollution in the current system change in the new Industrial Revolution?

11. How does cradle-to-grave (C2G) industry differ from cradle-to-cradle (C2C) industry?

12. Can technology alone save the day as world population, environmental, and energy problems continue to become more serious? Why or why not?

Suggested Readings

Barnett, Jonathan, ed. *Smart Growth in a Changing World*. Chicago: American Planning Association, 2007.

Benyus, Janine M. *Biomimicry: Innovation Inspired by Nature*. New York: HarperCollins, 1997.

Brown, Lester R. *Eco-Economy: Building an Economy for the Earth*. New York: Norton, 2001.

Chapin, F. S., and G. Whiteman. "Sustainable Development of the Boreal Forest: Interaction of Ecological, Social, and Business Feedbacks." *Conservation Ecology* 2, no. 2 (1998): 12, at www.consecol.org/vol2/iss2/art12/.

Edwards, Andres R. *The Sustainability Revolution*. Gabriola Island, B.C.: New Society Publishers, 2005.

Haughton, Graham, and Colin Hunter. *Sustainable Cities*. London: Routledge, 2003.

Manuel, John S. "Unbuilding for the Environment." *Environmental Health Perspectives* 111, no. 16 (December 2003): A880–A887.

McDonough, William, and Michael Braungart. *Cradle to Cradle: Remaking the Way We Make Things*. New York: North Point Press, 2002.

Rees, William. "Evaluation Criteria for a Sustainable Economy." Institut fur Verfahrenstechnik. Graz, Austria: Technische Universitat Graz, 1994.

Rohrman, Douglass. "How Brown Was My Valley." *Frontiers in Ecology and the Environment* 1, no. 6 (August 2003): 334.

"Turning Brownfields Green Again," *Environmental Health Perspectives* 104, no. 4 (April 1996): 371–72.

Wackernagel, M., and W. Rees. *Our Ecological Footprint: Reducing Human Impact on the Earth*. Gabriola Island, B.C.: New Society Publishers, 1996.

Wakefield, Julie. "Environmental Education: Teaching Sustainability." *Environmental Health Perspectives* 111, no. 5 (May 2003): A270.

York, Richard, Eugene A. Rosa, and Thomas Dietz. "Footprints on the Earth: The Environmental Consequences of Modernity." *American Sociological Review* 68, no. 2 (April 2003).

Internet Sources

U.S. Census Bureau. International Programs, at www.census.gov/ipc/www/idb/

WindEnergie, at www.wind-energie.de/

Energy Information Administration (consumption), at www.eia.doe
.gov/emeu/aer/consump.html

U.S. Green Building Council, at www.usgbc.org/

Population Reference Bureau. World Population Data Sheet, at www
.prb.org/Publications/Datasheets/2006/2006WorldPopulation
DataSheet.aspx

Carbon Footprint, at www.carbonfootprint.com/USA/calculator.html

U.S. Environmental Protection Agency, Municipal Solid Waste Generation, Recycling, and Disposal in the United States, 2008, http://
www.epa.gov/epawaste/nonhaz/municipal/pubs/msw2008rpt.pdf

PHOTO 4.1. Monterey, California. In the early 1850s, Monterey's Cannery Row was the center of Chinese fishing and export industry to China. Chinese enclaves flourished until the 1882 Chinese Exclusion Act stopped immigration until 1943. Today Chinese New Year is a celebration of tradition and the Chinese community.

4

POPULATION AND CONSUMPTION

Quantity versus Quality

Chapter Highlights

After reading this chapter you should be able to:

- Describe the growth of global population since 1900
- Explain carrying capacity
- Discuss the global issues of population and consumption
- Outline the demographic transition
- Describe the sectors of the national economy
- Discuss how the United States and Canada are similar regarding visible minorities
- Explain the difference between rate of growth and absolute growth
- Discuss the waves of immigration into the United States and Canada

Terms

absolute growth	center of population	multiculturalism	rate of growth
acculturation	conurbation	natural increase	replacement level
allophone	death rate	neo-Malthusian	rural
anglophone	demographic process	population density	secondary sector
assimilation	demographic transition	population pyramid	Sun Belt
baby boom	doubling time	postindustrial economy	tertiary sector
birthrate	francophone	primary sector	total fertility rate (TFR)
carrying capacity	Malthusian	quality of life	urban
	migration	quaternary sector	

Introduction

One of the basic themes underlying our analysis and policy recommendation is the substitution of quality for quantity; that is, we should concern ourselves with improving the quality of life for all Americans rather than merely adding more Americans.

— Commission on Population Growth and the American Future, 1972[1]

Human population and consumption are arguably the two largest concerns that if controlled would moderate many of our environmental and social equity problems. So easy to say, so difficult to achieve. The problem is exacerbated because population and consumption issues are unevenly divided globally. Population growth is most prevalent in the less developed countries; consumption is an issue in the developed world, and it is becoming more of an issue as the developing world copies the developed world's unsustainable fossil fuel–based living standards. Both are important subjects due to limited global resources, and neither is sustainable without serious social, political, and economic consequences. The interconnected nature of these issues will necessitate a global-scale discussion in this chapter before focusing on the United States and Canada.

Population growth and consumption are related to environment, resources, and the relationship of humans to each other and to the rest of the biotic and abiotic world. Some questions to ask of these relationships are:

- How do humans fit ecologically into the biosphere?
- How do humans maintain the delicate balance necessary for a healthy and rewarding life that respects all life and is within the carrying capacity of Earth?

Controlling population growth is a taboo subject almost anywhere in the world. There has been some indirect and ethical control of population, mostly through educating girls to their rights over their bodies. While education for females is common in developed countries, most of the world rejects limitations on reproduction, which is treated as sacred and often politicized. The matter becomes one of educating to a different worldview, one that is more ecological and supports an ethic so that the choice of how many children to have comes from within rather than being imposed. However, one country has imposed restrictions.

In 1978, China instituted a one-child policy to slow population growth and alleviate social and environmental problems. The policy helped China modernize economically and become a world industrial leader. However, the flaw is that China's booming economy is based on the cradle-to-grave economy of the first Industrial Revolution. The results are the same unregulated economic growth based on nonrenewable resources: rampant pollution, social ills, and demographic pressures on land, food, housing, and water. Those who have prospered in the Chinese economy are replicating the consumption patterns of the developed world.

While China may have controlled some population growth problems, it has not acted on global problems caused by human population growth and consumptive economies. In the past decade alone, an additional three hundred million Chinese have begun to attain a middle-class **quality of life**, as have an additional three hundred million subcontinental Indians. Neither they nor most developed countries have respected the ecological carrying capacity of the Earth. The Chinese and Indians see and want what the affluent world has. They are obtaining their consumer goods in the same manner as the developed world, dependent on nonrenewable resources based on the single profit-based bottom line.

World resource availability and population have changed since the first Industrial Revolution began in the 1750s, when the world had not yet reached a population of one billion. The developed countries were the first countries to undergo the Industrial Revolution. To attain similar standards of living, developing countries—China, India, Brazil—have been consuming their resources in a manner similar to the developing nations; however, the human impact on Earth's resources has multiplied since the Industrial Revolution began. The tenfold global population since 1750 continues to follow the same profit-oriented, short-term economic model, while pursuing an improved quality of life. However, quality of life has been measured by standard-of-living quantitative methods rather than by the immeasurable attributes of quality (happiness, social, environmental). The carrying capacity of Earth may already be overshot, so the new middle class can only last so long without pressuring economies and political power. If the United States and Canada were to adopt a mind-set that fosters happiness, health, and well-being rather than consumption, theirs and the EU's leadership in sustainable practices and renewable energy would provide a positive role model and shift the balance toward the Ecological Age.

While the meaning of quality of life differs among people, general indicators are economic, physical, psychological, and social well-being. To maintain a global quality of life requires a change in mind-set and transforming but not undermining the integrity of environmental, agricultural, or cultural systems.

Less Developed, Developing, and Developed Countries: Growth Rate and Consumption

The countries of the world are unequally developed. Lacking a standardized convention to define the less developed, developing, and developed countries, the terms will be defined as follows. Less developed are countries with low material well-being (e.g., Afghanistan, Somalia); developing countries have a higher standard of living and have adopted a manufacturing economy (e.g., China, India, Brazil); developed countries are those who first adopted the Industrial Revolution and fossil fuel dependence (e.g.,the United States, Canada, Western Europe, Japan).

Birthrates and consumption patterns evolve in relation to development. Generally, countries with high birthrates and low consumption patterns are less developed; countries with falling birthrates and higher consumption are developing; and countries with low birthrates and high consumption are developed.

A way to measure the birthrate in a country is the **total fertility rate (TFR)**, the number of children a woman has during her reproductive years. The less developed countries, such as Afghanistan (TFR 5.7) or Yemen (TFR 5.5),[2] have high but waning population growth rates.

Developing countries are pursuing developed-world standards. For example, the TFR in Brazil has dropped from 6 in the 1940s to 3.3 in 1986, and today it is below the 2.1 **replacement level**. As the TFR has dropped, the Brazilian economy and consumerism have risen, enabling Brazil to become one of the fastest-developing nations.

The developed countries are the largest consumers and are most aware and concerned about population growth. After years of environmental degradation, affluent countries now recognize the global cost and want developing countries to slow down or halt using their resources unsustainably. Developing countries have pointed to the developed world's consumption and greenhouse gas (GHG) emissions as the major problem, but some of them, like Brazil, are sometimes at the forefront of seeking more sustainable solutions.

While Brazil has exploited its vast rain forest, it has also begun to address Amazonian deforestation and growth without

BOX 4.1 POPULATION HISTORY

The Industrial Revolution was flourishing in Britain when Thomas Malthus wrote his treatise on population in 1798. His inspiration arose from his fear that unchecked population growth in Great Britain would lead to starvation for the masses. His fear turned out to be unwarranted because the second agricultural revolution (the first was the evolution from hunting and gathering to planting seed about ten thousand years ago) was taking place as he wrote. Land productivity increased due to changing cultivation methods and technological advances. **Malthusian** ideas were set aside until the 1960s when population growth fears rose again, and **neo-Malthusian** scientists such as Paul and Anne Ehrlich, Garrett Hardin, and the Club of Rome think tank called attention once again to world population growth and its effects.*

In the 1960s the global population surpassed three billion, doubling for the first time in the twentieth century, and in the shortest time ever: sixty years. It was a wake-up call, but the neo-Malthusians were not greeted as visionaries but as doomsayers, and their fears faded from public debate as a new agricultural revolution, the Green Revolution, seemingly saved the day and famine and destruction were averted. However, it took only forty years for the population to double again in 2000, accompanied by yet another agricultural revolution, this time genetically engineered food.

A pattern has been set. Technology and medical advances applied to food production allow population to grow. Many believe that population may continue to grow indefinitely as long as technology stays on track. But something is wrong. Population growth during the past two agricultural revolutions has been dependent on nonrenewable resources and may overshoot the carrying capacity of Earth. The vast majority of food grown in the world today depends on oil and its derivatives. The Green Revolution depends on fossil fuel–based fertilizers, pesticides, herbicides, and gasoline to plow, cultivate, irrigate, and transport crops. The dependence on nonrenewable fossil fuel resources has jeopardized future growth and prosperity.

The resources of Earth are limited. There is one Earth. It is not growing larger or replicating itself. Can developing renewable energy resources maintain a healthy quality of life over the long term?

---

* Paul and Anne Ehrlich published many articles and books, among them *The Population Bomb* (1968), *The End of Affluence* (1974), and *the Population Explosion* (1990). Garrett Hardin is best known for his "Tragedy of the Commons," and the Club of Rome published the environmental treatise *The Limits to Growth* (1972).

---

increasing dependence on fossil fuels. Rain forest destruction has been reduced almost 80 percent in the past decade, and Brazil has based much of its growth on using sustainable biofuel (based on sugarcane).

Consumption is often measured by gross domestic product (GDP) per capita, although GDP does not differentiate how money is spent. GDP equates with economic progress, including the costs involved with tackling social and environmental deterioration. In 2010, the United States and Canada were near $47,000 annually, developing Brazil was at $10,700, China was at $4,393, and less developed countries, such as Afghanistan, were well below $500 annually.[3] While these numbers indicate how much a country spends, it is not a fail-safe indicator of a sustainable lifestyle.

The complex population/consumption conundrum can be viewed from a systems perspective. Populations in less developed countries continue to grow rapidly, albeit more slowly than in the past, but their emphasis remains largely on purely economic progress and they seldom have educational opportunities or a local marketable economy. Developing countries have checked population growth and want to use their resources to attain a more consumer lifestyle, even while making strides toward sustainable growth. The developed countries have checked population growth to such an extent that many, including the United States, no longer have a substantial population willing to work in unskilled jobs, and thus have a large immigrant and often undocumented population to fill those jobs. Meanwhile, the developed world economy has been rocky since the 2008 economic meltdown. Regardless of the perspective, it is clear that a new economic model of global sustainable development needs to address both population growth and consumption patterns, not just GDP. Using systems thinking addresses the core problems on a global scale by examining multiple indicators of progress.

Population Size and Growth

Global and regional population distribution and size have changed since the beginning of the Industrial Revolution (Table 4.1). The changes have been dramatic and tell their own story. For example, world population was about 791 million at the beginning of the Industrial Revolution and has since multiplied almost tenfold. In the past decade alone (2000–2010), world population has grown by an additional billion, more than the total global population in 1750. This is significant because where one person impacted the planet in 1750, there are now ten. The growth has been due to dependence on nonrenewable fossil fuel resources.

Table 4.1 indicates where population has grown over periods of time. For example, the population of Africa was 13 percent of the total population in 1750, but during the nineteenth century to the mid-twentieth century the African population was much smaller (as low as 8.1 percent) because of lack of access to public health and modern medicine. Since the mid-twentieth century, though, African population growth has escalated, going from 8.8 percent in 1950 to an estimated 19.8 percent in 2050. And some of the highest TFRs in the world (5.2) are in sub-Saharan Africa.

TABLE 4.1. Population of the World and Its Major Areas, 1750–2050

Population Size (millions)

Major area	1750	1800	1850	1900	1950	2000	2010	2050 (est)
World	791	978	1,262	1,650	2,521	6,115	6,892	8,909
Africa	106	107	111	133	221	819	1030	1,766
Asia	502	635	809	947	1,402	3,698	4,157	5,268
Europe	163	203	276	408	547	727	739	628
Central and South America	16	24	38	74	167	521	544	809
North America	2	7	26	82	172	319	344	392
Oceania	2	2	2	6	13	31	37	46

Percentage Distribution

Major area	1750	1800	1850	1900	1950	2000	2010	2050 (est)
World	100	100	100	100	100	100	100	100
Africa	13.4	10.9	8.8	8.1	8.8	13.4	14.9	19.8
Asia	63.5	64.9	64.1	57.4	55.6	60.5	60.3	59.1
Europe	20.6	20.8	21.9	24.7	21.7	11.9	10.7	7.0
Central and South America	2.0	2.5	3.0	4.5	8.5	8.5	7.8	9.1
North America	0.3	0.7	2.1	5.0	5.1	5.2	5.0	4.4
Oceania	0.3	0.2	0.2	0.4	0.5	0.5	0.5	0.5

Source: United Nations Population Division, *The World at Six Billion*, at http://www.un.org/esa/population/publications/sixbillion/sixbillion.htm

North America's percentage of population distribution was very low during the nineteenth century but grew to its maximum in 1950. The population percentage has been declining since then, as the TFR has fallen below the 2.1 replacement level (Canadian TFR 1.7; U.S. TFR 2.0[4]). Europe has seen a marked decline in population distribution since 1950, as TFR has fallen below replacement level (European TFR 1.6).

These shifts in population size and distribution are also reflections of regional industrialization. Those countries that industrialized earliest (the United States, Canada, Europe and Japan) had higher growth rates during the nineteenth century, which declined as they entered the postindustrial stage. The growth pattern from nonindustrial to postindustrial growth is illustrated in the **demographic transition** model.

World, Canadian, and U.S. Population Growth

In the brief history of this nation, we have always assumed that progress and "the good life" are connected with population growth. In fact, population growth has frequently been regarded as a measure of our progress. If that were ever the case, it is not now. There is hardly any social problem confronting this nation whose solution would be easier if our population were larger.

— Commission on Population Growth and the American Future, 1972[5]

The growth in population may be the most significant issue the world faces, yet the United States has chosen not to recognize connections between population growth, deteriorated cities, economic malaise, and degraded environment. No national population policy has ever been adopted, despite numerous reports and books indicating the problems related to population

BOX 4.2 DEMOGRAPHIC TRANSITION

The demographic transition model describes in four stages how population growth changes in relation to industrial development over time (Chart 4.1). The development of a country from the first stage to the fourth usually requires several generations. The developed world has been undergoing the transition for 250 years, but the developing world is making the transition much faster. The resources used by the initial Industrial Revolution supported a population of less than 800 million. The first countries to achieve the second stage (est. 1750) occurred when world population was about 791 million. The impact on Earth of 791 million was one-eighth of the seven billion in 2011.

In the first stage of the model (pre-modern), countries are not industrialized. Birth and death rates are equally high and population growth is slow; doubling of population takes hundreds of years. The highest death rate is among children under the age of ten. All countries were at this stage into the eighteenth century, but public health and sanitation improvements have all but eliminated this category today.

Industrialization is the second stage of the model, during which people are forced from the farm, largely due to increasing farm mechanization. They move into cities and are employed in factories. The United States and Canada were at this stage in the mid-nineteenth century, and most developing countries are in this stage today. In the second stage the number of deaths drops dramatically, while the birthrate remains high. More children survive into adulthood, and the population average age grows older. Changes to the death rate can generally be attributed to improved health care, hygiene, and sanitation. Population growth is high.

In the third stage, the birth and death rates drop, but the birthrate remains higher than the death rate. The initial stages of the third stage have the highest birthrates. Later in the stage, as the population becomes more urbanized, people receive more education; women bear fewer children because educated women tend to have more rights over their body, can choose alternative career paths, may use contraception, or may rationalize the cost of children. Changes in social equity relieve children of being an additional labor supply or an old age security: in purely economic terms children go from being financial assets to being financial liabilities. Both fertility and infant mortality rates drop in relation to urbanization and education, and the population begins to stabilize. Several developing countries have entered this stage, including India, Brazil, Chile, and China.

The fourth stage is the current stage of the model for developed countries and indicates a stable or declining population in countries that have moved into the service-oriented **postindustrial economy**. Features include an aging population, high literacy rates, and a higher standard of living than in developing countries.

Industrialization and education can be measured by the total fertility rate (TFR). During the nineteenth-century stages of industrialization, an American woman had a TFR of seven children over the course of her childbearing years, similar to the TFR in 2009 for Afghanistan (TFR 5.7) or Somalia (TFR 6.7).* But when American women had a high TFR, the world population was less than a quarter of that in the twenty-first century and consumed far fewer resources. Developed countries evolved from high birthrates to a stabilized growth, but can the developing countries do the same today? Are there the resources for a highly consuming quality of life for all?

In many countries the TFR is below replacement level, so populations are declining. Most European countries have entered this stage. The United States and Canada are in the fourth stage, though their TFRs remain among the highest in the developed world (U.S. 2.1; Canada 1.6). An anomaly to this stage is Russia and the former Soviet republics. They have low birthrates, high death rates, and significantly shorter life expectancies than most developed countries, but they have not developed their economies or standards of living since they became independent states.

As sustainable economies become the new standard in the world, a fifth stage of the demographic transition may form.

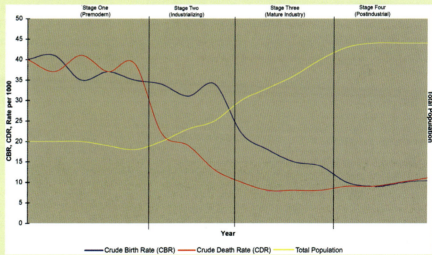

CHART 4.1. The Demographic Transition Model, describing population change over time. The model shows population growth from high birthrates and death rates in a pre-industrialized economy, where population growth is slow, to the low birthrates and death rates of a postindustrialized economy.

By "model" we mean that it is an idealized, composite picture of population change. The model is a generalization that applies to these countries as a group and may not accurately describe all individual cases. The transition began when today's developed countries began to industrialize in the nineteenth century. Whether or not it applies to less developed societies today remains to be seen.

* American fertility rates were not followed until the late nineteenth century, but families were generally larger during the nineteenth century in Europe. The first country to have lower fertility rates was France in 1830, followed by the rest of Europe by the 1870s and the United States in the 1890s. John C. Caldwell and Pat Caldwell, "Regional Paths to Fertility Transition," *Journal of Population Research* 18, no. 2 (2001); John C. Caldwell and Thomas Schindlmayr, "Explanations of the Fertility Crisis in Modern Societies: A Search for Commonalities," *Population Studies* 57, no. 3 (2003).

growth.[6] But by doing nothing the policy makers have indeed acted.

Despite its lack of leadership in population issues, the United States has the opportunity to become a role model by acting on one of the most important issues in the world today. To attain a sustainable nation, to attain a sustainable world, the population issue must be addressed. The first step in understanding population growth is to know:

- What population growth has been and how we got here
- The demographic process
- The makeup of the current population

After reviewing these points, we can begin to interpret the data and facts of population and consumption patterns and use that knowledge to begin to understand how to live in alliance with Earth rather than trying to conquer nature.

Population Growth

The world population experienced intense and continuing growth from 1900 to 2000. Rounding off numbers to make this easier, the world population in 1900 was approximately 1.5 billion, which doubled to 3 billion by 1960, and doubled again to 6 billion in 2000. The population of the world quadrupled during the twentieth century. By 2011 the world population had grown by another 1 billion people (Chart 4.2).

To put this increase in perspective, the previous **doubling time** (prior to 1900, from 750 million to 1.5 billion) was about 150 years (1750–1900), and before that the doubling time (1200–1750) was about 550 years.[7] But doubling of world population from 3 to 6 billion took only forty years (1960–2000), during a time when it was dependent on fossil fuels.

Each country's growth rate is determined by the **demographic process**: the number of births minus the number of deaths, plus the number of immigrants (or minus the number of emigrants). Developed countries tend to have lower growth rates, while developing countries have higher growth rates.

The United States and Canada have the highest growth rates in the developed world. The U.S. population doubled in fifty-six years from 150 million to 300 million (1950–2006), or 0.92 percent annually. Canada is growing at 0.9 percent annually, doubling from 16 million to its current 33 million in fifty-eight years (1950–2008). Between 2006 and 2011, Canada had a 5.9 percent increase. The United States had a 9.7 percent increase (2000–2010), the highest growth of the G8 countries.

Although the global population has doubled since 1960, the growth rate has slowed (Table 4.2). Population will continue to rise for at least another generation, because the average person in developing countries is much younger and still in their reproductive years. This will fuel population growth in the coming decades, until population tops out at about nine billion in 2050.

Another perspective on world population growth is the time it took to achieve it. It took all of human history to achieve a population of one billion around 1850. But because growth is exponential, the second billion took only 123 years, the sixth billionth 12 years, and little more than a decade for the seventh billion (Table 4.3).

Consumption Patterns

Consumption is a global problem but differs in the developed and developing world. The developed world consumes global resources at unsustainable rates that deplete supply; the developing nations extract resources for their own survival and to

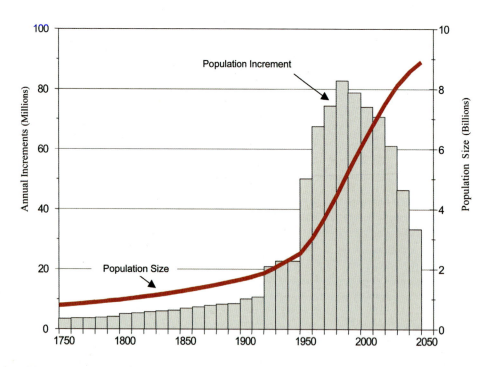

CHART 4.2. World Population Growth. The rapid increase since the Industrial Revolution has been unprecedented in human history and is linked to environmental issues.

TABLE 4.2. Population Growth, 2010

	World	U.S.	Canada	Developed	Asia	Africa	Europe
Percent natural increase	1.2	0.6	0.4	0.2	1.2	2.4	0.0
Percent population < 15 years	27	20	17	17	26	41	16
Years to double population	61	76	77.7	2,641	26	25	58

Source: Population Reference Bureau, at www.prb.org

TABLE 4.3. World Population, Years to Achieve

Population in billions (year achieved)	Years to achieve
1 (1804)	> 50,000
2 (1927)	123
3 (1960)	33
4 (1974)	14
5 (1987)	13
6 (1999)	12
7 (2011)	12

export to developed nations for their consumption, furthering direct environmental degradation. Globally, 20 percent of the world's people in the highest-income countries account for 76 percent of total private consumption expenditures, the poorest 20 percent a minuscule 1.5 percent. More specifically, the richest fifth

- Consume 45 percent of all meat and fish, the poorest fifth 5 percent
- Consume 58 percent of total energy, the poorest fifth less than 4 percent
- Have 74 percent of all telephone lines, the poorest fifth 1.5 percent
- Consume 84 percent of all paper, the poorest fifth 1.1 percent
- Own 87 percent of the world's vehicle fleet, the poorest fifth less than 1 percent[8]

Although the United States constitutes about 4.5 percent of world population, the country consumes about one-third of all processed minerals, 25 percent of nonrenewable energy, and creates about one-third of global pollution. The United States remains the world's largest producer of garbage and industrial waste. American consumption degrades resources worldwide because of its dependence on imported goods, often exporting its raw materials overseas to be processed in countries with low wages and fewer environmental regulations than the United States. This practice is the ultimate fragmented thinking of the status quo economy: exploit and pollute elsewhere, because pollution in one place is treated as disconnected from any other place—but everything is connected.

Humans have impacted all natural systems. It is estimated that 83 percent of the biosphere is now under the influence of humans and up to 36 percent is dominated by humans.[9] Human alteration of Earth has been substantial:[10]

- Human action affects one-third to one-half of land surface.
- Carbon dioxide (CO_2) increased 30 percent since the beginning of the Industrial Revolution.
- More than half of all accessible surface freshwater has been put to use by humans.
- One-quarter of bird species have been driven to extinction.
- Forty percent of the basic energy supply for all terrestrial animals is consumed or eliminated by humans.

These examples indicate how growth in population and consumption has been concomitant with natural resource depletion.

The U.S. and Canadian populations have depleted their readily available resources. New resource development within each country's borders is on less amenable terrain or is prohibited because of environmental constraints. Exploring new resource development areas, options, and technologies has become more viable as resources escalate in price. For example, mounting oil costs have pushed exploration into environmentally fragile areas that are only economical because of escalating oil production costs. New discoveries continue, as do the financial and environmental costs.

Growth since the Industrial Revolution has improved public health and the quality of life for some but has been a detriment to others. The exclusive preoccupation with technology and profit has led those who have benefited to believe that economic progress alone is the measure of quality of life. The Industrial Revolution's dependence on nonrenewable energy sources offered short-term boosts in production, but at the cost of pollution and unsustainable depletion of nonrenewable resources. Short-term benefits—improved public health, medicine, and elevated agricultural productivity—proliferate but are difficult to keep in perspective, as the end of inexpensive fossil fuel draws ever closer.

In and of themselves, each benefit has eased and saved lives, while other lives have been compromised. The current form of progress has produced profits for the few in the developed countries. Many in less developed countries or in the poverty-stricken areas of the United States and Canada have meager wages; they toil in environmentally degraded conditions for the short-term prosperity of moguls. However, in the end everyone pays for the neglected external costs. Additionally, the costs for resources have escalated as the population grows.

Gas, heating oil, food, and water have increased and will continue to increase in price, while quality often declines as does the worker's paycheck. The middle class and poor benefit least by the increases in price, causing the gap between wealthy and poor to grow. As prices rise and paychecks stagnate, the American status as the world's wealthiest nation is in jeopardy, and other questions come to the fore.

Carrying Capacity

Carrying capacity is defined as the maximum population size of a species that an area can support without reducing the area's ability to support the same species in the future. The carrying capacity of the biosphere with respect to the human species needs to be addressed globally. The carrying capacity can be measured for any biological life form, but this discussion concerns humans living in an ecologically balanced world. Long-term sustainability depends on how people live on the planet. There are two standards for measuring carrying capacity with regard to humans: biophysical and social.

The biophysical carrying capacity describes the maximum number of people that can live on Earth within technological capabilities. The biophysical carrying capacity has a higher maximum population than the social, but the standard of living is lower.

The social carrying capacity is based on how many people can live on Earth under a specific social system. The level of technological development determines the carrying capacity; the social carrying capacity is below the biophysical survival number. For example, if the entire world were to live at the Afghan standard of living, the carrying capacity would be considerably higher than if the entire world lived as Americans. Which brings up the question, how many people could the world hold if all people were to live as an average American?

If the world population were to live as Americans or Canadians, the global population would have to be less. According to the ecological footprint, at least five Earths would be necessary to provide the world population with the American or Canadian living standard. Therefore, the social carrying capacity for the North American standard of living would support 1.3 billion people (one-fifth of the current population). Any more people living at this standard would be unsustainable over the long term; it would rob future generations of resources.

Measuring standards of living is subjective, but some consumption criteria have been developed, such as per capita usage of energy. Energy use in the United States and Canada is the highest in the world—Canada has the highest at 422.4 million Btu per person, and the United States at 330.4 million Btu (2008).[11] (See Chart 4.3.) In comparison, Chinese average per capita consumption was 64.6 million Btu, about 15 percent of Canadian consumption.

Determining an ideal carrying capacity depends on the expected quality of life. Some quality of life measures are how land area is used, food production, and the usage rate of renewable and nonrenewable resources. To maintain a sustainable carrying capacity at current population levels requires increasing the use of renewable resources, decreasing the use of nonrenewable resources, and conserving energy use.

Numerous people have estimated Earth's carrying capacity.[12] Some estimates are based on a standard of living similar to that of developed countries (the social carrying capacity), others on the biophysical carrying capacity. Table 4.4 shows global carrying capacity estimates and assumptions calculated by population researchers. The result (median) indicates that a high quality of life carrying capacity has been surpassed and that the current path harms future generations.

Supporting sustainability at current world population levels will be difficult, but if consuming countries curtail consumption, all global inhabitants will move closer to sustainability. But will the United States and Canada change their consumption patterns and altruistically "turn green" to help alleviate world poverty? Past evidence shows the American mind-set has favored consumption and exploitation over conservation, perhaps because too few Americans or Canadians are aware of their disproportionate impact on resource use.

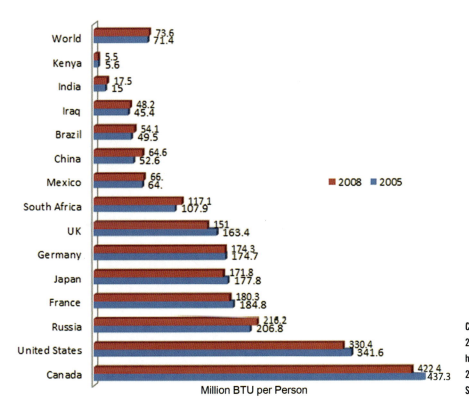

CHART 4.3. Per Capita Energy Consumption, 2005 and 2008. The G8 country with the highest per capita consumption of energy in 2008 was Canada, followed by the United States.

Population Basics: The Demographic Process

Population = Births − Deaths + Immigrants − Emigrants

Birthrate and Death Rate

Three factors—fertility (birthrate), mortality (**death rate**), and **migration**—define the demographic process and help explain changes in population. In the United States, there are about 4.1 million births each year and 2.4 million deaths—a **natural increase** (growth in population by births over deaths) of 1.7 million, or 5.2 percent (2005).[13] These numbers indicate national growth without taking migration into account. American and Canadian women have had the highest birthrates in the industrialized world and the G8,[14] but still, they are close to the replacement level of 2.1 children per woman (infant mortality accounts for the 2.1 number instead of 2.0). In the United States, the TFR is 2.0, while Canadians are at 1.5. The Canadian TFRs are below replacement level, yet the population continues to grow because of the third factor in population growth: immigration.

Migration Patterns

International Migration

Immigration is the most significant contributor to population growth in Canada and the United States. The immigration policies of both countries allow large numbers of legal immigrants to enter the respective countries. Each year, about one million people migrate legally to the United States (Chart 4.4);

however, an additional 500,000 migrants (approximately) enter illegally. Canadian immigration is about 250,000 annually, and another 8 percent arrive or stay illegally.[15]

About 15 percent of Canadian immigrants seek asylum or refugee status, of which 84 percent are accepted (versus 4 percent in the United States). A majority of Canadian immigrants arrive from Asia; China is the largest source, followed by India. Ontario and Alberta recorded the highest immigrant growth rates of 1.3 percent each (2000), but Ontario, Quebec, and British Columbia received 88 percent of all immigrants between 2002 and 2004.

The U.S. population continues to grow, both because of its TFR and because of immigration. The documented and undocumented immigrant birthrate is higher than that of the native-born citizens, which raises the overall birthrate.

More than half of the undocumented immigrants to the United States arrive from Mexico; others arrive from Central and South America or overstay their visas. Two-thirds of the undocumented immigrants settle in one of eight states: California (24 percent), Texas (14 percent), Florida (9 percent), New York (7 percent), Arizona (5 percent), Illinois (4 percent), New Jersey (4 percent), and North Carolina (3 percent).[16]

Internal Migration

Internal migration (migration between states) is common within the United States, especially among the young; more than half of those under forty live in a state other than their birth state. Between 1995 and 2000, only 54 percent of the

TABLE 4.4. Estimates of Socially Sustainable Carrying Capacity (billions)

Source	Low estimate	High estimate	Basis of estimate	Assumptions
Palmer, 1999	9	9	Ecological footprint	Standard of living lower than U.S. current (1 hectare per person) and requires improvements in energy efficiency, food production, pollution control.
Rees, 1996	4.3	6	Ecological footprint	4.3 B computed using 13 B ha of land and 3 ha/person, which is current European standard of living. 6 B using ecological footprint of current North American standards.
Pimental et al., 1994	1	3	Energy	Based on use of renewable solar energy. 1–2 B in relative prosperity, based on use of renewable solar energy. 3 B – adequate food supply.
Pimental et al., 1999	2	2	Energy	Optimal human population enjoying a relatively high standard of living.
Ferguson	2.1	2.1	Energy	Based on energy consumption and CO_2 emissions.
Smil, 1994	10	11	Food	Eliminate disparity in energy consumption of food production technology between developed and undeveloped world. A shift in Western consumptive mind-set toward a sustainable diet and lower quality of life would be necessary.
Brown and Kane	2.5	10	Food	Estimate depends on level of consumption. The lower estimate corresponds to U.S. level of consumption and the highest estimate to the level of people in India. Based on an estimated world grain harvest of 2.1 B tons in 2030.
Meadows et al., 1992	7.7	7.7	Systems model	Systems model results for supporting global population sustainably with enough food, consumer goods, and services. Includes increased technology, pollution reduction, and efficient use of nonrenewable resources.
Westing, 1981	2	3.9	Multiple factors	Based on total land area, cultivated land area, forest land area, cereals (grain), and wood, assuming technology and politics of 1975 and at affluent (average of 27 richest nations) to austere (average 43 nations of average wealth based on GNP) standards of living.
Ehrlich, 1971	0.5	1.2	Unknown	Best estimate of what the planet can maintain over long period of time.
Medians of estimates	2.1	5.0		

Source: Gigi Richard. "Human Carrying Capacity of Earth." ILEA (Institute for Lifecycle Environmental Assessment) Leaf, Winter 2002. Available online at http://www.all-creatures.org/hope/DOE/3%20-%20Human%20Carrying%20Capacity%20of%20Earth.htm

Note: This table is a truncated version of the original published in 2002, and therefore the medians will not be exactly the same.

population remained in the same house as during the previous five years. A quarter moved within their county, and the remainder moved out of state or abroad. Relocation varies regionally. Midwesterners tend to remain in the state of their birth, while in Nevada almost two-thirds move every five years and more than 40 percent are new arrivals in the state.

The internal migration pattern between states is dispersed; between 2000 and 2004 the Northeast and Midwest lost population, while the South and West gained population. In Canada, internal migration concentrates into Ontario and Alberta, where the young move to follow job opportunities.

Population movement has followed arrival areas and opportunities. The first European immigrants arrived on the eastern shore of both countries, the closest to the European homelands. Ninety percent of the colonial residents were farmers, and in time, many migrated west seeking better farmland. However,

BOX 4.3   DID YOU KNOW . . . U.S. AND CANADIAN POPULATION

	United States	Canada		United States	Canada
One birth every	7 seconds	1 minute 29 seconds	One international migrant every	31 seconds	2 minutes 29 seconds
One death every	13 seconds	2 minutes 14 seconds	A net gain of one person every	10 seconds	1 minute 36 seconds

Sources: United States Census, Statistics Canada

the ratio of **rural** to **urban** population began to shift with the onset of the Industrial Revolution.

During the early nineteenth century, waterways powered and transported the products of initial industrial output. Railroads dominated in the mid-nineteenth century. The United States completed the first transcontinental railroad in 1869, Canada in 1885. The transportation system conveyed people to new farming horizons and goods to markets. Ultimately, population growth shifted from rural to urban areas, while settlement continued moving westward. Half of Americans and Canadians were farmers at the beginning of the twentieth century, but less than 2 percent were farmers at the century's end. By 1890, about 35 percent were living in cities, and a century later 75 percent. More than 80 percent are now urban.

Push and pull factors affect migration patterns. California's jobs and warm climate were the pull factors that encouraged people to move there in the 1950s. Later in the century, people were pushed from their homes by age, cold weather, and industrial pollution for the warmer but air-conditioned southern

urban areas. In Canada, population also migrated south. Many retirees chose to settle in the mild and sunny Okanagan Valley of British Columbia. In both countries the economy has relocated or taken root in sunnier climes, and in areas with quality-of-life amenities fueled by nonrenewable resources. The first settlers were farmers who sought good farmland and were not deterred if the region had gray skies, flat marshes, and snow. Today the release from agricultural pursuits, the ease of transportation, and available technologies allow people to move to warmer, sunnier amenity-filled regions—but often in unsustainable numbers that consume at unsustainable rates.

The movement to western cities began in earnest in the 1950s, when televisions beamed Rose Parades in sunny January to the cold, dark Midwest. If the parents did not move the children did, leaving behind an aging population still in place today. The young moved from the Midwest to the Sun Belt—an area south of the 38th parallel.

Between 1990 and 2000, most of the internal migrants moved from the Midwest to one of the top ten Sun Belt

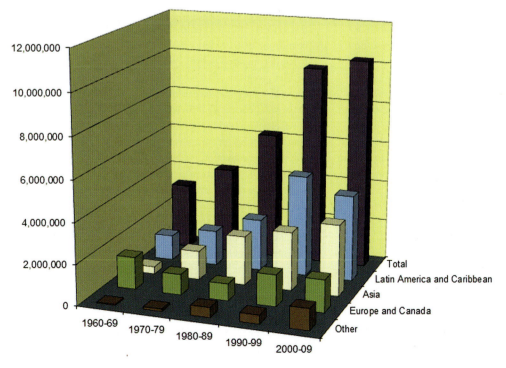

CHART 4.4. Annual Number of Legal U.S. Immigrants by Decade and Region of Origin, 1960–2009. Immigrants' homelands have shifted from Europe to Latin America and Asia.

Source: Homeland Security, 2010 Yearbook of Immigration Statistics, at http://www.dhs.gov/xlibrary/assets/statistics/yearbook/2010/ois_yb_2010.pdf

BOX 4.4 ASSIMILATION—ACCULTURATION

Both **assimilation** and **acculturation** have experienced nuanced changes in meaning since the 1960s. With this in mind, what follows is a generalized explanation.

Immigrants adjust to their new surroundings; however, that adjustment has changed since World War II. Until World War II, most immigrants were European, and their culture was usually somewhat related to the dominant culture; for example, most were white and Judeo-Christian. Though discrimination against various European ethnic groups was extensive at times, they eventually assimilated and were absorbed into the general white populace. The case has been made that these immigrants did not experience the type of racial profiling later immigrants would receive and therefore were more easily assimilated into the culture.

Those who did not fit the white, Judeo-Christian profile often faced discrimination. For example, many Japanese immigrated to the United States during the second half of the nineteenth century, and their thoroughly assimilated descendants were treated as alien terrorists during World War II. Despite their assimilation into America, they were still treated with suspicion and ultimately sent to internment camps.

Since World War II, immigrants have been more likely to go through the process of acculturation—that is, maintaining their own cultural characteristics yet changing superficial behaviors and values as a result of contact with the new culture.

Immigrants who have acculturated can function within the dominant culture but still retain their own cultural identity. Acculturation became dominant over assimilation as the demographics of immigration changed from European to Asian and Latin American. Acculturation grew into **multiculturalism** (an interest in more than one culture rather than only the dominant culture) during the 1960s in the United States and in Canada when it adopted Anglo-French bilingualism in 1971. Despite a multicultural course of action, both national immigration policies are fraught with discord and continue to be controversial.

cities—Phoenix, Atlanta, Las Vegas, Dallas, Austin, Tampa, Orlando, Denver, Charlotte, and Raleigh-Durham. In Canada, the young migrated to the Golden Horseshoe of Ontario and Alberta's booming oil-based economy.

Companies relocated to the Southwest once freed from the physical ties to place (raw materials, power supply, transportation routes). Young families followed. Postindustrial workplace flexibility allowed companies and employees to choose the Sun Belt's warm weather, youthful society, and new cities. The problem is that the Sun Belt's growth is largely due to nonrenewable resources and subsidized water.

The growth of the U.S. Sun Belt continued until the 2008 recession caused a population shift. Sun Belt state population growth slowed considerably. Texas was the state that grew the most, while Florida, Nevada, and Arizona (all states that had experienced large migrations during the boom years) slowed growth and even experienced small losses. The financial crisis created a different scenario in the Midwest, where the declining economy halted most home sales and the ability to move. Overall, the 2000–2010 decade showed a marked increase in the Sun Belt states, stability in the Megalopolis region, and loss of population throughout the Midwest (Map 4.1).[17]

Population Structure

Gender and age are the demographic characteristics that most define a population and in turn determine health care, education, and retirement infrastructures. **Population pyramids** graphically represent gender and age structures. The classic population pyramid, shaped like its name, has a bulging youth base (indicating a high birthrate) tapering to a narrow old age segment, and remains the structure of developing countries. In the mid-nineteenth

century, the population pyramid of the United States and Canada were developing economies with this classic pyramid shape.

The average age in developed countries is older. In the United States, the average age in 1820 was seventeen, in 1990 it was thirty-three, and in 2030 it is projected to be forty-two. By comparison, in 2000 the average age in Honduras—one of the poorest counties in the Americas—was twenty-two, so the age structure in Honduras is about equivalent to that of the United States in 1830, when it was a developing country (Chart 4.5).

The population pyramids for the United States and Canada have a similar age structure. In 2000 the largest group was forty-five to forty-nine, part of the **baby boom** generation (those born from 1946 to 1964 when the average growth rate was 1.7 percent, compared to 0.963 percent in 2011), followed by smaller groups in other age ranges. By 2030, retired baby boomers will be the largest segment of the population, and the classic shape will be somewhat inverted, resulting in a cultural change. For example, a senior population consumes less and requires an emphasis on health care; a younger population requires an emphasis on education.

Retired baby boomers' health care and Social Security costs will be supported by smaller succeeding generations. The large elderly population will be a challenge for the economy, especially if the United States continues to shun universal health care. Medicare only covers about 50 percent of health-care expenses and fails to cover long-term elderly care. Since most seniors live on a fixed income, they often cannot afford additional expenses. Medical care for the elderly will be a crucial concern throughout the twenty-first century.

The geography of population pyramids and the development of nations have changed over time. In the early nineteenth century, the first industrialized countries had youthful populations,

BOX 4.5 PRIMARY TO QUATERNARY SECTORS OF THE ECONOMY

Jobs and their locations have shifted, along with rural to urban growth patterns. Industry has developed over time from **primary sector** hands-on physical work—agriculture, mining, fishing, lumber—to the **secondary sector** of manufacturing, which grew rapidly as power sources changed from human and animal to water, steam, and fossil fuels. The next tier, the **tertiary sector**, specializes in services such as teaching, tourism, or insurance. The **quaternary sector** produces information (Table 4.5). The quaternary sector is still forming and reaches beyond national boundaries into the peer-to-peer (P2P) cyberworld, where people are valued for their connections with a variety of groups, each at a different level of expertise. Expertise is important but only when it is shared through coop-etition.

Historically, most people worked within the primary economy; the secondary economy dominated the Industrial Revolution; the tertiary the early- to mid-twentieth century; and the quaternary the late twentieth century. All continue to operate but in varying degrees. The primary economy employed about 95 percent in 1800; 7 percent work in the primary sector in the twenty-first century. The secondary sector dominated from the nineteenth into the mid-twentieth century but has declined in the United States and Canada; it now accounts for less than 20 percent of the jobs.

The tertiary or service sector employs the largest workforce in the United States today. Postindustrial quaternary sector employment no longer needs to be near specific natural resources or materials. Jobs can be anywhere, and many choose to be in the Sun Belt region, though advanced telecommunications infrastructure is still in larger cities, as are geographic concentrations of transportation. It has become important to be hooked into transportation networks, either located on an interstate or connected by air or rail. Cyberspace connections have become the fastest-growing medium in the twenty-first century, but it is still not focused on what it can do to improve the world situation.

TABLE 4.5. Economy Sectors

	Primary	Secondary	Tertiary	Quaternary
What the sector does	Obtaining raw materials from natural resources	Processing raw materials into goods	Wholesale and retail, banking, insurance, tourism, health, education	Inventing new products, research, science, information manipulation
Examples	Mining Fishing Agriculture Logging	Automobiles Steel Furniture Clothing Housing	Stores Transportation Schools Government	Science labs Inventors University research Computers

similar to developing countries today. They grew rapidly, with high birthrates and lower death rates, while less developed countries continued to have low population growth. By the twenty-first century, the developed countries have low population growth rates and developing countries have higher growth rates, following the same path as the developed countries followed during the nineteenth century, but at a time when the global population has multiplied sevenfold.

Developed countries grew when global population was one-seventh the current population. Countries developing in the twenty-first century also strive for the higher standards of living of the developed countries. However, global population growth and higher aspirations have led many to believe that humans have overshot resource availability and the long-term carrying capacity.

Twenty-first-century population structure and composition has diverged from the beginning of the twentieth century. The waves of migration and the shifting patterns of growth have created a very different ethnic composition in both the United States and Canada.

Population Composition

Historical Components

Until the late twentieth century, Europeans dominated the ethnic makeup of Canada and the United States; however, the countries of origin for immigrants have changed.

Canada

The majority of the Canadian population's forefathers emigrated from the British Isles, but the first immigrants were a significant French-speaking population occupying Quebec and the Maritimes. The 2006 census defines Canadian ethnicity as follows:

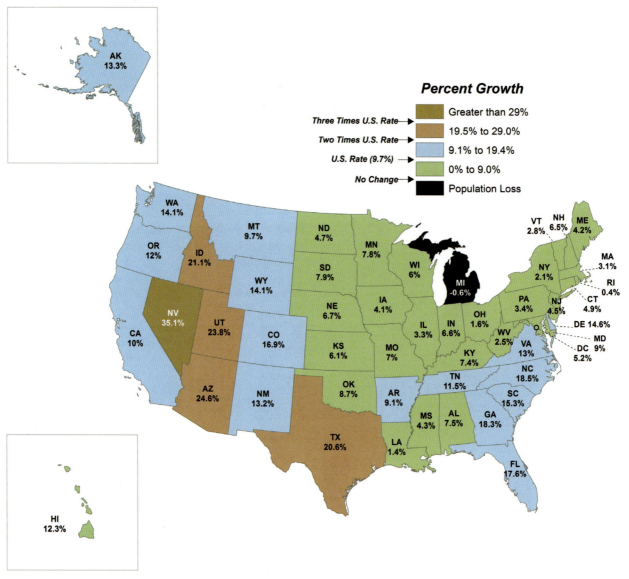

Percent Growth

Three Times U.S. Rate →	Greater than 29%
Two Times U.S. Rate →	19.5% to 29.0%
U.S. Rate (9.7%) →	9.1% to 19.4%
No Change →	0% to 9.0%
	Population Loss

MAP 4.1. Percent Change in U.S. Population by State, 2000–2010.

- Canadian, 32.2 percent
- English, 21.0 percent
- French, 15.8 percent
- Scottish, 15.1 percent
- Irish, 13.9 percent
- German, 10.2 percent

Most French immigration ended when France lost its North American colonies after the French and Indian War (1763). Canada remained a British colony until Confederation in 1867, when 3.6 million occupied Canada's eastern provinces. Manitoba, British Columbia, and the Prairie and northern territories known as Rupert's Land together had roughly 100,000—about 3 percent of the population. In 1870, Rupert's Land was annexed and settlement trickled onto the prairie.

Many Canadians migrated to the states, and there was fear that the United States would subsume the annexed land if it remained unsettled. Lack of transportation and severe climatic factors made settling the interior of Canada challenging. Before 1885, the rugged Canadian Shield topography provided no direct access from Ontario into Manitoba. Entering Western Canada was only possible via routes through the United States. In 1885, Canada blasted a transcontinental railroad route through the Shield and across the prairie.

After Confederation and until the Great Depression, many British immigrants and Canadians alike continued to migrate to the United States. Canada needed to attract new settlers and reached outside the British realm by creating a propaganda machine that promoted migration to Canada. The promotion forbade reference to the cold and snow in the prairies.

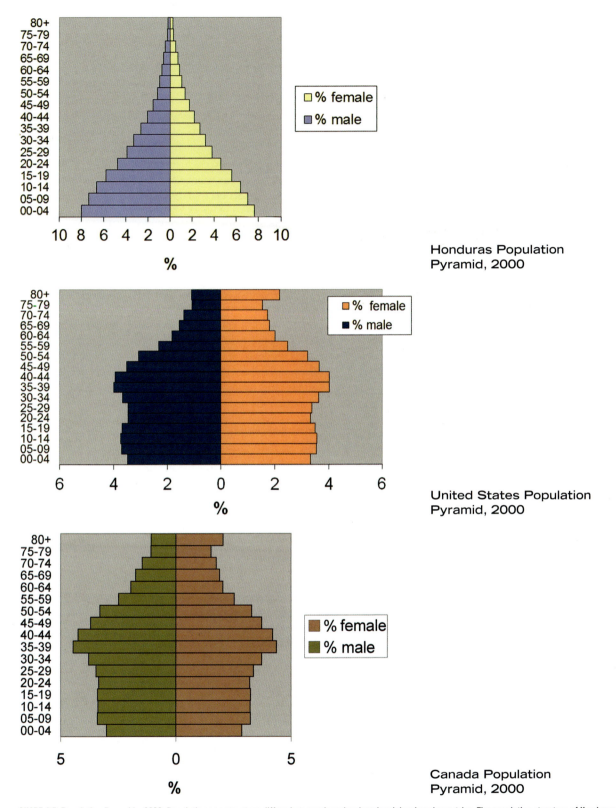

Honduras Population
Pyramid, 2000

United States Population
Pyramid, 2000

Canada Population
Pyramid, 2000

CHART 4.5. Population Pyramids, 2000. Population age structure differs between less developed and developed countries. The population structure of Honduras, one of the least developed countries in the Americas, is in the classic population pyramid form. The natural increase (2.8 percent) and the overall growth rate (2.16 percent) are much higher than those of the United States and Canada: More of the population is younger and less is older. Both the United States and Canada have the population pyramid shape of developed countries, with a bulge in the middle representing the "baby boom" generation, a smaller base of youth, and a larger population of seniors. These shapes are indicative of the smaller family size and longer lifespan in developed countries, but they also indicate new problems: the cost of health care for seniors and the smaller number of working-age population providing Social Security and public benefits for the larger older population.

Religiously persecuted immigrants—Mennonites, Doukhobors, and Hutterites—responded and fled their homelands for Canada. The immigrants, many from the Ukrainian steppes, were culturally preadapted (possessed adaptive traits in advance of migration) to cold climates. One and a half million arrived in Canada between 1900 and 1914, but the reality and harshness of the climate still forced half to leave within a short time. Those who stayed prospered in the face of hardship.

Canadian immigration patterns have undergone considerable changes in the late twentieth century. Both the immigrants and their destinations have changed. The largest immigrant group into Canada from 1995 to 2000 was Mainland Chinese (28.1 percent), followed by South Asian Indians (12.4 percent). Three other Asian countries (Philippines, South Korea, Taiwan) rounded out the top five, with an additional 22 percent of total immigrants. The overwhelming immigrant portal has been Toronto, where 50 percent of all residents are foreign born. Immigrants who speak French often choose to migrate to Quebec, while many Asians, especially Chinese, have chosen to migrate to Vancouver, British Columbia.

Canadians divide themselves linguistically into **francophones**, **anglophones**, and **allophones** (those who speak a language other than French or English). Most francophones occupy Quebec and New Brunswick, anglophones in the other provinces, but allophones are becoming a larger segment of the population. Ninety-two percent of allophones (2001) live in the most populated provinces: Ontario, British Columbia, Alberta, and Quebec.

United States

The initial American immigrants were Spanish and settled in St. Augustine, Florida (1565), and Santa Fe, New Mexico (1610). However, Spanish settlement within the United States in succeeding years was sparse and not the major thrust of the Spanish Empire. Beginning in the seventeenth century, the thirteen British colonies established the dominant Anglo culture along the eastern seaboard.

Today, the combined populations of United Kingdom ancestry (English, Irish, Scottish, and Scots-Irish) comprise 22.7 percent, but Germans comprise 15.2 percent, more than any other over time (Chart 4.6). Settlement of the United States was east to west, but the Great Plains region was usually bypassed and settled after the west and after the transcontinental railroad enabled transport of crops to markets.

Ethnic group settlement varies throughout the United States. The census divides the country into four regions (Northeast, Midwest, South, and West).[18] In the 2000 census, each region had a different primary ancestry group (Table 4.6).

The immigration policies of the United States and Canada have been contentious. From the nineteenth century to the present, waves of nativism (advocating the interests of citizens over immigrants) favored implementing strict immigration laws. The most recent, in the 1920s, were repealed beginning in the 1940s, when immigration policy was rewritten. Immigration continues to be controversial in times of economic stress; many residents continue to feel that new immigrants threaten harmony, cultural identity, and complicate national economic and security issues. Discrimination and racial and ethnic divisions have divided people rather than uniting them.

Ethnic Components

The majority population of both the United States and Canada has been non-Hispanic white, but since World War II global and multicultural immigration patterns have resulted in a more diverse population. In the United States, immigrant populations grew faster than the population as a whole, rising from 16 percent of the population in 1970 to 33 percent in 2005. The largest sources of current immigrants to the United States are Mexico

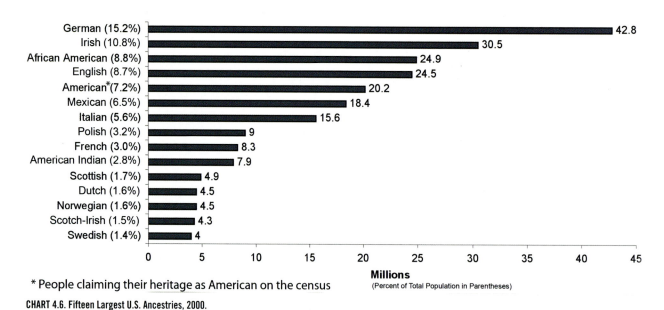

* People claiming their heritage as American on the census

CHART 4.6. Fifteen Largest U.S. Ancestries, 2000.

Source: Angela Brittingham and G. Patricia De La Cruz, "Ancestry: 2000, Census 2000 Brief," U.S. Census Bureau, June 2004

TABLE 4.6. U.S. Ancestry

	Total population (000)	Primary ancestry	Percent	Secondary ancestry	Percent
Northeast	53,594	Irish	15.8	Italian	14.1
Midwest	64,393	German	26.6	Irish	11.8
South	100,237	African American	14.0	American	11.2
West	63,198	Mexican	16.0	German	13.3

Source: Angela Brittingham and G. Patricia De La Cruz, "Ancestry: 2000, Census 2000 Brief," U.S. Census Bureau, June 2004, at http://www.census.gov/prod/2004pubs/c2kbr-35.pdf

(30 percent), the Philippines (4 percent), India (3 percent), China (3 percent), and Vietnam (3 percent). Each regional chapter will discuss specifics about the local migration patterns, but a general ethnic grouping is presented here.

Waves of Immigration

There were five waves of immigration in the United States, and Canada had two intense waves that occurred at approximately the same time as the final two in the states (Table 4.7). During the seventeenth and eighteenth centuries, the first wave of immigrants came from England, Scotland, or Ireland, although a few were Dutch or German. In Canada the earliest immigrants were from France and settled in Nova Scotia or Quebec.

The first wave in the United States consisted of perhaps a million mostly British settlers, who became the backbone of the nation's hearths and cultural mores. After the American Revolution, the British no longer immigrated in great numbers; they were replaced by Scots-Irish and then German settlers. As the War of 1812 and the Napoleonic era raged in America and Europe, immigration to the Americas almost ceased, but it began to increase again in 1820.

The second wave of settlers, from 1820 to 1860, was estimated at six million. Most immigrants were from Northern Europe, including Ireland, Germany, the Netherlands, France, Switzerland, and Scandinavian countries. Most were seeking new opportunities or fleeing religious or political persecution.

Immigration continued until the 1890s, interrupted only by the Civil War. The one exception to the halt of immigration during the Civil War was a flow of immigrants into the United States from Canada. The robust U.S. economy contrasted to a depressed Canadian economy where many, especially those from Quebec, chose to migrate into northeastern U.S. textile towns. Many towns in Massachusetts, Vermont, and New Hampshire still have large French Canadian populations.

TABLE 4.7. Waves of U.S. and Canadian Immigration

	Who	Why	Where
First wave (1600–1750)	British (U.S.) French, British (Canada)	Religious persecution, economic opportunities	Eastern seaboard
Second wave (1820–1860)	Irish, German, Welsh, Scots-Irish, Northern Europeans	Pushed by political and economic factors (crop failure, famine)	East coast cities, Ohio, and Appalachia
Third wave (1865–1873)	Belgian, Czech, Scandinavian	Pulled by political stability, economic growth, agricultural land	North Central United States
Fourth wave (1878–1890)	Southern and Eastern European (Canada: Eastern European from 1890–1921)	Religious persecution, access to land, rise of industrialization	Used transcontinental rail access to Great Plains, Canadian Prairie, Midwestern cities
Fifth wave (1890–1914)	Russian, Southern and Eastern European	Religious persecution, political unrest	New York, large cities
Sixth wave (1960–)	Latin American, Asian	Economic opportunity	West coast of both countries, large cities

Toward the end of this wave, the Canadian Prairies were opened to settlement, and many German Mennonite, Swedish, and Ukrainian farmers moved into the region.

The most significant immigration period occurred from 1890 to the onset of World War I (1914), when an average of one million immigrants, from Russia and from southern and eastern Europe, came to America. Between the world wars, 1918–1941, both the United States and Canada impeded immigration and discriminated against both southern Europeans and Asians. For a short period after World War II (1945–1950), the Displaced Persons Act authorized admission of refugees escaping persecution. They arrived from England, Germany, Italy, and eastern Europe, but the number of immigrants declined as the Soviet Iron Curtain tightened its grip on eastern Europe.

After 1960, the source of Canadian and American immigrants changed radically. In the mid-1960s, both countries liberalized immigration laws. European immigration dropped from 50 percent in the 1950s to 10 percent by 2000. In the United States, the largest groups were Latin Americans, accounting for about one-half of all immigrants, and Asians, constituting about one-third of the total. The Canadian visible minority population (those who are visibly not of the majority population) surpassed five million in 2006. Immigration rates have increased in both Canada and the United States. In the United States, about one million immigrate annually; the Canadian goal allows the equivalent of 1 percent of its total population to immigrate annually. In 2010, there were 280,681 immigrants to Canada.

The racial and ethnic mix in the United States and Canada has continued to change. A brief description of the major ethnicities and racial groups follows.

Native Americans and Canadian Aboriginals

The forefathers of North American Aboriginals began to migrate and spread throughout the continents from Asia about thirty-five thousand years ago.[19] Native Americans (or First Nations or Aboriginal peoples,[20] as they are called in Canada) were scattered in their settlements and were members of numerous linguistic and cultural groups. The estimates for the pre-Columbian indigenous population of Canada and the United States have varied widely (from two to eighteen million north of Mexico).

Contact with Europeans was traumatic for the natives, who lacked immunity to European diseases and were less technologically developed. Within a century, 90 to 95 percent of the indigenous population had died. The population has never recovered. In 2010, less than 1 percent (2,932,248) of the total U.S. population was indigenous. About one-third of Native Americans live on reservations, across the Southwest and in South Dakota, and the remainder live outside the reservation system, mostly in Oklahoma (former Indian Territory) and California.

In 2006, the Canadian Aboriginal and Métis population was 1,172,790 (3.8 percent). Many more Canadian Aboriginals claim native blood than a century ago, when only 127,000 claimed ancestry.[21] About one-half the Aboriginal population live on reservations.

Indigenous populations in both countries have higher birthrates than their respective national populations. The growth is a result of a drop in infant mortality and higher fertility rates among the Aboriginal groups. In Canada, the Inuit have the highest growth rate at 2.3 percent, First Nation 1.9 percent, and Métis 1.4 percent. From 2000 to 2010, the U.S. Native American population grew 18.4 percent. Life expectancy for Native Americans and Canadian Aboriginals remains lower than that of the general population.

African American Blacks

The involuntary immigration of Africans began early in the colonization period. While some northern colonies participated in the slave trade, the southern plantations required a large labor pool, and nine out of ten slaves were in the South by the time of the American Revolution. Emancipation came after the Civil War and changed life in the South for both plantation owners and the former slaves.

By 1900, nine million blacks lived in the South, but within a short period many left the South and its racist Jim Crow laws for jobs and opportunities in northeastern and midwestern industries. Fully one-third of blacks lived in the North, Midwest, or West by the late twentieth century; one in four lived in three states: New York, Florida, and Georgia (Map 4.2).

But after 1995, a new migration pattern was established, as blacks began to repopulate the South. Approximately three hundred thousand returned to the South between 1995 and 2000, about three times the number who returned from 1965 to 1970. They left their northern homes and returned to southern cities, especially Atlanta. Most of the blacks who returned had achieved middle-class prosperity and chose to return to neighborhoods where they felt they had roots.

About half of foreign-born blacks have arrived in the United States since 1990; about two-thirds arrived from the Caribbean, and most of the remaining from Africa. While many blacks have prospered, African American economic progress has lagged in relation to other ethnic and racial groups. (See Table 4.8.)

For four hundred years, the black population size has been modest in Canada; some arrived as slaves brought by Loyalist refugees, and some as free men. In 1901 there were 17,400 blacks in Canada, or 0.3 percent of the population. In 2006, the black population was 783,795, or 2.5 percent of the Canadian population. Forty-five percent of the blacks living in Canada are Canadian born, but since the 1990s almost half are immigrants who arrived from Africa, the Caribbean, and Central and South America. Blacks populate most Canadian cities, but almost half live in the greater Toronto area, where they represent 7 percent of the city's population.

TABLE 4.8. U.S. Ethnic and Racial Population Characteristics, 2010

Ethnicity/race	% of total population	% Change 2000–2010	Average age [a]	% Single mother[a]	Median income [a]	% Individual poverty rate [a]	% College degree [a]
African	12.6	5.7	31.2	53	$30,000	25.3	16.9
Hispanic [b]	16.3	43.0	27.6	28	$40,074	20.6	12.3
Asian	4.8	43.3	35.4	10	$72,305	10.7	49.2
White	72.4	5.7	38	19	$62,712	10.5	29.9
Indigenous	1.2	20.0	30.3	NA	$38,800	26.6	12.7
Total population [b]	107.3	9.7	36.6	25	$58,526	13.3	27

[a] 2007.

[b] Persons of Hispanic origin may be any race; therefore, the total population is more than 100%.

Source: U.S. Census Tables, 2010

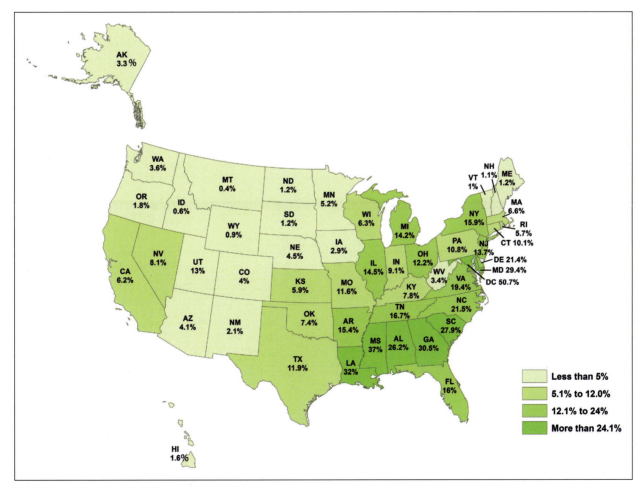

MAP 4.2. Percent Black by State, 2010.

Hispanic Population

The Spanish arrived in New Mexico at the beginning of the seventeenth century. Since that time, Hispanics have been a major settlement and cultural force within the entire Southwest. Prior to the immigration laws of 1920, Mexicans (and Canadians) had unrestricted access to the states. Since restriction quotas were enforced, the largest contingent of legal immigrants into the United States has been from Mexico, with additional immigrants from other Latin American and Caribbean countries. About ten million illegal Hispanic immigrants have also arrived.

Every state has a Hispanic population; however, two-thirds live in California, Texas, Florida, and New York. The states with the highest percentage of Hispanics are those bordering Mexico; New Mexico leads the nation with a 46.3 percent Hispanic population (2010) (Map 4.3).

The 304,245 (2006) Hispanic Canadians constituted 1.0 percent of the total population, with the largest proportions living in Manitoba and Ontario (2.2 percent each), followed by British Columbia (1.9 percent), and Quebec (1.6 percent). About half live in Toronto or Montreal. The majority of Canadian Hispanics are foreign born and arrived during the past twenty years. The largest groups of Hispanic immigrants are from El Salvador

and Mexico. In Canada, a higher percentage of Hispanics have a university degree than the general population (17.4 percent Hispanics, 16.0 percent Canadian). The average Hispanic income in 2000 was $24,917, whereas the median income for the general population was $29,769.

Asian Population

Asians have been a part of the U.S. population since the settlement of the West Coast; however, their numbers were few until after the 1960s. The Chinese Exclusion Act, which stopped Chinese immigration in 1882, was not repealed until 1943.

California had the earliest contingent of Asians. Chinese and some Japanese males mined gold or worked constructing the railroad. Most Asian immigrants lived along the West Coast, or later in Hawai`i, but some settled in Chicago and New York (Chart 4.7; Photo 4.1). Japanese immigrants were few in number prior to strict quotas after World War I.

After 1960, immigration policies opened the door to Asian immigrants. The first immigrants were Filipinos and Chinese from Taiwan and Hong Kong, but later immigrants came from many other Asian countries. Since the 1990s, Asians have constituted more than one-third of total U.S. immigrants. Thirty-five percent settled in California: Chinese in the San Francisco

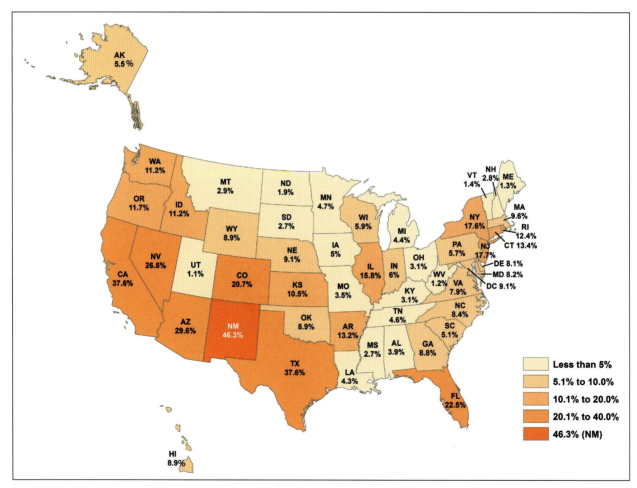

MAP 4.3. Percent Hispanic by State, 2010.

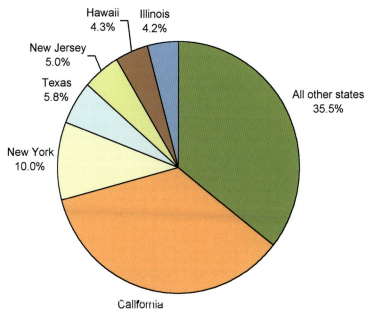

CHART 4.7. Asian Household Population by State, 2004.

Source: U.S. Census, "The American Community—Asians: 2004," American Community Survey Reports, February 2007

area; South Asians, mostly from India, along the southeastern shore of San Francisco Bay. Although Hawai`i's total percentage of Asians within the United States is small, 4.4 percent, 42.8 percent of all Hawaiians are of Asian ancestry.

In 2010, more than 17.3 million Asians lived in the United States (5.6 percent of the population). The largest contingent was from China, India, the Philippines, Korea, Vietnam, and Japan. Asian immigrants have a high rate of education and the highest per capita income (Table 4.9).

Asians began to arrive in Canada during the late nineteenth century. Small groups of Chinese and South Asians migrated to Vancouver. Many arrived from California, but later arrivals emigrated from China. The Chinese Immigration Act of 1923 restricted immigration until the 1940s, when a contingent of

Hong Kong Chinese began to arrive, along with Asians from Vietnam, India, and the Philippines.

The largest visible ethnic group in 2006 was South Asians, followed by Chinese and blacks. A majority of Canada's Asians have immigrated in the past twenty years. In 2001, about 70 percent of Asians in Canada were foreign born. The vast majority of Asians live in the urban areas of Ontario or British Columbia. The average income for Chinese was $25,000, compared to an average Canadian total of $30,000.

Population Distribution

The urban and rural populations of both Canada and America are disproportionately distributed due to employment. Most

TABLE 4.9. U.S. Ethnic Group Statistics

	Total pop. 2010 (million)	% Total	Fertility Rate (per 1000) 2008	% High School Graduates	Median Income 2010
Non-Hispanic white	196	63.7	67.8	89	54,620
Native American	2.8	0.9	64.6	76	35,062
Blacks	38.9	12.6	71.9	80	32,068
Asians	14.8	4.8	71.3	85	64,308
Hispanics	50.4	16.3	98.8	60	37,759

Source: U.S. Census; Kids Count, at http://www.aecf.org/majorinitiatives/kidscount.aspx

people today work in cities, and the population distribution is reflected in the denser urban and less dense rural population.

U.S. Distribution

The fastest-growing region in absolute numbers has continued to be California, but it is the most populous state, so its **rate of growth**—the rate at which the population increases or decreases expressed as a percentage of the base population size—is smaller than states that have less population but have a faster rate of growth, such as the surrounding Intermontane states. The states with the largest numerical increase in population, **absolute growth**, in the 2010 census were Texas with 4.3 million and California with 3.4 million (Table 4.10).

The ten most populous states contain 50.8 percent of the population (2010). The 2000–2010 rate of growth in the United States was 9.7 percent, but within the states, rates of growth vary widely. The states with the highest rate of growth for the past two census periods (1990–2010) were Nevada and Arizona. All of the fastest-growing states were either west of the Rockies or along coastal areas.

The South and West had the highest growth rates (2000–2010), but the South had the greatest share of the population (37.1 percent) (Chart 4.8).

The U.S. **center of population** has been traced since the country's birth, moving from Washington, D.C., in 1790, the year of the first census, to its 2010 location 2.7 miles northeast of Plato, Missouri, in Texas County. The mean center is "the point at which an imaginary, flat, weightless, and rigid map of the United States would balance if weight of identical value were placed on it so that each weight represented the location of one person" on the date weighed.[22] The path of the center of population has continued westward, and since the 1950s moved both west and south.

Canadian Distribution

Canada's largest absolute growth was in Ontario, which added 691,000 to reach 12.8 million in 2011, a 5.7 percent rate of growth since 2006. The province with the highest rate of growth (11.6 percent) from 2006 to 2011 was the Yukon, which added 3,525 people. However, the much larger population in Alberta had a 10.8 percent rate of growth, adding 355,000 to reach 3.6 million total population in 2011. Both the Yukon and Alberta experienced economic booms during this period based on natural resource extraction.

Urban, Suburban, and Rural Populations

The terms *rural* and *urban* have specific and different meanings in the United States and Canada. Until the 2000 Census, "urban" in the United States was defined as any town with 2,500+ people. The 2000 Census changed the ruling to reflect the expansion of suburban areas. No longer were counties within commuting distance of a large city considered rural. In the past, five contiguous towns with a population of two thousand each would still be considered rural. The new definition of urban does not recognize town boundaries but instead, urban clusters that account for people who live outside a city in a town

TABLE 4.10 Ten Most Populous States (2000, 2010)

	2000 (000)	2010 (000)	Absolute increase	Percent change
California	33,871	37,254	3,383	10.0
Texas	20,852	25,146	4,295	20.6
New York	18,976	19,378	402	2.1
Florida	15,982	18,801	2,819	17.6
Illinois	12,419	12,831	412	3.3
Pennsylvania	12,281	12,702	421	3.4
Ohio	11,353	11,537	184	1.6
Michigan	9,938	9,883	(55)	(0.6)
Georgia	8,186	9,688	1,502	18.3
New Jersey	8,414	8,792	378	4.5

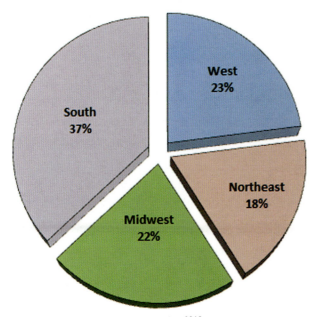

CHART 4.8. U.S. Regional Share of Population, 2010.

Source: U. S. Census

that is smaller than 2,500, but has become part of a sprawling urban metropolitan area. This change in definition in the 2000 Census reduced the rural population numbers from fifty-five million to forty-nine million.

Cities are noted by their population within city boundaries but also by their metropolitan statistical area (MSA) or their combined statistical area (CSA). MSAs are metropolitan areas lacking commuting ties with other large metro areas; CSAs are large cities that are tied together by commuting. In Canada, census metropolitan area (CMA) defines city agglomerations.

The United States and Canada have experienced rural depopulation. In 2003, nonmetropolitan areas of the United States contained 75 percent of the land and 17 percent of the people. About 20 percent of Canada's population lives in rural areas and small towns. The fact that so much land (especially in the West) is still considered rural or unoccupied is not to be mistaken to mean that there is much more land available for settlement. Most unoccupied land has limited access to water.

The last century's population shift was from rural to urban to suburban. Driven by the changes in transportation and employment, population has shifted from 60 percent rural in 1900, to less than 20 percent rural in 2007. Eighty percent of Americans are considered urban, but 60 percent are suburban. Population growth patterns have followed what many consider the American way—sprawl.

Urban and rural definitions do not describe overall density within the United States and Canada. In the United States, the East is more densely populated (Map 4.4), but clusters of density are spread throughout the country. The largest U.S. population cluster or **conurbation** in the twenty-first century is Megalopolis, situated along the Atlantic coast from Boston to Washington. Others include the Front Range of the Rocky

Mountains, Eastern Texas, the Southern Basin and Range, the Pacific Northwest, and California from the Mexican border through the San Francisco Bay area. U.S. coastal areas contain 51 percent of the population on 17 percent of the land, and are the principal concentration of population.

Despite the legalized end to racial discrimination and segregation, urban and suburban populations in the United States continue to remain segregated. In 2000, the core populations of the ten largest cities in America were either African American or Mexican, while the suburban populations tend to be non-Hispanic whites (Table 4.11).

Canada has followed a similar population trajectory; since 1901 the population has gone from 38 percent to 80 percent urban. The Canadian method of defining urban is different, though, so the comparison is not exact. Any town over one thousand inhabitants and a **population density** of at least one thousand people per square mile is considered urban. An urban core area is a city of at least one hundred thousand. Canada is also more suburban than urban; "peripheral municipalities" grew faster (11 percent) than central cities (4.2 percent) (2006). Eighty percent of all Canadians live in urban centers of more than ten thousand. Two-thirds live in the thirty-three largest metropolitan areas, where 90 percent of the population growth occurred from 2001 to 2006 (Table 4.12).

Aging Population

In affluent countries, the aging population is the most significant population phenomenon during the twenty-first century, because of low birthrates and long life expectancies. Aging baby boomers will shift the age structure for the G8 countries, including both the United States and Canada. The aging population and the percentage of elderly (over sixty-five) began to swell beginning in 2010 and will continue for the succeeding half century. In both the United States and Canada, about one in eight was sixty-five or over in 2000; by 2030 one in five will be. The consequences for Canada and the United States will be financial and political. For example, the ratio of the working population to those over sixty-five was 12:1 in 1950, but in 2050 it will be about 3:1 in the United States and it will be similar in Canada. This will have implications for Social Security taxes, retirement plans, and health care.

The problem of massive retirements from 2010 forward has been exacerbated by the 2008 financial crisis. Many people lost a large portion of their retirement funds or were forced into early retirement. Many nearing retirement age have lost their jobs and cannot get new jobs or rebuild their retirement accounts. Those nearing retirement age who have jobs may be forced to work longer, thereby decreasing jobs for the younger population, who would ordinarily fill the positions of the retired; therefore, the financial impact of the recession will have far-reaching effects. The aging population may continue working because they must make up for the losses in their retirement funds, and the younger generation will have a more difficult time finding work because of senior workers not retiring.

BOX 4.6 SPRAWL

Cities in the United States have grown in a different manner than European cities. In Europe, many people were unable to own land, and the opportunities in America were one of the driving forces to emigrate. However, the settlement of the Americas happened when there was a major shift in worldview, and individual desires became as important as if not more important than community. Instead of densely ordered cities with good transportation options, America sprawled across the landscape in a pattern that places demands on transportation, energy, infrastructure, and environment. Sprawl is the low-density, automobile-dependent, single-use neighborhoods found on urban peripheries throughout the states. The length and breadth of the continent have encouraged sprawl, but so have government policies, including socioeconomic and racial segregation and fragmented municipal authorities.

Sprawl resulted from an emphasis on growth for growth's sake, with little care about sustainable development. Growth in this case is likened to quantity—the "big is good" mentality that has been fostered in America; however, sustainable development is about quality of life and achieving energy efficiency. Some of the main costs attributed to sprawl include the following:

- Increased land costs
- Infrastructure (roads, sewers, water, education, fire and police services)
- Increased energy costs
- Increased fuel and water costs

Alternatives to sprawl that have been suggested include compact growth and transit-oriented development (TOD), both of which endorse public transportation systems.

By the 1970s, people were already questioning the costs of sprawl, but little was done to rectify the problems. Then new urbanism and smart growth evolved as answers. By the twenty-first century, sprawl was being reconsidered because of fossil fuel use, climate change, and infrastructure expenses.* However, sprawl continues, as evidenced by the 2010 census. All of the ten fastest-growing cities from 2000 to 2010 were outliers of metropolitan areas.†

* Robert Burchell, Anthony Downs, Barbara McCann, and Sahan Mukherji, *Sprawl Costs: Economic Impacts of Unchecked Development* (Washington, D.C.: Island Press, 2005).
† "Population Distribution and Change: 2000 to 2010," Table 5, at http://www.census.gov/prod/cen2010/briefs/c2010br-01.pdf

Reduced infant mortality has increased life expectancy (United States, 78, Canada, 80) over the past one hundred years, but during the past fifty years the gains were at the aged end of life spectrum, not in reduced infant mortality. A higher percentage of people are living longer than in the past (Table 4.13).

The shifting age structure will alter policies in both countries. The retired population requires more health care, does not consume at the same levels as the younger population, and therefore affects the gross domestic product. As the baby boom generation ages, many will relocate from the northern to southern cities, accenting already stressed environmental conditions in Sun Belt cities.

The Sun Belt attracts senior migrants, either over the winter as "snowbirds" or full-time, even though most seniors seldom move after retirement. Each year only 5 percent of seniors move, versus 20 percent of the general population. When seniors do relocate, more than half move within the same county. For example, the average age of farmers is about sixty-two (2011), and they stay on the farm, especially since most farms are no longer worked by the next generation. Many elderly are poor and cannot afford to move, and they remain in their home state. While Sun Belt states are attracting many elderly, the aging-in-place population is evident when comparing total state population percentages and total senior populations (Table 4.14).

The biggest expense for the senior population is health care. Health-care costs have continued to escalate over the past half-century, and with the bulge of baby boomers entering the "Medicare years," they will rise even more: In 1990 Medicare consumed 12 percent of the nation's GDP; in 2013 it will be 18.5 percent. Almost $1 out of every $5 spent will go to health care, with most for those over 65. Already by 2007, before the impact of baby boomer aging, seniors are declaring bankruptcy at rates far surpassing those under 55. One of the main reasons is a lack of national health-care coverage. The health-care reform of 2010 may alleviate some of the health-care issues.

Population and Environment

The Industrial Revolution and the concomitant rise in population are connected to environmental degradation. By 1850 the world population reached one billion people for the first time. By 2011 the population was seven billion. Not only are the numbers much larger, but our dependence on natural resources has had a tremendous impact on Earth's environment. The growth in human population to a degree that many consider beyond Earth's carrying capacity has accelerated resource depletion, the extinction of other species, as well as creating an array of political, economic, and social problems.

Environmental degradation has expanded from a local- to global-scale problem. Environmental degradation is not new; there are historical examples of deforestation and land depletion created by overpopulation. For example, during Greece's golden age, more and more forested land was cleared to feed ever more people, resulting in the unintended consequence of erosion, a problem that still affects Greece today.[23] In Guatemala during

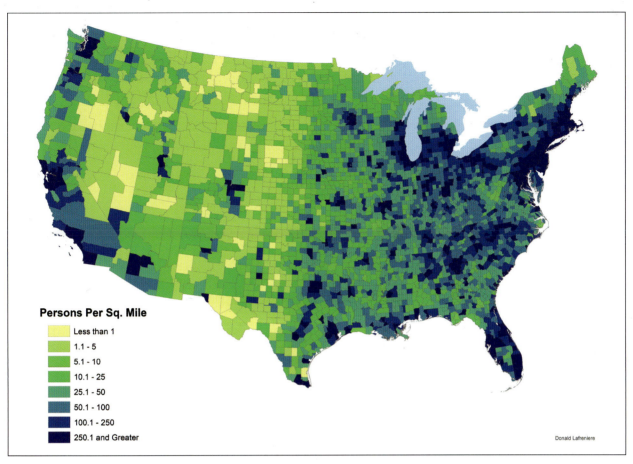

Persons Per Sq. Mile

- Less than 1
- 1.1 - 5
- 5.1 - 10
- 10.1 - 25
- 25.1 - 50
- 50.1 - 100
- 100.1 - 250
- 250.1 and Greater

Donald Lafreniere

MAP 4.4. U.S. Population Density, 2010.

TABLE 4.11. Largest Ancestry Group for Ten High-Population Cities, 2000

City	Primary ancestry	Percent
New York, New York	African American	11.5
Los Angeles, California	Mexican	26.6
Chicago, Illinois	African American	27.8
Houston, Texas	Mexican	23.9
Philadelphia, Pennsylvania	African American	32.5
Phoenix, Arizona	Mexican	24.2
San Diego, California	Mexican	19.9
Dallas, Texas	Mexican	25.8
San Antonio, Texas	Mexican	41.3
Detroit, Michigan	African American	63.0

Source: Angela Brittingham and G. Patricia De La Cruz, "Ancestry: 2000, Census 2000 Brief," U.S. Census Bureau, June 2004, at http://www.census.gov/prod/2004pubs/c2kbr-35.pdf

TABLE 4.12. Ten Largest-Census Canadian Metropolitan Areas, 1971–2006

	1971	Rank	1981	Rank	1991	Rank	2001	Rank	2006	Rank
Toronto	2,628.0	2	2,998.9	1	3,898.9	1	4,682.9	1	5,113.1	1
Montreal	2,743.2	1	2,828.3	2	3,209.0	2	3,451.0	2	3,635.6	2
Vancouver	1,082.4	3	1,268.2	3	1,602.6	3	1,987.0	3	2,116.6	3
Ottawa-Gatineau	602.5	4	717.8	4	941.8	4	1,067.8	4	1,130.8	4
Calgary	495.7	7	657.1	5	754.0	6	951.4	5	1,079.3	5
Edmonton	403.3	9	592.7	6	841.1	5	937.8	6	1,035.0	6
Quebec	480.5	8	576.0	8	645.6	8	686.6	7	715.5	7
Winnipeg	540.3	5	584.8	7	660.5	7	676.6	8	694.7	8
Hamilton	498.5	6	542.1	9	599.8	9	662.4	9	692.9	9
London	286.0	11	283.7	12	381.5	10	435.6	10	457.7	10

Source: Statistics Canada

TABLE 4.13. Percent of U.S. and Canadian Populations over 65

	% over 65	% over 85
United States		
1800	2.0	N/A
1900	4.1	0.2
2000	12.6	1.5
2009	12.9	N/A
2050 (projected)	20.2	4.3
Canada		
2006	13.2	0.9
2026 (projected)	21.2	1.5

Sources: U.S. Census, Statistics Canada

TABLE 4.14. Senior Populations, United States and Canada: Percentages and Locations

Country or state	% of population over 65 2000	% of population over 65 2010	Projected % of population over 65 2030
United States	12.4	13.0	19.7
Florida	17.6	17.3	27.1
Pennsylvania	15.6	15.4	22.6
West Virginia	15.3	16.0	24.8
Iowa	14.9	14.9	22.4
Maine	14.4	15.9	26.5

Source: 2000, http://www.census.gov/prod/2002pubs/01statab/pop.pdf; 2010, http://www.census.gov/compendia/statab/2012/tables/12s0016.pdf; projected 2030, http://www.census.gov/population/www/projections/projectionsagesex.html

the Mayan civilization, population increase eventually paired with soil depletion and resulted in the collapse of the Mayan empire.[24] Today the global population has multiplied far faster than ever before, and technology has enhanced the expansion. But human life is shared with and is dependent on other species; each time a species is lost due to human impact, the fabric of the web of life is weakened. A fish population collapses here, deforestation occurs there, a species is lost, an insect infestation devours crops, usable water becomes scarce, and land is ruined. All the while the human population increases, consumption levels rise, and more damage results.

Take one thread out and the fabric weakens, take ten threads out and holes develop, and people begin working to repair the holes. But in time and as more threads are removed, there are ten holes, a hundred, and the complexity of the consequences is more than human efforts or technology can handle while maintaining quality of life. At some point we may rip that fabric irreversibly and suffer horrific consequences.

A Sustainable Future

The time has come to speak more openly of a population policy. By this I mean not just capping the growth when the population hits the wall, as in India and China, but a policy based on a rational solution of this problem: what, in the judgment of its informed citizenry, is the optimal population.... The goal of an optimal population will require addressing, for the first time, the full range of processes that lock together the economy and the environment, the national interests and the global common good, and the welfare of the present generation with that of future generations. The matter should be aired not only in think tanks but in informed public debate.

—E. O. Wilson, 1999[25]

Population issues are seldom headline news unless to mark another milestone: seven billion in the world, three hundred million in the United States. However, traffic congestion, sprawl, and pollution headlines are related to population issues. Most people remain uneducated concerning the short- and long-term consequences of population growth. While outright population control is seldom discussed in most countries, this has already been done unconsciously. Birthrates in the developed countries of the world (those with the most education and affluence) are among the lowest. Children can be seen as "liabilities" that are expensive and impinge on lifestyles. Countries with less education and more poverty (those who can least afford more children) have the highest birthrates. Children continue to be viewed as "assets" and a form of social security for the parents.

Many people fight for environmental causes other than controlling human population growth. But the need to save the whales, the forests, or the tundra are all indirect effects of human population growth, overconsumption, and technologically and industrially produced pollution. The physical and living world deteriorates as the growth continues. We cannot save whales or any of the myriad species without acknowledging the imbalance that people have created on Earth—without seeing humans as part of the nature they strive to save, without understanding the interaction of all living systems. Whales can be saved if humans maintain a sustainable population and way of life. One way to accept our human place on Earth is to acknowledge the unintended consequences of our actions.

A place to begin is a population policy. Neither Canada nor the United States has a population policy. The last time the issue was addressed was in 1972, and the findings of that report were never implemented as policy.[26] Surely part of the reason is because the population issue is a powder keg, with social, racial, religious, and economic burning fuses. Some of this can be defused by education, including:

- understanding the demographic transition and processes
- understanding increase in population and consumption and their impact on ecological systems
- seeking the opportunities and making informed and healthy decisions about future growth

But the denial of the degradation to Earth's environmental fabric and the necessary cost for repairs is more than most people are willing to address.

The sheer number of people and the rates of consumption have made it difficult, if not impossible, for the environment to cleanse itself. Where there was one person living on a piece of land in 1850, there are now seven; where there was one person dumping their waste into a river, there are now seven; where there was one person seeking fuel, there are now seven. The signs are everywhere that something is not right.

- In the water: Fish are overfished, coral reefs are dying, and oxygen-depleted hypoxia zones no longer can support life.
- On the land: Acid deposition corrodes buildings and kills trees, erosion depletes soil, runoff pollutes waterways, and desertification reduces biodiversity and productive capacity of the soil.
- In the air: Greenhouse gas emissions are shifting the climate, and smog chokes the air and our lungs.

Population growth, consumption, and pollution are all a part of the environmental fabric in which humans live. Achieving a sustainable life, let alone healthy growth, must take all these variables into account. We need to accept that humans are a part of nature, not apart from nature. An attainable venue of change may be to find sustainable approaches to human consumption patterns and pollution. By accepting this premise, the United States and Canada can lead the way into a life of quality over quantity.

Questions for Discussion

1. How do population growth and consumption differ between developed and less developed countries?

2. What is the difference between assimilation and acculturation? What is the price paid by those who choose to assimilate today? By those who choose to acculturate? Which is better for the United States as a nation? For Canada?

3. Does the developed world have the right to call for a halt to population growth even though the major growth is in other parts of the world? Why or why not?

4. Does the developed world have the right to have profited from exploiting their own resources and then not allow developing countries to also exploit their resources for profit?

5. What is happening that indicates we may have exceeded the Earth's carrying capacity?

6. Do you think the United States and Canada should have population policies? What should they be like? What problems would be involved?

7. What is the relationship among population growth, consumption, resource use, pollution, environmental damage, and global warming?

8. Explain how humans are both apart from nature and a part of nature.

Suggested Readings

Allen, James, and Eugene Turner. *We the People: An Atlas of America's Ethnic Diversity.* New York: Macmillan, 1988.

Bailey, Adrian. *The Rise of a Modern Population Geography.* London: Hodder Education, 2005.

Brittingham, Angela, and G. Patricia De La Cruz. "Ancestry: 2000, Census 2000 Brief." U.S. Census Bureau, June 2004, at http://www.census.gov/prod/2004pubs/c2kbr-35.pdf.

Campbell, Colin J. "Petroleum and People." *Population and Environment* 24, no. 2 (2002).

Daugherty, Helen Ginn. *An Introduction to Population.* New York: Guilford Press, 1995.

De Souza, Roger-Mark, John S. Williams, and Frederick A. B. Meyerson. "Critical Links: Population, Health, and the Environment." *Population Bulletin* 58, no. 3 (September 2003).

Ehrlich, Paul. *The Population Bomb.* New York: Ballantine, 1968.

——. "Ecological Economics and the Carrying Capacity of the Earth." In *Investing in Natural Capital: The Ecological Economics Approach to Sustainability,* edited by AnnMari Jansson, 38–56. Washington D.C.: Island Press, 1994.

Ehrlich, Paul, and Anne Ehrlich. *One with Nineveh.* Washington D.C.: Island Press, 2004.

Hardin, Garrett. "Tragedy of the Commons." *Science,* 162 (1968): 1243–1248.

Kinsella, Kevin, and David R. Phillips. "Global Aging: The Challenge of Success." *Population Bulletin* 60, no. 1 (March 2005).

Lichter, Daniel T., and Martha L. Crowley. "Poverty in America: Beyond Welfare Reform." *Population Bulletin* 57, no. 2 (June 2002).

Martin, Philip, and Elizabeth Midgley. "Immigration: Shaping and Reshaping America." *Population Bulletin* 61, no. 4 (December 2006).

McFalls, Joseph A., Jr. "Population: A Lively Introduction, 4th edition," *Population Bulletin* 58, no. 4 (December 2003).

McKee, Jesse O. *Ethnicity in Contemporary America: A Geographical Appraisal.* 2nd ed. Lanham, Md.: Rowman & Littlefield, 2000.

Milan, Anne, and Kelly Tran. "Blacks in Canada: A Long History." *Canadian Social Trends* 72 (Spring 2004).

Moynihan, Daniel P. *Toward a National Urban Policy.* New York: Basic Books, 1970.

National Center for Health Statistics. "Revised Birth and Fertility Rates for the United States." *National Vital Statistics Reports* 54, no. 20 (2005).

Noble, Allen G., ed. *To Build a New Land: Ethnic Landscapes in North America.* Baltimore: Johns Hopkins, 1992.

Passel, Jeffrey S. *Estimates of the Size and Characteristics of the Undocumented Population.* Washington, D.C.: Pew Research Center, 2005.

Pimentel, David, Mario Giampietro, and Sandra G. F. Bukkens. "An Optimum Population for North and Latin America." *Population and Environment* 20, no. 2 (November 1998).

Population Reference Bureau. *World Population Data Sheet,* 2005, at http://www.prb.org/.

——. "Transitions in World Population." *Population Bulletin* 59, no. 1 (March 2004).

Richard, Gigi. "Human Carrying Capacity of Earth." Institute for Lifecycle Environmental Assessment. *Leaf* (Winter 2002).

Riley, Nancy E. "China's Population: New Trends and Challenges." *Population Bulletin* 59, no. 2 (June 2004).

Rockefeller, John D., III. "Population and the American Future: Excerpts." *Studies in Family Planning* 3, no. 5 (May 1972): 77–78.

Roy-Sole, Monique. "Keeping the Métis Faith Alive." *Canadian Geographic* 115 (March–April 1995): 36–46.

Statistics Canada. "Report on the Demographic Situation in Canada: 2003 and 2004." Canada's National Statistical Agency, 30 June 2006, at http://www.statcan.ca/bsolc/english/bsolc?catno=91-209-XIE.

——. "South Asians in Canada: Unity through Diversity." *Canadian Social Trends* 78 (Autumn 2005).

——. "Canada's Ethnocultural Mosaic, 2006 Census," Catalogue no. 97-562-X, 2006.

Thompson, John Herd, and Morton Weinfeld. "A Revolution inside Canada: Immigration and the New Canadians Entry and Exit: Canadian Immigration Policy in Context." *Annals of the American Academy of Political and Social Science* 538, Being and Becoming Canada (March 1995): 185–98.

Uitto, Juha I., and Akiko Ono, eds. *Population, Land Management, and Environmental Change.* Tokyo: United Nations University, 1996.

U.S. Census Bureau. "The American Community—Asians: 2004." *American Community Survey Reports,* February 2007.

——. "The American Community—Blacks: 2004." *American Community Survey Reports,* February 2007.

——. "The American Community—Hispanics: 2004." *American Community Survey Reports,* February 2007.

Wessels, Tom. *The Myth of Progress.* Burlington, Vt.: University of Vermont Press, 2006.

Wilson, E. O. *The Diversity of Life.* New York: Norton, 1999.

Internet Sources

U.S. Census. www.census.gov/

Canadian Census. www.statcan.gc.ca/

Population Pyramids. www.ageworks.com/course_demo/200/module2/module2b.htm#pyramid

Chinese Community in Canada. www.statcan.ca/english/freepub/89-621-XIE/89-621-XIE2006001.htm

Canada's Population Clock. http://www.statcan.gc.ca/ig-gi/pop-ca-eng.htm

Central Intelligence Agency, World Factbook. www.cia.gov/cia/publications/factbook/index.html

Population Reference Bureau, www.prb.org

CensusScope, www.censusscope.org/index.html

American Association for the Advancement of Science, Atlas of Population and Environment, atlas.aaas.org

Part Two

Moving toward Ecoregions

Places

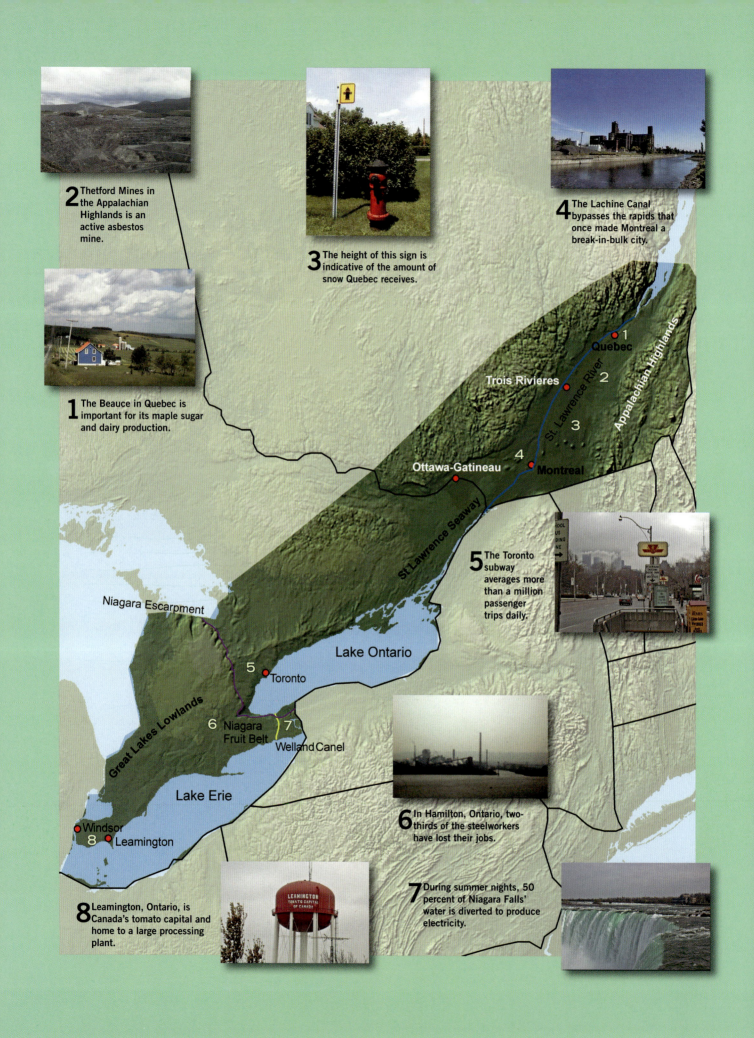

2 Thetford Mines in the Appalachian Highlands is an active asbestos mine.

3 The height of this sign is indicative of the amount of snow Quebec receives.

4 The Lachine Canal bypasses the rapids that once made Montreal a break-in-bulk city.

1 The Beauce in Quebec is important for its maple sugar and dairy production.

Appalachian Highlands

1 Quebec

Trois Rivieres

St. Lawrence River

2

3

4 Montreal

Ottawa-Gatineau

St. Lawrence Seaway

5 The Toronto subway averages more than a million passenger trips daily.

Niagara Escarpment

Lake Ontario

Great Lakes Lowlands

5 Toronto

6 Niagara Fruit Belt

7 Welland Canel

Lake Erie

Windsor

8 Leamington

6 In Hamilton, Ontario, two-thirds of the steelworkers have lost their jobs.

7 During summer nights, 50 percent of Niagara Falls' water is diverted to produce electricity.

8 Leamington, Ontario, is Canada's tomato capital and home to a large processing plant.

5
THE CANADIAN CORRIDOR
A Shift in Core Value

Chapter Highlights

After reading this chapter you should be able to:

- Discuss Inner and Outer Canada and how the relationships may be changing
- Identify francophone and anglophone Canada
- Describe how the Canadian manufacturing sector evolved
- Discuss Montreal and Toronto and their place in Canada
- Explain how Quebec emerged into the twentieth century with the Quiet Revolution

Terms

acid rain
break-in-bulk point
British North America Act
Canadien
cap and trade
Confederation
Corridor
Crown Land
cultural hearth

equalization payment
escarpment
General Agreement on Tariffs
   and Trade (GATT)
Golden Horseshoe
habitant
Inner Canada
locks
long lot
Lower Canada

Loyalist
Main Street
maîtres chez nous
National Policy
North American Free Trade
   Agreement (NAFTA)
Outer Canada
Québécois nationalism
Quiet Revolution
rang system

Reciprocity Treaty of 1854
rift valley
Royal Proclamation of 1763
seigneur
seigneuries
tariff
Treaty of Paris (1763)
Upper Canada
vernacular

Places

Appalachian Uplands
Frontenac Axis
Great Lakes Lowlands

Hamilton, Ontario
Lake Erie
Lake Ontario
Leamington, Ontario
Montreal, Quebec

Niagara Escarpment
Niagara fruit belt
Ottawa–Gatineau
Quebec City, Quebec
St. Lawrence Lowlands

St. Lawrence River
St. Lawrence Seaway
Toronto, Ontario
Trois-Rivières, Quebec
Welland Canal

PHOTO 5.1. Ville de Quebec, founded in 1608, was built in the style of a medieval walled French city, with steep-roofed and dormered sturdy fieldstone buildings. It is the only walled city in the United States and Canada. The homes in the city are also reminiscent of northern French architecture, and the influence of northern France extends even to the language and the food. Visiting Ville de Quebec is an inexpensive way to feel like you are in France, only better, because the people are friendly and gracious in their acceptance of less-than-perfect French.

Introduction

"Too much geography" is how former prime minister William Mackenzie King described Canada, the second-largest country on Earth.[1] While expansive in land area, the country has a relatively small, unevenly distributed population: 90 percent of the population is within 100 miles (161 km) of the U.S. border. A mere 2 percent of the land houses 60 percent of the entire country's population—hugging the southeastern border, the narrow but 700-mile (1,127 km) long **Corridor**, along the St. Lawrence River and Great Lakes. The Corridor land area is about the size of England and Wales, or two-thirds the size of France. Yet despite six of Canada's ten largest cities being situated along this strip,[2] most of the Corridor is open farmland and cities are hours apart.

"The Corridor"[3] is one of several terms that define this elongated region; others include "**Main Street,**"[4] "axis,"[5] "heartland,"[6] and "Central Canada."[7] Canada's core–periphery divide places the Corridor in **Inner Canada** and the rest of the country as periphery, **Outer Canada**. The Corridor is also the political, economic, demographic, and cultural core—the home of its two distinct European cultures.

Quebec remains francophone (French speaking), and it is a distinct cultural region, especially along the St. Lawrence Lowlands area (Photo 5.1). Ontario and most of the other provinces are predominantly anglophone, English in language and culture.

In 1867, the nation formed, with its core and authority in the St. Lawrence and Great Lakes Corridor. The Corridor, Inner Canada, has been accused of exerting its might over the rest of the country, Outer Canada.

Canada's view of itself has always been skewed by the United States, the world power with ten times the population. For most Americans Canada is a virtually invisible country, perhaps with a few trivial differences, but each day the importance of Canada, its worldview, and how it differs from America confirms Canada as its own entity. But Canada's image, power, and economy are changing in the twenty-first century. And the change is not necessarily good for Inner Canada's Corridor.

The Canadian identity has been shaped by four basic factors: geographic extent, northern climate, cultural history, and natural resources. Each continues to redefine Canada, and most especially the Corridor. Climate change and shifting commodity economies have partially destabilized and redefined the twenty-first century Canadian physical landscape.

The Corridor's dominant manufacturing economy has been replaced by the growth of the raw material resource economy in the northwest. With resources in the temperate zones depleted, people are looking to the abundant resources in the untapped north, but in the process creating more greenhouse gas emissions and turning the Inner Canada and Outer Canada economy on its head.

Canada has been more aggressive than the United States in addressing its sustainable future, but the provinces are not united in their aims. While seeking sustainability, Canada is also cashing in on the unsustainable oil sands bonanza in the north. Cap and trade seems a long way off in Outer Canada's resource-rich economies.

Physical Geography

Ninety-five percent of Quebec and Ontario, the Canadian Shield, is sparsely populated, but the other 5 percent, the lowlands Corridor, is the most densely populated region in Canada. Sandwiched between the Appalachian Uplands to the south and the Canadian Shield to the north, the Corridor strip is divided into the St. Lawrence Lowlands to the northeast, and the Great Lakes Lowlands to the southwest. Separating the two subregions

BOX 5.1 INNER AND OUTER CANADA

Politically and culturally, Canada has bifurcated between Inner Canada (lowlands of Ontario and Quebec) and Outer Canada (the rest of the country). Both have vied for political attention. Inner Canada, the Corridor, has been the core of the country industrially, politically, and demographically. Ottawa, the capital, positioned on the border between the provinces of Quebec and Ontario, is often accused by other Canadians of favoring the Corridor. Ontario and Quebec's seeming monopoly on population, political clout, manufacturing, service, and research and development leaves the rest of the country—98 percent of the territory and 40 percent of the population—with regional discontent. With a majority of the population, the Corridor is also disproportionately represented in the House of Commons.

Culturally, the division continues between anglophone and francophone Canada. Though most of the country is anglophone, the francophone population within the lowlands corridor is significant geographically, economically, environmentally, and culturally.

The balance of power within Canada is shifting, though. Alberta's and British Columbia's economies surpassed eastern cities in 2007, when the seven fastest-growing economies were all located in the west.* And power has shifted as well. No longer is the prime minister necessarily bound to the Corridor. Quebec's secession attempt, phrased as cultural separatism, has now been matched by Alberta's geographic separatism, where oil sand money has given them power to speak up about such matters as limiting the

federal government's authority and such issues as "forced" bilingualism, gun control, and energy policy. In 2008, Newfoundland also rocked the Inner Canada boat with its offshore oil deposits that have pumped new life into what had been a moribund economy since the 1992 collapse of the fishery.

The two distinct linguistic and cultural histories punctuate the Inner Canada favoritism. Quebec, once called Lower Canada, is mostly French speaking and Roman Catholic, while Ontario, Upper Canada, is English and initially settled by Loyalist Protestants. (The lower and upper designations are in relation to the St. Lawrence River, where Upper Canada is at the upper reaches of the river.) Despite their differences, the heavily populated portions of Ontario and Quebec have had political, economic, and demographic control of Canada since Confederation.

Despite western and Maritime alienation, Canadian policies favor economic, cultural, and political unification, though some may question Inner Canada's motivations for establishing a railroad early in its history or encouraging immigration and liberal land policies in the western provinces. All the while, though, the gorilla in the room has been the United States. Canada and the United States, which share what is still the longest undefended border in the world (though somewhat tarnished by 9/11), have also had a long, tortuous economic relationship in which the David of Canada has periodically succumbed and then triumphed over its Goliath-like neighbor.

* Eric Beaucchesne, "Western Canada Still Ahead of Eastern Cities," *Financial Post*, September 14, 2007.

is the Frontenac Axis, which connects the massive Canadian Shield with the Adirondack outlier across the border in New York (Map 5.1). The Corridor region is within the St. Lawrence River watershed (inclusive of the Great Lakes watershed), but it is not the entire watershed. The entire watershed of this ecoregion is divided by the U.S.-Canada border.

Corridor Lowlands

The Corridor, the southernmost part of Canada, is in the same ecoregion as the American Midwest, but to the north it is a subregion of colder climate.

The Corridor ecozone is the smallest in Canada, and although now populated and cleared, it was entirely forested when Europeans arrived. The Corridor deciduous mixed wood plain contained many sugar maples (Canada's national symbol) and moving north evolves into a boreal mixed and then coniferous forest (Map 5.2).

The St. Lawrence Lowlands live up to their name, except for the igneous intrusion of the Monteregian Hills, rising 800 feet (250 m) above Montreal. The earthquake-prone St. Lawrence Lowlands are part of a **rift valley** (a valley formed by the sinking of land between two faults) that has registered about ten earthquakes each century.

The Champlain Sea, of which Lake Champlain is a remnant, inundated the St. Lawrence Lowlands plain for about two thousand years at the end of the last ice age. Fertile sediment from the sea unevenly covers the flat plain between Montreal and Quebec City. The plain is widest at Montreal and along the south side of the St. Lawrence.

Continuing southwest, hugging the northern shores of lakes Erie and Ontario, the Great Lakes Lowlands' glacially derived clay deposits cover all, except the exposed Niagara Escarpment limestone. The Great Lakes Lowlands is both an important agricultural area and one of the most densely populated in Canada (Map 5.3).

Niagara Escarpment

The Niagara Escarpment is a geographic anomaly that begins in New York State, enters Canada at Niagara Falls, and then continues around the Michigan Basin (Map 5.4). Separating Lakes Ontario and Erie, the limestone and dolomite outcrop rises 200 feet (60 meters) above the Ontario Plain. Several gorges cleave the **escarpment**, the most notable being the 7-mile (11 km) Niagara Gorge, where Niagara Falls has eroded the escarpment at the rate of four feet a year (1.2 m). In a mere seventy-five thousand years, the two Great Lakes will merge.

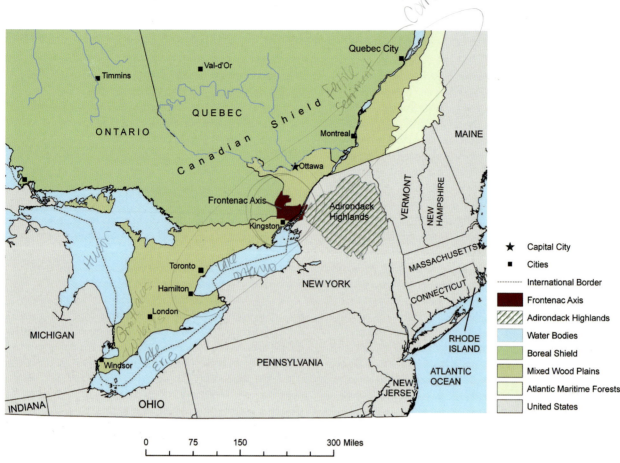

MAP 5.1. The Frontenac Axis, dividing the St. Lawrence Lowlands (north of the axis) from the Great Lakes Lowlands (south of the axis). The Frontenac Axis connects the Canadian Shield with the New York Adirondacks.

But meanwhile the escarpment creates a warming microclimate where fruit trees and wineries have flourished, although they now have given way to an increasingly suburbanized landscape.

Water

Canada has abundant freshwater. Much of that water feeds the St. Lawrence River, one of the continent's main natural transport routes, which connects the Atlantic and the interior. Both Natives and fur traders once portaged the river's two major obstacles, the Lachine Rapids and Niagara Falls. Later, the St. Lawrence Seaway bypassed the obstacles.

The St. Lawrence River begins near Kingston, Ontario, and courses along the ancient rift valley, draining into the Gulf of St. Lawrence estuary. The watershed includes the Great Lakes and reaches north into the Canadian Shield. Towns are positioned at river confluences, such as Kingston located at the northeastern end of Lake Ontario and Trois-Rivières located at the three mouths of the St. Maurice River.

Explorers LaSalle and Cartier sailed up the St. Lawrence River, hoping they had found the Northwest Passage. Cartier, obsessed with finding a route to China, followed the river and named the Lachine (China) Rapids in 1535.

Montreal, the head of ocean navigation, was founded at the rapids as a break-in-bulk city—all goods had to be portaged around the rapids to continue their journey. In 1825 the Lachine Canal bypassed the rapids and became the heart of Montreal's factory-laden industrial sector. The Lachine Canal launched the Corridor economy with lumber and wheat from the interior. The canal was also the first nail in the coffin of the Maritime trade, and its economy declined as Montreal's grew. But in 1959, the St. Lawrence Seaway opened and ended the Lachine reign. The canal closed for thirty-two years because of toxic sediment from years of industrial contamination. Since 1988, a prevention plan has eliminated the discharging of many industrial and agricultural chemicals into the river. The canal reopened in 2002 as a pleasure boat waterway.

The Niagara Falls presented a physical obstacle to transport. The falls were bypassed by a series of **locks** and have since been a lynchpin for the tourism and hydropower economies. The falls were first bypassed in 1829 with the completion of the first of five successive Welland Canals. However, the challenges of climate change include maintaining energy and shipping economies.

The Niagara River falls into the glacially formed Niagara Gorge, and in the process generates 2.4 million kilowatts (enough power to light twenty-four million 100-watt bulbs) of hydroelectric power for the Eastern United States and Canada. But

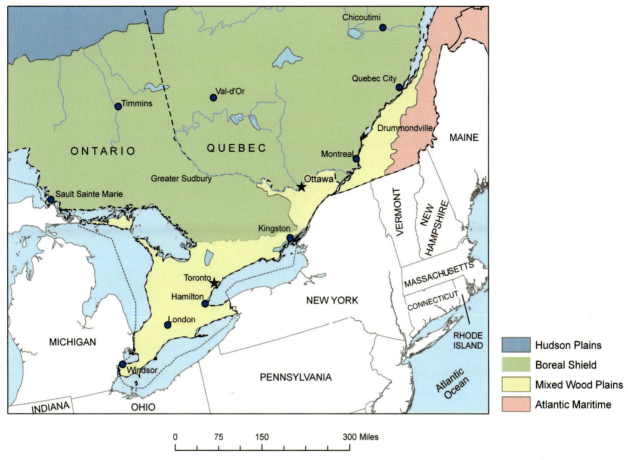

MAP 5.2. The Corridor Lowlands was a mixed wood forest prior to its current agricultural and urban use. Small portions of the forest remain and are protected.

Legend:
- Hudson Plains
- Boreal Shield
- Mixed Wood Plains
- Atlantic Maritime

maintaining the tourism economy and generating power was a problem, which was accomplished by cutting the Niagara's flow in half during the nighttime hours of the April through October tourist season. Hydropower's importance as an energy source has grown during the twenty-first century, as energy shortfalls and the pollution of coal-burning power plants become major impediments to reducing greenhouse gas (GHG) emissions. Private Canadian companies built hydropower generators on **Crown Land** (government-owned land) in order to expand waterpower production and reduce the carbon footprint.

The St. Lawrence water levels have always fluctuated, but climate change has exacerbated fluctuations and caused shipping problems. For example, lower water levels in the western portion of the river require increased dredging. Since the millennium, the Seaway and Great Lakes have already experienced a decrease in carrying capacity, an increase in the cost of moving cargo, and an increase in ship sizes.[8] Suggestions to improve the Seaway include conserving water, shifting energy production, reducing sprawl, and cleaning up industrial practices.

Climate

Most of Canada lies north of the 49th parallel, about the latitude of Frankfurt, Germany, but Canadian weather is usually colder than European cities at equivalent latitudes because the North Atlantic Drift and wind circulation patterns warm the European plains. Lower Canadian temperatures are due to the high western mountains blocking oceanic warmth, and the lack of large bodies of water to moderate the temperature leaves the region with the more extreme temperature fluctuations of a continental climate.

The Corridor seasonal climate of long, harsh winters and shorter warm, humid summers progresses north along the St. Lawrence Lowlands, where winters become extreme. Precipitation is ample, about sixty inches annually, much of it as snow. On the leeward side of the Great Lakes the water moderates the climate, including heavy lake-effect snow; some areas average 100 inches annually.

Along the St. Lawrence Corridor area, winter sets in by mid-December, when the river freezes leaving Montreal icebound. Unstable Gulf and Arctic winter weather systems can spawn major storms, blizzards, and ice storms.

Historical Geography and Settlement

Prior to European arrival, sixty thousand to eighty thousand Aboriginals lived in the Corridor lowlands. Algonquin lived

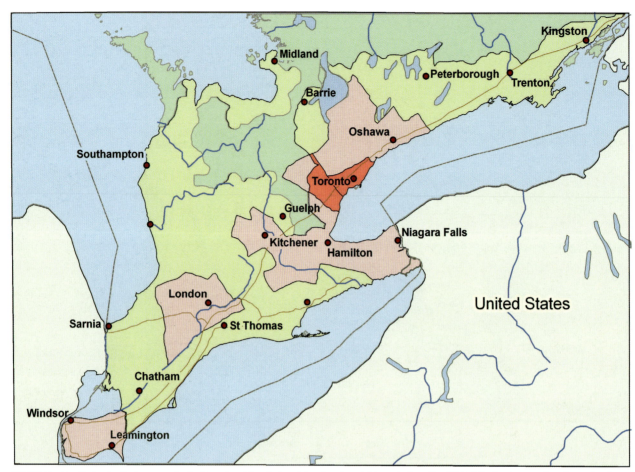

MAP 5.3. The Great Lakes Lowlands occupy the fertile region of Ontario from Lakes Ontario and Erie to the Canadian Shield. It is also the most densely populated part of Canada, with several large cities.

along the St. Lawrence waterway; the Iroquoian Confederacy lived near the Great Lakes. The small Algonquin bands lived as nomadic hunters and fishers, while the Iroquoian agricultural-ists lived in concentrated communal villages composed of up to three thousand residents. Today, about eleven thousand Algon-quin live in small communities across Quebec and eastern Ontario, and part of the Iroquoian Confederacy settled north of Lakes Erie and Ontario.

The French and Algonquins established early fur trade rela-tions, but this lasted only as long as the Natives were of use to the Europeans, and the Europeans to the Natives. Land loss for the Natives accelerated after the American Revolution, when many **Loyalists** migrated to Canada, necessitating land acquisi-tions from the Lake Ontario Aboriginals.

In 1867 the **British North America Act** created the Domin-ion of Canada, consisting of Nova Scotia and New Brunswick, and hugging the banks of the St. Lawrence were a much smaller Quebec (**Lower Canada**) and Ontario (**Upper Canada**) (Map 5.5). Soon after, Manitoba (1870), British Columbia (1871), and Prince Edward Island (1873) joined the decentralized federation called the **Confederation**. In order to keep peace within the

linguistically split country, Canada adopted a federalist govern-ment that granted political authority to the central government for foreign affairs and national and interprovincial communica-tions and transportation, while provinces protect their cultures by controlling education and language.

Quebec

The French were the first Europeans to colonize Canada. The initial French immigrants traded copper kettles and beads for furs to satisfy the European beaver felt hat fashion of the time. Catholics and Huguenots (French Protestants) initially immi-grated, but Cardinal Richelieu barred all Huguenot immigration after 1628.[9] Most Quebec settlers were Catholic, an imprint that remains on the landscape to the present day.

Fur traders eschewed agriculture, but the French Crown decided that permanent settlers would strengthen the French New World position and began encouraging families and women to emigrate. Few French were naturally inclined to immigrate to the hostile, harsh New France. Immigration was also hampered by the cost; the French lacked the subsidized passage practiced by the British. Indentured servants who

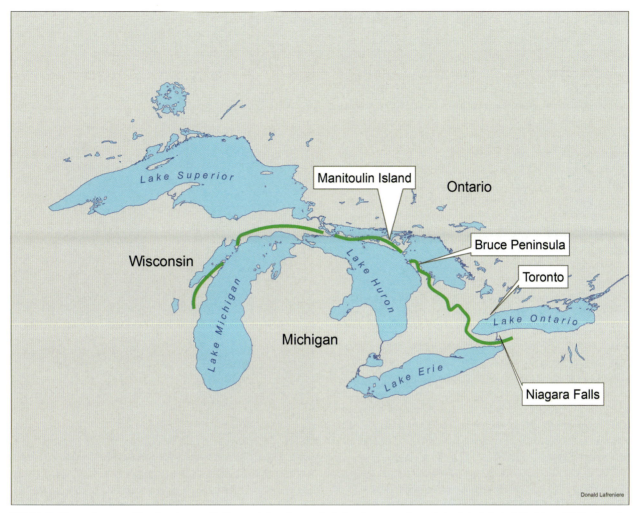

MAP 5.4. The Niagara Escarpment is a limestone cap that has eroded much more slowly than the surrounding rock. An obstacle for both the Erie and Welland canals, the escarpment was traversed by a series of locks.

immigrated worked for three years to pay their passage, but they were rewarded after with something unattainable in France—land. Many immigrant men stayed because of the access to land and the importation of poor, single women.

In the seventeenth century, the North American colonies had far more French immigrants than British. But the hard life, hostile Natives, and cold weather disenchanted many French settlers. About two-thirds returned to the mother country.

New France settlers were divided socioeconomically into a two-class model, the *seigneurs* and *habitants*. The **seigneurs** were aristocrats appointed by the king and given **seigneuries**, which were large swaths of land (the Seigneury of Beaupré, for example, was forty-eight miles long and eighteen miles deep). The *seigneurs* subgranted their land to the *habitants*, who were expected to pay rent with a portion of their crop. The *seigneurs* were enlightened by the new modern Baroque outlook. The **habitants** were peasants or lower-middle-class Roman Catholics from Normandy, conservative and

medieval in their thoughts. A wide cultural gap separated the *seigneurs* and the *habitants* from the beginning, and within that gap the New France culture formed. A few other settlers were minor government officials and a small merchant middle class, hoping that time spent in Canada would pay off in the future.[10]

French settlement established the region's population base and imprinted the St. Lawrence Lowlands landscape. Most of the *seigneuries* were located fronting the St. Lawrence and its tributaries. The French Canadians initially settled riverfront land in the distinctive long-lot style imported from Normandy (Photo 5.3). **Long lots** are about one-tenth as wide as they are long and consist of about seventy to ninety acres. The narrow width maximized the number of farmers with river frontage and created a village-like community. The lot depth encompassed a variety of uses: arable land, pasture, and timber for building material and fuel. As waterside lots filled, further *rangs* or rows were created away from the water, in what is known as the **rang** system.

BOX 5.2 THE ST. LAWRENCE SEAWAY

The St. Lawrence Seaway system stretches 2,038 nautical miles, connecting all the Great Lakes to the St. Lawrence River and the Atlantic Ocean. The first link in the chain was built in 1829, when the first of four sequential Welland Canals circumvented Niagara Falls. The canal was rebuilt each time to satisfy the ever-larger ships passing through the canal, much as today the system is once again under the same threat (Photo 5.2).

The St. Lawrence Seaway opened in 1959. The Seaway, a joint Canadian and U.S. project, opened the Great Lakes to ocean-going vessels during the ice-free season (usually March to December) and also enhanced power generation. The system allowed bulk carriers of the post–World War II era to pass from one lake to another, to the Atlantic, and back.

Since the late twentieth century, supertankers and ocean-going container ships have been too large to fit in the Seaway locks. These large ships must unload to smaller ships at Montreal or Atlantic ports, which increases the cost of shipping. Seaway shipping tonnage has declined for twenty-five years and continues to decrease. About 80 percent of the Seaway traffic is bulk cargo from the interior, grain, iron ore, and Powder River Basin low-sulfur coal, which is popular with European utilities. The remainder is smaller containerized "feeder" ships carrying manufactured goods. Additional problems include invasive species and the system's aging infrastructure, which requires maintenance. Research has examined upgrading and widening the Seaway to accommodate larger ships.*

The Great Lakes ecosystems have been significantly changed due to invasive species, which entered the ecosystems via ship ballast water. The Seaway has more than 180 invasive species, two-thirds of which have entered since the Seaway opened, despite regulations requiring exchange of ballast water prior to entering the Great Lakes.

There are both advantages and disadvantages to maintaining the Seaway. The Seaway competes with railways as the most efficient way to transport goods, because seagoing vessels burn less fossil fuel than land transport and both relieve congestion on highways. However, lake levels have been falling, partially due to climate change. A lack of funding has limited dredging so that ships

PHOTO 5.2. Welland Canal, St. Catherine's, Ontario. Since 1829, ships have been raised a total of 327 feet between Lake Ontario and Lake Erie. The canal has been rebuilt four times to accommodate ever-larger ships. It helped support a large manufacturing workforce in Welland until the 1990s, when globalization closed many companies and forced others to downsize.

have to reduce their cargo to accommodate the reduced depth in the waterway, thereby reducing profits.

The Seaway has advantages for a successful manufacturing economy, but the lack of investment in infrastructure and the potential for climate change shifts could threaten the continued success of the Seaway.

* Great Lakes St. Lawrence Seaway Study, Final Report, Fall 2007, at http://www.glsls-study.com/Supporting%20documents/GLSLS%20finalreport%20Fall%202007.pdf.

British and French both claimed land, with Natives caught between the two but usually siding with the British. In 1713 the British gained access to the Maritimes and the eastern seaboard; the French claims were superimposed on British claims, but French control was disputed and tenuous.[11] Both French and British sent troops, and military engagements led to the Seven Years' War. The war was ended by the **Treaty of Paris (1763)**, when the French relinquished their New World holdings to the British. The British and Scots established townships along the

outer edges of the southern *seigneuries*, south to the American border and west following the Ottawa River. Over time, English, French, and Aboriginals occupied the region.

While French immigration ended after the war, a high birthrate supported rapid population growth. The French expanded settlements onto British land or to the adjacent American Northeast. From 1840 until the twentieth century, push and pull factors prevailed, pushing many French Canadians away from the dominant agricultural life and pulling them

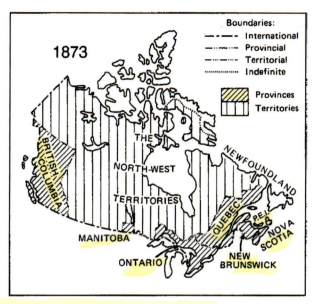

MAP 5.5. Canadian Confederation, 1867 and 1873. The four original provinces in 1867 were Ontario, Quebec, New Brunswick, and Nova Scotia. Manitoba, British Columbia, and Prince Edward Island joined by 1873. The Northwest Territories were still relatively unpopulated by Europeans. Ontario and Quebec grew to their current extent (at the expense of the Northwest Territory) by the beginning of the twentieth century.

to mill jobs in the burgeoning Industrial Revolution in the United States. Québécois heritage continues to influence many northeastern towns.

The Treaty of Paris also established Aboriginal "rights" to the New World, through the **Royal Proclamation of 1763**, which would later be used to determine the definition of Aboriginal title and rights in the territory west of Quebec. The proclamation, actually a strategic tool to retain Native and Aboriginal

PHOTO 5.3. The Long Lots of the Original French Settlers. The *rang* or range system differentiates Quebec from English grid pattern settlements. Long lots were narrow strips of land that allowed many farmers to have river frontage. As river frontage filled, another set of long lots would be made along a road parallel to the first, establishing a second *rang*, and later, a third, fourth, and so on.

allies during the colonial wars, recognized prior Aboriginal occupancy and permitted self-government and compensation for their land. However, over the ensuing years immigrants acquired land at the expense of the Aboriginals. In 1982, Canadian Aboriginals fought back and used the Royal Proclamation as the basis for Aboriginal title. They gained constitutional protection for fishing, logging, and hunting rights, as well as an inherent right of self-government.[12]

Ontario

Aboriginals and nomadic French fur traders inhabited Ontario's dense forests until the American Revolution, when ten thousand Tory Loyalists became the first permanent European settlers. With their land confiscated in the United States, Loyalists sought refuge in the remaining British colonies. They moved to Nova Scotia and New Brunswick, but most chose Quebec. Cultural differences—anglophone and Protestant versus francophone and Catholic—were enough impetus to carve a new, western colony, Upper Canada, located southwest of Kingston along Lake Ontario. Based on their Loyalist participation in the Revolution, the British gave the settlers provisions and land.

During the War of 1812 Americans, thinking Canadians desired liberty from British rule, attacked Canada and were thwarted, which effectively ended a stream of American farmers moving into Canada. Although the war itself was a stalemate, it demonstrated an early sense of an independent Canadian nationhood. Canadian immigration shifted from Americans to a wave of British and Irish settlers fleeing difficult economic conditions at home. The best agricultural land was settled by 1830. By Confederation, some 1.4 million migrants had settled in Upper Canada; another 1.2 million were split between Quebec and Atlantic Canada.

Upon Confederation, Upper Canada, renamed Ontario, occupied only the lowlands area, but it would expand four times in the succeeding years to incorporate newly acquired lands in the wild, rough-hewn Canadian Shield. However, the best farmland was along the Corridor, so when good Corridor land was no longer available, the sons and daughters of the large rural families migrated to the rich prairie farmland of Manitoba, while others populated the growing cities of Ontario. By the time of Confederation, Ontario had the largest population and had established a national industrial economy.

Cultural Perspectives

The Corridor has two distinct cultural landscapes. To the northeast, Quebec's landscape reflects French settlement patterns, from long lots to cultural artifacts. Although the culture has changed significantly since the 1960s **Quiet Revolution,** the artifacts remain and are cherished as an important part of the province's French history.

Southwest of the Frontenac Axis are the Great Lakes Lowlands, similar in physical landscape but anglophone culturally. The **Golden Horseshoe**—the agglomerated urban area surrounding the southwest end of Lake Ontario—highlights the Great Lakes Lowlands, which has become the most multicultural region in Canada.

The French Canadian Landscape

The French-Canadian presence along the St. Lawrence River has remained strong, despite the effective ending of French immigration in 1763. Of the thousands of French who had migrated to New France, less than ten thousand remained. They became the seed stock for the eight million francophones who live in the province today.

French-speaking Canadians from Quebec will often refer to themselves as Québécois. Through the 1990s, the term *Québécois* also indicated a preference for the Parti Québécois or separatist notions of **Québécois nationalism**, but that meaning has diffused into one indicating a more general and proud reference to the people, society, and nation. In November 2006, Prime Minister Stephen Harper supported the recognition of several Quebec cultural nations within a united Canada, including the Métis, the Canadian Aboriginals, and the Québécois. Today the term *Québécois* is more likely to mean a proud descendant of the original settlers in New France. The terms *French Canadian* or *Canadien* also refer to New France ancestry but without the separatist innuendos of *Québécois*.

The French **cultural hearth** is in Quebec, where more than 80 percent of the population is francophone. However, the French influence reaches beyond Quebec. In New Brunswick, 34 percent are francophone, mostly along its eastern shore. Ontario's eastern counties bordering Quebec also have a large French-speaking population.

The French have maintained their language despite the rest of Canada becoming English speaking. Montreal—the world's second-largest francophone city—is bilingual. It is possible to live one's entire life speaking English while living in the francophone hearth. Anglophones have congregated in Montreal, while Quebec's rural lowlands and Quebec City are generally francophone.

The French language in Quebec is quite different from Parisian French. The original French inhabitants came to Quebec in the seventeenth and early eighteenth centuries, and after 1760 the settlers had little contact with the motherland, so the language has evolved from the northern French dialect of the early settlers. The surrounding English-speaking populace, the Aboriginal contact, and Quebec's environment influenced the francophone Canadian vocabulary. Idioms and slang developed independently in both France and Quebec. The words and pronunciation of Quebec French and Parisian French differs more than the pronunciation of American English and British English.

Quebec City is the center of the francophone hearth. Almost everyone has been unilingual francophone, but slowly in the twenty-first century even this is changing, much to the chagrin of those who feel that bilingualism will be the downfall of the francophone landscape. For example, when entering a shop in Quebec City, one will be greeted initially with a friendly "Bonjour!" but if the customer proves to be less than fluent in French the college-age storekeepers will immediately break into an almost flawless English—a second language, yes, but spoken well. The youth seem to be both proud of their native language and cognizant that speaking English opens many opportunities. Only time will tell whether the French language will be diluted throughout the lowlands, but as of 2011 the city is becoming bilingual and the rural countryside remains francophone.

But of course, the francophones are not French people living in another land, but instead they have evolved their own French Canadian culture. Part of the **vernacular** (common style using local building materials) landscape is formed by the relationship of topography and housing, which has evolved to suit the countryside and includes steep roofs with flared eaves, porches, and colorful twin-gabled homes. Roman Catholic artifacts dot the countryside—life-size crucifixes, monasteries, and silver-towered churches—although all are slowly disappearing on the rural landscape, as both rural folk culture and the Church's influence diminish.

The Roman Catholic Church has been the most powerful social and cultural institution in Quebec. The Church regulated society and its social services, so it became the de facto state during the late nineteenth century until the 1960s, when dramatic changes occurred and the Church's influence declined. Multiple reasons for the decline of the Church include its failure to embrace birth control, the insular and limited educational system, and the emphasis on an agrarian lifestyle. But this all changed after World War II and the Quiet Revolution.

BOX 5.3 THE QUIET REVOLUTION

Quebec was an insular rural province until World War II exposed many veterans to new places and ideas that took shape politically during the 1960s. Modern communications diffused the Quiet Revolution sea change across the landscape. During this period the social, political, industrial, and population dimensions of Quebec changed radically, resulting in a modern urban society with two major urban centers: Montreal and Quebec City.

Quebec had always been a Roman Catholic province, where religion dominated society. But the Quiet Revolution secularized the province, and following the slogan of *maîtres chez nous* ("masters of our own house"), shed its dependence on religious education, its ideas of birth control, and its rural folk culture. The birth of an assertive French Canadian nationalism replaced Catholicism, favoring francophone business over anglophone, and supporting the ascendancy of the separatist Parti Québécois. The new Quebec valued its French identity, culture, and language, but without the Church.

Part of the effects of the Quiet Revolution and its industrialization was a shift in Quebec's population, from predominantly rural to urban. By 1990, only 3.8 percent of the population remained agricultural. The province industrialized and grew economically, as its birth rate plummeted from one of the highest to the lowest in the nation. There was a price to pay, though, as the Québécois feared losing francophone culture and possibly political power. Instead, the revolution spawned separatist ideals.

Over the ensuing years separatism spread, and through the 1990s the Parti Québécois gained Parliamentary representation and power. The separatist movement was split, though, between those who favored federalism (Prime Minister Trudeau) and those who favored secession from Canada. Among the separatists was an extreme element known as the Front de la Libération du Québec (FLQ), who both kidnapped and murdered to try to achieve their goals. These actions were answered by a crackdown on some Canadian freedoms during the 1970s, and eventually the FLQ leaders were arrested and brought to trial.

In 1976, Canada officially became a bilingual country, in order to appease those separatists who feared that the French language would be lost both because of their lower birth rate and because of an increase in immigrant populations. Despite the bilingual victory, the Quebec government enforced the almost exclusive use of French in Quebec. Today, provincial documents are in French alone, while national documents are bilingual. Many Canadians, including anglophone Quebecers, continue to grumble at the enforcement of French within the classroom and the strict use of French within Quebec.

Quebec developed an industrial base to support the economy. It has been active in the twenty-first century in supporting cap and trade policies and renewable energy. The province developed wind farms, and Hydro-Québec uses its greatest natural resource to generate hydroelectric power.

The Québécois separatist movement culminated in 1995 with a province-wide vote on succession. The province voted to remain within the Confederation by a slim margin. Since that time, occasional bursts of separatism still erupt, but Quebec has stayed the course and is working with Ontario especially to establish a more sustainable nation.

Regional Life

Population

Canada is a sparsely populated country, far less densely populated than the United Kingdom or France, and has about one-ninth the population density of the United States. Within Canada, both Ontario and Quebec are more densely populated than the country as a whole, and the majority live within the narrow Corridor (Table 5.1). Fully 60 percent of Canada's total population lives in the area from Windsor to Quebec City (Map 5.6).

The dual lowland cultures have grown independently. The initial French Canadian base population of about 9,000 had grown to 75,000 by 1760, and high birthrates led to population growth from 200,000 in 1800 to 1,488,535 in 1891. In 2010 the Quebec provincial population was the second largest in Canada at 7,879,167. Until the twentieth century, two-thirds lived in rural areas. Most of the riverside counties were Roman Catholic and francophone, while Appalachian Upland counties usually were anglophone and Protestant (Table 5.2). Although the Quebec population had grown rapidly by

TABLE 5.1. Population Density, 2010

	Canada	United States	France	United Kingdom	Ontario	Quebec	Golden Horseshoe
Per square mile	9.27	87.4	295	660	5.33	2.25	99
Per square kilometer	3.5	32	114	255	13.82	5.85	256

Source: U.S. Census; Statistics Canada

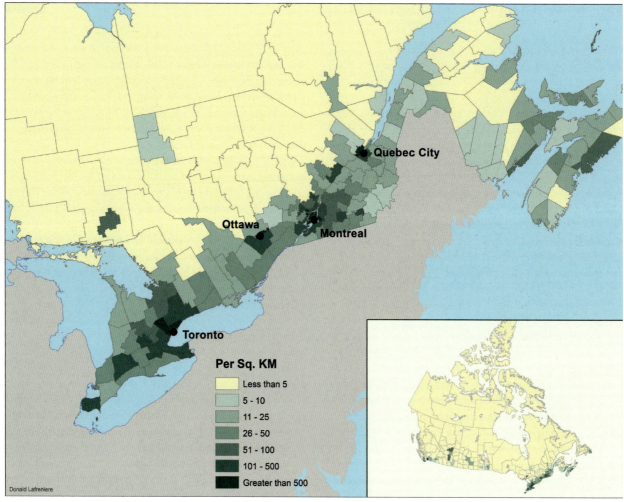

MAP 5.6. Canada's Population Density, 2001. The Corridor population density is highlighted.

Per Sq. KM
- Less than 5
- 5 - 10
- 11 - 25
- 26 - 50
- 51 - 100
- 101 - 500
- Greater than 500

Donald Lafreniere

natural increase, the English in Quebec grew more by immigration.

Ontario's Golden Horseshoe became the most densely populated, economically prosperous, and industrialized zone in Canada (Map 5.7). With more than eight million people, the Golden Horseshoe contains one-quarter of Canada's population, and 75 percent of Ontario's.

Emigration and Immigration

Historically, many Canadians have emigrated to the United States, especially prior to the beginning of U.S. immigration inspections in 1894. Up until this point, some Canadians and many European immigrants escaped stringent immigration inspections at U.S. ports of entry and freely crossed over from Canada into the United States.

Many Canadians continue to emigrate from Canada to the United States today, and many just stay over illegally. The entertainment industry has been enriched by Canadian immigrants including Joni Mitchell, Shania Twain, Neil Young, Alanis

Morissette, Jim Carrey, Mike Myers, Donald Sutherland, Dan Aykroyd, and Pamela Anderson.

Another emigrating group has been the Québécois; since 1960, an estimated 610,000 have left Quebec for other provinces (namely Ontario) and U.S. cities. Reasons for Québécois emigration range across Quebec's language laws, policies, and economic health. First anglophones left the province during the separatist regimes of the 1970s and 1980s, but francophone Quebecers have also pursued opportunity in Ontario or the United States. The émigrés are often in their prime earning years, leaving behind the aging, which increases the tax burden for those who remain. The more that leave, the higher the taxes for the remaining populace.

Early-twentieth-century Canadian immigration policies practiced segregation and discrimination, as did the United States. But more recent immigration has fueled regional population growth, although the sources of migrants have changed markedly since the 1980s. Asian and African immigrants have increased, and Europe and North American immigrants have decreased.

TABLE 5.2. Quebec Population and Number of Roman Catholics in Appalachian Uplands and St. Lawrence Lowlands, 1860

	Total population	Roman Catholic	% Roman Catholic
Appalachian Uplands			
Megantic	17,889	12,843	72
Sherbrooke	5,899	2,603	44
Stanstead	12,258	2,137	17
St. Lawrence Lowlands			
Drummond	12,356	9,088	73
Beauce	20,416	20,105	98
Montreal	90,323	65,896	73
Quebec	27,893	24,459	88
Ville Quebec	51,109	41,477	81

Source: Statistics Canada

Almost all immigration is to Canada's five largest urban centers: Toronto, Vancouver, Montreal, Calgary, and Ottawa–Gatineau.

The primary immigrant city is Toronto, where eighty-five thousand migrate annually. In Toronto, 150 languages are spoken and 50 percent of the residents are immigrants—perhaps the highest proportion of immigrants in either the U.S. or Canadian cities. Other cities are becoming more ethnically diverse, largely because of Canada's connection with the British Empire. Commonwealth of Nations status eases immigration for members of the former British Empire. However, over the years the nations sending immigrants have changed. During the nineteenth century, Irish Catholics migrated, but by the twentieth century the immigrant population was global and often outside of the British Empire, including Eastern Europeans, Caribbean, and Asian immigrants.

The primary city for French-speaking immigrants is Montreal. Haiti is the largest source, but others have arrived from Africa and South America. More than 50 percent of Canadian immigrants enter the economy at below the poverty level. Even those with good linguistic abilities and education are only slowly assimilated into the general populace and job market.

Since the defeat of the 1995 separatist vote, Quebec has redefined its immigrant identity from one of political separatism, a resistance identity as a nation, to one of accommodating distinct societies within greater Canada. The result is a transition from an ethnicized identity to a territorial, political, and national identity that is inclusive of Canada.[13]

Traditional and Sustainable Cities

Eighty percent of Canada's population is now urban, and eight of Canada's twelve largest cities, including the largest—Toronto and Montreal—are within the Corridor.

The Corridor includes four major cities:

- Quebec City, the French Canadian cultural hearth
- Montreal, the break-in-bulk city at the Lachine Rapids
- Ottawa–Gatineau, the capital city, located on the border between Ontario and Quebec
- Toronto, located at a shortcut to reach the interior; Toronto has also become a leading Canadian sustainable city

Other cities of note in the Corridor include Trois-Rivières in Quebec; and Hamilton, Kitchener–Waterloo, and London in Ontario. Trois-Rivières, whose economy is based on the pulp and paper industry, proved to be well situated for two reasons: (1) Trois-Rivières marks sea level for the St. Lawrence and tidal fluctuations affect points east, and (2) lumber could be easily transported down the subsidiary rivers to the St. Lawrence.

Hamilton, Kitchener–Waterloo, and London form a squat triangular area in the Great Lakes Lowlands south of Toronto and are in the most populated area of the province outside of Toronto. Hamilton is the former steel town of Canada, while Kitchener is a blue-collar, automobile-oriented city. Waterloo is

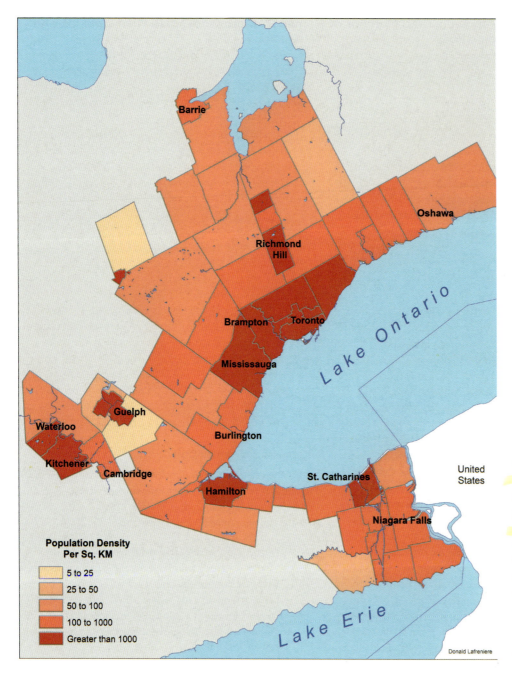

MAP 5.7. The Golden Horseshoe, at the western end of Lake Ontario, is the most densely populated and wealthy area of Canada. It includes the Greater Toronto Metropolitan area. Twenty percent of Canada's and more than half of Ontario's population lives in the Golden Horseshoe.

Source: Statistics Canada, at http://geodepot.statcan.ca/diss/highlights/page9/page9a_e.cfm

Population Density Per Sq. KM

- 5 to 25
- 25 to 50
- 50 to 100
- 100 to 1000
- Greater than 1000

Donald Lafreniere

a university town with high-tech industry. London is home to Western Ontario University and is a manufacturing city.

Quebec City, Ville de Quebec

(2011 pop. 516,622; CMA 765,706)

In 1608, Samuel de Champlain established the first permanent settlement of Quebec (*qebec* is a Micmaq word for "the narrows") on a defensive bluff overlooking the narrows of the St. Lawrence.

Originally established as a fur-trading outpost, Quebec City became the administrative and cultural center for New France. However, the city's importance waned for two reasons: (1) the

fur trade moved farther west, making Montreal the main outpost; and (2) the British gained control of Quebec in 1759. For a while, the province almost had a majority British population, but Quebec City has once again reclaimed its place as the cultural and political center for Québécois society. More than 90 percent of the residents speak French.

Quebec City is unique on the North American landscape because of its European appearance. Quebec was built as a typical early-seventeenth-century medieval French city and is the only preserved walled city in North America. Quebec City has grown well beyond the medieval walls, in the form of a typical North American suburban landscape, but the walled city

PHOTO 5.5. Underground Mall, Toronto. Despite hot and humid summers and long, freezing winters, Toronto shoppers have acres of underground malls. The subways, railroads, and many office buildings are connected to the underground system of stores and restaurants.

by lack of political will, but more likely because of lack of funding, and because laws—hamstrung by limitations—only suggest but do not explicitly demand cleanup.[18]

Economy

Historically, the Canadian economy has been based on trade with Britain and the United States. But British adoption of an open-trade policy in the mid-nineteenth century removed the preferential **tariffs** granted to the British protectorates, and Canada then focused on trade with its southern neighbor. The **Reciprocity Treaty of 1854** (also known as the Elgin-Marcy Treaty) reduced tariffs on natural resources between Canada and the United States in exchange for granting Americans navigational rights to the Great Lakes and fishing rights on the Grand Banks. Economically the treaty enriched Canada, providing a market for its abundance of timber and wheat. But the Americans canceled the treaty in 1865 for a variety of reasons, partially invested in their growing might and hubris (expecting Canada to join the United States), but also because the states were indebted by the Civil War and wanted to protect their industries by imposing high tariffs. Canada balked, and the cancellation of the treaty provided an impetus for Canadian Confederation.

Confederation came with challenges: to create a national economy and remain independent of the United States. The geographic realities of the second-largest country in the world created varying regional issues and forced economic and political competition between the far-flung Canadian regions.

The natural attraction between Canadian regions and their U.S. complements made Canadian unity more difficult. The Atlantic Provinces shared a trading history with New England. The Corridor had an industrial affinity with the nearby American industrial core. The Prairie region was geographically an extension of the Great Plains, and British Columbia's population resided mostly within the Pacific Northwest Puget Sound Basin. Each region often identified with its neighboring state more than it identified with Canada. Despite repeated attempts to renew a reciprocity agreement in the ensuing years, the United States was adamant in its trade demands, and Canada's response was to create the National Policy.

In 1879, the **National Policy** of high tariffs on imported manufactured goods effectively divided inner (core) from outer (periphery) Canada economically and politically. The National Policy was an act of "defensive expansionism" meant to build and protect Canada and to reduce reliance on the United States. Canadian firms declared independence in response to the high tariffs the United States had imposed on Canadian goods. From the late nineteenth century until the 1930s, the two countries assigned each other least-favored nation status, and trade fell off between the neighboring countries.

Tensions were also high between Inner Canada and Outer Canada because of the perceived economic and political favoritism toward the Corridor. Those favoring Inner Canada's strength believed in a strong federal government and industrial core located in the Corridor, while those favoring Outer Canada favored a more equitable division of power and decentralized trade, which empowers the provinces. The government continued the National Policy into World War II, but the policy was slowly dismantled after the war. A series of agreements—the General Agreement on Tariffs and Trade (GATT) and the Auto Pact of 1965, among others—reduced tariffs until the North

American Free Trade Agreement (NAFTA) opened up free trade in 1995.

Although the National Policy focused on protecting Canadian goods, it affected all aspects of the Canadian economy. Ontario's manufacturing grew, along with an urban workforce. While good for Ontario's economy, buying Canadian goods was more expensive than purchasing in the nearby American regions for two reasons: economies of scale, and geography—too much geography: long transit routes increased transportation costs. For example, farmers in the western provinces now had to buy Canadian equipment at higher prices than American goods, which kept the Canadian economy strong. But the farmers were at the mercy of the global economy, having to sell on a fluctuating commodity market.

The story continued in 2007, when the Canadian dollar reached parity with the U.S. dollar; the Canadian dollar had been at 60 percent of the U.S. dollar previously. Upon parity, Canadians flocked to the states for deals on everything from shoes to cars. The response from Canadian companies was to establish rules and regulations to halt the flow of capital into the states. For example, many people chose to buy their cars in the states, where they are less expensive, but Canadian dealerships retaliated by not honoring the warranties of U.S.-purchased cars. The Canadian dollar remained at 80 to 99 percent to the American dollar during the economic instability beginning in 2008.

In 2007, Ontario and Quebec represented 60 percent of the Canadian export market and gross domestic product. However, Canadian sentiment for a more robust information economy and the entry of the major Canadian cities into the global core economy will reshape and redistribute taxes; these may lift the largest cities into world-class economic euphoria but may also create more dissension between Inner and Outer Canada.

Primary Industry and Natural Resources

The traditional primary sector economy relied on agriculture, furs, fish, lumber, and mineral resources, and these have remained important exports despite a growing manufacturing sector. The Corridor played an important role in the primary economy.

Agriculture

The Corridor is a substantial Canadian agricultural region located near a majority of the population, thereby assuring an available market (Table 5.3). The Quebec and Ontario agricultural areas developed independently and specialized in crops and livestock that related to their distinct cultural and climatic conditions. While the average size of an Ontario and Quebec farm is the smallest in the nation, the farms practice more intensive production than Prairie farms.

Ontario agriculture has two distinct regions. The more productive is west of Toronto and produces grains, specialty crops, and livestock. East of Toronto is less productive. Quebec's agriculture is along the Lowlands Corridor, chiefly along the southern shore between Montreal and Quebec City. The short growing season limits crop growth, and so the region specializes in livestock production.

The Ontario Farm   Ontario's agriculture is dominant between Toronto and Windsor. The region is involved in specialty crops, livestock, and a growing organic market. The Ontario farm averages 233 acres, versus the 728-acre average Canadian farm (2006), but the Ontario farm is an appropriate size for the regional specialty crops—tobacco, tomatoes, stone fruits, and hemp. Crop production has ebbed and flowed over time in relation to changing agricultural laws, preferences, and styles.

Ontario grows 36 percent of all Canadian vegetables, many grown in greenhouses. Leamington, located on Lake Erie's north shore, has the largest concentration of greenhouses in Canada and a nine-hundred-employee Heinz factory for processing its chief crop, tomatoes. North of Leamington, along the Niagara Escarpment, is the Niagara fruit belt, located between lakes Erie and Ontario. The fruit belt benefits from the warmer air off the lakes and can therefore grow more crops than usually found at this latitude. Niagara Escarpment fruit has been a staple until the late twentieth century, when labor costs escalated and it became less economical to grow stone fruits. Vineyards capitalized by wealthy individuals became popular.

Ontario livestock production had been a staple for the region, but it contracted after 1996 when the century-long federally funded Crow Rate corn subsidy ended.

In 1998 legalized licensed growth of industrial hemp was inaugurated after a sixty-year ban. Industrial hemp is grown for fiber, food oil, meal, paper, and biomass. Hemp grows like the weed that it is, and it is used extensively in less developed countries. Demand exceeds supply for a number of uses. However, commercial hemp production lacks processing facilities; it experienced an uneven growth pattern, and hemp production declined until 2009. While production and processing are still lacking a clear national leader, many small companies are producing hemp food, health products, and clothing.[19]

The Quebec Farm   Prior to World War II, French Canadian Quebec remained a predominantly rural farming population. After the Quiet Revolution, the French Canadian agricultural economy became more specialized, intensive, and technologically developed. Quebec farms average about 279 acres, and the number of farms is ranked fourth in Canada.

Most agricultural pursuits were in the Lowlands area, especially along the flat and fertile right bank of the St. Lawrence. Other agricultural areas include the eastern townships and along the Montreal Laurentians. Production choices are limited in Quebec because of a brief growing season, from a miniscule three months in the Montreal Laurentians up to five months on the Montreal Plain.

Through the nineteenth century, Quebec grew grains, but as western Canada's more favorable growing conditions opened up, Quebec switched to forage and livestock. Livestock production, mostly dairy and hogs, remains the most important agricultural activity, accounting for almost half of all farming operations.

Because of a lack of suitable agricultural land in the province and because of increased urbanizing pressures, concentrated

BOX 5.4 NORTH AMERICAN FREE TRADE AGREEMENT (NAFTA)

In 1944, after World War II, the world economy began restructuring. At Bretton Woods (New Hampshire), the International Monetary Fund (IMF) and the World Bank were formed to oversee monetary systems. Over the ensuing years until the last decade of the century, the world, led by the United States, continued to pursue free trade among nations. The introduction of the **General Agreement on Tariffs and Trade (GATT)**, first introduced in 1947, was heralded as the beginning of a New World Economic Order. A series of eight GATT agreements over the next few decades liberalized trade and reduced tariffs in order to extend commercial advantage for the United States.

As Western Europe and Japan grew in their competition for trade with the United States, a new round of trade agreements began to lower tariffs, including the World Trade Organization (WTO) in 1994. U.S. policy entered a phase of protectionist policies, as global economies widened the gap between the wealthy and poor. In 1995 the **North American Free Trade Agreement (NAFTA)** was created to encourage trade among the three principal countries of North America by reducing and, within fifteen years, eliminating tariffs between the countries.

NAFTA has had periods of great growth and opportunity, but it has also experienced a steep decline in manufacturing jobs in the United States and Canada. Restructuring of manufacturing was augmented by a slowdown in domestic auto manufacturing and the loss of domestic labor-intensive jobs to relocation or technology. Though many jobs relocated to Mexico, the effects of NAFTA were mitigated when China entered the World Trade Organization (WTO) in 2000, shifting jobs from countries like Mexico to the lower-cost labor market in China.

One of the results of NAFTA and the WTO in Canada has been the loss of jobs in Ontario's automobile industry. Following in the trudging footsteps of the American Big Three manufacturers, the effect has devastated the local Ontario economy. The economy of Canada is tied not only to the auto industry but to the U.S. economy in general.

The United States remains Canada's largest trade partner, with more than 80 percent of all Canadian goods going to the states (21 percent of U.S. goods go to Canada). Questions abound about Canada's dependence on the United States, as Canada continues to seek new trading partners (Europe, Latin America). The mood is vulnerable though, as the end-of-the-millennium economy turned for the worse. Deregulation, lumber disputes, and oil in the Beaufort Sea and Alberta could bring Canada into protectionism or a further alliance with new trading partners.

---

animal feeding operations (CAFOs) practicing intensive livestock production have become the standard, resulting in environmental risks for air, land, and water. The growth in CAFO dairy and hog production resulted in a 2002 moratorium, which was lifted in 2005. A surplus of manure from the intensive production caused agricultural pollution, and the province has worked to manage its surplus sustainably.

An important part of hog production—Quebec produces the most hogs in Canada—is its export market, especially to the United States, but a fluctuating Canadian dollar since the millennium has hurt the hog export economy.

Quebec accounts for more than half of Canada's cheese production, and four companies account for more than 90 percent of Quebec's production. The remainder is divided among ninety specialty cheese makers who produce quality handmade cheeses, which are more sustainable and protect small farms.

Mineral Resources

The Canadian Shield is the most mineral-rich region of Canada; however, the Appalachian Uplands and St. Lawrence Lowlands area are also mineral resource areas. Ninety percent of Canadian aluminum has been mined in Quebec, making Canada the fourth-largest producer in the world and second-largest exporter behind Russia. Aluminum production thrives on the inexpensive and available hydroelectric power of Quebec. However, a lack of processing and dependence on importing semi-finished products, largely for the aircraft industry, have led Canada to begin developing an aluminum manufacturing sector to supply Montreal's aerospace industry.

TABLE 5.3 Canadian Farms, 2006

Province	Number of farms	Total farm area (acres)
Quebec	30,675	8,557,101
Ontario	57,211	13,310,216
Canada	229,373	167,010,491

Source: Statistics Canada, at http://www40.statcan.gc.ca/l01/cst01/agrc25a-eng.htm

Asbestos has been mined since 1847 in the eastern township towns of Asbestos and Thetford Mines. Production has continued, even as other mines have shut down due to health concerns with asbestos manufacturing. Most asbestos uses have been banned across the developed world, so most sales are to less developed countries. The health risks of asbestos found in Quebec mines—chrysotile—is played down within the towns. However, in April 2009 Health Canada concluded that there was a "strong relationship" between the chrysotile and lung cancer. Both asbestos and aluminum mining have negative environmental impacts. Environment Canada is working to reduce the fine-particle atmospheric pollutants from the industries.

Industry and Postindustrial

The Corridor shares manufacturing enterprises with neighboring U.S. industry. Until the 1990s, 50 percent of all jobs in the Golden Horseshoe were in the manufacturing sector, but an estimated 350,000 Canadian manufacturing jobs, mostly in the Corridor, were lost from 2002 to 2009.

The loss of so much of the manufacturing sector qualified Ontario in 2009, for the first time ever, to receive $347 million from the federal government as an **equalization payment**. Canada's Equalization Program transfers federal funds from wealthier to less affluent provinces and has caused continual discord between the wealthy and poorer provinces. The economic failure of primary industry has caused Canada's equalization payments to the Atlantic provinces to be disproportionately large; however, in 2008 a seismic shift occurred in Canada and the manufacturing-based historic core region grew more slowly than commodity-based provinces. The trend continued into 2011, when Ontario became the second-largest recipient of the funds; only Quebec received more. Inner Canada, the proverbial core region of Canada, is at the feet of the resource-rich provinces such as Alberta and Newfoundland.

However, sustainable industry has been growing. Ontario alone has more than 2,600 companies involved with environmental issues and is developing even more sustainable industries dealing with ecological balance and managing growth.

Auto Production

Manufacturing in Southern Ontario and Quebec developed hand in hand with the financial industry. Auto manufacturing developed as a crucial segment of the Corridor economy and was allied with industrial growth in neighboring Detroit. Until 1965, the Canadian auto industry developed with much smaller independent plants and smaller branch plants of U.S. companies. The United States opened Ontario branches and enjoyed reduced tariffs.

The signing of the 1965 Auto Pact was a major step that eliminated tariffs between the two countries. American and Japanese carmakers and car part manufacturing grew in the core region in alliance with Detroit industry. The industry profited on the low-valued but stable Canadian dollar. The car industry flourished from 1965 into the 1990s, when foreign competition began to affect the industry in both countries. By

2006, following the decline in American auto production and the escalating worth of the Canadian dollar, Canadian production also declined.

Steel

Canada's steel town is Hamilton, Ontario, situated on at the west end of Lake Ontario within the Golden Horseshoe. Available coal and Great Lakes iron ore created an auto production market. The greater Toronto market complemented the growth of industry and heavy manufacturing in the second decade of the twentieth century.

However, as with so many American and Canadian manufacturing industries, the steel companies hit hard times, and the major steel mills were in bankruptcy proceedings by 2004. A takeover and consolidation within American and Canadian steel companies followed, and by 2007 the two major steel companies—Dofasco and U.S. Steel Canada (formerly Stelco)—emerged from bankruptcy proceedings. Two-thirds of the employees had been laid off, and another two thousand lost their jobs in March 2009. Rehires began as the recession receded. In 2006 the two companies shipped over five million tons of steel worth more than $3.5 billion. The large steel mills may follow the lead of smaller mills and restructure at lower wages and with fewer employees.

Energy Production

Quebec and Ontario are both replete with energy options. Ontario's provincial electricity is produced by coal-burning power plants (22 percent), hydropower (33 percent), and nuclear energy (45 percent). In 2003, Ontario's Premier Dalton McGuinty promised to comply with the Kyoto Protocol by closing the coal-burning plants and replacing them with renewable energy sources by 2007. Although he only closed one plant by the deadline, the government passed legislation to close all coal-burning plants by 2014. Ontario became the first province to replace coal-produced electricity with conservation, natural gas, and wind power. In 2007 Ontario set up a Renewable Energy Act that promised contracts at set prices for renewable power. Although promising, the system has been stymied and relies on nuclear for more than half of its power.

There are two nuclear plants in Ontario, one near Toronto at Pickering, and another on the Bruce Peninsula. The Pickering plant alone can provide energy for a million and a half residents. Recent and unforeseen problems concerning climate change have periodically shut down the plants, a worrisome problem that may affect future production.[20] Despite the numerous options for power, Ontario remains dependent on Quebec for additional hydropower and on Alberta for oil.

Northern Quebec has extensive hydropower sources. Hydro Quebec provides power to the province and to the northeastern United States (Alaska and Canadian North Chapter).

A **cap and trade** program aims to reduce greenhouse gas (GHG) emissions in Canada. A cap and trade program involves capping GHG emissions by large companies, or purchasing credits from companies under the cap limits.

Provincial government programs set caps on emissions and tradable allowances. British Columbia was the first province to introduce cap and trade legislation, followed a few months later in 2008 by Quebec and Ontario, who agreed to continue integrating their economies. However, a proposed national carbon cap and trade program was tabled in 2011.

A federal program seemed imminent in 2009, but climate change and Canada's oil sands exports stymied improving the cap and trade policy. Canada has watched how the U.S. economy and its cap and trade policy has shifted. Canada seemed poised to favor a continent-wide cap and trade program that would allow the continuation of oil sand exports to the states.[21] Oil sands production from Alberta threatens Corridor aims for cap and trade and continues the long-standing tension between the core and periphery—but now the argument can be made that the Inner and Outer provinces have switched.

Pollution

Pollution affects the Corridor as it does the nearby Midwest. Sources include air pollution from acid precipitation, St. Lawrence Seaway water degradation, and the introduction of exotic species.

Acid precipitation is the most significant air pollutant. **Acid rain**—the result of coal-burning power plants in the United States and Ontario and the large steel smelter in Sudbury, Ontario—causes a loss of aquatic species and kills trees. In an effort to reduce acid rain, Ontario is turning away from coal-producing power plants.

The St. Lawrence has been the viaduct for exporting Canadian goods, but at the cost of contamination, invasive species, and pollution:

- In December 2006, an Ontario lawsuit was filed against General Motors and Alcoa regarding dumped PCBs, a known carcinogen, causing thyroid problems, learning disabilities, reproductive abnormalities, and liver cancer.
- Urban sewage and effluents from runoff are inadequately treated and then dumped into the St. Lawrence, where they are then absorbed by aquatic life that is later eaten by humans. Sewage treatment plants fail to remove many effluents—oils, grease, unused medications, and trace metals.
- Ballast water containing more than 180 nonnative species is flushed into the river and continues to plague the St. Lawrence Seaway. U.S. legislation to stem the flow of invasive species has been stalled.
- Nonnative species cause wildlife die-offs, destroy native fish populations, and create algae outbreaks that close beaches.
- The Ontario Medical Association says that air pollution causes 9,500 premature deaths and billions are lost annually to health costs and lost productivity.[22]

A plethora of laxly enforced laws protect the St. Lawrence River ecosystem. The St. Lawrence suffers from illegal toxic discharges from pulp mills and threatening species despite laws from Environment Canada. Canadian legislation to correct industrial waste, sewage, agricultural runoff, and lax shipping restrictions lacks enforcement, which strangles Canada as it does the United States.

Tourism

Canada aggressively pursues tourism. The most-visited places in the Corridor include Toronto, Montreal, Quebec City, and the outdoor tourist–based economy in the nearby Laurentian Mountains in the Canadian Shield.

Montreal and Quebec City tourism are attractive because of their francophone appeal and Old World feel. The walled city of Quebec is unsurpassed in North America for its location, European architecture, and cuisine. Even during the winter the city shines, with an annual February ice festival with snow sports and a unique ice hotel built for the Mardi Gras festival and melted on April 1 each year.

A Sustainable Future

The Corridor region will remain a center of Canadian power because of its population dominance, large cities, and capital. In many ways, the Corridor parades the essence of the bicultural and steadily more multicultural country. Canada feels it must continue to grow economically to prosper, and a large immigrant population augments Canada's low birthrate growth.

Canada is not a sleepy country to the north, but instead is finding its own way, without guns, with health care, favoring same sex marriage, legalizing marijuana production, and recognizing (however haltingly) how crucial sustainability is. However, frustrated cries for equality from Outer Canada are being heard, as Alberta with its oil sands and Newfoundland with its offshore oilfields gain more power, more control, and more of the export economy, even as manufacturing slows in the Corridor. Alberta and Newfoundland have periodically demanded independence from the Confederation in order to free themselves of what they perceive as inequality.[23]

To measure environmental and sustainable performance, the Canadian federal government began a reporting mechanism, which gives an annual snapshot of Canada's sustainable goals. The resulting report card displays the state of the environment in the seventeen most affluent countries in the world. Canada rates fifteenth. The United States places last (Table 5.4).

Canadian performance is above average on seven indicators:

- use of forest resources
- low-emitting electricity production
- Water Quality Index
- urban particulate matter (PM_{10}) concentration
- urban nitrogen dioxide (NO_2) concentration
- threatened species
- energy intensity (ratio of energy consumption and economic output)

BOX 5.5 GREAT LAKES INVASIVE SPECIES AND SYSTEMS THINKING

The greatest threat of the notion of wilderness is that there is a realm of "pristine" nature separate from humans, a dangerous quasi-religious myth that give us "permission to evade responsibility for the lives we actually lead."*

Invasive species are introduced to a habitat and thrive because they lack predators or parasites. This box will discuss the traditional way of addressing invasive species, which are usually transported by humans, often with unintended consequences. Change happens in the world, and humans are often the agent of this change, though other animals and weather can also be agents of change. What we call invasive species are part of the dynamic nature of ecology. Nature is not steady state. Invasive species have existed before human intervention, but humans have accelerated the changes. Humans are part of the natural world but need to accept responsibility for any of the complex and unintended consequences of their actions.

Unintended Consequences

The largest and most evident unintended consequence of invasive species is their pushing out native species, thereby upsetting the ecological order. For example, the introduction of plants, such as purple loosestrife, in the Great Lakes was intentional, but the full impact of the plant in its new habitat was not understood. This nonindigenous plant became invasive largely because it is a prolific seed producer.

The introduction of invasive species has accelerated since the globalization of trade. More than a third of the invasive species in the Great Lakes have arrived since the opening of the St. Lawrence Seaway.† Most invasive species arrived via ballast water discharged from ships, such as the zebra mussel, which was released into the Great Lakes from a Caspian Sea tanker's ballast water in 1988. Regulations requiring exchanging ballast water prior to entering the Great Lakes have been ineffectual.

Local and Ecoregional Impacts

Species brought into new ecosystems lack predators and proliferate far beyond their native habitat abilities, resulting in species that overrun native species. The Great Lakes have received more than 140 exotic species since the 1800s. The most recent Great Lakes invasive species threat, the Asian carp, is being held back by artificial means along the Chicago River. When a nonindigenous species flourishes in a new habitat, it upsets the ecosystem energy flow. The Asian carp could quickly become invasive because of their mobility and their voracious appetites. The effect of an invasive species on food supply was demonstrated when the zebra mussel reduced the available food and spawning habitat for local fish populations. The Asian carp entry into the Great Lakes ecosystems could result in a reinforcing feedback loop. With no controls to stop their entry, the carp begin to upset the ecosystem,

resulting in more carp. Without government intervention before the carp's entry, the fish will destroy the ecosystem and the fishing and tourist industry tied to the existing system.

External Costs

The economic and ecological impact of these invasive species has been significant, including reduction in the fishery and damage to water supplies. Control mechanisms run into the billions, although means of effective control or eradication of many of these species have not been found. When invasive species disrupt the food chain, the results are disastrous for sustainable development.

The following are a few of the significant invasive species, their damage, and the methods used to control them:

- Zebra mussel: This Black and Caspian seas native was first discovered in the Great Lakes in 1988, the probable result of ballast water discharged into Lake St. Clair. The mussel is now spread by currents throughout the Great Lakes system. The mussel prefers plankton-rich environments, where the prolific mussel anchors to hard substances (rocks, boats, buoys, water intakes) and reproduces quickly. While they filter and clarify water, they also remove nutrients required for healthy fish. The anchoring can create drag on boats, drown buoys, and overheat water intakes, creating motor failure. Decaying zebra mussels have reduced beach use because of the odor. Although many different control mechanisms have been tried, no viable means of eradicating the mussel has been found.†

- Sea lamprey: The sea lamprey is an eel-like vertebrate native to the Atlantic Ocean that entered the Great Lakes system in the nineteenth century after the opening of the Welland Canal. Unlike eels, the lamprey are a fish-feeding parasite, attaching with their suction-cup mouth and sucking out body fluids, killing six out of seven host fish. The lamprey has been a significant factor in the collapse of several native species in the lakes. A lamprey control program breaks the life cycle of the lamprey and has reduced their population by 90 percent.

- Purple loosestrife: This European wetland plant was introduced in the 1800s, when seeds were transferred through the ballast of ships. The plant produces 2.7 million seeds annually and outcompetes native plants. Species that depend on native plants are therefore also threatened. The plant is difficult to control. Burning does not destroy the underground root system and the plants reappear, and herbicides are environmentally degrading. Insects that control the plant in its native habitat are now being studied to possibly bring to the United States.‡

- Asian carp: First brought in by catfish farmers in the 1970s, the carp escaped the ponds into the Mississippi River basin during floods in the 1990s. They have become the most abundant species in the river and outcompete native species. They grow very large and have rapacious appetites, which could destroy local ecosystems. Carp are a food fish, but it is not popular in the United States. Most carp is sold to Asian communities, and there is a possible fertilizer market.§

Invasive species reduce the complexity of an ecosystem and therefore diminish its diversity, making the system more vulnerable. While species have migrated from their native habitats for centuries, the transport has accelerated due to technology and globalization. While some transports have been beneficial, such as the Columbian exchange (the transoceanic transmission of biota, culture, diseases, and ideas), other organisms threaten existing ecosystems and cause the décline or extinction of indigenous species. Prevention is the best course of action, but it requires education, respect, and cooperation among the nations.

---

* William Cronon, quoted in B. M. H. Larson,"Who's Invading What? Systems Thinking about Invasive Species," *Canadian Journal of Plant Science* 87 (2007).

† National Agricultural Library: National Invasive Species Information Center, at http://www.invasivespeciesinfo.gov/aquatics/zebramussel.shtml.

‡ Great Lakes Information Network, at http://www.great-lakes.net/envt/flora-fauna/invasive/loosestf.html.

§ Great Lakes Pollution Prevention and Toxics Reduction, at http://www.epa.gov/glnpo/invasive/asiancarp/index.html.

Canada's performance is below average on eight indicators:

- forest cover change
- urban sulfur dioxide (SO_2) concentration
- Marine Trophic Index
- greenhouse gas (GHG) emissions
- water consumption
- organic farming
- volatile organic compound (VOC) emissions
- municipal waste generation[24]

All is not green in Canada. Although all provinces have environmental issues, those with the most population or growth (Ontario and Alberta) are failing in sustainability for reasons that include the burgeoning population, waste management, urban sprawl, deindustrialization, regional disparities, and overconsumption. In general, the average Canadian is more aware and active in environmental sensibility than the average American, but there is more work to do. The national report card is useful to make people aware of their position in reaching the goals of Kyoto or any future protocols.[25]

TABLE 5.4. Environmental Report Card for Seventeen Developed Countries, 2008

Rating	Country	Grade
1	Sweden	A
2	Finland	A
3	Norway	A
4	Switzerland	A
5	United Kingdom	B
6	France	B
7	Italy	B
8	Austria	C
9	Germany	C
10	Ireland	C
11	Denmark	C
12	Belgium	C
13	Netherlands	C
14	Japan	C
15	Canada	C
16	Australia	D
17	United States	D

Source: The Conference Board of Canada, at http://www.conferenceboard.ca/HCP/Details/Environment.aspx#Indicators

Questions for Discussion

1. What is the traditional rivalry between Inner Canada and Outer Canada?

2. In what ways is Inner Canada now being challenged by Outer Canada?

3. Explain the shifting of population between Toronto and Montreal during the 1970s.

4. Why were there four Welland Canals built, and why might there be a fifth?

5. How is the Niagara Escarpment significant in the Corridor region?

6. How has the National Policy affected trade in Canada?

7. Why did the St. Lawrence Valley and not Acadia become the French cultural hearth of Canada?

8. What site and situation features made Montreal a prime center? Why did it become the economic center of Canada under British rule?

9. What was the effect of the Quiet Revolution? What grew from it?

10. What was Ontario called prior to Confederation, and who settled there?

11. What are the religious differences between Ontario and Quebec? When did it start and how did it evolve? How has it changed since the 1960s? Why?

12. Why is there the possibility of a shift in power between the Corridor and other Canadian regions in the twenty-first century? What other regions challenge the hegemony of the Corridor?

Suggested Readings

Chapman, L. J., and D. F. Putnam. *The Physiography of Southern Ontario.* 3rd ed. Toronto: Ontario Ministry of Natural Resources, 1984.

Craig, Gerald M. *Upper Canada.* Toronto: McClelland and Stewart; New York, Oxford University Press, 1963.

Dickinson, John Alexander, and Brian Young. *A Short History of Quebec.* Montreal: McGill-Queen's University Press, 2000.

Gayler, Hugh J. *Niagara's Changing Landscapes.* Ottawa: Carleton University Press, 1994.

Greenberg, Joel. *A Natural History of the Chicago Region.* Chicago: University of Chicago Press, 2004.

Greenwald, Michelle, Alan Levitt, and Elaine Peebles. *The Welland Canals: Historical Resource Analysis and Preservation Alternatives.* Toronto: Historical Planning and Research Branch, Ontario Ministry of Culture and Recreation, 1979.

Grenier, Fernand, ed. *Québec.* Toronto: University of Toronto Press, 1972.

———, ed. *Quebec Studies in Canadian Geography.* Toronto: University of Toronto Press, 1972.

Guindon, Hubert, ed. *Quebec Society: Tradition, Modernity, and Nationhood.* Toronto: University of Toronto Press, 1988.

Harris, Cole. "France in North America." In *North America: The Historical Geography of a Changing Continent,* edited by Thomas F. McIlwraith and Edward K. Muller. Lanham, Md.: Rowman & Littlefield, 2001.

———. *The Reluctant Land: Society, Space, and Environment in Canada before Confederation.* Vancouver: University of British Columbia Press, 2008.

——— [Richard Colebrook Harris]. *The Seigneurial System in Early Canada: A Geographical Study.* Madison: University of Wisconsin Press, 1966.

Kaplan, David H. "Population and Politics in a Plural Society: The Changing Geography of Canada's Linguistic Groups." *Annals of the Association of American Geographers* 84, no. 1 (March 1994).

Louder, Dean, ed. *The Heart of French Canada: From Ottawa to Quebec City.* New Brunswick, N.J.: Rutgers University Press, 1992.

Louder, Dean R., and Eric Waddell, eds. *French America: Mobility, Identity, and Minority Experience across the Continent.* Translated by Franklin Philip. Baton Rouge: Louisiana State University Press, 1993.

Martin, Virgil. *Changing Landscapes of Southern Ontario.* Toronto: Boston Mills Press, 1989.

McIlwraith, Thomas F. "British North America, 1763–1867," in *The Historical Geography of a Changing Continent,* edited by Thomas F. McIlwraith and Edward K. Muller. Lanham, Md.: Rowman & Littlefield, 2001.

Sundell, Paul, and Mathew Shane. "Canada: A Macroeconomic Study of the United States' Most Important Trade Partner." Outlook Report No.WRS-0602. U.S. Department of Agriculture, September 2006, at http://www.ers.usda.gov/Publications/WRS0602/.

Yeates, Maurice. *Main Street: Windsor to Quebec City.* Toronto: MacMillan, 1975.

Internet Sources

Great Lakes Commission, at http://www.glc.org/.

A Report Card on Canada, at http://www.conferenceboard.ca/hcp/default.aspx.

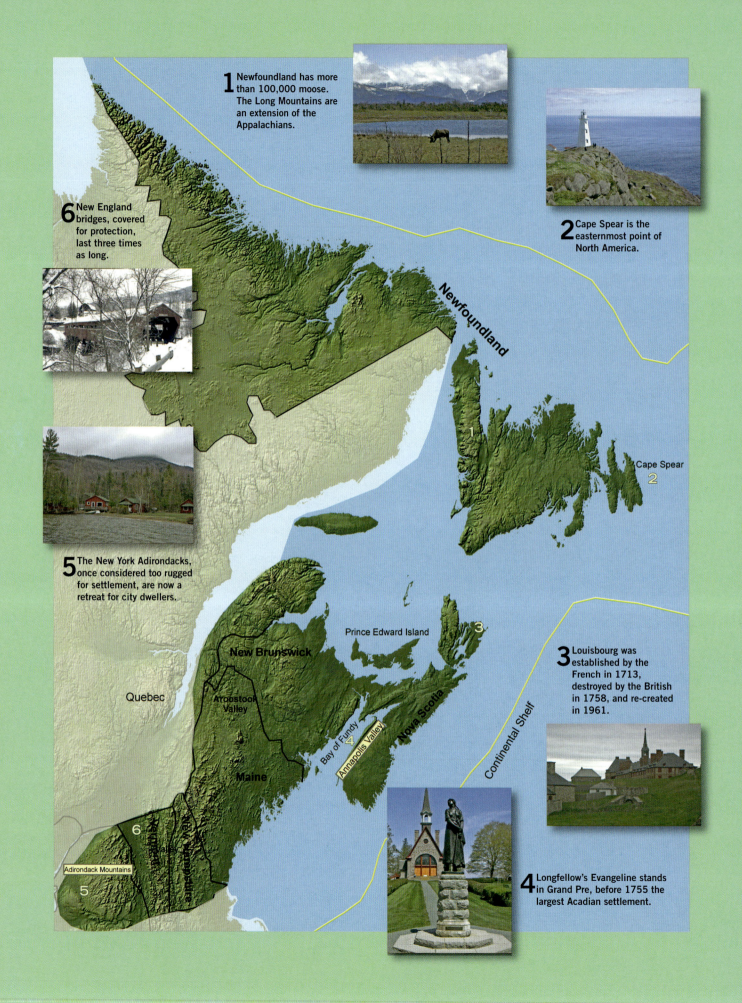

1 Newfoundland has more than 100,000 moose. The Long Mountains are an extension of the Appalachians.

2 Cape Spear is the easternmost point of North America.

6 New England bridges, covered for protection, last three times as long.

5 The New York Adirondacks, once considered too rugged for settlement, are now a retreat for city dwellers.

3 Louisbourg was established by the French in 1713, destroyed by the British in 1758, and re-created in 1961.

4 Longfellow's Evangeline stands in Grand Pre, before 1755 the largest Acadian settlement.

Newfoundland

Cape Spear

Prince Edward Island

New Brunswick

Quebec

Aroostook Valley

Bay of Fundy

Annapolis Valley

Nova Scotia

Continental Shelf

Maine

Adirondack Mountains

New Hampshire

6

THE NORTH ATLANTIC PROVINCES AND NORTHERN NEW ENGLAND

New Economic Hopes

Chapter Highlights

After reading this chapter you should be able to:

- Distinguish between the Maritime Provinces and Atlantic Canada
- Explain the collapse of the cod fishery
- Discuss how Northern New England interacts with Megalopolis
- Describe the resettlement of Newfoundland
- Give an overview of the importance of the Grand Banks
- Define the tragedy of the commons
- Describe the geographic limitations of the region

Terms

bank (geology)
brewis
capelin
cod
cultural preadaptation

Exclusive Economic Zone (EEZ)
fall foliage season
flake
Green Mountain Boys
maritime influence
maximum sustainable yield

milkshed
monadnock
North Atlantic Ocean Conveyor
outport
phytoplankton
polders
privateer

resettlement
resource hinterland
short sea shipping
thermohaline circulation
tidal bore
tragedy of the commons
trawler

Places

Acadia
Adirondacks
Annapolis Valley
Appalachian Uplands
Aroostook Valley

Atlantic Canada
Bay of Fundy
Continental Shelf
Flemish Cap
Georges Bank
Grand Banks

Gulf Stream
Halifax
Hibernia oil field
Labrador
Labrador Current
L'Anse aux Meadows

Maritime Provinces
Newfoundland
North Atlantic Drift
Northern New England
St. John's
Scotian Bank

PHOTO 6.1. Prospect, Nova Scotia. When the cod-fishing industry collapsed in 1992, North Atlantic regional town economies were devastated. Government support to maintain aging infrastructure in small Canadian coastal towns is dwindling.

Introduction

Nature has so arranged limited areas off our coast that they are veritable mines of self-perpetuating wealth and inexpensive food for the people. Shall we run the risk of losing one of the remaining natural sources of food supply which with judicious use may doubtless be saved for the future?

—George Curtis, 1913[1]

The North Atlantic region is as breathtakingly beautiful as it is economically and ecologically struggling. The dramatic beauty both invites and rejects human activities. The rock-strewn surface, the fjords, the bare, windswept summits, and the mile upon mile of nothing but rock, sea, and trees are glacial legacies left for humans to manipulate (Photo 6.1). With poor agricultural soils, only two natural resources make this region economically attractive: the fishery and lumber. The fishery provided both a food source and an income. Fish were once so plentiful that it was said that a bucket thrown in the sea emerged filled with fish. But the fishery collapsed in 1992. Only water fills the bucket today. Lumber, while plentiful, has been exploited in the past and then abandoned as regional manufacturing shut down, largely because of the region's isolated location. The loss of the fishery and lumbering industries left the Atlantic Provinces and Northern New England without their main sources of income.

Once upon a time, the Atlantic Provinces—Nova Scotia, New Brunswick, Prince Edward Island, and Newfoundland—were important economically. They were the major shipping ports to Europe and shared a reciprocity agreement with the adjacent New England states. Today the regional economy depends on limited natural resources, and Atlantic trade has become secondary to Pacific trade.

The Atlantic Provinces cling to political and economic stability as they lose population to Canada's urban centers. If Quebec had seceded in 1995, Atlantic Canada would have been severed from the rest of Canada. Tourism has become the economic base, but it affords meager recompense in relation to the national economy. With the 1992 loss of the **cod** fishery, their greatest source of income, the provinces floundered, until offshore oil production increased along with oil prices. But offshore drilling is a short-term answer to continued economic security, and so some, such as Prince Edward Island, have turned to alternative energy sources.

Northern New England is in similar economic shape. The once dominant shipbuilding industry and the fishery that gave its name to Cape Cod have both disappeared. The current economy relies on wealthy Megalopolis residents seeking solace in a scenic northern New England coastal home. However, a second-home economy based on retirement or vacations is unsustainable for the permanent populations.

The region's chief export, arguably emigrants—especially the vital young—hinders rebuilding the economy. Its small town and rural nature attracted some population growth from urban areas in the respective countries, but most were retirees or second-home residents. The small population makes for small internal markets, dependent on vulnerable primary industries—fishing, forestry, and mining. But population issues are only a part of the region's geographic limitations.

1. Physical fragmentation, adding to transportation costs and integration.
2. Political and cultural fragmentation from each other.
3. Geographic isolation from the rest of the continent. Distance from major markets, especially the distance of the Atlantic Provinces from the Canadian Corridor.
4. A limited resource base. The dramatic glacial landscape has rocky soils, limiting the ability to support large populations and industry.
5. A formidable climate. The region is prone to natural weather extremes like ice storms and nor'easters.

Physical Geography

The North Atlantic region has suffered a dramatic **tragedy of the commons** by seeking short-term profits while ignoring long-term sustainability in the Grand Banks fishery. Fishing techniques shifted from local **outport** fisheries to factory fishing, which ruined the local economies. Because of such tragedies, in the twenty-first century the region is building a sustainable paradigm to work with the environment instead of battling to control it.

The North Atlantic includes the northeastern United States, the Maritime Provinces of Canada, and Newfoundland. The northeastern United States lies north of Megalopolis and includes Vermont, New Hampshire, Maine, Massachusetts outside and the Boston metro area, and the Adirondacks and upstate New York. The four provinces of Atlantic Canada are Prince Edward Island (PEI), Nova Scotia, New Brunswick, and Newfoundland. New Brunswick and the two smallest provinces, PEI and Nova Scotia, are the Maritime Provinces. Newfoundland and its territory, Labrador, have a very different history, and are seldom included within the Canadian Maritime Province culture, but form their own cultural region.

Regions

The sea rather than land brought settlers and formed the economy of this fragmented, rugged landscape. The most lucrative subregion was offshore.

The North Atlantic has two distinct onshore physiographic regions, the Appalachian Uplands and the Canadian Shield, and one offshore region, the Continental Shelf. The North Atlantic Coastal Plain is all but submerged.

From Atlantic Canada down through northern New England, the Appalachian Uplands is a fjord-indented coastline with a rolling interior—the result of repeated glaciations. The rolling foothills of the Canadian Appalachian Uplands skirt the U.S. border, extending to the Gaspé Peninsula before terminating in Newfoundland. The portion between Lake Champlain and Maine is known as the Estrie or eastern townships. In the United States, the Appalachians are called the Green and White Mountains.

Shaped by glaciers, the Uplands' rock-strewn fields and scraped-bare mountains are clothed in hardwood and coniferous forests. About 90 percent of Maine and New Brunswick remain a roadless second-growth boreal forest.

The Labrador Canadian Shield is part of the ancient North American craton, upon which newer (only one to two billion years old!) crusts have accreted. In Labrador, glaciers sculpted the coastline fjords and exposed bedrock; inland remains forested. Tectonic forces embedded resource minerals into the shield rock. For example, Northern Labrador's Voisey's Bay nickel ore was intruded between two ancient and collided craton crusts. The site has become an important twenty-first-century mining site.

The North Atlantic Continental Shelf ranges between 200 and 350 miles from the shore and is called the Grand Banks.

Sunlight penetrates the relatively shallow, six-hundred-foot-deep **banks**, supporting abundant plant and sea life. The prolific fishery has attracted fishers from around the globe. The edge of the Grand Banks marks the end of the North American continent; beyond, the continental slope plunges two miles to the ocean floor abyss.

Nova Scotia

Virtually surrounded by the sea, Nova Scotia, originally named Acadia by the French, consists of a peninsula and island. The narrow Isthmus of Chignecto land bridge connects the peninsula to New Brunswick; Cape Breton Island, separated from the mainland by the two-mile-wide Strait of Canso, has been connected to the mainland by a causeway since 1955. The causeway also caused ecological imbalances within the Gulf of St. Lawrence, including changes in the tidal regime, sediment deposition, and upsetting ecosystems. For example, nonnative bobcats entered Cape Breton after the causeway was completed and forced relocation of the native but less aggressive lynx into the more isolated highlands.

The rugged Atlantic coastline is indented with countless bays, inlets, and coves. Marine sediment covers the straighter Fundy coastline and the low-lying and stone-free Annapolis Valley, one of the few places with fertile soil to support the province's agriculture.

Prince Edward Island (PEI)

From mud flats to marshes, a variety of red sand beaches border the coastal margins of the smallest province (2,185 square miles), the crescent-shaped Prince Edward Island, where one is never more than ten miles from the sea. The fertile seacoast prairies of PEI are reclaimed from the sea and now utilized as farmland. PEI, called the "Garden Isle," has had most of its forest cover converted to agriculture.

Tourism was inconvenient until the nine-mile-long Confederation Bridge linked the island to the New Brunswick mainland in 1997. The bridge's environmentally sensitive engineering respects local terrestrial and aquatic environments. Following the environmental theme, the island province has recently adopted the name "the Green Province," has endorsed wind turbine and biomass energy production, and practices a high rate of recycling.

New Brunswick

New Brunswick is divided into two general regions: a flat to undulating maritime plain occupies one-third, and the remaining area is the thickly forested Appalachian Uplands. The St. John River cuts through the highlands and flows alongside the larger cities: Edmundston, Fredericton, and St. John, a city famous for its reversing waterfalls caused by Fundy tides.

Newfoundland

The island of Newfoundland, affectionately called "The Rock," and its mainland territory, Labrador, compose Canada's most easterly province. Fjords and deep harbors indent the coastline; moss and lichens populate the tree-laden inland, while people populated the coastline. Inland, a hundred thousand nonnative moose have overrun the native caribou. Hunting moose is a popular and legal sport that provides meat for the subsistent Newfoundlander's diet.

A series of peninsulas divide the island. The most prominent are Avalon, home to the capital, St. John's, and the 180-mile-long Northern Peninsula, crested by the two-thousand-foot-high barren plateaus of the Long Mountains. On the west coast of the Northern Peninsula, the mountains drop to a small coastal plain, whereas the mountains along the east coast fjords plunge directly into the ocean.

Lying at a similar latitude, Newfoundland is colder than Vancouver, because the cold Labrador Current flows down from the Arctic and surrounds Newfoundland.

Northern New England

And Ahab was fairly within the smoky mountain mist, which, thrown off from the whale's spout, curled round his great, Monadnock hump; he was even thus close to him.

—Herman Melville, *Moby Dick*[2]

Over the past million years the White and Green Mountains of New Hampshire and Vermont (*vermont* means "green mountain" in French) have lost elevation to erosion. Today the elevation averages 2,500 feet; Vermont's Green Mountains top out at 4,500 feet, and Mount Washington in the White Mountains reaches 6,288 feet. Another type of peak is the stand-alone geological remnant **monadnock**. The best known is 3,165-foot Mount Monadnock in New Hampshire, where 1887 fires scarred the rocky summit, leaving it treeless despite its low peak (Photo 6.2).

The United States (Vermont and New York) and Canada (Quebec) share the fertile Lake Champlain Valley. The Lowlands hold Lake Champlain, North America's sixth-largest lake, which some proclaim as the sixth Great Lake. The lake has served as a commercial highway between Montreal and the Northeast. Along its shore are several regional cities: Ticonderoga and Plattsburgh in New York and Burlington in Vermont.

Water features—lakes, ponds, and wetlands—pockmark the Lake Champlain ecosystem, protected by a microclimate that extends the growing season. The fertile agricultural soils are marred by residential and commercial developments that have polluted runoff and diminished air and water quality. Habitat reductions, fire suppression, invasive species, and fragmented aquatic and terrestrial habitats have resulted. Numerous nonprofit groups are restoring riparian lands, managing erosion, and reducing phosphorus loads from agricultural runoff.

The Frontenac Axis cuts across the St. Lawrence Lowlands and connects the primeval Adirondacks and the Canadian Shield. The Adirondacks are part of the Canadian Shield, but for millions of years the igneous rock core was covered and deformed by sediment before emerging as a dome about sixty-five million years ago. The Adirondack wilderness contains two thousand glacial lakes and the headwaters of the Hudson River,

which along with thin eroded soils formed a formidable barrier to settlement and exploitation.

Water

The lumber, farming, and tourist economies profited from the glacial waterways and lakes, including Lake Champlain and Lake Placid, home to the 1932 and 1980 Winter Olympics.

Maritimes

While generally unnavigable, Atlantic Province waterways have played an important part in economic development. The waterways provided regional transportation and easy access to food and fresh water.

Northern New England

Years ago, there were so many salmon that, as an enthusiastic friend once assured me, "you could walk across on them below the falls;" but now they are unknown, simply because certain substances which would enrich the farms are thrown from factories and tanneries into our clear New England streams. Good river fish are growing very scarce.

—S. Jewett, 1881[3]

River power supported northern New England's initial Industrial Revolution. The smaller regional rivers were the perfect size for the technological capabilities of the nation's nascent saw and textile mills.

The Appalachian Plateau topography was critical to the movement of timber on Maine's largest rivers—the Penobscot, Saco, Androscoggin, Kennebec, and St. John. From the mountain flanks these swift-moving rivers carried timber from the westernmost corners to the sea, supplying ship builders and pulp and paper manufacturers.

The lumber industry depended on waterpower harnessed by dams, but not without consequences. Power generation grew and blocked salmon spawning grounds and created pollution. In 1800 an estimated eighty thousand salmon returned to spawn in the Penobscot, whereas in 2000 the salmon numbered less than two thousand. The Penobscot River became one of the most polluted in the nation by 1996, due to the paper industry's use of the toxic carcinogen dioxin.

By the second half of the twentieth century, dams along the Penobscot and Maine's smaller rivers were technologically obsolete but still blocked fish runs. Implementation of the 1972 Clean Water Act affected discharge of water by dams and resulted in cleaning up many riverine pollutants and the return of salmon runs. The Penobscot no longer occupies the most endangered list; however, salmon runs are still limited.

Bay of Fundy

The Bay of Fundy has the highest tidal fluctuations in the world. Twice a day, seawater surges in and out of the funnel-shaped bay, carving cliffs along the shoreline. The Bay of Fundy tides

erode, transport, and deposit sediment, forming tidal marshes along the Maritime prairies.

The tidal movement differs within areas of the bay. At the six-mile-wide mouth near the Atlantic, the fluctuations are slight, but further north the Minas Basin fluctuations are the largest, normally around fifty feet (Map 6.1). The Minas Basin is also the location of the **tidal bore,** where the incoming tide meets the outgoing freshwater**,** thereby changing the flow of the river. Spectacular peaked-wave tidal bores can form when one force meets the other.

Tidal power has been a partial source of energy since the nineteenth century, and interest in decreasing fossil fuel dependence has renewed interest. Since 1984, experiments in electrical generation have focused on bay area tidal power—perfecting underwater power by using the rising and falling tides. Tidal power may generate an instream potential of 300

megawatts—enough to power about a hundred thousand homes. Underwater turbines in the Bay of Fundy are an emerging technology that sources hope to operate by 2015.

Climate

The **maritime influence** along the coast of the North Atlantic moderates regional temperatures throughout the year, but because of prevailing winds does not reach too much into the interior. Regional temperatures are similar to the Great Lakes and the St. Lawrence but are somewhat lower than similar latitudes of Western Europe. North Atlantic temperatures rarely rise above 90°F (32°C) or drop below 1°F (–17°C). Winters are long with continuous snow cover.

Precipitation is 40–55 inches (100–140 cm) annually, with adequate amounts during the four-month frost-free growing

PHOTO 6 2. Mount Monadnock, New Hampshire. This isolated peak has a rocky summit that was severely glaciated and then eroded. Nineteenth-century fires left the peak bare and with an artificially low treeline.

BOX 6.2 THE ADIRONDACK PARK

The Adirondacks remained forested while most of the east coast was stripped of its wood. Known as the "Great Northern Wilderness," these mountains were not settled by either the Native Americans or Europeans until the late nineteenth and early twentieth centuries, when artists and writers discovered its natural beauty. Because of their relatively pure nature, the mountains were a perfect setting for the incipient conservation movement that began with George Perkins Marsh's *Man and Nature* (1865). By 1885, the Adirondacks emerged relatively intact and protected. The largest unlogged tract in the eastern United States is the forty thousand acres of virgin forest in the Five Ponds Wilderness Area.

Large-scale logging in other areas left bare, eroded slopes and sediment-filled streams, which taught those involved with the park's creation about environmental devastation and the actions necessary to protect the mountains. Ecologically tied to the Erie Canal and indirectly to New York City, the health of Adirondack waterways was imperative. The Adirondack Park declaration assured the Adirondacks would never be sold as timberland, its waterways would be protected, and the forests would remain "forever wild."

However, the park is beset with problems for its future and must resolve the question of the relationship of humans and nature. Many diverse groups depend on the region, and all cannot exist at the same time. Each group has a different set of values. Some need the natural resources, the wood; others rely on the same woods for tourism; developers want to build more; and conservationists want no building at all. Across America the forest, often called the "land of many uses" and unfortunately nicknamed the "land of many abuses," cannot be everything to everyone.

---

season. The cold climate often freezes the harbors of Atlantic Canada, Maine, and the Gulf of St. Lawrence.

Since air flows counterclockwise around these storms, the winds come out of the northeast as they move offshore. For that reason they're known as "nor'easters." Meteorologists have another name for them. They call them "bombs."[4]

The Gulf Stream–Labrador Current confluence transfers heat between the cold and warm currents, which sometimes results in penetrating fog and intense storms with gale-force winds—nor'easters. Newfoundland has the strongest winds, especially in winter. Low-pressure systems exit from the St. Lawrence River and create cloudy weather over the Atlantic, which can generate winds up to ninety miles per hour. Other conditions associated with the storms include a numbing-wind-chill spray and reduced visibility.

Climate Change

Climate change is not linear but complex. The seemingly chaotic patterns over time and space have so many variables that modeling to understand the system is still in an elementary stage. Climate change affects more than temperature, and indirect effects are still being discovered. For example, North Atlantic climate change was partially responsible for the collapse of the fishery.[5] Cod have a narrow temperature range for reproduction, and changing water temperatures may have altered their reproduction cycles. Water temperatures off Newfoundland were 1°C warmer in 2004, and while there were fewer icebergs that year, other years have been above normal. In 2010, a hundred-square-mile iceberg separated from northern Greenland, and while it caused issues with sea level rise, another issue is what is making the icebergs break off? The answer seems to be warming seawater. Examining the big picture of systems reveals the patterns of the seeming chaos.

Inconsistent temperatures in seawater disrupt ocean food chains, cod breeding cycles, and the entire ecosystem. Overfishing weakens the ecosystem from the top down, but climate change is changing the ecosystem from the bottom up.

There may be, though, a more devastating scenario. Climate change could, paradoxically, flip climate from interglacial to glacial within a generation—not quite the speed of glaciation in Hollywood movies (*The Day after Tomorrow*) but quick enough to see and feel within a lifetime. How will this happen? Scientific models predict that water circulation within the oceans may change, and with that will come perhaps another ice age.

Historical Geography and Settlement

The English, Irish, and Scots settled the North Atlantic region, while the French Acadians settled the Maritimes. Their cultural imprint has shaped today's landscape. Native Americans, while populating the region prior to European arrival, are a miniscule part of the current population.

Native American Algonquian and Iroquoian families lived in northern New England. The Iroquois lived in the lowlands near Lake Ontario and the Appalachian Uplands, and on occasion they hunted in the Adirondacks.

The Eastern Woodland Micmac were dominant in the Maritime Provinces, while the Beotuks dominated Newfoundland. The Micmac were among the first Aboriginals to have contact with the Europeans. Many of the Natives began trading with French fishers in the early 1500s. The story of their demise is somewhat different from the devastation of the other local tribes.

Prior to European arrival, the Micmac hunted and gathered during the summer and managed their accumulated food throughout the rest of year. After contact and trade with the

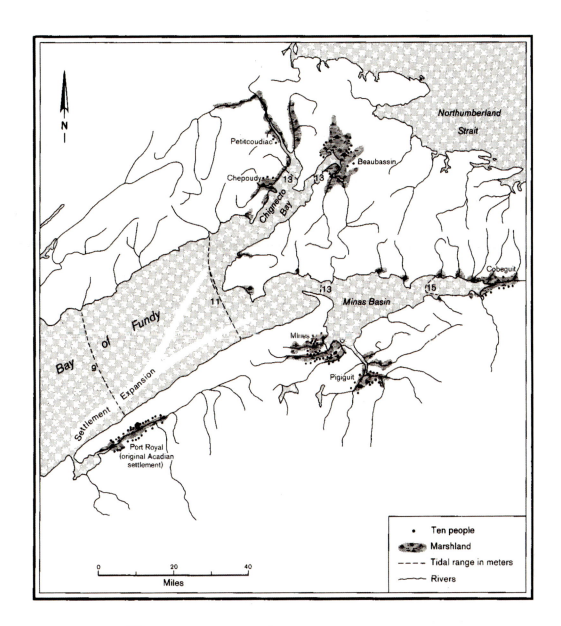

MAP 6.1. The Bay of Fundy was initially settled in 1604 by the French, who called the land Acadia. They settled and diked tidal marshlands for farming and pasture. The Bay of Fundy is known today as having the highest tidal range in the world, up to 50 feet as these two photos of the same boat illlustrate. The power generated by the tides is now being converted to electricity.

BOX 6.3 THE GULF STREAM AND THE LABRADOR CURRENT

The Gulf Stream originates in the Gulf of Mexico and then follows the wind north along the Gulf Coast through the Straits of Florida and up the East Coast continental slope (Map 6.2). The stream is 10°F warmer than the surrounding waters. Near Newfoundland, it turns toward Europe. Mid-ocean the current splits into the North Atlantic Drift, which moderates the high-latitude climate of Europe, and the Canary Current, which brings cool water to the Iberian Peninsula and beyond.

The cold Labrador Current (30°F, or 1.7°C) meets the northward-flowing Gulf Stream (68°F, or 20°C) off the coast of Newfoundland at the Grand Banks. The Labrador Current flows from Greenland's glaciers north into Baffin Bay and then south. Salt lowers the freezing temperature of water, so the Labrador Current—receiving freshwater from the Hudson Bay system—freezes more quickly than the saltier Gulf Stream Current. The Labrador Current usually freezes during winter, breaks up in May, and is ice-free by July. The Labrador Current delivers icebergs, which calf from Greenland's glaciers and seldom melt until they encounter the warm Gulf Stream, then melt rapidly, although icebergs have been reported as far south as Bermuda. Icebergs are now closely monitored because of their hazards to shipping—the *Titanic* was the victim of an iceberg.

When the two currents collide, they create advection fog (when warm air flows over cooler air below) and violent weather. The meeting place of the Gulf Stream and Labrador Currents is over the Grand Banks, one of the foggiest places in the world and formerly one of the richest fishing grounds.

The mixture of nutrients between the two currents has historically produced an abundance of plankton for feeding cod. However, the collapse of the cod fishery has created a domino effect for other species within the ecosystem, which in turn causes a decline in diversity, then a decline in the top predators, and finally, a decline in the plankton. Reduced diversity increases the chance of collapse of other species. Fishery management now seeks a sustainable harvest through the practice of **maximum sustainable yield**, the largest catch that can be continuously taken from a stock.

MAP 6.2. The meeting of the cold Labrador Current and the warmer Gulf Stream has numerous effects on the region, among them fog and the perfect conditions to grow phytoplankton. The fishing area includes a series of shallow areas—perfect for sunlight-spawned phytoplankton, the first link in the marine food chain—extending from the Grand Banks off Newfoundland to Georges Banks near Cape Cod. The Labrador Current also brings icebergs down from Greenland. Sometimes the icebergs anchor on the shallow continental shelf below and can become hazardous for shipping, as when the *Titanic* met its fate. The continental shelf of North America is widest near Newfoundland, where it extends more than three hundred miles.

BOX 6.4 THERMOHALINE CIRCULATION

Climate change can be an indirect effect of oceanic and atmospheric interactions.* The ocean contains 99.9 percent of the heat capacity of the climate system. Heat is distributed around the globe by way of the **North Atlantic Ocean Conveyor** current, a central part of **thermohaline circulation** in which heat is transferred from the equator toward the poles.

The conveyor circulates warmth and stabilizes weather patterns. The warm water increases evaporation, and the water becomes more saline (saltier). But the farther north it flows the more the water cools, until at a point off the coast of Norway gravity pulls the now salty, cool water (cold water is more dense than hot water) thousands of feet to the ocean bottom. The water is then pushed south within an undercurrent that wraps the world's oceans; it rises again in the Indian Ocean and makes its way back to the beginning of the conveyor along the coast of Africa.

The Gulf Stream is an important part of the conveyor. The ocean conveyor explains why places at the same latitude have different climates. England is at the same latitude as Labrador (54°N), but England's temperature is warmer, because the North Atlantic Drift extension of the Gulf Stream draws warm surface water from the tropical regions to the north. Conversely, the iceberg-filled water of the Labrador Current chills Labrador and Newfoundland. The conveyor is responsible for the warm Gulf Stream where it meets the Labrador Current, as discussed in Box 6.3.

Higher temperatures over the North Atlantic result in more precipitation, melt icebergs, and increase freshwater while decreasing water salinity. Dense water (cold and salty) tends to sink, while less dense water (warm and less salty) stays at the surface. The water in the North Atlantic is now cool and salty and sinks, but if freshwater continues to be added (icebergs melting and increased precipitation), the ocean's salinity will drop (making it less dense) and the water will no longer sink. This could even halt both the ocean conveyor and the Gulf Stream. The loss of salinity caused by additional freshwater (icebergs and increased precipitation) may trigger another ice age or ice event, such as happened during the Little Ice Age between 1300 CE and 1800 CE.

A decade ago this circulation scenario was dismissed as impossible, but scientists continually discover supporting evidence. The result of the shutdown could mean an increase in severe ocean weather, a major food chain disruption, and a rapidly advancing ice age, the duration of which no one can predict. Other effects of a shift in the ocean conveyor include the shift in salinity and warmer surface water temperatures; these could increase the number and intensity of hurricanes.

If these changes were to occur, the East Coast of the United States and Canada would be directly affected. The Atlantic and Gulf coasts have recently experienced more intense hurricane seasons than normal. If the ocean conveyor circulation were to halt, the land, no longer warmed by the Gulf Stream, would grow rapidly colder.† The interaction of each part of the climate system is more complex than current computer models can predict, but climate change is happening; what the models predict differs from the recent past and perhaps is a harbinger of things to come.

---

* Paul A. T. Higgins, Michael D. Mastrandrea, and Stephen H. Schneider, "Dynamics of Climate and Ecosystem Coupling: Abrupt Changes and Multiple Equilibria," *Philosophical Transactions of the Royal Society* 357, no. 1421 (2002): 647–55.

† A few of the many papers about thermohaline circulation are the following: W. S. Broecker, "The Biggest Chill," *Natural History* 96 (1987): 74–82; Peter U. Clark, Nicklas G. Pisias, Thomas F. Stocker, and Andrew J. Weaver, "The Role of the Thermohaline Circulation in Abrupt Climate Change," *Nature* 415 (February 21, 2002): 863–69; A. L. Gordon, "Interocean Exchange of Thermocline Water," *Journal of Geophysical Research* 91, no. C4 (1986): 5037–5046; N. G. Hogg, "A Note on the Deep Circulation of the Western North Atlantic: Its Nature and Causes," *Deep-Sea Research* 30 (1983): 945–61; Glen A. Jones, "A Stop-Start Conveyer," *Nature* 349 (January 31, 1991): 364–65; Andreas Schmittner, "Decline of the Marine Ecosystem Caused by a Reduction in the Atlantic Overturning Circulation," *Nature* 434 (March 31, 2005): 628–33.

Some websites discussing thermohaline circulation include the following: National Aeronautics and Space Administration (NASA), at science.nasa.gov/headlines/y2004/05mar_arctic.htm; National Geographic, at news.nationalgeographic.com/news/2005/06/0627_050627_oceancurrent.html; United Nations, at www.enviroliteracy.org/article.php/545.html; Woods Hole Oceanographic Institution, at www.whoi.edu/institutes/occi/currenttopics/ct_abruptclimate.htm.

Europeans, the Natives quit hunting and began depending on the dried vegetables, hardtack, and alcohol they received for their furs. The furs-for-food trade disrupted traditional winter food storage. Over the years the Micmac began to gorge during the summer, leaving few stores for the winter, because they depended on the European trade to provide winter provisions. Occasionally the Europeans did not arrive during the year, and the Natives starved. Mismanagement of food supply and the resulting diseases are most probably behind the 90 percent decline in the Micmac population, from thirty-five thousand in 1500 to thirty-five hundred in 1600.[6]

In Newfoundland, the Beotuk caused problems for the European fishers. The European travel pattern in the Atlantic North was migratory through the seventeenth century; Europeans arrived in the spring and returned to Europe in the fall. They sometimes built camps in Newfoundland and expected to return to them each spring, but the Beotuk scavenged the camps for wood and nails. Nails were so precious the Beotuk would often burn the camps just to acquire the nails, and so each year the camps had to be rebuilt. While many Natives died due to disease exposure, the Europeans viewed the Natives as a hindrance and systematically killed them for sport. By 1829 the last Beotuk died.

In Maine, the Malecite, Abenaki, and other tribal groups were hunter-gatherers and practiced agriculture. Little remains of their culture except the Maine tongue twister toponyms:

- *aroostook*: "beautiful river"; a county in northern Maine known for its potatoes and bilingual population (French and English).
- *passagassawakeag*: "a sturgeon's place" or "a place for spearing sturgeon by torchlight"; a river that runs through Belfast at Belfast Bay.
- *Penobscot*: "the rocky part" or "at the descending rock"; the name of a sovereign indigenous people and their language (mispronunciation of *Penawapskewi*), and Maine's longest river.

The Atlantic Provinces

While evidence remains of Viking visits, and many believe that pre-Columbian fishing crews plied the Grand Banks, the first Europeans to permanently settle the Atlantic Provinces were the Acadians. During the early 1600s, English, Scots, and Irish fishers settled in Newfoundland and along the North Atlantic coast.

Newfoundland

Europeans landed on Newfoundland in 988. The Viking Leif Ericsson founded Vinland, named after the wild grapes he found there, and in 1010, Thorfinn Karlsefni settled there for a few years. Archaeological evidence has documented a Viking settlement at L'Anse aux Meadows on the tip of Newfoundland's Northern Peninsula, but this was probably only a staging ground for other coastal forays, perhaps as far as the St. Lawrence River. The Vikings "discovered America," but their timing was poor. Europe was entrenched in the Dark Ages and lacked the tools, techniques, communication, and political motivations that popularized "discovery" in the fifteenth century.

Permanent European settlement of Newfoundland began in 1610, and by the mid-eighteenth century more than seven thousand settlers lived in hundreds of coast-hugging outports (out from St. John's) (Photo 6.3). St John's trading company vessels visited each outport twice annually, exchanging supplies for cod, which was shipped back to St John's and then exported. The credit system of trade was the only access to the outside world for this otherwise self-sufficient but isolated populace.

Newfoundland was ceded to Britain after the 1713 Treaty of Utrecht. When Canada confederated in 1867, Newfoundland had little reason to join, because its closest trade ties were with Britain. Newfoundland authorities were unsuccessful in brokering a deal with the United States, so Newfoundland became an independent country in 1855. But it failed to maintain a profitable economy. The island country fell into debt by the 1920s and went bankrupt during the Great Depression, and they rejoined the British Empire. After World War II, Britain, under its own financial stress, released the Newfoundland dominion. Newfoundland had to decide its fate as an independent country, a U.S. territory, or part of the Canadian Confederation. However, World War II had changed life for the poor and formerly insulated islanders.

During the war the island became a refueling stopover, and many Newfoundlanders were employed by American and Canadian military forces. The strategic importance of the island during the war fostered a belief in many Newfoundlanders that the island could remain independent. But more forces were at play than they fathomed. Premier Joey Smallwood was the man responsible for the choice of Newfoundland entering the Canadian Confederation in 1949 and for the still controversial agenda known in Newfoundland as the **resettlement**.

Acadia

In 1604, Northern French settlers arrived in the Bay of Fundy, a land they called Acadia. The land was marshy but similar to the

PHOTO 6.3. Salvage, Newfoundland. Newfoundland is still home to hundreds of picturesque but struggling outports that depend almost entirely on the sea for their livelihoods. Today, with the cod fishery closed, many are leaving their homes to find other opportunities. Salvage has earned a tourism economy because of its scenic beauty.

BOX 6.5 RESETTLEMENT

The settlement history of the Canadian Atlantic Provinces abounds with dramatic migration stories—the Acadian Grand Dérangement in Nova Scotia, the emigration of Scots to Nova Scotia after the Highlands clearance, and the resettlement in Newfoundland.

When Newfoundland became a province, the fishing-dependent economy was the poorest in Canada. The first premier, Joey Smallwood, who was instrumental in bringing Newfoundland into the Canadian Confederation, was dedicated to bringing Newfoundland industry "kicking and screaming into the twentieth century," but first he had to centralize and resettle the outports. The reasons for resettlement were largely economic. The fourteen hundred tiny outports (the average size less than two hundred people) were scattered along Newfoundland's shores. Canada was obligated to provide both education and medical attention to the new province. For Canada to efficiently provide these services to the outports was impossible. Resettlement was necessary to consolidate the tiny outports.

Resettlement began in the 1950s and was most active during the 1960s. During this time, three hundred outports were abandoned. More than thirty thousand people moved to new homes, in "growth centers." Resettlement remains controversial and has entered into local folklore through songs, poems, and pictures of homes being towed to their new outport (Photo 6.4).

In 1949, access to most outports was only by sea, because few roads connected outports to each other or to St John's. In addition, the fishery was already noted to be declining. Then in World War II the island became a strategic military base for the United States, and this break from the isolation of the island gave some Newfoundlanders a reason to leave the fishery for other opportunities.

The controversy stemmed from the "forced" removal of residents from their outports. Though portrayed as forced, it was not entirely so. Towns were given a vote. Often the vote was not unanimous, but a majority voted to move and the others succumbed to pressure and moved. The insulated people of the outports were removed from the only life they knew, and many had difficulty adjusting to their new towns. However, the next generation had more opportunities, and Newfoundland became more prosperous.

PHOTO 6.4. Floating Homes. During resettlement, many people moved to nearby outports. Rather than build new homes, about 20 percent floated their homes on rafts to the new outport. This practice has become a major folklore symbol in Newfoundland, found in every tourist area and postcard stand. The owner of the Newfoundland Emporium in Corner Brook was relocated as a child. This is his home being moved to its new location.
Source: Newfoundland Emporium

industrious settlers' homeland. Farming along the similar French coast landscape had taught them draining and diking techniques. Their **cultural preadaptation** to the new land gave them survival traits that allowed them to build a farming, fishing, and lumbering economy in the new environment.

Because of continued warfare and English **privateer** raids to seize goods, few immigrants settled in Port Royal, located along the well-protected Annapolis Valley harbor. However, the population grew because of a high birthrate. Acadian settlement later spread into New Brunswick, Prince Edward Island, and Maine.

The Maritimes were strategically important to both the French and English. In the first half of the eighteenth century, the two countries battled to control St. Lawrence trade. The land bounced between French and British control, but ultimately the French ceded Acadia to the British in 1713.

The Protestant British were uneasy with the Catholic French Acadians and their respect for, conversion of, and intermarriage with the Micmacs. Additionally, the Acadians refused to trade with or sign an oath of allegiance to the British. The result was the forced removal of the Acadians between 1755 and 1763.

BOX 6.6 GEO-TALES: GREAT HARBOUR DEEP

In 1999 I taught in Lethbridge, Alberta. While there I learned more about Canadian geography, including the collapse of the cod fishery. I was vaguely aware of the collapse, but access to Canadian journals (before digital databases!) allowed me to indulge my curiosity.

Fast-forward two years, when I was teaching in Michigan and still wondering how Newfoundland was doing after the collapse. Knowing there were still hundreds of outports, many with populations less than a thousand, and knowing that they were dependent on the fishery, I wondered how they were making it ten years after the collapse. With this question, I was awarded a grant to study outport population in relation to the fishery collapse. I was going to leave for points unknown at the end of the school year, but only a few weeks prior I received an e-mail from a colleague at Newfoundland's Memorial University informing me that the first resettlement in thirty years had just been granted to a small outport called Great Harbour Deep (GHD). My destination was now exact.

I spent my summer months in GHD, learning about the outport and how it was preparing for the resettlement, and in St. John's, where I gathered data at the Centre for Newfoundland Studies.

Great Harbour Deep had 420 residents in the 1980s but had lost half by 1996 and another 30 percent by 2001, leaving it with 136, most of whom had been born in the outport. GHD had grown during the original resettlement, when nearby outports had resettled in GHD, but it had been losing population and opportunities since (Photo 6.5). The school had twenty students from grades 1 through 8, but all ninth-grade students had to leave the outport during the school year for Deer Park, more than a hundred miles away. Fishing opportunities were limited by heavy quotas, and they were not nearly as lucrative as the cod had been. The outport petitioned the government to resettle and received their wish.

With no roads to the outport, I arrived via the available transportation: boat or plane, both subsidized by the government. Government subsidies to keep GHD viable cost about C$1 million annually. By paying the residents C$5 million to relocate, the Canadian government's investment would save the subsidy money after five years.

I made two trips to GHD. During the first trip, life was still at its usual pace in GHD (Photo 6.6). I met all the residents and interviewed them about their lives and their plans for the future. I left and did research at Memorial University in St John's. When I returned in late August, the outport was involved in moving. Those who had children in school were already leaving. Many heavy items had already been transported, but moving continued on the daily ferry. Interestingly, the ferry also contained a fair number of tourists, who came in each day to visit the resettling town. So the port area was busy with tourists and those who were moving each day as the school year commenced.

By October 31, 2002, the outport services were shut off and the last ferry left. The small lodge remains, mostly for hunting parties and the few who still fish the old ground, but without utilities or water the outport is abandoned.

PHOTO 6.5. Great Harbour Deep, Newfoundland, was protectively situated in one of the many Newfoundland fjords. In the past, several small outports were within each fjord, but now few remain. Great Harbour Deep was the last community in Harbour Deep fjord.

PHOTO 6.6. Boatbuilding in Great Harbour Deep. Outports were usually isolated, with their only access by the sea. Isolation made the people self-sufficient, often growing their own crops on the bare soil (using seaweed as fertilizer) and building their own boats.

More than six thousand Acadians were deported, their homes destroyed, and their lands confiscated. Many Acadians were deported to the American British colonies, others to France or other colonies, such as Quebec or Louisiana (*Cajun* is a corruption of *Acadian*); others became refugees in the inland forests of their former homes (Map 6.3).

In the meantime, British and Scots settlers replaced many Acadian farmers in the drained and diked Annapolis Valley, but their lack of knowledge about **polders** limited their success. The British needed assistance to farm the diked farmlands. Some Acadians returned and taught the new settlers how to manage the diked lands. Even more Acadians returned and resettled after 1763, although not on their old properties. Some were discouraged when they realized their land would not be returned and left again for Maine, the shore of New Brunswick, or Prince Edward Island.

The end of the French and Indian War in 1763 terminated the dream of a French North America. Soon after, the American Revolution impelled about forty thousand British Loyalists to resettle in the Maritimes. The contingent of Loyalists, along with new British, Irish, or Scots settlers, created an English-speaking majority in the 1760s, and Acadia became Nova Scotia. Loyalist settlement extended to the St. John River and New Brunswick in 1794.

In 1783, more than three thousand former slaves left the United States and created small communities in Nova Scotia; Birchtown, with more than fifteen hundred people, was the largest. They had difficulty adjusting to the harsh climate and rugged conditions, so most of the towns were short-lived. Many of the residents emigrated in 1792 to Sierra Leone.

Northern New England

The geographic factors of an embayed coast, narrow coastal land, and poor soil influenced coastal settlement. Fishing along the Grand, Scotian, or Georges banks, trade with Britain (closer than the southern colonies), and shipbuilding also influenced initial settlement. Shipbuilding deforested southern New England after 1750, and the industry relocated to northern New England, where forest resources supported the American shipbuilding center—building the cheapest and best vessels in the world—until the end of the wooden ship era in the 1850s.

In the 1600s, fishers and disgruntled Puritans from Massachusetts settled the commercial colony of New Hampshire, while French trappers and traders entered Vermont from the north through Lake Champlain. Today, many Vermont towns along the Champlain Valley bear French toponyms. Years later, crop failures and British anti-French discrimination caused

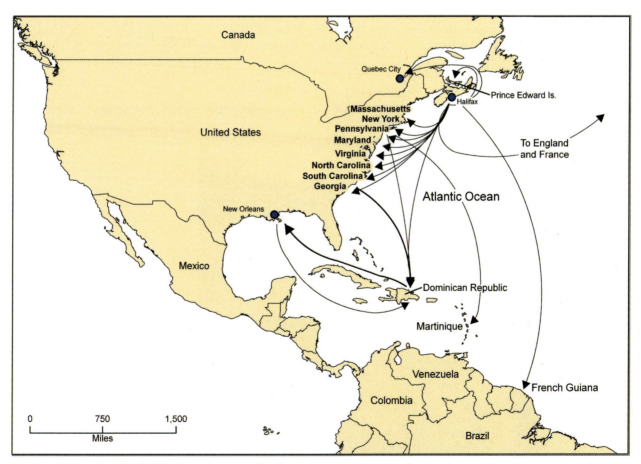

MAP 6.3 Acadian Expulsion, 1755–1763. During the French and Indian War, the British deported Acadians from their Nova Scotia home. They were deported to the American colonies, the Louisiana Territory, Prince Edward Island, and a few to Quebec, Martinique, French Guiana, England, and France.

more French to resettle from Quebec. Many found employment working in the textile mills.

Both New Hampshire and New York claimed Vermont and agreed to split it along the crest of the Green Mountains. The British prioritized New York claims over those of New Hampshire, and resurveyed New Hampshire land granted to settlers. The conflict agitated the settlers. Ethan Allen and the **Green Mountain Boys** fought the British and meted out vigilante justice upon New York surveyors. After the Revolutionary War, Vermont pursued independence. The Green Mountain Boys' actions and independent attitude led to the formation of the Republic of New Connecticut, then the Republic of Vermont, a safe haven for British and American deserters. The republic lasted from 1777 to 1791, when Vermont became the first state outside the original thirteen to join the United States, its ratification based on balancing its non-slaveholding status against slaveholding Kentucky.

Cultural Perspectives

The North Atlantic rural population lives in aesthetic but economically challenged towns. In the states, Northeastern towns are often arrayed in the classic village green crowned by a white-spired church, a symbolic pattern rather than a representation of the culture today. Manipulated cultural artifacts include lobster dinners and covered bridges. Almost two hundred covered bridges are in the North Atlantic states and another sixty-one in New Brunswick. The bridges are functionally obsolete except for their nostalgic significance.

"Lobstah"

Throughout the region, "lobstah" (the local pronunciation) is a common food. A delicacy in today's world, lobster has an indelicate past. Native Americans and early colonists applied the abundant crustacean as fertilizer, or lobster became an unwelcome and monotonous dinner several times a week. This is, of course, no longer the case. Today lobster has benefited by the decline of cod, one of its main predators. The lobster is a regular and high-priced menu item in numerous lobster shacks along the coast (Photo 6.7).

During the winter, lobsters retreat to deeper waters and are difficult to catch. To keep stocks of lobster available and provide a more consistent and sustainable market, Maine lobstermen have self-regulated conservation over the years. Many lobsters are "pounded"—caught in the previous peak season and held in blocked-off sections of bays for the winter season.

In the twenty-first century, pounding is most prevalent in Canada. Maine and Northern New England waterfronts have succumbed to high-priced, luxury housing, which raises taxes, limits beach access, and regulates what has been self-regulated by the locals for decades. Turning these Northern New England areas into the equivalent of Massachusetts, "Massification," has elevated prices, and those "from away" have compromised the cultural landscape that first attracted them.[7] Pounding has become a crucial tool for the northeastern lobster market. A cold spring results in a poor lobster catch, and because of decreased pounding, most Maine lobstermen go wanting, while Canada's pounded catch brings high prices.

Those who continue to fish lobster in Maine have suffered due to depleted stock and competition from mainlanders who come to fish the waters for sport during the summer season. Small island communities dependent on lobster fishing limit licensing to residents only.

Northern New England

The northern New England colonies were imprinted with Puritan values, morals, and frugality. New England's taciturn

PHOTO 6.7. Lobster is an abundant and popular food throughout the region. This is a local lobster restaurant in Antigonish County, at the Strait of Canso, Nova Scotia.

"Yankee" is a stereotype that contains grains of truth. This harsh land developed into a rooted homeland culture that maximized scant resources, often with picturesque results.

For example, the picturesque rock walls of New England are a valued cultural landscape feature treasured by a romantic urban population—but they were built by settlers to clear their rock-strewn fields (Photo 6.8). As time went by, most New England farmers migrated west, fished, or became traders.

Maritimes

Two cultural groups settled Nova Scotia—the Acadians and the Scots. In the early nineteenth century, Scotland's brutal highland clearances stripped tenants of the land they worked. They fled for the familiar feel of the highlands, bogs, and fog of Cape Breton.

Nova Scotia and Prince Edward Island have an abundance of Scottish toponyms, named by Scots who migrated to the provinces. Names such as Inverness, Strathgarney, and Cape Breton abound in the Maritimes. Acadian descendants live along the western Bay of Fundy coast, as well as in towns like Cheticamp along Cape Breton's western coast.

Two of Canada's cultural icons, both women and both in Atlantic Canada, are fictional characters. One was the heroine of the stirring epic poem Evangeline, by Henry Wadsworth Longfellow. The poem immortalizes the exile of the Acadians from their Nova Scotia homes. The other, the title character of Anne of Green Gables, originated on Prince Edward Island. In 1908, Lucy Maud Montgomery wrote of Anne growing up on a PEI farm. The island has become a mecca for those entranced by this childhood classic.

Newfoundland

Newfoundland settlers brought their European culture and dialects to the island. Isolated outports developed their own dialects, which were often unintelligible from one district to another. These distinctive dialects softened or disappeared as communication, transportation, and education equalized speech patterns, but even today the older inhabitants of outports speak a distinct English dialect that is almost unintelligible to those from outside the outport. Newfoundland language remains sprinkled with eighteenth-century speech patterns and distinctive Newfoundland words. Meanings of words such as gut (a narrow passage) and tickle (a pass) differ from the rest of English-speaking North America. These words are defined in a thick Newfoundland dictionary.[8]

Newfoundlanders were an uneducated and poor people who migrated for the fishery opportunities. Most inhabitants seldom left their outport and its fishing grounds except to find a mate. Outports were small affairs populated by few families, and finding a suitable mate often required visiting a neighboring outport, as long as both shared the same religion. Newfoundland outports were divided by denominations, Catholic versus several Protestant sects.

The isolation of Newfoundland and its almost complete dependence on the fishery created a food culture dependent on nonperishables. The traditional Newfoundland meal, **brewis**, includes the nonperishable salted codfish, hardtack, and salted pork. The lack of arable land, expense, and distance from markets make fresh fruit and vegetables rare in the outports even today.

Regional Life

Population

The North Atlantic regional population has been stable at best. Decreasing job opportunities and increasing emigration, especially by young adults, has been the standard since the 1920s.

PHOTO 6.8. New England Stone Wall. Farmers built walls with stones cleared from their fields. Many farmers chose to leave these stony fields for the better soils of the West. Today people pay more for homes with these nostalgic old stone walls. Some of the walls are dismantled and used as landscaping and house decoration.

The meager population supports few cities in Northern New England and Atlantic Canada. In Newfoundland and Nova Scotia, four out of five residents live in small dispersed coastal villages, and in PEI almost everyone lives within six miles of the coast. Only in New Brunswick do people live inland in cities along the rivers.

The population in Atlantic Canada and Northern New England states is older than the rest of their respective countries. All rural provincial areas in Canada continue to lose young adults but the Atlantic Provinces have lost the most; Northern New England is also losing its young. Few job opportunities and a high cost of living cause many young adults to migrate to urban areas. As baby boomers retire, the population will require costly social services, such as health care, but without a strong tax base these services will be underfunded. Older populations also have less discretionary income on which the consumer economy depends and are less inclined to fund school programs.

Maritimes

In 2011, the Maritimes and Newfoundland constituted 7.0 percent of Canada's population, down from 11.6 percent in 1949. Other than the territorial north, Atlantic Canada's 2.3 million population (2011) is the smallest in the nation. Population numbers have stagnated (Table 6.1). The collapse of the fishery continued to affect Newfoundland's population until 2007, when there was a slight resurgence of growth due to offshore oil drilling.

Most people in Atlantic Canada claim English, Irish, Scots, or French ancestry. New Brunswick received thousands of Loyalists who fled the United States after the American Revolution. During the latter part of the eighteenth century, fifty-five thousand British, Scots, Irish, and Welsh emigrants settled in Nova Scotia. Most of the immigrants began as farmers, but then turned to the sea.

The French-speaking populations of Nova Scotia, New Brunswick, and Prince Edward Island were Acadian exiles who returned to their homeland and live today in French-speaking towns. New Brunswick is 35 percent francophone; Nova Scotia has eight thousand Acadians who live in francophone villages,

and another forty thousand interspersed throughout the general populace. More than twenty-eight thousand Acadian descendants live on Prince Edward Island.

Newfoundland

Generally, the fishing industry and settlement patterns of Newfoundland are intertwined. The fishery collapse left most outport residents unemployed. Few jobs were in commuting distance because many outports are inaccessible by road. The demise of the fishery led to a population loss (1994 580,000; 2007 509,000), and the high unemployment rate left the province with only 45.2 percent with full-year employment (the Canada average is 59.4 percent). The overall population decline includes almost half of all young adults, who migrated toward areas with jobs. The birthrate is so low that in 2007 Premier Danny Williams offered a $1,000 financial incentive to the parents of every child born in the province.

Almost every small outport lost population, as well as the capital, St. John's (–2.7 percent), and Corner Brook (–8.2 percent). Many working-age residents have emigrated to other parts of Canada. So many Newfoundlanders live in Fort McMurray, Alberta, that they often joke that it (rather than Corner Brook) is the second-largest city in Newfoundland. This leaves the province aging in place; 14 percent of the population is over sixty-five, and this figure may reach 23.1 percent in the next decade.[9] Additional elderly are emigrating "home" when they near retirement.

In the days when the catch was prodigious and the fishing gear primitive, small fishing villages were strung one next to one another along the coast. But this has changed. The cod are gone. What remains of the industry is now fished from modern trawlers. The remaining quaint towns have become tourist attractions. Today the structure of society is around economies of scale— bigger is better. The picturesque outports are nostalgic and charming but no longer serve today's economic system. However, the economy has been rebounding as the price of oil escalates and more jobs related to the offshore oil rigs become available.

Oil resources caused the Newfoundland economy to grow 50 percent between 2000 and 2008, second only to Alberta.

TABLE 6.1. Atlantic Canada Population, 2011

	2011	2006	% Change
Newfoundland and Labrador	514,536	505,469	1.8
Prince Edward Island	140,204	135,851	3.2
Nova Scotia	921,727	913,462	0.9
New Brunswick	751,171	729,997	2.9
Canada	33,476,688	31,612,897	5.9

Source: Statistics Canada, Census 2006

Primary Industry and Natural Resources

A Natural Resource Periphery

The North Atlantic is a peripheral region dependent on natural resources; however, the primary resource industries (fishing, logging, mining, and agriculture) have been in decline, with the exception of oil production in Newfoundland. In 2008, for the first time since joining the Confederation, Newfoundland (a "have not" province) became more economically viable than Ontario (a "have" province).[13]

While Atlantic Canada welcomes the economic relief from oil production, the region is in need of a long-term sustainable economy. The collapse of the fishery was predicted decades prior to the moratorium, and yet Canadian officials were unable to create a sustainable fishery. Because oil is a nonrenewable energy source, it is short-term and will decline. Therefore, investing in renewable energy resources will provide long-term sustainable energy production.

History

As a part of a colonial empire, the Maritimes and Newfoundland were a **resource hinterland** for Great Britain until the markets opened to free trade in 1849. At that time, the Maritimes began a more earnest trade with New England until the Reciprocity Agreement was cancelled in 1866. The Maritimes were cut off from U.S. industry, and the fates of Northern New England and the Maritimes became independent of each other for over a century, until the North American Free Trade Agreement (NAFTA).

The 1867 formation of the Canadian Confederation shifted the North Atlantic provincial markets toward the core of the new nation.

Fisheries

Since the 1400s, the Grand Banks fishery was the catalyst for Atlantic Canada settlement. The original colonial fishery consisted of inshore fishing in small boats. By the 1960s, fishing trawlers changed fishing and the size of fishing vessels. Fishery boats now range from small owner-operated boats to **factory trawlers** with processing facilities.

An augmentation, or even maintenance of the present catch of sea-fish, however, is inconsistent with a policy of conservation. If New England wishes to fish in the future it must begin to harvest with discretion. Some restriction must be placed on the new unlimited fishing of certain species.

—Edward A. Ackerman, 1938[14]

Collapse of the Fishery   For the past five hundred years the Grand Banks, extending from the appropriately named Cape Cod to northern Labrador, has been among the world's most productive fishing grounds. Cod, the beef of the sea, was the most consumed fish in Europe.

In the fishing-dependent outports along the coastline of Newfoundland, cod was literally currency. In Europe, dried cod was a preserved food source, and in the West Indies it was an inexpensive food for feeding slaves. Cured and dried cod was a perfect, indestructible international trade commodity. Even after the invention of refrigeration, the favorite catch of fishers was cod—pure white, protein-rich, easy to catch, easy to fillet. Salted cod dried on the Newfoundland **flakes** (a platform for drying cod, built on poles on the foreshore of outports) were a global commodity (Photo 6.9). But this wealth of nature was exploited, resulting in a devastated fishery.

Unintended Consequences   Over the past several hundred years, the fishing industry depended on traditional line fishing in small dories along the outport coastline. But the Industrial Revolution and concurrent population growth supported ever larger ships plying the Grand Banks, until mammoth corporate freezer trawlers from every fish-trawling country were anchored in the Grand Banks. Despite warnings foreseen as

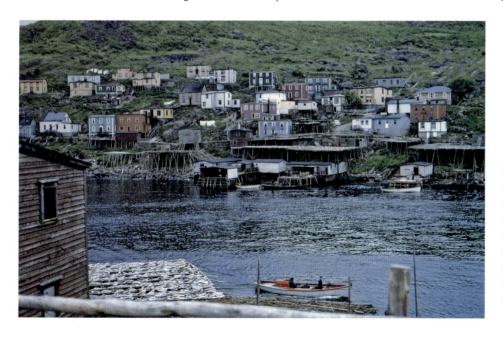

PHOTO 6.9. Flakes at St. John's, Newfoundland, 1964. The racks along the coast in the near area and across the neck are flakes, the standard technique for drying fish at the time. Modern refrigeration and the collapse of the fishery ended this traditional way to preserve cod.

Photo: Ed Badura

far back as 1871, the cod stock collapsed in 1992.[15] The fishers and the governments failed to act on the recognized changes in the ecosystem. The lack of connect-the-dots systems thinking incurred a classic case of tragedy of the commons.

By the 1960s, the government and fishers recognized that collapse was imminent, although little was done to limit fishing. Then in 1977, the **Exclusive Economic Zone (EEZ)** for fishing was extended from twelve to two hundred miles offshore, so maritime countries could control offshore foreign commercial fishing fleets. Canada had almost exclusive jurisdiction over the Grand Banks. However, the Grand Banks extend beyond the two-hundred-mile limit, and foreign trawlers continued to fish the area beyond the EEZ.

By the 1990s, the cod population had dropped 99.6 percent from 1505 estimates.[16] The ineffective regulation of the Grand Banks until it was too late left the region bereft of a recovery. The unintended consequences of industrial technology and greed may have eliminated this ecological niche. The cod have not returned. When there was still a chance to set a quota to regulate and maintain a sustainable catch, it was not done.

Local and Ecoregional Impacts   Atlantic cod proliferated because of sustained food chain conditions that supported the prey for cod: **phytoplankton**, crab, shrimp, and **capelin** (a small fish similar to a sardine or herring). Each level in the food chain depends on the next, and as the cod disappeared the effect cascaded down the food chain, so that the entire predator-prey relationship shifted. When a top predator, such as the cod, is removed from the food chain, then the predator's food increases—in this case, shrimp and crab. Many fishers turned to catching crab. But once again the food chain became vulnerable to additional imbalances.

Years after the collapse and closing of the cod fishery, the catch remains miniscule. The 2002 catch was only 2 percent of the 1988 catch, and the catch has remained flat in subsequent years. A slight resurgence of capelin has been noted, but cod remain in short supply. The cod may return, but in the meantime the prognosis is not good. Most global fishing zones have since collapsed, and commercial fishing has become problematic. To add to the problems, overfishing is also a victim of climate change, and as the ocean warms, marine ecosystems will be placed under ever greater pressure.

External Costs   The Atlantic cod disaster was and continues to be horrific, but the process is being repeated in other fishing grounds. The majority of Europe's fishing stocks are reported overfished and in need of a moratorium. Several other fishing grounds are also overfished. Placing moratoriums, though, is disastrous for fishing communities.

Commercial fishers throughout the world have yet to learn the lessons of overfishing. In the period from 2002 to 2005 following various scientists' warnings, the European Union (EU) halted commercial fishing in the North, Irish, and Baltic seas, and in the waters off the west coast of Scotland. Fished beyond reproduction levels, the fishing grounds approach collapse. The fishery collapse was caused by poor resource management, overfishing, and an additional environmental wild card—climate change.[17]

Additional external costs are the socioeconomic issues. Many families in Newfoundland have been dependent on the fishery for their livelihood. However, sad as it is, the livelihood of the individual and their family, whose best interest was to maximize their catch, was not in the best interest of society. The Canadian government's inability to face the unpopular consequences of shutting down the fishery earlier caused tremendous economic disarray in Newfoundland. The immediate effect of the 1992 moratorium was the unemployment of more than thirty-five thousand fishers in hundreds of outports. While the economic and industrial structure has changed, including growth of the snow crab and shrimp catch, it remains to be seen if a sustainable catch can be regulated.

Logging

American logging followed western expansion. The first commercially logged region was the North Atlantic, where settlers logged haphazardly, cutting down nearby forests but bypassing difficult-to-log areas.

For example, the Adirondacks escaped systematic logging because early-nineteenth-century waterpower and technology could only reach the margins of the remote Adirondacks. By the mid-nineteenth century, technology was capable of logging more mountainous terrain, but by that time the center of the logging industry had moved to the Great Lakes states. If the Adirondacks had been settled in the late nineteenth century instead of a century earlier, there would be little to protect in the Adirondack Park forest.[18]

Most of today's forests are the result of replanting. Some forests are protected as state parks and remain much as they were historically, although with second-growth trees.

In the past, extensive logging in Atlantic Canadian forests left only small and fragmented virgin forests. Areas that have been particularly threatened are across Newfoundland and Cape Breton, Nova Scotia.

New Brunswick logging flourished throughout the nineteenth century. Much of New Brunswick and western Maine remain forested with second and third growth (only 2 percent remains as virgin) in the twenty-first century. In 2002, New Brunswick adopted green environmental standards for the logging industry, the first North American province or region to do so.

The North Atlantic is not an important lumber source region. An exception arose during the early twenty-first century, when disagreements about lumbering in British Columbia shut down that timber area for a few years, resulting in the temporary increase in logging in the North Atlantic region.

Mining

Mining has been significant in the past, but few mines remain open and are inconsequential in the global market. The mining industry is important for the local economies.

BOX 6.7 TRAGEDY OF THE COMMONS

In 1968, Garrett Hardin wrote his tragedy of the commons essay regarding the exploitation of common shared resources, guided by self-interest and leading to destruction.* Though based on an equal distribution of any shared resource—air, land, and water—the distribution fails because of greed.

Hardin's essay begins by analyzing the assumption made in other arguments: All problems have technical solutions "demanding little or nothing in the way of change in human values or ideas of morality." But his analysis focuses on the size of the population and the amount of the resource limits to the commons. He applies his analysis specifically to the "population problem."

He develops his hypothesis within a hypothetical pasture commons, in which each herdsman traditionally operates within the carrying capacity of the land. Once uncontrollable factors—war, disease, famine—are eliminated and social stability is achieved, the entrepreneurial herdsman seeks to increase his herd: He acts for his own advantage and adds more animals. The difficulty, though, is that each entrepreneurial herdsman does the same. Garrett Hardin said it best:

Therein is the tragedy. Each man is locked into a system that compels him to increase his herd without limit—in a world that is limited. Ruin is the destination toward which all men rush, each pursuing his own best interest in a society that believes in the freedom of the commons. Freedom in a commons brings ruin to all.†

Hardin continued his essay by revealing the tragedy of the commons as seen from the 1968 point of view. He anticipates some of the larger tragedies we have encountered since: the collapse of fisheries, crowded national parks, accumulation of waste and pollutants in air, water, and land. He is, however, most concerned with the "freedom to breed"—overpopulation and its commensurate impact on the resource commons.

Despite recognition of this tragedy, only recently have responsibility and the common good been addressed through the auspices of sustainability. But human rights and responsibilities in relation to ecology are still not generally applied.

---

* Garrett Hardin, "The Tragedy of the Commons," *Science* 162 (1968): 1243–1248; at http://www.garretthardinsociety.org/articles/art_tragedy_of_the_commons.html.

† Hardin, "The Tragedy of the Commons."

Coal   Cape Breton had few cities until Sydney developed a coal and steel industry. Located on the northern shore of the island, Sydney (population 25,025) prospered as a major steel town from 1900 to the 1960s, when a variety of factors—the plant's changing hands several times, international competition, and modernized technology bypassing the town—closed the mills. More than twenty-three thousand jobs in the coal and steel industries have been lost since, leaving the Cape Breton region seeking new economic and employment opportunities, such as a proposed terminal for liquefied natural gas. Today, Sydney is best known as the terminus for the Newfoundland ferry and the city's "heritage" housing.

Nickel and Copper   Globally important nickel deposits were found in Voisey's Bay, Labrador, in 1993. About thirty million tonnes of nickel, copper, and cobalt ores have been extracted, worth $10 billion.

Voisey Bay mining commenced before land claims, work rights, and environmental issues had been addressed. The mining is on indigenous Inuit and Innu land; it was illegal until 1997, when a resolution gave the local Aboriginals rights to some land, royalty payments, a degree of self-government, cash for development, and agreements on employment.

The depressed region has few job opportunities. The historical Aboriginal occupation was seal hunting, but this declined when infrastructure and pollution caused by the mining and without consulting the Natives has destroyed former hunting grounds. The unemployment rate escalated, and Natives were shut out from mining employment during the initial years at Voisey's Bay. The latest and largest mine in Voisey's Bay has had to address Native Innu social equity and environmental justice claims and hire Native workers. By 2005, about 50 percent of the operation workforce was local Inuit.

Oil and Gas   Oil fields were discovered in the Grand Banks in 1878; however, production began in earnest in the 1960s, although still delayed because of offshore engineering problems. For example, the Hibernia oil field halted production until the late 1980s because of floating icebergs, severe storms, and shipwrecks.

Offshore oil and natural gas deposits near Newfoundland can only be profitable when commodity prices are high. They sat idle until 2005, when escalating oil prices supported high-risk oil production and helped diversify Newfoundland's economy. The additional jobs and oil revenue accrued to Newfoundland increased provincial investment in infrastructure, education, and medical facilities. Additional income from extensive gas deposits found off the shore of Labrador also benefited the province. Because of increased gas prices, oil revenues enhanced provincial GDP, and the province recorded a budget surplus in early 2008. For the first time since Newfoundland joined the Confederation, the poorest province shed its equalization payments and was in the black.

Stone Quarries   The folding, breaking, and crushing of rock formed the Appalachian Mountains and provided

BOX 6.8 WOMEN AND THE FISH PLANTS

In Newfoundland, most who fished were male, but women traditionally have been part of the fishery. For centuries, they worked at the flakes drying fish, and as technology changed after World War II they worked in the fish plants of small outports through the 1970s. The plant jobs gave the women a sense of independence and economic empowerment, although some theorize that the patriarchal economy actually victimized the women in their jobs rather than providing liberty. For example, despite their participation women were denied the same government benefits as men until 1981. When many plants closed after the 1992 cod fishery moratorium, the consequent job losses overwhelmingly affected women.

When the fishery collapsed, retraining efforts were concentrated on men, but for women in small outports retraining was a futile idea, because poor transportation networks limit outside opportunities. Losing the plants stripped the women of their jobs. After years of some independence, many women were unable to adjust to unemployment (Photo 6.10). The destroyed economy was destructive to families and often resulted in increased alcoholism and domestic abuse. Failure of the Canadian government to act on the precautionary principle and protect the people from the collision course of the fishing industry resulted in both the loss of the industry and the destruction of families.

For women, achieving self-reliance required inclusion in the decision-making process, improved access to training and education, improved gender equity, encouraging women entrepreneurs, and supporting women as they age.*

PHOTO 6.10. Weigh-in, Great Harbour Deep. Though the fish plant closed in Great Harbour Deep, some fishers still fish within the allowed quotas for lumpfish roe, seal, and crab. At one time the women of Great Harbour Deep worked in the local fish plant, but after it shut down, few women had jobs. In this photo, a local woman records the weigh-in for fishermen and stores the fish for a processing ship.

---

* Joanne Hussey, "The Changing Role of Women in Newfoundland and Labrador," Royal Commission on Renewing and Strengthening Our Place in Canada, March 2003, at http://www.gov.nl.ca/publicat/royalcomm/research/hussey.pdf.

---

abundant stone. The Granite State, New Hampshire, and the state of Vermont have operated large granite, slate, and marble mines. Up until the twentieth century, many building facades, interiors, and roofs were constructed of Vermont stone, but weight and expense limits the popularity of Vermont stone today. For example, replacing a slate roof on a house can cost more than $100,000. As the nation grew and expanded west, the peripheral location of Vermont and New Hampshire placed them geographically at a disadvantage in relation to centrally located stone quarries.

Agriculture

"There's no doubt that the land is more valuable as building lots than as a blueberry field," said Blue Hill real estate agent Jeff Allen.

Not only have land prices increased, but prospective Maine transplants like the look of a blueberry field, Allen said. To them, that's part of what living in Maine means.

"It's all about aesthetics," he said. [19]

Northern New England   Farming communities populated the earliest Northern New England settlements, but within one hundred years of settlement, farmers either abandoned their stony New England land for farms in the West or abandoned farming altogether and worked in the growing secondary industries of the burgeoning Industrial Revolution.

Prices fell as crop volume grew nationally, and the New England farm became unprofitable. From 1870 to 1920, New England farmers abandoned half of all farmland (Table 6.4). The

TABLE 6.4. Rockingham County, New Hampshire, Agricultural Land

Year	Acres in farmland
1870	235,605
1900	102,058
1920	86,336
1997	42,544
2002	31, 656
2007	33,570

Source: Smith, Russell, J. 1925, *North America: Its People and the Resources, Development, and Prospects of the Continent as an Agricultural, Industrial, and Commercial Area*, NY: Harcourt Brace; U.S. Agricultural Census 1997, 2002, 2007, http://www.agcensus.usda.gov/

farmers who remained grew specialized crops—potatoes, blueberries, and dairy—for the local market.

In Maine, the Aroostook Valley's soils are set apart from the inhospitable granites surrounding it. The cool, moist climate and sandy loam are ideal for potato growth. Aroostook was once the primary potato-producing area in the United States, but it is now ranked fifth. Maine potato production is developing crops for more niche-oriented markets, as it must, for it cannot compete with number one Idaho on a commodity basis.

Maine's glaciated landscape and acidic soil happen to be the ideal conditions for winter-hardy blueberries. Ninety percent of the world's wild blueberries are grown along Maine's coastal counties, although by 2008 rising fuel costs, the falling dollar, and a coastal real estate boom threatened the industry. Small, nonmechanized blueberry farms have been sold to developers, rather than owners investing the necessary capital to continue raising blueberries.

The Lake Champlain Lowlands' proximity to Megalopolis makes it a **milkshed** for the substantial Megalopolis markets. Its high-bulk, low-cost milk, a product with a short shelf-life, has serviced the New York City and Boston markets. Dairies in the Champlain Lowlands were once an economic mainstay for Vermont, and they still provide 90 percent of the state's agricultural income though only a small portion of the total economy. Atlantic North dairies are declining because of rising land values, regulated milk prices, industrial agribusiness, and increased competition from midwestern and western producers.

It's a national market, there are no provincial borders on chicken. . . . A great example would be the McDonald's McNugget. That is all made in a plant in Ontario; they service the whole Canadian market.[20]

The Atlantic Provinces Farmland occupies less than 5 percent of the Atlantic Provinces, and less than 0.1 percent of Newfoundland and Labrador. Although many subsistence farmers settled during the nineteenth century, most abandoned their farms during the first half of the twentieth century. In the twenty-first century, the remaining farms are in three small regions: Annapolis Valley in Nova Scotia, St. John River Valley in New Brunswick, and Prince Edward Island. These isolated agricultural areas have been economically stagnant at best.

The growing season, though short, is conducive to apple and potato crops. The warmer climate of the Bay of Fundy protected the fertile farming soils of Nova Scotia's Annapolis Valley. Early in the twentieth century, apples were a staple crop, but they declined after 1950 because of overseas competition and a lack of local markets. The local economy now depends on tourism and the environmentally problematic concentrated animal feeding operations (CAFOs). The CAFO is similar to U.S. chicken or hog farms, a centralized agribusiness that allows farmers to keep their farmland when traditional crops are unprofitable. (See Chapter 9, Southern Atlantic.)

The finest agricultural land on the northeastern coast is Prince Edward Island, which evolved into the picturesque "Garden Isle." The island had fewer stones than glacial till lands, and the red soil was perfect for potato farms, producing one-third of Canada's potato crop. New Brunswick also has a thriving potato-growing and processing industry near the Aroostook Maine border and on its northwestern coast.

Industry and Postindustrial

Secondary Sector: Manufacturing

American manufacturing and processing of goods began in the Northeast at the beginning of the nineteenth century. Textile mills and pulp and paper mills were located throughout the region.

The first part of the Industrial Revolution in the second decade of the nineteenth century was dependent on harnessing the power of local waterways to run textile mills. The mills thrived until after the Civil War, when the mill industry migrated to the Southern Atlantic states. The migration of the textile industry to cheaper production areas forced the old mill

PHOTO 6.11. Paper Mill at Berlin, New Hampshire, while the mill was still operating. The wood mill converted to a biomass power plant after the paper mill closed in 2008.

towns to redefine themselves in order to maintain population and economy.

Since the 1990s, the logging industry has also undergone changes. The pulp and paper industry was replaced by increased overseas production. The industrial logging and paper companies have sold their holdings and been replaced by landowners with different objectives. From 2006 to 2008, Katahdin Paper Company blamed high oil prices and globalization when they closed three paper mills in New Hampshire and Maine. By 2008, half of the 1970 manufacturing jobs had gone overseas (Photo 6.11).

As a response to the shutdown of Berlin, New Hampshire's primary industry, a deal was struck in 2008 to convert the paper mill to a wood-burning biomass power plant that will sell its power to the state's largest utility. It is hoped this deal will help Berlin, as well as supply a more carbon dioxide–neutral energy source for the state.

Tertiary Sector: Service

The loss of manufacturing has been compensated by a growth of jobs in education, health care, tourism, and business and professional services. However, many of these jobs pay less than the lost manufacturing jobs.

Tourism Since the end of World War II, tourism has replaced lost industry. The "pastoral" scenes of Maine and Vermont, the beaches of Prince Edward Island, the Bay of Fundy's tidal fluctuations, along with Atlantic Canada's picturesque fishing villages, turned the area into a nostalgic vacationland.

Additional cultural attractions include the Acadian past, folk art, fresh seafood, and restored historic landmarks like the fortress at Louisbourg.

The weather can also entice. Cool summers offer a retreat from the hot, humid Megalopolis summers, and winter offers skiing. During nineteenth-century summers, the White Mountains attracted both tourists and artists. The beauty of the northeastern ranges of Appalachia captivated artists, such as Alfred Bierstadt, Asher Durand, and other Luminists of the Hudson River and White Mountains Schools (Photo 6.12).

Today the Green Mountains of Vermont are a popular ski retreat, as is Corner Brook, Newfoundland's Marble Mountain, site of the 1999 Canada Winter Games. Northern New England has become a popular second-home location for Megalopolis urbanites. However, while serving the needs of the urban affluent, second-home economies favor the service sector over the higher-paying manufacturing or quaternary sector that locals need to support a family.

Exports

During the 1990s, 150 years after the Reciprocity Agreement lapsed, Maine and the Atlantic Provinces reestablished strong trade relations, much of it because of NAFTA. Exports to Canada, Maine's largest trading partner, have been resources: wood, potatoes, blueberries, and seafood. These commodities are then reimported from the Atlantic Provinces as processed goods, including lobster from New Brunswick or blueberries from Nova Scotia. This export-import market was

PHOTO 6.12. Lakeside Vacation Homes in Vermont, during **Fall Foliage Season**. Fall foliage is a North Atlantic tourist attraction; hotels are booked solid on October weekends, when chillier nights and shorter days decay chlorophyll, revealing the spectacular underlying earth-toned colors.

in many ways similar to the *maquiladora* export-import economy of the United States and Mexico. Exporting raw commodities and reimporting them as finished products takes advantage of inexpensive labor costs. Since NAFTA, Maine alone lost more than twenty thousand manufacturing jobs.

High-tech employment has also shifted to northeastern states, such as Vermont and Maine. The growth is in cost-savings and emerging technologies, such as the many sustainable technologic industries welcomed in Vermont. Value-added manufacturing (the higher price obtained after manufacturing), for example, auto suspension and telecommunication equipment, has also increased.

The glacially indented coastline created excellent harbors and access points to the sea, benefiting the Canadian cities of Halifax, St John, and St. John's, and Bangor and Portland, Maine. In the past these ports have serviced Mediterranean to Brazilian ports. The Atlantic Provinces were most prosperous during the nineteenth century when they were the center of trade. But Confederation and adoption of the National Policy shifted Canadian trade toward the heart of the Canadian economy. The Atlantic ports lost traffic to Montreal.

In the twenty-first century, conditions have changed. Transportation shifted from water to land routes, harming the water-dependent northeastern regions. Since 2002, in a move related to "smart growth," increased shipping has reduced highway traffic. The major twenty-first century ports are in the Pacific or use the Panama Canal and are at capacity. Atlantic trade, through the Suez Canal, could be an economic option, although pirating

in the Gulf of Aden is a continual problem. Cities like Halifax, with the necessary infrastructure for large shipping vessels, hope to profit from this, but at the expense of weaker environmental regulations; a continued fear is the loss of sovereignty with integrated trade blocs between Canada, America, and Mexico. Another possible economic boost may come from **short sea shipping**—promoting the use of waterways to ease traffic congestion on national highways.

Atlantica

The need for new economies within the North Atlantic is imperative, and a proposed answer is Atlantica: the International Northeast Economic Region (AINER), a trade bloc composed of the four Atlantic Provinces, eastern Quebec, and Northern New England.[21] The proponents believe that public policy is responsible for the region's lag behind national averages. Some policies Atlantica seeks to change are cross border interactions, transportation infrastructure, size of government, lowering the minimum wage, and reducing unions. The goal is to use Atlantic Canada shipping ports and highways to transport energy resources and Asian goods to the United States. The proponents cite other successful trading blocs as justification for this trade bloc.

Although some of the ideas are worthy of study, others are less so. Proposals such as lowering the minimum wage and removing the protection of unions from employees are not popular among people in economic doldrums. The ideals of a healthy Atlantica economy are worthy, but the methods—eradicating traditional trade regulations—favor corporate rather than sustainable interests. The leaders of Atlantica met in Halifax in June 2007 amid vociferous protest by those who will be penalized: workers who stand to lose union protection, receive lower wages, and lose human and environmental rights.

Atlantica is an idea from the past Industrial Revolution, one that disrespects the triple bottom line, and will result in social and environmental damage. It is based on historic precedent, but not on the sustainable industrial revolution.

A Sustainable Future

If picturesque equaled successful, the North Atlantic would be prosperous. But beauty is becoming accessible only to those who can afford it at the expense of the local population. Large corporate trade blocs that lower wages, or second homes and retirement living are attractions for the region's future. But these are based on the antiquated "modern" business models. There is, however, some hope on the horizon for an improved economy.

Being a resource hinterland has been unprofitable within the globalized economy. As long as a region depends on either the primary or tourist economy, in the current globalization it is creating its economic doom. With the future taking shape as a vertically integrated series of subcontracting industries, the losses incurred by the primary economy are subsumed in the larger corporate picture. It spells the end of the unionized worker, the independent farmer, or the fisherman. However, value-added industries are taking advantage of their locations and NAFTA trade opportunities with cross border trade between Canada and the northeastern states. The trade between Maine and the Atlantic Provinces broadened since NAFTA and may expand more if Atlantica proposals are achieved—but the question is, can it be sustainable?

The last resort for regions dependent on primary industry remains tourism. Historic preservation tourism has become so invasive in the postindustrial economy that virtually every city lacking postmodern accomplishments has become a city seeking historic preservation to attract tourists and high-end temporary or permanent residents. What is ironic, though, is that both purchasers of second homes and retirees choose to settle in the region because of the quaint fishing villages but live in high-priced condominiums or McMansions. They drive up the cost of housing and drive out the economy that attracted them.

The region's greatest geographical advantage may be its coastal location. A reliance on land transport is causing industry to improve transportation networks. Short sea shipping may relieve freight congestion and offer transportation advantages. But the booming seaport housing market hampers industrialized harbor growth and kills shipping opportunities. Finding the right combination of sustainable growth and progress remains elusive.

Nonetheless, both Nova Scotia and Prince Edward Island are in the forefront pursuing sustainable alternative energy. PEI has constructed nearly one hundred wind turbines, created an efficient recycling system, and turned to more biomass fuel to free itself of imported fossil fuel energy. Other provinces are beginning to notice and move further in their quest to become more energy efficient.

Let's stop subsidizing pollution and waste.

—Nova Scotia Premier Rodney MacDonald, 2007[22]

In 2007 Nova Scotian politicians were joining the green bandwagon, encouraging lower greenhouse gas emissions and solid waste and committing to green land and water use. Sustainability may stimulate the economy rather than devastate it. The government hopes to follow the lead of California and become "one of the cleanest and most sustainable environments in the world" by 2020.[23]

Which way does the region want to grow? One is short-term, single bottom line, profit-oriented, and dead-end (second-home luxury market). The region will remain a hinterland dependent on globalized values that do not include them. Social and environmental degradation will continue. Another option is to seek sustainable goals.

The fragmented North Atlantic region can develop a mutually cooperative local economy in order to be competitive. Sustainable ideas have this part of the equation right, but most sustainable projects within the region are small, provincial or statewide, and lack systems connections. Finding the right combination is the problem. While its backers push Atlantica as sustainable, the people have been omitted from the discussion and question its sustainability. Does sustainability equal economic dominance of the few paid for by the many, or is a sustainable future for all? One of the largest issues addressed is the concentration of power by corporate interests, rather than a more equitable distribution of wealth, education, and power. Education is important for a sustainable future, and it will need to change in this region of fewer university graduates and an overall income below the national average (Table 6.5).

Sustainability has become a buzzword, and every state and province in the region has added sustainability to their website. The idea of sustainability is becoming a standard, although there is no agreed-upon definition of sustainable. Local sustainable organizations and conferences focus on energy efficiency, local foods, natural resources, recycling, and a growing voice to reduce military spending in favor of renewable energy, thereby reducing the need to fight in oil-producing countries. Regional communities are distinctly different from each other and from the remainder of the respective countries, and sustainable ideas focus on how to profit from the unique nature of the region.

Sustainable ideas are new and have potential. Time will tell if the region will find sustainable industry, or profit short-term from oil production without a long-term and sustainable plan.

TABLE 6.5. Education and Income in North Atlantic

	% with university degree	Per capita income
Canada	28	C$29,769
Newfoundland	21	C$22,620
New Brunswick	22	C$24,091
Nova Scotia	26	C$25,297
Prince Edward Island	23	C$23,709
United States	24.4	$21,587
Maine	22.9	$19,533
New Hampshire	28.7	$23,844
Vermont	29.4	$20,625

Sources: Statistics Canada; U.S. Census
Note: Canada 2001, United States 2000

Questions for Discussion

1. What are possible sustainable growth areas for this region, both geographically and economically?

2. This region has been called the "bypassed east." What are reasons for this name, and why may it not apply today?

3. The population in Northern New England is growing, but how and why? What are the benefits/problems?

4. Explain the evolution of outports in Newfoundland and their relation to fishing.

5. After the collapse of the cod fishery in Newfoundland, the province was in economic decline. What replaced fishing economically?

6. Explain the evolution of Newfoundland from the 1400s to 1949.

7. Explain the controversy between Quebec and Newfoundland over Labrador. What is the agreed upon division?

8. How and why has the economy changed in Newfoundland since 2007?

9. Where did the Acadians first settle and where do they live now? Why has it changed?

10. What did Vermonters and the Green Mountain Boys need to do to get accepted into the United States?

11. What primary industries have dominated the Atlantic North and why have they been declining?

Suggested Readings

Bardach, John E., and Regina Miranda Santerre. "Climate and the Fish in the Sea." *BioScience* 31, no. 3 (March 1981): 206–15.

Bird, J. "Settlement Patterns in Maritime Canada: 1687–1786." *Geographic Review* 45, no. 3 (1955).

Clark, A. *Acadia: The Geography of Early Nova Scotia to 1760.* Madison: University of Wisconsin Press, 1968.

Copes, P. *The Resettlement of Fishing Communities in Newfoundland.* Ottawa: Canadian Council on Rural Development, 1972.

Cronon, William. *Changes in the Land: Indians, Colonists, and the Ecology of New England.* New York: Hill & Wang, 1983.

Finch, Robert. *The Iambics of Newfoundland: Notes from an Unknown Shore.* Berkeley, Calif.: Counterpoint, 2007.

Frideres, J. S. *Native Peoples in Canada: Contemporary Conflicts.* Scarborough: Prentice Hall, 1998.

Higgins, Paul A. T., Michael D. Mastrandrea, and Stephen H. Schneider. "Dynamics of Climate and Ecosystem Coupling: Abrupt Changes and Multiple Equilibria." *Philosophical Transactions of the Royal Society* 357, no. 1421 (2002): 647–55.

Holloway, Andy. "The Best Places to Do Business in Canada." *Canadian Business* 80, no. 18 (25 September 25, 2006): 26–30.

Innis, Harold A. *The Cod Fisheries: The History of an International Economy*. New Haven, Conn.: Yale University Press, 1940.

Kurlansky, Mark. *Cod*. New York: Penguin Books, 1997.

Mayda, Chris. "Resettlement in Newfoundland: Again." *Focus* 48, no. 1 (2004).

McGrath, C., B. Neis, and M. Porter. *Their Lives and Times*. St. John's, NL: Killick Press, 1995.

Mitchell, Robert. D. "The Colonial Origins of Anglo-America." In *North America: The Historical Geography of a Changing Continent*, edited by Thomas F. McIlwraith and Edward K. Muller. Lanham, Md.: Rowman & Littlefield, 2001.

Noble, Allen. *Migration to North America: Before, during, and after the Nineteenth Century*. Baltimore: Johns Hopkins University Press, 1992.

Wallach, Bret. "Logging in Maine's Empty Quarter." *Annals of American Geographers* 70 (1980): 542–52.

Warkentin, J., ed. *Canada: A Geographical Interpretation*. Toronto: Methuen, 1968.

Wright, Miriam. "Newfoundland and Labrador History in Canada, 1949–1972." Research Paper for the Royal Commission on Renewing and Strengthening Our Place in Canada. March 2003.

Internet Sources

Atlantica: The International Northeast Economic Region, at http://www.atlantica.org/default.asp

Newfoundland and Labrador Heritage, at http://www.heritage.nf.ca/home.html

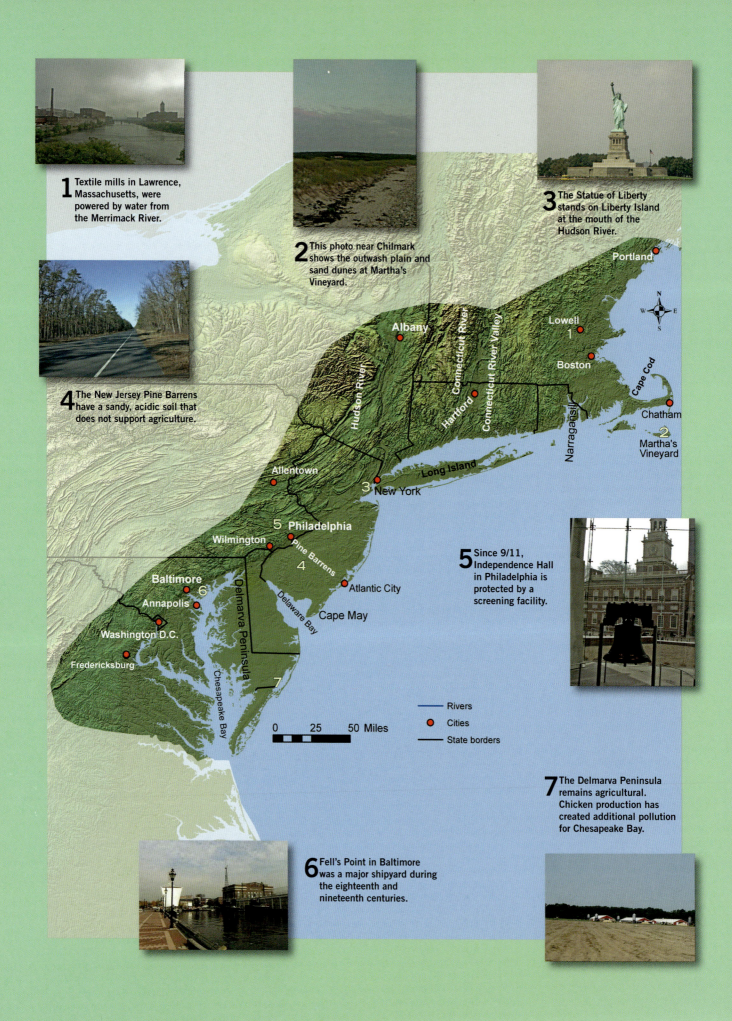

1 Textile mills in Lawrence, Massachusetts, were powered by water from the Merrimack River.

2 This photo near Chilmark shows the outwash plain and sand dunes at Martha's Vineyard.

3 The Statue of Liberty stands on Liberty Island at the mouth of the Hudson River.

4 The New Jersey Pine Barrens have a sandy, acidic soil that does not support agriculture.

5 Since 9/11, Independence Hall in Philadelphia is protected by a screening facility.

6 Fell's Point in Baltimore was a major shipyard during the eighteenth and nineteenth centuries.

7 The Delmarva Peninsula remains agricultural. Chicken production has created additional pollution for Chesapeake Bay.

Portland

Lowell
1

Boston

Albany

Chatham

Cape Cod

Martha's Vineyard
2

Hudson River

Connecticut River

Hartford

Connecticut River Valley

Narragansett

Long Island

Allentown

New York
3

Philadelphia
5

Wilmington

Pine Barrens
4

Baltimore
6

Annapolis

Delmarva Peninsula

Atlantic City

Cape May

Delaware Bay

Washington D.C.

Fredericksburg

Chesapeake Bay

7

0   25   50 Miles

—— Rivers
● Cities
—— State borders

N W E S

7
MEGALOPOLIS
Setting Sustainable Standards

Chapter Highlights

After reading this chapter you should be able to:

- Describe the Megalopolis region and its largest cities
- Compare urban and suburban growth patterns
- Identify the five boroughs of New York City
- Discuss the region's contribution toward sustainability
- Describe the three cultural hearths
- Explain the success of New York City over its rivals
- Discuss the lessons learned from Hutcheson Memorial Forest

Terms

basement rock
Beltway
borough
BosWash
drowned rivers
fall line
Megalopolis
Pennsylvania Dutch
technopole

Places

Albany, New York
Atlantic City, New Jersey
Baltimore, Maryland
Boston, Massachusetts
Cape Cod, Massachusetts
Cape May, New Jersey
Chesapeake Bay
Connecticut River Valley
Delaware Bay
Delmarva Peninsula
Long Island
Lowell, Massachusetts
Martha's Vineyard
Narragansett Basin
New York City
Philadelphia, Pennsylvania
Pine Barrens, New Jersey
Providence, Rhode Island
Washington, D.C.

PHOTO 7.1. New York City Skyscrapers. At the tip of the isle of Manhattan sits the financial capital of the United States, and one of the most important cities in the world. It is Manhattan's bedrock geology—a metamorphic rock called schist—that makes the high-rise skyline possible. Where the schist is close to the surface, it provides the structural stability needed for the skyscrapers.

Introduction

In 1957 Geographer Jean Gottman coined the term **Megalopolis**—Greek for "very large city"—an extended urban area with millions of people."[1] In the United States, the region from Boston to Washington, D.C., the **"BosWash"** corridor, populated by more than fifty-two million people, is Megalopolis, one of the largest conurbations in the world. It is a region where business and finance reign supreme. Regional superlatives include:

- Generates 20 percent of nation's total personal income
- Fourth-largest economy in the world, ahead of France and the UK
- Greatest wealth and greatest poverty
- One-quarter of all U.S. wholesale trade
- One-quarter of those working in finance and law
- Highest population densities in the nation
- Business and government center for the nation

Despite its superlatives, Megalopolis is a small region, encompassing about 1 percent of the continental land, but one out of six Americans (17 percent) reside there. Population, urban centers, and economy define Megalopolis more than its physical boundaries or watersheds. Its center, New York City, has been the largest city in the United States since the end of the eighteenth century, but other major cities within BosWash include Boston, Philadelphia, Baltimore, and Washington, D.C. The coastal plain is the site of the initial Anglo American settlements. Three separate groups established the cultural hearths where settlers imprinted the landscape with their cultural features, and it was along this coastal region that the new modern capitalist economy was established in the seventeenth century (Photo 7.1).

While Megalopolis is the historic and economic center of the United States, the tumult of change—the ecological age—is upsetting the traditional economic pattern. Cities in Megalopolis have begun to embrace sustainable ideals, to endorse a lighter, more efficient environmental impact, and to build green. A new generation of architects and graduates seeks sustainable methods, whether by greening buildings or following the corporate environmental path, a place where they can be "corporate hippies" from Yale and "actors of environmental sustainability."

The sustainable mind-set and thinking is infiltrating the staid and very short-term quarterly-report mentality. Increasingly, business reshapes itself, as pundits like Paul Hawken and Peter Senge envision a more holistic and long-term economically healthy future, where success and progress are no longer defined by the necessity to stay on top every ninety days regardless of the unintended consequences, impacts, or external costs of their actions.

Unintended Consequences

The unintended consequences of this human-dominated landscape have altered the ecology of the region, reduced wildlife habitat and natural vegetation, and created environmental issues. Changing climatic conditions have added to the complex mix. The economy, based on Adam Smith's eighteenth-century principles, requires updating to reflect the twenty-first-century circumstance. No longer can the "invisible hand" of self-interest be the sole guide to a healthy economy. There are too many unintended consequences (self-interest, environmental degradation, and the rise in population being major examples) to act the same today as we did three hundred years ago.

Local and Ecoregional Impacts

Seawater intrusion, the result of sea-level rise and groundwater pumping, has affected the low-lying coast and resulted in contaminated drinking water. Waterway conditions vary, from the partially reclaimed Hudson River, which was heavily polluted into the 1970s, to the contaminated Chesapeake Bay.

External Costs

In Megalopolis, the question remains whether or not a quarterly-report mentality can mix with green buildings, clean waterways, and a long-term sustainable future. Public companies must report their financial results every three

BOX 7.1

"'CORPORATE HIPPIES' SEEK THEIR BLISS IN A NEW ENVIRONMENTAL ECONOMY"

Felicity Barringer, *New York Times*, March 7, 2007

Change once came slowly to the job market for people seeking careers focused on the environment. No more.

There were signs as early as the 1980s, when the Rainforest Alliance began working with businesses to create a program for identifying environmentally sound wood products: more graduates were taking jobs outside traditional environmental arenas, jobs like engineering, waste management, policy development, law and resource protection.

The shift gathered steam in the 1990s, when companies like Starbucks and Nike started to integrate such concerns into everyday business practices.

Early this decade, Daniel C. Esty, a professor of environmental law and policy at Yale University, noticed changes in the goals of younger students and the kinds of jobs students took when they left the Yale School of Forestry and the Environment.

Law and science, which were traditional environmental specialties, still attracted many students; but a newer one, corporate environmental management, was growing. The latest ones—finance, venture investment, entrepreneurialism—barely registered.

"I am overwhelmed by how this has evolved," Dr. Esty said recently.

Students still gravitate toward nongovernmental organizations, advocacy groups and government, but a large plurality of the current generation interested in environmental work are looking elsewhere, particularly to financial firms, small businesses and even corporations. They seek employment there because, among other things, they think that is where they can have the greatest impact.

"It's extraordinary how many students see themselves as going into business as a place to have leverage on the issues," Dr. Esty said.

---

months. The pressure to show shareholders a profit forces company officials to sanction environmentally and socially damaging actions that will cause more economic harm in the long run but satisfy short-term predictions. Some companies have begun to issue self-regulated corporate social responsibility (CSR) reports that begin to address the ethics of incorporating the triple bottom line.

Physical Geography

Megalopolis occupies the elevated sea bottom of the Atlantic Coastal Plain. The plain continues offshore, gradually descending on the continental shelf until the continental slope drop-off. The embayed topography, indented coastline, and deciduous forests were a welcome sight to European immigrants. They set about clearing the land and began to farm. In southern Megalopolis, farms expanded into plantations, growing crops that England wanted but could not grow. But in the north, farming was less successful or lucrative; soon northern farms reverted to woodlands, as farmers either moved west toward better land or to the sea or cities of New England. Many nonurban areas of Megalopolis reverted to forest, although exotic species are often more prevalent than native.

However, the main attraction of Megalopolis is not its rural areas, but its cities, a conurbation where the edges of one city meet the edges of the next. This conurbation is ideal for sustainable transportation, but it also challenges living within natural resource limitations.

Boundaries

The boundaries of Megalopolis are not physical. They have changed over time, because the region is defined more by where people live, the growth in population, and the extent of sprawl than by the physical landscape of the Atlantic Coastal Plain. The Atlantic Ocean defines the eastern boundary, but the other boundaries are less distinct and change as populations grow and transportation changes. Today, traffic permitting, the Merrimack Valley, once more than a day's ride away, is incorporated into the Boston metropolitan area, as are the coastal areas of New Hampshire and southern Maine. The southern margin expands into counties beyond Arlington, Virginia. The western boundary is the least distinct of all and is best defined as where urban meets rural, seldom more than one hundred miles inland.

Physiography

Megalopolis extends from the Atlantic Coastal Plain into the Appalachian Blue Ridge and Piedmont. The rivers may be depressed below sea level, creating **drowned rivers** and converting them to estuaries and bays—Chesapeake, Delaware, and New York bays. Several Megalopolis BosWash cities lie near the deep bays of the convoluted coastline.

Subregions

New England

The Cape Cod to Hudson River portion of New England is a recently emerged part of the continental shelf. Glaciers flattened the land, leaving moraines that shaped the exposed ridge of Cape Cod and the islands of Martha's Vineyard, Nantucket, and Long Island. Climate change has already begun to raise sea levels and erode coastal areas lacking **basement rock**. In Cape Cod, oceanside sand cliffs have no resistance to rising sea level and waves. In Chatham, located on the elbow of the Cape, nine houses were lost to storms, and more are vulnerable to the capricious movement of sand. The Cape's Wellfleet or Chatham

BOX 7.2 MARTHA'S VINEYARD, NANTUCKET, AND THE SOUND

As the glacier retreated ten thousand years ago, Martha's Vineyard and Nantucket, located seven miles south of Cape Cod, were dry, inland hills on the coastal plain. As the ice melted and the water rose, they became islands on the continental shelf. All landscape features and waterways on the islands owe their origin to the glacier, wind, or waves. Sand dunes and beach deposits surround protected, low-barrier beaches and marshes, while wetlands have been filled, drained, and often developed. Altering the landscape has accelerated the effects of climate change, but other issues include declining fish stocks and lack of affordable housing.

Wampanoags settled the islands, perhaps as long as ten thousand years ago. Their diminished numbers occupy a small island reservation. They no longer depend on the fish and shellfish that were once staples of their diet.

Europeans settled the Vineyard in 1642 near the present site of Edgartown. Nantucket was settled in 1795. Settlers farmed and fished the bountiful waters until about 1800; whaling was the primary industry from 1800 until the 1870s, when petroleum replaced whale oil. The tourism economy followed, beginning slowly, with religious camp revival meetings in the Vineyard, while Quakers became the dominant force on Nantucket.

The real growth impetus was World War II and the evolution of mass transport. The Megalopolis population growth and the accessibility of the nearby islands made Martha's Vineyard and Nantucket a summer hideaway for the affluent. In the Vineyard, escalating prices and taxes have caused many of the fifteen thousand year-round local residents to lose their homes. During the summer months, more than a hundred thousand additional residents swell the population, and another twenty-five thousand visit on any summer day.

With the lack of affordable housing on the islands, the median home price on the Vineyard in 2010 was still $565,000, a 20 percent reduction from the $702,000 median in pre-crash 2007. The average price, though, was $923,500. In Nantucket, the median price for a home in 2010 was nearly $2 million. Two types of people inhabit the islands, the locals and those who have second or third homes. Between them is a world of difference. Almost all homes sold on the Vineyard are listed for more than $1 million and few for less than $250,000.*

The number of people on the islands has created a variety of environmental issues, from the aforementioned overfishing to pollution and energy needs. The growth in population and increasingly small lots for the less wealthy has added water pollution to the ills of the island, as septic systems may pollute water wells. The increased cost of constructing septic systems will make it more difficult and expensive for new homeowners. Another problem has been water quality in island ponds, forcing closure to a source of local income, shell fishing, because of low oxygen levels, the growth of algae, and a general degradation of the marine environment.

Sea level rise due to global warming is accelerating more quickly than was anticipated even at the millennium. Most homes are built a few hundred feet from the continually changing coastline, but nonetheless may be threatened as sea levels rise.

A proposal in Nantucket Sound for the first offshore wind farm in the United States had the island communities up in arms since 2003. Most opponents based their opposition on aesthetics and navigation, but in 2010 the wind farm was approved. The 130 wind turbine Cape Wind project will provide up to 75 percent of the Cape and island energy needs.

* In 2006 there were 9 houses sold on the island for under $250,000, and 188 homes listed for over $1 million.

---

shorelines accrete or recede randomly each year, but the continued sea level rise is washing away the sandy cliffs and threatening habitats and homes.

Southern Coastal Megalopolis

New York City's landscape has been altered since Henry Hudson landed. The biota were lost under tons of concrete—concrete supported by Manhattan's sturdy schist bedrock. The look of the land has changed so radically that few could imagine it prior to Anglo American settlement until the Mannahatta Project revealed in 2008 the ecological landscape seen by Henry Hudson.[2] The digital re-creation of the environment that Hudson found has planted the seeds to understanding the lost natural landscape. By knowing our land and what we have done to it, we can begin to live with the landscape instead of against it.

Just to the south and west of New York City lies New Jersey, the most densely populated state, which contains two

anomalous rural areas—Hutcheson Memorial Forest and the Pine Barrens. Southern New Jersey's soil, sandy and acidic, supports miles of pitch pine forests called the Barrens. This poor farmland was never settled to the degree of more productive soils, and today the drive from Atlantic City to Camden remains bucolic. The Pinelands are protected as a national reserve, due to threatening suburban encroachment.

Two major bays define the sites for major Megalopolis cities. The Delaware and Chesapeake bays are two submerged valleys that are now estuaries. The Delaware Estuary stretches from Cape May in New Jersey, inland past Philadelphia, and upstream to Trenton, New Jersey. Three large city ports—Philadelphia; Camden, New Jersey; and Wilmington, Delaware—now support petrochemical shipments and refineries. The Chesapeake Bay estuary is the largest in the nation, incorporating portions of six states and stretching two hundred miles from Havre de Grace, Maryland, to Norfolk, Virginia.

BOX 7.3 HUTCHESON MEMORIAL FOREST

The Hutcheson Memorial Forest is a remnant of northern New Jersey's heavily forested Piedmont region. During the late seventeenth century, European settlers cut most of the forest down as they settled their farmlands. Only sporadic woodlots were left, and they had also been cut and replanted by the mid-twentieth century. In 1954, the sixty-five-acre Hutcheson forest, located in the middle of densely populated New Jersey, was sold to Rutgers University and "rediscovered" as the last remaining old-growth Piedmont forest in New Jersey, a last remnant of "natural" land prior to Anglo settlement. Declared a static and unchanging climax forest, it became a cause célèbre.

During the succeeding years, the forest became one of the most studied ecologic resources in the world, documented by articles, numerous theses, and dissertations based on its climax status and the forest's historic provenance.

Dutch immigrants named Mettler cleared and settled the land, leaving a woodlot as most settlers did. Woodlots were a convenient source of fuel, timber, and hunting. In 1749, Peter Kalm, a student of Linnaeus of taxonomy fame, documented the area, including the woodlot. Among his notes were comments about the woodlot's canopy, so open a carriage could drive through. It was this comment that changed perceptions of the old-growth forest.

Only a single maintained trail traverses the open canopy forest, now overgrown and dark. The old-growth forest was mainly oak-hickory, with specimens up to three hundred years old. But the new forest was sugar maple, with few oak or hickory saplings. Twentieth-century researchers could not explain the change in species. If this was a climax forest, then why were the young tree species not in the same proportion to the older trees? Why was a different species prevalent?

The answers to these questions changed forest ecosystem theory: a steady state climax forest evolves in relation to surrounding influences. In the case of Hutcheson, a study of tree rings revealed that every decade prior to European settlement fire had spread through the forest, but none since. Native Americans had burned the understory periodically to open up forests for agricultural land and browse for game. Since European occupation, the forest had not been cut or burned and the species composition had changed. Why? Fire changes the composition of the forest. Fire helps propagate oaks and hickories but squelches sugar maples.

Studies also revealed new plant species in the forest since Kalm's eighteenth-century study. If the ecosystem was climax and undisturbed, why were these plants present? The answers lie in human disturbances in the forest. Development, agriculture, introduction of exotic species by air or animals, and climate change had changed the "pristine" forest.

Hutcheson Memorial Forest was indeed special, not because of its climax status but because it provided lessons in dynamism and the indirect effects of human activity.*

* Botkin, Daniel B., *Discordant Harmonies* (New York: Oxford University Press, 1992).

The Fall Line

A major geologic feature of southern Megalopolis is the **fall line**, where the harder rock of the Piedmont ends and the softer coastal soils begin. The inland barrier to navigation, the fall line was once the end of the continental shelf. Over time, sediment from the Appalachians was deposited and built up the coastal plain.

The fall line extends from New Jersey to Talladega, Alabama. The Rappahannock River in Chesapeake Bay generally divides the fall line topography; north is a distinct escarpment, south diminishes to rapids with little "fall" but a distinctive soil transition from the harder Piedmont to the sandy coastal alluvium.

Fall line rapids and waterfalls were the end of navigation up or down the rivers and therefore a natural place for break-in-bulk cities to develop as transfer points for portaging goods around the fall line obstructions until bypassed by canals. Megalopolis cities tend to be either at the rapids and waterfalls of the fall line (Trenton, Philadelphia, Baltimore, Washington) or at harbors (New York and Boston).

Water

Waterways are plentiful along the Megalopolis coast. Five major rivers—the Connecticut, Hudson, Delaware, Susquehanna, and Potomac—flow from their Appalachian headwaters to the sea. The Delaware and Chesapeake Bays offer safe ports and were the location for Anglo settlements. Barrier beaches extend from Long Island through New Jersey, where the landscape becomes one of drowned valleys or swampy tidal flats. The rivers and bays supported a fishing economy until the late twentieth century, when increased population caused runoff pollution and sea level rise began to threaten coastal areas.

Glacial Past, Sustainable Future

Today human artifacts hide the natural regional landscape. By understanding the underlying landscape, humans can work within the natural limitations rather than try to overcome them.

The Appalachian headwater rivers—the Hudson, Connecticut, Delaware, and Potomac—spawned the waterpower-dependent cities of the Industrial Revolution and may be a source of future power.

The Hudson River marks the southern extent of the last ice age glaciation. North of the river the topographic formations—drumlins, moraines, outwash plains, and fjords—are remnants of ice age glaciation. The river follows a fjord that thousands of years ago drained the meltwaters of glacial lakes of Iroquois,

BOX 7.4 THE POSITIVE AND NEGATIVE RESULTS OF DRAINING WETLANDS AND CLEANING ESTUARIES: MALARIA, TYPHOID, AND MARSHES

To comprehend this geography of health is thus to discover a surprising holism in the worldview of the bustling, rapidly industrializing nineteenth century.*

Seventy percent of Americans now live in coastal counties. Many of these areas, though, were originally tidal swamps, especially along the Atlantic and Gulf coasts. They are habitable today because the swamps were drained. They have been buttressed by billions of dollars of sand dredging and continually rebuilding beaches. The reasons for the draining were both agricultural and health related.

Draining swamps was intended to create agricultural land, not build sandy beaches and a leisure lifestyle. Along the Atlantic Coast and estuaries, industrious English and Dutch settlers used their knowledge of draining their homeland coastlines to build drainage ditches and create agricultural land in America, such as the extensive reclamation along Delaware Bay. Delaware's drained land was eventually abandoned and reverted back to the tidal marshes when better agricultural lands were found. In Delaware, the abandoned land has been transformed to reduce runoff and increase wildlife habitat,† but shopping malls and residential developments are often built on reclaimed land. The far heavier impact on the land destroys the soils of the altered landscape. Restoration of these lands is often impossible.

Another reason to drain the swamps was the so-called fevers of the nineteenth century, which today would go by the modern names of malaria, cholera, and typhoid. Draining the lands and spraying them with pesticides eliminated the causes of the diseases, but it also drastically changed the benefits of a swampy, marshy landscape and caused unintended consequences.

Unintended Consequences

All actions on the planet have positive and negative impacts for humans. Ridding the swamps of the diseases harbored in the fetid waters was certainly a positive impact, but it has been matched by negative and unintended consequences that became increasingly evident in the late twentieth century.

The swamps of yesteryear have been newly appreciated and renamed as wetlands. The coastal wetlands buffered and protected the inland areas from the worst effects of storms and flooding. Wetlands also filter polluted water and provide the habitats and rookeries for millions of aquatic species and birds. Removing the wetland areas along the coast has destroyed ecosystems and made the human population living in coastal areas more vulnerable to storms.

Region and Ecoregional Impacts

Most people living along the coast are unaware of the prior wetlands. They do not understand how the land has been altered, ecosystems destroyed, and their vulnerability to storms and floods increased. Knowing the history of the land you live on is an important part of becoming sustainable, especially when living in an area that is being affected by climate change. Sea-level rise and flooding in the heavily populated area will increase along with temperatures.

External Costs

Coastal land is some of the most expensive in the nation. However, the land is priced based on aesthetics, not on its vulnerability to storms or sea-level rise, both of which are indicators of climate change. Increased water vapor due to warmer temperature is fuel for stronger storms.

Over the years, coastal areas have been hit by numerous storms that have damaged infrastructure. An example in Megalopolis was in March 2010. The Narragansett region in Rhode Island was flooded when a rainstorm dumped nine inches of rain in a short period. Local rivers crested, and sewage plants overflowed. The low-lying and vulnerable Pawtuxet River rose twelve feet beyond flood stage and inundated Rhode Island areas that had not previously experienced flooding. In 2011, tropical storm Irene flooded the Atlantic coastal and inland areas, causing more than a billion dollars of damage. The increasing number of such events over a short period of time needs to be addressed in relation to rising carbon dioxide levels.‡

---

* Conevery Bolton Valenčius, *The Health of the Country: How American Settlers Understood Themselves and Their Land* (New York: Basic Books, 2002).

† An excellent report on Chesapeake Bay restoration is at http://www.conservationfund.org/sites/default/files/A_Sustainable_Chesapeake_The_Conservation_Fund.pdf.

‡ Climate Change: Health and Environmental Effects, at http://www.epa.gov/climatechange/effects/coastal/.

Albany, and Vermont. The deep fjord allows the salty Atlantic water to flow as far as Albany.

The Connecticut River, New England's longest river, evolved when glacial Lake Hitchcock drained thirteen thousand years ago after a moraine dam eroded, flooding the valley and blanketing it with fertile sediment. Today the river flows through the valley, now one of the few regional agricultural areas. Native Americans occupied the valley until they were subjected to

diseases brought by the Dutch and English settlers, who began arriving in 1620. By 1670, small Anglo towns extended along the river to Massachusetts.

The Connecticut River has been used and abused over the years, according to the zeitgeist (spirit of the times). During the Industrial Revolution, the river was used to dump waste, which polluted the water and ruined a once-thriving fishing industry. In the 1960s, deindustrialization, the environmental movement, and legislation such as the Clean Water Act rehabilitated the river. During the 1990s, as sustainability and renewable energy became the new zeitgeist, seventy additional watershed sites were identified as having hydropower potential.

Southern Megalopolis waterways have been less successfully renewed. The Chesapeake, Long Island, and Delaware estuaries continue to house ever-larger populations, while industrial waste, raw sewage, and hypoxia induce fish kills. Tidal action scours the estuaries clean, but pollution now overcomes the tide's ability to cleanse the water. Unsustainable environmental assaults, such as the aborted Broadwater Energy Project to pipe liquefied natural gas, continue to threaten the already contaminated Long Island Sound.

Progress continues to identify new hydropower energy sources. In New York City, a company attempted pollution-free underwater turbines in the East River in 2007. The excessive power of the river's tides overwhelmed construction, but the turbines were dismantled and will be reinstalled after more engineering. Underwater turbines are also being considered near Martha's Vineyard.

Across the nation, freshwater use is maximized. Overallocated freshwater along the entire eastern shoreline has caused saltwater intrusion that threatens coastal aquifers and results in a depletion of wildlife, aquatic sea life, and lack of water for the growing population. Freshwater supplies have hit crisis levels, and residents of Massachusetts, New York, and New Jersey have been periodically ordered to restrict water use.[3]

The New York City water supply system encompasses three reservoir systems. Much is upstate in the Catskill Mountains on land protected from development. New York City water has been proclaimed as among the best in the world and is one of the last unfiltered drinking water supplies in the nation, although it is treated with chlorine and fluoride to meet disinfection and contamination standards.

Several Megalopolis organizations seek environmental, ecological, and social equity in water use. For example, organizations that support sustainability worked to terminate the Broadwater Project and preserve the waterways for the future by calculating its environmental and social costs, thereby revealing the true cost of modifications.

Chesapeake Bay

Thirty-five million years ago, a meteor strike formed a crater at the mouth of Chesapeake Bay, creating a drowned estuary in the lower Susquehanna River. The former tributaries of the Lower Susquehanna—the Potomac, James, and Rappahannock—now empty into the drowned valley. Much of the area is shallow and a critical nursery habitat for aquatics. The Chesapeake has multiple habitats—forests, wetlands, tidal marshes, and open waters, for example—and each meets the needs of specific biota. Climate change has altered the existing ecosystems in ways not yet fully understood.

Climate change, for example, places habitats, beaches, and barrier islands at risk for sea-level rise along the Delaware and Chesapeake bays. An estimated two-foot rise by the end of the century could inundate up to four hundred square miles of the Chesapeake Bay coastline. The low-lying topography and increased population living along the shore make the bay one of the most vulnerable to sea-level rise.[4]

Unintended Consequences

The Chesapeake was once the healthiest estuary for fish and shellfish in the United States, but today the sixty-four-thousand-square-mile Chesapeake Bay watershed fishery has collapsed, the victim of population growth. Sixteen million people draining their refuse from the Delmarva Peninsula (Delaware and portions of Maryland and Virginia) to the bay has had the unintended consequences of toxicity and loss of aquatic life.

Healthy phytoplankton and grasses, the baseline for a healthy bay, trap sediment and improve water quality. The grasses at the bottom of the bay's food chain provide food for crabs and the bay's famous oysters. However, urban and CAFO runoff have polluted the waters of the Delmarva Peninsula. The runoff and manure disposal from CAFO poultry farms on the peninsula are responsible for causing phytoplankton toxicity.

Phytoplankton is food for oysters. An oyster will strain and filter up to fifty gallons of water daily. The millions of oysters in the Chesapeake Bay in the 1870s were capable of filtering the water in three days, but today there are so few oysters it would take more than a year to filter the water. In coastal areas known for local seafood, the restaurants sell imported oysters, clams, and crabs.

While the growing population produces much of the polluting runoff, the agricultural community of the Delmarva Peninsula is also maximizing its CAFO production in order to realize a profit, and leaving behind an environmental scar.

The regional population growth and the concomitant condos create polluting runoff when heavy rains hit the bay. Pollutants drain into the bay, and fecal coliform bacteria from human or animal waste closed the oyster grounds.

Local and Ecoregional Impacts

Runoff from city streets, air pollution, nitrogen- and phosphorus-rich inorganic nutrients from farmlands, and outflows from sewage treatment plants have choked the bay. The excess nutrients block sunlight, hampering grass growth, depleting oxygen from water, and creating a hypoxic zone that kills fish.

However, there are several reasons for the devastation of the Chesapeake oyster industry, including overharvesting, pollution, and population growth. In the 1940s, several million bushels of Maryland oysters were harvested annually, but in 2005, only 26,500 bushels were harvested. All aquatics are now under strict quotas or limits to preserve the stock. Pollution has forced the Maryland Department of Environment to issue warnings against eating locally harvested oysters.

External Costs

The collapse resulted in a loss of thousands of fishery jobs and the disappearance of the world-famous Chesapeake oysters and blue crabs. An oversupply of nutrients causes algae blooms, cutting off the oxygen supply and damaging the clam, scallop, and mussel fishery. The sick ecosystem has produced sick aquatics. The intensive industrial agriculture maximizes efficiently grown chickens, but does not measure the economic impact of the environmental damage caused by the runoff.

Solutions

The bay's pollution was so egregious that in 1983 the Chesapeake Bay Program was formed, with the goal of reducing nutrients by 40 percent by 2000. The deadline expired unfulfilled, but bay restoration has continued to be a critical investment to improve the environment and restore the ecosystem. One of the main obstacles is the fragmented watershed shared by several states. Tributaries often rise in areas not contiguous to the bay but still send pollution. While the Chesapeake Bay Program spends millions to restore the bay, far-away linkages are not connected to the program.

Climate

Weather in mid-latitude Megalopolis is humid in the summer; winter varies from cold in the north to mild in the south. Winds blowing from the west minimize the ocean's influence. Ample precipitation (forty to forty-five inches) is distributed throughout the year, with the occasional crippling snowstorm. During the summer, thunderstorms bring considerable precipitation, and the occasional hurricane can damage coastal areas.

Acid Rain (Acid Deposition)

Rain is naturally acidic (pH 5.6) but becomes more so when oversupplies of sulfur dioxide and nitrogen oxides react with the rain and lower the pH. Midwestern coal-burning power plants spew sulfur and nitrogen oxides into the air, which are carried east by the winds and result in acid rain (pH less than 5.6). While new power plants are equipped with scrubbers to minimize the pollution, older plants are grandfathered in without the pollution mitigation.

Acid rain leaches nutrients from soil, stresses plants, decays building materials, sterilizes lakes, and harms wildlife. Some of the direct consequences have been the death of red spruce trees, loss of sugar maples, and the long-term and life-killing acidification of lakes. Most acid rain is the result of coal-burning power plants, but other causes include automobile emissions, chemical reactions of water in rain, and volcanic eruptions.

Acid rain can be curtailed by reducing car usage and by reducing power plant emissions through technologic devices such as scrubbers, although most power plants will avoid scrubbers due to their half-billion dollar price tag (Photo 7.2). Catalytic converters and unleaded gasoline use have decreased atmospheric pollutants. However, catalytic converters have been criticized because they decrease fuel efficiency and increase nitrous oxide, a greenhouse gas. In Megalopolis, the main culprit causing acid rain is Midwestern power plant emissions.

During the 1980s, a flood of acid rain news stories resulted in regulation. The stories ended but the pollution did not. The

PHOTO 7.2. Cleopatra's Needle near the Metropolitan Museum, New York City. The obelisk had lain in the Egyptian desert for thousands of years before being transported to its current location. When the obelisk arrived in New York, the hieroglyphs were clearly visible, but a hundred years of pollution and acid rain have obscured the inscriptions. Acid rain can destroy irreplaceable cultural artifacts.
Photo: B. Christopherson

1980 and 1990 Clean Air Acts attempted but failed to eliminate Northeastern acid rain. In 1999, the attorney generals of New York, Connecticut, and New Jersey filed a lawsuit against one of the largest power plant polluters, the W.H. Sammis power plant in Steubenville, Ohio. In 2005, a billion-dollar settlement was used to reduce emissions of harmful chemicals and invest in alternative energy projects.[5] Additional legislation and an emphasis on more renewable energy sources have reduced some power plant emissions.

Historical Geography and Settlement

Numerous Native American tribes occupied the region prior to European arrival. Conflict and disease diminished their population rapidly, so by 1681 when Penn founded Philadelphia, the decline in the Native population minimized tribal interference with white settlement.

The founding settlers interpreted their new landscape in relation to the knowledge and culture they brought from their homelands. They regarded the Native Americans as savage and the physical environment as natural, untouched by the indigenous occupants. However, the indigenous occupants did impact the landscape. For example, the indigenous use of fire to round up game was alien to the settlers' culture and therefore was interpreted through the lens of the settlers' experiences. Europeans used fire for warmth and cooking and had no basis for understanding using fire for other means. It was not until many years later that dendrology scientists studied tree rings and began to understand how the Native Americans shaped the landscape through the use of fire.

In short, Native Americans who hunted game animals were not just taking the "unplanted bounties of nature"; they were using fire to harvest a foodstuff. Few English observers realized this. People accustomed to keeping domesticated animals lacked the conceptual tools to recognize that Native cultures lacking domesticated livestock practiced a different type of animal husbandry.[6]

Cultural Hearths

The principles of New England spread at first to the neighboring states; they then passed successively to the more distant ones; and at length they imbued the whole Confederation. They now extend their influence beyond its limits over the whole American world. The civilization of New England has been like a beacon lit upon a hill, which, after it has diffused its warmth around, tinges the distant horizon with its glow.

—Alexis de Tocqueville, 1839[7]

Megalopolis was the heart of transplanted European settlement and the home to the three East Coast hearths—Tidewater, New England, and Mid-Atlantic. The period of New World settlement was concurrent with a shift in Europe's economic structure from feudalism to capitalism. The new economy and the settlers' cultural backgrounds shaped the basic hearth characteristics, from land division systems to housing styles. The influences of these hearths spread across the continent and helped shape how the land was used.

The Tidewater hearth, along the barrier islands from Virginia south, was the first English settlement area. This temperate hearth was settled by a wealthier clientele, who had the king's favor. They were seeking to better their financial circumstances by raising coveted crops—tobacco, rice, indigo, and cotton—that did not grow in the mother country and could be exported there.

The New England hearth in the Massachusetts Bay area was established by twenty thousand Puritans who arrived on the colder and rocky northern coast from 1620 to 1635. The Puritans immigrated because of religious intolerance but were intolerant of others; they even fragmented among themselves, thus beginning other New England colonies. Farming was the presupposed economy, but the poor soils turned many people to trade, shipbuilding, or fishing the Grand Banks. Wood, a plentiful natural resource in New England but rare in deforested England, was the favored material for building ships and homes.

The religiously tolerant Mid-Atlantic cultural hearth was settled by several groups, beginning in 1637 when Swedes and Dutch settled the Delaware estuary south of New York. The changes in the economic system were in full swing by the 1681 settlement of Pennsylvania. Capitalism changed how that hearth was settled. Individuals over groups and speculation over religion shaped the last Atlantic hearth landscape.

The Mid-Atlantic hearth was a clearing ground for various ethnic and religious groups that were unwelcome in their homelands and in New England. English settlers in Pennsylvania were interspersed with Welsh and German Quakers, who settled in separate enclaves. Various religious and utopian sects settled and continue to occupy the Pennsylvania landscape, such as the Amish in Lancaster County and the Moravians in Bethlehem. The Scots-Irish also arrived through the Philadelphia portal beginning in 1718, but they funneled into the Great Valley seeking more affordable land.

Megalopolis established the settlement and cultural patterns of the eastern half of the nation. The three cultural hearths—Tidewater, New England, and Mid-Atlantic—each had distinctive features and represented ideas that would be copied and modified to fit the westward-moving settlers.

Cultural Perspectives

Urban Density and Sustainability

Megalopolis is the most urban and densely populated region within the United States, but the open space that abounds in the region has allowed the population to sprawl. Between 1983 and 1997, the urbanized space grew by 39 percent while the population increased only 7 percent. The reduced density in the suburban areas is not conducive to the sustainable attributes of compact housing and more efficient transportation patterns.

However, several Anglo American cities were more closely aligned with their European counterparts. The first cities settled—Boston and New York—were built following the feudal organic layout, which is still reflected in the oldest part of the cities. Only later did they adopt the more modern grid pattern that was first practiced in Philadelphia. The cities grew in relation to seventeenth- through nineteenth-century transportation methods—waterways and animal power—and therefore are more compact, like their European counterparts. This pattern serves them well as America moves away from fossil-fuel induced sprawl and toward more sustainable and technologically advanced living patterns.

The densely populated cities of Megalopolis are well entrenched in reduced carbon footprint mass transit systems and transit-oriented developments (TODs). For example, Boston and New York have reliable rail and bus systems that transport passengers from outlying suburbs and between regional cities. Following the triple bottom line, TODs encourage social, economic, and environmental benefits. Cities such as Boston and nearby Cambridge have adopted public investment policies and guidelines that attract private investment and improve property values. TODs are springing up across the nation, but the density of population in Megalopolis has capitalized on them.

Regional Life

Population

Five major metropolitan areas along the eastern seaboard contain more than fifty-two million people, and yet places such as the Pine Barrens of southern New Jersey remain forested (Map 7.1; Table 7.1). Still, New Jersey, the most densely populated state, has an average density of more than 1,000 people per square mile. In the north, the population of entire states—Massachusetts, Rhode Island, and Connecticut—have densities of more than 100 people per square mile. The least populated county in Massachusetts is Franklin, at 102 per square mile; in Connecticut, it is Litchfield at 206.6 per square mile. The average density in the United States is 87.4 per square mile (2010).

While the Megalopolis region is considered densely populated, its absolute population growth has been stagnant at best, and it has some of the lowest relative population gains in the United States. In the 2010 census, the growth rate for the Northeast was the smallest regional growth at 3.2 percent.

Traditional and Sustainable Cities

The major cities in Megalopolis were established during the colonial period and therefore used traditional site and situation locations. These included defensive and transportation sites, and situations in relation to local resources. Building on land in relation to its water and natural resources is more sustainable than building by relying on modern and fossil fuel–based resources alone. The cities and metropolitan areas of Megalopolis originated in relation to natural resources and landscapes.

- Merrimack Valley: established in relation to water used for manufacturing
- Boston: established on a defensive site that also was on a good harbor
- Narragansett Basin: water sites

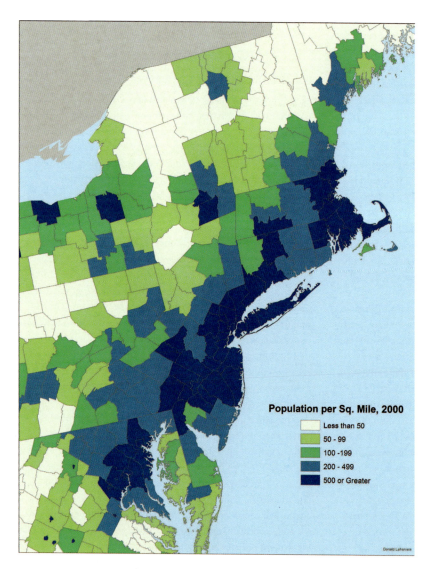

MAP 7.1. Megalopolis Population Densities. These are among the highest in the nation, but some counties have low population densities and even rural land.

TABLE 7.1. Megalopolis Population Densities, 2010

State	Persons per square mile	Rank
Washington, D.C.	9,856.5	1
New Jersey	1,195.5	2
Rhode Island	1,018.1	4
Massachusetts	839.4	5
Connecticut	738.1	6
Maryland	594.8	7
Delaware	460.8	8
New York	411.2	9

Source: U.S. Census (Puerto Rico is ranked number 3.)

- Connecticut River Valley: fertile agricultural land
- Albany and the Hudson River Valley: waterway into the interior
- New York City: harbor
- Philadelphia: between two rivers with access to ocean
- Baltimore: harbor
- Washington, D.C.: center of population, not north or south

Merrimack Valley

(2010 pop. Lowell 106,519; Lawrence 72,043)

The first industrialized towns in America, Lowell and Lawrence, were located north of Boston in the Merrimack River valley (Photo 7.3). The Merrimack River was the principal energy source for ten cotton and woolen textile mill complexes—Lawrence had the largest worsted wool mill in the world into the 1920s. The buildings still line the river, although they are no longer used as mills. In the early twentieth century, textile and shoe mills moved south in search of cheaper operating costs, which collapsed the regional economy.

Today the Merrimack populated area extends well beyond the valley into Portsmouth, New Hampshire, and Portland, Maine. In the twenty-first century, the Merrimack region is part of the greater Boston metropolitan region. The Merrimack Valley has attracted immigrants from its founding (the Irish) to the

PHOTO 7.3. Cotton Mill Reborn, Lowell, Massachusetts. Boot Mills processed cotton during the nineteenth century. By the late twentieth century, it was reborn as luxury apartments and condominiums.

present. Today's immigrants are largely Hispanic and Asian (Lawrence is 74 percent Hispanic, while Lowell is 16 percent Hispanic and 20 percent Asian).

Industry has focused on renewal as "Innovation Valley," concentrating on technology and green developments. Many of the old textile mills are morphing into retail and loft complexes, including the large green condo development at Wood Mill, which includes a massive geothermal heating and cooling unit. Today the Merrimack River continues to provide energy for the region, both the traditional dammed power and also innovative undammed hydropower technology such as underwater turbines.

Boston, Massachusetts

(2010 pop. 589,141; CSA 7,559,060[8])

Boston, founded in 1630, remains the economic capital of New England and for a century had the third-largest population in the nation. The Boston combined statistical area in 2009 is the fifth largest in the country and includes Cambridge, Quincy, Rhode Island, and extends north along the Massachusetts, southern New Hampshire, and Maine coastal areas. Most of the metropolitan area is urbanized, while western Massachusetts is more rural.

Settlements surrounded Boston's excellent protected harbor. The original landscape was hilly and compact. The original downtown complex contains the twisted, narrow, medieval roads common prior to the adoption of the modern grid (Photo 7.4). That pattern, as with other compact U.S. cities, has served it well in its environmental efforts. However, the city continued to grow beyond its peninsula beginnings. The hills were leveled and the fill used to extend the city into the marshes and bay. The result was a tripling in size of the narrow peninsula.

In the seventeenth century, the forests surrounding Boston were a resource for its shipbuilding industry. Boston traders roamed the seas from England to the Pacific and China. For example, Boston traders brought the first missionaries to Hawai`i.

But as the Boston hinterlands were tapped, people migrated toward better agricultural land. Traders sought out new enterprises for investment, leading them to create the textile industry during the Industrial Revolution. Later, as industry moved to the southern states, the city went into decline until the 1980s when technologic research at local universities—Harvard, MIT, and a host of other Boston schools—created the Boston **technopole**. Technological industries include electronics, computer, aerospace, and pharmaceuticals. Many major companies are located in both Boston (Liberty Mutual, Houghton Mifflin) and the greater Boston area (Bose, Novartis, and Raytheon).

Boston is also a cultural center with a strong elitist tradition, especially among those who have longtime roots in the community. The population was white until an influx of African Americans and Latinos in the late twentieth century. In 2010, the ethnic mix was 53.9 percent white, 24.3 percent black, 8.9 percent Asian, and 17.3 percent Latino. There is a wide discrepancy between socioeconomics and segregated residential areas that correspond with the socioeconomic divisions. While the 2009 per capita income was above the U.S. average ($31,856 Boston,

PHOTO 7.4. Old State House, Boston, Massachusetts (brick building in center). The oldest surviving public building, built in 1713, was once the tallest structure in the city, but today is dwarfed by the surrounding city. Inner-city Boston streets are medieval in style, laid out prior to the modern gridiron pattern.

$27,334 U.S.), one-fifth of the population lives below the poverty level (21.2 percent).

Boston and nearby Cambridge are national leaders in sustainable development. Boston is on the verge of a power revolution, using grass and leaves for methane production, while Cambridge aims to make 50 percent of its homes energy efficient by 2020.

Boston is the city most identified with the American Revolution. Its many historic buildings and sites include the Old North Church, the Paul Revere House, the Boston Commons, and the Freedom Trail. Other roads of note in the city are the two highways circumnavigating the city and the more recent "Big Dig," completed in 2005.

The Big Dig tunnel through the center of the downtown district replaced the clogged central artery. The Big Dig proved to be a public works project on the scale of the Alaska Pipeline or the English Channel Tunnel. Cost overruns (at $14.6 billion, about seven times the original estimate), corruption, and shoddy construction caused controversy over the Big Dig. In July 2006, a panel fell from the tunnel and killed a woman. As has happened in too many cases when profit alone is the goal, there have been calls for accountability on the errant project.

On a positive note, Boston has been a leader in adopting energy-efficient initiatives, such as encouraging with incentives for increased solar capacity and water-saving kits distributed to city residents. Water consumption is one of the lowest in the nation, averaging 74 gallons a person daily, versus the U.S. city average of 155 gallons.

Narragansett Basin

(2010 pop. 178,042 [Providence]; part of the Boston CSA)

Providence, Rhode Island, is both the second-largest city and second-largest industrial center in northeastern Megalopolis. The Narragansett Basin lowland emerges from the bay of the same name and is composed of Providence, Woonsocket, and Pawtucket and several small islands in Rhode Island, as well as nearby New Bedford and Fall River, Massachusetts.

The dissident Rhode Island colony broke away from Massachusetts and became an important ocean-faring state, dependent on fishing, whaling, rum-making, and the slave trade until it developed a textile industry. The nation's first water-powered textile mill was built in Pawtucket in 1793 (Photo 7.5). Other small textile mills allowed the basin towns to develop as mill villages. Larger mills were located on more powerful rivers in Massachusetts.

Cotton and textile mills were the investment standard during the nineteenth century, but from 1920 to 1968 the industry declined and almost half the workforce was unemployed. The current economy relies on trade, finance, and manufacturing of refined goods such as jewelry, silverware, and electrical equipment. Rhode Island's unemployment rate has been one of the highest in the nation during the economic recession beginning in 2008. This was due to a dependence on the manufacturing sector and small business enterprises, a high tax burden, and little investment in the quaternary economic sector.

The Rhode Island Bay area and its islands are filled with resorts and vacation homes. Sailing and boating are popular, highlighted with the America's Cup yacht race.

Connecticut River Valley

Connecticut's fertile and level land along the Connecticut River Valley is an anomaly in Megalopolis. The coastal and riverine cities—Hartford (2010 pop. 124,775), Bridgeport (144,229), and New Haven (129,779)—are medium sized in comparison to the Megalopolis metropolitan behemoths.

Historically, each town developed specialties, importing raw materials and producing highly finished products to justify shipment costs. Towns specialized in various textile industries or metal and machinery production. Central Connecticut produced brass clocks, silverware, and cutlery. Bridgeport, New Haven, and Waterbury were famous for hardware, tools, and small machinery. Other towns along the river produced machinery, electrical goods, and precision instruments.

The largest of the Connecticut River Valley cities is Hartford, situated at the head of ocean navigation. Dissenters from the Massachusetts Bay Company settled Hartford in 1635. Hartford became the insurance capital of America, but it also produced typewriters and Fuller brushes.

Sustainability has not been a priority within the valley. A 2008 report focused on the lack of sustainable housing, alternative transportation, and ecology. The report called the planning within the region "decentralized and haphazard without any long-term vision," a symptom of fragmented thinking. The report was a product of Dartmouth College, indicating how universities are leading the way to call attention to sustainability in America.[9]

PHOTO 7.5. Textile Mill, Pawtucket, Rhode Island. Slater Mill was built in 1793 on the Blackstone River. Modeled after English mills, it was the first water-powered cotton textile mill in America, marking the beginning of the American Industrial Revolution.

Albany and the Hudson River Valley

(2010 pop. 95,658; CSA 1,168,485)

The Hudson River Valley from New York City to Albany has been a center of transportation since Dutch settlement in the seventeenth century. Albany, the oldest continuously inhabited city in New England, was a Dutch fur-trading post established in 1619. In 1797, Albany replaced Kingston, New York, as the state capital. In 1825, the Erie Canal provided a low-lying continuous passage into the interior via the Great Lakes and elevated Albany's importance.

Regional towns specialized in specific industries until the middle of the twentieth century. Troy was known for men's shirts and detachable collars. Schenectady grew from Dutch beginnings into the home of General Electric in 1892. Albany was a wood-manufacturing center. The region's manufacturing industries declined after 1950 and have been replaced with trade, services, and government employment.

After years of preparation, Albany drafted its first long-range comprehensive plan, "Albany 2030," in 2011. The plan includes ideas such as neighborhood revitalization, redevelopment, and greenways. The plan is different from other plans because it is comprehensive, including all departments in the city, rather than the typical fragmented plans of the past. Therefore it is a step toward a more sustainable future for Albany.

New York City

(2010 pop. 8,175,133; CSA 22,085,649)

Since 1800, New York City has been the economic, commercial, financial, and cultural center for the nation. New York began in 1624 as a Dutch settlement on the southern tip of Manhattan. Its population bypassed Boston's in 1760 and Philadelphia's in 1800 to become the largest city, because of its deep harbor, coastal position, and access to the interior via the Hudson River and Erie Canal. Other cities competing for the premier position—Montreal, Halifax, Boston, Philadelphia, and Baltimore—all suffered from geographical deficiencies. Montreal is not an ice-free port; Halifax and Boston had lesser ports; and Philadelphia and Baltimore were less accessible, as they were located on narrow estuaries. New York Harbor was the major American port until the twenty-first century, when foreign trade shifted from Europe to Asia.

The waterfront extends over seven hundred miles of well-protected, ice-free piers surrounding Manhattan, Long Island, the East River, and along the northern Jersey shore. The Hudson scours the deep and wide port, enabling ships to come and go with ease. The New Jersey ports of Elizabeth, Newark, and North Bergen are the primary warehouse and intermodal shipping centers for the "Port of New York."[10] As one of the developed world's three major cities (the other two being London and Tokyo), New York anchors its international significance with one of the largest stock exchanges and the world headquarters for the United Nations.

New York City is the financial and corporate national leader. Stock exchanges are located in the Wall Street area, including the New York Stock Exchange (NYSE) and NASDAQ, the largest exchanges in the world. Manufacturing is minimal, but the fashion and garment industry remains central to the city. One-third of all clothing manufactured in the United States is designed and produced from 34th Street to 42nd Street, although this area's importance is declining because of local high rents and low-cost overseas production.

New York has the second most Fortune 500 corporate headquarters with fifty-five, following Texas' fifty-eight. Most headquarters in the state are in New York City. While many companies maintain a presence in the city, in recent years many others have left for the suburbs or nearby New Jersey because of high tax rates and costs in the city.

Among the several failings of the city is the waste situation (a low recycling rate) and the fragmented nature of the city. At the same time, the city has accomplished what seems impossible in a city so large: an excellent water system fed by reservoirs in the outlying counties, where development has been discouraged to protect the water. Water conservation has also been successful. Much of the city's environmental and sustainable goals have been because of strong support from local government and multiple environmental awareness campaigns, including a focus on schools and education.

New York City is fragmented: two **boroughs** are on islands, two others on Long Island, and one on the New York mainland (Map 7.2). The most populated area is Manhattan, a 13.5-mile by 2.3-mile island surrounded by the Hudson, East, and Harlem rivers, its southern tip facing the Upper New York Bay. Staten Island faces New York Bay and is separated from New Jersey by the Arthur Kill,[11] also called the Staten Island Sound. Both Queens and Brooklyn are located on the southwestern edge of Long Island, while the Bronx is on the mainland just south of Yonkers and Westchester County.

The fragmented nature and population densities of New York City required a supportive transportation network. The city is connected to its boroughs and New Jersey by a plethora of traffic-congested bridges and tunnels. However, there are multiple modes of travel, from autos to buses to local and commuter rail. The city has more miles of public transport than there are miles of city (1.8 miles to each 1 mile), so 37 percent of the workforce commutes by walking, cycling (doubling bike lanes in three years), or the extensive system of subways and hybrid buses.

The metropolitan area extends one hundred miles into four states, including New Jersey (Newark, Jersey City), Pennsylvania (Pike County, the fastest-growing county in Pennsylvania), and Connecticut (Stanford, Greenwich, Westport). North of the Bronx, Westchester County is an elite group of towns where the wealthy own homes in addition to their *pied à terre* (literally "piece of ground," apartments or coops) in the city. Beyond Queens, Long Island is now an interwoven mix of suburban communities with the exception of the north shore, which is still somewhat rural, and inhabited as second (third, fourth, or fifth) homes for the past century by the "à la Gatsby" wealthy.

Most of northern New Jersey is incorporated into the metropolitan complex. Since 1980, new luxury high rises tower where aging piers and warehouses once faced Manhattan. The Jersey shore is a popular weekend haven for many New Yorkers. The

BOX 7.5 GARBAGE IN THE CITY

For decades, New York City garbage disposal has been an ongoing environmental problem. During the nineteenth century, the filth from garbage was responsible for many cholera and typhus epidemics that killed thousands. Today the garbage is usually removed from the city streets, but disposing of thirty thousand tons of daily garbage remains a problem for the city and certainly highlights the unsustainable consumption issues that the United States still needs to address. U.S. garbage (1,600 pounds per person annually) compares negatively to European averages (1,100 pounds annually). Waste disposal is also handled less efficiently in the United States.

The United States has few incinerators that generate heat or electricity, largely because electricity costs have been relatively low. Few tax credits have been granted for renewable energy. In Europe, more than four hundred waste-to-energy plants emit few pollutants yet generate heat and electricity. Cities vie to have the energy plants, and many more are on the books.

While European incinerators are still not pollution free, they generate less pollution than the current diesel fuel trucks on New York's city streets. The fleet of diesel-burning garbage trucks is expected to be replaced by natural gas–burning vehicles as used in many EU countries. There are also plans to build a waterfront transfer system to reduce dependence on trucks.

In New York, garbage has periodically made the news. In 1987, a barge filled with New York garbage (the "Gar-Barge") was out at sea searching for a place to dump its garbage for six months before it finally returned to New York and the trash was incinerated. Sewer sludge has been dumped off the continental shelf for years, resulting in water and ecosystem degradation. Ocean dumping has been illegal since 1972, and other ocean dumping (e.g., construction debris) is no longer considered environmentally sound. The city has turned to landfills. The largest landfill in the world, Fresh Kills on Staten Island, opened in 1947. It leached toxic chemicals and heavy metals into waterways. In 2001, the landfill had closed, although it was still a recipient of 9/11 rubble.

Landfills are the victim of increased NIMBYism ("not in my backyard"). Local communities restrict or prohibit out-of-jurisdiction waste. Today most trash is disposed of out of state. Most New York garbage is collected and sent to New Jersey, Pennsylvania, Ohio, and Virginia landfills that are now near capacity. The cost has doubled since the exporting of trash began in 2000. The city plans to increase recycling, but the ongoing budget crisis has instead decreased recycling. In 2010, only paper and metal were recycled, though it is hoped that the increased interest in sustainability will support a full recycling program in the near future.

south coast of Connecticut has long been a suburban area for wealthy New York rail commuters.

Philadelphia, Pennsylvania

(2010 pop. 1,526,006; CSA 6,533,683)

Philadelphia was in many ways the nation's first "modern" city. Philadelphia was located for navigational purposes on a narrow peninsula between the Schuylkill and Delaware rivers. It was the first city in America to incorporate right-angle grid streets and several other modern amenities such as house numbering.

Religious and ethnic tolerance differentiated the city from the New England hearth. Most of America's Quakers, Mennonites, Germans, and Scots-Irish entered through the Philadelphia portal. By 1760, Philadelphia was the new nation's capital and the largest city in the new country. As the political center for the American Revolution, Philadelphia's iconic historic sites and features include Independence Hall and the Liberty Bell. Today, the Philadelphia combined statistical area is the eighth largest in America, but its city population is sixth largest and has been declining from its 1950 peak (Photo 7.6).

During the nineteenth century, Philadelphia was in the best position to compete with New York for the premier position for culture, population, and trade. However, its dreams of being the number one city in America were dashed with the success the Erie Canal brought to New York City.

Philadelphia remained an important port and historical city because of river access to fertile inland farms and later its

proximity to coal fields. But the city lacked New York's easy canal route to the west, and so after a failed attempt to compete in the canal arena, it turned its attention to the new railroad industry and became a hub for several rail companies. In the twenty-first century, Philadelphia's economy features manufacturing, food services, medical research, and finance. It is also recognized for its educational and cultural centers.

Philadelphia began issuing an annual Greenworks report in 2009. The report measures improvements in five goal areas: energy, environment, equity, economy, and engagement. Within the more than 150 initiatives are comprehensive plans and updating zoning codes. While the report shows how far the city has to go, it also is making people aware of how to make a difference and become more sustainable in the way they live.[12] Some of the areas where the city has excelled are in the comprehensive Greenworks program and its many green programs, from energy efficiency to including public input in its plans.

Southeastern Pennsylvania

The industrial cities of Allentown and Bethlehem lie in Lehigh Valley behind a row of ridges in the Ridge and Valley province. Canals and later railroads connected the long valley to the seaboard cities. Scranton and Wilkes-Barre anthracite deposits and limestone first attracted steel and cement production, followed by heavy machinery industry. Since the millennium, the southeastern cities have stabilized population despite a loss of manufacturing jobs.

MAP 7.2. Borough Map of New York City and Surrounding Area. New York's five boroughs (Manhattan, Brooklyn, Queens, Bronx, and Staten Island) are each an administrative subdivision of New York City. They were created in 1898 when the city consolidated.

Lancaster and its eponymous county are industrialized, but they have maintained the Amish **Pennsylvania Dutch**[13] farms. This fertile agricultural area near the city has been an important element of Philadelphia's economy.

Baltimore, Maryland

(2010 pop. 620,961; CSA 8,572,971)[14]

Baltimore, located on the Chesapeake Bay at the drowned mouth of the Patapsco River, was founded in 1729. Lord Baltimore's barony was meant to be a refuge for English Catholics, although religious toleration allowed many others to settle in the colony.

Baltimore's shipping advantages accelerated growth during the eighteenth century. The city was closer to Caribbean sugar producers than the more northern industrialized cities, and one hundred miles closer to the Ohio Valley than Philadelphia. During the twentieth century, the city's industry grew because of bulk shipping, grain elevators, coal piers, and fertilizer plants.

Baltimore grew to the sixth-largest American city by 1950, but in the 1970s harbor trade began to decline, and whites fled the city for the new suburbs. The harbor became the focus of redevelopment in the late twentieth century. Since gentrification of the narrow streets and brick row houses of Fells Point, the once tawdry harbor has become a tourist attraction and is reclaiming its importance.

The city of Baltimore remains at two-thirds its 1950 population, but population has stabilized; Baltimore lost 4.6 percent between 2000 and 2010, while the metropolitan area continues to grow. In the 1970s, Baltimore began to address environmental issues such as reducing air and water pollution, creating efficient land use patterns, and protecting streams, vegetation, and wildlife habitats in the surrounding area. However, sustainable ideals and growth have not infiltrated the city's many pockets of urban crime and poverty.

Washington, D.C.

(2010 pop. 601,723; CSA 8,572,971)[15]

Named for the father of the country (although George Washington referred to it as the Federal City), the capital was a planned city. In 1790, the new country needed a capital city, and

BOX 7.6 THE BOROUGHS

New York City has five administrative units called boroughs. Residents of the boroughs (which were originally independent cities) voted in 1898 to combine and form New York City. Each borough has retained its own personality. Though many Americans have not been to "the city," most people can identify the different boroughs through the many movies and television shows filmed in the city.

Manhattan

Manhattan is the core of the city and has the most skyscrapers in the nation. More than 40 percent of all office space in the nation is found in midtown Manhattan. The island's geologic structure allows the concentration of high-rises. The schist bedrock is close to the surface and provides structural support in the high-rise zones (midtown and Wall Street). In low-rise Greenwich Village and Chelsea, the bedrock lies hundreds of feet below the surface and therefore the land cannot support high-rises.

The 1,585,873 (2010) residents of Manhattan are divided into districts that any New Yorker is familiar with: Central Park occupies the center of the island and separates the liberal West Side from the more haute and affluent East Side. To the north Harlem, historically a Puerto Rican and African American enclave, has become an up-and-coming district in the early twenty-first century. To the south are the gentrified artist areas of Soho (South of Houston), Tribeca (Triangle below Canal Street), and the financial district, where the World Trade Towers once stood. The Lower East Side has historically been home to various ethnic groups and has many of the historic tenement buildings as seen in such movies as *The Godfather*. People who live in Manhattan can often have an elitist attitude about those who live off the island, the so-called "B&T" (bridge and tunnel) people, who commute to the island daily or for the nightlife.

Manhattan is often referred to as the media capital of the world, with national newspapers (*New York Times*, *Wall Street Journal*), literary magazines (*New Yorker*, *Harper's Weekly*), and advertising agencies, as well as corporate headquarters for such media giants as Time Warner, Condé Nast, and the Hearst Corporation. Major book publishers are also in the city, including Penguin, HarperCollins, Random House, and Simon & Schuster. All three of the major television networks (ABC, NBC, and CBS) are located in the city, as are many of the cable networks (e.g., HBO and MTV). Many movies have portrayed the city, such as many Woody Allen movies, *Taxi Driver*, and *The Devil Wears Prada*. Depictions of the city vary from violent to glamorous and are a geographic study in itself.

The Bronx

The only mainland borough, the Bronx consists of mostly residential land and commercial interests to service the communities.

Though there are single-family dwellings within the borough, it is known for its numerous housing projects, which have become notorious for drug use and poverty. During the 1980s, many of the housing projects fell victim to arson, for reasons not fully understood. The population in the borough is 1,385,108 (2010) with a density of 11,674 per square mile. The racial makeup is approximately 36 percent black, 20 percent white, and almost 50 percent Hispanic.* Most of the Hispanic population is Puerto Rican. About 30 percent of the population lives below the poverty line.

Queens

Queens is a residential borough. Its 2,230,722 (2010) inhabitants are almost 50 percent immigrants, and the borough is often considered the most diverse county in the nation. Both La Guardia and JFK airports are in Queens. The economy is based on tourism, the airports, and the headquarters of Jet Blue. Long Island City is a manufacturing and commercial center, with a growing artists' loft community.

Brooklyn

The most populous of the boroughs is Brooklyn, with 2,504,700 residents (2010). The borough has many well-known neighborhoods, such as Bensonhurst, Bedford-Stuyvesant, and Flatbush, along with Coney Island and Brighton Beach. Many Brooklyn neighborhoods are culturally distinct and house specific ethnic groups. In the past, Jewish and Italian immigrants lived in Brooklyn, and today it is home to a large Russian and Pakistani immigrant population. During the first decade of the twenty-first century, the artist community shifted from the now too expensive Soho to Brooklyn neighborhoods, such as Greenpoint and Park Slope. The shift brings a cool factor to the borough, and housing prices have escalated.

Staten Island

Staten Island, the most suburban of the boroughs, has the smallest but fastest-growing population of 468,730 (2010). It was not until 1960 that the island was connected to other boroughs via the Verrazano-Narrows Bridge. Until that time, the southern and central island maintained a rural atmosphere with poultry farms and dairies. Another feature on the island is the Fresh Kills Landfill—the largest landfill in the world at 2,200 acres—the repository of New York City garbage until 2001. It is currently being reclaimed for recreational use and for roads to ease traffic congestion. A regular and free ferry, offering excellent views of the Statue of Liberty, still connects lower Manhattan with Staten Island.

---

* Hispanics can be of any race. It is estimated that 14.5 percent of whites in the Bronx are not Hispanic.

PHOTO 7.6. Skyscrapers, Downtown Philadelphia. For many years the statue of William Penn atop City Hall was the tallest building, but skyscrapers such as One and Two Liberty Plaza, the Mellon Bank Center, and Bell Atlantic Tower (three towers on the left, and one to the right of City Hall) are now taller.

several cities vied for the title at congressional meetings. The cities with the most justified claims were Philadelphia and New York. However, their northern locations were politically unacceptable for the slaveholding South. James Madison, Alexander Hamilton, and Thomas Jefferson also discussed the need for a federal government and eventually agreed upon a more southern site. George Washington chose the Potomac site, because of its central location to the nation and his own predilection for all things Potomac.

Maryland and Virginia contributed land for America's Versailles, a ten-square-mile city built on a marshy and hilly terrace between the coastal plain and Piedmont. George Washington's friend, Pierre Charles L'Enfant, an American architect of French origin, designed the city. His plan worked within the constraints of the landscape and was considered genius, although his inability to compromise caused the surveyors of the federal district to eventually assume the architect function. But L'Enfant's inspired neoclassical ideals continued to influence the capital.

The city's broad boulevards housed only a few federal buildings in the nineteenth century, and few people lived in the city, so it seemed superfluous and grandiose. The city was only populated when Congress convened. Even at the dawn of the twentieth century, large expanses remained a thicket. But over time the city filled in around the federal buildings, until 1943, when the Pentagon became the first federal building built on the other side of the Potomac. In 1964 the **Beltway** circumferential highway was built to bypass the crowded streets of the capital city, but soon after the city experienced explosive growth and the Beltway became the primary thoroughfare and congested, which is still an issue today.

The city's 50.6 percent black population (2010) continues to reflect postwar migration. Many whites have chosen to live in the surrounding towns such as Georgetown or Arlington, Virginia. Between 2001 and 2006, the metropolitan area population swelled by four hundred thousand and northern Virginia

experienced a housing shortage, especially in the outer-ring counties of Loudoun and Stafford, which have grown by 96 and 51 percent respectively.

Washington's economy is based on the federal government. Although only 27 percent of jobs are directly government related, indirectly related jobs include government contractors, nonprofits, lobbyists, and law firms. Nongovernmental employment includes numerous educational and medical institutions and various media enterprises, such as National Public Radio and the *Washington Post*. The city's national mall is a stunning tourist attraction that contains national landmarks and monuments (e.g., the Jefferson, Lincoln, and Vietnam memorials, the Washington Monument) as well as major national museums (e.g., the Smithsonian, National Museum of the American Indian, National Gallery of Art).

Federal initiatives have been most evident in the capital city, where environmental policies are met with strong public support. Included in the policies are energy efficiency for buildings and many LEED-certified buildings incorporated within generous green spaces. Greenhouse gas emission reductions of 80 percent by 2050 have affected buildings, transportation, and land use.

Economy

Megalopolis was the birthplace of American manufacturing. The colonial New England economy evolved from the fishery to shipbuilding to water-powered textile mills. The Central Atlantic states of eastern Pennsylvania south to the Washington, D.C., metro area specialized in textiles, clothing, steel, and machinery.

Manufacturing in Megalopolis is no longer an important part of its economy, but Megalopolis is the financial heart of America. However, it is no longer the dominant region for Fortune 500 headquarters. In 2009, only sixteen of the top fifty companies were headquartered in the region.[16]

Primary Industry and Natural Resources

Primary industries are minimal in Megalopolis. Agriculture and fishing linger, but mineral resources and logging are no longer vital. Rural land and forests remain important for Megalopolis and its residents, because they literally provide the breathing space for the urban populations.

Agriculture

Agriculture has historically been a part of Megalopolis, but urban expansion sprawled over many former agricultural lands. Some farming still remains, but it caters to the local market (fruits and vegetables), chicken production (Delmarva Peninsula), or niche markets (mushrooms, organic, Amish).

The Connecticut River Valley, a wheat-producing and dairy area, specialized in a tobacco for cigar wrappers in the nineteenth century. After World War II, suburban development sprawled over the former dairies and tobacco fields. Most remaining farmers evolved into truck farmers, but sustaining a small farm is almost impossible today without outside income, so such enterprises cater to an urban family clientele with golf courses, cider mills, and pick-your-own fruit.

The Delaware and Chesapeake bay estuaries surround the relatively isolated Delmarva Peninsula, a mainstay in agricultural and CAFO chicken production. Egg production began in the 1920s, but it evolved into chicken production in the following decade because selling broilers was more profitable than selling eggs. The well-drained soil, low building costs, and proximity to large markets created a thriving chicken industry.

More than six hundred million chickens are grown on the peninsula, supplying 8 percent of American chickens and the majority of local agricultural sales. The chicken industry may be short lived, though, because of urban encroachment and environmental degradation. The peninsula generates more than eight hundred thousand tons of manure annually, which is a source of runoff and excessive nutrient buildup that is a major source of Chesapeake Bay pollution.

Many chicken growers unable to combat rising production costs are selling to developers and moving south, where production costs are lower. Those who remain must deal with the new suburban neighbors who complain about the chicken farm dust and smells.

Some farmers specialize in grain production for specific markets, but historically the most important crop has been tobacco, a crop subsidized so that a small-acreage farmer could realize a profit. Terminating tobacco quotas in 2004 blunted production, and finding replacement crops has been a priority. Organic farming and specialized crops, such as mushrooms, figs, and blueberries have been possible sustainable alternatives for the tobacco farmer.

The Amish settled and farmed the fertile land in Lancaster County west of Philadelphia, which brought prosperity to the city. The principal agricultural output of Amish farms is livestock and dairy products, but they also grow corn, hay, grain, and vegetables. The Amish are known for their old-fashioned, nonelectric ways, but little is known of their leadership in solar and wind power. Solar panels grace Amish barns, and wind power energizes their dairies, while compressed air runs machine shop tools and kitchen appliances.

Amish still live and farm in the county, drawing a large tourist population who come to view their quaint technology and attire. Other residents of Lancaster and the surrounding counties capitalize on the tourist trade, although the Amish do not, and dislike how they have become the center of tourist attention.

Fishing

Since the 1992 collapse of the fishery, strict quotas have limited fishing north of Boston. Pollution and overfishing have caused an annual decline in the Chesapeake Bay fishery.

Early Manufacturing

Southern New England

Early New England manufacturing was decentralized because of a dependence on waterpower. Towns specialized in producing one particular commodity and became known as one-industry towns or mill towns. They were seldom "company towns," as most towns had competitive companies producing the same ware. During the manufacturing era, New England and Mid-Atlantic towns were noted for their distinct specialties, such as Danbury, Connecticut, for felt hats, and silk and rayon goods in Mid-Atlantic towns (Table 7.2).

Water-powered mills were built in the late eighteenth century, but during the second decade of the nineteenth century New England's cotton and woolen textile mills dominated American industry. Towns sprang up along streams with sufficient waterpower to support mills—Waltham, Lowell, and Lawrence in Massachusetts; Manchester in New Hampshire; Providence in Rhode Island; and along the Connecticut River Valley.

The technological limitations of building dams and harnessing power determined the geographic situation of the mills. The first water-powered plants developed in New England were accessible to coastal transport. Falls were common, due to the granites of New England's bedrock; the south was far less accessible for transport because of the fall line, and so the early mills were located near the coast and in New England. During the initial industrial phase, harnessing and transporting the power was limited technologically on larger rivers, so falls at smaller streams dominated; hence the inland locations of many early textile mills. By mid-century, steam became the new form of power, and city growth reflected the new source.

Steam plants were coal powered, but heavy, bulky coal was most inexpensively delivered to ocean ports. The next generation of mills and factories were built along the coal delivery routes, such as Lowell, Salem, and Portsmouth. The mills remained important in the New England area until the 1880s, when electricity became a power source and cotton textile mills began to migrate closer to their southern commodity, where labor and land were less expensive. By World War I, the New England textile economy had severely declined.

TABLE 7.2. Late Nineteenth- and Early Twentieth-Century New England Cities and Their Specialized Industries

City	Commodity produced
Danbury, Connecticut	Felt hats
Woonsocket, Rhode Island	Handkerchiefs
Bridgeport, New Haven, and Worcester, Connecticut	Corsets
Peabody, Danvers, and Woburn, Massachusetts	Leather goods
Brockton, Haverhill, and Lynn, Massachusetts	Shoes
Hartford, Springfield, Waterbury, New Haven, and New Britain, Connecticut	Brass, hardware, electrical goods

Mid-Atlantic Manufacturing

Southern Megalopolis is dominated by the inland fall line cities—Philadelphia, Trenton, Wilmington, Baltimore, and Washington, D.C.—all situated on the two major estuaries. The Delaware River follows the fall line for fifty miles and contains the major cities of Philadelphia, Wilmington, and Trenton. Baltimore and Washington, D.C., are on Chesapeake Bay. With the exception of Washington, these cities developed as access points to both inland and ocean transport. With time, the waterpower advantage succumbed to coal-producing regions. Fall line cities were at first dependent on ocean access for shipping and importing, but in time railroads connected the cities to the interior. The cities evolved into distribution centers for manufactured goods. Both Philadelphia and Baltimore became major industrial cities; they reached their height of production during the 1950s, after which industry began to decline.

Tourism

Regional tourism is substantial, both for the residents who spend their vacations within the region and for visitors. Among the largest attractions are New York City, for the city itself and for its many museums and sites (the Empire State Building, the Natural History Museum, Ellis Island Museum, the Tenement Museum, and the Statue of Liberty); Washington, D.C., for its monuments, national museums, and the White House; Philadelphia, the city most identified with independence; and Boston's American Revolution sites.

The coast attracts local residents during the summer, when inland humidity can be stifling and ocean breezes a relief. The wealthy go to Montauk and surrounding communities at the end of Long Island, while gays and lesbians frequent Fire Island and families go to Coney Island. Martha's Vineyard and Nantucket are popular island getaways, as is the Cape Cod coast, led by Provincetown, a former whaling center that now supports a vibrant gay community. Atlantic City, New Jersey, a resort town known for its boardwalk, had declined and then reemerged in the late twentieth century as an East Coast gambling mecca.

A Sustainable Future

"Mr. Gates, I can deliver you an earth-, wind-, and solar-powered city built on entirely new construction and management principles. The technologies you need have been available since the late 20th century, but they've been stuck in underfunded startup companies, over-taxed, ignored, even laughed at."[17]

In many ways, Megalopolis is already the future of America. The densely populated multiple urban centers are the ideal for TODs, conservation, and energy efficiency. But Megalopolis has also been sprawling and needs to clean up its act and initiate green building and conservation methods that will reduce its impact on the surrounding area, as well as create new standards. It already leads the nation in available mass transit, but more rail lines and TODs can add efficiency. Environmentally conscious building structures must conserve resources, minimize pollution, and be energy efficient. Already, infrastructure collapse has caused temporary but cautionary halts to production.

In the second half of the twentieth century, New York City experienced several massive blackouts that called attention to infrastructure failure. In 2003, New York, the entire Northeast, and portions of the Midwest had an August blackout that left all residents in darkness for several days and caused a transportation shutdown. These blackouts and several others of shorter duration all show a need for upgrading infrastructure for more efficiency and conservation. Investing in energy-saving appliances can reduce energy demands, cogeneration systems can provide some energy during times of crisis, and experimental hydropower sources such as the East River tide-driven underwater turbines can provide new forms of power.

BOX 7.7 ATLANTIC CITY

In Las Vegas, they built a city to support the casinos. But in Atlantic City, they did it the other way around: they built the casinos to support the city.

—Baker, 1989*

The New Jersey coast had been New York's playground for decades before its post–World War II decline. New Jersey, seeking to renew a failing Atlantic City with an urban redevelopment project, passed legalized gambling in 1976 (after three failed attempts).

Atlantic City's boom-bust economy is a direct result of its geography. Speculators initiated the first boom. A railroad connecting the new town to Philadelphia allowed urban residents an easy escape to the Atlantic City seaside resort. But after World War II, easier transportation links to tropical Florida made the Atlantic City location obsolete as a resort destination. Corruption brought decline until gambling was legalized. The proximity to Megalopolis offered large casino gambling within an easy day's drive. The town had new hope.

Atlantic City evolved uneasily from the "Queen of the Coast" in 1900 to "South Bronx by the Sea" after World War II, into its present incarnation as a year-round gambling haven with fourteen casinos. The first casinos were built in 1978 along the famed boardwalk, but mostly drew day players. Hotels were largely vacant. Profit eluded the investors. Extensive promotions and "gambling clubs" built up the clientele, and in 1998 the gambling establishments finally became profitable. On paper, the city seems a tremendous success, with a high real estate value per capita. Though resorts and gambling have been successful at attracting more than 33 million bettors annually, the Atlantic City population (39,558 in 2010) has declined 1,000 since 2000.

There are now two Atlantic City's, in reality if not in fact. One is glitzy and monopolizes the coast. A few blocks inland the city remains ramshackle (Photo 7.7). Although the casinos created more jobs than residents, the residents are not doing well. Most jobs went to people who live outside the city. The city remains largely poor and black, with more than one-quarter of the residents living below the poverty line. There has been some reinvestment into the city, some low-cost housing units, but bridging the gap between the rich coastline and the poor city still has a long way to go.

PHOTO 7.7. A Study in Contrasts: Atlantic City, New Jersey. The legalization of gambling in New Jersey brought new life to this impoverished city, but though gambling is profitable, the money has not reached the residents. Almost one-quarter live below the poverty line. Within blocks of the high-rise casino-hotels are boarded-up row houses.

* Quoted in Paul Bela Sur Teske, "Winners and Losers: Politics, Casino Gambling, and Development in Atlantic City," *Review of Policy Research* 10, no. 2–3 (1991): 130–37.

Megalopolis has been active in sustainable issues, including renewable, sustainable energy and green power. Most state governments have agreed to purchase green power. For example, Connecticut, one of the most progressive states, has ordered state government agencies to purchase 23 percent renewable energy by 2020. In April 2007, New York City followed the carbon reduction standard set by California to reduce carbon emissions 30 percent by 2030. But these reductions are only for state agencies. Residential reduction and incentives are rare, even though residential use is the largest power user in the nation.

In addition, Megalopolis, along with fourteen states outside the region, has set standards to provide renewable energy by set dates (Table 7.3). State governments have pursued setting renewable and energy standards.

By mid-2009, New York City, reeling from the economic downturn, which was partially caused by the refusal to face energy efficiency or conservation, was starting to face the wind. Several companies began to purchase wind power. Companies began purchasing wind offsets, which reduced greenhouse gas emissions—the equivalent of taking cars off the road or planting trees. The interest in renewable energy continues to grow, and wind farms are springing up, such as an offshore farm at Rockaway Beach, Queens. Mayor Bloomberg passed a property tax credit that encourages green roofs. After a decade of opposition, the 130-turbine Cape Wind Project was approved in 2010, which will make it the first offshore wind farm in America. In October 2010, Google and a few other companies announced the 6,000-MW Atlantic Wind Connection, a Mid-Atlantic offshore wind farm. The proposed wind farm will stretch 350 miles from New Jersey to Virginia. The completion time is still unknown but could be far off. Cape Wind has been planned for a decade, and yet nothing has been built as of the end of 2010.

Although a broad regional movement has encouraged clean energy generation, it is but a beginning to a national energy conservation policy.

"Right now it's a boutique product that you pay premium prices for," Hovnanian told moderator Tom Brokaw, in response to a question about what "green" means to him. "If all is equal, consumers will choose green, but not all is equal and [most] consumers are not willing to pay more."[18]

Since 2003, New York City has been pursuing green design aggressively, but it requires government support (such as the subsidies given to nonrenewables) in order to become mainstream. The Leadership in Energy and Environmental Design (LEED) certification standards are expensive, as are upfront costs. Several commercial and residential buildings have attained LEED certification, but the high costs of certification, 4 to 8 percent above normal costs, while absorbed in energy savings over time, are difficult for many public companies to justify when restricted by quarterly reviews. There remains a need for

TABLE 7.3. Renewable Portfolio Standards for Megalopolis States

State	Standard (%)	Year
Massachusetts	15	2020
Rhode Island	16	2019
Connecticut	23	2020
New York	24	2013
New Jersey	22.5	2021
Pennsylvania	8	2020
Delaware	20	2019
Maryland	20	2022
Washington, D.C.	20	2020

Source: U.S. Department of Energy, "States with Renewable Portfolio Standards," at http://apps1.eere.energy.gov/states/maps/renewable_portfolio_states.cfm#chart

BOX 7.8   PLATINUM LEED IN CHESAPEAKE BAY

LEED certification has grown quickly. In 2008, the number of buildings certified doubled to twenty thousand, and double-digit growth continued through 2010 despite the depressed real estate market. Half of the buildings are governmental public buildings required to build to LEED standards, for example, the Environmental Protection Agency (EPA), General Services Administration (GSA), and the National Aeronautics and Space Administration (NASA).

In 2001, the Chesapeake Bay Foundation built the first Platinum-certified LEED building in Maryland, the Philip

Merrill Environmental Center, which endorses the environmental standards it demands from the bay it overlooks (Photo 7.8). Located just outside of Annapolis, the building features such green characteristics as rooftop cisterns for irrigation, solar components to generate electricity and hot water, composting toilets, geothermal heating and cooling, and at last, windows that open to allow in breezes. The energy-efficient building has been described as a "triumph of 'green' architecture."

PHOTO 7.8. Philip Merrill Environmental Center, Annapolis, Maryland. In 2001, the center became the first LEED Platinum building in the United States. Home to the Chesapeake Bay Foundation, the building is capable of using less than 70 percent of the energy of a typical office building.

strong residential incentives. Despite economic limitations, though, green buildings are popular, and they attract more educated and innovative employees.

New York City is a special case for green building. Building costs are high; land is precious. Despite the obstacle of higher costs, in 2007 Local Law 86 went into effect supporting sustainable standards. Any institutional building using more than $2 million in city funds must attain LEED certification. This is applauded as a step in the right direction by some, but others, especially those interested in affordable housing, feel that energy costs can be cut without using fancy, expensive gadgets or going through the costly red tape of meeting LEED standards. LEED does not work

everywhere equally. Using recycled goods, selling back excess energy, and recycling water to satisfy LEED requirements are difficult in New York City.

The attention to these sustainable issues in the nation's largest city will set some standards for the rest of the nation. In 2007, Boston joined seventy-four other localities and adopted some LEED criteria into its building code. Green building is the current trend and needs to become the standard, perhaps not following exact LEED requirements but maintaining conservation. However, Megalopolis did build the first LEED Platinum–certified green building in the nation. Perhaps with time, energy efficiency will become an important part of everyone's lives, as home and small businesses are supported in becoming more energy efficient.

Questions for Discussion

1. What were the early manufacturing industries in New England and how had they evolved by the mid-twentieth century?

2. What natural features have significance in explaining the distribution of cities in Megalopolis? How do New England features differ from the Central Atlantic region?

3. What were determining factors for the growth of Philadelphia and New York City?

4. What has been the historical importance of the Lehigh Valley of Pennsylvania? What has been its industrial history? Why?

5. Why has New York City surpassed all other American cities in population and economic importance?

6. What natural advantages favor New York Harbor over other Atlantic harbors? What human-made advantages favor it?

7. Population pressure and religious intolerance pushed people out of the original Boston settlement area. Where did they migrate?

8. Why did Boston not prosper as much as Philadelphia and New York after the Revolutionary War?

9. How did Philadelphia's urban planning differ from previous cities, and how did it affect later American urban development?

10. How did Boston's economy evolve from the colonial period to the present?

11. In what ways is Megalopolis best suited for a renewable energy future?

12. What role has hydropower played in Megalopolis's past, and what role will it play in its future?

13. How did Merrimack Valley industry evolve initially, and how has it changed since the 1970s?

14. How have Europeans changed the Atlantic Coast shoreline landscape?

15. What are some of the green ways that Megalopolis has led the nation?

Suggested Readings

Andersen, Tom. *This Fine Piece of Water: An Environmental History of Long Island Sound*. New Haven, Conn.: Yale University Press, 2002.

Bergman, Edward. *A Geography of the New York Metropolitan Region*. Dubuque, Iowa: Kendall/Hunt Publishing Company, 1975.

Borchert, John R. *Megalopolis: Washington, D.C., to Boston*. New Brunswick, N.J.: Rutgers University Press, 1992.

Conzen, Michael P., and George K. Lewis. *Boston: A Geographical Portrait*. Cambridge, Mass.: Ballinger, 1976.

Cronon, William. *Changes in the Land: Indians, Colonists, and the Ecology of New England*. New York: Hill & Wang, 1983.

Cunningham, John T. *This Is New Jersey*. New Brunswick, N.J.: Rutgers University Press, 2001.

De Souza, Anthony R., and Cotton Mather. *Capital Region: Day Trips in Maryland, Virginia, Pennsylvania, and Washington, D.C.* New Brunswick, N.J.: Rutgers University Press, 1992.

Ellis, Joseph J. *His Excellency: George Washington*. New York: Faber & Faber, 2005.

Gottmann, Jean. "Megalopolis, or the Urbanization of the Northeastern Seaboard." *Economic Geography* 33, no. 3 (July 1957): 189–200.

Harris, C. M. "Washington's Gamble, L'Enfant's Dream: Politics, Design, and the Founding of the National Capital." *William and Mary Quarterly*, 3rd series, 56, no. 3 (July 1999): 527–64.

Kieran, John. *Natural History of New York City*. New York: Houghton Mifflin, 1959.

Lippson, Alice Jane, and Robert L. Lippson. *Life in the Chesapeake Bay*. Baltimore: Johns Hopkins University Press, 2006.

Lotspeich, Katherine, Michael Fix, Dan Perez-Lopez, and Jason Ost. "A Profile of the Foreign-Born in Lowell, Massachusetts," The Urban Institute, October 2003, at http://www.urban.org/uploadedPDF/410918_Lowell_MA.pdf.

McDonough, Michael. "Newer York, New York." *Wired*, January 2000, at http://www.wired.com/wired/archive/8.01/futuretekture.html.

McManis, Douglas R. *Colonial New England: A Historical Geography*. New York: Oxford University Press, 1975.

McPhee, John. *The Pine Barrens*. New York: Farrar, Straus & Giroux, 1978.

Morrill, Richard. "Classic Map Revisited: The Growth of Megalopolis." *The Professional Geographer* 58, no. 2 (2006).

Oldale, Robert N. *Cape Cod, Martha's Vineyard and Nantucket: The Geologic Story*. Rev. ed. Yarmouth Port, Mass.: On Cape Publications, 2001.

Orton, Tom, and Joel K. Bourne Jr. "Chesapeake: Why Can't We Save the Bay?" *National Geographic* (June 2005), at http://environment.nationalgeographic.com/environment/habitats/chesapeake-save-bay/.

Rauber, Paul. "The Oyster Is Our World." *Sierra* 80, no. 5 (September–October 1995).

Sorkin, Michael. *After the World Trade Center: Rethinking New York City*. New York: Routledge, 2002.

Teske, Paul Bela Sur. "Winners and Losers: Politics, Casino Gambling, and Development in Atlantic City." *Review of Policy Research* 10, no. 2–3 (1991): 130–37.

Tuico, Elizabeth. "The Greenest Building in America?" *Constructor* (May 2002).

Warner, Sam Bass, Jr. *Greater Boston: Adapting Regional Traditions to the Present*. Philadelphia: University of Pennsylvania Press, 2001.

———. "Today's Boston: A History." *Massachusetts Historical Review* 1 (1999).

Wood, Joseph. *The New England Village*. Baltimore: Johns Hopkins Press, 1997.

Internet Sources

The Quest for a Capital, at http://www.capitolhillhistory.org/lectures/vlach/index.html.

Martha's Vineyard Gazette, at http://www.mvgazette.com/.

A Sustainable Chesapeake, at http://www.conservationfund.org/sites/default/files/The_Conservation_Fund_Chesapeake_Bay_Better_Models_for_Conservation_Chapt4_Patuxent_Greenway_Reforestation_Bank.pdf.

City Limits. "LEED-ing by Example: Green Building Grows Up," at http://www.citylimits.org/content/articles/viewarticle.cfm?article_id=3263.

Chesapeake Bay and Global Warming, at http://www.nwf.org/sealevelrise/chesapeake.cfm.

The Mannahatta Project, at http://welikia.org/.

Glaciers in New York City, at http://people.gl.ciw.edu/ecottrell/glaciers/Glaciers_in_NY_Intro.pdf.

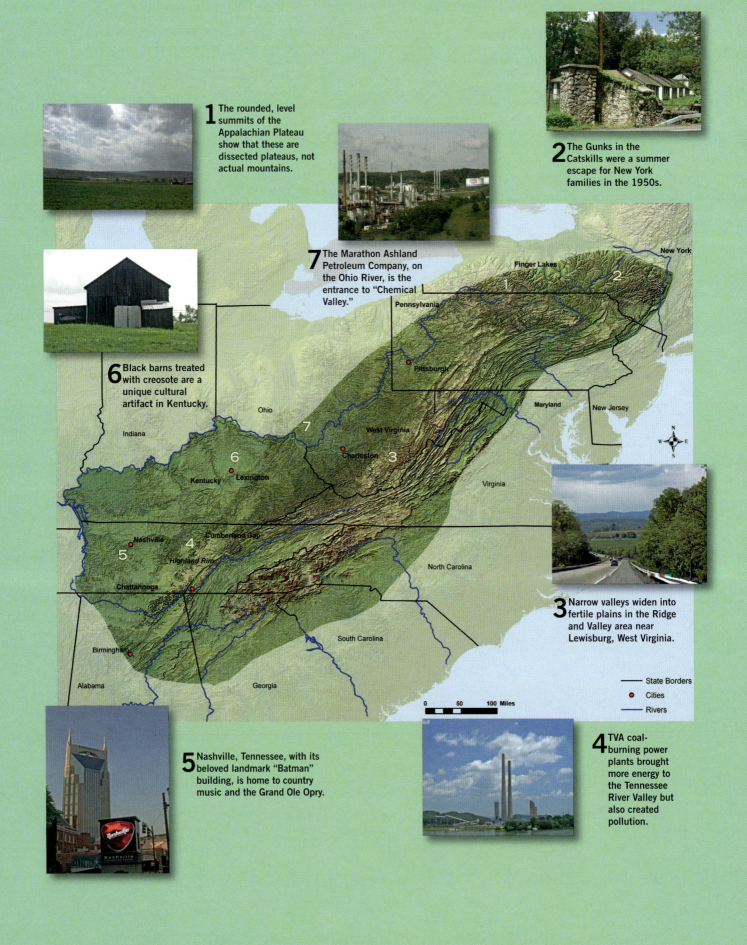

1 The rounded, level summits of the Appalachian Plateau show that these are dissected plateaus, not actual mountains.

2 The Gunks in the Catskills were a summer escape for New York families in the 1950s.

7 The Marathon Ashland Petroleum Company, on the Ohio River, is the entrance to "Chemical Valley."

6 Black barns treated with creosote are a unique cultural artifact in Kentucky.

3 Narrow valleys widen into fertile plains in the Ridge and Valley area near Lewisburg, West Virginia.

5 Nashville, Tennessee, with its beloved landmark "Batman" building, is home to country music and the Grand Ole Opry.

4 TVA coal-burning power plants brought more energy to the Tennessee River Valley but also created pollution.

New York

Finger Lakes

Pennsylvania

Pittsburgh

Maryland

New Jersey

Ohio

West Virginia

Indiana

Charleston

Kentucky

Lexington

Virginia

Cumberland Gap

Nashville

Highland Rim

North Carolina

Chattanooga

South Carolina

Birmingham

Alabama

Georgia

State Borders
Cities
Rivers

0   50   100 Miles

N
W   E
S

8

APPALACHIA

Trying to Love the Mountains

Terms

acid mine drainage
anthracite
Appalachian Regional
    Commission (ARC)
bituminous

canebrake
Clean Water Act (CWA)
cove
eco-industry
headwater stream
lignite
moonshine

mountaintop removal (MTR)
overburden
peat
Pittsburgh Plus
Second Great Awakening
strip-mining
subbituminous

Surface Mining Control and
    Reclamation Act (SMCRA)
Tennessee Valley Authority
    (TVA)
trace
water gap
wind gap

Places

Alleghenies
Appalachian Plateau
Birmingham, Alabama
Blue Ridge

Catskill Mountains
Charleston, West Virginia
Chattanooga, Tennessee
Cumberland Gap
Cumberland Plateau
Finger Lakes

Great Smoky Mountains
Great Valley
Highland Rim
Interior Plateau
Kanawha Valley

Lexington Basin
Nashville, Tennessee
Pittsburgh, Pennsylvania
Ridge and Valley
Shenandoah Valley

PHOTO 8.1. Billboard in Beckley, West Virginia. Billboards favoring the coal industry are plastered along all major roadways and in towns. Coal does provide the power for electrical generation, but it has also created a deep divide in West Virginia about the coal industry, especially mountaintop removal.

Introduction

A popular bumper sticker in Appalachia is "I ♥ the mountains." And love is what the occupants of this landscape have for their home—although these are not mountains but a dissected plateau. Years of water moving through the plateau have cut the mountainous shapes on the outside, but inside these "mountains" still show their geologic origins. Inside the layers are horizontal, not folded or uplifted as most mountains are. And inside these mountainous structures is their secret—coal, coal that is easy to access (Photo 8.1).

The horizontal geology has been important in shaping the regional economy, and more so as accessing natural resources becomes more expensive. Mining coal from horizontal layers is much easier and cheaper than underground mining. Scraping the horizontal coal layers is the cheapest way to convert the coal into electricity.

Coal is the least expensive source of electric power in America, but only if the destroyed environment and communities are not considered important. If you count communities and ecosystems as important, coal mining as it is done today is the antithesis of sustainable.

Although not all of Appalachia produces coal, it is the single most important resource within the region. Coal has been a source of wealth for some and steady employment for others. Mining coal has destroyed the landscape. The nation's incessant reliance on coal for electricity has caused portions of Appalachia to pay a disproportionate environmental price:

- The Great Smoky Mountains are enveloped in a permanent fossil fuel–produced haze that has nothing to do with the park's "Smoky" name.

- The Cumberland Plateau valleys have unprecedented environmental and social damage because of invasive coal extraction methods.
- Coal sludge, stored in makeshift impoundments, is susceptible to environmental disasters, such as the Kingston, Tennessee, disaster in December 2008.
- The biodiversity of the region has been compromised because of logging and mining.

The government has turned a blind eye to biologic and mining problems; if there are regulations, they are seldom enforced. However, many local nongovernmental organizations (NGOs) have formed to attend to the regional issues. The tide is turning to a healthier future for Appalachia and America.

The forested, rolling Appalachian landscape is filled with a rich biodiversity of plants and animals. Dispersed human communities living in the hollows are connected to the land. Access between communities is difficult, even with modern transportation and communication. But Appalachian life has been good, although quite different than what many other Americans experience. Appalachian folk have chosen to follow many old folkways and live a life based more on family and community than on consuming.

Holism is an important element among the people and how they live, but the regional biota have been fragmented by economic forces from outside the area. To live holistically within the region requires balancing regional ecological health with its functional uses.

Over millennia, numerous rivers and streams have dissected the undulating green plateaus of Appalachia. The plateaus have been more suitable as hunting grounds for wildlife than as a farming region. The ecologically wealthiest part of the region, the Cumberland Plateau, is exploited for its resources, providing wealth for those outside the region but leaving the residents poor. American industrial power grew because of Appalachian hardwood forests and the abundant coal, gaining a short-term, cheap, and polluted modern life at the cost of destroying a vibrant culture.

Physical Geography

The Appalachian cultural region follows the spine of the Appalachian Mountains through thirteen states. Only one state, West Virginia, is completely within the region. Portions of Kentucky, Tennessee, Mississippi, Alabama, Georgia, Virginia, Maryland, South Carolina, North Carolina, Ohio, Pennsylvania, and New York that are contiguous to the mountains are also included. The Interior Plateau, the region that connects Appalachia with its Ozark sister region, encompasses western Kentucky and Tennessee.

The Appalachian Highlands, between the Piedmont and the Midwestern lowlands, stretches from New England to the Gulf Coastal Plain. The Interior Plateau lies west of Appalachia and south of the Ohio River. The subregions contain five types of topography: mountains, valleys, plateaus, flood plains, and limestone prairie. The subregions are:

> The Blue Ridge Province, containing the Great Smoky Mountains
> Ridge and Valley Province, including the Great Valley
> Appalachian Plateaus: Allegheny, Cumberland
> Interior Plateau: Nashville and Lexington basins

The lush, green, mountainous expanse has provided solace for millions of Americans. But regional vegetation and wildlife have changed over the past century. During the early twentieth century, fungus blight virtually eliminated the once-dominant American chestnut; oaks now dominate. In higher elevations, spruce and fir share the landscape with oaks. Native Americans used fire to clear fields and open areas for agriculture, while Europeans altered the local vegetation through livestock grazing, agriculture, and logging. Only 1 percent of the pre-European forest remains intact; the remainder has been altered, cut, and replanted.

The local flora and fauna are unique in America. Thousands of years ago during the ice age advances, northern species were forced southward. When the ice retreated, many species remained in Appalachia, making the region one of the most biodiverse in the temperate realm. The many hollows and gorges in the dissected plateau provide microclimates that allow an unusual number of species to survive. But intense farming, logging, and extraction of resources have caused extinction of many species.

The Blue Ridge Province

The Blue Ridge Mountain ranges, the oldest part of the Appalachians, were created when the dominant Precambrian rocks thrusted over younger rocks. The Blue Ridge, east of the Piedmont and west of the Ridge and Valley, extends 550 miles. The northern Blue Ridge province extends into southern Pennsylvania, and the southern Blue Ridge includes the Great Smoky Mountains along the Tennessee–North Carolina border. Higher and wider in the south, the Blue Ridge varies from a single northern ridge to complex southern ridges near Asheville, North Carolina. The Blue Ridge Mountains are eighty miles wide at their widest and ascend over six thousand feet (Photo 8.2).

PHOTO 8.2. The Blue Ridge Mountains near Asheville, North Carolina. TVA coal-burning power plants have created a haze over the Blue Ridge Mountains and seriously impaired visibility.

Great Smoky Mountains

Air pollution is shrinking scenic views, damaging plants, and degrading high elevation streams and soils in the Great Smoky Mountains. Even human health is at risk. Most pollution originates outside the park and is created by power plants, industry, and automobiles.

—National Park Service website, 2009[1]

The Great Smoky Mountains are named for the natural mist—the Cherokee "place of blue smoke," and contain the nation's most visited National Park and the southeast's only national park. More than nine million visited in 2008—and therein lies the problem.

Park boundaries protect and preserve the Smokies' scenery and ecology but cannot stop pollutants, which cause air and land quality to deteriorate. Despite a number of legislative acts to protect the air, the Great Smoky Mountain National Park is being loved to death.

The former one-hundred-mile visibility has now decreased to about twenty miles on an average day. The loss of visibility is a sign of severe point source pollution (from industrial boilers, power plants, manufacturing facilities, and automobiles) and nonpoint source pollution. Coal-burning power plants generate electricity for the region but have the unintended consequence of acid rain caused by sulfur oxides and mercury, which affect the balance between ecosystems, vegetation, soils, and surface water.

Some pollution problems have been addressed. The Tennessee Valley Authority (TVA) has begun cleaning up its power plant pollution, and in 2005 emissions began to decline. Two-thirds of the power plant smokestacks have installed scrubbers that capture sulfur dioxide emissions. The remaining stacks are scheduled for conversion during the next decade. But scrubbers alone do not reduce all emissions.

Legislation and education to reduce pollution have lacked funding and staffing. Furthermore, the area around the National Park is a popular real estate investment area. Although conservation groups work to halt residential development, the surrounding counties' population grew at four times the national rate—23 percent from 1990 to 2000. Nonprofit environmental groups—Friends of the Smokies, Great Smoky Mountains Association—have contributed millions of dollars and hours of cleanup, but they still cannot solve the root of the problem: the dependence on coal.

Ridge and Valley

West of the Blue Ridge Mountains, the longitudinal Ridge and Valley ecoregion extends more than seven hundred miles from Canada to northern Alabama. The compressed and folded landscape alternates between limestone valleys and resistant sandstone and shale ridges. The regional profile resembles a rug buckling when pushed against a wall.

The easternmost valley, the Great Valley, extends from Canada to Alabama and has been one of the few north-south trending migration paths of American settlers. As settlers confronted the mountains, they followed the Great Valley to the south.

Some settled in the valley; others crossed through the Appalachians at the Cumberland Gap. The Great Valley is actually a chain of several valleys: from the Champlain Valley in the north, through the Mohawk and Hudson River valleys of New York, the Lehigh of Pennsylvania, Shenandoah and Roanoke valleys of Virginia, the Cumberland and Tennessee River valleys, and Coosa Valley at the southern end.

Appalachian Plateau

The Appalachian Plateau looks mountainous. Streams incise the green, wooded, and rolling landscape, leaving narrow winding valleys among steep-sided but level summits. The even height of the landscape is a clue to the origin of these dissected plateau "mountains."

The Appalachian Plateau is large, equal in size to the Piedmont, Blue Ridge Mountains, and Ridge and Valley combined. The plateau extends from Watertown in the Tug Hill section of New York at the base of the Adirondacks to northeastern Alabama.

Millions of years ago, sediments washed down from the original Appalachian Mountains and formed the two plateau provinces: to the north, the Allegheny Plateau covering southern New York to western West Virginia; and to the south, the Cumberland Plateau. The elevation rises from about one thousand feet on the western edge to three thousand feet at the Allegheny front. The four-thousand-foot-high Catskills, located about one hundred miles northwest of New York City, are the Appalachian Plateau's highest "mountains."

Allegheny Plateau

Glaciation divided the two Allegheny Plateaus. The glaciated northern plateau of northeastern Ohio, northwestern Pennsylvania, and southern New York is rounded, eroded uplands filled with small lakes and stony fields. Seventy percent of the glaciated plateau is forested, while the remaining area is devoted to dairying. The rugged landscape and higher elevations of the southern, unglaciated plateau is a transition to the Cumberland. European settlement left behind a legacy of irresponsible logging, mining, and waste, but the region still has potential for recreation and resources if managed in alliance with its natural ecology.

Regional rivers formed the rocky gorges of the southern plateau. The Kanawha is a major industrial river, while the New and Gauley rivers are both famous for white water adventures. In the glaciated Alleghenies, streams dissect and separate the Catskill, Shawanagunk, and Pocono ranges. The aptly named Finger Lakes district in upstate New York was formed by glaciation and is a transitional area between the Mohawk Valley and the northern edge of the glaciated Alleghenies.

Cumberland Plateau

The dissected and coal-laden Cumberland Plateau includes western West Virginia, eastern Kentucky and Tennessee, and northern Alabama. The Cumberland Gap cuts through the plateau into the Interior Plateaus of Kentucky and Tennessee.

BOX 8.1 COVES

The Great Smoky Mountain coves are small, oval-shaped, grass-floor valleys. Precambrian rocks completely surround the exposed and younger limestone and shale **coves**. Cove microclimates support an array of plant and animal species that differ from the surrounding area.

Cades Cove, Tennessee, is the most famous Appalachian cove. Cades Cove was once a junction of Cherokee pathways, but in 1820 it was settled as a farming community that prospered working the fertile limestone soil. Unfortunately, the community was forced to abandon their homes when they were taken by eminent domain in 1932. They had been promised that they could remain in their homes for life.

Today, Cades Cove is one of the most-visited sites within the Great Smoky Mountains National Park (Photo 8.3).

PHOTO 8.3. Cades Cove, Great Smoky Mountain National Park, Tennessee. The Carter Shields cabin is set against the wooded area. All cove residents were made to believe their community was safe when the park was created, but they were forcibly evicted by eminent domain in 1932.

In the Cumberland, elevation separated the people and the resources. The people live in the forested and rural bottomlands of the narrow, V-shaped valleys (Photo 8.4), and coal and logging companies own the higher-elevation resources.

Interior Low Plateaus

The Interior Low Plateau consists of the Highland Rim (Pennyroyal in Kentucky) escarpment surrounding the low-lying Lexington Plain and Nashville Basin. The region begins south of the Ohio River and extends more or less to the Tennessee River. The Interior Plateau vegetation regimes include the hardwoods of the Highland Rim, and in the basins the nearly impenetrable **canebrake** thickets composed of America's native bamboo. By 1799 the canebrakes had yielded to the axe and become grass and pasture lands.

Lexington and the Lexington Plain received their names in 1775 when patriotic hunters camping in the Kentucky clearing heard of the incipient revolutionary battle and commemorated the event by naming the clearing after the Massachusetts town. The Lexington Plain extends north to Cincinnati and west toward Louisville. The undulating limestone plain was transformed from a tangled canebrake to the excellent Kentucky bluegrass—an excellent and palatable turf grass for livestock.

The Nashville Basin in the central Tennessee rolling hills covers about six thousand square miles from Kentucky to the Alabama border. Karst topography underlies the former tobacco-growing region; today livestock (cattle and poultry) dominate farm production. The southern basin is also home to the Tennessee walking horse farms, although urban sprawl now envelops much of the land.

The karst terrain of underground streams, sinkholes, springs, or caves is the result of chemical weathering when slightly acidic rainwater dissolves limestone. The Interior Plateau's limestone layer has created more than a hundred caves, including the largest and best known, Mammoth Cave in Kentucky.

The subsurface water follows underground paths before reappearing along the valley floors. The water seeps and enlarges porous limestone fissures and develops an interconnected network of subsurface cavities and holes where rainwater

BOX 8.2 COAL

Coal was created when tropical plants decayed, compressed, and heated over millions of years. In the Appalachian Plateau, the repeated advance and retreat of seas 200 to 360 million years ago transformed the plants into peat layers, and with time and more pressure added by overburden and soil, harder coals formed. The coal ranks are **peat** (the softest and youngest), **lignite**, **subbituminous**, **bituminous**, and **anthracite** (the hardest). In the United States, 90 percent of the coal is subbituminous or bituminous (Map 8.1).

Canada and even more so the United States have abundant supplies of coal. Coal in Appalachia is either anthracite (found near Scranton, Pennsylvania) or bituminous (in the Appalachian Plateau and some Ridge and Valley areas). Appalachian coal is much older and more compressed than the other major North American coal deposit, Powder River Basin subbituminous coal. Lignite is located in Texas, Montana, North Dakota, Illinois, and the Gulf Coast. The low-rank and high-sulfur lignite is less attractive environmentally, but it has been used locally. Canadian coal ranges from bituminous to lignite and is located in the Prairie region and along the Canadian Rockies.

Plant types, the depth and chemistry of the water, and its organic and inorganic constituents differentiate the coal ranks. Anthracite has the fewest impurities and contains 86 to 98 percent carbon. When the Ridge and Valley folded, the heat and pressure applied to the bituminous coal turned it into the harder anthracite. Anthracite was the most popularly used coal until the 1930s when the Depression, cheaper fuels, and labor costs shifted coal production to the bituminous fields of the Cumberland Plateau.

Appalachian coal was formed in brackish swamps. Organic matter was deposited and accumulated in the stagnant water, forming the partially carbonized plant matter known as peat. Over time, layers of sediment buried the peat, subjected it to heat and pressure, and transformed it into harder coal. Appalachian bituminous coal, especially in the Cumberland Plateau, is sandwiched in flat layers: the region did not undergo the heat and pressure of the folded landscape of the Ridge and Valley, so the coal beds were less developed and softer than Scranton anthracite.

Bituminous coal was the source of power during the steel-making era. Its 45–86 percent carbon content produces less heat than anthracite. Most bituminous coal is laden with sulfur, a polluting impurity. Subbituminous coal of the Powder River Basin in Wyoming has a carbon content of 35–45 percent and lesser heat value than bituminous. But its lower sulfur content makes it the environmentally preferred and less polluting coal in the twenty-first century. Lignite has a low carbon value, 25–35 percent, and a lower heat value than subbituminous.

Coal when mined has many impurities. One of the most distinctive is sulfur content. Coal-fired steam plants convert sulfur to sulfur dioxide, a pollutant that causes acid rain. The higher the sulfur content, the more polluting. Appalachian high-sulfur coal must be "cleaned" to meet clean air standards. However, Appalachian bituminous coal is harder and more heat efficient than lower-sulfur subbituminous coal.

Coal is a carbon sink—a reservoir for carbon dioxide (CO_2). Stored CO_2 creates a balancing feedback loop that keeps the atmosphere within a steady state temperature range. As CO_2 is released by burning coal, it upsets the balance and becomes a major cause of climate change.

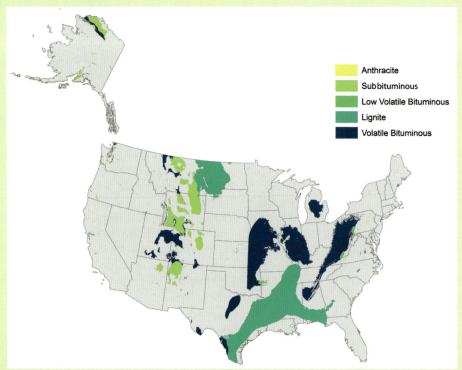

Anthracite
Subbituminous
Low Volatile Bituminous
Lignite
Volatile Bituminous

MAP 8.1. Coal Bodies in the United States. There are no significant deposits in Hawai`i.

PHOTO 8.4. Cumberland Plateau in Raleigh County, West Virginia. The "mountains" are heavily dissected, forested plateaus of roughly equal elevation.

replenishes groundwater. Karst has little ability to filter contaminants, so trash, farm waste, microbial contaminants, and septic systems pollute groundwater. Controlling pollution sources and treating water to remove microbial pollution protect karst waterways.

Water

Water is plentiful in Appalachia. The rivers, often older than the mountains, cut east-west wind and water gaps across the grain of the Appalachians. For example, the Delaware River's **water gap** carved a gorge through a ridge of the Ridge and Valley. **Wind gaps** were formed by water but are now dry. Gap usage has evolved from native trails, to forts protecting settlers from Indian attacks, to cities, roads, and railways.

Northern rivers in Appalachia—the Delaware, Susquehanna, Potomac, and James—have their headwaters on the Allegheny Plateau and empty into the Atlantic. The earliest European settlement occurred at the river mouths. Most southern rivers— the Nolichucky, Holston—flow to the west and into the Tennessee and Ohio rivers. Settlers followed the river valleys through the Appalachians, and communities developed around salt, coal, and chemical resources.

The Tennessee River headwaters in the Great Smoky Mountains flow more than eight hundred miles through the Cumberland and Interior plateaus to the Ohio River at Paducah, Kentucky. In 1935, President Roosevelt's New Deal program established the **Tennessee Valley Authority (TVA)**, building dams to tame the river, relieve flooding, stop erosion of topsoil, generate power, and provide navigation and recreational uses. The TVA became part of and the nation's largest public power

company. The goals of the TVA were ambitious but ultimately unachievable.

The TVA has successfully improved year-round navigation and offered affordable electricity and economic growth, but the multiple goals of the TVA system are often incompatible. TVA dams control the river and halt floods, but the river no longer free-flows but has effectively become a series of lakes (Map 8.2). Providing electricity and recreation and halting floods has also impaired water quality. Dividing water between industrial, agricultural, and urban use has become a serious water management issue.

Dams and flow diversions redirect about two-thirds of southern Appalachian water for industrial use. The TVA supports eleven coal-burning power plants, which supply over 60 percent of TVA electricity. Nuclear, hydropower, wind turbines, and solar installations supply the remainder. The coal-burning plants degrade the regional water and biota. For example, in December 2008, an earthen coal ash slurry dam in Kingston, Tennessee, collapsed and dumped over a billion gallons of watery sludge containing toxic heavy metals into the river. The spill flooded nearby homes and fields and prompted a national investigation on unregulated and unlined dams.

Settlement along the Central Appalachian Ohio, Kanawha, and Monongahela rivers began in 1774 at the Great Buffalo Lick along the Kanawha River. While salt is common today, it has not always been so. Sodium and chlorine are two essential elements for plant and animal life. Many of the old buffalo trails led to salt licks and evolved into important trade routes. The salt industry declined after the Civil War, when drilling reached richer salt brines, but the brines matured into a chemical product industry. The processing of brines and coal-burning power

BOX 8.3 CANEBRAKES

The pre-European river bottom landscape of the Interior Plateau basins and southern Appalachia was covered in tangles of native cane species—bamboo, sugarcane. The thick and seemingly impenetrable canebrakes were food for bison during prairie winters; were used variously by Native Americans, especially Cherokee basket weavers; were hiding places for attacking Native Americans; and were hunting grounds for intrepid frontiersmen.

American settlers cleared the canebrakes by fire or grazing. In one of the curious miracles of ecologic succession, the invasive species that replaced many of the canebrakes was bluegrass, offering an entirely different landscape than did the canebrakes. The bluegrass "prairie" was welcoming to the pioneers and encouraged the continued settlement of the cleared canebrake area on the Interior Plateau. However, canebrakes filled an ecological niche—curbing erosion, mitigating flood damage, and serving as wildlife habitat. Today many people see the canebrakes as an impaired ecosystem and have encouraged preserving and expanding the remaining canebrakes as valuable wildlife habitats.

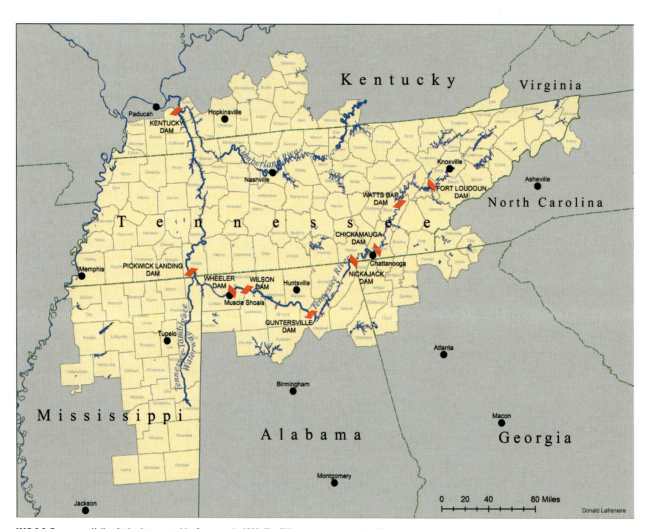

MAP 8.2. Tennessee Valley Authority, created by Congress in 1933. The TVA was meant to provide flood control, navigation, and electrical generation for the Tennessee Valley, but it has degraded water quality.

plants has polluted the Kanawha River and the Valley of West Virginia. Fallout, or "snow," from the chemical industry has led to the Kanawha Valley being nicknamed "Chemical Valley."

Since the late 1970s, grassroots organizations have urged cleaning up the waste dumps, dioxin, and other toxins discharged into the rivers, and results have been encouraging, although the work is still incomplete. Enforcing the 1972 **Clean Water Act (CWA)**, which federally governed water pollution, and Environmental Protection Agency (EPA) regulations made 20 to 30 percent of the polluted waterways suitable for human use.

Climate

The temperate continental Appalachian climate receives the third-highest precipitation, behind the Pacific Northwest and Gulf Coast. The windward western plateau receives between forty and fifty inches of precipitation, while the leeward rain shadow in the Ridge and Valley receives thirty to forty-five inches. About one-quarter of total precipitation falls in the form of snow. The Blue Ridge Mountains bordering the Piedmont receive the most rain in the eastern United States, about 80 inches annually. The growing season varies between 140 days in the north and higher elevations and 205 days in the south and in the lower elevations.

Historical Geography and Settlement

Native Americans

The earliest Appalachian settlement site, Russell Cave in Madison County, Alabama, was first inhabited by Native Americans around 6000 BCE. Several other Alabama and Kentucky cave sites have been dated to this period.

During the Woodland period (500 BCE to 1000 CE), settlements in the Mississippi and Ohio Valleys included the Adena and the Hopewell, who were known for their distinctive burial mounds and ornate jewelry. They practiced agriculture, built shelters and earthworks, and made pottery. Their extensive trading network extended through the Midwest and into the Deep South. For unexplained reasons, their culture declined around 1000 CE.

Algonquian tribes occupied the central Appalachians, and southern Appalachia was dominated by the Cherokee, who were linguistically related to the Iroquois. The Iroquoian Confederacy—a nation based more on diplomacy than on warfare—was strong throughout the eastern half of America and overpowered the Algonquian.

After European contact, the Cherokee organized the "Five Civilized Tribes" and adopted many "white" ways, although it ultimately did not protect their homelands. When gold was discovered on Cherokee soil, settlers encroached on their lands. The Indian Removal Act of 1830 forced abandonment of their Georgia Appalachian home territory so that whites could settle and mine their land. The Cherokee journey to their new home in Oklahoma became the infamous Trail of Tears (see Chapter 14).

The British promised to protect Native lands from encroaching settlers, so many Native Americans supported the British during the American Revolutionary War. After the war, the British abandoned their native treaties and relinquished their territory to the Americans.

European Arrival

Most Appalachian settlers arrived via the Mid-Atlantic hearth, but by the time they arrived the best land near the eastern seaboard was occupied, or the new settlers conflicted with local inhabitants. The Scots-Irish settled in the plateau valleys, and the Germans settled the more level farmland.

After the French and Indian Wars (1763), the British forbade white settlement west of the Appalachian crest in order to reduce Native war costs and control the colonial economy. The colonists objected, as they felt the war expedited settlement into Appalachia. For a short time, the land south of the Ohio River acted as an unsettled buffer zone between the natives and white settlers.

The Great Valley was easily accessible, because few permanent Native Americans occupied it at this moment in history. The Great Valley had been settled for thousands of years, but just prior to European arrival it evolved into a transitional buffer zone for Native tribes who used it for hunting. This quirk allowed Europeans to settle without fear of Native attacks—unlike western Pennsylvania and Ohio, where attacks on white settlements were common.

The Great Valley continued as a buffer zone, only now between Virginians, hostile natives, and the French further west. Wealthy Tidewater and Piedmont speculators received Great Valley land grants, which were subdivided and sold to land-hungry German, Scots-Irish, and Quaker settlers. Between 1745 and 1775, the Shenandoah Valley population rose from ten thousand to thirty-five thousand.

After the American Revolution, Indian attacks eased, and the region was settled. Many war veterans were paid with land, and by the end of the eighteenth century, population doubled again. Squatters who could not afford Great Valley land settled backcountry areas of western Pennsylvania, West Virginia, and the Carolinas. Good farmland was sparse in the mountainous Appalachian Plateau, but the land supported livestock and hunting grounds.

The most natural path through the Appalachians crossed the western tip of Virginia into Kentucky: the Cumberland Gap—where Daniel Boone cut the Wilderness Road for Judge Richard Henderson, a speculator seeking to set up his own trans-Appalachian empire. In 1775, he petitioned for recognition as the fourteenth colony.

During the late 1700s, trans-Appalachian pioneers ignored British settlement prohibitions, followed Boone's Cumberland Gap trail, and settled the grassy Nashville and Lexington basins. By 1800, the Ohio River Bluegrass south to the Nashville Basin was a continuous zone of settlement.

Appalachian Plateau settlement remained insulated well into the twentieth century. Although they seldom adopted the capitalistic interests of the rest of the nation, the Appalachian economy and culture were acknowledged as a national treasure, first because they maintained tradition, but later because they continued to live in what others strived for—a local economy. But modern influences have seeped into the region.

The major influence was World War II, when urban amenities and jobs in the war plants of Pittsburgh, Cleveland, and Detroit caused the "Great Migration." The migrants assimilated into the general culture, but they still hark back to Appalachia and often return to visit and later to retire.

Cultural Perspectives

Appalachia derives its name from the Apalache Indians, who lived in northern Florida but whose domain extended into southern Appalachia, and their name was applied to the entire mountain range. Scots-Irish, Celtic, English, and Germans created an Appalachian culture characterized by isolation, individualism, and distrust of government.

Folk Culture

Many Appalachian country immigrants settled in close proximity with one another. The largest ethnic group was the Scots-Irish, who often arrived as indentured servants and worked to pay their passage. When their term of service expired, they migrated to find their own land. The best land was spoken for or too expensive, so they moved to the less desirable land in the narrow stream-cut valleys of the plateaus. The area was remote, and in many ways remains so today. Although the terrain separated the population from most American progress, it tended to produce close-knit communities sharing common traits.

Over the past two hundred years, many of those traits remain intact. Among the retained traits are a strong sense of community, settlement patterns, dialects, music, food, and vernacular architecture. The unique regional culture remained separate from the rest of the nation until modern communication and transportation infiltrated. During the Great Depression, the TVA generated hydropower electricity and drew industry to this job-hungry area, connecting portions of Appalachia with mainstream American society. Later, in the 1960s, roads connected Appalachia with the surrounding regions.

The isolated small mountain towns fostered a sense of community that was once common throughout most of America, but was lost as towns grew into anonymous cities. In Appalachia, towns often struggled to survive, but surviving towns are filled with people who have grown and lived their whole life within the confines of the "holler"—the narrow valleys.

West Virginia, the only state entirely within Appalachia, still has this sense of community—a sense of survival among friends and family—but economic conditions have forced divides. Today, neighborhoods can be divided between those who are "Friends of Coal"—the few who still have high-paying coal industry jobs—and those who are fighting the long-term social and environmental damage caused by the coal industry. Families are torn when on one hand the father is working in a coal-processing plant, and on the other hand the mother watches daily as her child returns home from the only school in the valley with headaches or a bloody nose caused by the polluted and contaminated location. The father refuses to quit what both know is the best-paying job in the valley, but he watches as his child weakens.

Such is the case in West Virginia's Coal River Valley at Marsh Fork Elementary School. The school sits within feet of a coal silo where chemicals are sprayed on the coal for transport, and within a few hundred feet of a massive earthen dam holding billions of gallons of coal sludge containing the toxic chemicals removed from the coal (Photo 8.5). The coal company has refused to rebuild the school at an appropriate site that is nearby but out of the way of the coal sludge. A grant from the Annenberg Foundation in 2010 will allow a new school to be built at a new site.

The people of Appalachia have inhabited the region for generations. They value their community bonds and family more than they value the typical American Dream of affluent living, yet they are being forced to choose between the health of their family and their bank account.

Within the valleys are groups who have maintained their community and civic spirit and are protesting the continued assaults on the landscape and the people. They maintain and honor the many other cultural characteristics they share—their language, music, food ways, and heritage.

The colorful Southern Mountain dialect heard in Appalachian hollers is a remnant of seventeenth-century Elizabethan English. The Scots-Irish, Celts, and English who brought this dialect to the mountains built upon it in isolated circumstances and, until the twentieth century, had little access to American speech patterns developing in the surrounding area. The use of strange words and grammar ("I done finished," "his'n," "her'n," "I reckon hit don't never . . .") , often denigrated by other Americans, is a wealth of seventeenth-century linguistics, now cherished by those who revel in the origins of language.[2]

Traditional Appalachian music combines English ballads and American contexts that maintain an oral tradition of personal historical narratives. Musical influences were American religious gospel and African call and response. The fiddle initiated the music, later augmented by the banjo and then the guitar. Dance revolved around the reel, adapted from the Scottish highlands. Each area within Appalachia developed its own sound, but they melded as transportation and communication improved in the twentieth century. After the Great Depression and the beginning of commercial bluegrass, the sound evolved into country and western, but the hills and hollers still resound in the folk music played in impromptu gatherings.

Before Appalachian music became commercial, players would congregate at meetings where the main compensation was food. In Appalachia, food is more than sustenance; it is an act of sharing, generosity, and care. Appalachian food is as traditional and unpretentious as the dialect and the music, and it is influenced by the food ways of the original immigrants.

PHOTO 8.5. Marsh Fork Elementary School, Raleigh County, West Virginia. A coal-processing plant silo was erected directly behind the school. The silo is where railcars are sprayed with chemicals to limit coal dust during travel. The mountain saddle in the background is the location of a billion-gallon earthen dam holding coal waste sludge. NGO groups successfully fought to remove the silo and the plant, and to restore health to students sickened by the nearby toxins.

Appalachian meals center on corn—grits and cornbread—sweetened with honey and sorghum molasses. Meat favors either pork or hunted game. Local foods abound: rhubarb, sassafras, and ramps—the garlicky spinach-like shoots that flourish in the spring. Preserving food is still done by canning, pickling, drying, and salting. Although most residents now have electricity and refrigerators, these conveniences have been common for just over a generation; old traditions die hard in the hollers.

In Appalachia the quintessential one-room, single-pen log cabin flourished, surrounded by a cluster of rural buildings—corncribs, stock barns, and springhouses. The prototypical pioneer house, the log cabin originated in Delaware but was popularized in Appalachia and then diffused over the landscape.

Life was hard on the Appalachian backwoods frontier prior to the extraction of coal. Agricultural self-sufficiency ended when struggling farmers, eager to eliminate some of the rigor of life, moved to mine coal and live in the coal company towns.

Moonshine

To fund the military, an excise tax was added to alcoholic beverages in 1790. The tax resulted in the western Pennsylvania distillery revolt called the Whiskey Rebellion. The rebellion collapsed when troops quelled the dissenters, but the indirect result was the illegal **moonshine** industry. Working by the light of the moon, moonshiners evaded tax revenuers. The secluded hollows of Appalachia were a perfect location to practice making moonshine and to add value and longevity to the corn crop. Familiarity with the land was important: Moonshiners knew where to hide their stills and how to flavor their potent concoction with plant species from the hills.

The Scots-Irish brought over their customary drink—corn whiskey, a clear-as–water, 100+ proof drink—described as "swallowing sugar that was on fire." Although Germans, Irish, and English also participated, it was the Scots-Irish who dominated the moonshine-based barter economy.

The heyday of moonshine was during the twentieth-century Prohibition era. Producing or providing alcohol was a path to wealth during Prohibition. The bootleg mafia thrived, and fortunes were made smuggling illegal alcohol into the country, while whiskey moonshiners supplied the local country with their commodity.

Moonshine continues to be made in Appalachia. This region has many dry counties because of religious convictions, but illicit distilling is practiced more in dry than in wet counties.

Cultural Isolation and the Second Great Awakening[3]

The **Second Great Awakening** diffused from Europe to the Americas in the late eighteenth and antebellum nineteenth century. Evangelical conversion inspired Welsh, Scottish, Irish, and English immigrants to reinterpret the formal, elite practices of Protestant churches for the common man. The Methodist, Baptist, and Quaker religions characterized the religious revival and evangelicalism by reinvigorating stale, traditional methods to fit the settlers' real world. For example, Presbyterians required ordained ministers, which were in short supply in the New World, while the new religions bypassed official ordination, so backcountry circuit riders and farmer-preachers who felt the call could preach for less strict denominations.

The Second Great Awakening religion held the Appalachians together, despite their physical isolation from the rest

BOX 8.4 APPALACHIAN COAL COMPANY TOWNS

Steel, mining, and textile industries often built where all real estate was owned by the company. These company towns were typically isolated from other urban centers. Residents of company towns were employed by the industry sponsoring the town. The town lived for its industry. If the industry closed, the town usually went into decline. While some company towns were built as utopian visions (e.g., Hershey, Pennsylvania), many earned a reputation for exploiting workers.

The coal camp town thrived from the beginning of the 1900s until 1927, when the first coal boom ended. Prior to company towns, settlement was scattered throughout Appalachia and often far from the mines. Hastily erected coal camp towns solved housing shortages for mining areas. By the 1920s, each West Virginia and Kentucky coal-mining county had twenty or thirty new company towns.

Companies built identical houses in the industrial landscape for practical and economic reasons (Photo 8.6). The Appalachian hill people luxuriated in the five-room houses, which were much larger than the typical unfinished log cabins that were common. Local unskilled labor—farmers thrilled to earn daily wages of $1.50—built the towns using lumber from nearby forests. Appalachian farmers, black laborers, and eastern and southern European immigrants rapidly populated the towns

and earned stable and relatively high wages working in the mines. In the 1920s, during Appalachia's booming coal-mining era, up to 80 percent of the miners lived in the new towns and purchased goods at the only available outlet, the overpriced company store.

Exploitative company towns and the malevolent actions of company agents were exemplified by the violent union history of Matewan, West Virginia. During the 1920s, company policy forbade workers to organize to secure rights. The Matewan Massacre occurred on May 19, 1920, when company-hired detectives evicted union families from company-owned homes. The day ended with a melee between local residents and the detectives that left ten people dead and many wounded.

The company town flourished as long as an area was isolated and off the transportation grid. At their height in 1930, company towns were home to about 3 percent of the national population. By World War II, urban job opportunities opened for residents, drawing them away from Appalachia. Company towns declined when coal companies went out of business or laid off workers, and as workers became more mobile. Companies divested themselves of their real estate holdings by selling the houses to their inhabitants, and the towns became independent towns or unincorporated areas.

PHOTO 8.6. Company Town, Prenter, West Virginia. This company town was typical of the many coal camps in the state. When the local coal mining was no longer profitable, the mine was shut down and the homes were sold for a nominal fee to the residents.

of the country. Long camp meetings—multiple-act preachers or bands, crowds of people of similar background, and dancing and singing—sustained cultural ties. During the revivals, people vowed to change their lives. The first stirrings of the abolition, women's rights, and temperance movements can be traced to the awakening and contributed to the crisis that led to the Civil War.

Regional Life

Population

Appalachian ethnic stability created a multigenerational tie to the land, which was broken during the twentieth century when many migrated to Midwestern industrial cities for jobs. Often, though, the migrants returned "home," either to join family during the Depression or, later, to retire.

West Virginia provides an ethnic snapshot of the entire region. The earliest settlers were German or Scots-Irish, followed by a contingent of English, and some French Huguenots. In 2004, half the population of West Virginia claimed heritage in these groups, with another 15 percent who call themselves "Americans." Less than 1 percent is foreign born, compared to a national average of 11.1 percent. In 2000, 71 percent of West Virginia's residents were born in their home state, compared to an U.S. average of 60 percent. The racial makeup of the state was 94 percent white (2010); the next largest group was blacks, who comprised 3.4 percent of the population and lived in segregated towns in extreme southern West Virginia (Chart 8.1). The black population was recruited from the South during the nineteenth century to construct railroads. Many stayed to work in the coal mines.

Per capita income in West Virginia is $21,232, compared to a U.S. average of $27,334 (2010). Individuals below the poverty line constituted 17.4 percent of the population (2010), higher than the 13.8 percent figure for the United States as a whole.

Population Decline

After the initial European settlement, few others migrated to Appalachia. Population increased, with more births than deaths. A slow but steady growth from 1910 to 1950 (39 percent) was about half the national rate of growth (68 percent). States with Appalachian and non-Appalachian sectors grew more rapidly in the non-Appalachian sectors. Throughout the twentieth century, Appalachian population growth lagged behind the nation.

Coalfield jobs were plentiful during the early twentieth century, and many worked in the mines. But coal fuel energy lost favor to oil, resulting in fewer jobs and stagnated population growth from 1950 to 1960: The number of jobs fell by 15 percent, while the nation's employment expanded by 17 percent. Scarcity of work caused more than two million working-age people to emigrate from Appalachia during the 1950s. Population in many Appalachian counties has declined in every decade since 1950, although the largest drop in the region was between 1950 and 1970 (Table 8.1). Compounding the job loss problem, in 1960 only 11.6 percent of the population over the age of twenty-five had as much as a fifth-grade education, which was far below the U.S. average.

In the 1960s, the distressed region became a subject of economic development programs. The Tennessee Valley Authority (TVA) and **Appalachian Regional Commission (ARC)** were enacted to boost economic growth.

Alleghenies

After 1900, population in the Alleghenies expanded and retracted following the movement of manufacturing jobs. In upstate New York, Binghamton, the major Allegheny city in the 1920s, was known for its shoe manufacturing, but the 2010 population of 47,376 was less than half its 1920 population of 110,000, and 27.8 percent (2010) were living below the poverty line. The continued loss of manufacturing jobs has crippled this

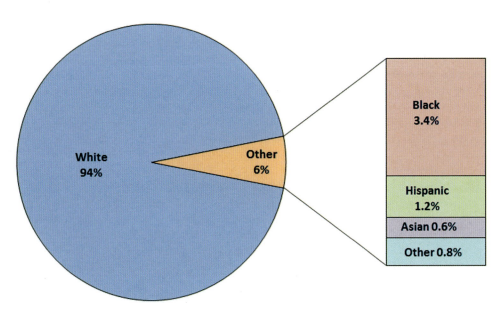

CHART 8.1. West Virginia Population, 2010

TABLE 8.1. Population Change in Appalachia and the United States, 1950–1970

Area	Number (000)	Percent change
Appalachia	840	4.7
Non-Appalachia	51,046	38.2

Source: U.S. Census

once-thriving area. The city has lost 48 percent of its factory jobs since 1990.

Traditional and Sustainable Cities

There are no large cities in Appalachia; the dissected plateaus and resultant narrow valleys preclude large agglomerations. The largest cities, Pittsburgh and Birmingham, are at opposite ends of the region. Both cities are nodes for regional resource convergence and distribution. While both have coal legacies, the cities that grew on coal mining were Scranton and Wilkes-Barre in Pennsylvania, where the first coal rush began.

Anthracite Life and Population

In the early nineteenth century, wood was the dominant fuel, and hard-to-ignite anthracite was shunned. But industrial and residential growth had deforested the eastern seaboard and Appalachia; another fuel source was needed. Technology and transportation innovations enabled anthracite to become the popular fuel. Transportation matured from canals to railroads during the period of anthracite production, and by 1900 all anthracite was shipped by rail. Anthracite mining employed 175,000 at its 1914 peak.

Today, fewer than two thousand people work in anthracite mines, and the loss of jobs has caused a regional exodus of educated adults. The population of the anthracite county of Lackawanna in northeastern Pennsylvania dropped from a high of 310,000 in 1930 to 214,437 in 2010. The anthracite-mining cities are Scranton and Wilkes-Barre. Both now have more people over the age of sixty-five than the national average, and fewer under the age of eighteen (Table 8.2).

The region continues to struggle, losing most of its jobs and much of the working population, while the land and water have suffered environmental damage from coal waste and **acid mine drainage** pollutes the groundwater and rivers, leaching iron and sulfates, making it more acidic than vinegar. Hence, water quality is lowered and aquatic life is killed.

Many small Appalachian communities are connected by generational and neighborhood networks where barter-oriented and personal economies maintain elements of sustainability that have been lost in larger towns. For example, Coal River Mountain Watch in Whitesville, West Virginia, is composed of local residents who have banded together to stop mountaintop removal but also provide community support. The core groups are lifetime residents of the valley who are there for each other. While the few remaining residents are strong supporters of their communities, towns such as Whitesville are empty, polluted shells of a once prosperous region.

Birmingham, Alabama

(2010 pop. 212,237; CSA 1,128,047)

The South had few antebellum cities, but the postbellum economy fostered the growth of new cities, such as Birmingham, Alabama's largest city. Although Birmingham can be called a southern city, it is geographically situated near Appalachia and its resources.

In 1871 Birmingham, established at the crossing of two railroads, was at the confluence of ore, coking coal, and limestone flux, all important resources for the development of a Southern steel industry. The city flourished as the "Pittsburgh of the South" because of accessible resources and low labor costs. But in 1901, U.S. Steel formed the **Pittsburgh Plus** pricing policy, forcing all steel to be priced based on its distance from Pittsburgh. The policy halted Birmingham's growth and locational advantage in steel production.

In 1907 U.S. Steel purchased the Birmingham steelworks, but although people rejoiced at the time thinking their jobs were saved, the purchase was made to eliminate competition. The Birmingham steelworks never grew as people expected. Birmingham's locational advantage was eliminated and the local steel industry was shut down. Government regulators rescinded the Pittsburgh Plus policy in 1924, but the damage to Birmingham's steel industry was complete (Photo 8.8). Today steel is a small part of the local economy.

The population within Birmingham has fallen about one-quarter since its maximum in 1960, but the surrounding suburbs have grown substantially. Birmingham has diversified into banking and to medical biotechnology research at its University of Alabama campus, and it is one of the cosmopolitan "New South" cities.

Pittsburgh, Pennsylvania

(2010 pop. 305,704; CSA 2,356,285)

Pittsburgh, the largest city near the Appalachian coalfields, was a site waiting for a city to happen. Established on the Appalachian Plateau at the headwaters of the Ohio River where the Allegheny and Monongahela ("the Mon") rivers meet,

BOX 8.5 CENTRALIA, PENNSYLVANIA

The main lesson from Centralia is not in the story of a fire; it is in the story of a coal town. Until the danger was obvious to everyone, Centralia was just like 50 other anthracite towns—old houses, a flabby economy, a broken landscape, and an aging population. The fire was just one more problem, getting in line with all the others, and the response was the same: convince yourself that the town is worth staying in and prove to yourself that you can stay.

—Ben Marsh, 1987*

About twenty miles south of Scranton, the small town of Centralia had eleven hundred residents in 1962. In 2010, the population was ten. The cause of the depopulating of Centralia was a 1962 trash fire in the mineshafts below the town. The legal trash fire began in an underground mine and soon lit a coal seam. Millions of dollars have been spent to stop the fire, but it continues to burn, leaking carbon monoxide into homes and causing sinkholes in areas where the fire has burned out. Town residents were in denial of the fire danger for years, until they sickened and gradually evacuated the town. A few remain, along with steaming cracks in the yards (Photo 8.7).

PHOTO 8.7. Slow-Burning Coal Fire at Centralia, Pennsylvania. This town of more than a thousand residents was situated in the center of the anthracite mining fields of eastern Pennsylvania. In 1962, a trash fire set in a mine caught in a coal seam and has continued to burn emitting lethal carbon monoxide and other toxins. The town was largely relocated by eminent domain. The current population of twenty remains despite the evictions.

* Ben Marsh, "Continuity and Decline in the Anthracite Towns of Pennsylvania," *Annals of the Association of American Geographers* 77, no. 3 (September 1987): 337–52.

TABLE 8.2. Changes in Population in Anthracite-Producing Cities

	Percent change 1990–2000	Population 2000	Population 2010	Percent change 2000–2010	Percent under 18	Percent over 65
Scranton, Pennsylvania	−6.7	76,415	76,089	−0.4	20.4 (24.5)	16.4 (12.6)
Wilkes-Barre, Pennsylvania	−9.5	43,123	41,498	−3.8	20.3 (24.5)	16.2 (12.6)

Source: U.S. Census
Note: Numbers in parentheses are U.S. averages.

PHOTO 8.8. Steel Production at Birmingham, Alabama. The proximity to raw materials for the steel industry fostered the initial growth of the city, which built a southern steel industry that competed with Pittsburgh. However, Pittsburgh and U.S. Steel passed a "Pittsburgh Plus" pricing policy in 1907 that added fees to eliminate southern shipping advantages. Today the city is home to the University of Alabama and has diversified.

Pittsburgh is an excellent example of a site-and-situation city. The site has been so important that it exchanged hands (and forts) between the British and French several times within a century, before it became the jumping-off point for western settlement. The town supplied boats and goods to pioneers heading west on the Ohio River. During the Industrial Revolution, Pittsburgh's steel industry growth was also due to nearby resources—importing Appalachian coal and Great Lakes ore and limestone.

Pittsburgh's "Mon" became a world-renowned, steel-based industrial complex. For a century, Pittsburgh was the heart of the steel-producing region, until cheaper labor, foreign competition, and declining demand slowed production in the 1970s. By the 1980s, over 150,000 jobs were lost, and the steel-making capacity had declined from 66 percent of the national output to less than 10 percent. Smaller specialty mills have replaced the large steel mills in the local area, as well as in Youngstown, Steubenville-Weirton, and Cleveland, but few jobs have been saved.

Pittsburgh's twenty-first-century renaissance relied on technology and many nonprofit organizations (with a strong arts and culture sector), and it was transformed into a medical center capped by the Carnegie-Mellon Institute. However, its population has continued to decline, losing 8.6 percent in the city between 2000 and 2010.

However, Pittsburgh, an Appalachian and Rust Belt city, has done the most in the Rust Belt sector to make it sustainable. While still suffering from the Midwestern city malaise of the continuing mentality of the original Industrial Revolution, it has adopted strong policies for building LEED-certified buildings, as well as offering incentives for retrofitting other buildings, including homes.

Kanawha Valley—Ashland (Kentucky); Huntington, Ironton (Ohio)

(2010 MSA 287,702); Charleston (West Virginia)
(2010 pop. 51,400 ; MSA 304,284)

The cities at the nexus of Ohio, Kentucky, and West Virginia lie in the Kanawha and Ohio valleys and share a common manufacturing base in chemical, nickel, oil refining, and steelmaking. The region's economy evolved from salt processing to chemical production.

Huntington provided nickel alloys, while Ashland and Ironton have been involved in steel and oil refining. Numerous coal-based, electric-power-generating plants and pulp chip mills also lie along the Ohio River and the Kanawha Valley rivers. The industries polluted this area, combining acid rain with air and water pollution. Cleanup has been an ongoing process.

Nashville, Tennessee

(2010 pop. 626,681; CSA 1,589,934)

Nashville, known today as "music city" for its country music stars and recording companies, was founded in 1779 in the Interior Plateau at the junction of water routes and the buffalo trail that became the Cumberland **Trace**. Nashville is a major southern city located on the fertile Nashville basin where Native Americans, French fur trappers, and settlers hunted and grazed cattle. Today in addition to the music industry, the city is an important meat, cotton, and tobacco-processing area.

Chattanooga, Tennessee

(2010 pop. 167,674; CSA 528,143)

Located in southeastern Tennessee on the Tennessee River at the transition between the Ridge and Valley and Cumberland

Plateau, Chattanooga evolved from a Native American settlement site to a steel-manufacturing dynamo, until its decline from the 1960s through 1980s. The city's industrial past caused Chattanooga to be named "America's Dirtiest City" in 1969. Industrial pollution, superfund sites, layoffs, and racial tensions tarnished the city, but decisions to rise again, led by sustainable choices to make the city livable, have reinvigorated Chattanooga. The TVA headquarters and several insurance and banking companies have located there.

Beginning in 1984, city leaders met and established Vision 2000, based on sustainable ideals, and they adopted "Economy, ecology, equity," as its slogan. Beginning with a riverwalk along the deteriorated Tennessee River area, the city built shopping areas, inner-city housing, and recreational spaces and walkways to draw people back. Green spaces, electronic mass transit, urban renewal, affordable housing, and recycling were additional cornerstones of the new and improved "green capitalism" sustainable city—but eco-industry was its shining star.

Eco-industry (providing goods and services that are environmentally protective) is more than just companies engaged in environmentally friendly industry. At its fullest (and not yet attained) level, eco-industry is a closed-loop, cradle-to-cradle industrial park where waste and the ecological footprint are minimized. Chattanooga has focused on cleanup of contaminated sites and replaced the famed "Chattanooga Choo-choo" with electric buses. The city became one of two American locations that manufacture the buses. In 2011 Volkswagen opened a billion-dollar, environmentally responsible plant in Chattanooga.

While the city has gained a sustainable reputation, it has also been said that "the development may be a shade of green, [but] the attainment of sustainability on the part of Chattanooga is simply not there, nor even near."[4] Racial and class biases and the inability to address roots of problems rather than short-term economic fixes have caused detractors to call the city unsustainable.[5] This may be true, but as of yet, no city in North America is considered sustainable, and trying to turn the economy around, even using the sustainability buzzword to do it, is a step in the direction of the new paradigm.

Economy

Appalachia is still a resource-based economy with limited secondary industry. The principal natural resource is coal. There has been and remains an agricultural backbone.

Agriculture

Ridge and Valley

The agricultural economy on the valley floors of the Ridge and Valley continues; however, suburban houses are now the most prevalent crop. The Shenandoah Valley is a dairying area, rotating corn, alfalfa, and small grains, and continues to produce the country's sixth-largest apple crop.

Appalachian Plateaus

Appalachia's urban population is about half the national average. Most of the rural population lives in plateau areas on small farms. Although the land is forested and mountainous, Appalachia has the most owner-operated farms, although many of the farmers are poor. The farms are undermechanized because the rugged undulating terrain limits farm size, which prevents using expensive, mechanized equipment. The farmers grow pasture crops or livestock, although most augment their income by gathering and selling various roots and herbs from the forested area or by working second jobs.

Interior Plateau

The Interior Plateau has been known for two distinct agricultural enterprises: tobacco and Kentucky bluegrass horse farms. One was the 2004 recipient of a radical change in production, and the other continues in a private world of the wealthy elite.

Kentucky Tobacco

The tobacco farmer averages nineteen acres of tobacco and has depended on the Agricultural Adjustment Act of 1933, which restricted the supply and set a minimum price stabilizing the tobacco earnings. Tobacco became one of the few crops by which a farmer could earn a living on so few acres. An acre of price-supported tobacco can net about $3,000 annually, whereas an acre of wheat nets about $30. Three-quarters of the regional small farmers depended on tobacco as the only profitable crop since the once major crop, hemp, was outlawed in 1937. However, in 2004 tobacco quotas ended and the bottom fell out of the American tobacco-crop market, despite a small buyout. Tobacco production accelerated in China.

About half of Kentucky's tobacco farmers halted tobacco production after the 2004 buyout. But exports exceeded production in 2005, and Philip Morris offered incentives to grow tobacco on contract. In 2006, tobacco acreage and production returned on a smaller scale. The prices were not as high as the price-supported quotas, but still they were higher than growing corn or wheat.

Kentucky Bluegrass

The Kentucky bluegrass around Lexington is known for its horse farms and gentleman farmers. The mineral-rich limestone soil produces grass that builds the bones and muscles of champion horses. This cultural landscape of wealth is rural, with lush, manicured pastures filled with purebred horses; well-maintained, color-schemed fences; antebellum mansions; and matching outbuildings. The culture of the horse set is separate from the rest of the region and revolves around the life cycle of horses and the racing season.

Kentucky bluegrass, a nutritious pasture and lawn grass that is not blue but decidedly green, replaced the native canebrakes. Kentucky bluegrass was the most important source of bluegrass seed in the world in 1939, but growing the seed is no longer economically feasible in the region. The primary region to grow bluegrass seed is in Idaho, Washington, and Oregon, where it helps reduce soil erosion.

BOX 8.6 HEMP AND TOBACCO

Hemp has been a traditional American crop, yielding twine, paper, oil, and of course, marijuana. Hemp and marijuana are the same plant grown for different uses, but undifferentiated legally. The federal government declared both illegal in 1937. But in recent years, fifteen states have authorized research and cultivation, and passed laws meant to test the federal ban, though none have yet to grow the crop. North Dakota has made the crop legal for commercial farming, and in 2007 attempted to be the first state to grow industrial hemp—not because of any legalizing interests, but because it is a practical crop that will grow on the rocky North Dakota soil. Bills have been introduced in Kentucky, though they have not yet been passed. Canada, which also had banned hemp, has reversed its laws and has harvested commercial crops since 1998.

Industrial hemp is an environmentally beneficial plant that is energy efficient, conserves forests (it grows rapidly and produces fiber), reduces toxins (requiring less chemicals to bleach for paper), is resistant to pests (hence requires less pesticide use), and replaces many polluting industrial feedstocks. Hemp has a much lower THC content than its more potent form, marijuana.

Kentucky has been the most tobacco-dependent state. One percent of the land produces more than 50 percent of crop receipts. Kentucky has the nation's highest death rate for tobacco use (1990–1994), reflecting its dependence on the crop. Tobacco quotas, the extremely regulated method of tobacco production, rose continually in the 1990s, averaging over $800 million annually. But foreign tobacco imports threatened tobacco production, and tobacco quotas were reduced by two-thirds and then dropped

altogether in 2004, halving farmer income. A tobacco settlement was paid to farmers, but they were left with few other profitable crop opportunities. Hemp would be one if legalized.

Wheat, corn, and soybeans yield a small percentage of tobacco income per acre and therefore are not viable alternatives for Kentucky's small farms. As tobacco quotas disappear, small farmers need a crop to provide an income on small land holdings (Chart 8.2).

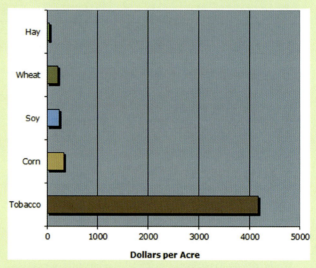

CHART 8.2. Kentucky Crop Values per Acre, 2006. Tobacco far outweighed any other crop grown in Kentucky. After the end of tobacco quotas in 2004, few other crops were capable of yielding as high an income.

Allegheny Plateau

The Finger Lakes microclimates favor dairy farms and vineyards. The region contains 85 percent of New York's winery acreage. Many Finger Lakes grape growers are prosperous gentlemen farmers. They are not tied to the old myth of the farmer who wins a million dollars and when asked what he will do with it, says, "Farm until it is all gone." Wine grape growers often have their millions and choose to farm glamorous crops because they can afford to (Photo 8.9).

Primary Industry

Coal

Appalachian coal supplies much of America's electricity and is the country's most plentiful energy resource. However, Appalachia's beautiful forested hills conceal layers of coal and have become a battlefield for an energy-hungry nation. Coal production waned in the late twentieth century, but twenty-first-century electricity consumption demands, along with higher costs for imported fuel, resulted in a return to coal. From 1960 to 2007, the number of people depending on coal-based energy doubled. But dependence on coal is waning. In 2010, coal

power provided 48 percent of the nation's electricity, versus the 52 percent generated in 2007.

Coal remains the most polluting, most profitable, and most inexpensive way to generate electricity, but only when environmental and social costs are not calculated. The preferred mining method in the Appalachian Plateau is a massive form of **strip-mining** called mountaintop mining (MTM) by mining companies, or **mountaintop removal** (**MTR**) by local residents who live with the damage. The coal is mined, processed, and shipped from Appalachian sites to generate electricity and provide heat for homes and industry.

National electricity needs are expanding, and the existing 599 coal-burning power plants are insufficient.[6] Despite the availability of cleaner energy sources, in 2006 the Department of Energy announced plans to build 129 new coal-burning power plants and committed to additional nuclear facilities. The decision to build the new plants was made without a national discussion of alternative energy sources or a discussion about reducing consumption. However, coal-burning power plant production came under intense scrutiny in 2009, and most states delayed if not stopped plans to build more coal-burning plants.

PHOTO 8.9. Lake Seneca, Finger Lakes Region, New York. The Finger Lakes are all named after the Iroquoian League of Five Nations tribes. The region has been agricultural, including dairies and wineries.

Nonetheless, the national hunger for energy continues to grow along with the population, and alternative energy sources are still expensive and rare.

Coal: Plentiful, Dirty, Cheap   The United States contains 25 percent of the world's coal reserves. The industrial age relied on coal power, but in the mid-twentieth century, industry turned away from dirty coal and toward cleaner nuclear and natural gas. But storing nuclear plant radioactive waste and dwindling natural gas supplies resulted in a doubling of gas prices and a return to coal. The cost of a megawatt of coal-produced energy is about one-half the cost of a megawatt produced by natural gas.

Every law written about coal mining was written in blood.
—Old coalfield saying, stemming from a 1945 lawsuit

Coal Mining: Mountaintop Removal   From the mid-nineteenth century to the 1972 Clean Air Act, West Virginia was the primary source of coal, supplying the Industrial Revolution's economic engine. The Clean Air Act regulated the amount of sulfur in coal, favoring the low-sulfur coal of Wyoming's Powder River Basin. Appalachian coal requires cleaning and processing to meet clean air standards. Wyoming has taken the lead in coal production, but West Virginia and Kentucky, which produce a higher-sulfur coal, still produce 37 percent of U.S. coal, and West Virginian coal still provides over half of Midwestern electricity. In West Virginia, Ohio, Indiana, and Kentucky, coal generates over 90 percent of the electricity.

Coal's legacy is engraved on the land and people of Appalachia's Cumberland Plateau, leaving them poor and the land polluted while creating wealth for outside corporations. Coal mining wars over unionization and health concerns such as black lung disease were the issues underwriting laws protecting coal miners and their families. The watershed year for mine safety was 1977, when two acts were passed: the Federal Mine Safety and Health Act (resulting in a decrease of accidental deaths) and the **Surface Mining Control and Reclamation Act (SMCRA)**, requiring mining sites to be reclaimed and restored to their original contours.

SMCRA requirements have not been strongly enforced. Most MTR land is never reclaimed or restored. Reclamation is attempted about 50 percent of the time; 5 percent is restored. By law, land should be restored to its former condition, which requires topsoil. Instead, the topsoil is never returned and the eroded sterile soils are planted with the only plant that will grow in such soil, nonnative *Lespedeza*. The plant limits the return of wildlife or using the land as pasture.

Enforcement of environmental protection laws has been lax. For example, the 1972 Clean Water Act (CWA) protected water against polluting substances, but the federal government has not enforced the law. Instead, companies sidestep the regulations or outright change them. For example, in 2003 after several lawsuits threatened to enforce the CWA definition of "valley fill," the law was changed. Valley fills became legal by redefining the term. "Waste" was redefined as "fill," thereby legalizing dumping **overburden**—the layer of rock and soil above a coal seam—into the valleys.[7] In 2009, the EPA reversed the valley fill definition and began to review valley fill permits, aiming to halt this practice.

Surface and underground mining are the most common coal-mining techniques. Surface or underground mining reveal coal seams of varying thickness, from an inch up to 100 feet (Photo 8.10). Surface mines produced over 65 percent of the nation's coal in 2000. West Virginia continues to be the national

BOX 8.7 DID YOU KNOW . . . SOURCES OF ENERGY

- Coal provides almost half of U.S. electricity.
- The United States has 104 nuclear reactors in sixty-five nuclear power plants.
- Nuclear power provides 20 percent of total U.S. energy generated.
- No nuclear plants have been built since the Three Mile Island nuclear accident in 1979.
- One nuclear plant is under construction in Tennessee and is expected to open in 2012.

- Renewable sources of energy provide 8 percent of total energy.
- Hydropower provides 6 percent of U.S. electricity, but 2 percent of total energy.
- Natural gas provides 25 percent of total energy.
- Wind provides less than 1 percent and solar less than 0.1 percent of total energy.
- The United States has less than 5 percent of world population but consumes 25 percent of world energy.

leader in underground production, while MTR surface mining now constitutes 33 percent of West Virginia mining.

MTR coal production in the twenty-first century has become the most profitable method of coal recovery, despite devastating environmental effects. The overburden is dynamited and then dumped into adjacent valleys, covering streams and destroying ecosystems, which in turn causes flooding, erosion, and air and water pollution. The artificial "flat" terrain created by MTR is called an advantage by the coal operators, who turn a blind eye to the pollution, destruction of habitats and communities, and the increase in respiratory disease (Photo 8.11). The reason for increasing MTR is economic; mechanization requires fewer laborers, increases productivity as it reduces long-term labor costs, and increases the economic bottom line. The environmental and social costs are borne by the local residents and the American taxpayer.

Unintended Consequences   The dependence on coal creates the unintended consequences of acid rain, respiratory disease, soil erosion and landslides, flooding, destruction of native habitats, damage to residents' property, and water pollution. All degraded the quality of life for the entire ecosystem. The burning of coal in power plants creates acid rain downwind over the Midwest, Northeast, and Canadian Corridor. When coal is burned, toxic chemicals from coal waste are spewed onto nearby residents and often inhaled, causing respiratory diseases. While the burning of coal is still not free from these consequences, the installation of scrubbers to clean sulfur dioxide has decreased the problem; but the use of scrubbers has resulted in another negative unintended consequence: water pollution.

Water Pollution   A major source of American water pollution is mining. Coal is not pure carbon but contains toxic by-products that need to be removed to meet clean air and water regulations. Many power plant stacks now have scrubbers installed to collect chemicals. The chemicals—lead, arsenic,

PHOTO 8.10. Coal Seam in Raleigh County, West Virginia. Strata in the Appalachian Plateau are horizontal, indicating plateaus, instead of the folded mountains in the Ridge and Valley. Coal seams vary in thickness throughout the Cumberland Plateau.

BOX 8.8 HOW TO REMOVE A MOUNTAIN

1. Raze and burn forest. Do not harvest wood.
2. Scrape land bare. (Remove topsoil and vegetation.)
3. Blast overburden to loosen rock.
4. Dump overburden into adjacent valley.

5. Scoop out the layers of coal.
6. Reclaim land to the minimum allowed by law, or commit to use for a public purpose.

mercury, and many more—are contained in wastewater and the wastewater is either solidified and sent to a landfill or dumped into rivers or lakes that provide drinking water. Some MTR mining companies build earthen embankments to block valleys, which are then filled with slurry or sludge.

Coal ash impoundments are the slurry from power plant coal waste. The slurry is a toxic watery mixture of impurities in the coal, while sludge is a semisolid ooze of concentrated coal waste material. Coal ash is the leftover toxic material from coal after it has been used in a coal-burning power plant.

The residue, if left alone, can filter into groundwater, but on occasion the impoundments, holding millions to billions of gallons, break and cause catastrophic floods in the valleys below, killing all life and ruining drinking water for hundreds of square miles.

Local and Ecoregional Impacts   The ecoregional impacts of MTR include destruction of streams at their headwaters, which destroys ecosystems, and periodic floods that rampage through valleys. The coalfield region houses the largest continuous forest in the United States. The trees provide shelter and warmth, and many animals are hunted for food. Over fifty-nine thousand

miles of streams provide water and aquatic life for residents and tourists.

Most streams in central Appalachia are primary **headwater streams**—capillary, origin rivulets for larger river systems. Headwater streams are important in the life of a river system, being the transition between water and land, where nutrients are broken down and recycled for other organisms. Burying headwaters destroys a watershed's quality. Some impacts of a poor headwater system are algae growth, floods, water-quality issues, and loss of floral and faunal diversity.

Flooding   Flash floods created by poor mining techniques threaten Central Appalachian communities annually. Filled areas have no topsoil and little to hold the rocky debris in place. Erosion gullies funnel storm water onto populated valleys below.

In 2000, a sludge dam in Martin County, Kentucky, failed, sending over 250 million tons of toxic sludge into the Big Sandy River. In 2001, three people were killed and parts of twenty-two counties in West Virginia were flooded because of erosion from MTR mining. In 2008, a slurry of coal ash flooded a portion of the Tennessee River Valley, sending 5.4 million cubic yards of

PHOTO 8.11. Kayford Mountain, Raleigh County, West Virginia. Mountaintop mining, as it is called by the coal companies, removes the overburden to access the coal. The overburden soil is dumped into nearby valleys as fill, creating a flat landscape that is spun by the coal companies as necessary flatland in the hilly plateau region. However, others claim that the filled valley destroys wildlife habitat and contaminates water. Another issue is the burning of trees from the scalped mountains (in the background) rather than recovering the logs for lumber.

Flight courtesy of Southwings.

sludge across the valley. This was estimated to be the largest environmental disaster of its kind, spewing dangerous chemicals into the river.

External Costs   Some of the human and environmental costs of MTR have already been mentioned: destruction of waterways, ecosystems, and local biota. Another environmental cost includes the constant explosions of the mountains to loosen the rock and reveal the coal seams. After the explosion the rubble, which was once part of an ecosystem, is bulldozed over the side of the mountain onto the ecosystems below. When the blasting is done and the coal removed, the coal companies deem the artificially flat mountaintop an improvement over nature. They plant useless plants on it (nothing else will grow as there is no topsoil) or "reclaim" it as a prison ground, as in Martin County, Kentucky.

Blasting also contaminates wells used for drinking, let alone causing numerous cracked foundations and structural damage to homes when the blasting commences in Boone County at 4 p.m. every working day.

Blasting destabilizes the earth and causes mud slides. The deforestation of each cleared area increases erosion and flooding. Lives and homes are lost in floods, and the cost is borne by not only the residents but by the American public, whose taxes support cleanup and restitution.

Solutions   America remains dependent on coal for electric power. Viable solutions to reduce pollution include government funding and subsidizing renewable energy to the same extent as fossil fuels have been subsidized. Consuming less and conserving energy may reduce indirect costs.[8] Part of the solution is education, so people have the data and facts about consumption. For example, burning one 100-watt light bulb continuously for one year consumes 712 pounds of coal. Turn off the light. Communities can also conserve by switching to LED lights, as several cities have done. People can ride a bicycle or take a walk, instead of another trip in the car, and thereby lessen the dependence on fossil fuels, and maybe as a side benefit reduce the obesity problem.

"Clean coal" has been discussed since the 1980s but is not considered viable because of the expense, although the "clean coal" alternatives are of questionable sustainability. To curb emissions, researchers are seeking ways to capture and store power plant carbon emissions. The cost, though, will be expensive, will be borne by the consumer, and is not sustainable.[9]

Current scrubber technology helps clean the air and improve air quality; however, power producers of older plants were exempted under a 2003 interpretation of the Clean Air Act, under the pretext that the older plants would soon be out of commission. Instead, the power producers placed more reliance on these older and more polluting plants rather than upgrade air quality. In 2005, the EPA reversed previous decisions and ordered power plants to reduce emissions. However, enforcement has been slow, because of expense. A scrubber, which takes several years to install, costs about half a billion dollars; scrubbers reduce sulfur dioxide but do not halt carbon dioxide greenhouse gas (GHG) emissions. Coal-burning power plants are the largest single source of human-made carbon dioxide output. They produce one-third of all CO_2. Scrubber waste is an additional pollutant that must be buried in hazardous waste dumps or processed for reuse. Carbon sequestration buries CO_2. Several locations in Appalachia are experimenting with sequestration.

Hydraulic Fracturing and Appalachia

In the twenty-first century, natural gas was hailed as a solution to reduce reliance on coal. Natural gas is a nonrenewable fossil fuel, but it burns cleaner than coal. In the 1990s, conventional[10] natural gas resources were limited and the price escalated, which allowed more expensive mining techniques to begin accessing unconventional, harder-to-reach natural gas. The technique known as hydraulic fracturing, or "fracking," has become common across the country but has been highlighted in northern Appalachia's Marcellus shale, located across the Allegheny Plateau and into the Ridge and Valley. The shale lies from four thousand to eighty-five hundred feet below the surface. The location has been of increased interest both because of the gas contained in the pores of the shale and also because of its proximity to Megalopolis.

The gas was formed and dispersed about three hundred million years ago. Horizontal drilling techniques can access more fractures than traditional vertical drilling, but it costs about four times as much. Vertically drilled gas fields that have played out can be reused for horizontal drilling, releasing trillions of cubic feet of gas. In 2010, almost two thousand wells were drilled and up to five thousand wells could be drilled in the Marcellus region alone. Many other states have now begun hydraulic fracturing.

Natural gas deep-shale gas drilling requires using up to three hundred thousand gallons of fresh water per day per well, and four to eight million gallons per well total. The extensive water withdrawals deplete the 1 percent of water available as fresh water. The withdrawals come from surface and groundwater and may affect drinking water sources. Essentially, all water used is lost to consumptive use and reuse, due to the multiple chemicals used to fracture the rock. While most of the water remains lost and below the surface, the water returned to the surface is wastewater.

Water-quality issues lead the environmental concerns about fracking. Despite potential human health and water-quality threats from the numerous chemicals and contaminants used in fracking, the Safe Drinking Water Act exempted fracking. A number of water-related incidents have raised concerns. For example, failure to seal off the drinking water in one well caused an explosion, and several other environmental hazards have caused damage. The amount of water used for fracking has also damaged ecosystems and caused drinking water impairment. The more water that is used, the more the quality of the remaining water is threatened.

> It is important to realize that water quantity and water quality are intimately linked. If the amount of water in a stream is reduced, any pollutants in the remaining water become more concentrated. . . . Development of the Marcellus shale for gas extraction may present a major economic expansion opportunity for Pennsylvania, but we need to learn from the legacy of coal mining in the state and ensure that environmental protections are in place up front, before drilling happens.[11]

In June 2011, a *New York Times* exposé revealed how insiders of the natural gas industry are expressing concerns about hydraulic fracturing techniques and production, even going so far as to call the expensive technique the equivalent of a Ponzi scheme or a dot-com bust waiting to happen.[12]

Logging

Wood is an abundant resource in southern Appalachia; however, a lack of transportation sheltered the forests from harvesting until railroads arrived in the mid-nineteenth century. Once accessible, the hardwood lumber was exploited. During the late nineteenth and early twentieth centuries, lumber companies purchased timber rights and stripped the lumber, leaving the land bare and prone to erosion and flooding. The hardwood and softwood forests were used for fuel, building homes, and for a variety of household goods.

Lumber companies came into areas offering money for lumber, but they purchased only the timber rights, leaving residents with worthless cutover land, property taxes, and multiple environmental problems. By 1910, outsiders owned and logged a majority of the land and mineral rights, leaving Appalachians with little choice but to migrate to the city or work in the coal mines.

By 1900, over half of West Virginia's ten-million-acre virgin forest was cut. Some areas were denuded. Hardwood stands had covered the Kanawha Valley, but by 1925 the commercial timber stocks were depleted, leading to the increased dependence on coal production.

Today second-growth logging is a part of the southern Appalachian economy. Many areas, such as the Great Smoky Mountains, are protected, but others are commercially logged. Logging has changed over the twentieth century from family-run sawmills to chip mills in southern Appalachia.

The controversial chip mills are efficient and satisfy global demand for pulp and paper. Private landowners prefer chip mills because they use poor-quality material, which allows owners to derive the most money from their land. Some local residents welcome logging jobs, while others disdain the clearcut methods and destroyed landscape. Those involved with

sustainable practices believe the replanted pine monoculture "managed forests" lack biodiversity, are vulnerable to disease or infestations, and are unsustainable.

Appalachian Regional Commission (ARC)

Appalachian coal fueled America's Industrial Revolution, but its resources and profits were exported from the region as raw material, rather than keeping the profits local with regional manufacturing. The reliance on taking resources and profits out of the region is a major cause of the high poverty rates and the devastated Appalachian landscape. In 1965, a federally funded economic development program—the Appalachian Regional Commission (ARC)—aimed to improve the regional quality of life by raising educational levels, building roads in inaccessible areas, and improving the job market.

Over the years, the ARC has built more than 2,100 miles of roads and spent more than $14 billion to industrialize the region and improve the economy. The ARC has successfully cut the poverty rate in half (from 31 percent to 13 percent), reduced the infant mortality rate by two-thirds, increased educational levels, and created more than 1.6 million jobs. More than 70 percent of adults now have a high school education and improved access to health care, clean water, and sewers.

But the gains have not been across the board. The Appalachia that benefited from the roads and industry were on the region's periphery. The core of Appalachia remains among the poorest in America.

Most small Appalachian towns are still isolated. Thirty-mile drives on narrow winding roads out of valleys and into towns can take an hour and a half. The largest cities are accessible via modern toll roads, but these traverse the Appalachians, connecting the East with the Midwest, not connecting cities and towns within the region. Towns that are only a few miles apart as the crow flies are hours apart because of the dissected terrain.

The shift in employment during the 1950s and 1960s caused jobs in agriculture and mining to go from 1:4 (1950) to 1:10 (1960). Some counties, such as McDowell County in southern West Virginia, lost half their population from 99,000 in 1950 to 50,000 in 1970, and halved again to 22,113 in 2010. Government programs like the ARC were created to make Appalachia like the rest of the national economy, instead of working with the beauty and culture of Appalachia. It is not what you have, but what you do with what you have.

Tourism

Tourism has become an avenue to an economic but possibly unsustainable option in Appalachia. Thousands of streams and rivers and the distinct rural population captivate tourists seeking natural beauty, folk arts, and crafts. The landscape is beautiful, if one can overlook the environmental scars and focus on the fall foliage, folk and artisan centers, and historic towns. From the Catskills of New York to Tennessee's Great Smoky Mountains, the region is now rife with tourist opportunities.

Local tourism began in the nineteenth century when wealthy North Carolina planters left the hot, mosquito-infested, low country for the Blue Ridge near Asheville, North Carolina. Later, regional health centers credited the mountain climate and springs with curing respiratory ailments. Healthy visitors accompanied those seeking a cure and recognized the beauty. Soon more roads were built, accelerating tourism.

The Catskill Mountains were popular with tourists in the late nineteenth and the first half of the twentieth century. The region has been in the public mind since settlement, for here slept legendary Rip Van Winkle in Sleepy Hollow on the eastern slope of panoramic North Mountain. The Hudson River and the Catskills were nineteenth-century tourist destinations for the New York urban population.

Jewish farmers settled in the Catskills in the late nineteenth century, but limited agricultural possibilities shifted farm production to summer boarders during the anti-Semitism of the 1950s and 1960s. The post–World War II years in the Catskills were a time of great growth, facilitated by automobile travel and the new highways to the "Borscht Belt," perhaps most popularly known through the movie *Dirty Dancing*. Discrimination toward Jewish comedians—Rodney Dangerfield, Lenny Bruce, Milton Berle, Woody Allen—led them to entertain at Borscht Belt hotels and bungalows. They migrated into mainstream comedy as segregation eased. After the 1960s, air travel, assimilation, and less anti-Semitism opened up other vacation destinations, and the era of the Catskills' popularity waned. Eventually, many of the wooden bungalows burned down. In the twenty-first century, the remaining bungalows are overgrown or converted to Indian casino establishments.

The Southern Appalachians contain the Great Smoky Mountains, America's premier tourist destination, attracting over nine million tourists annually. Access to the region through the Blue Ridge Parkway, as well as many of the buildings, was courtesy of New Deal agencies: the Civilian Conservation Corps (CCC), the relief program that conserved forests and parks, and the Work Projects Administration (WPA), responsible for many roads and public buildings. Resorts, casinos, and amusement parks catering to the tourist trade are now common throughout the region.

The Great Smoky Mountains Park has become an important part of the economy, but at a cost. Many local people were relocated in order to open the parks and throughways. Crime and air pollution have increased.

The abused Appalachian land has spurred additional tourist attractions. Logging has inspired several amusement park rides, including the newest—the lumber camp–themed area of Dollywood outside Pigeon Forge, Tennessee. In "reverse ecotourism," people concerned about environmental destruction are traveling to view mountaintop removal sites in Kentucky and at Kayford Mountain, West Virginia.

Tourism is not a panacea for the economy and is often unsustainable. Many second-home purchasers and retirees move to the region but do not participate economically. They are little more than tourists and offer little in the way of economic development, sustainable or otherwise.

A Sustainable Future

Appalachia can be a cultural world apart from the rest of America. Education, health, and road access have improved, thanks to the WPA, TVA, and ARC public works programs. But substantial work remains, including protecting the landscape from logging and coal resource industries. Appalachian folk life continues in the hills and valleys, and many people have remained or returned because they love the familiar friends, neighbors, and communities. The regional traditions maintain many sustainable elements. Although all Americans may not choose the Appalachian way of life, there is much to learn from the residents.

The rugged beauty of the Cumberlands is undeniable, but residents sit atop the cheapest and most plentiful energy source in America. As a result, local history and culture evaporates in the face of fossil fuel energy–dependent progress. As other fossil fuels escalate in price, the United States is dependent on coal for its energy, despite its external costs of a polluted environment and social inequities.

The Appalachian community lives in the heart of the mining zone. Reaching a compromise between King Coal and the poor but proud people of Appalachia has hardly been discussed. Only grassroots organizations focus on these aims, and little to no effort emanates from either the coal companies or the government. While this is happening, three national treasures are disappearing: the mountain folk, their culture, and the rolling, wooded landscape and its ecosystems.

On another Appalachian front, the Great Smoky Mountains are preserved as a National Park but suffer various environmental and cultural trials. In the past, logging companies were held at bay, but external invasive forces now threaten the park. Air pollution has restricted mountaintop views. Traffic crowds the roads, and kitsch fills the towns.

Appalachia is an American cultural treasure, much as the Native American cultures. But somehow many Americans are unable to understand that each culture—cultures that developed in relation to their surroundings—has knowledge specific to their landscape, and knowledge that can invigorate the mainstream culture. For all the knowledge we gain, we lose other knowledge. Traditional European heritages have been lost in the search for a fast-paced urban life. We do not have to stay in the past, but humanity can inform our hearts and help shape the future.

The outlook for Appalachia is as imperiled as it has ever been, but not hopeless. The region once isolated and considered

BOX 8.9 WIND FARMS IN APPALACHIA

In the late twentieth century, the Appalachian population was infused with new residents. This caused turmoil. Retirees and others who appreciate the Appalachian aesthetic landscape have joined the back-to-the-landers of the 1970s. But logging interests, MTR, and pollution have hampered the reverie. For example, residents in the valleys near Fayetteville, West Virginia, want to live with their view intact and fight efforts to build wind turbines to generate electricity. The various factions and agendas are mutually exclusive. Some want to be free of what coal has done to the Appalachians and seek renewable and pollution-free energy. In North Carolina, groups encourage building wind farms as a solution to end the smog and haze that coal-burning power plants cast over the region. Viewing the clear-cuts, the acid rain, and mercury pollution, they see wind farms as an answer to dependence on coal-burning plants. Others pushed to seriously limit wind farms along the North Carolina view shed.*

The second-home and retirement community fight the visual "blight" of the ridgeline wind turbines and see them as detrimental to their resale values. The back-to-the-landers see the wind turbines as just another form of city life infringing on their own, and they espouse conservation over more power options. MTR and wind turbines are why they fled urban life, which now arrives at their door and envelops Appalachia with the consumption demands of the rest of America. Groups have formed to fight what is seen not as an alternative energy source, but as another "carpetbagger" seeking to profit on Appalachian resources. Another group finds the extra-tall turbines creating additional problems: they may pose a danger to bats and birds.

Though those favoring and opposing wind farms have valid cases, both agree that conserving energy is much of the answer, and that smaller, locally owned generation; individual wind farms; and solar panels are more secure and friendly than another outside group taking from Appalachia.

* Kate Galbraith, "North Carolina Moves to Limit Wind Projects," *New York Times*, August 7, 2009.

---

backward, is no longer so. Several organizations are seeking and progressing toward a healthy economy and sustainable life within Appalachia.

The MTR coal situation and other environmental issues are closely followed and fought by several grassroots organizations, including Coal River Mountain Watch, the Ohio Valley Environmental Coalition, and Appalachian Voices. Each of these organizations champions education about their region, informing about MTR, economic and environmental sustainability, and litigation against nonsustainable or egregious environmental devastation. These organizations have fought to correct ills in the air, waste disposal, toxic leakage, violations of the Clean Air Act, and MTR. They have enjoyed success on shoestring budgets, but they can do much more if funded like their corporate opponents.

Appalachia is a region with a high percentage of rural communities and farms that understand the traditional food chain and the importance of sustainable agriculture and local foods. Yet the region is one of the unhealthiest in the nation. Throughout the region, groups such as Appalachian Sustainable Development in Virginia and Tennessee, and the Appalachian Sustainable Agriculture Project[13] in western

North Carolina seek to create a nutritious and healthy food system within Appalachia, while enhancing farming communities.[14] In 2010, famed chef Jamie Oliver turned his attention to this nutritionally impoverished region by starting the Food Revolution in Huntington, West Virginia.[15]

Sustainable economic development is important in Appalachia because its industry is headquartered outside the region and often favors unsustainable short-term versus long-term gain. Included within economic development is a burgeoning ecotourism industry, local resources, and self-reliance based on appropriate and green technologies. Other grassroots groups have educated the public about sustainable agriculture, including organic farming, growing gardens, and buying locally.

Appalachia also offers wilderness, something that becomes more precious as the population grows. A growing sense and practice of conservation is helping the region protect its wild areas but requires supporting public education. Appalachians have kept their way of life despite great odds, and hopefully Appalachia will become a source of pride for the country instead of being obliterated without the country ever appreciating its presence.

Questions for Discussion

1. Part of coal industry logic is that flattening the landscape of the Cumberland Plateau is advantageous because it makes the land accessible and usable, unlike the traditional Appalachian hollows. Are there advantages to preserving different physical geographies in different areas?

2. Although the TVA's damming of the river to generate power brought industry to the region and created many recreational sites, could the money have been used for more benefit? Was there a benefit to losing the valleys to flooding?

3. What is the difference between northern Appalachia and the Cumberland Plateau?

4. Who were the Scots-Irish and how did they come to settle Appalachia?

5. Why did cities appear at the north and south ends of the Finger Lakes and not along their sides?

6. How did coal mining affect the development of the Cumberland Plateau?

7. How will Americans get their electricity if not by coal? What does coal production mean for Appalachia?

8. How did Appalachian folk culture develop and what makes it unique? How is it threatened today?

9. What is Chemical Valley and how did it get its name?

10. What geographic factors combined to make Birmingham, Alabama, a center of steel production in the late nineteenth century?

11. In the Great Smoky Mountains, where will the increasing number of people live if development continues to be compromised? Can we afford to shut down power plants, admittedly the largest source of pollution, when the population is growing and more people are demanding more power?

Suggested Readings

Alvey, R. Gerald. *Kentucky Bluegrass Country.* Jackson: University Press of Mississippi, 1992.

Appalachian Rivers, Lakes and Streams: A Region's Life Reflected in Its Waters. Special issue, *Now and Then: The Appalachian Magazine* 18 (Spring 2001): 1–44.

Barney, Sandra. "Coming to Terms with Northern Appalachia." *Now and Then: The Appalachian Magazine* 14 (Winter 1997): 8–10.

Batteau, Allen. *The Invention of Appalachia.* Tucson: University of Arizona Press, 1990.

Berry, Chad. " 'Upon What Will I Hang My Hat in the Future?' Appalachia and Awaiting Post Postmodernity." *Journal of Appalachian Studies* 6, nos. 1–2 (Spring–Fall 2000): 121–30.

Boyd, Lawrence. "The Company Town." *EH.Net Encyclopedia*, January 31, 2003, at http://eh.net/encyclopedia/article/boyd.company.town.

Campbell, John C. *The Southern Highlander and His Homeland.* 1921; Lexington: University Press of Kentucky, 2004.

Caudill, Harry M. *Night Comes to the Cumberlands.* Ashland, Ky.: Jesse Stuart Foundation, 2001.

Commission on Geosciences, Environment, and Resources. *Coal Waste Impoundments: Risks, Responses, and Alternatives.* Washington, D.C.: National Academies Press, 2002.

Dabney, Joseph Earl. *Mountain Spirits.* New York: Scribner, 1974.

Davis, Leslie Martz. "Economic Development of the Great Kanawha Valley." *Economic Geography* 22, no. 4 (October 1946): 255–67.

Drake, Richard B. *A History of Appalachia.* Lexington, Ky.: University Press of Kentucky, 2003.

Hart, John Fraser. "Land Rotation in Appalachia." *Geographical Review* 67 (1977): 148–66.

Hofstra, Warren R. *The Planting of New Virginia: Settlement and Landscape in the Shenandoah Valley.* Baltimore: Johns Hopkins University Press, 2004.

Hsiung, David C. *Two Worlds in the Tennessee Mountains: Exploring the Origins of Appalachian Stereotypes.* Lexington: University Press of Kentucky, 1997.

Isserman, Andrew M. "Socio-Economic Review of Appalachia." Washington, D.C.: Appalachian Regional Commission, 1996.

Jones, L. *Appalachian Values.* Ashland, Ky.: Jesse Stuart Foundation, 1994.

MacNeal, Douglas. "How Can You Call Pittsburgh Appalachian?" *Now and Then: The Appalachian Magazine* 14 (Winter 1997): 10–13.

Marsh, Ben. "Continuity and Decline in the Anthracite Towns of Pennsylvania." *Annals of the Association of American Geographers* 77, no. 3 (September 1987): 337–52.

Meinig, D. W. *The Shaping of America.* New Haven, Conn.: Yale University Press, 1986.

Mitchell, Robert D. "The Shenandoah Valley Frontier." *Annals of the Association of America Geographers* 62, no. 3 (September 1972): 461–86.

Murphy, Raymond E., and Marion Murphy. "Anthracite Region of Pennsylvania." *Economic Geography* 14, no. 4 (October 1938): 338–48.

Pollard, Kelvin M. A. "New Diversity: Race and Ethnicity in the Appalachian Region." Washington, D.C.: Population Reference Bureau, September 2004.

———. "Population Growth and Distribution in Appalachia: New Realities." Washington, D.C.: Population Reference Bureau, January 2005.

Pudup, Mary Beth. *Appalachia in the Making: The Mountain South in the Nineteenth Century.* Chapel Hill: University of North Carolina Press, 1995.

Raitz, K. B., and Ulack, R. *Appalachia: A Regional Geography*. Boulder, Colo.: Westview Press, 1984.

Rehder, John B. *Appalachian Folkways*. Baltimore: Johns Hopkins University Press, 2004.

Shaver, Christine L., Kathy A. Tonnessen, and Tonnie G. Maniero. "Clearing the Air at Great Smoky Mountains National Park." *Ecological Applications* 4, no. 4 (November 1994): 690–701.

Thomas, William G., III. "The Shenandoah Valley." *Southern Spaces*, at http://southernspaces.org/2004/shenandoah-valley .

von Engeln, O. D. "Effects of Continental Glaciation on Agriculture." Part I. *Bulletin of the American Geographical Society* 46, no. 4 (1914): 241–64.

U.S. Environmental Protection Agency. *Final Programmatic Environmental Impact Statement on Mountaintop Mining/Valley Fills in Appalachia*, 2005, at http://www.epa.gov/region03/mtntop/eis2005.htm.

Webb, James. *Born Fighting*. New York: Broadway Books, 2004.

West Virginia Coal Association. Coal Facts, 2010, at http://www.wvcoal.com/201012182463/2010-coal-facts.html.

White, William B., Richard A. Watson, E. R. Pohl, and Roger Brucker. "The Central Kentucky Karst." *Geographical Review* 60, no. 1 (January 1970): 88–115.

Williams, John Alexander. *Appalachia: A History*. Chapel Hill: University of North Carolina Press, 2002.

———. *West Virginia and the Captains of Industry*. Morgantown: West Virginia University Press, 2003.

Wolfram, Walt, and Donna Christian. *Appalachian Speech*. Arlington, Va.: Center for Applied Linguistics, 1976.

Wright, Martin. "The Antecedents of the Double-Pen House Type." *Annals of the Association of American Geographers* 48, no. 2 (June 1958): 109–17.

Internet Sources

Tennessee Historical Society. *Tennessee Encyclopedia of History and Culture*, Version 2.0, at http://tennesseeencyclopedia.net/.

West Virginia Geology: Earth Science Studies. "Geology of the New River Gorge," at http://www.wvgs.wvnet.edu/www/geology/geoles01.htm.

National Park Service. "Great Smoky Mountains Air Quality," at http://www.nps.gov/grsm/naturescience/air-quality.htm.

Grist. Mountaintop Removal, at http://www.grist.org/article/reece/.

U.S. Environmental Protection Agency. Mid-Atlantic Mountaintop Mining, at http://www.epa.gov/region3/mtntop/.

Coal River Mountain Watch, at http://www.crmw.net/.

Mountain Justice Summer, at http://www.mountainjusticesummer.org/facts/steps.php.

Ohio Valley Environmental Coalition, at http://www.ohvec.org/galleries/mountaintop_removal/.

Appalachian Voices, at http://appvoices.org/?/site/mtr_overview/.

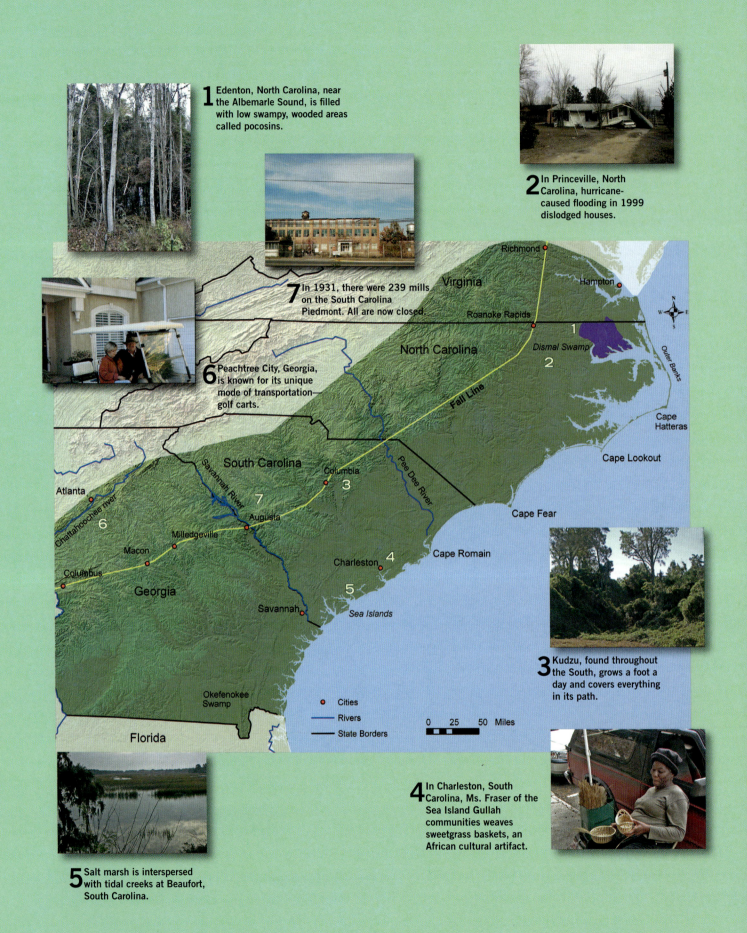

1 Edenton, North Carolina, near the Albemarle Sound, is filled with low swampy, wooded areas called pocosins.

2 In Princeville, North Carolina, hurricane-caused flooding in 1999 dislodged houses.

7 In 1931, there were 239 mills on the South Carolina Piedmont. All are now closed.

6 Peachtree City, Georgia, is known for its unique mode of transportation—golf carts.

3 Kudzu, found throughout the South, grows a foot a day and covers everything in its path.

4 In Charleston, South Carolina, Ms. Fraser of the Sea Island Gullah communities weaves sweetgrass baskets, an African cultural artifact.

5 Salt marsh is interspersed with tidal creeks at Beaufort, South Carolina.

Richmond

Virginia

Hampton

Roanoke Rapids

North Carolina

Dismal Swamp

Outer Banks

Fall Line

Cape Hatteras

Cape Lookout

South Carolina

Savannah River

Columbia

Pee Dee River

Atlanta

Chattahoochee river

Augusta

Milledgeville

Macon

Charleston

Cape Fear

Cape Romain

Columbus

Georgia

Savannah

Sea Islands

Okefenokee Swamp

Florida

Cities

Rivers

State Borders

0   25   50   Miles

9

SOUTH ATLANTIC

Gentry Tidewater, Hardscrabble Piedmont, and the Northern Invasion of Dixie

Chapter Highlights

After reading this chapter you should be able to:

- Identify the Low Country, Sea Islands, and barrier islands
- Compare the coastal plain and the Piedmont
- Discuss the fall line and its importance
- Identify the water war areas of the Atlantic South
- Discuss how the Gullah differed from other slaves
- Give an overview of the development of antebellum and postbellum Southern cities
- Explain textile manufacturing on the Piedmont after the Civil War
- Describe tobacco production and how it has changed over the past decades
- Discuss the evolution of hog and chicken production over the past twenty years
- Outline the development of the Southern economy prior to and after the Civil War
- List and describe the evolution of plantation crops
- Compare a yeoman and a plantation farmer
- Explain why logging is unsustainable in the South

Terms

barrier island
blackwater rivers
boll weevil
cape
Carolina bay
carpetbagger

coastal plain
concentrated animal feeding
   operations (CAFOs)
contract farmer
cotton gin
cracker
Gullah
industrial ecology

kudzu
lagoon
maroon
New South
Piedmont
plantation agriculture
Reconstruction
redneck

redwater rivers
right-to-work state
riparian rights
tidewater
triangular trade
vertical integration
yeoman

Places

Atlanta, Georgia

Charleston, South Carolina
Dismal Swamp
Low Country

Outer Banks
Research Triangle

Savannah, Georgia
Sea Islands

PHOTO 9.1. Fall Line on the Savannah River, Augusta, Georgia. The fall line is the point where the harder Piedmont rock ends and the sandy coastal zone begins; it is delineated by a drop in land level. The power created at the fall line was used to power the Piedmont textile mills during the late nineteenth century.

Introduction

My wound is geography. It is also my anchorage, my port of call.

Pat Conroy, *Prince of Tides*[1]

The South has changed. Depending on your point of view, this might be good or bad. The Old South has evolved into a **New South**. The Old South still exists, though, represented by a strong community-based sense of place and the beginning of American environmental degradation by Europeans. Both spell opportunities for a sustainable South that has yet to mature.

The evolution of the South differed markedly from that of the North. Prior to the Civil War, the self-sufficient plantation economy truncated urban development. After the war, the southern economy slowly evolved from rural to urban, and in the process began mirroring the North. By the late twentieth century, northern urban influences had reshaped the New South. In rural areas, agriculture shifted from time-honored crops (cotton and tobacco) to large-scale livestock production.

While rural areas maximized agricultural production, urban populations grew with northerners who fled the colder climes for the warmer South—once the humidity was controlled by technology. In the past, plantation owners had found more genteel ways of dealing with the environment's heat and humidity. Antebellum plantations were located in areas where the air flow limited the high summer heat and humidity. The architecture also reflected the awareness of place. Building materials were local. Foundations were raised and roof styles were shaped to work with the climate. Early design had many sustainable elements, a sense of place that worked with the climate, topography, vegetation, and local materials that was lost during the growth period of the twentieth century, when air-conditioning neutralized sustainable elements, but at an environmental cost.

Sustainability, living with the land instead of conquering it, remains elusive for those who call the South home. The cities were coopted by the North, but the mantra "the South will rise again" has helped maintain and reshape the values, politics, and culture of the twenty-first-century South. No northern invention or invasion will change the soul of the South.

Physical Geography

The Atlantic Coastal Plain extends from Cape Cod to Mexico's Yucatan Peninsula. Throughout history the seaward-dipping plain and marshy tracts have alternately emerged from and submerged into the ocean. The inland **coastal plain** gradually gains elevation, but it seldom rises higher than five hundred feet before it ends abruptly at the fall line where the **Piedmont** commences (Photo 9.1). The plain continues as the continental shelf more than one hundred miles out to sea. The gradually descending shelf dissipates wave energy; the mild waves differ from the dramatic waves along the steep descent of the Pacific shore.

Regional ecological systems include forests and marshy coastal grasslands. The soils, moisture, temperature, and geologic variations have created a regional mosaic of small-scale ecologic communities. The physical landscape and its difference from the English homeland have been important elements in regional economic development.

This chapter encompasses the three major subregions of the Atlantic coastal region between Virginia and Georgia, from the coast through the Piedmont.

- Southeastern Coast
- Southeastern Plain
- Piedmont

BOX 9.1 KUDZU

Kudzu (*Pueraria lobata*), a perennial of the legume family, entered the United States as a sample plant during the 1876 Centennial Exposition. The Japanese plant captivated gardeners and became an ornamental and then foraging vine by the 1920s (Map 9.1). During the 1930s drought, the Soil Conservation Service was seeking a plant to halt erosion in deforested areas. They chose kudzu. Farmers were paid by the government to plant kudzu.

By 1953, the government stopped advocating planting kudzu; it was successively named an invasive species, then a weed. The

fast-growing vine's only natural enemy is frost, which seldom occurs in the South. The vine overtakes everything and destroys other plants and forests in the process. The difficult-to-eradicate vine now covers more than seven million southern acres.

The vine does have many uses. In the 1920s, it was a fodder crop and later was used as the raw material for baskets. In China, kudzu is a medicine for dysentery, allergies, and diarrhea. Currently, chemicals in the root are being studied as a cure for alcoholism, and a few researchers are investigating how to convert the vine into a biomass feedstock.

MAP 9.1. Extent of Kudzu in the United States. This invasive species was intentionally planted in the 1930s to control erosion. Kudzu is difficult to eradicate.

The coast and the Piedmont are contiguous, but their geologic history and resulting soils have shaped their distinctive settlement, agriculture, and industrial development.

The Southeastern Coast and Plain

The coastal plain subregions include the **barrier islands** and the Sea Islands, the southeastern **tidewater** coast, and the rolling upland Southeastern Plain. Ancient geologic rhythms in the tidal areas have periodically submerged and then exposed the coastal bays, inlets, and islands. The plain is widest in the south and narrows to the north. Conversely, the submerged shelf is wider in the north and narrows in the south.

Inland from the marshy coast, the Southeast Plain slopes from the low, rolling sand hills of the fall line to the flat coastal plain. The narrow streams of the inland broaden and meander

as they near the coast. The region is two-thirds woodland; the remaining land is farms and pasture.

Appalachian sediment eroded onto the coastal plain and formed alluvial fans on the continental shelf. The alluvium travels a long distance, and along the way it leaves behind the heavier, coarser sand. Seaside sand is therefore white, pure, and much finer than the coarse Pacific sand that travels a shorter distance to the sea.

Barrier Island Coast

Winds, waves, and currents shape the long, narrow barrier islands along the Carolina coastlines. Barrier and sea islands together outline and protect about three-quarters of the Atlantic South mainland and continue along the Florida coast (Table 9.1). The islands buffer and absorb the shock of the

TABLE 9.1. Coastal Characteristic along Atlantic Coastal Plain

	Number of barrier islands	Length of coast	Percent coast
Virginia	9	112 m (180 km)	60
North Carolina	20	301 m (484 km)	95
South Carolina	18	187 m (301 km)	51
Georgia	12	100 m (161 km)	89

Source: H. Jesse Walker and James M. Coleman, "Atlantic and Gulf Coastal Province," in *Geomorphic Systems of North America*, edited by William L. Graf (Boulder, Colo.: Geological Society of America, 1987)

storms and waves. In the process, the sandbar islands are torn apart, then rebuilt in new configurations. The process is endlessly repeated.

The best-known barrier islands are the ever-changing ribbons of North Carolina's Outer Banks. In their natural state, the islands are marshy wetlands, but many have been drained. Today beaches are renourished with sand so million-dollar homes facing the Atlantic can be built. Understanding the relationship of the barrier island to their new beachfront property is lost in the property value equation. Everywhere there are reminders of the power of the sea. Triangular **capes**—Capes Hatteras, Lookout, and Fear in North Carolina and Romain in South Carolina—jut into the sea, shaped by alternating northeast-southeast storm patterns, and awaiting the next storm that will reshape them. Storms tear islands into pieces and bring jobs—but the jobs are cartographers to redraw the coastline and construction crews to rebuild the houses.

A reason for rising storm damage is the number of people living along the vulnerable coasts. When the barrier islands are developed, their effectiveness as storm and wetland buffers is reduced. Sea-level rise instigated by climate change now threatens the low-lying islands. The continual rebuilding and renourishment of beaches are expensive and have made insurance premiums rise. When the claims are more than the premiums, everyone pays more. When insurance no longer covers damages, FEMA and state taxes, by way of the American taxpayer, pick up the tab, not only for the houses but also for the infrastructure and the cleanup costs, thereby further subsidizing coastal area inhabitants.

Sea Islands Coast

Marshes separate the mainland from the small, closely knit rectangular Sea Islands that extend from Charleston, South Carolina, to Jacksonville, Florida. Salt-tolerant vegetation covers the miles of tidal creeks, salt marshes, and estuaries that muddle the line between the Low Country Sea Islands and the mainland.

Isolated from mainland activities, the hundreds of islands have harbored both wildlife refuges and the African American **Gullah** culture. The wildlife include deer, tacky horses, and aquatics, while the Gullah, once slaves on tobacco and cotton plantations, were the recipients of the "forty acres and a mule" promises for Sea Island freedmen.

Sea Island land was confiscated after the Civil War, during **Reconstruction**, as an experiment to redistribute land from the wealthy white owners to the freemen. Some Gullah maintained possession of small acreages, but most land remained populated by land-poor blacks. By the late twentieth century, the Gullah who owned land sold it on Hilton Head and St. Simons to developers who built lavish golf and destination resorts.[2] Many remaining Gullah residents have been forced out of their homes by rising rents and property taxes.

Swamps

Two well-known American swamps lie within the region: the Okefenokee Swamp along the Florida-Georgia border and the Dismal Swamp along the Virginia–North Carolina border.

The Okefenokee, the largest swamp in the United States, covers about seven hundred square miles on the lower coastal plain. Once part of the sea, the swamp is now inland. An old barrier island, the Trail Ridge, separates the swamp from the surrounding area. The Okefenokee is also the headwaters to the Suwannee River. The forested swamps have been assaulted by drainage, logging, and sawmills. By the late 1920s, a movement urged conservation, and in 1937 it became a wildlife refuge, preserving four hundred species of vertebrates and more than two hundred types of birds.

The Dismal Swamp, straddling the Virginia–North Carolina border, has shrunk to less than half its former size of nine hundred square miles. The heavily forested swamp was formed during the ice ages, when local climate and vegetation were similar to the current New England climate. As the seas rose and the ice melted, the swamp environment evolved into a hardwood forest in peat sediment. The rich organic sediment has tempted speculative developers of agricultural land since colonial times.

The speculators included the Dismal Swamp Land Company, organized by George Washington and other Virginia planters. Their agricultural goals were unsuccessful because of limited labor and capital, but by 1805 slave labor cleared and dug a twenty-two-mile canal that provided ships safety from the fierce Atlantic swells and treacherous sandbars between the Chesapeake and Albemarle bays. Later the swamp was an Underground Railroad hideout for runaway slaves called **maroons**.

The Dismal Canal was an important transportation route during the nineteenth century, but it fell upon hard times. In 1929, the canal was sold to the Army Corps of Engineers and refurbished as a pleasure-boat waterway. The swamp became a national wildlife refuge in 1974.

The Piedmont

The Piedmont, "foot of the mountains," stretches almost nine hundred miles from New Jersey into Alabama and is the effective divide between the fall line and the Appalachian Blue Ridge Mountains. One hundred to two hundred miles wide, the Piedmont was once mountainous but now has eroded into rolling hills and narrow stream valleys that end at the fall line as the streams drop to the sandy coastal plain. In the south, the original major cities were more likely along the fall line than the coast, due to the marshy shallow tidelands between the barrier islands and the mainland (Table 9.2). The fall line seldom stops travel upriver today but instead is the path for I-95 into South Carolina, then I-20 through Georgia.

Settlers exploited the characteristic red soil of the Piedmont, the result of iron oxides formed on the warm, moist land. The soil, climate, and rocks supported a native oak and hickory forest, but poorly managed tobacco and cotton plantations replaced the forest and resulted in erosion and the eventual abandonment of the plantations. The disturbed land reverted to pine forests and was never allowed succession to the more evolved hardwood forests, because the pine forests were continually logged for paper and chipboard products. The unsustainable practice of growing pine forests exclusively robs the soil of the humus and nutrients that a deciduous forest offers.

Water

The region receives ample precipitation throughout the year. About 70 percent of the rainwater is lost to evapotranspiration, and the remainder replenishes regional aquifers and streams. Groundwater storage is best along the coastal plain, but overpumping has led to saltwater intrusion along several coastal cities—Savannah, Georgia; Hilton Head, South Carolina; and Brunswick, Georgia—which contaminates the freshwater supply. Only by pumping less water can the saltwater intrusion end.

The few lakes along the coastal region from Delaware to Florida are called **Carolina bays**, named for the bay tree found near these oval, freshwater depressions. Most Carolina bays are small and shallow swamps that have been degraded or drained. The bays are thousands of years old, but their genesis is still theorized.

Pocosins, also called dismal swamps, occur near estuaries. Their impenetrable, vine-laden jungle muck is an excellent filter for water and flood control, but much of it has been lost to agricultural use and rising sea levels.

The fall line affects river flow. Along the Piedmont, **redwater rivers** carrying red Piedmont soil run straight, but along the softer coastal plain alluvium **blackwater rivers** meander over the lower-relief terrain.

TABLE 9.2. Middle Atlantic Fall Line Cities and Their Rivers

City	River
Washington, D.C.	Potomac
Fredericksburg, Virginia	Rappahannock
Richmond, Virginia	James
Petersburg, Virginia	Appomattox
Roanoke Rapids, North Carolina	Roanoke
Raleigh, North Carolina	Neuse
Columbia, South Carolina	Congaree
Augusta, Georgia	Savannah
Milledgeville, Georgia	Oconee
Macon, Georgia	Ocmulgee
Columbus, Georgia	Chattahoochee

Redwater rivers carry a higher concentration of clay-type soils than the sandier blackwater rivers, and therefore they are more fertile. Tidal forests flooded by redwater rivers receive more nutrients than those with blackwater rivers and therefore have more growth potential. The larger redwater rivers are Virginia's James and Roanoke, and Georgia's Savannah and Altamaha.

Blackwater rivers originate on the coastal plain, have wide floodplains, and flow into estuaries between the mainland and Sea Islands. The darkly stained waters of blackwater rivers are not polluted but obtain their dark color from the rich organic tannins leached from the poorly drained swamps. Blackwater rivers are some of the cleanest natural rivers because they carry little sediment but large amounts of decaying plant material that makes them acidic and oxygen starved. Low levels of dissolved minerals in the almost sterile waters inhibit insect populations and limit the diversity of other animal and tree species. Blackwater rivers include the Blackwater in Virginia, the Edisto in South Carolina, and the Satilla, St. Mary's, and Ohoopee in Georgia (Photo 9.2).

Water Wars

Water rights differ east and west of the Mississippi River. Riparian water rights rooted in English common law govern water east of the river. West of the river, water is governed by prior appropriation rooted in Spanish law. **Riparian rights** have protected South Atlantic waterways in the past, but recent population growth and the increased demand have created a series of water wars. Riparian rights allow all landowners with water frontage to have "reasonable" water use and access. Riparian features include (1) allotments in proportion to water frontage, (2) water cannot be sold separate from the land, and (3) water remains in its watershed.

Despite the protection of riparian right law, political borders rather than natural watersheds divide rivers. The political borders have created conflicts between Georgia, Alabama, and Florida over rights of the Chattahoochee River; Virginia and Maryland over the Potomac; and North Carolina and Virginia over Lake Gaston.

Georgia, Alabama, Florida, and the Chattahoochee River

Originating in the Appalachian foothills, the Chattahoochee River follows a fault line across the Piedmont north of Atlanta and then defines the Georgia-Alabama border before it joins the Apalachicola River and empties into the Gulf of Mexico. Thirteen water storage and hydropower-producing dams that flow through northeast Georgia obstruct the Chattahoochee. The largest dam—storing 65 percent of the water—is Lake Lanier, built in 1960. A favorite recreational lake for Atlantans, it also provides hydropower and drinking water.

During the 1950s and 1960s, poorly monitored urban and industrial growth caused the river's pristine northern waters to morph into a polluted dead zone south of Atlanta. However, pollution solutions since the 1960s—treating municipal sewage and industrial waters, reducing phosphorus and sediment loads, and increasing oxygen concentrations—have resulted in a return of fish to the river.

But Chattahoochee water issues reemerged after 1990. Atlanta was growing rapidly without sufficient planning, resulting in an increased dependence on Lake Lanier water. Fecal coliform (*E. coli*) and bacterial pathogens increased, as did claims for the water from neighboring states—Alabama for its agriculture and Florida for its Apalachicola Bay oyster and sturgeon industry.

Atlanta's wastewater infrastructure—an aging sewer system and a million septic systems—threatens water quality, and multiple uses threaten functionality. Agricultural water uses have increased. The EPA has continually fined the Atlanta wastewater

PHOTO 9.2. A Blackwater River near New Ellenton, South Carolina. Blackwater rivers are not polluted but gain their color from tannins leached from decayed vegetation.

system for spills and overloaded systems. Regional coal- and nuclear-powered plants increased water use as electric power consumption increased.

The region usually receives ample precipitation, but the early twenty-first century registered a multiyear drought. Farmers irrigated from overallocated aquifers, and urban demand strained intrastate allocations and other water uses. The drought intensified water disputes.

Georgia, Alabama, and Florida have battled for two decades over the rights to Chattahoochee River water. Court decisions have wavered between the states; the case continues to wend its way through the court systems. No one has enough water; usage is growing but the amount of water is not. Atlanta is expected to outgrow its water sources by 2030. Meanwhile, population growth and wasteful usage leaves downstream users with less water and more pollution. The regulation of Lake Lanier water by Georgia has satisfied Atlantans thirst in the past, but to the detriment of Alabama and Florida, who continue to claim rights to more water.

Virginia and Maryland and the Potomac River

The Potomac River divides Virginia and Maryland. The water is allocated to Maryland according to the 1632 colonial charter, although Virginia "owns" the mouth of the Chesapeake. A four-hundred-year dispute between the two states over water allocation has been exacerbated by rapid growth in metropolitan Washington, D.C. In 2003, the Supreme Court ruled that Virginia be given equal access to Potomac River water. Maryland held that suburban growth in Virginia was unsustainable, and therefore water and growth required regulation.

The Carolinas, Virginia, and Catawba Water Rights

South Carolina needs to get ready for water wars. [3]

Water wars have become a constant problem in North Carolina, a region that has plentiful precipitation but also has experienced tremendous population growth since the 1990s. First, a fourteen-year battle over Lake Gaston on the North Carolina–Virginia border favored Virginia and gave Virginia Beach access to Lake Gaston water. In late 2006, the conflict over water rights continued over Catawba River water.

The Catawba River begins in the North Carolina Appalachians and flows through the Piedmont into South Carolina, where it provides water to more than one million people, as well as for agricultural and forested land. Reservoirs impound the river for flood control and hydroelectric power purposes.

Rivers have been deemed economic panaceas to a region's growth and are used to within an inch of their flow. During the drought of the early twenty-first century, water issues mounted between North and South Carolina over use of Catawba River water. South Carolina, fearing economic loss due to lack of water, sued North Carolina over how the river's water was distributed. After millions of dollars spent in legal fees, the case awaited a Supreme Court judgment, when a regional cooperative settlement was reached in 2010.[4] The agreement strictly manages water during drought periods.

Drought has exacerbated water wars, and the reasons extend beyond local issues. The abundant regional precipitation from tropical storms and the Atlantic is insufficient to allay the combination of population growth, urban demands, and periodic drought conditions. The Southeastern water wars are bound to continue unless limitations are recognized and conservation is practiced.

Climate

The Southern Atlantic features hot, humid, rainy summers and mild winters in which temperatures rarely drop below freezing. Rain averages about fifty inches annually in brief thunderstorm torrents or cold winter drizzles. Snow is usually scant and occasional, except in the higher elevations. The coastal plain is generally warmer than the Piedmont, but the humidity is greatest inland, where 100°F summer temperatures are often matched with high humidity.

Between June and November, Southern Atlantic tropical storms and hurricanes can inundate both the shoreline and inland areas. Storm surges may drown and erode sea-level coastal and inland communities, such as in 1999 when Hurricane Floyd penetrated a hundred miles inland and flooded Princeville, North Carolina. The Outer Banks of North Carolina are constantly on the lookout for severe storms. From 1989 to 2011, the Outer Banks were hammered thirteen times.

Hurricane activity waxes and wanes in natural cycles. The current cycle of increased activity began in 1995 and lasted into the first decades of the twenty-first century. The relationship of hurricanes and climate change is still inconclusive, but sea-level rise will increasingly threaten coastal communities and barrier islands during the twenty-first century.[5]

Historical Geography and Settlement

Despite more than fifteen thousand years of habitation by the Eastern Woodland culture, artifacts are limited to toponyms—names carried by the rivers, plains, and towns. Disease and forcible removal from the area devastated the native population.

Mid-Atlantic Native American settlements followed physical and waterway landscape patterns. Generally, Algonquians lived along the coast to the fall line, the Sioux on the Piedmont, and Iroquois in the Appalachians. Warfare shaped many cultural traits, such as defensively oriented settlement patterns and tattooed body art signifying spiritual and warrior status. The hunting and agricultural economy featured deer, corn, pumpkin, squash, and tobacco. Early contact with Anglo settlers was positive. Many settlers survived by practicing native agriculture, but later wars erupted between natives and encroaching settlers. The South developed distinct European settlement patterns influenced by the physical environment and the settlers' cultural background. The first European settlements were along the Virginia and North Carolina coastline, the drowned valleys, and the heavily indented bays and harbors. Tidewater settlers were

BOX 9.2 PRINCEVILLE, NORTH CAROLINA

In 1865, Freedom Hill (the future Princeville, North Carolina) was founded on the Tar River's swampy flood plain, the only land available to the recently emancipated slaves. The white town of Tarboro occupied the higher ground on the opposite bank. Princeville was periodically inundated by flooding until a levee—built four feet higher than any previous storm surge—was built in 1967. More than two thousand residents lived in Princeville until 1999, when Hurricane Floyd broke through the levee and flooded the town for weeks. Fortunately, no lives were lost, but all the residents' possessions were washed away and the entire town was homeless (Photo 9.3).

FEMA reacted slowly to the disaster. Months after the storm, FEMA still insisted that the residents relocate, despite white towns' receiving immediate care and money. However, the spirit of Princeville was not broken. The mayor and community leaders sent out a countrywide call for help, and hundreds of faith-based and community organizations of all races responded. In mid-2000, hundreds of volunteers were rebuilding in the ruins. Eventually, FEMA set up a trailer village, and Congress gave $500,000 for the Army Corps of Engineers to rebuild the damaged levee. The government finally gave $2 million, far short of the $80 million price tag to rebuild Princeville.

PHOTO 9.3. 1999 Devastation in Princeville, North Carolina, shortly after Hurricanes Dennis and Floyd. The entire town was submerged for two weeks when a levee gave way. Reconstruction was slow due to a lack of government support, although many faith-based groups from across the country came to help rebuild the town.

less concerned with religious issues than the northern colonials and were often well positioned financially but out of political favor in their homeland. In the Tidewater, settlers had different priorities than colonists to the north.

The settlement of Jamestown represented an early, tenuous step away from feudalism and toward modern capitalism. The English settled this region with the intent to trade with the natives and to seek gold, and only secondarily to establish a settlement. The lack of food crops for the settlers had the indirect result of high death rates, and by 1618, the Virginia Company terminated because of grave management mistakes. Within a generation of establishing Jamestown, the settlers introduced new crops, plants, and processes to the Native American agricultural landscape, forever changing the

habitation of the land. Their first major crop was tobacco, and as European demand grew so did **plantation agriculture** and the labor force required for successful cultivation. The tobacco industry in the nascent plantations highlighted just how dramatically northern and southern economies, racial issues, and land uses diverged early in the settlement process.

The South's intensive agricultural methods harmed the land because Europeans brought with them preconceived agricultural expectations based on the European landscape. Developing agricultural methods appropriate for the American landscape evolved over decades. This new land was very different from the land they left. Europeans found themselves in a strange land and, to survive, at first they changed the land to reflect the world they had left behind rather than adapt themselves. They altered the ecological landscape and thereby hastened the decline of ecosystems and the indigenous population. Ever larger fields of tobacco, indigo, rice, and eventually cotton supplanted the ecological landscape of the natives. The resultant destruction extended beyond the land, ultimately destroying the indigenous way of life. Unable to fight off the encroaching settlers, the natives either fled or died out. When the Native American threat was eliminated, many planters moved to the Piedmont and then, as soil conditions deteriorated again, on to the Gulf Coast and farther west. The former plantation land reverted to wooded acreage.

The settlers envisioned an unlimited, easily exploited land, one that would be profitable, especially as the labor force evolved from indentured servants to procuring thousands of African slaves. But the land suffered as the settlers' nutrient-hungry crops leached and eroded the soil. Since land seemed abundant and endless, the settlers simply abandoned early plots and moved on to new land. The degraded land found today throughout the South began with the short-term, wasteful practices of the early planters, which in many ways have hardly matured to more long-term care.

In the uplands Piedmont, the **yeoman** farmers—former indentured servants, Scots-Irish, crackers, and rednecks—settled and eked out lives at odds with the tidewater whites. In the 1730s and 1740s, Swiss, German, and Scots-Irish settlers immigrated to the Carolinas through the Great Valley, before settling in the upland Piedmont. They became self-sufficient yeoman farmers who had few slaves and had different needs than the Low Country plantation gentry. The social and economic differences created regional antipathies; they were at first ignored by the Low Country aristocrats, but in the 1760s some yeomans' needs (e.g., roads, courts, protection from Native insurgencies) were addressed.

The last colony established was Georgia (1732), which James Oglethorpe settled as a buffer colony between the British and Spanish. Oglethorpe, a utopian idealist, set up alliances with neighboring Native American tribes and then progressed with his army to lay siege to St. Augustine, Florida. His assault was unsuccessful, but he did halt the Spanish at Florida's northern boundary.

The evolution of the antebellum South differed from that of the northern colonies. Transportation infrastructure lagged, as did growth in population. Immigrants entered through northern ports of entry; there was little need for laborers in the slaveholding South. The self-sufficient plantation system traded from private plantation docks, which truncated the need for cities. This system crimped southern urban development. While the North built an Industrial Revolution infrastructure, southern development stagnated within the slaveholding culture and remained agricultural until after the Civil War.

Textile mills began to relocate from the Northeast in the 1840s, accelerating after the Civil War. Northern textile factories urbanized the Piedmont, taking advantage of cheap labor, power, and the location near the cotton fields (Photo 9.4). A string of company towns, each with its own textile mill, spread from Augusta, Georgia, to Aiken, South Carolina. Mill jobs lured laborers, and the urban population grew. By 1874, Georgia had the most mills, but by 1900, South Carolina led textile production with 239 mills.

In the 1970s, the textile industry became one of the first U.S. industries to outsource manufacturing jobs. By 2006, the textile mills had shut down and left many small company towns without their main income source (Table 9.3). Some mill sites are making a comeback as retail, research facilities, or loft housing, especially if they are near a larger city. Others grow weeds and deteriorate.

PHOTO 9.4. Sibley Textile Mill, Augusta, Georgia. The obelisk is the last remainder of the former Confederate powder works on this site, which provided gunpowder for the Confederate Army. The mill decreased production over a decade and was retired in July 2006.

TABLE 9.3. Textile Mill Employment for the United States

State	March (000) 2005	March (000) 2006	March (000) 2009	Percent change 2006–2009
United States	223.9	203.4	127.6	−37.2
Alabama	12.0	11.4	5.1	−55.2
California	13.5	12.6	10.2	−19.0
Georgia	33.9	33.2	22.1	−33.4
Massachusetts	8.0	6.8	n/a	
North Carolina	56.9	50.5	n/a	
Tennessee	5.8	5.3	n/a	

Source: Bureau of Labor Statistics, May 2009
Note: Not seasonally adjusted

Cultural Perspectives

Gullah

Summertime, and the livin' is easy,
Fish are jumpin' and de cotton is high.
Oh, your daddy's rich, and your ma is good-lookin',
So, hush, little baby, don't you cry.

—Clara singing in *Porgy and Bess*[6]

The Gullah (called Geechee in Georgia) were African slaves who arrived on the Sea Islands to work the rice and indigo fields. In the twentieth century, the development of resort communities threatened Gullah land, culture, and language.

Most New World slaves lost both their rights and their culture, but the Gullah retained some of their African heritage. African language and cultural retention was most pronounced on the isolated and marshy Sea Islands; the malarial conditions kept most whites away, while many of the African slaves had a genetic tolerance to the disease. Therefore, the Sea Island plantations were occupied almost exclusively by native Africans and their descendants, and the culture and language that continued bore the marks of their African heritage.

One of the surviving African craft traditions is Gullah basket weaving. The Gullah basket designs are indistinguishable from their Senegalese counterparts. Other Sea Island crafts brought over from Africa are carving, quilting, and grave decoration. Gullah folk tales, such as Brer Rabbit stories, have also found their way into American folk culture. These cultural artifacts confirm that Africans did bring their culture to the New World.

The South Carolina Gullah language is a Creole mixture of African and English dialects that are disappearing from the landscape but still actively discussed in linguistic circles. In the late 1990s, about five hundred thousand people were estimated to speak Gullah, although people outside the Gullah community seldom hear the speech because it has been stigmatized. Additionally, as Gullah speakers leave their community, they often adopt the speech patterns of their new home areas. Nonetheless, there has been a resurgence of interest in Gullah language preservation.

Gullah was an arcane subject of study during most of the twentieth century. The major cultural artifact was Gershwin's *Porgy and Bess*, a musical that indirectly questioned the loss of Gullah folkways. Most people may be unaware that Gershwin wrote his folk opera about the Gullah and that it was based on his personal experiences on primitive Folly Island, South Carolina. With this one exception, most people were unaware of the Gullah.

Until the 1970s, the Gullah population lacked modern conveniences due to isolation and lack of support or recognition from the government. Since most Gullah land was held communally, they also lacked the traditional bundle of rights connected to land ownership. Once infrastructure was modernized, developers exploited the Gullah lack of clear title. Many Gullah were forced off their land and, sensing the end of their culture, sold their Sea Island land to the developers for less than its twentieth-century worth. The remaining Gullah residents were forced to sell and move because escalating prices increased property taxes. The valuable coastal property has been transformed into luxurious resorts. White populations have replaced the Gullah on the Sea Islands, especially commercialized Hilton Head or St. Simon, once Gullah communities, although whites seldom know of the once ubiquitous Gullah heritage on the islands.

In October 2006, the Gullah Cultural Heritage Corridor was officially recognized and given $10 million over the next decade to preserve the culture. The money will help the Gullah maintain their homes, their heritage, and correct at least one environmental problem: Sweetgrass, the main ingredient for their finely crafted baskets, has become scarce. Population growth and development has destroyed or privatized the land upon which the plant grows.

Food Geography: BBQ

Every region has a dominant food that reflects regional resources, culture, and sense of place. Today many unique regional cuisines are disappearing and being replaced by ubiquitous and unsustainable fast food franchises. Southern regional cuisine, however, survives. Slaves developed soul food cuisine featuring the unwanted or inexpensive food and meats—collard greens, black-eyed peas, corn, sweet potatoes, lesser cuts of pork, wild game, and fish. Fried catfish, pork chops, and chicken were popular. Included within the genre was the development of barbeque.

Many Southern locales claim to have the best barbeque (BBQ, or just "Q"). Barbeque's origins are unclear, but they include Spanish *barbacoa*, Native American roasting techniques, African influences, and various ethnic European origins. BBQ's prevalence in the South and the legacy of slavery ties it with less tender cuts of pork—shoulder and ribs—tenderized and preserved by being barbequed in the days before refrigeration. Often semiwild hogs were let out to root in the forest and then caught when the food supply was low.

However, barbeque varies (Map 9.2). Each Atlantic and Gulf South state claims the best Q, which is served in a variety of places, from roadside shacks to church fundraisers. Each state has its own barbeque claim, but in the South BBQ means slow-cooked and smoked, not grilled as outside the South. Certain recipes are ubiquitous—chopped, pulled pork, ribs, and sides of cole slaw and beans.

In the Carolinas, a base fire of oak with hickory BBQ is accompanied by sweet tea. Regional South Carolina savory sauces feature tomato, mustard, ketchup, or vinegar and pepper. North Carolina BBQ regions include Eastern North Carolina whole hog and a sharp apple cider vinegar–based sauce; chefs in

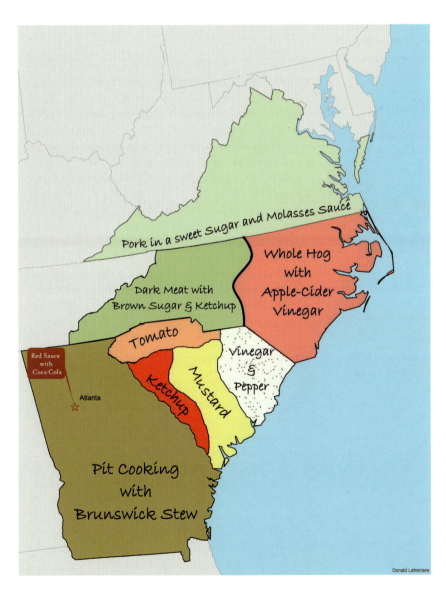

MAP 9.2. Barbeque in the South. States vary in their chosen method and sauce for the best barbeque.

western North Carolina prefer shoulder (dark meat) and sauce it with brown sugar and ketchup. Georgia cuisine favors pit cooking and often includes Brunswick stew, a combination of lima beans, onions, and potatoes with meat and grain. In Atlanta, a red sauce may include Coca-Cola (whose headquarters is in Atlanta). Virginia barbeque, more prevalent in the southern part of the state, favors pork with a sweet sugar and molasses sauce.

NASCAR

The National Association for Stock Car Auto Racing (NASCAR) has been identified in the public's mind as the quintessential southern sport, one that glorified cars, noise, and alcohol. The sport also has ties to moonshiners and flourished during the Prohibition era, when drivers raced their brew-filled cars to the nearby Piedmont cities. Races between the bootlegging runners were inevitable and evolved after WWII into NASCAR, but its roots reach farther and into a less romanticized history. NASCAR—currently headquartered in Daytona Beach, Florida—was already building its solid and profit-oriented reputation as cars developed and set up races at the turn of the twentieth century. NASCAR did rise in the rural Southeast, but it accepts its mythological past as important for the sport and its fans, not on its actual beginnings.[7]

In the 1990s, NASCAR spread across the United States; it became the largest motor sport and the second-largest sporting event on television (behind football). NASCAR has more than seventy-five million fans, and an average of 150,000 fans show up to any one race. The strongest fan base is in the South, but fans are found across the country. In 2004, about 38 percent of fans were from the South, 24 percent from the Midwest, 20 percent from the Northeast, and 10 percent from the West.

NASCAR races are run outside of EPA standards for emissions and fuel efficiency (cars average two to four miles per gallon). The cars have run on leaded gas in the past but transitioned to unleaded fuel in the 2008 series.

Crackers and Rednecks

Crackers

The **crackers** entered a region dense with longleaf Georgia Pine, sometimes called yellow pine, or most commonly, heart pine. Because wiregrass covered the forest floor, the area came to be known as Wiregrass Georgia, and its settlers were said to be as tough and wiry as the grass.[8]

Cracker and *redneck* are two derogatory terms for poor Southern white settlers, usually of Scots-Irish descent; the terms usually referred to a "white trash," uneducated person from the state of Georgia or perhaps northern Florida, although historic references also place them in the Virginia and Carolina backcountry. The term **cracker** has various possible origins: the tendency to crack whips while herding livestock or the practice of cracking rather than milling corn. Both were American adaptations of Scots-Irish culture; the livestock they herded were cattle and pigs, not sheep; and corn grits were the grain of choice, not oat porridge.

Both blacks and wealthy whites discriminated against poor whites, but in 1932 literary voices began defending their cracker ancestry with Erskine Caldwell's *Tobacco Road* and *God's Little Acre*, continuing in 1999 with Janisse Ray's *Ecology of a Cracker Childhood*. In each the plain, simple lives are recounted, and reason and context places these people within their milieu and way of life, rather than as caricatures.

Rednecks

The culture so dramatically symbolized by the Southern redneck [is] the greatest inhibitor of the plans of the activist Left and the cultural Marxists for a new kind of society altogether. From the perspective of the activist Left, [rednecks] are the greatest obstacles to what might be called the collectivist taming of America, symbolized by the edicts of political correctness. And for the last fifty years the Left has been doing everything in its power to sue them, legislate against their interests, mock them in the media, isolate them as idiosyncratic, and publicly humiliate their traditions in order to make them, at best, irrelevant to America's future growth.

—James Webb, 2004[9]

Rednecks—salt-of-the-earth "Joe Sixpacks"—can be found anywhere in the United States today, but the term comes from the South and could be derogatory or a source of pride, depending on its source. The redneck is the yeoman farmer who may well have arrived as an indentured servant or been dumped on the colonies to rid the mother country of undesirables. Today in an age of political correctness, the case has been made that the redneck is a scapegoat, the "other." The redneck can be termed the white underclass in the United States and has been pitted against the blacks and despised by wealthier whites. Traits tied to rednecks are loyalty to kin, mistrust of government, and fierce fighting.

The term *redneck* comes from Scotland, where Scot-Irish dissenters remained Protestant rather than join the Church of England. The redneck signed his name in blood and wore a red cloth around his neck to show dissent. When rednecks immigrated to America the name stuck. Some people, though, trace the name to a person from the South who worked in the sun and earned his red neck. Either way, the redneck's ethnic background can be traced to cracker, Scots-Irish, or Celtic roots.

Regional Life

Population

There were few Southern antebellum cities. Most people lived on self-sufficient plantations or farms. All of Georgia had but thirty-six towns on the 1860 census; North Carolina had twenty-five and South Carolina only fifteen, whereas northern states had hundreds of towns per state. For example, Vermont alone had more than 360 towns in 1860, although it had less than half the population of South Carolina. After the Civil War, the southern landscape became urbanized because the South could no longer maintain its plantation economy. But the South was so far behind northern development that it took a century to develop an urban infrastructure (Table 9.4).

Southern population and diversity has a distinct black-white racial profile. The regional black population remains more than double the national percentage. The southern black population is concentrated in the old plantation areas; however, many blacks migrated north during the twentieth century. Until the 1970s, blacks were pushed from the South to escape Jim Crow discrimination and civil rights injustices; they were pulled by employment opportunities in northern manufacturing industries. However, the Civil Rights movement resulted in reform laws against racial discrimination and natural justice; although rights continue to be unequal, conditions are slowly changing for the better. But diversity within the region is also changing. With few exceptions, both black and white population percentages have declined since 1990 in the Atlantic South. During the same time period, Hispanics replaced blacks as the largest minority in the nation (Hispanics 16.0 percent, blacks 13.6 percent [2010]). Blacks are still the largest minority in the southern states, but the Hispanic population in the Atlantic South rose from negligible in 1990 to 6.7 percent in 2009 (Table 9.5). Part of the reason for this demographic shift is the rise in hog and poultry **concentrated animal feeding operations (CAFOs)** in the South and the inexpensive labor needed to work these jobs. Another population shift during the past decade is the return of blacks from the Northeast to their southern roots. For example, 70 percent of the blacks leaving New York City since 1990 migrated to the Atlantic South or Florida. They were lured by the lower cost of living and better job opportunities in cities

such as Atlanta and Orlando. The South significantly gained black population during the 1990s, while every other U.S. region lost black population (Chart 9.1).

Traditional and Sustainable Cities

After the Civil War, the Southern economy and population shifted from rural agricultural to urban and from coastal to Piedmont. The few antebellum cities were on the coast, but currently, the two largest cities in the South are Atlanta and Charlotte, both on the Piedmont (Table 9.6). For example, population in antebellum Atlanta was 9,500 in 1860, but immediately after the Civil War, even after its destruction by General Sherman, the population was 21,780 in 1870 and 37,409 in 1880. By 1900, it grew to almost 90,000. Virginia's development differed from the Carolinas and Georgia, because the early cities were already along the fall line, with the exception of Norfolk. Urban growth followed the development of a manufacturing economy. Textile mills relocated from the Northeast to the Piedmont and created hundreds of company towns and several cities. Low-density non-farming development became common along the Piedmont and remains so today, but the rural population is dependent on urban employment. The Piedmont population, a southern version of sprawl, has more than four million residents spread across the region in what has been called "spersopolis."[10]

Cities are prevalent along the fall line (Richmond, Raleigh), on the Piedmont (Atlanta), or along the coastal drowned valley

TABLE 9.5. Percentage of Blacks, Whites, and Hispanics in Atlantic Southern States, 2010 (1990)

	Virginia	North Carolina	South Carolina	Georgia	United States
Blacks	19.4 (18.8)	21.5 (22.0)	27.9 (29.8)	30.5 (26.9)	12.6 (12.1)
Whites	68.6 (77.5)	68.5 (75.5)	66.2 (69.0)	59.7 (71.0)	72.4 (80.3)
Hispanics	7.9 (0.16)	8.4 (1.2)	5.1 (0.8)	8.38 (1.6)	16.3 (9.0)

Source: U.S. Census

TABLE 9.4. Number of Cities in the Atlantic South, 1860 and 1880

	1860	1880
Virginia	107	307
North Carolina	25	195
South Carolina	15	113
Georgia	36	200

Source: U.S. Census

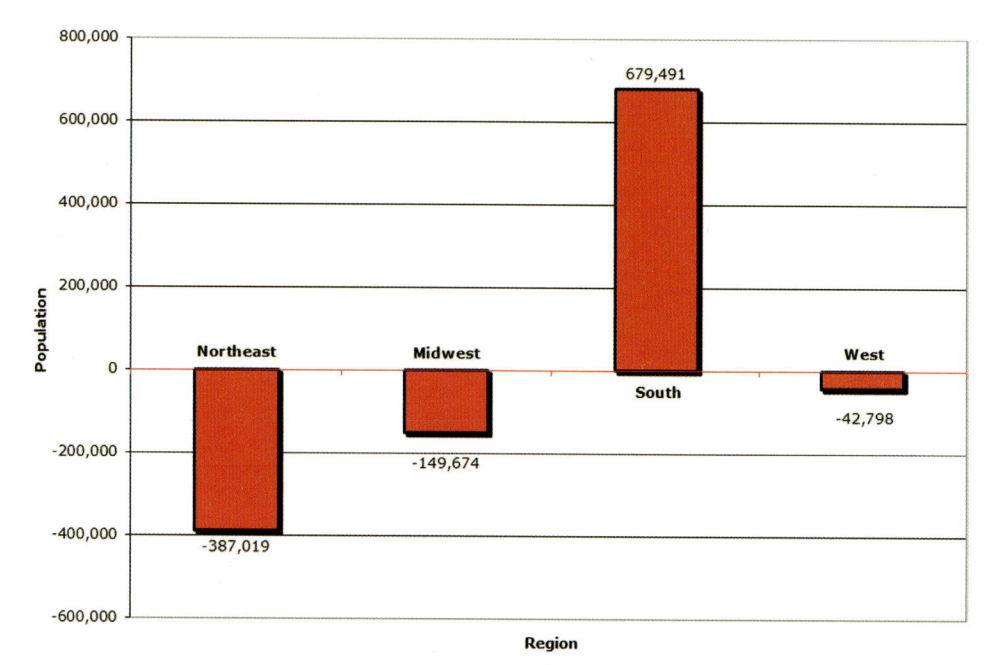

CHART 9.1. Black Net Migration from Regions, 1990–2000

Source: Based on William H. Frey's analysis of current population survey data, "Census 2000 Shows Large Black Return to the South, Reinforcing the Region's 'White-Black' Demographic Profile," *PSC Research Report* no. 01-473 (Ann Arbor, Mich.: Population Studies Center and Milken Institute, May 2001).

harbors (Norfolk, Wilmington, Charleston, and Savannah). Few significant cities are located within the coastal plain.

Richmond, Virginia
(2010 pop. 204,214, MSA 1,258,251)

Straddling the fall line at the James River, Richmond, the capital of both Virginia and the Confederacy, has been the break-in-bulk center of eastern Virginia's commerce and industry since colonial times. The city developed independent of Washington, D.C., but evolving transportation networks over the past century have drawn Richmond into the national capital's suburban loop. The economy reflects this, as it is primarily driven by law, finance, and government agencies.

Raleigh-Durham-Chapel Hill Triangle, North Carolina
(Raleigh 2010 pop. 403,892; Chapel Hill 48,715; Durham 228,330; CSA 1,749,525)

These three municipalities are known as the Research Triangle, or locally, simply as the Triangle. Major universities—North

TABLE 9.6. Population of Southern Cities, 1860–2010

	1860	1880	1900	1960	2010
Savannah, Georgia	22,292	30,709	54,244	149,245	136,286
Atlanta, Georgia	9,500	37,409	89,872	487,455	420,003
Charleston, South Carolina	40,522	49,984	55,807	65,925	120,083
Columbia, South Carolina	8,052	10,036	21,108	97,433	129,272
Wilmington, North Carolina	9,000	17,350	20,976	44,013	106,476
Charlotte, North Carolina	2,200	7,094	26,312	201,564	731,424
Raleigh, North Carolina	4,780	9,265	19,479	93,931	403,892
Norfolk, Virginia	14,000	21,906	46,624	305,872	242,803
Richmond, Virginia	37,000	63,000	85,050	219,958	204,214

Source: U.S. Census

Carolina State, Duke, and the University of North Carolina, Chapel Hill—form the basis for this technopole, the largest planned research and development park in the United States. Establishing the technopole in the 1960s helped reverse the North Carolina brain drain. Today the technopole's success can be measured by the presence of a high per capita rate of PhDs and MDs. The development was not easy.

In the 1960s, Governor Terry Sanford of North Carolina reversed the low per capita income figures for his state. He created Research Triangle Park, a partnership between business, government, and higher education. The major industries at the time revolved around tobacco, textiles, and furniture, all of which are still part of the economy. However, the economy has expanded into numerous research facilities, technology companies, and medical centers. In 1965 the first tenants were the National Institute of Environmental Health Sciences and IBM, followed by a number of technological and life science companies. The Triangle is now considered one of the best places to live and work in America.

Charlotte, North Carolina

(2010 pop. 731,424; CSA 2,402,623)

Charlotte is the second-largest city in the Southeast. Situated on the Piedmont, the city began as a cotton processing center and then a railroad hub after the Civil War. It gained fame as a financial center due to banking acquisitions in the 1970s and 1980s and became home to the Bank of America and other major banks in America.

Perhaps Charlotteans are thinking about climate change more than others, due to some unusual climate events. In 1989, although it is two hundred miles from the coast, the city was caught unprepared and suffered considerable damage from Hurricane Hugo. In 2002, an ice storm, unusual at its subtropical latitude, knocked out power for weeks.

Charlotte was granted a $6.8 million Energy Efficiency and Conservation Block Grant by the U.S. Department of Energy in 2009, which has allowed it to adopt more progressive integrated environmental policies that are supported by the administration, and to appoint a sustainable manager to oversee programs to reduce emissions and energy consumption.

Charleston, South Carolina

(2010 pop. 120,083; MSA 664,607)

English traders established Charleston in 1670, and it became one of the few antebellum southern cities. Charleston's location at the Ashley and Cooper confluence allowed planters to ferry between their plantations and the port. In an era when malaria and yellow fever raged through the coastal swamps, Charleston grew as an ocean breeze refuge and became the social center for southern Low Country planters (Photo 9.5). Since the "War of Northern Aggression," Charleston has gone its merry way, believing that it is the center of the universe (for example, to a Charlestonian the Ashley and Cooper confluence forms the Atlantic Ocean) and that all things Charleston are important. Certainly its downtown (the high ground in a marshy landscape) emphasis on historic preservation is impressive and draws many of the tourists it seeks, but it has become a multimillion-dollar investment that outsiders use for second or third homes and has lost its community and neighborhood charm. Outside the hallowed historic district, the rest of the town and the surrounding area are depressed, except for newly redeveloped but pricey sprawl.

The economy has been bumpy, especially when the Navy pulled out in 1996, leaving thousands without jobs and a hole in the city that has since undergone redevelopment, some with a more sustainable footprint. Charleston is also deeply involved in military defense and security centers, which draw a highly educated workforce.

Atlanta, Georgia

(2010 pop. 420,003; CSA 5,618,431)

Atlanta is Georgia's capital and the largest city in the Atlantic South. In 1837, railroad promoters established Terminus—Atlanta's original name—at the base of the Appalachians, giving it both East Coast and midwestern distribution connections. In 1864, Union troops occupied and burned the city to the ground, with the exception of churches and hospitals. It rebuilt and became the leading southern distribution point for goods up the Atlantic Coast.

The city has become a magnet of opportunities for blacks. Atlanta's inner city black population is middle class, but the city remains racially polarized. Ultimately, Atlanta became a majority black city (54.0 percent black, 38.3 percent white, 5.2 percent Hispanic, 3.1 percent Asian [2010]) with a white suburban ring. The power-play tension between the white outlying areas and the black inner core has been palpable.

Atlanta has become the economic center for the South, important in the technology sector, supported by a highly skilled workforce, regulatory incentives, and a political machine that works with research universities and the private sector. Atlanta is also a major tourist and convention destination. Hartsfield-Jackson Airport is the busiest airport in the world and is the Delta Airlines and AirTran Airways hub.

Metro Atlanta is third to New York and Houston in the number of Fortune 500 company headquarters; its largest corporation is Coca-Cola, invented for headache relief by a local pharmacist in 1886 as "French Wine Cola." Other major companies and institutions include Home Depot, United Parcel Service (UPS), and the Centers for Disease Control and Prevention (CDC). Turner Broadcasting media headquarters (CNN) is in Atlanta, and the Weather Channel is located in nearby suburban Marietta.

Sprawl From 2000 to 2010, Georgia was the seventh-fastest-growing state and has continued its growth.[11] Currently, only 10 percent of Atlanta's metropolitan population live in the city. The remainder sprawl unchecked across twenty counties.

The north-south distance across the sprawling city has grown from 68 miles in 1990 to 121 miles in 1997, and the city continues to spread. The unobstructed geography—flat with no large bodies of water, natural boundaries, or federal land—has created a low-density pattern inconvenient for mass transit (Photo 9.6). Atlanta is the least densely populated city in America, with 1,370 persons per square mile, compared to 5,400 in Los Angeles. The seemingly endless sprawl has created traffic and environmental problems.

Commute times in the Atlanta region are second only to Los Angeles. Zoning separates residential from office and retail use, so people depend on cars and walkability is low. Commutes of only ten miles can take an hour, and many live up to thirty miles from the city.

Metro city planning lacks consideration of water or air quality. The amount of green space and trees is negligible—the city lost 38 percent of its greenery between 1982 and 1992—creating a heat island effect and more air pollution, especially vexing during an already hot, humid summer.

However, beginning in 1996 with the Olympics and progressing since, several areas in Atlanta have become more sustainable. Atlanta has supported energy efficiency and building; it has the most LEED-certified buildings in the Southeast, but it has done little to encourage retrofit incentives or public participation. The transit-oriented developments (TODs) downtown along the MARTA perimeter rail line have created several walkable communities that have escalated in price. But public transport and bicycling serve only 5 percent of the population, so congestion remains near impossible. Connect Atlanta, a new transportation plan, hopes to give more residents access to public transport.

Savannah, Georgia

(2010 pop. 136,286; CSA 425,528)

Savannah is a city with a reputation, in many ways it is quintessentially southern, personifying the dank, subtropical eccentricities that attract those seeking a real southern experience.

Savannah was founded as a utopian community by James Oglethorpe on the Savannah River in 1733. His idealism led him to create a unique urban plan and to outlaw slavery and drinking—fearing the vices would weaken the colony in the face of the Spanish enemy. Both laws were overturned by mid-century, because settlers believed that the slavery and drinking restrictions, in a turn of irony, weakened the colony. However, the city's original urban plan—with open space and multiple squares—continues to attract those seeking a more convivial atmosphere.

During the Civil War, the city surrendered rather than undergo the ignominy of destruction by Sherman's troops. This allowed the city to maintain its southern charm and historical buildings, but it took another move in the mid-twentieth century to preserve a fading glory. Historic preservation in Savannah has helped the city become a popular tourist city. In 1994, John Berendt's *Midnight in the Garden of Good and Evil* assisted the city by portraying the eccentric nature of its citizens within the story of a sensational murder.

Savannah continues to seek economic isolation and favors maintaining its unique image. But Savannah is an important part of the Georgia economy: it is the main port for Georgia, a main processor of paper pulp from Georgia's vast pine forests, the home to Gulfstream (a leader in corporate jet production,) and its dominant industry is historic preservation cum eccentric-oriented tourism.

PHOTO 9.5. Rainbow Row, Charleston, South Carolina, is a beautiful example of the restored historic district. Eighteenth-century Charleston society was more interested in replicating British society than were the more northern cities. Its buildings were first built with brick but later stuccoed over and still later painted in Caribbean-influenced colors.

PHOTO 9.6. Atlanta, Georgia, is considered one of the fastest-growing and most sprawling cities in America. The lack of physical boundaries or nearby federal land allows the city to continue to sprawl in all directions.

Economy

In a sense colonial economy is just the right description of the South's condition, a distinct economy located within the political jurisdiction of a larger country, subject to laws, markets, polities, and technologies that it would not have chosen had it been independent. . . . The "colonial economy" no longer exists because "outsiders" have so thoroughly penetrated the South that both the people and the economy have lost their distinct identities, economically speaking. [12]

After the Civil War, the southern economy veered from plantation to industrial; the South evolved into a "colony" of the North and then into the current northern-influenced economy. The South never developed its own technology adaptable to its particular geographic and economic realities, and so it has relied on northern manufacturing methods to process raw southern goods.

The plantation economy's self-sufficiency discouraged cities, infrastructure, settlers, and manufacturing. Development was retarded until after the Civil War, when northern money and **carpetbaggers** moved south to take advantage of the raw materials and cheap labor. The carpetbaggers invested in railroads, steel, cigarettes, and liquor. The textile industry grew after the Civil War.

A bright spot in the local economy is the growth in the southern carpet industry, especially in Georgia. From humble beginnings in the 1930s—selling homemade tufted bedspreads—the industry has increased its jobs, from thirty-two thousand to forty thousand since 1997, even as the state lost manufacturing jobs. Part of the reason it has maintained its stability in the face of jobs fleeing elsewhere is the mechanization of the industry and its bulk. Less than 10 percent of costs are labor, and its bulk is a disadvantage for overseas shippers. [13]

After the Civil War a New South emerged, but the Southern economy remained regional and low wage for blacks and for textile workers (nearly all white). A second "New South" emerged after World War II, when racial tensions and segregation began to ease and southern industrial growth was invigorated. Spurred by the national wage and labor laws of the 1930s, a new ease in transportation, and the advantages of the warmer climate (largely made amenable because of air-conditioning), the New South developed cities that mirrored northern urban plans.

Much of the new growth is in the automobile industry. During the late twentieth century, the industry devolved from the unionized North, and new auto factories opened in the Southern nonunion **right-to-work states** where low land and labor costs beckoned. Spartanburg, Greenville, and Anderson in South Carolina now manufacture automobile parts, tires, or silicon chips. Incentives of $150 million lured BMW to Spartanburg, while North Carolina benefited with lucrative jobs and contracts for auto suppliers. In Virginia, while some manufacturers closed, others received new orders. Roanoke satisfies the demand for railcars as rail traffic escalates. In Greensboro, North Carolina, part of the Carolina Triad (Winston-Salem, High Point, and Greensboro), regional jobs once focused on tobacco and then furniture, but now are shifting to new industries. Honda opened a business-jet-manufacturing facility, while others pursue the biotech industry and research rather than manufacturing.

However, despite the new jobs and manufacturing facilities, the Piedmont economy is frail. Manufacturing jobs are relatively scarce; they pay less than union jobs, but still better than the proliferation of poor-paying service jobs. People are

BOX 9.3 SUSTAINABLE CARPET

One of the most renowned American sustainable industrial stories is the conversion of Interface Inc., headquartered in Atlanta, Georgia. Interface's founder and chairman Ray Anderson read Paul Hawken's *Ecology of Commerce* and had an epiphany on the environmental actions of companies. He vowed to make his company one of the most sustainable in America.

His company has become a leader in **industrial ecology**—a network of industrial processes that interact and live off each other, economically, while eliminating waste. The waste of one company becomes the resource of another company, or it is recycled within the original company. Industrial ecology aims to work as nature works, rather than trying to conquer nature.

Since Mr. Anderson's epiphany, the company has become more sustainable and aims to achieve zero emissions by 2020. In its redefinition of industry, the company has identified seven fronts that define the climb to "Mount Sustainability." In order, they are as follows:

1. Eliminating waste: Reduce and simplify the amount of resources used.
2. Benign emissions: Eliminate toxic substances used.
3. Renewable energy: Operate facilities with solar, wind, geothermal, and other renewable energy sources.
4. Closing the loop: Redesign processes and products to recover materials for reuse and to return organic materials to their natural systems.
5. Resource-efficient transportation: Reduce pollution and greenhouse gas emissions to offset CO_2 emissions.
6. Sensitizing stakeholders: Educate all involved in the company about sustainability, and share environmental and social goals.
7. Redesigning commerce: Create a new business model that is sustainably based.*

* Interface Global, at http://www.interfaceglobal.com/getdoc/224de860-bf76-4d2f-973c-80af60a4addd/7-Fronts-of-Sustainability.aspx.

---

employed but for less money. Median household income dropped 20 percent from 1999 to 2005.

Primary Industry and Natural Resources

The Atlantic South was dependent on agriculture prior to the Civil War and the textile industry into the mid-twentieth century. The regional paucity of minerals is offset by rich endowments of lumber and fish.

Rural Areas and Agriculture

The South depended on an agricultural economy much longer than the rest of America. The long frost-free periods and soil types were conducive to specific crops: tobacco, indigo, rice, sugar, and cotton. Livestock gained importance when the tobacco crop began to decline in the 1950s. Southern entrepreneurs seeking other agricultural pursuits revolutionized chicken and then hog production and changed the American livestock landscape. Since that time, both tobacco and cotton have undergone transitions as crops. Tobacco quotas have ended, which exacerbated problems for the small tobacco farmer, while cotton has returned to the Atlantic Coastal states after the regional eradication of the **boll weevil** (Map 9.3).

Historically, the Atlantic South had two types of farmers: the plantation owner and the yeoman farmer. They were separated socioeconomically. The plantation owner was deemed a member of the powerful aristocracy, while the yeoman farmer was relegated to a lesser socioeconomic order, the redneck, cracker, or "trash."

After the Civil War, many plantation owners retained their land by renting to tenant farmers. Freed slaves and poor whites rented and sharecropped the land, with contracts favoring the landowner interests. The owner provided the land, mule, plow, and seed; the sharecropper provided the labor. Often the costs exceeded crop profits. In a way, this kept the "practice" of slavery alive, as often the sharecropper was in perpetual debt to the owner. Thus the plantation changed from a singly owned and operated economy to multiple producing families living on the land and "sharing" the crop and "wealth." The poor yeoman farmer continued to farm his marginal upcountry soil into the early twentieth century, when most left the farm because competition from mechanization was destroying any hope of profitability.

Tobacco

Tobacco is longing, tobacco is desire, tobacco is a dream. That makes it perfect for a southern landscape that has long made dreaming a prerequisite for survival. . . . Even as the modern South moves slowly into the smoke-free zone, the haunting aroma of tobacco longing hangs on, lingering like the whiff of a dream.[14]

Tobacco brought the southern colonies their first economic success. In Jamestown the English adopted imported West Indies varieties over the local because it was a smoother, less biting smoke. Trade began with England within a decade of settlement.

Tobacco brought wealth to the Tidewater landed aristocracy. First grown along the Chesapeake Bay estuaries, tobacco was one leg of the **triangular trade**—tobacco to England, manufactured goods to Africa, slaves to America. Tobacco cultivation spread from the Tidewater to the Piedmont and eventually to Kentucky. Tobacco's labor-intensive workforce evolved from indentured servants to slaves and then, after the Civil War, to tenant farmers who farmed small plots. But labor was not the only problem: Tobacco exhausts the soil and requires an intimate knowledge of its physical requirements.

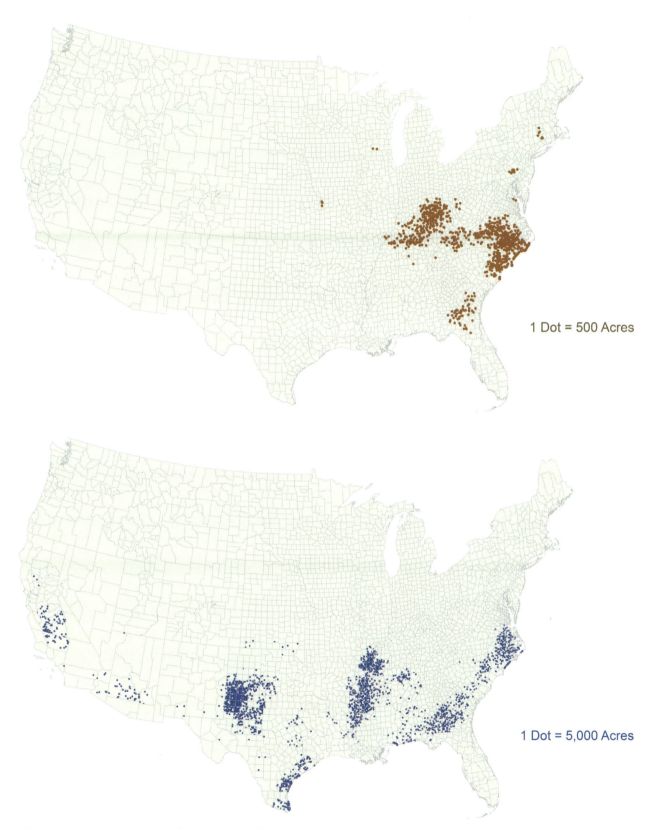

1 Dot = 500 Acres

1 Dot = 5,000 Acres

MAP 9.3. Tobacco (top) and Cotton (bottom), Harvested Acres, 2002. Two of the most important crops in South Atlantic history have been tobacco and cotton. Both have undergone changes in the recent past. Tobacco is no longer a quota crop, and cotton has returned to the Atlantic coast after elimination of the boll weevil.

Virginia was the center of the early tobacco trade, but the colonies developed different varieties and methods to cure the leaf. Air curing (drying of the leaf) was used in Maryland and Kentucky, fire curing on the Piedmont. Flue curing evolved in the 1840s, and along with new methods of growing tobacco for milder flavor developed the modern industry along the Virginia–North Carolina coastal plain.

The industrialization of tobacco began in the 1880s. For the farmer, mechanization reduced field labor 80 percent, although tobacco remains more labor intensive than other crops. Cigarette factories were constructed near the crop, because raw tobacco is most profitable when processed locally and then shipped. Until the 1970s, most tobacco products were shipped within the large domestic market where smoking was perceived as "cool."[15] Then the market moved overseas, mostly to China, where U.S. tobacco companies promoted their product to the tune of $15 billion in 2006. Nearly three-quarters of all Chinese men smoke.

At the beginning of the twentieth century, the American Tobacco Company controlled 90 percent of the industry, but it was forced to break up the monopoly due to a 1911 antitrust suit. Emerging from the breakup were four companies (in order of market share): a reshaped American Tobacco Company, R.J. Reynolds (Camels), P. Lorillard (Newport), and Liggett and Myers (Chesterfield). R.J. Reynolds and the American Tobacco Company were founded by the Dukes (after whom the university is named) and were centered in Winston-Salem and Durham, North Carolina. Another company, Philip Morris (now Altria Group; makers of Marlboro), would later emerge from the breakup.

Rice, "Carolina Gold"   Neither tobacco nor sugar grew well along the swampy, mosquito-infested Sea Islands, but once the land was drained and irrigated, rice became the staple crop of the Low Country. By 1730, the South Carolina coast was a center of rice production. Charleston exported ten thousand pounds in 1698 and more than twenty million pounds by 1730.

Lacking laborers for the burgeoning rice plantations, early-eighteenth-century planters turned to slaves, as had their Virginia tobacco-growing neighbors. The most-sought-after slaves were from the West African Rice Coast, where Africans had grown rice for thousands of years. The arduous work and high mortality rates for whites kept the area almost entirely black for the duration of the rice-growing industry.

Most rice was exported to Northern European countries. But rice was also consumed in the South, and in many Southern cuisines rice remains the staple starch.

Rice growers became very wealthy during the antebellum period and aligned themselves with the Charleston elite. They built grand plantations and gardens, even using Versailles as their model. Their wealth also made them confident that they could break free of colonization and become an independent nation.

After the Civil War, rice production declined in the Atlantic South, while it expanded into the Gulf South. Early in the twentieth century, large-scale rice production ended in the Carolinas. Arkansas is the number one producer of rice in the United States today.

Indigo   Before synthetic dyes were developed, natural dyes were the only way to dye clothes, but most natural colors were muted browns and grays with few colorfast or bright colors. The leaves of the spindly indigo plant created a brilliant blue that was cherished among ancient people and became a favored crop and trade commodity in the subtropics, supplying the "royal" blue that denoted wealth and social standing. The plant grew wild along the South Carolina, Georgia, and northern Florida coasts, but it was war that made indigo a valuable crop.

During the first half of the eighteenth century, England was at war with Spain and France, ending indigo trade with colonial India, Central America, and the East Indies. Britain needed the deep blue dye for its textile industry and paid a bounty for American indigo. The American "indigo bonanza" from 1740 to 1790 doubled investment every three to four years. The American Revolution ended trade with Britain, and after Britain resumed trade with its other colonies, the market was glutted. Indigo planters in the South shifted to growing cotton, a judicious choice as the **cotton gin** had just been invented and the period of King Cotton began. Cotton exports increased from one million to six million pounds from 1797 to 1800, while indigo went from more than a million pounds exported in 1775 to 3,400 pounds in 1800.

Indigo dye (the color used for denim) is almost completely synthetic today, but wild, perennial indigo plants still bloom in the spring along the roadsides of South Carolina, two hundred years after the industry was abandoned.

Cotton   From the late eighteenth century until World War II, cotton was the single most important crop in the South's agricultural economy. Cotton became the major crop when American and British textile mills demanded more than the plantations could supply, and the labor-intensive process of separating the seed from the boll had been mechanized.

The Atlantic South grew two types of cotton: Sea Island and upland cotton. Sea Island cotton was imported from the West Indies. It had a longer fiber and was easier to clean, but the finicky plant only grew on the small offshore islands and demand exceeded supply. Upland cotton grew inland but was difficult to clean. The cotton gin automated the labor-intensive process in 1793 and was the first of numerous inventions that helped increase cotton production from 1.5 million pounds in 1790 to 673 million pounds in 1840. This period was the slave-dependent era, when nearly 75 percent of the 2.5 million slaves in America worked in cotton fields.

Cotton production was dominant in the Atlantic South but migrated west over time. Production spread into the Piedmont region in the 1830s, when the Indian Removal Program cleared the region of Native Americans.

Continuous cotton production exhausted already poor soils, and the resulting erosion caused the large plantation owners to move their Atlantic South cotton plantations to the Gulf Coast and up the Mississippi River Valley. After the Civil War, large-scale plantation cotton production ended and sharecropping began. Cotton production dropped radically after 1960 due to boll weevil infestations but has rebounded in the twenty-first century. However, cotton has several other environmental and social issues (Table 9.7).

Cotton production ranks third behind corn and soybeans for the amount of fossil fuel–based chemicals used, several of which are carcinogenic. Some farmers are now avoiding this problem by growing organic cotton, but the vast majority of cotton is conventionally raised.

The United States is the leading exporter of cotton. There have been several cases of illegal and unfair cotton subsidies brought to the attention of the WTO (World Trade Organization), in which it is claimed that the subsidies given to American farmers undermine developing world farmers' livelihoods and destroy their export markets.

Other Crops   Other Southern crops include peanuts in Georgia (Jimmy Carter was a peanut farmer) and peaches. The "Georgia peach" is a classic, but it is also popular in South Carolina's Ridge region, located between the Piedmont and Sandhills near Aiken. However, California is number one in peach production, followed by South Carolina and Georgia.

Livestock

Both poultry and hog production have changed radically in the latter twentieth century, resulting in an increase in meat consumption without a huge increase in price. The cost of plentiful meat, though, came at the expense of ethical and environmental problems.

Poultry   "A chicken in every pot" seems strange in the twenty-first century as a saying indicating wealth and prosperity, but before World War II chicken was luxury meat. The 1928 Republican presidential slogan (along with "a car in every backyard") was an American Dream for continued prosperity. This dream came to fruition after World War II through the introduction of **vertical integration**—a single large company controlling a commodity, in this case chicken, through the entire highly mechanized process "from semen to cellophane." Prior to vertical integration, each stage of production was owned by a different entity—the farmer, the miller, the processor, the transporter, etc. This method was not providing profit at most levels. Improvement came through vertical integration, which improves supply chain coordination, reduces transportation costs by having all production in geographic proximity, and captures profit margins at all stages of production.

In vertical integration, farmers own the land and the barns where thousands of chickens are raised every six weeks, but the company owns the chickens, the food, and any other part of the production process. The **contract farmer** follows precise instructions for raising the chickens to earn about $7.50 an hour, but it is a guaranteed income rather than the erratic income of tobacco or other crops. Contracting for a vertically integrated company has become an attractive alternative for many farmers, but the contracts are not always renewed. Growers may renew their contract with each flock of poultry, but each new flock brings the chance of insecurity. Vertical integration, while stabilizing incomes, has taken advantage of farmers, so many join poultry owners' associations and unions for income protection.

Insecure as the contract farmer's life can be, the advent of the vertically integrated poultry industry changed the 1910 luxury meat into an inexpensive and readily available meat in the twenty-first century (Table 9.8).

Tyson initiated contract chicken production in the 1950s, but several companies in the Atlantic South were also moving toward vertical integration. Georgia emerged as the top producer of chicken, with more than 6.5 billion pounds in 1998.

TABLE 9.7. Acres of Upland Cotton Harvested in the Atlantic South and Texas, 1960–2008

	Virginia (000)	North Carolina (000)	South Carolina (000)	Georgia (000)	Texas (000)
1960	15.5	390	—	653	6,303
1970	4.3	160	—	375	4,870
1980	0.3	65	120	160	6,850
1990	5.3	200	154	350	5,000
2000	108	925	290	1,350	4,400
2008	60	428	134	920	3,250

Source: U.S. Department of Agriculture, National Agricultural Statistics Service, at http://www.nass.usda.gov

TABLE 9.8. U.S. per Capita Meat Availability, 1910–2007

Year	Pounds of chicken	Pounds of beef	Pounds of pork
1910	11.0	48.5	38.2
1920	9.7	40.7	39.0
1930	11.1	33.7	41.1
1940	10.0	42.6	45.1
1950	14.3	44.6	43.0
1960	19.1	59.1	48.6
1970	27.4	79.6	48.1
1980	32.7	72.1	52.1
1990	42.4	63.9	46.4
2000	54.2	64.5	47.8
2007	59.9	62.2	47.3

Source: USDA/Economic Research Service

Processing chickens is the number one agricultural commodity in Georgia. Turkey and egg production also thrive in the South. North Carolina produced the second-largest amount of turkeys in 2005 (behind Minnesota). Egg production in the South is a secondary market, following the Midwest.

Hogs   Vertical integration also changed hog production, although integration occurred a few decades after chicken integration. Once again, the dying tobacco industry spurred changes in hog production from dirt-floored pigpens to plastic slats in metal concentrated animal feeding operations (CAFOs). Concentrated vertically integrated hog production added new industry to the Atlantic South. North Carolina became the second-largest hog-producing state despite a lack of the dominant feed, locally produced corn.

The person who changed hog production was a tobacco farmer, Wendell Murphy, who was seeking another form of income as the tobacco industry failed around him. He established Murphy Family Farms and brought the traditional southern meat, pork, to the South again, from its hiatus with pork producers in the Midwest. Centered in Duplin and Samson counties in eastern North Carolina, Murphy began his rise as the king of CAFO in the 1970s and by the 1990s became the largest individual producer of hogs in the nation.

There were thousands of farmers just like Murphy who lacked a profitable crop but wanted to stay on the land. Murphy provided them a livelihood, the hog—not the few hogs that nearly every farmer raised, but a thousand confined hogs per low-slung metal-roofed holding pen. Murphy's company owned the hogs, but the contract farmers raised them. Contract hogs replaced tobacco as the commodity of choice and provided farmers with a steady income. By 1997, hog production passed tobacco as North Carolina's number one agricultural commodity.

Murphy's method changed hog production across the nation, from thousands of small producers who produced variable-quality hogs to fewer, more regulated hog producers who produced uniform and consistent CAFO hogs of median quality. In 1949, there were 70,496 hog producers in North Carolina who produced about eleven hogs each. By 2007 there were 1,700 hog producers, and 75 percent of them had more than five thousand hogs apiece. Nationally, the number of hog producers declined from more than 600,000 in 1980 to fewer than 100,000 in 2005, although total inventory remained relatively constant.

American pork consumption has remained fairly stable, but to maximize profits the highest-quality meat is exported, most notably to the high-paying Japanese market. Hogs raised in North Carolina are often on the dinner plate in Japan, hardly supporting local production or sustainable practices.

While CAFO hog production has allowed many farmers to stay on their land, it has also had a host of unintended consequences and environmental impacts.

Unintended consequences. While vertically integrated companies have emphasized the economic benefits of CAFO hog production, many people believe that the environmental and social consequences of CAFO production have outweighed the benefits. CAFO hog farms have polluted groundwater and air, and they are raising human and animal health issues. Fertilizing fields with CAFO waste often results in overfertilization and water table contamination. Waste stored in euphemistically named **lagoons**—often unlined and inadequately constructed—leaks into the groundwater. Air pollution has resulted in respiratory diseases in workers and nearby residents, as well as being infamously malodorous. Additionally, the overuse of antibiotics to stop the spread of disease in pigs has been tied to increased antibiotic-resistant germs in humans. And many define the cheek-to-jowl crowding in CAFO farms as animal cruelty.

Local and ecoregional impacts. Starting in the 1990s, North Carolina hog production exploded from 2.6 million hogs in 1988 to almost 10 million hogs in 2010. The growth has been in large-scale hog production facilities that have had a local and ecoregional impact on water and air.

Hog manure has been stored in open-pit lagoons and disposed of by spraying on fields, a troublesome method that at times is extremely hazardous. North Carolina lagoons are built on sandy soil in areas with high water tables. Because water tables are near the surface, hog lagoons often have to be built with berms to keep the depth out of the water table and protect the groundwater. Nonetheless, the feces-laden water can and often does leak into the groundwater and contaminate drinking water. During hurricanes, as in 1999 during Hurricane Floyd, flooding caused the lagoons to overflow and dump the hog waste into rivers, causing massive fish kills.

In Samson and Duplin counties, North Carolina, where hog production is most prevalent, ammonia and methane give off foul odors that waft to surrounding communities and decrease the quality of life for residents.

External costs. CAFO hog production endangers public health. Widespread administration of antibiotics to confined hogs has contributed to antibiotic resistance in humans. In the United States, 70 percent of antibiotics are fed to healthy livestock to promote growth and relieve health concerns with closely confined animals. The antibiotics used for the animals are closely related to those used in human medicine and have decreased the effectiveness of standard antibiotics in humans.[16]

Land located near CAFO facilities decreases in value because of degraded air quality. Most hog farms are located in lower-economic-strata areas; the loss is disproportionately borne by those who can least afford it. The towns that have been saddled with CAFOs are told that the farms will help the economy; in fact they do not, but they help destroy small-scale farmers. Where large hog farms are the standard, it has been unprofitable for local communities, as commodities are often purchased from outside the local area. Rural communities do better socially and economically when there are more farmers rather than having production in the hands of a few. The result is deep-seated rifts between CAFOs and their neighbors.[17]

Solutions. Sustainability in North Carolina's hog industry would benefit all, and research has begun to maximize profits while introducing some sustainable practices. Capturing the methane produced by the lagoons can create additional fuel that can be sold as a by-product. Manure management systems to capture biogas are expensive (about $250,000 minimum per hog farm), but they have the advantage of helping maintain clean air and water, reduce GHG emissions, and provide biogas to operate the facility. Incentives have helped manure management gain acceptance. However, a lack of government incentives has limited the number of biogas operations to less than 1 percent.

While manure management can improve air quality, the CAFO method of hog production is an unsustainable system that has many environmental and social ills. Sustainable livestock production can reduce pollution, clear the air, and provide a more healthful environment for workers and those who live near the farms. Sustainable production is holistic and incorporates human labor rather than depending solely on mechanization, while maintaining animal health and nutrients in the environment.

There has been a trend among consumers toward more natural, organic, and locally grown food. Although the amount of meat produced will be less, it will be a higher quality and sold locally. Reducing the amount of meat produced will also reduce the dependence on corn for livestock production, which in turn will reduce the use of fresh water for growing excess corn crops.

Logging

The presettlement Atlantic South was forested. The land was cleared and used for crop production, mostly cotton, but improper soil use caused erosion and reversion of the land to forest or pasture. The forests of Georgia and North Carolina were stripped in the nineteenth century for use as the nation's naval stores—lumber, rosin, and turpentine to build sailing ships—providing 70 percent of the world supply by the twentieth century. The region was logged during the 1890s, and then the industry left for the more lucrative forests in the Pacific Northwest. A reforestation plan was initiated in the 1940s and has continued, so that the woodland acreage is larger but of less quality today than in the 1930s.

The pulp and paper industry shifted back to the South from the Pacific Northwest in 1982 for two reasons: the spotted owl crisis in the West and the accelerated growth pattern in the warmer southern climate.

Today Georgia is the number one state for lumber production, and lumber processing has provided 23 percent of manufacturing jobs and 2 percent of all jobs in the state. At $24 billion, lumber is the second-largest industry behind food processing. However, the current lumber industry is unsustainable.

Rows of loblolly and slash pine plantations have replaced the native longleaf forests along the coastal plain. Longleaf pines are more resistant to insect and disease pests; however, loblolly can be cut in twenty-five years and used as low-grade lumber or plywood. Farms along the plain disappeared, replaced by uniform and managed tree plantations that lack the natural nurture of fire and the ecological diversity so important for the life of the land.

The logging industry as practiced today is unsustainable and does not support the triple bottom line. It is unhealthy for long-term forests, pays poorly, and provides relatively few jobs.

Fishing

The tidewater has been a prime regional commercial and sport fishing area. Fishing in the tidal areas has yielded blue crabs, shrimp, oysters, clams, and southern flounder. North Carolina's Pamlico-Albemarle Sound system is the largest estuary. Historically, many Gullah made their living collecting oysters, and a few still land oysters along the tidal estuaries, but both the oysters and the Gullah are disappearing (Photo 9.7).

Overfishing has been a problem. The Sustainable Seafood Initiative in South Carolina and similar initiatives in other states adhere to U.S. regulations to improve the fishing stocks and promote eating local seafood. However, the fish and shellfish served in the restaurants are no longer assumed to be from the region because of decreased stocks and pollution.

Tourism

The Atlantic South has increasingly relied on its heritage and good weather to attract tourists. Tourism was the largest or second-largest industry in each state at $59.1 billion regionally in 2005. Tourism accounted for more than 10 percent of all jobs. Civil War battlefields and forts, along with antebellum cities such as Williamsburg, Virginia, or Charleston, South Carolina, are major attractions. Added to these historic sites are the

formerly isolated but now developed Sea Islands. Many islands are now connected to major highways, and some islands, such as Hilton Head or St. Simon's in Georgia, are major tourist attractions, while others offer sporting activities such as kayaking and fishing. National Parks, such as the Okefenokee National Wildlife Refuge and the Cape Hatteras and Cape Lookout seashores, also lure visitors.

Hunting is another form of tourism popular in the South. The South Carolina Low Country deer-hunting season adds more than $240 million to the state's economy. Many old rice plantations have been converted into hunting preserves and wildlife habitats.

In 2005, the tremendously successful aquarium and the World of Coca-Cola added $200 million to the local economy and boosted urban tourism in Atlanta.

A Sustainable Future

In new rebellion we stand together, black and white, urbanite and farmer, workers all, in keeping Dixie. We are a patient people who for generations have not been ousted from this land, and we are willing to fight for the birthright of our children's children and their children's children, to be of a place, in all ways, for all time. What is left is not enough. When we say the South will rise again we can mean that we will allow the cutover forests to return to their former grandeur and pine plantations to grow wild.

—Janisse Ray, *Ecology of a Cracker Childhood*, 1999[18]

The twentieth century changed the South. Many changes followed northern development patterns, and others have been

PHOTO 9.7. Gathering Oysters at Harris Neck, Georgia. Along the Sea Islands, Geechee blacks still make a living harvesting oysters along the tidal estuaries. The region is becoming gentrified, though, and soon the gatherers will be gone.

more sustainable. Dense urban settlement is more sustainable than current settlement patterns but change will not be easy; it contradicts the "wide open spaces" of the American Dream. The Atlantic South was almost totally rural in 1900, but now is much closer to the national urban/rural norm, and follows the distinctly American pattern of a nonwhite inner city and white suburbs, which enforces the difference between more sustainable and diverse European cities and sprawling and racially segregated American cities.

As cities grow, the rural areas wither, or those close enough to urban areas sprout into extended suburbs. But reducing GHG emissions and carbon dioxide levels or conserving fossil fuels will only happen as sprawl and the concomitant use of fossil fuels is reduced. Yet Atlanta is one of the most sprawling and racially polarized cities in America, forcing long commutes and wasted energy. Atlanta's planned perimeter rail line and series of TODs would be a positive step toward density, if the city can overcome its racial tensions.

The agricultural economy has also changed. Large CAFOs have replaced the mom-and-pop livestock farms of the 1900s, and a growing Hispanic community works the low-paying CAFO and processing jobs. While CAFOs have become a prime economic factor in the region, they are destructive to the environment and exploit the wages and health of workers. Rather than eat ever more meat, Americans need to rethink their diet. By eating less meat, they can help preserve the environment and help workers have a healthier workplace.

The future of this region and of the South is a mixed bag. While the region grows as a part of the globalized economy, it does so assimilating into another clone of fast-food, homogenized America. And still the community and idea of a genteel South remains, but it is fractured along racial and economic lines. Even as the New South blossoms, the legacy of the Old South—segregation, racism, and poverty—continues to hold it back from attaining a sustainable culture for all. The city of Charleston, South Carolina, is aesthetic and soothing—until you step out of the historic district and the pastel single houses fade quickly into rundown tenements.

Many people of the Atlantic South have become more aware of population's impact on the environment. In Georgia, attention is being paid to land use and transportation issues, as the cities grow. Atlanta showed a return to growth in the 2000 census after years of decline. Although the city is one of the most sprawling in the nation, people are paying attention to the problems and coming up with solutions to sustain their way of life.

Some southern states are turning to renewable energy to increase energy availability, while others lag. North Carolina—where 95 percent of the electricity is nuclear or coal-fired—has begun to overcome the North Carolina Ridge Law, which was passed in 1983 to protect "unsightly developments" for mountaintop homes and has been a barrier to wind generation. In 2006, as many residents were experiencing high energy costs and seeking renewable energy alternatives, a bill was introduced into the house to expand renewable energy. Wind turbines have been addressed on a county-by-county basis, with some prohibiting the renewable energy because of the viewshed and others encouraging wind power.

South Carolina is attempting to implement renewable energy policies and offer financial incentives. Additionally, some developments, such as Dewee Island in South Carolina, have adopted sustainable development policies, such as building infrastructure using natural drainage and landscaping instead of traditional lawns, but problems exist. They have not developed into the self-contained communities promised; traffic snarls the outgoing highways; and they are affordable for only the wealthy, with home prices starting at $650,000. This is part of the problem with sustainable housing: it is fashionable and not considered essential, therefore it is out of the price range for most people.

Sustainable building does not have to be expensive, but because it is fashionable many sustainable houses are the size of McMansions, rather than less consumptive sizes. Sustainable cities need to accommodate everyone. The large houses were built to satisfy the American need for everything bigger, and the higher property taxes of McMansions are important sources of revenues for cities. While smaller homes may be the future, especially after the economy rebounds, tax income for cities will be affected negatively. Other sources will need to be found or new formulas developed.

Industry has also committed to using alternative fuels. In South Carolina, J.W. Aluminum will be heating its new smelter with methane obtained from rotting trash. The forest industry in Georgia is hoping to become the "Silicon Valley of ethanol," converting tree waste to biomass.

Across the region, universities are involved in clean energy initiatives, sustainability, and going green. Both Duke and the University of North Carolina have worked to become more environmentally friendly in construction, landscaping, and water use.

While there are scattered instances of sustainable action, the Atlantic South has a long way to go to become sustainable. Even Interface, the leading sustainable company, admits, "No individual and no company is truly 'sustainable' yet,"[19] but there are many companies, farmers, and people who see the future and the possibilities for the region to find jobs, profit, and environmental health in sustainable development.

Questions for Discussion

1. Why did textile manufacturing develop in the southern Piedmont region in the late 1800s?

2. Why did textile mills begin to close in the 1970s?

3. How has tobacco production changed since 2004? How has the change affected the tobacco farmer?

4. What has been the impact of poultry and hog production in the southern environment?

5. What is the Gullah language, and where and why did it develop?

6. What is the fall line, and how did it influence the development of the Atlantic South?

7. Is the fall line as important for the location of cities today as it was in the eighteenth century? Why or why not?

8. What factors influenced the location of Atlanta?

9. What do Charleston, Savannah, and the Hampton Roads areas share, and how do they differ from the rest of the coastal plain?

10. What factors led to the demise of cotton in the Atlantic South?

11. Will cotton continue to be an economically viable crop as WTO talks increasingly call for a level playing field?

12. Where was cigarette manufacturing concentrated? Why?

13. Can CAFO production last in the long term?

14. Read the Web pages on sustainability for Interface (http://www.interfacesustainability.com/whatis.html) and comment on the advantages and disadvantages of a sustainable future for the carpet, CAFO, or automotive industry in the Atlantic South.

Suggested Readings

Baird, Keith E. "Guy B. Johnson Revisited: Another Look at Gullah." *Journal of Black Studies* 10, no. 4 (June 1980): 425–35.

Berendt, John. *Midnight in the Garden of Good and Evil: A Savannah Story.* New York: Random House, 1994.

Brown, R. Harold. *The Greening of Georgia: The Improvement of the Environment in the Twentieth Century.* Macon, Ga.: Mercer University Press, 2002.

Calhoun, Daniel L., Elizabeth A. Frick, and Gary R. Buell. "Effects of Urban Development on Nutrient Loads and Streamflow, Upper Chattahoochee River Basin, Georgia, 1976–2001." *Proceedings of the 2003 Georgia Water Resources Conference,* April 23–24, 2003.

Carney, Judith A. *Black Rice: The African Origins of Rice Cultivation in the Americas.* Cambridge, Mass.: Harvard University Press, 2001.

Conner, William H., Thomas W. Doyle, and Ken W. Krauss, eds. *Ecology of Tidal Freshwater Forested Wetlands of the Southeastern United States.* New York: Springer, 2007.

Conroy, Pat. *Prince of Tides.* Boston: Houghton Mifflin, 1986.

Egerton, John. *The Americanization of Dixie: The Southernization of America.* New York: Harper's Magazine Press, 1974.

———. *Southern Food: At Home, on the Road, in History.* New York: Knopf, 1987.

Frey, William H. "Census 2000 Shows Large Black Return to the South, Reinforcing the Region's 'White-Black' Demographic Profile." *PSC Research Report* no. 01-473. Ann Arbor, Mich.: Population Studies Center and Milken Institute, May 2001.

Grantham, Dewey W. *The Life and Death of the Solid South,* Lexington: University of Kentucky Press, 1992.

Hart, John Fraser, and Ennis L. Chestang. "Turmoil in Tobaccoland." *Geographical Review* 86, no. 4 (October 1996): 550–72.

Hilliard, Sam B. "Antebellum Tidewater Rice Culture in South Carolina and Georgia." In *European Settlement and Development in North America,* edited by James R. Gibson. Toronto: University of Toronto Press, 1978.

Hinderaker, Eric, and Peter C. Mancall. *At the Edge of Empire: The Backcountry in British North America.* Baltimore: Johns Hopkins University Press, 2003.

Lander, Ernest M., Jr., and Robert K Ackerman, eds. *Perspectives in South Carolina History: The First 300 Years.* Columbia: University of South Carolina Press, 1973.

The New Georgia Encyclopedia, at http://www.georgiaencyclopedia.org/nge/home.jsp.

Olwell, Robert. *Masters, Slaves, and Subjects: The Culture of Power in the South Carolina Low Country, 1740–1790.* Ithaca, N.Y.: Cornell University Press, 1998.

Prunty, Merle C., and Charles S. Aiken. "The Demise of the Piedmont Cotton Region." *Annals of the Association of American Geographers* 62 (1972).

Ray, Janisse. *Ecology of a Cracker Childhood.* Minneapolis, Minn.: Milkweed Editions, 1999.

Reed, John Shelton, James Kohls, and Carol Hanchette. "The Dissolution of Dixie and the Changing Shape of the South." *Social Forces* 69, no. 1 (September 1990): 221–33.

Royster, Charles. *The Fabulous History of the Dismal Swamp Company: A Story of George Washington's Times.* New York: Knopf, 1999.

Smith, C. Wayne, and Robert H. Dilday, eds. *Rice: Origin, History, Technology, and Production.* Hoboken, N.J.: Wiley, 2003.

Twining, Mary A., and Keith E. Baird. "Preface: The Significance of Sea Island Culture." *Journal of Black Studies* 10, no. 4 (June 1980): 379–86.

Walker, H. Jesse, and James M. Coleman. "Atlantic and Gulf Coastal Province." In *Geomorphic Systems of North America*, edited by William L. Graf. Boulder, Colo.: Geological Society of America, 1987.

Watson, Harry L. "Front Porch." *Southern Cultures* 12, no. 2 (Summer 2006): 1–5.

Webb, James. *Born Fighting: How the Scots-Irish Shaped America.* New York: Broadway Books, 2004.

Whitehead, Donald R. "Developmental and Environmental History of the Dismal Swamp." *Ecological Monographs* 42, no. 3 (1972): 301–15.

Wilkerson, Isabel. *The Warmth of Other Suns,* New York: Random House, 2010.

Wright, Gavin. *Old South, New South.* New York: Basic Books, 1986.

Internet Sources

Federal Reserve Bank of Atlanta. "Carpeting on a Roll in Georgia," at http://www.frbatlanta.org/pubs/econsouth/econsouth-vol_8_no_4-carpeting_on_a_roll_in_georgia.cfm?redirected=true.

U.S. Environmental Protection Agency. Nonpoint Pollution, at http://www.epa.gov/watertrain/nonpointabstr.html.

Indigo Development. "Industrial Ecology," at http://www.indigodev.com/IE.html.

U.S. Department of Agriculture. Economic Research Service. Types of Tobacco, at http://www.ers.usda.gov/Briefing/Archive/Tobacco/.

1 Florida residents build "Florida rooms" for protection from insects and even gators.

2 Clustered karst lakes are numerous in central Florida, here near Orlando.

3 Florida is the second-largest producer of orange juice concentrate, after Brazil.

4 Worth Street is the Rodeo Drive of Palm Beach.

5 After the 1982 blockade by the Border Patrol, residents of the Keys declared independence.

6 More than 50 percent of the population of Miami are Cubans, among whom dominoes is a popular sport.

7 Disney's Epcot Center was originally designed as a city of the future.

Florida

Jacksonville

St. Augustine

Swanee River

St. Johns River

Orlando

Celebration

Lakes District

Florida Coastal Plain

Tampa Bay

Florida Coastal Plain

Fort Myers

Lake Okeechobee

Palm Beach

Fort Lauderdale

Miami

Everglades National Park

Florida Bay

Florida Keys

Straits of Florida

WELCOME TO THE CONCH REPUBLIC
BEACH MAINTENANCE FUNDED BY MONROE COUNTY TOURIST DEVELOPMENT TAX DOLLARS

State Border
Cities
Rivers

0   25   50 Miles

10
FLORIDA
A Victim of Its Own Geography

Chapter Highlights

After reading this chapter you should be able to:

- Discuss Florida's unique geologic history
- Distinguish the subregions and basic topography, including the shoreline and karst
- Explain Florida's population growth since the beginning of the twentieth century
- Give an overview of the state of the Everglades and list its environmental problems
- Describe the agricultural areas of Florida and their environmental impact
- List Florida's major agricultural products
- Identify major urban developments in Florida and discuss their economies

Terms

artesian spring
coquina

hammock
imagineer
mangrove

new urbanism
saw-grass

sinkhole
slough

Places

Everglades
Florida Bay

Intracoastal Waterway
The Keys
Lake Okeechobee

Miami
Orlando

St. Augustine
Tampa

PHOTO 10.1. Everglades Marsh. At the southern tip of Florida, the Everglades is the only tropical climate in the contiguous United States. The fragile Everglades ecosystem has been damaged during the past century by channeling the water, by irrigation, and by levees on Lake Okeechobee. Included in the damage is a loss of about 90 percent of the Everglades wetland habitat and its large diversity of species, among them over 350 bird species, many with dwindling populations. The birds pictured are snowy egrets, which were almost hunted into extinction in the late nineteenth century because of the popularity of their plumes. Other factors contributing to dwindling numbers of birds are toxic waste dumping, pesticides, dredging, and urbanization.

Introduction

In Florida, the environment is the economy.

—Al Gore, 1997[1]

Peninsular Florida is an immigrant. The Florida platform was once part of Africa, but when Pangaea rifted apart about two hundred million years ago, Florida remained attached to North America. The population, like the state, has also migrated from other cultures and continents to their new home. Both the land and the people have vacillated. For millions of years the peninsula rose, then returned to the water, only to emerge again. Half the population moves every five years or so. One out of six is a foreign-born immigrant, but many, many others are just seeking warmth in their retirement years. Florida has been one of the fastest-growing states, but physical, cultural, and demographic problems have made the state unsustainable. The climate of the Sunshine State glazes over the problems, but more than 90 percent of Floridians now live in the coastal counties—the hurricane counties. The population growth and FEMA policies are unsustainable.

Florida's warmth attracts northerners escaping the winter cold. Tourism has trumped the state's original agricultural economy. First the city of Miami swelled, but then as transportation evolved, the East Coast wealthy established winter homes from Palm Beach to Boca Raton; middle-class retirees soon followed, infilling the remaining coastlines.

Florida has attempted to implement more sustainable programs (health care, reduced emissions, and alternative energy), but several issues stand in the way of a sustainable future: the population growth rate (more than double the nation's average); the distribution of population (along vulnerable coastal counties); agricultural subsidies and quotas (sugar and citrus); vulnerability to hurricanes; and the need for clean water.

Settlement patterns combined with climate change reveal the weaknesses to achieving a sustainable future.

Physical Geography

The topography and formation of Florida differs from the other southern coastal regions. Florida was once geologically part of North Africa. The peninsular part of the state broke off from Africa and has only recently (geologically speaking) emerged from its latest submarine foray; it may submerge again due to sea level shift caused by climate change. Some computer models predict that southern Florida could be underwater by 2100.[2] Several times during the Pleistocene, the continental shelf of Florida was exposed and the land area was twice the state's current size, but then once again the land submerged, drowning much of the state. The geologic structure makes one wonder about the wisdom of the majority of the population settled in the coastal counties.

The entire peninsula is a shallow, sediment-covered limestone shelf. Currently, the eastern edge has emerged (the continental shelf is just off the coast), while the western continental shelf is submerged for miles beyond the current coastline.

Florida is an extension of the Atlantic Coastal Plain, but its unique geology, cultures, and physical features set it apart, and it will be examined separately as the Floridian Coastal Plain, Lake District, Everglades, and Keys. Florida's subregion north of Jacksonville is part of the Sea Islands section in the South Atlantic chapter, and the Florida Panhandle is part of the Gulf Coastal Plains.

The Floridian Coastal Plain

Peninsular Florida extends east to west across sand-covered limestone strata. The elevation averages less than one hundred feet above sea level. Water is plentiful, with a plethora of

BOX 10.1 KARST

Karst topography is found across the globe and underlies about 20 percent of the United States, especially large areas of Florida and Texas and 60 percent of Missouri (Map 10.1). The karst landscape is formed when slightly acidic groundwater dissolves limestone and opens spaces, cavities, caverns, or sinkholes. Most water flows in karst-ridden areas are subsurface, flowing through underground springs and issuing from fractured rock, underground rivers, caves (more than 9,200 in the Ozarks), and sinkholes in the barren, rocky karst soil. Spectacular rock formations often result.

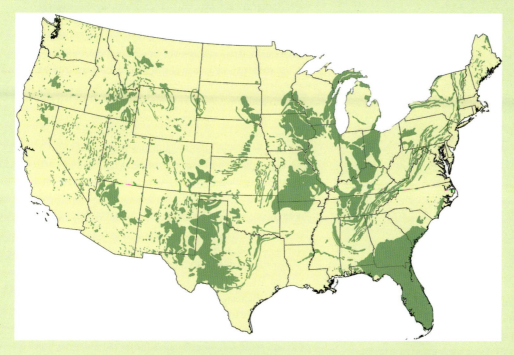

MAP 10.1. Karst Coverage of the United States. Karst topography forms when rainwater combines with carbon dioxide forming carbonic acid, which flows over and through limestone fractures, dissolving the rock and creating caves, springs, and sinkholes.

karst—where water has dissolved limestone bedrock—and produced underground springs and sinkhole lakes, as well as multiple wetlands and swamps.

Most of the seven million southern Florida residents live along the Gold Coast ridge in urban Miami, Fort Lauderdale, and Palm Beach. South of Miami at Florida City, the ridge disappears into the Everglades. The Gold Coast ridge is built on a solid rock foundation. The land is a bit higher than the surrounding area and benefits from warmer water and air, because the warm Florida Current sweeps up from the Caribbean, past the Keys, and along the southern coast. Flatwoods, cypress swamps, tidal salt-marshes, and mangrove forests dominate the southern landscape. A string of barrier islands and sand bars protects the east coast, while western coast bays and inlets, the largest being Tampa Bay, provide protection from the open sea.

The Lake District

The central region surrounding the Orlando urban complex is sandy with undulating dunes and an underlying karst terrain. Water courses through and dissolves the limestone into a system of channels and pockets reminiscent of an enlarged sponge. The pockmarked drainage systems recharge the Floridian Aquifer, the largest aquifer in the southeast, which supplies water to cities from Savannah, Georgia, to Orlando.

The Lake District vegetation of interior grasslands, flatwoods, and coastal pine forest abounded with native animals such as the endangered Florida panther and the once endangered but now recovered American alligator. Today the landscape is agricultural, grazed pasture, and the Orlando Disney complex.

The Everglades

The natural Everglades was not quite land and not quite water, but a soggy amalgamation of the two.[3]

The last of Florida's land to emerge from the sea was the flat Everglades, barely above sea level (Photo 10.1). The subtropical Everglades originally extended from Kissimmee south, but during the twentieth century humans drained much of the swamp (Map 10.2). The Everglades swamp was a quicksand-like river of sharp, serrated saw-grass on a mattress of peat and muddy sediment with little topographic or vegetative relief. Then human activities altered the landscape. For example, cattails have replaced the saw-grass due to the phosphorus-rich pollution near Lake Okeechobee, where a toxic chemical stew has also altered the fisheries and wildlife. A few inland trees grow on isolated

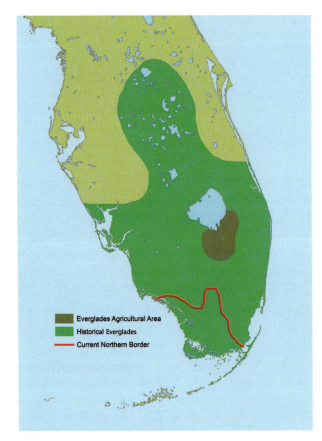

MAP 10.2. The Everglades Ecosystem. Historically, this ecosystem and water flow originated in the Lakes District near Orlando. Today the system is managed to service the Okeechobee agricultural district (shown in brown). The national park at the southern tip of the state is only a remnant of the Everglades ecosystem. Historical flow was to the southwest, but today much of the flow is diverted to the populated areas along the eastern coast.

Everglades Agricultural Area
Historical Everglades
Current Northern Border

hammocks—small tree islands rising a few feet above the ridges. Enveloping the coastal areas are saltwater cypress and mangrove swamps. The sense of place is unique: primitive; inhabited by a seemingly infinite variety of insects, reptiles, and rodents; and quiet except for the occasional wildlife screech or howl.

The Everglades were designated as federal land when Florida achieved statehood in 1845. Congress granted the "utterly worthless" Everglades to Florida in 1850, when the state was offered the opportunity to gain title to all drained swampland. The state set about draining the Everglades swamps near Lake Okeechobee, although draining and reclaiming land was more difficult than originally anticipated. The draining destroyed ecosystems, but it also created a fertile cropland that reduced U.S. dependence on tropical crops from the West Indies.

Sloughs (stagnant swamps), muck, and hammocks saturate the land between the parallel, low ridges of the Everglades. Historically, Lake Okeechobee, which lies slightly below sea level, regularly overflowed its southern banks and inundated the Everglades, almost one-fifth of Florida. Because the land is flat from Okeechobee to Florida Bay, a shallow sheet of water drained the entire landscape, a natural process that replenished the

Everglades' waters. But during the 1920s, two hurricanes flooded the land and killed two thousand people, resulting in building protective dikes, levees, and canals around Lake Okeechobee. By the 1950s, extensive levees and canals had drained the land south of Lake Okeechobee, and 65 percent of the Everglades had been converted into sugarcane fields. Converting the land to agriculture desecrated the remaining Everglades biome.

The Ten Thousand Islands southwestern coast is a brackish-water **mangrove** and cypress swamp. The mangrove tropical evergreen grows in salt water and protects shorelines from storm, wave, wind, and flood hazards, and it is valuable as rookeries for crustaceans and fish. Mangroves provide homes for endangered and threatened species, such as the green and loggerhead sea turtles, the American crocodile, and West Indian Manatee.

The islands are part of the Everglades Park today, but park regulations limiting fire have decreased ecosystem productivity. The mangrove swamps and saw-grass marshes along the edges are no longer burned annually to renew nutrients. Today, regulations against burning have created a deep and matted saw-grass that has reduced wildlife habitat and feeding grounds.

The Keys

The only living coral reef ecosystem in North America is the seventeen-hundred-island Florida Keys archipelago, which curves 150 miles into the Gulf of Mexico. Separating the Gulf from the Atlantic Ocean, the Keys are a series of flat, coral and limestone islands—the highest point on the Keys is only eighteen feet above sea level. The Keys are represented as a tropical zone; however, the low-lying Keys are too flat to effect airflow rains and are in fact desert islands. Imported water has transformed them to their present, faux-tropical state.

The approximately six thousand coral reefs grow slowly, about sixteen feet every thousand years, and are protected from harvesting or even touching, although every year boaters inadvertently damage them, especially when anchoring (Photo 10.2). Millions of tiny coral polyps form a protective coastal breakwater, which provides shelter and breeding sites for plants, animals, and other organisms. The coral are also important sources of food and reduce wave energy, thereby protecting beaches from erosion. But coral reefs are threatened by habitat destruction, unsustainable fishing, invasive species, and climate change. Coral, which is susceptible to warmer ocean temperatures and pollution, has weakened and become more vulnerable to diseases.

Like a string of pearls, the Overseas Highway connects the islands to the mainland. The islands are, however, at the mercy of hurricanes, which can cut them off from the mainland, disrupt water supply, and cause coastal erosion.

Water

Florida has plenty of freshwater; however, many water features are poorly drained due to the slight gradients of the flat topography. Florida is waterlogged, but draining the wetlands, lowering water tables, and overconsumption have caused water

PHOTO 10.2. Florida Bay at Sunset. The bay's interconnected basins average three feet deep, and allow only shallow-draft boats. The bay supports sea grass vegetation that provides habitat for many aquatic species. Due to the shallowness of the bay, many motor boat propellers have damaged the sea grass, corals, and habitats.

shortages. In southern Florida, per capita water use is about 50 percent above the national average and unsustainable.

Water has become such an issue that Tampa Bay is home to the nation's largest water desalination plant. The plant became fully operational in 2007, six years behind schedule and $40 million over budget, yet it still does not produce at capacity. The plant reduces the stress on Tampa's aquifers but at the cost of enormous energy consumption, emitting yet more CO_2 and devastating fisheries and aquatic habitat. Desalination plants are becoming popular as national water wars increase. Several have been proposed in California (as of 2011), but all are economically and environmentally expensive due to the fossil fuel energy required to run a plant. Previously, only oil-rich countries relied on desalination (70 percent of Saudi Arabia's water is desalinated).

Subsurface Water Features

The karst topography is characterized by subsurface drainage, high water table, artesian springs, and many sinkhole depressions—Florida has more sinkholes than any other state. **Sinkholes** form when the roof of a cavern or cave dissolves and collapses. Sinkholes are both human induced and naturally formed. Human-induced sinkholes are the result of overpumping groundwater or drilling new water wells. Natural sinkholes are formed in one of three ways: subsidence, solution, or the most common type in Florida, collapse of a limestone layer above a cavity.

Artesian springs are formed when pressurized groundwater is released through faults from a confined aquifer. Fully one-quarter of U.S. artesian wells and springs (seven hundred springs) are in Florida. Silver Springs is the largest, discharging about five hundred million gallons daily. The artesian springs are crucial to the freshwater supply, and yet the flow is declining in many and a few have stopped flowing altogether. Reasons for the decline include consumption through drawdown, increased nitrates due to agriculture and urbanization, and the destruction of

ecosystems by such modifications as dams. Water conservation, reduced nitrogen fertilizer use, and improved wastewater reuse will help reverse past damage and protect springs in the future.

Intracoastal Waterway

The Atlantic and Gulf coasts are connected by the three-thousand-mile Maine to Mexico Intracoastal Waterway, which consists of natural and human-made features. The sandbar barrier islands along the eastern coast separate the mainland from the ocean. Between the barrier islands and the mainland, the Intracoastal Water Project connects a series of lagoons as one long, safe navigation canal between Jacksonville and Miami.

Recreational boaters and barges hauling commercial products use the waterway. Along the route, several inlets enter the waterway. The Army Corps of Engineers maintains and dredges the route.

Dredging

Beaches erode. Migration and recession of sands are part of the natural cycle of coastal environments. Nature is not static, so acceptance of a dynamic coastline should be part of living with nature. Beach erosion has accelerated due to sea-level rise, which in turn is due to climate change. Barbara Culliton pointed out in 1992, "It hardly seems sensible that people build houses on shifting sands,"[4] yet eroding beaches are popular building sites and the most expensive properties in the state. The dense and growing population along Florida beaches has encouraged dredge and fill operations to create land for development, which has created additional erosion. Saving beaches at any cost is expensive, including destroying habitats and accelerating the erosion that techno fixes are meant to stop. Maintaining the artificial beaches protects expensive oceanfront properties at taxpayer expense, and the environmental impact is detrimental and has unintended consequences.

PHOTO 10.3. Dredging at Palm Beach, Florida. The delicate balance of the shoreline on the eastern coastline is often protected by artificial means. Dredging and placing boulders to protect the shoreline from erosion is a common site. The dredging is often at taxpayer expense.

Unintended Consequences

Many sandy beaches are continually rebuilt from dredged sand (Photo 10.3). The dredged sand is discharged through a pipeline and then bulldozed across the beach.

Protecting beaches and renourishing them with sand have the unintended consequence of destroying marine habitats and coral reefs. Siltation and the indirect effects of renourishment have buried reefs along Miami Beach. Continued vacuuming of fill material from twenty to fifty feet deep in the ocean has disturbed many organisms—shrimp, crabs, mollusks, juvenile fish, and sea grasses—along the ocean bottom, which in turn affects game fish habitats. The fill leads to additional and unintentional environmental problems, including the possible collapse of the marine and coastal ecosystems.

Marine algal blooms, led to eutrophication, degraded coastal water quality, and deterioration of coral reefs indicate environmental problems at least as serious as beach erosion.[5]

Sediments stirred up by renourishment are structurally different from fine quartz sand and easily migrate into the surf, turning the water milky, halting photosynthesis, interfering with the feeding process of fish, and obscuring the habitat and reefs, thereby destroying scuba diving and fishing.

Local and Ecoregional Impacts

In some Florida communities, "beach armor" seawalls were built, especially when buildings are too close to the shore. Where sand is insufficient to protect the shoreline, a grid or a seawall is formed and filled in with boulders to protect it from erosion. But seawalls destroy natural beaches and have been outlawed in five states (Oregon, North Carolina, South Carolina, Maine, and Rhode Island), which prompted the increased reliance on dredging. Dredging is an unsustainable practice because the dredged fill is not truly "sand" but strip-mined offshore mud and

fossil fragments that destroy the continental shelf fish habitat and biomass. Both the act of dredging and the mud destroy the local habitat.

Several other techno fixes (artificial reefs, jetties, and sand-trapping systems) have been used to save beaches, but all are short-term and ultimately lead to more erosion. All are done at taxpayer expense, and done in areas where the beach sand problem was known beforehand.[6]

External Costs

Every year the Army Corps of Engineers spends millions of taxpayer dollars to renourish Atlantic beaches. The beaches have been "saved," because developers and landowners don't want to see their buildings or land washed out to sea and because of special interest groups who are invested in shoreline renourishment. As such, the protection becomes political and agenda driven. It may be that the short-term nature of the current political process cannot find a way to live with nature.

The highly erodible dredged sand is not a long-term solution, and it leads to a never-ending parade of expensive beach-renourishment projects. A few places, such as Stuart Rocks, were stripped to the limestone mantle and have been replenished with quality inland sand in an environmentally sustainable manner, but this has not been the general rule. Nature is not static but ever changing, and yet building on beaches, in search of an ocean view, has been done in a never-ending renourishing to protect "private property."

The Everglades

During the twentieth century, the Everglades were intensely modified and hydrologically and ecologically degraded. Most of southern Florida is now drained, and only the southern tip—a mere 7 percent remnant of the Everglades system—remains a swamp.

One of the major alterations in the Everglades system is the diking of Lake Okeechobee after severe floods in the 1920s. A twenty-foot-high dike surrounds the shallow lake to protect the people, but it has also endangered the complex ecosystem and waterway relations. Pesticide-laced runoff from agriculture produced muck at the bottom of the lake. The muck was removed during the drought of 2007; however, arsenic was found in the muck, creating additional pollution problems.

Although the agricultural potential of the Everglades was recognized in 1848, draining did not begin until 1907. By World War II, more than four hundred miles of canals dissected the Everglades, and by the 1960s over seven hundred thousand acres had been drained.

The Everglades ecosystem has been named a UNESCO Biosphere Reserve,[7] but it is now endangered because Lake Okeechobee levees halt the natural flooding that renourished the Everglades. Habitats have been destroyed, invasive species abound, saltwater intrusion inundates freshwater, and polluted runoff contaminates drinking water supplies. The human impact on the land has been immense. The "worthless" swamp and marsh are now water deprived. The land is being used, but multiple issues now environmentally challenge the Everglades:

- The ridge and slough low-lying relief has become more uniform, and water no longer has a directional flow.
- Fishery and rookery have experienced losses as sloughs fill in with saw-grass and hammocks.
- Construction of canals, highways, and flood-control channels has affected water flow.
- Competition for freshwater has risen, as urban encroachment, tourism, and agriculture deplete the Everglades to less than 50 percent of its previous flow.
- Chemicals from agricultural areas have degraded the ecosystem.
- Lake Okeechobee has experienced eutrophication from dairy and agricultural runoff.
- Invasive species, such as the melaleuca tree, have proliferated.

Restoration efforts on the Everglades began in 1984, but perhaps is too little too late, because population growth has damaged the region. Between World War II and 2000, Florida's population increased sevenfold.

Current plans are not to return the Everglades to its former water regime and health, but to find a sustainable plan providing for the health of the population, agriculture, and ecosystem. The largest ecological restoration project—the Comprehensive Everglades Restoration Plan (CERP) — began in 2000, incorporating wetland science, ecosystem modeling, and restoration ecology. Goals of the $12 billion restoration project are to:

- Increase water flow
- Increase water-storage capacity
- Improve water quality
- Improve water deliveries to maintain estuary health
- Improve system connectivity by removing some infrastructure, such as canals

The CERP goal is to find compromises between the divergent Everglades interests: Urban land planners seek fresh water to support the growing population; environmentalists seek ecological restoration; and agricultural users wish to continue growing crops on the drained areas around Lake Okeechobee.

In 2008, the CERP was at a standstill, when Governor Charlie Crist announced a deal that enabled Florida to buy out the nation's largest sugarcane producer, United States Sugar, which had been repeatedly fined millions of dollars for illegal and improper disposal of hazardous waste in the Everglades. The deal could have helped restore the natural flow of the Everglades (Map 10.3), but the deal was partially rescinded later in the year due to the depressed economy. Documents revealed that the deal was political and more about saving United States Sugar than the Everglades, but it is still the best offer to return water flow to the Everglades.[8]

Florida Bay–Everglades Estuary

Florida Bay, wedged between the southern tip of Florida and the Keys, is the largest estuary in the state. The shallow bay's low tides expose muddy, grassy flats, which act as a rookery and feeding area, as well as a home to dolphins, manatees, American crocodiles, and an array of other aquatic species.

The bay was known for its clear, warm waters until the 1980s, when the ecology changed: The water became turbid, sea grass died, algae blooms proliferated, and aquatic life—shellfish, sponges, pink shrimp—were decimated. The estuary—at the bay and Everglades boundary—is considered extremely sensitive to salinity, nutrients, and freshwater changes.[9] Studies in the 1990s researched the reasons behind the destruction of the bay and its relation to the Everglades water system.

The studies revealed that the saline content had changed considerably since the 1800s. Core samples showed a stable saline system without noticeable human disturbance. But in 1900, the salinity became irregular; curiously enough, plants and sea life declined during the period of stable salinity and increased after. The increase was during a period of human activity. These anomalies are not yet understood and seem to oppose logic.

Human activity and changes in the natural environment can account for salinity level variances. The interrelations between irrigation canal construction, climate change, and perhaps El Niño events are not entirely understood. Human activities alone are not responsible for environmental change; other causal agents play a role, but the code has not yet been deciphered. The "natural state" of the ecosystem is difficult to evaluate when the ecosystem continues to change.[10]

Climate

The first rule of hurricane coverage is that every broadcast must begin with palm trees bending in the wind.[11]

The almost tropical "Caribbean light" peninsula weather is a transition zone between the Caribbean and the temperate mainland. Florida is unique climatically, agriculturally, and geologically.

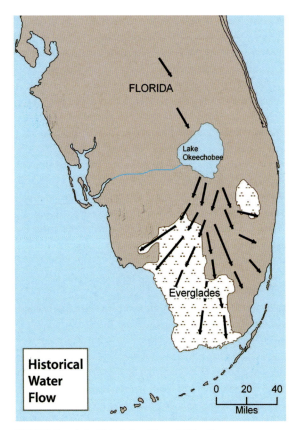

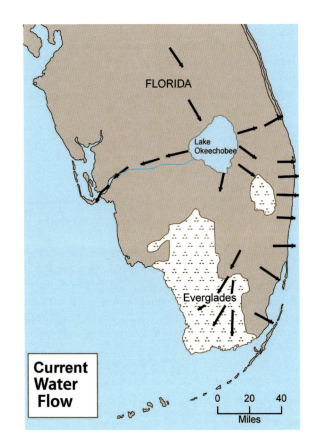

MAP 10.3. Everglades Historical and Current Water Flow.

Source: Remote Sensing Tutor, "The Everglades: America's Most Threatened Ecosystem," at http://rst.gsfc.nasa.gov/Sect3/Sect3_8.html

The climate has affected the crops, cities, vegetation, soil, and of course, the people.

Florida has benefited from its subtropical location and accompanying temperatures, first agriculturally and then later accommodating millions of annual tourists. The three-hundred-day growing season supports year-round citrus and vegetable production, although occasional frosts threaten crops. Annual rainfall is fifty to sixty inches a year, and along the west coast of Florida thunderstorms are more frequent than anywhere else in the United States. Rain can fall in any season but favors the hot and humid summer and autumn. Southern Florida has many bright, warm, and dry days during winter and spring, which supports a winter playground with temperatures regularly in the seventies and eighties, while the North is well below freezing. Northern and central Florida winters are cooler and receive more precipitation.

The Gulf Coast atmospheric pressure patterns affect the southern Florida wet season (May through September). The Bermuda high-pressure system shifts annually, sometimes resulting in drought. Decreasing temperatures in winter and spring and the Pacific-based El Niño affect Florida, bringing more wet days but fewer hurricanes, the state's big atmospheric pressure story.

Hurricanes

The northern hemisphere hurricane season extends from June through November, with the prime months being August and September. Hurricanes are violent storms that circulate rain and wind (more than 64 knots, or 73 miles per hour) and move heat from the tropics to cooler areas.

Florida is annually in the path of at least one hurricane, if not several. In southern Florida, hurricanes have struck on average once every 5.5 years and have caused extensive flooding, loss of property, and loss of beaches. The storm damage losses are a tax burden placed on the entire population of the United States.

In Florida, as we said many times before, there's two trillion dollars of risk out there and we're collecting inadequate premiums to cover this risk."[12]

If Florida were to get a direct hit from a Category 4 or Category 5 hurricane, the damage would dwarf the damage done to New Orleans after Katrina. Even now, the cost of insurance to live in the hurricane-prone state is exorbitant. In July 2008, after repeated hurricanes in 2004 and 2005, insurance giant State Farm sought a 47.1 percent rate increase on homeowners' policies, while scaling back on the number of policies. The state-run insurer now insures a quarter of the homeowners, but at a reduced rate because of lobbies by those who live along the coast—the wealthy—which means that everyone else, those with less resources, pay the difference if Florida is hit by a big hurricane.[13]

Historical Geography and Settlement

Native Americans

Indigenous nomads roamed Florida at least since 7500 BCE, although little else is known about them. At the time of European encroachment, the Timucua lived in western Florida, the Apalachee in the Tallahassee Hills, the Calusa in southwestern Florida, and several smaller bands along the eastern coast. The early indigenous preferred the narrow coastal zone for settlement, as the Everglades was a mosquito-infested swamp of little interest to humans.

The tribe most associated with Florida, the Seminoles, did not arrive until the early 1700s. The Seminoles were members of different Creek tribal affiliations (the name may have come from either a corruption of the Spanish word for runaway, *cimarron*, or from their own term for "free people"). The Seminoles were initially hunters and developed into farmers, but fear of slavery and attacks by whites led them to a half century of Seminole Wars, which resulted in the 1835 removal of many Seminoles to Indian Territory in Oklahoma. About three hundred Seminoles remained in the Everglades; however, they had to fight to maintain land because of settlers' claims. The Seminole descendants now live on reservations, and the tribe is officially recognized, allowing them certain rights. Their former sustainable hunting-and-gathering way of life disappeared with fixed land ownership, so the Seminoles have pursued alternative incomes. Some Seminoles have chosen to use their reservation lands to help preserve their culture; others derive income from gaming, tourism, land leases, and various agricultural pursuits.

Europeans

During the sixteenth century, the "island" of Florida was explored and ascertained to be a peninsula. The attractions of its peninsular location and climate have shaped its destiny and how people came to the land. First ships brought riches or pirate marauders, then rails brought speculators seeking other riches, and finally the automobile brought hordes of retirees plundering the wealth of sunshine.

The Spanish were the first Europeans to establish a permanent settlement in what is now the United States; however, they were more concerned with seeking gold and riches than settling. Their methods of exploration were often brutal and alienated native tribes, making the few settlers uneasy occupants.

The Spanish started exploring the Florida coast in 1513, but by 1561 they were losing interest. A year later, French Huguenots claimed and established a short-lived settlement, but they were routed in 1565 when the Spanish renewed their interest and established St. Augustine.

Settlement remained uneasy, and over time was governed by a succession of three countries. From the time of the French and Indian War (1763) until the first decades of the nineteenth century, Florida was governed by Spain, France, or England. In 1819, Spain ceded Florida to the United States.

The Americans found the French, Spanish, and American land claims difficult to unravel. The peninsula was sparsely populated, but resolving the land claims was divisive. Many Spanish settlers chose to abandon and burn their homes rather than leave them to the American settlers. From 1821 to 1845, when Florida gained statehood, political maneuvers among the Americans led to establishing Florida's northern counties as an "Old South," slave-holding, cotton plantation economy. Peninsular Florida was not as lucrative agriculturally, and few settled there.

Americans built forts to protect settlers and to establish their claim to the land. Former fort sites are today's cities—Miami (Fort Dallas), Tampa (Fort Brooke), Fort Lauderdale, and Fort Myers. Natives retreated into the Everglades. Through 1858, they continued guerilla warfare against invading settlers and American forces. Even after the Seminole threat was removed, Florida remained the least populated state east of the Mississippi. The economy and population grew when speculators dredged the peninsula swamplands and imported citrus, agriculture, and cattle. Soon after the Civil War, railroad barons seeking a warm retreat from the cold eastern winters were attracted to the area.

Florida's popularity began with dreams and speculators, such as Henry Flagler and Henry Plant. Flagler, a Rockefeller partner in Standard Oil, initiated Florida tourism by bringing the railroad down the east coast and in 1902 building his house on the barrier island of Palm Beach (Photo 10.4). He eventually continued the railroad to Miami, and then over islands and water to Key West. On the west coast, Henry Plant promoted his South Florida Railroad and eight hotels, beginning with the Tampa Bay Hotel in 1891, a mere three years after Flagler's first hotel—the Ponce de León in St. Augustine. Both Flagler and Plant were zealous promoters of their vision for Florida, and the coastal populations grew. In the decade from 1900 to 1910, southeast Florida's population quadrupled to seventy thousand.

The rail lines exported the state's agricultural and resource largess—citrus, sugar, cattle, and phosphates—and imported tourists. The "worthless" swampland was drained, and farmers immigrated, lured by reports of a frost-free, year-round crop. In the 1920s, the Lake Okeechobee area commenced draining, settling, and cultivating winter crops for the northern states.

During the early 1920s, automobiles transported middle-class Americans to the first Florida land boom. Land sales of empty lots and speculative developments prospered, and many chose to move and enjoy the "Florida lifestyle." The Gold Coast—Hollywood, Coral Gables, and Boca Raton—was developed along the southeastern shoreline counties. The first land boom ended with a triple hit: inflated prices; the 1926 hurricane across Miami and Okeechobee; and the citrus destructor, the Mediterranean fruit fly. The Depression further compromised an already slow economy. The economy recovered after World War II.

Cultural Perspectives

Coquina

Along the barrier islands between Jacksonville and Lake Okeechobee, the coastline has a soft, coastal rock called

PHOTO 10.4. Whitehall, Palm Beach, Florida. Built in 1902, Whitehall was Henry Flagler's winter home. Flagler was instrumental in establishing Florida's agricultural and tourist industries. He built the Florida East Coast Railway and hotels to accommodate tourists.

coquina, composed of shells and limestone from marine reefs. The material is soft in the ground, but it hardens when exposed to the open air; it makes an excellent local and common vernacular building material that was used in colonial foundations and chimneys and industrial structures, such as sugar mills.

The Spanish and British used coquina, such as the still-standing Castillo de San Marcos built in 1695 in St. Augustine; however, many buildings were deserted during the upheavals of the eighteenth and nineteenth centuries, and few were preserved. Those surviving the period were often destroyed intentionally when modern styles were built. During the Depression, the Conservation Construction Corps built a few coquina structures in Daytona Beach.

What has been used, and destructively so, is limestone gouged from Florida reefs and used in federal and institutional buildings. The resulting gaping holes of the quarries became dumping grounds for consumer detritus.

The Conch Republic (The Florida Keys)

The Conch Republic was proclaimed on April 23, 1982, when a border patrol blockade cut the Keys off from the rest of the United States, while agents searched for locally problematic illegal immigrants and drugs. Many residents now claim to be both Conch Republic and U.S. citizens, although they also boost tourism by celebrating their annual Independence Day—creating more problems by bringing in more tourists.

Florida Keys residents have been independent and individualistic since they started to populate the *cayos (keys* is a corruption of this Spanish term for small island). Some colonial residents prospered by living off the shipwrecks along the treacherous coastline. But this too changed. By 1931, local fishers and an intellectual crowd grounded by Ernest Hemingway, enticed by the Caribbean appeal and New Orleans–influenced architectural styles, settled in Key West, then the largest city in Florida. The few natives of the Keys were called Conches, named for the tasty local seafood housed in large seashells found along Caribbean coastlines.

Living in Key West was more sustainable in those days: Electric light did not pollute the skies, and water cisterns gathered fresh water. The vegetation and fauna differed as well. The current tropical vegetation only began after a water line was brought in from the mainland. Ornithologist John James Audubon, drawn by the plethora of tropical birds, was one of the early visitors, but the number of birds decreased due to spraying for mosquitoes. Nonetheless, the birds and tropical vegetation attracted more people to the Keys after World War II.

The laid-back style with an anything-goes attitude has attracted many to the Keys and thereby threatened the local culture. Within the past forty years, the population of the Keys doubled, and more than three million tourists visit the islands annually. In 2002, only 45 percent of the residents had lived in the Keys more than five years, and less than 25 percent for ten years. The Keys have the highest median house price in Florida and are one of the most expensive areas to live in the United States. Living expenses have forced locals out. The commercial area has also changed from one of individual quirky shops to national chains, and annoyingly familiar visual pollution along Highway 1 now threatens the once unique cultural landscape.

Another environmental impact of the increased population on the Keys is water pollution due to the reliance on septic systems, which was a poor choice for waste management on porous limestone. Beach closures due to fecal microbe contamination have become a regular part of the Keys' waterways.[14] The continued growth of the Keys has surpassed sustainable standards. Several local and national conservancy groups are working to conserve land and protect the natural resources.

Boom-Bust Florida

Florida real estate speculation—"if you buy that then I have some land for you in Florida"—used its tropic-like location and climate to build dreams. The boom-bust growth was once again brought to a screeching halt in 2008, when Florida led most of the states in mortgage fraud, foreclosures, and even losing population.

Flashy Florida developers have been hustling swampland and undredged ocean "land" for almost a century, beginning with the first big boom in 1920. After five heady years of building cities on bubbles—Miami, Tampa Bay, and St. Petersburg—the collapse brought speculation and flipping to an abrupt end. Easy credit and rapidly spiraling property values—often quadrupling in a year—reached a fever pitch, as get-rich-quick speculators looked for get-fleeced-quick winter vacationers to buy the undeveloped and often swampy land; the buyers then tried to flip the property before the first overleveraged payment was due. But it could not and did not last.

In the 1920s, railroad congestion caused by transportation of too many construction materials forced an embargo, and prices for transport escalated, beginning a spiral of increased cost of living. Land prices began a downward trend. Hurricanes in 1926 and 1928 created more bankrupt development projects, and the Crash of 1929 ended the first boom. But more were to come. From World War II until the 1960s, Florida developed rapidly. Another expansion continued until the recession of 2008. Many of the recent busts are due to the lack of good available land (the best was already taken). Commercial developers built on less-than-viable tracts and lost their investment when they lacked good construction, good tenants, or a good location, location, location.

Regional Life

Population

Florida's population changed dramatically during the twentieth century, from just over a half million residents in 1900 to 18.8 million in 2010. The population has continued to grow at almost double the nation's rate—17.6 percent, adding 2.8 million inhabitants from 2000 to 2010. In 2000, Florida was the fourth most populous state and the most populous state in the South; however, the following recession affected growth, and by April 2009, the state experienced its first decline in population (outside of wartime years) in a century. Florida is highly urbanized (over 85 percent) and contains some of the fastest-growing cities in the nation.

Population Distribution

The 2010 racial and ethnic breakdown for the entire state of Florida was:

- 75.0 percent white
- 22.5 percent Hispanic
- 16.0 percent black
- 2.4 percent Asian.
- 0.4 percent Native American
- 2.5 two or more races

The state's minority populations surged, led by a 57.4 percent increase in Hispanics and a 25 percent increase of blacks. While the white population has continued to increase (4.1 percent), it is at a much slower pace than in the past decade. Most of the growth for the state has been from domestic migration.

About 90 percent of Florida's population lives in Florida's coastal counties, which are among the fastest-growing counties in America (Map 10.4). Between 1980 and 2010, Florida's population more than doubled, with most growth occurring within the coastal counties.

Florida is well known for two demographic groups: Cubans and retirees. Cubans have settled throughout the state but are most concentrated in Miami, which has the state's highest percentage (60 percent) of foreign-born residents. Two-thirds of all Cubans living in America live in Florida, and three-quarters of Cubans in Florida live in Miami's Dade County (Table 10.1). The two demographic groups merge, as many elderly Cubans have retired in Miami. Thirty-four percent of Miami's population is Cuban immigrants (137,301 [2010]). The median age of Miami's Cuban population is fifty-five, while the median age in Miami is thirty-nine. The Cubans did not assimilate into Miami but acculturated, remaking the city in their own image.

Historically, some Cubans migrated to Florida, but they arrived en masse after Fidel Castro overthrew the Cuban government in 1959; an additional flood of immigrants arrived after Cuba lost the support of the defunct Soviet Union. The U.S. policy toward Cuban emigrants has been amended. The most recent policy, adopted in 1994, allows up to twenty thousand visas annually and includes a "wet-foot, dry-foot policy": Cubans who reach dry land are allowed to remain, while those who are caught at sea are repatriated. The United States has had a Cuban travel and trade moratorium, which eased in 2009 when restrictions were removed for Cuban-Americans on family visits and remittances. In 2011 restrictions were further eased for educational and religious travel.

The other major demographic group in Florida is retired U.S. citizens. In four counties, population of those over the age of sixty-five exceeds 30 percent, and in three cities, 35 percent of their population is over the age of sixty-five (Table 10.2). The most people over sixty-five live between Miami and Palm Beach. The largest state-to-state migration

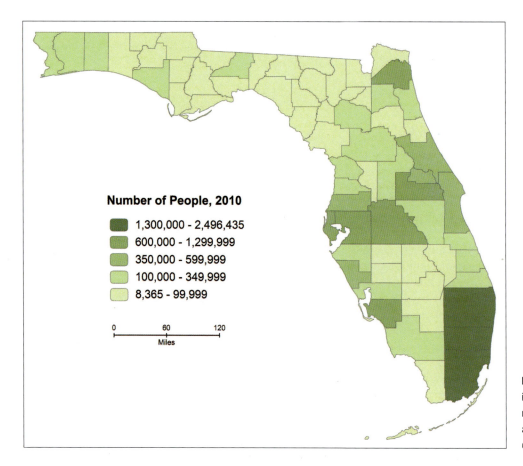

Number of People, 2010

- 1,300,000 - 2,496,435
- 600,000 - 1,299,999
- 350,000 - 599,999
- 100,000 - 349,999
- 8,365 - 99,999

0   60   120
Miles

MAP 10.4. Population of Florida, 2010. Florida's population more than doubled since 1980 and is heaviest along the coastal counties.

between 1995 and 2000 was retirees moving from New York to Florida. The retired population has affected and will continue to affect the south Florida environment because their living pattern needs—housing, transportation, recreation, and health care—differ from those of the rest of the population.

Retirees have developed their own style of urban sprawl, both in rings around the major cities and in thousands of hurricane-vulnerable mobile home parks. Increasing density in the ring cities has been a priority for developers, and urban high-rise suburbs, such as Aventura, are the result.

Population and Environment: The Everglades

Real and sustainable controls on sprawl are not practicable without vigorous national and local efforts to attack half the source of sprawl by moving toward population stabilization.[15]

Nine million southern Floridians are beyond the region's long-term carrying capacity. The dominant terrestrial feature in southern Florida is the Everglades, which was inundated with water prior to European settlement. Today, mismanaged policy leaves water in short supply for residents, agriculture, and the natural environment.

TABLE 10.1. Florida Residents' Background

Residents	Hialeah	Miami-Dade County	Florida
Foreign-born residents	71.6	50.2	16.7
Residents of Hispanic or Latino origin	94.4	61.7	21.0
Language other than English spoken at home	92.6[a]	70.6	23.1

Source: U.S. Census
Note: Hialeah, just inland from Miami, is the state's fifth most populous city (2008).
[a] 2000

TABLE 10.2. Florida State, Counties, and Cities Population over 65, 2010

		Percent population over 65
State		17.3
Counties		
	Charlotte	34.1
	Hernando	25.8
	Highlands	32.2
	Sarasota	31.2
Cities		
	Aventura	36.6
	Palm Beach	55.8
	Tamarac	27.5

Source: U.S. Census

In the late 1800s, the thirty thousand people in southern Florida received their water from drained Everglades projects. Over the first three decades of the twentieth century, both the population along the eastern coastal ridge and the water projects grew. In 1990, the population had reached six million, and another million were added by 2000; the population is expected to rise to twelve million by 2050. Miami's extended East Coast counties, consisting of about 7 percent of the land, contain 31 percent of the population. An additional thirteen million visit annually.[16] To accommodate this population, Everglades water management schemes have drained and rerouted water for human use, while damaging the ecosystems.

Traditional and Sustainable Cities

Florida's cities have experienced several growth spurts during the twentieth century. From 1980 to 1990, Florida contained nine out of the ten fastest-growing cities in America. In the twenty-first century, many retiring baby boomers are expected to retire in Florida. Miami and Dade County is expected to double its current population (2.5 million) by 2050, although many current occupants are against further growth.[17]

In 2001 Florida, among several other states, took the initiative to promote smart growth to "foster economic vitality, preserve natural resources, and enhance the quality of life."[18] Governor Jeb Bush promised neighborhood revitalization, open space preservation, efficient transportation, and matching school density to population density. Smart growth initiatives have since been adopted by many cities and groups within the state. Despite the intentions, reports issued in the following years envisioned Florida with massive development, doubled population, and loss of habitat for wildlife.[19] Clearly Florida has room to grow—toward sustainability.

Miami

(2010 pop. 399,457; MSA 5,564,635)

The Miami–Fort Lauderdale metropolitan complex is the nation's eighth-largest metropolitan area and has grown another 11 percent since 2000. It sprawls fifty miles from Miami through Fort Lauderdale to Palm Beach. Miami has been a commercial and tourist destination throughout the twentieth century.

Miami is a gateway city. Since the 1970s, it has emerged as an important banking center for Central and South America, and it may become a major international banking center. Miami has a large, busy airport and the busiest cruise ship port in the world.

During the middle of the twentieth century, the barrier island across Biscayne Bay was developed as Miami Beach and was bedecked with hotels luring luxury-seeking tourists. But tourism waned due to changing demographics and left a crime-ridden reputation memorialized in such shows as *Miami Vice*, which paradoxically enhanced the island's reputation again.

Since the 1980s, the classic Art Deco hotels have been refurbished and have become popular with the wealthy.

The population structure of Dade County underwent radical change since the mid-1950s, when thousands of wealthy Cuban refugees flocked to Miami, reinvigorating what was by then a fading resort town and turning it into the Cuban capital of America. A continued stream of refugees from Cuba and other Spanish-speaking countries followed. Today, Miami is a trade entrepôt for the Caribbean and Central and South American countries, because of its location and the influx of Cubans.

Miami has little industry outside of tourism, and that has benefited the city; its CO_2 levels are among the lowest in the nation, and it plans to continue reducing CO_2 by supporting public incentives. However, incentives for building greener are missing, as are incentives to retrofit.

Tampa

(2010 pop. 335,709; MSA 2,783,243)

The Spanish considered colonizing Tampa Bay during the sixteenth century. The exploration had two side effects: the harrowing eight-year survival tale of Cabeza de Vaca's wander across the continent to Mexico ending in 1536, and the almost-complete annihilation of Tampa's native population due to European diseases.

In 1824, Tampa was a military trading post. Tampa grew in the 1850s with the Cuban cattle trade and cigar-making. During the mid-nineteenth century, Tampa was a Wild West frontier town ruled by a rough breed of gamblers and misfit vigilantes practicing a lynch-happy form of justice.[20] The Wild West attitude continued in Tampa until the 1930s.

Today, Tampa's metropolitan complex, including Clearwater and St. Petersburg, is second in population to the Miami metro area. The economy revolves around tourism and resources, such as phosphate and fisheries. An active shipping port serves Central America and the Panama Canal.

Jacksonville

(2010 pop. 821,784; MSA 1,345,596)

Located at the mouth of the St. Johns River in northeast Florida, Jacksonville is the state's largest city and fourth-largest metro area. It includes within its borders St. Augustine, the oldest permanent settlement in America. Jacksonville was first settled by French Huguenots in 1562, and it changed hands between Spanish, British, and Americans before the city was chartered in 1832. St. Augustine did not become the nexus city for the metropolis, because it was hemmed in by a barrier island and lacked the deep-water harbor that made Jacksonville a regional distribution hub. The city diversified into such industries as research, information, and financial and insurance services. It is also the most industrialized city in Florida.

Orlando

(2010 pop. 238,300; CSA 2,818,120)

Orlando specialized in distribution, high-tech aviation, and citrus before the 1965 Disney transformation. Disney chose the inland Florida city to avoid the hurricane-threatened coast. Today, Orlando is the sixth-largest city in Florida, the third-largest metropolis, and the largest inland city. The Orlando complex of cities stretches across four inland contiguous counties; most have at least doubled in population in the past three decades.

Orlando, a city with a Jim Crow past, remains economically but not legally segregated. Wealthy whites live in the new urban developments, and poorer blacks and a rising number of Hispanics live in the outlying rural areas in the face of the diminishing stock of urban affordable housing.

Orlando and its environs have become a tourist destination. Following Disney, several other amusement parks also opened in the nearby area, as well as the nation's largest convention center. Orlando maintains its original citrus and livestock economy, but it has developed a video gaming industry and capitalizes on its proximity to the coastal Kennedy Space Center. The space center created thousands of well-paid professional jobs, juxtaposed to the low-paying tourism sector. The city's airport was developed in 1970 and is one of the largest in the nation.

The per capita income is lower than the U.S. average (and with a higher poverty level, at 16.6 percent [2010]), due to the low wages of the tourist economy, and this in turn has affected building standards. Energy consumption is high due to a reliance on air-conditioning.

It has been argued that the Orlando-Tampa conurbation is not a "normal city" but instead a "geographical city" or even an **"imagineered** city," a multi-nuclei city model popular in late-twentieth-century America.[21] The Disney stamp was incontestable in the imagineered town of Celebration.

The Orlando complex is dependent on cars and has few public transport options, although it is ramping up on charging stations for electric cars. What there is of public transport is converted to cleaner fuels, but still its CO_2 emissions are only aligned with national standards, instead of the more progressive standards set by many other sustainably aware cities.

Economy

Florida's economy is based on tourism and retirees. Tourism has been an important part of the economy since the first railroads arrived and remains the number one industry in the state.

But there are also some natural resources such as fisheries and phosphates and large agricultural production. The small quaternary-sector, high-tech economy contributes about 8 percent of the gross state output. The state's ability to attract

BOX 10.2 CELEBRATION, FLORIDA

Nostalgia is memory with the pain removed.

— Herb Caen, 1975*

Celebration (2010 pop. 7,427) is the quintessential Disney-imagineered city—a plastic and vinyl–infused re-creation of Walt Disney's childhood home in Marceline, Missouri. Disney died before his dream was realized, but in 1995 Michael Eisner (the chairman of Disney) began constructing the faux-urbanism dream.

The town of Celebration simulates a nostalgic past. Features include covered front porches so that neighbors can greet each other as they stroll by, garages that are not visible on the front streets, and rigid CCRs (conditions, covenants, and restrictions) thick enough to keep away the riff-raff (those who do not care about property values). Porches are seldom used because air-conditioning obviated their use, and everything is sanitized and clean, so many who visit the town come away feeling that they just entered some strange warp that revolves around property values. But shortly after the construction began so did the problems.

Beneath the pastel colors and Mickey flags is shoddy McMansion construction, using unskilled workers whose daily work changes to whatever trade is necessary—electrician, gardener, or painter. Little is said about the poor construction publicly, because a main reason that residents moved to the community is the "In Disney we trust" maintenance of high property values.† Things

went wrong, though: Alligators crawled into residents' pools—the town is built on a swamp that was Disney World's dumping ground for alligators. All homes were forced to screen in "Florida rooms." Schools were supposed to be special for Celebration children, but the county, notably poorer than the town, would not allow only the Celebration public school children to receive special benefits. Nonetheless, property values continued to rise, doubling in five years, until the recession of 2008 when values halved and foreclosures began, Then in 2011, the first murder occurred in the town, leaving occupants realizing that Disney was not an envelope of safety from the real world.

The town does not feel real. Owners—mostly corporate executives and golden parachuters—know it; they have posted signs outside their houses indicating that "real" people live there and that they do not want to be bothered.

The town has become a tourist attraction. Main Street is subsidized by developers and sports antique shops, restaurants, and tourist art galleries (Photo 10.5). No full-service market or local services are located in the Main Street area. Shopping is done along the garish and unsightly Highway 192, just outside the entrance to Celebration. A big box store is just across the street.

And while the town is a landmark for **new urbanism**, it was not built to be sustainably oriented. It sits apart from the surrounding area on a brownfield site, and it fails any energy efficiency test.

PHOTO 10.5. Celebration, Florida. Built by Disney, the town is known for its unreal feel. Many who purchased homes in the community did so in the belief "In Disney we trust" and placed a high importance on property values. Unfortunately, many reports reveal poor construction and failure to live up to its proposed goals. Although it is a new urbanist community, there is little community feel, and most people seen on the street are tourists.

---

* Herb Caen, Editorial, *San Francisco Chronicle*, April 15, 1975.

† Andrew Ross, *The Celebration Chronicles: Life, Liberty, and the Pursuit of Property Values in Disney's New Town* (New York: Ballantine, 1999).

high-tech skilled jobs has been impeded by high housing prices. A notable exception has been Cape Canaveral Space Center; however, the space shuttle phaseout during 2010–2011 led to a glut of high-paid and skilled workers without opportunities for similar jobs.

Primary Industry and Natural Resources

Agriculture

Florida is capable of growing vegetables throughout the winter, making it an agricultural savior for the colder northern states. But the national importance of Florida's agricultural crops has changed since globalization, WTO, and NAFTA, and many of its crops are no longer competitive with imported goods.

Florida has had a long history of agricultural output dominated by open-range cattle, citrus, sugarcane, and warm weather specialty and nursery crops. Between November and February, Florida grows about one-half of the nation's fresh vegetables, despite encroaching urban sprawl and population growth.

Nursery Crops   Florida nursery and greenhouse sales are second to California. Over three-quarters of sales are container plants. Deciduous flowering and tropical foliage plants and evergreen shrubs equal 83 percent of nursery sales.

Specialty Crops   Florida's southern location gave it a unique agricultural status during the twentieth century. The long growing season and ample precipitation allow out-of-season crops—tomatoes, cucumbers, green beans, and peppers—to grow when most of America is enduring winter. Florida continues to have a thriving citrus industry in the interior counties.

Citrus   Oranges are native to Asia, but Columbus brought them to the Americas. By 1579, citrus fruits were already well established in St. Augustine, Florida. Orange exports began in 1887, as railcar refrigeration became available.

Until the middle of the twentieth century, most of peninsular Florida land was in cattle or citrus orchards. The north was dedicated to grazing grassland, and south of Orlando the sandy, well-drained soil, unsuitable for grasses and cattle, was perfect for citrus. Florida became the nation's number one producer of oranges in 1945 for three reasons: (1) Florida grew more Valencia oranges, preferred by the incipient frozen-concentrate industry (whereas California grew navel oranges); (2) Florida focused on the new frozen-concentrate technology; (3) California's urban growth from 1950 to 1980 replaced orange trees with housing tracts, while Florida expanded its citrus industry in the less populated interior of the state.

The Florida citrus crop produces about 68 percent of the nation's oranges and 73 percent of its grapefruit, about twice

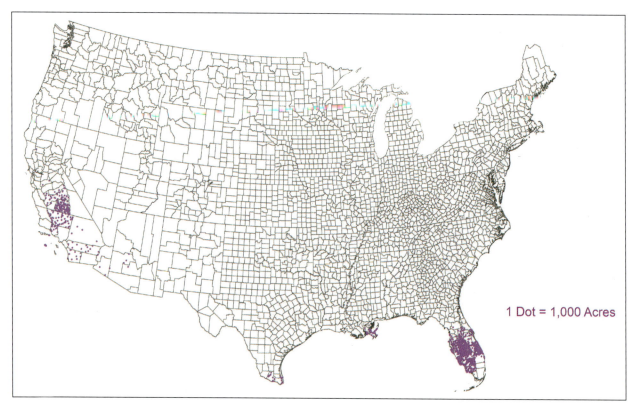

MAP 10.5. U.S. Orange Crop, 2002. Florida is the second-largest (Brazil is number one) producer of juice oranges in the world; however, stateside orange juice is given preferential treatment over imported juice. Brazilian companies have invested in Florida groves to escape paying steep and litigated excise taxes.

California's, the next-largest producer (Map 10.5). Internationally, only Brazil grows more oranges than Florida.

Today the territory between Tampa and Orlando produces about half of the state's citrus. Commercial acreage has declined 25 percent since 1996 because of urban encroachment. Citrus also suffered incalculable losses during the 2005 hurricane season. Hurricane damage weakened trees, destroyed nursery crops for replanting, and caused diseases, reducing the crop almost 50 percent from prehurricane production (2010 produced 133.6 million boxes, 2011 produced 139 million boxes). Farmers have sometimes chosen to sell to developers rather than invest more money in their trees and crops, but the recession of 2008 ended development speculation and left farmers without options.

Sugarcane   Sugarcane production within the contiguous forty-eight states has been limited to the Gulf Coast states of Florida, Louisiana, and Texas. In Florida, sugarcane is a field crop, the third most important in the agricultural economy, behind nursery and citrus crops. About half of American sugar is produced from cane, the other half from sugar beets (Map 10.6). About half of all U.S. cane is grown in Florida. It is subsidized, politically corrupted by lobbyists, and unsustainable. Quotas on sugar have kept the price of sugar above the world market and discouraged imports, which has resulted in higher consumer prices and damages countries that depend on sugar exports.

Prior to the Cuban Embargo of 1962, most Cuban sugarcane was owned by U.S. companies and imported. Florida grew only fifty thousand acres, but after the embargo Florida production expanded to four hundred thousand acres.

The best place to grow sugarcane is in the tropics. Florida is subtropical and therefore less than ideal for sugar growth, but since Cuban sugar is off limits, Cuban growers migrated to Florida and expanded sugar production (Photo 10.6). The cane grows in one of the wealthiest counties in America, Palm Beach County; however, few people in Palm Beach are aware of it. The cane grows inland in a sparsely populated area near Lake Okeechobee, far from the luxurious beachside community. Sugar mills are located near the cane fields, because the cane is too heavy and bulky to ship.

The polluting and subsidized crop is protected by government controls that limit imports, especially from Caribbean nations, whose economies have been crippled because of U.S. tariffs and quotas. However, the American sugarcane and sugar beet producers, Big Sugar, have been indefatigable lobbyists for price supports and lowered water-quality standards. About one-fifth of the sugar used in America is imported; however, strict quotas and price supports keep the American price for sugar about double the world price.

The American sugar crop is the result of political maneuvering for profit, and it is grown in a climate and on soil that is marginal for sugarcane production. The weather is not quite warm enough for cane, and the land is too wet without drainage, so new varieties that require use of extensive chemicals were developed for Florida. The chemical runoff into the

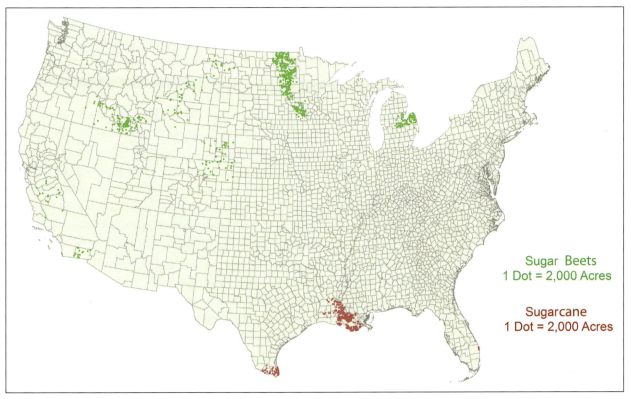

MAP 10.6. Sugarcane and Sugar Beets, 2002. Sugarcane is grown in extreme southern locations of the United States along the Gulf Coast. In Florida, sugar is grown south of Lake Okeechobee, although some of the land will be returned to the more natural wetlands. Sugar beets are grown in more northern climes.

PHOTO 10.6. Sugarcane Fires at Belle Glade, Florida. Fire burns off debris and creates a more efficient sugarcane harvest. Fires are set mechanically, supervised by the Department of Forestry. Each fire last about fifteen minutes, and the smoke and fire can be seen throughout the area. After the fire, the cane is mechanically harvested and then transported to nearby mills.

Everglades has created additional damage, such as toxicity and the loss of biodiversity. As noted earlier, the rise in sugarcane production began with the draining of the northern Everglades, which is an area not conducive to growing crops, yet taxpayers continue to pay billions to subsidize growers.[22] In 2009, a political deal with United States Sugar returned some of the less profitable agricultural land south of Lake Okeechobee to the Everglades.

Livestock: Cattle

Cattle have been an important part of Florida's agricultural production since the mid-1800s. Florida cattle descended from Spanish breeds introduced in the sixteenth century. The mangy, underweight Florida cow, called the "4-H type" (hide, hair, hoofs, and horns),[23] was unacceptable to most Americans' taste, therefore the market for Florida cattle until the early twentieth century was either local or Cuban, except for supplying Confederate troops during the Civil War. The cattle were immune to Florida diseases and parasites and roamed central Florida's free range until after World War II, when the range was fenced to eradicate a scourge of ticks (blocking Florida cattle from the American market). After World War II, the cattle industry introduced new breeds, changing land ownership techniques, taxation, and fencing laws. Today, Florida is the third-largest cattle producer east of the Mississippi and eleventh in the nation.

Fishery

The fishery concentrated in northeastern Florida targets brown shrimp in the summer and white shrimp in the fall and winter. Most shrimping occurs in state waters (three miles on the east coast of Florida and nine miles on the west coast). Quotas regulate other commercial fisheries. There is also an active sports fishery for a variety of fish. Dredging along the beaches has decimated the commercial fishery.

Minerals

Florida supplies 75 percent of America's phosphates and about 25 percent of the world's phosphates. Most phosphates are located to the east of Tampa Bay, but as deposits diminish mining has moved south to lesser quality and more technologically challenging areas. Phosphates are formed by the precipitation of dissolved phosphorus and fossils in sedimentary layers of Florida when it was beneath the sea millions of years ago. Phosphorus, which is locked within phosphates, is required by every animal and plant cell and is a primary nutrient for plant growth. Phosphorus is a nonrenewable resource that cannot be artificially produced.

Phosphorus is one of the main causes of nutrient-polluting water eutrophication. In Florida, more than 50 percent of its lakes are overly rich in natural phosphorus. However, decades of nutrient loading by Floridian agriculture, residents, and industry have caused algal blooms and low oxygen levels, resulting in fish kills.

Industry and Postindustrial

Space Economy

Florida's fair-weather launching location established a vital role in the space program. The Cape Canaveral "Space Coast" has supported over 180 businesses along the Atlantic coastline and has contributed more than $4.5 billion to the state economy. The more than twenty-three thousand jobs generated are considered environmentally clean and are high-paying technical jobs.

However, space launchings have been in decline. In 2011 the space shuttle and thousands of employees were retired. Therefore Florida's space companies are looking to diversify, offering incentive programs to high-tech space industry companies wishing to relocate in Florida and working with universities to develop further research opportunities. In August 2008, Space Florida signed a deal for an unused public-private launch pad at Cape Canaveral. The deal will allow Florida to stay in the competition, as private companies begin to compete for space launches.

Tourism

Tourism is the number one industry in Florida, bringing in more than eighty million visitors annually. Domestic visitors made up 54 percent, foreign 46 percent (2007). Snowbirds, seniors who relocate during the prime winter season, account for 818,000. Tourists arrive for its climate (winter in southwestern Florida), and human-made (Disneyworld) and natural attractions (the Everglades and Keys). Florida's tourism industry has an economic impact of $57 billion annually (2007) and therefore pays a large portion of Floridian taxes (paying for Florida's education and infrastructure), while providing 12 percent of all nonfarm jobs.

Although tourism brings in cash and employment, it also has an effect on the local economy, increasing traffic, health care for retirees, public safety (crime), and environmental destruction. An additional burden for Florida residents is the minimum wage jobs in the tourist industry.

A Sustainable Future

Still, the biggest factor in the attacks is the continuing encroachment of humanity. For eons the critters had the wetlands to themselves, and now the wetlands are subdivisions, and the subdivisions are full of people. . . .

As primitive as they are, gators have adjusted to our presence far better than we've adjusted to theirs. . . . The smartest way to deal with gators is to avoid them, which isn't always easy in Florida. They were here first, and obviously they're not going anywhere. . . .

But they're also killing machines. In millions of years they haven't changed their agenda, and they're not going to change for us.[24]

The future of Florida depends on population: what happens in Cuba, and how many foreigners and retirees move to the region. As the baby boom generation retires, many more could find their way to the state, but will they be welcome? The developed region found itself overbuilt with speculative real estate when the market soured in 2008. The faltering economy halted retiree immigration and the tourist industry.

Some future issues facing Floridians are climate change and its relation to hurricanes, property insurance increases, and government funds for hurricane damage. Florida expects the population to double in the next forty or fifty years, but many residents scorn new residents or want them congregated in specific areas with up to twenty-one units per acre. Low-cost housing is disappearing quickly, although the housing crunch beginning in 2008 has eased prices.

Another issue, emphasized by Carl Hiassen, is Florida's reputation of failures and frauds. Elian Gonzalez, wet-land/dry-land immigrants, hanging chads, security frauds, swamp swindles, and people-eating gators—these are common occurrences past and present found in a state that has been said to be "a victim of its own geography."

Florida's environmental problems include the following:

- Vulnerability to hurricanes
- A high rate of population growth
- Dependence on natural gas and coal for 86 percent of its energy
- Dependence on outside sources for fossil fuel
- Ranking third nationally in total energy consumption

A main focus is Florida's high per capita energy use due to a dependence on air-conditioning. Less than 1 percent of state energy is renewable. Yet by 2008, Florida was the state that offered the most tax incentives for solar power, and homeowners were able to recoup up to $20,000 in solar costs. Additional sustainable issues address water treatment and discharge, which reduces nitrogen, reduces discharges to rivers, and eliminates failing septic tank systems.

Until 2005, Florida was dependent on traditional fuel sources for home and vehicles. In 2005, a state energy plan was enacted to build a more sustainable Florida. Despite the potential, Florida's reliance on solar power was negligible until the largest solar photovoltaic power plant in the United States was completed in 2010. The plant will generate enough electricity to power three thousand homes and avoid 575,000 tons of GHG emissions annually—still a drop in the bucket, but a beginning. One biodiesel facility operates within the state, but all ethanol is imported.

Florida has joined other states in executing orders that mirror California's plan for climate change policy, including reducing emissions from utilities, clean cars, and energy-efficient appliances. Florida is beginning to move toward sustainability, but can it operate sustainably with eighteen million residents, a lack of water, and increased energy costs?

Questions for Discussion

1. Explain why eighteen million people is or is not a sustainable carrying capacity for Florida.

2. Is restoring previous ecosystems really a path toward environmental health? Is nature static?

3. Explain how the Everglades and Lake Okeechobee have changed since the early twentieth century.

4. The dramatic decline in aquatic life and changes in plants and turbidity have been occurring over the past two hundred years. What do you think is the "natural" ecosystem that needs to be restored? Why?

5. Give an explanation of Florida's coastal disasters and the reasons Florida is prone to them.

6. What was Florida's geologic origin? How is this origin related to the economic development of the region?

7. Where is agriculture most important in Florida? What are the most important crops and why?

8. Discuss the two largest immigrant groups and why they have chosen Florida as their home.

9. What measures has Florida taken to ensure a more sustainable future?

Suggested Readings

Barnett, Cynthia. *Mirage: Florida and the Vanishing Water of the Eastern US.* Ann Arbor: University of Michigan Press, 2007.

Blake, N. M. *Land into Water—Water into Land: A History of Water Management in Florida.* Tallahassee: University Presses of Florida, 1980.

Brooks, H. K., and J. M. Merritt. *Guide to the Physiographic Divisions of Florida.* Florida Cooperative Extension Service Institute of Food and Agricultural Sciences. Gainesville: University of Florida, 1981.

Clark, Alice L., and George H. Dalrymple. "$7.8 Billion for Everglades Restoration: Why Do Environmentalists Look So Worried?" *Population and Environment* 24, no. 6 (July 2003).

Cronin, Thomas. "Increased Salinity in Florida Bay: Nature or Man?" Paper presented at Florida Bay and Adjacent Waters Science Conference, Taverner, November 1998; Florida Bay Research Project Files.

Fourqurean, James W., and Michael B. Robblee. "Florida Bay: A History of Recent Ecological Changes." *Estuaries* 22, no. 2B (June 1999): 345–57.

Grunwald, Michael. *The Swamp: The Everglades, Florida, and the Politics of Paradise.* New York: Simon & Schuster, 2006.

McHugh, Kevin E., Ines M. Miyares, and Emily H. Skop. "The Magnetism of Miami: Segmented Paths in Cuban Migration." *Geographical Review* 87, no. 4 (October 1997): 504–19.

Mealor, W. Theodore, Jr., and Merle C. Prunty. "Open-Range Ranching in Southern Florida." *Annals of the Association of American Geographers* 66, no. 3 (1976): 360–76.

Smith, Stanley K., and Mark House. "Snowbirds, Sunbirds, and Stayers: Seasonal Migration of Elderly Adults in Florida." *Journals of Gerontology: Series B: Psychological Sciences and Social Sciences* 61, no. 5 (September 2006): S232.

Water Science and Technology Board (WSTB). Board on Environmental Studies and Toxicology (BEST). Committee on Greater Everglades Ecosystem. *Does Water Flow Influence Everglades Landscape Patterns?* Washington, D.C.: National Academies Press, 2003.

Wilkinson, Alec. *Big Sugar: Seasons in the Cane Fields of Florida.* New York: Knopf, 1989.

Internet Sources

Florida Museum of Natural History. "Mangroves," at http://www.flmnh.ufl.edu/fish/southflorida/mangrove/Introduction.html.

ThinkQuest. "Everglades Facts," at http://library.thinkquest.org/CR0214223/facts.html.

Florida Department of State. "A Brief History of Florida," at http://www.flheritage.com/facts/history/summary/.

Flagler Museum (Historic Landmark), at http://www.flaglermuseum.us/.

Tampa Bay Seawater Desalination Plant, at http://www.water-technology.net/projects/tampa/.

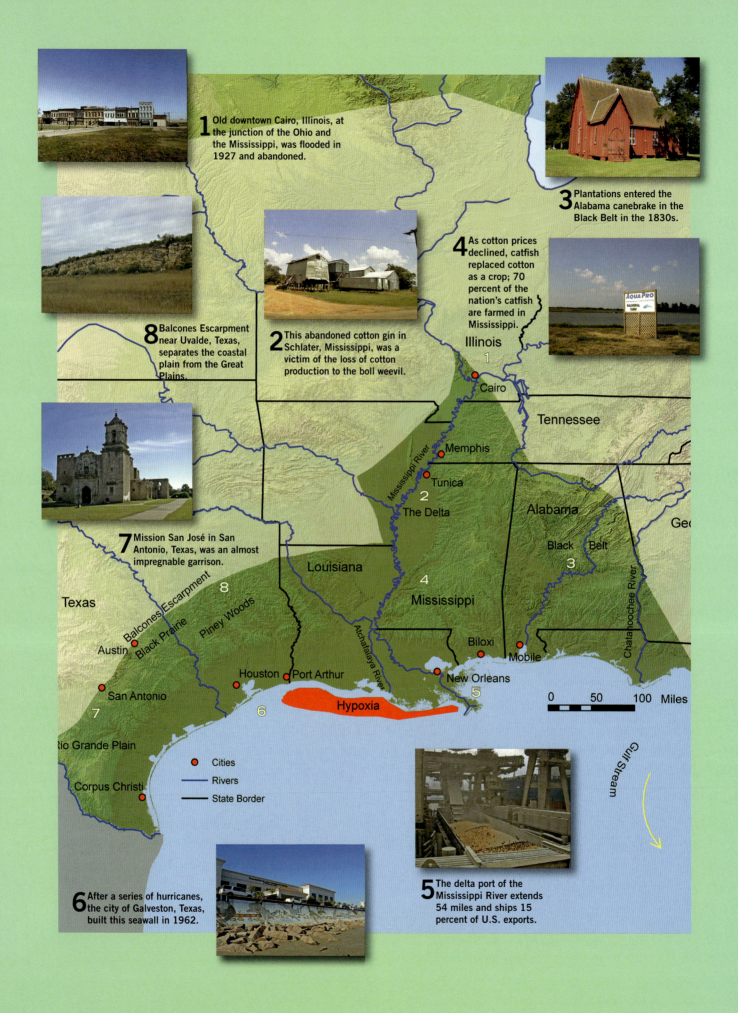

1 Old downtown Cairo, Illinois, at the junction of the Ohio and the Mississippi, was flooded in 1927 and abandoned.

3 Plantations entered the Alabama canebrake in the Black Belt in the 1830s.

4 As cotton prices declined, catfish replaced cotton as a crop; 70 percent of the nation's catfish are farmed in Mississippi.

8 Balcones Escarpment near Uvalde, Texas, separates the coastal plain from the Great Plains.

2 This abandoned cotton gin in Schlater, Mississippi, was a victim of the loss of cotton production to the boll weevil.

7 Mission San José in San Antonio, Texas, was an almost impregnable garrison.

6 After a series of hurricanes, the city of Galveston, Texas, built this seawall in 1962.

5 The delta port of the Mississippi River extends 54 miles and ships 15 percent of U.S. exports.

Illinois

Cairo

Tennessee

Memphis

Tunica

2

The Delta

Alabama

Black Belt

3

Louisiana

4

Mississippi

Texas

Balcones Escarpment

Black Prairie

Piney Woods

8

Austin

Biloxi

Mobile

San Antonio

New Orleans

5

7

Rio Grande Plain

6

Hypoxia

Corpus Christi

Houston   Port Arthur

Atchafalaya River

Mississippi River

Chatahoochee River

Ge

Gulf Stream

0   50   100   Miles

- Cities
— Rivers
— State Border

11

GULF COASTAL PLAINS AND MISSISSIPPI VALLEY

Juxtaposition Squared

Chapter Highlights

After reading this chapter you should be able to:

- Explain the importance of the wetlands along the Gulf Coast
- List the subregions and identify their similarities and differences
- Discuss how landscape change has affected the force of hurricanes
- Give an overview of how the Mississippi River has been altered and its effect
- Describe the relationship between fertilizers and hypoxia
- Outline the evolution of plantations from the antebellum to Reconstruction periods
- Define colonias and their impact on the border region
- Discuss the reasons for and impact of disease and pestilence in the Gulf region
- Explain the strategic importance of New Orleans
- Compare and contrast the Old South and the New South
- Identify the Black Belt both topographically and culturally
- Describe the impact of oil and gas on the Gulf Coast economy and environment
- List the major crops along the Gulf Coast and Mississippi alluvial area

Terms

antebellum	Creole	hurricane	pulpwood
Army Corps of Engineers	cuesta	hydrocarbon	push and pull factors
bayou	delta	hypoxia	salt dome
bosque	embayment	Jim Crow	sharecropper
Cajun	environmental justice	levee	subsidence
chain migration	estuary	Mardi Gras	sustainable hazard
colonia	eutrophication	melting pot	mitigation
	flatwoods	oxbow lake	sustainable yield
	Great Migration	petroleum	

Places

Atchafalaya River	Black Prairie, Texas	Memphis, Tennessee	Rio Grande Plain
Black Belt	Cairo, Illinois	Mississippi River	Riverwalk
	Gulf Stream	New Orleans, Louisiana	San Antonio, Texas
	Houston, Texas		

PHOTO 11.1. Mardi Gras, New Orleans, Louisiana. Mardi Gras ("fat Tuesday") is so named because it is the last hurrah for Roman Catholics before the spare days of Lent prior to Easter. The roots of the end-of-winter-beginning-of-spring season reach back to pagan times, as do many of the holy days celebrated today. Louisiana and especially New Orleans are known for over-the-top Mardi Gras celebrations and numerous parades.

Introduction

. . . that doomed wilderness whose edges were being constantly and punily gnawed at by men with plows and axes who feared it because it was wilderness.

—William Faulkner, *Go Down, Moses*, 1942[1]

In the passenger car every window was propped open with a stick of kindling wood. A breeze blew through, hot and then cool, fragrant of the woods and yellow flower and of the train. . . . And then, as if a hand reached along the green ridge and all of a sudden pulled down with a sweep, like a scoop in the bin, the hill and every tree in the world and left cotton fields, the Delta began.

—Eudora Welty, *Delta Wedding*, 1945[2]

The belly of the states, the underside of America, the Gulf, the South—the Mississippi Delta sense of place fills the landscape. This is the "most southern place on Earth,"[3] the "quintessential South."[4] After both the 2005 Hurricane Katrina and the 2010 Deepwater Horizon oil spill, the Gulf Coast became known as the most ecologically devastated region in America. This region of extremes is a jumble of juxtapositions: slaves and plantations; black and white; cotton and oil; segregation and integration; Caribbean **Creole** and Canadian **Cajun**; extreme wealth and extreme poverty; thick, black soils and thin, piney sands.

The heavy, dank Gulf Coast has inspired impassioned art and been memorialized in literature, by William Faulkner, Harper Lee, Eudora Welty, and Tennessee Williams, among others. Their stories reflect Gulf Coast life, one of racial disease and rebirth, one of dependence on cotton in a swampy, bayou-ridden tangle of quasi-land. This same land is also a laid-back, joyous, and culinary treasure filled with good and friendly people and their corrupt counterparts.

The American South includes the Atlantic and Gulf Coasts, and while they share a subtropical climate, marsh-ridden coastline, and slaveholding past, the two coasts developed dissimilar economies pegged to their regional landscapes. Although the region remains one of the poorest in America, it is also home to coastal wealth, new industries, and opportunities.

The Gulf Coast's most engrossing city has always been New Orleans, but even more so since the debacle of Hurricane Katrina. The Gulf Coastal Plain has long been a target for hurricane destruction because of natural and human events. Climate change has only increased susceptibility to severe storms and hurricanes. Despite academic and environmental warnings, the government has ignored how human interventions—population growth, pollution, destruction of wetlands, and controlling the river—have affected the landscape. The levee system had been in dire straits since Hurricane Betsy in 1965, but still it was not fixed when in roared Katrina.[5] The follow-up of the Deepwater Horizon oil spill was the proverbial icing in the form of an oil slick.

New Orleans, the "inevitable city on the impossible site,"[6] is a shadow of its prior grace, but it is also a city of great wealth and poverty. While wealth remains intact, including the famed French Quarter built on the natural levee of the river, there were many other levees that protected those who lived below sea level in **subsidence**-prone areas. Those residents were inundated and have scattered from what is no longer their home, at least physically. The losses were disproportionate. Although black and white alike lost their homes to Katrina, it was the poorer black population who lost everything and had no insurance or support. The oil spill damaged the fishing and tourism industry. Katrina's destruction and the oil slick added to the Gulf's problems of providing **environmental justice**—fair treatment for the economically disadvantaged areas and residents.

The Gulf Coast, from Alabama to Texas, lost delicate, over-populated coastal properties, but there may have been a silver lining. The next chapter in the Gulf's life is yet to be written. The cost—to those who lived there and to the rest of Americans who will pay for the loss—is beyond dollars and a mighty blow to the country's health and welfare, but a "tabula rasa" benefit was that the damage came at a time when a sustainable mind-set to rebuild long-term was possible.

It has been a long road for the Gulf Coast. Recovery from the Civil War took decades. Discrimination and segregation policies encapsulated the "Old South" awaiting the "New South"—a South that blended with the lockstep consumerism and economy of the nation. But the transition was uneven. By the end of the twentieth century, coastal areas transformed into opulent McMansions, while the interior Black Belt remained mired in illiteracy and poverty, emphasizing the wealth and poverty gap. Per capita income in Mississippi's Gulf Coast cities rose more than 50 percent in the past decade; those in the Delta and Black Belt saw no such gain. Money for these long-term needy areas was funneled to Katrina victims, many of whom are wealthier than the Black Belt poor.

But environmental destruction is not the only change: The chemical industry is leaving, while the auto industry is abandoning Detroit and choosing the cheaper labor and climatically warmer right-to-work nonunion Gulf states. The Gulf Coast has evolved from seafood and lumber to chemicals, computers, cars, and tourism—especially gaming casinos. Most growth has been along the wealthier coastal area, which was most affected by Katrina (Photo 11.2). In some strange balancing act between humans and nature, the most fragile places environmentally are the same as those that prosper economically.

Physical Geography

Finding a sustainable balance in the Gulf Coast will be difficult. The fragile physical landscape has now suffered its most feared disasters. The coastal wetlands buffered the inland areas before human intervention based on short-term profit eroded the wetlands and exposed the interior. To find a dynamic balance, the Gulf Coast must first learn to live within the natural landscape.

The Gulf Coast from the Florida Panhandle to the Mexican border shares humidity and rainfall, abundant marshy areas, and a low-lying and once submerged coastal plain. The Gulf Coastal Plain, a continuation of the Atlantic Coastal Plain, is an elevated sea bottom that barely emerges from the 75-mile-wide continental shelf. Varying from 10 to 150 miles wide, the low-lying and swampy coastal plain seldom rises above fifty feet. It is one of the continent's richest ecological regions. The complex ecological communities in the river's brackish wetlands sustain the local economy as long as pollution is checked. The mixed fresh and saltwater **estuary** habitats shelter species on barrier islands, mangroves, and reefs.

Spanish moss–shrouded oaks, magnolias, and bayou cypress live along the marshes and coastal plain, while inland along the extended Black Belt, the swampy **flatwood** forest featured deciduous oak and maple mixed with southern pines, until the forest landscape was removed for crops, urban development, or tree plantations. What remains are ecologically sterile loblolly tree plantations that are harvested about every thirty years.

More than four hundred species of wildlife and 40 percent of North America's migratory waterfowl live within the Mississippi River basin, but erosion, pollution, and climate change disrupt existing ecosystems and habitats, and introduce pests and new species.

PHOTO 11.2. Post-Katrina Destruction, Ocean Springs, Mississippi. Ocean Springs was an affluent suburb of Biloxi. After Hurricane Katrina, the houses closest to shore were completely demolished. The renewal of the region brought to the fore many issues that were already brewing in America, but Katrina victims had to deal with them first, including the growing gap between the haves and have-nots.

Natural disasters are exacerbated by human folly. Land is sinking and still the infrastructure is rebuilt, and rebuilt again. While losing a billion dollars a week to disasters, it may be time to think about **sustainable hazard mitigation** that assesses physical vulnerabilities and plans accordingly. At some point, bailing out vulnerable regions should no longer be an option. To live in hazard zones sustainably is to live locally, honestly, and improve the environmental quality—to be an integral part of the place.

What follows is the physical landscape of the Gulf Coast. The region contains four subregional plains, all edging the gulf but all displaying their own personalities:

- East Gulf Coastal
- Mississippi Alluvial
- West Gulf Coastal
- Rio Grande

East Gulf Coastal Plain

The eastern coastal plain is characterized by a belted, concentric band of lowlands and **cuesta** ridges, steep on one side, gently sloped on the other. The forested swampy lowland extends over beaches and barrier islands. The northern edge extends to the Alabama Black Belt, just south of the Appalachians and west of Montgomery, Alabama (Map 11.1).

The popularity of oceanfront property has caused a plethora of second homes to be built, all open to the destruction of Gulf hazards. For example Orange Beach, Alabama, sits on a barrier island with thousands of high-rise units sitting empty due to overbuilding and destruction from the 2010 oil spill.

Mississippi Alluvial Plain

10,000 River Commissions, with the mines of the world at their back, cannot tame that lawless stream, cannot curb it or confine it, cannot say to it, Go here or Go there, and make it obey; cannot save a shore which it has sentenced; cannot bar its path with an obstruction which it will not tear down, dance over and laugh at.

—Mark Twain, *Life on the Mississippi*, 1883[7]

The Mississippi Alluvial Plain extends five hundred miles from the **delta** northward to Cairo, Illinois, where the Mississippi meets the Ohio River. The fifty-to-one-hundred-mile-wide plain leaves sediment replenishing the soil as it descends to the

MAP 11.1. Traditional Counties of the Alabama Black Belt. The name was first applied for the rich, dark soil, but later became synonymous with the large, poor black population living in the area.

coast. For thousands of years the river has followed the easiest gradient, changing course multiple times, leaving behind natural levees, back swamps, and the large, graceful, curving commas—cutoff or **oxbow lakes**—demarcating old river routes.

An important part of the alluvial plain, "the Delta" lies between the Yazoo and Mississippi rivers, between Memphis and Natchez. The Delta has engendered its own persona. Alluvial floods laid down the flat pan of the Delta's storied soils, which mutated into slave-run cotton plantations and became the birthplace of the blues, a music form that expresses the longtime tenor of the place.

Just north of the Delta and on the opposite bank is Crowley's Ridge—named after the region's first settler. The ridge is the most prominent topographic feature along the alluvial plain. The loess ridge may have originated as an island within the river, or it may be the result of uplift (the New Madrid earthquake zone is nearby). Jonesboro and other Arkansas alluvial towns are protected from flooding because of their location on the higher ground of Crowley's Ridge.

West Gulf Coastal Plain

The flat West Gulf Coastal Plain topography contains numerous barrier islands and salt domes. The West Gulf Coast bay-estuary-lagoon complex—the largest is Galveston Bay—separates the mainland and Gulf. **Salt domes**, the buried remnants of a shallow sea, dot the coast and coastal plain, demarcating **petroleum** traps.

The West Gulf Coastal Plain has two subregions: the eastern Texas Piney Woods and the Coastal Prairie. The Piney Woods are a sandy, agriculturally poor area, whose natural pine-hardwood vegetation has been converted to loblolly pine plantations. The Coastal Prairie grasslands from Houston south to Corpus Christi are all but gone and now grow cotton or graze cattle. The plain spreads inland to the Balcones Escarpment, where the Great Plains begin. At the southernmost edge is the Rio Grande Plain.

Rio Grande Plain

The Rio Grande Plain, occupying the Texas border region south of San Antonio to the Rio Grande River, is a lowland with occasional limestone-capped hills, buttes, or volcanic necks, a transition zone from the coastal plain to the Great Plains. The landscape varies from the intensively farmed flat, fertile flood plain in the south to the drier, semiarid grassy shrub area that sprouts the ubiquitous Texan mesquite.

The cottonwood-mesquite (**bosque**) ecosystem along river bottoms has adapted well to the local arid climate and occasional flood patterns. The bosque ecosystem requires no fire suppression, but invasive salt cedar and Russian olive trees have crowded the natural species out, swilled water, and expanded flammable debris that is vulnerable to human-made fires. To rid the bosque of the fire-prone nonnative tinder, management programs have reintroduced goats that browse the tinder as a sustainable conservation measure.[8]

Modern civilization has been unkind to the Rio Grande Valley. First the Spanish grazed too many sheep and caused erosion; Americans followed, overstocking the animal and human population and building dams and levees to serve urban areas. Land is grazed, cultivated, and, along the Mexican border, urbanized. Cities thrive along the river, while native plants, such as the Texas palmetto, languish. Water continues to be a major problem, as populations grow and agriculture continues to provide winter season fruits and vegetables. Many farmer cooperatives and conservation-minded groups work to achieve sustainable practices to maintain the valley's economy.

Water

It is entirely in the power of man to control all the water of the Mississippi and Missouri, and compel every river to flow with an even current, from its source in the Allegheny or Rocky Mountains, to its home in the Ocean, forever free from the hurtful effects of floods and droughts.

—Charles Ellet, 1851[9]

The Mississippi River system is the dominant water source for the continental interior, while the Rio Grande divides a portion of the United States from Mexico. Oxbow lakes are the natural lakes in this part of the country, but dam reservoirs form artificial lakes. Another important water feature is the extensive, poorly drained coastline, much of which has subsided, been reclaimed, or developed.

Mississippi River

You can easily imagine that there is nothing permanent upon the banks of this part of the Mississippi. Whoever builds upon it will find himself like the "foolish man who built his house upon the sand."

—Edward Fontaine, 1872[10]

Before human intervention, the sinuous lower Mississippi River meandered in 180-degree turns, losing elevation slowly as it made its way to the coast. The river shifts some of its channels ten to twenty times a century as it courses at four miles per hour, ninety-six miles per day. The entire basin from Cape Girardeau, Missouri (the geologic head), was once a submerged part of the Gulf **embayment**, but as sea levels dropped it emerged as an alluvial plain.

The river's course was cast during the Precambrian when the supercontinent of Rodinia fractured North America. The Mississippi embayment was formed as the ocean flooded and then retracted. During the Pleistocene, drainage patterns reconfigured, and the Mississippi changed its directional flow from north to south.

The middle Mississippi River region between the confluences of the Missouri and Ohio rivers has been an important settlement area. Native Americans settled in Cahokia, and later the French established the trading and farm towns of Cape Giradeau, Kaskaskia, and St. Genevieve. Along the Missouri confluence was St. Louis (see chapter 12), a city well situated to command trade between the east and west. Along the Ohio confluence was the less successful city of Cairo, Illinois.

BOX 11.1 SALT DOMES AND HYDROCARBONS

The foundations for salt domes were created in ancient evaporated seas. A deep, less dense salt formation lies miles below the surface and moves upward, pushing the surrounding sediment layers upward and forming bumps five to eighty-three feet high on the surface of the otherwise flat Gulf Coast. The uplift truncates horizontal layers near the rock and traps reservoirs of migrating **hydrocarbons**—petroleum (literally from Latin, "rock oil") and natural gas.

Geophysicists seek out salt domes for their potential oil-based energy sources.

The 1901 discovery of Spindletop oilfield—a salt dome formation—sparked the birth of the modern oilfield industry. That discovery verified the theory of salt dome–oil relationships. Beaumont, Texas, boomed, and soon intense technologic innovation mastered salt dome exploitation and initiated oil companies such as Texaco, Exxon, Gulf Oil, and Sun Oil.

Controlling the Mississippi River: Wetlands, Levees, and Flooding

The meandering Mississippi River deposits sediment across the broad alluvial valley and delta. As the river approaches the Gulf, sediment shapes the wide "bird's foot" delta below New Orleans, but over millennia, river sediment has also covered about one-fourth of Louisiana's coastline. The river's mouth has shifted several times over the past thousand years, each time finding the path of least resistance and greatest efficiency of flow.

Upon European arrival, Louisiana's coastline was a water-filtering, storm-buffering wetland providing homes for migratory birds and ducks, and supporting about one-third of the nation's commercial fish and shellfish harvests. Louisiana continues to have more coastal wetlands than other Gulf Coast states, but since the 1930s, human intervention has caused unintended consequences that have devastated the regional economy.

Unintended Consequences

Loss of Wetlands   The tidal wetlands along the Louisiana coast have been dissolving into the Gulf despite natural resource management. The wetlands loss is due to coastal development and because the Mississippi River has been channelized for flood control and to "correct" its path. Human intervention interfered with the natural cycle of sediment deposition that created the wetlands. The wetlands starved, resulting in the state losing over a million acres of coastlands at a rate of one football field of land every fifteen minutes (Table 11.1). This is typical of how problems have been solved in the past with single-issue "answers," acting on one issue in an ecosystem without taking into consideration its impact on the rest of the system. This fragmented approach has caused many of the problems that systems recognize, such as interconnections, revealing choices more amenable to not only humans but the physical and biotic landscape. While far more complex, a systems-thinking answer to such problems seeks answers within an integrated whole rather than piecemeal. Additionally, the complexity of the solution will create many jobs that do not currently exist.

An example of a solely anthropocentric single-issue answer is the 1920s crisscrossing of the wetlands by canals connecting energy sources for the oil and gas industry. The intended consequences all favored humans: high-paying jobs, taxes for the state, and profit for the corporations. These benefits operated, though, on a boom-bust cycle. When the bust arrived, the jobs were lost and state and corporate revenue declined. There was little thought to the long-term relationships between the canals, saltwater intrusion and the loss of land.

The unintended consequences of the canals were a study in how the triple bottom line can improve human interactions. The canals destroyed ecosystems, eroded wetlands, and infiltrated salt water into freshwater marshes (environmental degradation). These consequences all diminished protection to human habitations (social equity) but increased profits for companies. Under natural conditions, wetlands sediment and nutrients are converted to biologically useful materials and serve as fish and shellfish nurseries. Wetland losses increase inland area susceptibility to salt water and hurricanes. Eroded wetlands allow the water level to rise and expose the coast to flooding.

Attention has been paid to the destruction. By the 1940s, the industry was charged for polluting oyster beds, and some changes reduced the impact. But when the industry moved offshore in the 1950s, the wetland environment was seriously impacted by miles and miles of pipeline and canal systems to support them. Since that time, many improvements in wetland restoration have been made, but the corrections were too little, too late. The April 2010 Deepwater Horizon oil spill revealed the weakness of protection.

Unintended Consequences of Artificial Levees

Sediment builds modest natural **levees** protected by wetlands that lie opposite the levees. The wetlands absorb water after flooding events and then dry. Humans have attempted to protect populated areas by building artificial levees, but these levees do not have wetland buffers. Normal flooding outside natural levees is gradual; artificial levees raise the crest in anticipation of great floods, but ultimately create more dramatic devastation when the levees are breached, rather than the more gradual flooding of natural levees and their wetland buffers.

Regional and Ecoregional Impacts

The Many Mississippi River Deltas   Devastating floods occur periodically. The first recorded flood was described by the 1543 Desoto expedition, but of course, many floods preceded European occupancy. Floods do not dissipate quickly. They

BOX 11.2   DID YOU KNOW . . . LOUISIANA WETLANDS

- More than 40 percent of the salt marshes in the contiguous United States are in Louisiana.
- It took five thousand years to build the Louisiana coastline lowlands, yet 20 percent was lost in a hundred years as a result of coastal erosion.
- About forty square miles of land are lost annually, which amounts to an acre every fifteen minutes, or a football field every forty to forty-five minutes.
- Over the twentieth century, the state of Louisiana lost more than nineteen hundred square miles of land.

- Coastal Texas to Mississippi and inland about fifty miles, the Mississippi and other rivers naturally built the coastal ridges from the silt washed down from the river.
- Human alterations have caused land loss, deteriorated wetlands, and greater susceptibility to storm damage.
- The Mississippi River brings about a half million tons of silt to the delta, but the controlled delta washes most of the silt out to sea.

often crest for a month in March and then do not recede until May—almost three months lost to flooding.

After numerous commissions and reports in the mid-twentieth century, a plan was inaugurated to control the Mississippi by a combination of levees, outlets, cutoffs, and dams. More than two thousand miles of levees, constructed to prevent the river from flooding, proved unsuccessful.

Included within the plan was a structure to control the river's course. Prior to the massive 1927 flood, the Atchafalaya River had been widening, accepting more Mississippi River water. After the flood, it became obvious that the Mississippi was changing its course to flow down the Atchafalaya.

Over the past nine thousand years, the river has formed at least seven different deltas discharging the Mississippi waters along the Louisiana coastline. Still another shift of the delta began in the twentieth century. While shifts of the river have been known, this shift would have huge economic impacts because of the infrastructure along the current delta path. If the mouth of the delta were to shift down what is now the Atchafalaya it would cripple the coastal and national economy. So in 1963, the **Army Corps of Engineers** completed the Old River Control Structure to restrain the course of the river and protect the delta infrastructure. However, alternating the river flow only satisfied the human economy and ignored ecological considerations, such as sediment deposition.

The Atchafalaya delta currently receives about 30 percent of the river's flow, and its delta is growing and building new wetlands. But the Mississippi bird's foot–delta no longer builds much wetland area, because it extends so far onto the continental shelf that it now descends into the deep waters of the

continental slope rather than building new wetlands and barrier islands.[11] If the river flowed down the Atchafalaya, as its natural course now dictates, the sediment would be deposited on the shallow continental shelf and build additional wetlands and barrier islands.

To protect human habitation and commercial navigation, the river and its silt deposits have been modified and channeled to continue the use of the current infrastructure. But interfering was done in a piecemeal and unsustainable fashion and seldom considered the added complexity of climate change. The lack of a holistic plan has degraded the Louisiana coastline. More long-range and holistic plans have since been formulized in academic studies, but they have not been endorsed by government policy.[12] The plans include the entire river system and the offshore hypoxia. Acting on holistic plans would benefit the region and its surroundings.

The Current Mississippi River Delta

Louisiana's coastal wetlands, tied to Mississippi River oscillations, absorb the shock of Gulf storms and protect the low-lying areas, but the delta is subsiding and has stopped silting. The coastal delta is disappearing.

The disappearing wetlands expose oil industry infrastructure to open water conditions. The infrastructure—pipelines, roads, ports, and wells—services thousands of Gulf platforms. Wetland loss, infrastructure exposure, and deep drilling in fragile areas lead to more oil spills and have been a factor in inflating oil prices.

Twentieth-century wetland loss accelerated because of human impacts—marsh subsidence, levee construction, and

TABLE 11.1. Wetlands Loss in the Gulf Coast

	Alabama	Louisiana	Mississippi	Texas
Coastal acreage loss	121,603	3,910,664	64,805	412,516

Source: Zhu H. Ning, R. Eugene Turner, Thomas Doyle, and Kamran Abdollahi, *Preparing for a Changing Climate: The Potential Consequences of Climate Variability and Change. Gulf Coast Region* (Baton Rouge, La.: Gulf Coast Regional Climate Change, June 2003)

grazing nutria (an invasive rodent brought in by fur ranchers)—although little attention was paid to the loss until 1970. The Army Corps of Engineers constructed confining levees, altered nutrient distribution to wetlands, and altered sediment accumulation patterns.

External Costs

If the Mississippi River is allowed to complete the change of its course, the cost will be monumental. New Orleans would be superfluous and Morgan City would be engulfed by the raging Atchafalaya River. A new port city would have to be built. The offshore oil and gas industry infrastructure would require rebuilding. The delta fisheries could all be altered and oyster beds destroyed. The infrastructure built around the current Atchafalaya would no longer be sufficient to meet the needs of the new and much larger river.

New Orleans and all other cities along the Mississippi would still exist but in much different circumstances. Shipping patterns would change, and drinking water would have to come from another source, as the lower level of water in the river would allow more salt water to enter the channel. All petrochemical infrastructures would also be affected by the saltier water, which would corrode pipes. The cost for our control of nature would be in the many billions of dollars and would interrupt commerce for decades.

The economic cost of these damages is beyond dollars and cents. The social equity costs of the oil and gas industry along the Louisiana coastal area have only begun to be understood. They include the numerous towns of Louisiana's chemical corridor from Baton Rouge to New Orleans, polluted by the oil industry's waste disposal. On a per capita basis, Louisiana has the highest volume of toxic chemicals in the country.

Gulf of Mexico

The origin of the Gulf of Mexico is still debated and studied. A prevalent theory says the basin was formed during the Triassic period (230 million years ago), as Pangaea broke up and the North American Plate drifted away from the African and South American Plates.[13] Several times, sea water inundated the region and deposited salt, which emerged later as the Gulf region's salt domes.

The warm water Loop Current, a segment of global oceanic patterns, dominates the Gulf of Mexico water flow. The current flows from the Yucatan Peninsula toward the Mississippi delta and then continues out to the Atlantic or returns to the Gulf (hence the phrase "loop current"). The current's only escape funnels through the Straits of Florida between the Florida Keys and Cuba and connects to the Gulf Stream, the warm ocean current that flows northward along the Atlantic coast. Loop Current studies increased after the April 2010 Deep Horizon oil spill opened the possibility of oil reaching the Atlantic coast.

Coastal areas along the Gulf are low and prone to subsidence and flooding. Galveston, located on a barrier island, has been flooded several times, resulting in the town's building a seawall to stop the relentless ocean. However, hurricanes continue to cause destruction, such as a section of Baytown that was inundated in 1983 during Hurricane Alicia or the direct hit and devastation to Galveston in 2008.

Hypoxia

Shrimp and fish require oxygen. Excess nitrogen from runoff reduces oxygen for aquatic life. Nitrogen is essential for making amino acids, proteins, and DNA; it also boosts crop yields, and added to fields expands productive land. Natural nitrogen conversion by bacteria is no longer the main source of nitrogen; instead, nitrogen is combined with hydrogen under heat and pressure to create anhydrous ammonia, which can be applied directly to fields. In trying to both have healthy plants and to maximize yields, overfertilization of nitrogen has become common. Human coastal habitation, urbanization, industrial effluent, and runoff of nitrogen-based fertilizers from watershed farms cause **hypoxia**—too much nitrogen, not enough oxygen. Hypoxia is a step-by-step process:

1. The polluted freshwater flowing from the Mississippi River is less dense than salty Gulf water, allowing prime algal bloom conditions.
2. Algae die, sink, and are eaten by bacteria.
3. The loss of algae depletes the oxygen needed by fish and shellfish.

Several hypoxic "dead zones" are found annually along the Gulf Coast and along Atlantic inlets, but the largest is west of the Mississippi Delta along the Louisiana coast. The summertime hypoxic zone fluctuates annually, but it averages around eight thousand square miles (about the size of New Jersey) of dead zone **eutrophication**—nutrient pollution. The overenrichment of nutrients in the dead zone, which are ten to twenty feet below the surface, upsets the natural balance of aquatic ecosystems and can lead to algal blooms, fish kills, and eventual ecosystem collapse.

The main cause of the hypoxic zone is a classic reinforcing feedback loop that affects Midwestern farmers and crop yields. Midwestern farmers use nitrogen-based fertilizers, which are washed into the river, flow to the Gulf, and create the hypoxic zones. If the farmers stop using or filter the pesticides, their yields will decrease. Diminishing yields would affect the financial viability of the already threatened family farmer. Ultimately, unsustainable human intervention on the natural system causes the present system of interrelated problems.

Attempts to correct this problem have come from the new field of ecotechnology—the use of natural ecosystems to solve environmental problems—an example of a long-term solution offered by systems thinking. For example, rather than concentrating on the hypoxic zone itself, researchers are now thinking holistically and seeking long-term solutions not short-term fixes. They are studying the entire watershed and its influence on the discharge zone. By eliminating problems at the source, the discharge zone will be less affected. Some of the new techniques include modifying farm practices so nitrogen will be used more efficiently; and diverting Mississippi floodwaters to wetlands where they will be filtered, thus slowing the flow of polluted water to the Gulf.[14]

Rio Grande

The only perennial stream on the Rio Grande plain is the border-defining Rio Grande, which rises in Colorado and flows through New Mexico to El Paso, Texas, where it begins its journey as the border between the United States and Mexico. Industrialization along the border has increased chemical pollution, and increased population has caused sewage issues in the river. Pesticides from the farms also make their way into the river. By the time the river reaches the Gulf, irrigation withdrawals and overuse relegates the mouth to a mere trickle of water.

Climate

The global landscape at 30° north latitude is generally arid and includes major deserts—the Sonora in the United States and the Sahara in Africa. The climate is a result of trade winds circulating warm, dry air, except in the Gulf Coastal region, which is influenced by the Gulf of Mexico and the Atlantic Ocean. Moist winds blow onshore, boosting winter and spring precipitation from a high of ninety inches along the Eastern Gulf Coastal Plain tapering to seven inches along the southernmost Rio Grande Plain. During the growing season, thunderstorms and accompanying lightening are almost daily occurrences. The warm, humid region experiences occasional frosts that limit the growing season to 200 to 240 days. The warm humidity and the ocean mix to bring the most spectacular of its climatic characteristics, the hurricane.

Hurricanes

June through November is **hurricane** season and a cause for concern along the Gulf Coast. Massive tropical storm systems pound the region with high wind speeds, thunderstorms, and storm surges that can flood the low-lying coast.

On average about five hurricanes every two years hit somewhere within the Gulf Coastal region, but hurricanes vary both in intensity and in periodic activity. During the twentieth century, hurricanes were intense from 1941 to 1965, then calmer until intensifying again about 1990. In August 2005, Hurricane Katrina slammed into the Gulf Coast just east of New Orleans, broke the human-made artificial levees, destroyed large portions of the city, displaced a million people, and killed more than thirteen hundred, while inflicting over $200 billion in damages.

Katrina redefined the meaning of natural disaster, but natural forces were not the only causes. Human intervention contributed greatly to the extensive damage and loss of life. The results of human activity created regional effects and consequences.

In the years prior to the hurricane, coastal wetlands decreased from Mobile, Alabama to New Orleans.[15] The ingredients for the destruction of New Orleans were a recipe for destruction: a lack of wetland buffers, weak infrastructure (breachable levees), densely packed homes in the lowland areas, and a poorly planned evacuation plan for all residents. A few weeks later, Hurricane Rita damaged the region again near Port Arthur, Texas.

In 2008, Hurricanes Gustav and Ike wreaked destruction on the barrier island city of Galveston, Texas. Galveston built a seawall after the devastating 1900 hurricane to protect against further hurricane damages, but it was little relief against the power of Gustav and Ike. The city received the brunt force of the storm, with storm surges that easily overcame the seawall.

Climate change may play a role in hurricane intensity, frequency, and the increase of temperatures and sea levels. However, the lack of hurricane records over long periods of time hampers long-term climate change causality or predictions.

Historical Geography and Settlement

Gulf Coast cultures can be divided into four periods: Native American, plantation, Reconstruction, and New South. Each had a different settlement pattern and impact on the landscape.

Native Americans

Native Americans occupied the Gulf region by 5000 BCE but flourished after 1300 BCE. From 1000 to 1600 CE, the alluvial valley flourished with mound cultures, such as Moundville, Alabama, and the Plaquemine and Poverty Point in Louisiana. These less populous cultures lived concurrently with the larger Cahokia Mississippian culture to the north. The mound cultures built flat-topped ceremonial or burial site mounds over one hundred feet wide and ten feet high. These hunter-gatherers also practiced agriculture. The culture declined after contact with European diseases. The "five civilized tribes"—Cherokee, Chickasaw, Choctaw, Creek, and Seminole—migrated into the area after the mound builders' demise.

As land opened to white settlement, Native American treaties were dishonored, Indian wars broke out, and ultimately the native inhabitants were relocated to Indian Territory in Oklahoma, where they were forced to live on land and in climates that differed from their cultures and native homelands. Migrating cultural groups do best when they move to regions that approximate their homeland, such as most European migrants did in America. Cultures that were cast into unknown areas had difficulty adjusting to the new and very different environment. Those Native Americans who survived the initial diseases were then sent to unfamiliar landscapes and climate. Their culture and way of life floundered and struggled to survive.

European Immigration and Settlement

The Spanish, English, French, and Americans colonized and fought to control the area of the Florida Panhandle to the Mississippi coast until the 1820 and 1832 Indian treaties, when Americans prevailed. The Gulf population grew slowly. The significance of its seaports went unrealized until later in the nineteenth century, whereas during the second and third decade of the nineteenth century the interior agricultural areas, especially those suitable for cotton production, increased in population courtesy of homestead acts and cheap land.

The Gulf French

The first French settlements in 1699 occurred concurrently along the Gulf Coast and Mississippi River regions, and consisted of Biloxi, Mississippi, built on an ancient Native American site and settlements along both sides of the Mississippi in Illinois and Missouri (Photo 11.3).

The Spaniard Hernando Desoto was the first European to document the Mississippi River, but he misinterpreted its worth because only the southern extremity was explored. Meanwhile, the French entered the Mississippi River from the north and settled near the heart of the recently extinct Mississippian culture.

Unlike Louisiana, the Illinois colony was an extension of French Canada and received settlers via the Great Lakes. French colonization connected the Great Lakes and Canada to the Gulf Coast. The Illinois and the Louisiana colonies opened trade to Biloxi in 1717 and New Orleans in 1718. The first colonists were Roman Catholic French, who were later joined by Huguenots and German-speaking Protestants. During the colonizing period, Native Americans warred and skirmished to maintain their land but ultimately were relocated.

The French and Indian War ended the French North American colonies.[16] Canada and Florida were relinquished to the British, and the Louisiana colonies became Spanish to compensate for the Spanish loss of Florida. But Louisiana was remanded to the French in 1801 and then, when French Caribbean interests were threatened, offered to the Americans in 1803, resulting in the Louisiana Purchase. French and French Creole cultural traits remain in the region, such as the French Quarter of New Orleans, the exiled Cajuns, and toponyms (Detroit, Michigan; St. Louis, Missouri; and Baton Rouge, Louisiana), along with administrative units, the Mississippi River long lots and Louisiana's parishes (equivalent to counties). The French also gave the region its southern pride "Dixie" name. Several theories abound as to the origin, but a popular one is that the French circulated ten-dollar banknotes that were inscribed with the French word *dix* ("ten") and the South became the land of dixies.

East Texas Settlement

In the seventeenth century, Spanish settlement moved from Mexico into Texas, establishing missions along the Texas Gulf Coast. Catholicism spread to the Native people via a mission system. The first and best-known mission was the Alamo—San Antonio de Valero—built in 1718, followed in 1720 by Mission San José.

The San Antonio missions received land grants from the king of Spain, and the monks became the first successful Texas cattle ranchers. After 1750, East Texas Spanish ranchers sued the missions over land rights, and by 1787 the mission ranches waned in importance. However, by the 1821 commencement of Mexican rule, the Spanish ranchers' rule had dissipated. Despite the small Spanish population, Spanish cultural traits— equipment, dress, saddles, and terminology—influenced the cattle industry.

In 1820 Spain, unable to attract its own colonists, opened settlement of East Texas to Anglo-Americans, who were attracted to the inexpensive land (four cents per acre). The Mexican Republic continued the policy as long as Anglo recruits were Catholic, industrious, and willing to become

PHOTO 11.3. French-Creole House, Ste. Genevieve, Missouri. Both the French and Germans settled along this stretch of the Mississippi, bringing with them their cultural architectural models. The architectural style of wraparound porches was adapted to the warmer climate of the Mississippi River Valley. The Bequette-Ribault house is a French-Creole vernacular structure constructed from vertically placed (*poteaux en terre*) timbers forming the walls. The Bequette-Ribault house is one of five U.S. buildings built in this manner.

BOX 11.3 ATCHAFALAYA BASIN: FRENCH ACADIAN "CAJUN"

The Cajuns (a corruption of the word *Acadian*) settled the bayou-ridden coast west of New Orleans. After being exiled to various British colonies between 1755 and 1763, some of the remaining Acadians chose to emigrate to then Spanish Louisiana. Once in Louisiana, they moved west to the unoccupied swamps and bayous along the coastal parishes from the Texas border to the edges of the Atchafalaya Basin (Map 11.2).

The Cajuns adapted to their life in the bayous, fishing, hunting, and trapping in their *pirogues*—canoe-type boats fashioned from native bayou cypress. They trapped muskrat, nutria, or alligator and also farmed on the natural levees and coastal grasslands. The isolated backcountry life forced adaptation to the local topography and resources, including affecting their French patois, which is peppered with relevant words from their new landscape.

The Acadians sustained cultural and linguistic contortions before they emerged as culturally distinct Cajuns. Other ethnic influences were incorporated into their life and their population. Spaniards, Germans, Native Americans, and African Americans lived among and became acculturated with the Cajuns.

After the Civil War, discrimination against Cajuns reduced many to tenant farming, resulting in forced migration to other regions. By the twentieth century, the ascendancy of English in Louisiana pitted the New Orleans Creole whites against the Cajun French. Cajuns almost lost their language and culture; they were denigrated and forced to learn and speak English in schools. This changed in 1960, and French immersion schools are now part of the Cajun parish curriculum. Cajun assimilation was enhanced by twentieth-century improvements in transportation and communication.

Cajun music and cuisine has become popular within the American ethnic mosaic and is now widespread outside the Atchafalaya Basin. The music is lively and features the fiddle and accordion. The cuisine has changed significantly from the blander Acadian food of Nova Scotia, adopting local ingredients— crawfish, peppers, and gumbo.

A dominant fishing resource was the lowly crawfish, used as bait until the 1960s, when Cajuns and then Louisianans incorporated it into their cuisine. The crawfish are still an important part of the fishing economy, but now instead of netting or trapping, some sixteen hundred farmers grow them in human-made ponds.

The Cajun population was counted separately for the first time in the 1990 census; 432,000 in Louisiana claimed Cajun ethnicity, 50,000 in east Texas, and an additional 190,000 in other states. In the Cajun heartland, Vermilion Parish was more than 50 percent Cajun, while in New Orleans less than 1 percent claimed Cajun heritage.

MAP 11.2. Cajun Parishes of Louisiana. The Acadians settled to the west of New Orleans. Vermillion Bay and the Atchafalaya Basin are the heart of Cajun country. The Cajuns adopted and were adopted by many other ethnic groups that settled in the country, including the Native Americans. They evolved as a French-speaking but diverse group of people with a distinctive culture and cuisine.

Mexican citizens. An early Anglo recruit was Moses Austin, father to Stephen Austin. When Moses died in 1821, Stephen fulfilled his father's land grant and established a colony on the Brazos River in what became Austin County, Texas.

In the 1830s and 1840s, Germans and Czechs fled unsettled political situations at home and migrated into the Texas Hill Country. Many town names and architectural styles reflect the region's ethnic origins. German immigrants settled inland from Houston, establishing Hill Country towns such as New Ulm, New Braunfels, Millheim, and Berlin. Few Slavic migrants entered the United States during the period of homesteading and relatively free land, but the Moravian Czech immigrants began settlement in 1851 near Corpus Christi; because land was still cheap, they became the major Slavic population to farm in the United States.

Gulf Plantations

The plantation settlement pattern was established on Delta and Black Belt land. A change in banking practices in 1830 enabled state banks to lend "easy" money on western lands. Many Carolina and Georgia plantation owners had farmed their land unsustainably, and they abandoned their leached and eroded coastal and piedmont lands for the Gulf Coast.

The rich Black Belt, Delta, and Black Prairie soils became the new cotton-growing region. The Delta was swampy and overgrown, but once cultivated, the land was fertile and grew cotton. Slaves worked the cotton crop and often outnumbered the whites. In the Black Belt, the population multiplied from 9,000 in 1810 to 310,000 in 1830.

The region's largest cities—New Orleans and Mobile—exported cotton, but they contained regionally insignificant populations. In Alabama, only 2.2 percent of the population was urban in 1840. The rural plantation ruled the Delta and Black Belt economic and political life for generations.

The Civil War devastated many plantations. With the men at war, women ran the plantations as best they could. Many slaves left to fight or heeded the call of freedom. Some plantation families lost everything and were unable to adapt to postwar circumstances; other families thrived, but often because they smuggled and sold their crop to the northern enemy. After the war, labor was in short supply. Freed slaves left to seek their fortunes, while others stayed on the plantations but now in different circumstances.

Blacks who stayed after the war were uninterested in working on a plantation; they wanted to work their own land, become independent, and exercise their political rights. But owning land was seldom an option, and many blacks became **sharecroppers**—tenant farmers who gave a share of the crop to the desperate plantation owners, who lacked both funds and labor to work the land. In the Black Belt, slave cabins were relocated on small plots of land, and former slaves sharecropped cotton and grew subsistence gardens on the plantation owner's land. By 1910, sharecropping constituted 92 percent of the farms, and 95 percent of the sharecroppers were black.

While many planters continued their society life, blacks faced hardship after the Civil War, and discrimination was rampant, as were lynchings. When **Great Migration** (1910–1970) opportunities opened in other regions, many blacks left. In Mississippi, more than a hundred thousand left between 1915 and 1920. The Great Migration peaked in the 1950s and 1960s, with **push and pull factors** pushing them away from the South and pulling them toward jobs in northern industry.

During the Great Migration, black population in the South dropped from 77 percent (1940) to 50 percent (1970). Blacks migrated north following regional rail lines and roads—those from the Mississippi area moved to Chicago, those from Alabama and Kentucky to Detroit, and those from east of the Appalachians to New York or other Megalopolis cities. Once relocated, another pattern of migration, **chain migration,** followed, in which friends or family followed earlier émigrés. Black migration routes reversed in the 1990s, when many middle-class families chose to return to the South (Table 11.2).

Blacks who remained in the Gulf South had few opportunities to prosper and little control or profit from the cotton they grew. Few owned Delta land—ownership shrank from 7.3 percent in 1900 to 2.5 percent in 1925.[17] Even successful towns, such as Mound Bayou, Mississippi, called the "Jewel of the Delta" by its founders and lauded by Theodore Roosevelt, lost its optimism when the local bank was forced to reorganize and farmers had to return to tenancy. Delta planters once again had a firm grip on cotton production.

Despite emancipation, southern blacks were denied the vote and subjected to **Jim Crow** laws that enforced racial segregation in employment and housing, voting discrimination, and violence toward blacks.

With more blacks than whites in the South, whites denied the vote to blacks so they could maintain control. Segregation ended officially with the 1960s civil rights movement, which focused along the Black Belt Selma-Montgomery Freedom Road. Since that time, slowly but surely, civil rights have improved for blacks.

New South

When change finally came to the South, it came with a mighty rush.

—John Egerton, *Southern Food*, 1987[18]

Southern black living conditions improved with the 1950s and 1960s Supreme Court decisions and the activism of the civil rights movement. Racism and segregation declined, and hope dawned among southern blacks. Among the changes was the removal of Jim Crow laws. The results were politically dramatic for southern blacks. Before the Voting Right Act (1965), 72 blacks held elected office in the South; a mere five years later, 711 held elected office. Some migrated blacks, having realized the underlying racism of the North, returned to the South where they felt they had a better chance of furthering the black cause.

The lack of transportation and the self-sufficient plantation system kept the **antebellum** South rural and isolated from the North. After the Civil War, the plantation system changed, cities grew, and railroad networks extended into the South, bringing high-wage jobs. During the Great Migration, southern white culture changed and northern corporations spread into southern cities, transferring employees from the North to the South and further diluting southern white racism.

Cultural Perspectives

A wide range of influences formed the Gulf Coast cultural landscape. The oldest and longest-lasting influence is the interaction of the physical landscape with pestilence and pests, taken for granted today when many diseases are no longer a threat. In addition, three cultures are each tied to this region's racial divisiveness, the blues of the Delta, Creole, and the Black Belt.

Disease and Pests

Man imagines himself to be the dominant power on the earth. He is nothing of the sort. The true lords of the universe are the insects. While it is true that man has invented and perfected so many destructive agencies that he has attained to predominance over the fiercest and most powerful mammals and the most deadly reptiles, it is also true that in face of an attack of insects he and all his works are set at naught.

—James Buckland, 1913[19]

The Gulf Coast subtropical wetlands favor insects that spread disease and destroy crops. In the past, disease was the result of the interaction of the marsh with insects, humans, or wildlife, but the twentieth century brought its own forms of ecological destruction.

TABLE 11.2. Black Migration to and from the South, 1965–2000

	Northeast	Midwest	West	Total
From South to				
1965–1970	143,000	182,000	103,000	428,000
1970–1975	79,000	123,000	86,000	288,000
1975–1980	84,000	130,000	117,000	331,000
1980–1985	101,000	105,000	123,000	329,000
1995–2000	63,115	77,024	40,046	180,545
To South from				
1965–1970	76,000	60,000	41,000	177,000
1970–1975	158,000	122,000	22,000	302,000
1975–1980	208,000	144,000	87,000	439,000
1980–1985	132,000	171,000	110,000	413,000
1995–2000	233,149	125,760	79,514	438,423
Net for South				
1965–1970	(67,000)	(122,000)	(62,000)	(251,000)
1970–1975	79,000	(1,000)	(64,000)	14,000
1975–1980	124,000	14,000	(30,000)	108,000
1980–1985	31,000	66,000	(13,000)	84,000
1995–2000	170,034	48,736	39,108	257,878

Source: Adapted from John Cromartie and Carol B. Stack, "Reinterpretation of Black Return and Nonreturn Migration to the South, 1975–1980," *Geographical Review* 79, no. 3 (July 1989), and U.S. Census

Disease

The indirect effects of regional climate and physiography are often overlooked. During the eighteenth and nineteenth centuries, virulent killers—smallpox, malaria, dysentery, cholera, yellow fever—swept periodically through the region. The interrelationships between disease, epidemics, contagion, and landscape were not understood, so the causes—viruses (smallpox), unclean water (cholera, dysentery), and mosquitoes (yellow fever, malaria)—were unknown.[20]

Yellow fever epidemics killed thousands during the nineteenth and early twentieth centuries. For example, a wave of yellow fever outbreaks swept through the Mississippi Alluvial Plain in the 1870s. In 1878 alone, Memphis lost half its population of forty thousand to the disease; many fled and thousands died.[21] All diseases were treated by bleeding, quinine, opium, a mixture called Calomel (mercury and chloride), and the chief preventative and cure: whiskey.

With opium retailing from fifty cents to a dollar an ounce and whiskey going for forty to fifty cents a gallon, it is easily understandable which painkiller was most frequently used.

—John Duffy, 1959[22]

Treatments were ineffective, and mortality often reached 60 percent during periodic epidemics. Urban density and poor sanitation elevated death rates. Epidemics were usually feared,

BOX 11.4 GEO-TALES: MOUND BAYOU, MISSISSIPPI—SOUTHERN HOSPITALITY

The 1970s movie *Easy Rider* influenced me—I didn't think I'd be welcomed in the South. But by 2000, it was time for me to get past this and head south. I booked a flight to Memphis and headed down the Blues Highway toward Cleveland, Mississippi, planning to visit aqua farms and plantations and attend a few blues festivals. One thing I did not plan on was what happened.

My predeparture research revealed a bit about the towns that I would be traveling through, one of which was Mound Bayou. Freed blacks had settled the small town after the Civil War, and it remained virtually all black (2010 population 1,533; 98.5 percent black). The town was struggling, losing population slowly, and poor; 45.6 percent of the population was below the poverty level. The average per capita income was $8,227 (2000).

It was late afternoon on a Friday when I entered Mississippi for the first time. In just a few minutes, I was struck by the cultural landscape. Tunica, Mississippi? Never heard of it. Roadside barbeque (BBQ)? While these roadside barbeque stands were nonexistent where I come from, I was willing to give this regional cuisine a try.

I am always a sucker for BBQ (even during my vegetarian days), and in the South every state has its own style and flavors. Every town I drove through had a BBQ joint, augmented by weekend roadside BBQ entrepreneurs. So when I got to Mound Bayou, I pulled over and went shopping for ribs.

So there I am a white woman in an all-black town standing on the side of the road and talking to the cook as he prepares my BBQ rib package. We are doing the usual small talk—he asks me where I am from (how could he tell I wasn't from there?) and I ask him how long he has lived in Mound Bayou (all his life). A few hundred feet away a gathering—men, grills, cars—are cooking their weekly get-together BBQ. One of the men wanders by, catches a portion of my story, and then returns to his friends.

Shortly after, I get my ribs, pay, and start to drive off—but wait. As I head onto the road I glance over to the riverside encampment, and eight men are waving, gesticulating, and calling to me: Come down, talk.

I stop the car. I walk over to them.

They are stunned, but pleased. "Do you know what you are doing, a white woman, and all these black men—in the South?"

I don't know why I did it. I was well past any rebellious stage, and I wasn't particularly aware of black culture or black people. But it felt right. My gut said yes.

It *was* right—one of the most memorable moments in my life.

We introduced ourselves. The snippet of my story that the one man had heard was enough for them to try to signal me down to their Friday night BBQ lair and share stories and BBQ. The five smoky BBQ grills were each devoted to a meat, a technique, a sauce. They cut various slices and offered me samples. Try this, try that, and all the while we were trading stories. I found out that they were all professionals—schoolteachers, social workers, police, fire, and correctional officers—all people who, as they said, "are trying to erase the image of the South to outsiders."

They were the best welcoming party to the South that someone like me, who feared the South, could have possibly conjured up—as if they were placed there for me and me for them. I now think fondly of the South, of Mound Bayou, and of them (Photo 11.4). If any of them should ever read this, thank you again for welcoming me to your New South, and to the warmth of your humanity. My vision of the South was changed that day, and I have since returned several times to explore southern landscapes.

PHOTO 11.4. Barbeque at Mound Bayou, Mississippi. A Friday night ritual in Mississippi is BBQ. Roadside stands open up for travelers, where friends gather and discuss the week's events while cooking BBQ.

but during the Civil War New Orleans residents wished and hoped that yellow fever would return to decimate the occupying northern troops. But as luck would have it, the Union commander ordered a major cleanup of the city sewers and drainage canals, and no fever besieged the city during the war, although periodic epidemics continued to kill thousands in Gulf Coast cities until 1905.

Louisiana and especially New Orleans were subjected to more than their share of disease, because of their numerous swamps, **bayous**, wetlands, and unsanitary public health conditions, such as open sewage for human waste and lack of a clean water system. Clearing the land and draining the swamps helped rid the towns of mosquitoes, but clearing was irregular until the twentieth century.

At times, the death toll was hidden from the outside world so trade would continue; at other times, those in power considered the loss small because those who died were immigrants and "usually voted Democrat," or checked "the tide of immigration."[23] Wealthy residents had better access to sanitation and could flee to healthier surroundings during the disease-ridden hot and humid months.

In early New Orleans, death was a constant visitor and graves required special arrangements. The high water table forced the first graves to be shallow. Later, dirt topped the graves to facilitate additional burials. Still later, the indigent were buried below ground, while most others were buried in aboveground tombs, the better not to float to the surface (Photo 11.5). The tombs could be elaborate, depending on the wealth of the deceased, and funerals became a regionally distinctive cultural display and even extravaganza. Black cultural influences, the "funeral with music" (the jazz funeral) began somber and grew raucous as the body was laid to rest.

The funeral procession marches down the street to the cemetery wearing white and returns dancing, singing, and celebrating life.

Pests

Hey, boll weevil,
Don't sing them blues no more,
Hey, hey, boll weevil,
Don't sing them blues no more,
Boll weevil's here, boll weevil's everywhere you go.

—Ma Rainey, "Boll Weevil Blues"

The warm and marshy landscape of the Gulf Coast is perfect for the mosquito to lay its eggs and develop. The adult mosquito transmits infectious disease and was the primary insect to affect Gulf Coast residents until the twentieth century, when a solid connection was made between the mosquito and disease.

The cattle tick and boll weevil also affected animals and crops. The cattle tick was prevalent in Florida and in Texas, where cattle carried the tick but were immune to the effects of the Texas fever ticks carried. In 1868, when thousands of cattle died in the Midwest, the source of the problem was traced to tick-infested Texas cattle driven north. This led to excluding southern cattle from the north, which crippled the southern industry. An eradication program ended the infestation in 1943, when once again the herds could be mixed.

The boll weevil, boring into cotton bolls and eating cotton fibers, caused more than $45 billion in damage before it was controlled. The beetle spread into Texas from Mexico in 1892 and then moved through the cotton-growing areas around sixty miles annually, reaching Virginia in 1922. When the weevil

PHOTO 11.5. Southern Louisiana Cemetery. Tombs in southern Louisiana are often above ground because of high groundwater levels, which cause the graves to fill with water or float to the surface. Modern drainage has allowed graves to be below ground, but the tradition often prevails.

struck Texas, many cotton farmers emigrated to the supposedly immune Delta region. But their escape was short lived, as the weevil infested the entire Gulf region and then the Carolinas. Some regions have only recently returned to planting cotton. The weevils' influence in infected areas was so pronounced that it entered popular culture through music: Many Delta blues songs feature the weevil.

Pesticide use on cotton is three to five times greater than on corn, but little has been studied about the environmental effects of pesticides on the land and human population. An alternative to direct pesticide application is genetically modified seed; however, many farmers have rejected this seed because of lower yields and poor seed quality.

The Blues

Well, the blues am a achin' old heart disease,

Well, the blues am a low down achin' heart disease,

Like consumption, killin' me by degrees.

—Robert Johnson, "Preachin' Blues"

The blues, a new music form rising from the Delta's steam and heat, verbalized emancipated black farmers' disillusionment over segregation, Jim Crow discrimination, and endless share-cropping debt. The blues combines African roots (call and response), southern field hollers, and spirituals, played with a guitar, wailing the promises and letdowns blacks found after the Civil War—and turned it all into a music that brought respect and fame to many Delta blacks, such as B.B. King and Muddy Waters. Blues was a dominant influence in the evolution of rock and roll, including its most famous white singer from Yazoo County, Mississippi—Elvis Presley. Black musicians lived what the blues (or R&B) lamented, but it was years later when white musicians like the Rolling Stones ("Little Red Rooster") and the Animals ("House of the Rising Sun") brought their music to mass audiences.

The blues evolved along Mississippi's Highway 61—from Memphis to Natchez— the birthplace and home of many blues artists. Today, summertime blues festivals enliven the dusty lots and chained-in yards of small towns and villages. But changing times have many people fearing that the blues may be dying, because cotton no longer requires the manual labor that once inspired the songs. However, along the highway the forlorn plaints arise anew each year and grab a heart or two.

Creole Culture

The Creole arose from the Gulf and West Indies slave sugar plantations where Spanish, French, African, and Anglicans interbred in the seventeenth century. The Creole culture dominated the region until American annexation. Then the Gulf Coast states joined the Confederacy, and with that sealed their fate to keep separate from the mainstream until well into the twentieth century.

Creole is a term still bandied about with several definitions: a mixture of several cultures, a free person of color, a mixed-

race person. The designations are not clear, and many an argument has erupted over the various definitions of Creole.

Why the argument? Initially, the term meant one who was born in the New World. Now, did that apply to just Europeans or did it include Africans? To some, you had to have French or Spanish ancestry and speak French or Spanish. To others, Creole was not restricted to just Europeans as Creole identified locals of all colors. In the late nineteenth and early twentieth century a totally different Creole designation evolved in Louisiana. Creoles could be White Creole (Europeans descendants), Black Creole (African descendants), or mixed-race Creoles (light-skinned). So, "Who is a Creole?" In today's world, it probably would identify a person of an ancestral mixture living in South Louisiana or having family ties to South Louisiana. [24]

Creole culture has left a significant mark on the gastronomic landscape. Caribbean methods were imported, and pork, barbeque, rice, and the ever-present red-hot chiles were cooked into a hundred varieties of hot sauce. Rum, distilled from native sugar, was the potent alcohol of the region.

The Cultural Black Belt

Alabama's Third World

—Auburn University, *Bridging the Divide*, 2004[25]

The Black Belt core crosses Alabama, but the Black Belt can be extended, spreading across the South incorporating the areas that have a high percentage of blacks. Before the Civil War, the Black Belt supported a wealthy, slave-holding plantation economy, and it remained a strong political force and source of wealth into the twentieth century. The regional economy eventually succumbed to the boll weevil, migration of African-Americans, and Jim Crow politics, and in the end it became a racially polarized region. African Americans are poverty ridden, poorly educated, and have a higher unemployment rate and less adequate social services than the rest of the state.

The Civil War destroyed the Black Belt cotton-growing plantation economy when slavery, the economic lynchpin of the system, ended and many young, promising Confederate soldiers were killed. The lack of natural resources and transportation (few roads and no railroads) confined the owners and their freed slaves to the region after the war, and helped isolate the Old South mentality.

Alabama's Black Belt was central to the civil rights movement, in which some of its most remembered leaders and battles emerged—Martin Luther King Jr., Rosa Parks, and the Selma March—all of which led to the 1965 Voting Rights Act and the beginning of black political activism. Today, the former cotton-growing region depends on pine tree plantations, cattle, hunting leases, and continued educational segregation. Private Christian academies are almost exclusively for whites, leaving Black Belt blacks with underfunded public schools (Table 11.3).

TABLE 11.3. Comparison of Poverty and Education in the Black Belt Region of Alabama with the State and Country, 2007

	Black Belt	Alabama	United States
% Poverty level	29.5	16.6	13.0
Median household income	$21,432	$40,596	$50,740
% High school graduates over 25 years old	55	75.3	80.4

Source: U.S. Census

Regional Life

Population

The Gulf Coast population has burgeoned, especially along the coastal areas where sea breezes make the humid climate tolerable and the casinos offer other pleasures. But it was not always so. The antebellum Gulf Coast attracted few immigrants because the economy operated on the slave-powered plantation system, and yeoman farmers and others had little economic opportunity. After the Civil War, the situation was somewhat different, and for a time immigrants, chiefly Italians, were welcome to fill the lacuna left by slave labor. But soon the immigrants realized that they were considered inferior by the gentry and were unwelcome in society.

Today people pick their home based on aesthetic rather than farming parameters. Since most of the coastal pestilent diseases have been controlled, coastal areas are considered attractive (Table 11.4). Gulf Coast population density has doubled and has grown faster than the national average. For example, in Mississippi, coastal county density is up to 334 per square mile, whereas the Mississippi average is 63.2 per square mile.

Texas settlement patterns vary regionally. The Rio Grande Valley's proximity to Mexico predicted the Latino population southwest of San Antonio. Although many Latinos in the region are legal, many undocumented workers populate the Texas border regions, living in unincorporated rural communities called **colonias** (Spanish for a settlement of homes, a neighborhood).

TABLE 11.4. Mississippi State, Coastal Counties, and Tunica Population Density and Economics, 2010

	Population density	Per capita income (2009)	Median home value
Mississippi	63.2	$19,534	150,000
Hancock County	91	$22,168	150,000
Waveland	844[a]	$20,237	117,000
Harrison County	326	$22,444	149,000
Pass Christian	643[a]	$27,663	225,000
Jackson County	181	$22,256	145,000
Ocean Springs	1,487[a]	$30,543	160,000
Tunica County	21	$14,818	170,000
United States	87.4	$27,041	190,000

[a] 2009

Source: U.S. Census; Zillow for home prices (http://www.zillow.com, December 2010)

BOX 11.5 COLONIAS

This is the place you land when you cross the river.*

Along the New Mexico-Texas-Mexico border, more than fifteen hundred small, unincorporated towns called colonias are home to more than five hundred thousand residents, many of them poor, undocumented immigrants. Colonias are built by speculators who exploit the immigrants. For exorbitant prices, they sell bare land that lacks basic services—paved streets, running water, legal electricity, or sewers. The lots are sold as land contracts, where the title stays with the developer until the last payment is made. The immigrants are unaware of their legal rights, unable to pay for legal services, and vulnerable to losing their homes because of conditions favoring the title.†

Residents build their houses incrementally as they can afford materials, which often results in makeshift structures similar to those found in Mexico; they are illegal in the United States but are tolerated along the border (Photo 11.6). Cities are reluctant to incorporate the colonias for several reasons, among them lack of financial viability. However, several governmental agencies now include colonias in their strategic plans, because they affect the region's overall welfare.

Residents of colonias have considerable hurdles to overcome before they reach American standards. Annual wages ($10,000) in the colonias are about one-third the Texas average, and unemployment rates are the highest in the state. Most employment is part of the informal economy, such as day laborers or ice cream vendors. Another hurdle along the border region is health care. Colonias have higher rates of tuberculosis, hepatitis, and HIV than the surrounding area.

PHOTO 11.6. Colonia along the Rio Grande border, Texas. Most residents are illegal immigrants, who often make their living through the informal economy; they build their homes in the Mexican style, as they can afford it.

* Cecilia Ballí, "Bottom's Up," *Texas Monthly*, January 2003.

† "Legal Issues in New Mexico's Colonia Communities," at http://nmpovertylaw.org/WP-nmclp/wordpress/wp-content/uploads/2009/12/Report-Legal-Issues-in-NM-Colonias-FINAL-DRAFT-2010-7-2.pdf.

Traditional and Sustainable Cities

Gulf Coast cities are located in four principal areas: along the coastal margins, the rivers, the Balcones Escarpment, and the Rio Grande River. Generally, coastal cities are split between agricultural core ports—Mobile and Biloxi—and the industrialized west—New Orleans and Houston-Galveston. River cities along the Mississippi include Memphis, Baton Rouge, and the geographically curious Cairo, Illinois. Both San Antonio and Austin, Texas, are positioned at the foot of the Balcones Escarpment. Brownsville and Laredo are along the Rio Grande. Most are traditional cities, but Austin and New Orleans have gained special distinctions: Austin as a city working toward sustainability, and New Orleans as a city capable of rebuilding sustainably after Hurricane Katrina.

New Orleans, Louisiana

(2005 pop. 454,863 [pre-Katrina]; 2007 pop. 239,124; 2010 pop. 343,829; CSA 1,214,932)

New Orleans has been a multicultural racial and musical **melting pot**. The "Big Easy" is the birthplace of jazz and home to the most famous of American **Mardi Gras** celebrations

(Photo 11.1). New Orleans is also the "inevitable city on the impossible site,"[26] a sobriquet whose time has come.

Swampy, malaria-ridden New Orleans was always at the river's mercy, but a city was necessary to service the mouth of America's largest river. To survive, the city depended on human intervention. Ditches to drain the annual floodwater surrounded the city's first streets, making New Orleans an American Venice. The Army Corps of Engineers constructed a massive levee system that was incapable of resisting a Category 3 hurricane. But improvements were not funded, and a battle was waged to contain the Mississippi River. The battle against nature was lost in August 2005.

Hurricane Katrina ravaged 80 percent of the city. Rebuilding has been slow. Years after the levees broke, several hundred thousand people remain displaced. The sub–sea level part of the city was submerged when the levees broke. Only areas built on the natural levees were left intact, such as the French Quarter, the oldest part of the city and main tourist attraction—one that may be bypassed by the newest attraction, disaster tourism. Tour companies, answering popular demand, began to include the devastated sections of the city in their standard tours in 2007.

New Orleans' population and demographics changed after Katrina's flooding. By June 2006, population estimates in the New Orleans metropolitan area had dropped from over a million to 700,000 and the city was at one-third of its pre-flood population. Slowly the city repopulated, adding an additional 104,000 between 2007 and 2010; however, repopulation rates have decelerated. Half of the population lives in nonflooded areas, but some of the flooded districts are also repopulating.[27]

The racial makeup of the city has also changed. The population in 2008 was whiter (34 percent in 2008, up from 28 percent in 2000), older (33.1 median age in 2008, up from 31 in 2000), and wealthier ($21,985 in 2008, up from $17,258 in 2000) than before the storm. It is uncertain how many evacuees will return, and much of that uncertainty depends on rebuilding public housing.

A Sustainable New Orleans?

Hurricane Katrina gives us the chance to build "green" buildings and to build energy-saving buildings.

—Laura Bush, National Design Awards, July 2006

In general, in order for the Lower Ninth Ward to come back, you've got to change the culture of the people living there, and you've got to get people with the economic means to move into the Lower Ninth Ward to make it a sustainable area."

—Wendell Dufour, 2007[28]

Katrina's destruction of New Orleans presented the city with a unique opportunity, to build from the ground up—green. Building in a sustainable manner would also allow the city to right many wrongs of the city's past. Rebuilding the city requires a respect for its past, recognition of environmental problems, and a focus on the long-term growth of the city.

But rebuilding a city is expensive in the short term. And so New Orleans has been rebuilt with the same short-term methods; few buildings have been constructed in a sustainable and long-term manner. Building in a sustainable manner may be a bit more expensive in the short term, but in the long term it is far more economical.

Green buildings are most cost efficient when constructed from the ground up, using the site to its advantage and using ecologically based materials. The opportunity to use the destruction to advantage was a huge benefit to the storm surge–flooded areas along the hurricane-ravaged Gulf Coast. The all-new construction could have been a model for the greening of entire cities across America. However, government incentives and benefits were seldom redirected toward sustainable growth. But the demographics of the flooded areas may not change if substantial funding is not offered to previous residents, most of who can ill afford sustainable construction.

Coastal rebuilding has been inequitable and uneven. In Mississippi, the governor opted to rebuild first in the more affluent areas and stagnated poorer areas' rebuilding efforts. In New Orleans, many of the new homes are no safer than those that were destroyed.

However, several sustainable-oriented companies and organizations—U.S. Green Building Council, Enterprise Foundation, Habitat for Humanity, the Trust for Public Land, and Architecture for Humanity—have addressed the possibilities of sustainably rebuilding the Gulf Coast communities (Photo 11.7). Others were concerned with storm-related energy problems. Local residents, though, have found fault with the architectural integrity of the new designs, citing a break with New Orleans tradition. Rebuilding has not been easy for the city, and many poor and middle-class residents cannot afford the new trendy and therefore more expensive construction. The conventional utility grid needs to be rebuilt by renewable energy systems, with plenty of local solar radiation and smaller, geographically dispersed energy plants.

Although the devastation of New Orleans was horrible, it need not be repeated. Building smart—constructing strong levees, building homes on stilts in case of flooding, following green designs and efficiencies—has been a unique opportunity. New Orleans provided the opportunity to be the first green city at a time when sustainable assets were becoming more available and economical.

Oil Cities

The oil industry spurred the growth of several west coast Gulf cities and waterways: Houston, Galveston, Lake Charles, New Orleans, Baton Rouge, Corpus Christi, Beaumont, and Port Arthur. New Orleans and Baton Rouge were established cities prior to the twentieth-century boom. Lake Charles was a mid-nineteenth-century lumber mill town that evolved into petrochemical refining after World War II. Corpus Christi grew from a small shallow port and resort town into a dredged deepwater port that distributes local agricultural goods and petrochemicals. Beaumont and Port Arthur both grew after the turn-of-the-century Spindletop oil strike.

BOX 11.6 PUBLIC HOUSING IN NEW ORLEANS

by Gerald McNeill

The key to rebuilding the population of New Orleans lies in public housing. After Katrina, former residents of four World War II–era public housing projects (B. W. Cooper, C. J. Peete, Lafitte, and St. Bernard) have expressed their desire to return to the City of New Orleans, but their homes have been deemed unlivable.

In December 2007, the New Orleans City Council decided the public housing projects' future. In a unanimous decision, the council approved demolition, but not without controversy. The new mixed-income housing developments will not be completed until 2012 at the earliest, a long wait for those who still lack housing. Many believe that the old public housing projects might have served as short-term residences until other affordable units were built.

By 2011, parts of three of the public housing developments were demolished and some buildings refurbished and rebuilt, with most of the buildings newly constructed. Different housing or architectural styles are being used, with some following the patterns of old New Orleans houses. The eye-catching new developments are taking on new names as well—Harmony Oaks (C. J. Peete), Faubourg Lafitte (Lafitte), and Columbia Parc (St. Bernard). The key in the eyes of many of the developers is to ensure that all of the buildings do not look the same but are unique to New Orleans and the residents that occupy them. Having your own upstairs porch certainly makes residents feel safer compared to the old shared downstairs porches that anyone could access. The best news is that all of these public housing developments should be completed by the end of 2012. The fourth public housing area, the B. W. Cooper public housing development, has been mostly demolished, but no new buildings adorn the landscape as of summer 2011.

Houston, Texas

(2010 pop. 2,099,451; CSA 6,051,363)

Sprawling across a flat, marshy inland plain, Houston is the largest city in Texas and the South, and the sixth-largest metropolitan area in the United States. A world-famous shipping port and oil, energy, and medical center, Houston is home to such companies as Shell, Conoco, Reliant Energy, Dynegy, and Halliburton, and former home to bankrupt Enron.

Despite the occasional torrential rain and periodic epidemics, the boosters advertised the town as healthful and were willing to do anything to bring residents to the hot, humid town. Houston has had a plethora of environmental problems during the twentieth century, including subsidence, flooding, sewage problems, and air pollution. As one of the most air-conditioned cities in America, it flies in the face of sustainable energy.

Houston's earliest trade was in cotton, agriculture, and livestock. The shallow and narrow shipping channel limited access for oceangoing vessels. Houston competed with Galveston for shipping traffic, until dredging deepened and widened its waterway in 1914 and Houston bypassed Galveston in size and importance. The Port of Houston, the second-largest shipping

PHOTO 11.7. Rebuilt Home in the Ninth Ward, New Orleans, Louisiana. Rebuilding in the Ninth Ward is sometimes done with green and sustainable construction, but this type of construction is usually out of the financial reach of the people who live in the ward.

Photo: Warren Hofstra

BOX 11.7 SUBSIDENCE

Subsidence, the downward settling of the earth's surface, is common in both New Orleans and Houston. Subsidence increases flooding, decreases wetlands, and impairs industrial and transportation infrastructure.

The sea-level location of Houston accentuates the subsidence caused by hurricane flooding and the withdrawal of groundwater, oil, and gas. Groundwater subsidence is common throughout the region, while oil and gas subsidence is directly below pumped fields.

Houston–Galveston Bay area wetlands filter pollutants and protect inland areas from flooding. The rising sea and subsidence accelerate erosion and wetland loss. Along the edges of the bay, near rivers, and next to estuaries, up to three feet of land erodes and converts to open water annually. At times, encroaching seawater enters inland woodland areas and suffocates vegetation.

Petrochemical industry intrusion caused Houston Bay to subside up to ten feet between 1940 and the 1970s. Subsidence was reduced when local communities switched from groundwater pumping to using surface water from Lake Houston. However, suburban Houston continues to rely on groundwater and has subsided an additional 2.5 feet through the 1990s.

Hurricane floods and subsidence have destroyed some coastal areas, such as Brownwood near Galveston. The original 1938 community was built ten feet above sea level, but by 1978 the area had subsided eight feet. In 1983, Hurricane Alicia eradicated the community, which has since been converted to the slough-ridden Baytown Nature Reserve (Photo 11.8).

Annually, homes, infrastructure, and wetlands have been lost to subsidence. Although some areas have slowed subsidence, many others still sink, and others await another Katrina-type hurricane to end their tenure. A sustainable and scientific response to subsidence has endorsed flood-controlling levees built to sustain long-term sea-level rise.

PHOTO 11.8. Post-Alicia Baytown, Texas. The Baytown Nature Reserve was the Brownwood development until 1983, when Hurricane Alicia flooded the area and caused subsidence and its permanent evacuation. Today, all that remains are the slabs and remnant docks.

port for America in total tonnage and tenth-largest in the world, is also home to the world's second-largest petrochemical complex.

The protected inland channel made Houston a prime shipping port and refinery location. Petrodollars fueled the city's growth until the oil bust in the 1980s, when the city lost population, which it has since regained and surpassed, helped by more than 130,000 Katrina refugees.

Houston has adopted many energy-efficient and retrofit standards to reduce energy consumption, although relative to its size it has few LEED-certified buildings. Public transportation is also inefficient and made more so by the city's sprawl and low population density. While the city does coordinate its departments in relation to environmental standards, it has poor air quality and has had little interest in recycling. It has the worst recycling rate (2.6 percent) of the major cities in America. The lack of recycling is tied into the city's lack of zoning and sprawling nature, which makes the cost to recycle prohibitive. Fewer than half of households have recycling bins and pickup. The lack of zoning also encourages businesses at the cost of healthy residential areas. Although zoning is an unsustainable practice for community development and transportation ease, the manner that zoning has been banned in Houston is not about community development but about economic might. Several attempts to create zoning have failed. Deed restrictions govern the city's development.

River Cities

The Mississippi River's largest cities were founded when water traffic was the dominant means of transportation. The cities serviced mining and agricultural production. Below Cairo the eastern bluff cities—Baton Rouge, Natchez, Memphis—prospered, while the western bank flood plain cities—Cairo, Greensville, and New Madrid—had limited growth and were victims of periodic flooding.

The Rio Grande Valley has several expanding cities along the border region. The largest city, Brownsville, is near the mouth of the Rio Grande. In the interior are several border-sharing twin cities, such as Laredo/Nuevo Laredo and Eagle Pass/Piedras Negras.

The Balcones Escarpment separates the coastal areas from the Great Plains. Faults create a natural divide, which forced the inland area up while the coastal areas downwarped. Saturated water draining from the uplifted block created springs and artesian wells. The water from the springs and wells determined the locations of San Antonio and Austin.

San Antonio, Texas

(2010 pop. 1,327,407; MSA 2,142,508)

San Antonio was established along the escarpment at San Pedro Springs in 1709. The city still depends on the springs, now reduced due to pumping and agricultural use. San Antonio is the largest city in America dependent on groundwater. The Edwards Aquifer is the source of the groundwater, and the city has learned how to use its water wisely.

The battle of the Alamo in 1836, when Mexican General Santa Anna's army massacred a band of Texans, placed San Antonio on the map of consciousness. The Alamo became the decisive battle for Texan independence a few months later, when Americans angered at the massacre poured into Texas and defeated General Santa Anna.

San Antonio is among the fastest-growing and most Hispanic cities in America, with a 60 percent Latino population. During the 1990s, Latinos constituted more than three-quarters of the population growth.

In the late 1980s, the fallout in the petroleum industry damaged the city's economic growth, which has since rebounded. The service sector, tourism, and real estate construction drive the economy. The main tourist attraction, the world-famous Riverwalk, celebrates the city's Mexican heritage (Photo 11.9). Once the dumping ground for shops, the Depression-era Works Progress Administration (WPA) cleanup project transformed the riverside into a model walkway, an idea that has been adopted by many other cities.

Austin, Texas

(2010 pop. 790,390; MSA 1,716,289)

Austin was founded at Barton Springs on the Balcones Escarpment. In 1839, Austin was chosen as the capital of Texas. Despite the presence of the University of Texas, the city's growth was slow until after World War II. In the 1950s and 1960s, the economy expanded into high-technology sectors, when companies such as IBM and Texas Instruments moved in. In the 1990s, Motorola, Dell Computers, and more than eight hundred high-tech companies established Austin and the University of Texas as a technopole, and Austin evolved into a city with a high quality of life. But it has not come easy. Closures of Barton Springs due to high bacteria levels made many citizens aware of sprawl over the recharge zone and spurred environmental awareness.

In the 1990s, Austin vowed to become the "Clean Energy Capital of the World" and to grow in a more responsible way.[29]

PHOTO 11.9. Riverwalk, San Antonio, Texas. In 1921, a deadly flood caused many people to rethink the river. In the 1940s and 1950s, riverside establishments faced the street and the river was a dumping ground. But starting in the late 1960s, more than fifty restaurants, along with major hotels, opened up facing the river, instead of backing to it. The Riverwalk idea has become a redevelopment inspiration for many other cities.

Austin has set renewable energy goals, including the installation of 165 wind turbines that power twenty thousand homes, and has committed to a 20 percent renewable electricity supply by 2020, with the most successful utility-sponsored green building program in the country. So far, the utility has saved enough energy to eliminate the need for additional coal-burning power plants. In 1991, Austin adopted the nation's first green building program. LEED Silver Certification is required on all city buildings, and residents and contractors are encouraged to build green. In 2004, more than 25 percent of all residential construction was green.

While Austin has been at the forefront of the sustainable curve, the city agencies are decentralized. As with many administrative structures in America, the agencies and planning departments have little coordination. Nonetheless, the city has created an annual State of the Environment Report that helps measure progress.

Economy

Primary Industry and Natural Resources

The Gulf Coast natural resources support primary, processing, and shipping industries—from eighteenth-century fur trapping to more current forestry, fish, oil-gas, and agriculture. The sole dependence on the economic bottom line created unsustainable conditions in the oil, forestry, and fishing industries. Hurricane destruction has been partially due to ignoring long-term care of resources, and it has resulted in continued unsustainable methods and higher prices for lumber, gas, oil, fish, and food.

Agriculture

European settlement altered the pine forest, the alluvial floodplain, and the semi-desert Rio Grande Valley: Gulf Coastal forests were cut, and farms were established on former marshes along the Louisiana Coast or the arid lands of the Rio Grande Valley.

The Port of New Orleans handled the regional crop production, progressing from plantations growing monoculture crops—rice, indigo, and tobacco in the eighteenth century and sugarcane and "King Cotton" after the 1793 invention of the cotton gin.

Instead of following long-term cropping patterns, plantation owners chose to relocate and repeat the damaging process. These patterns, minus slavery, continue today. Cotton, rice, and sugarcane dominate current production along with significant corn and soybean crops.

Most agricultural land in the Rio Grande Valley is pasture, and cultivated "crop islands"[30] utilize ideally suited soils and climate for specific crops. The mild, frost-free winters allow farmers to grow winter specialty fruits and vegetables to supply northern cities.

Cotton   Cotton requires summer precipitation, two hundred frost-free days, and plenty of water during the growing season but little rain in the fall. These requirements have limited the American crop to the South, where cotton was the Gulf Coast economic staple until the boll weevil infestation. Antebellum cotton was cultivated on Delta and Black Belt slaveholding plantations, but the labor pool shifted to sharecroppers after the Civil War. After World War II, regional farms consolidated and mechanized.

The Mississippi Alluvial Valley, especially the Delta, still grows cotton, but the cotton market changed when American textile mills shut down; more cotton was exported, especially to China, prompting the alteration of ginning techniques to respond to foreign mill demands. Recently, nonlocal agribusiness has accrued profits and invested elsewhere, while the remaining farmers rent their land and "retire."

The Delta depends on irrigation for its crops despite more than forty inches of annual precipitation, because summertime drought can reduce crop yields. Although the boll weevil is almost eradicated, the cotton crop is problematic because of unstable market prices and unsustainable groundwater irrigation and soil renewal. The alluvial soil is no longer renewed by periodic flooding of the river. Levees block the river's annual enrichment, and nitrogen-rich fertilizers are added to the crops that wash into streams and rivers, before discharging to the Gulf of Mexico where it causes algal blooms and hypoxia.

In 2001, cotton production regained its title as king of production, but in 2008 cotton acreage plummeted almost 50 percent; it continued to decline through 2010 because of the global economy. Cotton prices stabilized, but fertilizer prices inflated. At the same time, ethanol, the need for feed grains, and the market for domestic vegetable oils have boosted corn and soy prices. Many farmers have traded growing cotton for corn or soy.

Rice   While rice production in the United States began in South Carolina, cultivation continued in the mid-nineteenth century in the swampy, watertight claypan of the Mississippi Alluvial Valley and southwestern Louisiana. Rice requires constant irrigation and flooding during its growing cycle, in order to alleviate water depletion and soil salinity.

Cajun rice production began during the eighteenth century. By 1900, rice was grown along the western Louisiana and eastern Texas coastlines. These areas continue to grow rice, but by the latter half of the twentieth century the prime rice-growing region became the Grand Prairie of southeastern Arkansas, where the solid, flat land was perfect for mechanized rice production. Arkansas now cultivates 45 percent of U.S. rice—three times the next highest state, California. The Gulf Coastal area, including Arkansas, grows about 75 percent of American rice, but all the rice grown in America is less than 2 percent of global rice production.

Sugarcane   Sugarcane is cultivated in only three U.S. regions: the Rio Grande Valley; south of Baton Rouge, Louisiana; and near Lake Okeechobee in Florida (see Chapter 10). The Louisiana crop prospered first near New Orleans and then in the South Central Cajun Bayou Teche and Bayou LaFourche country, where it remains today.

Sugarcane earned its foothold in Louisiana. Indigo had been the major eighteenth-century crop but failed when locusts inundated it in 1793, by which time the market was already flooded with good dye and, fortuitously, the cotton gin was invented, changing the course of southern agriculture. But not all lands were good for growing cotton.

In antebellum Louisiana, sugar was the right crop for planters, but the worst conditions for slaves (which spawned the expression "sold down the river"). Being sent to the Louisiana sugar plantations was the fate of incorrigible slaves, who were deported to what was considered the most deplorable colonial job. Slaves faced unending work on the first agro-industrial economy in America, huge sugar plantations and the nearby processing plants. Processing plants were built near the fields, because the sugar juices would sour if not processed immediately. The sugar plantations and local economy were ruined during the Civil War.

Before the Civil War, smaller plantations were the norm, but when railroads arrived in the 1880s, sugar plantations and mills consolidated and created large sugar plantations. The number of plantations diminished from a high of 1,549 in 1849 to 82 in 1969.

The evolution of industry and trade. After the Civil War, many emancipated slaves remained on plantations and worked as laborers. Some former slaves founded villages, such as Oakville, Convent, and Alsen, near the river plantations, but over time the landscape and industry changed. The remaining sugar plantations bear little resemblance to the old plantations. New plantations are mechanized, offer few jobs, and run by absentee ownership. New industrial concerns have replaced many old plantations, but problems also exist within sugarcane production.

Louisiana is the second-largest producer of cane after Florida, but rising fossil fuel costs threaten sugarcane profits. Additionally, Mexican cane imports have increased because trade restrictions and limits were lifted in 2008. Imported sugar from Mexico almost doubled between 2007 and 2008.

The dependence on sugar in the American diet offers great opportunities for profit, but the lack of tropical regions to grow sugarcane continues to hamper U.S. production. The United States is the ninth-largest producer in the world, far behind the number one producer, Brazil, and half of the number six producer, Mexico. But as trade restrictions are removed from Mexico, American production costs cannot compete with Mexico's ideal sugarcane climate.

U.S. corn conglomerates push high-fructose corn syrup (HFCS) usage in the beverage industry, resulting in a decline in the imported sugar market. Only continued subsidies for corn and for cane allow U.S. sugar production to continue.

Forestry

The Gulf Coast is the largest pine forest in America. The acidic soil complements the native piney woods, but the natural vegetation and species are now rare. The native forests have succumbed to single-crop pine plantations.

In the eighteenth century, Gulf Coast lumber—cypress, cedar, and pine—and its by-products were exported to the West Indies sugar plantations. Prior to the Civil War, forest land was cut and converted to plantations. However, poor management left the land eroded, exhausted, and diseased. The plantations were abandoned, reverted to forest, or were planted as pine plantations. The arrival of railroads after the Civil War allowed Mobile, Alabama, and new ports, such as Gulfport, Mississippi, to ship lumber. New Orleans led southern ports in wood exports into the twentieth century.

The Gulf Coast forest industry provided wood for the development of the U.S. market after the Great Lakes forests were cut over, and then again after the 1980s, when Pacific Northwest forest clearance was halted for environmental reasons.

Settlers cut over the old growth as they "tamed" the wilderness, so most lumber logged today is second or third growth. Sawed lumber can be attained in forty years, but the ground-up timber called **pulpwood** can be cut in twelve to fifteen years. Today's small-diameter trees, unsuitable for most lumber uses, are pulverized into paper and chipboard, which relies on chemicals that pollute water and cause health problems for industry workers. For example, the most common pollutant is formaldehyde, the source of many common ailments such as asthma and cancer. The reliance on small-diameter logs for chipboard is short-term and unsustainable.

Pulp and paper mills convert lumber to plywood, paper, and chipboard. The number of mills and board feet magnified as the forests grew. In 1953, there were 60 pulp and paper mills; in 1998 there were 103, each three times as large as a 1950s mill. Lumber was no longer the mill's major product, but instead "engineered wood products"—first plywood, then oriented strand board (OSB), and particleboard, small trees glued and pressed into wood chips.

From 1950 to 2000, the Gulf Coast forest grew from two million to thirty-two million acres. Temperate climate and a longer growing season have caused logging companies to focus more on these forests than northern forests. Alabama and Texas alone account for more than 10 percent of national wood inventory and half of Gulf Coast production.

Since the mid-1990s, the U.S. Fish and Wildlife Service, the U.S. Forest Service, and several private organizations have promoted diversity in the natural forest. They have worked to restore the longleaf pine forest ecosystem and practiced controlled burns to encourage propagation of pine and the regional vegetation.

In 2005, Hurricanes Katrina and Rita slammed this region, destroying from fifteen to nineteen billion board feet on five million Gulf Coast acres. The wood will be salvaged, but the remaining young trees need at least a decade to mature, resulting in an inevitable rise in home prices because of wood costs.

The aim of the industry is a **sustainable yield**, in which trees can be harvested without diminishing the stock. Perhaps returning to a more quality-built home, at whatever size, over the poorly constructed homes of the twenty-first century, will allow wood to be used in a more sustainable and long-term fashion.

Fishery

The marshy coastal water of the Gulf has been an excellent fishery for oysters, crab, shrimp, and plankton-eating fish. The multi-billion-dollar Gulf Coast seafood industry employs more than a million people, despite hurricane damage, upturned oyster beds, lost docks, and destroyed boats. The 2010 oil spill added to the destruction.

The Gulf port shrimp fleets have been the nation's largest, but they were already threatened before the hurricanes. The traditional generational shrimper runs a small family-owned boat but is disappearing as American shrimping declines (Photo 11.10). In the 1990s, 50 percent of the consumed shrimp were from American waters, but in 2006 only 10 percent of consumed shrimp were American. Most shrimp are now from Thailand and Vietnam, where they are grown in areas of coastal degradation and pollution. Reasons for the decline in American shrimp are multiple—high fuel prices, low shrimp prices, increased environmental regulation, and overshrimping. Many shrimpers no longer encourage their children to follow in their footsteps.

The Gulf Coast leads oyster production, but oyster beds are doing little better than shrimping. Half the nation's oyster stock comes from the Gulf Coast, with Louisiana alone supplying 30 percent of the nation's oysters. Louisiana oysters, raised on public property in long-term leased private beds, have maintained a healthy environment, in contrast with Chesapeake Bay's depleted public oyster bed. Privatizing oyster beds in the late nineteenth century allowed the Louisiana industry to thrive, passing Maryland as the number one producer in 1982. However, the oyster industry along the Louisiana coast has been under assault since the mid-twentieth century, because of silting, changing salinity, industrial waste, oil production pollution, and biological factors such as predators, bacteria, diseases, and red tides.

Oysters are being asphyxiated, poisoned, and overfished, and people are eating fewer of them because of the fear of bacteria. Hurricanes have added to Gulf Coast fishery problems. For example, in September 2008, Hurricane Ike slammed into Galveston, spreading sediment that covered surfaces that oysters need for adherence and eliminating half of the oyster habitat. By the end of 2009, the damage threatened to end the long-standing industry. Despite efforts to restore the habitat, oystermen left the industry in droves because of poor oyster harvests.[31]

Aquaculture

The American aquaculture industry efficiently and profitably converts catfish, tilapia, redfish, eels, and crawfish into seafood. Most U.S. fish farming is in fresh water, but international fish farming is saltwater based—Canadian, Scottish, and Chilean salmon, and Thai shrimp. This may be changing, though, as attention and support lean toward future fish farms located at abandoned oil and gas platforms arrayed in the Gulf of Mexico. The thirty-eight hundred platforms, some more than two hundred miles offshore, may operate as feed storage, and help raise and lower the fish pens.

Several onshore fish farms are located in the Gulf Coastal region. Mississippi has the most catfish farms, spreading from its inception in the Delta to eastern Mississippi. Over a hundred thousand acres of fish farms produce 70 percent of the nation's catfish catch, with the remaining catfish also grown in the South, all farmed and processed in their native region and providing much-needed capital for the local populace. Catfish, long a staple

PHOTO 11.10. Shrimp Boat, Dauphin Island, Alabama. Most shrimp boats are small, family-operated enterprises. Since the double blow of Katrina and the BP oil spill, shrimping has been in jeopardy.

BOX 11.8 SHRIMPING IN PORT ARTHUR, TEXAS

Located on a deep channel along Sabine Lake near the Louisiana border, Port Arthur peaked during the early-twentieth-century oil boom and crashed in the 1980s. Today, the city feels abandoned, and the chief industry is seafood—processing, shrimping, crabbing, and wholesaling, which is also under attack. Most of the work is controlled by Vietnamese immigrants.

Making a living by fishing has never been lucrative, so when experienced Vietnamese fishers migrated to Port Arthur after the Vietnam War they were not welcomed by white fishers. A series of murders, firebombs, Klan activities, and curfews preceded a grudging truce. Today, a quarter century later, 95 percent of the shrimpers are Vietnamese—but they are battling another interloper, global trade. Shrimp from foreign ports costs much less than U.S. shrimp.

Reasons for the decline vary, ranging from Asian and Latin American countries that are either dumping shrimp at below-market values or have cheaper production costs and improved aquaculture methods of raising shrimp. The market price of wild shrimp has fallen in relation to farmed shrimp. The costs of

farmed shrimp, though, do not reflect the environmental damage of antibiotics, growth stimulants, contaminated fishmeal, the constant flushing of manure pollutants into the sea, or the cancer-causing antibiotics found in imported Chinese shrimp.* By 2009, 11.5 percent of shrimp were from China.†

Shrimping along the Texas Coast may end soon, but the Vietnamese who arrived in the 1970s have prospered and now own much of the industry. Their children are leaving the town, going to college, and pursuing other, more rarified lives.

The assault on the industry continues. In 2005, Hurricane Rita hit Port Arthur directly and destroyed 80 percent of the boats; Hurricane Katrina took a toll on Vietnamese shrimpers in other Gulf ports; and in 2008, Hurricane Ike hit the coast again. The hurricanes, combined with low prices and increasing regulation (making the cost of shrimping even higher), may spell the end of American shrimping. But not all have given up. Those who remain after the hurricanes are identifying niche markets and selling high-quality shrimp directly to farmers' markets and restaurants—if not yet in New Orleans, then in Manhattan.

---

* U.S. Food and Drug Administration, "Safety of Chinese Imports," July 18, 2007, at http://www.fda.gov/NewsEvents/Testimony/ucm110728.htm.

† U.S. Food and Drug Administration, "Questions and Answers on FDA's Import Alert on Farm-Raised Seafood from China," at http://www.fda.gov/Food/FoodSafety/Product-Specific-Information/Seafood/ucm119105.htm.

---

southern fish, became a popular replacement "crop" when cotton prices declined in the 1970s; its use was further augmented when the Pentagon adopted a program to serve the fish to the military. Cotton acreage was converted to shallow ten- to twenty-acre catfish ponds, although the increased cost of feed has hurt profits and reduced the number of farms.

Farmed catfish occupy an anomalous place: they are healthier than wild catfish but have a worrisome unintended consequence. In the wild, the bottom-feeding catfish has succumbed to pollution. Although there are some environmental issues with catfish farming, it is generally environmentally sustainable. The unintended consequence, however, is the Asian carp, the large invasive fish brought in by catfish farmers to eat the algae in their fish farms. The carp escaped and are now threatening the Great Lakes.

Along Louisiana's Atchafalaya River about twelve hundred crawfish farms and fisheries produced 113.5 million pounds (2009) and 96 percent of the national catch. Ninety percent of the catch is farmed but not in the ordinary hatchery and feed of other aquatic farms. Crawfish are grown during the rice or sorghum off-season, because the vegetation provides a natural food source for the crawfish.

America imports 70 percent of its fish from overseas fish farms, but there is now basis for increasing American fish farms to employ people who have lost jobs in the traditional fishing industry. However, fish farming in the United States faces environmental challenges and competition with lower labor costs. Fish farming in the Gulf or in freshwater has environmental problems, including discharge of waste, pesticides, antibiotics, and chemical

use. Lax environmental laws allow other countries to use aquaculture far more cheaply than is possible in the states. For example, antibiotics, now banned in the states, are used to prevent disease in their crowded habitat, and as a growth stimulant.

Mineral Industry

Oil and Gas Gulf Coast states provide about 25 percent of the nation's total crude oil output; however, the largest source of oil is from offshore platforms near Texas and Louisiana. Stateside production has been dropping while offshore production has expanded. The United States provides 25 percent of its domestic oil supply. Of that, Texas provides 21 percent and Louisiana 3 percent (Chart 11.1). The U.S. oil supply has been shrinking since 1990. The 2005 and 2008 hurricanes shut down Gulf oil and natural gas production for months. For example, after Katrina in November 2005, 46 percent of Gulf Coast oil and 40 percent of its natural gas remained closed, and 10 percent were still shut down in June 2006. A shrinking supply, the loss of Gulf Coast production, and increased global demand have escalated oil and gas prices.

Beginning with Spindletop in 1901, oil and gas have been important revenue sources for Louisiana and Texas. By 1909, Louisiana was home to Standard Oil refineries, and multiple pipelines were built across the state. Currently nineteen refineries provide jobs but also harm the health of nearby communities.

For example, the Mississippi River bottomland between Baton Rouge and New Orleans is called the chemical or industrial corridor by industry, and Cancer Alley by environmentalists.

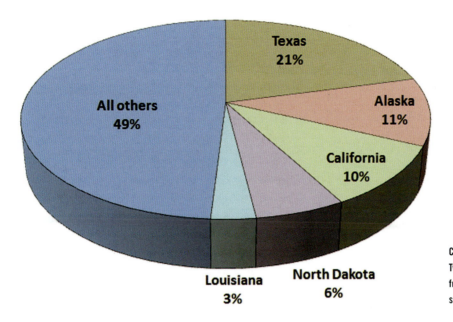

CHART 11.1. Crude Oil–Producing States, 2011. Two regions that formed large stores of fossil fuels as Pangaea broke up are the Arabian Peninsula and Gulf of Mexico offshore basins.

Between these two cities, more than 7 percent of all chemicals and 13 percent of the nation's hazardous waste is produced. This stretch is also home to a poor black populace mired in the toxic soup of their environment and home to the environmental justice movement.[32]

In the 1940s Louisiana, seeking more industrial activity, offered generous tax breaks to polluting industries. These industries replaced the old sugar plantations and surround the environmentally and economically devastated villages. After years of environmental and health assaults, the residents of these small African American communities fought for environmental justice; there were a few successes, though much still needs to be done. To achieve a sense of sustainability, the fight has entered the courts and the political system with the aim to achieve the

social, environmental, and physical well-being of the community for future generations.

Chemical Industry The chemical industry was built on former sugar fields along the Mississippi River and Louisiana coastline. During the boom years—1978 to 2000—the lucrative industry ran on cheap natural gas with little environmental oversight. For example, a Cytec methanol plant built in 1994 for $100 million paid for itself in one year. In 1978 alone, over $2.5 billion was invested in sixty-six new plants and 442 expansions. Louisiana produced over two hundred chemical products, such as ammonia and methanol (Table 11.5). Since 1978, employment, environmental, and competitive concerns have rocked Louisiana's chemical industry, resulting in many moving

TABLE 11.5. Chemicals Produced in Louisiana Plants

Chemical	Uses
Ammonia	Fertilizer, paper manufacturing, refrigerant, household cleaner, pharmaceuticals, fungal control on citrus fruits
Methanol	Plastics, plywoods, paint, explosives, auto gas additive, solvent or antifreeze in paint strippers, aerosol spray paints, carburetor cleaner
Urethane	Refinishing automobiles, refinishing industrial flooring
Melamine	Industrial coatings, paints
Polymers	Aviation and automotive lightweight composites, structural adhesives, water treatment, durable and weather-resistant plastics, safety glass, paper coatings
Specialty resins	Rubber and tire industry, bonding steel-belted tires
Monomers	Coatings, adhesion of latex paints

offshore where environmental regulations are nonexistent. By 2002 the United States, a former exporter of chemicals, became a net importer.

Typically, new chemical plants offered jobs and built towns near the industrial complexes, and at first local residents were pleased with the opportunities. The industry initially welcomed the residents, mostly blacks who had worked in the sugar fields, but as computers mechanized the industries the local skill set was surpassed, leaving many unemployed. Chemical companies were criticized from a variety of angles, from jobs to worker training to neighborhood aesthetics. The companies began training through community colleges, and they improved their community image by becoming more sensitive to historic areas and houses that had been destroyed by the companies in the past.

Additional areas of concern were the sources of pollution. Chemicals dumped into streams and rivers polluted hunting and fishing grounds and emitted caustic pollutants into the air. Chemical companies reduced emissions and complied with environmental laws; however, enforcement is lax and the chemical industry is still not considered a clean source of jobs for a healthy quality of life.

Chemical companies are reliant on natural gas, both to provide energy and as feedstock for its products. Natural gas is a local resource, but the demand and the price have escalated dramatically. In 1999, a thousand cubic feet of natural gas was $2, in 2002 it was $3, and in December 2005 it was $10.02 (prices also escalate during the critical winter months when home heating is important). In May 2006 prices were $6.19. By 2010–2011, the prices had fallen to the $3 to $4 range. Nonetheless, U.S. prices are higher than international competitors (Saudi Arabia $0.60, Trinidad $1), where labor costs are also very low, making Louisiana uncompetitive. The result has been a flurry of layoffs and shifting of investments overseas, which cost Louisiana high-wage jobs and tax revenues. Stressed companies and legislators adjusted natural gas access while maintaining low labor costs. Already environmental damage to nearby towns has initiated an environmental justice movement. Future growth in the industry will rely on conservation, niche markets, and adopting sustainable techniques.

Industry

Lower land and labor costs attracted shipbuilding and automobile industries to the Gulf Coast. However, international competition has caused layoffs.

Although bright spots remain in the information economy, the only Gulf Coast technology-driven quaternary economy is near Austin, Texas, a center for computer chip manufacturing. Austin continues its goal to be the most sustainable city in America, with companies dedicated to cutting electricity costs.

Shipbuilding

Historically Texas and Mississippi built ships, but only the Mississippi operation continues. Texas shipbuilding companies,

between Houston and Port Arthur, thrived during World War II, but they retracted to one-tenth their thirty-five thousand employees by 1960. They now construct offshore drilling platforms.

The largest employer in Mississippi is Ingalls Shipbuilding, now a division of Northrop Grumman. Ingalls was lured to Pascagoula by a corporate grant in 1938; it builds ships and fulfills naval combatant, cruise, and commercial ship contracts. In the 1950s, the company began to also construct drilling rigs.

Automobile Industry

Alabama, "Detroit South," is the new automobile capital of America. Beginning in 1997, the first of seven auto assembly plants opened in various stateside locations. Four companies in separate rural Alabama locations—Mercedes-Benz near Tuscaloosa, Honda near Lincoln, Toyota near Huntsville, Hyundai near Montgomery—are giving Detroit a run for its money because they are new and flexible, and Alabama has right-to-work laws that prohibit compulsory union membership (Photo 11.11). The wages, averaging $26 per hour plus benefits including 401(k)s—not pensions—are considerably higher than the local labor market, and they are meant to keep unions out.

Hundreds of millions of dollars in subsidies have influenced the choice of plant locations. The subsidies are sweetened by inexpensive land, the temperate climate, nonunion environment, tax abatements, and supportive infrastructure. In addition, the plants are built in rural areas where unemployment rates are higher than in urban locales. For example, the Hyundai plant is built on the edge of the poverty-stricken Black Belt region, and therefore offers new employment opportunities to impoverished local residents.

Car assembly plants have also opened in Georgia (Kia), Mississippi (Nissan), Tennessee (Nissan and Volkswagen), and South Carolina (BMW). Foreign car companies have more than forty-five thousand employees, mostly nonunion, and they account for about one-quarter of all U.S. automobile production.

Tourism

Tourism is a significant portion of the Gulf Coast economy. Mardi Gras, the French Quarter, offshore casinos, hunting and fishing, and historical plantation tours are a few attractions people enjoy. By 2006, tours were already burgeoning along the ravaged coast, including disaster tours of New Orleans and Biloxi, ecotours of wetlands, community tours for volunteer aid by church groups, and casinos.

Casino gaming has been a moneymaker for struggling Gulf Coast economies, especially as it recovers from hurricane damage. Among the first buildings reconstructed were the casinos, which reopened in 2008. Mississippi, although it has grown and diversified, remains at the bottom in per capita income and has focused on reopening its profitable casinos.

However, the largest casino area is along the Mississippi River. Tunica, Mississippi, a Delta town an hour south of

PHOTO 11.11. Hyundai Plant, Montgomery, Alabama. The Hyundai plant opened in 2004 was the first North American plant built by foreign car manufacturers. Three other companies—Mercedes, Honda, and Toyota—have also chosen to build in the South. All are nonunion shops that pay well for the area but do not have pension plans, thereby saving money on car costs.

Memphis, was among the poorest counties in the nation, until 1992 when a group of farmers, Tunica-Biloxi tribal leaders, a Las Vegas gaming company, and the Mississippi gaming commission activated a plan to open its first casino. Many more casinos followed, and Tunica changed from being a place where 50 percent of the population lived below the poverty line to having an abundance of jobs. The Tunica gambling area became the third largest in America; Highway 61 from Memphis to the casinos had to be widened from two lanes to four—too many people on too small a road.

Since the casinos arrived, Tunica has new public buildings, schools, and an arena. Desoto County, between Tunica and Memphis, is about to convert former cotton fields for an "urban" master-planned community complete with lakes, golf courses, and ninety-five hundred expensive homes, which has been called "the largest tourism project to come to Mississippi that is not connected to the casino market."[33]

A Sustainable Future

The Gulf Coast developed much more slowly than the northern areas, partially because its self-sufficient plantation made cities superfluous, and because of poor transportation infrastructure. The low cost of land and labor has influenced Gulf Coast development, but the region still depends on primary industries (logging, fishing, and aquaculture) or the secondary economy (auto production, oil, plastics, and chemical industries). Only the Balcones Escarpment area is part of the tech-oriented "creative class" profit centers.

But the Gulf Coast is also home to exciting American cities and an important shipping and industrial network. Although hurricanes have devastated the area, much can be learned from past mistakes. A new Gulf Coastal region can incorporate sustainable industries and reduce pollution. The opportune time is now, as the area rebuilds.

The rebuilding of the Gulf Coast region is auspicious, just at the time that sustainable cities are becoming accepted for the future of America. Several green building groups have endorsed and invested in creating a green Gulf Coast, and conferences abound dedicated to green building. Architects, geographers, and geologists call for rebuilding in a sustainable and scientifically based manner so that future storms will not cause the devastation of recent storms. Now all they need are the political will and the government support that the oil companies receive.

Questions for Discussion

1. Explain the evolution of the plantation economy from antebellum to Reconstruction and the New South.

2. Why has environmental justice been an important issue in this region?

3. Discuss the issues and problems with colonias and how traditional cities deal with them.

4. How has the Black Belt of Alabama changed since the antebellum South?

5. Why has the auto industry moved into the Gulf Coast region?

6. How did the Great Migration change America's demographic distribution?

7. How did black migration change in the 1990s?

8. Describe the evolution of agriculture in the Gulf Coast. How did the climate and geography affect the choice of crops?

9. How did the boll weevil affect southern cotton production, human life, and the environment? How did farmers and government agencies deal with the weevil?

10. How did life change for blacks after the Civil War?

11. How did agricultural systems change in the South after the Civil War?

12. Why did Houston develop into a major city? What is its geographic association with Galveston?

13. Why has the location of New Orleans been strategic for commercial development?

14. How has Mobile, Alabama's situation helped it grow? How has it fared since Katrina?

15. How is the Mississippi River below Baton Rouge threatened?

16. Who are the Cajuns and what is their migration history?

17. After learning about the disease that was prevalent in the New Orleans and coastal areas, and knowing what you do about the hurricanes, why do people choose to live in this region during the warmer months? Should those who do be subject to the motto "Buyer, beware!" and accept the responsibility for their actions?

Suggested Readings

American Geophysical Union. "Hurricanes and the U.S. Gulf Coast: Science and Sustainable Rebuilding," at http://www.agu.org/report/hurricanes/.

Austin, Diane, Bob Carriker, Tom Mcguire, et al. *History of the Offshore Oil and Gas Industry in Southern Louisiana*. Interim Report. vol. 1, *Papers on the Evolving Offshore Industry*. (New Orleans: U.S. Department of the Interior, Minerals Management Service, Gulf of Mexico OCS Region, July 2004).

Baker, Oliver E. "Agricultural Regions of North America: Part II—The South," *Economic Geography* 3, no. 1 (January 1927): 50–86.

Barry, John M. *Rising Tide: The Great Mississippi Flood of 1927 and How It Changed America*. New York: Simon & Schuster, 1997.

Brandfon, Robert L. "The End of Immigration to the Cotton Fields." *Mississippi Valley Historical Review* 50, no. 4 (1964): 591–611.

Christensen, N. L. "Vegetation of the Southeastern Coastal Plain." In *North American Terrestrial Vegetation*, edited by M. G. Barbour and W. D. Billings, 317–64. Cambridge, UK: Cambridge University Press, 1988.

Cisneros, Ariel. "Texas Colonias: Housing and Infrastructure Issues." Federal Reserve Bank of Dallas, June 2001.

Cleland, Herman F. "The Black Belt of Alabama." *Geographical Review* 10, no. 6 (December 1920): 375–87.

Colten, Craig. *An Unnatural Metropolis: Wresting New Orleans from Nature*. Baton Rouge: Louisiana State University Press, 2004.

Cromartie, John, and Carol B. Stack. "Black Migration Reversal in the United States." *Geographical Review* 77 no. 2 (April 1987).

——. "Reinterpretation of Black Return and Nonreturn Migration to the South, 1975–1980." *Geographical Review* 79 no. 3 (July 1989).

Gibson, Jon L. *Poverty Point: A Terminal Archaic Culture of the Lower Mississippi Valley*. Baton Rouge, La.: Department of Culture, Recreation, and Tourism, 1996.

Hall, Gwendolyn Midlo. *Africans in Colonial Louisiana*. Baton Rouge: Louisiana State University Press, 1995.

"Louisiana Chemical Manufacturers Struggle in the Global Economy." *MacNeil/Lehrer Newshour*. Donna Lafleur and Al Godoy, research. October 4, 2004.

Mattera, Philip. "Gone South: Decline and Renewal in the U.S. Auto Industry." Corporate Research Project, 2006, at http://www.corp-research.org/e-letter/gone-south.

McGowen, J. M., L. E. Garner, and B. M. Wilkinson. "The Gulf Shoreline of Texas—Processes, Characteristics, and Factors in Use." University of Texas, Bureau of Economic Geology's *Geological Circular* 75–76 (1977).

Meek, Andy. "Counties Adjust to Growth, Growth, and More Growth." *Daily News (Memphis)*, January 10, 2006.

Meitrodt, Jeffrey, and Aaron Kuriloff. "Thanks to Lease Arrangement, Louisiana Leads Nation in Oyster Production." *The (New Orleans) Times-Picayune*, May 11, 2003.

Mileti, Dennis. *Disasters by Design: A Reassessment of Natural Hazards in the United States.* Washington, D.C.: National Academies Press, 1999.

Mileti, Dennis S., and Julie L. Gailus. "Sustainable Development and Hazards Mitigation in the United States: Disasters by Design Revisited." *Mitigation and Adaptation Strategies for Global Change* 10, no. 3 (July 2005): 491–504.

Mulholland, Patrick J., G. Ronnie Best, Charles C. Coutant, et al. "Effects of Climate Change on Freshwater Ecosystems of the South-Eastern United States and the Gulf Coast of Mexico." *Hydrological Processes* 11, no. 8 (1997): 949–70.

Ning, Zhu H., R. Eugene Turner, Thomas Doyle, and Kamran Abdollahi. *Preparing for a Changing Climate: The Potential Consequences of Climate Variability and Change. Gulf Coast Region.* Baton Rouge, La.: Gulf Coast Regional Climate Change, June 2003.

Padgett, Herbert R. "Some Physical and Biological Relationships to the Fisheries of the Louisiana Coast." *Annals of the Association of American Geographers* 56, no. 3 (September 1966): 423–39.

Penland, Shea. "Taming the River to Let In the Sea." *Natural History Magazine*, February 2005.

Robinson, Isaac. "Blacks Move Back to the South." *American Demographics* 40 (June 1986).

Tullos, Allen. "The Black Belt." *Southern Spaces*, April 2004, at http://www.southernspaces.org/2004/black-belt.

Walker H. J., J. M. Coleman, H. H. Roberts. and R. S. Tye. "Wetland Loss in Louisiana." *Annales de Geographie* 691 (1987): 89–200.

Wilson, Charles Reagan. "Mississippi Delta." *Southern Spaces*, April 2004, at http://southernspaces.org/2004/mississippi-delta.

Internet Sources

Energy Information Administration. Petroleum and Other Liquids, at http://www.eia.gov/petroleum/.

Body Burden. Case Study: Mossville, Louisiana, at http://www.chemicalbodyburden.org/tools.htm#Community%20Case%20Study1:%20Mossvil

U.S. Environmental Protection Agency. "Environmental Justice," at http://www.epa.gov/environmentaljustice/index.html.

U.S. Geological Survey. "Nutrients in the Mississippi River Basin," at http://toxics.usgs.gov/hypoxia/mississippi/index.html.

National Aeronautics and Space Administietration. "Using Landsat, USGS Reports Post-Katrina and Rita Land Change Estimates for Louisiana Coast," at http://landsat.gsfc.nasa.gov/news/news-archive/sci_0006.html.

1 Big Spring, Missouri, has an average flow of 276 million gallons per day.

2 Grand Gulf State Park, Missouri, features the collapsed remains of a major cave system.

3 The double pen dogtrot house was a Scots-Irish vernacular home designed for cool comfort before air conditioning.

7 These chickens are headed for a processing plant.

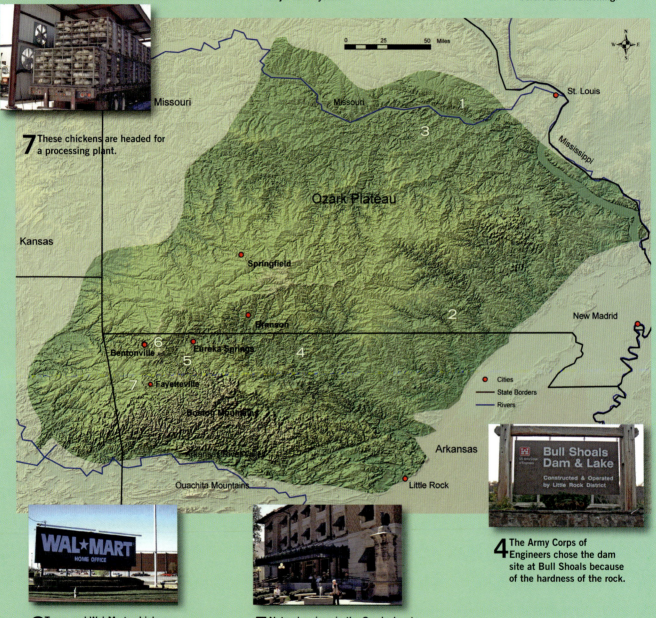

Ozark Plateau

Kansas

Missouri

Missouri

Mississippi

St. Louis

Springfield

Branson

Bentonville

Eureka Springs

Fayetteville

Boston Mountains

Arkansas River Valley

Ouachita Mountains

Arkansas

Little Rock

New Madrid

0   25   50   Miles

● Cities
— State Borders
— Rivers

Bull Shoals Dam & Lake
Constructed & Operated by Little Rock District

4 The Army Corps of Engineers chose the dam site at Bull Shoals because of the hardness of the rock.

6 Tyson and Wal-Mart, which changed how Americans eat and shop, are headquartered in northwest Arkansas.

WAL★MART HOME OFFICE

5 Natural springs in the Ozarks karst formations appealed to tourists in the 1800s and are still popular today.

12
THE OZARKS
Unexpected Economic Miracles

Chapter Highlights

After reading this chapter you should be able to:

- Discuss the advantages and disadvantages of CAFO chicken production
- Describe the various ethnic groups that have settled in the Ozarks recently and why
- Identify the subregions that have become economically viable in the past fifty years
- Define and discuss the importance of "mountain medicine"
- Describe the role of religion in the region
- Discuss the cultural quirks found in the Ozarks
- Describe where major urban areas are in relation to the Ozarks and the reasons why
- Explain how logging has changed in the Ozarks and the effect of the changes
- Describe the traditional primary economies in the Ozarks
- Explain why the Ozarks have been sustainable until the late twentieth century

Terms

bald
Bald Knobbers

Bible Belt
broiler chicken
geothermal spring

hillbilly
limestone
losing stream

shut-in
spring

Places

Bentonville, Arkansas
Boston Mountains

Branson, Missouri
Courtois Hills, Missouri
Eureka Springs, Arkansas
Fayetteville, Arkansas

McClellan-Kerr Waterway
New Madrid, Missouri
Ouachita Mountains
Ozark Plateau

Springfield, Missouri
St. Francois Mountains
St. Louis, Missouri

PHOTO 12.1. Ozark Landscape, Van Buren, Missouri. The origin of the term *Ozark* is possibly an English corruption of the French *aux arcs* (at the river bend), in relation to the Arkansas River meanders. The Ozark Plateau shares rock types, structure, and landforms with Appalachia.

Introduction

"Son, you want to study the Ozarks? You're twenty-five years too late. The Ozarks is over, it's done with."[1]

It's better to be poor than to be beholden.
—Ozark saying

Regional success can be as elusive as winning the lottery—who knows who will be the winner? By the 1950s, the Ozarks were known locally as a land of opportunity, although outsiders considered the region backwards—one where a main attribute was its self-sufficient remoteness (Photo 12.1). But by 2000, the Ozarks region had overcome its stereotype, outgrown its self-sufficiency, and in the process joined as well as changed America. The region, once joked about in comic strips and newspapers, now dictates the uniform and consistent retail and food industries.

But has the region lost its former sustainable lifestyle in its newfound success? Has the Ozarks region traded its colorful, eccentric past for a big-box, processed-food future? Or do both exist side-by-side: one the shallow, moral face that most Americans will recognize, the other living within the brutal moral code of the hills and hollers?

The traditional "down in the Ozarks" life was sparsely populated, laid-back, old-fashioned, and quaint—it was the "hillbilly" region, where people were more interested in noodling or hand-grabbin' a catfish than revolutionizing the American lifestyle. Two definitive Ozarks companies, Tyson and Wal-Mart, and one tourist town, Branson, changed this. In 1950, the region was remote, but it is now a well-connected

geographic and demographic center. In 2010, Texas County, Missouri, was the national center of population, the point at which an equal number of Americans lived to the north, south, east, and west.

Appalachian folk migrated to the Ozarks seeking a topographically similar but less populated region where they could continue to live surrounded by family and unmolested by the outside world. Midwestern and Southern migrants were also attracted by promotional literature from the railroads or dreams of red-apple orchards. The settlers shaped the landscape with their cultural imprint until the mid-twentieth century, when Ozark industry bifurcated. One shed the primary economy and adopted the more uniform cultural landscape of the American dream (tertiary retail, tourism, and religious revivalism); the other seeks out a dram of the American dream in one get-rich-quick scheme after another.

Regional religious beliefs remain a basic tenet but have changed since the 1950s. The small, old-timey congregations with roots in the Second Great Awakening have been replaced by industrial-sized churches and televised, globalized evangelical religion. The region's homespun ways attract those seeking the nostalgic good old days in vinyl churches based on big-box economies of scale.

The Ozarks lacked an agricultural bounty but provided a sense of security and familiarity for people emigrating from Appalachia. Later, the regional isolation, water, and beauty provided Midwestern urbanites relief from urban ills, but at the cost of turning the countryside into the rural equivalent of urban environmental degradation. The pristine beauty of the Ozarks has given way to polluted waterways, mismanaged forests, industrial chicken farms, and crank.

Now many in the Ozarks reminisce about what was lost and pursue a more sustainable future. Progress is being made in sustainable forest management. Wal-Mart has adopted energy-efficient standards in its buildings but has done little to create social equity for its employees. Social equity and crank, the cheap and even more devastating form of methamphetamine, do not belong in the same sentence. If there were social equity, there might not be the current need for methamphetamine (or "meth") among those who feel there is no other option.

The region is still basking in the sunshine of conquering stereotypes, but it has yet to calculate the full cost. There is plenty of room for additional sustainable growth in the Ozarks.

Physical Geography

The Ozarks' physical landscape called for a low-impact lifestyle, which is what most people lived until the second half of the twentieth century. Then the human cultural landscape began to change the physical landscape.

This remnant of a five-hundred-million-year-old inland sea left behind a karst landscape pockmarked by caves, sinkholes, and water discharging from rock as springs. Karst-formed features are an important part of the tourism economy, but they also cause water pollution problems.

Plains surround the higher-than-hills, lower-than-mountains, dissected-and-uplifted Ozark plateaus. The core is an ancient volcanic rock in the St. Francois Mountains; sedimentary rock overlays the rest of the plateaus.

The Ozarks lie in the middle of the continent and form a rough parallelogram over about fifty thousand square miles of southern Missouri and northern Arkansas. To the north, the transitional Missouri River flood plain separates the glacial plains of northern Missouri from the upland Ozarks. The eastern border drifts into the Central Lowlands, but the southern uplifted edge contrasts with the Mississippi embayment. The western border is geologically but not visually differentiated.[2] The Ozark bioregion has three major divisions: the Ozark Plateau, the Arkansas River Valley, and the Ouachita Mountains (Map 12.1).

Ozark Plateau

The Ozark or Central Plateau dominates the southern half of Missouri and extends into northern Arkansas. The plateau blends into Kansas prairie in the west and fades south of the Eureka Springs escarpment in Arkansas. Along the northern edge and bounded by the Missouri River, the small subsistence farms of the Osage-Gasconade Hills are scattered through forested, river-carved ridges and valleys. Farther east is the poorest, most rugged, isolated section of the Ozarks, the Courtois Hills, where timber in the steep-sided **limestone** hills provide the region's principal resource. The hills and hollers kept the plateau culturally insulated until the late-twentieth-century interstate highway system integrated the region with the nation.

The St. Francois Mountains' igneous knobs peek through the forest in southeastern Missouri. These Lead Belt rocks are also infiltrated with iron ores, zinc, and other minerals, all deposited when the region was surrounded by seas 1.5 billion years ago.

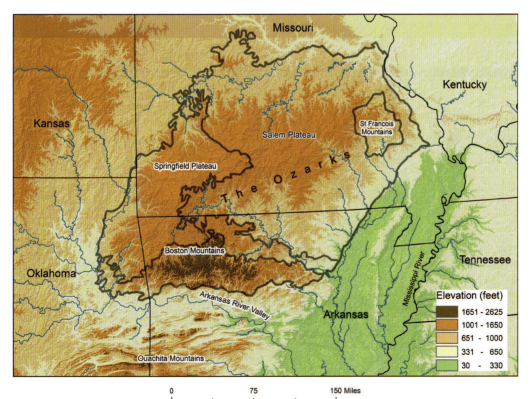

MAP 12.1. Ozark Plateau Subregions

Mineral deposits have been mined since 1720. The regional landscape is a mixture of unusual topographic features. Unnavigable gorges called **shut-ins** are deep, narrow channels carved into hard rock. Another regional feature is **bald** knobs—hilltop grasslands devoid of trees. Prior to European arrival, the balds were an open refuge from the forests for bison, deer, and other wildlife.

Separating the Ozark Plateau from the Arkansas River Valley, the Ouachita and Boston mountains are two of the few east-to-west ranges in the United States. The hills contain some of the more spectacular sinkholes and springs, the region's highest elevations, and a pleasing forest and glade landscape. The region once grew corn and cotton, but soil erosion and a lack of level land hampered production. The scenic White River Hills have metamorphosed from farmland into a tourist area boasting large human-made lakes, limestone caves, and country music.

Arkansas River Valley

The Arkansas River Valley trough, a transition zone between the Boston and Ouachita mountains, defines the southern extent of the Ozarks. Fort Smith marks the western entrance to the river valley, which extends eastward to Little Rock. The natural east-west valley corridor connects the coastal plain, the Mississippi Valley, and the Great Plains. The fertile bottomlands support a wide range of agricultural crops.

Ouachita Mountains

South of the Arkansas River Valley, the Ouachitas extend westward from Little Rock, Arkansas, into eastern Oklahoma. The rounded features of the low-elevation Ouachita Range were once connected to the Appalachians and as high as the Swiss Alps. Over time, the Mississippi embayment rift separated the Ouachitas from the Appalachians. Tectonic processes have geothermally activated the region and produced areas such as Hot Springs, outside of Little Rock.

Native Americans and Europeans alike have bathed in the **geothermal springs**, but the water's potential energy source has been wasted and considered a nuisance. However, the water may be a future source of renewable heat for space heating and, when potable, hot water, thereby decreasing dependency on fossil fuels.[3]

Water

Water is plentiful throughout the Ozarks. Water oozes out of karst seeps, peeks out of karst windows, or disappears underground in **losing streams**, which then reappear out of seemingly solid bedrock. Although water is plentiful, the porous limestone increases the possibility of contamination, because of the regional dependence on intensive livestock production, especially chickens and hogs, whose manure compromises water quality and the ecological balance of aquatic species.[4]

Managing Ozark water began after the Depression. The Army Corps of Engineers built dams, and flooded and altered rivers to meet the demands of the increasing human,

agricultural, and industrial sectors, but at the cost of environmental degradation. For example, changing the hydrographic profile resulted in wider, shallower stream channels and eliminated deepwater species. For all its forested areas, the Ozark regional ecosystems are fragile and became fragmented when virgin timbers were cut, and then later the remaining forested area was exploited for wood chemicals such as charcoal and methanol, a solvent and chemical feedstock. The resulting environmental damage to the soil, game, timber, and minerals was the result of a lack of systematic thinking patterns that reveal the connections between water and intervention.

Rivers

The navigable Mississippi and Missouri rivers define the northeastern periphery of the Ozarks, but smaller rivers—the Arkansas, Gasconade, Meramec, and White—flow through steep-sided river valleys that require dredging and damming to make them navigable. In the second half of the twentieth century, eighteen dams were built along Ozark rivers. The wilderness morphed into second-home lakeside retreats when dammed rivers created artificial lakes. River water was also reconfigured to improve navigation and agricultural use.

Navigated since 1820, the Arkansas River connects the Great Plains with the Gulf Coast; however, beyond Little Rock the river was too shallow for navigation by larger and heavier ships. In 1971, the McClellan-Kerr Waterway opened navigation from Little Rock to the Port of Catoosa near Tulsa. The system expanded industrial opportunities through the Arkansas Valley and Oklahoma, but not as much as originally predicted. Still, workers call the port "extremely busy" (Photo 12.2). Grain is shipped south, whereas petroleum, coal, and chemicals are major northbound commodities.

The Arkansas River is the water source for local agricultural and urban areas. However, groundwater withdrawn for irrigation evaporates, leaving behind mineral salts. The increased salinity has caused declining water quality and lowered crop yields. Studies continue to evaluate water quality protection strategies.

Springs

More than twenty million gallons of water from six hundred Ozarks **springs** feed rivers daily, adding up to billions of gallons of water annually. The rainwater-fed springs follow a maze of underground faults before emerging as springs from caves or sinkholes.

Southern Missouri's Big Spring is the largest and once recorded a peak flow of one billion gallons a day. The Arkansas mineral waters include Eureka Springs, but the most popular geothermal springs are in Hot Springs, in the Ouachita Mountains.

Springs were popular with Native Americans and as pioneer settlement sites. Several saline and geothermal springs have been developed commercially for medicinal use. Hot Springs, Arkansas, a popular nineteenth-century spa, was fashioned after

PHOTO 12.2. Offloading Cargo at Tulsa, Oklahoma. Port of Catoosa is the Tulsa port on the McClellan-Kerr waterway. These metal spools came from Japan by way of New Orleans and will be used in refrigeration units.

the great spas of Europe. The forty-seven springs produce over a million gallons of 143°F geothermally heated water daily.

Geothermal springs are scattered throughout the United States. There are more than 190 therapeutic geothermal spas, including Saratoga Springs, New York; Warm Springs, Georgia; Hot Springs, Virginia; White Sulfur Springs, West Virginia; Hot Springs, Arkansas; Thermopolis, Wyoming; and Calistoga, California. The regional health benefits are not limited to the water, though; the Ozarks have been one of the regions most dependent on natural remedies and cures.

Climate

The Ozarks' four distinct but temperate seasons range from 80°F average, humid and rainy summers (annual mean precipitation is forty to forty-eight inches) to average January temperatures of 34°F. Winter snows are brief because of diurnal temperature variations. The growing season varies between 180 and 200 days. Periodic droughts can be severe and destructive to the economy.

Climate Change

Several climate models estimate how climate change will alter the Ozark environment, ranging from average temperature rising from 1°F to 7°F. But the models do not agree if the climate will be wetter or drier and how carbon dioxide levels will affect the vegetation. While the models vary in their predictions, all agree that changes will reconfigure the forest vegetation. The models indicate that changes could be:

- Pines replacing the oak/hickory forest (warmer and wetter)

- Forests retreating and being replaced by a grassland (warmer and drier)
- Undergrowth of vines choking out trees by mid-century (rising carbon dioxide levels)[5]

Historical Geography and Settlement

Native Americans have occupied the Ozarks from the Woodland period (100 BCE–900 CE) through the Mississippian period (900–1200 CE). Remnants of these tribes were first encountered by Desoto's 1540 foray into the region, but by 1673 when French explorers Marquette and Joliet entered the region, the Sioux Nation Osage tribe inhabited the area between the Missouri and Arkansas rivers.

Most who settled the Ozarks in the nineteenth century were Scots-Irish and Germans. The uplander Scots-Irish often left the "overpopulated" Appalachian region to settle in the hills and hollows of the Ozark Plateau. Into the first decades of the twentieth century, they practiced a self-sufficient lifestyle—hunting; pasturing farm animals; growing corn, sorghum, wheat, and vegetables; and hiring out for lumber work to augment their income. A few farmers owned slaves, but most did not.

During the Civil War, Ozark allegiance was divided: Missouri stayed with the Union, while Arkansas seceded; however, many in each state followed their heart, while others felt forced to fight for something they did not believe in. The result was a war torn and devastated region, battle worn and filled with refugees.

After the war, the bald mountaintops acted as signal outlooks for the **Bald Knobbers,** a Reconstruction vigilante group named for the topographic feature. From 1864 to 1885, Bald

BOX 12.1 WATER UTILIZATION

Public policy dictates that dams must have multiple uses: rural electrification, flood control, tourism promotion, and economic development. However, these uses are not mutually compatible. Water level fluctuations caused by flood control and electricity generation are not compatible with development aims. To maintain high property values, the region needs to maintain scenic amenity values and high lake levels for deepwater watersports activities. But to maintain electricity levels and continue flood control requires water levels to change periodically, regardless of amenities and water-sports activities. Rural electrification, flood control, and tourism are not possible at the same time.

Knobber ceremonies and patterns became an Ozark stereotype; they were characterized as a group of violent, ignorant hillbillies, who seemed indiscriminant in clearing the land of people whom they deemed criminals.

German farmers immigrated to the United States between 1850 and 1880. Many Germans who had settled in Kentucky continued their westward movement into northern Missouri and the fertile bottomlands along the Missouri and Mississippi river flood plains. In time they purchased additional land from American farmers. Many Germans maintained ethnic communities, and they purchased land from footloose American farmers who moved on.

Cultural Perspectives

The colorful people of the Ozarks are one of America's most recognized rural groups. They share cultural traits such as self-sufficiency, traditional lifestyles, reluctance to accept change, suspicion of outsiders, and political conservatism. The Ozark population pursued hunting, fishing, and home crafts more than in other farming areas.

The Ozark and Appalachian cultural roots differed from the rest of America. Few pursued technological advancement or education. Lacking the tools of industrial progress left them impoverished, but with a strong wealth in kinship and self-sufficiency that set them outside mainstream America. Their independent ways earned them the nickname hillbillies.

Hillbillies

In 1960, the Springfield, Missouri, Court of Appeals ruled on a divorce case involving the use of the term **hillbilly**. Judge Justin Ruark, in the case of Moore v. Moore (337 S.W. 2d 781) made the following statement in his decision:

An Ozark hillbilly is an individual who has learned the real luxury of doing without the entangling complications of things that the dependent and over-pressured city dweller is required to consider as necessities. The hillbilly foregoes the hard grandeur of high buildings and canyon streets in exchange for wooded hills and verdant valleys. In place of creeping traffic he accepts the rippling flow of the wandering stream. He does not hear the snarl of exhaust, the raucous braying of horns, and the sharp, strident babble of many tense voices. For him instead is the measured beat of the katydid, the lonesome, far-off complaining of the whippoorwill, perhaps even the sound of a falling acorn in the infinite peace of the quiet woods. The hillbilly is often not familiar with new models, soirées, and office politics. But he does have the time and surroundings conducive to sober reflection and honest thought, the opportunity to get closer to his God. No, in Southern Missouri the appellation "hillbilly" is not generally an insult or an indignity; it is an expression of envy.

Today Ozark tourism and music capitalize on the stereotypical hillbilly moniker. Hillbilly music evolved from Celtic and English folk songs into today's country music. However, many people of the Ozarks are not hillbillies. Advancements in communication and transportation increased connections and consumer ideals. Now, those who choose the simpler hillbilly lifestyle do so by choice and not only because of geographic location.

Religion

Many American areas proudly proclaim themselves to be the "Buckle of the **Bible Belt**," because of the dominance of provincial, often fundamentalist or Pentecostal Christian religions that are often evangelical (emphasizing the authority of the Bible). Springfield, Missouri, is home to many individualistic conservative sects.

Several religious denominations are headquartered in the Ozarks. Springfield is home to fundamental Christian colleges and conservative publishing houses. Sharing a basic Christian faith in Jesus and a hope for eternal destiny, the evangelical leaders preach various biblical interpretations and apocalyptic events, sometimes reaching fanatical proportions. For example, some follow white supremacist teachings; others adamantly maintain their bonds and beliefs despite the jailing of their wayward leaders. These marginalized groups are small in number, but their existence highlights the religious fervor of the Ozark region.

Although Christian religions dominate the Ozarks, other pockets of faith exist, from Baha'i to Buddhist, and such imported religions as the animist shamanism of the Hmong, many of whom have migrated to the Ozarks in search of a quality of life similar to their former farming culture.

BOX 12.2 MOUNTAIN MEDICINE

An Ozarker went to Wyoming to herd sheep. He spent long days in the saddle, days that stretched into years. In his eighties he began to have severe back pain. On a visit to Denver, kin there insisted he go to the doctor. The physician, looking at the patient information sheet, said, "Sir, you're eighty-three years old! You can't continue to work the way you do and expect to avoid pain." Afterward the old man complained disgustedly, "I gave him ten dollars to fix my back, and all he did was tell me how old I am!"

Cancer, high blood pressure, heart disease, stroke, and diabetes occur in the rural Ozarks at above-average rates. A Federal Government study will seek to find out why.
—News story out of Springfield, Missouri, October 18, 1994*

Ozark residents have long preferred old-fashioned healing traditions over modern medicine. Ordinary people administered health care with home remedies available from the "pharmacy" in the fields. Health cure-alls purchased through magazine ads usually contained a high percentage of alcohol or opiates. Cures were found in plants and homemade whiskey.

The chemical properties of plants made some mountain medicine—foul-smelling poultices and teas, concocted with skunk oil or onions—effective. For example, springtime sassafras and molasses were used as blood thinners after blood "thickened" over the inactive and fat-eating winter. Modern medicine discounted the relief derived from mountain medicine, but many of the active ingredients in plants are curative. Today, some people eschew modern doctors and favor the more "natural" medicine rather than depend on the pharmaceutical industry.

Numerous springs and mineralized waters created another Ozark cure, "taking the waters." During the late nineteenth century, local spa towns blossomed, offering a healing cure for a stressful urban life (Photo 12.3). The Ozark lifestyle, natural cures, treatments, and baths became and remain attractive. During the late nineteenth century, the main streets of towns like Hot Springs or Eureka Springs were lined with bathhouses, similar to European bathhouses. Both attracted a wealthy clientele.

In the nineteenth and early twentieth century, trained doctors were uncommon in the hills, and traditional methods prevailed. Modern medicine, along with doctors and dentists, was a last resort. A dentist extracted teeth, regardless of the problem. Still

PHOTO 12.3. Sanitarium Ruins, Welch Springs, Missouri. In 1855, homesteader Thomas Welch built a grist mill, which he operated until he sold the property to Dr. Christian Diehl in 1913. Dr. Diehl built this building as a sanitarium and rest camp for asthma sufferers. He claimed the spring and cave air were medicinal and healthful. The sanitarium, never a monetary success, is now part of the Park Service.

today, many Ozark people lack a full set of teeth because of either poor oral hygiene or traditionally practiced dentistry. Of course, as more outsiders and retirees move into the Ozarks, modern medicine and dentistry are becoming more acceptable, and managed health care is common. Still, many of the old-timers prefer the traditional Ozark remedies.

The Ozark reputation as a natural region—unspoiled, uncivilized, and clean—was fed by the unpolished but honest people. The naturalness and the spring-fed land highlighted what was considered a healthy atmosphere, which preached the curative properties of hot mineral baths, herbs, and organic therapies. These features helped bring the Ozarks to the forefront of the Midwestern mind that sought solace from urban ills, and they helped begin the Ozark tourism industry.

* Robert Flanders, "Health and Healing in the Ozarks," *OzarksWatch* 8, no. 1 (1995), at http://thelibrary.springfield.missouri.org/lochist/periodicals/ozarkswatch/ow801b.htm.

Regional Life

Population Distribution

The U.S. Census taker might have been puzzled at the ages of children presented as "one creeper, one walker, two pallet babies, one suckling, and an apron child."[6]

Historically, the Ozarks have been an area of sparse, dispersed population that grew by two means: large families and chain migration. The traditional Ozark family produced a child a year, usually born at home because of a lack of health facilities or state services. Chain migration operated when word was sent back to their former home of a good life, prompting family members to migrate to the Ozarks.

After the 1960s, Ozark immigration expanded to groups without regional ties. By the 1980s, the number of commuters and retirees moving to the Ozarks exceeded national growth averages and continued; between 1990 and 2000, the region grew by more than 25 percent. Large towns expanded, but the fastest growth was in seasonal homes and retirement communities.

BOX 12.3 SALT AND ORGANOCHLORINES

Salt is essential for regulating body functions in animals and humans. Historically, wealth and power came to those knowing and controlling salt production. The former importance of salt is hidden in the words "soldier" and "salary" both having their roots in salt's root, *sal*, a form of payment for work.

In the United States, several early settlements in Virginia and New York were based on salt production, and farther west new settlements grew around areas of salt production. A salt tax was instrumental in funding the Erie Canal. The Erie Canal made the Syracuse, New York, salt works prosper and gave the city the name "Salt City"; its population tripled in the next twenty years before the industry declined in the 1860s.

Salt commanded a high price and was in demand in the Ozarks until the 1820s. In Ste. Genevieve, Missouri, the earliest authenticated occupation was salt making. When Daniel Boone lived in Booneslick, Missouri, he made salt by evaporating weak brine water from springs. The next closest location known at the time was the salt spring near Syracuse, New York, and the shipping cost was prohibitive. After the 1820s, other salt sources were discovered, and prices fell as river transport improved.

Salt also has played a role in the modern chemical industry. Natural salt deposits were also the location of brine springs, from which many chlorine derivatives, the essential building blocks of the chemical industry, were developed. Chlorides are formed when the chemical bonds of salt (NaCl) are broken. The resulting chlorine is then bound with organic matter (carbon and hydrogen—the building blocks of life), forming organochlorines. The chemical industry has basically been a combination of chlorine and organic substances, most of which are petrochemicals, used for pesticides, herbicides, plastics, paints, and any number of what have become everyday substances of the modern world. The organochlorine industry arose in places such as Missouri (Monsanto), the Kanawha Valley of West Virginia (Union Carbide), and Midland, Michigan (Dow Chemical).

Organochlorines are bioaccumulative toxins that do not degrade in the environment. They are linked to birth defects, reproductive failure, tumors, cancer, and development problems. While some have been banned (PCBs and DDT), others like dioxin are still produced.*

* Judy Ehlen, William C. Haneberg, and Robert A. Larson, eds., *Humans as Geologic Agents* (Boulder, Colo.: Geological Society of America, 2005); Paul Hawken, *The Ecology of Commerce* (New York: Harper Collins, 1993).

The population in the Ozarks is over 95 percent Caucasian and approximately 20 percent are age sixty-five or older (U.S. average over sixty-five is 14 percent). In many small towns, the younger population migrates to well-paying jobs, leaving the elderly behind. Retirement communities such as Bella Vista, Kimberling City, and Branson, Missouri, establish their own programs favoring senior over family interests.

Overall, settlement is sparse in the uplands and dense in the river valleys. The underpopulated areas often have high poverty and unemployment rates. A recent anomaly, though, is the northwest quadrant of Arkansas where Tyson and ConAgra became food processing giants; Wal-Mart reinvented retailing; and trucking dynamo J. B. Hunt took advantage of lenient trucking laws. In this area, the population boomed.

Traditional and Sustainable Cities

The center point of the U.S. population now lies in the Ozarks; however, few urban centers are in the region. Ozark cities lie along the regional perimeter: St. Louis, Little Rock, and Kansas City. The dissected Ozark topography accounts for the lack of cities. Urban growth is often linked to tourist amenities—the natural environment, infrastructure, lakes, health-care facilities, and retirement centers. Other cities have grown as gateway cities.

Fort Smith, at the entrance to the Arkansas River Valley, had retarded growth because of its location at the edge of Oklahoma's Indian Territory, but it grew after Oklahoma opened to

settlement. Poplar Bluff in southeastern Missouri is billed as the gateway to the Ozarks. America has been impacted by several other Ozarks towns:

- Branson, Missouri: This small town that has a big impact in the country music industry almost tripled between 1990 and 2010.
- Bentonville, Arkansas: Home to Wal-Mart, the world's largest retail chain.
- Springdale, Arkansas: Home to Tyson, the world's largest chicken producer.
- Lowell, Arkansas: Home to J. B. Hunt, the fourth-largest national trucking firm.

The most important regional city, St. Louis, draws a great deal of its commerce from the Ozark hinterland.

St. Louis, Missouri
(2010 pop. 348,189; CSA 2,754,328)

As long as sprawl continues unchecked, St. Louis City will continue to lose. Population will continue to drain from the city, leaving fewer people to pay the increasing costs for construction and/or maintenance of public facilities and services.[7]

Strategically located on a bluff near the confluence of the Mississippi and Missouri rivers, St. Louis has served as a break-in-bulk point, fulcrum of east-west movement, and wholesale outlet for the Ozarks. The city's prosperity and location can be

BOX 12.4 NEW MADRID AND THE EARTHQUAKES

In 1788, New Madrid, Missouri, was founded in what was then Spanish-ruled Louisiana Territory. The settlers were Kentucky discontents who lacked faith in the new American government and feared the loss of economic and political security. Many considered seeking that stability with the Spanish and their control of the Mississippi River. A primary reason to settle along the Mississippi was river access to transport their produce.

The Spanish—lacking the settlers necessary to stabilize the region from American or British attack—welcomed the group and the grand plans drawn up for the New Madrid settlement. The American settlers were willing to claim allegiance to Spain in exchange for freedom of trade, land grants, and religious tolerance. New Madrid was envisioned as the primary Mississippi town that would open the Ohio Valley markets to New Orleans and beyond. The marsh-filled town survived Mississippi River flooding and disease problems. By 1810 the all-but-vanished town, now a part of the United States after the Louisiana Purchase, awaited the next cataclysm.

Mid-Continent Earthquakes

Most earthquakes are along tectonic plate boundaries. However, during 1811–1812, more than eighteen hundred earthquakes, many in the 7 to 8 magnitude, occurred far from any plate boundaries, near the small Missouri boot-heel town of New Madrid. A fault line separating the region from the Mississippi Delta passes from New Madrid through Arkansas and then south to the Balcones Escarpment in Texas. The fault line is essentially a scarred weakness from a failed rift formed when Rodinia broke apart 750 million years ago.

The New Madrid earthquakes were strong enough to change the Mississippi River's course, but few humans or their structures were lost in the sparsely settled region. Today, the visible remnant of the quakes is the seventy-mile-long Reelfoot Lake, an oxbow in Western Tennessee, formed when subsurface water and sediment were ejected to the surface, creating subsurface voids that subsided during the violent quakes.

New Madrid has survived as a sleepy town on the Mississippi River, which is still occasionally rocked by earthquakes (Map 12.2).*

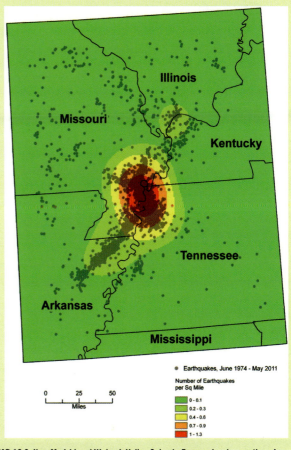

MAP 12.2. New Madrid and Wabash Valley Seismic Zones, showing earthquakes that occurred between June 1974 and May 2011. The intensity of earthquakes centers on the New Madrid Zone, where there were a series of major earthquakes in 1811–1812.

---

* John W. Reps, "New Madrid on the Mississippi," *Journal of the Society of Architectural Historians* 18, no. 1 (March 1959).

---

compared to that of another city located at another junction, low-lying and oft-flooded Cairo, Illinois (pop. 2,831), where the Mississippi meets the Ohio River. The site and situation of St. Louis has everything to do with why it flourished (sitting above flood level) and why low-lying and often-flooded Cairo, stagnated.

In 1764, French traders established St. Louis, a trading post that became the gateway city to the West. When the city lost the gateway raison d'être, growth diminished. Until the Civil War, St. Louis competed with Chicago for midwestern trade, but St. Louis's dependence on river traffic was no match for Chicago's railroad network. It remains, though, the second-largest inland

port city. After the Civil War, St. Louis became an important distribution center for the Missouri Iron Belt, but the industry declined as the richer Mesabi mines north of Lake Superior expanded. St. Louis remains a financial and commercial center that encompasses much of the upper Great Plains, Ozarks, and Mississippi Valley.

By 1918, St. Louis was America's fourth-largest city, and it grew to more than 1.3 million by 1930. Today, St. Louis is the nation's eighteenth-largest metro area. The city population has declined, and building has stagnated. The growth has been in eight hundred sprawling square miles supporting almost three million residents. This has left the city proper in the familiar

BOX 12.5 METH

The seemingly hopeless and bleak rural life has created a backlash culture in places like the Ozark hollers of southern Missouri. These Ozark counties are a region plagued by unemployment and dead-end jobs in nonlocal industry, and residents may enter into the excitement of producing "performance-enhancing" methamphetamines (also called meth or crank).

One night, when Ree was still a bantling, dad had gotten crossways with Buster Leroy Dolly and been shot in the chest, clear out by Twin Forks River. He was electric on crank, thrilled to have been shot, and instead of driving to a doctor, he drove 30 miles to Westable and the Tiny Spot Tavern to show his assembled buddies the glamorous bullet hole and the blood bubbling. He collapsed grinning and the drunks carried him to the town hospital and nobody thought he'd live to see noon, until he did.*

The backwoods are found down rutted roads that lead to the hopeless poverty and hardscrabble lives of the people seeking the only way they see to make ends meet, cooking up the addictive, illegal meth. While taking an additional toll on the local populace, meth leads to desperate measures that further undermine the economy and the future (Photo 12.4). When local cultures are overwhelmed with outside exploitation industries, where humans are no more than producing machines, the level of depression can lead to extreme measures of escape, such as lucrative meth labs. Since the millennium, Missouri has been called the meth capital of the United States. In 2010 Missouri had 1,917 meth lab seizures out of a national total of 11,239.†

PHOTO 12.4. Methamphetamine Warning. Rural America has been under the influence of methamphetamine, manufactured in thousands of small labs across the countryside. The ills of meth can be found in some unusual locations, as this sign in a field in eastern Montana indicates.

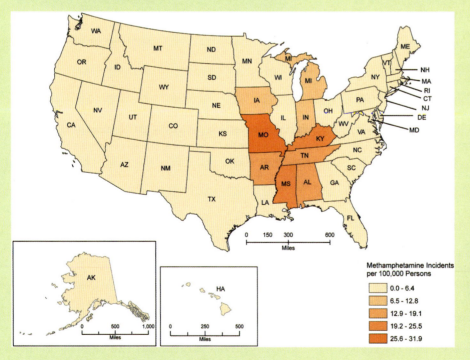

Methamphetamine Incidents
per 100,000 Persons

	0.0 - 6.4
	6.5 - 12.8
	12.9 - 19.1
	19.2 - 25.5
	25.6 - 31.9

MAP 12.3. Methamphetamine Incidents, 2010. The total number of clandestine laboratory incidents reported by the Drug Enforcement Agency (DEA) in 2010 was 11,239. The number of incidents in Missouri was 1,917. Meth has become a national problem, especially in rural areas.

Source: http://www.justice.gov/dea/concern/meth_lab_maps/2010.jpg

---

* Daniel Woodrell, *Winter's Bone* (Boston: Little, Brown, 2006).
† U.S. Department of Justice, at http://www.justice.gov/dea/concern/meth_lab_maps/2010.jpg.

pattern of interior America, with an eroding tax base, fewer resources, and aging infrastructure in a time when higher-density cities and personal transportation efficiency have become imperative for American cities.

One of the weaknesses in building a sustainable city is the lack of integration among administration levels. Decisions are scattered among the city, county, and region, making cohesive plans next to impossible. The city suffers from poor air quality and needs to institute a recycling program and education for residents to improve recycling rates (3 percent).

In an attempt to address some of the ills in St. Louis, a Sustainable Neighborhood Program was adopted in 2005, along with a Confluence Greenway as a heritage and sustainable tourism project approved by voters. The city is yet to be a leader in sustainability, but it has begun addressing the negative environmental impact of sprawl.

Fayetteville, Arkansas

(2010 pop. 73,580; MSA 463,204)

Fayetteville is located near the three largest industries in Arkansas, the Ozarks, and arguably, even the nation—Tyson, Wal-Mart, and J. B. Hunt Trucking. Fayetteville is also home to the University of Arkansas. The location—growing at twice the state rate—has made Fayetteville a magnet for other companies and a retirement center. The metropolitan area has almost doubled since 1990. The growth, while welcome, has also led to sprawl, traffic, and environmental concerns, leading to a controlled growth plan emphasizing infill areas and attainable housing.

Economy

Primary Industry and Natural Resources

The Ozark economy has been based on primary industry: hog-corn subsistence agriculture, lumber, mining, hunting, and fishing.

Rural Areas and Agriculture

While many local residents rely partially on agriculture, crop production in the Ozarks is poor. Most farmers who have depended on crops for their complete income have migrated from the poor soils of the Ozarks to richer land.

Only 10 percent of the Ozarks is good cropland; another 20 percent produces livestock and hay; the remaining 70 percent of the uplands is forested. The good cropland is on the Mississippi and Missouri flood plains, while runoff or thousands of karst pits and sinkholes limit the nutrient-poor plateau soils. Agricultural production and grazing are further deterred by the chert (flint) rock that has broken off from the limestone strata and is now scattered throughout the area.

As agriculture on large and fertile farms prospered in other regions, Ozark farmers were unable to survive economically. Tyson's chicken production methods saved many poor farmers, but at an environmental price. Those who were in the far

backwoods areas were left out of a steady economy, and many insulated folk chose what they saw as their only escape and source of income: the quick and easy money of meth.

Chicken Production

John Tyson rescued the ailing Ozark agricultural economy. A century of raising cotton and corn or a few chickens or hogs had left farmers poor and dependent on unstable commodity prices. John Tyson mechanized and consolidated chicken production in the 1950s. Under Tyson's intensive production methods, raising chickens became an industrial enterprise entailing contract farming and processing. Instead of raising a few chickens, farmers began to adopt the intensive methods that Tyson perfected. Concentrated animal feeding operations (CAFOs) house ten thousand chickens in one building and grow them to slaughter weight in six weeks. CAFO chicken farms earn farmers a steady but meager income, but they remove most of the commodity market risk. A $125,000 poultry house provides $4,000 to $6,000 income per year, a 4 to 5 percent return on investment. Farmers who signed contracts with Tyson received loans to build two or three CAFO buildings, which provided the necessary income to stay on the land.

Today, **broiler chicken** and turkey production is the Ozarks' major agricultural enterprise. Tyson and a few other CAFO-oriented companies have vertically integrated owning the chicken production process "from semen to cellophane." The chickens, the feed mills, the hatcheries, and transportation are owned and controlled by the corporation, while seven thousand contract farmers provide land and labor. The farmers grow the company's chickens according to exacting instructions from the company. Virtually the entire broiler industry is now contract farmed.

Arkansas is the second-largest chicken producer in the United States (Chart 12.1). Headquartered in Arkansas, Tyson is America's largest processor, with forty-two plants nationwide. While the CAFO industry has grown and profited the economy, it has also caused environmental and social equity issues.

Chicken Industry: Nutrient Load

Between 1992 and 1999, concentrations of fecal coliform bacteria in water samples collected by the Missouri Department of Natural Resources from the upper reach of Shoal Creek averaged more than 5,000 colonies per 100 mL (milliliters). These concentrations greatly exceed the Missouri limit of 200 colonies per 100 mL for the stated uses of Shoal Creek and have resulted in the upper Shoal Creek basin being placed on the 303(d) list of impaired water bodies in Missouri.[8]

The chicken industry saved many Ozark farmers from losing their farms, but at the cost of environmental damage. CAFO-related environmental issues include the following:

- Nonpoint pollution from nutrient load fertilizer on soil and in groundwater
- Litigation over carcinogenic matter in manure dust
- Antibiotic resistance

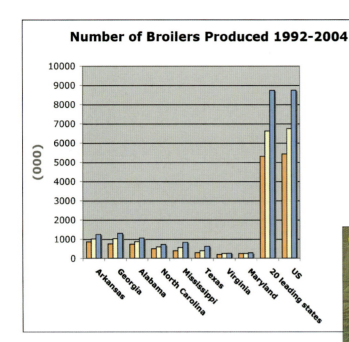

Number of Broilers Produced 1992-2004

Legend:
- 1992
- 1997
- 2004

Y-axis: (000), scale from 0 to 10000

X-axis categories: Arkansas, Georgia, Alabama, North Carolina, Mississippi, Texas, Virginia, Maryland, 20 leading states, US

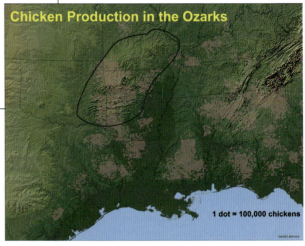

Chicken Production in the Ozarks

1 dot = 100,000 chickens

CHART 12.1. Chicken Production in the Ozarks. John Tyson changed the way chickens were grown in America, from a few in the yard to large-scale concentrated animal feeding operations (CAFOs). Tyson began in Arkansas; Arkansas and Georgia are the largest producers of broilers in America (see map above).

These problems have restricted the growth of American CAFOs.

Thousands of CAFO poultry houses were built in the Ozarks during the past half century. Arkansas produces more than 1.2 billion broilers annually, each contributing about 2.5 pounds of manure. Traditionally applied to land as fertilizer, manure has become a significant source of nutrient loading in waterways and raised phosphorus levels in soils. In karst terrain, the limestone formations connecting groundwater with surface water are susceptible to contamination from CAFO lagoon leakage or overflows. In Missouri, one-third to one-half of all streams and creeks test so high for coliform bacteria they are unsafe to touch.[9]

Conservation practices can reduce these problems and keep soils healthy. However, although a number of proposed bills address manure management, protect water quality, and establish renewable energy standards, new rules only apply to new operations. Old operations are grandfathered in.

Mineral Resources

While the Ozarks lack abundant natural resources, mineral resources were a catalyst for some Ozark settlements. Lead and zinc have been mined throughout southeastern Missouri for 250 years and still contribute to the nation's total production of these ores (Photo 12.5). The primary ore, galena lead (the state mineral), was originally important for making ammunition and pewter, but it is used today in batteries and as protection from radioactivity and X-rays.

The New Lead Belt, or Viburnum Trend, located in Reynolds and Iron counties is the current lead-producing area. These lead, zinc, and copper mines began producing in the 1960s but are close to being played out. The toxicity levels of lead

BOX 12.6 HMONG POULTRY FARMERS

The Hmong, a small Laotian tribe who sided with American forces during the Vietnam War, were forced to leave their homeland for the United States after the war. Many were shocked into the American culture by way of California, then Minnesota, then the Ozarks. The adults from this isolated tribe first migrated to urban areas, but their agricultural background led them to migrate to chicken CAFOs in the Ozarks. The families wanted their children to prosper in the new country, but unfortunately many of the youth responded poorly and entered a gang lifestyle. The parents hoped the rural life would help the children adjust. But moving to a chicken farm required saving money for twenty years to purchase the farm, and it was not until 2000 when several hundred Hmong took their life savings and bought CAFO chicken farms.

The adults have tried to emulate their former agricultural life. The Ozark landscape felt familiar and the Hmong knew chickens, so the possibility of raising CAFO chickens for Tyson or similar companies was a seeming return to what they knew; it kept their

children away from gang influence, and it was a step up from the low-wage and mundane factory jobs that were often the only source of income for their large families.

The Hmong often assumed existing contracts with chicken producers. What they did not know was that raising CAFO chickens was not the same as raising chickens in Laos. They also were unaware that the reason the chicken farmers were selling was that the farms were unprofitable. The banks and appraisers were supported by the government* and therefore may have taken advantage of the refugees and not shown them accurate income projections and expenses. The Hmong farmers would be unable to make the payments for the farms and any type of living at all as a contract farmer.†

Hmong farmers began to go bankrupt in the twenty-first century, and they brought their grievances to the courts. A few are beginning to find their way clear of the debt and out of bankruptcy, and they are setting up agencies to warn other farmers with similar dreams.

---

* Congress designed the Farm Service Agency to guarantee loans to help family farmers purchase farms. The federal government will pay up to 90 percent of any loss on these loans. So if the Hmong farmers defaulted, the banks, appraisers and real estate agents were covered for their expenses, but the farmer lost all. Many Hmong farmers are not in litigation and fighting bankruptcy because of the poor representation they received in purchasing their farms.

† Laura Yuen, "Farm of Failed Dreams" *St. Paul (Minnesota) Pioneer Press*, May 17, 2006.

---

exposure (causing lifelong learning disabilities or behavioral problems in children) have affected local residential yards along the trucking routes to processing plants. In 2005, the EPA began a cleanup of lead-contaminated soils.

Logging

Hardwood forests covered almost three-quarters of the Ozark plateaus, but in the early eighteenth century the forests were cut over to supply building material for St. Louis and nearby railroads. After the Civil War, the need for timber increased, both for railway ties and for fuel for steam locomotives. After the original forest was cut, second- and third-growth forests were planted. These immature forests were cut as soon as economically feasible and used for pulp; therefore, most of the new cutovers have been by the temporary facilities used to convert wood to pulp and wood chips—chip mills. No longer are logs transported to pulp mills, but the mills are brought into the forest so the complete tree can be milled and hauling costs are reduced.

Unintended Consequences   Most forests are no longer grown as natural ecosystems. They are now managed monocultures. The forests that Europeans found when they arrived have long ago been cut and used. In the Ozarks, only about 3 percent of the forested area is intact as it was when Europeans arrived. European arrivals found shortleaf pine forests, but today the region has been converted to loblolly pine plantations—miles

and miles of the same species planted row upon row. Pine plantations are economical because they shorten the harvest rotation. The unintended consequences of these short-term profits, though, are multiple: depleted nutrients from the soil, polluted waterways, and destruction of wildlife and fishery habitats. For example, songbirds become more susceptible to predators and parasites when they lack large forested areas or when they are victim to mismanaged forests. And in the twenty-first century, climate change has added to the consequences and affected forest management and practices.

Improperly managed water systems can result in water quality and quantity issues such as increased flooding and an increase in wildfires. An additional unintended consequence is the chemical toxins used to manufacture chip mill wood, which result in polluted water.

Local and Bioregional Impact   The poor soil of the Ozarks limited cotton production. Soon the clear-cut land was no longer farmed and was open to large-scale erosion, which led to the loss of topsoil. The creation of a National Forest System helped preserve the remaining Ozark forests, only to be threatened again in the 1990s when chip mill logging arrived in the Ozarks.

Public forested lands are managed to protect wildlife habitat, biodiversity, watersheds, and resource production. However, most of the forested Ozarks are privately held.

PHOTO 12.5. Nineteenth-Century Iron Furnace, Maramec Spring, Southeastern Missouri. Iron production helped St. Louis prosper in the early nineteenth century. In 1826, the site was the first iron furnace west of the Mississippi River. Production continued for fifty years, supplying pig iron and wrought iron.

The most important thing that must be done to preserve and maintain both water quantity and water quality is to ensure that forested watersheds remain forested. When forests are replaced by urban sprawl, suburban development, or other non-forest uses, watershed functioning can change drastically and often for the worse. Given increasing financial pressures to sell or develop forestlands across the country, providing financial incentives for landowners to keep and maintain forests should be a crucial component of any policy or strategy that seeks to protect water supplies.[10]

Many landowners of Ozark forests are poor, and they often make choices based on short-term profit, at the expense of long-term, healthy forested areas. Often regulations, meant to further sustainable forestry practices, are interpreted as bureaucratic. Being educated to the effects of selling wood to mills is the best choice for a timber owner and for the health of the land.

A few private landowners and foundations in the region have begun to conserve the forested natural resources and assure long-term yields supporting sustainable forest management. For example, the Current River and Pioneer Forest area of southeastern Missouri developed a long-term strategy in the 1970s to protect its watershed and timber reserves by practicing uneven-aged management, cutting trees based on quality, over the dominant clear-cutting method of even-aged management.

External Costs: Chip Mills   Using chip mills provides short-term benefits at the cost of long-term health of the forests. For the past 150 years, improperly managed timber harvests have been part of the Ozark economy. Since the 1990s, some owners have sold their forested land to short-term oriented chip mills.

Sawmills had been the standard for wood production until chip mills entered the region. However, with the decline in mature wood, the industry relies on chip mills that use ten times as much wood as a regular sawmill. The chip mills grind entire but immature trees into chips and furnish the pulp and paper industry with low-grade fiber for particleboard or grocery bags.

Chip mills are temporary industries in Missouri's Ozarks. Two large chip mills were built in the late 1990s in Missouri's Ozark region, and by 2005 one had already relocated. The mills pay landowners for their wood, but they also pose a threat to the continued health of the forest ecology. Eighty-five percent of the forested land is in private hands, and few owners seek professional help in clearing their land or maintaining a sustainable forest.

The various participants interpret forest management techniques according to factional agendas, not the holistic health of the region. The logging industry claims clear-cutting is beneficial for forests because it maintains long-term health, allows light for new growth, and utilizes scrap wood that might otherwise be burned or discarded. Landowners are interested in the money for their wood. Environmentalists believe clear-cutting disrupts the ecological balance by fragmenting forests, exacerbating soil erosion, and reducing fertility, water quality, and biodiversity.

Feedstock provided by wood waste and thinning forests can meet some of the needs of renewable energy goals rather than continue the unsustainable practices of chip mills.

Achieving sustainable forests requires participation from both public and private landowners to improve and manage growing stock. The demand of chip mills for wood increases clear-cuts, which in turn increase erosion, decrease soil fertility, impair water quality, and accelerate forest fragmentation. Attempts to professionalize and regulate the forestry industry and to develop best management practices have often been stymied due to short-term profit over long-term forest health. The traditional Ozark economy maintained a sustainable landscape of healthy woods, water, and wildlife while practicing within the local economy, but the short-term profit of a globalized economy became the status quo in the forested areas.

Food Processing

With the advent of Tyson Foods and Wal-Mart, northwest Arkansas took on the world. By the late twentieth century, manufacturing was declining in America, although in rural America resource-based manufacturing—from lumber to food processing—retained a local presence. Now Tyson Foods dominates Arkansas industry. Late-twentieth-century food processing enterprises offered dangerous, low-skilled jobs that many local residents shunned. So most workers have been immigrants, usually Hispanics, but in the case of Tyson many workers came from the Marshall Islands, a U.S. territory that allowed legal emigration without visas.

Wal-Mart, the world's largest retail company (with annual sales of more than $300 billion), is headquartered in Bentonville in northwestern Arkansas. In the 1950s, Sam Walton located his first stores in America's underserviced rural areas. Using his marketing techniques, the company grew into a global enterprise. Wal-Mart has adopted many energy-efficient procedures and features in its stores to increase profitability, but it has failed to recognize and act on the social and other environmental responsibilities that accompany a sustainable economy. For example, Wal-Mart has been accused for years of discrimination in paying women less than men.

Tourism

During the late nineteenth century, Ozark health spas capitalized on natural springs and built health spas, such as Eureka Springs and Hot Springs, Arkansas (Photo 12.6). However, the spa health claims diminished when the Food and Drug Administration (FDA) formed in the early twentieth century and enforced truth-in-advertising laws.

By 1950, springs tourism had faded, and Missouri and Arkansas were better known for their rural appeal: more pitching horseshoes than sales. Mineral-spring health spas were no longer fashionable, so the Ozarks reinvented its tourism. When the Army Corps of Engineers constructed Table Rock Dam for flood control and hydroelectric power, it also offered lakeside lots, enhanced an already thriving fishing and recreational economy, and helped secure Branson, Missouri's entertainment complex. As the rest of America grew more urban, the scenic, laid-back lifestyle made the Ozarks popular as an inexpensive vacationland and retirement community.

A Sustainable Future

The Ozarks are no longer considered backward, but instead they are located at the center of the country's population and the center of food processing, discount retail, retirement communities, and tourism consumer industries. The Ozarks traded their backwoods past for the same environmental problems as the rest of America, namely urban sprawl, point and nonpoint pollution of streams, loss of biodiversity for plant and animal life, and the logging, mining, and hydropower influences on the land and the people. Nonlocal industries, such as chip mills, have exploited the Ozarks landscape to the detriment of the local people.

Although the karst topography attracts tourism and provides the spring-fed water supply, during the past half century these features have been degraded because of increased population. Because the water rushes through the karst network, filtration is low. Therefore, industrial or residential waste is more damaging than in less porous areas. Among the many water pollution issues are nitrogen and phosphorus nutrients from chicken and

PHOTO 12.6. Hot Springs, Arkansas. There are forty-seven thermal springs that flow at 147°F. The natural springs and baths were popular health resorts in the late nineteenth century. Their popularity declined after the formation of the Food and Drug Administration.

BOX 12.7 BRANSON, MISSOURI

Early in the twentieth century, author Harold Wright Bell sought refuge from urban ills in the Ozarks. His surroundings so impressed him that he wrote *Shepherd of the Hills,* a thinly veiled fiction about the tribulations of local pioneers. The book was instantly successful and attracted thousands to southwestern Missouri. Some locals profited from the ensuing tourism; others bemoaned the loss of their privacy and natural area.

Thus began the Branson tourist complex. Until the novel's publication, Branson was a small logging community. In the 1930s, Branson became more accessible and popular when dams supplied electricity and running water and roads provided access. By the 1960s, Branson began attracting local musical talent that has grown to sixty nighttime venues. Music and water sports helped the town blossom into a midwestern tourism capital. Unlike the large halls of Nashville, Branson has smaller theaters, which cater to fans seeking more intimate gatherings to see their favorite stars (Photo 12.7).

Every year more than seven million visitors seek traditional and family entertainment values in Branson.

PHOTO 12.7. Branson, Missouri. The entertainment complex of Branson, in the middle of nowhere, is testament to the power of transportation access. Presleys' Country Jubilee was among the first local production groups to locate in Branson. Today, many nationwide music groups have built theaters in the town. Branson can seat up to fifty thousand people at its shows on any day. It rivals Nashville as the capital of country music.

hog manure, chemical spills from the mining industry, and sewage sludge from residential septic systems.

Although population growth was never an issue in the Ozarks before the 1960s and for many is now a blessing (though some regret the loss of their natural homeland), population pressure has indirectly caused pollution and sprawl.

In many ways the traditional Ozark economy, which many urban Americans might describe as "poor," is a self-sufficient and sustainable economy. Perhaps the initial Ozark economy has something to teach the rest of America. Some, of course, realize what has been lost and are working to maintain the quality of life and live within a more sustainable economy.

The Ozark population has become more aware of sustainable ecosystems. Fishers realize that runoff and septic systems affect the water and the fish within them. Chip mills have an impact on erosion and soil fertility and have slowly adopted sustainable forest management systems, and some farmers search for more sustainable methods and local crops.

The land of opportunity has briefly segued into another mode of production, but perhaps the reason that so many chose this natural area is that it unwittingly provided some answers for a sustainable America. The naturalness that brought people to the Ozarks after *Shepherd of the Hills* is ironic: people came bringing with them the very things they wanted to leave.

Questions for Discussion

1. Tainted water from chicken waste has been the source of many environmental lawsuits. But chicken farms have enabled many small family farmers to keep their land. If environmental restrictions add to the farmers' cost of chicken production, many may lose their income and farms. What are some options for addressing this problem?

2. Where do the workers in the chicken plants come from, and why are they there?

3. What part of the Ozarks did the Germans settle? What was their chief occupation?

4. Are earthquakes a danger in this region? Why or why not?

5. How have the Ozarks changed economically over the past fifty years?

6. How did the creation of Oklahoma's Federal Indian lands affect growth in Fort Smith and the Arkansas River Valley?

7. How has the White River region of Arkansas changed since the 1980s?

8. How did logging change in the twentieth century, and what were the consequences?

Suggested Readings

Burgess, Stanley. "Perspectives on the Sacred: 'Religion in the Ozarks.'" *OzarksWatch* 2, no. 2 (Fall 1988): 4–7.

Embree, David. "The Ozarks: Buckle of the Bible Belt or Haven for Religious Diversity?" *OzarksWatch* 12 (2005): 3–4.

Farley, Gary. "The Wal-Martization of Rural America and Other Things," *OzarksWatch* 5, no. 3 (Winter 1992), at http://thelibrary.org/lochist/periodicals/ozarkswatch/ow50329.htm.

Flanders, Robert. "Where Is the Ozarks? You Wouldn't Want to Live There—Would You?" *OzarksWatch* 5, no. 3 (Winter 1992).

Gerlach, Russel L. *Immigrants in the Ozarks: A Study in Ethnic Geography*. Columbia: University of Missouri Press, 1976.

Gilmore, Robert K. *Ozark Baptisms, Hangings, and Other Diversions: Theatrical Folkways of Rural Missouri, 1885–1910*. Norman: University of Oklahoma Press, 1984.

Glassie, Henry. *Pattern in the Material Field Culture of the Eastern United States*. Philadelphia: University of Pennsylvania Press, 1968.

Hartman, Mary, and Elmo Ingenthron. *Baldknobbers: Vigilantes on the Ozark Frontier*. Gretna, La.: Pelican Publishing Company, 1988.

Kersten, E. W. "Changing Economy and Landscape in a Missouri Ozarks Area." *Annals of the Association of American Geographers* 48, no. 4 (1958): 398–418.

Martin, Gladys, and Donnis Martin. *Ozark Idyll: Life at the Turn of the Century in the Missouri Ozarks*. Point Lookout, Mo.: School of the Ozarks Press, 1972.

Miller, E. Joan Wilson. "The Ozark Culture Region as Revealed by Traditional Materials." *Annals of the Association of American Geographers* 58, no. 1 (1968): 51–77.

Otto, J. S., and A. M. Burns III. "Traditional Agricultural Practices in the Arkansas Highlands." *Journal of American Folklore* 94, no. 372 (1981).

Rafferty, Milton. *Missouri: A Geography*. Boulder, Colo.: Westview Press, 1983.

———. *The Ozarks: Lands and Life*. Fayetteville: University of Arkansas Press, 2001.

———. "The Ozarks as a Region: A Geographer's Description." *OzarksWatch* 1, no. 4 (1988).

Sauer, Carl O. *The Geography of the Ozark Highland of Missouri*. Chicago: University of Chicago Press, 1920.

Wright, Harold Bell. *The Shepherd of the Hills*. Book Supply Company, 1907.

Internet Sources

U.S. Department of Agriculture. Rural Development. Contract Farms, at http://www.rurdev.usda.gov/rbs/pub/jul02/farm.html.

OzarksWatch, at http://ozarkswatch.missouristate.edu/.

Sierra Club. "Chip Mills: Industrial Logging Returns to the Ozarks," at http://missouri.sierraclub.org/SierranOnline/mayjune2000/chipmill.htm.

Forest Stewardship Council–U.S. *Forest Stewardship Standard for the Ozark-Ouachita Region*, at http://www.scscertified.com/docs/oo_6.4_NTC.pdf.

1 Dairy Belt farms are growing larger to compete with CAFO dairies.

2 Iowa's economy revolves around agriculture; corn and hogs play an interrelated role.

Lake Agassiz

Lake Superior

U.P.

Red River Valley

Fargo

Dairy Belt

1

Great Lakes

Lake Huron

Minneapolis

Lake Michigan

Sioux Falls

Madison

Driftless

6

Detroit

Dissected Till Plain

Black Swamp

Cleveland

2

Chicago

Des Moines

Rust Belt

Omaha

Corn Belt

Till Plain

Osage Plains

3

Indianapolis

5

4

Mississippi River

Cincinnati

St. Louis

N
W   E
S

Ohio River

3 Native midwestern grasses were long ago plowed up for cropland, but some areas have begun restoration.

0   75   150 M

● Cities

Rivers

State Border

Cross Timbers

5 Relict wood lots stand out as dark spots in the fertile farmland of Ohio's Till Plains.

6 Declining Rust Belt cities such as Detroit have many vacant buildings and homes.

4 This canal in Indianapolis, meant to connect the Wabash River with Lake Erie, was never completed.

13
THE MIDWEST
Corn, Cars, Conundrums, and Hope

Chapter Highlights

After reading this chapter you should be able to:

- Describe the formation of the midwestern landscape
- Compare and contrast the Driftless and the Till Plain
- Identify the subregions of the Midwest
- Discuss how the Green Revolution and GMO crops have changed agriculture and food
- Explain how coal-burning power plants impact the environment
- Describe the evolution of the region's two major economies, agriculture and manufacturing
- Give an overview of the population dynamics in the Midwest in relation to the rest of the country
- Name the major cities and discuss their economies
- Identify the location, relationship, and importance of the Dairy, Corn, and Soybean belts
- Discuss the relationship between vertical integration, contract farms, and CAFOs
- Define wetlands and how perceptions have changed about them over the past twenty years
- Discuss the midwestern industrial belt and auto industry
- Explain the importance of the Great Lakes
- Describe the impact of the Erie Canal

Terms

agglomeration
bike station
brownfield
community-supported
   agriculture (CSA)

ethanol
family farm
Five Civilized Tribes
genetically modified
   organisms (GMOs)
Green Revolution

Indian Removal Act (1830)
kettle
lake effect
Land Ordinance of 1785
loess

portage
prairie
township and range system
Trail of Tears
urban village

Places

Black Swamp
Chicago, Illinois
Cincinnati, Ohio
Cleveland, Ohio

Corn Belt
Cross Timbers
Dairy Belt
Detroit, Michigan
The Driftless

Erie Canal
Great Lakes
Lake Agassiz
Minneapolis, Minnesota
Ohio River

Osage Plain
Prairie Peninsula
Red River Valley
Rust Belt
Till Plain

PHOTO 13.1. Ohio Rural Landscape. Agriculture is the most conspicuous human activity in the Midwest and covers most of the land, especially in the Corn Belt.

Introduction

The Midwest is flat.[1]

Because of the great cultural diversity of the region, perhaps the Midwest is less a region than a sense of place. . . . At the very least, the Midwest is what people say it is, that is, what they perceive it to be, and boundaries are important however they are defined or there would be no region.[2]

The Midwest became the heartland of America during the nineteenth century, when transportation connected its agricultural bounty to the more populated eastern markets. During the first half of the twentieth century, regional industry structured the American future with the automobile. But the heartland became the flyover Midwest and lost its way— temporarily.

The pastoral culture—silos, cornfields, and red barns (Photo 13.1)—and steel age factories of the Midwest still occupy a unique place within the United States and the American psyche, but in many cases, not in terms of a sustainable culture. The flat, glaciated Great Lakes landscape shaped its use and perhaps its people, but the culture was short lived, and many locales have stuttered for more than half a century.

The midwestern pace is a slower-paced America. The Midwest became the regional glue holding the more frenetic and equally vulnerable coasts together, but Midwesterners became complacent in their sense of place. Traditional American values are still midwestern family values (stability, modesty, honesty, industriousness, self-reliance, and morality), but the Midwest is split in applying them to a long-term sustainable future or remaining within the short-term-thinking modern mind-set.

For inhabitants on the East and West coasts, "Midwest" conjures up a hard-working blue-collar American image. But the physical-labor economy has dissipated from the American landscape, and the Midwest is divided in adopting the postindustrial economy—if in fact, this is the economy to adopt. The western areas—Wisconsin, Minnesota, Iowa, and eastern borders of both the Dakotas and Nebraska—were not the heart of the industrial complex; they have survived and even lead the way into the ecological economy, but the Great Lakes industry has not.

Minnesota, for example, is progressive, and was an early adopter of statewide sustainability principles. Minnesota's economy is healthy, and the Minneapolis metro area receives high marks in technology, innovation, and as a magnet for young, educated, and alternative groups. Chicago has also adopted many green elements into its city structure, energy production, and transportation patterns.

The eastern Midwest's brawny values are still present, but that memory is fading as the initial manufacturing economy fails and young adults leave. The home to "the heartbeat of America," the nation's manufacturing sector, is now the Rust Belt, which embraced the economic shift from agriculture to industry but failed in the postindustrial transition. Although some cities and states have emerged economically, many have not. The Rust Belt has lost its family-based rural economy, its manufacturing foundation, and its jobs, and many Midwesterners have also been losing hope, their homes, and their economic place in the United States in relation to the wealthier coastal areas. Hope fades in the Midwest when the old remain economically tied to the location, and young college graduates, finding little opportunity at home, migrate to Sunbelt cities.

Midwestern rock-solid values crumble beneath some of the worst U.S. employment and job creation statistics. American agriculture has morphed into agribusiness; manufacturing jobs, the heart of the midwestern economy, now flow offshore. The Midwest's inability to reconfigure its assembly-line mentality has left it bereft of sustainable thinking.

Even the remaining agricultural and manufacturing workers are unsettled. The rural economy was thrust into the twenty-first-century agribusiness regime, in which small family farms must identify a niche, contract with a corporation, or be unprofitable. The union worker no longer dreams he will retire with a pension; many who can afford to leave, do. When two of the Big Three (General Motors, Chrysler, and Ford) declared bankruptcy in 2009, hopes of a funded retirement, even for those already retired, evaporated.

As the service industry surges ahead, the nuts-and-bolts infrastructure of the last economy has diminished. Rusting industrial hulks sit on contaminated **brownfields** in the gritty Rust Belt cities, which suffer today by losing their young adults to cities with jobs. Cities that depended on the automotive industry have bled jobs, but other cities—Madison, Indianapolis, and some small cities such as Sioux Falls and Fargo—have begun to find their way onto "best cities to live" lists, attracting residents with their low cost of living and healthy lifestyles.

The conundrum is: How does an economy change and become more environmentally healthy, while at the same time maintain the hard-working middle class so cherished in the heartland?

The booming midwestern economy was formed prior to widespread environmental consciousness. Agriculture flourished in its fertile soil. Industry exploited natural resources and then used the waterways to build the economic engine that put the United States on the world map. But agriculture and industry have left indelible marks on the landscape. Agricultural issues include soil erosion, loss of wetlands, and groundwater contamination from fossil fuel–based pesticides and fertilizers. Industry and power plants spewed industrial toxic pollutants into the water, onto the land, and up in the air.

The Midwest needs to preserve its natural endowments and improve the surroundings by creating more ecological cities. But the Midwest must do it in its own way and use its resources, including its human capital. Manufacturing jobs can return, but they can no longer be polluting and based on crass consumerism. The entrepreneurship that made the industrial economy needs to return, but in a new and more sustainable form.

Physical Geography

The Midwestern Central Lowland landscape can be described as flat. But as with the detail of almost anything, there is variety: lakes, rivers, trees, rolling hills, glaciers, grass, dairy, corn, and rust. Broad-stroke definitions emphasize the flatness, but the physiographic subregions subtly vary, mostly in relation to their glacial history, which in turn affected economic development. Building a more sustainable midwestern landscape is possible, given industry's preference for abundant water and flat land. As water becomes more precious as a resource, the richly endowed Midwest should develop sustainably, not retract.

The regional industry and agriculture developed in relation to the physical landscape, but instead of working with it, the original Industrial Revolution only served human demands and ignored the environmental destruction to the rest of life and land. The midwestern glacial landscape was reconfigured to satisfy the short-term goals of industry, not the long-term goals of sustainability.

The lake states, one of the major sources of freshwater in the world, rendered their flat and fertile glacial soils into the Corn Belt and the Dairy Belt, two of the most important agricultural regions in the world. The soil, the climate, and the moisture are perfect for corn and dairy, but the pollutants used to grow them endanger the ecosystems. Maintaining this part of the country sustainably, while still maintaining the integrity of the ecological landscape, has challenged the widely divergent interests of industry and sustainable agriculture.

Physical Regions

The Midwest . . . suffers from the lack of geographically defined borders and specific stereotypes. When it comes to definition, the Midwest is a mushy place; experts cannot even agree on where it begins and ends.[3]

The Midwestern open grassland **prairie** landscape is the product of glacial weight. The Midwest begins in eastern Ohio and fades into the transition zone between the 98th and 100th parallels, where precipitation falls below twenty inches annually. The Canadian Shield and the Niagara Escarpment denote the northern borders, while the southern border follows the southern extent of glaciation, the Ohio River.

Presettlement vegetation ranged from hardwood forests in Ohio and Indiana to tall grass on the Illinois-Indiana Prairie Peninsula. Forests fell before the farmers' axes, and plows planted corn and hay from the mid-eighteenth century onward.

During the Pleistocene, no mountains halted the advancing glacial lobes over the Central Lowlands, so the stone-free glacial deposits were a more attractive agricultural workplace than the rocky New England soil. As the glaciers retreated, wind-blown **loess** accumulated over the prairies, creating a fertile, moisture-retaining soil. Rolling ridge moraines offer welcome relief to the flat landscape.

The Midwestern Central Lowlands is made up of six physiographic subregions:

- Great Lakes
- Till Plain
- Dissected Till Plain
- The Driftless
- Red River Valley
- Transitional Osage Plain

Commonalities between the subregions include some glacial history from the last ice age, an abundance of water, and the lack of mountainous terrain.

Great Lakes

The Great Lakes region and watershed includes all of Michigan and portions of Wisconsin, Minnesota, Illinois, Indiana,

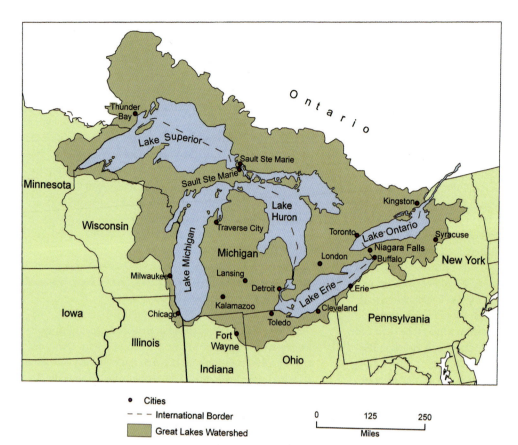

MAP 13.1. The Great Lakes Watershed. With the exception of Michigan, the watershed is narrow around the surrounding states and provinces.

Source: http://www.epa.gov/glnpo/atlas/images/big01.gif

- • Cities
- – – – International Border
- Great Lakes Watershed

0	125	250

Miles

Pennsylvania, and New York (Map 13.1). Ten thousand years ago, the Pleistocene glaciers retreated from the Great Lakes region, leaving behind thousands of lake and wetland features. For example, **kettle** lakes were formed when a large block of ice calved from a receding glacier, was buried by glacial outwash, and then filled with water as the ice block melted. Smaller kettle lakes, called prairie potholes, are abundant across the northern prairies. Many wetlands on the glacial landscape have been subsequently drained for agricultural production, but at the cost of ecological degradation.

Till Plain

Glaciers deposited Till Plain soil across eastern Ohio into southern Illinois. Europeans found a hardwood forest landscape, but in a century agriculture replaced the forest; by 1940, only 12 percent remained. The grass fields that had been the result of prairie fires, such as the Prairie Peninsula jutting across Iowa to Ohio, were also replaced by agriculture (Map 13.2).[4] Today, agriculture dominates the tall grass prairie.

Across the northern edge of the Till Plain, the Black Swamp was a remnant of ancient Lake Maumee, precursor to Lake Erie. Only a few sand ridges allowed sluggish passage through the muddy, insect-infested area to the north. Michigan settlement was deterred until the swamp was drained in the 1840s. Once drained, the land became prime for agriculture. However, when rains come or spring thaws are large, the old Black Swamp wetland soils are one of the first to be inundated.

Dissected Till Plain

Four major glacial stages incised the Pleistocene landscape. The first two stages covered Iowa and northern Missouri, but the later glacial advances stopped farther north and the unglaciated Iowa and Missouri till eroded and formed the drainage systems of the Dissected Till Plain. Thick loess deposits blanketed the undulating terrain, making it a perfect land for corn—humid and flat, with hot summers and cold winters—although it is not considered perfect by most people.[5] The Missouri River flows through the western plain, and along it are the leading regional hubs, from Sioux City to Kansas City.

The Driftless

The southwestern corner of Wisconsin and sections of adjoining states are together called the Driftless, a landscape that escaped glaciation during the last glacial episode. The Driftless pre–ice age landscape of rough, steep hills and sandstone or limestone formations is reminiscent of the Southwest, only more verdant (Photo 13.2). The rough-hewn Driftless topography, while aesthetically appealing, has left it less fertile than the surrounding areas and therefore not as agriculturally productive.

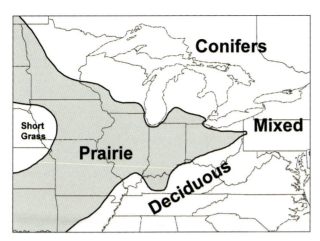

MAP 13.2. The Prairie Peninsula, Extending across the Midwest. Forests surround it on three sides. It has been theorized that the peninsula remained grassy because of prairie fires that retarded forest growth.

Red River Valley

The Red River Valley is a remnant of ancient Lake Agassiz, which was larger than all the Great Lakes combined. Lake Agassiz receded when Hudson Bay became ice-free about 7,700 years ago, leaving behind Lake Winnipeg, the Red River, and the flat and fertile Red River Valley.

The Red River has the distinction of being the only major north-flowing river in the conterminous United States; it flows into Manitoba and Hudson Bay. However, the northern route also accounts for the valley's major geographic problem—floods. The northern plains become ice-free later than the southern areas. As the southern river melts, the frozen north can block runoff. In years of abnormal snowfall when the thaw is rapid, as in 1997 and 2009, the flooding is monumental.

Transitional Osage Plain

The Osage Plain on either side of the Kansas-Missouri border is a transition between the eastern tall grass lowlands and the western short grasses. Within the Osage Plain are the Flint Hills, formed two hundred million years ago. The Flint Hill limestone and chert were deposited when inland seas periodically inundated the area. The Flint Hills are a remnant of the native grassy plain that received glacial dust (loess). The Osage Plain agricultural landscape is also transitional, with corn to the east and wheat to the west. The Flint Hills are too rocky for good agricultural crops, and so they are grazed.

The rolling Cross Timbers tract is a remnant of an ancient deciduous forest found cutting across east central Oklahoma and north central Texas. The Cross Timbers occupies a transitional zone between the eastern forests and the western grassland. The stunted post oaks were unsuitable for lumber production, but access to wood was limited across the plains, so settlers used the wood for wagon repairs. Small settlements sprang up along the trails to provide food and water, but few people settled the area until the late nineteenth century.

Water

The continental interior includes two major North American drainage systems, the Great Lakes and the Mississippi River. Both are remnants of the ice ages.

PHOTO 13.2. The Driftless, Southwestern Wisconsin. The Driftless was not glaciated like the surrounding Midwestern area. Its landforms, such as the Three Chimneys, are unlike the rest of the Midwest.

BOX 13.1 BLACK SWAMP

The Black Swamp was once the lakebed of glacial Lake Maumee, a remnant of the ancestral Great Lakes. Upon European arrival, the flat, forested Black Swamp surrounded the Maumee River from present-day Toledo west to Fort Wayne, Indiana, and then south to Findlay, Ohio (Map 13.3).

The swamp was nearly impassable, so settlement to the north lagged behind surrounding regions. It took six days to cross the oozing, muddy swamp from Cleveland to Detroit, a three-hour drive today. In the 1830s, canal building encouraged some settlement, but draining the swamp using clay-drain pipes called tiles brought consistent settlement in the 1840s.

Settlement hinged on draining the swamps, but draining the swamps required easy access to the clay for pipes. In the 1870s, clay was found beneath the swamp, and by 1880 fifty tile factories were producing inexpensive clay pipes in the Black Swamp region alone. Once tiled (drained by hand-dug ditches and lined with perforated pipes), the drained land became fertile agricultural land. By 1930, it was almost entirely farmland. Most large towns are located along the less fertile swamp periphery.

However, the swamp is not entirely gone. The area is dry when there are no extreme precipitation events, but the soil is still wetland soil, and heavy rains still flood the region. Such is the case in Findlay, Ohio, at the southern edge of the old swamp. Findlay floods regularly due to its location at the edge of the Black Swamp.

MAP 13.3. The Black Swamp. A remnant of ancestral Lake Maumee, this swamp was drained in the late nineteenth century for agricultural use, but the area is still subject to flooding.

The abundance of freshwater in the Midwest secured agricultural and industrial enterprises, but only after intensive infrastructure—canals, tiling, dams, and locks—controlled the waters. Canals and locks were built when waterways were the main mode of transport. They became secondary after railroads became dominant.

Wetlands

The regions with the highest percentage of total wetlands are those that were glaciated during the most recent ice ages. Wetlands are an integral part of the thousands of midwestern lakes and ephemeral ponds (Photo 13.3). Wetlands covered about 20 percent of the midwestern land area prior to European occupation, of which about 85 percent have been drained and converted to agricultural use.

Fifty-three percent of U.S. wetlands have been drained, going from 221 million acres in 1780 to 104 million acres in 1980. The Midwest lost the most; about 36 million acres were converted to agricultural or urban use.

Wetlands filter excess nutrients from agricultural fields. The typical ways to drain Midwestern wetlands were to tile fields or dig ditches; the water from both empty into nearby streams. Many fields have become productive because of draining wetlands and dependence on fossil fuel–based pesticides, herbicides, and fertilizers since the 1960s **Green Revolution**, but the tiling has increased the amount of nitrogen and phosphorus flowing into streams and rivers.

The dead zones in the Gulf of Mexico are related to the loss of midwestern wetlands. Fertilizers flow into the Mississippi

PHOTO 13.3. LeFurge Woods Wetland Creation Project, Southeastern Michigan. This restored wetland was formerly in agricultural production. Michigan had eleven million acres of wetland prior to American settlement, but now has about three million acres.

watershed because wetlands have been drained and can no longer buffer between fields and the watershed. Tiles drain wetland fields, but they send nitrogen, phosphorus, and other chemicals directly into the watershed and cause excess vegetative and algal growth, which results in the low-oxygen eutrophic water bodies. Restoring wetlands will increase filtration, reduce flooding, reestablish habitats, and provide better drinking water, but it will also decrease the amount of productive agricultural land. There is a price to pay to feed a growing population that may have exceeded a sustainable carrying capacity.

The swampy shorelines of water-laden midwestern cities were filled, stabilized, and polluted. In Chicago, the Chicago River had been a dumping ground for urban waste. In 1887, the flow of the river was reversed from Lake Michigan into the Mississippi River in order to maintain the lake water for drinking. In 2009, the Chicago River waterway became a political issue when invasive Asian carp threatened to enter the Great Lakes system via the Chicago channel and destroy the Great Lakes fishery.

The Great Lakes

The Great Lakes hold nearly 20 percent of the world's freshwater. The five lakes—Superior, Michigan, Huron, Erie, and Ontario—span 750 miles along the U.S.–Canadian border. Lake Superior is the only Great Lake with underlying Canadian Shield rock. It is the largest (10 percent of global surface freshwater), deepest, and youngest of the Great Lakes. Sedimentary rocks glacially scoured the remaining lakes, including Lake Michigan, the only Great Lake to reside completely within the United States.

There are several theories on Great Lakes evolution, but all theories agree that glacial movement was involved A billion

years ago, a horseshoe-shaped rift cut across Iowa into the future Great Lakes states, creating the Michigan Basin and intruding copper and silver deposits on the Keweenaw Peninsula. Then, only twenty million years ago, the Great Lakes were formed.

Rapids and falls between the interconnected lakes made continuous passage through the system hazardous. Historically, Native Americans and later the French fur trappers **portaged** (carrying canoes between navigable waterways) through the lake system. The interior developed agriculturally and industrially, creating a need for an uninterrupted Great Lakes transportation network. This network evolved through the nineteenth century until its completion in 1959 (see Chapter 5).

The Great Lakes region dominated the national economy during the Industrial Revolution, a period that created and left a legacy of waste. The Great Lakes have undergone a series of cleanups, only to be polluted again. One of the most spectacular pollution accidents occurred in Ohio's Cuyahoga River and Lake Erie, where extreme pollution in the late 1960s caused the river to catch fire several times, most spectacularly in 1969. The river became a symbol for the deteriorating environment and was a catalyst for the Clean Water Act and the formation of the Environmental Protection Agency (EPA). The river debris was cleared, but other problems continue along the waterways, including nonpoint pollution, sewer overflows, and stagnation of water from dam storage.

Numerous pollution accidents have inspired people to clean the waterways. Although cleanup successes are paraded, only three sites of forty-three Great Lakes toxic harbors had been cleaned by 2008. Deep lake sediments are infiltrated with PCBs, which affect hormones and disrupt the endocrine system. The PCBs bioaccumulate as they ascend the food chain; by the time they reach humans the effects are huge. While some Great Lakes areas, such as Ontario, focus on controlling wastewater discharge systems, maintaining sustainable fisheries, and monitoring diversity and water quality, the lakes remain some of the most polluted in the hemisphere.

Lake levels have fluctuated throughout history, but recent declines are consistent with climate change forecasts.[6] Other reasons for the drawdown include rising lake temperatures (more than 3°C warmer than the beginning of the twentieth century), higher wind speeds that reduce ice cover, and accelerated evaporation. Human modifications such as dredging and building shoreline structures keep sand on the beaches but alter ecosystems and water flows.

The lower water levels affect the regional economy by reducing cargo capacity for freighters and by decreasing tourism. Other environmental issues include numerous invasive species, beach closings, and the loss of wetlands.

The Great Lakes freshwater resource became political in 2007, when drought-stricken areas of the Basin and Range began to publicly thirst for Great Lakes water. However, while the quest to transport the water was on, the Great Lakes were at their lowest levels in recorded history.

Smaller Lakes

Each Great Lakes state and province has innumerable glacially formed lakes. Michigan, Minnesota, and Wisconsin have up to ten thousand lakes each; Ontario and Quebec have millions of glacial lakes, wetland marshes, and bogs that pockmark regional drainage patterns. The extensive wetlands were viewed negatively and delayed settlement. In Michigan, the original land survey, the Tiffin Report, was so negative it discouraged settlement and farming for years. Today, the wetlands are drained, and most residents are unaware of the former landscape and how it still affects local landscape patterns. While the land may feel dry, artificially drained landscapes exacerbate flooding and negatively affect water quality.

The Upper Mississippi River Basins and Ohio River

The Upper Mississippi River basin begins at Cairo, Illinois. The rich loess-covered basin was originally part of the tall grass prairie but today is an important corn and soybean producer. The river in the upper basin was inadequate for shipping purposes, until twenty-nine locks, twenty-eight dams, and numerous channelization structures transformed the river and facilitated navigation for agricultural commodities to the south and fossil fuel commodities to the north. The human-built structures have adversely affected riverine ecosystems. An unintended consequence of human impact is decreased water quality, which requires managing and regulating restoration projects.[7]

The Ohio River drainage basin encompasses fourteen states, including the majority of Ohio, Indiana, and Illinois, and includes 9 percent of the American population (twenty-seven million people). Beginning at the confluence of the Allegheny and Monongahela at Pittsburgh, the Ohio flows west to meet the Mississippi at Cairo, Illinois. Along the way, the river receives 95 percent of its runoff from tributary channels, such as the Scioto (Ohio), Wabash (Illinois/Indiana), Tennessee, and Cumberland rivers.

When Europeans arrived, the Ohio River was relatively free of obstacles, excepting the minor falls and rapids at Louisville, Kentucky. But as communities and industry developed along the river, a series of disastrous floods through the area's narrow valleys forced the construction of protective floodwalls. The levees were built to protect human communities, but in the process they destroyed many ecosystems, and subsequent major flood events destroyed communities.

During the initial period of western expansion, the Pittsburgh-Cincinnati portion of the Ohio River was the nation's most important river and transportation corridor. The river was also an important cultural boundary, separating slave-free Ohio and slaveholding Kentucky, and so became an important crossing for the Underground Railroad.

The river corridor changed. In the early twentieth century, the Army Corps of Engineers constructed locks, dams, and power-generating facilities to control the quantity and quality of flow. A total of twenty dams tame the entire length of the 981-mile-long river.

After World War II, industrial and residential traffic on the Ohio River has continued to increase, with each lock averaging ninety million tons annually. Heavy reliance on the river has strained the navigation system. The infrastructure has deteriorated and requires upgrades.

Updating infrastructure on the Ohio began in the 1950s. The final and most expensive project is the Olmsted Lock at the border of Illinois and Kentucky, near the New Madrid Fault. The aged 1920s-era structures are being replaced with state-of-the-art water level controls. However, the Olmsted has been twenty years in the making, and its completion depends on additional funding. The nation's decaying infrastructure—as the breakdown of the levees in New Orleans and the 2007 collapse of the I-35 bridge into the Mississippi River in Minneapolis have revealed—is in need of attention to rebuild the economy for the long term (Photo 13.4).

Both the Mississippi and Ohio river systems have suffered water-quality issues from pesticide use, artificial levee construction, sediment buildup, and navigation. Pesticide runoff pollutes the watershed and eventually flows into the Mississippi River and Gulf, creating the hypoxic dead zone (see Chapter 11).

Climate

The Central Lowlands humid continental climate fluctuates more than coastal areas, because land both gains and loses warmth more quickly than water. The lack of natural barriers

BOX 13.2 NATURAL AND ARTIFICIAL RIVER LEVEES

Steep-gradient rivers flow straighter than meandering, gentle-gradient (losing elevation) rivers. The meandering river has a tendency to flood, often spreading the waters across flat, wide flood plains. The flooding process slows the river and continues the meandering process, finding the easiest path to the mouth. Successive floods deposit sediment along the channels that form natural levees.

The Mississippi River meanders across its wide alluvial floodplain. The slight gradient over its course below Cairo, Illinois, creates meander belts. The river constantly finds the path of least resistance, changing courses during floods. In the process, the river shifts over the alluvial plain, and the river undercuts one bank and deposits sediment on the opposite bank, building natural levees. Over thousands of years, the river forms one meander belt and abandons another. On the Mississippi River, the natural levees can be up to fifteen feet high. Typically, the natural levees are the highest points in the alluvial plain and the most protected areas during floods.

Humans build artificial levees to control floods and protect human structures. Artificial levees are usually built on top of natural levees, further confining river water. People build structures behind the protection of the levees. There are unintended consequences of building the levees.

Unintended Consequences

Natural levees overflow from time to time, adding sediment to natural levees and then slowly flowing over the flood plain, dropping finer-grained sediment and enriching the topsoil. Some of the richest agricultural plains in the world are flood plains of major rivers—the Nile, the Yellow River—that have been farmed for thousands of years. When an artificial levee fails, though, the floodwaters are much more powerful, and instead of replenishing the topsoil, they erode it. Topsoil is carried away, and gullies form in the plain.

Artificial levees do save towns and fields during minor floods, but every time a levee is artificially built up it raises the level of the river. When a natural levee is breached, it slows the speed of the river by dissipating the water over the flood plain, and high levels of water do not build up downstream. Artificial levees do not allow the dissipation; the constricted river will be more powerful. The faster and deeper river will eventually breach the levees and be more damaging than if it were allowed to naturally spread over the flood plain.

Ecoregional and Regional Impact

Flooding is hard on artificial levees that are built higher and higher to protect the surrounding area. Each time the levees are built higher to protect local land, it increases the chances of flooding downstream. The regional effect of failed levees on the Mississippi River is now well known, after the levees broke during Hurricane Katrina in 2005. New Orleans had built its levees so high that ships floated above the city. When the levees broke, the results were catastrophic.

Less known is the Red River, which flows north into Hudson Bay. The river is also heavily protected by levees because the region is regularly flooded due to the northern flow. The spring snowmelt has the highest probability of flooding. The river breaks up in the south earlier than the north, and the river has nowhere to go until the ice breaks up farther north. Since the levees have continually been built up artificially, the river is constricted, and when the levees break the results are more damaging than if the natural flooding were allowed. Cities along the Red River—Morehead, Fargo, and Grand Forks—find themselves fighting the river periodically.

The Red River has exceeded flood stage 43 years of the past 108 years, including every year from 1993 through 2010.*

External Costs

Building the levees and then rebuilding after breaching are expensive. In New Orleans, the costs are in the billions, but even the more moderate Grand Forks flood of the Red River in 1997 was $325 million. The average flood costs annually are $193 million. Cities like Fargo have extensive flood plans that include building temporary levees and sandbag levees, as well as pumping to protect infrastructure. People are flooded out and then a decade or so later flooded out again. Rebuilding is federally funded and therefore at taxpayer expense, and it incurs more stress on natural resources used in the rebuilding.

Social costs include the repeated destruction of homes, towns, and agricultural fields. Alternatives to the current flood situation along the Red River include ideas within the same mind-set that created the artificial levees. However, there are also those who envision more sustainable solutions, such as increasing the removal of structures where flooding is most probable and allowing more wetlands that sponge up floodwaters along the back of levees. These solutions would help alleviate flood problems in affected areas.

---

* Flood Risk Management: Fargo-Moorhead Metro, North Dakota and Minnesota, U.S. Army Corps of Engineers, at http://www.mvp.usace.army.mil/fl_damage_reduct/default.asp?pageid=1455.

PHOTO 13.4. Bridge Collapse in Minneapolis, Minnesota. This bridge crossing the Mississippi River collapsed in August 2007, killing thirteen people. Since the collapse, the bridge has symbolized the decline in U.S. infrastructure and its maintenance.

allows winds to blow freely across the prairie. The continentality and winds account for the abrupt diurnal temperature variation, as well as the pronounced four seasons, from the short, dramatic, transitional spring and fall to the longer, hot, humid summer and seemingly endless, cold winter.

Since 1960, weather stations have noted changing weather patterns, including more extreme event rain and hotter temperatures, resulting in increased evaporation and drought.[8] Fearing a loss of heartland agriculture, scientists continue to study climate patterns.

Through the 1960s, rain became sulfate-intensive acid rain, affecting aquatic animals, plants, lakes, and infrastructure. Acid rain emissions decreased after the 1990 Clean Air Act amendments, and lakes have shown signs of recovery.

The lack of topographic barriers means that weather can come from many directions: cold Arctic flows, hot humid Gulf winds, and westward air movement across the continent. However, proximity to large bodies of water, in this case the Great Lakes, has other effects. The Great Lakes stabilize the local climate, allowing fruit production on their leeward side during the spring and summer, and they produce the abundant **lake effect** snow in winter (when evaporating water forms clouds and falls as snow). Although Buffalo and Rochester, New York, are famed for their lake effect snow, New York's Tug Hill Uplands, between the Adirondack Mountains and the leeward (east) side of Lake Ontario, receive the most lake effect snow in the United States, more than two hundred inches annually. The snow, in addition to poor agricultural soil, has kept this area sparsely settled.

Historical Geography and Settlement

Mound Builders

Archaeological evidence suggests that prehistoric Adena, Cahokia, Hopewell, and Woodland Period Iroquois and Huron were active in the Midwest for more than twelve thousand years, culminating during the Mississippian period.

The Late Woodland Mississippian culture began around 800 CE. The largest Mississippian site was located at Cahokia, near the confluence of the Mississippi and Missouri rivers. Mound Builders practiced agriculture and traded widely with other Native Americans, as evidenced by the many artifacts found throughout the northern hemisphere. The Mississippian mounds were large, flat-topped, and often served ceremonial purposes. The largest is Monk's Mound. More than a hundred mounds have been identified.

Cahokia flourished in the twelfth and thirteenth centuries, but during the fourteenth century residents dispersed for unknown reasons, perhaps because of ecological changes in soil fertility, supply of woodlands, or a decrease in wild game.

Iroquoians

Just prior to European contact, the Great Lakes Iroquoian tribal family was composed of the Hurons (Ontario and Michigan) and the New York area–based League of Five Nations (Seneca, Cayuga, Onondaga, Oneida, and Mohawk). Generally, the sedentary Iroquoian tribes lived in longhouses in semipermanent villages and practiced agriculture, growing corn, beans, squash, and tobacco.

Pre-Columbian Native Americans are often perceived as peaceful; however, there were territorial disputes among tribes, and later conflicts arose when alliances were formed with various colonial groups.

European Settlement

French fur trappers were the first Europeans to traverse the midwestern landscape. Beginning in the late seventeenth century, the French colonized a few places along the main Great Lakes transport routes (Detroit, Mackinaw) and along the rivers (St. Louis, New Orleans, and Kaskaskia).

Inaugurating midwestern settlement, French trading posts and protective forts—Fort Ponchartrain (1701; Detroit), Fort Duquesne (1754; Pittsburgh)—stopped British movement and monopolized the fur trade. The U.S. government also built a series of protective forts at key geographic sites. Many became major cities: Fort Snelling (Minneapolis), Fort Washington (Cincinnati), and Fort Dearborn (Chicago).

The trans-Appalachian territory was French until the Proclamation of 1763 ended the French and Indian War and the territory was ceded to Britain. The British promised the territory to the native tribes and forbade colonists to settle west of the Appalachian Plateaus, but settlers felt a sense of entitlement and continued to move into the region and, eventually, revolt for their independence. The British claimed the trans-Appalachian land until 1783, when the land was ceded to the new American Confederation government.

By 1763 there were already 120,000 settlers living west of the Appalachians, but by 1800 there were 1 million living west of the Appalachians, 2.5 million by 1820, and 3.5 million by 1830. Colonists gained security when the Ohioan Miami Native American tribe was defeated in 1794 and more so at the end of the War of 1812. The colonist population multiplied, while Native Americans were denied land.

Trans-Appalachian settlement followed natural routes along the Ohio River, the Cumberland Pass, or later the newly constructed Erie Canal. The trans-Appalachian Northwest Territory land was claimed by eight of the original thirteen states, both as reward for veterans of the revolution and for speculative profit.

However, the new government needed a source of income to pay off debts, and after much debate, the Northwest Territory was ceded as public domain to the U.S. federal government, which established the **Land Ordinance of 1785** to alienate the land from the government to individual owners. The **township and range system** allowed a quick distribution of land in private sales, group deeds, or homesteading.

Kentucky and Tennessee achieved the required population for statehood (sixty thousand population) in 1790 and joined the union, and Ohio joined in 1803. The Midwest drew its population from all parts of the Atlantic seaboard. Traces of the three cultural hearths (New England, Mid-Atlantic, and Upland South) are visible on the midwestern landscape.

The completion of the Erie Canal in 1825 facilitated easier passage through the Great Lakes, enabling Michigan settlement, which had been truncated due to the impassable Black Swamp. The New York canal allowed many New Englanders and upstate New Yorkers to settle in Michigan and points west.

Beyond Ohio's forests, pioneers were confronted with the treeless Prairie Peninsula grassland, a landscape for which they had no cultural precedent. The pioneers initially settled in transition areas near the forest, which gave them access to lumber for houses and heat. Later, when the grasslands proved fertile, the open prairie was also settled, although the rich but heavy soil, very different from the sandier soil of New England, was difficult to plow. An ingenious blacksmith, John Deere, developed a new steel plow for these soils in 1837. Once the plains could be plowed, farms spread throughout the lowlands.

Midwestern railroad trunk lines followed the westward direction of population growth. The major growth cities during the late nineteenth century were along rail lines; Chicago became the preeminent rail center. The railroad transported midwestern agricultural and manufactured products to the nation. For example, in 1850 there were 575 miles of railroad in Ohio, but a decade later there were 2,946 miles connecting field crops to city use. Other states expanded and revolutionized national transportation, trade, and the direction of population growth.

European immigration peaked in the 1880s, and by 1920 one out of six Americans was foreign born. As most of the farmland was already settled by 1880, the immigrants settled in urban areas. They tended to follow chain migration patterns and settle in cities with a significant ethnic group: the Polish in Detroit, the Germans in Milwaukee, and the Scandinavians in Minneapolis. The Midwest heartland became the melting pot of the assimilated peoples of the United States and the home to all things identified as American.

Indian Territory, Oklahoma

In the early nineteenth century, settlers spread throughout the Southeast, displacing and ignoring Native American reserves and violating Native American treaties. In 1830, the **Indian Removal Act** exiled tribes east of the Mississippi River to Oklahoma Indian Territory on the Osage Plains. The U.S. government considered the forcible confinement in Oklahoma a good solution to the Native American "problem" but failed to consider the cultural disarray it caused the Natives. Native Americans were relocated without any say and without respect to their culture and habitat. They were expected to adopt a sedentary agricultural lifestyle, despite their dependence on hunting.

An example of the relocation was that of the **Five Civilized Tribes**, who had distinguished themselves by adopting European ways. In 1838, more than four thousand Cherokee died when they were forcibly removed a thousand miles from their homeland, along the **Trail of Tears** to Indian Territory in Oklahoma. Most Cherokee were relocated, although a few retreated into the hills of North Carolina, where their descendants still live.

BOX 13.3 LAND ORDINANCE OF 1785

Colonial land division followed European style: irregular parcels shaped by metes and bounds. However, once the colonies became independent and had gained new lands, they needed to alienate the land from the government to individuals as quickly as possible. The new country also had Revolutionary War debts to pay off. Prior to independence, land speculation and illegal claims were legion; several people claimed or squatted on the same land. To accomplish alienation and pay the debt, the original thirteen states needed to divide land securely and keep litigation to a minimum.

After the French and Indians Wars (1763), Britain obtained Canada and the Northwest Territories (Ohio, Indiana, Illinois, Michigan, Wisconsin, and part of Minnesota), the latter of which were granted to the new nation with the 1783 Treaty of Paris. Virginia, Connecticut, New York, and Massachusetts claimed the lands immediately, but the land was also home to several indigenous tribes, creating a problem between overlapping claims and the new government's need for money. The Confederation Congress struggled to maintain control over the public domain, and it made compromises to attain the government's goal. Amid several possible systems, Thomas Jefferson's township and range system was adopted as the Land Ordinance of 1785. The states ceded their claims, and the federal government had its sorely needed income source.

After the land ordinance was adopted the way was not easy, straight, or clear. Many were still claiming lands, and Congress had adopted Jefferson's plan without adopting his vision of the yeoman farmer. Hence, speculators began to obtain title. Ultimately, the first land divided according to the land ordinance was along the Seven Ranges at the point where the Ohio River enters eastern Ohio. The land was initially sold for small farms, but eventually much of the territorial land went to speculators, as the government needed more and quicker money than small yeoman farmers could afford to pay. Jefferson's township survey is used in thirty states today.

Today more than 20 percent of Native Americans live on reservations amid poverty, unemployment, abuse, alcoholism, and disease. Native Americans are U.S. citizens, but their tribes are semiautonomous nations regulated by tribal communities and minimally by the laws of federal or state governments.

Most tribes were left with few economic resources on land that settlers regarded as distant and worthless. Few Native Americans had acquired the skills required to prosper in the modern world. But technology and transportation changed during the late twentieth century.

Starting with bingo in 1988, the Native American Indian gaming industry has created more than three hundred tribal facilities that cater to ever more sophisticated gambling. In 2004, gaming revenues generated over $19 billion.[9] Several tribal reservations have begun to generate wind power. Gambling enterprises and alternative energy have given many Native Americans hopes for a brighter future and some financial freedom, although often at the cost of cultural integrity.

Cultural Perspectives

Farmsteads and Industry

Three contradictory midwestern images capture the American perception of the Midwest: red barn farmsteads, steel industries, and main street small towns. They represent a nostalgia-ridden American psyche.

Two-story clapboard farmhouses and red barns are dispersed across the Corn Belt landscape. In the nineteenth century, barns housed draft animals, but on the postmodern farm, traditional barns are seldom useful, except for nostalgia or for non-farm applications. No longer does every farm have a cow, pig, and a chicken or two along with hay, wheat, and cornfields. Today, in the name of economic efficiency, farmers have large farms where they raise livestock or a single monoculture crop, rather than a mix. The small family farm, like so many other memories, is now a part of history. "Old McDonald's farm" is seldom the reality in the twenty-first century. Farms are rarely about agriculture anymore, but instead are about agribusiness.

Germans were one of the major ethnic groups to settle across the midwestern farming landscape, and the German barns of Ohio and Indiana represent the region's last remnant of traditional rural architecture (Photo 13.5). The white, red, or black wooden barns are being replaced with, if anything, either a uniform-sized pole barn, or a concentrated animal feeding operation (CAFO) hog, dairy, or chicken barn.

The midwestern industrial landscape is also vanishing, although its nostalgia differs from that of agriculture, except for those who can find beauty in rusted hulks or the struggle of the unionized working class. Many buildings are abandoned empty shells, while others have been converted into trendy, industrial lofts.

The midwestern small-town landscape with Victorian, tin-ceiling storefronts lingers, but the storefronts are peripheral anomalies in a big-box world. All three images have faded into memory: Red barns are often near collapse, industrial towns bear rusted factory shells, and Main Street is no longer main. However, historic preservationists find value in respecting and learning from history, retaining the symbolic wooden barns, the rusting behemoths that rest on polluted brown fields, and the facades of Main Street towns. These

BOX 13.4 FIVE CIVILIZED TRIBES

The Five Civilized Tribes (Cherokee, Creek, Choctaw, Chickasaw, and Seminole) were called civilized because of their nonviolent adoption of many European cultural traits, but this was not enough for Anglo American acceptance. Despite practicing agriculture, holding slaves, and living within and adopting laws similar to the southern states where they originated, the tribes were removed one by one to Oklahoma's Indian Territory, beginning with the Choctaws in 1820 and continuing to 1837. Encroaching settlers on Native land began the exodus as the Native Americans tried to maintain their lifestyles, but in time forcing the tribes out of their native areas became a political issue. Squatters settled on tribal land, and when gold was found the settlers grew from a trickle to a rush, and miners demanded the land be taken from the tribes.

Three factors led to rescinding the Native American land: (1) the political relationship with Spain and the ceding of Florida to the United States, (2) the increased value of land as cotton became a serious industry, and (3) the discovery of gold on Cherokee land in 1828 just as Andrew Jackson became president. Jackson favored the removal of Native Americans and endorsed the 1830 Indian Removal Act. In 1831, forced removal began along the infamous "Trail of Tears," resulting in the death of one-quarter to one-third of the Cherokee migrants. By 1840, the tribes were established on reservations in Oklahoma Indian Territory, outside the domain of the states.

artifacts of the past also represent a period when our buildings and towns were indeed more sustainable and sturdy, and they can be adapted for new uses rather than being demolished.

Regional Life

Population

For the first time in a hundred years, the 2000 census showed that every state in the Union gained population; however, the growth was unevenly distributed. The 2010 Census indicated continued growth in every state except Michigan, but the Midwest stagnated while the southern states grew. Midwestern states lost congressional seats or stayed even, while the Intermontane and southern states gained representation. Growth in the Midwest has been slow; cities lose population to suburbia, outlying rural areas, and other regions.

The Midwest grew at 3.9 percent, as compared to a national growth rate of 9.7 percent (2010). The fastest-growing states in the Midwest since 2000 were Minnesota (7.8 percent) and Indiana (6.6 percent). The percentage of population for the seven midwestern states (Illinois, Indiana, Iowa, Michigan, Minnesota, Ohio, and Wisconsin) has decreased. In 1960, the midwestern states held 23.5 percent of the national population: 42.3 million residents. In 2010, 17.5 percent of the national population, about 55 million people, lived in the Midwest (Table 13.1).

The slow growth is attributed to the loss of employment in all sectors and to jobs moving to the more amenities-based southern climates. Increased imports and outsourced jobs

PHOTO 13.5. Round Barn near Muncie, Indiana. Round barns were more economical to build and operate than rectangular barns; however, traditional barn uses are now obsolete agriculturally. Indiana has the most round barns, but only 100 of the original 225 remain.

TABLE 13.1. Population and Growth Rates: Midwest, Regional, and U.S., 2010

	2000 (millions)	2010 (millions)	Percent growth
Illinois	12.4	12.8	3.3
Indiana	6.1	6.5	6.6
Iowa	2.9	3.0	4.1
Michigan	9.9	9.88	−0.6
Minnesota	4.9	5.3	7.8
Ohio	11.4	11.5	1.6
Wisconsin	5.4	5.7	6.0
Northeast	53.6	55.3	3.2
Midwest	64.4	66.9	3.9
South	100.2	114.6	14.3
West	63.2	71.9	13.8
U.S. Total	281.4	308.7	9.7

Source: U.S. Census 2010, Resident Population Data, at http://2010.census.gov/2010census/data/apportionment-pop-text.php

caused the United States to lose almost three million jobs from 2001 to 2004, and the rate accelerated after the 2008 recession. The employed sector continued to lose jobs monthly through 2010, with the heaviest toll in midwestern automobile and associated industries.

Midwestern unemployment totals were well above the national level (Table 13.2). Three of the midwestern states (Ohio, Indiana, and Michigan) had the lowest per capita income growth in the country from 2004 through 2010.[10]

The midwestern Snow Belt cities have continually lost population since their 1950s peak (Table 13.3). Industry fled high union wages and environmental regulations, and it moved offshore or to less regulated states. The continued emphasis on economic profits alone and short-term economic benefit forced the United States to outsource industry and degrade other countries' environments and labor, rather than mature and develop a triple bottom line economy. To bring back jobs and create a sustainable economy will require rethinking the design of the current system to include ecological balance and social equity issues.

In the Midwest, out-migration has been higher than immigration. Many young adults leave seeking better job opportunities and more career choices. When young families leave the Midwest, what remains is an aging population, higher healthcare costs, and slow economic growth.

Traditional and Sustainable Cities

Once the physical barrier of the Appalachians was overcome, the midwestern lowlands were easy to traverse and settle. Frontier fur trading posts and forts developed during the Industrial Revolution into national transportation hubs. Industrial cities contributed to the United States becoming a hegemonic power during the twentieth century, but most of these cities have ill-adjusted to the twenty-first-century global economy. Today, the industrial shells of the Rust Belt no longer embellish their output with "Made in America." The unused factories oxidize and rust.

Cities were first situated along waterways: the Ohio and Mississippi rivers, the Great Lakes. Cities along the Ohio River include Pittsburgh, Cincinnati, and Louisville, while the Mississippi had Minneapolis and St. Louis. Major cities along the Great Lakes include Cleveland, Toledo, Detroit, and Chicago (Table 13.4). All but Chicago and Minneapolis are suffering economically.

The population decline in these cities has become an infrastructure headache. Some Rust Belt gap-toothed city blocks survive with

TABLE 13.2. Midwestern Economics and Unemployment

	Illinois	Indiana	Iowa	Michigan	Minnesota	Ohio	Wisconsin
Total population, 2010 (millions)	12.8	6.5	3.0	9.9	5.3	11.5	5.7
Population percent change, 2000–2010	3.3%	6.6%	4.1%	−0.6%	7.8%	1.6%	6.0%
Median household income, 2007	$54,141	$47,422	$47,324	$47,931	$55,664	$46,645	$50,567
Unemployment rate, July 2002	6.8%	5.1%	4.0%	6.2%	4.5%	5.8%	5.2%
Unemployment rate, October 2007	5.3%	4.6%	3.9%	7.7%	4.7%	5.9%	5.2%
Unemployment rate, November 2008	7.3%	7.1%	4.3%	9.6%	6.4%	7.3%	5.6%
Unemployment rate, January 2011	9.0%	9.1%	6.1%	10.7%	6.7%	9.4%	7.4%
College-educated, 2000	26.1%	19.4%	21.2%	21.8%	27.4%	21.1%	22.4%

Sources: U.S. Census Bureau; U.S. Bureau of Economic Analysis; U.S. Department of Labor, Bureau of Labor Statistics
Note: All unemployment rates are seasonally adjusted.

TABLE 13.3. Population Growth/Decline in Midwestern Snow Belt Cities

	2000	2010	Percent change	1990	1950	Percent change
Chicago, Illinois	2,896,016	2,695,598	−6.9	2,783,726	3,620,962	−22
Detroit, Michigan	951,270	713,777	−25.0	1,027,974	1,849,568	−53
Indianapolis, Indiana	781,870	829,718	4.8	731,311	427,173	+84
Minneapolis, Minnesota	382,618	382,578	−0.01	368,383	521,718	−29
Cleveland, Ohio	478,403	396,815	−17.1	505,616	914,808	−51
Milwaukee, Wisconsin	596,974	594,833	−0.4	628,088	637,392	−10

Sources: U.S. Census; Proximity, at http://proximityone.com/msa03us

only one or two remaining houses. The city-size footprint remains, but services are limited and infrastructure decays.

Facing the decline, a city like Youngstown, Ohio, a former steel mill city, has committed to recast itself with a smaller, energy-efficient footprint. Youngstown at 66,982 (2010) is less than half its 1950 population. With excess infrastructure and a declining tax base, the city leaders decided to downsize. By consolidating neighborhoods, Youngstown has focused on open green spaces and is re-creating itself as a "garden living" suburb for Cleveland or Pittsburgh. By keeping infrastructure in a concentrated area and using its distinctive sense of place downtown, Youngstown has opportunities for better transportation options (maybe rail to the nearby cities?) and city services. Tightening up the living area has been difficult and is still considered unproven, but shrinking cities, downsizing infrastructure and creating innovative ideas for open space, may be what many cities should be thinking about as more sustainable, localized economies prosper.[11]

TABLE 13.4. Midwestern City Matrix

	Year founded	Founded as	Location
Chicago, Illinois	1833	Fort Dearborn 1803	Lake Michigan and Chicago River
Detroit, Michigan	1701	French trading post	Detroit River and Lake St. Clair
Indianapolis, Indiana	1821	State capital	Center of Indiana
Minneapolis Minnesota	1820	Military post	St. Anthony Falls, Mississippi River
Milwaukee, Wisconsin	1846	Trade	Lake Michigan and Milwaukee River
Columbus, Ohio	1812	Intentional state capital	Confluence Scioto and Olentangy rivers
Cleveland, Ohio	1796	Speculative city	South shore Lake Erie and Cuyahoga River
Cincinnati, Ohio	1789	Fort	Ohio River
Kansas City, Missouri	1821	Trading post	Missouri and Kansas rivers
Omaha, Nebraska	1854	Speculative railroad	Missouri and Platte rivers

Source: U.S. Census
Note: Dates are estimates.

Chicago, Illinois

(2010 pop. 2,695,598; CSA 9,804,845)

Hog Butcher for the World,
 Tool Maker, Stacker of Wheat,
 Player with Railroads and the Nation's Freight Handler[12]

Mayor Richard M. Daley's objective is to make Chicago the greenest city in the United States.[13]

Chicago's location was favorable, but the soil was not. Buildings and transportation infrastructure sank into the glacial lakebed. Most wastewater was dumped into the Chicago River, and the resulting pollution caused typhoid and cholera epidemics. Chicago amended this problem by taking the unusual step of raising its streets six to ten feet, laying sewer and other utility lines in the intervening space. Building owners were expected to follow suit. However, soon after, in October 1871, a fire destroyed one-third of the city. The cause remains uncertain, but the conditions (wood construction material and a drought) allowed the fire to claim three hundred lives. The city rebuilt using less combustible Indiana limestone.[14]

The three largest cities in America are located on water. Chicago grew because of its location at the south end of Lake Michigan. The city depended on the Great Lakes waterways and the expanding railroad network. As the world's largest railway center, Chicago distributed agricultural and timber commodities.

The Chicago Commodities Board of Trade flourished on Corn Belt, cattle, and hog meatpacking products. Chicago became a job mecca for immigrants and the model for Upton Sinclair's *The Jungle*.

In 1830, Chicago had one hundred people, but by 1890, the population exceeded one million; most of the growth was supplied by European immigration and African American migration from the South. Today, Chicago has one million African Americans, more than any other city in the United States. Most live on the south side of the city.

Chicago was the second-largest city in the country, until Los Angeles surpassed it in the 1970s. Today, the Chicago metro area is one-half the population of metro Los Angeles but still the largest city in the Midwest. Chicago is the city where Midwesterners find large-city excitement with the flash and panache of the coastal cities, and although it has the dirt, grime, and poverty that disfigure all big cities, it also has a vital, walkable central city and good public transit, including a progressive program to encourage bicyclists. The economy is no longer dependent on meatpacking, but instead concentrates on midwestern banking and finance, automotive parts, food products, and aerospace technologies (Boeing moved its corporate office to Chicago from Seattle in 2001), and it continues to function as a center for agricultural trade.

Chicago is also rated as one of America's more sustainable cities. After the 1998 blackouts, with Mayor Richard M. Daley's blessing, the city established a green presence. Since then, the city has planted half a million trees, encouraged green roofs (including one on City Hall), and is reducing greenhouse gas emissions by embracing solar and wind power, as well as supporting the simultaneous generation of electricity and heat in a new cogeneration plant. Green projects range from a Green Exchange building that sells environmental goods and services, to schoolyard programs that offer organic food. Mayor Rahm Emanuel has promised to continue Chicago's commitment to energy efficiency and cleaning up pollutants.

Detroit, Michigan

(2010 pop. 713,777; CSA 5,218,852)

Detroit was founded in 1701 as a French trading post at the straits of the Detroit River and Lake St. Clair (Detroit was founded as *Ville d'etroit*, "town at the straits"). The city's growth was slow at first because access from the south was limited due to the Black Swamp. The opening of the Erie Canal in 1825 eased access, and by 1837 the population had grown to a respectable 212,000.

During the Industrial Revolution, Detroit was a steel town, along with several other smaller industries, but it was the automotive boom (thanks to Henry Ford and the auto assembly line) that put Detroit on the map. By 1920, the population exceeded one million, and by 1950 Southeastern Michigan boomed, and Detroit had almost two million inhabitants. Detroit remains the largest city in Michigan, but the population has declined 60 percent since its 1950 peak and continues to shrink. Between 2000 and 2010, the city lost an additional 25 percent of its population. The suburban population has grown (Table 13.5).

Detroit is the largest African American–majority city in the United States. The city was 83 percent white and 16 percent African American in 1950, but by 2000 it had done a complete reversal to 83 percent African American and 12 percent white. Detroit is one of the most segregated cities in the United States. Whites fled the city for the suburbs after the 1967 riots, a steady increase in crime, and discriminatory redlining of building projects. Redlining is an illegal and discriminatory practice of denying credit based on ethnic background or neighborhood.

In 1941, a wall built along a section of 8 Mile Road divided black and white settlements (Photo 13.6).[15] The name "8 Mile" refers to its distance from the center of the city, but it has greater significance because it marks the end of Detroit and the beginning of the suburbs, and remains a racial divide.

Detroit has remained dependent on manufacturing and unionized labor, even as unions weakened in the U.S. economy. Some of the reasons for Detroit's failure to rebuild its economy are geographic isolation (it is a peninsula outside the main interstate highway system), the loss of population, the Big Three automotive companies' lack of concern about fossil-fuel efficiency, a poor mass transportation network, and white flight. The city's inability to attract or keep young professionals with a college education has left it with the lowest percentage of young professionals in the Midwest.[16]

Detroit has remained the third-largest industrial center in the United States, but Michigan continues to fight high unemployment rates, the continued loss of jobs (780,000 lost from 2000 to 2009), the loss of its urban tax base, and infrastructure deterioration. Detroit is one of the three poorest cities in America, with a poverty rate of 37.6 percent (compared to 15.1 percent for the United States [2010].)

While Detroit faces multiple challenges, there has been light shining on improving the quality of life. Low-income residents have some incentive plans to weatherize homes, but little is offered to the embattled and disappearing middle class. The roads are abominable, although traffic is hard to find, and public transport is almost nonexistent. Only 4 percent travel by public transport or bicycle, although new bike paths and lanes are slowly being added through nonmotorized master plans adopted by Detroit and neighboring communities. Urban gardens have been a highlight to greening the Detroit landscape, and they provide fresh fruits and vegetables in an otherwise lackluster food environment.

Minneapolis–St. Paul, Minnesota

(2010 pop. (Minneapolis) 382,578; (St. Paul) 285,068; CSA 3,615,902)

The Twin Cities developed along the only major waterfall on the upper Mississippi River, St. Anthony Falls. They used the waterpower of the falls to saw lumber, process meat, and after the Civil War, mill flour (Photo 13.7). Presently, none of these industries remain important to the metro area.

The Twin Cities are known for their youthful population, creativity, and tolerance. The cities have together become the nation's fifteenth-largest CSA and the Midwest's fastest-growing urban center. The cities coexist with their harsh continental weather. They were among the first in the nation to embrace enclosed malls and a series of skyways connecting stores and offices. The largest enclosed space is the five-hundred-store regional tourist attraction, the Mall of America, which is now connected to the airport by light rail. At the same time, 20 percent of the city is devoted to green space; it still has fairly good population density but has been lax in building a good public transit system. Bicycling is encouraged, and new bike paths and trails are being built, but still only 8 percent travel by public transit or bike to work.

Minneapolis was one of the first cities to integrate sustainability within its city planning programs. Minnesota and the Twin Cities have been leaders in protection and restoration of natural habitats, adopting policies to reduce greenhouse gas emissions, increasing renewable energy use, and establishing incentives for citizens to encourage energy-saving ideas.

Cleveland, Ohio

(2010 pop. 396,815; CSA 2,881,937)

Founded in 1796 on the southern shore of Lake Erie at the mouth of the Cuyahoga River, Cleveland remained a small town (in 1820 there were only a hundred houses) until the Civil War,

BOX 13.5 BICYCLING IN AMERICA

Biking is definitely fashionable in Chicago.*

The Great Downturn may have its first real status symbol.†

Bicycling facilities are common in several bike-friendly European cities and have even become trendy and fashionable in New York City or Seattle, but they are not generally common in the United States.‡ While New York City has sprouted 170 miles of new bike lanes and the Dutch have opened a location for their famous bike brand in Seattle, the Midwest has its own example of bicycle chic.

Chicago, a proclaimed "sustainable city," according to former Mayor Richard M. Daley, has redefined itself. One of the changes is the **bike station**, a city-owned facility for bicycle commuters to store their bikes, take a shower, and get the occasional repair.

The Windy City has taken both sustainability and bicycling to heart. A network of bike paths is available for the intrepid bicycler. About 7 to 10 percent of the city's employees bike to work, and the trend is growing and becoming fashionable. It has been so successful that other midwestern cities (Cleveland and Louisville) are also considering biking. Albuquerque, Washington, D.C., and Boulder have adopted bike lanes and bike stations. Universities across America are also bike friendly. Biking has grown to the extent that a small part of one of the federal bailouts of 2009 included a biking subsidy.

As of January 1, 2009, the Bicycle Commuter Act, which promotes bicycling and reduces fossil fuel use, allows companies to give bikers $20 monthly while deducting the same amount from the company federal taxes.

---

* Allison Krueger in Kevin Helliker, "Cycling Commute Gets Chic," *Chicago Sun Times*, May 16, 2006.
† David Colman, "Riding the It Factor," *New York Times*, April 15, 2009.
‡ Colman, "Riding the It Factor."

TABLE 13.5. The Shrinking of Detroit

	1950	2000	2010
Detroit	1,849,668	951,270	713,777

Sources: U.S. Census; *Detroit Free Press*

PHOTO 13.6. Eight Mile Road, Detroit, Michigan. The Birwood Wall was built in the 1940s near 8 Mile Road. The Federal Housing Administration (FHA) told a white developer that financing was unavailable for a white development in an area where blacks lived, unless his development separated the races. The developer built the six-foot-high, half-mile-long concrete wall and received his financing. The mural was painted in 2006, to help erase the ugly memory of racism.

PHOTO 13.7. St. Anthony Falls, Minneapolis, Minnesota. The head of navigation for the Mississippi River, St. Anthony Falls was also the site of numerous Minneapolis flour mills.

when industry boomed and many immigrants moved into the city. Cleveland grew due to navigational access to the interior and flat and buildable land near the Erie shore.

The city's mélange of ethnicities included German, Irish, Polish, Italian, and Hungarian immigrants; they settled in separate neighborhoods, but all worked in the industrial city at the foundries, port, or textile mills. However, similar to other midwestern cities, Cleveland's manufacturing base suffered an economic collapse in the late twentieth century and lost more than half its manufacturing jobs. This has resulted in a decline in population.

Today, Cleveland's economy is based on health/medicine, science/engineering, biotechnology, manufacturing, and education. Twelve Fortune 500 companies are headquartered in the greater Cleveland area. Cleveland invested billions of dollars revitalizing its downtown in the 1980s and 1990s, including public space and tourism attractions such as the Rock and Roll Hall of Fame. However, Cleveland has also invested in a major sustainable project, the EcoCity.

Cleveland has continued to lose population during the past decade. It lost 17.1 percent of its population between 2000 and 2010 but is pinning its hopes on moving toward a more sustainable city mode to improve its economic future.

Midwest Sustainable-Green City: Blue Lake   EcoCity Cleveland was built from the bottom up in a redevelopment zone. Ten rundown homes were replaced with higher-density, state-of-the-art, energy- and resource-efficient townhomes. The site selection for the **urban village** project was steered by a preexisting local rail station, but as plans progressed, the station announced it would be closing. Following a storm of protest, the station was redeveloped as a "vintage sustainable

neighborhood station." Since the completion of the first part of the project, plans are to extend it into artist's lofts and cohousing. Other projects include decreasing dependence on cars, more bicycling, and encouraging a healthy economy that includes triple-bottom-line accountability.

The EcoCity is not the first foray into sustainable projects in Cleveland. Shaker Square, a 1929-built coordination of public transport, community development, and private investment, became one of the first transit-oriented developments (TODs) in the nation, containing a mixed-use and walkable environment centered on public transportation light rail and buses.

Economy

Primary Industry and Natural Resources

Midwestern agricultural production has been a key component of the national economy. However, increased reliance on fossil fuels and larger monoculture enterprises have created an unsustainable agricultural industry.

Agriculture

The Midwest was large and varied enough to be both the U.S. center of agricultural production and the home to its industrial expansion. While industry concentrated and thrived at river and lake ports, the interior areas were quintessential family farms with a reasonable growing season, ample precipitation, and markets for dairy and agricultural products.

The midwestern agricultural landscape has evolved from forests to late-twentieth-century monoculture. When Europeans settled the forested midwestern Till Plain, farmers felled trees and removed stumps before they could cultivate the land.

They transformed the forest into productive cropland. Over the past half century, farms have grown larger, farmers fewer and older, and crops and livestock have shifted geographically. Farming is no longer about country living but rather about big business, razor-thin profit margins, and subsidies. Farming is a lifestyle that many prefer, but the economic circumstances are such now that few young farmers remain, leaving an aging and dwindling farming population.

The Midwest Farm Operation   Few Americans are farmers today. The high cost of farming and its low returns have contributed to a rural decline, while unstable weather and changing climatic conditions have increased farming risks.

Technologic improvements have increased output but support fewer farmers. In the 1960s, the Green Revolution increased crop production but also raised dependence on fossil fuel–based fertilizers and chemicals, which increased water pollution.

The Green Revolution and **genetically modified organism (GMO)** seed modifications achieved short-term success feeding the growing world population; however, both systems have unanswered questions about sustainability. Unsustainable use of aquifer water and the development of high-yield crops have shifted food growth from a system based on natural manures and fertilizers to one based on fossil fuels.

The Agricultural Past   Traditional agricultural production in the United States has been based on a cash market economy. Only the earliest settlers were subsistence farmers. Midwestern farmers transported their crops to eastern urban markets via muddy roads over the Appalachians, such as the National Road, or down the Mississippi River to New Orleans. Both were expensive and unprofitable modes of transport. Farmers needed a more efficient system to transport their goods to market, which was answered in 1825 by the Erie Canal.

Midwestern farms developed in relation to the landscape, precipitation, and growing season and were more sustainable than the current chemically altered, fossil fuel-dependent crops. The Midwest adopted a three-year crop rotation anchored by corn, along with small grain, hay, and livestock. Each rotation completed a nutrient cycle that was healthy for the land, and was therefore sustainable, but rotation is no longer practiced.

Nineteenth-century farmers realized that the Till Plains landscape grew the best corn and that other locations were better suited for dairy or wheat. Dairy replaced grains in sections of Wisconsin, Minnesota, and portions of Ohio and Michigan because weather and growing season limited the corn crop. The shift from grain to dairy proved advantageous, as nearby population centers were a ready market for milk, a perishable commodity. In some areas, notably Wisconsin, much of the milk was converted to inherently more stable cheese products.

Wheat production was best in areas where precipitation was insufficient for corn production. Minneapolis used its Mississippi River waterpower at St. Anthony Falls to provide energy to operate flour mills. and by 1870 the growing railroad network improved distribution (Photo 13.8).

Mixed farming on a few hundred acres was typical through the early twentieth century. However, in the 1950s production mechanized, yields increased, crops specialized, and monocultures became the dominant form of agricultural production. Traditional value-added methods of raising and feeding corn to livestock were abandoned. Most farmers now concentrate on either a crop or livestock.

In the 1980s, grain embargoes, drought, and overproduction depressed crop prices, causing agricultural assets and income to decline. Many farmers declared bankruptcy; farms were foreclosed. The number of farms in the United States declined, while their relative size increased, from 213 acres in 1950 to 441 acres in 2002. Canadian farms have followed a similar pattern.

The Agricultural Present   The **family farm** has been a staple of American food production. In 1900, about half of Americans were farmers, but by 2000 family farmers accounted for less than 2 percent of the population. According to the 2008 Agricultural Census, 90 percent of all farms were considered family farms. However, the story is more complex than what the graph indicates (Chart 13.1). The idea of the seemingly dominant family farm is deceptive for three basic reasons:

- The average age of the family farmer is now over sixty. Few farmers want their children to farm, and even fewer children want to farm. As a result, the demographics of the family farm are very likely to change in the future.
- While family farms still own the farmland, most crops and livestock are now contract farmed. Corporations own the crop or livestock, and family farmers use their land and labor to satisfy corporate interests. The farmer will not have a market unless crops are grown to corporate specifications and livestock raised in a uniform and consistent manner to satisfy mechanized processing guidelines. Consolidation of both buyers and suppliers leaves farmers with few options other than to sell to vertically integrated agribusiness corporations.
- Increasingly, farmers are "retiring" by leasing their land to other farmers ("get big or get out"); if they are near a city they sell their land to developers, or they simply sell and move. The 86.5 percent small family farms receive about 74 percent of government subsidies, the 8 percent large family farm partnerships receive 13 percent of all subsidies, and the 4.4 percent corporate farms receive 11 percent of subsidies.[17]

Many remaining farmers and a new group of young and sustainably oriented farmers have established niche markets that turn their back on agribusiness and embrace healthier and

PHOTO 13.8. Flour Mill, Minneapolis, Minnesota. Wheat grown in the Midwest and the Dakotas came to Minneapolis for milling after 1860. By 1880, the city was the site of numerous mills, but by the 1930s, three major mills (Pillsbury, General, and Standard) controlled national flour production. In 2003, the last of the flour mills closed. Many have fallen to ruin.

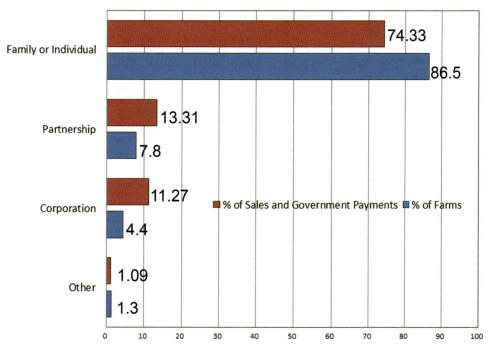

■ % of Sales and Government Payments ■ % of Farms

"Other" includes cooperative, estate or trust, institutional, etc.

CHART 13.1. Farm Organization Types. Ninety percent of farms are still owned by families, but subsidies and sales are increasingly corporate.

BOX 13.6 GENETICALLY MODIFIED ORGANISMS (GMOs)

A genetically modified plant is altered by inserting specific genes into an unrelated species. The benefits of GMO transgenic plants are a longer shelf life and resistance to a variety of factors, such as insects, disease, or herbicides. The development of GMOs is aligned with the globalized transport of food. The average food in the United States travels about fifteen hundred miles from field to table, which uses more fossil fuel calories than the food delivers. Goals of GMO food follow the cultural zeitgeist: it must look good, be profitable, and have a long shelf life. Taste is sacrificed for shelf life and profit.

The major monoculture crops have been altered genetically, and GMO crop acreage has expanded rapidly, with 4.3 million acres grown in 1996, and over 153 million acres in 2011 (Table 13.6). The United States grows 50 percent (2011) of global GMO crops, and it continues to lead the world in absolute increase and range of GMO crops.

Genetically modified crops (GMOs) are favored by most farmers because of:

- The saved labor costs
- Plant disease resistance
- Insect resistance

But GMOs are controversial because:

- The ecological consequences of spraying have unintended results, such as superweeds and gene transfer.
- Yields have not increased substantially.
- They have harmed soil productivity.
- There are health consequences, including allergic reactions and diminishing antibiotic efficacy.

GMO food is a controversial subject. GMO crops may improve farmer profit and ease world food shortages, but on the other hand, GMO crops may contaminate traditional or organic crops and cause unwarranted risk to humans, animals, or the environment. In the European Union, genetically modified food has been rejected for human consumption, though in 2005, the EU changed two of its former stances, allowing GMO corn for animal feed and implementing a risk assessment program to study the effects of GMOs. The slow acceptance of GMO crops by the EU has slowed exports of U.S. crops.

TABLE 13.6. GMO Crops Grown in the United States, 2011

Food	Modification	Percentage of total U.S. crop
Soybeans	Herbicide resistant	94
Corn	New genes Bt bacterium added	88
Cotton (cottonseed oil)	Bt protein gene added	90
Rapeseed (canola)	New genes added	90
Sugar beets	Herbicide resistant	95

Sources: http://www.ers.usda.gov/data/biotechcrops/adoption.htm; http://www.ncbi.nlm.nih.gov/pmc/articles/PMC3187797/; http://www.ncbi.nlm.nih.gov/pmc/articles/PMC2910966/

sustainable food systems. Included with the niche markets are farmers who raise organic, grass-fed cows and organic and local dairies. Other farmers have established **community-supported agriculture (CSAs)** featuring local-farm-to-resident produce throughout the growing season. CSAs are most popular in the Midwest and along the eastern seaboard.

Traditional agriculture relied on crop rotation that reduced diseases, weeds, and pests while it replenished soil. In the second half of the twentieth century, genetic improvements increased crop yields for short periods of time, but they also increased the cost of production. Growing high-yield corn now depends on petrochemical feedstock and depletes usable water. Using fossil fuels and petrochemical feedstock has been a short-term, cheap way to maximize grains and livestock yields. The

long-term costs—lower food value, environmental damage, and social inequity—have been excluded in the pricing of food.

As the price of oil increases, however, so do the prices of oil products and subsequently food. Yields in organic or traditional crops cannot match petrochemical crop yields, but organic systems are better for the soil, the crops, and the water table.[18] Traditional and organic systems are far more sustainable methods of farming, more nutritious, and use renewable resources. Fossil fuel–dependent methods are less expensive in the short term, but they destroy the soil and therefore decrease crop yields. Sustainable methods are more expensive in the short term, but they create long-term viability for crop production. One of the major reasons that current short-term production methods are pursued, though, is because of the growing population.

BOX 13.7 THE IMPACT OF THE ERIE CANAL

Transportation methods shifted when the Erie Canal was completed in 1825 and the American canal craze began. The Erie Canal followed the Mohawk Valley along the southern shore of Lake Ontario, thereby connecting New York City and the Midwest (Map 13.4). The canal followed the lowest trans-Appalachian route between the St. Lawrence River and Atlanta along the glacially formed valleys between Buffalo and the Hudson River, and then continued on to New York City. The canal cut transport time, and it also cut transportation costs by 90 percent.

By today's standards, the Erie Canal is surprisingly narrow (Photo 13.9). Mules pulled barges filled with passengers into the region and brought coal, crops, and furs out. The Erie Canal proved successful economically, and it also demonstrated to many European doubters that the United States was a country capable of major engineering feats.

Canals were at the time the most economical transportation method, connecting farmers to the Great Lakes or the Ohio River. For example, the frontier state of Ohio was settled throughout the period of the canal craze. More than a thousand miles of canals were built to the Ohio River or Lake Erie, which allowed farmers' agricultural goods easy access to markets.

When railroads became viable in the 1850s, canal traffic slowed and then halted. Today, bikeways and hiking trails line

PHOTO 13.9. The Erie Canal began in Rome, New York, and continued the first ninety-eight miles to Syracuse along level land that required no locks. The canal is forty feet wide and four feet deep.

many canal routes. However, the Erie Canal has recently been rehabilitated and is now a state barge canal with moderate traffic; it experienced a surge of traffic during the oil price increases of 2008.

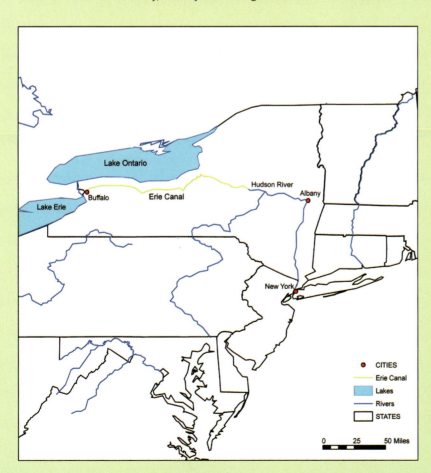

MAP 13.4. The Erie Canal, New York. Following the natural lowlands through the Hudson and Mohawk Valleys, the canal was hugely successful, cutting the cost of shipping farmers' goods by 90 percent and starting a canal phase of U.S. transportation from 1825 to 1850.

Population has continued to grow along with dependence on fossil fuels. One way to break the dependence has been to create biofuels. The growing American dependence on corn-based biofuels has been popular with farmers because it has more than doubled the price they receive for corn, and it is a possible way to be less fossil fuel–based.

Biofuels

Biofuels are produced from renewable sources. Food crop biofuels, especially corn, have been most prevalent in the United States. Using corn for biofuels has interrupted worldwide food supplies and raised prices since 2007. Food makers and livestock producers have scrutinized corn subsidies for **ethanol**, a renewable, high-octane grain alcohol that has led to huge price increases for corn.

Unstable fossil fuel prices have increased interest in alternative fuels. Sugarcane has been the primary source of fuel in Brazil, the largest producer of ethanol in the world, but corn is currently the dominant crop for bioethanol in the United States. However, there is continued controversy regarding the energy efficiency of corn ethanol plants. Reports vary about efficiency. Many U.S. agricultural specialists believe that corn is an inefficient biofuel crop and favor cellulose-based ethanol; other reports indicate a continued rise in efficiency of corn-based ethanol.

Ethanol is meant to reduce U.S. dependency on foreign oil and decrease harmful emissions; however, controversy rages over mandated usage and subsidies. For example, many critics believe that subsidized ethanol production is nothing more than an agribusiness subsidy; Archer Daniels Midland, a heavily subsidized agribusiness giant, produces about 40 percent of U.S. ethanol. Ethanol subsidies have come under increased scrutiny, especially since fuel blenders are required by law to purchase the fuel.

Another controversy revolves around fossil fuel consumption in the ethanol-making process. Some believe that the amount of fossil fuels used in making ethanol is higher than the quantity of ethanol it produces. Many researchers question whether using coal-powered electricity to produce ethanol actually cuts fuel consumption or pollution at all. The sustainability of ethanol production is also being questioned in regard to land use, water consumption, refining methods, and the fuel used for production. Many scientists question whether ethanol, touted as saving 15 percent in carbon dioxide emissions, is saving anything at all. For example, corn is raised using many fossil fuel–based fertilizers and fossil fuel–pumped irrigation water. The carbon footprint of raising corn and converting it to ethanol may well be more than gas tank savings. Additional concerns are the return of some environmentally sensitive lands, such as in the Conservation Reserve Programs (CRP), to crop production to grow corn for ethanol production.

Finally, food prices inflated in 2007 as a result of (1) the diversion created by corn-to-ethanol production and (2) the increased cost of oil. The overproduction of corn for ethanol, and the decrease of corn for food, nearly tripled the cost of corn and carried over and affected the production and cost of other crops. The prices of wheat, rice, and other grains increased within the United States and throughout the world in 2008 and continued into 2011.

Department of Energy incentives have set a 10 percent goal for transportation biofuels by 2020, and additional biofuels will supply industrial and utility power demands. Much of this production will be in the Midwest, where biomass crops are grown and refined.

Agricultural Production and Livestock

Corn The midwestern physical environment, known as the Corn Belt since 1850, is ideal for corn. In 2007, eight of the top ten areas for corn production in the United States were in midwestern states: (1) Iowa, (2) Illinois, (3) Nebraska, (4) Minnesota, (5) Indiana, (6) South Dakota, (7) Wisconsin, (8) Ohio (Map 13.5). The United States alone produces almost half of the world's corn. The high prices for corn (due to ethanol regulations) have elevated corn acreage since 2007.

The Corn Belt also contributes to livestock production. Livestock consume about 60 percent of cultivated corn. Historically, farmers favored either corn or livestock, depending on which had the better market price. If the market for corn was low, it was fed to the livestock to add value. This value-added relationship changed in the late twentieth century, when most farmers chose to specialize in either corn production or livestock, and changed again in the twenty-first century when much of the corn crop went into biofuel production.

Soybeans The Soybean Belt overlaps the Corn Belt. However, corn spread east to west while soybean growth trends in a north-south direction, predominantly along the Mississippi and Red River valleys. The number one county for both corn and soy is McLean in central Illinois.

In the late twentieth century, soybeans bypassed corn production in volume and were second only to corn in value (Map 13.6). The United States now produces half of the world's soybeans, while China produces about one-tenth of the total harvest. The United States is the leading exporter of soybeans, and China imports much of the U.S. soybean crop.

Soybeans, an inexpensive form of protein, contribute to animal diets and are an ingredient in many processed foods. Less than 10 percent is used in the manner many Americans think of soy: as tofu or soy sauce.

Soy is controversial because 89 percent of all soy in the United States is genetically modified and is known amongst farmers as Roundup-ready soy—able to withstand regular doses of the herbicide Roundup, which kills weeds. Prolonged use of Roundup decreases the effectiveness of glyphosate, the active chemical in Roundup, which is highly toxic to plants and fish. The almost exclusive use of genetically modified soy and its rapid adoption (since 1996) could decrease long-term crop yields and decrease the effectiveness of the herbicide.

Fruits and Vegetables Fruits and vegetables are not among the top five midwestern crops, but significant amounts are

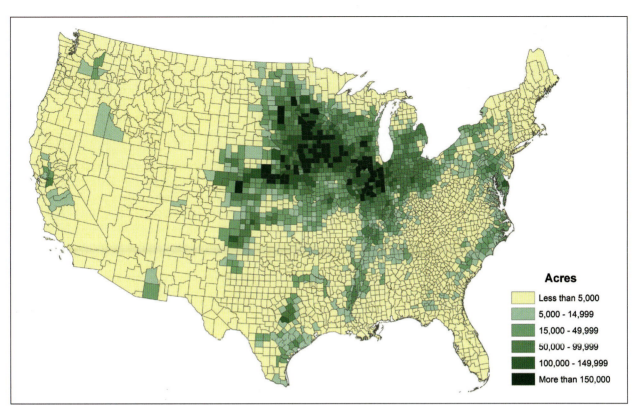

Acres

Less than 5,000
5,000 - 14,999
15,000 - 49,999
50,000 - 99,999
100,000 - 149,999
More than 150,000

MAP 13.5. Corn for Grain, Harvested Acres, 2002. Corn is still the most important crop in the Central Lowlands, but it has become increasingly important where the Ogallala Aquifer irrigates the fields. The water table for the Ogallala Aquifer has been dropping, partly because of growing crops, such as corn, that require much more water than the local climate provides.

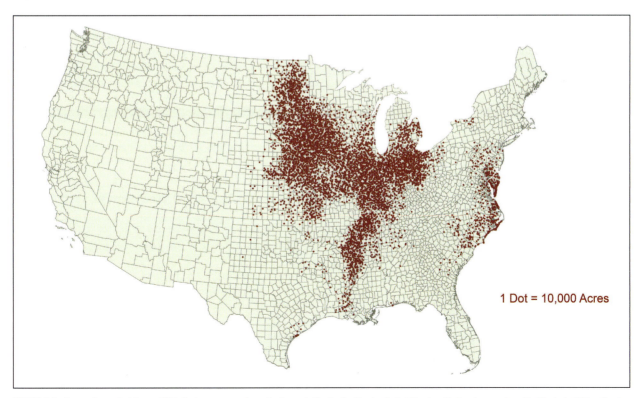

1 Dot = 10,000 Acres

MAP 13.6. Soybeans, Harvested Acres, 2002. Soybeans are an important crop in the Central Lowlands, but they tend to trend more along the Mississippi River flood-plain than the corn crop.

concentrated along the lake effect edges of northern Ohio and in Michigan's Lower Peninsula. These tender crops require a more exacting climate, with minimum frost danger in late spring or early fall. Westerly winds moderate the Great Lakes shoreline climate, making it conducive to fruit production. Apples, cherries, and wineries thrive along the eastern Lake Michigan shore. Other Great Lakes leeward shores share a similar effect, illustrated by the recent increase in wineries along Lake Erie's shoreline.

Livestock   Traditionally, Corn Belt feed grains fattened midwestern livestock; however, a shift in feed grain production areas has affected livestock production and processing. Today, irrigated corn is raised in areas lacking sufficient precipitation, although methods are short term and have evolved unsustainably. Livestock production, especially hogs, has also shifted from traditional midwestern bases into the South and Great Plains. Limited corn production in these areas has increased transport costs for corn.

Beef. Midwestern cattle production thrives where row crops are less productive. Only one midwestern state, Iowa, remains among the top ten (number six) beef producers in America.

Midwestern feedlots were common during the late nineteenth and early twentieth centuries, when slaughterhouses were located in Chicago and St. Louis. However, as slaughterhouses moved to the High Plains, feedlots moved closer to the slaughterhouses. Cattle are still fattened on a corn mixture prior to slaughter, but instead of cattle being shipped from the plains to the corn-producing states, the grain is now grown or shipped to the High Plains, where cattle are raised, finished, and slaughtered.

Most midwestern areas now have ranchers growing grass-fed beef that service those who support locavore foods. Grass-fed beef is raised without corn finishing, hormones, or antibiotics. Grass-fed beef has less total fat and more omega-3 fatty acids.

Dairy Belt. Dairying is one of the top agricultural commodities in seven midwestern states and is Michigan and

Wisconsin's number one commodity (Table 13.7). Dairy provides about half of the agricultural sales in Wisconsin.

Dairy was the center of Wisconsin's family farm until large corporate dairies developed in the late twentieth century. California became the number one milk producer in 1993. Wisconsin remains the nation's leader in cheese production.

In order to compete with California and other new dairy regions, Wisconsin and other midwestern dairies must identify and maintain niche markets, or multiply their herds by ten, matching California's seven-hundred-cow average size. Due to location, resources, and transportation, Wisconsin may not regain its previous market position. The expense of upgrading infrastructure is prohibitive, but between 2000 and 2006, 10 percent more dairy farmers in Wisconsin had more than 499 head. By 2006, 51.6 percent of all national dairies had more than 499 head of cattle, up from 35.8 percent in 2000.[19] The slowing domestic economy caused milk production and exports to slow after 2008.

Some midwestern farmers have identified niche markets such as the artisan cheese market. Most niche diaries belong to cooperatives, which allow them protection in numbers and cut costs. Niche markets focus on the higher-quality milk required by cheese producers. Jersey cows, for example, produce less quantity, but offer higher butterfat and protein content. Niche markets also avoid hormones and graze their cows longer, resulting in a subtle, more natural flavor. Many niche dairies are organic, and most are family run. Eighty five percent of Wisconsin milk is converted to more than three hundred cheese varieties, many of which are niche market specialty cheeses.

New dairy facilities have moved into the Midwest. Most are in Ohio and southern Michigan, and they are usually financed and built by immigrant Dutch farmers, who seek more opportunity than the Netherlands can offer. These new farms are large CAFOs using the most recent technology. Many residents living near CAFOs fight to eliminate the pollution, odor, and traffic inherent in the CAFO operations.

Hogs. Hogs are the perfect match for Iowa, a corn-producing state. Hogs are an efficient and quick converter of corn to meat. A hog grows from 1 to 250 pounds in six months. Until the

TABLE 13.7. Significance of Dairy Products: Lake States, California, United States, 2007

	Number of operations	Number of farms with 500+ head	State rank	Average number of cows (000)	Annual milk production per cow
California	2,200	1,100	1	1,813	22,440
Wisconsin	14,200	280	2	1,247	19,310
Minnesota	5,100	90	6	460	18,817
Michigan	2,700	115	8	335	22,761
United States	69,995	3,320		9,189	20,447

Source: National Agricultural Statistics Service, at http://www.nass.usda.gov

1980s, Iowa and other midwestern states dominated the traditional hog farm industry, raising 80 percent of commercial hog farms, but in 2007 the top midwestern states (IA, IL, IN, MN) produced 52 percent of all hogs (Table 13.8). Although Iowa remains the number one producer of hogs, the top three counties for hog production are now in the CAFO-reliant states of North Carolina and Oklahoma.

Vertically integrated corporations now own and contract most of the nation's pork (Map 13.7). Hogs are raised in CAFOs, where a thousand hogs are raised in each concrete-slatted, metal CAFO barn. In 2011, 45 percent of all contracted hogs were in operations with more than five thousand hogs. In the hog industry, this is succinctly described as "from birth to bacon" or "from conception to consumption."

Profitable CAFOs practice economies of scale and rely on hormones, antibiotics, and pesticides. CAFOs cause aquifer depletion, reduction of genetic diversity, air and water pollution, and have augmented human antibiotic resistance despite numerous reports urging a limitation of routine antibiotic use in the United States because of antibiotic-resistant strains developing in humans.[20] The unsustainable CAFO system currently produces the overwhelming majority of meat, at a tremendous environmental and social cost.

Chickens. Chicken broiler production is limited in the Midwest; however, layer hens and egg production are important. In 2010, Iowa, Ohio, and Pennsylvania were the nation's top three egg-producing states.[21]

Egg production has also changed. Chickens roaming and pecking in the yard have been replaced by commercial caged-egg production systems with more than 335 million laying hens producing over 6.51 billion eggs per year (2010). Seventy-five companies each have more than one million layers. More than 80 percent of all layers are in flocks of more than thirty thousand layers. Iowa capitalizes on its position as number one in soybeans by feeding the soy meal to chickens, thereby directly adding value to their crops.

Mineral Resources

Most minerals discussed in this chapter are actually a part of the Canadian Shield area in location, but their importance and relations are more midwestern. A floristic tension zone (Map 13.8) runs through central Michigan, Wisconsin, and Minnesota, dividing the agricultural land to the south and where many deciduous trees reach their northern limits, creating a transition to the boreal forest in the north. Most of the midwestern minerals are located within this transitional region.

The natural resources needed for the Industrial Revolution were abundant in the north central region that used the Great Lakes corridor to transport resources between its cities. Copper and iron ore were from the Canadian Shield. The resources later contributed to industrial production in cities bordering the lakes, including Chicago, Gary, Duluth, Detroit, Toledo, and Cleveland in the United States, and Toronto and Hamilton in Ontario, Canada.

The Midwest also has significant and locally important mineral deposits; among the more important of these are limestone and salt.

Copper   Michigan's Upper Peninsula provided the United States with the copper necessary to conduct the entire nation's

TABLE 13.8. Hog Inventory Rank in Top-Ranked States, 1987–2007

	1987	1992	1997	2002	2007
Iowa	1	1	1	1	1
North Carolina	7	3	2	2	2
Minnesota	4	4	3	3	3
Illinois	2	2	4	4	4
Indiana	3	5	5	5	5
Missouri	6	7	6	6	7
Nebraska	5	6	7	7	6
Oklahoma	—	24	9	8	8
Kansas	10	10	10	9	10
Ohio	8	9	8	10	9

Source: http://usda01.library.cornell.edu/usda/nass/SB986/sb1020.txt

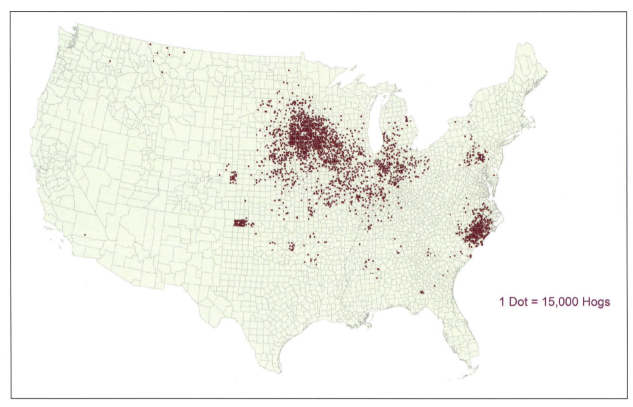

MAP 13.7. Hogs and Pigs, 2002. The relationship of corn and hogs has made Iowa and the Midwest the traditional main hog-producing states, but the Midwest resisted corporate CAFO production methods, and hog production and inventory grew in other regions.

1 Dot = 15,000 Hogs

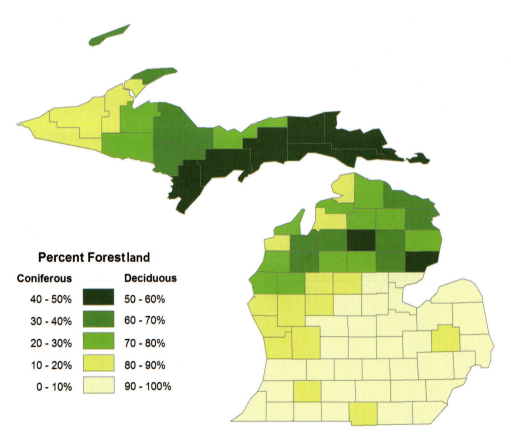

Percent Forestland

Coniferous	Deciduous
40 - 50%	50 - 60%
30 - 40%	60 - 70%
20 - 30%	70 - 80%
10 - 20%	80 - 90%
0 - 10%	90 - 100%

MAP 13.8. Predominant Forest Types, Michigan. Southern and up-north Michigan have different vegetation zones, separated by the floristic tension zone. The zones are differentiated by climate and soils. The southern heavy glacial soils are characterized by deciduous forest. These soils are supportive of agriculture. The northern zone has sandy, acidic soils and supports a mixed forest, which includes coniferous softwoods and can be considered a transition to the boreal forest farther north. These soils usually are not good agricultural soils.

electricity. Upper Peninsula copper mines produced more than thirteen billion pounds of pure native copper from 1846 to the 1900s, when Butte, Montana, mines became the dominant source. Keweenaw copper became less accessible as the underground mines grew deeper. However, the copper mined was so pure that it needed little or no refining, which contrasts sharply with today's low-grade Intermontane ores.

Copper explorations continue in Michigan. In late 2007, Kennecott proposed opening a copper and nickel mine in Michigan's Upper Peninsula. It is scheduled to begin operations in 2013. While the mine may reinvigorate a sluggish economy and provide jobs, it could also cause significant air and groundwater pollution, which Kennecott recognizes and is working to keep at a minimum.

Iron   Iron ore (hematite) from Lake Superior mines built the industrial core of the United States. From 1840 to 1887, Michigan's western Upper Peninsula was the main source, and from 1887 into the twentieth century, northern Minnesota's Mesabi Range boomed.

Minnesota and Michigan's Upper Peninsula iron ranges expose the iron ore through erosion, although some iron has been mined underground or in open pits.

By the 1950s, the highest-quality iron ore had been removed from the mines, necessitating new mining techniques, such as grinding rock and removing taconite iron to form pellets. Declining mining prices in the mid-1970s slowed production. At one time, six mines operated; today only Mesabi and Marquette Range open pits are operating, and the towns of Hibbing, Minnesota, and Ishpeming, Michigan, remain involved in the industry, although they have diversified into logging, pulpwood, and tourism. Today the United States produces about 5 percent of world iron ore and is the seventh-largest producer. The largest and also most actively growing producer is China.

Limestone   Eighty percent of the U.S. limestone for buildings has been quarried from the Bedford-Bloomington area of south central Indiana. This buff-and-gray-colored limestone is fine-grained and easily sawn; however, competition from other, less expensive building materials has dampened demand. In the nineteenth century, many churches, city halls, office buildings (the Empire State Building), and federal buildings used Indiana limestone. Postmodern buildings in the late twentieth and early twenty-first centuries, such as the Holocaust Museum in Washington, used limestone in their construction.

Dolomite (magnesium-rich limestone) was prevalent and exposed in Michigan along the northern shores of Lakes Huron and Michigan. It is used for chemicals, steel making (as a flux), and to refine beet sugar. Rogers City, Michigan, contains the largest limestone quarry and processing plant in the world.

Salt   The importance of salt licks in relation to settlement has been lost in our era of easily available salt, but historically, salt determined many settlement sites. Salt licks provided an important nutritional ingredient for the sequence of buffalo, Native American, and western settlement. Game proliferated near the licks, and the salt was used to preserve beef jerky and salt pork, which was a source of fat for the pioneer diet.

The remains of an evaporated sea lie beneath Michigan and the province of Ontario. Michigan leads the states in salt production. The two forms of salt are brine (water saturated with salt) and rock salt, used for melting snow or refined for table salt. Rock salt mines are located twelve hundred feet below the city of Detroit. The mines have been operating most of the twentieth century, except for a shutdown in 1983, the victim of falling prices. The mines reopened in 1989 as the Detroit Salt Company.

Brine   Brines, heavy accumulations of salt deposited from ancient seas, were the basis for developing the Midland, Michigan, chemical industry. In 1891, chemist Herbert Henry Dow discovered a way to extract chemicals from the brine, and Dow Chemical was born. The first chemical made was potassium bromide, used in photography, followed by chlorine, which was made into bleach.

Dow has created a profusion of toxic organochlorine products and toxic waste dump Superfund sites, many of which have been cleaned, while other cleanups, such as the Tittabawassee River, have been negotiated for more than thirty years. While continuing a legacy of pollution, the company has won awards for energy efficiency.

Coal   The major coal-mining regions remain the Powder River Basin of Wyoming and the Appalachian states, but the Midwest has about 15 percent of the nation's high-sulfur bituminous coal deposits, mostly in the Illinois Basin encompassing northern Kentucky, Indiana, and Illinois. Regional coal was important in local industrial development, mostly because of its location to midwestern industry. Its sulfur content is far more than either Appalachian or Powder River Basin coal, and therefore production is limited by Clean Air Act standards.

Industry and Postindustrial

Midwestern waterways were at the heart of the Industrial Revolution, during the mid- to late nineteenth century. Cheap land, raw materials, low taxes, good water, rail connections, and a hardworking and unionized labor force drove the economy. The Midwest remains a stronghold of union authority, especially in manufacturing (Map 13.9). The cities are proud of the industrial grit that made this region famous the world over; however, since globalization, regional manufacturing jobs have evaporated, leaving many without secure incomes. The unions have been forced to adjust their contracts due to the 2008 recession. However, the Midwest still needs to reanalyze its position in the postindustrial and coming economies.

During the first half of the twentieth century, Chicago and Detroit were the nation's fastest-growing cities, both in population and industry. Great Lakes natural resources fed Chicago's sprawling steel industry along its southern shore, and spread into nearby cities like Gary, Indiana. Iron ore from Minnesota and coal from West Virginia were fashioned into steel and

BOX 13.8 COAL-BURNING POWER PLANTS AND INDUSTRIAL AIR POLLUTANTS

Midwestern industry grew when environmental pollution was not legally recognized as a health risk, and the results—Dickensian dirty cities, disease, respiratory disorders—were considered a part of life, especially for the urban poor. Today, technology is capable of cleaning up the pollutants, but the cost and the lack of political will have halted progress and placed the burden on consumer health, but without a national health care system.

Unintended Consequences

The Midwest was once the heart of industrial America at a time when there were no environmental regulations. Some industries still spew pollutants and toxic chemicals, and the Midwest continues to drown in gaseous toxins and pollutants from industrial waste. Many of the responsible industries continue: metal casting—melting and casting metal into objects, such as automobile frames and parts and plumbing (industrial waste, air emissions, wastewater discharges, and solid waste) and the steel industry (water pollution, industrial waste, heavy metal dust pollution causing respiratory illness, CO_2 emissions). Minimization of pollutants has been enacted, largely by the Environmental Protection Agency (EPA), but has suffered setbacks in enforcement. For example, air pollution regulatory control has increased, but control systems capture only some of the gases, and many control regulations have been overturned in favor of increased production. One of the continuing major polluters is coal-burning power plants, the source of about half of the nation's electric power and source of several pollutants responsible for acid rain, respiratory illness, and contributing to climate change.

Several coal-burning plant pollutants—sulfur dioxide, nitrogen oxide, carbon dioxide, and mercury are a few—damage the environment and health. Sulfur dioxide is the major ingredient in acid rain. Nitrogen oxide is a major ingredient in smog and causes respiratory problems, lessens visibility, deteriorates water with overfertilization causing algae blooms, and contributes to acid rain and climate change. Carbon dioxide is the primary climate change pollutant, not because of its intensity but because there is so much emitted. Mercury particulates from power plants enter water and the food chain, causing learning disabilities and neurological damage, especially to fetuses and children. Mercury bioaccumulates in the food chain, so larger species such as humans get

larger doses. Adults may not get sick for years, but babies and small children can be affected quickly. There are ways of lessening the intake of mercury. In Michigan, for example, pregnant women and children may avoid mercury poisoning by eating very limited amounts of fish from the local waterways and the Great Lakes.

Regional and Ecoregional Impacts

Midwestern air, water, and land pollution are a legacy of the industrial period. Some contaminated areas have been cleaned up and laws changed, but many industries and plants were grandfathered in and continue to pollute. There is movement, though, for reducing coal-burning power plant emissions.

The Midwest depends on coal-burning power plants for much of its electricity. Power plants are one of the largest emitters of greenhouse gases (GHGs) in America, because many coal-burning plants are not required to meet current emission standards and pollute the local region and the entire Northeast quadrant.

Midwest power plant pollution is unevenly distributed. The largest midwestern environmental polluters are Ohio, Indiana, Illinois, and Michigan, all within the top twenty toxic polluters in the nation (Table 13.9). All four of these states are also ranked in the top eleven nationally for energy consumption and in the top ten for coal usage (Table 13.10). Ohio power plants are the number one producer of sulfur dioxide and nitrogen oxide and the number two producer of carbon monoxide. One of the worst polluters on the Ohio River is the General Gavin power plant next to the former town of Cheshire (Photo 13.10).

External Costs

The external costs of heavy industry continue to mount, even though many of the industries are now gone. While studies take stock of the environmental damage from industry and coal-burning power plants, a lack of political will has stymied corrections. Following are a few examples:

- Emissions from coal-burning power plants include sulfur dioxide (SO_2), nitrogen oxide (NO_x), carbon dioxide (CO_2), and mercury. Between 14,000 and 26,000 premature deaths are caused annually by emissions, as well as 38,000 nonfatal heart attacks and respiratory problems, such as asthma.

TABLE 13.9. National Rankings of the Top Four Polluting Midwestern States

	Ohio	Indiana	Illinois	Michigan
Total environmental pollution	5	9	16	20
Air pollution	1	8	14	15
Water pollution	10	2	11	35
Energy consumption	5	11	7	9
Coal consumption	4	1	6	9

Source: Energy Information Administration, at http://www.scorecard.org

TABLE 13.10. Coal-Burning Power Plants

	Sulfur dioxide	Nitrogen oxide	Carbon dioxide	Mercury
% Industry emissions	97	92	86	100
% National emissions	67	23	40	41

Source: Environmental Protection Agency, Clean Energy, at http://www.epa.gov/cleanenergy/energy-and-you/affect/air-emissions.html; http://www.mass.gov/dep/toxics/stypes/hgfact.doc; U.S. Energy Information; http://www.eia.gov/cneaf/electricity/page/prim2/chapter3.html
Note: Fifty-six percent of power plants are coal burning. They create these percentages of emissions for the entire industry.

PHOTO 13.10. Pollutants in Cheshire, Ohio. This town along the Ohio River was purchased by the AEP Power Company in 2002 because of pollutants from the nearby General Gavin coal-burning power plant. Inhabitants received about three times the going price of their homes if they signed a health release.

- Although air scrubbers reduce sulfuric air emissions on coal-burning power plants, they do not reduce CO_2 emissions, which contribute to climate change.
- Fine particle pollution from power plants causes thousands of deaths annually.

- Superfund was established in 1980 to clean up many of the industrial pollution sites; however, companies continually found ways to not pay for their cleanup. Those that did only participated in paying the cleanup through 1995, after which the burden was placed on the American taxpayer. Estimated cost to the taxpayer is $1 billion annually.*

Rather than clean up the environmental pollution and protect American workers, industry decided to move overseas. The result was increased industrial pollution in other countries and a loss of manufacturing jobs for the American worker.

Solutions

Midwestern states are beginning to build wind turbines, which hopefully will reduce coal burning within power plants. Near Buffalo, New York, on the shore of Lake Erie, the Lackawanna wind turbine project is juxtaposed against an old rusting Bethlehem Steel site. Minnesota has several wind turbine projects, with many more on the drawing board. In the thumb of Michigan, thirty-two wind turbines rise over sugar beet fields. Ohio is discussing the advantages of wind turbines—employment, property taxes, and clean air—and is planning several wind farms. While wind farms are not a panacea, they are indicators of the changing mindset in America.

* U.S. Public Interest Research Groups, at http://www.uspirg.org.

machinery in Chicago. Detroit boasted the economically advantageous assembly line. The genius of Henry Ford provided cars for the average family, in "any color as long as it was black!" Many cities, such as Pontiac, Ypsilanti, and Dearborn, Michigan, along with Windsor, Ontario, supplied parts for the auto industry. In Ohio, Toledo and Akron provided glass and tires for the automobiles. Most of these plants are now closed.

By the 1980s, nonunionized labor in the South and West challenged midwestern growth and stability. Foreign automobile manufacturers built plants outside of the

midwestern core. Factory shutdowns and layoffs became common midwestern occurrences into the twenty-first century. Low-cost foreign competition, shoddy workmanship, and lack of fuel-efficient American cars diminished domestic demand. This changed the regional employment pattern from well-paid union members to laid-off workers who were undereducated for the postindustrial economy. The industrial region, the Rust Belt, has been slow to reinvent or reinvest in its assembly line labor force to create one focused on education, training, and technology.

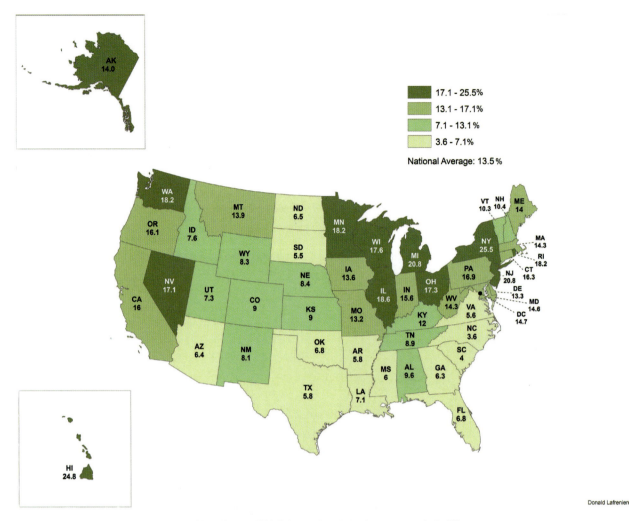

Legend
17.1 - 25.5%
13.1 - 17.1%
7.1 - 13.1%
3.6 - 7.1%

National Average: 13.5%

Donald Lafreniere

MAP 13.9. Union Membership as a Percentage of Total Workers, 2000. Union membership has been strongest in the Midwest.

Auto Industry

The midwestern auto industry grew during the first half of the twentieth century, spurred by Ford's assembly line and vertical integration methods. The industry's large size and broad scope are critical to the continued stability of the manufacturing sector.[22]

Currently the domestic automotive industry is shifting away from the upper Midwest toward the mid-south, posing a structural threat to the midwestern economy. About one in six manufacturing jobs in the Great Lakes states has been in this sector.

The auto industry was geographically concentrated in the early twentieth century; it formed an **agglomeration** in the Midwest. Detroit and Flint, Michigan, and other midwestern areas (Indianapolis: Dusenberg; Toledo: Jeep) built a new industry, and automobile suppliers agglomerated around the factories.

The heart of the old automobile industry was Detroit, "Motor City," the home to the Big Three automobile manufacturers: Ford, General Motors, and Chrysler. Fully one-sixth of the nation's jobs were related to the Detroit-based auto industry. During the first half of the twentieth century, Detroit was home to the largest factories in the world, but in 2009 the industry

suffered a long-expected meltdown. The change was evident long before but was effectively ignored by the Big Three. In the 1960s, overseas auto manufacturers began entering the U.S. market and building foreign-owned, U.S.-based plants outside of the unionized Midwest in such places as Alabama and Tennessee.

Two major reasons the Big Three lost their grip on the automobile industry are the high cost of union contract labor and poor fuel efficiency. For example, union-enforced benefits add an additional $1,500 to the cost of each car sold by the Big Three. Foreign manufacturers have eliminated labor contracts and pensions, replacing them with 401(k) retirement plans. In addition, or perhaps because of, the quality of automobiles from the United States and the continued insistence on manufacturing big cars such as the ubiquitous SUV, the domestic auto companies showed little interest in fuel economy and were late in moving from petroleum-based energy while other auto companies moved toward alternative fuels. By the end of the twentieth century, Detroit was still the Motor City, but more than half of the auto jobs were gone; GM went from 482,000 employees in 1978 to 47,330 in 2009. The city was

BOX 13.9 IOWA AND WIND

Iowa has been known for its corn and hogs, but in 2008 Iowa took advantage of its level topography, access to electric transmission lines, and wind energy potential. Iowa is now the second-largest producer of wind energy, surpassing California (Texas is first). The largest wind farms are in the northern part of the state, where winds speeds are highest.

In 2010, Iowa wind farms generated 15.4 percent of all electricity in the state, and Iowa became the first state to generate more than 10 percent of its electricity from wind power. The goal is for 50 percent of electricity to be generated from wind power. The total installed capacity in 2010 was 3675 megawatts, which is the equivalent of about 10 percent of the U.S. total, and Iowa has continued to build new wind farms since.

A number of wind power companies have established offices and manufacturing facilities in the state. For example, Siemens (the largest German engineering company) opened a large manufacturing facility in 2007 that produces wind turbine blades and employs 260 people.

---

economically devastated. In 2009 two of the Big Three companies, Chrysler and GM, declared bankruptcy; they reorganized as smaller companies.

Tourism

Midwest tourism is largely within state, such as the allegiance of people from southeastern Michigan to travel "up north." One exception to this, however, is the rise of tribal gambling.

Tribal gaming began with bingo parlors in the 1980s and escalated during the 1990s after court rulings allowed state-sanctioned legal gaming. From 1995 to 2004, revenues in the industry escalated almost 400 percent. The number of gaming establishments has risen to more than four hundred in thirty states. The operations began in Florida and California; however, the Midwest leads with 117 tribal casinos. It has made many tribes wealthy but has also caused alarm, as more tribes, and their financial backers, seek more land to on which to build casinos. Many now believe that the tribes are but pawns to the outside interests that control them. Included in the worries are the possibility of money laundering and a loss of tribal autonomy.

A Sustainable Future

The end of the twentieth century was a mixed bag for the Midwest. The western states of the region have remained healthy, but the eastern region has suffered. Dependence on industry, manufacturing, and the family farm remained steadfast, but economic and resource activities were either outsourced or agglomerated within the global market. The region has excellent agricultural land as well as hard-working laborers, but the skills of the workforce in the declining cities are outdated and the much-needed entrepreneurs and the technical ability to produce their ideas are in short supply, as many of the college educated have left the region.

The engine that once drove the midwestern economy, if not the national economy, is stagnant. Many midwestern cities were unable or unwilling to move toward energy efficiency when the nation was turning to sustainability and conservation of resources. The old mind-set led to the downfall of the auto industry in 2009. Fighting to stay afloat, the Midwest maintains the old manufacturing paradigm rather than adopt sustainability. The old cradle-to-grave Industrial Revolution is over, and a new Industrial Revolution waits in the wings, focusing on waste-free cradle-to-cradle (C2C) industry. But shifting paradigms will be difficult, as few workers have been educated in C2C thinking, and the innovative entrepreneurial young people are leaving the region in search of jobs, leaving an older and more conservative population.

A few cities and states have emerged as leaders by overcoming a manufacturing past and entering the technological and progressive economy. For example, Minnesota (along with Massachusetts and Washington) has taken the lead in sustainable policy and embraced the triple bottom line. It has also attempted a universal health care system—something that is essential for a sustainable and healthy future.

In late 2008 the rest of the nation caught the malaise that had captured the Midwest and entered into a major recession capped by the fall of the auto industry, the loss of millions of jobs, and a nagging high unemployment rate.

The bounty of Great Lakes freshwater could be a ray of hope attracting future populations weary of the continual water wars of the South and West. The abundance of this natural resource could foster an industry based on distributing freshwater, one that brings money and bright minds into the region, not sending them or the water to outside companies or cities (Photo 13.11). Of course, there will have to be increased attention to water pollution issues, especially in the Great Lakes. The Midwest needs to reassess its human and physical resources and take bold, brave chances to change—or risk forever being left sitting at the side of the road.

The Midwest may rise again, but under a different internal engine, one that a few cities—Chicago, Minneapolis, Indianapolis, Madison, and Sioux Falls—have identified. Others have yet to make the transition. Two Michigan cities, Flint and Detroit, round out the least desirable places to live in the nation. The powerhouse cities of the industrial age struggle at best and are handicapped at worst. The venturesome have fled to places where people are rewarded, not chastised, for taking chances—places that encourage higher education, not hinder it. The states

BOX 13.10 RUST BELT

America's manufacturing sector is greatly diminished. Beginning in the 1960s and accelerating in the 1990s, the loss of industry deprived cities like Pittsburgh, Cleveland, and Detroit of thousands of blue-collar jobs. The jobs were outsourced to less developed countries where workers were paid far less and environmental laws were nonexistent. No longer was the American dream built on a high school education and well-paying union jobs. It was replaced by a low-wage service economy and high unemployment rates.

Industrial cities became pariahs, as people became aware of pollution and realized the environmental and social costs of the industrial economy. Some cities and states made halting recoveries. Cleveland redefined itself and looked beyond its dependence on dirty resources and began seeking sustainable goals. Pennsylvania always had the megalopolis region to give it locational advantages, and Pittsburgh reinvented itself. But the rusting industrial complex of the early twentieth century is now no more than twenty-first-century museum fodder. The hardest-hit state has been Michigan, which experienced what was called a one-state recession, when the rest of the national economy was still positive. Michigan led the rapid rise in unemployment rates and layoffs in the twenty-first century.

Michigan's and Detroit's time of greatness was partially based on geography. The region had tremendous natural resources, and Great Lakes transportation facilitated industrial progress. The region's nineteenth-century lumber and grain production was ebbing when the next opportunity arrived. The genius of Henry Ford and the investment money of the lumber barons saved Detroit from fading into history at the beginning of the twentieth century, but the same cannot be said for the twenty-first century.

Michigan's recuperation has been delayed for several reasons, including a severe racial divide, a high rate of poverty, a lack of support for higher education, a smug auto industry (which led to bankruptcy for two of the Big Three), and a brain drain. A geographical reason is that the state's peninsula configuration blocked its inclusion within the main transportation arteries along the southern shore of lakes Erie and Michigan, although it is a main port for Canada. As the importance of water transportation declines, the peninsular advantage becomes a disadvantage.

Detroit continues to lose population and per capita income. Those who can, move out of the city (or the state). Many of the college-educated move out in search of jobs in other areas. Those who remain are the poor, the aged, and those who still have jobs. In 2001, 9.4 percent lived below the poverty line; in 2002, 11.6 percent did, an increase of over 25 percent in one year. In 2010, the statewide poverty level was 16.8 percent, one out of six in the state. The number of bachelor's degrees in the state, 24.5 percent, is below the national average, with Detroit having only 11 percent with bachelor's degrees. Despite the low education rate, the state continues to cut education support.

Detroit leads the nation in the Rust Belt bust economy, and it has been hampered by a brain drain, a failing automobile industry, and the continued strength of unions throughout the state. The state of Michigan has suffered the most job losses in the nation for manufacturing. From 2000 to January 2009, Michigan lost 45.5 percent of its manufacturing jobs (Table 13.11).

TABLE 13.11. Manufacturing Job Losses, January 2000 to January 2009

	% Job loss
Michigan	45.5
North Carolina	37.2
Ohio	35.1
New York	33.5
South Carolina	31.9
Massachusetts	30.2
Georgia	29.7
Illinois	27.9
United States	26.8
California	25.6
Florida	25.2
Arizona	18.7
Texas	15.8

Source: Center for Continuing Study of the California Economy, "Why Are Manufacturing Job Losses So Large?" March 2009, at http://www.insightcced.org/uploads/nnsp/Why%20Are%20 Manufacturing%20Losses%20So%20Large.pdf

BOX 13.11 PRINCIPLES OF SUSTAINABLE DEVELOPMENT IN MINNESOTA

The Round Table's recommendations are based on the recognition that Minnesotans do not need or want to choose between good jobs, vital communities, and a healthy environment. They want all three.*

A 1996 poll of Minnesotans revealed a disinterest in repealing environmental laws to attract jobs and investment. This poll stimulated a group of statewide leaders to form the Minnesota Round Table on Sustainable Development, in order to incorporate ecological, economic, and equity concerns into an interconnected web of possibility and growth. Its goal was to create a working strategy for sustainable, green goals by including public, private, and individual interests in a long-term plan. A three-legged stool of economy, community, and environment became the basis for the following five-pronged sustainability guidelines.†

1. *Global Interdependence.* Economic prosperity, ecosystem health, liberty, and Justice are linked, and our long-term well being depends on maintaining all four, and local decisions must be informed by their regional and global context.
2. *Stewardship.* Stewardship requires recognition of the environment and economy for the benefit of present and future generations— finding a balance of the impacts of today's decisions with the needs of those who will follow.
3. *Conservation.* Minnesotans must maintain the essential ecological processes, biological diversity, and life-support systems of the environment; harvest renewable resources on a sustainable basis; and make wise and efficient use of renewable and nonrenewable resources.
4. *Indicators.* Minnesotans need to have and use clear goals and measurable indicators based on reliable information to guide public policies and private actions toward long-term economic prosperity, community vitality, cultural diversity, and the maintenance of healthy ecosystems.
5. *Shared Responsibility.* All Minnesotans accept responsibility for sustaining the environment and economy, with each being accountable for his or her decisions and actions, in a spirit of partnership and open cooperation. No entity has the right to shift the costs of its behavior to other individuals, communities, states, nations, or future generations. Full-cost accountability is essential for assuring shared responsibility.

The group issued priorities in order to attain their goals.

1. Raise awareness and understanding by incorporating sustainable goals in statewide educational institutions, and educating the public in sustainable ideas.
2. Measure progress toward sustainable development by instituting a statewide report card and encouraging communities to measure their own progress.
3. Encourage sustainable communities.
4. Engage and empower business so that it would be profitable to become sustainable. (Included in the reforms were tax incentives, and the incorporation of the full-life costs of corporate products.)
5. Create new institutions and approaches such as a Sustainable Center, and engender the support to pass more sustainable laws within the legislature.
6. Understand connections between long-term economic and environmental health, and the issues of liberty and justice.

Minnesota's actions in sustainability are being used across the country as a sustainability template.

* Minnesota Round Table on Sustainable Development, *Investing in Minnesota's Future: An Agenda for Sustaining Our Quality of Life* (St. Paul: Minnesota Planning Environmental Quality Board, May 1998), at http://www.mnplan.state.mn.us/pdf/inv-v3.pdf.

† Minnesota Round Table on Sustainable Development, *Investing in Minnesota's Future.*

with the highest percentage of college-educated residents are those that are also working with sustainable ideas.

Sustainable ideas and government support are needed to reinvigorate the Midwest's cities and its agriculture. Unfortunately, though, many Midwestern cities are mired in corrupt governments or conservative politics that fear change. However, the midwestern sustainable horizon has a few bright spots: niche markets, green roofs, university students, an EcoCity, and even a statewide plan for sustainability.

Many midwestern farms and dairies have chosen to be independent from large conglomerates and to pursue smaller, high-quality niche markets. These producers offer organic foods and community-supported agriculture, and they view a more sustainably oriented future.

Sustainable agriculture has three integrated goals: environmental health, profitability, and equity. Key issues include the reduction of chemical use, conserving resources, and providing social and economic equity to laborers. The sustainable niche market farm is small and meets the needs and tastes of people who are dissatisfied with the industrial food system. Most farms participating in sustainability are run by families who have made a choice in their way of life, one of "humans working with nature," rather than the more prevalent "man conquering nature," as practiced in corporate agribusiness.

Green roofs have caught on in the Midwest (Table 13.12). There was an 80 percent increase in green roof projects from 2004 to 2005. The midwestern city with the most green roofs is Chicago. By reducing air pollution and storm runoff, thereby

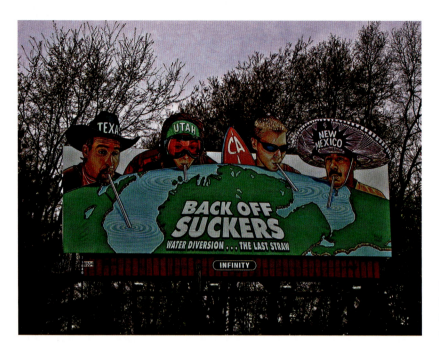

PHOTO 13.11. Protest Billboard near Lansing, Michigan. Diverting water from the Great Lakes is a controversial subject in Michigan and became a national subject during the 2008 presidential race.

reducing floods and runoff into rivers, green roofs also moderate the temperatures of nearby buildings and reduce noise, while requiring less maintenance and providing landscaping jobs.

There is a sign of hope in one of the most devastated cities, Detroit. Some corporate and educational structures have adopted green roofs and fields as an environmental and aesthetic response to environmental problems (Photo 13.12). But in energy efficiency, the city stutters. In 2008, the two largest

electric utilities insisted on virtual monopolies, limiting competition to 10 percent of the market, thereby guaranteeing higher rates and the creation of more coal-burning power plants and limiting renewable options.[23] But there is a rising star in Detroit: urban gardens. The city is a virtual food desert, with few opportunities to purchase fresh goods, yet the surrounding area is filled with empty lots and once occupied houses that are now being converted to urban gardens. However, one of the problems with the urban garden solution is the toxic pollutants that

TABLE 13.12. Top Ten American and Canadian Cities for Green Roofs, 2008

Rank	City	Square feet
1	Chicago, Illinois	534,507
2	Washington, D.C.	501,042
3	New York, New York	358,986
4	Vancouver, British Columbia	320,000
5	Philadelphia, Pennsylvania	196,820
6	Baltimore, Maryland	150,032
7	Montreal, Quebec	75,700
8	Grand Rapids, Michigan	74,784
9	Princeton, New Jersey	56,250
10	Newtown Square, Pennsylvania	48,130

Source: Green Roofs for Healthy Cities, at http://www.greenroofs.org

PHOTO 13.12. River Rouge Plant, Detroit, Michigan. The two-thousand-acre Ford plant has reinvented its brownfield image in the past few years by adopting environmental ideas such as fields of sunflowers and the world's largest green roof. At its height in the 1930s, the plant employed more than a hundred thousand workers, but labor unrest and globalization left the plant with only six thousand workers in 1990. The plant has been retooling itself to current industrial trends in flexible manufacturing, in which the production line is capable of producing variations of cars by changing the computer program.

have been dumped on the land over the years. Many urban gardens must be built on raised beds to avoid the toxic soil.

Perhaps the most hope in sustainable thinking comes from the youth, tomorrow's leaders, many of whom see the writing on the wall, that becoming sustainable is the only way to give them a future, as the United States reshapes the meaning of progress. Across the land, student groups at universities have been creating sustainable classes, positions, and curriculums. Studies of green roofs have been ongoing at Southern Illinois University and at Lawrence Technical University in Southfield, Michigan. Michigan State University and Grinnell College in Iowa have been at the forefront of agricultural and sustainable progress, as well as offering alternative studies in sustainable development.

However, midwestern states are losing their college graduates. Illinois, Michigan, and Ohio are losing many college graduates to growing states. To rebuild these states, they need to stop the brain drain.

The Midwest, like the rest of the nation, has in many ways lost its sense of place. This region is regaled for its abundant water. The glacial lakes are considered a regional amenity, but the water is polluted, the aquatics stressed by invasive species. Most people do not know the ground under their feet. They do not know how much of the land has been drained, the water wasted, and they do not recognize the physical fragility of the region. Until the relationship with the land is reestablished, an honest assessment for a sustainable future will not be accomplished.

Questions for Discussion

1. Why is the northern Great Lakes region not a cash-grain region?

2. Why has dairying been more profitable than grains in the northern Great Lakes?

3. Is the production of ethanol from corn a feasible answer to the region's economic malaise? Why or why not?

4. The Midwest has been losing population and jobs for the past fifty years. What are the reasons for the losses?

5. Wetlands have gone from having a negative to a positive connotation over the past half century. The irony is that as wetlands are being appreciated and less land is available for development, population has doubled and more land is needed to accommodate the American lifestyle. Is the maintenance of this lifestyle something that can be accomplished, or is it something that should be?

6. How did Michigan make the transition from a lumber to an automobile economy?

7. What was the role of the Great Lakes in relation to the development of the steel industry?

8. Why did the iron and steel industry evolve in the Pittsburgh-Cleveland area?

9. What was the strategic importance of the location of Buffalo?

10. What did Chicago do to become the regional center for the Midwest?

11. How do the western and eastern midwestern states differ in economy and sustainability?

12. How has Minnesota separated itself from the rest of the Midwest in its sustainable actions? Explain.

Suggested Readings

Abler, Ron. *The Twin Cities of Saint Paul and Minneapolis.* Cambridge, Mass: Ballinger, 1976.

Adams, John S., and Barbara J. van Drasek. *Minneapolis–St. Paul; People, Place, and Public Life.* Minneapolis: University of Minnesota Press, 1993.

Cayton, Andrew, Robert Lee, and Susan E. Gray, eds. *The American Midwest.* Indianapolis: Indiana University Press, 2001.

Chappell, Sally Anderson. *Cahokia: Mirror of the Cosmos.* Chicago: University of Chicago Press, 2002.

Cronon, William. *Nature's Metropolis: Chicago and the Great West.* New York: Norton, 1991.

Grady, Wayne. *The Great Lakes: The Natural History of a Changing Region.* Vancouver, B.C.: Greystone Books, 2007.

Hart, John Fraser. "Change in the Corn Belt." *Geographical Review* 76, no. 1 (January 1986): 51–72.

———. *The Land That Feeds Us.* New York: Norton, 1993.

———. "The Middle West." *Annals of the Association of American Geographers* 62, no. 2 (1972): 258–82.

Hess, Jeffrey, and Camille Kudzia. "St. Anthony Falls Waterpower Area; St. Anthony Falls Historic District" (Hennepin County, Minnesota) National Register of Historic Places Registration Form. Washington, D.C.: U.S. Department of the Interior, National Park Service, 1991.

Hudson, John C. *Making the Corn Belt: A Geographical History of Middle-Western Agriculture.* Bloomington: Indiana University Press, 1994.

Hymowitz, T., and W. R. Shurtleff, "Debunking Soybean Myths and Legends in the Historical and Popular Literature." *Crop Science* 45 (2005): 473–76, at http://extension.agron.iastate.edu/soybean/documents/Historypaper.pdf.

Johnson, Hannibal B. *Up from the Ashes: A Story about Building Community.* Austin, Tex.: Eakin Press, 2000.

Jones, Larry Eugene, and Georg G. Iggers. *Crossing Boundaries: The Exclusion and Inclusion of Minorities in Germany and the United States.* New York: Berghahn Books, 2001.

Kaatz, M. R. "The Black Swamp: A Study in Historical Geography." *Annals of the Association of American Geographers* 45, no. 1 (1955).

Kane, Lucile M. *The Falls of St. Anthony: The Waterfall That Built Minneapolis.* St. Paul: Minnesota Historical Society, 1966.

Lampard, Eric E. *The Rise of the Dairy Industry in Wisconsin.* Madison: State Historical Society of Wisconsin, 1963.

Martin, Lawrence. *The Physical Geography of Wisconsin.* Madison: University of Wisconsin Press, 1965.

Mayda, Chris, Artimus Keiffer, and Joseph W. Slade. "Ecology and Environment." In *The Midwest*, edited by Joseph W. Slade and Judith Yaross Lee. Westport, Conn.: Greenfield Press, 2004.

Misa, Thomas J. *A Nation of Steel: The Making of Modern America, 1865–1925.* Baltimore: Johns Hopkins University Press, 1995.

Opie, John. *Order on the Land.* Lincoln: University of Nebraska Press, 1987.

Richter, Fe. "The Copper-Mining Industry in the United States, 1845–1925." *Quarterly Journal of Economics* 41, no. 4 (1927): 684–717.

Rubenstein, James M. *The Changing U.S. Auto Industry: A Geographical Analysis.* London: Routledge, 2002.

Sauer, Carl O. *The Geography of the Ozark Highland of Missouri.* Chicago: University of Chicago Press, 1920.

Schaetzl, Randall. "Underlying Hard Rock Geology: Geography of Michigan and the Great Lakes Region." *Earthscape* (January 2002).

Shortridge, James R. *Cities on the Plains: The Evolution of Urban Kansas.* Lawrence: University Press of Kansas, 2004.

———. *The Middle West: Its Meaning in American Culture.* Lawrence: University Press of Kansas, 1989.

Zakrzewska, Varbara. "Valleys of Driftless Areas." *Annals of the Association of American Geographers* 61, no. 3 (1971): 441–59.

Internet Sources

Greenroof Project Database, at http://www.greenroofs.com/projects/plist.php.

U.S. Poultry and Egg Association. "Economic Data," at http://www.poultryegg.org/economic_data/.

Scorecard: The Pollution Data Site, at http://www.scorecard.org/.

Minnesota Round Table on Sustainable Development. *Investing in Minnesota's Future*, at http://www.mnplan.state.mn.us/pdf/inv-v3.pdf.

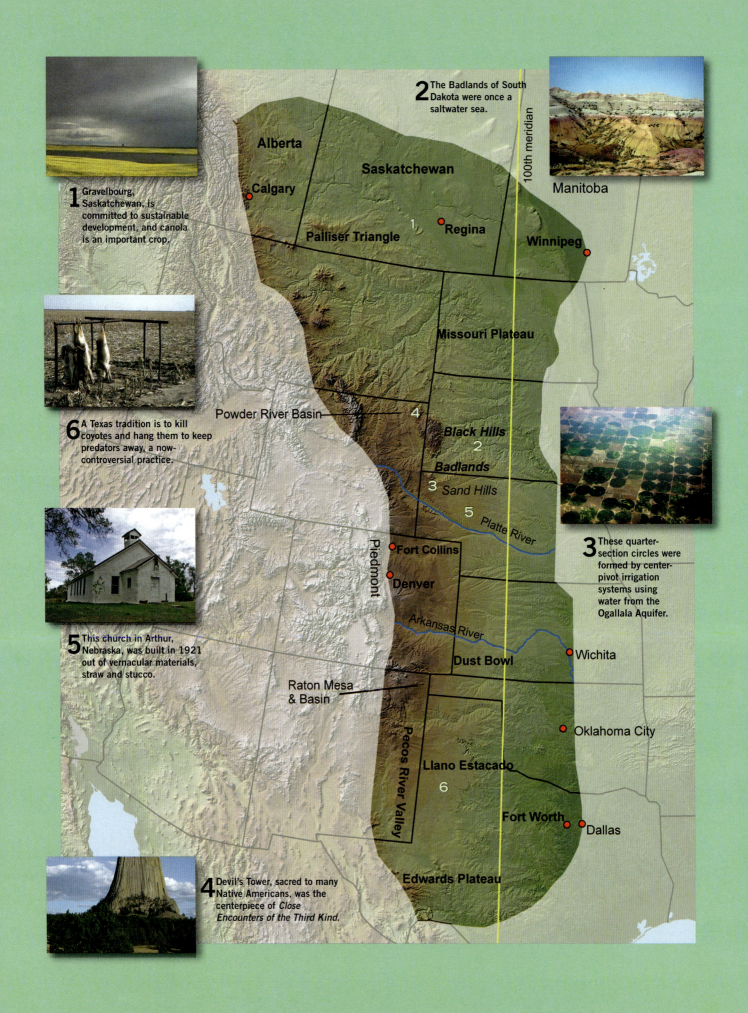

2 The Badlands of South Dakota were once a saltwater sea.

Manitoba

1 Gravelbourg, Saskatchewan, is committed to sustainable development, and canola is an important crop.

Alberta

Saskatchewan

100th meridian

Calgary

Palliser Triangle

1

Regina

Winnipeg

Missouri Plateau

6 A Texas tradition is to kill coyotes and hang them to keep predators away, a now-controversial practice.

Powder River Basin

4

Black Hills

2

Badlands

3 Sand Hills

5 Platte River

3 These quarter-section circles were formed by center-pivot irrigation systems using water from the Ogallala Aquifer.

Piedmont

Fort Collins

Denver

Arkansas River

5 This church in Arthur, Nebraska, was built in 1921 out of vernacular materials, straw and stucco.

Dust Bowl

Wichita

Raton Mesa & Basin

Oklahoma City

Pecos River Valley

Llano Estacado

6

Fort Worth

Dallas

4 Devil's Tower, sacred to many Native Americans, was the centerpiece of *Close Encounters of the Third Kind*.

Edwards Plateau

14

THE GREAT PLAINS AND CANADIAN PRAIRIE

Land of Opportunity, or Where the Buffalo Roam?

Chapter Highlights

After reading this chapter you should be able to:

- Identify and label U.S. and Canadian Great Plains and Prairie subregions
- Discuss the importance of the Ogallala Aquifer
- Explain the relationship between corn, hogs, and cattle on the plains
- Describe the settlement process and how it differed from settlement on the West Coast
- Give an overview of the major Plains cities
- Identify the historic range of the buffalo, and explain the theory of the Buffalo Commons
- Distinguish the dividing line between the Great Plains and the Midwest and its connection to climate and agriculture
- Explain how cattle ranching and processing has changed from the late nineteenth century to the present on the Plains
- Contrast farmers and ranchers and discuss the concept of range war
- Describe the place of the Hutterites and the Métis in Canada
- Explain the importance of the Palliser Triangle on the Canadian Prairie

Terms

aging in place
agribusiness
badlands
Bureau of Land Management (BLM)
caliche
center pivot irrigation (CPI)
chinook

coalbed methane (CBM)
Conservation Reserve Program (CRP)
Crow Rate
Dominion Lands Act
dryland farming
Dust Bowl
Exodusters
Frontier Thesis
frost-freeze cycles

grassland
Homestead Act
Hutterites
meander
Métis
New Homestead Act
open-range ranching
panhandle
prior appropriation
"Rain follows the plow"

range war
sod house
steppe
subsidy
suitcase farmers
tornadoes
volcanic plug
water table
windmill

Places

100th meridian
Badlands
Black Hills
Calgary, Alberta
Dallas–Fort Worth, Texas

Edwards Plateau
Great American Desert
High Plains
Llano Estacado
Missouri Plateau
Ogallala Aquifer
Paha Sapa

Palliser Triangle
Peace River Valley
Pecos River Valley
Powder River Basin
Prairie provinces
Raton Mesa and Basin
Regina, Saskatchewan

Rupert's Land
Sand Hills
Winnipeg, Manitoba

PHOTO 14.1. Oklahoma Panhandle. The High Plains of Oklahoma are a quintessential regional landscape. The flat, endless expanse of "wide open spaces" is appealing. Windmills pump shallow groundwater for livestock, and winds blow across the open grasses.

Introduction

The Great Plains are not an Eden, but neither are they an impossible land in which to develop a stable society of people with a decent level of living. Their tragedy is the result of general ignorance as to how best to manage them and misunderstanding of their real nature, plus a system of values brought from entirely different areas. Given understanding treatment, they can become a place where honest, hard-working men can make homes and raise families in the security of a stable society.

—Earl Bell, 1942[1]

Driving eighty miles an hour through the Great Plains is too slow for most people, while others enjoy the subtly revealed landscape. There is much to see in this so-called boring but ancient landscape. Seas, glaciers, and mountains left their imprints, so that the endless vanishing point ahead is, in fact, diverse and far more complex than it seems at a casual glance.

The Great Plains climate, topography, and vegetation signify a transition zone between the wet and forested Midwest and the dry, scruffy West. Arriving from the humid East, the first explorers and settlers found dry **grassland** filled with millions of buffalo.

But the perception of the plains varied with the weather. The farmers or ranchers who settled there depended on rain to define their crops and profits. Sometimes rain fell in the "proper" proportions, and crops were bountiful. Sometimes there was too much rain, other times, no rain; both brought despair. Farmers tried to farm the plains in the same manner they farmed the Midwest, but the land and the weather demanded their own regimen, which was not practiced until after the 1930s Depression and drought.

After the drought, Great Plains and Prairie farmers and ranchers developed more sustainable agricultural methods (Photo 14.1) until pressured to increase yields. Today, the Great Plains and Canadian Prairie are major agricultural and livestock regions, but they are also resource hinterlands where the few remaining independent farmers and ranchers struggle to maintain the dream of independent production, land ownership, and profit. Today, unsustainable production supported by industrialized agriculture has increased yields for the short term, but at the cost of environmental degradation, diminishing water resources, and social injustice.

Since World War II, the region's agricultural bonanza is paired with outside corporations exploiting Great Plains resources. The profits leave the region, instead of being reinvested, resulting in spiritual and economic devastation in the Plains. However, all is not lost. Producers on the land have banded together and offer more sustainable and local agricultural options. And then there is the idea to return the plains to the buffalo.

Physical Geography

A sustainable landscape works with and does not attempt to conquer the physical features. While the Great Plains' relatively flat terrain is perfect for modern mechanized agriculture, the minimal surface water cannot support massive **agribusiness** investment without drilling for underlying groundwater. But to achieve the yields that are wanted, farmers drill beyond the recharge rate, so each year the water table drops. Furthermore, the native grass structure has changed since the days of the free-roaming buffalo. Today's closed-range cattle ranching system has overgrazed many areas, resulting in erosion and a loss of soil moisture and carbon storage.

If an ecological balance were maintained, the region would become less sensitive to drought and more resilient to climatic change. While exploiting the plains for human benefit alone, we have caused unintended consequences. To become sustainable, the land needs to be accepted, understood, and then worked for what it is.

The flat, treeless, and dry landscape may seem monotonous and even endless, until it is more closely inspected. The High Plains, for example, feel flat but incline toward the Rocky Mountains from 2,500 feet at the 100th meridian to 4,500 feet at the Oklahoma–New Mexico border 180 miles away, an increase of about 11 feet per mile. The treeless short-grass prairie relies on less than twenty inches of precipitation annually and has a nest of integrated ecosystems that have been degraded.

Modern agricultural methods have fragmented the land and its ecosystems and left native species in a discontinuous pattern threatened by invasive species, such as the Eurasian leafy spurge introduced by humans in the nineteenth century. The deep-rooted plant infested the Great Plains and crowds out native species, reduces crop yields, and is difficult to control. Humans are not the only culprits, though; seeds can be dispersed through the air or by animals from one ecosystem to another, making for constant instability in ecosystems. Still, despite its limitations, this geologically youthful landscape is among the most valuable agricultural land in the world.

About sixty-five million years ago, the Great Plains lay beneath a shallow sea. Thousands of feet of sedimentary rock calcified and accumulated over the Precambrian bedrock. Millions of years later, the Rocky Mountain uplift wrenched the nearby flat topography into the rolling Colorado Piedmont. Stream flows accelerated, washing down alluvial soils from the newly formed mountains and covering the Plains seabed in fertile soils.

Each Great Plains state is part of at least two ecoregions. Some states are partially humid in the east and dry in the west; other states are divided between the Rocky Mountains and Plains climates and topographies. Most of the state or provincial borders are straight lines, ignoring ecoregional patterns. The exceptions along the Texas, Mexico, and Oklahoma borders follow rivers, but not the natural watersheds. Therefore the states are fragmented between watersheds and ecological systems. No Great Plains state is within a single major ecoregion or watershed. For example, Oklahoma includes portions of the Gulf Coast South, the Ozarks, the Central Lowlands, and the High Plains. Colorado is part of the Great Plains, the Rocky Mountains, and the Intermontane. The Missouri River divides North Dakota into the Great Plains to the south and west, and the wetter, glaciated Central Lowlands to the north. The Canadian Prairie provinces share the Canadian Shield to the east, the Rocky Mountains to the west, and the boreal forest to the north. The ecological needs of each state or provincial ecoregion are often ignored, and therefore valuable and balancing ecosystems are destroyed.

These human-induced fragmented landscapes make an ecologically balanced region almost impossible. Watersheds and ecosystems are not honored or protected beyond state or provincial borders. For example, the latitude line that separates Oklahoma and Kansas has nothing to do with the physical landscape, and yet each state maximizes its water use for its own purposes without working toward the greater whole and the common good.[2]

While the Great Plains is generally a semiarid flat expanse, physical and precipitation patterns define the subregions. The subregions include:

- Canadian Prairie and Northern Great Plains
- Dissected Missouri Plateau
- Sand Hills
- High Plains
- Raton Mesa and Basin
- Pecos Valley
- Edwards Plateau and Central Texas Uplift

Canadian Prairie and Northern Great Plains

The Canadian Prairie and Northern Great Plains were glaciated north of the Missouri River, with a few unglaciated areas, such as the rugged Cypress Hills on the Alberta-Saskatchewan border. The rolling Alberta Plains are a mixture of glacial sedimentary deposits and sediment washed from the Rocky Mountains. The Northern Great Plains extends into southern Saskatchewan and contain glacial reminders—thousands of small Prairie pot hole lakes and rough badland topography (Photo 14.2). The northernmost Prairie, the Peace River Valley, straddles the Alberta–British Columbia border just south of the boreal forest. The valley is a former lake bottom, a twenty-five-thousand-square-mile fertile agricultural area, a warm microclimate region of good soils that has been homesteaded since World War II.

Ninety-five percent of the native Canadian Prairie grasslands have been converted to wheat farms or rangelands. In the process, wetlands were drained to create a uniform farming landscape. Only about 20 percent of the original wetlands remain.

Dissected Missouri Plateau

West of the Missouri River, the Central Lowlands open into the big-sky West. The Missouri Plateau, a transitional landmass north of the High Plains, begins at the Pine Ridge Escarpment along the Nebraska–South Dakota border. In southern South Dakota, the Badlands and Black Hills punctuate this semiarid, eroded, and rolling plain. The underpopulated plain is dryland farmed (not irrigated) or grazed.

Near the meeting place of South Dakota, Wyoming, and Nebraska, the contorted Badlands plateau offers a visual break from the High Plains. The **badland** gullies, towers, canyons, and mesas are the result of seasonal downpours and **frost-freeze cycles** that loosened and cracked rocks into fantastic shapes.

The scenic Black Hills are named for the forests that darken the slopes. The hills are sacred to the native Lakota, who call them Paha Sapa ("the hills that are black"). The Black Hills boom-bust region of gold, tin, and lead mining camps currently depends on tourism, featuring Mt. Rushmore and the Crazy Horse monument honoring the chief who fought to preserve the Lakota way of life. The area is too rough for farming but acceptable grazing land.

Also sacred to Native Americans is the nearby columnar **volcanic plug** called Devil's Tower. Its igneous core was exposed

PHOTO 14.2. Big Muddy Badlands, Saskatchewan. These compressed clay and eroded sandstone outcrops are just north of the U.S.–Canadian border. Stone circles and effigies mark symbolic and sacred places and perhaps graves of native chiefs. During the late nineteenth century, the Badlands were an outlaw hideout for the Sundance Kid, Sam Kelly, and Dutch Henry. Today, cattle graze the Badlands.

after its sedimentary rock covering eroded over millions of years.

Sand Hills, Nebraska

North America's largest sand dunes— the Sand Hills—are composed of sand left behind after the finer silt and clay loess were blown and deposited eastward. Wind and rain shaped the maze of sand dunes into their irregular, grass-covered shapes covering almost twenty thousand square miles north of the Platte River in west-central Nebraska. Lakes in the basins of the dunes replenish the Ogallala Aquifer below.

Buffalo once grazed the land but were hunted to near extinction by the time of the Civil War. After the war, ranchers invested in cattle, and a boom-bust economy prevailed. Grazing remained the prevalent use of the land until the 1960s. Since the 1960s, some of the native Sand Hills grassland was altered by Ogallala Aquifer–supported center-pivot-irrigation farming.

High Plains

The treeless, flat landscape, more often traversed than settled, is the quintessential Great Plains, the region marked on early maps as the Great American Desert. The unfamiliar landscape did not fit midwestern settlers' perceptions. The lack of trees and the lack of surface water denoted a land unfit for farming, and therefore it was called a desert.

The slight elevation gradient and high evaporation rates left a semiarid landscape with few streams or rivers. The uplifted limestone plateau, as wide as the Oklahoma and Texas **panhandles**, extends almost featureless from the South Dakota–Nebraska border south to Texas's Edwards Plateau. Only the colorful buttes and mesas of the Gypsum Hills of southwestern Kansas (Photo 14.3) punctuate this "boring" transition to the drier West.

The southern High Plains plateau begins south of the Canadian River in western Texas. Explorers named these treeless plains the Llano Estacado ("Staked Plains") for the buffalo-bone stakes that served as rudimentary milestones. The Ogallala formation—limestone rock debris washed down from the southern Rocky Mountains—once extended to the foot of the mountains, but rains, streams, and the Pecos River have eroded it into the Pecos River Valley.

Pecos River Valley

Nestled between the Llano Estacado and the Guadalupe Mountains, the sluggish Pecos River runs almost parallel to the Rio Grande until they meet near Del Rio, Texas. The river may be sluggish, but the need for water has caused water wars between Texas and New Mexico throughout most of the twentieth century. The river valley is a transitional landscape between the Great Plains to the east, the Basin and Range to the west, and the Rocky Mountains to the north.

At the eastern edge of the valley is Carlsbad Caverns, the largest cavern system in the world and one of many local limestone sinks and caves. The formation was a reef in an inland tropical sea 250 million years ago. Over time, the sea evaporated and the remaining reef was buried under salt deposits. A few million years ago, the area was uplifted and water seeped into cracks, dissolving the limestone and creating spectacular stalagmite and stalactite formations.

Raton Mesa and Basin

Named for local rock rats, the Raton Mesa in southeastern Colorado and northeastern New Mexico is one of the few forested areas within the Plains. Capped by lava flows and riddled with dissected mesas, the transitional landscape lies between the Great Plains and the Rocky Mountains. At eight

thousand feet, the steep and narrow Raton Pass cuts below volcanic peaks and above grassy valleys. Raton Pass was one of the Santa Fe Trail's most difficult traverses, but that was overcome in 1879 by the Atchison, Topeka, and Santa Fe Railroad.

Edwards Plateau and Central Texas Uplift

The limestone Balcones Escarpment separates the Gulf Coastal and Great Plains regions and is the defining feature of south central Texas's Edwards Plateau. The Edwards Aquifer—recharged from local rivers and lakes—supplies water for more than two million San Antonio and Austin residents, although overdevelopment has caused pollution that threatens the supply.

West of the escarpment is a deeply dissected canyon land commonly known as the Hill Country, a favored recreational getaway for Texas residents. Shrubs, oaks, and junipers populate the grazed land.

Water

The lack of surface water has compelled humans to modify the Great Plains water systems by building reservoirs, wells, windmills, pipelines, and ditches to use the limited surface water and deep groundwater.

Great Plains waterways are usually small and often ephemeral. The gentle slope of the land allows even the largest of the perennial rivers—the Missouri, Platte, and Arkansas—a sluggish **meander** across the Plains toward the Mississippi Basin and into the Gulf of Mexico. Even shallow draft canoes had difficulty navigating the lazy braided riverbeds. Another waterway

PHOTO 14.3. Gypsum Hills, Kansas. The hills near Medicine Lodge are red from iron oxide and are capped by gypsum.

into the Gulf is the Rio Grande, which has been a victim of drought and poor water management. Mexicans, Americans, and Native Americans all seek court approval to obtain water rights on the drought-stricken river.

Missouri River

Prior to the last ice age, Northern Plains rivers drained into Hudson Bay. But glaciation blocked the northern routes; with each glacial advance the rivers were routed south; until the edge of glacial advance formed the Missouri River, which drained into the Mississippi River and eventually into the Gulf of Mexico.

Navigating the "Big Muddy" Missouri was difficult for traders, because frost cut the season short and sand bars, snags, and logs impeded the flow. Over time, the Army Corps of Engineers constructed controlling dams, which improved navigation and protected against flooding, but bureaucracy has caused the Corps to operate at cross-purposes to serve multiple agendas. The river cannot be made to serve all those who have an interest in the river at once—farmers, towns, tourists, wildlife, and environmentalists. For example, environmental groups seek to repair imbalances and restore the river, while economic pressure continues to seek profitable solutions. Clearly, the river cannot be returned to its former "natural" state, but can the river be ecologically balanced, profitable, and sustainable?

North Platte River

The "mile-wide, inch-deep" North Platte River, named after an Omaha tribal word for "flat water," is a major tributary of the Missouri River. Westward-moving pioneers and their prairie schooners depended on the Platte for water and direction. Near Ash Hollow, Nebraska, the Platte splits to a southern and northern branch. Oregon Trail pioneers followed the northern branch into Wyoming along the Middle Rockies to South Pass.

To utilize the snowmelt water of the Platte for irrigation and electric generation, Kingsley Dam was built in 1941 in western Nebraska's North Platte Valley. The earthen dam forms Lake McConaughy, "Big Mac." However, a decade-long drought introducing the twenty-first century reduced lake levels by 82 percent, thereby eliminating power generation and reducing irrigation by 60 percent. In 2010, snowmelt was above normal and the lake returned to near capacity levels. The lake, sometimes called Nebraska's ocean, has been an economic boon attracting a million visitors annually, but the drought hurt the recreational economy (Photo 14.4). Numerous disputed claims over water rights to the lake have been the source of litigation between the states that share the watershed area. In 2001, courts granted Colorado, Wyoming, and Nebraska limited irrigation use, but the region has not yet adopted a sustainable standard.

Arkansas River

The Arkansas River commences in the Rockies near Leadville, Colorado, and flows east over fourteen hundred miles to the Mississippi River southeast of Little Rock. From 1820 to 1846, the Arkansas River marked the boundary between the United States and Mexico.

The river flow varies from major whitewater near its Colorado headwaters to the wide, meandering Arkansas River Valley following the Santa Fe Trail through Kansas. The Kerr-McClellan commercial waterway altered navigation from Tulsa to the river's confluence with the Mississippi.

The Arkansas River Valley near Pueblo, Colorado, has traditionally supported agriculture, but increased urban demand, power generation, and salinity have cut agricultural water in half over twenty-five years. By 2007, the reduced water supply severely impacted the service economy of rural communities. The Arkansas River has also lost surface flow and irrigation potential because of Ogallala Aquifer drawdown.

Ogallala Aquifer

The Ogallala Aquifer underground reservoir lies one hundred to four hundred feet below eight High Plains states (Map 14.1). The aquifer provides about 30 percent of the nation's groundwater, and 95 percent of the aquifer water is used for irrigation.

The Rocky Mountain uplift both created the aquifer and then cut it off from its original water source. Only scant regional precipitation recharges the aquifer's fossil water from the last glacial period. Ogallala water is overdrafted, and the inability to replenish is a source of concern for the agricultural community.[3] Although in the past regional crops were limited to dryland crops, today aquifer water supports extensive cornfields and CAFO hog farms, as well as the multiple cattle feedlots. The aquifer is being used at unsustainable rates and growing unsustainable crops.

Climate

The Great Plains climate is extreme, dramatic, and decidedly western in its aridity. Four physical factors differentiate the Great Plains from the eastern United States.

- **Climate**. The Pacific air mass moves eastward, losing moisture as it passes over mountain ranges. The Great Plains are in the rain shadow of the Rocky Mountains. The western Plains lack precipitation because of the rain shadow, while the eastern Plains are more affected by the Gulf Coast air mass and consequently more humid.
- **Precipitation**. A dry climate regime beginning around the 100th meridian has less than twenty inches of precipitation.
- **Soil**. The scant precipitation cannot leach carbonates from the soil, often leaving a calcium carbonate soil horizon locally called **caliche** (or hardpan). The topsoil is fertile, but precipitation limits its production.
- **Vegetation**. Only scruffy grasses with long, moisture-seeking roots can survive the climate, soil, and precipitation limits in the west; farther east the grasses grow taller due to increased precipitation. The few trees in most Plains areas are limited to riverbed areas.

The Great Plains have a continental climate—a lack of large water bodies that moderate land temperatures. Because land

BOX 14.2 MISSOURI RIVER DAMS AND NAVIGATION

In 1936, the dam-building era began on the Missouri River. Seventy-five dams now control floods on the Missouri, but with unintended consequences.

Unintended Consequences

Increases in cultivated and irrigated land came at the cost of diminished wetlands, sandbars, and grasslands. Uncontrolled sediment deposition in the reservoirs causes operational, environmental, and economic problems. Reservoir fish are negatively impacted by falling water levels, particularly during spawning, and interruptions in the food chain. Fish are in turn weakened, and they are susceptible to nonnative species, such as Asian carp. Of sixty-seven species of fish, fifty-one are endangered.

Regional and Ecoregional Impacts

The system of locks and dams operates differently than the system on other U.S. rivers because of the muddy Missouri's silt load. A system of wing dams, rock structures built from the floodplain into the river channel, promote slowing river velocities.

The channel is listless along the edges because of sediment deposition, but it is scoured and rapid through the center, allowing larger barges to pass. The wing dams are responsible for numerous changes in the ecosystem and natural processes. Among the changes are these:

- Straightening of meanders and alteration of floodplain
- Altering sediment transport, changing the river's form and life
- Loss of floral and faunal biodiversity
- Changes in vegetation caused by altered peak flows and impoundments
- Recreational opportunities, not considered when the dams were built, have become important for the small-town economies along

the river. In 2009, fishing along the Dakotas section of the Missouri River had an economic impact of $77 million.

External Costs

Building the dams caused the sediment load on the river to change. Small amounts of gravel deposited over a twenty-year period have ultimately led to degradation and erosion of the river, which in turn have negatively affected wildlife habitats and the ability to control floods. Costs to stabilize the banks of the river are large.

The river would be healthier and not suffer navigation distress if the wing dams were removed. Environmental studies have shown that riverine fish and wildlife will be severely damaged if the dams are not removed or more water released. But the economic gains for wildlife of a free-flowing river will be countered by flooding and the loss of hydropower for humans.

Solutions

An alliance between the Sierra Club and the Army Corps of Engineers has worked to restore ecological health to the river. Among the declarations are: no new dams; no human-made levees built beyond the hundred-year flood stage; mitigation of wetlands; reconfiguring dams to allow fish spawning; and supporting setbacks for human infrastructures.

Despite hundreds of reports documenting the river's fragmented ecosystem, managing the system as a whole has yet to be accomplished. The management of only one species, or one area of the river, is not possible unless the entire system is comprehensively integrated. Working within a systematic approach can only be successfully addressed on all levels at once because it is all connected. This requires a new mind-set in our approach to solving environmental problems.

PHOTO 14.4. Declining Lake McConaughy, Nebraska. The lake is a source of irrigation and power generation for the state. The lake has declined more than 80 percent during the twenty-first century, affecting irrigation, the Nebraska corn crop, and the tourist industry. The shore has retracted hundreds of feet, and launching boats in what is left of the lake has become increasingly difficult.

BOX 14.3 DID YOU KNOW . . . HIGH PLAINS AND OGALLALA AQUIFER

- The High Plains aquifer is the largest groundwater system in North America.
- The Ogallala is three-quarters of the High Plains Aquifer groundwater under the Great Plains region.
- The amount of water in the High Plains Aquifer is approximately 3.25 billion acre feet, larger than Lake Huron.
- More than 170,000 wells pump aquifer water, 90 percent of which is used for irrigation.

- Thirty percent of all irrigated water in the United States is from the Ogallala.
- The aquifer is divided among eight Great Plains states. Nebraska has the largest share with about 65 percent, Kansas 10 percent.
- Aquifer consumption rates are ten to forty times the recharge rate.
- Aquifer water application increased after World War II, using technology and the development of center pivot irrigation.
- Technology has improved irrigation efficiency, although pumping rates remain unsustainable.

loses heat faster than water, land far from water bodies tends to have more extreme weather: very cold winters or hot, windy summers, along with the periodic and opposing extremes of drought or flood.

The rain shadow limits precipitation along the Rocky Mountain front. The precipitation increases near the 100th meridian, affected by the Gulf of Mexico.[4] East of the 100th meridian the increased precipitation augments agricultural production. To the west of the 100th meridian is the wheat-growing Great Plains, to the east the corn-growing Midwest.

Precipitation and temperature averages have the greatest seasonal variation of any region, and they become more pronounced farther north (Table 14.1). Precipitation can fall in one thunderous storm that produces flash floods or not fall for years on end. The Northern Plains are affected by winter's frigid Arctic air masses, causing blowing snowstorms.

Extreme weather on the Great Plains includes thunderstorms and hail that can precede the violent rotating **tornadoes** (Map 14.2). The extreme weather occurs during the spring and early summer, when Arctic and Gulf fronts meet over the Great

MAP 14.1. Ogallala Aquifer. The High Plains aquifer, of which the Ogallala is the largest part, underlies portions of eight Great Plains states. Since the 1960s, fossil fuel–pumped irrigation water has been pumped onto the fields at a rate at least four times faster than recharge.

TABLE 14.1. Average Temperatures in the Great Plains and Prairies

	July high	January high	Yearly average
Lemmon, South Dakota	85°F	26°F	42.9°F
Guymon, Oklahoma	93°F	43°F	57°F
Gravelbourg, Saskatchewan	80°F	−2°F	37°F

Source: CLRSearch, at http://www.clrsearch.com

Plains. Oklahoma and southern Kansas receive the most tornadoes, although tornadoes also batter the midwestern states.

Hail, a spectacular form of precipitation, forms in unstable air during severe spring or summer thunderstorms. Damaging hailstorms are most frequent in the Great Plains. Hail consists of ice and water in alternate layers that adhere and grow in size and collide with supercooled water in a cumulonimbus cloud. Hail usually falls for about fifteen intense minutes, damaging crops, buildings, and livestock. Cars pockmarked by hail are common sights in storm areas.

On the Canadian Prairies immediately east of the Rockies, dry winds called **chinooks** or "snow eaters" descend the mountains in winter bringing warm Pacific air, capable of melting two feet of snow and raising temperatures 40°F in fifteen minutes. For many people, the chinooks are a welcome relief to the normal snow cover and Arctic cold. But the winds

remove soil moisture (causing "chinook burn"), increase the risk of forest fires, and remove winter snow insulation from plants.

Historical Geography and Settlement

The physical landscape and climate of the Plains have always limited settlement. Because the Plains lacked surface water, permanent Native American settlements were unusual; most Plains tribes lived a nomadic lifestyle following the buffalo. The semiarid lands were unappealing to American settlers while lucrative lands elsewhere were available. Later economic and political incentives, such as the Homestead Act, and propaganda, such as "**Rain follows the plow**," aroused interest. In recent years the controversial Buffalo Commons theory

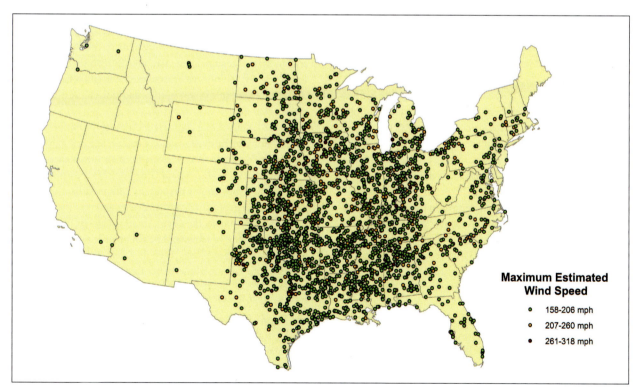

Maximum Estimated Wind Speed

- 158-206 mph
- 207-260 mph
- 261-318 mph

MAP 14.2. Tornadoes by Severity, 1950–2004. Tornadoes occur where there are no obstacles stopping cold Canadian air meeting moist Gulf air, usually in thunderstorms. Wind speeds up to three hundred miles per hour can result, destroying everything in the tornado's path.

BOX 14.4 SUSTAINABLE BUFFALO?

In 1987 an academic couple, Frank and Deborah Popper, made a case for the Buffalo Commons—returning the Great Plains to the buffalo—and restoring the Plains grasslands to their pre-European condition, without fences or permanently settled people. The Buffalo Commons theory questioned the ecological and environmental right thing to do in a boom-bust region of impermanent settlement. The theory introduced a continuing debate about sustainability and the suitability of Plains settlement.*

In 2000, Ernest Callenbach added fuel to the fire by not only supporting a return of buffalo but also adding wind power, calling them "an elegant combination." The traditional Plains windmills have used the ever-present wind to sustainably pump water in the past. Why not convert energy using modern wind turbines and the same wind?†

If millions of buffalo once roamed the Plains causing less environmental harm than cattle, why was this natural ecosystem destroyed and the current cattle system favored when the current system has degraded the landscape? The debate regarding the Buffalo Commons is ongoing. There are, however, many cattle ranchers who have banded together to form stewardship alliances to conserve the prairie grasses and prevent overgrazing. With proper care, cattle can be raised and used to maintain healthy grasses, but ranchers must work with the ecosystem and not rely on only economic motives for short-lived success at the price of long-term disaster.

* D. E. Popper and F. J. Popper, "The Great Plains: From Dust to Dust," *Planning* 53, no. 6 (1987).

† Ernest Callenbach, *Bring Back the Buffalo! A Sustainable Future for America's Great Plains* (Berkeley: University of California Press, 2000).

hypothesized a return of the plains to the buffalo because their grazing patterns were more amenable to a healthy plains environment.[5] This theory endorses removing humans from the landscape so the ecology may prosper. However, as humans are part of the ecological cycle, it is imperative for humans to learn to work within their landscape rather than fence it off as if it were a zoo. Another theory for using the Great Plains is to convert to biomass energy crops to reduce greenhouse gas emissions.[6]

Native Americans

Plains Indigenous Peoples

Twelve thousand years ago as the last ice-age glaciers retreated, the Plains indigenous tribes led a seminomadic life revolving around where they could walk in a day to gather berries and seeds, practice elemental agriculture, and hunt wooly mammoths and buffalo. In the sixteenth century the Spanish arrived, introducing horses and firearms to the Natives. The Native culture was changed forever. By the early eighteenth century, horses and firearms had expanded Native mobility and warfare. Tribal groups repositioned across the Midwest and Plains: the Sioux Lakota from Minnesota to the Plains, Shoshones into the Intermontane. The Lakota and the Crow became powerful horsemen, secure in hunting, trading, and waging war, although at the cost of cultural loss; the dependence on the horse shifted their social structure, degraded the Plains ecology, and intensified warfare.

Spanish Period

Spanish exploration of the Plains was limited. Coronado covered the largest area searching for the Seven Cities of Cibola in 1541.[7] However, the golden cities were illusory. Spanish settlement remained sparse and developed a contentious relationship with the Native population.

The Great American Desert

Two lines of sand-hills, broken often into the wildest and most fantastic forms, flanked the valley at the distance of a mile or two on the right and left; while beyond them lay a barren, trackless waste [the "Great American Desert"], extending for hundreds of miles to the Arkansas on the one side, and the Missouri on the other. Before and behind us, the level monotony of the plain was unbroken as far as the eye could reach. . . . Skulls and whitening bones of buffalo were scattered everywhere.

—Francis Parkman, 1849[8]

Lewis and Clark traveled along the Missouri River through the "Great American Desert," reporting of dry creek beds in a "desert and barren" region. Lieutenant Pike in 1806 visited and wrote of a vast interior American desert. He and others attributed the treeless area to soil sterility and lack of moisture, fuel, and vegetation.

In 1820, Major Long concurred, claiming the entire region "wholly unfit for cultivation, and of course, uninhabitable by a people depending upon agriculture for their subsistence."[9] In Timothy Flint's *The History and Geography of the Mississippi Valley* (1833), the country beyond the 98th meridian "may be likened to the great Sahara of the African deserts." The region remained perceptually the Great American Desert until the 1870s, when general settlement began because no other lands were affordable or available. Then the Great Plains began to be farmed in the fashion of the wetter East.

From Nomadic to Reservations

The United States acquired most of the Great Plains from France in the 1803 Louisiana Purchase. By 1851, a series of treaties redefined Lakota territories and allowed westward wagon train passage. However, few pioneers settled on the Plains until the passage of the Homestead Act (1862) and the end of the Civil War (1865).

BOX 14.5 JOHN WESLEY POWELL AND HIS VISION FOR THE WEST

John Wesley Powell, the second director of the U.S. Geological Survey, led several expeditions west of the 100th meridian, the dividing line between the drier West and the moister East. His experiences led him to devise theories of the West that differed from those of his contemporaries. He believed that a lack of water and insufficient rainfall made the West unsuitable for eastern land uses. His policies have not been followed to this day.

Powell's 1878 study of the region, *Report on the Lands of the Arid Region*, described a realistic but ultimately politically unacceptable settlement pattern, one where watersheds were respected, conservation enforced, and cooperative self-reliance was practiced, rather than depending on government-subsidized water projects. Powell also stated that western state boundaries should follow watersheds instead of politics. When Congress was delineating western water, he was asked to speak "against the grain of accepted theory and practice." He said:

Now, what I wish to make clear to you is this. There is not water enough, runoff water enough to irrigate all the lands. When all the rivers are used, when all the creeks and ravines, when all the springs are used, when all the reservoirs along the streams are used, when all the canyon waters are taken up, when all the artesian waters are taken up, when all the wells that are sunk or dug that can be dug in all this arid region, there is still not sufficient water to irrigate all this arid region. There is still not sufficient water to irrigate all the land.

During Powell's tenure in government posts, he consistently spoke and wrote for developing the West based on judicious water rights that went with land titles, but his vision, though prescient, was not followed. He was booed when he took the podium. For example, in 1893 he spoke to Los Angeles boosters in favor of growth despite limited water:

What matters it whether I am popular or unpopular? I tell you, gentlemen, you are piling up a heritage of conflict and litigation over water rights, for there is not sufficient water to supply the land

Powell understood then what many still do not see: Water must be treated in a different manner in the West than in the East. Water is a scarce commodity and requires adjusting the water policy to correspond to western realities.*

* William deBuys, ed., *Seeing Things Whole: The Essential John Wesley Powell* (Washington, D.C.: Island Press, 2001).

As settlers encroached on tribal hunting grounds, Native American tribes fought to save their nomadic lifestyle. Uprisings and massacres continued as late as the 1870s, when most tribal groups were assigned to reservations. Europeans continued to settle and exploit Native lands, such as the Black Hills, Paha Sapa.

The Cowboy and Cattle

How odd it is that for more than a hundred years it was the employees of a ranch who were lauded in popular literature. . . . While a cowhand is a worker separated . . . from ranching's financial complications, the rancher is another matter entirely. Fundamentally, the rancher is an entrepreneur. While it is the "hands" that work on a cow outfit, it is ranchers who own livestock, grazing animals over extensive acreage, in a market–oriented modification of traditional pastoralism.[10]

The cowboy rode horseback and herded cattle on the Great Plains. He exploited available grass for unfenced, free-ranging cattle and became an American icon—but cowboys are hired hands. The rancher owns the land, the cowboy works it. But the potent cowboy persona lures wealthy ranchers today to look "authentic" in cowboy getups of denim and old pickup trucks while living in log cabin mansions. They are not the real cowboy—paid $800 a month, living in a mobile home next to the feedlot.

Four cultures—Spanish, Anglo, Gulf Coast, and subcontinental India—created the American cattle industry. The cattle drive diffused the Spanish-Anglo cattle-raising traditions across the West. Spanish words— *ranch, lasso,* and *corral*—were adopted into English. In the mid-nineteenth century, Brahman cattle from India—capable of withstanding heat, grazing large areas, and immune to insects and diseases—were introduced into the Gulf Coast. Brahman were then crossbred with European cattle to create the climatically suited Texas longhorn and then bred with other varieties to accommodate the western landscape and the Anglo palate.

The legendary cattle drive and horseback cowboy originated in Texas. The cattle drive delivered millions of longhorn cattle to rail yard cow towns such as Abilene or Dodge City, Kansas, where they were shipped sequentially to the corn-rich midwestern feedlots, the slaughterhouses of Chicago or St. Louis, and finally to East Coast markets. A cattle boom ensued across the Plains and was the favored "get rich quick" investment of the 1870s. In 1867, thirty-five thousand cattle were shipped at $4 to $5 a head; in the East they were worth $50. By 1871, Abilene alone shipped more than seven hundred thousand cattle to Chicago.

During the 1870s, the cattle-grazing industry boomed on the open plains, displacing the millions of native buffalo that were relegated to near extinction. The boom-bust-cycle cattle ranches had undisputed possession of the Plains, and everyone was either a cattle rancher or wanted to be one. When the

BOX 14.6 PAHA SAPA

The 1851 and 1868 Treaties of Fort Laramie promised the Lakota their sacred Paha Sapa land (*paha sapa* means "the hills that are black" in Lakota). However, in 1874 the Black Hills gold rush turned Paha Sapa into a battleground between miners and the Lakota. Cavalry arrived to protect miners on the reservation land. Eventually, skirmishes led to the Battle of Little Big Horn. Although the Native Americans won this battle, the "war" was lost, and soon Native Americans were confined to reservations.

But reservation lands were violated. The 1887 Dawes Severalty Act and Sioux agreement redistributed and allotted specific land to the Native Americans and allowed additional settlements on reservation lands. But the indigenous nomadic way of life was disappearing along with its source, the buffalo. The antidote was the messianic Ghost Dance, a last-hope religion for the beleaguered Sioux wishing a return to their former life. The Ghost Dance did

not, though, make the white man disappear or return the buffalo. It ended with the 1890 massacre of hundreds of unarmed natives at Wounded Knee Creek. After Wounded Knee, tribal authority was attacked by English-only educational policies, abandonment of communal lands in 1897 because of the Dawes Act, and other federal laws.

The Lakota Sioux and the federal government have had a hundred-year dispute over Paha Sapa. In 1934 the Dawes Act was rescinded and tribal ownership was again legal, but only after the loss of one hundred million acres of tribal land. In 1980, the Supreme Court awarded the Lakota over $100 million in compensation for the illegal taking of Paha Sapa. The Court told the Sioux that money, not land, was the only compensation available to them. The Sioux have not accepted the money and continue to fight to have their sacred land returned to them.

---

market collapsed in the 1880s from drought, blizzards, and overinvestment, the western cowboy and the cattle drive crashed like more recent dot-com debacles. Meanwhile, Great Plains ecosystems were profoundly altered by killing the buffalo for sport and replacing them with cattle.

Fourteen million buffalo had roamed freely, following the perennial grasses and the seasons. They did not overgraze areas because they moved on when the grass was sparse. Buffalo were a sustainable biotic system for the Plains, but the buffalo's nomadic grazing was unfit for the rigid and permanent European agricultural and ranching system, where fenced-in cattle eat introduced species of annual grass, often to the point of destroying the root. Many perennial grasses became scarce, as was noticed by ranchers and scientists alike. Range management became a primary concern for ranchers wishing to sustain ecologic diversity and health.

Canada's cowboy heritage is sometimes difficult to disentangle from the American version, but it lives on, especially in Alberta. The late-nineteenth-century cattle-ranching industry began with large ranches granted to an elite few. Cattle ranching and its perceptual aura continue, although in muted form. By 1906, frontier settlement replaced the open range, and today "cowboys" are more likely to be working in Alberta's oil fields than on the ranch. Nonetheless, Alberta and especially Calgary, where the cattle industry was the initial economic stimulus, is replete with cowboy everything—roundups, stampedes, blizzards, barbed wire, songs, and rodeos. Calgary, a place where a cowboy hat is almost de rigueur, is home to the largest cowboy rodeo anywhere, the Calgary Stampede.

With the exception of dude ranches and artificial cattle drives in both countries, the cattle-drive cowboy has disappeared, although the heroic legend remains. Throughout the Great Plains, indeed throughout America, people still dream of

having a "home on the range"—although today the "ranch" is five acres in suburbia.

Farming and Ranching

Farming and ranching on the Great Plains did not begin until other areas became populated and too expensive. The Great Plains landscape was misunderstood. Settlers from humid areas were unfamiliar with the arid, grassy plains. **Dryland farming** (without irrigation) required adjusting farm implements to break the thick sod. Wet years brought bounty, dry years despair. Nonetheless propaganda transformed the image of the "Great American Desert" and attracted settlers who believed they could tame the plains. As luck would have it, the 1870s, the period of greatest settlement of the U.S. Plains, proved wetter than the norm. "Rain follows the plow" seemed plausible, until trees planted and fields plowed during wet periods suffered when precipitation waned. This period was a prelude to the Dust Bowl debacle fifty years later.

Plains settlement became political when the North and South went to war. The dry Great Plains land seemed marginally productive but was heralded as otherwise in a government propaganda campaign that encouraged land settlement and productivity. Congress passed the **Homestead Act** in 1862, offering quarter sections for almost nothing if the land was settled. Although it has been perceived by later generations as a great giveaway, the act was a last-ditch effort by Congress to produce income while ridding the government of excess poor land. The best land had been already settled or granted to the rail companies. Agricultural settlement was drawing to a close, though, because the nation's attention was drawing away from the farm and toward industry. Still, some areas attracted settlers.

After the Civil War, a new group of farmers were seeking land for the first time. Freed black families, the **Exodusters**, were pulled to the Plains after the Klu Klux Klan and Jim Crow racial oppression pushed them out of the South. In Kansas, slavery was a hot political debate during the 1850s, after abolitionist John Brown had taken up arms against pro-slavery Kansans and established the name "bleeding Kansas." After the Civil War, the abolitionist legacy was enough to support rumors of free land, mules, and plows for freed slaves. Twenty thousand freed blacks migrated seeking their fortunes. They formed more than thirty independent farm communities in Kansas, and about three-quarters of the migrants eventually owned their own farms. Some towns still exist but are dying, such as Nicodemus in north central Kansas. Seeking respect and opportunity, other freed African Americans joined the military; they were dubbed "buffalo soldiers" by their Cheyenne and Comanche opponents.

"Free" land, though, was not an easy answer. On the surface, the lack of water, wood, and tools to work this dry land often drained settlers' resources. Western land was almost free except for the cost of fencing, which was a source of irritation for both farmer and rancher. Fencing land often cost more than purchasing land in the East. Eventually, fencing the Plains became a major component of the range wars.

Range Wars

Friction between ranchers and farmers caused the **range wars**. The question of the highest and best use of this dry land was answered in numerous, mutually exclusive ways. Cattlemen, sheepherders, and farmers clashed in how they used the fragile landscape. Cattlemen with large spreads inhibited the small farm operators and often cut through fences to access free range. Farmers wanted cattle fenced out of their fields. Ranchers wanted unwelcome farmers to bear the fencing cost, since the farmers arrived after the ranchers. Shepherds allowed the grazing sheep to crop grass close to the ground, preventing regrowth and therefore ruining the grass for cattle grazing.

The cost of fencing was a major settlement obstacle. The treeless plains offered no inexpensive way to fence until the 1874 invention of barbed wire. Billed as "cheaper than dirt and stronger than steel," barbed wire was strung on a minimum of wooden posts. But although it solved one dilemma it caused another: the cost of labor.

Labor costs for fencing and the loss of open waterways for their cattle were irritants for ranchers that caused many to "go to war," against the barbed wire fence. Eventually, states adopted fencing laws that shifted the burden of fencing to one party or another. At first, most western states allowed livestock to roam at will. **Open-range ranching** allowed cattle to graze on unfenced range. The farmer was expected to fence the cattle out. Eventually, states adopted a closed-range fencing policy, which effectively ended the cattle drives. The cost and time of "riding fence" has continued to be a large expense and a source of irritation and litigation. Some old-time ranchers still complain about the loss of the open range.

Northern Plains

The Northern Plains settlement pattern differed from the High Plains since the Northern Plains were far from the cattle trails, and the Europeans who settled the Dakotas were more culturally preadapted to the regional landscape. Settlers from Sweden and Finland understood the long, cold winters and the agricultural conditions. They brought with them four valuable tools for the Northern Plains: (1) a Protestant work ethic, (2) seed adapted to the northern latitude, (3) a winterproof mentality, and (4) cold-weather traditions that included festivals and saunas that broke the monotony of long winters.

The Canadian Prairie

Métis and Louis Riel

"There was a time when we were told that the Métis were not a nation, that they did not have a culture or language. A Métis was a Heinz 57, a mongrel. Now we realize that the Métis were not Heinz 57s, but that in effect they were the creation of a new nation, of a new people in Western Canada. . . . Today, being Métis means identifying oneself with the group that was responsible for the founding of the province."

—Lieutenant-governor and Métis Yvon Dumont, 1995[11]

The **Métis** (a French term meaning "mixed," akin to the Spanish *mestizo*) are a people of mixed Aboriginal and European descent, the descendants of Native women and French trappers. Métis hunted, trapped, and traded in the Great Lakes wilderness of Canada and the northern United States, and they were fundamental in the settling of Manitoba's Red River Valley. The ten thousand Métis of the late nineteenth century formed their own culture; they lived more like a Native nation than European, adopted Catholicism, and spoke French or their mixed language, Michif. They depended on the buffalo and traded animal pelts with Hudson Bay posts. Their sense of nationhood developed under the leadership of Louis Riel.

In 1870, Canada purchased Rupert's Land (renamed the Northwest Territories) and European settlers began to arrive in Manitoba's Red River Valley where many Métis were settled. The new settlers disputed the earlier Métis claims. The Métis were starved by loss of their land claims, drought, and the loss of the buffalo herds.

The Métis appealed to Louis Riel, who had been instrumental in obtaining the Manitoba Métis Indian Treaty land. But mistreatment by the Canadian government led him to retreat to a quiet life in Montana. After entreaties to return and lead his people, Riel reluctantly returned and fought for their treaty-promised land. Canadian forces quashed the uprising and forced the Métis to surrender. Riel was tempted to return to Montana but chose instead to surrender and stand trial. He hoped his presence and trial would bring attention to his people's predicament. He surrendered, was tried, and was executed in what can only be called a death of political expediency. He died a martyr for his cause and remains a hero in Canadian lore.

His death was more than a loss to the Métis; his French-Canadian roots represented a loss for Quebec as well, and his death widened the gap between French-speaking and English-speaking Canadians. Today, Métis and First Nations peoples live on reservations and experience the same societal ills as American tribes.

The Métis have become the fastest-growing ethnic group, although some of the growth can be attributed to awareness of Métis issues and rights. Not that long ago, claiming to have Métis blood was unpopular, but this has changed. In 1982, the Métis were granted legal status as Native people. About 30 percent of all Aboriginals (292,310) were reported in the 2001 Canadian census to be Métis. Two-thirds live in the Prairie provinces and make their living by fishing, guiding tourists who hunt, procuring seasonal jobs, and a bit of subsistence farming.

Canadian Prairie Settlement

The Canadian Prairie was settled after the 1870s, despite early explorers' disparaging analyses of the landscape. John Palliser explored Canada's prairie in 1857 to assess settlement possibilities. Palliser concluded that the grassy, dry "Palliser Triangle" extending from southwestern Manitoba to southern Alberta was unsuitable for agriculture.[12] Nonetheless, Canada purchased Rupert's Land in 1870 (Map 14.3).

Canadians asserted their sovereignty over the newly acquired land with the **Dominion Lands Act** (1872), which closely resembled the 1862 U.S. Homestead Act; but although the Dominion Lands Act was meant to provide an impetus for settlement, relatively few settlers were attracted. Success increased when the government offered additional incentives: loans, larger acreage, reserves of land, and military exemptions. For example, several thousand pacifist Mennonites and Icelanders fleeing Icelandic volcanic eruptions settled Manitoba and the upper Midwest beginning in the 1870s. But still the

expansive West had too few settlers, many of whom migrated from Canada into the states (Table 14.2).

The Canadian Shield was a barrier to transcontinental transportation. Traveling to the Canadian Prairie could only be accomplished by crossing the American Great Lakes states. The Canadian transcontinental railroad (1885) provided a direct route through Canada's Shield from northwestern Ontario into Manitoba and tied British Columbia to the rest of the fledgling country.

With the railroad complete, populating the Prairie region became the mission of Canadian Prime Minister Sir Wilfred Laurier, who came into office at the dawn of the twentieth century. The "Laurier boom" (1896–1911) was a perfect storm for immigrants at an opportune time.

A push and pull migration followed. The push was from political, religious, and economic repression. Eastern Europeans and landless American and Canadian immigrants were pulled by free land on the Canadian Prairies. Another pull factor was a shift in economic well-being; both the United States and Canada emerged from the 1890 depression amid rising wheat prices that brought settlers to the last frontier on the Canadian Prairies.

Laurier's Minister of the Interior, Sir Clifford Sifton, devoted his attention to populating the Prairies. He eased immigration restrictions and land acquisition, and developed a publicity/propaganda campaign to encourage settlement. He advertised the Prairies throughout the United States and Europe by sending promotional agents with lantern slide shows and bright, beautifully illustrated ads showing the golden fields of

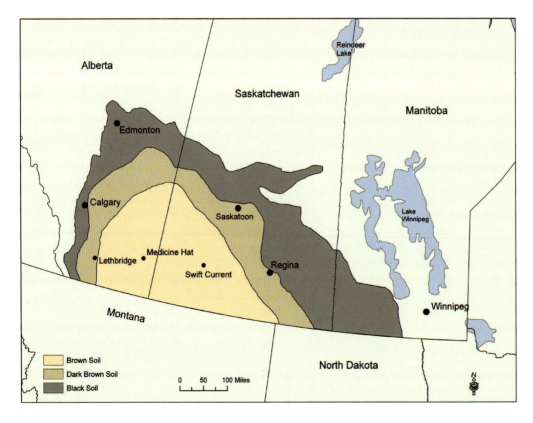

MAP 14.3. Canadian Prairie. The Palliser Triangle is the northern extension of the Great Plains. These fertile prairies produce the most grain in Canada.

TABLE 14.2. Net Immigration in Canada, 1871–1920

Census period	Excess of arrivals over departures
1871–1880	(40,000)
1881–1890	(154,000)
1891–1900	(115,000)
1901–1910	794,000
1911–1920	306,000

Source: Carl E. Solberg, "Peopling the Prairies and the Pampas," *Journal of Interamerican Studies and World Affairs* 24, no. 2 (1982); Duncan M. McDougall, "Immigration into Canada, 1851–1920," *Canadian Journal of Economics and Political Science / Revue canadienne d'economique et de science politique* 27, no. 2 (1961)

the Prairies. Sifton "spun" the wording, though, preferring "bracing" to "freezing" temperatures, "invigorating" over "desolate." Publishing winter temperatures or mentioning snow or cold was forbidden in the ads.

Up to this time Palliser's analysis had deterred settlement, but Sifton's "Last Best West" publicity tours became the most successful immigration device in Canadian history. Between 1896 and 1911, more than two million land-seeking Canadians, Americans, and exiled **Hutterites** and Ukrainians settled the Prairie region. Among them were six hundred thousand midwestern tenant farmers seeking their own land; they reversed the previous trend of immigration to America. Many of the immigrants would not stay; the climate was far harsher, the land more marginal than advertised. But many did stay, and in time, improved technology, such as quickly maturing strains of wheat that fit the short growing season, made life bearable.

In 1897, the **Crow Rate** subsidized the transportation of crops to market. It reduced the cost of transporting grain over Crow's Nest Pass to Vancouver in the West and to the Great Lakes in the East. The subsidy was a benefit for prairie farmers and supported the development of the railroad in Western Canada, but it hindered the development of western industry because the Crow Rate distorted production costs. The Crow Rate was abolished in 1995, and thereafter prairie farmers' exposure to unstable economic conditions increased as environmental conditions degraded. Climate change became more pronounced, and severe droughts marked some ensuing years. Wheat price instability left farmers with erratic incomes, at a time when transportation costs escalated by as much as 40 percent. After the demise of the Crow Rate, policy shifts were unable to compensate for the climatic shifts and the inflexibility of the rate over its century of operation.

Ultimately the Prairie land was settled, and although many left, others built a life. The Palliser Triangle morphed from unusable to becoming Canada's greatest wheat-growing area, while Alberta and then Saskatchewan evolved from cattle to oil, becoming the economic engine of Canada during the twenty-first century. The farmer, though, was left with environmental degradation.

Cultural Perspectives

Dwellings: Vernacular Architecture

The lack of transportation and the scarcity of wood on the Plains and Canadian Prairie forced settlers to build their initial homes with local materials—sod and hay. Because of superior insulation qualities, both hay and sod buildings have made a comeback since 1970, mostly by environmentally green–oriented people who see the advantages of building with well-insulating local materials.

Sod Buildings

Sod houses were well adjusted for the semiarid climate. The short, tufted grasses were supported by a deep root system that improved the soil, prevented erosion, and served as a building material because the grass roots held the sod blocks together. Sod house construction varied in relation to the culture adapting the building material. Some houses were cut directly from the sod, built brick upon brick; others dug into the ground; while others were built from rammed earth or wattle and daub, a construction technique intertwining branches and twigs and then smearing them with mud.

Although cramped and uncomfortable, the sod houses were well insulated, a necessity for the continental climate extremes. Among the many inconveniences of living in a sod house were insects and snakes living in the walls and the inevitable washing away of the walls with each rain. Few of the original sod houses remain today, due to the temporary nature of their unbaked soil construction (Photo 14.5).

Straw Bale Buildings

For hundreds of years, Europeans built straw bale homes and many still stand. They are inexpensive to build, use local material, and their insulating qualities make them energy efficient. The bales are stacked like bricks and then held in place

PHOTO 14.5. Sod House in Texas County, Oklahoma. The last sod house in the county is protected from cattle by a fence, has a metal roof, and is whitewashed to maintain its structural integrity. This sod house was a semidugout, with a front door and excavated walls.

with rods driven through the bales. The Sand Hills of Nebraska in the Great Plains were the birthplace for American straw-bale homes during the late nineteenth century, driven by the invention of the steam-powered baler.

Today, straw bale buildings have become a favorite for "greens" seeking a sustainable building material. People who build these homes aim to be off the grid as much as possible, so solar heating, rainwater collection, and solar hot water are part of the straw-bale package. The U.S. Department of Energy has also endorsed this energy efficient and renewable house form.[13]

The 49th Parallel

The goal of the Convention of 1818 was to establish a permanent border to end Great Plains border disputes. The ideal was to have waters flowing into the Gulf of Mexico (Mississippi-Missouri rivers) for the United States and waters flowing into Hudson Bay for Britain. Up to that time the land had been divided along watersheds: Hudson Bay in Canada and the Mississippi-Missouri in the United States. However, the watersheds were difficult to survey in 1818, so a compromise was chosen: the 49th parallel.

Although many Americans feel there is little difference between Canada and America, Canadians know that there is a cultural chasm that perhaps is growing wider in the twenty-first century. Although Canadians share the English language and colonial past, the political and social stances of the two countries are remarkably different. Still, the sharing of a common language (despite differences of spelling such as *color* and *colour*, *centre* and *center*), similar socioeconomic profiles, and the undefended border make the two countries more aligned than the United States and Mexico.

The physical region continues beyond the 49th parallel into the Canadian Prairie region with little to physically divide them

other than the International Boundary Commission's twenty-foot-wide (six-meter) swath marking the border. Yet on either side of the border the crops usually differ, matching each country's agricultural policies. The Montanan farmer may plant wheat, while his Albertan neighbor directly north is a rancher and will have nothing to do with farming; yet they share common climate and soil. Government policies and tariffs often determine whether a farmer will grow canola or wheat or be a rancher. Generally, Canadian beef and hogs flow south as exports, unless the supply threatens American farmers' incomes. For example, between 2003 and 2007 Canadian beef was not accepted by the American government because of a BSE (mad cow disease) cow found in Alberta. Later, the disease was found in American cows.

Another similarity of border culture is that residents of both countries flock to their southern borders, and their perceptions of the 49th parallel differ widely. Southern Alberta has a milder winter than other interior provinces because of the chinook winds, and the relatively warm and sunny climate has drawn people to the region. The same winds across the border in Montana are not celebrated for their warmth, and the idea of advertising eastern Montana as "sunny and warm" would be laughable in the states.[14]

Regional Life

Population

Historically, the Great Plains Native American population was sparse and nomadic. The Native American followed the buffalo herd, the cowboy followed the cattle, and the settler followed (in historic sequence) trails, rails, and highways. European Americans were slow to settle the Plains, until the 1870s when the population in Nebraska more than tripled to almost half a million and in the 1880s when population in Kansas reached a million. Every Great Plains state grew during the late nineteenth century but lost population since 1920.

In 1893 the national population density reached two people per square mile, and the Wisconsin historian Frederick Jackson Turner in his **Frontier Thesis** declared the frontier and a chapter of American history closed. The thesis identified powerful American psyche images, among them the cowboy and the pioneer's rugged individualism. Using statistical data from the 1890 Census, a first in modern social science, Turner analyzed the data and told a politically charged story, identifying a shift in demography from rural agricultural settlement to urban. By 1900, half of all Americans were living in urban settings, and the percentage of farmers was in a continual decline.

While the Dakotas reached Turner's critical population of two people per square mile in the 1890 census, the population density has declined since. In North Dakota, for example, only six of its fifty-three counties gained population between 1990 and 2000; most counties in the western part of the state were below two people per square mile, despite a boom economy beginning in 2007 when oil field work in the Bakken formation brought a flood of RVs and campers filled with temporary workers into the small towns.

Current Population Issues

The rural population of the Great Plains and Canadian Prairies has the highest percentage of Americans and Canadians over the age of sixty-five. **Aging in place** creates demographic and economic dynamics that place strains on social services. The constrained budget of an elderly population does not support the consumer economy as much as a fully employed youthful population. An economic structure based on the gross domestic product (GDP) and consumer spending ill-fits an older population and may signal a new economic order. Older populations also require additional health-care facilities that further restrain limited budgets, especially when health care is not universal.

In the Great Plains, many elderly are isolated in low-amenity rural settings, a situation very different from higher-income areas such as Florida and Arizona. Aging in place hinders population growth on the Plains, because while the older population remains, the younger population often chooses to migrate outside the area and further alters the population balance (Table 14.3).

Living on large, dispersed farms made sense in the nineteenth century when transportation was limited; however, fewer people live on their farms now that transportation allows more freedom. "**Suitcase farmers**" plant and harvest the farm but live in the city. They farm their land using capital-intensive, technology-dependent mechanization, unlike the 24/7 life of the traditional farmer. Assembly-line farming production breaks the tie to the land that has been the hallmark of the American farmer. Technology frees farmers from the fields and from labor-intensive chores. For example, the time-and-labor-intensive operation of manually moving irrigation pipes has been replaced with automated **center pivot irrigation (CPI)**.

TABLE 14.3. Population in Low-Population-Density Counties in North Dakota, 2000 and 2010, Showing Aging in Place, Low Percentage of Youth, and Overall Loss of Population

County	Population density per square mile (2010)	Population (2000)	Population (2010)	Median age (2000)	% < 18 (2010)	% > 65 (2010)	Vacant housing (2010)
Slope	0.6	767	727	42.5	20.0	18.6	44.7
Billings	0.7	888	783	41.9	17.6	19.3	26.0
Grant	1.4	2,841	2,392	46.5	19.0	26.9	33.3
Sheridan	1.3	1,710	1,321	48.1	16.0	30.0	27.9
Divide	1.6	2,283	2,071	49	17.1	26.6	26.2
Dunn	1.7	3,600	3,536	40.9	22.0	17.4	34.3
North Dakota	9.8	642,200	672,591	37a	6.6	14.5	11.4
United States	87.3	282 M	308M	35.3a	24.3	12.9	9.0

a 2010
Source: U.S. Census

Canadian Prairie Populations

The Canadian Prairie has been an underpopulated resource hinterland, separated politically and geographically from the heartland. In 1870, the newly acquired Rupert's Land was surveyed in a rectangular grid pattern and opened to homesteading. Still, population remained sparse. Rural settlement increased after 1900 and peaked in the mid-1930s; it has since waned as technology has enabled land-use changes, the reorganization of farms, and movement into the city.

Prairie settlers included Canadians and Americans. Eastern and northern Europeans were the largest ethnic groups immigrating during the Laurier boom period at the turn of the twentieth century. Pacifist German Mennonites and Hutterites fled religious persecution first into the Russian Ukraine and then, when threatened with conscription, onto the Canadian Prairie. Immigrating to the harsh climatic conditions of the Canadian Prairie was not quite as onerous for the Hutterites as for other groups, because the climate resembles the Ukrainian steppes and the Hutterites understood that landscape. Hutterites continue to live in isolated, agricultural, communal settlements, while many Mennonites have assimilated into Canadian society.

The Canadian Prairie and the Great Plains share rural changes: Farms are growing larger, the workforce is growing smaller, and small towns are disappearing. Fewer people equates to a loss of political influence for the remaining farmers and ranchers.

Between 1998 and 2006, Saskatchewan lost population while Manitoba grew slightly. By 2006, Alberta had grown substantially, and by 2008, Saskatchewan joined Alberta as one of the fastest-growing provinces in the nation because of crude petroleum production. However, farms and ranches benefited little from the economic growth.

Urban Life

The Great Plains is not known for its urban centers but for its dispersed farms and ranches. Large urban centers located on the region's periphery are juxtaposed to hundreds of withering towns, which reflect the changed economy and transportation patterns.

Small Towns

The Great Plains was settled in a dispersed pattern. The towns have been small and served the local farming population, but the economic, social, and political viability of these towns is waning. Pockets of wealth surround poverty, because most of the middle class has left for urban areas. The region's agricultural and manufacturing economy cannot support large populations. Economic enterprises are controlled by a few, and all others have the choice to be at the mercy of those in power or to move from the area.

Historically, U.S. and Canadian speculators planned Great Plains towns every fifteen miles—a day's round-trip journey—along the railroad lines. The centerpiece of each town was the grain elevator (Photo 14.6). As long as the grain elevator was operating, the town remained viable. Local farmers brought their grain to the elevator and their business to the town. When a town lost its grain elevator, the town's reason for existence went with it.

Reliance on local community was further weakened when rural electrification became a priority and reality in rural America and Canada. Although over 90 percent of urban dwellers had electricity in 1930, only 10 percent of rural residents did. By 1939, 35 percent of the rural populace had electricity, and by 2000 over 90 percent. Electricity changed the way farming was done, allowing more mechanization and extending working hours. But electricity did not halt the migration of rural families into cities or stop the growth of corporate farming control.

Numerous Great Plains towns have tried economic development ideas in order to save their small and aging towns. For example, Guymon in the Oklahoma Panhandle has continually run after the most popular economic panacea of the times. In

PHOTO 14.6. Grain Elevators, Southern Saskatchewan. Grain elevators, originally designed for nineteenth-century operations, stood in each town about fifteen miles apart, a day's travel. Newer elevators are much larger and more widely spaced, accommodating modern travel. Towns bypassed by the newer elevators lose their identity when the local elevator closes.

the 1990s, Guymon courted a pork-processing plant. After its success, the immigrant workers increased crime levels and caused new problems. By 2011, the city was working to attract wind power companies to exploit the Panhandle's most abundant natural resource, wind.

As an antidote to population loss, Plains towns' residents are creating opportunities for families to repopulate withering Great Plains towns. Two of these opportunities are small-town land giveaways and a proposed New Homestead Act.

If enacted, the **New Homestead Act** would offer incentives to move into small Plains towns. Proposed by Senator Dorgan of North Dakota, himself a great-grandson of an 1860s homesteader, the new act would fight emigration by offering tax credits and capital for starting businesses in these towns. It would also forgive college loans and offer home-buying assistance. First introduced in 2003, the bill has been reintroduced annually but has not passed.

Traditional and Sustainable Cities

The Great Plains metropolitan areas are on the periphery of the region. Denver and the Front Range complex (see Chapter 15) and the Calgary-Edmonton corridor in Alberta are gateway cities. Dallas–Fort Worth, the largest metropolitan complex, is located along the eastern margin of the Plains, while on the Osage Plain, Oklahoma City and Kansas City are both transitional cities between the Central Lowlands and the Great Plains.

Canadian Prairie Cities

The capitals of each prairie province are located in the more populated southern part of the provinces. Winnipeg is a wheat distribution center, while Regina is a center for natural resources. But the major urban centers in the Canadian Prairie are in Alberta. Both Calgary and Edmonton are gateway cities to other regions, Calgary to the Rocky Mountains, and Edmonton to the boreal north and its booming oil sand economy. The energy sector supports their booming economies.

Calgary

(2011 pop. 1,096,833; CMA 1,214,839)

Calgary is the fifth-largest, and the second-fastest-growing city in Canada, with a growth rate of 12.6 percent between the 2006 and 2011 census. Immigrants and Canadians from outside the province fuel the growth to the oil-rich province. Calgary's population is skilled and educated; 60 percent have a postsecondary education, the highest in the province. They seek local quality-of-life amenities and low tax rates, and they have the highest employment rate in North America.

Calgary started as a cattle ranching center and evolved into the Prairie's financial, natural resource, and transportation center. In 1883, the Canadian Pacific Railroad chose the southern route through Calgary over Edmonton, thereby assuring Calgary's growth. The 240-mile urban corridor between Calgary and Edmonton contains 2.2 million people (about 72 percent of the provincial population).[15] Calgary is Canada's second-largest center of corporate headquarters (behind Toronto).

Calgary has been recognized as a city working toward sustainability, especially in water efficiency. Calgary sits in the rain shadow of the Canadian Rockies and receives only about sixteen inches (41 cm) of precipitation annually. The city has depended on local rivers, the Bow and the Elbow, but the resources are finite and service not only the human population but a variety of plant and aquatic life. Recognizing the city's growth and its high water consumption, the city adopted "30-in-30 by 2033." The goal of the plan is to keep water consumption at the same level in 2033 as it was in 2003, despite the expected population growth of about eighteen thousand people annually. The population is being asked to reduce water consumption by 30 percent over thirty years. By 2010, the population was cooperating and the goal was on track.

Cities on the Eastern Margin

Great Plains agricultural and resource wealth has supplied eastern markets. Transitional cities—Minneapolis–St. Paul, Kansas City, Omaha (see Chapter 13), and Dallas–Fort Worth—developed along the eastern margins, distributing Plains commodities and livestock to eastern markets.

Dallas–Fort Worth

(2010 pop. [Dallas] 1,197,816; [Fort Worth] 741,206; CSA 6,731,317)

Dallas–Fort Worth was founded at a transportation junction in the 1860s. Dallas and Fort Worth began as separate cites with separate hinterlands, but they coalesced over time into the sprawling metropolis (called the Metroplex locally) it is today. While Dallas is not known as being especially aware of its sustainable options, it has begun to recognize the problems with sprawl and is working to institute a mass transit system that will serve the populace.

Dallas's hinterland is to the east in the Texas Blacklands, where 40 percent of U.S. cotton was grown in the nineteenth century. Dallas was the distribution city for cotton, hence the naming of the Cotton Bowl football classic. In the 1930s, the discovery of oilfields near Dallas provided a future beyond cotton. Today, Dallas is a regional center for transportation and finance and a gateway for wholesale trade.

Fort Worth's history is tied to western cattle, oil, and railroads. The Chisholm Trail was Texas's major cattle trail through Fort Worth and on to Abilene, Kansas. Fort Worth remains tied to cattle and agricultural production and its distribution. Today, the combined "twin" cities are the second-largest population in Texas after Houston.

Economy

The Great Plains economy revolves around agricultural production, but it has experienced a sea change. Traditionally, the Great Plains distributed their crops and livestock to eastern U.S. population centers. By the late twentieth century, however, another "East" emerged as the main market for Great Plains

TABLE 14.4. Great Plains Agriculture and Livestock Variables

	Major crops	Livestock	Water source
Canadian Prairie	Spring wheat, barley, flax, canola	Cattle, hogs	Irrigation dryland
Northern Plains	Spring wheat, barley	Cattle	Dryland irrigation in river valleys
Nebraska Sand Hills	Corn	Cattle	CPI irrigation
High Plains	Wheat, corn, milo	Cattle, hogs	Dryland, CPI
Edwards Plateau		Cattle, sheep, goats	Irrigation dryland

crop production. Successful Asian economies invested in Great Plains crops and livestock. Technology and shifting transportation patterns augmented this change. The transportation patterns are dependent on fossil fuel use and may require reconsideration as new transportation patterns emerge in a more sustainable economy.

Primary Economy and Natural Resources

The Great Plains and Canadian Prairie are major resource hinterlands for their respective countries. The primary economy of this region is essential for both countries, and yet it is often unsustainable. Primary sector industries have been taken for granted but are the economic building blocks of both countries.

Agricultural Landscape

Migrating settlers from the Midwest misunderstood the Great Plains landscape and its demands. The lack of trees, abundant heavy sod, and grasses were unfamiliar features. The sod was rich in nutrients but a lack of water limited crop production until irrigation brought water.

America and Canada have supported a family farm agricultural economy that remains a standard in name, although most farmers are no longer independent family operations. The family farm is tied to corporate inputs (feed, mechanical, and technological) and unless they have identified a niche market, it is also tied to corporate buyers. In order to remain in business, the family farm must produce according to corporate demands. Little is left to chance or the open market. Eighty percent of farmers now operate on negative income and would go out of business providing food for America if not for agricultural **subsidies** and off-farm jobs.

The average age of a U.S. farmer today is over sixty years, and less than 8 percent are under the age of thirty-five. The young farmers have a much different background than the previous generation did. Today's young farmer is more often a graduate of business school and agribusiness than a farmer working in agriculture. Every year there are larger farms and fewer farmers; less than 2 percent of the total population now claim farming as their major occupation.

Without government subsidies and corporate contracts, Canadian and American family farmers may disappear in the next generation. Farms are getting bigger and more expensive to operate; technological improvements are capital intensive and often require government-subsidized megafarms.

Although both the United States and Canada have prided themselves in maintaining a cheap food policy, subsidies are hidden costs that consumers pay with tax dollars. Subsidies have become a controversial subject both within America and within the globalized economy. Americans who are aware of the subsidies often feel that if farmers were any good they would not need subsidies. Farmers in less developed countries feel subsidies interfere with their right to compete. Yet without subsidies, American farmers would be unable to compete with the lower prices from abroad and food security would be weakened.

The fertile Great Plains and Canadian Prairie traditionally grow wheat, sorghum, and other dry-farmed crops; however, corn has become an important crop on the aquifer-watered plains during the last half of the twentieth century because of two shifts: irrigation and the evolution of seed (Table 14.4).

Irrigation

[Water management in the West is a] techno-economic order imposed for the purpose of mastering a difficult environment. People are organized and induced to run, as the water in the canal does, in a straight line toward maximum yield, maximum profit.

—Donald Worster, 1985[16]

Irrigation artificially waters fields from sources other than precipitation. It is usually used in dry areas, or in areas with insufficient precipitation during the growing season. In the United States, irrigation is common in the major agricultural areas of the Mississippi River Valley of Arkansas, the High Plains, the Snake River Valley, the Columbia Plateau, and the Central, Coachella, and Imperial valleys of California.

On the Great Plains, unreliable natural precipitation has forced farmers to try several methods to stabilize water access. The lack of surface water has turned attention to larger water projects including unsuccessful diversion projects, such as the Trans-Texas Canal, and the successful Rocky Mountain

BOX 14.7 THE DUST BOWL AND SOIL CONSERVATION

Since the nineteenth century, the iconic Great Plains windmills provided water from shallow aquifers for livestock but not enough for crops. The limited water supply, however, did not halt a demand for wheat during World War I.

The 1929 stock market crash signaled the start of the Great Depression that dominated the American economy until the start of World War II. To compound farmers' problems, a nationwide drought began in 1931 and continued for most of the "dirty thirties," the **Dust Bowl** decade. The drought brought intense heat; grasshoppers multiplied and swarmed, destroying what the heat or lack of rain did not.

After World War I, the grasslands west of the 100th meridian, once considered too dry to grow crops, were plowed for agricultural use. The Wheat Belt expanded across Oklahoma and into Texas, as new farm implements—the tractor and Hoeme plow—broke the heavy but fertile sod. In the Northern Plains, dryland crops stretched beyond the Missouri River to northern Montana.

During the economic expansion of the 1920s, grazing areas shrank while farm size grew to satisfy food demands. The natural deep-rooted sod that had held the topsoil in place was destroyed along with a fragile ecologic balance, but few paid attention. The focus on economic factors alone drove the environmental and social factors to ruin. The short-term benefits were not applicable long-term and were unable to support the farming methods. Farmers became refugees, as the land dried up and literally blew away. The "American Dream" of agricultural bounty became an ecological tragedy of soil degradation and falling market prices.

The extensive root systems of native sod held the soil in place and returned nutrients, but overgrazing from cattle ranching and the replacement of perennial grasses with annual wheat and corn crops left the land bare after harvest and prone to soil erosion. When soil moisture fell, the topsoil began to blow, creating zero visibility in the infamous High Plains dust storms. The remote panhandle of Oklahoma was the hardest hit, with sixteen million acres of topsoil blown hundreds of miles during black blizzards. Farmers left their land or lost their farms to foreclosure, as documented by John Steinbeck in *Grapes of Wrath* or by Woody Guthrie in his songs.

The newly formed Soil Conservation Service introduced tillage methods to halt the Dust Bowl disaster and prevent future occurrences. The new techniques—growing cover crops, shallow plowing, and no-till fields—limited soil exposure to the wind. A Shelterbelt Project of planting trees along fencerows between properties to cut wind force and erosion was proposed by President Franklin D. Roosevelt. When the rains returned in 1939, wheat once again covered the Plains but utilized the new soil protection methods.

---

transmountain diversion (see Chapter 15). Dams built on the upper Missouri River and in Nebraska controlled flooding, provided irrigation, and generated power. But accessing the Ogallala Aquifer water has been the single most important resource for Great Plains agricultural production.

Crop irrigation changed western settlement patterns and local climates. Irrigation in the United States accounts for the agricultural viability of 26.8 percent of all land on farms and 64.8 percent of the nation's total harvested cropland.[17] West of the 100th meridian, 55 percent of all harvested cropland has been irrigated since the 1980s.

Water remains the single largest determining factor for crop yields. Technology-driven irrigation systems support the High Plains' corn, cow, and hog production.

Irrigation systems have increased efficiency and conservation of water over the years, but the growth has exceeded the savings. Irrigation farming is most efficient and economical in flat country, such as the High Plains, so more than two hundred thousand wells were installed since Ogallala irrigation became viable in the 1960s, and water-efficient CPI circles now dot the otherwise dry landscape (Photo 14.7). Irrigated fields yield two to three times what dryland fields produce, but the challenge to maintain agricultural production for future generations requires analyzing current irrigation practices to determine sustainability.

The availability of irrigation water has also changed the choice of crops. While wheat and sorghum require little water, they are marginally profitable. More profitable crops such as corn require consistent water. Dryland corn yields 48 bushels per acre; irrigated corn yields 115. Irrigation supports water-intensive crops such as alfalfa, corn, and cotton, which have replaced many dryland crops.

Sustainability of the Ogallala   Farmers maximize profits and growth in order to maintain their way of life. One of the keystones of successful farm operation is access to water. In the Plains, this has been a source of stress. Since the 1960s, extensive irrigation with Ogallala Aquifer water seemed to answer the problems. However, the long-term sustainability of the aquifer is now questioned.[18] Towns from Kansas through the Texas Panhandle have lowered the **water table** (level at which ground is saturated) and overpumped the aquifer, so irrigation is no longer possible.

European American farmers settled the Plains, but incomplete knowledge and tools for dryland cultivation subjected them to a boom-bust cycle. Settlers prospered or despaired depending on the annual precipitation. In the 1960s, the Green Revolution and access to the Ogallala Aquifer ended the previous cycle and provided a steady source of water for crops, but began unsustainable fossil fuel–dependent farming operating on the underlying water rights pattern.

In the United States, water rights differ in the East and West. East of the Mississippi, riparian rights allocate water rights to all

BOX 14.8 SUBSIDIES

To stabilize food prices, agricultural subsidies (government payments to support food producers) are common in developed countries. The European Union's largest expense is agricultural subsidies, averaging $17,000 per farmer; in the United States subsidies average $48,000, but the majority of subsidies go to 10 percent of the farmers, usually the larger farmers, far different than the original purpose of subsidies: to help the small farmer.*

Developed-country food subsidies have been a target at World Trade Organization (WTO) talks. Developing countries in the WTO challenge American agricultural subsidies, because they disable both competition and a free-trade network. But although these claims hold some truth, if agricultural subsidies were to end, prices for American agricultural products would increase or reach a point where agriculture could disappear in America, placing the country in a tenuous food-security position. Additionally, shipping food over large distances does not create the best nutritional and transport value for food. Limiting food production so that the United States is no longer self-sufficient can also be a security threat, because of possible embargoes or a dependence on non-regulated foreign food.

America has supported a cheap food policy, and in order to continue this policy, subsidies have been an important factor in maintaining American food production. However, the distribution of subsidies among farmers is problematic. The largest subsidies go to the largest producers. The top 10 percent of recipients receive 66 percent of subsidies, and the bottom 80 percent receive 16 percent. Large farms use the small farmer as a ploy for continuing subsidies, but the small farmer is not the main recipient. About two-thirds of all farmers receive no subsidies because they are either too small or do not grow subsidized crops.

Most subsidized crops are grains, but cotton, sugar, and sorghum are also supported. Fruit, vegetable, and nut crops have not been directly subsidized, which has proved controversial. The price of grain remains low because of subsidies, while fresh fruits and vegetables increase in price. Since the subsidized grains are the raw goods for most processed foods, the grain-heavy subsidies are also affecting obesity levels in America.

Agricultural subsidies have been politically controversial and have been consistently cut with each new farm bill since the 1990s. In 2007, a new farm bill suggested a radical change, which favored independent farmers by limiting subsidies to those who make less than $200,000 annually, with a maximum of $360,000 per payment. The savings, which are estimated at $10 billion over five years, would subsidize healthier food like fruits and vegetables, alternative fuels, and land preservation. However, little has been done to undo the grain-heavy subsidies (feeding the meat-heavy American diet), and large farmers continue to be the ones benefiting from subsidies (although most large farm companies favor less government intervention). The next farm subsidy bill is due in 2012. Will it fund more research into our farming methods? Will it attract the new farmers we need to replace the ever aging farming population?†

Subsidies can take many forms, such as direct subsidies with price-support loans on commodities, land conservation subsidies, and energy usage subsidies. Land conservation subsidies under the **Conservation Reserve Program (CRP)** pay farmers to reduce their acreage and allow land to remain fallow. Energy subsidies take the form of low-cost loans for irrigation systems, and the corn-based ethanol program.

Subsidies are controversial because they are only represented from the economic side, instead of including environmental and social costs. Many people believe that farmers should not be paid for growing food, but the high cost of labor and land, and a commitment to low food prices necessitate subsidies within the United States. Under the current economic system, the elimination of subsidies could bankrupt the American farmer because the cost of growing food would be much higher than in less developed countries that have lower land and labor costs. However, when the cost of shipping and fossil fuel carbon emissions are included in the cost of imported food, local food may be more economical and a smarter choice.

---

* "Most U.S. Farm Subsidies Go to 10% of Recipients, Group Says," *Bloomberg Businessweek*, May 4, 2010.

† http://grist.org/food/2011-02-02-how-the-next-farm-bill-could-plant-a-new-crop-of-farmers/.

---

owners of water frontage land. Western water law revolves around "first in time, first in right" principle of **prior appropriation**, which allows "usage for any useful or beneficial purpose." In the West, water rights law relegates water as a commodity that can be sold separate from the land. Senior rights holders may use or sell what they want, without regard to junior rights. Western water rights encourage those with first rights to waste water so they do not lose their rights. Current water rights laws are not national or regional, but statewide, and they often contradict the laws of surrounding states, which is adverse to sharing and water conservation. The current state of

water rights is a tragedy of the commons, in which no one is responsible for the use of water for the common good. Water rights laws and unsustainable farming practices could make pumping water from the Ogallala Aquifer economically unfeasible in fifteen to twenth-five years.[19]

Legal and regulatory frameworks need to be established for sustainable water management; this has become increasingly important as climate change alters the water landscape.

Climate Change   Climate change and the Ogallala Aquifer are related because they are long-term commitments that have been disregarded as the conditions become more serious and cumulative.

Climate change alters the temperature, precipitation, and distribution of crops, and it is therefore monitored in fields across America. Climate change will impose additional expenses to already slim agricultural profits.

Two parameters studied on the Plains are atmospheric warming, which produces the greenhouse effect, and the introduction of Ogallala water. The greenhouse effect changes the location of crops and the choice of seed. For example, North America's growing season (the time of plant growth from the last frost to the first) has been increasing over the past twenty years, and is now about twelve days longer than twenty years ago.

Seed is specific to several variables, such as temperature range and growing seasons. As global warming progresses, regional seed preferences will shift with the temperature and require ongoing research to find the most viable alternatives.

Large-scale irrigation modifies climate, although the long-term impact is still unknown.[20] The ability to forecast realistic and sustainable models is an important element of a long-term sustainable food supply. Despite advances in water-saving technology, present levels of CPI irrigation allow more water to leave the aquifer than enter. Additional environmental consequences of irrigation dependence are increased soil salinity, water pollution, and destruction of ecosystems. If the Ogallala continues to be pumped at an unsustainable rate, dryland farming will be the only alternative, which will decrease the food supply as the population continues to grow.

Several options have been discussed to improve water availability, such as increased aquifer management, increased storage, reduced consumption, and conservation. Water management needs to respect watersheds more than geometric political boundaries and end the fragmentation of this most precious resource.

Crops

Great Plains crops range from intensively grown cotton and sugar beets to extensive monocultures of grains, wheat, corn, and soy. The region produces over 60 percent of the wheat, 87 percent of the sorghum, and a third of the cotton, and it also raises over 60 percent of the nation's livestock. Crops are grown with capital-intensive tilling methods promoted by the Green Revolution, genetically modified crop (GMO) production, and fossil fuels.

Wheat   The United States grows about one-eighth of the world's wheat, and two-thirds of wheat production is on the Great Plains. Two types are grown, winter and spring wheat (Map 14.4). Winter wheat is grown in the southern Great Plains and spring wheat north of the Nebraska Sand Hills. Wheat has been a dryland crop grown where precipitation was inadequate for thirstier corn.

At 50 percent, the American wheat crop is the most exported crop. Genetically modified (GM) wheat is due on the market soon, although many world markets, including the lucrative European market, have refused GM crops. Many farmers are worried about the consequences of GM wheat and the export market.

Corn   The United States produces more corn than any other country in the world. Today, Ogallala water irrigates corn grown on the arid land once used for dryland sorghum and wheat (Map 14.5). Corn requires thirty inches of growing season precipitation, which was impossible on the Plains until fossil-fuel pumping of groundwater was introduced in the 1960s. Great Plains corn production damages the landscape because growing corn in a region with more evaporation than precipitation upsets the water balance equilibrium. The fossil fuels used to grow corn and process it into food and other products far outstrip what it supplies in calories and energy.

Traditionally, about 70 percent of all corn is for livestock consumption, although in the twenty-first century increasing

PHOTO 14.7. Irrigation. Left: The High Plains is too dry for corn without center pivot irrigation (CPI) supplied by the Ogallala Aquifer. Corn requires about thirty inches of water during the season, and the High Plains receives about twelve to fifteen inches. Right: CPI circles in the Texas Panhandle. Each circle is one-quarter of a section (160 acres). Feed corn has become the dominant crop in the Panhandle.

BOX 14.9 ENERGY AND FOOD

Agriculture has been described as a process that uses land to convert petroleum into food.*

Traditionally, crops were raised with renewable solar energy. Throughout history and into the twentieth century, most people depended on solar energy and animals for power and fertilizer. The Industrial Revolution was based on deriving energy from fossil fuels instead of solar power. Mechanized agriculture dependent on fossil fuels increases carbon dioxide production and makes food production also fossil fuel dependent. Agriculture has evolved in a series of revolutions, each seeking to improve food production to feed an increased population.

The first agricultural revolution occurred about ten thousand years ago, when the planting of seed established a more sedentary population. The next three agricultural revolutions occurred in the past two hundred years in order to accommodate population growth.

The second agricultural revolution occurred around 1800, as Thomas Malthus queried the future of humanity as he watched the growth and shift of population from rural to urban, from farm to industry. His query was indirectly answered by technology, the enclosure of fields in England, and a new privatized agriculture that increased crop production, but one which continued to rely on renewable solar energy and animal power.

The third agricultural revolution, in the 1960s, was also in relation to an increased population and the fear of famine. At the time that human population achieved three billion people, the Green Revolution increased agricultural production. The Green Revolution depended on fossil fuel energy to increase food supply. Fossil fuels provide energy to grow, plow, irrigate, and transport crops, as well as to provide feedstock for fertilizers.

The fourth agricultural revolution, genetic engineering, followed a doubling of world population from 1960 to 2000. It continues the dependence on fossil fuels. Fossil fuels have increased Earth's agricultural production and supported a growing population. However, current agricultural production practices release greenhouse gases (GHG) into the atmosphere.

The U.S. food system is complex and heavily dependent on fossil fuels, which are used in every stage of food production including seed production, cultivation, planting, growing, harvesting, processing, distribution, and storage, all before the food reaches the family table.† As fossil fuel availability reaches its peak consumption, fuel and food costs are escalating. Additionally, food costs do not reveal the environmental and social costs necessary to obtain a sustainable system. Companies profit by passing on the external costs to the populace.

Energy-intensive farming and ranching convert imported fossil fuel energy (fertilizer, herbicides and pesticides, equipment and its fuel supplies, animal feed) into meat and the four primary crops (corn, wheat, hay, and soybeans). None are produced in an energy-efficient manner but are grown to satisfy a singular bottom line. None of the crops are eaten raw, but all are the main ingredients for a processed food industry.‡ The health of the American landscape and of Americans pays the external costs with environmental pollution and many modern-day health issues.

---

* Dan Campbell, "Unstable Farm Markets Prompt More Growers to Look to Bargaining Co-ops," *Rural Cooperative Magazine*, July–August 2002.

† The Leopold Institute, "Foodmiles," at http://www.leopold.iastate.edu/pubs/staff/ppp/foodmiles.htm.

‡ Michael Pollan, *The Omnivore's Dilemma* (New York: Penguin Press, 2006), provides an excellent introduction to what has happened to corn in the process of processing.

---

amounts have been converted to ethanol. The remainder is used for human consumption in processed foods or as sweeteners (high fructose corn syrup). Most corn grown is feed corn, not the sweet corn that is eaten on the cob.

The increased demand for ethanol changed the corn market. The 2007 corn crop was the largest since World War II, because increased ethanol production created a need for more corn, at the expense of other crops, especially soy. Corn prices spiked. The choice has affected world markets, and the long-term effect, including impact on the Ogallala Aquifer, has yet to be measured.

Canola   In 1974, Canada satisfied a shortage of monounsaturated domestic oil by engineering a new crop, canola, from rapeseed. Used for industrial purposes, rapeseed oil is toxic to humans because of erucic acid. Canola was created and later genetically modified to substantially reduce the toxic acid. Canola is a cooking oil, a margarine, and a feed grain for sheep and cattle when there is a shortage of other feed grains. Fields of bright yellow canola grace the Northern Plains and the Canadian Prairie, where it is a major cash crop on a par with wheat production.

Sorghum   Sorghum is indigenous to Africa, where it is a food crop, but in the United States, sorghum is a High Plains feed grain. The plant is similar to corn in appearance but is drought resistant and requires far less water than corn.

Cotton

The Ogallala Aquifer is the most intensively used aquifer in the U.S. . . . Without question, the future for [the Llano Estacado] will not be a continuation of past practices. Water in sufficient quantities will not be available to support the irrigation practices and cropping systems that came to characterize this region during the last century.[21]

After the boll weevil debacle in the Cotton Belt, cotton production moved to western Texas. From 1900 until 1929, the Llano Estacado received above average rainfall and cotton was extensively cultivated, but cotton production ended with the Dust Bowl era and then resumed after World War II. About 25

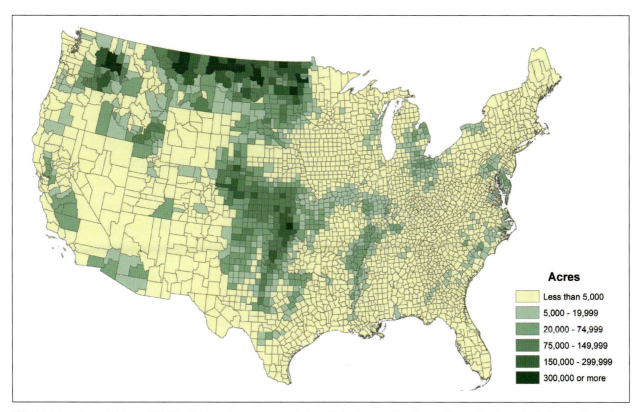

MAP 14.4. Wheat, Harvested Acres, 2002. Wheat is the main crop grown in the Great Plains, because wheat is naturally suited to the semiarid climate and precipitation. Winter wheat is prevalent in the southern plains and spring wheat to the north.

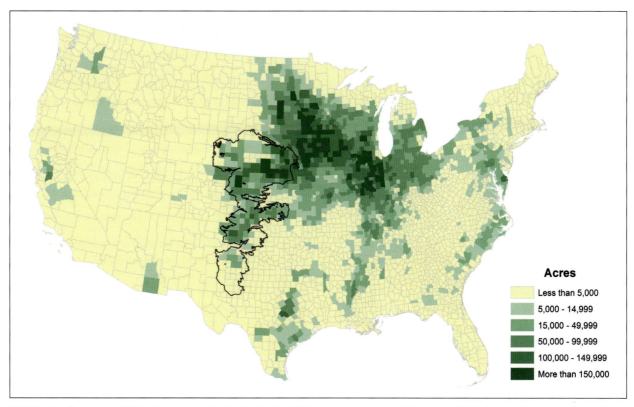

MAP 14.5. Corn Harvested and Water Dependency on the Ogallala Aquifer, 2002. Corn is not grown naturally in the Great Plains because of a lack of moisture. After tapping the Ogallala Aquifer, corn crop production increased using aquifer water, but unsustainably. By 2025, it is estimated that aquifer water will no longer be economically feasible.

percent of U.S. cotton is grown in the Llano Estacado, augmented by Ogallala water and increased mechanization.

The southwestern states dominated cotton production from the 1970s into the twenty-first century, led by California's San Joaquin Valley and the Llano Estacado. However, falling water levels in the Ogallala have caused many large cotton growers to migrate back to the Mississippi Delta region or other points in the South. Falling prices have further depressed cotton production.

Farms continue cotton production because of government subsidy programs. American cotton subsidies are one of the most controversial on World Trade Organization (WTO) markets, accused of destroying less developed markets in a free trade economy. To make matters worse, low prices hinder cotton, while other crops are receiving bonus subsidies. Mississippi Delta cotton production declined 50 percent in 2008 from 2007 levels because of low prices for cotton and high prices for corn. Farmers chose to grow corn.

Despite the unsustainable impact of ethanol corn and the subsequent drop in cotton production, since 1997 ongoing studies seek more sustainable methods to continue cotton production. Included in the findings has been reduction of water use and a more integrated system that includes all three aspects of the triple bottom line.[22]

Sunflowers   The Plains have increased sunflower production for both oil and seed. Sunflowers are popular crops because they require about one-third less water than corn and half the water needed to grow hay. The Dakotas grow the most sunflowers, followed by Kansas, Minnesota, and Colorado.

Other Crops   The glaciated plain of Montana, Saskatchewan, and Alberta grows irrigated feed grains and sugar beets. Canadian barley and flax grow in areas that are too cold or dry for corn. Beer is produced from barley, which is also the principal livestock feed in the Northern Plains. Flax has the health benefits of omega-3 fatty acids and is also spun into linen or made into linseed oil, a paint additive.

Livestock and the Meat-Processing Industry

Grazing land is usually unsuitable cropland because it lacks either fertility or water. The U.S. and Canadian Plains have been long-time livestock producers, but they have accelerated production since the 1990s. The Plains supply 60 percent of grain-fed cattle and have over half of all U.S. and Canadian beef-processing plants. The cattle, dairy, and hog industries have grown apace with access to the Ogallala.

Cattle   Cattle have been an important industry on the Plains. However, the patterns have changed. Shipping beef to slaughterhouses in Chicago is no longer necessary. Refrigeration and transportation allows meat to be grown, fattened, and processed within miles of each other and then shipped globally. All three segments of beef production are now located on the High Plains. In Canada, 40 percent of beef

cattle production is in Alberta, where feed and processing are combined.

Turning cattle into beef is a three-step process. Cows are grass-fed for six months, finishing in feedlots for eight months; then they are taken to the slaughterhouse. Feedlots are used for two reasons: feedlot cattle gain weight rapidly, and Americans have been told they like the taste of corn-fed meat over grass-fed. However, cattle are not genetically disposed to eating corn, as they are ruminants, but the fast weight gain for corn-fed meat has made this method almost ubiquitous.

A grass-fed beef niche market has evolved for those who prefer the health benefits and more direct transfer of solar energy to humans. Grass-fed beef are far less reliant on fossil fuels and are high in saturated fats and low in omega-3 fatty acids; corn-fed beef is responsible for increased heart disease. And cattle raised on grass and moved so as not to overgraze are similar to buffalo in relation to environmental health.[23]

Livestock use only about 3 percent of regional water. However, corn, a main ingredient of feed, is now grown locally due to access to Ogallala water. When the water requirements for growing irrigated corn on the Plains are factored into livestock production, over 90 percent of water withdrawal from the aquifer is for livestock production. This pattern reflects short-term thinking and is unsustainable. Additional environmental questions concern the intensive cattle-processing industry, manure disposal methods, and air and water pollution.

Dairy   Dairying had not been a large component of Great Plains agriculture until the 1970s when the New Mexico dairy industry began growing. From 1970 to 1995, the number of New Mexico dairies grew fifteenfold, concentrating along the Texas border. New Mexico entered the 1990s as thirtieth in overall milk production, exited the decade ranked tenth, and was seventh and eighth respectively in milk and cheese production in 2005.

The New Mexico dairy herd averages more than two thousand cows each. The dairies are dependent on Ogallala water, increasing the possibility of contaminated groundwater and concentrating manure in a small land area, which then suffers from overfertilization.

Hogs   In 1995, CAFO hog production began in the Oklahoma and Texas panhandles and then diffused across the Plains states. The rapid and intense growth of Texas County, Oklahoma, saw the county grow from the 797th largest hog producer to third largest between the years of 1992 and 1997, increasing annual hog production from four thousand animals in the early 1990s to over a million hogs by the decade's end (Photo 14.8).

The pork industry rationalized its move to the Plains by saying it would create jobs, stimulate a moribund rural economy, increase the tax base, and create a more efficient method of pork production. Other unstated reasons included the economic benefits, the availability of Ogallala water, the access to feed, a sparsely populated space, and lax environmental regulations. CAFO hog production in vertically integrated companies

PHOTO 14.8. Texas County, Oklahoma. Hog barns and lagoons are a common site on the Panhandle fields. Each hog barn holds a thousand hogs, whose waste is flushed into the lagoon. Lagoon wastewater fertilizes nearby fields, sometimes resulting in overfertilization and water pollution.

has prospered economically but has had dire environmental and social consequences.

Unintended Consequences. The unintended consequences are as follows:

- "More jobs." The CAFO industry does indeed create more jobs, but they are low-wage, dangerous jobs with high rates of accidents.
- "Stimulate the rural economy." CAFOs dislocate farm families and cause many businesses in the community to close.
- "Increase the tax base." Billions of dollars of government subsidies support CAFOs in such ways as subsidized feed. Guymon, Oklahoma, subsidized the building and operation of a new pork-processing plant with $21 million in incentives.
- Hog production facilities produce hogs in the most economical and cost efficient manner.
- CAFO hog production stinks. Although the propaganda insists that the odor (the smell of money) is not that bad, the lagoons and barns are malignantly odor intensive and cause land, water, and air pollution. They are also only economically efficient when environmental and social costs are not included.

The odor is caused by gases created when manure decomposes. The interaction between compounds creates the gases and has proved difficult to eradicate. Phosphorus- and nitrogen-rich manure spread over relatively small areas contaminates water. Although applying manure to farmland is a tried-and-true method of increasing crop production while managing waste, it must be applied at the proper rate. Too many nutrients result in fish kills, degradation of water quality, and contamination of drinking water.

Local and Ecoregional Impacts. Animal waste runoff from CAFO production is one of the major contaminants of waterways. Agricultural runoff has polluted Chesapeake Bay (chickens), Pamlico Sound, North Carolina (hogs), and the Ogallala Aquifer (corn feed production). The hypoxic dead zones (see Chapter 11) are also the result of agricultural runoff.

Odor and contamination have pitted rural neighbors against one another and disenfranchised many hog farmers from their communities.

External Costs. Processing plant communities experience a shift in demographics and increased community discord. People who work in the plants are often undocumented immigrants from Mexico and Central America. The rural communities where they are based are seldom prepared to integrate the new population. The immigrant workers fill the need when few locals want these low-wage and dangerous jobs.

Originally, the region was home to individual farmers and ranchers, but nonlocal, vertically integrated corporate food companies have become the main source of hogs. Production and pollution are located in the Great Plains, but the corporations are nonlocal and the profits leave the region, so the local populace benefits little from the industry.

Health costs for CAFO farmers and workers include heart disease, stroke, diabetes, cancer, and respiratory illness. Antibiotic resistance caused by overusing antibiotics for growth promotion has increased human vulnerability to infection. The combined costs increase social services for immigrants without insurance, increase insurance costs for those who are covered, and reduce productivity.

BOX 14.10 SUSTAINABLE MEAT

Americans eat an average of about two hundred pounds of meat annually, sixty pounds more than in the 1950s (Chart 14.1).* The increased meat production along with a larger population increases greenhouse gas emissions (GHGs) and places stresses on the land, water, and economy. For example, it takes about seven pounds of feed (mostly corn) to grow one pound of beef, and three to four pounds of feed to grow one pound of pork. Estimates for the water used to grow one pound of beef vary according to the agenda being pushed: from 441 gallons (beef industry) to 2,500 gallons (vegetarians). Feed production is dependent on fossil fuels used in the fertilizers, herbicides, pumping, irrigation water, and transporting the meat to market. The land becomes polluted from overfertilization and pesticide use. An additional GHG caused by the increased meat production is methane from cows. Methane is capable of trapping twenty-one times the heat of the most prevalent form of GHGs, carbon dioxide. The methane is created when feed is fermented in the ruminant digestive system and then belched by

the cow. The one hundred million cattle cause 20 percent of methane emissions.†

Feeding the populace has essentially become a study in the unsustainable use of water and fossil fuels. About 60 percent of the corn crop feeds livestock. Corn is a water-hungry crop; it requires eighty gallons of water to grow one ear of corn, which is then fed to cattle, hogs, or poultry. Petroleum-based fertilizers support high-yielding hybrid corn, which has traditionally been grown in the Corn Belt, but today may be grown in irrigated areas dependent on groundwater pumped by fossil fuels.

The livestock industry's unstable roller coaster ride in profits and losses has caused many livestock producers to seek the stability of contract livestock as a risk management tool. Though it does provide the stability ranchers seek, it also has decreased per head profits and consolidated the industry. The economics of the current livestock industry depends on continued increase in consumption, making the per capita growth of meat consumption ecologically unsustainable.

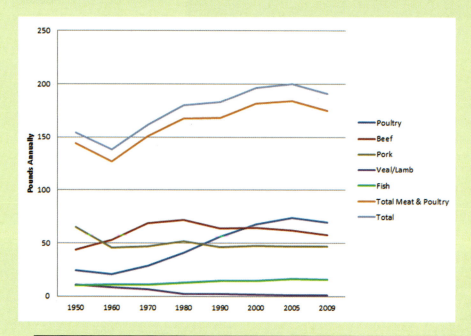

CHART 14.1. U.S. per Capita Meat Consumption, 1950–2009

* Profiling Food Consumption in America, 2001–2002, at http://www.usda.gov/factbook/chapter2.htm.
† EPA, Ruminant Livestock, at http://www.epa.gov/rlep/faq.html.

U.S. Agricultural Exports

Agricultural exports have historically been a large part of U.S. trade. The shift to GMO, though, has affected this trade, because many countries, such as the European Union, have restricted acceptance of GM products. Agricultural exports have shifted to Asian countries, such as China and Japan, but some are due to shifts within the U.S. economy, such as the growing interest in ethanol and its effects on corn production.

China, the current largest export market, is changing its use of agricultural land and water. Facing water shortages, China has moved away from water-hungry grain crops toward more water-efficient fruits and vegetables that produce a higher income per pound. In the process, China has upset several fruit and vegetable markets in America and become increasingly dependent on foreign grains. China receives much of the U.S.-grown GM canola, corn, cotton, and soy products. Half of China's soy consumption is with U.S.-grown GM soy, although the

BOX 14.11 CONTRACT FARMING

Why own farms if you can own the farmers?

—Neil Hamilton, agricultural law expert
(commenting on corporations owning farms)*

Agribusiness favors contract farming, in which a farmer raises crops or animals for a much larger, usually corporate concern. Contracting standardizes cost, quality, and reduces market and environmental risks for the corporation, while the contract farmer owns the land and accepts a steady but small wage over the less stable commodity economy.

For family farmers, the story is different. American family farmers are now more fragile than their land. As farms grow larger, the small farmer survives with difficulty. In fact, most small farmers in America find it impossible to survive economically if they do not receive subsidies or work at outside jobs.

Family farmers save their farms by choosing the more stable income of contract farming. The corporation owns the product, makes the decisions, and the farmer follows explicit production instructions, supplying the labor and the land. In hog production, the contract farmer receives financing from banks and builds large metal hog barns, costing $200,000 each. Banks will only finance farmers with CAFO contracts.

The advantages of the contract system for farmers are risk reduction and receiving a steady paycheck, rather than dependence on cyclical weather patterns and market fluctuations. The disadvantage is that farmers are at the mercy of corporations, which may change or cancel the contracts and often make decisions that are not environmentally healthy or sustainable.

For example, in 2002 Tyson Foods' hog production cancelled the contracts of Oklahoma contract farmers because the company deemed them unprofitable. The CAFOs had become a major source of income for the farmers, so they were victimized by the cancellation. The contract farmers took Tyson to court in 2002 and received a $42 million settlement in 2005.†

The growth of vertically integrated agribusiness often depends on the small family farmer to supply the needed product, and the family farmer often chooses contract farming as the only way to save the family-farm land. Contract farming reduces risk and uncertainty, but at the cost of a limited income and environmental damage to the farmer's land.

---

* Dan Campbell, "Unstable Farm Markets Prompt More Growers to Look to Bargaining Co-ops," *Rural Cooperative Magazine*, July–August 2002.

† "Tyson Settles Suit over Live Swine Operations: Settlement Resolves 2002 Lawsuit by Contract Growers," at http://foodandfarm.org/agribusiness_records.cfm?nID=861.

---

market may have peaked due to more U.S. farmland raising corn for biofuel production.

Since the 1990s, the highest quality CAFO pork has been exported to the Japanese, who pay up to eight times more than Americans for fresh pork. In 2005, almost 45 percent of all pork exports went to Japan; however, by 2008 China, a market ten times as large as Japan, became the largest importer of U.S. pork because of increased demand from a larger middle class, decreased Chinese production, and the weak American dollar.

Canadian Agricultural Policy

By the late nineteenth century, the Canadian Prairie region had been settled and farmed, but farmers were constricted in their ability to sell wheat, their most important crop. Grain elevator ownership had consolidated, offered uniform crop prices, and had developed a speculative market that often hurt the farmer's price. By the 1920s, farmers formed cooperative elevator companies to gain a competitive position and stabilize prices. But the fall of wheat prices in 1930 ended many of the farmers' pools, and the government became increasingly involved in marketing grain.

Canadian wheat farmers created cooperatives to influence the National Policy that favored the Corridor. Farmers both rejected the open market and eliminated competition and price manipulations, while attempting to gain economic independence. Ultimately the farmers were unable to control market speculations. The only way farmers may receive an equitable price on their crop has been government-controlled subsidies; however, in the global agricultural economy less developed countries consider trade distorted when developed countries subsidize crops.

Canadian farmer cooperatives gained bargaining strength for a while, but they were often overpowered by the Corridor and the National Policy, which does not fully address their needs. Farmers were further limited by their place in the global wheat economy. During the early twentieth century, the inner versus outer Canadian policies affecting agriculture culminated in the rise of separate political parties in the Prairie region.

Carbon Sinks and Sequestration in Canada

Grasslands are carbon sinks; they remove carbon dioxide from the air (carbon sequestration). Canadian agriculture accounts for about 15 percent of Canada's total greenhouse gas emissions. In an effort to reduce its ecological footprint, Canada signed the Kyoto Protocol but was unable to meet its goals, largely because of rising carbon dioxide levels. Converting grasslands to agriculture has increased the carbon dioxide level. The Canadian government supports carbon sinks (sequestering carbon in soil) for limiting carbon dioxide buildup and improving agricultural soil. Good land management practices carbon sequestering, such as no-till seeding, reducing fallows, and cultivating forage crops.[24]

Carbon sequestration is a controversial subject, especially when attempting to define carbon sinks, but it has many benefits, such as improving soil quality and nutrients, improving filtration and moisture, and thereby improving waterways by decreasing runoff pollution. Carbon sequestration improves soil quality and ensures food security, while decreasing dependence on fossil-fuel fertilizers. Canada moved closer to sustainability in 2000, when it actively began to sequester carbon, improve soil, and increase food production.

In 2000, Canada also invested in the first commercial carbon capture project near Weyburn, Saskatchewan. This heralded plant injects millions of tons of CO_2 into permanent storage, although expectations have been dampened by reports that fizzy-pop CO_2 leakage on a nearby farm's soil have killed animals. A technological fix will not be easy.

Mineral Resources

The quest for gold and other extractive minerals and possible riches is part of North America's legacy, and it has created numerous boom-bust stories. Coal and gold created boom-bust cycles that had geopolitical and environmental impacts in the Plains.

Coal and Coalbed Methane (CBM)   Coal seams run throughout the Great Plains, usually near Rocky Mountain outcrops. The Wyoming-Montana Powder River Basin and the North Dakota Williston Basin are currently the largest producers, and in the nineteenth century the Raton Basin of New Mexico was an important coal production area.

The Clean Air Act of 1970 emphasized using cleaner-burning coal, and the nation's chief coal source moved from Appalachia to the Powder River Basin of Wyoming and Montana. The thick, low-sulfur coal seams of the Powder River Basin lie under a thin overburden, which is stripped away to supply 30 percent of American coal. To the northeast, the coal-laden Williston Basin has been mined periodically since the early twentieth century.

In 1873, mining began in the Raton Basin. Peak production was from 1911 to 1920, but it continued until 1956. The coal supplied the steel mills of Colorado, California, and Utah. Today Raton Mesa coal is used for **coalbed methane (CBM)** and generating electricity.[25]

Coalbed methane, a by-product of coal formation, was once considered a hazard and vented, but in the twenty-first century it is increasingly captured as natural gas. Natural gas is the main source of home heating. CBM requires no refining and is less polluting and less expensive to recover than coal, but it has large environmental costs.

Access to coalbed methane on a large scale came about when the **Bureau of Land Management (BLM)**, a government agency that administers public lands, accessed the mineral rights. The BLM was created in 1946 by joining the General Land Office (formerly in charge of distributing homestead lands) with public grazing land regulated by the 1934 Taylor Grazing Act. During the first half of the twentieth century, many farmers and ranchers under duress sold their mineral rights to speculators or to the BLM. The farmers did not realize how selling their mineral rights would ultimately affect their surface land.

CBM recovery methods place environmental burdens on ranching and farming. Methane recovery methods require stripping the land bare and removing water from coal seams in order to access the methane gas. Wastewater from gas recovery is saline and results in a decline in water quality, which alters the ecology, stunts plant growth, and causes erosion. CBM development has also affected the quantity of water available for local residents. The aquifer has dropped several hundred feet and will continue to decline as CBM capture continues.[26]

While coalbed methane has been an active area for natural gas production, another method has recently become more active, hydraulic fracturing, or "fracking," which has become common throughout the Powder River Basin and the Williston Basin. Fracking requires horizontal drilling at depths of thousands of feet, using tremendous quantities of freshwater contaminated with proprietary fracking fluids. Water used in the process is contaminated. Fracking is also questionable for the large amounts of fossil fuels used to access the natural gas. Social costs include contaminating water wells with natural gas and destroying drinking water.

Oil and Gas   Oil booms shaped the economies of Texas and Oklahoma from the 1920s to the 1960s, when natural gas and oil fields across the Oklahoma Panhandle and Texas's Permian basin provided about one-sixth of U.S. petroleum production. Oil-well production boomed again in the early twenty-first century, when gasoline prices rose.

Two areas have increased oil and gas production: the northern Alberta oil sand fields (see Chapter 18) and North Dakota's Williston Basin Bakken formation. North Dakota became the fourth major oil production site in the United States in 2008. Three to four billion barrels are estimated in the formation, and drilling has accelerated in the North Dakota–Saskatchewan region (Map 14.6).

Gold   The discovery of gold in 1874 led to the breaking of the 1868 treaty giving the sacred Black Hills, Paha Sapa, to the Lakota Sioux. A massive migration of gold miners ensued. The Homestead Mine in the Black Hills operated until 2001 and was the nation's largest gold mine, yielding about one-tenth of the nation's gold.

The Lakota refused to renegotiate the treaty, so the land was forcibly purchased from them, beginning the chain of events that would lead to the Battle of Little Big Horn. The Lakota have since been offered millions to pay for the land, but they have refused. They want their sacred land back.

Wind   Traditional Great Plains **windmills** are used to pump water for cattle and homes. However, since the 1990s, more powerful wind turbines generate electricity. Texas, Iowa, and California remain the leaders in wind energy production, but northern Great Plains states and the Alberta Prairie are investing heavily in this abundant and sustainable resource.

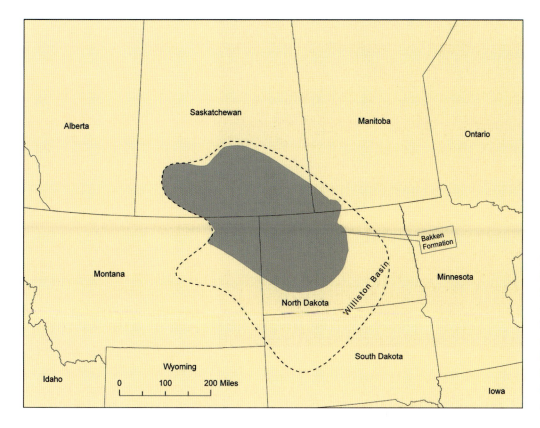

MAP 14.6. The Bakken Formation, North Dakota. Oil production dependent on hydraulic fracking has been booming since 2007, making North Dakota the fourth-biggest oil producer with more than four billion barrels of recoverable oil.

North Dakota alone has the potential to generate 36 percent of the nation's electricity.[27]

Rural towns and farmsteads have found wind farms beneficial. A single tower producing a megawatt of electricity costs more than $1 million; however, towers also increase property taxes, farm incomes, tourism, and construction jobs. Wind farms provide jobs in aging farm communities that are losing young families. At first, companies built turbines on leased land that provided farmers with royalty payments, but farmers are now forming cooperatives to build and own turbines outright. Native Americans have also taken advantage of wind power.

The Standing Rock and Spirit Lake Sioux and the Turtle Mountain Chippewa are generating wind turbine electricity. In 1996, the Spirit Lake Sioux installed a wind turbine at Fort Totten, North Dakota, to power the Spirit Lake Casino. The purpose was to evaluate and establish the feasibility of wind power. In an area of high unemployment, wind farms also provide about 66 percent more jobs than either gas- or coal-fired power plants.

A checkered history of tax credit support has constrained wind power development. In Germany, continued support of wind power has enabled secure investment and resulted in producing 7 percent of German electricity. But in the United States, federal production tax credits have been enacted and expired three times since 1992, disrupting projects in progress. Some states, such as Oregon, have embraced renewable sources of energy, but continued support at the federal level could provide about 6 percent of U.S. electricity by 2020.[28]

Canadian wind generation is growing rapidly but as of 2009 only provides 1 percent of electricity demand, although it may produce up to 20 percent of total generation if a federal wind-energy subsidy is enacted.

Alberta has been at the forefront of Canadian wind generation. Since 1996, windy Pincher Creek, just outside of Lethbridge, Alberta, and at the junction of the prairie and the Rocky Mountains, has supported several large wind farms using the typical wind turbines along with the Canadian eggbeater turbines (Photo 14.9). The wind farms provide some of southern Alberta's energy and give residents the option of buying green energy.

While both countries have the potential to provide 20 percent of their power from wind energy, this goal has the additional barrier of transmission of power. Adding renewable energy to the grid will require updating the current system to reflect the multiple sources of power and their reliability. Sources of generation in remote areas will require transmission line investments. Updating current control and monitoring capabilities using state-of-the-art technology would enable an integration of transmission companies and renewable energy suppliers to coordinate the formation of a robust transmission grid.[29]

A Sustainable Future

John Wesley Powell understood in the nineteenth century what the West still struggles with today: regional water is insufficient for a large population or for large-scale irrigation. Yet from the

PHOTO 14.9. "Egg Beater" Wind Turbines, Pincher Creek, Alberta. Vertical-access, "egg beater" wind turbines generate power, and tax money for the small town. Seventeen percent of Pincher Creek's 2006 revenue came from its wind farms. The federal and Alberta governments offer incentives to boost wind power production.

time of "Rain follows the plow" to the present, the Great Plains uses unsustainable amounts of water. Across the western states from the 100th meridian west, water conservation should be a priority, but few, Calgary excepted, have practical plans to institute conservation.

The Great Plains remains a primary producer of agricultural and livestock goods, producing approximately 55 percent of the nation's wheat and 30 percent of animal product value. Maintaining this production has forced farms to change, and in the process has changed what we eat. The decline in family farms is contrasted with the rise in the more economically efficient contract or corporate farm, but at the cost of environmental integrity and increased social injustices. While this trend continues, many programs are seeking more sustainable answers.

Sustainable agriculture has been an important subject on the Plains for the past quarter century. Groups supporting Great Plains sustainability include the Grassland Foundation, Powering the Plains, the International Institute for Sustainable Development (IISD) in Winnipeg, Manitoba, and the venerable Land Institute in Kansas. The Land Institute has been working on developing sustainable agriculture, especially perennial over annual grains, since 1976. A primary aim of the institute is to redesign agricultural methods to follow natural ecosystems while maintaining high yields.

The Grassland Foundation seeks to regenerate devastated grassland ecosystems that have converted to agriculture. Another project is to develop arrangements with cattle ranchers to improve and create sustainable grazing grasslands.

Powering the Plains is a regional effort by Manitoba and the northern Great Plains and Prairie states to address climate change while promoting economic development. The regional scale allows the states to work cooperatively in economic activities, including renewable and carbon-neutral energy sources. They seek to reduce carbon dioxide emissions to 80 percent of 1990 levels by 2050 and thereby create a more sustainable environment.

The IISD has been working on sustainable development globally and at multiple levels. Members work with international groups and help form national strategies on sustainable development and to further work on sustainability, climate change, and biofuels.

The Great Plains still struggles to be economically viable and successful. Perhaps the Great Plains needs to listen to its past and learn to work with the land, rather than following standards set outside the region. Perhaps the Great Plains is developing its niche in the current society, or perhaps it is showing that the human dimension does matter, and that a long-term sustainable future is more profitable than a short-term present.

In this light, New Homestead ideas demonstrate that many Americans want rural community values. They want their children to attend nonurban schools and want to settle in small towns. A small but growing movement finds more satisfaction with less materialism and more spirituality.

Ironically, it is in choosing the stability of the . . . Plains, [a place] where nothing happens, [a place] the world calls dull, that we discover that we can change. In choosing a bare bones existence, we are enriched, and can redefine success as an internal process rather than an outward display of wealth and power.[30]

Questions for Discussion

1. How is the Great Plains a land of opportunity and a region of tragedy in America?

2. What was the original vegetation on the Plains and how does it differ from its current use? Is the current use sustainable? Why or why not?

3. Discuss the unique physical and ecological features of Great Plains topography, climate, water, and grasses. What features made European settlement of the Great Plains different from settlement of the eastern seaboard region?

4. What was the Dust Bowl and what was learned from that period of time?

5. What can still be learned about using the Great Plains?

6. What suggestions have been made toward the future use of the region?

7. Describe the cattle industry in the past and in the present. How has irrigation affected the location of cattle feeding?

8. How did the environmental impact differ between bison and cattle on the Plains? Why do you think cattle predominated as the commodity?

9. Locate the two wheat areas of the Plains. How are they different?

10. Where is the land irrigated on the Plains? What is grown on these areas? Is it sustainable?

11. How did railroad access affect regional production?

12. Can mineral resources be extracted without destroying nearby land and life, and can it be done in a way that the nation can remain healthy and progressive?

13. How has the Missouri River changed since European settlement?

14. What are the advantages and disadvantages of altering the course of rivers?

15. Why are subsidies offered to American farmers?

16. Should Americans become dependent on imported crops? Do terrorism and political instability effect the importation of food?

Suggested Readings

Abbott, Carl, Stephen J. Leonard, and David G. McComb. *Colorado: A History of the Centennial State.* Niwot: University Press of Colorado, 1994.

Andruss, Van, Christopher Plant, Judith Plant, and Eleanor Wright, eds. *Home! A Bioregional Reader.* Gabriola Island, B.C.: New Society Publishers. 1990.

Arreola, D. D. "The Mexican American Cultural Capital." *Geographical Review* 77 (January 1987): 17–34.

Beatty, C. B., and G. S. Young. *The Landscapes of Southern Alberta: A Regional Geomorphology.* Lethbridge: Alberta University at Lethbridge, 1975.

Bonanno, Alessandro, and Douglas H. Constance. *Stories of Globalization: Transnational Corporations, Resistance, and the State.* University Park, Penn.: Pennsylvania State University Press, 2008.

Bowden, Martyn. "The Great American Desert and the American Frontier, 1800–1882: Popular Images of the Plains." In *Anonymous Americans: Explorations in Nineteenth-Century Social History,* edited by Tamara K. Hareven. Englewood Cliffs, N.J.: Prentice-Hall, 1971.

Brooks, Elizabeth, and Jacque Emel. *The Llano Estacado of the U.S. Southern High Plains.* Tokyo: United Nations University Press, 2000.

Callenbach, Ernest. *Bring Back the Buffalo! A Sustainable Future for America's Great Plains.* Berkeley: University of California Press, 2000.

Griffiths, Mel, and Lynnell Rubright. *Colorado: A Geography.* Boulder, Colo.: Westview Press, 1983.

Gutmann, Myron P., William J. Parton, Geoff Cunfer, and Ingrid C. Burke. "Population and Environment in the U.S. Great Plains." In *Population, Land Use, and Environment: Research Directions,* edited by Barbara Entwisle and Paul C. Stern. Washington, D.C.: National Academies Press, 2005.

Hamalainen, Pekka. "The Rise and Fall of Plains Indian Horse Cultures." *Journal of American History* 90, no. 3 (2004).

Hamilton, Marie Albina, and Zachary Macaulay. *These Are the Prairies.* Regina, Saskatchewan: School Aids and Text Book Publishing Co., n.d. (approximately 1950).

Hart, John Fraser, and Chris Mayda. "Pork Palaces in the Panhandle." *Geographic Review* 87 (1997).

Hewes, Leslie. *The Suitcase-Farming Frontier: A Study in the Historical Geography of the Central Great Plains.* Lincoln: University of Nebraska Press, 1973.

Hudson, John C. *Crossing the Heartland: Chicago to Denver.* New Brunswick, N.J.: Rutgers University Press, 1992.

Jordan, Terry, John L. Bean Jr., and William M. Holmes. *Texas: A Geography.* Boulder, Colo.: Westview Press, 1984.

Leonard, Stephen J., and Thomas J. Noel. *Denver: Mining Camp to Metropolis.* Boulder: University Press of Colorado, 1990.

MacLachlan, Ian. *Kill and Chill: Restructuring Canada's Beef Commodity Chain.* Toronto: University of Toronto Press, 2001.

Mather, E. Cotton. "The American Great Plains." *Annals of the Association of American Geographers* 62, no. 2 (June 1972): 237–57.

McIntosh, Charles Barron. *The Nebraska Sand Hills: The Human Landscape.* Lincoln: University of Nebraska Press, 1996.

Meinig, D. W. *Southwest: Three Peoples in Geographical Change, 1600–1970.* New York: Oxford University Press, 1971.

Merchant, Carolyn. *American Environmental History.* New York: Columbia University Press, 2007.

Milne, Brian, and Terry Johnson. "Against the Grain." *Canadian Geographic* (September–October 1997).

Mutel, C. F., and J. C. Emerick. *From Grassland to Glacier: The Natural History of Colorado.* Boulder, Colo.: Johnson Books, 1984.

Norris, Kathleen. *Dakota: A Spiritual Geography.* Boston: Houghton Mifflin, 1993.

Opie, John. *Ogallala: Water for a Dry Land.* Lincoln: University of Nebraska Press, 1993.

Pimentel, David, and Mario Giampietro. "Food, Land, Population, and the U.S. Economy." Carrying Capacity Network, November 21, 1994, at http://www.dieoff.com/page55.htm.

Popper, D. E., and F. J. Popper. "The Great Plains: From Dust to Dust." *Planning* 53, no. 6 (1987).

Potyondi, B. *In Palliser's Triangle: Living in the Grasslands.* Saskatoon, Saskatchewan: Purich Press, 1995.

Roy-Sole, Monique. "Keeping the Métis Faith Alive." *Canadian Geographic* 115 (March–April 1995): 36–46.

Smith, P. J., ed. *The Prairie Provinces.* Toronto: University of Toronto Press, 1972.

Spry, Irene M. *The Palliser Expedition.* Toronto: Macmillan, 1963.

Starrs, Paul. *Let the Cowboy Ride: Cattle Ranching in the American West.* Baltimore: Johns Hopkins University Press, 1998.

Webb, W. P. *The Great Plains.* Lincoln: University of Nebraska Press, 1931.

Welsted, J. E., C. Stadel, and J. C. Everitt, eds. *The Geography of Manitoba.* Winnipeg: University of Manitoba Press, 1997.

Worster, Donald. *Dust Bowl: The Southern Plains in the 1930s.* New York: Oxford University Press, 1979.

Internet Sources

U.S. Geological Survey. "America's Volcanic Past: South Dakota," at http://vulcan.wr.usgs.gov/LivingWith/VolcanicPast/Places/volcanic_past_south_dakota.html.

Great Plains Nature Center, at http://www.gpnc.org/.

Statistics Canada. Calgary-Edmonton Corridor, at http://geodepot.statcan.ca/Diss/Highlights/Page9/Page9d_e.cfm/.

Kansas Department of Agriculture, Ogallala–High Plains Aquifer, at http://www.ksda.gov/subbasin/content/204.

Northern Prairie Wildlife Research Center, at http://www.npwrc.usgs.gov/.

Regelson, Ken. "Sustainable Cities," Sierra Club, at http://www.rmc.sierraclub.org/energy/library/sustainablecities.pdf.

The Nature Conservancy, at http://www.nature.org/.

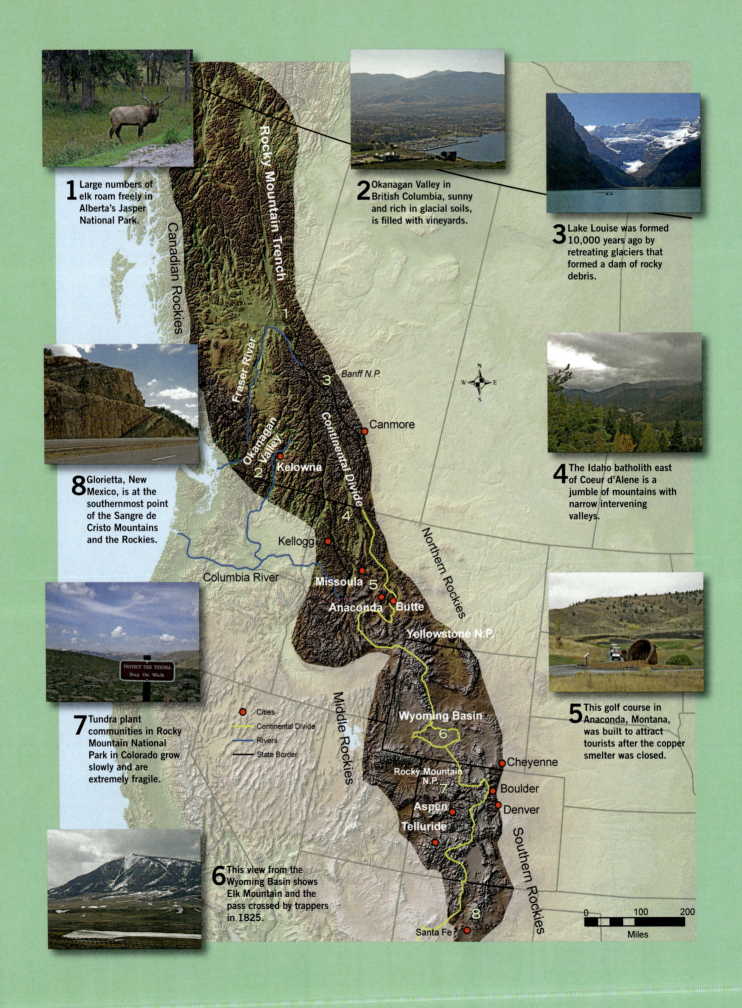

1 Large numbers of elk roam freely in Alberta's Jasper National Park.

2 Okanagan Valley in British Columbia, sunny and rich in glacial soils, is filled with vineyards.

3 Lake Louise was formed 10,000 years ago by retreating glaciers that formed a dam of rocky debris.

4 The Idaho batholith east of Coeur d'Alene is a jumble of mountains with narrow intervening valleys.

8 Glorietta, New Mexico, is at the southernmost point of the Sangre de Cristo Mountains and the Rockies.

7 Tundra plant communities in Rocky Mountain National Park in Colorado grow slowly and are extremely fragile.

5 This golf course in Anaconda, Montana, was built to attract tourists after the copper smelter was closed.

6 This view from the Wyoming Basin shows Elk Mountain and the pass crossed by trappers in 1825.

Canadian Rockies

Rocky Mountain Trench

Fraser River

Okanagan Valley

Continental Divide

Banff N.P.

Canmore

Kelowna

Kellogg

Columbia River

Missoula

Anaconda   Butte

Northern Rockies

Yellowstone N.P.

Middle Rockies

Wyoming Basin

Cheyenne

Rocky Mountain N.P.

Boulder

Aspen   Denver

Telluride

Southern Rockies

Santa Fe

- Cities
- Continental Divide
- Rivers
- State Border

PROTECT THE TUNDRA
Stay On Walk

N
W   E
S

0   100   200
Miles

15
THE ROCKY MOUNTAINS
High in Elevations, Aspirations, and Appreciation

Chapter Highlights

After reading this chapter you should be able to:

- Label and identify the major subregions of the Rockies in the United States and Canada
- Explain the Mining Law of 1872 and the environmental issues with abandoned mines
- Describe the location and importance of South and Crowsnest passes
- Define a boom and bust town and an Aspenized town
- Identify and discuss the importance of the Okanagan Valley
- Compare and contrast Canmore and Banff
- Discuss the recent population growth in the Rockies and its relationship to environmental health
- Identify and describe the importance of the Canadian Rockies areas and major ice fields
- Describe the significance and location of the Rocky Mountain continental divide
- Portray the historic and current settlement patterns within the Rockies

Terms

batholith
boom and bust town
continental divide

cordillera
ghost town
hogback
hot spot
land trust

Law of the Indies
Mining Law of 1872
park
transhumance

transmountain diversion
tree line
vertical zonation
Wilderness Act (1964)

Places

Anaconda, Montana
Aspen, Colorado
Banff National Park
Boulder, Colorado
Butte, Montana

Canadian Rockies
Canmore, Alberta
Cheyenne, Wyoming
Colorado Mineral Belt
Columbia Icefield
Denver, Colorado
Fort Collins, Colorado

Front Range
Kellogg, Idaho
Kelowna, British Columbia
Middle Rockies
Northern Rockies
Okanagan Valley
Rocky Mountain Trench

Santa Fe, New Mexico
Southern Rockies
Telluride, Colorado
Wyoming Basin
Yellowstone National Park

PHOTO 15.1. Front Range, Rising behind Denver, Colorado. The drama of the elevated Rockies after miles of the flat Plains is a stunning sight.

Introduction

Nature obtained a hold over me in those Rocky Mountains. . . . The very sense of living was an absolute delight, which cannot be realized by those who have never experienced the buoyancy of this electric air.

—Emily Faithfull, 1884[1]

Late-nineteenth-century Americans imagined the West . . . as the premodern world they had lost. In it life was primitive but also simple, real, and basic. . . . Life in the West could restore authenticity, moral order, and masculinity.

—Richard White, 1991[2]

The sight of the Rocky Mountains exhilarates almost everyone who has driven the hours and miles of the flat Great Plains (Photo 15.1). Here is where the boom-bust western world begins.

The physical barrier of the Rockies governs the weather, precipitation, and—most importantly for the West—the flow of water (Photo 15.2). Before World War II, water was not as much an issue because few people had settled in the region, but that has changed; water became a critical commodity to assuage the growing population. Paying little heed to the entreaties of John Wesley Powell, everything west of the Rocky Mountains has grown by stealing water and altering ecosystems for the benefit of humans alone.

While the population of the Rockies has been on a boom-bust pattern since the mid-nineteenth century, the current population boom has been exactly where the water is not. The Great Plains lie in the rain shadow of the Rocky Mountains, and the largest cities of both the Plains and the Rockies lie in that rain shadow, along the Front Range. Providing water for the Front Range population has required major diversions that have impacted entire watersheds and their ecosystems. The Rocky Mountains are also a flashpoint for climate change and its effects, which may further enforce repeating the boom-bust pattern.

Boom and bust populations in regional towns have oscillated due to the mining and logging extraction industries. The booms and busts are cyclic: property is worth nothing one day, a fortune the next, and nothing again the day after. Today boom (and bust?) may be repeating.

Different political agendas are pushed onto the landscape. Federal policies push development of extraction industries; environmentalists push static preservation; the recreational public wants the mythic West; the affluent have made the Rockies home to two of America's wealthiest counties. Ranchers have grazed their livestock on federal land for a century, and now development and new residents with different agendas challenge the ranchers. The result has been clashes between ranchers, environmentalists, industry, the recreationally oriented public, and new inhabitants. Does sustainability stand a chance, with so many agendas and stresses on the land? Why is it that none of the agendas seek a systems approach of what is best for humans and ecosystems?

Physical Geography

The regional stresses and perceptions have changed over time. The Native Americans used the Rocky Mountains as a hunting ground. The first Europeans arrived as fur trappers and mined beavers almost to extinction when, luckily for the beaver, the hats using their fur went out of fashion. Next, miners exploited the resources, resulting in toxic pollution from the mining methods. When mining was played out, the region went into hiatus, awaiting economic and technologic changes. Value arrived again in the guise of an aesthetic landscape

PHOTO 15.2. Bighorn River, Alberta, Canadian Rockies. The river is named for the bighorn sheep in the area.

that fragmented the habitat and failed to recognize ecological relationships. Both exploitation and aesthetics have perturbed the region, environmentally and socially. Americans have yet to sustainably manage the region.

The many ranges of the Rocky Mountain **cordillera** stretch from Alaska to New Mexico, rising above the Plains to the east and melding into the western plateaus. The narrow mountain system in the south widens in Colorado (300 miles), tapers in the Northern Rockies of Montana (150 miles), and widens again into the multiple ranges of the Canadian Rockies. The **continental divide** separates the Atlantic and Pacific watersheds along the crest of the Rocky Mountain system, dividing ecoregions and yet not dividing most of the states. In the Canadian Rockies, the divide separates British Columbia and Alberta for a considerable distance, as does the border between the Yukon and the Northwest territories.

Formation and Ecological Issues

The Rocky Mountains abutted the original craton mass. The multiple ranges and rock types were formed in stages over millions of years. Uplift, deposition, and erosion along with tectonic activity shaped the mountains and the distribution of surface water and groundwater. During the most recent uplift, deposits eroded, tilted, and exposed ancient core rocks, such as the steeply tilted **hogbacks** along the Piedmont of the Front Range.

For example, Rocky Mountain runoff discharge once fed the Ogallala Aquifer, but uplift cut the aquifer off from its water source, and today the recharge is limited to the scant precipitation. Aquifers underlying the Denver Basin are also cut off from rivers and are difficult to recharge, making water conservation ever more critical in a region that has been one of the fastest growing in America. While Denver relies on surface water,

growth areas outside of Denver depend on aquifers and are withdrawing water far more quickly than the aquifers are being recharged. This has forced the transport of water and affected environmental areas far beyond the immediate area.

Rocky Mountains ecosystems have been affected in multiple ways due to the changing climate. For example, whitebark pine is not a lumber tree but is valued for its seeds (pine nuts), which are a source of fats for grizzly bears preparing for winter hibernation. Fire suppression has caused the number of whitebark pine to diminish, and now firs and spruce grow in former whitebark habitats. Diseases are killing the pine where the natural cycle has been interrupted.[3] In Glacier National Park, almost half of the pines have died, and 80 percent of the remainder are infected. The loss of the pines affects grizzly populations, which in turn affect others in the ecosystem. Wildlife has also been affected because of human intrusion into the mountains. Grizzlies, aquatic species, and wolves have all suffered losses or are near extinction.

Rocky Mountains

The Rocky Mountains are divided into five latitudinal subregions:

- Southern Rockies (New Mexico and Colorado)
- Middle Rockies (Utah and Wyoming)
- Northern Rockies (Montana and Idaho)
- Canadian Rockies (Alberta/British Columbia)
- Brooks Range (part of the Alaska/North; Chapter 18)

Southern Rockies

The Southern Rocky Mountains extend from New Mexico into Wyoming, but the core and highest peaks are in Colorado, "the Rocky Mountain State." The glaciated peaks range from six

BOX 15.1 DID YOU KNOW . . . THE ROCKIES

- The Rocky Mountains extend about 3,000 miles (5,000 km), from New Mexico to the Yukon Territory.
- They are composed of many ranges. For example, Wyoming alone has twenty ranges.
- They range in elevation from 4,500 ft. (1,500 m) to 14,000+ ft. (4,267+ m).
- Most 14,000-ft. peaks are in the Southern Rockies.
- Range width is between 70 and 400 miles (120 and 650 km).
- Climate change is altering vegetation and wildlife.

thousand feet to more than fifty peaks over fourteen thousand feet. The high-elevation Southern Rocky Mountains deflected immigrant trails to the north or south. Regional travel is still interfered with by the undulating rhythm of ranges and **parks**, the treeless, broad, grassy plateaus between the ranges. The mountains surround the high elevation parks, and although the surrounding ranges have deep snowpack, the rain shadow protects the parks from heavy snowfalls, allowing ranchers to graze their livestock and grow a few crops.

The fifty-mile-wide swath of the Colorado Mineral Belt (pyrite, gold, silver, and copper) stretches between the Four Corners area (Arizona, New Mexico, Utah, and Colorado) and Boulder, Colorado. Most of the boom-bust towns in the Southern Rockies are within this belt.

Dividing the Southern Rocky Mountains from the High Plains is the transitional Colorado Piedmont basin. The gateway cities to the Rockies—Denver, Colorado Springs—lie along the Piedmont's South Platte and Arkansas rivers and their tributaries.

Middle Rockies

The Middle Rockies occupy most of Wyoming, northern Utah, and edge into eastern Idaho. The Middle Rockies are not as impressive or as tall as the southern ranges, but they contain the majestic Tetons and the transition to the Northern Rockies, Yellowstone National Park. Other distinctive features are the Wyoming Basin, South Pass, and the Great Divide. The gradually ascending Wyoming Basin (six thousand to eight thousand feet) connects the Great Plains and the Colorado Plateau through the gap between the Laramie and Bighorn mountains. The basin divides the Middle and Southern Rockies and can be approached from the east at the headwaters of the North Platte and Green rivers. The Wyoming Basin provides entry to the Intermontane without ever crossing a mountain range.

The Great Divide Basin splits the Wyoming Basin near Rawlins, and it contains numerous sand dunes and alkali flats. Water from the Great Divide Basin stays within the divide, as it loses more water by evaporation than it gains in precipitation. The basin has been a primary mining site for oil and gas deposits and uranium.

Northern Rockies

The isolated Northern Rockies span western Montana, the Idaho Panhandle, and the northeastern corner of Washington to the Canadian border. Twenty-one percent of Idaho and

Montana land is national forest, most of it within the Northern Rocky Mountain system. The national forest has multiple uses, many of which are mutually exclusive but are usually only measured anthropocentrically. Human interests include lumber, the environment, oil, mountain biking, and hiking, each seeing the forest from his or her own agenda-ridden point of view, but none ecologically. The "right" use of a forest is a weighty decision. While cutting the forests down completely may not be "right," neither is leaving the forest untouched by humans. Humans are part of the natural world and use the wood, but they need to find a balanced way to use this resource.

The Idaho **batholith** (intrusive igneous rock) lies north of the Snake River Valley. Rivers have cut and eroded multiple uneven and narrow valleys (Photo 15.3). The only linear range, the Sawtooth Range, is located just north of the Snake River Valley. Across the northern panhandle, only one major road traverses the jumble of granitic mountains.

Montana's Bitterroot Mountains frame the eastern edge of the batholith. The downfaulted Bitterroot Valley once held a lake, but it drained through a river-cut gorge. The lake alluvium and temperate climate have supported farming and ranching economies, supplemented by logging in the nearby mountains. However, the lifestyle was disrupted in the late twentieth century, when the valley became a favored retreat for the wealthy, resulting in socioeconomic imbalances.[4]

Additionally, the Bitterroots were the site of a controversial logging of burned-over forest, pitting environmentalists against the local job-seeking population. Human population continues to grow, but Earth does not. Wilderness resources become lucrative areas for exploitation. As resource availability in other areas becomes stressed and as prices rise, more people extract resources from the wilderness. But can it be done sustainably, in a healthy way that leaves resources for future generations? Should a burned-over forest be logged, or is it healthier to allow it to evolve with the ecosystem in place? Agenda-ridden views, from multiple groups interested in the timberland, muddy the decision for the healthiest and most objective way to work with wilderness logging and burned-over areas.

Canadian Rockies

The Canadian Rockies extend across the interior ranges and plateaus of British Columbia. Along the Yukon border, the mountains are interspersed with plateaus, lowlands, and valleys. The Liard Plateau at the Yukon border breaks the Rocky Mountain continuity, and some believe terminates the Rocky

BOX 15.2 REINTRODUCING GRAY WOLVES

Wolves are so common on the plains and in the mountains that the hunter never cares to throw away a charge of ammunition upon them, although the ravenous animals are a constant source of annoyance to him.

—George Frederick Ruxton, 1915*

"Montana needs wolves like we need another drought."

—Rep. Ron Marlenee, 1988†

Wolves and humans once vied to be the most prevalent mammals in North America. But by the 1960s, wolves were hunted to near extinction: The only gray wolves remaining in America were in the woods of northern Minnesota and on Michigan's Isle Royale. In an effort to reestablish a natural balance of native species, the gray wolf was earmarked for recovery within the Northern Rocky Mountains.

Rocky Mountain gray wolves were eliminated in the 1920s because they threatened domestic livestock. But during the 1960s, endangered species attracted the attention of environmentalists, who inaugurated protected areas for these species, among them the wolf. The first wolf rebound was in Canada, where between 1970 and 1990, their numbers escalated from twenty-eight thousand to fifty thousand. By 1985, wolves had migrated south and entered Montana and Idaho. In 1995, 118 Canadian gray wolves were reintroduced to Yellowstone and 141 in central Idaho.

Controversy follows the wolf as surely as the wolf follows its prey. The wolf was part of the ecosystem; when they were eliminated from the landscape, the ecosystem changed to reflect the gap left by the wolf. The predator-prey balance shifted, lacking the wolves' presence. Elk, deer, and moose multiplied, overgrew their range and starved over winter because their natural predator, the wolf, was no longer present to check the populations. The wolf's subsistence diet is mainly elk, white-tailed deer, mule deer, moose, and bison, but the wolves only attack those who are sick, old, or defenseless.

Wolves have been successfully reintroduced to the protected areas, such as Yellowstone Park. By 2005, the wolf population had reached 1,020.‡ Since the reintroduction of wolves, both elk and the wolf are flourishing, and kills seem to depend on climatic conditions: When winter weather is severe, elk are weakened and wolves attack, but in milder years fewer elk are lost to wolves. By 2009, wolves were removed from the endangered species list and set for the first authorized hunt in more than thirty years. Hunters were happy, environmentalists angry, ranchers caught in between.

Humans could not agree on the reintroduction. Each group had its own agenda. Environmentalists believed that reintroducing the wolf created a more natural animal habitat for all the animals. Ranchers believed wolves would prey on domestic livestock, leading the ranchers to kill wolves. In 2008, 264 wolves were killed by ranchers, which enraged environmentalists. Hunters feared that neither elk nor wolf could withstand the reintroduction and game would diminish. Compensation programs were established to address ranchers' concerns, and hunters were assured that the few wolves would not destroy their hunt.

Reestablishing a "natural" ecosystem is complex and requires extensive research and study. The multiple agendas of different human groups complicate matters. Wolves often interfere with human profits, hence their past elimination. But the rest of the biotic world lives within ecological systems, based on survival. Upsetting the equilibrium of an ecosystem, often accomplished by human interaction, may profit humans, but it affects the survival of the rest of the biotic world and ultimately human occupance.

Prior wolf populations were part of an ecosystem with relatively few humans. As the human population grew, their economy has interfered with the natural instincts of wolves. The two species collided. Humans won in the short run, but they interfered with delicate ecological balances. Mere reintroduction of wolves does not reestablish those old balances unless humans also include themselves as part of the ecosystem and act accordingly.

* George Frederick Ruxton, *In the Old West*, ed. Horace Kephart (New York: International Fiction Library, 1915).

† Rep. Ron Marlenee, 1988, in Jeffrey P. Cohn, "Endangered Wolf Population Increases," *BioScience* 40, no. 9 (October 1990).

‡ http://westerngraywolf.fws.gov/; http://www.fws.gov/midwest/wolf/.

Mountain system, although others contend that the system ends in Alaska's Brooks Range. Two major passes—Crowsnest and Yellowhead—along the Alberta–British Columbia border provide rail and highway access between the coast and the Plains. Crowsnest, near the U.S. border, is the lowest-elevation pass across the Canadian Rockies.

Between the 49th parallel and the 54th parallel, more than thirty of the ruggedly handsome mountains surpass ten thousand feet, the tallest being Mount Robson (12,989 feet) near Yellowhead Pass. The narrow, folded, and faulted ranges tower above long, flat-floored valleys. The Alberta valleys contain the tourist towns of Banff, Jasper, and Canmore, while British

Columbia contains several valleys, including the Okanagan and the Rocky Mountain Trench.

The westernmost valley in the cordillera is the long, narrow Rocky Mountain Trench (one thousand miles by fifteen miles), which stretches north from Flathead Lake in Montana. The trench is of uncertain origin, although both glaciers and faulting played a part in its formation. Numerous rivers—the Kootenay, Columbia, and Fraser—have their headwaters in the trench.

To the west of the trench, the Columbia Mountains are composed of the Purcell, Selkirk, Monashee, and Cariboo ranges. The glacially derived Kootenay, Arrow, and Okanagan lakes lie in valleys between the ranges.

PHOTO 15.3. The Idaho Batholith. This photo of this jumble of mountains with narrow intervening valleys was taken east of Coeur d'Alene along Highway I-90, the only major highway across the Panhandle. Notice the clear-cuts on the mountainsides.

The United States and Canada share the slender, mountain-ringed Okanagan Valley (Canada spells it Okanagan, the United States Okanogan) along the Okanagan Lake and River. The sunny Okanagan Valley interior plateau separates the coastal mountains from the Rockies; it extends hundreds of miles north and also south into Central Washington. At the border in Osoyoos is Canada's celebrated and only desert, a northern outlier of the Sonoran Desert.

Seventeen icefields crown the Canadian Rockies. The largest, the Columbia Icefield, lies between Banff and Jasper, feeds six glaciers, and is the largest glacial agglomeration south of the Arctic Circle. The snow dome atop the icefield straddles three continental divides, so water from the dome may flow into the Pacific, Atlantic, or Arctic oceans. The Athabascan glacier is the largest glacier in the icefield, but it has retreated more than a mile over the past hundred years and continues to retreat about six feet annually (Photo 15.4).

Water

The Rocky Mountain river watershed drains about two-thirds of the continent into three continental drainage basins (Table 15.1); the Southern Rockies drain two-thirds of its runoff to the Atlantic, whereas 80 percent of the Northern Rockies and southern Canada drain to the Pacific (with the remainder draining to the Arctic).

Rivers

The Rocky Mountains serve as the wellspring for the major western rivers. The Missouri, Platte, and Arkansas rivers all have their headwaters in the Rockies and drain into the

Mississippi watershed. The Colorado River begins in Colorado and is the main water source for the driest part of the United States; it drains into the Gulf of California. The Columbia, Snake, and Fraser rivers all begin on the Pacific slope of the continental divide.

Lakes

Faulting, glacial deposits, and structural depressions form Rocky Mountain lakes. For example, faulting, glacial deposits, and volcanic action formed Yellowstone Lake, the largest lake in the Middle Rockies. It once drained southward into the Snake River, but faulting blocked the outlet; it now drains into the Yellowstone River, eroding the Grand Canyon of the Yellowstone in the process.

Many of the lakes on the western slope of the Rocky Mountains are artificial, formed by damming waters for water storage and diversion. These reservoirs, such as Shadow Mountain, Willow Creek, and Granby lakes on the western slope and Carter Lake and Boulder Reservoir on the eastern slope, are part of the Colorado Transmountain River Project (see below).

Water Transfers

The Great Plains and the West lack their own water sources and depend on Rocky Mountain water, most of which flows to the sparsely populated West, not the more populated and drier Front Range cities (Map 15.1). Supporting the growing Front Range population requires controlling the water for irrigation projects. This has been accomplished with dams and interbasin water transfers.

Water transfers were also attempted in Canada, with disastrous results. In 1966, British Columbia built the Peace

PHOTO 15.4. Athabasca Glacier, Columbia Icefield, Jasper National Park, Alberta, Canada. The glacier has retreated more than a mile since 1890 and continues to retreat about six feet per year. The drift between the glacier and the sign are moraines.

River Valley WAC Bennett Dam, which transmits its power six hundred miles to Vancouver. The adverse environmental impact and social damage to the local West Moberly First Nation peoples was unrecognized for decades and led the tribe to destitution and primitive living conditions that killed many. In 2008, the affected tribal groups accepted a multimillion-dollar settlement.

Colorado Transmountain Water Projects

Colorado has a water problem. Most of the water is west of the continental divide (the windward side of the mountains) but most of the people live along the drier Front Range. Colorado's Front Range cities contain about 80 percent of the state's population; however, they are in the rain shadow and receive little precipitation and only 15 percent of stream runoff. Agriculture claims most Front Range water, leaving little for the urban population. Since water rights can be sold in the West, and since western slope water was not being entirely "used," urban Front Range Coloradoans created water markets to transfer western water to their homes. Claims for water rights in urban developments often require a water broker and must go through water court. It gets expensive.

Deals for urban water are made privately, without government help. In Colorado, the Front Range Piedmont residents must pay a tap fee to receive water. While Idaho residents may pay $325 per acre-foot of water (326,000 gallons = 1 acre-foot), Colorado residents pay as much as $20,000 per acre-foot. The water deals are made with the private right holders, and prices have escalated as demand grows on the populated Front Range. The major water source to the Front Range cities has been western slope "unused" water. More than 20 **transmountain diversions** ship water over the mountains.

The Colorado River Basin, located along the western edge of the Southern Rockies, has 97 percent of its water diverted for agricultural use, mostly in the Colorado Plateau, and yet it also provides 35 percent of Denver's and 65 percent of Colorado Springs' water supply via transmountain diversion.

In 1957, the first and largest of these diversions opened. The Colorado–Big Thompson Project (the Big T) serves thirty cities and includes twelve reservoirs and thirty-five miles of tunnels. It also irrigates 693,000 acres in northeastern Colorado. The project delivers more than sixty-nine billion gallons of water annually and generates more than 670 million kilowatt-hours of electricity.[5] Tunnels transport water from the western slope of Colorado River Basin under the continental divide to eastern slope reservoirs. Water then generates electricity and is allotted for agricultural and urban uses.

The transmountain diversions have caused tragedy, raised storms of protest, and impacted the environment. Reservoir failures resulted in flooding and death; western slope communities protested losing their water and altering ecosystems. Reservoirs were built to protect future growth on the western slope, but stream flows have diminished. Western communities send water to Front Range communities but have diminished their own water allocations, which has affected hunting, fishing, and boating. A settlement between the western and eastern slopes in order to avoid future acrimony is still incomplete.[6]

Colorado's transmountain diversion continues to be an unsustainable problem. Several court cases have challenged further diversions or reservoir contracts because they jeopardize endangered species and alter the western slope. The claims pit the Bureau of Reclamation against Front Range water

TABLE 15.1. Major Rivers Whose Headwaters Are in the Rockies

River	Length (miles)	Watershed basin (square miles)	Subregion	Headwater near
Columbia River	1,243	260,000	Canadian Rockies	Columbia Valley, Rocky Mountain Trench, British Columbia
Fraser River	850	89,962 (233,000 km²)	Canadian Rockies	Yellowhead Pass, Mount Robson, British Columbia
North Saskatchewan River	800	15,830 (41,000 km²) Branch of Saskatchewan River, confluence near Prince Albert Sas.	Canadian Rockies	Saskatchewan Glacier, Columbia Icefield, Alberta
Snake River	1,038	72,000 Tributary of Columbia River	Middle Rockies	Jackson Hole, Wyoming
Missouri River	2,315	500,000	Middle Rockies	Yellowstone National Park, confluence of three rivers (Madison, Gallatin, Jefferson)
Green River	730	30,000 Part of Colorado	Middle Rockies	Wind River Range, Sublette County, Wyoming
Colorado River	1,450	246,000	Southern Rockies	Rocky Mountain National Park
Arkansas River	1,459	247,000	Southern Rockies	Leadville, Lake County, Colorado
Platte River	990	90,000	Southern Rockies	Routt National Forest, Park Range, Colorado
Rio Grande	1,900	185,000	Southern Rockies	San Juan Mountains, San Juan County, Colorado

interests, neither of which takes an objective systems view of the entire situation.

Climate

The temperature differential between the Rocky Mountain peaks and the adjacent Great Plains is 35°F, about the same as between the Great Plains and Alaska. Although the Rockies adjoin the Plains, the difference can be accounted for by the air temperature decrease when elevation increases—**vertical zonation**.

Vertical zonation and latitude characterize Rocky Mountain climate patterns and the distribution of plants and wildlife. In the southern ranges, plants and animals are desertlike at the lower elevations and tundra at the highest elevations, whereas in the high-latitude ranges, especially in the Brooks Range of Alaska, even the lowest-elevation vegetation is limited

to matlike tundra. For example, in the Southern and Middle Rockies, ponderosa pine populates low-elevation forested areas, and as elevation increases Douglas fir, pines, and aspen grow sequentially up the slopes to timberline (9,000–9,500 feet), where tundra, consisting of bare rock, fragile lichens, and mosses, ekes out a harsh existence.

The Rocky Mountain climate is generally warm and dry in summer, and cold and wet in winter. Considerable summer showers are mediated by winds, low humidity, and evaporation. The winter snowpack provides most of the measurable precipitation. The westerly winds influence precipitation, sending the western ranges ample summer rain. The accompanying valleys and parks are in the rain shadow, receiving only six or seven inches of precipitation annually. During the winter, the weather is both cold and dry, so snow is powdery and may lie until spring thaw.

Ice age climate superimposed glacial features on the landscape. However, warmer temperatures have been

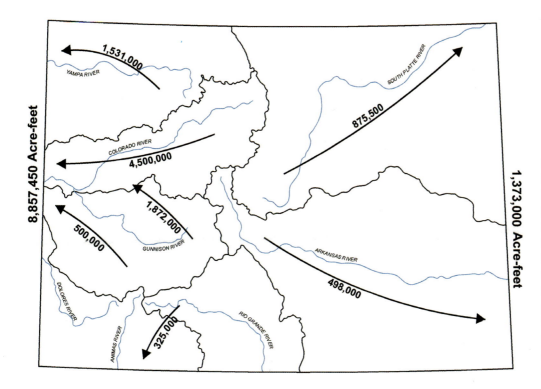

MAP 15.1. Historical Annual Stream Flow, Colorado. Water in the Rocky Mountains has a stream flow that naturally flows mostly to the west, rather than to the Front Range where most of the population lives. Large water diversion projects like the Big Thompson have changed this flow to the Front Range, at great economic and environmental cost.

melting glaciers, some of which may disappear within the next twenty-five years. Climate change may also reduce snow and water, increase drought, and bring higher temperatures at lower elevations. For example, if climate change continues, Aspen may be as warm as Flagstaff is today and Missoula as warm as Denver.[7]

Climate Change

The Rocky Mountain peaks have experienced rapid and nonlinear change that has affected plants, fire, and water flow. At the **tree line**, where forest gives way to tundra, increased nitrogen levels subject the spruce—like Ingleman spruce—to insect infestation and disease. Other plants react to warmer temperatures with erratic growth and diebacks, or in the tundra, more grasses and fewer wildflowers. The erratic nature of these changes makes predictions uncertain.

Throughout the Rockies the tiny mountain pine beetle has infested pines, killed trees, and threatens the boreal forest—all a legacy of long-term fire suppression. The erratic temperatures of climate change have lacked the sustained cold weather necessary to keep the beetles in check.[8] The federal government has supported large-scale burns to halt the progress of the beetle, but it may be a futile battle.

Climate change can causes intense and fast-spreading fires. The changes may be connected to El Niño, an interaction between ocean and atmosphere that occurs over the Pacific Ocean periodically and alters global weather patterns. In the Rockies, El Niño brings more rain, which influences the brush-tinder ratio in subsequent drier years. The feedback causes climatic change that amplifies the initial disturbance. As temperatures rise, river headwaters gorge early in the season

and upset ordinary water flow; the result is drought, floods, or moisture robbed from the soil.

The West has been in a seesaw between drought and flooding for most of the twenty-first century. Snowpack has been below average or way above. The margins of the mountains receive more rain than snow, and spring melt starts earlier. Drought can affect the tourist-dependent ski industry. Winter ski season is shortened, although ski areas have lengthened their season by making artificial snow. The environmental impact of using fossil fuels to create artificial snow, or the additives used in the snow-making process, has seldom been accounted for.

Weather involves multiple variables, which complicates predictions. Climate change adds variables to the already complex equation. The more stable and continuous patterns of past climate are disturbed; in their place, the new dynamic was initially interpreted as chaotic but has matured into complex system science. The infinitesimally small variables, nanogeographies, are being discovered, as people begin to decipher how to live sustainably. It is these shifts that account for how nature works and the broader scope of past human interventions. Today, nanogeographies, manipulating individual atoms and molecules, are a glimpse into a more sustainable future, but only if done using appropriate technology and honesty.

Historical Geography and Settlement

At length the Rocky Mountains came in sight like shining white clouds on the horizon, and as we proceeded they rose in height, their immense masses of snow appeared above the clouds and formed an impassable barrier, even to the Eagle.

—David Thompson, 1787[9]

BOX 15.3   YELLOWSTONE NATIONAL PARK

For millions of years, the North American plate has inched over a stationary **hot spot**—a persistent heat source from the mantle—from the lava fields of the Columbia Plateau in eastern Oregon over the Snake River Plain to its current position over the Yellowstone Plateau spanning the Middle and Northern Rockies at the Wyoming-Montana border. The hot spot has been beneath Yellowstone for more than two million years, building pressure in the underlying magma, which released in the last volcanic eruption about six hundred thousand years ago and then collapsed into the Yellowstone caldera (basin). The hot spot is the source of the park's various hot springs, geysers, and mud pot volcanic features.

The volcanic features are geothermal vents that release pressure either intermittently or periodically. Irregular or constricted vents cause geysers to spout periodically, while hot springs and mud pots can vary, erupting water or mud, sometimes many feet into the air.

After surveying the area in 1871, Ferdinand Hayden urged Congress to preserve the area as a park. In 1872, Yellowstone became the world's first national park, and the park's unique features were protected for the public in perpetuity.

More recently, as noted in Alston Chase's excellent *Playing God in Yellowstone*, the National Park system has come under criticism for its handling of the ecosystem and how politics have forced poor environmental decisions on issues like fire suppression and the destruction of habitat and species. One of the major problems is the possible exposure of cattle to brucellosis, a disease that nomadic buffalo may carry, and which may abort cattle fetuses. The Park Service and the nearby ranchers do not know what to do with roaming buffalo, and some have been killed amid fears of spreading the disease. The National Park Service has been unable to enforce a holistic way to deal with the many animals and issues within what they call an "intact" ecosystem, but which is defined by the park's arbitrary borders, at least as far as animals are concerned.

The Rocky Mountains were one of the last American regions to be systematically studied. Explorers concentrated on finding passages through rather than into the mountains. In the late nineteenth century, explorers and scientists entered thinking they were bringing progress, and in many ways they did, but at the expense of the environment and social equity for others.

The region has always had few people but many resources. Native Americans hunted but seldom lived in the region; whites exploited furs followed by minerals and water. Each came and went, taking what was important to them, and leaving the problems behind. Even today many high-country inhabitants are part timers, using regional amenities during the favored season and then departing. But over time the favored seasons and reasons have changed. Whereas Native American inhabitants hunted and foraged during the warm season, today winter sports dominate how the Rockies are used.

Mountain Men

It was the trader and trapper who first explored and established the routes of travel which are now, and always will be, the avenues of commerce in that region. . . . No feature of western geography was ever discovered by Government explorers after 1840.[10]

Native Americans hunted and traded beaver pelts with the settlers since the seventeenth century, but by the beginning of the nineteenth century Americans and French Canadians trapped the Rocky Mountains to satisfy the need for hats made from felted beaver fur. They engendered the legendary mountain men.

Four countries—Spain, Russia, Britain, and the United States—claimed territory from the Rockies to the Pacific, but only Britain and the United States seriously explored the high country. Britain, under the auspices of the Hudson's Bay Company (HBC) claimed the Columbia River drainage basin and dominated trapping during the second decade of the nineteenth century. The era of American mountain men began around 1825 and lasted until 1840.

British trapping was a monolithic enterprise meant to profit the stockholders, control trapping, and occupy the West. Between 1823 and 1841, HBC employees trapped entire watersheds with the intent of exhausting the resource supply—making a "fur desert"—and keeping American trappers out of the lucrative Northern Rockies and British Columbia hunting grounds. Across the Plains to the Rockies, the 49th parallel had been defined as the border during the Convention of 1818, but west of the Rockies remained disputed territory between the British and Americans until 1846.

The first American trappers were French Canadians who responded to newspaper ads for employment or explorers who left expeditions to join fur companies. John Colter, a member of the Lewis and Clark expedition, left in 1806 to join two fur trappers in one of the first American fur-trapping companies. American trappers were seldom independent; most joined a company for security. Most mountain men trapped out of economic necessity; they saw a way to profit in the lucrative fur trade.

Trappers explored the unknown territories and discovered geographical features (holes, rivers, springs, and passes), establishing a knowledge base for the Rocky Mountains and points west. Later, after the decline of the fur trade, some trappers remained as guides; one of the better known was Kit Carson. Other trappers, such as David Thompson and Jedediah Smith, were well known as both trappers and geographers.

The British relied on a permanent fort system to claim and ship the annual fur bounty. Forts were difficult to defend on the frontier, so beginning in 1825 Americans traded at the annual rendezvous. The trading and social function revolved around trapping near the South Pass trail at a series of "holes"—Cache

BOX 15.4 JEDEDIAH SMITH AND GEOGRAPHY

Jedediah Smith was only thirty-one years old when he was killed by Comanche on the Santa Fe Trail. But his years were full. In his eight years of trapping, he traveled over more territory, much of it unknown to white men, than any other mountain man. He mapped and recorded his travels, widening geographic knowledge. Up until his travels and recordings, maps of the West were still fanciful, showing all rivers rising from a single source in the Rockies and flowing into the Pacific.

Born in 1799 in upstate New York, he grew up in Ohio; in 1819 he left for St. Louis and the fur trade. He proved worthy of the job and became a leader and owner of one of the fur-trading companies in 1826. He worked hard trapping and had some narrow escapes with death, but he was drawn to explore.

I wanted to be the first to view a country on which the eyes of white man had never gazed and to follow the course of rivers that run through a new land.*

In 1823, Smith led a group of trappers into unknown Crow country to open new hunting areas for the Americans. He took his men through the Black Hills and almost met an earlier death when he was attacked by a grizzly bear. The bear's claws scraped open his scalp, broke ribs, and mangled an ear. Undeterred, Smith continued on after a fellow trapper stitched his scalp back on, and it

was said that after he afterward wore his hair long in order to cover up the scars from the attack.

After the attack, he continued across the Powder River Basin around the Wind Range and emerged at South Pass. Although it had been discovered before, it was his discovery that would open up regular travel through the pass. His reporting back to the trapping company would help establish the rendezvous system that characterized American trapping. He also traversed the unknown West.

In August 1826, he led a group of trappers to the Spanish missions of California. He left from Idaho and traversed the Utah and Nevada desert to enter San Gabriel Mission three months later; they were the first white men to enter California overland. They stayed the winter, despite some suspicions by the Spanish that Smith was an American spy. He left most of his men in California and returned for the April rendezvous in Bear Valley, Utah (1827), promptly recruiting more men and returning to California. This time his arrival was more problematic, as the Spanish were wary, and maybe with reason; Smith's role in California is still a matter of debate. He remained for much of the year before leaving for Oregon. While in California, Smith wrote prolifically of his travels across the deserts and over the Sierras. In addition, he made many maps and kept journals, both of which were later used by settlers.

* Quoted in Barton H. Barbour, "Jedediah S. Smith and Marcus and Narcissa Whitman: Mountain Men and Missionaries in the Far West," in *Western Lives,* edited by Richard W. Etulain (Albuquerque: University of New Mexico Press, 2004).

Valley, Utah; Jackson Hole, Wyoming; and Pierre's Hole, Idaho. The rendezvous system continued until 1840, at which time the demand for beaver fur declined and silk hats became the rage. By this time, though, the beaver was almost extinct due to overtrapping.

Exploration

In 1793, Alexander Mackenzie first crossed the Canadian Rockies through the Peace River Valley of northern Alberta–British Columbia. Shortly after, David Thompson surveyed the Canadian and Northern Rocky Mountains, becoming the first European to explore and map the Columbia River from source to mouth. In 1858, the Palliser Expedition explored, analyzed, and mapped western Canada. Three explorers from the expedition entered the Rockies, searching for suitable railroad passes.

American exploration of the Rockies began after the Louisiana Purchase, when President Jefferson sent the Lewis and Clark Expedition (1803–1806) across the continent to explore its potential. The American government ordered continued surveying of the Rocky Mountains during the mid-nineteenth century. John C. Fremont's 1845 *The Report of the Exploring Expedition to the Rocky Mountains* discusses a possible railroad route through the Southern Rockies. In the 1870s, geologists

Hayden, King, and Powell roamed and documented landforms, glaciers, flora, and fauna in the West, including the Rocky Mountain area, and published their findings in geological reports. In total, these explorers set the stage for the following waves of migrants: farmers, ranchers, and capitalists.

Settlement

With the exception of the Front Range and a few small, wealthy enclaves of part-time residents, the Rocky Mountains remain a sparsely settled region. Nineteenth-century mining or logging camps inhabited the region for resource exploitation, but most towns were abandoned after their boom period. A few towns continued haltingly and a few others boomed again as elite Rocky Mountain enclaves, when powdery snow and aesthetic views became important settlement attributes.

Cultural Perspectives

Geography of Wealth: Aspenization and Community Development Needs

A town [Crested Butte] with such attractions is a natural target for what people in Colorado call Aspenization: the upscale living death that fossilizes trendy communities from Long Island's Hamptons to California's Lake Tahoe. Aspen was a splendid place, too, before it was discovered by the rich and famous—and the greedy and entrepreneurial. Now it's a case study in overdevelopment. Its lavish second homes sit empty for most of the year while three quarters of the work force, who can't afford to live there, commute from 40 miles down-valley—a two-hour trek at rush hour.[11]

Aspen, Steamboat Springs, Breckenridge, and Crested Butte all began as remote mining towns cut off by annual snows. Before railroads reached the small towns, "Norwegian snowshoes" were used to traverse the deep snows. In the early twentieth century, rails reached the towns, highways became the prevalent Rockies transportation routes, and the "Norwegian snowshoes" were renamed skis.

Skiing grew in popularity during the 1970s and reached an apex when 1980s tax reforms dropped tax rates for the wealthy from 55 percent to 28 percent, and in the process indirectly changed the skiing landscape. The new disposable "trickle down" income gave more wealth to the wealthy, who invested in homes in the quaint "ski villages." Today, the isolated mining towns with worthy ski slopes have become secluded world-class second hometowns for the wealthy. Pitkin County, Colorado (Aspen), and Teton County, Wyoming (Jackson Hole), are two of the wealthiest counties in America. A mixture of social and environmental problems—"Aspenization"[12]—challenges the popular Rocky Mountain towns. The benefits enjoyed by the wealthy leave everyone with the unintended consequences of their actions.

Unintended Consequences

Tourists often destroy the very things that attract them—wilderness, beauty, and peace. Additionally, wealthy newcomers build and move into their "dream home" with only aesthetics in mind. They ignore or do not understand their impact on the local traditional economy or their own impact on the wilderness.

The wealthy will often close off or place in "land conservation" fishing and hunting areas that the less wealthy locals have used for generations. An example is described in the opening chapter of Jared Diamond's *Collapse*, in which wealthy Californians have established second or third homes, arriving on private jets at the beautiful but struggling Bitterroot Valley. With their money, the Californians purchase trout streams that have been part of the local commons for generations and shut out the people who have been living in and using the area responsibly.[13]

Extractive mining leaves environmental scars that repel the new wealthy residents, who are willing to spend their money to stop these economies without understanding the important role they play in the local economy, both for the residents and the nation. The country depends on many of the resources that public lands provide. Instead of shutting down local and extractive economies, seeking more sustainable extractive methods and more efficient resource use would allow the local economy to thrive. Changing to a more sustainable economy will result in a shift in the types of jobs; more sustainable extractions emphasize ecologically restoring the land.

Local and Ecoregional Impacts

The shift from extraction to aesthetic amenities has altered regional economies. Towns like Aspen are small, private landholdings surrounded by large swaths of protected wilderness—public land that cannot be developed and hence becomes an investment amenity. The limited available land skyrockets in price, and full-time locals who service the economy are unable to afford homes in the community (Table 15.2). Such towns become more corporate than community. They lack affordable housing, and tax revenues become unequally apportioned, forcing the local economy out of the town in favor of resort economies.

External Costs

Aspenization has spread across the continent from Nantucket, Massachusetts, to the San Juan Islands in Washington state. The wealthy homeowner in these exclusive areas aims to

TABLE 15.2. Wealthy Counties in the Rockies, 2010

	Per capita income (2009)	Housing median value (December 2010)
Pitkin County, Colorado (Aspen)	62,544	$1,430,000
Eagle County, Colorado (Vail)	35,104	$695,000
Colorado	29,679	$250,000
Teton County, Wyoming (Jackson)	38,588	$575,000
Wyoming	26,925	$213,000
United States	27,041	$190,000

Source: U.S. Census; Zillow for housing values, at http://www.zillow.com

control growth and keep space open. Attempts to control growth include placing caps on building permits or creating land lotteries. Controlling growth has had the side effect of devastating local economies and eliminating affordable housing. The same can be said of open space programs, in which large amounts of land are taken off the market, thereby driving up the price of the remaining land and increasing property taxes.

Other costs to an Aspenized economy are overcommercialization, in which everything is for the tourist, and a weak job market, either because most of the homeowners have no need of jobs or because the jobs that exist do not pay nearly enough to support living in the area. The entire effect is one of a growing gap between rich and poor and the elimination of the middle.

Boom and Bust Towns

It is the attitude of the extractive industry—get in, get rich, get out.[14]

Dreams and Swindles

Boom and bust towns usually rely on natural resource extraction. Most Rocky Mountain mining towns prospered and then withered in relation to the price and quality of their ores. Many towns fade into history, visited only by those who seek out the past in the moldering remains of ghost towns; others renew and boom again, following commodity exchange rates. They rise phoenixlike after years of decay before the precipice leads to another decline, while still others boom-bust and then boom again.

Boomtowns are unstable, chaotic, energized, stressful, and dangerous. Quick growth fosters primitive and uncomfortable shelters where people make do in whatever housing they can secure: shacks, tents, and in the modern boomtown, mobile homes. When the boom ends, the shelters are abandoned as workers migrate to the next boomtown. But while the boom is on, everyone feels the adrenaline rush, and money flows freely. Prices may be out of control, but money is also. Real estate prices can be astronomical one day and crash the next. Boomtowns often revel in gambling and prostitution, to quench the money-in-the-pocket freedom.

When the boom is over, the town transforms into economic and often environmental decline, unable or unwilling to deal with or pay for employment, housing, and schooling. The Rocky Mountains boom-bust towns began their transitory assemblages in the 1870s, and most had undergone their first transition by 1900.

Ghost Towns

Hundreds of Rocky Mountains **ghost towns** are spread throughout the Southern Rockies Mineral Belt. Outside the Mineral Belt are other ghost towns, such as the Alberta coal-mining towns of Nordegg and Bankhead, or Garnet, a well-preserved gold-mining town high in the Northern Rockies near Missoula, Montana.

Garnet evolved after the Sherman Silver Purchase Act of 1890, when silver prices fell. The discovery of gold in the granite veins of the nearby mountains in this steep-sided mountain valley brought more than a thousand to the town within three years of its 1895 settlement. In the time-honored tradition of ghost towns to be, Garnet was not built to last. The wooden buildings provided the temporary shelters needed while working the twenty mines. By 1905, gold extraction became more elusive or expensive, and the town population dwindled to only 150 residents. A commercial-district fire and World War I halted population growth, and by the 1950s the last inhabitants abandoned the new ghost town. Small mining revivals occurred several times when gold prices warranted, but only those who appreciate historic preservation now travel the rough gravel road to Garnet (Photo 15.5).

Ghost Towns Redux

The perfect example of ghost town returned is Aspen. Two more modest redux examples (among many) are Telluride, Colorado, and the most recent, Kellogg, Idaho.

Telluride, Colorado Telluride was a hard-drinking 1880s southwestern Colorado mining town set in an avalanche-prone box canyon. The area's numerous silver- and gold-mining towns are mostly ghost towns today. Telluride shut down also and was ghostly after the 1920s, a hippie hangout in the 1960s, and then was reborn in the 1970s with a new gold—snow. The overabundance of snow that threatened the community at the century's beginning became its savior at the century's end.

Victorian homes that went for $300 in 1960 were $30,000 in 1970 and $900,000 by 1990. In 2010, while the recession continues for millions, exclusive Sotheby's and Christie's have real estate offices in Telluride—average price is $1.5 million.[15] Now an annual skiing crowd of 190,000 shop and après-ski along the Victorian Main Street, and the tourism continues throughout the year, highlighted by the thirty-year-old Telluride Labor Day film festival.

In Telluride, housing is limited by the surrounding Forest Service and BLM land. The town's isolated geography—forty miles of steep, windy roads to the next town—limits affordable housing. For years, town employees opted to camp out in the surrounding woods, until it was made illegal and replaced by too few affordable units. Now most town workers must navigate the treacherous road down the mountain to "home." In town, the smaller old and somewhat affordable homes are purchased, torn down, and replaced with megasized second homes. Since 2000, the situation has only been exacerbated: more homes are owned by second-home owners, per capita income has increased, and the median price of homes has almost doubled (Table 15.3).

Kellogg, Idaho Kellogg was a silver boomtown founded in 1885. Over the decades, Silver Valley mining employed many families, but the environmental cost left the town with polluted water, smokestack emissions, and lead buildup. In 1981, the price of silver fell, the mines shut, and the town went into an economic and demographic tailspin. Population fell 28 percent

PHOTO 15.5. Ghost Town, Garnet, Montana. This late-nineteenth-century boom town was completely abandoned by 1950. Today it is a well-maintained ghost town, where students study the relics of the past.

to three thousand during the 1980s. In 1983, Superfund began to clean up the lead and zinc in the water and chemically denuded hills.

Not to be undone by their circumstances, the town taxed themselves to construct "the world's longest gondola" on their recently completed Superfund ski hill, which they then sold in 1996 to an investment company that started building condos for $100,000 (Photo 15.6). Several condo series sold out, and by 2007 condos in the old mining town were selling for $800,000, although little in the still hardscrabble town, best known for its giant automobile dealer, calls for the luxurious condos. But developers saw only a future Vail or Aspen; they even discounted its Superfund status by calling it "superfun."[14]

But as boom and bust towns will do, the story is not yet over for silver-mining Kellogg. Rising prices in silver prompted two mines to reopen in December 2007. Mining jobs, averaging more than $60,000 annually, encourage long-term residency and trump the $10,000 average tourism jobs and its transient population. The recession of 2008 hampered growth. Empty storefronts brought a campaign to give away free rent to encourage a return of business, and prices fell into late 2010.

The median sales price for a home went from $190,000 in early 2009 to $102,000 in late 2011.

As of 2011, both tourism and the silver mines were ongoing. New mines continue to open as the price of silver remains high enough to make them profitable. However, the condo boom has come to a grinding halt, with no new building and hundreds of foreclosures of these second-home condos. Whether the current economy is sustainable is questioned. Mining is cyclic, and the tourist economy is both fickle and aging in the valley. The 2010 census shows Shoshone County as losing population and an increase in those over sixty-five (20 percent in the 2010 Census).

Regional Life

Population

While the Front Range population has been booming since the 1960s, by the 1990s rural and resort developments experienced population explosion in northern New Mexico, western Montana, and the province of Alberta. The entire region has grown, but rural area sprawl supported the American dream of a

TABLE 15.3. Telluride, Colorado, Facts, 2000 and 2010

Year	Population	Total housing units	Single-family owner-occupied homes	Vacant housing units (second homes)	Per capita income (2009)	Home median value
2010	2,325	2,070	495	35.0%	$49,121	$1,000,000
2000	2,221	1,776	244	47.7%	$38,832	$566, 500

Source: U.S. Census

private mini-spread within an hour's drive of main cities, especially along the panoramic Front Range.

Since the 1990s, Front Range growth has been unprecedented; land was converted from agricultural to residential along the valleys or in aesthetically pleasing "ghost towns." In Colorado alone, each year more than ninety thousand acres of land are converted from agricultural to residential use. The open space symbolizes a better quality of life to suburban residents, but at the expense of wildlife and longtime ranchers.

In the past, extractive economies attracted pockets of population, but over the latter half of the twentieth century, population growth was oriented toward an amenity-filled leisure landscape. The growth affected the local economies and often damaged the very amenities people were seeking. Often the "not in my backyard" mentality (NIMBY) froze development. New occupants often want the door closed behind them. The landscape represents a countrified ideal, but it does not represent the reality of country living. For example, the Roadless Acts passed during the Clinton administration protected millions of acres of national forest from future road building or commercial development. These acts were either regaled because they provide the privacy that new residents were seeking, or were renounced because people wanted to develop the areas. Often the two groups are the very same people, just at different periods of their lives.

Ranchers populated the Front Range prior to the current suburban sprawl. The ranching economy has evolved with the times, but the public perception remains mythic—the cowboy and horse. The public desires to be part of the myth and not part of the reality.

Most relocating residents are nonranching retirees, telecommuters, and second homeowners who live on miniranches, while long-term owners are traditional livestock ranchers. Most residents of both groups prefer the open space landscape and have an interest in the abutting federal- or state-protected forests. The ranchers, though, use the protected lands as grazing grounds, whereas the new residents see the public lands as providing them anonymity, privacy, and higher property values.

The continued decline in beef prices has made it difficult for any but the largest ranchers to be viable and has resulted in consolidation; only 10 percent of the ranchers have more than one hundred head, and they control 50 percent of the inventory. Consolidation has benefits: lower production costs for the rancher and lower food prices for the consumer; this makes the United States more competitive globally, but it also destroys rural communities and local businesses, favoring large-scale corporate concerns and outside control.

Economies of scale have forced many of the remaining small ranchers to turn to alternative income, such as dude ranches or hunting preserves; others have sold their land to developers or to preservation **land trusts** that do more than preserve open space—they also limit available land, which effectively escalates prices so only the wealthy can afford land. Neither is healthy for the overall ranching economy. The American dream of wide-open spaces was good for the nineteenth century, but more sustainable lifestyles are needed to accommodate extreme population growth and consumption.

Traditional and Sustainable Cities

No major cities lie within the Rockies, but gateway cities border the mountains. Santa Fe, Denver, and Salt Lake in the Southern Rockies; Spokane and Boise in the Northern Rockies; and Calgary and Edmonton, Canada, have benefited as distribution points for mountain resources.

In the United States, Pueblo, Colorado Springs, Denver, and Fort Collins are the largest cities between Chicago and the West Coast. All depend on Rocky Mountain source water. Provo, Salt Lake City, and Ogden along the western side of the mountains also depend on high-country water (see Chapter 16).

PHOTO 15.6. Gondola in Kellogg, Idaho. A Superfund site, tagged by developers to become the next Vail, has a luxurious development plopped in the middle of a dilapidated and struggling town with high lead pollution and high unemployment. Seeking a tourism industry to replace the closed mines, Kellogg residents voted to tax themselves and build the world's longest gondola, which they sold to developers. The mines have since reopened.

BOX 15.5 GHOST TOWN BOOM, BUST, BOOM, BUST

Half an hour west of Denver, Central City and neighboring Black-hawk are carved into the Gilpin County mountainside. These gold mining towns flourished from 1859 until the 1920s, long enough to evolve from wooden buildings (which burned) to granite structures. Finally, the gold could no longer be profitably mined.

Central City's population dropped from 3,114 in 1900 to 335 in 1990. Several times, the remaining residents attempted to save the town from oblivion. In the 1930s, they pursued attractions and built an opera house. While the opera house was successful, it did not attract new settlers but highlighted the town's dependency on outside speculators. The "quaint" opera house attracted visitors from sophisticated Denver, who only came for entertainment, not to settle. Central City continued to seek a more sustainable and fitting way to grow economically.

In the 1970s, the skiing boom fostered growth in nearby towns, but Central City, lacking skiable mountains, had to seek other avenues for development. Harking back to the mythical western boomtown mythology and its gold-mining aura, the town was designated as a National Historic Landmark District, but it still was depressed until gambling was legalized and rationalized as "consistent with the 'Western' history of the mining region."*

In 1991, a statewide referendum legalized low-stakes gambling (mom-and-pop gambling houses) in Central City and Blackhawk and sparked the third boom.† A local real estate rush ensued. Between 1990 and 1991, there was a 600 percent increase in sales in Central City, and by 2007 population grew to 544. Assessed valuation on commercial property went from $3.6 million in 1991 to $109 million in 1994, but the wanted panacea was elusive. Despite buttons that proclaimed "The boom is back in Gilpin County," residents learned that gambling, once part of booming gold-mining towns, is not the economic salvation for small-town America.

Instead, residents found corporate manipulation and social engineering of the small town's attitudes, such as whitewashing the negative impacts of gambling. They found that gambling was an unprofitable sham for the residents, but it profited outside interests who owned the casinos. The promised mom-and-pop gambling structures never happened, and the 2 a.m. curfew low-stakes gambling (less than $5 bets), which was also promised, was voted out and replaced by 24/7 operation and $100 limits. Under

the banner of the "old West," the town had invited in traffic, parking problems, pollution, and a landscape that altered their lives. But Central City still tried to maintain its folksy, small-town feel, despite the corporate deluge.

While Central City corporate gambling grew and became profitable at the residents' expense, Blackhawk gambling enterprises grew seven times faster and larger because of geography and preservation attitudes. The easiest access to Central City was through Blackhawk. A new highway funded by local property taxes connects Central City with the trunk highway, but leads gamblers directly to Blackhawk.

Blackhawk adopted the "anything goes" attitude for ubiquitous franchises and profitable construction, including blowing up mountainsides for casino development. Blackhawk construction flies in the face of Central City's strict adherence to "sense of place" historical preservation. In 2009, the casino score was Central City six, Blackhawk, nineteen going on twenty, as a thirty-three-story casino hotel was being added (Photo 15.7). The state of Colorado has profited from taxes collected from the gambling establishments, and people who are invested in the casinos see the move to gambling as positive. But local residents who tried to save their town saved it and lost it at the same time.

PHOTO 15.7. Casinos in Blackhawk, Colorado. The mom-and-pop gambling casinos that Central City (in the background) was hoping for have been overridden by large gambling interests in nearby Blackhawk, including the construction of this thirty-three-story hotel/casino.

---

* Patricia A. Stowkowski, *Riches and Regrets: Betting on Gambling in Two Colorado Mountain Towns* (Niwot: University Press of Colorado, 1996). Most of the information on this section is drawn from this excellent book. See also Lionel Beehner, "A Rockies Casino Town Preps for the Big Time," *New York Times*, April 17, 2009.

† Proceeds from gambling support historic preservation throughout the state.

The Wyoming Basin has a different population pattern. Laramie, Rawlins, Rock Springs, and Cheyenne were developed as Union Pacific Railroad "hell on wheels" towns, known for their loose morality and ethics when they were established. A few other towns were built along river valleys: Casper on the North Platte and Cody on the Shoshone River.

In British Columbia, the Rocky Mountains have been protected from development because most mountain areas are within national park boundaries. However, development has increased outside park boundaries.

Denver, Colorado

(2010 pop. 600,158; CSA 3,090,874)

Situated along the South Platte River on the Colorado Piedmont, Denver was founded as a supply town for the mountain mining camps and has evolved into the undeniable gateway to both the Plains and the Rockies, serving the agricultural and meat industries of the Plains, the mining interests of the Rockies, and also employing a major federal workforce. But it had to fight to earn these titles.

The transcontinental railroad bypassed Denver, which supposedly doomed it to second-class status. The Union Pacific chose the easy summit of the Wyoming Basin and founded Cheyenne as the Rocky Mountain supply center. A successful nineteenth-century city needed rail access, which lowered production costs. So in 1870, the Denver boosters built the Denver Pacific line to the main transcontinental rail trunk and so secured its place as the gateway to Colorado mining areas. Population tripled over the next four years.

When extractive industry crashed in the 1980s, it brought Denver down along with them, but the city diversified its economy with a university research focus on IT and health-care services. Denver grew beyond a regional hub based on these industries, augmented by a highly educated population and local amenities—hiking, skiing, climate, and scenery. Denver continued its growth into the biotech and renewable energy sectors.

In 2006, the mayor announced sustainable plans for "Greenprint Denver," a coordinated effort across city agencies that includes more energy-efficient city vehicles and by 2012 a 10 percent reduction in greenhouse gases relative to 1990 levels. These choices were supported by statewide initiatives that have made Colorado a leader in clean energy. Power plant emissions were cut 47 percent between 2000 and 2010. Included are a solar plant, numerous wind turbine farms, and a commitment to convert coal power plants to natural gas. In early 2012, Greenprint Denver is revising its goals through 2020, including adding energy efficiency rebates for thousands of homes.

Santa Fe, New Mexico

(2010 pop. 67,947; CSA 184,416)

The Pueblo Indians lived on the Santa Fe site as early as 1000 CE. By 1608, the abandoned site was chosen as the Spanish Nueva Mexico capital, and Santa Fe became the oldest continuously settled city in Spanish America. The city was a natural site for settlement and a gateway—lying on the boundary between the Basin and Range, the Great Plains, and the Southern Rockies. Santa Fe functioned as the trading post for the Plains and Pueblo Indians; it was the end of the eponymous trail and a terminus for the first southern railroad route.

The town of Santa Fe was centered around a plaza in the traditional Spanish **Law of the Indies** style that regulated architectural, social, political, and economic life. But in the ensuing years, as Santa Fe developed, it looked like other American cities, until citizens realized in the early twentieth century that the city's popularity was declining. To maintain the city's heritage and attract tourism, the Spanish Pueblo or Territorial architectural styles were enforced (Photo 15.8). Today, the city and surrounding area are an artists' colony, tourist center, and wealthy enclave.

Boulder, Colorado

(2010 pop. 97,385; part of Denver CSA)

Boulder attracts people for its beauty and its progressive, sustainable outlook. Its beautiful setting, flanked by the Rocky Mountains, bohemian air augmented by its university, and forward-thinking residential ideals have set it apart from most of America. It implemented an antisprawl stance well before others (1959), began to purchase open space for greenbelts in the 1960s, and allocated 20 percent of its transportation budget away from automobiles and toward alternative transport methods.

Increased parking rates and doubled fines in the downtown area encourage more than half of the residents to use alternate transit; there is an active bike program, such as "Bike to work" weeks and free bike use in the central business district. Boulder's 1987 Greenways program was designed to encourage bicycle and pedestrian trails along Boulder Creek while enhancing fish and wildlife habitat. Boulder's initiatives have impressed surrounding areas, which are now implementing the ideas in their own cities.

As Boulder became more popular, it limited commercial growth, but it also built an innovative relationship between the public and private sectors. Businesses are encouraged to work toward sustainability through the city's Partners for a Clean Environment (PACE) program. Boulder's city council supports environmental and economic sustainability, and the city is awash in sustainable projects and living opportunities, including a transportation and mixed-use development that reduces auto dependence and increases local integration. But although Boulder stopped sprawling into its mountains and established a greenbelt, it could not stop Denver from sprawling toward the town and contributing its smog.

Okanagan Valley, British Columbia

Three cities have developed along Lake Okanagan: Vernon (population 58,584) in the north, centrally located Kelowna (population 179,839), and southern Penticton (population 42,361).[17] The economy's mainstay has been agriculture, but it has diversified into a tourist and retiree destination.

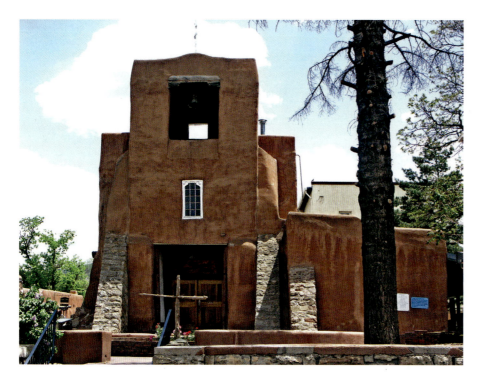

PHOTO 15.8. San Miguel Mission, Santa Fe, New Mexico. This mission was constructed in 1610 and is the oldest church in America. Santa Fe architectural styles were based on antecedent structures like this, reflecting Spanish and Pueblo influence.

A favorable climate highlighted by many sunny days and a deliberate self-reinvention has made Kelowna the largest Okanagan city and the fastest-growing retirement area in Canada. Its traditional agricultural economy has diversified into forestry, aerospace, food processing, engineering/environmental technologies, and tourism. Since the 1980s, the reinvention has been argued to be a "place making, place selling" campaign geared to attract "white" consumption over agricultural production. It is meant to attract those who seek a lifestyle and to exploit those who service the lifestyle.[18]

Fort Collins, Colorado

(2010 pop. 143,986; MSA 299,630)

Fort Collins has been a leader in habitat protection, affordable housing, growth management, and green energy investment. More than 50 percent of Fort Collins adults have at least a college degree. They have invested their time and energy in inventing sustainable and renewable businesses and ideas.

The city grew rapidly since 1970 and began to purchase open spaces after passing a one-cent capital improvement sales tax. In 1998, Fort Collins was the second utility in the nation to offer a green wind program and has since added other green programs; it is active in reducing greenhouse gas emissions and increasing renewable energy use. In 2004, Fort Collins supported 2.4 percent renewable energy and plans to have 15 percent renewable energy by 2017. To encourage energy efficiency, the city provides zero-interest loans for energy improvements and offers rebates on several energy-saving devices.

New city-owned buildings are LEED Silver, and homeowners are guided toward interest-free, energy-efficient building. City, developers, and Colorado State University work together to create sustainable services and green practices. Students at the college work on sustainable entrepreneurship, and Fort Collins tourism packages feature bike tours, local foods, and wines.

Economy

Primary Industry and Natural Resources

The Rocky Mountain economy has been based on primary sector industries—mining, timber, and livestock ranching—but has shifted to a tertiary service economy of tourism. As profits and employment in primary industry decline, the low-wage tourism economy accelerates.

Agriculture and Livestock

Rocky Mountain agriculture flourished during the boom and bust nineteenth century when food costs to miners were high, which allowed local farmers to profit from growing and selling their fruits and vegetables. Today, few farmers grow fruit and vegetable crops; they are replaced by irrigated hay or niche markets, such as chiles in New Mexico and ginseng in British Columbia.

Livestock Grazing   The basin and park bottomlands grow irrigated hay and graze cattle and sheep. **Transhumance** grazing, where livestock are moved to high pasture during the summer and low during winter, is on private and BLM land. Valley land produces supplementary hay in summer and supplies low-elevation pastures during the winter.

Okanagan Valley Agriculture   The Okanagan Valley of British Columbia is a 125-mile-long semiarid valley in the rain shadow of the Coast Mountains. The valley was dry until after

World War I, when irrigation turned the brown soil to green apple orchards. The valley is changing again in the twenty-first century, as Canadians flock to Canada's sunniest and longest growing season (175 days).

Until railroads arrived in 1892, most settlers were cattle ranchers, because it was the most economically viable. Fruit, especially apple orchards, became profitable after irrigation and rail access, but orchards are being razed in the twenty-first century because of high production costs and low market value. In the 1970s, there were more than 24,710 acres of apples, but by 2001 apple orchards had declined to 1,779 acres, replaced by either the more profitable and popular vineyards or by housing developments (Photo 15.9).

The winery industry has been growing in the Okanagan and nearby valleys. Since the late 1980s, three dozen wineries have opened in the Okanagan Valley alone. The wineries are a tourist and retiree attraction, and they are one of the reasons for the population growth. The Okanagan Valley has excellent vineyard conditions: Sunshine is abundant; glacial benches rich in till line the valley walls; and the lake in the valley floor moderates temperatures and nearby climatic extremes, creating microclimates that benefit the vineyards, which are at the same latitude as the wineries of north Germany and France.

Ginseng, a perennial herbaceous plant that looks like parsnip, grows in arid areas such as the Okanagan. The root is grown on small acreages (often under five acres), with occasional farms in the hundreds of acres. Maturing in four years, the crop is then dried and sold to ginseng brokers at about $25 per pound. Ninety percent is shipped to Asian markets, where it is used in tea, soups, candies, drinks, and capsules.

The Okanagan faces several sustainable challenges in the future. Since it is the only desert in Canada, its biodiversity is unique and threatened by development and water use. The number of homes being built, agriculture, and climate change place heavy demands on the limited water supply. Recent geographic information system (GIS) models indicate that an increase in evapotranspiration due to climate change will increase crop water demand. The research also indicates a lack of water to satisfy future needs.[19]

Mineral Resources

Both the Canadian and American Rocky Mountains have rich mineral deposits. Rocky Mountain mining reached its pinnacle in the nineteenth century.

Mining is easiest in mountainous areas because the rock veins are closer to the surface, but not all mountains share in the mineral wealth. Most of the mining in the Southern Rockies has been in the Colorado Mineral Belt (Map 15.2). The Northern Rockies also had significant mining districts, as did the Cariboo and Kootenay districts of British Columbia.

Miners heading for the California gold fields did some preliminary panning in the Rockies, then returned after the California rush had subsided. The first metal to be mined in both the Southern and Northern Rockies was gold. By 1859, gold was found near Pikes Peak in Colorado; the Idaho batholith near the Salmon River; and in Virginia City, Montana.

The long history of mining has left abandoned mines, released chemicals into watersheds, left swaths of displaced land, cut roads through wilderness, and tore up land. These activities displace wildlife and damage ecosystems. Additionally, global climate change affects alpine vegetation and human-made features such as road and hiking trails. Mining damage lasts for decades after the activity has ended, and it necessitates governmental cleanup.

Private companies have free access to metallic minerals on public land because of the **Mining Law of 1872,** which was

PHOTO 15.9. Kelowna, Okanagan Valley, British Columbia. A housing boom and rising prices have been a hallmark of the Okanagan Valley in recent years. The region has been known for its apple orchards historically, but it now supports a retirement community and a growing wine industry.

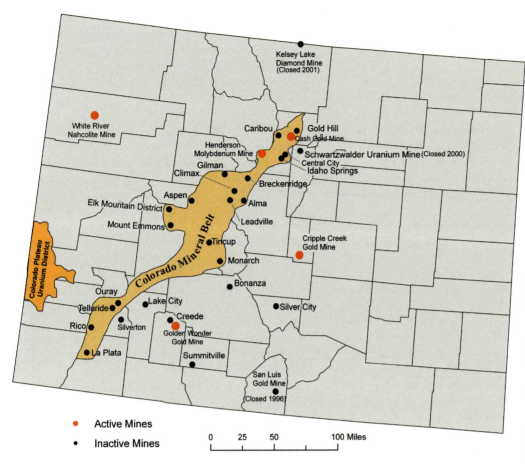

MAP 15.2. The Colorado Mineral Belt lies within a system of faults that trend about 250 miles from the southwest to the north central part of the state and is the site of most of Colorado's major mining areas. Ores found in this zone include gold, silver, lead, zinc, uranium, and molybdenum.

originally written to bring order to chaotic exploitation in the mountainous West. In the late 1990s, climate change and its impact on the tundra and glaciers increased the ecologic fragility of the Rockies and increased concerns about current mining practices. Today controversy continues around the law's lack of environmental protection.

Colorado. Denver, Pueblo, Golden, and Colorado City vied to be the gateway city into Colorado's Mineral Belt country, but Denver prevailed because of proximity to placer mines (Cherry Creek and Central City). The mines evolved slowly and lacked technology, but access improved with the railroad in the late 1860s. The boom-bust mining towns experienced quick growth and quick abandonment when the metal was played out or the commodity market fell. The initial mining boom, which was dependent on easily accessed shallow mines, ended during the 1920s.

Often multiple ores would be found in one site. At Leadville, Colorado, the original strike was silver, but it evolved into gold in the 1890s and then lead, zinc, and molybdenum.

Northern Rockies. In 1876, the Butte, Montana, mining boom began, first in silver, then gold, and finally in copper. The copper-mining process required power to refine the ore. Dams built along the Missouri River provided cheap electricity, but a smelter was necessary to process the ore. In 1884, the town of Anaconda built up around a copper smelter.

Copper is an excellent conductor of electricity and was immensely important for the development of American energy, but processing is toxic. The toxins used during the mining operation affected Butte residents' health: Between 1949 and 1971 the death rate from related illnesses was among the highest in America.[20]

Canada. Eighty-nine percent of all Canadian land is Crown Land, which is managed and protected by the federal or provincial governments. In British Columbia, 92 percent of the land is provincial Crown Land, 1 percent federal, and the remaining private land. Much like BLM land in the states, Crown Land is leased to mining and logging companies for resource extraction. Crown Land was once available for homesteading, but it is now either leased or sold to interested parties at fair market value.

The 1860s gold rush in the Cariboo Mountains of British Columbia created several boom and bust towns, such as Barkerville and Quesnel. Other towns, such as Wells, mined gold from the 1930s until the 1960s. In the Kootenays, the Sullivan mine in Kimberley was mined for lead, zinc, and silver until 2001.

Mining continues in British Columbia. The world's largest zinc- and lead-smelting complex is located in southeastern British Columbia at Trail, originally a silver-mining town established in the nineteenth century. Other mines include copper and molybdenum, the largest located in Highland Valley, southwest of Kamloops in the interior plateau.

BOX 15.6 MINERAL EXTRACTION IN MONTANA

Pro-industry advocates were given a boost when the 9/11 terrorist attacks increased the need for western minerals in the name of energy security. By December 2001, several new mining commitments and land giveaways had already gelled.

The Mining Law of 1872 allows the federal giveaways of public land. Over the years Mining Law controls, such as the federal protections of wilderness land in the 1964 **Wilderness Act**, have not halted the land giveaways. Though some new claims are denied, one may purchase a previous claim that has been grandfathered in.

By 2007, mining interests controlled 77 percent of Montana's public land. For example, the Rock Creek Mine in the Cabinet Mountain Wilderness of the Kootenai National Forest, one of the few remaining grizzly and trout habitats, was seeking permits to mine copper and silver. The mine's owner purchased claims filed a generation ago, prior to Wilderness Act protection. Rock Creek Mine would be the largest such enterprise in America, and the first under a national wilderness area.

The Rock Creek Mine had staked its claim in the 1980s, but in 2001 the time and federal policy were right for passage. Billing the mine as "you won't even know we're there," the underground mine would provide needed metals for the national economy and more than three hundred jobs over a thirty-year period. The mine has caused a rift among local residents, with some favoring the jobs and others favoring environmental care.

The environmental consequences of the underground mine are multiple. Two alpine lakes beneath the mineral deposit could be drained because faults running through the deposit may generate new rifts due to mining blasts. A buffer zone was added, but a loophole denied the subsidence threat. Although other mining in the area has resulted in subsidence, the threat does "not present significant new environmental concerns."* Mining water polluted with heavy metals will be discharged into the Clark Fork River. Wildlife in the area is fragile at best, especially the grizzlies, who only exist in the area because of continual transplanting. Only five grizzly bear females are known in this region, and yet the Forest Service defended losing one or two. Bull trout have been in decline, and water pollution may disturb restoration efforts. In Idaho, residents oppose it because of possible water contamination to Lake Pend Orielle.

Federal leasing arrangements allow mining companies access to land at minimal prices (often less than $1 per acre) and do not respect the costs to wildlife habitat, industrial and water pollution from chemicals, and cleanup standards. Residents in the area are aware of lax cleanup standards, because in 1998 Montana taxpayers footed a $33 million bankrupt mine clean-up of cyanide spills and acid mine drainage, which will require continual water treatment into the far future.

Seeking only economic benefit and not the triple bottom line objectives, the Rock Creek Mine has had ten lawsuits against its operation, but in December 2007 the U.S. Forest Service and the Montana Department of Environmental Quality approved the underground silver and copper mine. In July 2011, a Montana state court blocked construction of Rock Creek Mine because of violations of the Montana Water Quality Act. However, the mine is still on track to open in 2018, perhaps spurred by the elevating costs of copper.

* U.S. Department of Agriculture, *Rock Creek Supplemental Information Report: Subsidence* (FSH 1909.15 section 18.1), January 25, 2007.

Coal   Rocky Mountain coal is lower quality but is used to generate local power. Most Rocky Mountain coal-mining operations have closed in both the United States and Canada.

Canada ranks tenth in the world for coal reserves, and Alberta coal represents 60 percent of Canadian coal reserves. Alberta's coal reserves are found to the west of Lethbridge along the eastern Rocky Mountain front. Since the late nineteenth century, Alberta coal production dominated Canadian coal reserves. Several foothill Rocky Mountain towns—Canmore, Nordegg, and Hinton, for example—were once coal-mining towns. All these mines are now closed, and the economies have changed. Canmore and Nordegg rely on tourism. Hinton reliance on lumber has also shifted toward tourism, due to its proximity to Jasper.

High coal prices have supported metallurgical coal mines (for making steel) in the Peace River and Kootenay districts of British Columbia. Near Fernie, five mines continue to mine coal. Much of this coal is exported to Asian steel mills.

Oil and Gas   Domestic oil and gas drilling proliferated in the 1970s when foreign prices escalated, but when oil prices fell the boom ended, only to be revived in the early twenty-first century. Oil and gas recovery methods that are economically impossible when oil prices are low become feasible when prices escalate beyond $50 a barrel.

The Rocky Mountains contain vast oil shale deposits, estimated as high as eight hundred billion barrels. During the 1970 oil crisis, the deposits seemed an energy find, but as oil prices fell so did interest in shale. Interest has picked up again since 2001 (Table 15.4). Drilling in the Rocky Mountains boosts domestic oil supplies but remains a controversial subject in the twenty-first century due to environmental concerns.

Controversy continues between the need for oil and gas and damages to environmentally sensitive areas, such as ecosystem disruption, air pollution, road building through roadless areas, and defiling landscapes while generating tons of mining waste. Oil shale mining uses vast amounts of water that leach into the groundwater supply. Many of the oil and gas recovery sites are located in wilderness areas used by hunting and fishing guides, who feel they will lose their livelihood should drilling proceed.

BOX 15.7 ANACONDA, MONTANA

[They'd work] their heads off to have a nice yard . . . and the smelter fumes were killing it as fast as they could plant it. Everybody in town worked for the ACM [smelter] but me. And I was independent, I could say whatever I darn pleased. . . . A person would say, "look at my lawn how yellow it's getting', just what's the matter with it?" I'd say . . . "It's the smelter fumes." And he shut up like a clam. He wouldn't talk about it anymore. They're hard on anybody that tried to make it look like the smelter fumes were doing it.

—Eric White, U.S. Forest Service*

Anaconda was a working-class smelter boom town that ended abruptly in September 1980, when Arco closed the smelter, citing the high cost of environmental legislation, although global competition and production costs were as much to blame. The single-industry-resource town was left without its primary source of income. The shutdown was devastating—in one day a community of ten thousand lost a thousand of its highest-paying jobs—followed by years of indirect results: divorce, abuse, and poverty.

The widespread environmental damage was ignored until the shutdown. The site became the largest Superfund site in the nation. The heavy metals spewed from the famous Anaconda "Big Stack" that towered 585 feet in the air scourged land and befouled water for miles around, and sulfur dioxide and arsenic denuded the entire forested area between Anaconda and Butte (Photo 15.10).

The environmental cleanup relocated residents and caused homes to be torn down. Soil was removed or capped and revegetated, and in 1994, a signature golf course opened. Several elements of the old mining complex embellished the golf course, which used slag for the sand traps, and left old mining equipment as decoration. Mining is no longer part of the town's economy, other than as historical tourism.† The golf course does not reflect the town's working-class background but sets it on a tangential trajectory.

The cleanup was not without its critics. Some hoped for another smokestack industry to keep the town in business; others

PHOTO 15.10. Smokestack, Anaconda, Montana. The smokestack is the country's tallest, rising 585 feet above the town and overlooking a mountain of slag. During the last years of the smelter's operation (it closed in 1980), workers would look up at the stack each morning seeking the smoke, which told them the plant was open and they still had a job.

fought the reclamation project, claiming that the capped soil may not stop the contamination, or that the soil would be exposed in the event of flood. Many agreements and mitigation efforts were implemented to make the golf course work and the inhabitants at ease in the town.

The golf course and its surrounding development are considered reclamation successes, augmented by several casinos to create new industry. Yet the population of this former smelting town and county dropped from 10,278 in 1990 to 7,734 in 2010.

---

* Quoted in Laurie Mercier, *Anaconda: Labor, Community, and Culture in Montana's Smelter City* (Urbana: University of Illinois, 2001).

† Brian Shovers, "Remaking the Wide-Open Town: Butte at the End of the Twentieth Century," *Montana* 48, no. 3 (September 1998): 40–53.

Abandoned Mines The legacy of mining has left the Rockies with abandoned mines containing physical and environmental hazards, such as acid mine drainage, metal leaching, destroyed aquatic habitats, contamination, open shafts, and steep pit walls. Cleanup of these sites has been ongoing, involving the EPA, Superfund, and various state agencies. Sites include seventeen thousand mines throughout the Colorado Mineral Belt, the copper mines of Montana, and radioactive uranium mines. In Canada, ten thousand mines have been abandoned.[21] Some sites have been cleaned or are in the process, but many others still require remediation. In some areas environmental rules are being rolled back or are not fully implemented.

Clear Creek, Colorado. About thirty miles west of Denver is the Clear Creek drainage basin, containing 1,343 abandoned mines, tailings, waste rock piles, and more than a hundred abandoned mine tunnels that drain into the watershed. The region was an important mining area from 1860 to 1890, when Leadville mines dominated. Clear Creek mining continued at a lesser level until about 1950. In 1983, the area was declared a Superfund site.

The most significant impact has been from acid mine drainage. About 250,000 people in Denver depend on Clear Creek water, which is contaminated from water flowing through the waste piles and mining tunnels. Other contributing factors are heavy metals (cadmium, arsenic, lead, zinc, copper) and mine wastes (Photo 15.12). The drainage has also degraded fishery and aquatic habitats.

Cleanup began in 1993 and is ongoing. The cleanup involves groundwater contamination remediation, identifying other

BOX 15.8 CANMORE, ALBERTA

Banff and Lake Louise are in Banff National Park, a premier tourist attraction since the early twentieth century. But since the 1980s, Canmore, Alberta, just sixteen miles from Banff and sixty miles from Calgary, has evolved from a 1930s coal company town into a world-class climbing and winter sport resort.

Fast-growing Calgary is close to Banff and Canmore. Both are situated within the Bow River Valley between the Front Range of the Canadian Rockies and the continental divide, but there is one major difference: Canmore is on private land and occupies about 80 percent of the developable land in the Banff region.

Canmore's last coal mine closed in 1979, at which time residents feared the town would become another ghost town. However, some residents saw an advantage to Canmore's geography—it is just outside the park limits, and it is close to Calgary. Owning resort vacation homes inside national parks is prohibited in Canada, so Canmore's location outside the park boundaries allowed thousands of condominiums to sprout on former dairy farm land, and thousands more are promised. Prices have escalated, and Canmore's fear of becoming a ghost town faded. In its place, environmentally friendly, sustainable development–supporting energy-efficiency ideals grew, although prices averaging more than $500,000 left little affordable housing. The town grew 10 percent annually until 2006, when the town restricted population growth to 6 percent annually. Growth slowed in 2009 but rebounded in 2011. The Bow River Valley may be built out by 2020 (Photo 15.11).

Developments now block the magnificent Rocky Mountain backdrop. The growth affects wildlife populations. Like Banff in

PHOTO 15.11. Condominiums in Canmore, Alberta. Canmore was a company coal-mining town; its last mine closed in 1979. The town was faced with desolation, until it realized its locational asset. Located near Calgary and outside Banff Park boundaries, the town built condominiums and began to satisfy a pent-up demand for recreational tourism.

the 1990s, Canmore is experiencing aggressive and growing elk populations. Wolves, the elk's natural predators, have been chased away by human activity. Canmore has become a heli-skiing center, and that activity is stressing caribou populations. Other towns adjoining national parks—Nordegg, Hinton, Rocky Mountain House, Pincher Creek—are beginning to experience the same growth interferences.

TABLE 15.4. Western States Oil Drilling, 1993–2004

Type of land	Total land area (acres)
2001–2004	
Lands protected from drilling	511,201
Lands opened to drilling	45,057,180
Net drilling	(44,545,9779)
1993–2000	
Lands protected from drilling	64,006,146
Lands opened to drilling	862
Net drilling	64,005,284

Source: Environmental Working Group from Federal Register, "Who Owns the West: Oil and Gas Leases," at http://www.ewg.org/oil_and_gas/dataindex.php?fips=00000&data=protection

PHOTO 15.12. Old Stanley Mine, Idaho Springs, Colorado. The Stanley Mine was mined for gold, silver, copper, and lead, bringing in more than $3.6 million in 1910. The mine is a probable source of mine waste, low pH groundwater, and mine tailing contamination in the Clear Creek watershed, which provides water for part of the Denver metro area. The numerous mines in the area have created traffic snarls when abandoned mine shafts create sinkholes on nearby I-70. As of 2010, the mines have not been cleaned up.

sources of drinking water, capping tailings piles to minimize leaching, and purging waste piles. An increase in gambling in Central City and Blackhawk has brought more people and increased contamination exposure, but signs of health are apparent, such as the return of trout to formerly contaminated streams.[22]

Logging **American Rocky Mountains**. The U.S. Rocky Mountains have approximately two hundred million acres of fir, pine, and spruce alpine forests, mostly protected from logging. The Northern Rockies harbor 58 percent of the American Rocky Mountain growing stock, and they provide about 10 percent of U.S. timber cut.

Nineteenth-century development in the United States required lumber to build its structures. The first massive clear-cuts began in Michigan in the nineteenth century. When Michigan timber was cleared, logging enterprises moved west. By the early twentieth century, huge tracts of Idaho white pine supplied sawmills, but the land was stripped of forests until laws required replanting. Forests are now harvested as a crop every thirty to forty years. Small-diameter trees lack the high-quality wood of old-growth forests, and therefore much of the wood is now produced into lesser wood products, such as plywood and oriented strand board (OSB).

Idaho has the most National Forest land in the contiguous states and has master-planned its logging. In 2008, a roadless plan covered a portion of the area, but another 405,000 acres were opened to logging and road construction.

Canadian Rockies. Both British Columbia and Alberta operate significant pulp and sawed lumber mills for global markets. British Columbia coniferous forests provide about half of Canada's total softwood inventory. Rocky Mountain lodgepole pine and spruce is used throughout the world for lumber, pulp, paper, shingles, and plywood.

Alberta forestland is 59 percent of the province land and 87 percent Crown provincial land, and 9 percent Crown federal land. Fifty foothill communities depend on forestry in Alberta, and twelve depend on it exclusively. Poplar and aspen wood from northwestern Alberta Rocky Mountain foothills contribute to the growing OSB market.

Tourism

The drivers of the Rocky Mountain economy are tourism and recreation, ranging from scenic viewing to hiking and climbing in the warm months and winter sports in the cold months. Major Rocky Mountain travel destinations include national parks, towns dependent on ski resorts, and the Front Range cities. The challenge to these complexes is to maintain their "sense of place" character while promoting sustainable tourism and recreational use.

In the Canadian Rockies, Banff National Park has pioneered environmental protection, with some developments adopting the cradle-to-cradle ethos of recycling and regeneration. Banff has invested in energy-efficient LED lighting to reduce energy consumption. While sustainability has become popular, most ski industry towns continue to rely on the single bottom line, profit.

The ski industry is famous throughout the Rockies, from Taos, New Mexico, to Banff and Jasper in Canada, but Colorado has been the most influential ski tourism state. Many skiers favor the dry, powdery, Rocky Mountain snow, the result of a continental climate and high elevation. The major ski resorts occupy a path along the Colorado Mineral Belt, since many of the cities are revived ghost towns. Vail and Aspen, the largest complexes with more than twenty-five miles of ski trails, each sells more than eleven million ski tickets annually (at daily prices averaging $90). Both became known as high-priced developments, where wealthy "owner's clubs" offer first-class amenities—no ski lines, coveted parking, and gourmet restaurants—that the average skier cannot afford.

The longtime competition between Vail and Aspen now includes who is the "greenest." However, being green does not equate to being sustainable, as it does not endorse the triple bottom line mentality. Green continues to favor consumption. Both towns claim that they run on wind power and are developing solar power, because it is trendy and currently popular in elite crowds to be green. Being green is a first step in recognizing the problem. Corporations are noticing that global warming is beginning to affect their business. On the one hand, they advocate "green" renewable energy, and on the other they artificially make snow. Snowmaking is dependent on fossil fuels and exerts pressure on water resources. Making artificial snow withdraws water from streams, stressing aquatic life, and increases energy use.

The terrain in the Southern Rockies is perfect for ski runs for all levels of expertise at ski resorts. During the summer months, peaks can be reached by strenuous hikes, but the less energetic may reach the tops of Pikes Peak and Mount Evans by road. Fishing and hunting have long been a reason many of the local residents came to the communities, but as large developments purchase more land, local hunting and fishing grounds are often closed and wealthy newcomers, who destroy or remove the natural amenities with preserves or development, are resented by the local populace.

Tourism has a variety of positive and negative influences. It can bring people to areas where local extractive economies have failed, but it can also damage the environment. Towns dependent on extractive industry often turn to tourism to revive their economy. Tourism is usually not as environmentally damaging as extractive industry, although it too can wreak havoc on fragile rural landscapes. Golf and ski industries, for example, can fragment ecosystems and wildlife habitats, as well as pollute water and land.

The Rocky Mountain allure varies with the visitors and the time of year. Each visitor profile has different needs: The hunter seeks open space; the skier, après-ski amenities; the hiker, rustic infrastructure and a trail system. Towns seeking to satisfy all or one of these groups may damage the environment for the others, or may harm the landscape by trying to satisfy all groups. Another environmental impact is when "clash cultures" (locals and affluent newcomers) have different perceptions about local development and industry. Newcomers often want to save the environment after they have arrived, stop what they see as overdevelopment, and truncate the opportunities of longtime residents who are not as affluent as their new neighbors. Extractive or tourist industries, frowned upon by the newcomers, provide income for the local residents, who may find that newcomers

overdevelop hunting and fishing grounds, or ruin the authenticity of the town and its attraction to other tourists.

Tourism is encouraged not only for the local economy, but also because it places part of the local tax burden on nonresidents. Colorado, well aware that its many tourist towns face economic hurdles, partially because of a poorly paid tourism workforce, find that higher taxes for lodging, rentals, and airport fees help reduce the residents' tax base—but higher taxes also discourage tourism.

A Sustainable Future

The future of the Rocky Mountains may be troubling. Although mineral extraction has not been the reason for recent growth, escalating prices and a favorable federal administration can change this scenario. The major industries today are tourism and recreation, but they also face challenges, such as traffic, growth, immigration, and climate change. The third challenge to the Rocky Mountains is polarized population growth.

The Rockies demographics has changed from extractive industry miners, to one where the magnificent scenery is the main commodity and is now home, or more likely second home, to the wealthy. This switch in population dynamics has affected the local population and workers who are squeezed out by upscale homes, land prices that have escalated tenfold, and have been shut out of their own backyards for hunting and fishing. As prices for the "beautiful" areas escalate, the grown children of local residents can no longer afford to live in their hometown and are forced to relocate. Service industry employees are also priced out of the market. The landscape changes into one where preservation, a static and zoo-like amenity of scenic beauty, becomes paramount and important to maintain property values for the new residents.

Many people move to the Rocky Mountains to experience the lifestyle of the rancher, even if on a five-acre "spread." It is an urban-sprawl lifestyle. One of the ways that people conserve this lifestyle is through land trusts and reserves, although these have the additional effect of increasing land prices because less land is available for everyone.

In Canada, mining has continued, but only after sustainability issues are addressed before the mining begins. Mining permits are only issued if the impact is balanced between the ore extracted and the damage to the environment. However, unsustainable drilling for oil and gas continues relatively unabated throughout the United States and Canadian Rocky Mountain Front, destroying air and water quality, wildlife habitats, and landscapes. Alliances such as the Coalition to Protect the Rocky Mountain Front work to protect the landscape.

Environmental groups, such as the Nature Conservancy and the Freshwater Initiative, along with provincial and statewide groups, join forces to provide annual ecoregional assessments analyzing all aspects of the ecological subdivisions and their interactions, and to lay out plans for the future. Included within their analyses are threat assessments (fire management, forestry practices, invasive species, etc.) and climate change.[23]

Communities, companies, institutes, and universities advocate for sustainability. Throughout the region, cities and towns are seeking economic development while integrating holistic thinking. For example, Alamosa, Colorado, an agricultural community located in the San Juan interbasin near the Sangre de Cristo Range, has reinvented itself with alternative crops, fish farms using local hot springs water, the nation's first biodiesel refinery in 2004, and an 8.2-megawatt photovoltaic solar plant, which opened in December 2007.

Companies committed to the triple bottom line are investing in recycling and biofuels, while institutes, such as the Rocky Mountain Institute, are engaging in renewable energy research, resource planning, and green buildings. Universities, led by the University of Colorado, Boulder, and at Fort Collins, have embraced sustainable goals and sustainable education to prepare students for their future. In 2007, four institutions in Colorado (the University of Colorado, Boulder; the National Renewable Energy Laboratory [NREL]; Colorado State University; and the Colorado School of Mines) teamed up to research more efficient renewable energy options. For example, they are researching how to double the efficiency of the Alamosa solar plant.

High energy prices, climate change, and reduced water consumption are some of the reasons that companies, universities, and towns are considering sustainable practices in the Rocky Mountains. However, sustainable practices need to extend to the second-home complexes and the extraction industries, and they need to allow social equity to local residents so that all can benefit now and in the future.

Questions for Discussion

1. Why were the endangered or threatened wolves reintroduced into the Rocky Mountains? What have been the advantages and disadvantages?

2. Should oil and gas drilling be allowed in environmentally sensitive areas? Why or why not?

3. Is tourism the right industry for the Rocky Mountains? If so, why; if not, why not? What would be alternatives?

4. Is it better to let wildlife roam free, killing what they need, including cattle or sheep, or should wildlife who roam onto cattle ranges be shot by ranchers?

5. Tax laws currently allow full mortgage interest deductions on second homes, which generates towns with more empty second homes than full-time residents. Additionally, many local residents cannot afford to live in the town because of the second homes. Is this type of tax deduction sustainable for the entire community?

6. Can primary industry exist along with increased population growth and environmental issues?

7. Land preservation and trusts have become big business, but what are the advantages and disadvantages socioeconomically? At what point do the rights of one animal or human begin and end?

8. The debate over what should be kept as wilderness areas is not simple. Explain the reasoning for both sides and what some of the related issues are.

9. How has the Mining Law of 1872 been controversial and affected current mining operations?

10. Explain how tourism and recreational use are both boon and bane to a sustainable economy.

Suggested Readings

Aguiar, Luis L. M., Patricia Tomic, and Ricardo Trumper. "Work Hard, Play Hard: Selling Kelowna, BC, as Year-Round Playground." *Canadian Geographer* 49, no. 2 (Summer 2005).

Barbour, Barton H. "Jedediah S. Smith and Marcus and Narcissa Whitman: Mountain Men and Missionaries in the Far West." In *Western Lives,* edited by Richard W. Etulain. Albuquerque: University of New Mexico Press, 2004.

Baron, Jill S., ed. *Rocky Mountain Futures.* Washington, D.C.: Island Press, 2002.

Lorah, Paul, and Rob Southwick. "Environmental Protection, Population Change, and Economic Development in the Rural Western United States." *Population and Environment* 24, no. 3 (January 2003).

Mathews, Daniel. *Rocky Mountain Natural History.* Portland, Ore.: Raven Editions, 2003.

Mercier, Laurie. *Anaconda: Labor, Community, and Culture in Montana's Smelter City.* Urbana: University of Illinois, 2001.

Morgan, Dale L. *Jedediah Smith and the Opening of the West.* Indianapolis: Bobbs-Merrill, 1953.

Sprague, Marshall. *The Great Gates: The Story of the Rocky Mountain Passes.* Boston: Little, Brown, 1964.

Stowkowski, Patricia A. *Riches and Regrets: Betting on Gambling in Two Colorado Mountain Towns.* Niwot: University Press of Colorado, 1996.

U.S. Environmental Protection Agency. Abandoned Mine Lands Team. *Reference Notebooks*, September 2004.

Utley, Robert M. *A Life Wild and Perilous: Mountain Men and the Paths to the Pacific.* New York: Holt, 1997.

Veblen, Thomas T., William L. Baker, Gloria Montenegro, and Thomas W. Swetnam, eds. *Fire and Climatic Change in Temperate Ecosystems of the Western Americas.* New York: Springer, 2003.

Wyckoff, William. *Creating Colorado: The Making of a Western American Landscape.* 1860; New Haven, Conn.: Yale University Press, 1999.

Yorath, Chris. *How Old Is That Mountain? A Visitor's Guide to the Geology of Banff and Yoho National Parks.* Rev. ed. Madeira Park, B.C., Canada: Harbour Publishing, 2006.

Internet Sources

U.S. Fish and Wildlife Service. "Gray Wolves in the Rocky Mountains," at http://westerngraywolf.fws.gov/annualreports.htm.

National Park Service. "Rocky Mountains System," at http://www2.nature.nps.gov/geology/usgsnps/province/rockymtn.html.

Rocky Mountain Climate Organization, at http://www.rockymountainclimate.org/.

Rocky Mountain Institute, at http://www.rmi.org/.

1 Dry Falls in eastern Washington, formed during the Missoula floods, were once the world's highest falls.

2 Potatoes thrive in the soil, climate, and irrigation of Idaho's Snake River Plain.

3 The Mormon Temple is the center of Salt Lake City and the initial node for the state's baseline and meridian.

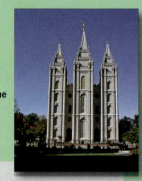

7 This central Arizona aqueduct was built to supply water from the Colorado River to the state's cities.

4 The Anasazi may have abandoned Colorado's Mesa Verde in the thirteenth century for environmental reasons.

Washington
Spokane
Channeled Scablands
Palouse
Columbia River
Montana
Bend
Oregon
Boise
Idaho
Snake River Plain
Wyoming
Nevada
Great Basin
Salt Lake City
Colorado
Basin & Range
Utah
Reno
Canyon Lands
Death Valley
Colorado River
St. George
Four Corners
Las Vegas
Arizona
Santa Fe
California
Grand Canyon
Albuquerque
Mogollon Rim
New Mexico
Coachella Valley
Phoenix
Imperial Valley
Sonoran Desert
Tucson
Mexican Highland
Texas
Central Arizona Project
Rio Grande River
Pecos River

Central Arizona Project
Cities
Rivers
State Borders

N W E S

6 The Anza-Borrego Desert in southeastern California gets less than 2 inches of rain a year.

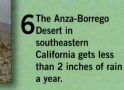

5 The Great Basin conceals many possible secrets, such as those in the movie *Independence Day*.

16
INTERMONTANE
Baked, Beguiling, and Booming

Chapter Highlights

After reading this chapter you should be able to:

- Discuss how the region has changed since 1960 and why
- List the fastest-growing cities
- Identify the major water sources and explain their relationship to the region
- Compare and contrast western versus eastern water rights
- Discuss ranching and its relationship to the Bureau of Land Management
- Explain the influences of Hispanic, Basque, and Mormon cultures within the region
- Discuss the major environmental issues
- Describe what makes the Great Basin unique
- Explain the economic structure of the region

Terms

alluvial fan
arroyo
basin
Basque

butte
canyon
Colorado River Compact
Columbia Basin Project
coulee
ecological balance

exotic stream
flash flood
Gadsden Purchase
glacial erratic
grass banking
haboob

Manifest Destiny
mesa
Mexican Cession of 1848
open pit mine
playa
scabland

Places

Anza Borrego
Basin and Range
Bonneville Salt Flats
Canyonlands
Central Arizona Project

Channeled Scablands
Coachella Valley, California
Colorado Plateau
Colorado River
Columbia Plateau
Columbia River

Death Valley
Four Corners
Grand Canyon
Great Basin
Imperial Valley, California
Las Vegas, Nevada

Mogollon Rim
Palouse
Phoenix, Arizona
Snake River Plain
Spokane, Washington
Sun Belt

PHOTO 16.1. The Basin and Range. This subregion contains a series of dry, north-south-trending faulted mountains and valleys between the western ranges and the Rocky Mountains.

Introduction

He would have said there is a difference between using a resource and mining it. He would have said the future has a claim on us. He would have said that on the evidence of several generations of exploitative freedom no one could guarantee the future its share of the American earth except the American government.

—Wallace Stegner on John Wesley Powell[1]

Between the Sierra Nevada and the Rocky Mountains lies the driest and most beguiling region in the United States (Photo 16.1). For years this "empty quarter," this "ghost region" was dry, rough-hewn, unproductive, and sparsely populated.[2] While portions of the region thrived aeons ago, the occupants disappeared mysteriously. Now the region is once again thriving, spending resources freely, but some cast a wary eye toward the past and wonder, why did the old societies vanish?

By 1950, Americans were no longer choosing where they lived based on agricultural production but instead on aesthetics, desirable climate, and affordable housing. Desert areas became attractive when air-conditioning became common in the 1960s. By 1990, the hot, arid metropolitan areas of Phoenix and Las Vegas boomed, and each surpassed one million residents. The spectacular population growth in a region comprised of too many people and too little water makes the Intermontane a modern miracle—but is there really a free lunch?

The Intermontane's leisurely urban lifestyle evolved in air-conditioned comfort following a round of golf. The few remaining farmers and ranchers profit more from selling their land to developers than working the land.

Many Intermontane residents abandoned the harsher climates and gritty cities of the Midwest for Sun Belt swimming pools. This lifestyle depends on seemingly plentiful water resources in a dry region. As American consumers, Intermontane residents depend on technology as their savior and spend rather than conserve. Living a sustainable lifestyle is only just entering the regional public consciousness.

Physical Geography

The Intermontane, that region between the Rocky Mountains and the Sierra Nevada, is challenged climatically. Hot and dry, it will sustain a small population indefinitely, but a large population is a short-term strategy. Life requires water, so the harsh, dry desert is more vulnerable than its tough-looking exterior might suggest. The human impact over the past century has caused harm that will only be remedied slowly because of the intense climatic variables.

The Intermontane's entry into the world was tumultuous. Tectonic and volcanic forces deranged and contorted the Intermontane into a combination of arid plateaus, deep-gorged **canyons**, and a series of dramatic ridges and valleys that continue to reconfigure in a planetary timeframe indifferent to human occupation. Human habitation depends on nature, but nature does not need humans.

The Intermontane region is composed of three major subregions. They are:

* the Columbia Plateau
* the Basin and Range
* the Colorado Plateau

The Columbia Plateau is divided into two provinces: the Palouse and the Snake River Plain. The Basin and Range is divided into three provinces—the Great Basin, the Sonoran Desert, and the Mexican Highlands—and the Colorado Plateau is a jumble of mesas and canyons, highlighted by the Grand Canyon.

Columbia Plateau

Approached from any direction the visible change [at the Great Plain of the Columbia] is striking: the forest thins then abruptly ends, the mountains lower then merge into a much smoother surface, and a different kind of country, open and undulating, rolls out before the viewer like a great interior sea.

—D. W. Meinig[3]

Mountains surround three sides of the two-hundred-thousand-square-mile Colombia Plateau. Intense and repeated lava flows over a ten-million-year period (ending about six million years ago) left behind a six-thousand-foot-thick blanket of alternating basalt and soil. While basalt defines the foundational plateau, it was only the canvas for a more dramatic progression of events.

Roughly fifteen thousand years ago, toward the end of the last Ice Age, an ice dam plugged Idaho's Clark River, creating Lake Missoula, which was as large as Lakes Ontario and Erie combined. Over time, the ice dam cracked. The cracks grew until a cataclysm of water—estimated at ten times the combined flow of all of Earth's rivers—burst through the dam and thundered across the Columbia Plateau. The wall of water gouged lava beds, scoured huge pothole lakes, eroded the soil to its basalt base, and formed the Columbia Gorge as it rushed toward the Pacific Ocean. The process was repeated from eighty to one hundred times over the next three thousand years, and so the descriptively named Channeled Scablands were shaped.

The combined lava flows and the repeated floods sculpted the broken landscape and carved deep canyons, creating a **scabland** of exposed lava rock. The Missoula floodwaters scraped the Columbia Gorge walls bare. The gorge wall dropped hundreds of feet, and streams that once flowed peacefully into the Columbia became dramatic waterfalls into the gorge. The floodwaters settled in the Willamette Valley as far south as Eugene, exposing sand and debris bars that molded the northern bend of the Columbia River where Portland, Oregon, is located. Floods laid down fertile soils through the Scablands, the Palouse, and the Willamette Valley and also deposited huge **glacial erratics**, which settled near places like Lake Oswego. Today, the floodwaters are long gone. Left behind are dry gulch **coulees** and the Columbia River, the only perennial river through the bare Scablands.

The Palouse

Floods, lava flows, and deposition of hundreds of feet of windblown loess (finely ground glacial sediment) formed the now peaceful, undulating hills of the Palouse subregion—south of Spokane, Washington, and west into Idaho. The Palouse was once open grassland, but over 90 percent is now cultivated. To the east are the rippled Camas Prairies.

Snake River Plain

Idaho is a mountainous state, with the exception of southern Idaho's flat crescent Snake River Plain, which was shaped as the North American Plate migrated over a stationary hot spot (Map 16.1). The Snake River rises in the Wyoming Tetons and flows through the eponymous plain, joining the Columbia River at Pasco, Washington. The hot spot now underlies Yellowstone, but as the continental plate journeyed across the Snake River Plain the hot spot caused basalts and other volcanic rock to be deposited on the surface. Fresh lava flows are sterile and barren, but over time vegetation colonizes the rock, which breaks down into a rich soil. The Snake River Plain is Idaho's best agricultural land, and it contains most of the state's population.

Basin and Range

Averaging less than ten inches of precipitation annually, the nation's most arid region is exactly what it is called, a basin and range, with topography composed of more than 150 short, north-south-trending ranges interspersed with broad, flat desert **basins**. The five-hundred-mile-wide expanse, hemmed in from Utah's Wasatch Range to the Sierra Nevada, widens to nearly seven hundred miles along the southwestern border of California, east into Texas near El Paso. In the north the indefinite boundaries blend into the Columbia Plateau, and in the south they continue into Mexico.

The major subregions in the Basin and Range are:

- the Great Basin
- the Sonoran Desert
- the Mexican Highlands

0	30	60	120	180	240

Miles

MAP 16.1. Snake River Plain, Idaho. The distinctive crescent-shaped swath was created by the hot spot moving beneath the plain.

The Great Basin

The Great Basin consists of most of Nevada, the western half of Utah, and surrounding areas. Named for its closed internal drainage system, the Great Basin is confined east and west by mountain systems that keep the water from ocean outlets. It is dry and drier because evaporation exceeds precipitation. What water there is sinks into the ground to the water table, emits from groundwater springs along fault lines, or evaporates, leaving high-mineral-content water in saline lakes. Water is regionally important, not because of its prevalence but because of its scarcity. Access to water allows agricultural and urban growth, while the lack leaves the land stark, parched, and capable of providing for few humans, although many other species abound.

The land has not always been so dry. The wetter and cooler Pleistocene climate supported over a hundred lakes, but today, most are **playas** (dry lakebeds). The two largest Pleistocene lakes were Bonneville and Lahontan. The Great Salt Lake and Pyramid Lake are remnants of those former lakes. Some lakes accumulate water during the spring runoff, evaporate and leave behind salts, and then repeat the cycle annually; other lakes are more ephemeral, appearing irregularly in relation to precipitation.

This region of solitude has been earmarked for the original nuclear test sites: Area 51—the loneliest road in America—and Yucca Mountain, the once designated storage area for nuclear waste. After more than twenty years of work and billions of taxpayer dollars, the controversial site was not funded in 2010, effectively shutting it down and leaving America without a permanent repository for nuclear waste.

Mojave Desert The southern Great Basin consists of a maze of uplifted mountains and downfaulting basins.

Ephemeral streams deposit sediment, shaping **alluvial fans** at the base of the ranges. Regional vegetation varies from low desert xerophytic plants (resistant to drought) (Photo 16.2), including creosote bush, ocotillo tree, and the cholla cactus, and high desert plant life, featuring the distinctive Joshua tree.

Owens Valley, in the rain shadow of the Sierra Nevada, receives scant precipitation, but the abundant runoff from the mountains allowed valley residents to raise cattle and orchards until duplicitous agents for the Los Angeles water department changed the local economy in the early twentieth century, robbing the Owens Valley of its agricultural livelihood. The valley remains dry and depends on outdoor tourism to support the local economy. Owens Valley and Los Angeles water rights remain controversial and are highlighted in the battle surrounding Mono Lake (Photo 16.3).

The Sonoran Desert

The Sonoran Desert extends from southeastern California, across southern Arizona, and south into Mexico. Subregions include the Salton Trough, Anza Borrego Desert, California's Coachella and Imperial Valleys, and Arizona's Gila Desert. Intense summer heat limited habitation to the desert edges or the few water oases, until air-conditioning enabled regional growth.

Lower-elevation native plants in the Sonoran Desert are xerophytic; the saguaro cacti are the indicator species. Higher elevations support chaparral and evergreen trees.

The Mexican Highlands

The Mexican Highlands are sandwiched between the Sonoran Desert and the Colorado Plateau and spread from

PHOTO 16.2. Death Valley, California. The lowest elevation in the United States, Death Valley is part of the Mojave Desert and lies within the Basin and Range subregion. In the background are the Sierra Nevada, with the highest elevation in the conterminous United States.

PHOTO 16.3. Mono Lake, Southeast California. Lake water levels began to decline after 1941, when Los Angeles began diverting its streams. The lake water levels dropped and the salinity doubled, causing the ecosystem to collapse. For twenty years, the Mono Lake Committee took it upon themselves to protect the lake and its ecosystems. Since their success, water levels continue to rise, minimizing the salt flats (white areas at lake margin) and protecting islands from predators.

Arizona to Big Bend, Texas. Volcanic activity faulted and deformed mountains between the higher-elevation plateaus and the desert. Torrential **flash floods** cut **arroyos** (Spanish, "dry creek") into the plains, creating a physiographic anomaly: People drown in the desert.

The Mogollon Rim, a series of high escarpments that run from Sedona, Arizona, to the New Mexico border, separates the Colorado Plateau from the Sonoran Desert. The rim was home to western storyteller Zane Grey, who featured this "Tonto Rim" in his books. Forests dominate the mountains, while grasslands, creosote bushes, mesquite trees, and sagebrush inhabit the basin.

The easternmost Basin and Range province is a transition zone holding the tension between the Intermontane, Great Plains, and Rocky Mountains. The thin, fractured crust of the Rio Grande rift zone may eventually widen into a gulf or ocean basin, but it currently separates the Great Plains and the Intermontane; to the north, distinctive hogback formations introduce the southern extent of the Rocky Mountains Sangre de Cristo range (Photo 16.4).

Colorado Plateau

[The Plateau Province] is scenically the most spectacular and humanly the least usable of all our regions.[4]

A maze of uplifted, eroded mesas and canyons shapes the mile-high, 150,000-square-mile Colorado Plateau, leaving a rocky, difficult-to-traverse region of colorful sedimentary layers. The Colorado River cuts through the layers, creating the Grand Canyon and draining 90 percent of the plateau (Photo 16.5). To the north and east rise the Rocky Mountains, and to the west and south, bold escarpments overlook the Basin and Range.

Within the plateau are the Canyonlands, a maze of colorful slickrock-sandstone arches, and the flat-topped **mesa**s and **buttes** that are home to four national parks, monuments, and several national forests.

The lower-elevation mesas are wooded with piñon and juniper cedar, and spruce, pine, and fir at higher elevations. However, the attractive grasslands of the lower plateau have been overgrazed and reduced to desert scrub due to poor range management.

Water

Intermontane rivers—the Columbia, Colorado, and Rio Grande—are **exotic streams** (originating in a humid area but flowing through an arid area) and have been a battleground for water rights. John Wesley Powell realized that the regional water policies were ruinous and tried to alter water usage. His prophecies went unheeded in the late nineteenth century, but people are now beginning to understand his concerns.

The Intermontane West was divvied up by speculators and a Congress that wanted to populate the West quickly. The results are evident today in river water policies. For example, dams along the Columbia and Colorado rivers supply irrigation water for agriculture and provide half of the nation's waterpower resources, but at a cost of overallocation and destruction of natural habitats.

Columbia River

The Columbia River, second in size only to the Mississippi River system, is the largest North American river to enter the Pacific Ocean. Mountain snowpack supplies the water for the thirty dams that provide irrigation and generate power. Beginning in the 1930s, the **Columbia Basin Project** converted dryland crop

areas into higher-yielding irrigated land. The project centerpiece, Grand Coulee Dam, irrigates more than six hundred thousand acres of land and is the largest producer of hydroelectric power in the United States. The Snake River flows from near Jackson Hole, Wyoming, across Idaho's Snake River Plain into Oregon, passing through deep, dark canyons, the Palouse, and then joining the Columbia. The Yakima River flows from the Cascades to eastern Washington. Both irrigate the surrounding dry but fertile agricultural land.

Colorado River

The Colorado River is the most important river in the arid southwestern United States. The Colorado flows fourteen hundred miles from the Rocky Mountains through the Colorado Plateau and the southern Basin and Range. Seven western states depend on the river's water for their agricultural and urban needs. Beginning in 1935, Hoover Dam transferred the river's water to irrigate Los Angeles, the Coachella and Imperial valleys, and later Las Vegas. Other dams and the Colorado River Aqueduct followed, continuing to irrigate more than five hundred thousand acres of land.

From Glen Canyon to Lake Mead, dams divert and control river waters and diminish flow into the Mexico borderlands. Serious droughts in the twenty-first century depleted the flow and reduced the amount of water in Glen Canyon and Lake Mead (Photo 16.6)[5] but were followed in 2011 with unprecedented snowpack, displaying the irregular and nonlinear effects of climate change. If drought returns, Lake Mead may be

PHOTO 16.4. Three Regions Meeting at Galisteo, New Mexico. This region is a junction of three major regions. To the east is the Great Plains' Llano Estacado, to the north the Southern Rockies.

The Salton Sea was created in a 1904 irrigation accident that caused the Colorado River to overflow into the Imperial Valley Trough. Thousands of years previously, the trough had been covered with Lake Cahuilla, whose wave-cut shoreline can still be seen along the hillsides. The mud left from the lakebed is the fertile soil now farmed in the Imperial and Coachella valleys. The trough was formed by the earthquake-prone rifting system that stretches from the Gulf of California to north of San Francisco.

The Salton Sea—a closed hydrologic basin where evaporation exceeds precipitation, resulting in salty water—has gone through a number of transformations, from accident to seaside resort in the 1950s to ecological wasteland since the 1970s. Today, the sea has three uses: a drainage basin for southeastern California irrigation, a wildlife refuge, and a settlement site. Agricultural drainage from irrigation maintains volume, despite loss of water to evaporation, but polluted agricultural runoff contaminates the water and affects both the wildlife and the settlement. Today, broken concrete slabs and the occasional motel sign mark the past resort community, along with a scattering of current mobile home settlements.

dry by 2021.[6] The Colorado River ecosystems have been drastically altered because of the dams and drought, but scientists are working to return **ecological balance** to the region despite the dichotomy of more people and less water. Water conservation is essential but has not been fully enforced.

By the early twentieth century Colorado River water was usurped by a booming Los Angeles, to the chagrin of other states. In order to secure future rights to the river's water, the seven western states agreed in the 1922 **Colorado River Compact** to divide the waters between them. California received one-quarter of the water and unused surpluses until the 1990s, when population growth and drought in the southwestern states forced a reallocation. In 2003, after years of arbitration between the compact states, a resolution was negotiated and the growing Intermontane states claimed their full allotted water rights, which forced California to relinquish its overallotted surplus. How a continually growing California will adjust to losing significant portions of its former water resources remains to be seen.

Rio Grande

The Rio Grande originates in the San Juan Mountains of southern Colorado and flows for almost two thousand miles before it becomes navigable near the Gulf of Mexico. Gorges and mountain slopes flank the torrential river from its source to the Albuquerque, New Mexico, plain, where the river enters a desert environment and the Rio Grande rift trough. For approximately two-thirds of its course, the river serves as the boundary between the United States and Mexico.

PHOTO 16.5. Grand Canyon, Arizona. The Colorado River carved the canyon into the Colorado Plateau. The Grand Canyon exposes one of the most complete sequences of rock, aged from two billion years to the present.

PHOTO 16.6. Hoover Dam and Lake Mead, Nevada, in April 2005. Notice the white "bathtub ring" around the edges of the lake, indicating the lower water level due to drought. Between January 2000 and 2010, Lake Mead water levels dropped 138 feet, although snow accumulation during the winter of 2011 offered a reprieve.

Salt Lakes

Salt lakes are the termini of inland drainage basins, where evaporation exceeds precipitation, leaving behind concentrated salts and minerals. The interior basin remnant lakes are three to five times saltier than ocean water.

The Great Basin has several dry lakes. Historically, the largest of these was Lake Bonneville, which was thousands of feet deep and ten times larger than its fluctuating remnant, the shallow Great Salt Lake. Today, Lake Bonneville is a dry, flat salt bed, where alkaline minerals are mined industrially. Bonneville Salt Flats have been the location of land speed records, although they have been overused, which has necessitated other salt flats being used for these purposes.

The Great Salt Lake water levels have been erratic. During the 1980s, erratic climate produced heavy snows in the Great Salt Lake, resulting in rising lake levels. The relatively shallow land doubled its surface area, inundating buildings and highways. However, in the early twenty-first century, a period of drought reduced the Great Salt Lake water level, leaving whole arms of the lake dry.

Sinks

Many Great Basin streams are ephemeral or disappear into sinkholes, where they leach into groundwater or evaporate, leaving behind salts and minerals. Within the Great Basin are two major sinks: the Humboldt River, which disappears into the Humboldt Sink near Lovelock, Nevada; and the Carson Sink, once the deepest part of ancient Lake Lohantan. The saline sinks are the only source of local water and are a stopover for migratory wildlife. The sinks were the last source of water for pioneer wagons until the Sierra Nevada.

Humboldt River

The humble Humboldt River is the only stream of consequence crossing the Great Basin. As such, fur trappers, immigrant wagon trains, the railroad, and today's Interstate Highway 80 have followed the river's route. The largest towns in northern Nevada—Winnemucca, Battle Mountain, and Elko—are located along its banks. The regional economy is currently ranching and mining.

Central Arizona Project

The Central Arizona Project (CAP) was formed in 1946, when Arizona became the final signatory to the Colorado River Compact. The CAP is the latest in a historic series of Arizona irrigation projects, beginning with the Hohokam people (300 BCE–1400 CE).

The federally funded CAP aqueduct was completed in 1993. The project was allocated to Arizona's portion of the Colorado River, 336 miles from Lake Havasu to Tucson. The aqueduct supplemented agricultural water, but a serious groundwater overdraft due to increased population shifted the use from agriculture alone to municipal and industrial use, creating deleterious effects downstream. Agricultural water usage and the high rate of population growth have strained the region's water resources. Many ephemeral lakes have become permanently dry, negatively affecting local ecosystems. The overdrawn Phoenix water system used CAP as the last resort for securing usable water. The system lacks backups for protection when drought again comes to the area.[7] In early 2008 a new reservoir was planned to "capture water that now flows unused into Mexico."[8]

The Sustainable Use of Water

"This would be good country," a tourist says to me, "if only you had some water."
He's from Cleveland, Ohio.

"If we had water here," I reply, "this country would not be what it is. It would be like Ohio, wet and humid and hydrological, all covered with cabbage farms and golf courses. Instead of this lovely barren desert we would have only another blooming garden state, like New Jersey. You see what I mean?"

"If you had more water more people could live here."

—Edward Abbey, 1968[9]

The bones of the Intermontane are dry. The physical and climatic geography of the region have interrelated over time to create a baked and dramatic landscape. However, many Intermontane residents immigrated to the region because of the artificially wet, green landscape in a dry, warm climate. That their lifestyle was robbing from the future was seldom a concern. For example, this region of North America has more pools and golf courses per capita than any other region, and so it follows that the Intermontane population explosion of the 1990s only served to further exacerbate long-term water problems. Damming and irrigation networks allow short-term, extensive agricultural production and population growth, but undermine ecologic systems and long-term solutions.

A prolonged twenty-first-century drought has forced the Intermontane to tighten its water belt. The wastewater system of Phoenix, which was financially incapable of updating its infrastructure, continued as usual while the city continued to sprawl.[10] The dry Phoenix area sports vast greenbelts, and nearby affluent Scottsdale sports noontime sprinklers despite temperatures over 90°F through October. The region remains seemingly oblivious to the concept of water conservation and sustainability.

The Intermontane continues to rely on irrigated agriculture. Arizona, the Imperial Valley, and the Columbia Basin continue to grow water-hungry, irrigated cotton and corn, where dryland cropping or less water-thirsty crops may be a wiser water choice. Western water rights—the law of prior appropriation and the law of beneficial use (both ignoring the "rights" of instream life)—contort water usage for both agricultural and urban use. Historically, prior appropriation was adopted due to the initial amount of time and work necessary to irrigate the dry land. While at one point it made sense to reward the initial irrigators, the system has since become unbalanced.

Despite the past decade of drought and continued population growth, water conservation has been uneven. Cities are going to great lengths to procure water for their commercial enterprises. Las Vegas requires more water than it is allocated, so the city is deep in negotiations to construct a water pipeline that extends from northern Nevada (causing many ranchers to cry foul, owing to memories of the Owens Valley water grab for Los Angeles) to provide water to the city. The Phoenix area, where residents are often complacent and in denial, accesses an overdrafted underground aquifer that has dropped the water table and caused subsidence. While the city touts that it is conserving water, its efforts are not visible.[11]

In late 2007, a presidential candidate opined that a Great Lake state was "awash in water," making Great Lakes states ever more protective about their greatest resource, the resource sorely lacking in the dry Intermontane.[12] This kind of thinking is an example of the fragmented thinking pattern that has created the American short-term mind-set and ignores the interrelated geographic processes of a place. Bringing water to a desert does not re-create ecology; it disturbs the existing balance. Nature seeks a balance in all places, regardless of human wants.

Climate

The lack of precipitation is the defining attribute of the Intermontane. The rain shadow of the Cascade Mountains and the Sierra Nevada halts most coastal moisture from the west, and the Rocky Mountains block any connection to eastern humidity. The result is a dry region, from the barren Anza Borrego Desert, receiving less than two inches of precipitation annually, to the loess-covered Palouse, with its beneficent six to sixteen inches annually. Even that scant precipitation often evaporates, leaving the region even drier.

Cloudbursts rain on the thinly vegetated land and then run off, eroding and transporting soil. The continental climate oscillates between hot summers and cold winters, although diurnal summer patterns result in hot days and cold nights.

The Colorado Plateau averages fifteen inches of precipitation annually, mostly through summer thunderstorms that produce runoff and a little groundwater recharge. During the winter, the high plateau receives some snow, which nourishes the plant life.

The Sonoran Desert temperatures, winds, and moisture govern a sporadic summer monsoon season of higher humidity. Large and sometimes dangerous dust storms called **haboobs** may precede short, intense monsoon rains. In July 2011, the largest dust storm in memory razed the Phoenix landscape as it awaited an end to an extreme drought.

Historical Geography and Settlement

The first inhabitants of this rugged region lived in relation to the land, but they still struggled and sometimes lost the battle to survive on this harsh land. European occupation battled against the natural landscape and destroyed the adaptive cultures, while razing the land to provide beyond its ability to sustain.

Native Americans

In the Intermontane, the major indigenous tribes were the Nez Perce in the Columbia Basin; the Paiute in California, Nevada, and Arizona; and the Navajo and Hopi and the historic Anasazi, Hohokam, and Mogollon across Arizona and New Mexico. Each had a distinct culture that adapted to their natural habitat.

The Nez Perce arrived in the northern Intermontane around twelve thousand years ago. They lived in scattered villages and developed a salmon-harvesting culture along the rivers. They hunted wildlife, harvested the local camas bulbs to make bread, and traded goods with Natives from both the coastal and interior areas. After contact with Europeans in the late eighteenth century, smallpox and other deadly epidemics decimated the Nez Perce.

The Northern and Southern Paiute were only related linguistically. The Northern Paiute lived in the Great Basin, where they fished and gathered roots and seeds. The Southern Paiute lived

BOX 16.3 ANCESTRAL PUEBLOANS (ANASAZI)

For more than a thousand years, the Ancestral Puebloans lived in permanent abodes set into the Colorado Plateau cliffs. They were mainly hunters and gatherers but also practiced agriculture and crafts. Their artistry weaving intricate baskets earned them the name "basketmakers." Around 1300, they abandoned their settlements.

Many scholars have theorized about the disappearance of this advanced civilization. One popular theory established by studying tree-rings is that a prolonged drought in the late 1200s caused the group to move elsewhere on the Colorado Plateau. Other theories include a religious upheaval, unsustainable land-use in an arid landscape, or more likely a combination of these factors.*

* Margaret C. Nelson and Michelle Hegmon, "Abandonment Is Not as It Seems: An Approach to the Relationship between Site and Regional Abandonment," *American Antiquity* (2001): 213–35.

along the Colorado River and Mojave Desert. Wars, slavery, and smallpox eventually devastated both Paiute groups.

In the Basin and Range, ancestral Native groups had attained a high stage of civilization, but these tribes had disappeared prior to European contact. When the first Europeans arrived, the Navajo, Hopi, Pueblo, Apache, and Utes were living on the landscape, growing maize and creating pottery and weavings.

European Incursion

The Spanish arrived in New Mexico in 1598 and quickly forced rule over the local tribes. During the seventeenth century, Pueblo revolts about religion, the destruction of their culture, and abusive labor practices disrupted Spanish occupancy, but ultimately the Spanish prevailed. American dominance began in the mid-nineteenth century.

Initial geographic information about the Basin and Range came from Spanish exploration, followed years later by information from American fur trappers. In the northern Intermontane, the British Hudson's Bay trappers dominated the regional

landscape. However, despite these nineteenth-century incursions, the Intermontane was settled slowly; it was bypassed during the mania for continent-wide **Manifest Destiny** (divinely ordained expansion) and later infilled (Map 16.2).

The Intermontane region entered the Union as territories in the 1840s. In 1846, the Oregon Country was defined along the 49th parallel. The Treaty of Guadalupe-Hidalgo ended the Mexican American War, and the **Mexican Cession of 1848** ceded 525,000 square miles of New Mexico, Arizona, California, Colorado, Utah, and Nevada to the United States for the bargain price of $15 million. Following annexation, the California Gold Rush and the Silver Lode in Nevada drew settlers into these areas and speeded their statehood. Despite the gold and silver rushes, most of the Intermontane remained a sometimes traversed but sparsely settled area into the mid-twentieth century.

Opening Up the Intermontane

Trails marked the dry and difficult passages through the Intermontane (Map 16.3). The Oregon Trail crossed the Wyoming

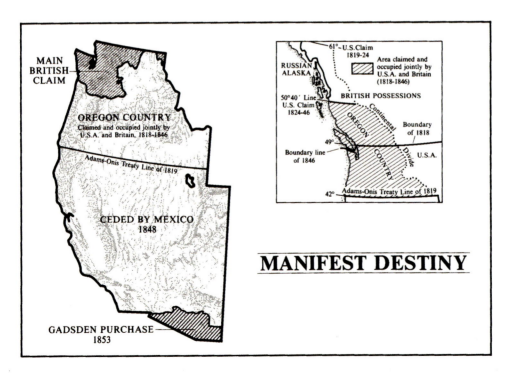

MAP 16.2. Manifest Destiny Territorial Acquisitions in the Far West.

Source: Thomas F. McIlwraith and Edward K. Muller, eds., *North America: The Historical Geography of a Changing Continent*, 2nd ed. (Lanham, Md.: Rowman & Littlefield, 2001).

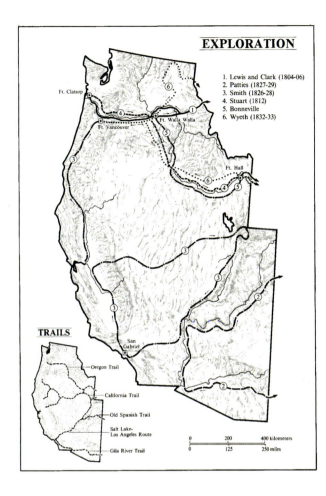

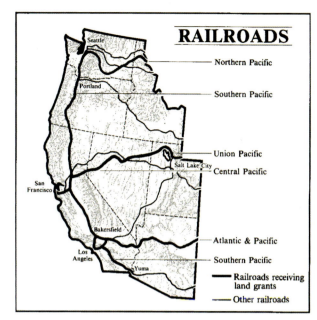

MAP 16.3. Intermontane Exploration. The Intermontane was explored by Lewis and Clark and several others before settlers began to arrive via the various wagon train trails. Many settlers traveled beyond the Intermontane on trails that led to the far West. As transportation for crops and livestock via the railroad became available in the 1870s, farmers and ranchers began to settle the dry area.

Source: Thomas F. McIlwraith and Edward K. Muller, eds., *North America: The Historical Geography of a Changing Continent*, 2nd ed. (Lanham, Md.: Rowman & Littlefield, 2001).

Basin and Utah, and then followed the trickling Humboldt River to the Sierra Nevada. The Santa Fe Trail traversed desert terrain south of the Rocky Mountains. On the Columbia Plateau, traveling down the Columbia Gorge to the Willamette Valley was treacherous.

When a transcontinental railroad was first contemplated, the most feasible Pacific-bound route was not through the higher elevations of the Wyoming Basin but through the more easily traversed Southwest. With this in mind, Secretary of War Jefferson Davis pursued a route along the 32nd parallel, a route that, coincidentally (he would later be the president of the Confederacy), favored the southern rather than the northern economy.

The most obvious southern route followed the tributaries of the Gila River—an area south of the Mexican Cession. In 1853, Davis sent James Gadsden—who championed a southern railroad system—to negotiate the purchase from Mexico of this barren thirty thousand square miles, which he accomplished for $10 million. The **Gadsden Purchase** was a strategic political move viewed in one of three ways: a coup for the southern railroad route, a waste of money on nonagricultural desert land, or conscience money for those who felt that Mexico had not been properly reimbursed for the Treaty of Guadalupe-Hidalgo land.

As Americans considered building a transcontinental railroad, a congressional battle ensued between the northern and southern

route, which remained unresolved until the secession of the southern states. The first transcontinental railroad line was completed in 1869, across the more northerly Wyoming Basin route. The route reflected the bias against the South after the Civil War. The Southern Pacific line, through the Gadsden Purchase land, was completed in 1881, long after the end of the war.

The progression of transportation and technology transformed Native American trails into rail lines and later highways. The Industrial Revolution and reliance on fossil fuels transformed the Intermontane from supporting marginal populations in the nineteenth century, to a lifestyle region for millions in the twentieth century. The region that had blossomed and then disappeared hundreds of years ago with the Anasazi and Hohokam may be repeating the pattern.

Cultural Perspectives

Over time, five distinctive cultures have populated the region: Native Americans, Hispanics, Mormons, Basques, and retirees. Native Americans settled first, and for the most part remained after European settlement. The Hispanic culture arrived in the seventeenth century and strongly influenced the southern Intermontane. The Mormons escaped persecution by relocating to culturally disparate Utah, whereas the Basques were culturally preadapted to their new mountainous homeland. Retirees comprise a cultural phenomenon of pensioned seniors who relocate for climate, lifestyle, and amenities.

Native American Culture

About 23 percent of the three million Native Americans living in the United States continue to live on reservations. Although scattered throughout the region, the largest concentration is in the Four Corners region of the southwest Basin and Range.

Thirteen percent of the national Native American population, Ute, Hopi, Jicarilla Apache, and Navajo, occupy reservations in the Four Corner states. The Navajo Nation occupies the largest reservation, consisting of sixteen million acres of land spread throughout Arizona, New Mexico, and Utah. The Navajo (*Diné Bikeyah*, meaning "Land of the People") are also the largest recognized Native American tribe, with more than 270,000 people claiming ethnicity (2010); two-thirds of them live on the reservation.[13]

The Apache and Navajo are related to the Athabascan family of Native Americans. They migrated to the Southwest from the Athabascan territories in Canada about a thousand years ago. The Navajo have maintained their more sedentary lifestyle living in their homeland after European settlement, although they were relocated for a short time in the mid-nineteenth century because of mining interests on their land. The Jicarilla Apache were seminomadic, living in southern Colorado and into New Mexico. Their reservation land is rich with oil and gas, which along with casinos and ranching supports the people—although they continue to be known for their intricate basketry.

At present, over half of the Navajo live below the poverty level, with a per capita income of $6,217 and an unemployment rate of 43.65 percent. Living facilities often lack kitchens, plumbing, and telephone service.[14] Navajo income sources include pastoral herding, Black Mesa mineral rights, and tourism.

The agricultural Hopi reservation is surrounded by the Navajo reservation (Map 16.4). Hopi and Navajo lands have been adjacent, but contentious land disputes between the tribes predate European contact. Since the 1950s, differences in traditional land use systems and the Black Mesa coal deposit within the reservation area exacerbated the disputes, until an agreement was reached in 1996.

The Mountain Utes occupy southwestern Colorado and have progressed from hunters and gatherers to livestock raiders. Currently, the Utes are known for their beading work and have entered the casino industry.

Hispanic Culture

For four hundred years, Spanish culture has influenced the southwestern landscape, creating the following cultural artifacts:

- The Law of the Indies plaza-style city pattern, built to work in harmony with the sun's rays.
- Hispanic livestock-raising methods that set the standard for cowboy culture.
- The southwestern architectural style, using adobe and tiles made from local sources, which is ubiquitous in Arizona and New Mexico
- The Western water policy of "first in time, first in right," based on Spanish law

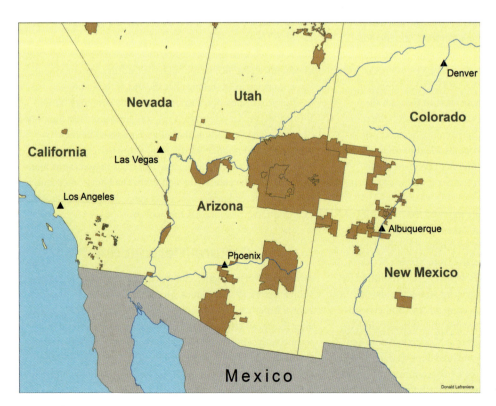

MAP 16.4. Four Corners Reservations. Native American reservations in the Four Corners region of the United States. The Navajo have the largest reservation in the states, 27,635 square miles. The Hopi reservation is completely surrounded by the Navajo reservation, which is the largest brown area near Four Corners.

BOX 16.4 BLACK MESA

Somewhere far away from us, people have no understanding that their demand for cheap electricity, air conditioning and lights 24 hours a day have contributed to the imbalance of this very delicate place.

—Nicole Horseherder, Navajo, Black Mesa*

Black Mesa has been a traditional grazing area for Navajo livestock and a cultivation area for Hopi corn, but since the 1970s Black Mesa coal mining has been an important source of income for the poverty-stricken Navajo and Hopi. Coal production has also scarred the earth and made water a scarce commodity for the residents.

The remote coal mines required using clean aquifer water to transport slurried coal 273 miles to a power plant in Mojave, California. The power plant furnished about 3 percent of California's electricity, or enough for 1.5 million homes. The aquifer is the sole source of water for the Navajo nation. Navajo elders made the initial deal in the 1960s but were unaware of the environmental impact on reservation water and how absurdly low the price paid to the tribes, $1.67 per acre-foot (an acre-foot equals 325,851 gallons). It was only in 2002 that younger, more educated Navajo and Hopi pointed out the unfair and unsustainable nature of the coal deal.

The Navajo claimed that using aquifer water for coal transport has decreased the availability of agricultural water. For many tribal ranchers, the only access to water was to drive to water stations to fill up fifty-five-gallon tanks. The Peabody Company claimed their mining did not interfere with tribal water. They claimed the Natives have no idea what they are talking about, that science tells the truth and their science shows no relation. The Navajo and Hopi, though, are approaching the subject from more than one cosmology. Unlike western science, their cultural

heritage and beliefs interrelate life and Earth. Nicole Horseherder stated this view:

We had an opportunity to go to school, and now I have a master's degree. . . . I am able to research and draft technical documents, but at the same time I am from this area. So we carried the wisdom of both worlds with us in this effort. We did the kind of work that a lawyer could do for us, and at the same time we sought the knowledge, the teaching and the prayers our elders told us we needed in order to tackle this.†

In 2004, the Navajo and Hopi accepted a December 2005 deadline to correct environmental problems or to shut down the plant. The Mojave plant, a serious environmental polluter producing more than a million tons of carbon dioxide annually, chose to shut down rather than retrofit its pollution-control devices. Meanwhile, the Navajo and Hopi have their water, but they have lost more than $7 million annually in tribal income, and Native employees have lost mining and power plant jobs. The power plant owners have since sold sulfur-dioxide-emission credits making $9 million annually, which was not shared with the Native Americans.

Although the tribes lost a polluted source of income, they were not undone. A trust was established in Black Mesa that is investing in renewable energy, both wind farms and solar-powered generating stations. It will bring thousands of needed jobs to the communities and provide a clean source of energy, and the tribes will have their water once again.

There are lessons to be learned that I would like to share with the outside world. Never doubt the power and wisdom of our ancestors. That is how we made the difference with Peabody.

—Vernon Masayesva, fighter for Hopi Water and founder of the Black Mesa Trust‡

* Quoted in Sean Patrick Reily, "Gathering Clouds," *Los Angeles Times Magazine*, June 6, 2004.
† Reily, "Gathering Clouds."
‡ John Dougherty, "Wisdom of the Ancestors," *Phoenix New Times*, December 1, 2005, at http://www.phoenixnewtimes.com/2005-12-01/news/wisdom-of-the-ancestors/1.

- The introduction of horses to the Native Americans, which changed their cultures permanently
- The influence of the Spanish language in speech and toponyms
- The world-famous Mexican cuisine, which is based on local ingredients and emphasizes the importance of community through the enjoyment of food

The National Council of La Raza (from the Spanish *la raza*, "the race") is a Hispanic American ethnocentrist organization. La Raza, often criticized for its exclusive use of Spanish, has symbolically been used as both a separatist movement and as a means to reduce poverty, discrimination, and to improve the Hispanic American quality of life. The La Raza philosophy emphasizes family unity over education. This cultural difference

slows acculturation between the Anglo and Hispanic cultures, while calling attention to the successes and failures of both cultures and what can be learned from each.

Mormon Culture

In the mid-nineteenth century, Mormon settlers fled religious persecution and migrated from New York sequentially to Ohio, Illinois, and Missouri, searching for their promised land. John C. Fremont's Great Salt Basin reports influenced their leader, Brigham Young, to settle in Deseret (the state of Utah) in 1847, and establish Mormon outposts throughout the Intermontane. Their towns are modeled upon their primary city, Salt Lake City, which was planned as the biblical Zion, with a rigid settlement pattern that enforced social interaction among the settlers.

Utah was settled as a religious theocracy, the New Zion. Under the leadership of Brigham Young, the Mormons systematically colonized Utah and a constellation of regional oases by establishing community-based but hierarchically formalized irrigated farms. The desert bloomed for the industrious Mormons. Utah remains a Mormon stronghold. Utah statehood was delayed until 1896, when the Mormon practice of polygamy was banned. Despite the ban, some fundamentalists in Utah's hinterland areas still practice polygamy today, although officially the Mormon Church disowns them for continuing this practice.

The Basques

The **Basque** homeland in the Pyrenees of Northern Spain was near both the mountains and the ocean. They worked with the physical landscape in a fishing and sheep-raising economy. Basques migrated to California's Gold Rush originally, but after their mining foray many Basques settled in the Intermontane, which physically resembled their mountain homeland and allowed them to continue their sheep-based livelihood. They settled in northern California, Nevada, eastern Oregon, and southwestern Idaho.

As latecomers to these areas, the Basques contributed few visible cultural landmarks in the Intermontane. However, a Basque influence can be found in regional restaurants that feature communal-style meals that specialize in cuisine featuring lamb and seafood.

Retirement Culture

Americans have gravitated toward more nuclear rather than multigenerational homes and families. Even traditional multigenerational families have become more nuclear because of escalating costs.

The breakup of multigenerational families has been accompanied by the rise in financially and physically able retirees moving to amenity-rich areas. Since 1960, the preferred destination for retirees has been the Sun Belt. Arizona is second to Florida in having the largest percentage of those over the age of sixty, a number which is expected to double in size to 26 percent of the state's population by 2050.

Retirees move either to planned retirement communities, where entry is limited to those over age fifty-five, or to Sun Belt cities that have become retirement meccas with a larger senior population—Lake Havasu (25.5 percent), Oro Valley, Arizona (22.7 percent), and St. George, Utah (19.3 percent) (the U.S. average is 12.9 percent [2009]). The fifty-five-to-sixty-four-year-old baby boomer demographic is expected to add to Sun Belt retirement suburban areas, such as Phoenix and Las Vegas. Retirees affect the cultural landscape because their social requirements and decisions are based on different criteria than that of the younger population. For example, their needs tend to include more health care facilities, specialized housing, transportation, and social services.

Regional Life

Population

The Intermontane rate of growth since the 1990s has been much higher than in the United States as a whole (Table 16.1). In 1950, five states within the region (Arizona, Idaho, Nevada, New Mexico, and Utah) contained 1.9 percent of America's population. In 2010, those same states held 5.1 percent of the total population. Three Sun Belt states—Arizona, Nevada, and Utah—have the nation's highest rate of growth (percentage increase over last census), although all the states in the Intermontane were above the average. Growth occurs as a result of

TABLE 16.1. Intermontane Rate of Growth

Area/state	Percent population growth, 2000–2010
United States	9.7
Arizona	24.6
New Mexico	13.2
Utah	23.8
Nevada	35.1
Idaho[a]	21.1
Washington[a]	14.1
Oregon[a]	12.0

Source: U.S. Census
[a] Entire state included.

internal migration to warmer climes by retirees, and by young midwestern Americans seeking more job opportunities, better weather, and more active cities.

Reasons for internal migration vary. For example, racial issues and increased housing costs fueled emigration from California after the 1970s. At present, more than a third of Nevada's population growth is the result of Californian emigration. In fact, Nevada, Arizona, and Oregon can all claim domestic migration as their main source of growth, while other states, such as Idaho, New Mexico, Washington, and Utah (with the highest birthrate in the nation), owe much of their population rise to natural increase.

Population statistics indicate that white non-Hispanics have been the largest contingent of recent legal migrants, although ethnic group representations are growing disproportionately. For example, the black population remained at 3 percent in Arizona's 1990 and 2000 census, and rose to 3.7 in 2010, whereas the Hispanic population grew from 18.7 percent to 25.3 percent from 1990 to 2000 and increased to 29.6 in 2010. In the Columbia Plateau, population is mostly white, but 10 percent are diverse population groups, mostly residing within the cities. For example, the population of Spokane, Washington, the largest city in the Columbia Plateau, is 87 percent white (2010), and the remainder of the populace is a mix of other ethnic groups.

Forty-two percent of the Basin and Range population are of Hispanic descent, with the highest percentage living in the Albuquerque–Santa Fe region, which historically was 90 percent Hispanic—but after 1900 the percentage declined as Anglos migrated to the region. Other states in the Southwest (including southwestern Texas and Southern California) also have both a large legal and undocumented Hispanic population. The Hispanic population increased in all of the Intermontane states, with the largest number settling along the border states and counties (Table 16.2).

Across the Intermontane are population "islands"—isolated cities that have access to water and amenities such as jobs, recreation, and retirement housing. Sparsely populated areas surround these islands, and groundwater irrigation supplies most of the water. The number of irrigation wells has grown substantially since the 1960s when technology allowed deepwater access, but in recent years, continued growth and the lack of water conservation have stressed wells.

Beyond the growth rates and the population islands, most land in the Intermontane is still the "empty quarter," as it was dubbed by Joel Garreau.[15] Much of the land is still "frontier" with a population below two people per square mile, including 80 percent of Nevada, 44 percent of Idaho, 41 percent of Utah, 27 percent of New Mexico, and 27 percent of Oregon.[16] This is the land of the rancher and the cowboy, where concerns center on whether cattle are grazing on public or private land, although concerns are changing as cities seek water rights from rural areas.

Traditional and Sustainable Cities

City development patterns have varied within the Intermontane. Although the Southwest expanded, federally owned land has hampered Great Basin growth. The Columbia Plateau remains a farming region, although the Spokane metropolitan area has grown faster than national averages.

Despite mandates for LEED-certified state buildings in several of the states, Intermontane cities are not leaders in sustainability. In a ranking of sustainable cities, no Intermontane city earned a place in the top fifteen, which is surprising for a region awash in the sunlight needed for solar power.[17] The highest sustainable ranking for an Intermontane city in 2008 was Albuquerque (number 18), where 20 percent of the city government electricity is wind powered.

TABLE 16.2. Hispanic and White Population

State	Percent white non-Hispanic (2010)	Percent Hispanic (2010)	Percent white non-Hispanic (1990)	Percent Hispanic (1990)
Arizona	57.8	29.6	71.6	18.7
New Mexico	54.1	26.5	50.4	37.6
Utah	80.4	13.0	91.1	4.9
Nevada	55.1	26.5	78.7	10.3
Idaho	84.0	11.2	92.0	5.2
Washington	72.5	11.2	86.7	4.4
Oregon	78.5	11.7	90.8	3.9

Source: U.S. Census

Southwest

The Sonoran Desert is a seldom-heard name within its own region; instead, the Sonoran is known as the Southwest, as if changing the name of the place would change its climate. The Southwest grew slowly until the 1960s advent of air-conditioning.

Southwestern growth from 2000 to 2010 was in double digits. In contrast, many Rust Belt and midwestern cities lost population: Phoenix gained 35.2 percent, while Cleveland lost 2.65 percent, and Pittsburgh lost 3.13 percent (Table 16.3).

Southwest settlement patterns feature sprawl and lower population densities than east of the Mississippi River. Las Vegas, hemmed in by public lands, has expanded faster than available land and has adopted a high-rise profile. Phoenix's uncontrolled sprawl has resulted in air pollution and gridlocked streets, and it has become one of the five worst traffic knots in the nation.[18]

Las Vegas, Nevada

(2010 pop. 583,756; CSA 1,995,215)

No American city has ever ceased to grow because of a lack of water, and it's unlikely that Las Vegas will be the first.

—Hal Rothman, *Neon Metropolis*[19]

Las Vegas (in Spanish, "the meadows") began as a desert oasis watered by springs that seeped from a groundwater aquifer. The city has grown from five thousand people in 1930, to almost two million in the metro area in 2010, an increase of 38 percent since 2000.

The first settlers in 1855 were Mormons, but they were recalled to Salt Lake City and the official city began in 1911 as a desert railroad stop. When the railroad pulled out of Las Vegas in 1925, the town seemed doomed, but in 1931, the city's location near the Hoover Dam construction site and the legalization of gambling caused significant expansion. In the late twentieth century, Las Vegas grew quickly (83 percent from 1990 to 2000), and by 2003, seven thousand to eight thousand new households were being added each month, in a city which lacks both land and water (Photo 16.7). City growth has slowed considerably since the 2008 recession.

The city of Las Vegas has reached the limits of its available land. The federal government controls 80 percent of Nevada land—more than in any other state. On occasion, the government sells land to developers, but the cost is extreme because so little land is privately held in Nevada (in June 2004 the BLM sold 2,532 acres at $280,000 per acre).[20] The result has been a high-rise "Manhattanization" of Las Vegas hotels and condominiums. The cost of housing also increased from $150,000 in 2000 to $315,000 in mid-2006, before the subprime housing debacle beginning in 2008. As of early 2011, more than thirty thousand homes remain vacant and on the market. Home prices dropped 21 percent in the first half of 2008 to a median price of less than $250,000 and continued their downward trend to $112,000 average in July 2011.

Water shortages have become a part of everyday Las Vegas life. By 2010, the West was in its thirteenth year of drought, and Las Vegas residents faced cuts in water usage and demanded more water from the Colorado River, which already provides 90 percent of its water. A progressive conservation program instituted by the Las Vegas water manager has forced the city to face its water denial and enforce conservation measures. Cutbacks on the water allotted for personal domestic use have been augmented with a moratorium on green lawn plantings. Lawn watering is illegal between 11 a.m. and 7 p.m., and water recycling and conservation measures have been instituted for casinos. Xeriscaping (a way of landscaping that negates the need for extra irrigation) has become de rigueur. The inability of some people to accept the "monotonous" desert landscape has resulted in a blossoming of artificial turf cropping up on former lawns, but in general, Las Vegas is accepting some of its prior desert denial.

TABLE 16.3. U.S. Metropolitan Statistical Area (MSA) Population, 2000–2010

Rank	Metro area	2010	2000	Percent growth
14	Phoenix-Mesa, Arizona	4,192,887	3,251,876	28.94
30	Las Vegas, Nevada	1,995,215	1,375,765	41.83
50	Salt Lake City–Ogden, Utah	1,124,197	968,858	16.03
52	Tucson, Arizona	980,263	843,746	16.18
86	Boise, Idaho	616,561	464,840	32.64
91	Provo-Orem, Utah	526,810	376,774	39.82
107	Spokane, Washington	471,221	417,939	12.75

Source: U.S. Census

PHOTO 16.7. Aerial View of Las Vegas, Nevada. One of the fastest-growing cities in America, Las Vegas has sprawled despite a severe lack of water, high summer temperatures, and its desert location. The line where water is available and where it ends is obvious on this aerial view.

Phoenix, Arizona

(2010 pop. 1,445,632; MSA 4,192,887)

Phoenix's growth is recent and fast. Arizona's capital city entered the ranks of the top one hundred cities in population in 1950 (as number 99, pop. 106,818) (Table 16.4). More than 90 percent of the city's population has moved to the city since 1950. In 2006, Phoenix surpassed Philadelphia as the fifth-largest metropolitan area in the United States.

Prior to the invention of air-conditioning, Phoenix was just a small desert town based on Salt River Valley–irrigated agriculture. Since the 1960s, the city has been one of the fastest growing in the nation, increasing 35 percent in each of the past two decades. Three of the major migration groups to the Phoenix area are Hispanics (many of whom are undocumented), retirees, and blue-collar midwesterners, all searching for better climate, job, and lifestyle.

Since 1990, Phoenix has been ranked among the top ten cities in the nation in employment growth, and it has received more than three-quarters of Arizona's population and job growth between 1996 and 2006. The capital city and its surrounding area are home to government, education, and high-tech jobs that have relocated to Arizona because of its highly educated workforce and desirable quality of life, despite a lack of a workable public transit system. Only 5 percent of city workers use public transport or bicycles. The city residents are not interested in providing more; legislation to fund more was not passed in 2006.

The economy also depends on a strong tourist and retirement population. More than ten million people visit the region annually, including snowbirds—northerners escaping winter. Arizona had more than three hundred thousand snowbird visitors in 2008.

Phoenix has made some movement in sustainable issues, but it lacks a strong commitment despite the fact that the city is located in a desert. Energy consumption has been emphasized, and city buildings have been mandated to use 15 percent renewable energy by 2025. Water consumption, as noted, is above U.S. averages, although treated wastewater is 90 percent recycled as drinking water or used in agriculture.

Great Basin, Utah

Utah's population has grown, but it is no longer only Mormon. In 2004, 62.4 percent of the population in Utah was Mormon; this percentage continues to decline. By 2030, Mormons may no longer be a majority of the state population.[21] The Mormon majority in Utah declined for two reasons: the non-Mormon birthrate (Utah still has the highest birthrate,

TABLE 16.4. Population Growth of Phoenix, Arizona

Year	1890	1920	1950	1960	1980	2000	2010
Population	3,152	29,053	106,818	439,170	789,704	1,321,045	1,445,632

Source: U.S. Census

though, because of a high birthrate among Mormons) and the influx of non-Mormon aerospace and defense workers who come to the region for such amenities as ski resorts and mountain recreation. St. George was the second-fastest-growing metro area (52.9 percent) in the nation from 2000 to 2010 (Palm Coast, Florida, was first at 92 percent). The growth was fueled by nearby booming Las Vegas, which in turn is fueled by those leaving Los Angeles (Table 16.5).

Salt Lake City, Utah

(2010 pop. 186,440; CSA 1,744,886)

Certainly Salt Lake City itself has no lack of intriguing social problems, air pollution, traffic jams, or angry adolescents, and very soon the Latter Day Saints will be forced to directly confront the symptoms of discontent and desperation with which most Americans are now familiar: from LDS to LSD, even unto the Land of Moab.

—Edward Abbey, 1968[22]

Salt Lake City (SLC) is the capital of Utah and the Latter Day Saints (Mormons) core city. The city is just east of the Great Salt Lake, which is located on the lakebed of Pleistocene Lake Bonneville. Prior to Mormon settlement, local Shoshone, Paiute, and Ute tribes used the area for temporary gatherings.

The city population is only 10 percent of the 1.7 million combined statistical area (CSA), which is more than 80 percent of the total state population. SLC lost population to the suburban front from 1980 to 2000, but it has since begun to grow again. The population is about 75 percent white, 22 percent Hispanic, 4 percent Asian, and 3 percent black (2010).

The broad-based economy's strong service sector contains high-tech jobs. Also important is mining in the nearby mountains, an example of which is the Kennecott Copper Mine, one of the largest open pit mines in the world. Other employment markets include government, church, and tourism. Many move to Utah for amenities such as the mountains, which provide world-class skiing, summertime hiking, and camping opportunities. Pollution is a big concern, as some of the worst smog in the nation is trapped in atmospheric inversions, especially in the winter.

Salt Lake City is dependent on the Rocky Mountain snowpack for its water, and the unevenness of the snowpack each year (Table 16.6), a result of climate change, has made the city adopt some sustainable goals, such as the 2005 vow to cut greenhouse gases by 21 percent, as well as to conserve electricity and transportation costs, and to build green. The city now uses compact fluorescent light bulbs and LED lights at traffic signals; has purchased smaller, more fuel-efficient cars for the city's fleet; and converted commercial vehicles to run on natural gas. All future state buildings will be energy-efficient designs incorporating recycled materials. The savings from these initiatives have been invested in wind power.

TABLE 16.5. Population Increase, Washington County, Utah (St. George Metro)

	Population	Percent increase
1970	13,669	33
1980	26,065	90
1990	48,560	86
2000	90,354	86
2010	138,115	53

Source: U.S. Census, at http://www.media.utah.edu/UHE/w/WASHINGTONCT.html

TABLE 16.6. Rocky Mountain Snowpack

	2003	2004	2005	2006	2007	2008	2009	2010
Grizzly Ridge, Utah	N/A	N/A	N/A	N/A	91	99	91	91
Lake Fork, Utah	N/A	N/A	N/A	N/A	111	117	88	87
Ripple Creek, Colorado	208	220	145	167	85	160	199	136
Grand Mesa, Colorado	143	101	220	136	113	197	141	145

Source: U.S. Geological Survey, Colorado Water Science Center, "Rocky Mountain Snowpack Physical and Chemical Data for Selected Sites," 1993–2008; 2009; 2010
Note: Snow depth (cm), April

Economy

Since the 1990s, the Intermontane led the nation in both population growth and job creation. While the area generally was not as devastated as other areas during the economic downturn of 2008, some areas suffered both in housing value and unemployment rates (Table 16.7). The Columbia Plateau and Basin and Range continue to support primary industries; however, the more populated southwestern region has diversified and contains significant tertiary and quaternary economies.

Primary Industry and Natural Resources

The Columbia Plateau and portions of the Basin and Range are important agriculturally. The Basin and Range remains an important mining region. Early settlers mined gold and silver, but trends have changed, and at present, copper is the main ore mined in the Intermontane. The Colorado Plateau is rich with strip-mined coal deposits.

Agriculture

Historically, Intermontane agriculture has been devoted to ranching, with only a fraction of the land growing crops because of the rugged terrain, lack of water, and remoteness of the area from population centers. However, the Desert Land Act and Mormon immigration spurred irrigation projects and more farming. Ranching is still a major enterprise, but the region now boasts some of the nation's most productive farmland. Both ranching and irrigated farming are currently unsustainable, although efforts persist toward sustainable production methods. For example, exercising sustainable methods of crop rotation, such as planting no-till crops over conventional tillage areas, has prevented the eroding of topsoil.

The southeastern Californian Coachella and Imperial valleys enjoy a year-round growing season, while the higher-latitude or higher-elevation Columbia and Colorado plateaus are frost-free for less than 120 days per year. However, both of these fertile subregions depend on irrigation to produce profitable yields.

Irrigation and Water Rights   Without irrigation, the Intermontane would have remained the "empty quarter." Irrigated agriculture has been historically significant: Native Americans in the Southwest irrigated their fields hundreds of years ago; the Mormons became the first modern irrigators. Both groups practiced irrigation cooperatively, balancing environmental, social, and economic interests—a fusion considered essential for sustainable irrigation. That balance is precarious, however, and must be adjusted for variables such as climate change and population density.

As population has grown in the Intermontane, water rights laws have made equitable distribution of water to the area nearly impossible. Mormons abandoned English riparian rights and adopted the Spanish "first in time, first in right" water laws that became the standard for the West.

Currently, more than forty-three million acres of western cropland are irrigated, which accounts for 90 percent of regional freshwater consumption. Crops in the American West depend on irrigation (Table 16.8; Map 16.5.). Only grasses and wheat can be grown as dryland crops, and irrigation increases their yields.

Subregions and Crops   **Snake River Plain**. Southern Idaho's lava-covered Snake River Plain is dependent on irrigated agriculture for its survival. The plain's long summer days and cool nights are the perfect conditions for growing root crops, such as sugar beets, and the nation's largest potato crop, which includes the potatoes used for McDonald's french fries.

Columbia Plateau. Once dismissed as a wasteland, the Columbia Plateau, thanks to the Columbia Basin Project, is now a fertile agricultural area that grows wheat, hay, corn, potatoes, and wine grapes.

The physical geography of the land has created an ideal foundation for wine grapes. The Lake Missoula floods left behind loess-covered benches, which augment the good air circulation and warm days with natural drainage for the vineyards.

Palouse. The fertile Palouse receives the most rain in the region, but it is still dependent on irrigation to grow crops. The loess soils produce the highest-yielding winter wheat on the continent. Three-quarters of this wheat is exported to Japan and India, where it is made into noodles. Other crops cultivated in the Palouse include peas, lentils, barley, and clover alfalfa.

TABLE 16.7. Percentage of Intermontane Unemployment Rates

	Arizona	Idaho	New Mexico	Nevada	Utah	United States
December 2007	4.3	3.6	3.6	5.2	3.0	5.0
December 2008	6.6	6.1	4.7	8.4	4.1	7.4
December 2009	9.1	9.1	8.3	13.0	6.7	10.0
February 2011	9.6	9.7	8.7	13.6	7.7	8.9
August 2011	9.3	9.2	6.6	13.4	7.6	9.1

Source: U.S. Bureau of Labor Statistics, at http://www.bls.gov/web/laus/laumstrk.htm

TABLE 16.8. Intermontane Irrigated Areas and Their Crops

Area	Location	Specifics	Crops
Columbia Plateau	Rain shadow of Cascades, Yakima, Washington	Columbia Basin irrigation Project Water diverted from Columbia River	Apples, hay, field corn, hops, potatoes, vineyards, cherries, onions
Snake River Plain	Southern Idaho above Snake River	Irrigation projects and well irrigation Large farms, corporate, capital intensive	Hay, potatoes, sugar beets
Palouse (subunit of Columbia Plateau)	Southeastern Washington, southwestern Idaho	More rain than rest of Columbia Basin, thick layer of fertile loess	Cereal grain, field crops
Salt Lake Oasis	Great Salt Lake, Wasatch Mountain valley	Established by Mormons	Hay, grains, wheat, sugar beets, fruits, apples, peaches, cherries. Livestock, chickens
Salton Trough	Imperial and Coachella valleys	Depend on migratory labor Water from the Colorado River	Alfalfa, lettuce, carrots, vineyards, citrus, dates
Salt River Valley	Central Arizona	First major federal irrigation project Highest cost of irrigation	Cotton, hay, wheat, barley, citrus
Rio Grande	Near El Paso, Texas, southern New Mexico	Oldest irrigation on continent, pre-Columbian	Cotton, poultry, pecans, grapes Feed grains, dairy
Colorado Grand Valley	West central Colorado	Rocky Mountain water, Colorado and Gunnison rivers	Corn, small grains, alfalfa, fruit crops, peaches

Coachella and Imperial Valleys. The southern locale, sunny weather, and fertile soil of southeastern California's Imperial and Coachella valleys support year-round farming on over six hundred thousand irrigated acres. Although the region receives only three inches of precipitation annually, irrigation provides the commercial crops with up to thirty-six inches of water annually (Photo 16.8). The desert valleys (a region that would be barren without Colorado River irrigation water) produce the nation's specialty crops, including lemons, table grapes, nursery stock, and dates (Table 16.9).

Arizona. Cotton requires irrigation when grown in dry western regions like the Salt River Valley of Arizona, and yet cotton production in Arizona is the eleventh highest in the nation. The water was the result of pork barrel politics that secured the Central Arizona Project in 1968. Cheap water, subsidies, and cotton prices on the world market make cotton farming profitable. While cotton is still grown, urban development has taken over more than half the cotton acreage.

Rangelands

The Bureau of Land Management (BLM) administers the multiple uses of federal land and mineral rights for the public good. The Department of Interior's BLM has stewardship responsibility for this land belonging to all Americans, but it has been consistently underfunded and unable to raise revenues, resulting in unintended consequences from land use and management, to disposition of mineral rights and overgrazing.

Unintended Consequences **Human Influence on Vegetation.** The first nonnative settlers in the Intermontane found a rugged, dry land. What has evolved is an excellent example of unintentional alteration of the ecological balance.

Prior to nonnative settlement, the natural vegetation was perennial grasses in wetter areas and sagebrush in the drier areas. There were few hoofed animals. As settlers and their domesticated animals arrived, the grasses switched from perennial to annuals, which is a less sustainable grass sequence. Perennials are the plants of most natural ecosystems, and yet agriculture has become dependent on annuals, although they are less efficient at using water and maintaining soil fertility.[23]

Ranching techniques evolved when Spanish herdsman unfamiliar with the drier Intermontane climate increased the number of cattle and sheep and overgrazed the land. The loss of grasses encouraged invasive species such as cheatgrass and leafy spurge. Cheatgrass is slightly edible to cattle but has lower protein content, is a fire hazard, and affects biological diversity. Cheatgrass does best where cattle have disturbed ecological systems by overgrazing and may have been intentionally introduced to stabilize damaged grazing lands. Climate change may increase the spread of cheatgrass because it creates more favorable fire season conditions.

The noxious leafy spurge spreads by an extensive underground root system and left uncontrolled will outcompete the native grasses. Some ranchers have supported multiple grazing techniques (cattle and sheep), so if the cattle do not eat the

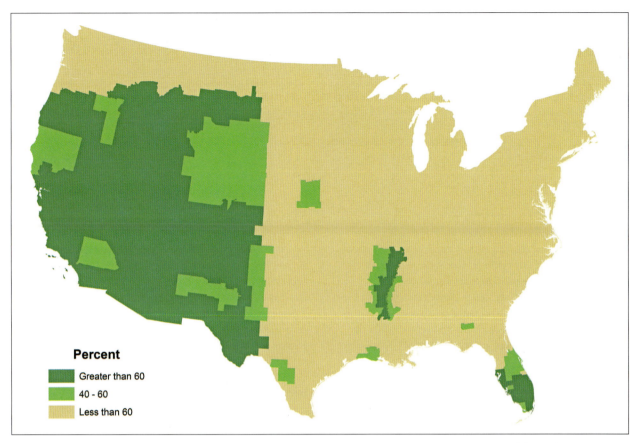

MAP 16.5. Acres of Irrigated Harvested Cropland as Percentage of All Harvested Cropland Acreage. Most cropland in the Intermontane is irrigated.

Percent
- Greater than 60
- 40 - 60
- Less than 60

PHOTO 16.8. Coachella Valley, Southeastern California. The desert valley receives about three inches of precipitation annually; crops and date palms require irrigation. Over six hundred thousand acres are irrigated in the Coachella and Imperial valleys. Eighty-five percent of water in California is used for agricultural irrigation. The irrigation method shown in the photo is inefficient, allowing much of the water to evaporate.

TABLE 16.9. Crops, Imperial Valley, California

January–March	April–June	July–September	October–December
Alfalfa, asparagus, broccoli, cabbage, carrots, citrus, lettuce, onions, romaine, summer squash	Alfalfa, artichokes, asparagus, cantaloupes, eggplant, flax, garlic, grapes, honeydew, okra, onions, peppers, Sudan grass, sugar beets, summer squash, sweet corn, tomatoes, watermelon, wheat	Alfalfa, banana squash, casaba, flax, okra, onions, sugar beets, sesbania, sorghums, tomatoes, watermelon, wheat	Broccoli, cabbage, cantaloupes, carrots, casaba, cucumbers, dates, honeydew, lettuce, okra, onions, rapine, romaine, summer squash, sorghums

plant, the sheep will. Since leafy spurge comes from Europe and has a host of natural predators there, many researchers have argued for biological controls in the United States. But failures in controls have had dire consequences in the past. Think kudzu, which was brought in to control erosion.

Both cheatgrass and leafy spurge can be controlled, but they require extensive and long-term range management, including fossil fuel–based pesticides. By far the best vegetation for the region is the native perennial grasses that existed prior to western ranching techniques.

Local and Bioregional Impacts. The Intermontane is generally an arid, sparsely settled region due to the limitations of water. Ranching and urbanization have negatively affected the availability of water.

Overgrazing and Range Management   The U.S. government controls about 70 percent of all western land (Map 16.6). For example, more than 80 percent of Nevada's land and 72 percent of Arizona's land is federally owned; other government agencies control additional land, which is usually hot, dry, rocky, or steep land that is undesirable for farming.

Unsettled land in the West reverted to the government. The land remains in the care of the BLM and other public agencies. The BLM leases land to mining and ranching enterprises, and it is responsible for more than 250 million acres, more land than any other agency in the United States.

Ranching has changed considerably over the years. The number of ranchers has declined precipitously, and most remaining ranchers are very large or corporate entities. About 5 percent of the ranchers control 58 percent of BLM grazing areas, and pricing and regulation of these grazing areas have been controversial. BLM land was already heavily overgrazed when the BLM assumed management, and the agency had little say in grazing fees.

Government grazing fees are charged per animal unit per month (AUM). The formulaic fees are less than private grazing fees and do not cover the costs for maintaining the land in a healthy condition.[24] The result has been overgrazed, eroded land depleted of the natural vegetation, beginning a domino effect of deterioration in the entire ecosystem. The complex system of ranching is often only addressed from a single variable—grazing fees for ranchers—rather than addressing the foundational problems with the systems. The unintended consequences can be seen throughout the ecosystem, throughout the bioregion.

External Costs. Grazing fees on BLM land have never aligned with actual costs. Ranchers effectively pay grazing fees equivalent to a tenth of private land costs. The BLM spends more money to protect against overgrazing than it receives in income, and the U.S. taxpayer supports the shortfall. In 2004, grazing fees, which had remained constant since 1978, accounted for only one-sixth the cost of federal land management.[25]

The BLM contends that raising grazing fees will allow better land management and protection from overgrazing. Cattle ranchers maintain that grazing fees cannot be raised because of low cattle prices and razor-slim profits. Environmental opponents believe that public land is unprotected, and that raising grazing fees to fair market value will end the subsidizing of the largest owners, who benefit from the current policy at taxpayer expense. Taxpayer subsidies of large ranching operations are a continued debate; however, debates about ranching and food are equally problematic.

Cattle ranching requires understanding the connections between land, habitats, soils, water, energy, and land management, because ranching is much more than putting cows on the range and then driving them to market for profit.

Some cattle ranchers practice a form of cooperative conservation called **grass banking**, in which ranchers pool their herds and move them from ranch to ranch. Grass banking allows land to rest for long periods, which provides relief from stresses on grazing land such as in times of drought. Large herds of cattle are grazed on grass-banked land but are moved often to allow the land to rest and recover.[26] Benefits include forming conservation easements to halt development and prevent land fragmentation, an increased awareness of perennial native grasses, and strength in numbers for the traditionally individualistic ranchers who now must market their cattle together in order to receive better prices. A unified ranching voice has been influential politically in conservation and ranching.

Grass banking has been successful from New Mexico to Oregon into the Great Plains of Montana. But it is not a panacea. Its use on public lands can still result in overgrazing; however, grass banking encourages ecological restoration and is a more sustainable use of private and public grazing lands.

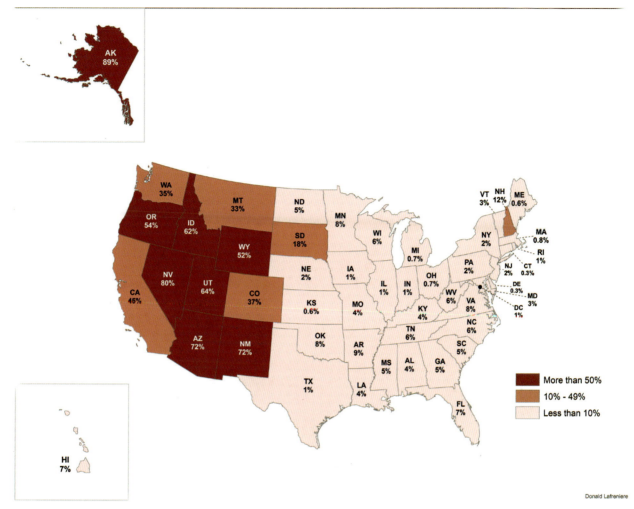

MAP 16.6. Federal Land as a Percentage of Total Land Area. Federal land ownership is overwhelmingly in the drier western region, with 55.5 percent of land federally owned, compared to, for example, 0.2 percent of the Northeast.

Source: Bureau of Land Management, Public Land Statistics, at http://www.blm.gov/public_land_statistics/pls10/pls10_combined.pdf

Mineral Resources

Boom and bust mining operations have been an important part of the Intermontane economy from the mid-nineteenth century to the present.

Copper   Copper is currently the most-mined resource in the Intermontane. The United States is the second-largest producer of copper in the world (Chile is the largest); however, it also consumes more copper than any other country. The major copper-producing states are located in the southern Basin and Range region. The largest single copper producer in the world, the **open pit mine** in Bingham, Utah (near Salt Lake City), produces about 25 percent of the nation's copper, while Arizona and New Mexico account for the remaining copper ore. Arizona had several copper districts, but only Morenci continues to mine copper. The few copper boomtowns that remain, such as Jerome, survive on tourism.

Copper mining requires enormous capital investments for machinery and the processing of low-grade ore. Most copper mines are open pit, some are underground, and a growing number leach under weak acid conditions to dissolve copper. Methods of removing metal from rock are environmentally dangerous, and they require rethinking in order to maintain environmental health. Costs for mined resources have escalated rapidly in the twenty-first century. Since 2000, copper prices have doubled and doubled again, and caused new forms of environmental destruction. Thieves now recycle copper to sell as scrap, but in the process of stripping the copper often ruin intact infrastructure.

The hard rock mining industry is America's largest source of toxic pollutants. More than 90 percent of open pit mining rock removed is broken and crushed to extract the copper, and then stored in a toxic-laden lake.

The extraction of copper from the Kennecott Copper Mine west of Salt Lake City (Bingham) produces toxic leachate solutions and tailings, which are disposed into streams and contaminate groundwater aquifers for many miles around. These actions, among many more, have created problems for local flora and fauna, and they have produced high rates of cancer in copper-mining communities. The Bingham mines have worked to minimize their waste, and they have met government standards for contaminated soils in most of their exposure sites. They have also remediated former mine sites by building sustainable development projects.

Over the years, Kennecott purchased surplus mining land, some of which was contaminated, and cleaned these areas up. Kennecott is developing its properties into large-scale master-planned communities (ultimately to house five hundred thousand people) that will generate less greenhouse gases and operate in an environmentally responsible and energy-efficient manner.

Coal   The southern Intermontane—Utah, the Colorado Plateau, and Arizona—is well endowed with coal. The world's largest open pit strip mine in Black Mesa, Arizona, contains high-grade, low-sulfur coal. Unregulated burning of coal pollutes the air and water, and as prices of electric generation rise, the use of plentiful and inexpensive coal also rises.

Uranium   Mining companies continue to seek sources of uranium, oil, oil shale, and natural gas on the Colorado Plateau. Uranium, used in nuclear reactors, generates electricity, but it fell out of favor in 1979 because of nuclear accidents and the perpetual danger of radioactivity.

The uranium mill waste equals six times the debris taken from the collapsed World Trade Center. Along with the mildly radioactive uranium, it contains ammonia and other pollutants—threats to several endangered species and the Colorado River water supply used by 25 million people downstream.[27]

Uranium was originally considered a nuisance mineral found with gold. Once Madame Curie discovered the uses of radiation—X-rays, and irradiation of foods—old gold mines were reworked to recover uranium. The need for nuclear reactor fuel and the U.S. government's purchase of all mined uranium sparked a 1952 uranium boom. Boomtowns like Moab, Utah, burst upon the Colorado Plateau and provided the labor force for the more than eight hundred mines.

The boom fizzled out in 1962 when accidents deflated interest, and the government had already acquired ample reserves of the mineral. Today, Moab depends on a tourism economy, although in 2006, another boom began when the nation's uranium source was depleted; prices escalated from $7 to $138 per pound in June 2007, following possible nuclear reactor construction in Russia, India, China, and possibly the United States. The price began to fall after the Fukushima nuclear plant disaster in Japan and continued to decline to $52 in December 2011. In 2012, President Obama banned uranium mining around the Grand Canyon for twenty years. The move enraged mining companies but was praised by environmental groups.

Toxic tailings from uranium mines are located throughout the area, and some exist on the Colorado River flood plain, which were being removed starting in 2009. People throughout the Moab area still suffer radiation poisoning from the mines, and lawsuits have been filed and await settlement. If nuclear reactors become a standard form of energy in the United States instead of fossil fuels, more uranium will be mined, and this will cause clashes with various environmental groups who lobby to close mills, stop tailing leakage, and clean up operations.

Renewable Energy

Perhaps the most ignored Intermontane resource, especially in the southern regions, is renewable energy. At present, the Intermontane relies on coal to produce 60 percent of its electric power; petroleum is not used in the region to produce electricity. Renewable resources (without hydro) produce just 1 percent of the region's energy (Chart 16.1; Table 16.10; Table 16.11).[28]

Although the region now depends heavily on nonrenewable sources of energy, the Intermontane is beginning to take notice of fossil fuel limitations. The Intermontane is geographically well situated to foster renewable energy sources

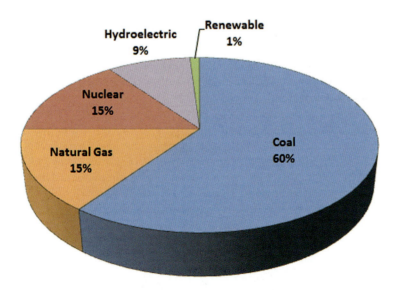

CHART 16.1. Energy Consumption in the Intermontane, 2005

TABLE 16.10. Electric Power Net Generation by Primary Energy Source, 2008, Intermontane Percentage Share

	Arizona	New Mexico	Utah	Nevada	Idaho
Coal	36.7	73.0	81.6	22.3	0.8
Natural gas	33.9	21.5	15.8	68.3	14.2
Petroleum		0.1	0.1		
Nuclear	24.5			15	
Hydroelectric	6.1	0.8	1.4	5.0	78.2
Renewables	0.1	4.5	0.6	4.4	6.3
Othera	0.1		0.1		0.6
Total	100	100	100	100	100

Source: U.S. Energy Information Administration (EIA), State Electricity Profiles 2007, Table 5, at ftp://tonto.eia.doe.gov/electricity/stateprofiles/07st_profiles/062907.pdf
a Includes municipal solid waste, batteries, chemicals, hydrogen, pitch, purchased steam, sulfur, tire-derived fuels, and miscellaneous technologies

TABLE 16.11. Renewable Electricity Generation, 2009

	Arizona	New Mexico	Utah	Nevada	Idaho
Total percent state renewable net generation	5.9	4.7	3.0	11.3	86.3
Breakdown of renewable					
Geothermal	—	—	0.6	4.3	0.6
Solar		—		0.5	—
Wind	—	3.9	0.4	—	2.4
Wood/wood waste	0.1	—		—	3.6
Landfill gas	—	—	0.1	—	—
Other biomass	—	0.1		—	—
Conventional hydro	5.7	0.7	1.9	6.5	79.6
Rank nationally	14	40	43	23	7

Source: U.S. Energy Information Administration (EIA), "Renewable and Alternative Fuels," at http://www.eia.gov/cneaf/solar.renewables/page/state_profiles/r_profiles_sum.html

such as geothermal, wind, and solar power; however, these lack government and popular support. For example, Arizona, a state awash in sunshine but also awash in a traditional conservative culture, receives less than 1 percent of its energy from solar power, although that began to change with the 2009 announcement of two solar plants in the state and an increase of support for renewable energy in 2011.

In June 2007, Arizona passed a law requiring its utilities to generate 15 percent of its energy from renewable sources by 2025. New Mexico requires at least 5 percent be renewable, and Nevada has the highest solar generation per capita in the nation. However, renewable energy operations, such as utilizing wind power with turbines, are still negligible in fast-growing Nevada and Arizona. However, in 2009 Arizona built its first wind farm near Holbrook, and many more, supported by federal energy incentives, are expected.

Industry and Postindustrial

Since the 1970s, Arizona and Utah have invested in and profited from the postindustrial economy, while manufacturing has continued to decline since the approval of NAFTA. Much of its business has gone to *maquiladora* assembly plants across the border.

Universities contribute both research expertise and graduates to build the postindustrial economy in information technology, optics/photonics, biotechnology, aerospace, environmental technologies, and advanced composite materials. Utah focuses on health services, as well as computer systems design, aerospace, and software publishing. Despite their investment and overall success, state economies have suffered declines in the new millennium, and job recovery has been slow, low-wage, and marred by outsourcing.[29]

Tourism

Tourism has been an important part of the Intermontane economy. The Colorado Plateau is a major American tourist destination, offering a colorful landscape that awes and inspires visitors. In the Basin and Range state of Nevada, the gambling meccas of Las Vegas and Reno form the major industry.

The Colorado Plateau has the nation's greatest concentration of national parks, which are mostly located along the Colorado River. The most popular parks are the Grand Canyon in Arizona, and Zion, Bryce, and Arches in Utah (Photo 16.9). These treasures are located in sparsely populated areas, with the exception of Moab, Utah, which has resurrected itself from a uranium mining town into a hiking, biking, sport enthusiast capital.

National park features are wonders, but they are also socially constructed landscapes—zoos of the land—"Look but don't touch." The parks are the simulacra idea of those who want to preserve something natural as constant and static, not allowing the land to change naturally. Public use of parks for example, is measured in relation to maintaining a habitat, yet just outside the park there will be no measurement at all. There are set standards to maintain vegetation, soil, and wildlife, which are measured in relation to recreational use. Increasingly, the number of people visiting many parks is limited due to their impact on the land. The dual objectives of maintaining the habitat and ecology and providing recreational experiences are often mutually exclusive.

Las Vegas attracts more than thirty million visitors annually. The original tiny desert town was financed by organized crime, until a 1969 law significantly altered the city's character by allowing major hotel chains and entertainment conglomerates to operate gambling casinos. "Sin City" evolved into a

PHOTO 16.9. Arches National Park, Moab, Utah. The park is one of eight national parks within the Colorado Plateau. Arches is famous for its more than one thousand red sandstone arches and natural bridges.

BOX 16.5 COSANTI AND ARCOSANTI, ARIZONA

In 1956, Paolo Soleri began a lifelong urban planning project, which he named Arcology (*architecture + ecology*). It highlights minimizing the use of energy, reducing waste, and preventing pollution. Soleri believes that the environment and habitat should interact. For example, his architectural style incorporates both concrete precast panels and solar greenhouses (Photo 16.10). The results are two projects: the original Cosanti, in Scottsdale; and Arcosanti, the prototype town for five thousand built an hour north of Phoenix. Few others in this region of great possibility have committed to or invested in long-term sustainability.

PHOTO 16.10. Arcosanti, Arizona. Arcosanti is an experimental "arcology" community north of Phoenix, which uses local building materials and the natural locale to create a livable space. This is the main community building.

family-oriented theme park. In the transition, Las Vegas evolved into the epitome of the postmodern simulacrum, a replica of the original. One can now visit New York, Egypt, Paris, and Venice, all in the air-conditioned comfort of the Las Vegas Strip. Laughlin, Nevada, along the Colorado River, is also casino laden, strategically located to take advantage of the river's recreational crowd.

A Sustainable Future

The Intermontane has undergone an extreme makeover since the mid-twentieth century when it was a hot, dry, and relatively empty section of the United States. Now hot, dry, air-conditioned, and populated, it needs to address the interrelationship of people, energy, and water. It remains a drought-prone region dependent on irrigation and dams. The reality is that the carefree lifestyle of swimming pools, green lawns, and golf courses that bring so many people to this area may also be its undoing.

The West has been in drought since the millennium, a fact that may reflect why Native American settlements were abandoned long ago. Today, water is more important than ever, and it is being closely measured and transported through canals and irrigation ditches. But wars over water have already begun.

Agriculture uses most of the region's water, but the population boom that has occurred since the 1960s has accelerated energy and water usage so that the current lifestyle in the Intermontane could be in serious jeopardy as a result of water shortages.

Livestock still graze on millions of acres of public land controlled by powerful ranching lobbies, who work to keep land lease prices low but increase public expense. Sustainability within the ranching world has a long road ahead, although some ranchers now see the worth of healthy ranching practices and have introduced grass banking and other conservation practices.

The Southwest has been an attractive area for winter residents for most of the twentieth century, bringing in such notables as Frank Lloyd Wright, who built his signature-style winter home, Taliesin West, in Scottsdale, Arizona, during the 1930s. The home respects nature, and it is built to withstand fire and use sunlight efficiently. A school of architecture continues at Taliesin West, spawning ideas among new generations of architects following in Wright's footsteps. Paolo Soleri was a Wright student who stayed in the area and made his lifework building a sustainable local landscape. As more people with the ecological mind-set settle in the Intermontane the landscape will evolve more sustainably.

Questions for Discussion

1. As this region continues to grow, it will require more water. Where should this water come from?

2. Will the region "do a California," as Las Vegas is now proposing, and divert water from other less populated areas? Should it?

3. Is a desert-like region sustainable when water is artificially introduced?

4. Is the current Intermontane population growth and water use rate sustainable? If yes, how? If no, what would make it sustainable?

5. Can the lopsided growth in the driest part of the United States continue and be sustainable within the nation?

6. A highly civilized grouping of peoples (Anasazi, Mogollon, and Hohokam) lived and farmed in the extended Four Corners region until 1300, at which time they dispersed, and possibly became the Pueblo tribe. However, the Pueblo way of life is radically changed from their historical antecedents. What are some of the reasons this dispersion happened? If the reasons are environmental, what can be learned today, if anything, from their travails?

7. What is the Great Basin, and what is significant about it?

8. Where did the Mormons settle, and how did they affect the region?

9. One of the largest questions on everyone's mind in the West and across the wetter regions of the United States is, How much energy and water will be needed, and should it be used to keep the West green?

10. What was the relationship to the land of each of the cultural groups that settled the region? What were sustainable elements of these cultures?

11. What are the site and situation of Reno and Las Vegas? Why are these factors not enough to explain the growth of these cities?

12. What historically has been the transportation problem on the Colorado Plateau?

13. What are the reasons for using Yucca Mountain for the storage of nuclear waste? What are the problems?

14. How has the region approached alternative energy sources?

15. Technological inventions such as air-conditioning have changed the landscape and population of the Intermontane. Do geography and natural obstacles matter any longer?

16. How was the Snake River Plain formed and how is it used today?

Suggested Readings

Abbey, Edward. *Desert Solitaire*. New York: Simon & Schuster, 1968.

Acrey, Bill P. *Navajo History: The Land and the People*. Shiprock, N.Mex.: Department of Curriculum Materials Development, 1994.

Arrington, Leonard J. *Great Basin Kingdom: An Economic History of the Latter-Day Saints, 1830–1900*. Cambridge, Mass.: Harvard University Press, 1958.

———. *History of Idaho*. 2 vols. Moscow: University of Idaho Press, 1994.

Baker, Oliver E. "Agricultural Regions of North America. Part X: The Grazing and Irrigated Crops Region." *Economic Geography* 7, no. 4 (October 1931): 325–64.

Beatley, Janice C. "Climates and Vegetation Pattern across the Mojave/Great Basin Desert Transition of Southern Nevada." *American Midland Naturalist* 93, no. 1 (January 1975): 53–70.

Beheiry, Salah A. "Sand Forms in the Coachella Valley, Southern California." *Annals of the Association of American Geographers* 57, no. 1 (March 1967): 25–48.

Black, Anne E., J. Michael Scott, Eva Strand, et al. "Biodiversity and Land-Use History of the Palouse Bioregion: Pre-European to Present." 2003, at http://biology.usgs.gov/luhna/chap10.html.

Bogardus, J. F. "The Great Basin." *Economic Geography*. 6, no. 4 (1930): 321–37.

Boswell, Thomas D., and Timothy C. Jones. "A Regionalization of Mexican Americans in the United States." *Geographical Review* 70, no. 1 (1980): 88–98.

Canham, Matt. "Mormon Portion of Utah Population Steadily Shrinking." *Salt Lake Tribune*, July 24, 2005.

Commission on Geosciences, Environment, and Resources. *A New Era for Irrigation*. Washington D.C.: National Academies Press, 1996.

Dougherty, John. "Wisdom of the Ancestors." *Phoenix New Times*, December 1, 2005, at http://www.phoenixnewtimes.com/2005-12-01/news/wisdom-of-the-ancestors/1.

Durrenberger, Robert. "The Colorado Plateau." *Annals of the Association of American Geographers* 62, no. 2 (June 1972): 211–36.

Fahys, Judy. "Tailings Create a New Kind of Fallout," *Salt Lake Tribune*, August 24, 2005.

Fifer, J. Valerie. "Transcontinental: The Political Word." *Geographical Journal* 144, no. 3 (November 1978).

Fonaroff, L. Schuyler. "Conservation and Stock Reduction on the Navajo Tribal Range." *Geographical Review* 53, no. 2 (1963): 200–23.

Foy, Paul. "Climate Expert: Rocky Mountains Snowpack Shrinks at Margins." Associated Press, December 1, 2006.

Fradkin, Philip L. *A River No More: The Colorado River and the West.* Berkeley: University of California Press, 1996.

Garreau, Joel. *The Nine Nations of North America.* Boston: Houghton Mifflin, 1981.

General Accountability Office (GAO). *Livestock Grazing.* Report to Congressional Requesters, September 2005, at http://www.gao .gov/new.items/d05869.pdf.

Griffiths, Mel, and Lynnell Rubright. *Colorado: A Geography.* Boulder, Colo.: Westview Press, 1983.

Hansen, Dan. "Grazing Costly to Taxpayers." *(Spokane, Wash.) Spokesman Review,* February 14, 2000.

Harris, Chauncy D. "Location of Salt Lake City." *Economic Geography* 17, no. 2 (April 1941): 204–12.

Jefferson, Mark. "Utah, the Oasis at the Foot of the Wasatch." *Geographical Review* 1, no. 5 (May 1916): 346–58.

Larson, Daniel O., Hector Neff, Donald A. Graybill, et al. "Risk, Climatic Variability, and the Study of Southwestern Prehistory: An Evolutionary Perspective." *American Antiquity* 61, no. 2 (1996): 217–41.

Meinig D. W. *The Great Columbia Plain.* Seattle: University of Washington Press, 1995.

———. "The Mormon Culture Region: Strategies and Patterns in the Geography of the American West, 1847–1964." *Annals of the Association of American Geographers* 55, no. 2 (June 1965): 191–220.

Merchant, Carolyn. *Major Problems in American Environmental History.* Lexington, Mass.: Heath, 1993.

Miser, H. D., K. W. Trimble, and Sidney Paige. "The Rainbow Bridge, Utah." *Geographical Review* 13, no. 4 (October 1923): 518–31.

Moehring, Eugene P., and Michael S. Green. *Las Vegas: A Centennial History.* Reno: University of Nevada Press, 2005.

Nelson, Margaret C., and Michelle Hegmon. "Abandonment Is Not as It Seems: An Approach to the Relationship between Site and Regional Abandonment." *American Antiquity* (2001): 213–35.

Nostrand, Richard L. "The Hispanic-American Borderland: Delimitation of an American Culture Region." *Annals of the Association of American Geographers* 60, no. 4 (December 1970): 638–61.

Oregon Department of Fish and Wildlife. "Northern Basin and Range Ecoregion," at http://www.dfw.state.or.us/conservationstrategy/ docs/document_pdf/b-eco_nb.pdf.

Parfit, Michael. "The Floods That Carved the West." *Smithsonian* 26, no. 1 (April 1995): 48–59.

Reff, Daniel T. "The 'Predicament of Culture' and Spanish Missionary Accounts of the Tepehuan and Pueblo Revolts." *Ethnohistory* 42, no. 1 (Winter 1995): 63–90.

Robbins, Jim. "Where the Cattle Herds Roam, Ideally in Harmony with Their Neighbors." *New York Times,* July 11, 2006.

Roberts, David. "The Long Walk to Bosque Redondo." *Smithsonian* 28, no. 9 (December 1997).

Rothman, Hal. *Neon Metropolis.* New York: Routledge, 2003.

Schmandt, Michael J. "Postmodern Phoenix." *Geographical Review* 85, no. 3 (July 1995): 349–63.

South, Robert B. "Transnational 'Maquiladora' Location." *Annals of the Association of American Geographers* 80, no. 4 (December 1990): 549–70.

Starrs, Paul. *Let the Cowboy Ride.* Baltimore: Johns Hopkins University Press, 1998.

Starrs, Paul F., and John B. Wright. "Great Basin Growth and the Withering of California's Pacific Idyll." *Geographical Review* 85, no. 4 (October 1995): 417–35.

Stegner, Wallace. *Beyond the Hundredth Meridian.* New York: Penguin Books, 1992.

Thomas, Benjamin E. "The California-Nevada Boundary." *Annals of the Association of American Geographers* 42, no. 1 (March 1952): 51–68.

Vance, James E., Jr. "The Oregon Trail and Union Pacific Railroad: A Contrast in Purpose." *Annals of the Association of American Geographers* 51, no. 4 (December 1961): 357–79.

Waitt, Richard B., Jr., and Robert M. Thorson. "The Cordilleran Ice Sheet in Washington, Idaho, and Montana." In *Late-Quaternary Environments of the United States,* edited by H. E. Wright, Jr., vol. 1, *The Late Pleistocene,* edited by Stephen C. Porter, 53–70. Minneapolis: University of Minnesota Press, 1983.

Wauer, Roland. *Naturalist's Big Bend.* Austin: Texas A&M University Press, 1980.

Weaver, Glen D. "Nevada's Federal Lands." *Annals of the Association of American Geographers* 59, no. 1 (March 1969): 27–49.

Works, Martha A. "Creating Trading Places on the New Mexican Frontier." *Geographical Review* 82, no. 3 (July 1992): 268–81.

Wycoff, William. "Creating Colorado: The Making of a Western American Landscape." New Haven, Conn.: Yale University Press, 1999.

Internet Sources

U.S. Geological Survey. "Water Quality in the Central Columbia Plateau, Washington and Idaho, 1992–95," at http://pubs.usgs.gov/ circ/circ1144/nawqa91.3.html#14330.

U.S. Department of Energy. "Energy Efficiency and Renewable Energy," at http://www.eere.energy.gov/.

U.S. Energy Information Administration. 2005. State Energy Data System, at http://www.eia.doe.gov/emeu/states/_seds.html.

U.S. Environmental Protection Agency. "Kennecott Mining Site," at http://www.epa.gov/aml/tech/kennecott.pdf.

Imperial (Calif.) Irrigation District. "Water," at http://www.iid.com/ Water.

National Public Radio. "Stakes High for Las Vegas Water Czar," at http:// www.npr.org/templates/story/story.php?storyId=10939792.

U.S. Geological Survey. "Changing Water Use and Demand in the Southwest," at http://geochange.er.usgs.gov/sw/impacts/society/ water_demand/.

Navajo Nation, at http://www.nnwo.org/.

SustainLane. 2008 U.S. City Rankings, at http://www.sustainlane.com/ us-city-rankings/.

City of Portland. Portland Water Bureau. Water Costs, at http:// www.portlandonline.com/water/index.cfm?a=behgie&c=26426.

Arizona Department of Water Resources, at http://www.azwater.gov/ azdwr/default.aspx.

Phoenix Business Journal. "Arizona Second in Population Growth," at http://www.bizjournals.com/phoenix/stories/2003/03/03/ daily7.html.

Arcosanti Project, at http://www.arcosanti.org/project/main.html.

Arizona Water Crisis, at http://www.uswaternews.com/archives/ arcsupply/tarifac7.html.

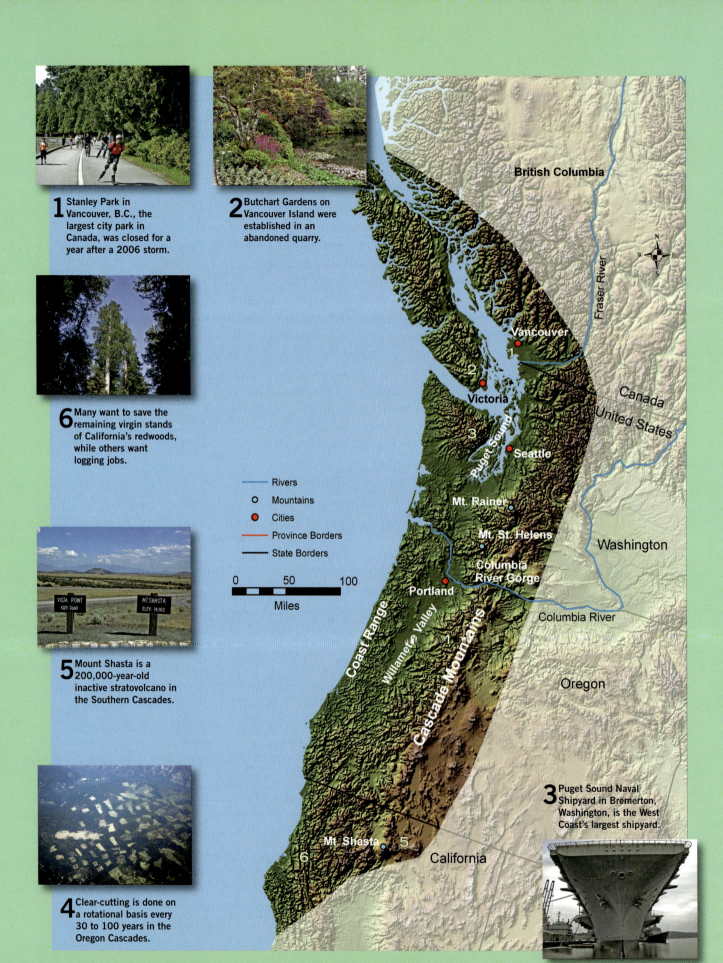

1 Stanley Park in Vancouver, B.C., the largest city park in Canada, was closed for a year after a 2006 storm.

2 Butchart Gardens on Vancouver Island were established in an abandoned quarry.

6 Many want to save the remaining virgin stands of California's redwoods, while others want logging jobs.

5 Mount Shasta is a 200,000-year-old inactive stratovolcano in the Southern Cascades.

4 Clear-cutting is done on a rotational basis every 30 to 100 years in the Oregon Cascades.

3 Puget Sound Naval Shipyard in Bremerton, Washington, is the West Coast's largest shipyard.

British Columbia

Fraser River

Canada
United States

Vancouver

Victoria

Puget Sound

Seattle

Mt. Rainer

Mt. St. Helens

Washington

Columbia River Gorge

Portland

Columbia River

Oregon

Coast Range

Willamette Valley

Cascade Mountains

Mt. Shasta

California

Rivers
Mountains
Cities
Province Borders
State Borders

0   50   100
Miles

17
PACIFIC NORTHWEST
Environment as Lifestyle

Chapter Highlights

After reading this chapter you should be able to:

- Identify the subregions within the Pacific Northwest
- Compare and contrast the eastern and western parts of Washington and Oregon in relation to climate and precipitation
- Describe the major mountains in the region and their impact on the climate
- Discuss the importance of the Inside Passage
- Compare and contrast farmed salmon with wild salmon
- Discuss the important cultural traditions of the Pacific Northwest Native Americans
- Describe population growth in the region
- Describe the major cities and their relationship to environmental issues
- Explain the past and present economies in the subregions
- Define the Ring of Fire
- Discuss the level of sustainability in the region

Terms

anadromous fish
bioaccumulation
clear-cut

cutover
fish farm
fish ladder
hatchery
keystone species

lahar
managed use
marine climate
old growth
potlatch

selective cut
shelter wood
stratovolcano
strip cut

Places

Cascade Mountains
Coast Mountains
Coast Range

Columbia Gorge
Columbia River
Fraser River
Inside Passage
Mount Rainier

Mount Shasta
Mount St. Helens
Olympic Mountains
Portland, Oregon
Puget Sound

Ring of Fire
Seattle, Washington
Vancouver, British Columbia
Victoria, British Columbia
Willamette Valley

PHOTO 17.1. Mount Rainier, Washington. Located in the Seattle-Tacoma metro area, Mount Rainier rises more than a mile above the surrounding Cascades and dominates the skyline. It is one of two dozen towering volcanoes in the Pacific Northwest Cascade Range. Pollution often mars viewing Mount Rainer from the metro area.

Introduction

The mountains dominating the Pacific Northwest (Photo 17.1) form a barrier separating the region from the rest of the country, and sire a distinct geography and culture. The physical landscape evokes dreams of an ecological utopia, an ecotopia. The region was used as a prototype in Ernest Callenbach's *Ecotopia*, as well as in Joel Garreau's *Nine Nations of North America*. *Ecotopia* favors ecological land-use policies versus overdevelopment and industrialization, a sensible decision in this verdant region of dramatic coastlines and volcanically punctuated timberland slopes.

Regional residents lead the nation in controlling urban sprawl and securing a quality of life that features local foods and a healthy, green, environmental attitude. The Pacific Northwest may not be the fabled Ecotopia, but it could be argued that more people in this region are aware of sustainable issues than anywhere else in America.

Once the mountainous barrier was overcome and its timberland resource exploited, the region benefited from its location. By the late twentieth century, the region evolved further along with the burgeoning Pacific Rim economy. The natural resource economy transformed into a postindustrial technology and services economy. Although affected by the dot-com crash, the alternative, healthy lifestyle has retained residents.

The three major cities of the region—Portland, Seattle, and Vancouver, British Columbia—have been growing at a rate well beyond the national level. Outbound migration is almost nil, even as spiraling land costs infect Portland; as traffic, pollution, lumber, and economic imbalances affect Seattle; and as gridlocked Vancouver reflects its lack of a highway system. People

want to call this place home, and they remain hopeful that an environmental utopia is still around the corner.

Environmentalism is almost synonymous with the Pacific Northwest lifestyle. The residents' green psyche revels in outdoor living, hiking, biking, and horticulture. But it has not come easily or evenly. Despite its Ecotopia reputation, the Pacific Northwest has severe environmental problems just like the rest of America. Only the specifics differ. While the Northwest respects the countryside aesthetic and clean, postmodern industries, and although residents have fought urban sprawl, the natural world conflicts with urban living.

Logging, fishing, and water pollution top the Pacific Northwest list of environmental concerns. The three ills are interrelated and together create a plethora of environmental problems, including diseases, pests, habitat loss, land fragmentation, invasive species, agricultural grazing, coastal pollution, fishery destruction, water quantity and quality issues, and forest management practices. However, the regional emphasis on sustainability is highlighted by several of the most notable environmentally oriented groups and individuals—Greenpeace, Sightline, and David Suzuki—who address specific issues and are working toward a more sustainable future.

Physical Geography

Nestled between the Intermontane and the Pacific Ocean, the Pacific Northwest spans two thousand miles from the Alaska Panhandle to northern California. The region is wet in the west, moist in the trough, and divided from the dry Intermontane by rugged, snow-covered mountains. The region, part of the Pacific Basin Ring of Fire, is volcanically active and delineated by a north-south line of steep-sided and occasionally explosive **stratovolcanoes.**

The moderate climate and visually stunning landscape have attracted those seeking a healthy lifestyle, but the increased population and the volatile nature of the volcanoes causes ecological issues.

The Pacific Northwest topography defines the three subregions:

- the Washington and Oregon Coast Ranges; the British Columbia Coast Mountains
- the Puget Sound Trough, Willamette Valley, and the Inside Passage
- the Cascade Mountains

Coast Ranges and Coast Mountains

The Pacific coastline is dramatic: Mountains rise abruptly from the ocean, and the continental shelf plunges into the abyss just a few miles offshore. For example, British Columbia's Queen Charlotte Island Basin descends more than three thousand feet only four miles from the shore. The evenly crested Oregon and northern California Coast Ranges hover over the narrow coastline (Photo 17.2). The action of waves and tectonics through the ages has eroded and then lifted the stepped terraces sixteen hundred feet above the sea.

The coastal mountain systems include British Columbia's Coast Mountains, Olympics, Klamath, and Coast Ranges. Unlike the flat coastal plain of the Atlantic, the coastal ranges are a spectacular backdrop to the ocean—but are the primary evidence that all is not calm on this edge of the continent. The region is much younger than the East Coast and still tectonically active.

In British Columbia, the rugged and fjorded Coast Mountains rise precipitously ten thousand feet above the ocean, blocking interior access while offsetting the modest elevations of Vancouver Island and other Inside Passage islands. But they also set the stage for the numerous alternating mountain ranges and trenched valleys between the Cascades and the Rocky Mountains (Chapter 15).

Washington's glacier-clad Olympic Mountains dominate the steep glacial cuts of the Coastal Range. Mount Olympus surmounts the four-thousand-square-mile rainforest wilderness. The Olympic Peninsula coastline contains numerous sea cliffs and offshore rock pillars.

The Olympic Peninsula and Vancouver Island receive the most rain in their respective countries, although the moisture is fickle, drowning some areas (in the west) in moisture and leaving others relatively dry.

The Oregon Cascades and Coast Ranges converge at the Klamath Mountains, and then diverge at California's Central Plateau into the California Coast Range and the Sierra Nevada. The California Coast Ranges rise from the coast in a complex mélange of faulted valleys and bold escarpments. A jumbled mountain-valley rhythm continues inland, restricting transportation between valley troughs.

The forested mountain habitats share a mild, maritime climate and ample rainfall. The dominant species in the Oregon and Washington Cascades and coastal mountains is Douglas fir. The dominant tree species in the wetter Olympics and Vancouver Island and along the Pacific Northwest Coast are Sitka spruce and western hemlock, but thousands of species from towering trees to ferns and mosses cover nearly every inch of the ground. Timber is still cut in the temperate rain forest; however, twenty-first-century U.S. logging is about one-tenth of

PHOTO 17.2. Arch Cape, Oregon. The Pacific coastline is much younger and more rugged than the Atlantic coastline. Flat land along the coast is at a premium.

previous decades. Canadian logging has been more active, but managed.

In northern California, the majestic redwood tree is the dominant tree (Photo 17.3). The oldest redwoods are two thousand years old. Periodic flooding and fog account for the redwoods' successful growth. Redwoods rely on the fog for moisture during the dry summer months. They are a good example of the inner workings of ecosystems and how every plant fits within its natural habitat. Remove fog from the trees, and the result would be a drier site, poorer mineral recycling, and a changed ecosystem, one that is sans redwoods.[1]

Understanding the natural evolution of forests is still a work in progress. The past policy controlled insect and rodent damage and halted fires, but researchers found that halting human control may be healthier. Insects and rodents are integral parts of the ecosystems. Fire leaves char and adds nutrients. Forest management is complex and not totally understood.[2]

Puget Sound

Nestled between the Coast Range and the Cascades, the Puget Sound waterway extends from the Inside Passage south to Olympia, Washington. Puget Sound is an estuary fed by freshwater coming from the Cascades and the Olympics. Washington's largest cities—Seattle, Tacoma, and Olympia—occupy the trough.

Inside Passage

North of Puget Sound, the Inside Passage is protected from the turbulent Pacific Ocean by Vancouver Island's Insular Mountain Range. The eight-hundred-mile-long Inside Passage has been the preferred shipping route since the 1897 Klondike Gold Rush. Today, thousands of cruise ships annually bring tourism and the accompanying pollution to the delicate passage environment.

The Puget Trough

The Pleistocene ice sheet depressed Puget Sound under a mile of ice. About ten thousand years ago, the glacier retreated and left glacial drift, thousands of islands, the deeply gouged Puget Trough, and the Inside Passage channel. Seattle and Tacoma edge the dramatic Puget Trough landscape.

The Puget Trough extends into Oregon, where the Willamette River drains the broad Willamette alluvial valley. The Columbia Gorge connects the Trough with the interior. The trough encompasses only 5 percent of Washington and Oregon land, but half their population resides there.

Cascade Range

Seven hundred miles long and fifty miles wide, the Cascade Range extends from northern California to southwestern Canada. The Cascades' elevation varies from 3,000 to 9,000 feet, but the volcanic peaks within the range are much higher, the most massive being the majestic 14,415-foot Mount Rainier (Map 17.1). The Columbia River divides the rugged volcanic crustal mass of the northern Cascades from the gentler but still volcanic southern Cascades. The volcanic action is created by the subduction of the Juan de Fuca tectonic plate beneath the North American plate. The subduction increases temperatures and pressure, which melts rock and forms magma that rises to the surface, erupts, and creates the Cascade volcanoes.

Northern Cascades   The northern Cascades are a granitic mass thrusted amid lava flows and volcanic debris and then carved by streams and glaciers. The range holds hundreds of small glaciers, including twenty-eight on Mount Rainier.

PHOTO 17.3. Humboldt Redwood State Park, Northern California. The Rockefeller Forest was donated by John D. Rockefeller in 1931. It is the largest remaining stand of virgin redwoods in the world.

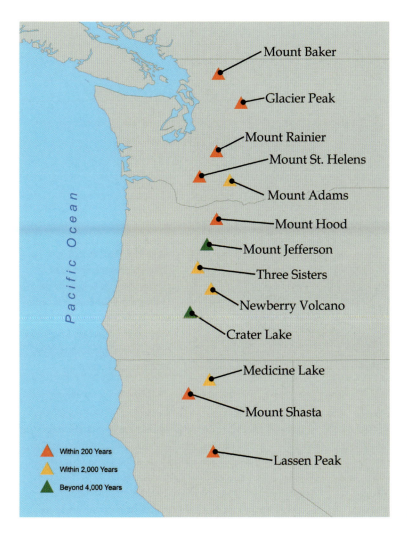

MAP 17.1. Volcanoes in the Cascade Mountains. The Cascades are punctuated with many volcanoes, some of which are still active.

Southern Cascades Over 120 volcanoes and numerous cinder cones, lava flows, hot springs, and mud pools blanket the southern Cascades from Lassen Peak to Mount Hood. Rising abruptly from the Cascades, the volcanoes, including Oregon's Mount Hood, Crater Lake (the remains of Mount Mazama), and California's Mount Shasta, are locally spectacular sights.

Mount Hood, a still active snow-covered stratovolcano, is located along the Columbia River between Portland and The Dalles (Photo 17.4). The last major eruption occurred in 1782, but since then several smaller eruptions sent muddy **lahars** down the mountain.

The remains of Mount Mazama form the intensely blue Crater Lake (Photo 17.5). The original nine-thousand-foot peak collapsed about 5700 BC, in an eruption forty times as powerful as the 1980 Mount St. Helens explosion. Continued lava flows sealed the opening of Mazama and sired the lake within the caldera.

Located about two hundred miles north of Sacramento, fourteen-thousand-foot-high Mount Shasta soars more than ten thousand feet directly from the base. Its old-growth, incense cedar forest was cut over, cleared of timber, and ingloriously made into pencils.

Water

Although water is usually abundant in the Pacific Northwest, the region became mindful of water use in 2005 because of extended drought, population growth, and the concomitant growth in energy and water consumption.

Important rivers in the Pacific Northwest include the Columbia, the Willamette in Oregon, and the Fraser River in British Columbia.

Snowmelt provides about 70 percent of the western water supply. The abundant rain and snow delineate Pacific Northwest waterways through the Coastal Ranges, although only the Columbia River dissects both the Coastal Range and the Cascade Mountains. The two major cities in the Puget Sound—Seattle and Vancouver, British Columbia—depend on Cascades snowmelt for their water. Because no rivers transverse California's coastal ranges, northern California coastal towns remain isolated from the interior, which has slowed regional population growth.

Columbia River

The Columbia River is the major regional source of water and power. The river originates in the Selkirk Mountains of British

PHOTO 17.4. Mount Hood, Oregon. The Mount Hood volcanic peak rises abruptly above the Cascade Range. Seen here from The Dalles, it occasionally is still visible through the Portland haze. The Dalles has been and remains a busy railroad route connecting the Northwest with the interior.

Columbia and flows through the Rocky Mountains, the Intermontane, and the Pacific Northwest to the Pacific Ocean. The Columbia has the third-largest flow in America, and the steep gradient provides hydropower to the region.

In the United States, the Columbia is dammed for all but 50 miles of its 632-mile course, and in Canada, only the 140 miles nearest the headwaters are not dammed. Thirty dams generate hydropower, stimulating industrial growth and irrigating land, but they also disturb the salmon runs.

Astoria, at the mouth of the Columbia, was bypassed as the major Oregon port because of the hazardous, ship-sinking waters that earned it the name "Graveyard of the Pacific." The shipping channels are dredged regularly so ever larger ships can enter the river on their way to Portland. But dredging upset the crab fishery, and after the earlier loss of the salmon fishery and the canneries, added to Astoria's woes (Photo 17.6). Today, Astoria is a quaint tourist town (background for the popular *Goonies* film of the 1980s). Portland thrives on the dredging that helped kill Astoria's economy.

Portland's port is entangled with its own water woes. Despite extensive cleanup work on the Willamette River in the 1960s, inspiring the rest of America to wake up to environmental

PHOTO 17.5. Crater Lake, Oregon. The Crater Lake caldera, the deepest lake in the United States at 1,932 feet, is about six miles in diameter. The Wisdom Island cinder cone emerged later from explosive eruptions in the caldera.

BOX 17.1 COLUMBIA RIVER POWER

Should you schedule flows to maximize survival of salmon or set them aside to cover . . . California?*

During World War II, Oregon and Washington built vast war plants and produced approximately half of the nation's aluminum. On the Columbia River, the turbines of Bonneville and Grand Coulee dams satisfied power needs. Funded by the 1937 Bonneville Power Administration, the

dams provided below-market-price power to fledgling Pacific Northwest industries, such as aircraft, aluminum, and farming. Columbia dam power also provided about one-seventh of California's electricity.

The aluminum plants laid off workers in 2000, and in 2003 two major aluminum plants closed permanently. The aluminum plant closures were due to the lower labor and electricity costs and lower environmental standards of foreign competitors.

* Robert McCullough, *Energy Consultant*, April 17, 2005.

issues, the river had become a toxin-filled sump again by 2000, the result of wood creosote factories, shipyards, and coal and oil storage facilities. The Willamette became a Superfund site. Toxins in the river have harmed fish (people are warned not to eat the fish) and cause cancers. Actions to decrease pollution since the Superfund designation include the port's commitment to clean up contaminated sediment. Portland's century-old sewer lines carried both waste and storm runoff, but they have recently been augmented by Big Pipe, which treats 96 percent of sewage formerly dumped directly into the river.

Fraser River

Southwestern British Columbia's Fraser is the largest and longest river in the province (850 miles), flowing from Mount Robson to Vancouver. The river drains about 25 percent of the province and is a major salmon producer, containing five types of salmon and other fish species. Environmental pressures

include urbanization and agriculture development, punctuated by Vancouver population growth.

Water Pollution

Increased Pacific Northwest population, logging, and tourism have polluted water and decreased wildlife habitat. Although protection has been implemented to stop pulp mills from polluting Puget Sound, much work remains to be done.

Puget Sound

Aquatic life in the Sound is dying due to toxic chemicals and climate change. PCBs, PDBEs (flame retardants), lead, mercury, and dioxins discharged into the Puget Sound threaten residents and plant, animal, and aquatic ecosystems. The **bioaccumulation** (a process where toxic levels become more concentrated as they move up the food chain) has been linked to developmental effects in children. The marine bird population has halved since

PHOTO 17.6. Cannery Remains at Astoria, Oregon. Located at the mouth of the Columbia River, Astoria was once a major salmon cannery, but the canneries are now gone. All that remains in the place of one of the old canneries is the pilings, the old boiler, and an office building.

BOX 17.2 HOOD CANAL

The Hood Canal, on the western side of Puget Sound Basin, was formed millions of years ago, but only fifteen thousand years ago, glaciers carved its elongated shape (Map 17.2). The Hood Canal fjord has traditionally been a spawning ground for finfish and an excellent breeding ground for shrimp, clams, oysters, and crab. However, since the 1930s the canal has been hypoxic (oxygen starved), which resulted in sporadic fish kills that became severe in the twenty-first century.

Reasons for the hypoxic conditions are both natural and human induced. A sill blocks the narrow entrance, slowing deepwater flushing and circulation in the sixty-mile waterway. Increased

sunlight, along with nitrogen and phosphorus, and warmer temperatures stimulate algal growth, which increases the phytoplankton in the system.

Adding to the hypoxic conditions are human activities, including nitrogen loads from septic systems, animal waste, storm water, and agricultural and residential runoff. The continual population growth along the canal has exacerbated problems. The southern portion is now hypoxic year-round, and the northern end is now oxygen starved about half the year. Several studies and groups are working to restore health to the canal, but progress is slow.*

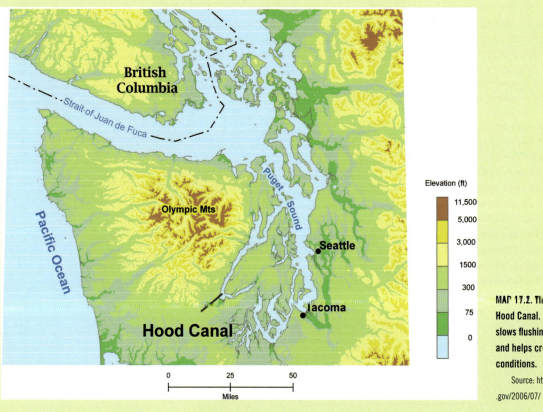

MAP 17.2. The Glacially Created Hood Canal. Its narrow entrance slows flushing and circulation and helps create its hypoxic conditions.

Source: http://soundwaves.usgs .gov/2006/07/

* http://pubs.usgs.gov/sir/2006/5106/.

the 1970s, and 20 percent of shellfish beds have closed since 1980. The loss of fish has resulted in a dramatic decline in fish-feeding marine birds. Thousands of fish species and aquatic mammals are on the Sound's endangered list. A 2005 study blamed warmer water for a two-hundred-thousand-salmon kill in Puget Sound. Average summer surface water temperatures have risen about 4°F in the past thirty-five years. The Hood Canal has been plagued with hypoxia, killing crabs, shrimp, and finfish, and along the Pacific coast of Washington a

summertime low-oxygen zone extends down the entire length of the state.

The busy Tacoma and Seattle shipping lanes transport more than fifteen billion gallons of oil, and sometimes there are oil spills. Even small oil spills, such as in 2004 and 2005, reveal system weaknesses and require millions of dollars to clean up.

Several governmental and nongovernmental groups in the Puget Sound Basin address pollutant issues, including a partnership formed by the governor of Washington to clean up the sound by 2020, making it one of the most environmentally ambitious cleanups in the nation.[3] Cleanup groups focus on studies alleviating population and health issues for fish and humans, studying storm intensity models, flood areas, and levees to minimize losses in the future. Wastewater systems and reclaimed water are now built into the planning process.

Inside Passage

The Inside Passage has been a vital seaway and home to the many tribal groups dependent on the forest and salmon for their livelihood. But beginning with the Klondike Gold Rush in 1897, the passage sequenced through salmon canneries, logging, tourism, fish farms, and oil. Along the way the passage took a beating.

In high season, cruise ships carry more than a million passengers through the waterway. Many ships ignore pollution regulations and dump their waste, bilge water, and untreated sewage into the water. U.S. environmental laws that prohibit waste dumps and require onboard treatment have been unenforceable; few ships are checked. Canada, however, has no laws stopping ships from dumping into its water. The polluting chemicals and oil-laden bilge water threaten several Inside Passage whale species.

Jobs along the Inside Passage—forestry, fishery, and cruise ships—pay low wages. Hopes for a better economy hang on more ecotourism or mining oil from the Queen Charlotte Basin. The basin, estimated to hold almost ten billion barrels of oil and twenty-six trillion cubic feet of gas, is within the continental shelf and therefore fairly shallow and accessible. If oil production is pursued, a future challenge will be protection of the Passage from the mining, while maintaining the ecotourism economy. Separating the sound from the ocean is a group of islands, the Queen Charlotte Islands (Haida Gwaii). They are renowned for their flora and fauna, as well as for harboring a traditional Haida village.

Climate

The moist, gray climate is not as ubiquitous as its reputation. For three seasons, the temperate **marine climate** receives plentiful precipitation. The northwest corner of Vancouver Island is inundated with 250 inches annually, and Mount Olympus on the Olympic Peninsula receives more than 200 inches annually.

In the Cascades, westerly winds cause abundant orographic precipitation on the windward side and much less on the leeward rain shadow side (Map 17.3). But regional precipitation varies widely. From the Olympics to the eastern Cascades town of Wenatchee, a distance of about a hundred miles, the annual rainfall diminishes from more than one hundred inches to less than ten inches.

Cold ocean air decreases air pressure, and storms move up the mountains and release the moisture as rain or snow, depending on elevation. The Puget Trough receives less rain than the coast because the Coast Range acts as a moisture

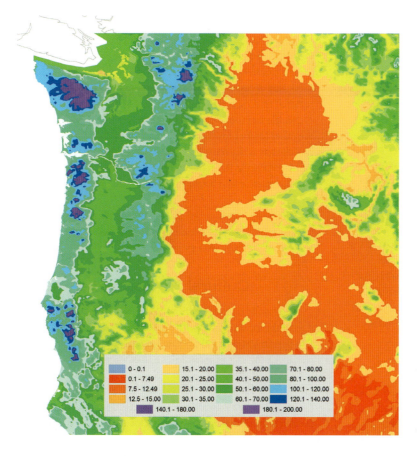

0 - 0.1	15.1 - 20.00	35.1 - 40.00	70.1 - 80.00
0.1 - 7.49	20.1 - 25.00	40.1 - 50.00	80.1 - 100.00
7.5 - 12.49	25.1 - 30.00	50.1 - 60.00	100.1 - 120.00
12.5 - 15.00	30.1 - 35.00	60.1 - 70.00	120.1 - 140.00
	140.1 - 180.00		180.1 - 200.00

MAP 17.3. Precipitation in the U.S. Pacific Northwest. Although precipitation is heaviest along the Olympic Peninsula, Seattle and Portland receive around forty inches of rain annually and have many drizzly days. The eastern side of the states is in the rain shadow, and the precipitation drops off rapidly.

barrier. The Seattle area receives about forty inches of rain, three-quarters of it from October through March. However, less than a hundred days a year are clear, and jokes abound when the overcast days extend well past May into "Junuary."

Nestled between the Coast and Cascade Ranges, the Willamette Valley is sunnier and drier than the coast, but is wetter and cooler than eastern Oregon.

Climate Change

In April 2005, residents of Seattle were asked to conserve drinking water. The 1998 to 2005 drought in the Pacific Northwest halved the average snowpack, which provides more than half its water. The reduced snow and increased rain may be a result of long-term climate change, but it also may be an anomaly; tree rings show alternating wet and dry periods in the past. Average snowpack returned during the winter of 2006, and conservation worries ended, for the time being. Forecasts for the future, though, include higher temperatures (about 1.8°F [1°C] every twenty-five years), an increase in precipitation, and more rain than snow. Climate change, along with steady increases in population and consumption, will continue to stress local water sources.

Historical Geography and Settlement

Native Americans

Humans migrated into the region about ten thousand years ago, some three thousand years after the glacial retreat. The inhabitants lived in fishing villages and depended on abundant natural resources, including coniferous timber, shellfish, and salmon.

Prior to European arrival, the region was the most densely populated Native American region. Coastal tribes—Algonquian in northern California, Chinook in Washington and Oregon; and Haida, Tlingit, and Tsimshian in British Columbia—lived in permanent villages.

After mid-eighteenth-century European discovery, smallpox and other European diseases devastated the indigenous population. Today, despite environmental problems, the remaining Aboriginals continue their cultural traditions, including a salmon-based lifestyle, potlatch, and totem poles.

The long-term existence of these local groups has depended on communal land and a sustainable fishery, in contrast to the practices of western civilization. However, since the late twentieth century, native fishing rights have been a source of contention, because native use is no longer only subsistent. Numerous problems have devastated the fishery over the past century, including overfishing and for-profit fishing by the natives, warming waters, El Niño, dams, and sea lions.

Hudson's Bay/Fort Vancouver

Lewis and Clark were the first white explorers in search of a transcontinental water route. Their published works influenced John Jacob Astor to extend fur trapping into the territory.

Astor's fur-trading company established the western trading post of Fort Astoria (1811). The trading post languished until the Oregon Trail was established and immigrants settled the area. The British Hudson's Bay Company (1824) erected the competing Fort Vancouver, Washington, across from present-day Portland. The trading companies competed, and both claimed land to the mouth of the Columbia River.

The Oregon Trail symbolized America's credo of Manifest Destiny and the expanding power over the British. In the early 1840s, settlers followed the trail to its end at The Dalles in Oregon. The way to the fertile Willamette Valley was treacherous, requiring either traversing the Cascades or portaging past the waterfalls on the Columbia. In a classic example of push-pull migration, thousands of settlers left disease and poor economic conditions in the East to seek a more promising life two thousand miles to the west.

American settlers in the Willamette Valley soon outnumbered the Canadian Métis settlers. Both American and British claims on the valley remained unresolved until the 1846 Oregon Treaty extended the 49th parallel boundary to the Pacific Coast, establishing the border for the United States and the British.

Settling the Pacific Northwest Cities

The Pacific Northwest supplied commodities to California during the gold rush. California outgrew its own natural resources, so businesses eyed Oregon and Washington resources, especially timber. Several small company towns along Puget Sound, such as Port Townsend, Port Gamble, and Seattle, all competed and prospered, cutting timber for the California market.

Portland also benefited from gold rush demands and distributed Willamette River and Columbia River crops. Steamboats navigating the Columbia to the Willamette River established a market-based lumber and agricultural economy. Portland grew from a handful of houses in 1850 to a population of 2,874 in 1860. Rail access in 1883 sealed Portland's position as the regional trading center.

Seattle was founded on a deep harbor in 1851 and resembled the other lumber towns except for its pluck. When tiny Tacoma was chosen as the most profitable choice for the terminus of the Northern Pacific Railroad (1883), Seattle built its own railroad into the interior and became the gateway to the 1897 Klondike gold rush.

Vancouver was founded as a sawmill settlement in 1886. The fortunate timing of the Klondike gold strike positioned Vancouver as Canada's Klondike gateway.

Cultural Perspectives

The Pacific Northwest tribal cosmology has evolved in relation to the local resources. The tribal groups have tried to maintain their traditional culture, but necessary adjustments have cost them socially, economically, and environmentally.

Salmon Culture

It all started with the banning of the potlatch. And then they implemented the residential school because this government of ours has a hundred year plan for Canada

BOX 17.3 THE LEWIS AND CLARK ROUTE AND THE OREGON TRAIL

Lewis and Clark opened Oregon Territory trade for both the United States and the British. Heading west past the Missouri River, the continental divide, and the Columbia River, the presidentially appointed expedition explored to the Pacific Ocean. The following year, 1805, the Lewis and Clark expedition followed the Columbia to the Snake River along a well-traveled Native American buffalo trail. This was the shortest route, but skirmishes between the Lewis and Clark party and the Blackfoot tribe halted most future passage. Instead, settlers tracked another route west over what became the Oregon Trail, through the Green River Basin, the North Platte, and the Wyoming Basin.

The first explorers were followed by religiously zealous Atlantic seaboard settlers who arrived to "tame" the West Coast Natives. The settlers' experiences on the Willamette (1834) and at Walla Walla, where the Snake and Columbia rivers meet (1836), proved disastrous.* But continued use refined the Oregon Trail. The first small parties of settlers arrived in 1839. Nine hundred settlers arrived in 1843, and 11,500 settlers braved the Oregon Trail in 1849. The Oregon Trail became the standard route for quick access to the Pacific.

* Pioneers of the Oregon Trail, Marcus and Narcissa Whitman were massacred in 1847 as martyrs bearing the blame for a measles epidemic that swept through Native American villages. From the Native point of view the killings were defensive. To the Cayus mind, the Whitmans brought what we would call "germ warfare" and were the cause of the Natives' hunger after the arrival of settlers. C. Addis, "The Whitman Massacre," *Journal of the Early Republic* 25, no. 2 (Summer 2005).

and Natives are not included. That wasn't successful, what other option do they have? They are going to the very substance that sustained us throughout our history: our food supply.

— Art Dick, Namgis First Nation, hereditary chief, Mamalilifulla tribe

To me, this wild fish is who we are, what we are.

— Stan Hunt, Alert Bay, Namgis First Nation [4]

Gift-giving kept potential encroachers away and avoided mutually destructive warfare.[5]

A visual survey of Pacific Northwest airport concession stands reveals salmon's local iconic status. Every shop sells boxes of smoked or dried salmon. Salmon is seemingly everywhere, but perhaps not. The salmon may be farmed instead of wild. Most First Nation people believe farmed salmon destroy their way of life and their relationship with the Pacific Northwest environment.

The Pacific Northwest indigenous cultures continue to depend on two natural resources: salmon for their diet and lumber for their structures. Salmon need cold water to survive. The cold, oxygenated Pacific Northwest water has been an ideal habitat.

Europeans overwhelmed the region while Natives continued their traditional salmon hunts until 1866, when whites opened the first salmon cannery. Soon, the tribal groups worked for and in the canneries. In the 1930s, the canneries became obsolete when refrigeration enhanced the market for fresh fish. After 1950, salmon migration routes were disrupted due to overfishing, habitat degradation, and dammed rivers. Tribal fishing grounds were eliminated.

Treaties guaranteeing Native American fishing rights were repeatedly ignored, and fishing was outlawed in "usual and accustomed" waters after 1900. A pivotal 1974 court decision finally restored Northwestern tribal rights.

The salmon culture continues today, though greatly modified. Tribal groups continue to rely on salmon as their chief food source and have tried to maintain a culturally consistent salmon fishery. The number of fishing boats has decreased because of quotas on salmon and other fish stock. Salmon hatcheries and **fish farms**—commercially bred fish in sequestered areas—have all but replaced wild salmon. Maintaining a sustainable commercial and tribal salmon fishery is the ideal, but so far has been unachievable.

An additional and thorny problem is the influence of the dominant society on the indigenous population. Although tribes continue to practice their traditions and the salmon continues to be an important local food, many Natives have taken advantage of tribal privileges for catching salmon; catches can far exceed their needs. Many sell their excess salmon. This adds fuel to environmentalists' claims of tribal abuses and furthers sustainability worries.

Regional Life

Population

As the region connected to the rest of the nation and the Pacific Basin became economically important during the latter third of the twentieth century, the regional population grew. Washington's rate of growth was highest surrounding Seattle's King County. In Oregon, the greatest surge was in counties west of Portland and in the Willamette Valley.

An anomalous growth pattern includes Willamette-area retirees east of the Cascades in Bend, Oregon. Bend is located in Deschutes County, the state's fastest-growing county. From 1990 to 2000, Bend more than doubled in size, reaching 52,000 in 2000 and 76,639 in 2010; it is expected to continue growing as the national population ages.

Southwestern British Columbia has 60 percent of the provincial population. Other population centers in the province are Vancouver Island, the Okanagan Valley (Chapter 15), and the

BOX 17.4 POTLATCH, ABORIGINAL RIGHTS, AND TITLE

Potlatch was a misunderstood ceremony of the Pacific Northwest gift-giver cultures. In 1884, the Canadian and American misunderstanding of the potlatch's cultural importance for sharing culture and peace led the two countries to outlaw the practice. But the essential ceremony was practiced covertly until the ban was lifted in 1951.

Historically, many Pacific Northwest tribal groups distributed lavish gifts in potlatch feasts and ceremonies. But potlatch was more than gifts; it also conveyed oral histories among illiterate societies and marked a rite of passage for tribal members. Potlatch displayed wealth and power that held the expectation of future reciprocation. The potlatch created alliances, vanquished rivals, was closely tied to the rights for salmon streams, and was a method of avoiding war between the haves and have-nots.* Potlatch maintained peace, and it was not a display of social rank, which was how anthropologists—only capable of understanding the practice in relation to their own social systems—first explained the phenomenon.†

In British Columbia, Aboriginal claims were treated differently than in the rest of Canada, and Native groups lost most rights, so

that the maximum land could be opened for settlement and resource development. Natives were allotted individual claims of ten or twenty acres, rather than the larger communal claims that allowed the continuation of hunting and fishing as a way of life.

Aboriginal groups sustained a long-term battle to secure several rights—potlatch, legal counsel on land claims, land claims, the vote—even as their traditional lands were being subsumed by the rights given large resource development projects. The inconclusive state of Aboriginal rights left First Nations groups in British Columbia economically impoverished and with numerous social ills. Following a series of court cases in the 1970s, the federal government realized they needed to recognize Aboriginal title as first recognized in the Royal Proclamation of 1763, and the tide slowly began to turn in favor of the Aboriginals.

In the 1997 Delgamuukw Case, the Canadian Supreme Court firmly established Aboriginal title and reestablished the Royal Proclamation as the precedent to Aboriginal title in the province. The case was a watershed for Native groups, who rapidly sought to negotiate treaties to hold their land communally in accordance with Aboriginal title.

---

* Bruce D. Johnsen, "A Culturally Correct Proposal to Privatize the British Columbia Salmon Fishery," in *Self-Determination: The Other Path for Native Americans*, edited by Terry L. Anderson, Bruce L. Benson, and Thomas E. Flanagan (Stanford, Calif.: Stanford University Press, 2006).

† Franz Boas, *Fighting with Property: A Study of Kwakiutl Potlatching and Warfare, 1792–1930*, American Ethnological Society Monograph 18 (New York: J. J. Augustin, 1966).

---

northern towns of Prince Rupert and Prince George along the Canadian National Rail line.

Two population groups, immigrating Chinese and retirees, have elevated Vancouver's population density. Vancouver's 1,905 people per square mile (2006) far outweigh the British Columbia average of 12 people per square mile.

The Chinese are British Columbia's largest visible minority. They compose 10 percent of the population. Most live in Vancouver and nearby Richmond. Chinese originally arrived in the late nineteenth century and worked in sawmills. The most recent Chinese immigration was prior to the 1997 transfer of Hong Kong to China. Unsure of their future in the People's Republic of China, many left Hong Kong and moved to the Vancouver area, capitalizing on a shared British Commonwealth status that eased immigration requirements. Hong Kong immigrants brought with them knowledge of living in densely populated areas, and they helped convert Vancouver's transit stations into more densely populated urban marketplaces.

Many Canadian retirees migrated west to sunny British Columbia, which has caused concern over senior health-care issues for the provincial system. Between 1980 and 2004, over twenty-four thousand moved to the province, and more are expected as baby boomers retire. In 2002, British Columbia seniors accounted for 13 percent of the population but accounted for 50 percent of prescriptions and 55 percent of hospitalizations. Twenty-five percent of British Columbia's

population will be over sixty-five by 2031, increasing prescription and hospitalization costs.

Traditional and Sustainable Cities

Polls cite Seattle and Portland as favorite places to live in the United States because of their reputations for a healthy quality of life. They are typically listed within the top U.S. cities in sustainability.[6] Vancouver is consistently rated one of the world's best-quality-of-life cities.[7] Each of these cities has a stronger sustainable community practice than is found in most U.S. and Canadian locales, including a commitment to compact neighborhoods, but Pacific Northwest cities still have multiple sustainability issues.

Seattle, Washington
(2010 pop. 608,660; CSA 4,199,312)

[Seattle] . . . probably represents one of the most infilled, graded, and leveled of all North American cities.[8]

Seattle, the Emerald City, is green both in its thinking and its foliage. The thinking stems from the love of the aesthetics of this place, while the foliage flourishes because of ample precipitation (Photo 17.7).

But green does not mean natural. The flat portions of the downtown Seattle landscape are artificial. Located on a narrow isthmus between Puget Sound and Lake Washington, Seattle's hills blocked growth, travel, and ease of construction. The city

PHOTO 17.7. Downtown Seattle on the Puget Sound was originally interspersed with marshes and hills. In the early twentieth century, the hills were sluiced and the marshes drained, developing a more amenable cityscape for the growing metropolitan area.

quickly outgrew its original purpose as a timber resource hinterland and evolved into the Alaskan gateway. As the hilly city grew during the late nineteenth century, it was regularly flooded and in need of reclamation. The Great Fire of 1889 provided the impetus the city needed to rebuild by improving nature. It began hydrosluicing hills and filling in lowlands to improve the landscape.

Seattle developed its port and large industrial areas by filling in the tidal flats during the early twentieth century. The city continued to grow and become more important for the national welfare during World War I, providing Puget Sound lumber, fish, and shipbuilding. During World War II, a small local aircraft company, Boeing, took off, along with the aviation industry, and Seattle boomed. Today Boeing is still important, supporting 3 percent of the economy and supplying eighty thousand jobs, but the Pacific Northwest economy is now diversified and no longer dependent on Boeing.

During the 1990s, the Puget Sound economy grew at twice the national rate, and per capita income was 20 percent above the national average. But Seattle has not been immune to millennial issues. The city that spawned Starbucks, Microsoft, and Amazon entered the new millennium with a staggering Asian economy, a dot-com bust, a Microsoft antitrust suit, WTO riots, and a downturn in the airline industry, especially after 9/11. However, the Pacific Coast location has helped the port economy.

Two days closer to Asia than Los Angeles, the Seattle and Tacoma harbors are deepwater ports capable of handling large container ships. Container traffic increased 40 percent in Seattle and 19 percent in Tacoma between 2004 and 2006, and it has formed bottlenecks when distributing the containers to rail or truck lines. The overflow of Asian imports has stressed local ports and traffic infrastructure.

Constructed in the 1950s, U.S. port infrastructure is not as modern as that of Chinese and Indian ports. The lack of modern infrastructure in America has hindered the flow of goods and added to shipping costs. Ships have grown larger than American ports can handle. Although deepening channels is an option, the environmental consequences are negative and require a global agreement regarding shipping practices. Additionally, port congestion affects the environment by releasing more harmful diesel emissions into the air and water, and truck traffic is hard on local roads and increases congestion. Despite the environmentally sensitive problems, the Puget Sound allure and belief in its continued success remains, partially because of its commitment to sustainability.

Seattle is grounded in the nonprofit "Sustainable Seattle" organization formed in preparation for the 1992 Earth Summit in Rio. Seattle focuses on the long-term health and vitality of the city through links between economic prosperity, environmental vitality, and social equity.[9] Seattle is also home to the Sightline Institute, a northwestern think tank addressing regional sustainable development and a model for bioregional awareness of sustainable issues.

Through an active program of grants and community participation, city administrators have internalized sustainable goals more successfully than in any other U.S. city. The city has many LEED-certified buildings and has implemented a retrofit program that has created thousands of jobs. Seattle has worked to improve its carbon footprint by revamping its transit system, using buses, a new light

BOX 17.5 LIFESTYLES: THE COMPACT NEIGHBORHOOD

Portland, Seattle, and Vancouver have been at the forefront of transit-oriented developments (TODs) and have attempted to halt urban sprawl with smart growth. Smart growth cities are walkable, bicycle-friendly, and have compact neighborhoods (Table 17.1). Smart growth and the compact neighborhoods it encourages have been popular choices to thwart urban sprawl, but they also have shortcomings: increased housing prices, reduced property rights in rural or undeveloped areas, and planning codes that prevent innovative ideas, a few examples of which follow.

Portland

Portland, Oregon, is the kind of city where a "greener-than-thou" restaurateur's dilemma over what to do when Monsanto executives make a dinner reservation is a lead story in the local "newsmakers" column, where local chefs are celebrities and have their own cooking shows, and where a neighborhood BBQ joint feels the need to advertise its vegetarian fare.*

Portland, the healthy dream of California transported hundreds of miles north, is all about bicycle riding, hiking, green gardens, healthy lifestyle, and local foods. But the liberal city's popularity and attraction may have become its undoing. Portland grew rapidly in the 1960s and 1970s, doubling in size to over one million auto-dependent residents. Portland's central business district decayed as suburban areas grew. Efficient transportation became untenable as low-density development sprawled across the Portland landscape.

In 1973, Oregon passed a land-use law mandating urban growth boundaries, thereby restricting sprawl and forbidding rural development in the state. Portland eschewed sprawl for infill, and it featured walkable, low-rise urban units accessible to shopping and public transportation. Growth was not entirely eliminated but was strictly controlled, in 2002, the city added 10,700 acres to accommodate its growing population. Public transportation systems, such as light rail, were developed. The central city has free public transit, bicycling is encouraged, and bike lanes connect communities.

Limiting urban sprawl escalated Portland's cost of living. In five years, permitted-growth-zone prices increased more

than 500 percent and controlled sprawl. Smart growth had other unanticipated effects. Metropolitan growth shifted north to Vancouver, directly north of Portland but in the state of Washington, where the law had no effect.

Land-use restrictions reduced property value for many rural residents. To address these losses, ballot initiative Measure 37 was passed in 2004 and began ungluing smart growth. Measure 37 requires the government to compensate landowners whose property values were reduced and whose ownership predates the measure. If the government cannot pay, then the owners may develop the property for permitted uses. By early 2006, almost three thousand claims across the state requested $4 billion, an unaffordable amount for state and local governments. Although Measure 37 mostly affects rural areas, it also influences Portland's land.

In a classic case of hidden agendas, Measure 37, which spawned copycat measures in other states, was sold to the public as providing justice for the small landholder, even though the initiative was financed by large lumber companies seeking development rights. The measure also threatened the loss of cherished landscapes, such as Columbia Gorge vineyards and orchards. Landowners in popular and scenic areas were seeking to cash in on their property, to the chagrin of neighbors.

The star witness at the hearing was John M. Benton, whose family has been growing fruit near Hood River for nearly a century. This town, a destination resort for Columbia River wind surfers, has experienced a steep rise in real estate values caused, in large measure, by land use laws that prevent orchards on the edge of town from turning into subdivisions.

To take advantage of this market, Benton wants to convert 210 acres of his family orchard into housing. The resale value of his orchard, if it continues to be zoned exclusively as farmland, would be about $8,000 an acre. But if it were sold for housing, Benton said, it would fetch $284,000 an acre.†

In 2007, the Courts ruled that the Columbia Gorge was protected as a federal scenic area, and so Measure 37 compensation did not apply. In a special election in 2007, Measure 49 modified

TABLE 17.1. Percentage of Residents in Compact Neighborhoods

	1990	2000
Vancouver, B.C.	51	62
Victoria, B.C.	33	34
Seattle, Washington	21	24
Eugene, Oregon	10	12
Portland, Oregon	20	25

Source: Sightline Institute

Measure 37 by protecting forests and farmlands from excessive development.

Seattle

At the millennium, Seattle was sprawling in every direction. Traffic was outrageous, housing prices skyrocketing, and the natural resources, including the almighty salmon, deteriorating. Numerous nongovernmental organizations and the public began to follow smart growth compact city design.

Since that time Seattle has built more cohesive transit-oriented neighborhoods and a public transport system to remove autos from the road. Many compact homes are being built along the numerous bus routes. The bus routes into the downtown area keep it alive, vibrant, and a favorite for local residents and visitors alike.

Vancouver

Vancouver is the champion of compact neighborhoods in the Northwest. Vancouver's population has grown over 50 percent since it hosted Expo '86. Sprawl is restrained, though, because of land use policies fashioned to preserve agricultural land. Though West Vancouver sprawled, most growth has concentrated in the dense, pedestrian-oriented neighborhoods near the downtown area or in northern Vancouver. Sixty-two percent of Vancouver's residents live in compact neighborhoods of high-rise condominiums, compared to 24 percent in Seattle (Photo 17.8).

PHOTO 17.8. Vancouver, British Columbia. Vancouver witnessed four building booms. The first two were between its 1860 founding and World War I and the last two since the 1980s. The most recent was after Expo '86, when glass and steel condominiums took over the main streets. The Expo brought new investors to the beautiful setting of the coastal city.

---

* Martha Works and Thomas Harvey, "Can the Way We Eat Change Metropolitan Agriculture? The Portland Example," *Terrain* 17 (Fall–Winter 2005), at http://www.terrain.org/articles/17/works_harvey.htm.

† Blaine Harden, "Anti-Sprawl Laws, Property Rights Collide in Oregon," *Washington Post*, February 28, 2005.

rail, an extensive ferry system, and bicycle lanes (Map 17.4). In 2005, the mayor implemented a program to cut carbon dioxide emissions in alignment with the Kyoto Protocol, despite the federal government's lack of commitment. Since that time, more than a thousand other mayors have joined Seattle's resolve.

Portland, Oregon

(2010 pop. 583,776; MSA 2,226,009)

Built at the confluence of the Columbia and Willamette rivers, Portland's location benefited from access to the Pacific and to Willamette Valley agriculture. Later, an intercontinental rail connection established Portland as a main distribution point for the Northwest. But today Portland is best known as the "greenest city in America," because of its dedication to renewable energy, commuting patterns, and healthy buildings.

In 1994, Portland was among the first to adopt a global warming policy to reduce carbon dioxide emissions. In 2005, the city had achieved its goal of cutting carbon emissions below 1990 levels. The strategy for this achievement included adopting long-term sustainability principles, which are fully integrated within city administration operations, including an incentive program for using public transport or building green. Portland's successful light rail and bus systems have a ridership level of seventy-six million annually. Free downtown public transport,

the venerable Powell's Bookstore, numerous public gardens, and the perfect climate for blooming plants, added to an outspoken civic stance and strong laws against sprawl, makes the "City of Roses" many people's favorite city.

Portland's urban growth control has attracted large companies, such as Hewlett-Packard, Intel, and Hyundai, and educated workers who seek a high quality of life. The riverside location has substantial geographic and economic advantages for freight shipment. Portland is ranked as the third-largest-volume port on the West Coast, the nation's largest wheat exporter, seventh-largest export gateway, and fourteenth-largest container port.

Portland has been at the forefront of sustainable issues, but there has been a price, including price differentials between undeveloped land and land that is allowed to be developed and the widening gap in jobs. Portland and Oregon have had higher-than-average rates of unemployment since 2005. In January 2011, Oregon unemployment was at 10.4 percent (Portland at 10.0 percent), above the national rate of 9.8 percent. But people are still moving to the city. Jobs in manufacturing, even high-tech manufacturing, are down, and so is the median income, and yet the city has jobs, although at opposing ends of the pay scale: low paying or highly skilled. People move to the city to enjoy the quality of life and sense of place. Many are wealthy and work outside the city, commuting weekly by air,

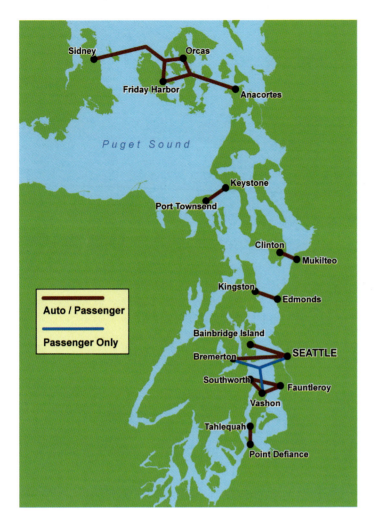

MAP 17.4. Washington Ferry System. Ferries are a way of life for many people in the Puget Sound Basin. Costs have escalated rapidly in the past decade.

returning on weekends to play in their private utopias. They move to Portland because they can afford to, and in so doing they economically squeeze many locals out.

Victoria, British Columbia

(2011 pop. 80,017; CMA 344,615)

Victoria began its existence in 1843 as a Hudson's Bay outpost to protect British interests on Vancouver Island and in 1848 developed sawmills for timber bound for San Francisco. When gold was discovered along the Fraser River, Victoria (Vancouver did not yet exist) was the dominant city in the Canadian Cordillera and the transshipment point for miners. Vancouver eventually competed with Victoria for economic and political power. Despite being overshadowed by Vancouver, the older and more established Victoria became the capital when British Columbia joined the Confederation in 1871.

Situated at the southern end of Vancouver Island, regular ferries from Washington State or Vancouver provide access. Once in the town, the genteel atmosphere of hanging flower baskets, Butchart Gardens, and the fairy-lit domed capitol is a world away from the high-tech power of Vancouver (Photo 17.9). As the capital, the city economy is largely governmental, augmented by tourism and services.

Vancouver, British Columbia

(2011 pop. 603,502; CMA 2,313,328)

Vancouver, the economic core of British Columbia, is one of the most livable and green cities in both the United States and Canada; it has spawned the buzzword *Vancouverism*, such is its appeal to numerous cities imitating its sustainable resolve. The fast-growing Canadian city was intentionally founded as a terminus to the Canadian Pacific Railroad, which received and shipped goods from Canada's interior. Although it was founded thirty years after Victoria, a mere fifteen years after its founding Vancouver in 1901 became the largest city on Canada's West Coast, with a population of thirty thousand.

Sitting at the mouth of the Fraser River, the city is the largest port in Canada, shipping lumber, western Canadian crops, and minerals, such as potash from Saskatchewan and coal from the Rocky Mountains. Biodiesel and ethanol plants have increased the need for oilseeds, so canola exports have been on the rise. The city is also a major port for cruise lines.

Vancouver has weathered recessions, but Expo '86 boosted the economy and renewed optimism and links with Asia. One of Vancouver's main resources is this long-established link. The Port of Vancouver is a destination for many Asian goods, and Asian developers fund many buildings.

PHOTO 17.9. The Capitol, Victoria, British Columbia. Victoria won the provincial capital, but Vancouver is the larger and more economically important city.

The city thrived economically until a downturn in the 1950s and 1960s, when suburbanization sapped energy and the rail and port manufacturing economy flagged. During this time, the city considered standard renewal programs, building freeways through the city and into the suburban sprawl, but instead arrived at a more locally based, participatory land use and planning policy. The policy separated Vancouver's growth from the rest of Canada and the United States. Vancouver's postindustrial knowledge-based economy replaced the resource and manufacturing economy. Today, central Vancouver is a densely populated compact city—the only large North American city without freeways bisecting the core.

The lack of freeways leaves the city with traffic congestion, but neighborhoods remain whole. Vancouver modeled a new paradigm, one based on density, public transport, walking, and bicycle paths. The city developed into an innovation storehouse for Canada and the world. It adopted a Livable Region Strategic Plan in 1996 and a one-hundred-year plan that anticipates climate change, pollution, sprawl, disease, and terrorism, all the while conserving energy and water and aiming to become a thoroughly sustainable city.

The appeal of Vancouver and its lifestyle is marred by becoming one of the least affordable cities in the world, especially in housing. Although the city has increased affordable housing for low-paid service economy employees, the amount does not nearly meet the needs.

This is a trend in cities that value sustainable goals. Affordability and sustainability are often mutually exclusive. While living sustainably itself is not out of reach for the average person, sustainable housing is available in so few places and the demand is so great that it decreases affordability.

The Greater Vancouver Regional District aims for sustainability in waste management, air, land, energy, density, water, and green design. A few of their accomplishments have increased water quality; reduced chlorine and removed microorganisms from drinking water; reduced sewer overflows; and created Skytrain, an elevated train transportation network. Skytrain stations have become dense, mixed-use urban village nodes. The lack of freeways, the Skytrain system, and the commitment of Vancouver's policymakers to a green and densely populated city has limited reliance on the automobile and made the city one of the most desirable and sustainable in North America.

Economy

Lumber, hydropower, and fish anchored the Pacific Northwest economy. While the Washington and Oregon economies have moved from reliance on primary industries, British Columbia still depends on them, although it too is developing the quaternary economy. But the regional economy is at a crossroads: The lumber industry has an environmental and political crisis; hydropower is no longer competitive; wild salmon is expensive, while farmed and hatchery fish—with their environmental issues—are cheap, plentiful, and short-term oriented.

During the 1990s the economy flourished, led by a flurry of dot-com companies, Seattle-built airplanes, and the Columbia River dams that provided cheap power for ancillary industries. The dot-com and 9/11 crashes ended the economic euphoria but not the livability. The computer industry is rebounding, but outsourced, although both countries still have profit centers. Microsoft remains near Seattle but hires from a global human resource pool. No longer economically isolated, the Pacific Northwest reaches outside its boundaries and into the global market.

Primary Industry and Natural Resources

Farmland in Oregon and lumber in Puget Sound attracted the first settlers. Both of these activities are still influential, but they have evolved into one of the most sustainable and innovative in either country, although still largely dependent on fossil fuels and therefore unsustainable in the long run.

Agriculture

The coniferous forested hillsides of the Pacific Northwest are unfit for farming. The Willamette Valley became the regional agricultural heartland because of the plentiful rain, fertile soil, and temperate climate. Dominant farming activities are dairying, truck farming, vineyard culture, and forage crops.

Oregon grows more than 225 crops, the third most diverse in the nation (after California and Florida). Two million acres of crops dominate Willamette Valley agriculture. The location and climate enhance its specialized crops, including fruits and berries grown for local consumption. Specialized farms in the Willamette Valley also provide grass seed and such nursery products as roses, irises, and grafted fruit trees for the national market. A recent trend has replaced old orchards with vineyards. Oregon had about 350 wineries in 2008, and the Puget Sound area of Washington has 50 wineries.

The Western Washington Bellingham Plain and Cowlitz Valley specialize in dairying, and the Puyallup area specializes in daffodil and tulip production, followed by berry and truck gardening for local markets. As growth continues in the Seattle Plain, farms and CAFO dairies are moving farther afield, such as Skagit Valley north of Everett. However, the bulk of Washington agricultural production remains east of the Cascades.

The British Columbia coast produces crops for local urban markets and has a thriving marijuana industry, taking advantage of laxer Canadian laws.

California also has a thriving but illegal marijuana industry, especially in the northern areas near Humboldt University, known for its mixed demographics of hippies, loggers, and fishers. Approximately one-third to one-half of marijuana consumed in the United States is grown domestically. California grows and harvests as much as $5 billion of marijuana annually. Law enforcement estimates that 10 to 20 percent of the domestic crop is seized. In 2004, $2.5 billion of marijuana (621,000 plants) were seized in California.[10] California passed and implemented a medical marijuana program in 2005. Patients and dispensaries have spread significantly since. There is no statewide regulation standard regarding cultivation of medical marijuana. Legal and illegal plants cannot be distinguished, and federal authorities continue a program of eradication.

Logging

Forests are called the "land of many uses" in the United States and are used similarly in Canada. The uses include food for humans and livestock, building materials, fuel, oil, gas, and industrial forest uses including lumber, pulpwood, paper, charcoal, and construction material. Ecological uses include carbon sinks, watershed protection, and biodiversity. The forest, however, cannot be all these things simultaneously and also be a natural treasure, so there are often battles between the government, corporations, and environmentalists over managing forest resources.

Forests cover about 29 percent of the United States and 43.7 percent of Canada. These forests are equivalent to one-quarter of the world's forests, and they are therefore crucial as a large carbon sink sequestering carbon dioxide. In the United States, large lumber companies privately own 72 percent of this land. The remaining 28 percent lie within the National Forest system. Crown Land holds 90 percent of Canadian forests and leases them to logging companies. Environmentalists in both countries claim that logging methods are unsustainable. Corporate logging is done within a management system meant to gain the most profit at the least cost, without taking long-term viability, sustainability, and ecology into account.

Throughout the windward side of the Pacific Northwest, mountain conifers, such as the Douglas fir, dominate the ecosystem; they are the primary habitat for many species. The Douglas fir, a large tree capable of living five hundred years, has always been part of the ecosystem, naturally complemented by western hemlock and western red cedar. The logging industry favors Douglas fir, because it grows quickly, yields the most timber per tree, and regenerates readily in clear-cuts because they thrive in full sunlight.

The **old growth** forest stands natural and unplanned, but commercial stands result in even-aged managed forests. **Managed use** is a contentious phrase, whose definition varies between anthropocentric and environmental points of view. To a lumber company, managed use rationalizes **clear-cutting** (removing all trees in an area at one time) as beneficial to the forest and their logging interests; however, environmental activists endorse preserving the entire ecosystem as is. Environmentalists' efforts have saved many acres of forest but perhaps at the cost of an unhealthy ecologic stagnation. A sustainable point of view would allow wood to be cut, but only at a rate that will ensure long-term productivity. The best forest to maintain ecosystems is a mixture of old growth and younger varieties that would allow the complex ecological communities to evolve. A mixed-forest ecosystem is also healthier for biodiversity and fire protection.

Since 1990, lumber imports have risen. The United States imported over 18.5 billion board feet of Canadian softwood in 2001, as well as 26.8 billion pounds of paper.

While environmental concerns "saved" U.S. forests, America's unabated consumption of wood continued—about 718 pounds per person annually, the highest in the world by a factor of three. American forests had reduced their logging, but Canadian logging increased, with most wood exported to the United States.

Northern California   California's timber production has dropped 80 percent since 1990, and many mills have closed because of pressure from environmental groups. The surviving companies must wade through environmental regulations and lawsuits regarding sustained yield, clean water, and

BOX 17.6 DAIRYING

The coastal town of Tillamook is an unlikely place for dairy production, but it remains Oregon's major milk producer and has developed into a tourist industry since the lumbering and commercial fishery industries declined. Agriculture remains the largest single source of income in the county. Dairy cooperative owners built a consumer-friendly production facility, best known for their annual one hundred million pounds of Tillamook Cheddar. Tillamook Cooperative dairy sales were $260 million in 2004. The cooperative has been a leader in healthy and more sustainable production of cheese.

The Tillamook Cooperative has demonstrated environmental awareness by erecting fences to stop erosion, using manure instead of commercial inorganic fertilizers, and in 2005, in response to consumer complaints, the cooperative members voted to ban the use of synthetic bovine growth hormone (rBGH), a genetically engineered hormone that stimulates cows to produce more milk. Monsanto, sole producer of rBGH, fought the Tillamook Cooperative over its decision, citing free choice, but ultimately lost because the Cooperative chose to represent a niche and voted to lose some of its free choice in order to maintain that niche. The ban on the hormone remains in place. Since that time, many other dairies have also chosen to ban rBGH because of contamination of the milk, including possible cancer-causing agents. The hormone is banned in Canada, twenty-four European nations, Japan, and Australia.

---

habitat-sensitive cuts while maneuvering around issues like the spotted owl, old growth, and pollutants.

Washington and Oregon   The Pacific Northwest was 90 percent forested and an important resource when the first non-natives arrived. Native Americans built wooden houses and dugout canoes from readily available wood. European explorers found cedar logs made excellent masts for their ships. Most cities and many smaller company towns were founded on the timber trade. Only recently has the warmer Southeast, where trees grow twice as fast, bypassed Washington and Oregon in lumber volume.

During the nineteenth century, the government paid railroad companies with four-hundred-foot rights-of-way plus ten-square-mile land grants for every mile of track built. Grants were sold to such companies as Weyerhaeuser, who maximized their profits by waiting until the market was right. The Northwest rail network helped lumber production open internal markets.

After the spotted owl controversy in the 1980s, lumbering jobs declined, but the timing was perhaps fortuitous for the region, if not the lumbermen. The economy was diversifying, and the net loss of jobs in lumbering was made up for in other parts of the economy. Logging was a regional source of income and jobs, but during the 1980s the typically small-owner industry changed.

Big corporations and huge sawmills operate vertically integrated production facilities based on efficiency and economies of scale. A typical vertically integrated company owns the land, mills, and all production from raw material to the finished product: "from primeval to paper." The U.S. government subsidizes these globalized producers, which, in turn, further destroys smaller local markets.

It is difficult to satisfy both animal habitats and human desires when dealing with policies based on politics or economics. The northern spotted owl cause célèbre

of the environmentalists was ostensibly to keep many of the old-growth forests and to protect the owl, but the environmentalists failed to examine the overall repercussions of their action. Protecting the northern spotted owl in the 1980s shut down many mills, and U.S. timber production dropped precipitously. Cutting old-growth forests on public land was virtually eliminated. By 1993, the timber harvest was reduced by 80 percent, and the regional lumber economy was in shambles. A new concept, ecosystem management, attempted to rebuild biodiversity, forest health, and sustainability.

Shifts in forest policy favored timber interests, and the removal of old-growth forests streamlined timber removal during the Bush administration; but policies have changed again under Obama. The increased subsidies for lumber companies, opening up wilderness areas to logging roads, and allowing commercial logging in the Californian sequoia groves have effectively ended.

The commercial logging industry considers clear-cutting to be a long-established, sound, silvicultural practice. The advantages are its efficiency and the ease of replanting, but its disadvantages are a scarred landscape, erosion, and a monoculture "forest" that is ecologically unstable. Natural forests are complete ecosystems with multiple interactive species, but lumber companies plant trees as forest crops chosen for their genetic disposition to quick growth and return on investment.

Several issues have environmentalists concerned, including the following:

- Taxpayer subsidies used for short-term profit in the commercial logging industry
- Dismantling of protected wild forests
- Opening up old-growth forests to logging
- Loss of diversity

British Columbia   Lumber is Canada's chief export product to the United States. British Columbia has half of all Canadian

BOX 17.7 LUMBER MANAGEMENT SYSTEMS

Lumber companies have not always replanted recently cutover timber areas. The Great Lakes region lumber companies tried unsuccessfully to sell the flat cutover land as farms, despite the fact that the soil and weather were generally not conducive to farming. Most lumber companies simply moved on to the next forest rather than replant **cutovers**. When the Great Lakes region was logged, the timberland magnate Weyerhaeuser moved on to a million and a half acres of timberland in the Pacific Northwest.

Dependence on Pacific Northwest lumber evolved into a system in which forestry officials studied reforestation and healthy forest systems. During the 1930s, replanting became common as part of the Civilian Conservation Corps (CCC), and many unemployed workers were hired to plant trees. In Washington, the Forest Practice Act, passed in 1946, required all lumber companies to reforest logged areas. Clear-cutting has not always been the standard; other management systems have been popular at different times. But generally, planned management of forests was lax until the middle of the twentieth century.

PHOTO 17.10. Clear-Cuts in Oregon as Seen from the Air (43.649°, −123.048°). Clear-cuts are difficult to see from the ground because the lumber companies usually leave a line of trees along highways.

Clear-Cutting

In a clear-cut area, an entire patch of evenly aged mature trees is removed, leaving a path of bare ground in the forest. Planned management clear-cutting began in the 1950s in the Pacific Northwest, and since 1969 two-thirds of all wood has been clear-cut (Photo 17.10). Clear-cutting is done on a rotational basis, so an area will be "harvested" every thirty to one hundred years. Clear-cutting is the preferred method for some tree species, but there has been a renewed interest in other, more sustainable systems: selective cut, shelter wood, and strip-cutting. However, sustainability is still a long-term goal, and current market conditions are inconsistent with sustainability. Financial markets and the short-term-oriented politicians still favor profit only, over the triple bottom line of environmental and social benefits. It is as if we said, "Let the future deal with what we leave them."

Selective cutting—removing mature trees progressively from a stand—was considered the most economically profitable in the 1930s and 1940s. It remains more environmentally sensitive, and it protects forests against blowdown. Disadvantages are that Douglas fir, the dominant cut species, does not react well to the shade provided in selective cut, and smaller trees are bruised and damaged, affecting profitability.

Shelter wood cutting requires thinning and cutting poor-quality trees. Larger trees provide shelter for the seedlings. Shelter wood is best used in small plots with a homogeneous tree species.

Strip-cutting—removing narrow strips of mature trees of a desirable species—leaves open-space corridors about 250 feet wide, which are used as seed sources for regrowth. This method is prevalent in mixed-species hardwood forests favoring a desirable species composition, but it is more expensive than clear-cutting. All of these methods still require a replanting of the forest to provide for future lumber needs.

Most forested areas in the United States are second and third growth, and are relatively small in size compared to those found by the first European settlers. While today's trees are much smaller than the first-growth forests, all the wood is used and there is little waste. Traditional logging was highly unsustainable, with less than a third of the wood from a tree used as lumber, and more than 30 percent left in the woods. Additionally, the land was left bare and subject to erosion. Today, cutover land is reforested in one of four ways: by allowing natural growth, leaving a few seed-bearing trees, aerial seeding by helicopter, or replanting small trees. Although land is reforested and the wood used more efficiently, the methods of use, such as making paper, are toxic. The pulp and paper industries are a major polluter of air and water.

BOX 17.8 THE SPOTTED OWL

Since the 1960s, old-growth forests have become a battleground. Seeking an angle to gain concessions from Congress, the environmental movement seized on the Endangered Species Act to forward their old-growth agenda. After petitions were denied and appealed, something needed to be done to protect the old-growth forests, or so environmentalists believed. Their answer was the northern spotted owl, which has since become synonymous with the old-growth fight and the Endangered Species Act. As a political instrument, the owl symbolized a forest protector indicator species for environmentalists, but loggers saw it only as a symbol for the destruction of their industry.*

The uproar about the spotted owl began in the Coastal Ranges. During the 1980s, the owl became the focus of a debate between logging and environmentalist factions, resulting in listing the owl as a threatened species. Its habitat was closed to logging, resulting in destroying the local logging industry. But despite the "win" of stabilizing the old-growth forests, the owl population has declined about one-half since 1990.

Environmentalists' efforts to save the owl were simplistic, focusing only on its habitat and not on a stable ecosystem. Several factors reduced spotted owl numbers. The barred owl, an East Coast native, has invaded and now dominates the spotted owl's habitat.† Fires and the West Nile virus also played a part in changing the ecosystem. Saving the spotted owl is a larger issue than merely manipulating the habitat. While the political agenda was served, it ignored the fact that ecosystems are interrelated, and their health requires more than simplistic manipulation.

---

* Mark Moore, "Constructing Irreconcilable Conflict: The Function of Synecdoche in the Spotted Owl Controversy," in *Landmark Essays on Rhetoric and the Environment*, ed. Craig Waddell (Hillsdale, N.J.: Erlbaum, 1998).

† Elizabeth G. Kelly, Eric D. Forsman, and Robert G. Anthony, "Are Barred Owls Displacing Spotted Owls?" *The Condor* 105, no. 1 (February 2003): 45–53.

---

spruce, pine, and fir forests. The lumber industry has been important and the leading employer in the early twentieth century.

In Canada softwood lumber—used to frame buildings—was the fifth-largest export to the United States in 2003, and had been a long-standing source of trade disputes. When American logging was virtually halted during the 1980s, lumber still was plentiful and available but was imported from Canadian forests, especially those of British Columbia. The bulk of the old-growth forest remained in British Columbia, where logging interests, First Nations, and environmentalists fought over regulating logging in Calyquot Sound on Vancouver Island. A 1999 agreement limited the cut and preserved the forest, which was soon declared a UNESCO biosphere site.

From the 1980s until 2006, a lumber dispute between the United States and Canada slowed timber trade, because Canada was accused of dumping lumber at less than the cost of production. A 2006 agreement ended the dispute, and Canada began shipping lumber into the United States under agreement policies.

British Columbia forest policies have been severely criticized both for damaging rural economies and for not providing sustainable forest systems. People seeking rural economic improvement depended on local answers over provincial or national policies. The argument has been made and continues that economy alone is not the answer to a thriving community, and that stability is dependent on sustainability.[11]

Fishing

Regulations to commercially fish salmon, tuna, shrimp, and crab on the North Pacific Coast have tightened, resulting in a 90 percent drop in fishing incomes. Commercial fishing fleets are as endangered as the fish. The Oregon fishing fleet, for example, declined from 3,000 boats in the 1980s to 467 in 2003. Commercial, sport, and Native American fishers have endured quotas and other limitations resulting in drastic reductions. The salmon fishing season has shortened each year, and it was completely shut down in California and Oregon in 2008. The revenue loss devastated the commercial fleet and the charter-fishing industry. Ocean-dependent areas have gradually turned to tourism, such as whale watching and cruise ships.

Many Pacific Northwest tribes identify heart and soul with the Pacific salmon and are culturally and economically tied to its fate. However, mismanagement, exploitation, and ethnic discrimination have spoiled many salmon habitats. Pacific salmon disappeared from about 40 percent of their breeding grounds and run sizes declined up to 90 percent. Columbia River salmon stock is down 80 to 90 percent, of which 70 percent are bred in a **hatchery**, an enclosed area where fish are artificially bred.

The potential ecological importance of these fishes is so great that we have ventured to call them . . . a "cornerstone species" because we think that these fish provide a resource base that supports much of the coastal ecosystem.[12]

The problem has been trying to fix the problem. Salmon play an important role in complex Pacific Northwest ecosystems. Flora and fauna depend on the salmon, a cornerstone or keystone species. A **keystone species** is important because it acts like a keystone in an arch: If it is taken out, the arch fails. Salmon affect the entire food chain, and they, in turn, are also affected. Polluted and overfished ocean habitats upset a healthy food chain, and climate change, now an accepted reality, disrupts habitats more.

BOX 17.9 DID YOU KNOW . . . SALMON PRESERVATION

- Salmon fishery research started in the 1920s.
- By the 1960s, three key factors to decline were identified:
  - Dam construction
  - Ocean fishery
  - Habitat damage

- An early response to the decline was the establishment of the two-hundred-mile fishery economic zone.
- Native American rights to fisheries were established in the Pacific Northwest before they spread across the nation.

People have to realize that things are connected—the state of coastal temperatures and plankton populations are connected to larger issues like Pacific salmon populations.

—Bill Peterson, National Oceanic and Atmospheric Administration, July 2005

The surrounding area and wildlife influence salmon populations. Human activities in forests can increase soil erosion, reduce woody debris in streams (used to hide from predators), add contaminants, and reduce available water. The spawning salmon, eggs, and future stock deteriorate and upset the entire Pacific Northwest ecosystem. Forty wildlife predators, such as gulls, eagles, and bears, feed on salmon. Diminished salmon stocks upset the ecosystem balances, including the salmon-reliant Native American food supply.

During the twentieth century, opposing groups of resource users blamed each other for habitat destruction. The threatened users offer many simplistic answers, because all try to protect their use while blaming others. The complete and interrelated fish habitat remains unacknowledged. Blame is placed on harvesting fish or the dismal hatchery fish results, but not the habitat, because it is personal, specific, and political. When the habitat is sick, then so are the fish. A healthy habitat means healthy fish, and healthy fish mean a healthy economy and water.

Salmon are an **anadromous fish** that live their early lives in freshwater before migrating to salt water, where they live most of their adult lives before returning to their natal ground to spawn and die. This seemingly simple life course is actually a complex set of relations that tie together freshwater, land, and ocean habitats, each of which modern technology has violated.

Many salmon species have been listed as either endangered or threatened, because damming of rivers made their freshwater habitat inaccessible. For example, **fish ladders**, a series of shallow pools built around dams to facilitate fish migrations, sometimes are ineffective or absent altogether, resulting in dramatically reduced salmon fisheries. Other degradations are a result of logging activities, farming, and urbanization.

Hundreds of Pacific Northwest dams have restricted returning and spawning salmon in their home ground, which in turn limits ocean-bound juvenile salmon. Spill water from the dams simulates the necessary currents directing salmon to the ocean as juveniles and to their breeding ground as adults. Regulating the currents leaves salmon open to predators, but allowing more spills decreases hydropower potential. In 2005, activating spills for the benefit of the salmon elevated the cost of regional power $75 million, and power rates increased 2 to 3 percent.[13]

Salmon habitats are disproportionately disturbed. Coastal salmon are generally healthier than inland, and the Pacific Northwest American salmon fishery suffers more than in British Columbia or Alaska. Warmer weather in the twenty-first century stresses the vulnerable fish. Salmon thrive best in water that is below 68°F. Washington's Puget Sound water temperatures exceeded 70°F in 2004. At 77°F, the salmon die.

There have been several examples of fish kills. Warmer water may have caused more than 1.3 million sockeye salmon to not return to their Fraser River spawning grounds. In 2002, the multiple agendas of farmers, fishers, and environmentalists led to a massive fish kill on the Klamath River.[14] Maintaining a healthy ecosystem will become increasingly complex as climate change progresses.[15]

A Sustainable Future

The Pacific Northwest remains a quality-of-life mecca that tries to live up to its Ecotopia nickname. The local economy was blessed with a wealth of old-growth timber and a healthy, robust wild salmon fishery. The economy, though, has changed. It has stabilized since the challenges of the millennial dot-com bust, but the stability of the salmon and timber industries is of questionable duration. Old-growth wood and wild salmon have become precious commodities.

The Pacific Rim position and the growing Chinese and Indian economies enable regional port growth. Seattle remains Washington's largest port, while Portland continues to increase its share of containerized shipments. Vancouver is Canada's largest port and second-largest (behind Los Angeles) on the West Coast. Continued trade with the Pacific Rim will benefit all these ports, but only if pollution problems, shipping bottlenecks, and infrastructure renewal are addressed and if long-distance shipping is sustainable.

The Pacific Northwest takes sustainability seriously. Sense of place is meaningful to residents, and lifestyle choices indicate that people are thinking about their impact on the land and how to deal with economic and population issues while maintaining a high quality of life. Still, many mistakes have been made.

Cities have attempted different solutions to control sprawl and population growth. Measure 37 in Oregon and the many copycat proposals indicate how putting a finger in the dam stops one flood but diverts the flood elsewhere.

Vancouver, British Columbia, has become known for its walkable neighborhoods. Vancouver and Seattle work to

BOX 17.10 HATCHERIES

While wild salmon have existed in the Pacific Northwest for millions of years and supplied Native American tribes for thousands of years, the wild salmon numbers have dwindled since the late nineteenth century. Hatchery fish, artificially propagated, were raised to regulate the salmon harvest.

Hatchery salmon have been propagated in order to continue the harvest of salmon, reduce human intervention impacts such as dams, and reintroduce salmon into empty habitats. Hatchery fish are genetically wild salmon, but they are often a mix of several different stocks that are not in the specific streams where that stock breeds and are often hatched beyond a stream's carrying capacity. In a hatchery, over 90 percent of the eggs survive, versus the 5 to 10 percent that survive in nature. Currently, 80 percent of Columbia River salmon are hatchery raised.* Because hatchery fish are propagated, there has been less care to regulating the salmon harvest or to protecting the habitat.

Unintended Consequences

Hatchery fish released in streams are vulnerable to outside influences, so that their return to the hatchery produces an illusion about the health of the salmon fishery. The abundance of hatchery fish alludes to a nonexistent healthy wild salmon population. Hatchery salmon are not indigenous wild salmon; instead, the huge hatchery stock depletes the remaining wild salmon.

In 2004, the federal government bowed to development interests and adapted a method of counting wild salmon that included hatchery fish, and therefore it seemed like wild salmon were increasing.† In 2006, the administration qualified policy again,

closing some hatcheries, as saving wild salmon was not working. Some believe that the action was a red herring to divert attention from the killing of salmon at hydropower plants.

Hatchery fish are not an answer to the root causes of wild salmon decline but a cover-up.

Local and Ecoregional Impacts

Wild salmon populations have suffered because of hatchery fish and fish farms. Wild salmon develop in freshwater in streams that they will return to for spawning after a several-year ocean existence. Each salmon type has evolved in relation to the specifics of their home stream. Hatchery fish are raised independent of the watershed ecosystem they are released to. Hatchery fish are not specific to a stream as are wild salmon, and their genetics do not match the particulars of the wild salmon. Hatchery fish can therefore become confused when they return to spawn. They upset the local habitat and compete with wild salmon for food.

Hatchery salmon can overpower an ecosystem beyond its carrying capacity. Competition with wild salmon in an ecosystem can destroy the wild salmon because of predation or dietary limitations.

External Costs

Hatchery fish are a short-term answer to a long-term problem and have caused wild salmon to decrease in numbers. Since commercial and tribal catches increase when hatchery fish are available, the chances are better to decrease the wild stock by overfishing.

* U.S. Fish and Wildlife Service, "Salmon of the West," at http://www.fws.gov/salmonofthewest/wild.htm.

† Timothy Egan, "Shift on Salmon Reignites Fight on Species Law," *New York Times*, May 9, 2004, at http://www.nytimes.com/2004/05/09/us/shift-on-salmon-reignites-fight-on-species-law.html; Union of Concerned Scientists, "Scientific Advice on Endangered Salmon Deleted," at http://www.ucsusa.org/scientific_integrity/abuses_of_science/deleting-scientific-advice-on.html.

---

improve their transportation network by encouraging better public transport, including using hybrid bus engines, cycling networks of greenways, and developing TODs aiming to improve transportation networks, all of which have the goal of reducing greenhouse gas emissions, congestion, air emissions, and transportation costs.

As a leader in sustainable living and conservation, the Pacific Northwest continues to espouse lofty goals of a healthy economy, a healthy ecosystem, and a quality of life

that other regions strive to attain. Despite critical sprawl and population issues, the region has performed poorly by its own standards, largely because of continued growth, its inability to keep sprawl in check, and a growing income gap.[16] Yet it continues to seek innovative methods of sustaining a large population, a good employment record, and a high quality of life. Although its overall sustainability still has room to grow, it is far beyond what most U.S. and Canadian regions have attained.

BOX 17.11   FISH FARMS: FLOATING FEEDLOTS?

The presence and possible establishment of feral Atlantic salmon may further jeopardize the continued persistence of already fragile native Pacific salmonids through competition for resources and occupation of niches that are currently underutilized.*

Some prehistoric societies, such as the Hawaiians, farmed fish for their own use. Today, farmed fish is a global enterprise and an answer to the diminishing stocks of wild fish.

Modern fish farming began with salmon in Norway and Scotland in the 1960s, and by the 1970s the practice reached the east coast of Canada. When the wild salmon population crashed in the 1990s, the response was an increase in salmon farms. In 2007, dire reports about the state of wild sea life caused attention to turn increasingly toward aquaculture (fish farms).

There are freshwater fish farms spread over the interior of the United States raising catfish, tilapia, and several other varieties. The major North American saltwater fish farms are salmon farms located in British Columbia, especially in the Broughton Archipelago across from the northern tip of Vancouver Island. Salmon farming is meant to protect the remaining wild salmon and to provide reasonably priced food. In theory, the salmon are raised in controlled conditions and then sold, alleviating pressure on the wild salmon catch while creating jobs in locations that often lack opportunities. British Columbia salmon farms produced 96,000 tons worth $387 million annually (2005), the largest agricultural export for the province. Most B.C. fish farm salmon are exported to the United States.

A number of controversies cloud aquaculture, including fish subject to disease, sea lice transfer to migrating wild stocks, and mercury-laced fish pellets that are fed to the carnivorous fish. Foreign fish, especially Atlantic salmon in the Pacific (90 percent of B.C. farmed fish are Atlantic salmon), may escape into the wild and interbreed with wild stock or situate themselves in the Pacific

salmon's habitat. Interbreeding may weaken the native wild salmon. Additionally, wild salmon also suffer because farmed fish deplete the natural food stock and spread diseases. In December 2007, a study estimated that the wild stock of pink salmon, the most abundant Pacific salmon and a keystone species, would be 99 percent extinct in the Broughton within four generations (eight years) because of sea lice attacking from the densely crowded fish farms. The Pacific Coast ecosystem could be destroyed if the pink salmon goes extinct.† In 2008, the number of salmon was down 90 percent from 2006 runs, and only 2 percent of runs in 2000.‡

Although some people claim that aquaculture helps world hunger issues, salmon is an expensive fish; wild salmon can bring up to $30 per pound, and farmed salmon is in the $8 range. Additionally, farmed salmon are an inefficient use of energy: It takes about four pounds of smaller fish to produce one pound of farmed salmon.§

An additional issue, aside from fish farms, is the idea of a sustainable product. The word "sustainable" has been used and overused in the past few years. It has become a buzzword that ensures a higher price, but what is a sustainable salmon? According to the Monterey Bay Seafood Watch, the most respected source on the fisheries, aquaculture in general can be sustainable:

> But the environmental impact of fish farming varies widely, depending on the species being farmed, the methods used and where the farm is located. When the environment is considered and good practices are used, it's possible to create sustainably farmed seafood. Such operations limit habitat damage, disease, escapes of non-native fish, and the use of wild fish as feed. . . . The aquaculture industry is growing quickly. Innovative practices as well as careful oversight are needed to reduce impacts on the environment and ensure a sustainable future.**

---

* John P. Volpe, Eric B. Taylor, David W. Rimmer, and Barry W. Glickman, "Evidence of Natural Reproduction of Aquaculture-Escaped Atlantic Salmon in a Coastal British Columbia River," *Conservation Biology* 14, no. 3 (2000): 899–903.

† E. Stokstad, "Parasites from Fish Farms Driving Wild Salmon to Extinction," *Science*, December 14, 2007, 1711.

‡ Scott Simpson, "Collapse of Pink Salmon Runs Reopens Debate over Fish Farms," Canwest News Service, October 31, 2008.

§ Glen H. Spain, "Fisheries Issues for the Pacific Northwest," presentation for the U.S. Commission on Ocean Policy, Seattle, Washington, June 13–14, 2002, at http://www.newscientist.com/channel/life/mg19225724.600-farmed-salmon-put-wild-cousins-at-risk.html.

** Monterey Bay Aquarium, "Aquaculture," at http://www.montereybayaquarium.org/cr/cr_seafoodwatch/issues/aquaculture.aspx.

Questions for Discussion

1. What is the general attitude toward sustainability in the Pacific Northwest? How does it differ from the rest of America?

2. What did Portland, Oregon, do to change the sprawl of the city? What was the result?

3. How did Seattle establish itself as the leading city in Puget Sound?

4. Explain the life of a salmon and why they have declined in numbers over the past century.

5. How does a wild salmon differ from a fish farm salmon? Where are most salmon aquaculture farms located (geographically)?

6. How has Vancouver differentiated itself in sustainability? What has been the outcome of this choice?

7. What role has timber played in the Pacific Northwest's development? What have been some turning points in the timber industry?

Suggested Readings

Ambrose, Steven. *Undaunted Courage: Meriwether Lewis, Thomas Jefferson, and the Opening of the American West.* New York: Simon & Schuster, 1996.

Ashbaugh, James G., ed. *The Pacific Northwest: Geographical Perspectives.* Dubuque, Iowa: Kendall/Hunt, 1994.

Barnes, Trevor, and Roger Hayter, eds. *Trouble in the Rainforest: British Columbia's Forest Economy in Transition.* Victoria, B.C.: Western Geographical Press, 1997.

Beckey, Fred. *Range of Glaciers: The Exploration and Survey of the Northern Cascade Range.* Portland: Oregon Historical Society Press, 2003.

Berelowitz, Lance. *Dream City: Vancouver and the Global Imagination.* Vancouver, B.C.: Douglas & McIntyre, 2005.

Berg, Laura, ed. *The First Oregonians.* 2nd ed. Portland: Oregon Council for the Humanities, 2007.

Callenbach, Ernest. *Ecotopia.* New York: Bantam, 1990. First published in 1975 by Banyan Tree Books, Berkeley, Calif.

Cooley, Richard A. *Politics and Conservation: The Decline of the Alaska Salmon.* New York: Harper & Row, 1963.

Egan, Timothy P. *The Good Rain: Across Time and Terrain in the Pacific Northwest.* New York: Vintage Books, 1991.

Fick, Steven, and Elizabeth Shilts. "Mixing Water and Oil." *Canadian Geographic* 124, no. 4 (July–August 2004): 52.

Freedman, B. *Environmental Science: A Canadian Perspective.* Scarborough: Prentice Hall Canada, 1998, Chapter 12.

Garreau, Joel. *The Nine Nations of North America.* Boston: Houghton Mifflin, 1981.

Goble, Dale D., and Paul W. Hirt, eds. *Northwest Lands, Northwest Peoples: Readings in Environmental History.* Seattle: University of Washington Press, 1999.

Hammond, Paul E. *Guide to Geology of the Cascade Range: Portland, Oregon, to Seattle, Washington.* Washington, D.C.: American Geophysical Union, 1989.

Harris, Cole [Richard Colebrook Harris]. *The Resettlement of British Columbia: Essays on Colonialism and Geographical Change.* Vancouver: University of British Columbia Press, 1997.

Hume, Stephen, Alexandra Morton, Betty Keller, et al. *A Stain upon the Sea: West Coast Salmon Farming.* Madeira Park, B.C.: Harbour Publishing, 2004.

Jackson, Philip, and Jon Kimerling, eds. *Atlas of the Pacific Northwest,* 9th ed, Corvallis: Oregon State University Press, 2003.

Johannessen, Carl L., William A. Davenport, Artimus Millet, and Steven McWilliams "The Vegetation of the Williamette Valley." *Annals of the Association of American Geographers* 61, no. 2 (June 1971): 286–302.

Mackie, Richard. *Trading beyond the Mountains: The British Fur Trade on the Pacific, 1793–1843.* Vancouver: University of British Columbia Press, 1997.

Manning, Richard. *Inside Passage: A Journey beyond Borders.* Washington, D.C.: Island Press, 2001.

McKee, Bates. *Cascadia: The Geologic Evolution of the Pacific Northwest.* New York: McGraw Hill, 1972.

Montgomery, Charles. "Futureville." *Canadian Geographic* 126, no. 3 (May–June 2006): 44–60.

Robb, James, J., ed. *Atlas of the New West.* New York: Norton, 1997.

Robbins, William G. *Landscapes of Promise: The Oregon Story, 1800–1940.* Seattle: University of Washington Press, 1997.

Weisheit, Ralph A. *Domestic Marijuana: A Neglected Industry.* New York: Greenwood Press, 1992.

Williams, Hill. *The Restless Northwest: A Geological Story.* Pullman: Washington State University, 2002.

Wood, Colin J. B., ed. *British Columbia, The Pacific Province: Geographical Essays.* Victoria, B.C.: Western Geographical Press, 2001.

Internet Sources

David Suzuki Foundation, at http://www.davidsuzuki.org/.

Ecotopia, at http://www.ecotopia.com/.

New Scientist, Farmed salmon issues, at http://www.newscientist.com/search?doSearch=true&query=farmed+salmon.

Bureau of Planning and Sustainability, Portland, Oregon, at http://www.portlandonline.com/bps/index.cfm?.

Sightline Institute, at http://www.sightline.org/.

State of Jefferson History. at http://www.jeffersonstate.com/jeffersonstory.html.

Metro Vancouver, at http://www.metrovancouver.org/Pages/default.aspx.

1 About 1,200 seasonal employees live and work at the Unisea fish processing plant in Dutch Harbor.

2 Kotzebue is an indigenous trading post located 30 miles north of the Arctic Circle.

3 Spruce bark beetles have killed millions of trees in Alaska and the Yukon.

Beringia

Shishmaref

Nome

Bering Sea

Pribolof Islands

Dutch Harbor

Aleutian Islands

Seward Peninsula

Yukon River

Arctic Slope

Brooks Range

Prudhoe Bay

Arctic National Wildlife Refuge

Fairbanks

Mt. McKinley

Alaska Range

Anchorage

Kenai Peninsula

Prince William Sound

Chugach Mts

Alaska Pipeline

Yukon

Klondike

Whitehorse

Tongass National Forest

Alexander Archipelago

Juneau

7 Many caribou are killed for their antlers alone; 500,000 of them migrate between Canada and Alaska.

5 The Inside Passage between Seattle and Alaska was once used by gold seekers, now by cruise ships.

6 Turnagain has the second-highest tidal fluctuation in the world.

4 Skagway, Alaska, entrance to Klondike Gold Rush National Historical Park, is almost entirely dependent on cruise ship tourism.

18
ALASKA, PACIFIC BORDERLANDS, AND ARCTIC BOREAL CANADA
Feeling the Heat

Chapter Highlights

After reading this chapter you should be able to:

- Label on a map the Alaskan subregions and Canadian territories and subregions
- Identify the location of the Pacific panhandle, boreal forest, and Arctic Slope
- Identify and discuss the Aleutian Islands
- Explain why Alaska and the North are called the bellwethers of global warming
- Explain the relationship of Inuit to the land and how westernization has changed it
- Describe population trends in Alaska and the Canadian Territories since 1960
- Discuss the importance of the primary economy in the North
- Describe the mining industry in the Arctic regions
- Explain the importance of the various fishing industries in Alaska and the Canadian North

Terms

Aboriginal	caribou	James Bay and Northern
archipelago	Dene	Quebec Agreement
Berger Inquiry	ice roads	lichen
bush	Inuit	Mackenzie Valley Pipeline
cache	island arc	muskeg
	isostatic rebound	oil sands
		permafrost

seismic line
subsistence economy
syncretism
territory (Canadian)
thaw lake
White Paper on Indian Policy

Places

Aleutian Islands	Brooks Range	Mackenzie River	Ring of Fire
Alexander Archipelago	Canadian Shield	Mount McKinley	Seward Peninsula
Anchorage	Dutch Harbor	North Slope	Shishmaref
Arctic Circle	Fort McMurray	Northwest Passage	Tongass National Forest
Arctic National Wildlife	Iqaluit	Northwest Territory	Whitehorse
Refuge (ANWR)	James Bay Project	Nunavik	Yellowknife
Bering Sea	Kenai Peninsula	Nunavut	Yukon
	Klondike	Prince William Sound	Yukon River
	La Grande River	Prudhoe Bay	

PHOTO 18.1. Tormented Valley, Northern British Columbia. This glacially scraped landscape along the Klondike Highway to the Yukon is pockmarked with lakes and wetlands. The 2,800-foot elevation is just above tree line, so the only trees that grow are stunted.

Introduction

Alaska and Northern Canada's territories—Yukon, Northwest Territory, and Nunavut—were home to **Aboriginal**[1] peoples who adapted to the harsh environment for thousands of years before the late-eighteenth-century arrival of Europeans. The indigenous Arctic population hibernated, migrated, and learned how to resist the cold. The Aboriginals used local resources to establish a healthy way of life. The Europeans arrived seeking to exploit the natural resources. Resource extraction began with animal resources and escalated to mineral and energy resources. The industrial expansion left the finely honed Aboriginal culturally assaulted and fragmented. The long-term and sustainable culture was devastated.

The first European interlopers arrived to exploit beaver and sea otters. The Russians (otters) and Hudson's Bay Company (beaver) annihilated these resources and then sold off the "worthless" land to the United States and Canada respectively. However, in the twentieth century, abundant natural resources—lumber, fish, oil, and diamonds—vindicated the American and Canadian purchases. The exploitation continued.

The resources have enriched both countries for the short term, but climate change and its effect on the indigenous population presents a new shared experience for the two countries, one which has the potential to be the largest Canadian-American disaster in history. Rising sea levels, permafrost melt, and receding glaciers have assaulted the northern latitudes, making them the bellwether "canary in the [climate change] coal mine" region. The first people affected by climate change are those who did not cause it.

The indigenous peoples' traditions, already weakened by Western intrusion, are now further endangered, as the effects of climate change destroy villages and undermine traditional hunting practices. Yet the governments have been slow to recognize and act upon these new threats, leaving indigenous groups in peril.

Alaska

Aleutian Natives, the Unangan, named Alaska the "great land," referring to the large mainland in relation to the much smaller Aleutian Islands.[2] Alaska is one-fifth the size of the entire contiguous United States, and it is also great in its expansive, raw beauty. Resource exploitation progressed from furs to gold to oil, and it still provides 80 percent of Alaska's revenue.

America caught a glimpse of the Alaskan mind-set from the 2008 Republican vice-presidential candidate. The "drill, baby, drill" governor of Alaska expressed a dominant Alaskan dream of resource extraction without any care for the environmental damage it might cause. But it also indicates social inequity, the desperation of people who have little other economy to replace their former subsistent lifestyle. "Drill, baby, drill" equates to "Jobs, baby, jobs." Jobs are important, and more so when unemployed. However, continuing to create jobs for economic reasons alone is a sure path to destruction. The jobs of the future need to support the triple bottom line economy.

Canadian Territories

The northern wilderness Canadian territories differ from the rest of Canada in two ways: the sparse population is largely Aboriginal, and the economy revolves around resources. The Aboriginal population and settlement have historically been sustainable. However, during the second half of the twentieth century, the federal government contorted Aboriginal lives to

BOX 18.1 GOOD FRIDAY EARTHQUAKE, 1964

Prince William Sound, Alaska, was rocked by a four-minute earthquake registering 9.2 on the Richter scale at 5:30 in the evening, March 26, 1964 (Good Friday). The earthquake released tectonic pressure, offset the land surface by as much as thirty-eight feet, and caused a tsunami.

Prince William Sound, a sheltered body of water within the Gulf of Alaska, is filled with glacially formed fjords and islands. Within the sound is the town of Whittier, home port to cruise ships bound for Anchorage. The sound is also the terminus of the Alaskan Pipeline (Valdez). The intensely faulted sound has been deformed several times over millennia, attested to by numerous rock fractures, the uplift of the adjacent Chugach Mountains, and earthquake activity.

Damage from the 1964 quake was extensive, ranging from landslides to avalanches to severe destruction in populated areas. Considering the magnitude of the quake, relatively few people died (130), which was attributed to the overall sparse population, holiday timing, and wooden buildings. Most of the deaths were caused by the tsunami, which struck coastal areas of Alaska, Oregon, and California.

Anchorage, seventy-five miles northwest of the epicenter, lost large buildings, such as the J.C. Penney store and the local high school. Nearer the epicenter, the small town of Portage dropped eight feet below the high tide level and was subsequently abandoned. Over time the encroaching seawater killed conifers and cottonwoods, leaving behind a "ghost forest" (Photo 18.2).

PHOTO 18.2. Portage, Alaska, and Its Ghost Forest after the 1964 Earthquake.

---

simulate southern Canadian lives. The seminomadic Aboriginal life, developed over millennia and fitting the environment, was scrapped and replaced with permanent communities, compulsory education, social programs, and an economy that disregarded the fragile landscape and subsistence cultures.

Modern conveniences—rifles, metal knives, and snowmobiles—have seduced the Aboriginal cultures. Few Natives could refuse the temptations, but modernity is a poor fit for replacing the Aboriginal economy, lifestyle, or cultures honed in this harsh climate. By the late 1970s, the devastation of the Aboriginal lifestyle was recognized by the Ottawa-based federal government, and in an attempt to retain some semblance of a healthy culture, treaties and agreements granted Native groups more sovereignty and created several autonomous regions.

Physical Geography

The northern regions may be divided into three broad landscapes:

- the Pacific borderlands of British Columbia, Alaska, and the Aleutians
- the boreal forest, or taiga, cutting a swath across the continent from Labrador to the Bering Sea
- the Arctic Slope tundra in the northernmost region

Pacific Borderlands

From the Alaskan Panhandle to the western end of the Aleutians, coastal mountains hem in the Pacific Borderland region. Two physical forces—tectonics and glaciers—molded this region: The faulting thrust of colliding tectonic plates built mountains, and glaciers eroded them, leaving behind dramatic fjords and islands. Between the coastline and the turbulent open sea are mountaintop islands of the Alexander Archipelago and the protected Inside Passage. The region is part of the tectonically active Ring of Fire that partially encircles the Pacific Ocean. Some of the largest earthquakes ever recorded have been along the Alaskan coastline.

Aleutian Islands

Extending a thousand miles west beyond mainland Alaska, the Aleutian **archipelago** (large group of islands) separates the Bering Sea from the Northern Pacific Ocean. The volcanic **island arc** delineates the boundary between the North American and Pacific plates (Map 18.1).

Tectonic Activity

The northern part of the Ring of Fire consists of the Aleutian Islands, one of the most tectonically active margins in the world and the scene of powerful earthquakes. The dense Pacific plate subducts beneath the floating North American plate along the deep Aleutian Trench south of the islands. In

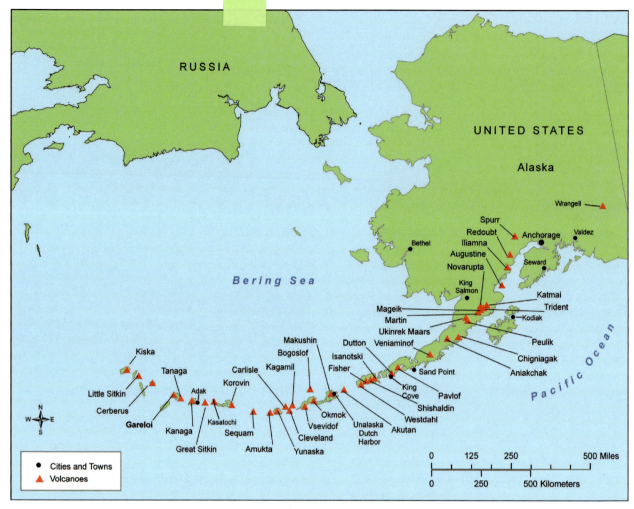

MAP 18.1. The Aleutian Archipelago and Volcanoes. The Aleutians are a volcanically formed chain of islands called an island arc.

the process the oceanic plate, exposed to great pressure and heat, will melt and form magma, which erupts as the Aleutian volcanoes.

Alaskan and Canadian Mountain Ranges

The numerous mountain ranges are divided between the Pacific Borderland mountains, the Alaskan interior, and the Canadian Arctic Cordillera. The Pacific Borderland mountains stretch from the Aleutian archipelago through the Gulf of Alaska, and then south four hundred miles through the Alaskan Panhandle and into the Pacific Northwest.

Glaciers

Most North American glaciers are located along the Pacific Coastal Mountains from Anchorage to Seattle. Alaska's 100,000 glaciers cover 5 percent of the state. Most glaciers form along the relatively warm coastal zone, influenced by ocean currents. Glaciers form when winter snow exceeds summer melting. The Alaskan glacial mass has been shrinking, a telltale sign of global climate change.

Boreal Forest—Taiga

The Canadian boreal forest, the largest contiguous forest remaining on Earth, covers 35 percent of Canada and consti- tutes about 30 percent of the global boreal forest. The boreal forest makes oxygen, distills water, fixes nitrogen, makes com- plex sugars and food, is habitat for hundreds of species, and is a carbon sink that stores some ninety billion tons of carbon. For- ests are more than just wood and trees.

The boreal forest has been called the lungs of the planet, because it offsets the carbon dioxide made by humans and their interventions. The boreal forest is also one of the largest filters of freshwater; peatlands filter water through the area's estimated 1.5 million lakes. Clean, fresh water, breathing forests, and the sequestration of carbon maintain stable atmospheric carbon levels and global temperatures.

The forest extends from Alaska across Canada to Labrador, passing through the western cordillera, the Mackenzie River Valley, across the shield, and dipping south into the Superior Uplands of Michigan, Minnesota, and Wisconsin. Low plateaus and river valleys composed of meadows, peatlands, and barrens form the boreal interior. The Brooks Range (blocking polar weather) and the Alaska Range (blocking Pacific precipitation) shape the taiga climate. The taiga has more snowfall than the Arctic, but less than the Pacific Borderlands.

The eastern boreal forest lies over the exposed Canadian Shield craton. The western forested area continues into the prairie along the Manitoba-Ontario border, follows the northern prairie line into the cordillera of British Columbia and the Yukon Plateau, and then follows the Yukon River drainage basin through interior Alaska.

The exploitation of lumber, oil, gas, and minerals supports taiga cities—Fairbanks, Alaska; Dawson and Whitehorse, Yukon; Yellowknife, Northwest Territory; Fort McMurray, Alberta; and Sudbury, Ontario.

Permafrost

Permafrost (ground that is continually frozen for at least two years) underlies more than two-thirds of Alaska and all Canadian territories (Map 18.2). Permafrost is up to half a mile thick in the north, but the thickness decreases to the south. Low-lying and very fragile vegetation protect and insulate the permafrost. Most permafrost is overlain by an active layer of soil, which freezes in winter but thaws each summer. The low-lying bogs and ponds called **thaw lakes** are formed when the top layer of the permafrost melts, because the water cannot seep into the frozen ground below. The lakes are a water source for vegetation and fauna in a region with little precipitation.

A sign of climate change in the bellwether northern latitudes is the discharge of greenhouse gas (GHG) as permafrost melts. For example, as permafrost thaws due to climate change, carbon sinks release potent GHG into the atmosphere, creating a positive (amplifying) feedback loop that in turn further increases global warming, as well as increasing wildfires and insect outbreaks.[3] The permafrost thaws because of increased CO_2 in the atmosphere, releasing methane, which in turn causes more warming, which releases more methane—and the cycle, the positive feedback loop, goes on and on.

The melting permafrost has several disadvantages, including shorter development seasons for oil and gas exploration and drilling; changing ecosystems; and the loss of biodiversity, Native villages, and traditional lifestyles.

Canadian Shield

The Canadian Shield, whose core is 80 percent igneous granite, spreads across six provinces and territories (Newfoundland, Quebec, Ontario, Manitoba, Nunavut, and the Northwest Territory), composing over 40 percent of Canada's total land area (Map 18.3). The horseshoe-shaped landmass around Hudson Bay, extends across the taiga of the eastern provinces, and ends near the eastern Manitoba border. It also stretches north through the Arctic archipelago and south into the Adirondacks of New York.

The ancient shield was once a mountain range, but numerous glaciations removed soil; reduced the mountains to a rough, rolling landscape; and left millions of pothole depressions that became lakes and wetlands. Glacial movement formed hills and mounds of till, sand, and gravel, which are sometimes capable of agricultural production but are usually just cold marshes.

The Hudson Bay and its lowlands extend along the southwestern edge of Ontario and into Manitoba near Churchill. The bay is experiencing **isostatic rebound** since last glaciated and is calculated to resurge another three hundred feet, causing most of the shallow bay to be aboveground in the next ten thousand years or so. The lowland surrounding the bay is a **muskeg** (a permafrost region dominated by an undrained, spongy sphagnum moss and a few stunted trees) with only a few small settlements, the largest being Churchill, Manitoba (pop. 1,000), an old Hudson Bay trading post. Recently, Churchill has become a conservation site for that harbinger of climate change—polar bears. While the theory of polar bear demise is controversial, it appears that as the temperature warms it reduces snow and ice cover and limits access to the bear's preferred diet, ringed seal.[4]

The Canadian Shield rock has been both hindrance and advantage. The rugged shield landscape obstructed travel and

Treeline
Continuous
Discontinuous
Patchy

MAP 18.2. North American Permafrost. The dotted line is the current Arctic tree line, the northernmost latitude capable of supporting tree growth. Farther north is too cold for the sap lifeline to continue flowing, and permafrost can halt root growth.

BOX 18.2 NORTHERN MOUNTAIN RANGES

Alaska

Six Pacific mountain ranges—the Coast Mountains, St. Elias, the Fairweather Range, Wrangell, Chugach, and the Alaska Range—are thrust together along the coastal arc of Alaska. In the interior, the Brooks Range divides the boreal interior from the Arctic Slope.

Coast Mountains

The one-hundred-mile wide Coast Mountains rim the Pacific and extend north from British Columbia through Alaska's Panhandle. The metamorphic mountains drop precipitously into the Pacific Ocean in deeply indented fjords cut by glaciers and rivers. The temperate rain-forest territory is one of the wettest places in North America. Portions of the Coast Mountains are within Alaska's Tongass National Forest.

St. Elias

Located at the oceanic arc where Alaska and the Yukon meet, the coastal St. Elias Range is the root of two other ranges; to the north is the Wrangell and to the south is the Fairweather. The St. Elias, the highest coastal range in the world, features Mount Logan (19,550 feet), the highest Canadian mountain.

The St. Elias Range also has the largest ice field in Alaska, the Malaspina, larger than Rhode Island (at 850 square miles) and fed by more than twenty-five glaciers.

Fairweather Range

Captain George Vancouver named the peninsular Fairweather Range in 1778 when he encountered them on a rare fair-weather day. In reality, the range has some of the worst weather, including over one hundred inches of precipitation. The peninsula is a southern continuation of the St. Elias Mountains. The Fairweather Range, located southwest of Glacier Bay—a frozen, impenetrable bay when Vancouver first sailed by—is testament to the effects of global warming since that time. The frozen bay Vancouver found has receded more than sixty-five miles. Cruise ships on glacier tours now venture into the bay to view deeply fjorded rock walls and sixteen tidal glaciers.

Wrangell

The rugged, volcanic Wrangell Mountains, the northern extension of the St. Elias Mountains, are nested between the Coastal Chugach to the south and the high ranging Alaska Range to the north and west. The active shield volcano Mount Wrangell (14,163 feet) last erupted in 1902. Glaciers cover the higher elevations of the Wrangell Range. The caldera of Mount Wrangell contains more snow and ice than any other active volcano in the world, and if another eruption should occur it would melt and create huge floods and mudslides.

Chugach

The Chugach Mountains form a coast-hugging crescent from the Wrangell Mountains to near Valdez, where they continue as the Kenai Mountains westward through the Kenai Peninsula. The claim to fame of these thickly forested mountains is ample precipitation in the form of snow. At higher elevations, the range has set world records with over six hundred inches of snow annually.

Alaska Range

Dividing the coast from the colder interior plateau, the heavily glaciated Alaska Range extends for about four hundred miles. The young system has twenty peaks exceeding 10,000 feet and is capped by Mount McKinley (Denali), the highest peak in North America (20,300 feet). East of Mount McKinley, the range divides the Yukon and Pacific drainage basins. The extreme weather on the mountains is augmented by the location between the warmer coastal region and the colder interior continental regime.

Brooks Range

Dividing the Arctic North from the continental interior of Alaska, the Brooks Range trends east to west from the Chukchi Sea, north of the Bering Strait, into the Yukon. At seven thousand to nine thousand feet, they are the highest mountains within the Arctic Circle.

The Brooks Range, which some call an extension of the Rocky Mountains, has relatively little snowfall, and although severely glaciated historically, the scant snow today has hindered glacial development. The high-latitude location makes for a short growing season (less than forty days). Stunted trees can be found along the south slope, but throughout the range sparse tundra vegetation is most common.

Canada

The Canadian North is occupied by the Arctic Cordillera, consisting of the multiple ranges of the Innuitian Mountains along the northern edges of Nunavut and the Northwest Territory and the Torngat Mountains of northern Labrador and Quebec. The Arctic Cordillera is located north of the Arctic tree line. The economic impact of the Arctic Cordillera has been limited because of its extreme northern location and remoteness. Most minerals, while present, will probably not be exploited until southern resources are exhausted.

BOX 18.3 DID YOU KNOW . . . TUNDRA AND TAIGA

- The word *tundra* comes from a Finnish word meaning "barren land."
- Tundra is the youngest biome, approximately ten thousand years old.
- Tundra is about 20 percent of the Earth's surfaces and circumnavigates the North Pole.
- The tundra is a region of continuous permafrost .
- The Inuit live in the tundra and the Dene (Athabascan) live in the taiga.
- Taiga and tundra have no landform dividing them. They are divided by the 50°F July isotherm in the warmest month.
- *Taiga* is a Russian word for "forest." *Taiga* and *boreal forest* are synonymous. *Boreal* means north.
- Taiga is the largest biome in the world.

- The taiga permafrost is continuous in the north and discontinuous in the south.
- Taiga is the largest North American region.
- Taiga is a forested area, largely populated with needle-leaf varieties.
- Taiga is home to the caribou herds of Canada, and resource exploitation has caused them to retreat as they decrease in numbers.
- The many insects of the taiga attract migrating birds during breeding.
- Pulp mills and seismic lines have been laid throughout the taiga, fragmenting forest areas and wildlife.
- The tundra and the taiga are the first ecoregions to be severely affected by climate change.

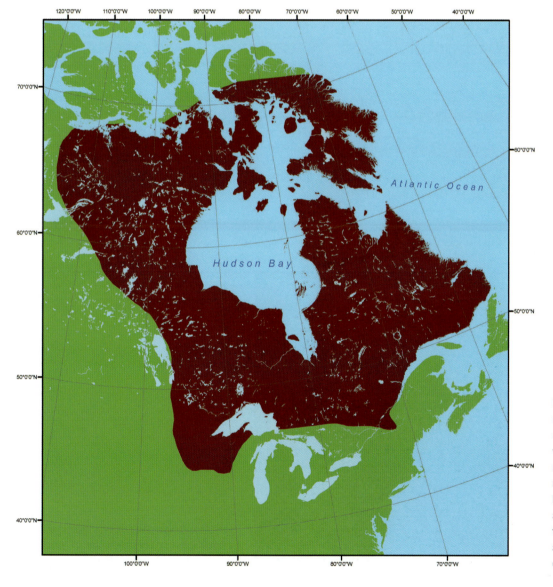

MAP 18.3. The Canadian Shield has the oldest rocks in the world, and they have remained permanently above sea level. The last ice ages created more than a million lakes and removed much of the soil.

BOX 18.4 CLIMATE CHANGE AND THE TAIGA

Climate change has caused terrestrial vegetation to shift from tundra to taiga in far less time than originally theorized. The shift was expected to take much longer than a 1993 model forecast of a 150-year response time from tundra to taiga and has altered estimates of the impact of the present global climate change and its possible effects.*

The biological effects of the transition are also not proceeding as theorized. Climate change was expected to extend the range of the boreal forest north, but also to extend the season of the existing boreal forest. Instead of growing healthier, the forest has been browning, suffering disease infestations and more fires and slowing growth.† This was expected eventually, but not within a decade of the original theory about high-latitude growth. One result of these disturbances is decreased carbon dioxide absorption. The carbon sink of the forest would be less efficient, and it would instigate a reinforcing feedback loop: The more the forest did not absorb carbon dioxide, the faster it would warm.‡

---

* Glen M. MacDonald, Tom W. D. Edwards, Katrina A. Moser, et al., "Rapid Response of Tree Line Vegetation and Lakes to Past Climate Warming," *Nature* 361 (January 1993): 243–46.

† Jonathan T. Overpeck, David Rind, and Richard Goldberg, "Climate-Induced Changes in Forest Disturbance and Vegetation." *Nature* 343 (January 1990): 51–53.

‡ Holli Riebeek, Holli, "Forest on the Threshold," 2006, at http://earthobservatory.nasa.gov/Study/BorealThreshold/.

exploration from Ontario to the western provinces, until the granitic rock was blasted out while building the transcontinental railroad in the 1880s (Photo 18.3). In the twenty-first century, as natural resource mining in temperate areas was exhausted or became unprofitable, the shield has been exploited for resources.

Arctic Slope—Tundra

The Arctic Plain is a paradox. Literally a desert, this inhospitable land receives less than six inches of precipitation annually, yet it is also classified as a permafrost wetland because of its low evaporation rate. The region extends from northern Quebec's Canadian Shield (Ungava Peninsula) to the Arctic Slope of Alaska, interrupted only by the Hudson Bay and the Mackenzie Delta.

Limited plants, sluggish drainage, lakes, marshes, and resources define the fragile permafrost environment above the Arctic tree line. Fragile vegetation hugs the relatively warm ground, avoiding the colder air temperatures. The plants have adapted to the Arctic environment by retaining leaves through winter so that in spring they may photosynthesize sunlight as soon as possible. The moss, fungal **lichen**, and grass vegetation in the active layer of permafrost can support small herbivores and large, migratory animal populations, such as **caribou**, although the extreme climate and vegetation variety limit the ecosystem. Beyond the 70th parallel, even tundra vegetation becomes scarce, and the land is barren.

Across the tundra landscape, ice-cored *pingos* (an Inuit word for small hill) appear to be small volcanoes, but they are frost-heaved mounds caused by frozen water expanding and pushing up the soil. They are most prevalent along the Mackenzie River delta.

The northernmost Arctic includes a sea ice cap and the Arctic Archipelago on the continental shelf. Farther north,

PHOTO 18.3. Canadian Shield, Ontario. Shield rock is some of the oldest rock in the world. This part of the craton was heavily glaciated and is covered by a thin soil layer.

the Arctic cordillera includes the remote Innuitian Mountains, hovering over the extreme northern islands. The Arctic ice cap encased the polar region during the modern era, but its melting has become a harbinger of climate change. Since the 1970s, the Arctic ice cap has shrunk approximately 30 percent. Ice thickness in the Northwest Passage has declined between 4 and 10 percent per decade; the ice is melting at the rate of 9 percent per decade.[5] By 2007, the Northwest Passage shipping lanes and fishing grounds were open and predictions were for an ice-free Arctic within a decade.

In 2007, Canadian Prime Minister Stephen Harper claimed that the long-sought northwest passage was open, as was part of Canadian waters. Other countries claim them as international waters,[6] seeking possible oil and mineral rights.

Water

Water is plentiful in the north. Shifting glacial drainage patterns have left a landscape with seemingly more water than land. Permafrost prevents water from percolating downward, and therefore it lies on the surface and creates impassable muskegs during the brief summer period. During the winter, the frozen landscape becomes more accessible. In the past, Natives used dog sleds, but today's transportation options range from riding snowmobiles to driving ice roads.

Freshwater covers about 9 percent of Canada's landmass, making it one of the world's largest freshwater reservoirs. Canadian rivers discharge 7 percent of the world's renewable water supply. Twenty-five percent of the world's wetlands cover about 14 percent of Canada's land area.

Rivers

The Arctic North has two major rivers—the Mackenzie and the Yukon—and many smaller rivers, as well as millions of lakes. Additionally, the Anchorage complex depends on the Susitna River, which rises from the Susitna glacier in the Alaska Range and flows into Cook Inlet west of Anchorage. Alaska's populated area near Anchorage depends on local agriculture from the glacially derived silt deposited by the Susitna, Matanuska, and Knik rivers in the Matanuska-Susitna Valley (Photo 18.4).

Alaska

Yukon River   The two-thousand-mile-long Yukon River, the third longest in America, has headwaters in northern British Columbia and flows through Whitehorse and Dawson City, Yukon Territory, before turning west through Alaska's interior into the Bering Sea. Many of Alaska's rivers are Yukon tributaries.

During the gold rush era and until the Alaska Highway opened in the 1940s, the Yukon served as a transport link between Whitehorse and the Bering Sea. More recently, the Yukon is a popular sporting river for canoeing, kayaking, and fishing.

The river has served as a transport artery between interior villages and a crazy-quilt ice highway during the winter. Extreme winter temperatures freeze the river. The river's course is altered

each time the ice breaks at a weak point; the water spreads across the flat river plain until it too freezes, causing huge ice buildups.

Copper River   The salmon-rich Copper River begins at a Wrangell Mountain glacier and flows south into the Gulf of Alaska east of Cordova. The Copper drains much of the Wrangell and Chugach ranges. The river's ecological variations shape vegetation. For example, the lack of nutrients in glacial soil limits the forest vegetation to black spruce.[7] As an organic mat accumulates, it promotes other deciduous species and moss growth.[8]

Canada

Mackenzie River   The Mackenzie River, also called Deh Cho by the local Athabascans (who call themselves the **Dene**), is the longest river in Canada and the world's tenth largest (Map 18.4). It channels one-fifth of Canada's water supply and is almost unique among the world's largest rivers because it has no major dams or diversions along its course.

The Mackenzie flows north through various ecoregions from the glacial meltwater–fed Great Slave Lake in the Northwest Territories into the Arctic Ocean. The southern headwaters are within temperate coniferous forests but flow north through the boreal forest/taiga to the tundra at its mouth. The taiga extends farther north as the river flows through the protected river valley. But permafrost and Arctic climatic extremes leave the trees skinny; their branches reach only a foot or so beyond their trunks and the trees are heaved in odd directions; they are known locally as the "drunken forest."

The Mackenzie basin was the Dene homeland for ten thousand years before fur trappers arrived in the nineteenth century. Since the 1920s, the Mackenzie has been an oil-producing region, but in the twenty-first century the much larger Mackenzie Project will produce both energy and a new Aboriginal rights policy (see below).

Hydropower   Hydro-Québec generates two-thirds of Canada's electricity and produces 13 percent of the world's hydropower.[9] The drop in elevation from the Canadian Shield into Hudson Bay and its drainage basin has more potential for hydropower than anywhere else in the country. The La Grande River hydropower project, part of the James Bay Project (see below), lies in the remote Quebec side of James Bay.

Lakes

Alaska

Alaska has thousands of lakes that range from uncultivated, sparsely settled **bush** lakes used for fishing expeditions to thaw lakes along the Arctic coastal plain. Thaw lakes are the major surface feature on the coastal plain and may be a help (sequestering carbon) or hindrance (releasing CO_2 into the atmosphere) as they are affected by climate change. What happens to the lakes will also affect the vegetation, fauna, and human habitats of the region.

The largest of Alaska's many lakes is Iliamna Lake (1,033 square miles), southwest of the Cook Inlet. Accessible only by

BOX 18.5 CARIBOU, REINDEER OF THE AMERICAS

The ungulate caribou roam throughout the Yukon, Northwest Territories, and eastern Alaska. Similar to Eurasian reindeer, caribou are larger, and both males and females have antlers. Caribou have genetically adapted to the Arctic environment. Their hooves are shaped to walk on the tundra and act as shovels digging out their diet of edible grasses. Caribou skin has air cells insulating them from the cold; their fur is structured to repel blizzards, making them waterproof and buoyant for Arctic Ocean migrations between islands and the mainland.* Textile and clothing companies are learning through biomimicry about caribou genetic adaptations so they can incorporate the knowledge into their products.†

Subsistence indigenous and western hunters hunt caribou as a source of food. In the early twentieth century, twenty to fifty million caribou roamed the Arctic, but in 2011, herd size was estimated at 378,000; despite strict controls, the herd continues to diminish. Environmental issues limiting caribou herds include reduction in grazing land, large-scale oil exploration, and global warming. For example, global warming can upset island caribou migration patterns; they swim each year from islands to the mainland when ice melts; climate change means freezing times change, thus making the passage treacherous.

The caribou presence on the Arctic Slope has been contested in an ongoing debate between environmentalists, oil companies, and the local population. The Porcupine caribou herd uses the coastal plains of the Arctic National Wildlife Refuge (ANWR) for spring migration calving because of the nutritious moss and lichens. It is possible that oil-company drilling will upset the coastal plain and thereby disturb or destroy the caribou calving area. The debate is answered by widely varying responses, and further complicated by the herd migrating each year to the best location for forage and snow cover, regardless of politics.

* P. Soppela, M. Nieminen, and J. Timisjàrvi, "Thermoregulation in Reindeer," *Rangifer* 1 (1986): 273–78; Sally Foy, Oxford Scientific Films, *The Grand Design: Form and Colour in Animals*. Lingfield, UK: BLA Publishing for J. M. Dent & Sons, Aldine House, London, 1982.

† http://www.biomimicryguild.com/guild_service_reference_09_10.pdf; http://www.patagonia.com/us/patagonia.go?assetid=2063; http://www.etracc.net/index.php?module=16&m=10&ttimes=15.

PHOTO 18.4. The Braided Susitna River, North of Anchorage, Alaska. Glacial braided rivers deposit gravel from one side to the other, creating new channels; thus the river continually changes its flow pattern. The Susitna's fluctuating discharge and variable sediment loads braid the glacially carved river and have formed broad floodplains.

MAP 18.4. The Mackenzie River is the longest in Canada and the tenth largest in the world.

air or water, the bush lake is known for its scenery, incredible fishing, and possibly a nearby large and controversial gold and copper mine. Studies are being done to see if a sustainable fishery can exist with a large-scale mining operation. For example, the mine would require roads, which would interfere with salmon spawning sites and with a caribou herd's territory and calving site.[10] The lake has been a site for scientific research that aims to understand the systems dynamics of the remote lake, polluted by industrial PCBs. Results from this work reveal the interrelationships between the industrial world and remote Alaskan lakes.[11]

Turnagain Arm The Cook Inlet separates the mainland from the Kenai Peninsula. At its head, the inlet splits into Turnagain and Knik arms, which have the second-highest tidal variations after the Bay of Fundy. During low tide, the bottom of the silt-laden Turnagain Arm becomes an exposed quicksand-like mudflat and is subject to a strong and treacherous tidal bore. Turnagain Arm was named by Captain Cook, who "turned again" to exit another failed attempt at finding the northwest passage (Map 18.5).

Canada

Canada has more than two million glacial meltwater lakes, especially in the glacially scoured, poorly drained north, where water acreage may exceed land. The Northwest Territory has both the largest (Great Bear at 12,095 square miles) and deepest (Great Slave) lakes in the country. Quebec's shield contains a million lakes and also has more waterways than any other region in Canada.

Climate

Arctic and subarctic climates dominate. The dividing line between Arctic and subarctic conditions is defined as:

1. The region where the average July temperature is 50°F (10°C)
2. The area where the vegetation taiga gives way to tundra
3. The place where cold and short growing seasons no longer support the growth of trees

This climatic dividing line follows the northeastern edge of the Great Bear and Great Slave lakes and continues upward to

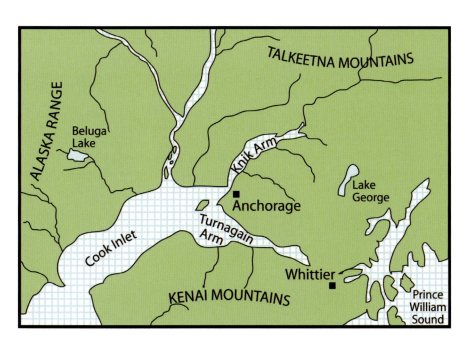

MAP 18.5. Cook Inlet. Anchorage sits at the point where Cook Inlet separates into the Knik Arm and Turnagain Arm. The Anchorage metropolitan area depends on water from the Susitna, Matanuska, and Knik rivers.

the Arctic coastal slope. The Arctic begins more or less where the annual mean air temperature is 14°F (–10°C), which is close to the northern limits of trees.

The Arctic and interior regions are colder than the Pacific Borderlands, which are warmed by the Kuroshio/Alaska Current. The Pacific Borderlands temperatures and precipitation patterns keep the weather mild in winter and cool in summer (Table 18.1). The warm Kuroshio Current flows to southeastern Alaska, where it splits (Map 18.6). The northern arm, renamed the Alaska Current, flows toward the Gulf of Alaska. Winds pick up the warm air, carry it to the mountains, and condense the water vapor, which results in heavy precipitation and the creation of Alaska's snowiest region. The Aleutian Low, where the Kuroshio Current meets the cold Bering Sea water, is the birthplace of Pacific storms, which follow prevailing winds tracking from west to east along the Aleutian archipelago.

The Arctic interior has a continental climate with extreme seasonal temperatures, because the Alaska and Brooks mountain ranges block the interior of Alaska from moderating maritime influences. Long, dark, cold winters and rainy Pacific air masses dominate most of the year. Summers are short and warm. The mosquito-filled summer temperatures can rise to 100°F (38°C) north of the Arctic Circle (latitude 66°32' N), where the sun never sets from May until August and never rises during winter. Across Canada, the boreal forest interior experiences similar weather conditions and poor drainage, resulting in an expansive area of marshes and bogs.

The Arctic Slope has cold, dry air with scant annual precipitation, making it a polar desert; snowfall stays on the ground most of the year, broken only in the heart of summer when continuous daylight melts the snow and stimulates vegetation. The Arctic Ocean keeps the coastal areas colder during the summer, but during the long, dark winter the frozen-over ocean provides heat, because it is warmer than the ground.

Climate Change

Americans have been alerted to the dangers of global warming so many times that volumes have been written just on the history of efforts to draw attention to the problem.

—Elizabeth Kolbert, *The New Yorker*, April 2005

Things are melting pretty fast around here. Climate change has become one of the major new themes for this park.

—Jim Ireland, chief ranger for Kenai Fjords, August 14, 2005

The North is the harbinger of climate change. Over the past forty years, the average Arctic atmospheric temperature has warmed 3.5°F to 5°F (1.5°C to 3°C) versus the 1°F (0.6°C) worldwide average. Scientific evidence of warming has left few doubting the changing climate, although the U.S. and Canadian governments have reacted to these changes differently. Despite intense research confirming climate change, the United States has been in denial for many years, while Canadian public policy has been more accepting, though not entirely. Examples of the U.S. denial can be seen in the fact that the United States did not sign the Kyoto Protocol, or in the crumbling climate change initiatives—cap and trade, and a renewable energy standard. In 2007, Canada reneged on its Kyoto promise and implemented a new program, "Turning the Corner," with less demanding requirements to reduce global warming.[12]

TABLE 18.1. Alaska and Canadian Territories Average Weather Conditions

	January (°F)	July (°F)	Annual precipitation (inches)
Anchorage, Alaska	14.9	58.4	15.9
Barrow, Alaska	−13.4	45	5
Fairbanks, Alaska	−10.1	62.5	10.9
Juneau, Alaska	24.2	56	54.3
Iqaluit, Nunavut	−13	46	16.2
Resolute, Nunavut	−23	39	5
Whitehorse, Yukon	0	57	10.5
Yellowknife, Northwest Territory	−17	62	11
Unalaska, Aleutian Islands (Alaska)	36	54	57

Source: http://www.climate-zone.com/climate/united-states/alaska/; Statistics Canada, at http://www40.statcan.gc.ca/l01/cst01/phys08a-eng.htm

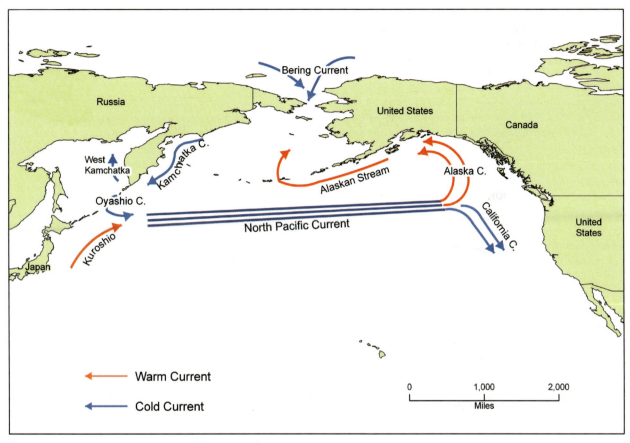

MAP 18.6. Northern Pacific Ocean Currents. Currents that flow along the western edges of oceans are warm, along eastern edges, cold. The Kuroshio Current flows along the western edge of the Pacific and then splits into two currents at the eastern edge. The Alaska Current is warm and moderates the Pacific Borderlands climate.

Source: http://www.pmel.noaa.gov/np/pages/seas/npmap4.html

Climate change has traumatized Arctic and Antarctic glacial regions.[13] In 2004, the Inside Passage, Anchorage, Fairbanks, Nome, and Juneau all recorded their warmest summers. In 2004 in Barrow, Alaska, the northernmost city in the United States, the earliest snow-free day, May 10, was a full forty days earlier than its traditional mid-June average.[14]

Alaska

Unintended Consequences   Climate change is largely due to the dependence on fossil fuels for energy, which has been most prevalent in the heavily populated world south of the Arctic. But the effects of climate change in Alaska and the Canadian Arctic have been responsible for numerous unintended consequences of the Western way of life, including shrinking glaciers, melting permafrost that turns into a miasma of mud, buckling roads and structures, and erosion and flooding in more than 180 Native Arctic villages.

Other effects of climate change range from insect infestations to forest fires and loss of sea life. Forest fires have almost tripled, destroying as many as 2.5 to 7 million acres since 1970. Warmer temperatures have allowed spruce bark beetles on the Kenai Peninsula to reproduce at twice their normal rate. The beetle infestation has resulted in killing nearly 4 million

acres of trees. The infestation has now spread south into Colorado.

Populations of whales, sharks, salmon, and marlins have plummeted 90 percent. The diminishing Arctic sea life and ice cover disrupt Inuit subsistence hunting. Hunters now have to literally tread on thin ice when hunting for seals. Some have changed their mode of transportation from snowmobiles to boats, after unsuspecting snowmobilers have fallen through the fragile ice to their deaths.

Local and Ecoregional Impacts   Climate change has disproportionately affected Alaskan Native villages, perched along river and ocean shores. The permafrost thaw comes earlier each year and wreaks havoc on infrastructure. As the climate warms, damage becomes more widespread and expensive to prevent or repair. Unless specialized building techniques are used, most structures built on permafrost conduct heat into the ground, causing the permafrost to melt. Buildings in permafrost areas should be constructed on pilings or insulated from the frozen ground below the active layer. Elevating buildings on pilings allows air to circulate below them so that the ground remains frozen. Piling construction is more expensive than construction in more temperate regions. But if structures are not properly

BOX 18.6 INUIT VILLAGES AND CLIMATE CHANGE

Two Inuit groups affected by global warming are the Yup'ik and the Inupiaq. Both groups live along the Bering Sea and have been competing for funding to move their villages to safer grounds.

The Yup'ik live along the Bering Sea coastline near the mouth and up the Yukon River. There are about twenty-two thousand living in Alaska, spread between seventy small communities. Prior to Western incursion, the Yup'ik were seminomadic, although regional goods allowed them to be more self-sufficient and permanently settled than the Inupiaq or similar groups.

Newtok, a village of 340 on the Ninglick River near the Bering Sea, is one of the many Native villages where a seasonal camp of the Yup'ik became the permanent settlement in the 1950s because of compulsory education. Permafrost is defrosting and can no longer protect the village from storm surge thaws. Newtok is falling into the river; most buildings are sinking into the ground as the permafrost melts.

In November 2008, the U.S. Marines, Navy Seabees, and other branches of the military agreed to provide assistance to moving the village to higher ground over the succeeding four years. It is hoped that the military-assisted move will cut the high costs.* By 2010,

the first of the infrastructure for a new village located nine miles away was built, with plans to relocate other buildings on barges.

The Inupiaq settled along the Seward Peninsula and the Bering Sea coastline. The group's practice of harpoon hunting brought them in contact with Europeans, whose diseases eventually devastated the Inupiaq. Today's Inupiaq continue to partially subsist on their traditional food sources, but most now live in Western-style permanent villages instead of traditional summer camps and winter semi-subterranean earthen structures.

Shishmaref, located along the northern edge of the Seward Peninsula, has 600 people hoping to move from their permanent settlement. They, like the Yup'ik, were once seminomadic and chose their island location when compulsory schooling became mandatory. Over the past twenty years, storm surges and warmer temperatures have eroded up to three hundred feet of coastline, damaging the village's land and buildings. The natural ice caches where their food is stored have melted, and lives have been lost due to the thinning ice. The Native Inupiaq pleaded for relocation money but have been denied. Estimated costs are over $100 million to move this village.

* http://www.fortmilltimes.com/124/story/344347.html.

constructed, the thawed ground buckles and destroys buildings, roads, and rail lines.

Thawing permafrost has affected numerous Arctic and Bering Sea villages. The ice pack has decreased 2 to 3 percent each decade since the 1970s, handicapping subsistence hunting. Alaska's interior weather has less snow and more rain, affecting hunting habits and age-old cultures.

External Costs   In the United States, climate change has been most evident in Alaska. Many of the Native villages are experiencing infrastructure damage. According to a 2003 General Accounting Report, it would require more than $130 million to relocate each of the 320 Native villages.[15] About 183 of 213 Native villages will require funds for flooding and erosion problems.[16]

Estimates for the cost of replacing public infrastructure alone are between $3 billion and $6 billion by 2030. Moving the villagers will add to the cost. Many people want the villagers to move into public housing in Fairbanks or Anchorage, but the destruction of indigenous cultural life has already taken a large toll in alcoholism, violence, and suicide; villagers want to maintain what they can of their communities and identities.

Canadian North

More than half of Canada lies north of the Arctic Circle, where climate change has been most extreme. In Canada, northern warming is "one of the most significant environmental

challenges the world has ever faced."[17] The Canadian government encourages energy efficiency and conserving fossil fuel resources, even while it mines the profitable **oil sands** in northern Alberta. The foci of Canada's concerns are the past decade's extreme weather (Prairie drought, British Columbia forest fires, the 1998 ice storm, and Hurricane Juan in 2003); an imperiled Aboriginal way of life; and economic costs, particularly to the primary sector industries.

Historical Geography and Settlement

Native Peoples and Initial European Contact

Archaeological and genetic research has extended so-called Clovis migration to the Americas beyond the Bering Land Bridge crossing from approximately thirteen thousand years ago to more than twenty thousand years ago.[18] New theories will continue to hypothesize Amerindian migration patterns. Over time, northern Aboriginal groups grew to include the Arctic Inuit, the Interior Dene, the Shield Cree, and the Inside Passage Haida and Tlingit.

Arctic Slope

Alaskan and Canadian **Inuit** occupy the Bering Sea and Arctic Ocean coastline. They are linguistically and culturally related to the Inuit of Russia. Arctic Circle natives have lived seminomadic subsistence lives as hunters, fishers, and gatherers

BOX 18.7 KOTZEBUE

The largest and oldest of the Inupiaq villages is on a spit named after a Russian explorer, Kotzebue Sound, but to the Natives the town was *Qikiqtagruk* ("shaped like a long island," matching its appearance). The location—near the Russian mainland, and at the mouth of three rivers, giving it additional interior access—was a logical choice as a trading post, which it was for hundreds of years before Western contact in 1818. Today the population of Kotzebue is 3,201 (2010) of which 74 percent are Inupiaq. It is the trading and transportation center for nearby villages. The economy is centered on mineral and oil production, including the world's largest zinc mine, Red Dog Mine.

Kotzebue depended on polluting and expensive diesel engines for electric power until 1997, when the town constructed the first three wind turbines in Arctic conditions. The bountiful winds scoured the treeless tundra, but Arctic extremes challenged the construction. After extensive research, wind turbines to meet the extremes of Arctic conditions were installed.

By changing the source of energy production, the town reduced air pollutants and greenhouse gases, and saved money. Eventually thirteen turbines were constructed; they saved the town $190,000 annually, and since 2001 have displaced more than 300,000 gallons of diesel fuel. Now diesel is only used when wind energy is insufficient.

The success of the project has encouraged other Arctic villages to study wind power. By the end of 2008, nine remote communities in Alaska had wind power, and additional projects are planned along the rail belt, from Fairbanks to Homer.*

* "There's a Crisp Wind Blowing in Alaska," *Northwest Public Power Association Bulletin*, January 2006.

---

and have successfully adapted to the harsh surroundings with innovations that include the kayak, the dog sled, and the igloo. Today, Inuit retain many traditions, which are perhaps the best manner to live in this extreme region; however, Western appliances such as cable TV, cell phones, and snowmobiles have entered everyday Inuit life and caused cultural disjunction. There has been a trading of cultural information—the Western cultures learn to respect traditional knowledge; the natives learn from the West—but finding a balance of the old and new has caused tumult in the Native cultures.[19]

The Aboriginals of Alaska's Aleutian Islands are called Unangan; they are distant linguistic relatives of the Inuit, from whom they separated roughly ten thousand years ago. Like the Inuit, the Unangan were village-sized tribal groupings of similar cultures, each adapting to their homeland. Historically, Unangan were a sea-hunting culture dependent on the whale, seal, and walrus, which provided them with food, shelter, and clothing. Life on the Aleutian Islands was stressful, dependent on a marine-based diet, and punctuated by regular volcanic eruptions, earthquakes, and long bouts of isolation.

The first European contact for the Unangan was brutal. Russian fur traders enslaved the sea-faring Unangan and forced them to hunt seals and sea otters for the benefit of the Russians. Within a century, 90 percent of the Unangan were dead because of sickness and harsh treatment. The archipelago population was approximately fifteen thousand upon Russian arrival. After years of brutal occupation and deaths from disease, the Unangan population has revived to about 2,000 of the 8,100 living on the islands.[20]

In Canada, most Inuit live in Nunavut Territory. Western trading routes and government programs transformed the Inuit hunting lifestyle. The Canadian government encouraged the seminomadic Inuit to adopt a sedentary lifestyle, which caused an erosion of their traditional hunting practices and survival skills, both of which are important underpinnings of their traditional culture.

Interior

The Dene are composed of many subgroups living in the Alaskan and Canadian boreal forest. Archaeological evidence suggests that all Dene lived in the Mackenzie River area roughly two thousand years ago, when a catastrophe (possibly the White River volcanic eruptions around 310 CE) dispersed the population. The Navajo and Apache, who are linguistically related, moved south from the subarctic into their current homelands, while others dispersed into more local sub-Arctic regions, such as the Slavey near the Great Slave, and the Tli Cho or Dogrib, who live between the Great Bear and Great Slave lakes.

The Dene nomadic hunters and gatherers became dependent on French fur traders. The fur trade and religious missionaries disrupted the Dene lifestyle, and various epidemics and toxins decimated the population. Today, most Dene live in cities or in permanent homes near the trading posts. They have, however, learned to adapt, live, and maintain a sense of cultural uniqueness in the industrialized world.

Pacific Borderlands

The Haida, Tsimshian, and the dominant Tlingit populated the Pacific Borderlands. Salmon dominated the rich natural resources in this temperate environment and supported a more sophisticated and advanced culture than farther north. The culture expressed itself in the practice of artistic crafts, in which they excelled. The Tlingit and Haida, known for their carvings, such as totem poles, were among the first to trade with the Russians and Europeans. Most Tlingit and Haida still live along the Alexander Archipelago, especially near Prince of Wales Island, and continue to fish, work in fish-processing plants, or practice traditional crafts.

Canadian Shield

Aboriginals of the Algonquin (east), Athabascan (west), and Inuit (north) tribal groups populate the shield area of Quebec and the territories. The Athabascans arrived first; Algonquin arrived about eight thousand years ago; and the Inuit, who settled along the northern shore and Hudson Bay, arrived about three thousand years ago. Most Aboriginals still practice traditional activities such as hunting, trapping, and fishing.

Evolution of the Alaskan State

U.S. Presence and Gold

Russia's involvement in the Crimean War weakened its hold on the Alaskan territory, although interest had been already waning due to overfishing. Since the Russians were fighting the British, they chose to sell Alaska to their American allies. Negotiations began in 1854 but were disrupted by the American Civil War. Secretary of State William Seward promptly renegotiated after the war. In 1867, the United States purchased Alaska from the Russians for $7.2 million, a purchase that was derided as "Seward's Folly." While the economics of the sale are no longer derided, the sale of Alaska as a commodity, ignoring the Native peoples, has continued to be questioned.[21] For the first thirty years of U.S. rule, Alaska was left to fend for itself with only a sporadic military presence. Although Seward's goal in purchasing Alaska had more to do with control over the Pacific trade routes, his "folly" was vindicated by the Alaskan and Yukon gold rushes.

From 1867 until statehood in 1959, Alaska was an American territory that was owned and exploited like a colony. The "Alaska Syndicate," a consortium supported by J. P. Morgan, the Guggenheims, and various Seattle enterprises, invested in mining, salmon canning, and steam and rail transportation. Seattle companies still control most of Alaska's salmon and fishing industry.

During the period before statehood, the price of living in Alaska escalated because of discriminatory legislation that favored outside control over the territory and allowed profits to flow out of Alaska, mostly to Seattle. This situation remained until World War II, when many soldiers who had been shipped to Alaska stayed after the war and helped strengthen the movement toward statehood and economic control.

Alaskan statehood was a controversial subject for years, because outside interests insisted the territory was poor and unable to support itself. Upon gaining statehood in 1959, the state, which was required to provide an economic base and financial security, claimed 104 million acres of land along with mineral rights from the federal public domain.

Alaska Native Claims Settlement Act (ANCSA)

Following Alaska's annexation, Native land claims remained in limbo. Although a few congressional bills addressed Native land claims, no specifics were delineated. Native land claims were defined in 1884 as those "actually in their use or occupation or now claimed,"[22] but they were vague, as most Natives were semimigratory and each year ranged over the most advantageous route for their survival (a sustainable tactic), much as the caribou continue to do today. In 1968, the discovery of Prudhoe Bay oil prompted a quick resolution to Native land claims because many Native claims crossed the pipeline route. Passage of the Alaska Native Claims Settlement Act (ANCSA) in 1971 was the largest land claim settlement in U.S. history.

ANCSA settled longtime land claims and helped Native areas develop economically. It gave Alaskan indigenous groups a special identity as shareholders in regional corporations, managing community land and resources while revitalizing their cultures, languages, and identities. Claims stipulated rights to land near the villages, and both hunting and subsurface mineral rights.

The formation of ANCSA was and remains controversial. All Native claims were extinguished, and in return, thirteen ANCSA regional corporations were allocated $962 million and forty-four million acres of state land to develop their resources and become self-sufficient. The formation of these corporations was done without a general vote of tribal groups. Many felt that the regional corporations leaned toward supporting corporate more than tribal interests, and that the timing of ANCSA was forced because of oil development speculations. The political nature of the formation and the continued politics have created varied rates of success in the corporations.

Evolution of the Canadian Territories

Western Canadian land north of the 60th parallel is federally controlled territory with limited rights and privileges. The original Northwest Territory once included the Yukon, Nunavut, and much of Alberta, Saskatchewan and Manitoba. The Northwest Territory was part of the Hudson's Bay Company fur-trapping empire, until Canada purchased the company in 1869 and subsequently annexed the land. No landform divides the northern territories from the rest of the country, so the boundary was established at the 60th parallel.

Territorial Canada had a rapid wake-up call in the fall of 1897, when the Klondike Gold Rush began along the Yukon River near Dawson. Within a year, forty thousand would-be miners trudged up the highest coastal mountains in the world enroute to the goldfields. The Yukon's Dawson and Alaska's Skagway and Dyea became boomtowns during the gold rush period, only to shrivel or die after the rush until they were revived by late-twentieth-century cruise ships.[23]

The sudden inundation of people in the Klondike required more legislative representation in the boom region. In response, the Canadian government carved the Yukon Territory from the Northwest Territories, with gold boomtown Dawson City as its capital. Once the gold rush was over, the population decreased. The capital shifted from Dawson City to Whitehorse in 1952.

As Westerners moved into the region, the northern Aboriginal and Métis lifestyles changed. The Royal Canadian Mounted Police (RCMP) and religious missionaries enforced the rule of law and challenged the native nomadic culture. Westerners wanted the Native children to attend schools and learn English or French rather than their native languages. The Aboriginals understood that their children's future required a Western education, but attending a permanent school interfered with their traditional hunting activities and seasonal migrations. Parents were forbidden to abandon their children to go hunting. The loss of their traditional hunting patterns dealt a severe blow to Native cultures. Parents were deprived of their livelihood and their children never learned how to hunt. The northern way of life changed forever when World War II arrived. Economic development for oil, gas, and minerals to carry out war-related production brought more Westerners and their influences to the indigenous land.

Relocation of Arctic Inuit

By the late 1950s, the Inuit were starving because of a lack of game to support their subsistence diet. The Canadian government's response to this crisis was to move the Inuit into trading posts and villages, essentially ending their previous lifestyle. Children living in the trading post villages assimilated into the Western culture and lost the close relationship that their parents had with the land. The disruption of Native life contributed to the Natives' hard-fought battle to establish Native territories, which focused on reorganizing the lost lifestyle of the Aboriginal people and creating a livable economy.

The Canadian Territories and Alaska from 1939 to the Present

The strategic value of Alaska and the Canadian Territories was realized when the United States entered World War II as an ally of Russia, and the region remained valuable because of the proximity to Asia. However, the established relationships between Alaska and the Canadian Territories are based on geopolitics more than geographical constraints. Connections between the northern regions are limited and more apt to connect to the mother country rather than with each other. The Aboriginals in Alaska and in the northern territories of Canada were seldom included in political and economic decisions that affected their lives and livelihoods.

Alaska was a U.S. territory until statehood in 1959, but in Canada the north remains territorial. A Canadian **territory** operates under the legislative authority of the federal government and has fewer rights than a province. A territory receives a lesser share of natural resource income than a province. However, power has begun to shift away from Ottawa and toward the territories in an attempt to right the Aboriginal cultural devastation.

During the end of the twentieth century, the Canadian government agreed to varying levels of independence for several Native cultures; however, neither country volunteered to right the wrongs of Native land claims. The Natives had to fight for them. From Nunavut to the Ungava Peninsula to Alaska, various tribal groups began to patch together some hope to renew their cultures.

Nunavut and Other Native Enclaves

Carved from the eastern Northwest Territory and established in 1999, Nunavut (Inuktitut for "our land") had been a twenty-year-long dream and battle for the eastern Inuit. The reasons for creating this new territory date back to the Natives' original loss of their subsistence-based hunting economy

without a Western economy replacement. High unemployment rates (60 to 80 percent), few children who complete high school, and low incomes have devastated the once self-reliant people.

Nunavut comprises about 20 percent of Canada's total landmass, most of it in the Arctic Canadian Shield. Nunavut consists of three regions and twenty-eight communities run by local people. The Inuit were granted self-rule and a territorial settlement grant of $1.2 billion, allowing them control over 18 percent of the territory, which included some subsurface and mineral rights. The Canadian government granted one-tenth of their total mining area rights, which has encouraged Inuit-based mining, including the development of a diamond mine.

Nunavut is somewhat different from other Canadian territories because the Native heritage and culture in Nunavut have been incorporated into the government. The federal government transferred many powers to the territory, although about 90 percent of the budget is provided by the federal government. The indigenous people speak their native languages and utilize English as their second language. The economy is still based on trapping, mining, and natural resources, although a noteworthy crafts industry featuring Aboriginal carvings has augmented local financial welfare.

Despite the high hopes of the Inuit people after the formation of Nunavut, regional reports remain dismal. Alcoholism, drug abuse, and suicide are common, and still only 25 percent graduate from high school. Nunavut has consistently had the highest birthrate in the country, which has resulted in 38 percent of the population being under fourteen. The lack of basic skills has left the Inuit unable to fill available government jobs. Only 45 percent of public jobs are filled by Inuit, although 85 percent of the population is Inuit. There are reports of widespread financial mismanagement.[24]

The Dene Tli Cho, like the Inuit of Nunavut, have also gained self-governance as part of a 2003 territorial agreement, although they are not a separate territory like Nunavut. The Tli Cho control hunting, fishing, resources, and industrial development, as well as rights to a share of energy development revenues along the Mackenzie Valley. Thus, the discovery of diamonds in the local area has influenced the economy. As part of their territorial deal, the Tli Cho are now being trained to work in the industry.

In December 2007, Phase One of a move toward a new Quebec regional government, Nunavik, was signed. With the creation of Nunavik, the Inuit on the Ungava Peninsula, the land from the 55th parallel and north, have been granted a self-governing territory within Quebec. The Inuit have been negotiating for such a deal for twenty-five years, and it is hoped that autonomy will improve their standard of living. The fourteen villages, containing ten thousand people, have had their culture destroyed. There are few jobs and multiple social problems, such as suicide and drug and alcohol abuse.

Self-governance alone, though, may not be enough. Native village life and culture have been damaged and the people discriminated against, while abuse problems are often the result of few jobs and opportunities. People are poor, bored, and depressed. Teenagers have few activities to occupy them, and they often turn to sexual encounters, resulting in the high birthrate. The devastation of Native cultures and imposition of the federal government leaves the cultures with few workable scenarios. If they stay in the village, maintain traditional family relations, and try to maintain traditional cultural practices, they're faced with chronic unemployment, poverty, and social problems. If they leave, they face cultural and social isolation, discrimination, and competition in a world for which village life never prepared them. The poor educational offerings in the villages put them at even more of a disadvantage. The high rates of substance abuse, suicide, domestic abuse, and violent crime are predictable when the social structure has been so impaired.

James Bay Project

The James Bay hydroelectric project for Hydro-Québec is located in Northern Quebec on traditional Cree and Inuit lands. When project plans were first announced in the 1960s, the local Aboriginals were excluded from the process, even though the project would flood much of their traditional hunting territory. The Aboriginal groups banded together, sued the government, and won an injunction to block the construction.

The project was timely for two reasons: (1) it heralded the realization of Quebec's modernization during the Quiet Revolution, and (2) it resulted in the first treaty since the 1920s favoring Aboriginals in Canada. It was also the first treaty since the government rescinded the disastrous 1969 **White Paper on Indian Policy**, which abolished most Native land claims and eliminated special status in an attempt to "assimilate" all Natives. The new Quebec government envisioned the James Bay Project as critical to Quebec's entry onto the world stage. The Aboriginals fought to establish the **James Bay and Northern Quebec Agreement** (1975), which gave the bands exclusive rights to land for subsistence hunting and fishing, a say in future developments, an educational program in their native language for Aboriginal children, and $225 million for economic development. The agreement has served as a model for multiple treaties since that time.

By 1986, the first phase of the hydroelectric project had been completed successfully. The gargantuan project incorporates an area the size of the state of New York, produces more than three times the power of Niagara Falls, and although environmental groups continually censure the project, it is relatively pollution free. Phase Two was completed in 1996. In 2002, La Paix des Braves ("Peace of the Braves") was signed, which established environmental assessments for further construction. As of 2011, the Cree favor the construction of wind turbines over further water projects.

Aboriginals claim that agreed-upon obligations remained unmet; there are disputes over pollution of drinking water and mercury poisoning. The local Cree and Inuit have struggled for autonomy with some success, but the fight for economic development outside of resource exploitation is difficult in a region that has derived most of its economy from exploiting natural resources.

Mackenzie Valley Pipeline Project

The **Mackenzie Valley Pipeline** is a proposed energy corridor extending across the Northwest Territory from the northern gas fields in the Mackenzie delta to the Athabasca oil sands of Alberta. The pipeline will be the longest and largest development project in the Arctic.

In the 1970s, the Canadian government, composed of southern Canadians, began to listen to Aboriginal complaints. When the Mackenzie Valley Pipeline project was announced, the government adopted a new stance and launched a groundbreaking inquiry under Justice Thomas Berger. Inquiry members traveled to the sites and interviewed the Aboriginals about the threat to long-term resources and the ensuing social problems. The release of the 1977 **Berger Inquiry** documented for the first time the lack of care toward renewable resources and the lack of Aboriginal representation in Canada. It was a turning point in Canadian Aboriginal policy. A ten-year moratorium was imposed on the pipeline while the government negotiated with the Natives and gave them a voice and a financial interest in the development.[25] In 2000, the project was revived when Aboriginals supported the project.

Major oil companies own two-thirds of the gas and oil fields, and presently, the Aboriginal Pipeline Group (APG), formed in 2000, owns one-third. APG represents the interests of Northwest Territory Aboriginals, who have been seeking economic independence and benefits.

The gas pipeline continues to be fraught with controversy about the potential effects on hunting, fishing, and the environment, such as habitat destruction in the roadless wilderness, sediment deposition, increased greenhouse gas emissions, depletion of Arctic mammals, and increased insect infestations. While the Native groups are included in the development process and for the first time look to have real economic returns, the fear of continued destruction of the traditional way of life and continued drug and alcohol abuse dampens enthusiasm. The opportunity to participate in the economic advantages presents a conundrum: choosing profits over culture and environmental preservation.

By 2005, Natives threatened to block the pipeline's passage through Inuit reservations unless they received adequate compensation. Continued consultation resulted in a more positive outlook for the project. In November 2007, Aboriginal groups agreed that the prospect of economic development trumped expressed environmentalist concerns. The $16.2 billion project may be further delayed because of the volatile cost of natural gas; in December 2005 the cost was $15.38/MMBtu,[26] in July 2011 $4.57, and in January 2012 $2.50. The project will be the first to include Canadian Aboriginals as major owners in a large industrial project. The pipeline's development and socioeconomic and environmental assessments approaches triple bottom line sustainability.

Cultural Perspectives

Contact with Europeans changed the Alaskan and Canadian Territory cultures. However, the Natives have fared somewhat better than most southern Native groups. Arctic Native groups have had more Western education and have developed a greater capacity to fight for their ignored rights; in addition, governmental bodies have been more responsive to Native claims. As a result of numerous court battles, treaties, and agreements, Arctic and Alaskan cultural traditions are finally being addressed.

After years of negotiating with the Canadian government, many Inuit, Dene (Great Slave Lake), and Cree (James Bay) leaders fought to maintain control and autonomy of their people and cultures. Northern industrialization threatened and destroyed many cultural practices and traditions, so that cultures often lost their sense of place.

Age-old cultures have been fragmented in a generation. Western culture imposed on the Native peoples exploited natural resources and cared little about the legacy left for future generations. Western laws, education, and health care have replaced traditional standards, not always for the worse, but often without measuring what is lost against what is gained. Natives who lived in traditional sod igloos a generation ago are now on the Internet, driving snowmobiles, and experiencing consumption-based lives, but they have often lost the meaning of the North and of their own lives. Life in the North had been harsh but meaningful.

Habitat Destruction: The Inuit

The Canadian and American indigenous populations have not fared well. Thus, the cultural destruction of the Inuit people is not surprising but disappointing. The Inuit culture was imperiled in the second half of the twentieth century. The hegemonic culture exploited their region and failed to respect Native rights until forced by court order.

The Inuit seminomadic life relied on hunting, fishing, and following game throughout the year. But in the late twentieth and early twenty-first centuries, the Inuit were caught between their traditional culture and a Western consumer economy.

During the 1960s, the adult generation was expected to make the cultural leap from a seminomadic life living in sod igloos to permanent southern-type housing, from hunting and fishing to a cash economy of grocery stores and fast food. The northern indigenous bands were settled in centralized villages so that Western education, health care, and welfare were more accessible—but at the cost of losing their place-based cultures.

In Canada, the Inuit lost more than their freedoms; they also lost their dogs, an important part of the Inuit transport system. According to Inuit sources, the government killed thousands of sled dogs between 1950 and 1970 in order to achieve the goal of centralization.[27] The slaughter is still being investigated.

The Aboriginals could no longer follow the annual migrations of prey, whose habitat was fragmented by oil drilling, hydroelectric dams, deforestation, mining, and climate change. Toxins like dioxins, PCBs, pesticides, and heavy

metals bioaccumulate as they work their way up the food chain, contaminating Arctic Ocean fish and eventually causing a serious health hazard for those who eat the fish, especially for pregnant and nursing indigenous mothers, who pass the chemicals to their children through breast milk.[28] The contaminants are produced in industrialized countries but reach the Arctic waters via water and air currents. The pollutants are incorporated through the fatty tissue of the cold-weather animals. The pollutants concentrate tenfold at each level of the food chain, reaching a millionfold for top predators and humans.

Solving the problem of Arctic pollution is difficult, and related to global-scale issues. For example, DDT has been illegal in the United States and Canada for years, but DDT continued to be used by other countries and continues to enter the food chain and the air, affecting Arctic waters.

In the 1990s, those who continued to hunt and fish as their forefathers found that climate change had thinned and depleted the sea ice, leading to the decline of Arctic prey such as seals, walruses, and polar bears. These hunters lost their "living off the land" **subsistence economy** and their connection to the environment. The current Inuit food supply is deficient in game, nutritionally poor, and considered out of balance—yet another reason for the endemic cultural decline of the Inuit people.

However, losing the Inuit hunting grounds was more devastating to the people than the loss of their subsistence economy. The value system associated with hunting was decoupled from their ethics and values as a people. Living in the harsh Arctic environment was only possible if they all held common values of courage, patience, tenacity, and boldness. The 1960s generation was deprived of its cultural core and way of life. But few opportunities exist in a northern wage economy, and many Inuit have fallen into despair. These problems are multigenerational, as their children also have a high incidence of drug use, suicide, alcoholism, and depression.

In order for the culture to regain meaning, the economic outlook needs to adopt the social equity implicit in the triple bottom line. By focusing on economics alone, places that do not fit the norms of more temperate regions are left out of the loop and will spiral into oblivion unless the economy respects environmental and social equity.

Homes

Traditional Inuit housing, the igloo, has become an icon. Some people still think that all Canadians live in snowhouse igloos, but the Inuit igloo was one of several types of shelters, including the temporary shelter that used the icy local resources. The Inuit also built sod igloos and igloos that combined snow with other materials. During the hunt, temporary igloos were built by Inuit hunters, who cut and shaped the ice into blocks. The more permanent Arctic and boreal forest sod igloos of the Inuit provided warmth in a cold climate. Aboriginals built a variety of different "pit" houses, using whalebone or driftwood for the structure and sod for insulation (Photo 18.5). The houses were one-room affairs, built into the ground for

PHOTO 18.5. Indigenous Sod "Pit" House in Alaska. This house was built with whalebone structure and sod covering. Seldom seen today on the landscape, this one is at a museum site.

further protection against the elements. A hole covered by semitransparent animal intestine provided light to the shelter.

Today, the average house in a northern Native village is similar to U.S. and Canadian homes; however, they differ because of climate (more insulation) and landscape. Modern homes in permafrost locations are built on pilings for air circulation and to stabilize home foundations (Photo 18.6).

In Alaska, some Native groups are returning to more traditional local materials and energy-efficient building methods, because the high costs of Western-type homes and heating with imported energy are making Natives appraise more sustainable and culturally appropriate options. For example, Anaktuvuk Pass in the Brooks Range has had a long-term housing shortage, and existing houses inefficiently use air and energy. Several projects of the Cold Climate Housing Research Center were completed in 2009, using traditional earth-berming techniques combined with solar power, green roofs, and passive ventilation to build an energy-efficient home. Another was designed in Quinhagak on the Yukon delta in 2010.[29]

Food Resources and Subsistence Hunting

In the twenty-first century, subsistence or "country" food remains prevalent in indigenous diets, similar to 1980 levels.[30] Eighty percent of the men still hunt, and 50 percent of families still eat traditional foods daily, because imported foods are at least twice the price of the average Canadian food budget. Food

is obtained by subsistence hunting or fishing, and it is interrelated with Native family life. Men hunt; women preserve meat, sew hides for clothing or household goods, and are involved in Native crafts. The subsistence lifestyle was once a full-time occupation and rewarded the family with a healthy diet and life experience. This system, although superficially intact (most Natives still live in villages and are dependent on subsistence food), has experienced a detrimental cultural shift. While the subsistence culture continues, the manner has changed, unraveling those parts of the culture that remain.

As Native lifestyles have changed and the North has been exploited, subsistence foods are no longer bountiful or local. Contaminants and fishing limitations on the depleted animal population have disrupted the Inuit diet of seal, walrus, and, most importantly, whale. Inland Natives were traditionally dependent on caribou and salmon. Many bands, such as the Inupiaq, were dependent on food from the sea in summer and caribou in the winter. In the past, they lived a seminomadic life revolving around summer and winter home sites. However, the methods of hunting have changed. For example, few Natives still use dog sleds to hunt caribou, but instead use the ubiquitous "snow machine" (snowmobile).

Not that long ago, the village men hunted caribou for days if not weeks at a time. Reaching game animals even only a few miles away was slow compared to current methods. Today the herd may be 50 or 60 miles (80–100 km) away, but rapid access by snowmobiles and hunting with high-powered rifles procures the entire winter's food in a much shorter timeframe—a few days. A Native family of four may consume up to one caribou a week, eating it three times a day. In the past, the women cleaned and preserved the meat, storing it in permafrost **caches** designed to store food and as protection from animals, but today many of the caches have defrosted due to melting permafrost.

Today the women are often more involved in the cash economy, making masks and Native artifacts for tourists, thus altering the family economic complex. Men no longer have much to do once the hunt is over, and women now earn most of the money. They may still eat subsistence food, but the traditional food system has changed. Gaping holes left in the culture are now often filled with depression, alcoholism, and domestic violence.

Language

When cultures assimilate, two traditional features—food and language—are the last to go. Many Alaskan Native groups have maintained fluency in one of the twenty recognized indigenous languages. The Tlingit and Haida languages and dialects still survive along the Alaskan Panhandle, but others such as Eyak have all but disappeared. In the Aleutians, Native languages were discouraged fifty years ago, and few elders speak the languages today, although the current generation has been learning their native tongue in school. One-half of the more isolated Yup'ik along the southwestern coast of Alaska still speak one of several Native dialects at home. Native languages reflect the adaptations of the culture, and specifics cannot be easily replaced with a Western language that does not share the same environment.

PHOTO 18.6. Building on Permafrost in Nome, Alaska. This house was built on pilings, but the garage was not. Permafrost melting has caused movement. Notice the board holding up the door and keeping the roof from further buckling.

Nunavut native languages have been encouraged since the region became a territory. According to Statistics Canada (2006), the mother tongue for 75 percent of the northern population is not the official English or French languages, but an indigenous language, especially Inuktitut/Inuinnaqtun (Table 18.2).[31]

Religion

The Alaskan and Canadian Native American bands worshipped animistic deities, whose spirits were imbued within animals and landscape features. Closely tied to Native religion, but separate,

were the shamans, who these bands believed worked with dangerous and mysterious powers beyond the human realm. They divined hunting rituals, were central sources of wisdom, and diagnosed and treated diseases.

Many Natives had little reason to adopt the religion of their oppressors, but devoted Russian missionaries often won the Natives' faith. For example, the Tlingit of Southeastern Alaska were wary of the Russians until a smallpox epidemic swept through the area in 1830, killing 40 to 50 percent of the Tlingit; the Russians suffered considerably less because they were vaccinated. The power of the Russian "medicine" swayed many

TABLE 18.2. Alaskan or Arctic Canadian Language Spoken at Home

Language family	Population	Number of speakers
Aleut	5,000	605
Yup'ik	22,100	11,000
Inuit (Alaska)	13,500	3,100
Inuit (Canada)	30,500	24,500
Tsimshianic/Haida (U.S./Canada)	8,820	<1,500
Tlingit (U.S./Canada)	11,000	575
Athabascan (U.S./Canada)	8,575	1,477
Inuktitut (Nunavut) [a]	29,325	21,170

Source: Michael Krauss, "The Indigenous Languages of the North: A Report on Their Present State," in *Northern Minority Languages: Problems of Survival*, Senri Ethnological Studies 44, edited by H. Shoji and J. Janhunen (Osaka, Japan: National Museum of Ethnology, 1997), 1–34; Statistics Canada, 2007, at http://www12.statcan.ca/english/census06/data/profiles/community/Index.cfm?Lang=E
[a] 2007

Tlingit toward the Russian church, especially in light of the shamans' inability to combat the disease.[32] Another example of missionary religious conversion was the development of written languages and translation of the Bible into the Native languages.

The Church was a lasting cultural influence of Alaska's Russian occupation. The American and Russian Orthodox missionaries Christianized the Alaskan Natives by the early 1920s. Today, the Orthodox Church has forty Alaskan parishes and over fifty thousand indigenous followers. The onion-domed churches are visible in many communities.

While Arctic Aboriginals converted to Christianity, **syncretism** imbued their Christian vision with their past religious expressions, such as in the Athabascan spirit houses in Eklutna and on occasion along roadsides (Photo 18.7). The spirit houses are shrines to the deceased, where the living can bring offerings to the spirits and the spirits can visit the living.

Regional Life

Population

The vast and sparsely populated North is the Inuit, Athabascan, and Algonquin homeland, along with the Métis of Canada and a sprinkling of whites. Many Native groups have retained cultural integrity despite grievous losses in the past and have increased their population in the twenty-first century.

Alaska

Alaska, one of the least populous American states, has been growing faster than the national average. The population was 710,231 in 2010, a 13.3 percent increase over its 2000 population. The sources of this growth are natural increase, adventurous spirits, and petroleum industry in-migrations during the 1970s and 1980s. However, petroleum industry opportunities dried up in the mid-1980s, and many areas lost population as oil revenues declined.

Population growth was stunted during Alaska's colonial period (1867–1959), because laws made it almost impossible for settlers to secure title to land. Ninety-nine percent of the land was in the public domain, and the artificially high cost of living deterred white settlement. The increased military presence after World War II altered Alaska's settlement patterns. Before the war, only 1,000 of 75,000 residents were military, but by 1943, 152,000 of the 233,000 total Alaskan residents were military. After the war, many decided to stay.

The Anchorage metropolitan area has the largest population in the state. Anchorage is also the most ethnically diverse area, with 66.1 percent white, 5.4 percent black, 6.4 percent Asian, 7.5 percent Hispanic, and 7.9 percent Native American or Alaskan Native (2010).

The ethnic breakdown of all Alaskan inhabitants is about 66.7 percent white, 3.3 percent black, 5.4 percent Asian, and 14.8 percent Native (2010). This has changed radically since the 1930s, when the Native population was the majority (Table 18.3).

Canadian Territories and Shield

Ontario and British Columbia have the most First Nations people numerically, but they only represent a small portion of the total population: less than 2.0 percent of Ontario's population (188,315) and 4.4 percent of the population of British Columbia (170,025). In the territories, the Native groups have the highest population concentrations. Eighty-five percent of

PHOTO 18.7. "Spirit Houses" at Eklutna, Alaska. The colorful spirit houses (graves) occupy the cemetery of the local Russian Orthodox church. The spirit houses meld Athabascan and Russian Orthodox beliefs. Colors identify clans, and crosses represent the Church.

TABLE 18.3. Alaska Natives as Percentage of Total Population, 1930–2010

Decade	Percent Native
1930	50.6
1940	44.8
1950	26.3
1960	19.0
1970	16.9
1980	16.0
1990	15.6
2000	15.6
2010	14.8

Source: U.S. Census

the 29,474 Nunavut population (2006) are Aboriginal; they make up about one-half of all Canadian Inuit. In the Northwest Territories, First Nations people are 51 percent, composed of Dene, Métis, and Inuvialuit, and about 11 percent are Inuit. In the Yukon, 23 percent are Aboriginal.

The Inuit birthrate is about twice Canada's national birthrate, making the Inuit the fastest-growing group relatively. The Inuit are also the youngest compared with other First Nations peoples, and with a median age of 23, much younger than the median age of the Canadian population at 39.5 (Table 18.4).

The overall populations in the Northwest Territories and the Yukon have been declining, as are the populations in the largest cities and capitals, Yellowknife and Whitehorse. Driven by a high birthrate, Nunavut and its capital, Iqaluit, are gaining population (Table 18.5).

The shield represents 40 percent of the Canadian landmass but holds only 8 percent of Canada's population. Most of Ontario and Quebec's land is in the shield, but only two million of the twenty million people in those provinces live in the shield, mostly along the rail lines or the transcontinental highway.

Traditional and Sustainable Cities

Urban centers in Alaska and the Canadian Territories are small in comparison to temperate-climate cities. There are, however, seven communities of significant size in Alaska, and each Canadian territory has a regional center, populated by about half the territory's residents. In Alaska, the largest city by far is Anchorage, followed by Fairbanks (pop. 31,535) in the interior, and in the Panhandle region Juneau, the capital (31,275), Sitka (8,881), and Ketchikan (8,050). The three Panhandle cities have no road

connections outside the Panhandle, yet all are crowded with automobiles (all of which have to be transported in by water or air). Although the past Panhandle economy has been forestry and fishing, increasingly it is tied to the cruise ship trade. Several other communities—Barrow, Nome, Valdez, and Seward—are regional centers.

The Canadian North has few people, but nonetheless the urban structure is discrete, divided between three types of communities: the government-service communities, such as the capitals; resource communities, such as the oil sands town of Fort McMurray in northern Alberta; and the small Native communities.

Anchorage, Alaska

(2010 pop. 291,826, MSA 380,821)

Anchorage in south central Alaska is set against the scenic Chugach Mountains (Photo 18.8). Situated in a protected area of the Cook Inlet, the city sits on glacial silt and rock between the Knik and Turnagain arms. Anchorage and Stockholm, Sweden, sit at about the same latitude and share similar weather moderated by water. In Anchorage, average summer temperatures range from 55°F to 80°F (13°C to 27°C), and winter temperatures from 5°F to 20°F (–15°C to –7°C).

Founded in 1915, the railroad construction camp consisted of plank sidewalks and rows of tents. Anchorage grew during World War II, when Alaska became a strategic location in response to the Japanese threat. Military installations and infrastructure shaped the city for its future development, as the city grew from eight thousand before the war to forty-three thousand after. Today, half of Alaska's population lives within twenty-five miles of Anchorage.

TABLE 18.4. Age Structure of Canadian Territories

	Yukon	Percent increase	Northwest Territory	Percent increase	Nunavut	Percent increase
2001 population	28,674		37,360		26,745	
2006 population	30,372	5.9	41,464	11.0	29,474	10.2
0–19	5,720		9,915		9,995	
20–64	18,730		29,570		18,660	
65+	2,280		1,975		815	
Median age[a]	38.4		31.2		23.1	
% under age 15	19.8		24.9		33.9	

[a] The median age is an age x, such that exactly one half of the population is older than x and the other half is younger than x.
Source: Statistics Canada, Age Characteristics, 2006

TABLE 18.5. Population of Canadian Territories and Capital Cities

	2001	2006	Percent change	2011
Northwest Territories	37,360	41,464	0	41,462
Yellowknife	16,541	18,700	2.9	19,234
Yukon	28,674	30,372	11.6	33,897
Whitehorse	19,058	20,461	13.8	23,276
Nunavut	26,745	29,474	8.3	31,906
Iqaluit	5,236	6,184	8.3	6,699

Source: Statistics Canada, 2011 Census

Anchorage's transportation links helped it become the region's most important city and the oil production business center. After World War II, suburban developments in the Matanuska River Valley, Wasilla, and down the Kenai Peninsula alleviated housing shortages. Anchorage is a gateway into the interior, serviced by a railroad, two highways, and Alaska's largest airport. It is also the service and distribution center for farming, oil production, and military and governmental activities, and it is the dominant tourist stopover. Anchorage also provides a local shopping area for many Alaskans, including a mall filled with familiar American stores.

Anchorage has adopted a number of sustainable features, including a handful of LEED-certified buildings and street lighting. The city has changed a quarter of the streetlights to energy-saving LEDs, which is expected to save the city about 30 percent on street lighting costs. Since Anchorage has very long periods of darkness during the winter, the savings are welcomed.

Canadian North

The combined Canadian territorial population (107,265 in 2011) is less than the population of Anchorage. The largest city in each territory (Whitehorse, Yellowknife, and Iqaluit) is also the capital.

Whitehorse (23,276 pop. [2011]) has been the Yukon capital since it replaced Dawson City in 1952. Whitehorse was founded in 1900 upon completion of the White Pass and Yukon Railway. Whitehorse accounts for three-quarters of the territorial population, and it is the territory's tourism, transportation, and freight hub.

PHOTO 18.8. Downtown Anchorage, Alaska. During the spring and summer, Anchorage looks like many other American cities, except for the dramatic backdrop of the Chugach Mountains. Half of Alaska's population lives in the Anchorage area.

Yellowknife, Northwest Territories (19,234 [2011]) was founded as a gold-mining town in the 1930s and is now a center for diamond-mining operations. The town, accessed via the Mackenzie Highway, is located about nine hundred miles north of Edmonton.

Iqaluit, Nunavut, located on Baffin Island (6,699 [2011]), was formerly called Frobisher Bay after the sixteenth-century Northwest Passage explorer Sir Martin Frobisher. Frobisher Bay was a U.S. Air Force base linking North America and Europe during World War II; it became Nunavut's capital, reverting to its Inuit name (meaning "many fish") in 1987. This least-populated Canadian capital is more than three times the size of the next largest Nunavut town, and the only territorial capital currently gaining population. It is the transportation and service focus for the territory. Only local roads service the town. Outside access is by air.

Fort McMurray, Alberta, is an oil sands boomtown that has averaged six new people daily, growing from 20,000 in 1977 to 61,374 in 2011.[33] Fort McMurray is expected to grow at about 9.5 percent annually, drawing from eastern and less prosperous Canadian provinces. Since the collapse of the Atlantic cod fishery, many from Newfoundland migrated to work in the Fort McMurray oil sand industry, giving it the colloquial title of the "second-largest city in Newfoundland." This may be changing, though, as the Newfoundland economy picks up with its own oil industry.

Fort McMurray's escalating cost of living and continued growth has caused the cost of an average house to increase from $100,000 in 1995 to more than $740,000 in 2010.[34] Fort McMurray has the highest median income for families in Canada at $164,122 in 2009.

Economy

One cannot fail to see that Canada is greatly handicapped thro' her geographical position, in trying to hold her own against the States. Someday geography will be the determining factor in North American relations.

—William Lyon Mackenzie King, April 3, 1923[35]

Alaska and territorial Canadian economies have been resource based. Agriculture is unimportant economically, although both crops and livestock are grown in southern areas.

Mining became a primary source of income in the North in the twenty-first century, when commodity prices escalated, making northern investments lucrative. Mineral and fossil fuel production has become substantial; however, the friction of distance functions as a deterrent.

Primary Economy and Natural Resources

Agriculture

The vast and sparsely populated Canadian territories and Alaska have limited agricultural production. Whites have practiced agriculture, while Native Americans have been involved in herding.

In Alaska, the Matanuska Valley near Anchorage has drawn the most agricultural attention. The glacial outwash valley exits at the Cook Inlet and is set against the backdrop of the magnificent Alaska and Chugach range. During the 1930s Depression, a Department of the Interior program was enacted to prove that Alaska was capable of supporting agriculture and colonization. Thousands of farmers in the lower forty-eight applied to resettle, but the government chose about two hundred families from the cutover lake states (Wisconsin, Minnesota, and Michigan)

BOX 18.8 ALASKA TRANSPORTATION

Permafrost and rough terrain force most Alaskan transportation to be on water or in the air. Today the most economical means of transport remains the Inside Passage, which is serviced by the Alaska Marine Highway and the ferry system.

Alaskan interior roads were opened by the military and government intervention early in the twentieth century. The Richardson Highway was the first, connecting the port city of Valdez with the interior boomtown of Fairbanks in 1919. Rail access from the tent city of Anchorage to Fairbanks opened the interior in 1915.

In 1942, the United States and Canada felt vulnerable after the Japanese attack on the Aleutians. In response, the 1,523-mile Alaskan Canadian Highway (AlCan), running from Dawson Creek, British Columbia, to Fairbanks, Alaska, was hurriedly built in eight months from 1942 to 1943, despite construction difficulties through permafrost, muskeg, and extreme climate. The AlCan provided military access and the first road to the lower forty-eight states. It was opened to the public in 1946.

PHOTO 18.9. Bush Plane. Bush planes are a vital part of the transportation network in the bush wilderness areas of Alaska and the Canadian Territories.

Air

An unusual aspect of the Alaskan and territorial network is the dependence on air transport serviced by bush pilots. Seventy-five percent of Alaska is inaccessible by road. Bush pilots have achieved legendary status flying small, light planes anywhere within the region, from fishing enclaves to mining operations (Photo 18.9). They land on almost any surface, such as gravel bars, water, and glaciers. Hundreds of Alaskan bush flights take off daily. Lake Hood, near Anchorage, has the most, with five hundred flights a day.

Both Anchorage and Fairbanks were refueling stations for trans-Pacific flights prior to World War II; however, no central Alaskan line existed. Starting in 1945, several bush airlines merged and eventually formed Alaska Airlines. Anchorage today has a major international airport.

Shipping

To control Alaskan resources and protect his constituency, Seattle-based Senator Wesley Jones sponsored the 1920 U.S. Maritime Act, commonly called the Jones Act, which stipulated that all commercial ships traveling between two American ports needed to be American-built, staffed, and owned. Alaska, at the time only a territory and underrepresented in Congress, was singled out as the only place in America where foreign ships were forbidden. The act was political. Alaska became the vassal of the state of Washington. All ships had to be routed through Seattle.

The act is still in force today and affects Alaskans on a daily basis. Most goods are not driven into the state, which is far more expensive than shipping, but the limitations of the Jones Act disallow inexpensive shipping practices. Most shipping and fishing companies today remain based out of Seattle rather than in Alaska, which takes away from the local economy. The major port for Alaska cruises is now in Vancouver, which has been a boon to their tourism business but has hurt American ports. Additionally, oil tankers shipping Trans-Alaska Pipeline System (TAPS) crude must all be built in America and of American components. The shipping industry remains one of the major uses of American steel.

The domestic tankers carry approximately four million barrels of oil per day; half are shipped from Alaska. The Alaskan crude oil fleet consists of forty-four tankers with a total capacity of 4.8 million deadweight tons (DWT). Many existing tankers are single hulled, which were outlawed in 1990 after the Exxon Valdez oil spill. All must be replaced with double-hulled tankers by 2015.* The current tanker fleet is considerably older than the world fleet, as most ships were constructed during the peak years of TAPS (late 1970s). Between 2004 and 2007, the number of double-hulled ships increased significantly; replacement is expected to be complete by 2012.† The Jones Act has made it nearly impossible to compete with overseas ship-building techniques and costs.

---

* Committee on Oil Pollution Act of 1990, Implementation Review, National Research Council, *Double-Hull Tanker Legislation: An Assessment of the Oil Pollution Act of 1990* (Washington, D.C.: National Academies Press, 1998).

† U.S. Department of Transportation, Maritime Administration. "Coastal Tank Vessel Market Snapshot, 2009," at http://www.marad.dot.gov/documents/Coastal_Tank_Vessel_Market_Snapshot.pdf.

because they were more likely to be culturally preadapted to Alaska's climate and farming conditions. The program was established in Palmer, Alaska, which became and remains the Matanuska Valley agricultural production center. The Matanuska Valley today is a successful agricultural community, but the New Deal reforms are often considered failures (Photo 18.10). Most people who moved to Alaska after World War II did not come to farm but to live an urban life. The American farming experience was no longer part of the American dream.[36]

Alaska's agricultural potential is unusual. The growing season is short, from 90 to 120 days, but the long daylight hours produce oversized produce: seventy-pound cabbages and twenty-pound carrots. Due to high transportation costs, most crops are sold locally. Farms extend their growing seasons with greenhouses, especially for warm-weather crops like tomatoes and herbs.

Herding

Northern and central Alaska [is] capable of supporting over 9,000,000 head of reindeer. To reclaim and make valuable land, otherwise worthless; to introduce large, permanent, and wealth-producing industries, when none previously existed; to take a barbarian people on the verge of starvation and lift them up to a comfortable self-support and civilization, is certainly work of national importance.

—Sheldon Jackson, 1890[37]

After 1850, whaling ships on the Arctic Chukchi Sea interfered with the traditional Inupiaq lifestyle. Sailors slaughtered whales, walrus, and seals and diminished the local subsistence food supply, leading to widespread starvation in the scattered villages. In an effort to provide food, reindeer were imported from Siberia in the 1890s, and Natives were taught to herd.

Despite the good intentions of missionaries, their attempts to convert Inupiaq into reindeer herders showed a lack of cultural understanding. Western logic and rationales were used to colonize the Natives, and Native cultural knowledge was discounted.

At one point in the 1930s, the reindeer thrived, reaching a population of over six hundred thousand. However, changes in lifestyle and government policies ended the experiment in the 1950s. Many Natives abandoned the traditional lifestyle and earned a living in a wage economy, while those who remained within the traditional way of life found the herding too confining, and questioned the applicability of ever-changing government policies. Herding is no longer practiced.

Mineral Resources

Mining, fishing, and lumber overshadow the northern agricultural economy. The lowland slope and forest areas are accessible and rich in hydrocarbons. Many of the world's largest producing mines are located in the Arctic and boreal regions.

The taiga economy depends on mining, which is the basis for most of the settlements. However, mines and their towns are usually boom-or-bust propositions that follow world market prices and demand.

Oil and gas continue to be important Alaskan sources of income, while diamonds are the lead mining story in the Canadian North. Other significant minerals include gold, zinc, copper, and coal. Historically, mineral production has been limited because of the distance; however, decreased resources, increased prices in temperate climatic zones, and technological advances have caused boreal and Arctic resources to become economically viable.

Hydrocarbons

In 1945, we were exporting oil to our allies. By 1970, we were importing 24 percent of our oil. By the 1980s, it was 37 percent, and, in 1991, during the Gulf War, it was 42 percent. Today, we are approaching 70 percent.

—T. Boone Pickens, July 24, 2008[38]

PHOTO 18.10. Matanuska Valley, Alaska. The Alaskan Range looms beyond the valley north of Anchorage. The long daylight hours produce oversized vegetables in this successful Alaskan farming venture.

We have to adjust to progress; we have to stop dreaming about tradition and living off the land. We can't turn back the clock.

—Doug Cardinal, Deh Cho, 2005[39]

Gas and Oil   Parts of the Arctic Slope contain major deposits of petroleum and natural gas, which were formed about two hundred million years ago when the area was submerged in a shallow sea and the organisms (which are the source material for oil) died and were pressurized and heated until they were transformed into hydrocarbons.

In 1967, Alaska sold leases in the Prudhoe Bay area to oil companies, and in 1973 the oil crisis accelerated investment in Alaskan oil production. The Trans-Alaskan Pipeline System (TAPS) began commercial production in 1977. It was built to transport crude oil from the North Slope to Valdez, where tankers were loaded and the oil shipped to Washington and California refineries.

Oil company profits have been taxed numerous times, the most recent being a 22.5 percent tax. Over the years, the state economy has yo-yoed in relation to the collected taxes. Low oil prices and reduced production kept the state near bankruptcy in the 1990s, but a rise in oil prices in 2003 created a boom that brought more money into Alaska despite the continued decline in production.

Since nearly all mineral rights are on public land, the state set up a Permanent Fund Dividend (PFD, as it is called in Alaska) derived from oil production revenues. The PFD gives every state resident an annual check derived from the amount of oil produced. In 2001 the PFD check was $1,500, but it has varied in the intervening years. In 2010 the PFD was $1,281; in 2011 the PFD was $1,174.

The boom went bust when oil prices began to decline in late 2008; prices remain unsteady in 2011 due to the weak economy.

In the Canadian North, oil and gas production mostly depends on Alberta oil sands production, located in three major oil sands deposits: Peace River, Cold Lake, and the largest near Fort McMurray.

Coal   Alaskan coal reserves are an insignificant part of the economy; Alaskan coal is low rank and located under permafrost, and therefore expensive to mine and transport. Two operational mines yield about 0.2 percent of total U.S. production. Coal bed methane, a source of natural gas, is more abundant in Alaska than it is in the lower forty-eight. Approximately 50 percent of all American coal bed methane resources are in Alaska. As natural gas prices escalate, there is increased interest in recovering other sources of gas, such as coal bed methane.

The Yukon and Northwest Territory have significant possibilities in the coal industry, although little gas has been recovered in these areas. Most coal bed methane is found near remote villages, and if developed, could be significant as a rural energy source.

Minerals

Gold   Alaska has had several significant gold rushes including:

- Gastineau Channel in the 1880s, which established the capital, Juneau, named after a prospector in the region
- Nome in 1899 and 1900, at which time Nome was the largest city in Alaska
- Ester, near Fairbanks, in 1902

Nome's gold rush was known as the "poor man's gold rush," because small-time prospectors could find gold on the town's beaches. In other areas, the cost of extraction limited gold production to large operations.

In 2006, the price of gold surpassed $600 per ounce and rose in 2011 to more than $1,800 per ounce. The price jump has rekindled interest in gold mining. The beaches of Nome were once again filled with placer prospectors and dredgers mining gold (Photo 18.11). Gold mining has also begun again north of Fairbanks at the Fort Knox open-pit mine.

Northern Dynasty Mines and Anglo American U.S. (LLC) propose to open Pebble Mine, located about fifteen miles north of Lake Iliamna in the southwestern part of Alaska. The proposed open-pit and underground mines, which would be the largest gold and copper mine in the United States, could potentially contain more than thirty-one million ounces of gold and

PHOTO 18.11. Dredging for Gold in Nome, Alaska. Many miners dredge the beaches or water for gold in Nome. While many miners dredge with small suction devices on the public beach mining area, this dredge goes into the water equipped with a camera on the vacuum pipe to see dredged material. This dredging outfit cost approximately $250,000 to construct.

BOX 18.9 TRANS-ALASKA PIPELINE SYSTEM (TAPS) AND CAFE

The American dependence on fossil fuel has been supported by oil companies sponsoring weak legislation for automobile efficiency and by strong automobile company lobbying to build bigger, low-efficiency cars and "light truck" SUVs that are not required to meet automobile fuel economy standards. Both the low Corporate Average Fuel Economy (CAFE) standards for the United States and increasing dependence on foreign oil have created unintended consequences; as Thomas Friedman points out, the U.S. economy includes the "everything is connected" idea of Saudi money from oil profits funding Islamic fundamentalists.*

The construction timing of the pipeline after the oil crisis of 1973 was purely political, but that does not take away from the construction as a twentieth-century engineering marvel. It was also a time of growing environmental awareness, and the pipeline taught engineers several geographical and environmental lessons (Photo 18.12). Some of the lessons learned were.

- Warm crude oil flowing through the pipeline would harm the fragile permafrost.
- The pipeline was originally conceived to be underground, but as permafrost and its ecosystem relation were understood, the pipeline became about 50/50 under and above ground.
- Construction costs in permafrost areas are double those in non-permafrost areas.
- Seismic and vehicle trails over tundra destroy vegetation. Winter snow cover and ice roads are usually the least damaging methods to move over the tundra.
- Road construction has been both a positive and negative influence for the pipeline route.

The pipeline had both positive and negative consequences.

Positive: It increased communication within the region and among its residents; it brought jobs and also brings tourism.

Negative: It alters animal habitats, increases competition for subsistence resources, and brings tourists, who damage fragile tundra. It has endorsed relying on nonrenewable natural resources over conservation of resources.

PHOTO 18.12. The Trans-Alaska Pipeline System (TAPS). The pipeline runs eight hundred miles from Prudhoe Bay to Valdez. This section is between Glenallen and Valdez.

Alaska is the second-largest oil-producing state after Texas and accounts for more than 25 percent of American oil production. North Slope production has declined from its peak of 2 million barrels per day in 1988 and has steadily declined to 1 million barrels daily in 2002 and 0.644 million barrels in 2010.† The decline has meant fewer jobs, so most Alaskans now back an initiative to open the Arctic National Wildlife Refuge (ANWR) to further oil extraction.

CAFE standards of 27.5 mpg for cars (lower for light trucks—SUVs) set in 1974 were lowered during the 1980s to 26 mpg and not raised again to the original 27.5 mpg until 1989. Raising the fuel standard by 10 mpg would have saved the United States about 1.1 billion gallons per day, but the United States remained in denial about long-term investment and ended up wasting an amount equivalent to ANWR by not raising the fuel standard. The automobile lobby pushed to keep the standard at the wasteful level through 2008 and to keep gasoline taxes low to limit reinvestment in more efficient energy practices. In 2008 (after the American automobile meltdown), CAFE standards were boosted to current European standards of 35 mpg, but not until 2020. In 2011, the CAFE standard for cars was raised to 54.5 mpg by 2025.

* To read more about unintended consequences, see Thomas Friedman, *Hot, Flat, and Crowded: Why We Need a Green Revolution and How It Can Renew America* (New York: Farrar, Straus & Giroux, 2008).

† Alaska Department of Revenue, Tax Division, at http://www.tax.alaska.gov/sourcesbook/AlaskaProduction.pdf.

BOX 18.10 ARCTIC NATIONAL WILDLIFE REFUGE (ANWR)

The nineteen-million-acre Arctic National Wildlife Refuge (ANWR) was created in 1960 and is America's largest wildlife preserve, supporting 169 species of birds, 28 species of fish, 44 species of mammals, and an unknown number of plants and lichens. Located on the North Slope of Alaska along the Arctic Ocean, it includes a portion of the coastal plain. In 1980, oil and gas development were prohibited unless specifically authorized by an act of Congress.

In the early twentieth-first century, debate grew about whether to open the reserve to oil and gas exploration along the 1.5 million coastal plain acres, 8 percent of the refuge. It is both the most likely place to find oil and the most fragile area for habitat preservation. The alleged benefits would decrease dependence on foreign oil and would augment American oil and gas production in a time of escalating prices.

Environmental groups criticize the possible destruction of the fragile tundra ecosystem. The ANWR coast is the last part of Alaska's North Slope closed to drilling. Environmentalists believe that the amount of oil is nowhere near the stated claims of those favoring development. Comparative oil industry test drilling results are unavailable to the public.

The effects of drilling are controversial and wide ranging. Those who favor ANWR oil production believe that as little as 0.1 percent of the preserve would yield more than one million barrels of oil a day for thirty years. Drilling the preserve would bring in more jobs, but environmentalists have fought these initiatives, citing destruction of the Alaskan coastal plain, caribou migration routes, and calving patterns. They also point out that drilling within ANWR is a short-term answer that will not free America of oil dependence. In 2006, a crisis of escalated oil and gas prices brought the issue to the forefront again, and U.S. and Canadian companies agreed to develop the Beaufort Sea area.

Some oil companies continue to invest in Alaskan oil production and found new reserves in the Cook Outlet, Kenai Peninsula, Chukchi Sea, and along the North Slope. The government and oil companies focus on efficient production and development of new oil fields. Oil has been explored in the Beaufort Sea along a disputed international boundary between the United States and Canada.

Price escalations have prompted an increased interest in North Slope and Cook Inlet natural gas field development, which provides heating and electricity for Alaskan communities. The Alaskan government and many residents favor developing a pipeline to the lower forty-eight. The proposed pipeline would run about thirty-six hundred miles from Prudhoe Bay to Calgary and then to Chicago, delivering about four billion cubic feet of natural gas daily.

---

eighteen billion pounds of copper. The current Alaskan administration and the mining industry favor opening the mine, but fishers and local residents who may lose their subsistence way of life oppose it because of the mine's location at the headwaters of the world's largest sockeye salmon fishery. Additional environmental issues include adding road access in an inaccessible area and transporting power to the site, which would have a major impact on fragile habitats.

Hard-rock mining sites are the largest source of pollution in the United States. This project has advanced from its proposal stage in 2007 and is in the process of completing extensive social and environmental research relating to the proposed mine and how it will affect the local area. Despite continuing protests, the Pebble Mine Company has continued to pursue permits in 2011.

Several gold mines operate in the Canadian North. Placer mines are in the Yukon, while the Northwest Territory and Nunavut continue to mine gold near the Great Slave Lake.

Nickel The center for nonferrous mining and smelting in Canada is located in Sudbury, Ontario (106,840 pop. [2011]), whose fifteen Canadian Shield mines produce nickel, copper, and gold, among other metals. Sudbury mines produce about 10 percent of the world's nickel. The production site is a crater created from a meteorite that impacted the earth about 1.8 million years ago, leaving behind a rich deposit of metals.

Mining and smelting the metal cause the landscape to be ecologically damaged. After years of sulfur buildup, the town was left with acid soil where few plants grew. The soil eroded. Increased cancer rates and respiratory problems are common local ailments. The mining industry's severe environmental damage has been cleaned up since the 1970s. Neutralizing the soil and planting grasses and trees has turned the landscape from barren to flourishing. To disperse acid-rain-causing emissions, the tallest stack in North America was built in 1972 in Sudbury. The stack dispersed its toxic gas emissions over eastern Canada and was instrumental in affecting the biology of about seven thousand lakes. Continued upgrades to the stack have reduced 90 percent of acid-rain pollution.

Another nickel-producing area is in the Canadian Shield on the Atlantic shore: Labrador's Voisey Bay. The deposit, discovered in 1993, may contain 150 million tons of ore-grade material, making it one of the most significant geologic discoveries in Canada since the 1970s. Development of this area began in 2002 and has encountered controversy about the environmental impact of the mine and the protection of local Inuit social and cultural values. The original mining company, Toronto-based Inco, promised to develop the mine safely and to hire local Inuit, thereby solving some of the area's unemployment problems. But in 2007 the mine (along with the mine in Sudbury) was purchased by the Brazilian mining conglomerate Vale, the world's second-largest mining company. After a year-long strike by union workers in 2010 in both Sudbury and Voisey Bay was settled, Vale was voted the worthy recipient of the world's worst company in 2012 due to its record of destroying communities and the environment.[40]

Zinc   The Red Dog open-pit mine, located in the western Brooks Range of northwest Alaska about ninety miles north of Kotzebue, produces lead and is the largest zinc concentrate producer in the world. The mine employs about six hundred people. The extracted ores are shipped to a smelter in British Columbia and then to Asia and Europe.

Copper   Despite hundreds of copper-mining sites, only the J. P. Morgan–run Alaskan Syndicate (1908–1938) mines were profitable, because they had railroad access. The ore was shipped from Alaska to Tacoma, Washington, for smelting. Over $200 million in copper ore was mined, making it the richest copper mine in the world at the time. The abandoned mines have become tourist destinations. Currently, little copper is produced in Alaska, although the proposed Pebble Mine near Lake Iliamna may yield significant copper concentrations.

Silver   The largest underground silver mine in Alaska is Greens Creek Mine, located in the Tongass National Forest on Admiralty Island near Juneau. This important economic resource for the city has gone through boom-bust cycles during its operation: it opened in 1975, closed in 1993 as a result of low metal prices, and then reopened in 1996. Several other metals are mined at this location, including zinc, gold, and lead.

Diamonds   In 1991, diamonds put the Northwest Territory on the economic map. The dogged persistence of Charles Fipke, a British Columbian geologist, culminated in the discovery of gem-quality diamond mines and another mining rush. In 2004, the Northwest Territories produced about 12 percent of the world's diamonds by value, and in the ensuing years northern Quebec and Nunavut also opened diamond mines. Yellowknife became a diamond sorting, polishing, and selling facility, and it has diversified its economy, adding about seventeen hundred jobs to the area's market.

The diamond mine's open pits, roads, and utilities damage the fragile tundra ecosystem. Finding a balance between the benefits and liabilities of such an operation is the challenge. Applying technologic innovations, such as scrubbers, to the mining process has reduced emissions produced by mining activity but not the carbon dioxide.

Logging

Canada's Boreal North Logging   Logging, oil, and gas interests exploit the boreal North. When environmental politics gutted Pacific Northwest stateside logging, the practice accelerated in Canada. In 1970, 1.6 million acres of trees were cut down, increasing to more than 2.5 million acres in 2001. Forests are carbon sinks, so cutting them decreases the ability to store car-

bon dioxide, increases the level in the atmosphere, and contributes to climate change.

One of the collective oil and gas exploration and forestry issues in northeastern Alberta's boreal forest has been **seismic lines**, thirty-foot-wide strips bulldozed across the taiga landscape to facilitate drilling and dynamiting. Almost as much land is cleared for seismic lines as for logging, but seismic lines remain deforested, which affects natural habitats and fragments the forests. These disturbance corridors aggravate soils, vegetation, and aquatic systems and give hunters and poachers forest access.

Pulp mills harvest Alberta and British Columbia forests. The wood is then exported: 60 percent to the United States, a growing market in China, and much of the remainder to Japan. The mills, built on the Athabascan and Peace rivers, dump mill effluent, cause pollution, and contain carcinogens, such as dioxin. However, some companies are addressing ecosystem pollution. Abitibi Consolidated, a large paper mill supplying newsprint to the United States, is working with the Aboriginal Kaska Dena to establish an environmentally sensitive logging operation.

Alaska Logging   The Tongass National Forest spreads across almost seventeen million acres of southeastern Alaska and the Inside Passage. As the largest temperate rain forest in the world, the Tongass contains about 29 percent of the planet's total unlogged temperate rain forest. The near-perfect conditions for the conifer forests are the result of air masses coming off the Pacific and rising against the mountains.

The Alaskan forests were not cut over like Great Lakes forests, because of the distance from lumber markets and the time period of possible development. By the 1950s, many lower-forty-eight forests were logged, and Forest Service and state territory campaigns were focused on building an Alaskan logging industry to ensure economic development and local employment. In the late nineteenth century, Tongass wood was cut and used for local production and cannery needs, but building the necessary infrastructure for an international market required substantial capital and was never achieved.

Congressional subsidies allocated most of the forest to logging and pulp mills to provide local employment in the 1960s, but global competition, high labor costs, falling prices for wood, and a rising environmental movement hindered the success of Tongass pulp mills. The Tongass Timber Reform Act of 1990 reduced the amount of trees available for logging and halted most timber production. In 2003, only fifty-one million board feet were logged, about one-tenth of previous cuts. A subsequent study shows that nontimber uses such as recreation, subsistence food, and carbon sequestration may be more valuable economic drivers.[41]

The rise of environmental consciousness in the 1970s and 1980s changed how people viewed the Tongass. Some Alaskan areas were set aside as wilderness areas, while logging peaked in other areas. By 1997, the government imposed cut restrictions that left nearly 80 percent of the forests protected. Increased

BOX 18.11 FORT McMURRAY AND OIL SANDS

A sea once covered the plains of Alberta. Over time the plants and animals from that sea were heated, pressurized, and converted into the extensive oil and gas fields that account for 85 percent of Canada's oil and gas. Alberta has reaped profits from these deposits in the last half of the twentieth century. In the process, the balance of political power shifted toward the Outer Canada Prairies for the first time since Canadian Confederation.

As conventional oil production declines, the biggest news and fastest-growing industry is oil sands, whose largest reserves are north of Edmonton at three sites: Peace River, Athabasca, and Cold Lake (Map 18.7). The largest and most accessible reserve is the Athabascan oil sands, along the Athabasca River near Fort McMurray. In 2002, Fort McMurray provided one-third of Canadian production; in 2010, it provided to one-half. Only Saudi Arabia has larger oil reserves than Canada. Almost one-quarter of all oil imported into the United States is from Canada.

Alberta oil sand deposits contain 1.7 trillion to 2.5 trillion barrels of oil. The oil sands produce more than one million barrels daily, which is expected to grow to three million barrels daily by 2020. Technologies to extract the oil from the sands are more expensive than conventional methods and are only profitable when the price of oil is high. Saudi oil costs about $2 to $3 per barrel to pump, whereas Alberta bitumen (the molasses-like crude extracted) costs from $8.50 to $12 per barrel. The crude oil leaves Fort McMurray by underground pipeline to Edmonton or to the United States, where it is refined into gasoline, home heating oil, and jet fuel. The Keystone Pipeline and Keystone XL extension is a proposed system of transporting the thick oil through the United States to the Gulf Coast. The proposed pipeline has been controversial due to potential environmental impacts, including passing over the Sand Hills of Nebraska and the Ogallala Aquifer and the potential harm of a pipeline leak.

The extreme environmental impact of oil sands mining has affected land, air, water, and health. The oil is mixed with sand and clay; separating the oil takes heat, pressure, and chemicals, all of which cause additional problems for the climate and environment. The oil removal process, the number one source of greenhouse gases in Canada, is two to three times more polluting than conventional oil development. Two tons of oil sands produce one barrel of crude oil (Photo 18.13).

The current pit surface mining methods have displaced more than 150,000 acres that must be reclaimed, including resurfacing and planting trees and greenbelts for wildlife habitat. The disruption to the land and the cost to reclaim it are immense, and reclamation has yet to be satisfactorily fulfilled, although the companies have invested millions to attempt reclamation with little success. The adjacent rivers, which run north to the Arctic

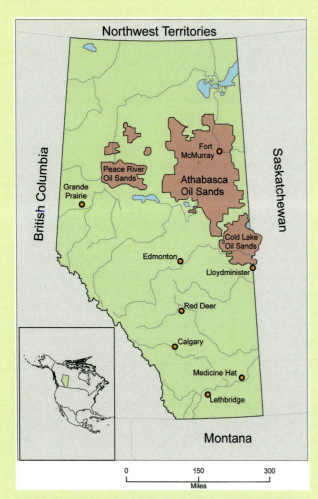

MAP 18.7. Canada's Oil Sands Deposits. These deposits are found mostly at three sites. The Peach River and Athabasca sites are in Alberta, and the Cold Lake site is within Alberta and Saskatchewan.

PHOTO 18.13. Syncrude, Fort McMurray, Alberta. The boomtown region has more than eighty thousand people, plus another ten thousand who live in the multiple work camps on oil company sites, as seen here. Traffic jams and need for infrastructure—including a widening of the "killer highway," the single road that runs from Edmonton—are part of the price of growth for this twenty-first-century boomtown.

Ocean, are heavily polluted. Few dare to eat the fish, though not that long ago they were a source for subsistence food.

Oil sands extraction uses Athabascan River water, causing water quantity and quality problems. The water is seldom recycled but dumped in unrecoverable toxic ponds. Residents downriver from the oil sands have reported high incidences of asthma and respiratory illness, but even more disturbing is the high incidence of cancer, as reported in Alberta's oldest settlement, Fort Chipewyan. The fort sits on the shore of Lake Athabasca—the Athabasca River drains into the lake. Among the carcinogenic chemicals in the water are benzene and arsenic, while fish have high mercury levels. A 2006 study by Alberta Health and Wellness found no higher risk of cancer, but the local community doubted the findings; the results of a new study were reported in 2009. The results showed a higher incidence of cancer than expected, but it did not go so far as to blame the oil sands industry, saying that the increased cancers could be due to chance.*

The oil sands have brought an economic boom and political power to Alberta, but at the price of unsustainability and pollution.

* Alberta Cancer Board, "Cancer Incidence in Fort Chipewyan, Alberta, 1995–2006," February 2009, at http://www.ualberta.ca/~avnish/rls-2009-02-06-fort-chipewyan-study.pdf.

global competition (the opening of the Russian-Siberian market) affected the remaining forest's profitability, and by 1997 the pulp mills were closed.

The logging industry plays a minor role in the Alaskan economy. But increased pressure to reopen Tongass logging has been a popular sentiment, although the industry now faces increased global competition. The region still has an abundant forest, but its location and high American labor costs are unfavorable.

Alaska needs more jobs, but the dependence on natural resources places these jobs in direct conflict with environmental concerns. The Tongass and Chugach national forests have become political hot potatoes in the new millennium, and each administration has forwarded its agenda over logging. In 2009 the Obama administration reversed Bush-era logging by protecting roadless areas of national forests; however, conservation and logging interests continue to battle their interests in court.

Fishing

Here was Alaska's greatest natural resource. Here was the nation's greatest fishery resource. . . . The result is written in figures that spell tragedy for Alaska's coastal communities whose economy has long depended on fisheries. The tragedy has deepened year after year. So grave has become the plight that the administration found it necessary to declare the fishing villages to be disaster areas. It is a disaster caused by colonialism . . . (that) has preferred to conserve the power and special privileges . . . of a politically potent absentee industry.[42]

The average value of Alaska's annual wild salmon harvest fell from $500 million between 1990 and 1995, to below $200 million in 2001 and 2002, due mostly to the competition posed by cheaper farmed salmon.[43]

Upon statehood, Alaska's primary industry was the fishery. After oil production grew in the 1970s, fishing became Alaska's second- and then third-largest industry (after tourism), but it continued to provide nearly six billion pounds of seafood annually. Most attention has been on the lucrative salmon fishery, but low salmon prices and dwindling fish stock, along with quotas, have curbed the wild-fish commercial fishery. The largest-volume fishery, dominated by species other than salmon, remains in the Bering Sea.

The commercial salmon fishery has been a staple of the Alaskan and Canadian West Coast economy, but historically outside interests and legislation have favored the Alaskan syndicate and Seattle profiteers who controlled Alaska's fishing industry and denied profits to local fishers. By 1918, the local commercial fishery and the livelihood of many fishers became obsolete.

Salmon has remained important in the Native diet, but it is also an American delicacy. However, for years little attention was paid to salmon sustainability; instead, the anadromous salmon's homing instinct was exploited. Presently, Pacific Northwest fishing resources are down 90 percent, due to overfishing and dam construction. To combat this shortage, fish farms proliferate and threaten the viability of the Alaskan wild fishery.

The per-pound price for salmon waned in the 1990s as the result of increased competition from Norwegian, Chilean, and Scottish farm-raised salmon. A small rebound in wild fish occurred in the twenty-first century but remained lower than in the past. Fishery experts believe the rebound is the result of increased environmental awareness of antibiotic, insecticide, and colorant use in farmed fish.

Ninety-eight percent of the world salmon supply was wild in 1980. By 1997, farm-raised salmon exceeded the wild salmon catch in value, and by 2001, 62 percent was farmed. By 2005, wild salmon was seldom available in markets outside Alaska and the Pacific Northwest. The largest customer for Alaskan fish has been Japan, but their purchase of farm-raised salmon is increasing. The relationship of the Japanese yen to the American dollar also controls Japanese purchases of Alaskan fish. Since 2000, the weakened American dollar has enhanced Japanese fish purchases.

Salmon continue to account for the largest share of Alaskan fishing receipts, but king crab, snow crab, halibut, cod, pollock, and several other fish are also valuable. Strict quotas control and restrict fishing. The principal fishing grounds are in the panhandle area, the Gulf of Alaska, Kodiak, Bristol Bay, and the Bering Sea. The Bering Sea alone accounts for one-half of the U.S. catch, but it is overfished. Dutch Harbor in the Aleutian Islands has become the number one port in the nation for seafood volume (Photo 18.14).

Local fish-processing plants employ thousands of nonresidents, who live in dorms near the plant during the processing seasons. The two main seasons are during the winter (crab,

PHOTO 18.14. Unalaska, Alaska, on the Aleutian Islands. Unalaska has become the primary fishing port by volume for the United States. Its history goes back to Unangan Natives, who were followed by Russian fur traders. Today Unalaska remains influenced by its Russian past and the port town of Dutch Harbor.

halibut, and pollock) and summer through fall (halibut, cod, turbot, and pollock). The processed seafood is converted to surimi (restructured fish flesh or fish paste, colored and reshaped to resemble more expensive seafood, such as crab) and shipped to Japan. Other fish are processed into bone-free blocks and cut into patty shapes to be used by fast-food chains. All fish parts are processed. Fishmeal is made from by-products. Fish oil was once an unprofitable by-product until experiments in the late 1990s perfected another use: green energy. Biodiesel fuel is used approximately fifty-fifty with fossil fuel in the plant generators and in the powerhouse. The fish oil is biodegradable and less polluting than diesel.[44]

The Alaskan fishery, the largest in the United States, struggles with continued out-of-state ownership, decreasing fishery profits, and the annual closure of canneries. Many towns along the Alaskan Peninsula and the Aleutians depend on the fishery, and they have been protected by quotas implemented in 1992.

Arctic Fishery—Canada   Commercial and sport fishing industries have caused a decline in the Arctic fishery and have influenced the native diet, as have environmental contaminants.

Commercial whaling throughout the nineteenth century depleted whale populations, until commercial operations were no longer viable by the century's end. The population of bowhead whales, estimated at fifty thousand in the sixteenth and seventeenth centuries, was reduced to five thousand by 1900 because of extensive Western whaling, but it has begun to recover due to protection and conservation efforts. In 2004, the number of bowhead whales had grown to ten thousand, mostly in Canadian Arctic waters. The Arctic Inupiaq "people of the whale" are dependent on the whale, but only limited indigenous hunting is allowed for bowhead whales, both because of their depleted numbers and because of the inability to harvest the large mammal efficiently.[45]

Industry and Postindustrial

Government

The government sector employs eighty thousand Alaskans. In Juneau, the state capital, the pay structure is lopsided; well-paid jobs within the government provide two-thirds of the employment, but reduced oil revenues have curtailed the abundance of government jobs. The remainder is made up of low-paying tourism-related jobs. Government jobs are also important in the Canadian Territories, where jobs are scarce outside the mining industry.

Tourism

Alaska Tourism

Alaska tourism emphasizes a Disneyland-like romanticized and simplified Alaska that contrasts with the reality; however, tourism is one of the largest sources of income in Alaska. Cruises along the Inside Passage began during the late nineteenth century but intensified during the late twentieth century. While fishing and logging are important, most Alaskan towns profit from tourism.

Places like Whittier, Alaska, have transformed from a military to a contemporary tourism-based economy. In 2010, the state received 1.78 million visitors, more than 742,700 of whom arrived on cruise ships. After September 11, 2001, tourism dropped significantly; it rebounded and then dropped again due to the economic slump of 2008. The decreased value of the American dollar has encouraged foreign tourism, but the depressed dollar has also boosted the number of American tourists who choose to vacation in Alaska, because European travel is too expensive.

Keeping tourist dollars within the local economies and not exporting profits to outside corporations is a continuing challenge. Profits leave the locale and leave locals with low-paying jobs and reduced community services. However, Seattle has been the headquarters for many Alaskan companies for the past century. For example, Princess Cruises and Tours are headquartered in Washington, as are the large fishing companies. Princess Tours controls nearly all the tourist dollars it generates with its own ships, hotels, bus lines, and tour packages.

Alaska has many scenic and outdoor sites with over fifty-one million acres of national park land, including Denali (Mount McKinley) and Glacier Bay. Towns on cruise-ship lines rely on tourism for their sustenance. Skagway, for example, was a ghost town until cruise ships reinvigorated the town of eight hundred. Over four hundred cruise ships visit annually, up to five per day visit during the May to September tourism season. During the off-season, the town shuts down.

Canadian Territories Economy and Tourism

Income in the Canadian territories has traditionally been either subsistence- or resource-based. Mining accounts for 99 percent of total exports from the Northwest Territory and 80 percent of Yukon exports. Preserving regional environmental integrity has become a growing concern. Territorial wilderness landscapes are among the last on the continent and as such have attracted increased tourism. Hunters and fishers fly into remote areas on bush planes, or they arrive on the few existing roads into the territories.

Transportation across the tundra has always been difficult. Natives and early Western inhabitants traveled the Mackenzie River by canoe or barge in the summer, but mosquito-infested bogs and marshes limited the ability to carry the heavy equipment needed by extractive industries. Winter travel by dog sleds and snowshoes was in many ways easier than summer travel. In the late nineteenth century, the railway came into Dawson City, Yukon, but the costs of infrastructure to maintain a permafrost railway were enormous. Roads have slowly developed in the North, but few penetrate the Arctic. The Northwest Territory and the Yukon have a combined total of thirty-six hundred highway miles (Photo 18.1). Nunavut has no long-distance highways.

Permafrost roads are built with a thick insulating gravel layer built atop the tundra mat, because cutting into the tundra results in muck. An elevated gravel road can withstand the changing active layer better than a permanent roadbed. The two major Arctic highways, built to support mineral and petroleum extraction, are the Alaska Dalton Highway from Fairbanks to Prudhoe Bay, which services the oil pipeline, and the Dempster Highway, which provides the required road to reach petroleum deposits in Canada's territorial North.

Travel through the Arctic to resource sites, such as the diamond mines, is best done in the winter trucking over **ice roads** made of compacted snow, because in the summer the muskeg makes the route impassable. Although the ice roads have been rebuilt each winter since the 1980s, they may soon become impractical. Climate change is shortening the ice-road season.

A Sustainable Future

The highly vulnerable geography of Canada's Arctic has been experiencing growing pressures due to climate change, contaminated sites, persistent organic pollutants and economic development based on non-renewable resource industries, such as diamond mining and oil and gas extraction, increased recreational boating or commercial shipping and ecotourism.[46]

Although written about Canada, most of the preceding paragraph can also apply to Alaska. The "pristine North" is an illusion. Many environmental ills originating in the industrialized South have found their way into the Arctic, and many are now generated in the North and wreak bioaccumulation havoc on the region. The reality of Arctic climate change has resulted in ecosystem and habitat destruction. The Arctic role in global resources is recent; as temperate-climate resources reach their economic limits, Arctic resources are being tapped. Additionally, a significant discovery of diamonds in the Northwest Territory has realigned the worldwide diamond cartel; this discovery ensures the region's economic viability at least temporarily, it but also requires mitigation to reduce environmental damage.

Arctic oil is a contentious issue. Local residents want the resource to be developed because they want the jobs provided by the industry. However, mounting evidence in environmentalists' reports indicates that oil development in the Arctic National Wildlife Refuge would damage local flora and fauna, including the declining Porcupine caribou herd that supplies local residents with food. Ultimately, the question of Arctic oil development and the short-term benefit it offers the U.S. oil supply (possibly a year's worth of oil) becomes a less important issue than the question of when and how the United States will evolve beyond its fossil fuel dependence.

Sustainability studies are now common in Alaska and territorial Canada, because of the "canary in the coal mine" role the region plays regarding climate change. Halting this progression and achieving environmental sustainability is essential, and some small actions have taken place toward this end. Environmental issues have been addressed with the Alaskan Pipeline, the Keystone Pipeline and Extension, and the possible construction of a natural gas pipeline. However, Canada has pulled out of the Kyoto Protocol and joined the United States in refusal to participate. The much-ballyhooed Copenhagen meetings in December 2009 were ineffective.

Inuit and First Nations bands have pursued sustainable research to support the continuation of their culture and to document environmental changes. At the University of Alaska, Fairbanks, the Alaska Native Knowledge Network and the Cold

Climate Housing Research Center are studying cultural resources and investigating renewable energy options and local housing materials.[47] In January 2009, the state energy policy was facing the inevitable—cheap energy was over and renewable energy cannot (at least within a short period of time) replace what fossil fuels have provided: It was time to conserve.[48] Geothermal power has been pursued on Unalaska in the Aleutians. First discovered in 1982 on the flank of Matushin Volcano, the hot-water source has yet to be tapped for use. Geothermal

opportunities are rare in Alaska, except along the volcanic subduction zones.

In Canada, several organizations favor seeking sustainable methods and management. The work involved in protecting the Stellar sea lion is among the projects, as is monitoring the Porcupine caribou herd; this work is being led by the Arctic Borderlands Ecological Knowledge Co-op.[49] Technology can align human activities with nature, instead of for profit alone. Sustainability is in the people's hands; they form the hope for the future.

Questions for Discussion

1. Why is Alaska called the bellwether state in regard to climate change? Give an example.

2. What are the issues for drilling in the Arctic National Wildlife Refuge?

3. What have been the issues of building a gas pipeline in the Mackenzie River area?

4. What are the advantages of mining in the North and the Canadian Shield? What are the disadvantages?

5. Who is in charge of Alaska's fishery, and how does it affect the state?

6. What are the political, economic, and cultural implications that have made the James Bay Project controversial?

7. What is permafrost, and how is it an impediment to construction? How does the construction industry get around the impediment?

8. How have Inuit lifestyles changed in recent decades, and what problems do they face today?

9. Why was the Trans-Alaska Pipeline considered environmentally sensitive? How did the oil companies work to protect the environment?

10. What are ANCSA Corporations (Alaska Native Corporations) and what has been their impact?

11. What is the relationship and effect between the Mackenzie Valley Pipeline project and the Berger Inquiry?

Suggested Readings

Abel, Kerry. *Drum Songs: Glimpses of Dene History*. Buffalo, N.Y.: McGill-Queen's University Press, 1993.

Alaska Energy Authority. "Alaska Energy: A First Step toward Energy Independence." January 2009, at http://chpcenternw.org/Nw ChpDocs/AlaskaEnergy_AFirstStepTowardEnergyIndependence .pdf.

Bone, Robert M. *The Geography of the Canadian North: Issues and Challenges*. Toronto: Oxford University Press, 2003.

———. *The Regional Geography of Canada*. Toronto: Oxford University Press, 2000.

Bourassa, Robert. *Power from the North*. Scarborough, Ontario: Prentice Hall of Canada, 1985.

Canadian Arctic Resources Committee. "On Thinning Ice." *Northern Perspectives* 27, no. 2 (Spring 2002).

Charndonnet, Ann. *On the Trail of Eklutna*. Chicago: Adams Press, 1991.

Collier, Robert. "Fueling America: Canadian Oil Showdown." *San Francisco Chronicle*, May 23, 2005.

Committee on the Alaska Groundfish Fishery and Stellar Sea Lions, National Research Council. *The Decline of the Stellar Sea Lion in Alaskan Waters: Untangling Food Webs and Fishing Nets*. Washington, D.C.: National Academies Press, 2003.

Davis, Neil. *Permafrost: A Guide to Frozen Ground in Transition*. Fairbanks: University of Alaska Press, 2001.

French, Hugh M., and Olav Slaymaker, eds. "Canada's Cold Environments." Canadian Association of Geographers Series in Canadian Geography. Montreal and Kingston: McGill-Queen's University Press, 1997.

Gibson, James R. "Russian Expansion in Siberia and America." *Geographical Review* 70, no. 2 (April 1980): 127–36.

Goulden, M. L., S. C. Wofsy, J. W. Harden, et al. "Sensitivity of Boreal Forest Carbon Balance to Soil Thaw." *Science*, January 9, 1998.

Gruening, Ernest. *The Battle for Alaska Statehood*. Fairbanks: University of Alaska Press.

Hensley, William. "What Rights to Land Have the Alaska Natives? The Primary Question." May 1966, at http://www.alaskool.org/ projects/ancsa/WLH/WLH66_2.htm.

Huberman, Irwin. *The Place We Call Home: A History of Fort McMurray as Its People Remember 1778–1980*. Fort McMurray, Alberta: Fort McMurray Historical Book Society, 2001.

Jablonski, Nina G., ed. *The First Americans: The Pleistocene Colonization of the New World*. San Francisco: University of California Press, 2002.

Keith, Robert F., Terry Fenge, Peter Jacobs, and Shelagh Jane Woods. "Arctic Fisheries: New Approaches for Troubled Waters." *Northern Perspectives* 15, no. 4,(November 1987).

Kolbert, Elizabeth. "Disappearing Islands, Thawing Permafrost, Melting Polar Ice. How the Earth Is Changing." *The New Yorker*, April 25, 2005, at http://www.wesjones.com/climate1.htm.

Krim, Arthur. "Fort McMurray: Future City of the Far North." *Geographical Review* 93, no. 2 (April 2003): 258–66.

Lischke, Ute, and David T. McNab, eds. *The Long Journey of a Forgotten People: Métis Identities and Family Histories.* Waterloo, Ontario: Wilfrid Laurier University Press, 2007.

Lucier, Charles V., and James W. Vanstone. *Traditional Beluga Drives of the Inupiaq of Kotzebue Sound, Alaska.* Fieldiana, new series, no. 25. Chicago: Field Museum of Natural History, 1995.

Naske, Claus M., and Herman E. Slotnick. *Alaska: A History of the Forty-Ninth State.* Norman: University of Oklahoma Press, 1987.

Shortridge, James R. "The Collapse of Frontier Farming in Alaska." *Annals of the Association of American Geographers* 66, no. 4 (December 1976): 583–604.

Sokolowski, Thomas J. "The Great Alaskan Earthquake and Tsunamis of 1964." West Coast and Alaska Tsunami Warning Center, Palmer, Alaska, December 1976, at http://wcatwc.arh.noaa.gov/64quake.htm.

Stager, J. K., and Harry Swain. *Canada North: Journey to the High Arctic.* New Brunswick, N.J.: Rutgers University Press, 1992.

Tarr, Ralph Stockman. "Glaciers and Glaciation of Alaska." *Annals of the Association of American Geographers* 2 (1912): 3–24.

United Nations Environment Programme. "Melting Permafrost May Accelerate Global Warming, UNEP Scientists Warn." United Nations Environment Programme, February 7, 2001, at http://www.unep.org/Documents.multilingual/Default.asp?DocumentID=192&ArticleID=2763

U.S. General Accounting Office. "Alaska Native Villages." GAO-04-142, December 2003, at http://www.gao.gov/new.items/d04142.pdf.

Welsted, John E., Christoph Stadel, and John C. Everitt, eds. *The Geography of Manitoba: Its Land and Its People.* Winnipeg: University of Manitoba Press, 1996.

Wynn, Graeme, and Mark Stoll, eds. *Canada and Arctic North America: An Environmental History.* Santa Barbara, Calif.: ABC-CLIO, 2006.

Internet Sources

Alaska Department of Natural Resources. Division of Oil and Gas, at http://dog.dnr.alaska.gov/.

Carbon Dioxide Information Analysis Center. Global, Regional, and National Fossil Fuel CO_2 Emissions, at http://cdiac.ornl.gov/trends/emis/em_cont.html.

North Country Public Radio. Hydro Power in Cree Country, at http://www.northcountrypublicradio.org/news/hydrocree.html.

United Nations Environment Programme. Population Pyramid for Nunavut and Canada, at http://www.grida.no/publications/other/geo3/?src=/geo/geo3/english/fig58.htm.

U.S. Geological Survey. Sea Level and Climate. http://pubs.usgs.gov/fs/fs2-00/.

Statistics Canada. Family Income, at http://www40.statcan.gc.ca/l01/cst01/famil106a-eng.htm.

Statistics Canada, at http://www.statcan.gc.ca.

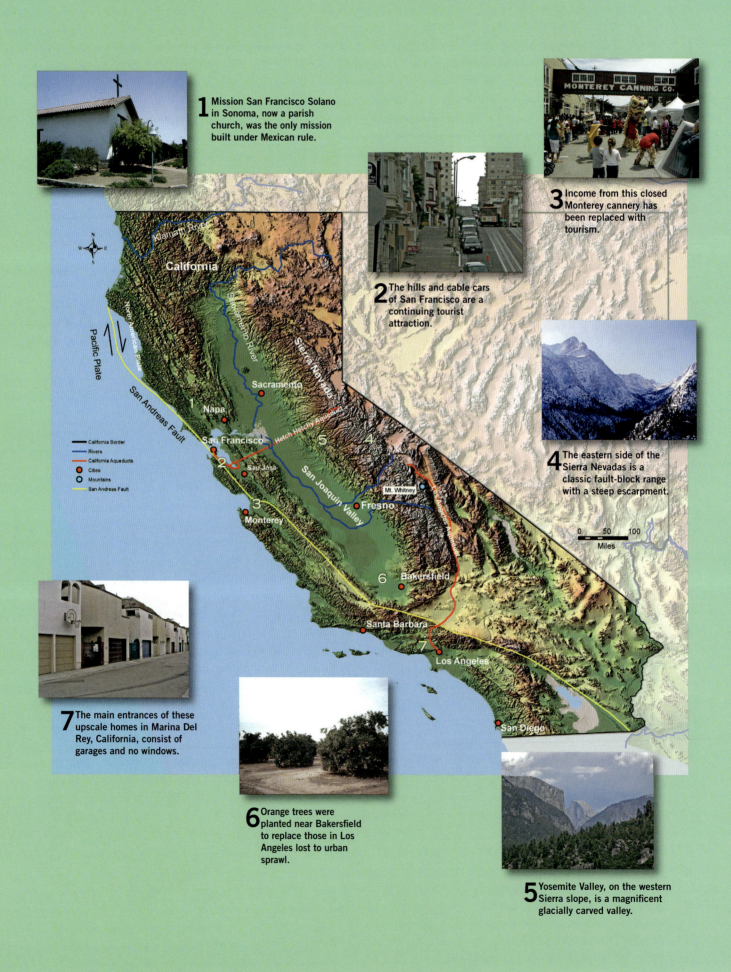

1 Mission San Francisco Solano in Sonoma, now a parish church, was the only mission built under Mexican rule.

3 Income from this closed Monterey cannery has been replaced with tourism.

2 The hills and cable cars of San Francisco are a continuing tourist attraction.

4 The eastern side of the Sierra Nevadas is a classic fault-block range with a steep escarpment.

7 The main entrances of these upscale homes in Marina Del Rey, California, consist of garages and no windows.

6 Orange trees were planted near Bakersfield to replace those in Los Angeles lost to urban sprawl.

5 Yosemite Valley, on the western Sierra slope, is a magnificent glacially carved valley.

Map labels: California; Klamath River; Sacramento River; Sierra Nevada; Pacific Plate; North American Plate; San Andreas Fault; Sacramento; Napa; San Francisco; San Jose; Monterey; Hetch Hetchy Aqueduct; San Joaquin Valley; Fresno; Mt. Whitney; Bakersfield; Santa Barbara; Los Angeles; San Diego

Legend:
California Border
Rivers
California Aqueducts
Cities
Mountains
San Andreas Fault

0   50   100
Miles

19
CALIFORNIA
Having It All, and Then Some

PHOTO 19.1. Mission San Juan Capistrano. This is one of twenty-one missions built by the Spanish beginning in 1769. Spanish-style architecture remains popular in California.

Introduction

California is complex, diverse, and extreme. The state has a complex topography, diversified demography and economy, and extremes in elevation, climate, vegetation. The highest and lowest elevations, Mount Whitney and Death Valley, are within view of each other and experience glacial cold and extreme heat, respectively. Climate ranges from always-sunny, Southern California to the colder, foggy interior and north; rainfall ranges from less than three inches in the desert to one hundred inches in the northern Coastal Ranges. The state's vegetation varies from xerophytic cacti and shrubs to giant redwoods. The extremes do not end there. California, the most populous state, has water problems exacerbated by periodic droughts. And in 2011, California also had mounting foreclosures, job loss, and one of the nation's highest unemployment rates

Despite its extremes, California's effect on the nation and the world is significant. Nearly everyone knows where California is located and what it signifies—sun, sand, money, and beautiful people—but it also is a bellwether for diversity. There has been a provocative shift in the state's demographics. For many non-Hispanic whites, the shift signaled emigration; for many remaining Californians, the shift is viewed as either a cultural boon or a sore point of discussion. Regardless, California's diverse demographics embody large populations of every major ethnic group and are representative of the future of America.

In the 2000 Census, California realized a sea change shift in population since 1960. The census disclosed that the majority white non-Hispanic population was shrinking. **Hispanics** (or **Latinos**, depending on who is referring to them) were the fastest-growing segment of the population. While many Hispanics are legal, many are not, which has created multiple problems.

The undocumented Hispanics seek a better life, but their lack of legal status, education, and English skills leaves them exploited. Hispanic cultural differences and expectations often disengage them from the more affluent mainstream, acculturated but not assimilated into the land they chose to enter. An additional demographic change has been the many Asian cultural groups who have migrated to the state, sought out education, and become successful.

Overall, the population shifted within a generation, creating tension among white non-Hispanic Californians. In a special election in October 2004, this tension was revealed by Proposition 54, which would have restricted the government from "classifying" (collecting and using) information on an individual's race, ethnicity, color, or national origin. The proposition failed to pass, and classification by these categories continues, but one-third of the populace voted in favor of the proposition—in other words, one-third feel serious discrimination exists and chose a "colorblind" society.

The changes in demographics have changed how people live in California. Gangs and drive-by shootings were rare prior to the current mass of immigrants entering California. Is the increased violence and crime the result of the immigrants? Or perhaps they were the result of the crush of thirty-seven million people living in a water-challenged state? Regardless, California was at the forefront for living isolated and gated lives. America's fortress-living, gated communities began in California. The mass of immigrants has exacerbated the ever-widening gap between wealthy and poor. The Golden State enters the twenty-first century as the most multicultural of all the states, containing what may be the most multicultural city in the world—Los Angeles.

California has led the nation in a variety of ways, but in the twenty-first century California is a leader in another vital area, sustainability—although California's role is at odds with itself. California has been at the forefront of renewable energy with wind farms, solar power, and a commitment to reducing greenhouse gases. But California lacks sufficient water for the vaunted California standard of living, and rather than rethink its water policy it has decided to augment the water system by expensive and fossil fuel–dependent desalination. The state needs to seek new conservation methods and to rethink its access to water and its relation to continued population growth.

Physical Geography

The topography and almost everything else about California's geology are complex and diverse. California spans more than 770 miles from Mexico to Oregon and 250 miles from the West Coast to its eastern boundary. At its most basic, California's topography is mountains–valley–mountains: Coastal Range–Central Valley–Sierra Nevada and Basin and Range. Parts of the state are included in three major regions: Pacific Northwest, Intermontane, and this chapter's concentration, the core where more than 95 percent of the people live (Map 19.1). The core contains the Sierra Nevada and Coastal Range, the Coastal urban conurbations, and the Central Valley.

Sierra Nevada and Coastal Range

The steep, rugged Coastal Range parallels and edges the Pacific Ocean. Structural depressions, such as Salinas Valley and San Francisco Bay, separate the series of linear northwest-to-southeast-oriented coastal mountains. The local physiography is a jumble of igneous-infused sedimentary rock, liquefaction soils, and microclimates such as the hot and dry **chaparral ecosystems** with their moisture-retaining shrubs that are fire and drought resistant.

Farther south, near the intersection of the San Andreas and Garlock earthquake faults, are the east-west-trending Transverse and Tehachapi ranges. The San Gabriel and San Bernardino mountains encompass that part of the populous Los Angeles Basin that does not face the sea. San Gorgonio (11, 490 feet) towers over its pass, which connects the Inland Empire extension of the Los Angeles Basin with the Basin and Range city of Palm Springs. To the south of the Los Angeles Basin, the Peninsular Range separates the San Diego watershed basin from the much drier Anza Borrego Desert within the Colorado River watershed. The coastal mountains separate the coast from the Central Valley, which is separated from the Basin and Range by the Sierra Nevada.

South of the Cascades, the Sierra Nevada, 350 miles long and 60 miles wide, divide the Intermontane Basin and Range from California's core region. The pine-forested Sierras rise

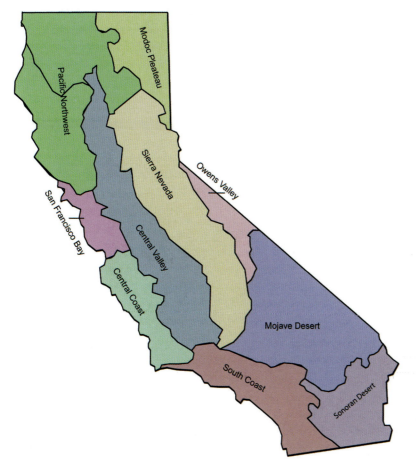

MAP 19.1. California Regions. The state of California is included in three major regions: the Pacific Northwest; Intermontane Basin and Range; and California. The northern coast is part of the Pacific Northwest. The eastern sections are part of the Basin and Range (Modoc Plateau, Owens Valley, Mojave Desert, Sonoran Desert), and the area with the most population, agriculture, and largest economy is the core of California: the San Francisco Bay, Central Coast, Central Valley, Sierra Nevada, and South Coast.

some nine thousand feet above the five-thousand-foot valley floor, culminating in 14,494-foot Mount Whitney. California's few major rivers originate in the Sierras. The fault-block granitic escarpment tilts sharply upward in the east and gradually descends west under Central Valley sediments. The abrupt rise of the eastern face of the mountains is related to the underlying geology and the number of earthquakes that uplifted the mountains and continue to shake California.

South Coast and Los Angeles Basin

The South Coast encompasses the skinny coastal plain to the Mexican border. Coastal ranges separate Los Angeles from the Inland Empire counties of San Bernardino and Riverside (part of the Intermontane), which are included in the greater metropolitan area (including Los Angeles, Orange, and Ventura counties), known as the Southland.

Tectonics shaped the Los Angeles Basin fifteen million years ago. The resulting crust collapsed into a sediment-filled bowl, until another tectonic event uplifted the basin about five million years ago. The bowl contains thirty thousand feet of gravel, sand, and clay sediments over the bedrock.[1] The lack of bedrock close to the surface explains the gelatin-like **liquefaction** of soil during seismic events, and it leaves Los Angeles Basin prone to earthquake damage.

Central Valley

The four-hundred-mile by fifty-mile Central Valley, wedged between the Coast Ranges and the Sierra Nevada, is flat, fertile alluvium converted from grassland and marsh to the richest agricultural plain in America. Today the native grasslands are less than 6 percent of their original extent. The valley has two significant rivers (but small when compared to the mighty rivers of America): the Sacramento in the north and the San Joaquin in the south. Both empty into the San Francisco Bay. Water is a major issue in the valley and in California. Rainfall diminishes from north to south, from twenty inches to less than ten. The rainfall was sufficient for ranching operations as the Spanish practiced them, but irrigation became the norm as Anglos assumed control.

West of the Central Valley, the Salinas Valley is hemmed in by the Coastal Mountains east of the Monterey Peninsula. The valley emerged from an ancient inland sea. The Salinas River drained the valley and deposited the sandy, well-drained alluvium soil that now grows bountiful specialty crops.

Water

Water is a problem in California. The state is drought prone, and the water is unevenly distributed. The northern third of the state has 70 percent of the water, while the southern two-thirds have 80 percent of the need. California's three major drainage basins, the Sacramento, San Joaquin, and Tulare, all drain into the San Francisco Bay, but their flow is modest in relation to the state's current needs. The state water system is complex and political, with constant battles between agricultural and urban uses.

Southern California has grown into the second-largest conurbation in America. It has more than one-half of the state's population, but only 2 percent of its natural runoff. Southern California's lack of water has been a long-standing and expensive problem; more than $12 billion has been spent on water systems and studies continue to seek water access.

Southern California receives two-thirds of its water from various nonlocal water aqueducts and reservoirs. The balance is met with groundwater and runoff. In 1922, the Colorado River Compact apportioned the river's water between the western states, but California claimed more than its share of water with little competition from the less-populated contiguous states. However, the Basin and Range Intermontane states have grown considerably since 1990 and have now claimed their legal share of water.

The water-starved south has also diverted Northern California water, which is unpopular among Northern Californians. Many dams were built for Southern Californian use, but in the twenty-first century, dams have fallen out of favor. Rather than build more, the current trend is to remove established dams, such as the Hetch-Hetchy.[2]

Some possible solutions to the lack of water include conservation, recycling, mandatory restrictions, desalination, and building more storage facilities. While conservation, recycling, and restrictions are now commonplace, they are insufficient to satisfy the water needs; so California has pursued desalination possibilities since the 1980s.

Desalination (desal) has become a popular consideration because of population growth, industrial and agricultural needs, and changing climate patterns. Desal removes the salts from ocean water, but exorbitant costs and fossil-fuel-energy use has limited its appeal. Desalination is at least four times the cost of urban water and ten to twenty times the cost of California's agricultural water. Cheap oil or alternative energy sources are required to desalinate water, so historically only places like Saudi Arabia can afford the process. Desal plants have been the subject of environmental scrutiny, raising concerns about fossil-fuel dependence, fish kills and aquatic ecosystems disturbed by the pumping process, and return of brine to the ocean.

In energy- and conservation-conscious California, desal plant proposals have caused uproars in local communities. For example, desalinated water is at the heart of price increases and water shortages in Monterey, California. The peninsula lacks access to state water projects. Proposed rate increases brought a storm of protest; water will go from an average of $38 monthly to $80, despite the 80 percent drop in desal cost in the past twenty-five years. Most desal plants require an adjacent coal-burning power plant to provide the additional energy. Residents fear the continued dependence on coal-powered energy and the destruction of their coastal environment. A 2004 study estimated the cost of Monterey's desal plant at over $250 million, but by 2010 the cost estimate ballooned to $400 million. However, Monterey continues to research options, and is now considering an offshore shipboard facility that will be less destructive to the coastal region.

BOX 19.1 SAN FRANCISCO BAY

A series of valleys are tucked between California's coastal ranges. San Francisco Bay was once one of the valleys, but the estuary has been inundated with saltwater multiple times in the past fifteen million years, until the present shallow bay was created about ten thousand years ago. The elongated bay is also a major West Coast estuary, receiving freshwater from the Central Valley and saltwater from the gap spanned by the Golden Gate Bridge. Native Americans lived along the bay for thousands of years but left little evidence of their occupancy, whereas Europeans affected the bay's appearance within a few years of their arrival.

Unintended Consequences

The Gold Rush was located inland near Sacramento, but by 1869, the mines, development, and runoff had already had a deleterious environmental effect on the entire Bay Area. Hydraulic gold mining dumped debris into the streams, and as a result large areas of the bay silted up.

In the subsequent years, the Bay Area has become densely populated and land costs have skyrocketed. To satisfy the need for more land, many wetland areas have been filled in. The bay is in an earthquake zone, and the filled areas are subject to liquefaction, which makes soil behave like a liquid during earthquakes and causes more damage, especially to underground pipelines, airport runways, and road surfaces. Liquefaction has been indirectly blamed for about 85 percent of the total damage due to broken pipelines in the 1906 San Francisco earthquake.*

Local and Ecoregional Impacts

When Europeans first arrived, the bay was about 680 square miles, but today it is less than 400 square miles (Map 19.2). Airports, freeways, and development have reclaimed land and shrunk and polluted the bay, while killing many endemic organisms. Urban and agricultural runoff, along with industrial sewage, has contaminated the estuary. Within the remaining bay area, the Army Corps of Engineers began dredging the bay, thereby subsidizing the shipping industry, but the disposal of the dredged material has had an effect on the fishing and environmental communities. Over the years, the Army Corps of Engineers has dredged materials and enacted the most beneficial use for both wetland construction and the fishery.†

External Costs

The effects of fill and dredging have destroyed biologically productive estuarine zones and altered weather patterns. In the nineteenth century, 90 percent of West Coast wetlands were in the bay. Tidal marshes covered an area nearly twice the size of the bay itself. Today, over 95 percent of the tidal marshes have levees or are filled in. The bay was also a natural air conditioner for the Bay Area; with less water, inland towns have warmer weather.

Prior to the 1960s and the environmental movement, the bay's economic benefits were paramount. Schemes were proposed to maximize land use and even to eliminate the bay. Few people thought of the bay's ecology and how the modifications—land reclamation, wastewater discharge, and a decline in the fishery—impacted their life.

Fisherman's Wharf in San Francisco has long been a tourist landmark, but the catch of local fish—chinook salmon, clams, striped bass, Dungeness crabs, and oysters—has declined dramatically. Existing fisheries have switched from commercial to recreational, because of laws regulating and diminishing the commercial catch.

Since the 1960s, the bay has been studied to rectify damage. A plethora of federal programs and local conservation networks work to acquire, restore, and study the bay. Some of the goals encourage compact and infill development near transit hubs, especially in brownfield or low-income areas.

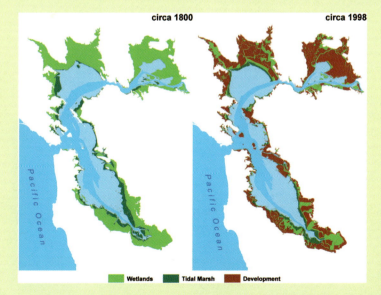

circa 1800   circa 1998

Pacific Ocean

Wetlands   Tidal Marsh   Development

MAP 19.2. San Francisco Bay, Filled-In Lands. Dikes, levees, and land reclamation reduced the bay in size from 680 square miles in 1850 to less than 400 square miles today. Over 95 percent of the tidal marshes have been drained.

---

* Association of Bay Area Governments, "The Real Dirt on Liquefaction," February 2001; T. L. Youd and S. N. Hoose, "Historic Ground Failures in Northern California Triggered by Earthquakes," U.S. Geological Survey Professional Paper 993 (Washington, D.C.: U.S. Government Printing Office, 1978).

† "Long-Term Management Strategy," May 2006, at http://www.spn.usace.army.mil/conops/LTMS6-yrReviewReport.pdf.

BOX 19.2 MONTEREY SUBMARINE CANYON

The largest and deepest submerged canyon in North America is incised into the Pacific continental shelf and almost reaches the shore at Monterey Bay (Map 19.3). The canyon begins near Moss Landing at a depth of fifty feet and extends more than sixty miles seaward reaching a maximum depth of ten thousand feet, with steep, six-thousand-foot walls in a classic V-profile. Researchers at the Monterey Bay National Marine Sanctuary study the many deep-water marine mammals that live in the canyon and near the shore. Marine animals populate the shoreline because of cold up-welled, nutrient-rich water that brings nutrients to the surface and creates plankton blooms that establish the marine food chain. Among the many marine animals in the canyon are porpoises, dolphins, sea otters, seals, and three whale species: killer-gray, humpback, and minke.

During the nineteenth century, the submarine canyon provided a seafaring livelihood for the Monterey Peninsula whaling and processing port. By 1910, low-wage Chinese laborers worked on Cannery Row processing sardines, until they were overfished in the 1950s. A fishing moratorium was declared in 1967. Today, the commercial fishery is gone, replaced by a tourist economy featuring the Cannery Row Antique Mall and the world-famous Monterey Aquarium.

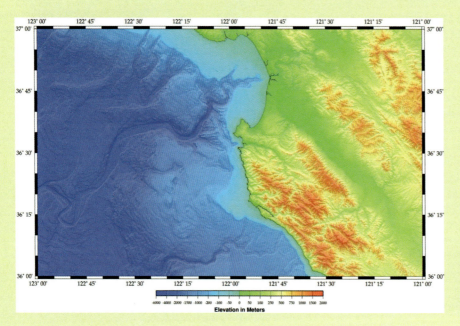

MAP 19.3. Monterey Submarine Canyon. This canyon begins close to shore and extends more than sixty miles seaward, reaching a depth of over ten thousand feet

In 2009, a $320 million desalination plant was approved for Carlsbad, a town north of San Diego. The plant has yet to break ground and will not begin operations until at least 2015.

Meanwhile, twenty California areas such as Long Beach, Marin County, Santa Cruz, and Huntington Beach are also considering desal to cure their water woes. The increased pressure to find freshwater has driven technology in the desalination industry, making it more efficient and economical but still expensive and environmentally challenging.

The Los Angeles Metropolitan Water District also imports water from the Colorado River and Owens Valley, enforcing a long-term Integrated Resources Plan for the eighteen million people it services. The water district conserves some water and deposits surplus water in groundwater basins as insurance in the driest weather. About 520 billion gallons can be stored. The conservation program incorporates financial incentives, public affairs programs, and best-management practices. On the local level, homes are encouraged to reduce overwatering and promote native and water-conserving xeriscape plants.

Water access allowed the Southland to grow in the twentieth century. The lack of access may either halt growth or begin honest conservation, such as addressing the verdant but semiarid Southland.

Climate

California's mild weather and Mediterranean precipitation pattern have been prime attractors. Annual coastal temperatures average between 50°F and 80°F (10°C and 27°C), so neither heating nor air-conditioning is usually required. Inland valleys have more temperature variation; they often climb over 100°F in the summer and on occasion freeze in the winter.

The Mediterranean semiarid wet winter–dry summer climate seldom experiences more than twenty inches of

BOX 19.3 DID YOU KNOW . . . WATER USAGE

Did you know how many gallons of water it takes to produce

- A serving of lettuce? 6
- A serving of steak? 2,600
- An eight-ounce glass of milk? 49
- A day's food for a family of four? 6,800
- An average American's food for a year? 1.5 million*

U.S. water usage remains the highest in the world, despite a 2 percent drop in water usage since 1990. An American uses over 100 gallons a day, whereas their French or German counterparts use 55 to 60 gallons per day. Californians consume between 100 and 140 gallons of water daily. In California, an average home uses over 384 gallons daily, and an average apartment or condominium 256 gallons. Many homes have xeriscaped (landscaped with drought-resistance plantings) their outdoor area, and many apply water-saving methods to their kitchen and bathroom uses, but still the overall usage is above national averages.

In the United States, 45 percent of all water goes to industry, 42 percent to agriculture, and 13 percent to domestic uses. Between 1950 and 1990, industry reduced its water usage by a third, largely because of recycling and reusing water. Agricultural water conservation has improved, using 98 percent efficient drip irrigation and precision irrigation techniques. The equation differs in California.

In California, 85 percent of the water goes to agriculture, and only 15 percent to household and industrial use. California has the largest population and leads the nation in agricultural production. Some crops are "thirsty" crops—rice, alfalfa, and cotton—that consume 40 percent of the water but produce less than 1 percent of the income. At $8 per acre-foot versus $200 per acre-foot† for urban use, agricultural water is sold much cheaper to farmers. The wide discrepancy in water cost has its roots in western water laws where "first in time, first in right" laws enforce "beneficial" use as long as the water is continually used; this may result in irrigating pastures or growing alfalfa in a desert, so the holder of water rights will not lose them.

---

* http://www.nwf.org/nationalwildlife/article.cfm?issueID=68&articleID=928.

† An acre-foot of water equals 326,000 gallons of water, the equivalent of what two families of four would use annually.

---

precipitation annually, except in the Sierras, where snow packs of ten feet or more are common.

San Francisco Bay

On the coast of California there is a city justly famed for the abnormalities of its climate. Overcoats and heavy wraps are worn in midsummer, while the lilies bloom in December.

—Alexander McAdie, 1903[3]

The San Francisco Bay estuary cools the surrounding area and keeps the temperature mild. A well-known saying (wrongly attributed to Mark Twain) captures the mood of many people's favorite city: "The coldest winter I ever spent was a summer in San Francisco."

The city does have an unusual weather pattern, which is caused by the currents and pressure zones. During the summer, the Aleutian Low accompanies the south-flowing California Current. Cold water upwells along the coast and mixes with the warmer summer air, producing fog and keeping the weather cool and gray. During the winter months, the ocean current flows to the north, bringing warmer water and air to the bay.

But the city's weather is part of a much larger and more complex pattern of microclimates formed by the interaction of the hill and valley features and the bay's oceanic winds and currents.

Central Valleys

Central California's multiple valleys are increasingly drier and more continental as one moves eastward. The Central Valley proper has blistering hot days and nights during the summer, and cooler "tule fog" days during the winter, named after the tule reeds that grow in the Central Valley marshes. The regular winter fog rolls in on clear, windless nights, limits visibility, and often causes multiple car accidents. The semiarid climate and precipitation pattern reflects its Coastal Range rain shadow position. Only five to twenty inches of rain fall on the valley floor. Crops require irrigation because of the scant Mediterranean precipitation patterns during the summer growing season.

Sierra Nevada

The plentiful Sierra precipitation follows the Mediterranean weather pattern. Air masses bring the wet winter season over the lower-elevation Coastal Range and over the valleys, and then the air is forced upward on the western slopes of the Sierras causing precipitation, usually in the form of snow. Precipitation is more episodic and of higher intensity than in the Cascades. The erratic Sierra weather patterns depend on elevation and on hill and valley wind patterns. The eastern leeward flank of the mountains is in the rain shadow, where the dry Basin and Range environment commences.

Smog

Many places in America now experience **thermal inversion** (warm air trapped between cool air layers) smog, but in the 1950s Los Angeles made smog an American household word. Smog is the result of millions of gas-powered automobiles in Southern California's enclosed basins, along with airports, power plants, industrialization, and port facilities.

BOX 19.4 LOS ANGELES WATER

The Owens Valley, the most westerly section of the Basin and Range, is located just east of the Sierra Nevada. In the early twentieth century, Eastern Sierra Nevada snowmelt watered the Owens Valley and allowed the residents to raise cattle and orchards. However, Los Angeles had other plans for the valley.

Los Angeles has a semiarid environment that receives about fourteen inches of precipitation annually, and it has no major freshwater source. Although the city had only about sixteen hundred residents in 1850, it was fast becoming the most profitable agricultural county in America by the 1880s. Boosters of the city realized that the city would require additional sources of water. They accomplished their goal during the first decades of the twentieth century, when agents for the city surreptitiously purchased the valley's water rights and built the L.A. aqueduct, diverting the water to fruit orchards and agricultural fields. Soon land was converted to suburban developments.

By 1930 Los Angeles, a city with natural water for only a few hundred thousand, had a million people, and in 2009 the metropolitan area had about seventeen million people—all dependent on water from external sources.

Smog is created when carbon monoxide (CO) and nitrogen oxide (NO_x) emissions cook in the sun and react chemically. Photochemical reactions create ozone and particulate matter (PM)—tiny particles of soot, smoke, and dust—that lodge in the lungs and impair the respiratory system.

Children suffer from respiratory problems, burning eyes, and asthma due to the ozone levels on hot, smoggy days and face long-term health problems.[4] Asthma affects one in eight Los Angeles County children, although it is but one of the many respiratory problems. Los Angeles schools regularly have smog days, when no one is allowed outside to play.

Geography, wind patterns, and the local weather compose the toxic chemical stew sitting over the basin and cooking in the sun. The confined thermal inversion airflow in Los Angeles is nothing new. The Native Americans called the region the "Land of Smoke" for the same entrapment reasons. The flow layers the air in the mountain-enclosed basin. Warm air hovers over the cooler marine air. The usual light winds are unable to clear out pollutants. The coastal winds blow the pollutants from the coast inland and against the mountain barrier. For example, the San Gabriel Mountains trap the smog in Pasadena and the San Gabriel Valley. Only the coast is pollution free, because of onshore and offshore winds.

In 1965, California was the first state to tighten vehicle emissions standards. The state has continued to pursue clean air by setting new standards. However, the smog problem has spread, and six of the ten most polluted cities in the nation are in California: Los Angeles, Bakersfield, Visalia, Fresno, Sacramento, and El Centro.[5]

While smog pollution caused by auto emission restrictions has decreased, it still defines residence choices in Los Angeles. Coastal areas—free from smog and with mild temperatures—are in demand. Inland areas, such as Riverside and San Bernardino counties, are warmer, more polluted, and less expensive.

Natural Hazards

For all its beauty, California's apocalyptic side includes erratic but devastating natural hazards such as earthquakes, fire, and landslides, making it essential to connect the dots of the relationship between geography and urban land use. Most of California's major cities are built near or on earthquake faults. Fire is an indirect hazard of the Mediterranean climate, and landslides often are the result of exposing the bare, fire-scarred soils to the winter rains.

In California, hillside view lots are premier home locations—but there is a hidden cost. Half of the region's scant precipitation may fall in a single rainstorm and cause landslides. If the previous winter is wet, the threat of landslides multiplies. Landslides occur in two situations: when massive amounts of rainfall and rock separate from steep cliffs, or along California's many fault zones. As a result, hillside home foundations become unstable, and homes may slide down the mountain. Autumn fires can accelerate erosion, while winter rainfall destabilizes already weak foundations and may trigger additional landslides.

Most of America occupies the North American Plate, but Southern California lies on the Pacific Plate west of the world-famous San Andreas Fault. Faults riddle the meeting place of the North American and Pacific plates. The San Andreas extends on land seven hundred miles from the Gulf of California to Mendocino. The Pacific Plate moves two inches per year in a northwest direction. This movement creates the stresses and friction that trigger earthquakes, especially in the mountains near the San Andreas.

California is always waiting for the "big one." The state averages about two hundred earthquakes a week; most are small and only felt by seismographs.[6] Earthquakes are so normal that residents greet them casually with comments like "That felt like a 4.0. What do you think?"

The most recent large quake occurred in the predawn of January 17, 1994, and was named the Northridge earthquake. Registering 6.7 on the Richter scale, it lasted forty-five seconds and woke those living within a fifty-mile radius. It killed fifty-one people; California State University, Northridge, and the surrounding area were heavily damaged (Photo 19.2). It was the largest earthquake in a populated area since the 1933 Long Beach earthquake.

Fire and the Mediterranean climate are related in California. Fires rage during the dry months when the hills are golden and the dry Santa Ana winds blow from the desert to the coast. The

PHOTO 19.2. Northridge Earthquake Damage. Apartments built over garages fell on cars in the magnitude 6.7 Northridge earthquake of 1994. The earthquake caused over $44 billion in damage.

winds desiccate vegetation and raise the possibility of wildfires. Each year some part of California has a wildfire, usually in October at the end of the dry season when the vegetation is driest. However, frequent droughts can increase wildfire danger. In June and July of 2008, extreme drought and years of fire suppression caused more than eight hundred lightning-induced fires and scorched more than eight hundred thousand acres in the northern hillsides and the Big Sur coast.

The common practice of forest fire suppression in California allows understory brush to proliferate and fuel fires. Americans have treated fire as an enemy that must be halted, but fire is a natural pattern that regenerates forest health. The anthropocentric view of fire excludes the overall ecology of natural vegetation and wildlife. Today, some of the most preferred residential areas are in fire-sensitive, mountainous viewsheds. The expensive homes in these areas can be burned out, rebuild, and burned out again. Directly or indirectly, taxpayers support this unsustainable practice.

Historical Geography and Settlement

Effectively, there have been two Californias, divided approximately by Monterey Bay. The separate demography and culture of each half evolved in relation to the physiography, vegetation, and climatic patterns.

Native Americans

Northern and southern California Native cultures were distinctly different, each aligned culturally and linguistically more with their tribal neighbors than each other. The northern tribes were similar to the Klamath and Modoc, while the southern were similar to southwestern tribes. The tribal cultures evolved in relation to the mild weather and temperate vegetation, which provided a comfortable and laid-back lifestyle.

The approximately 310,000 Natives in California at the beginning of the Spanish mission period (1769) were reduced to less than 10,000 by the end of the period (1848), the result of disease and forced tenure at the Spanish missions.

The Spanish Period

The Spanish built twenty-one **missions** along the California coastal region to secure possession of the territory. The Spanish were aware of the Russians progressing southward from Alaska in search of otter fur. The Russians came as far south as Mendocino County, where they established Fort Ross on the Russian River.

The Spanish established four **presidios** (military fortifications) to protect the missions and establish their political claim to California. The presidios were in geographically strategic locations and would become a population center for California (San Diego, Monterey, San Francisco, and Santa Barbara). The Spanish also established agricultural towns called **pueblos**, two of which were San Jose and Los Angeles.

Spanish rule in California ended with the establishment of Mexico in 1822. Spanish rule had imprinted the landscape with its land tenure system, urban plans, architecture, and toponyms, but few people occupied the California region (Photo 19.1). Far from the center of Spain's New World holdings, California's residents were retired presidio soldiers who were granted land grants for their service. The *Californios* **rancho** and grazing culture was similar to that of the semiarid Spanish homeland. The Spanish and later the Mexican governments granted more than ten million acres as ranchos. Each grant ranged over several square miles and established the soldiers as *dons,* landowners in the under-populated territory. California ranchos raised

BOX 19.5 THE GOLD RUSH

California's Sierra Gold Rush began in 1848 and lasted into the early 1860s.* The Mother Lode gold occurs in veins that fractured the rock millions of years ago. Glacial or alluvial deposits containing bits of the valuable mineral were most simply extracted by placer panning.

Hydraulic mining began on a small scale in 1852 in Placer County. The process, washing away topsoil and revealing the underlying gold-veined bedrock, was efficient in isolating the gold, but it was environmentally devastating. The method choked rivers and their habitats, ruined farms, caused flooding, and was the source of the first environmental court case. In 1884, farmers whose land had been ruined by the process finally legally halted hydraulic mining, and the industry was shut down. The case, heralded as an environmental win today, was not about environmentalism, but it was more a case of using private property to ruin the property of someone else.†

The Gold Rush made San Francisco the dominant California city. In the Central Valley, Sacramento was the largest city to service the Gold Rush region, while other towns, such as Placerville, Jamestown, and Sonora were established in the Mother Lode hills and valleys. Over $2 billion of gold were found in the Mother Lode, and additional wealth was retrieved from the silver found in Nevada near Virginia City. The immense wealth was of great importance to the country at the time and hastened the entry of both states into the Union.

---

* The 1842 gold strike in Southern California's Placerita Canyon had little impact.

† Norris Hundley Jr., *The Great Thirst: Californians and Water, 1770s–1990s* (Berkeley: University of California Press, 1992)

---

cattle only for their hides and tallow, as the isolated region was far from populated markets until the 1848 **Gold Rush**.

In 1848, the Mexican Cession granted California and much of the Southwest to the Americans. The **Treaty of Guadalupe Hidalgo** promised to respect the property rights of Mexican landowners, but because Mexico had been "conquered," the public ignored Mexican rights and believed the California ranchos would revert to the public domain. Additionally, the American land-tenure system legally rejected the rights of the Mexican system. The American patent process averaged seventeen years, all at the expense of the land-rich but cash-poor ranchero. Proving Spanish land claims was expensive and often futile. Most rancheros lost their land to the Americans.[7] The shift in land tenure from one culture to another continues to be a point of conflict relevant to supporters of Hispanic organizations such as the National Council of La Raza (known as La Raza).[8]

The Anglo Period

By the 1880s, Anglos controlled California. The growth began in the north near the Gold Rush areas, where San Francisco became the largest city and economic hub. Later, the Mediterranean climate, dry heat, and sunshine made Southern California attractive to Americans seeking an escape from the ague and fevers of the humid East. The completion of the Southern Pacific Railway line in 1876 and the Santa Fe line in 1887 encouraged transcontinental travel and triggered fare wars. The transcontinental link connected California to the nation and enhanced immigration, trade, and the agricultural industry. Los Angeles County became one of America's most productive agricultural centers.

During the first half of the twentieth century, California-dreaming became a national obsession, and many relocated to the sunshine land of orange trees and red-tiled mission houses. The motion picture industry accentuated and enhanced the unreal realities of the Golden State. The site of the sunny, warm Rose Parade on a frigid midwestern January morning was enough to cause a cascade of midwestern migrations to California. During the dirty thirties, farmers from Oklahoma and Arkansas sought refuge picking orchard fruit in the Central Valley.

The Multicultural Period

California has been a multicultural and discriminatory land from the beginning of European settlement. The Russian and Spanish incursions were prologue to the Gold Rush global influx, which included white Americans and a contingent of Asians. Chinese arrived to work on the transcontinental railroad in 1864 and continued to arrive until the **Chinese Exclusion Act** of 1882 limited their employment and then even their immigration. Few Chinese immigrated between 1882 and 1965, when the Civil Rights Act allowed further immigration. Since 1965, two segments of Chinese—educated Chinese and political refugees—have immigrated to America, usually through the portals of San Francisco or Los Angeles.

The Japanese arrived in America a few years after the Chinese. Most were either railroad workers or domestics, but soon they moved into agricultural work and settled in Southern California or the Central Valley. Japanese were discriminated against, especially after the attack on Pearl Harbor, when more than 110,000 Pacific Coast Japanese were forced into ten internment camps in remote areas despite the fact that over half were U.S. citizens.

Large-scale black immigration began during World War II, when President Roosevelt ordered defense industries to hire blacks. About eight thousand blacks lived in California between 1900 and the beginning of WWII. By 1943, more than ten thousand per month arrived in Los Angeles, eager to earn over ten times their southern wages. By the end of the war, California's black population had increased 272 percent, while Mississippi's black population had dropped by 8 percent.

However, California was also mired in civil rights discrimination. In the 1920s, Los Angeles enacted exclusionary zoning that restricted black settlement. Blacks were limited to purchasing property in South Central Los Angeles until 1947, and they remained discriminated against well into the 1960s, when only twenty thousand of three hundred thousand blacks lived outside the segregated area. Black population today remains concentrated in South Central Los Angeles.

Cultural Perspectives

At Least Two Californias

Northern and Southern California are culturally divided. The physical attributes and population of the two Californias differ: Most of the water is in the north and most of the people are in the south.

During the Mexican period, the north and south favored different political rule. During the 1830s and early 1840s, Southern California kept its Mexican allegiance, while the north aligned and connected with the United States. In 1848, Mexican General Vallejo favored the U.S. annexation granted with the Treaty of Guadalupe Hidalgo, while southern forces favored remaining with Mexico. The Gold Rush diverted attention from seeking separate governance.

The two Californias remained conjoined into the 1960s, although each developed distinctive cultures and cuisines. Southern Californians worshiped under the Beach Boy surfing sun, and Southern California was called a "neon wasteland,"[9] while the north found psychedelic solace with Jimi Hendrix and Janis Joplin. The hippies of Berkeley and Mendocino inaugurated the healthy and vegetarian California cuisine, while Southern California benefited from its Mexican heritage and invented its own Mexican cuisine.

The separation continued during the 1980s. Northern and Southern California each influenced American cultural patterns. Los Angeles initiated and defined sprawl, decentralization, and illegal immigration for America, while Northern California reinvented itself with a new gold in Silicon Valley. Two scholarly Bay Area universities, Stanford and Berkeley, fueled the transition from tubes to chip,s and the "SoCal" sprawl style overwhelmed the Bay peninsula. Today, the area around San Jose is home to some of the priciest real estate in America, even after the 2000 dot-com crash and the 2008 housing crunch.

Northern and Southern California continue to develop contrarian cultures. The more populated, water-poor south contains a large contingent of Hollywood-type "plastic" people, while the wealthy, water-rich north is known for its laid-back style. Both Californias are multicultural, but they are occupied with different cultures and ethnic groups.

Throughout its statehood, California has at times supported separating into two or three states. During the 1990s, an informal advisory vote was taken in Northern California, and two-thirds of the population living north of San Francisco voted to divide the state. In 1993, a bill to place a measure on the ballot passed the State Assembly before it died in the Senate. More recently, politics separated the state. In 2007, California considered dividing its electoral votes for president instead of the winner-take-all system giving all fifty-five votes to the leader. And in 2011, the Inland Empire of Southern California passed a resolution to secede from the rest of the state.

Homes and Homeless

Homes

Since the 1960s, a widened socioeconomic gap makes it difficult for ordinary people to purchase homes in the close-in metropolitan areas. Sprawl resulted. Living two hours from work is common but affordable. Eight of the ten California high-income counties are in the north, six in the Bay Area alone. By 2005, it was near impossible to find a house in Northern or Southern California for under $250,000, and in Northern California the prices were closer to $1 million within fifty miles of most jobs. Only 16 percent of Bay Area households and 7 percent of Napa and Sonoma county residents could afford the average-priced home in close-in areas.

In July 2005, the median-priced home in California was $451,000, an increase of 16 percent from the previous year. In Los Angeles, the average-priced home in 2006 was $604,000, while in Orange County, the average price was $692,000. The housing credit problems that began in 2007 hit the lower end of California's market first, but by midyear 2008 many California residential markets were realizing significant downward shifts. The median-price home in the state was $252,000 in July 2011, but the hardest hit was in the far-flung sprawl areas. The median sales price for homes in Los Angeles was $295,000; Orange County homes continued to slide, averaging $437,500 in July 2011. Cities in the Central Valley were the hardest hit: Stockton went from an average price of $360,000 in 2006 to $115,000 in July 2011, which is representative for Central Valley home prices. The premier areas (coastal, Silicon Valley, Mendocino) have retained most of their value. For example, the average home in Malibu was $1.8 million in 2006 and $1.57 million in 2011.[10]

Fortress L.A.

In a city of several million aspiring immigrants (where Spanish-surname children are now almost two-thirds of the school-age population), public amenities are shrinking radically, libraries and playgrounds are closing, parks are falling derelict, and streets are growing ever more desolate and dangerous.[11]

Los Angeles introduced **fortress living** to America, and it has diffused pandemic-like across the nation.[12] Although gated communities increased nationally after 9/11, Los Angeles enforced a socioeconomic and racial divide. The wealthier were seeking security and shelter from violence and rampant crime well before the rest of the nation. Gated communities are common, alarm systems or barred entrances are considered essential, and architectural entrances have turned away from public spaces. For example, in Marina del Rey few windows faced public spaces, and garages were the main entries into million-dollar houses (Photo 19.3).

PHOTO 19.3. Fortress Living in Marina Del Rey. Homes in this oceanside community were built so the main entrance was from the garage, creating a very sterile environment. While "front doors" were on the other side of the buildings, they were seldom used.

Homeless

Although California is a rich state, the wealth is unevenly distributed, and a widening gap separates the haves from the have-nots. The haves live in expensive homes, and the have-nots range from those living in small but still expensive apartments to the **homeless**. On any day in California, between five hundred thousand and 1.1 million people are homeless, many working but earning less than rent. Many were displaced in the late 1970s when federal institutions shut down, and people with mental illnesses, disabilities, or addictions were abandoned. Although the states were supposed to pick up the slack left by the federal government, few were able to afford to house those with disabilities.

Los Angeles's large homeless population, up to eighty-two thousand nightly, may choose Los Angeles because of the year-round temperate climate. The nucleus of its homeless area is Skid Row, the largest in the nation, where people live either in shelters or on the street, often in cardboard boxes lined up along sidewalks and within sight of the affluent offices on Bunker Hill (Photo 19.4).

The fortunate homeless live in one-room SRO (single-room occupancy) hotels that provide rental assistance and communal bathrooms and kitchens. However, SROs and most affordable housing are threatened with extinction because of the rising cost of land. Developers have threatened Skid Row with redevelopment, such as converting the SROs into high-priced lofts. Some SROs are protected, having been purchased by nonprofit agencies, but others could fall prey to developers, thereby making affordable housing more difficult to find.

Downtown Los Angeles's office center is Bunker Hill, located a few blocks from Skid Row. However, in order to maintain its affluent clientele, the city does everything it can to discourage the Skid Row occupants from walking up the hill. Bunker Hill's street-side appearance excludes those who do not belong—there are no street benches, no windows, and no entries other than for cars—only blank concrete walls. Office workers congregate in open-air patios several floors above street level and only accessible from inside buildings (Photo 19.5).

Gangs

Before the 1980s, gangs existed in Los Angeles, but they were invisible to the vast majority of residents. The rise in gangs occurred at the same time as deindustrialization in Los Angeles. Plants closed and workers were laid off. The resulting poverty, disaffected youth, and female-headed households were factors in the rise of gang culture.[13]

Since that time, gangs have become more visible throughout the city, and graffiti, violence, and shootings occur even in "good" neighborhoods. California leads the nation in street gangs, and Los Angeles is the originating city for many gangs in other American cities. In the mid-1990s, the United States had approximately 650,000 gang members, mostly in large cities; about 150,000 were in Los Angeles alone. By 1992, more than 769 U.S. cities had gang activity.

Los Angeles was the nation's homicide capital for a time, mostly because of black, Latino, and Asian gangs. They control their turfs and live by rules and signs. Wearing a bandana, the wrong gang colors (red or blue), or being in the wrong neighborhood can lead to a violent death. Knowing the city's geography is imperative, or chances of violence increase dramatically.

The Bloods and Crips are the most widely known Los Angeles gangs. They organized in the late 1960s after the Watts riots. By 1996, the Los Angeles area had 274 black gangs. Since the 1980s, an additional 600 Hispanic gangs, and Asian gangs with

PHOTO 19.4. Los Angeles Skid Row. "Skid row" was originally a street in Seattle, Washington, named Skid Road, which was used to skid logs into the water. Over time, the road went into decline, and the term *skid row* became synonymous with a bad neighborhood.

a total of twenty thousand members have formed. They are located throughout the city, but most are in pockets following the Harbor Freeway through South Central Los Angeles.

Regional Life

Population

In the near future, people will look at California and Mexico as one magnificent region.

—Gray Davis, governor of California, 1999

In the mid-1960s, California became the most populous state. Approximately one out of every eight Americans lives in California. The population is overwhelmingly urban and coastal, living along the Pacific Plate section of the state (Map 19.4). The state is perhaps also the most diverse, but it is also self-segregated. The unprecedented influx of both Hispanic-Latino and Asian immigrants highlights the California demographic shift. Hispanics now populate almost half of Los Angeles County, while 30 percent of San Francisco's population is Chinese, the city's largest ethnic group. In Fremont, along the southeastern bay, nearly 40 percent of the residents are Asian American. Juxtaposing this demographic shift is the emigration from California by non-Hispanic whites.[14]

The complexity of ethnicities in the state results in a widely divergent set of cultures and values. Hispanics number about

PHOTO 19.5. Los Angeles Business District. Figueroa Street, in the heart of the Bunker Hill business district, is not welcoming to the homeless, many of whom live less than half a mile away on skid row. Bunker Hill has no street benches, windows, or street entrances other than through garages.

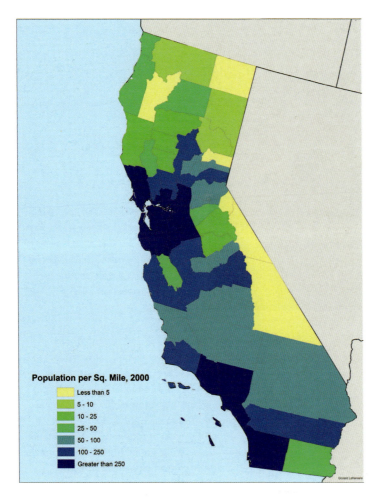

Population per Sq. Mile, 2000

- Less than 5
- 5 - 10
- 10 - 25
- 25 - 50
- 50 - 100
- 100 - 250
- Greater than 250

MAP 19.4. California Population Density, 2000. Most of the population lives in two of the largest conurbations in America, Southern California and the Bay Area. Northern California is the least populated, although it has the most water. The portion along the Nevada border is part of the Basin and Range desert area.

fourteen million and continue to immigrate from Mexico and Central America. There is continued tension between the various cultural groups with different values. For example, the Hispanic community tends to favor traditional family values, including higher birthrates, which outweigh educational priorities. On the other hand, Chinese immigrants prioritize education for their children, and they are changing the San Francisco school system by promoting a diversity index for education to end discrimination.

Fremont has become one of the nation's most diverse cities (137 languages are spoken in Fremont homes), but the city's immigrant experiences are different from those experienced by Los Angeles immigrants, because most of Fremont's immigrants are affluent. Many Fremont residents are from India, and their festivals and Bollywood extravaganzas create near riots and mounds of trash, thereby becoming a source of community strife.

The California Latino population fluctuated from dominance before annexation in 1848 (with only 6,900 residents in the entire state), to only 9 percent of the much larger population in 1960, to 37.6 percent of 37,253,956 in 2010. Seventy percent of the Hispanic growth was attributed to natural increase, while the remaining stemmed from immigration, largely undocumented.

Hispanic culture differs from American Anglo culture. Several **la raza** (literally "the race," but vernacular "the people") groups address poverty, the continued discrimination against Latinos, and the loss of ownership during the early American period.

Hispanic immigration and non-Hispanic emigration defined state population during the 1990s. From 1992 to 1999, over 1.8 million more whites left than entered the state. The non-Hispanic white population was 57.6 percent, a 6.4 percent increase from 2000 to 2010. During this time, several southern counties had majority Hispanic populations, while Central Valley populations continued to grow (Table 19.1). Shasta and Trinity counties, both in the northern part of the state, had the smallest Hispanic populations.

Asian and Pacific Islander populations increased from 2000 to 2010, growing from 12 to almost 13 percent. Unlike the Hispanic population, Asian population growth was the result of migration and extended throughout both Northern and Southern California counties. By 2000, San Francisco had the highest proportion of Asians, comprising almost one-third of the total population, while other Bay Area counties also grew by 20 percent or more.

The Anglo American population declined by nearly one million from 1990 to 2000, and for the first time since statehood,

TABLE 19.1. Central Valley Hispanic Population Growth

City	Population 2010	Population 2000	Percent Hispanic 2010	Percent Hispanic 2000
Fresno	494,665	427,652	46.9	39.9
Bakersfield	347,483	247,057	45.5	32.5
Stockton	291,707	243,771	40.3	32.5
Modesto	201,165	188,856	35.5	25.6
California	37,253,956	33,871,648	37.6	32.4

Source: U.S. Census

whites were no longer the majority. The trend continued from 2000 to 2010, when the non-Hispanic white population declined to 40 percent. Many whites emigrate from Southern California to the Intermontane, where four out of ten settlers are now transplants from California. The emigration was unequal between Northern and Southern California.

In Northern California, fourteen counties were more than 80 percent white, while four Southern California counties were less than 44 percent white. Los Angeles County was 28.9 percent non-Hispanic white and 47.7 percent Hispanic in 2010 (Table 19.2).

Segregation continues in property values. The areas where whites live in the Los Angeles metropolitan area—the Westside, the beach cities, or the Santa Monica Mountains—have the highest property values and the least amount of smog. The San Fernando Valley demographics have changed since the 1970s, when most of the areas were non-Hispanic white. In an attempt to maintain their property values, a secessionist movement led by whites was rife in the San Fernando Valley for years. If successful, the movement would have saddled the city with increased socioeconomic and racial divisions in a Detroit-like situation.

The average Hispanic household income is 50 to 85 percent below that of non-Hispanic whites and about the same as African Americans. The variance is generational for Hispanics; successive generations earn more. Asian household incomes are just below that of white incomes.

The state's racial composition continues to divide California's north and south. Hispanics are the fastest-growing group in California, but an overwhelming majority live in the south. Despite the diversity, most ethnic or racial groups tend to live near others who share their culture, and the state continues to be self-segregated.

Assimilating the multiple cultures is a difficult proposition. Riots in 1967 and 1992 centered in the city's South Central area, where many disenfranchised blacks live, victims of manufacturing job loss. The tension in the area has increased since the 1980s, as Hispanics, now outnumbering the blacks, have also made South Central their home.

Traditional and Sustainable Cities

Ninety-five percent of California's population is urban. The two coastal conurbations, one from the Mexican border to Santa Barbara and the other surrounding the San Francisco Bay, contain twenty-five million people, approximately 70 percent of the state's population.

Most Californians define themselves in relation to the Los Angeles Basin or the Bay Area. The Central Valley and Central Coast are also growing (with about 3.5 million people in 2007) and might well be included in either of the north or south

TABLE 19.2. Percentage of Ethnic and Racial Groups in Los Angeles County, California, and New York City, 2010

	Total population (millions)	White	Black	Asian	Hispanic
Los Angeles County	9.8	50.2	8.7	13.7	47.7
California	37.3	54.9	6.2	13.0	37.6
New York City	8.2	44.0	25.6	12.7	28.6

Source: U.S. Census

conurbations (depending on proximity); some in the Central areas also have separatist ideals and disassociate from either conurbation. Both population and wealth are concentrated in the two conurbations. The Central Valley has become the state's final affordable housing outlier and has grown rapidly in the twenty-first century, although it was hit the hardest during the housing crunch in 2008.

California has distinguished itself for its environmental attitude and regulations. Some say this has also been its downfall. The state has undergone serious budget shortfalls since the 2008 economic crash. But still, the state's cities have been steady in their pursuit of green initiatives, far outweighing the slow-to-move federal government. Among the successes in California is the diversion of waste from landfills. Among U.S. cities, California has led the diversion, with San Francisco and Los Angeles (at 69 and 62 percent respectively) at about double the 33.8 percent national average. San Diego and San Jose are also well above national averages.[15]

Southern California Conurbation

The Southern California conurbation is one of the largest in the world, both in population and in square miles; it extends almost continuously (Camp Pendleton, a Marine base, being the major exception) over 200 miles to the north from the Mexican border and another 150 miles inland to Palm Springs. Included within the conurbation are many city nodes; the largest and most identifiable is Los Angeles–Long Beach, followed by San Diego, Anaheim–Santa Ana, Riverside–San Bernardino, Oxnard–Ventura, and Santa Barbara–Santa Maria. All are interconnected with freeways and airport complexes (there are six major airports in the conurbation).

The conurbations are among the most favored places in the nation to do business and to start companies. They are the most wired in America. Southern California shares a high quality of life and good incomes for the educated.

Los Angeles

(2010 pop. 3,792,621; CSA 17,877,006)

Los Angeles (L.A.), the second-largest city in America, occupies hundreds of miles of Mediterranean, semiarid land, whose dominant color is brown. Although green emerges for a short, glorious period after the winter rains, the city and the state would be brown without the elaborate water schemes. Of course, today there are new definitions of green, and Los Angeles emerges as one of the leaders in America, with green initiatives to cut greenhouse gas emissions, including retrofitting of buildings; greener public transport (what there is of it); and incentives to buy energy-efficient appliances. In so doing, the city on its own was able to surpass the Kyoto emissions cuts of 7 percent in 2008.

Los Angeles's average skin color is also brown, and the language most heard on the streets is no longer English. Radio and TV stations are seemingly more Spanish than English, to the point where in 2005 a controversial billboard celebrated the new majority populace and "*Viva la reconquista*" ("Long live the reconquest") was commonly heard on the streets. The takeover attitude was emphasized in 2008 when Absolut vodka created a campaign in Mexico that showed the Mexican Cessation as part of Mexico.

Founded in 1781, Los Angeles was a small village situated on the ephemeral Los Angeles River. When California became a state, the village had a mere 1,600 people. Los Angeles grew slowly; by 1870, the population was only 5,700. Los Angeles experienced its first population boom from 1880 (30,000) to 1890 (100,000). By 1930, the city had over a million people and was one of the largest in America.

Prior to World War II, Los Angeles County was California's leading fruit and vegetable producer, but suburban home tracts replaced the orchards and fields after the war. In 1955 alone, 135,000 new homes were built.

The growth of the city was due to the first aqueduct that brought water to the semiarid city in 1913. Water has supported the growth and has continued to be an important part of growing up in Los Angeles. Water efficiency is high, and water conservation is promoted. (Don't drain that bathtub water—and no salts or toxic bubble baths!—but use it to water your plants.) Water consumption is still high, but people are aware. Yet many still want their private swimming pools and green lawns.

Today, Los Angeles remains a **polynucleated city**—a jumble of edge cities, each with its own downtown and shopping area. The metropolitan area includes eighty cities and five counties (Los Angeles, Orange, Ventura, San Bernardino, and Riverside), with a total of about eighteen million people (half of California's population).

The city's complexity can overwhelm the first-time visitor. Options include a plethora of eight-lane freeways (and how to drive them), suburbs galore, beaches, ghettoes, ethnic communities, extreme affluence or poverty, and alternative lifestyles.

Los Angeles is also recognized as an automobile capital because of its size, dependence on automobiles, and its general lack of public transportation. Freeways connect Los Angeles as a system of free highways, mostly built and completed by the early 1970s. Since that time, traffic has doubled, but few freeway miles have been added and the city has become known for its monumental traffic jams. Los Angeles shows no political will to build new or larger freeways. Despite public opposition, the freeways have been recently augmented by toll roads.

Although Los Angeles may lead the nation in a variety of ways, it has also followed some national economic development patterns. For example, although Midwestern industrialization led the nation in the late nineteenth century, Los Angeles led the nation in agriculture until 1950, at which time it transformed into manufacturing aircraft, automobiles, and steel. However, California easily made the transition from manufacturing to the postindustrial economy. Today, mergers and acquisitions and outsourcing have caused industry and corporate headquarters to depart Los Angeles. Manufacturing has been replaced with services, high-tech industry, electronics, a diverse service economy, the motion picture industry, and computerized special effects.

BOX 19.6 LARGEST CALIFORNIA CITIES, 2010

Four of the largest cities in the United States are in California:

    Number 2: Los Angeles, with 3.79 million in the city (17.8 million in the CMSA)

Number 6: San Diego, with 1.31 million (3.0 million CMSA)

Number 10: San Jose, with 945,942 (7.427 million CMSA*)

Number 14: San Francisco, with 810,235 (7.427 million CMSA)

* San Francisco and San Jose are considered part of the same CMSA.

The motion picture industry originated in nearby Hollywood and is still significant. Most major studios are within the Los Angeles metro area, but actual filming has often relocated to less expensive venues. Southern California still has about one-third of worldwide motion picture employees (only about 2 percent of the total metro employment), and a majority of recording businesses.

The Los Angeles economy also reflects the demographic shift. Immigrant labor, especially in the informal economy, bolsters the economy (see below).

San Diego

(2010 pop. 1,307,402; CSA 3,095,313)

San Diego, the nation's sixth-largest city, is located south of Los Angeles very near the Mexican border (Photo 19.6). Today, the two large cities' peripheries melt into one conurbation, broken only by Camp Pendleton Marine base. San Diego was the site of California's first mission (1769) and evolved into a pueblo during the Mexican regime (1834). When the first southern rail line was discussed, San Diego was the expected southern terminus, because of its natural harbor. However, the lack of a

Peninsular Mountain pass forced the terminus north to Los Angeles, and San Diego settled as a military "Navy town." San Diego's naval fleet is the largest in the world, and the city's largest employer, adding $13 billion annually to the economy. The nation's largest number of retired military personnel lives in the metro area. The city is consistently listed as a top place to live in America. The dry, cool climate has drawn many wealthy residents, who live in elite enclaves such as La Jolla.

The city grew slowly until the twentieth century, when the nearby Imperial Valley became agriculturally productive and San Diego began shipping the valley's produce, as well as developing into the world's largest tuna-fishing center. In 1980, the fishing economy disappeared because it submitted to environmentalists' demands for "dolphin-safe" tuna, and because the Magnuson Act of 1976, which established the two-hundred-mile boundary, cut off the fishing fleet's access to South American waters.

San Diego has its own identity, with an economy based on high-tech telecommunication, biotechnology, and tourism. The San Diego metropolitan area, like many of the largest cities in the West, is a polynucleated city with several core cities,

PHOTO 19.6. U.S.-Mexico Border near San Diego. The metropolitan area of San Diego extends close to the border, but it is separated from the border area by a state park with no buildings. The Tijuana side, though, reaches right to the border.

including Chula Vista, Coronado, La Mesa, El Cajon, and National City.

San Jose

(2010 pop. 945,942; part of San Francisco CSA)

San Jose, at the southern extremity of the Bay Area peninsula, evolved in the shadow of San Francisco. In the 1950s, San Jose in the Santa Clara Valley was the nation's largest fruit and vegetable canning center, but under the influence of Stanford University in nearby Palo Alto and the University of California at Berkeley across the bay, technology redefined the city. The metropolitan area of the city grew to 1.8 million in 2005, displacing Detroit as the tenth-largest city in America. Since 1950, Detroit lost half of its population, while San Jose and Santa Clara County increased by a factor of twenty.

In 1939, Bill Hewlett and Dave Packard, who had met as students at Stanford, began a small technology enterprise in a garage. From these humble beginnings grew Silicon Valley, the nation's leading producer of semiconductors and software development. The archetype for America's new industry offered high salaries and campus-like office parks. Today, San Jose anchors the wealthy enclave that spreads north into San Mateo County. Silicon Valley has become a magnet for the technologically educated. In 2009, 35.7 percent of San Jose's residents had bachelor's degrees (versus 27.5 percent in the United States). The area has become the national leader in generating patents. Santa Clara County is also one of the most expensive places in America to live. But the county has also worked at overcoming some of the more vexing problems of urban living, and it has become more sustainable.

For example in Mountain View, just north of San Jose, a dying shopping center was rebuilt as a transit oriented development (TOD) called the Crossings. A commuter rail line anchors the 540 compact housing units (30 units per acre) that are a mixed-use and walkable community. Such urban villages are beginning to be visible on the landscape, and they represent a sustainable way to live in the city.

San Francisco

(2010 pop. 805,235; CSA 7,468,390)

San Francisco became the first major metropolis after the Gold Rush and California's largest city until World War I. Despite its short tenure, the city has a colorful history beginning with its Spanish settlement, blossoming during the Gold Rush, and followed by the downturn and rebuilding after the 1906 earthquake. The city remains a major metropolitan area, and its cosmopolitan feeling and setting, along with its wide acceptance as one of the most sustainable cities, has made it a favorite city, highlighted by a well-known skyline featuring the Golden Gate Bridge. One in six acres in the city is devoted to green space, and nonrecyclable plastic bags are banned, along with plastic toys with toxic chemicals.

The city is fortunate in several ways geographically. The setting is unparalleled—it is surrounded on three sides by water—and although this limited its space to grow, it encouraged something that many U.S. cities now crave: a vibrant inner city with the second-most-dense population in the nation (after New York). Using the density, the city has set high standards for reducing CO_2 in its closely spaced and increasingly green buildings, energy use, and transportation. Cars are not the average city transportation. Almost half of all San Franciscans do not take cars to work.

San Francisco and the Bay Area were almost completely dependent on the auto until, after twenty years of planning and construction, the Bay Area Rapid Transit (BART) electric train system opened in 1972, connecting the East Bay (Walnut Creek, Richmond, Oakland, and Berkeley) with San Francisco. A San Francisco International Airport extension opened in 2003, amid competition from Baby Bullet trains from San Jose to San Francisco. The Baby Bullets are faster and cost less, and the BART train from San Francisco to the airport costs about one-eighth the taxi fare. Despite these alternative transit options, San Francisco, a peninsula city, still suffers from intense traffic. In 2010, San Francisco considered following London's lead and charge each car a fee for entering the city.

The West Coast's largest natural harbor predetermined the location of San Francisco. The Spanish established a presidio at the northern point of the San Francisco peninsula, near the Golden Gate Bridge (Photo 19.7). The presidio remains a national park and historic landmark.

The city is the financial center for the state and the chief port for the Central Valley. San Francisco, one of the least industrialized cities in America, has a large financial and government workforce, and has moved into the biotechnology field by housing the state's stem cell institute. More than half of the highly educated workforce has at least a bachelor's degree. The city has been a birthplace of and supported various counterculture **alternative lifestyles**, including the City Lights Beat Generation, hippies, and a large LGBT (lesbian, gay, bisexual, and transsexual) population.

The city and its environs have very different physical geographies. San Francisco is the hilliest city in America, renowned for cable cars and steep streets. The original plat for San Francisco was filled with narrow, windy streets and paths into the hills. After the 1906 earthquake, the city straightened and widened many of the streets, and Market Street was laid out as the main street. The East Bay is almost entirely on level land, with much of it being reclaimed marshland.

East Bay Cities

The East Bay cities—Oakland, Berkeley, and Richmond—have an advantage San Francisco lacks: easy access into the interior valleys. East Bay growth was augmented with the 1936 opening of America's most traveled bridge, the Bay Bridge (Photo 19.8). It was the first of eight bridges connecting the Bay area. It partially collapsed during the 1989 Loma Prieta Earthquake and has since been rebuilt. The Golden Gate Bridge, completed in 1937, connects the northern coast to the city and remains a West Coast icon.

Oakland (2010 pop. 390,724), the Bay area's workhorse, is a blue-collar city and the seventh-largest port in America. The

PHOTO 19.7. San Francisco Presidio (Golden Gate Bridge, Background). The presidio was underdeveloped in recent years. In 2005, Skywalker Studios (George Lucas of *Star Wars* fame) made a $350 million investment and relocated from its isolated Marin County location to the presidio, transforming the area in the process. The relocation was a coup, geographically for the studio and economically for the presidio.

city also has a radical political legacy based on a large black population (27.9 percent in 2010) that galvanized in the 1960s around the Black Panther movement.

Today Oakland is better known for its rising star in the green movement, largely thanks to then Mayor Jerry Brown, the returned Governor of California. Mayor Brown gathered with other mayors to commit to a more sustainable city by bringing in renewable energy, achieving zero waste in landfills, and building green buildings, making Oakland— a city that is known for its port and heavy industry—one of the greener cities in America.[16] Oakland, Richmond, Emeryville, and Berkeley are the East Bay Green Corridor.

Berkeley (2010 pop. 112,580) is home to the famous and infamous flagship campus of the California university system, where dissent reached its maximum volume during the 1960s. Berkeley is a wealthy city now, known for its continual influence from the university and for its aging, esoteric hippies who continue to support healthy living. Berkeley was one of the first cities to adopt curbside recycling, convert its public transit fleet to biodiesel, and embrace solar power and green-collar jobs. In November 2006, Measure G, a plan to reduce emissions within the city, passed with 80 percent of the vote. This was followed with a Climate Action Plan in 2008 that laid out the strategies to reach the emissions goal.

Central Valley Urban Areas

The Central Valley, to the east of the Bay Area, has several medium-sized agricultural towns. The largest city in the Central Valley is Fresno (2010 pop. 494,665; CSA 1,081,315). The state capital is Sacramento (2010 pop. 466,488; CSA 2,461,780), founded by John Sutter of Gold Rush fame. The city became the

main supply point for gold miners and eventually a major railroad connection. Other cities in the Central Valley are Stockton and Modesto. The southern San Joaquin Valley is less populated but more devoted to irrigated agriculture. The largest city is Bakersfield (2010 pop. 387,483), which grew more than 40 percent from 2000 to 2010.

Economy

The gross state product (GSP) for California in 2010 was $1.9 trillion, making it the eighth-largest economy in the world (Chart 19.1). The next-largest state economy, Texas, is only 60 percent of California's size. While California has one of the largest economies in the world, its years of economic health slowed in 2008, largely due to tax reform, the informal economy, and a housing meltdown.

In 2011, the California economy had one of the highest unemployment rates (12.1 percent in August 2011) in the nation (which stood at 9.1 percent), and jobs continued to evaporate. The state dealt with a budget shortfall much as other states, but economic decline continued, largely due to the large informal economy and to tax reforms such as Proposition 13 in 1978 that limited the property tax rate. The economy stagnated in its most productive sectors—agriculture, motion pictures and media, technology, biotechnology, and services (real estate, financial services, tourism, and health care).

Primary Industry and Natural Resources

California leads the nation in cash farm receipts, the backbone of its diversified economy. Additionally, California produces oil and, of course, was the Gold Rush state. Historically, the Gold Rush gave the state its Golden State nickname, and it pushed

PHOTO 19.8. San Francisco Bay Bridges. The upper bridge in the picture is the famous Golden Gate, spanning the entrance to the bay and connecting northern California to the peninsula. In the center of the photo is the Bay Bridge, connecting the peninsula to the East Bay cities of Oakland, Berkeley, and Richmond. The dark area to the left of the Golden Gate is the original presidio area.

the state's entry into the Union a mere two years after gold was discovered.

Agriculture

California is a farmer's paradise where almost any crop can thrive, but it capitalizes on more profitable **specialty crops**, leaving most grain staples to the Midwest and Great Plains. California is the largest producer of fruits, vegetables, nuts, nursery goods, and dairy; it ranks second in livestock but fifteenth in grains. The top five agriculturally productive counties are all in the Central or Salinas valleys (Chart 19.2). The principal market crops are fruits and berries, with 34 percent of market value, followed by vegetables and melons, with 19 percent of market value. Overall, four hundred

crops are grown in the state, but its top twenty crops and livestock commodities account for 74 percent of state's gross farm income.

In the late nineteenth century, technology and transportation developments facilitated the distribution of California fruits and vegetables nationally. The availability of fresh food has also influenced the healthy California cuisine. However, to remain the number one agricultural producer in America, California must overcome several obstacles, such as high labor costs, limited water resources, population growth, foreign competition, and tough environmental regulations.

California combines its long, sunny growing season, fertile soils, and water resources for high-value agricultural crops in several distinct agricultural districts.

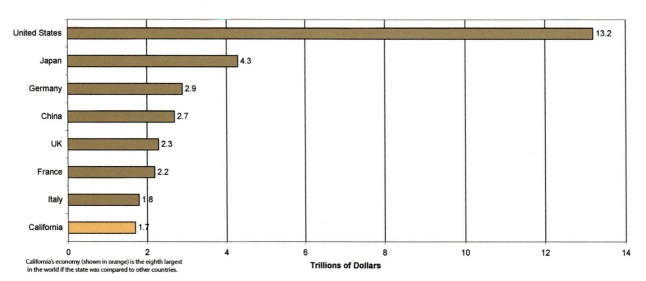

California's economy (shown in orange) is the eighth largest in the world if the state was compared to other countries.

Trillions of Dollars

CHART 19.1. Gross Production, California, 2006. California's economy is rated as the eighth largest in the world.

the refrigerated railcar made it possible to ship perishables, such as the orange, over long distances. By 1920, California grew 75 percent of the nation's orange crop.

After World War II, the orange industry repositioned to Florida. California replaced orange groves with tract homes. As more houses were built and land prices escalated, farmland near urban areas became too expensive. Farmers sold their land and moved into the Central Valley, where land was about one-fifth the price they received for their Southland orange groves. California oranges today are mostly in the southern Central Valley. Seventy-five percent of the oranges are navel oranges and are sold fresh, unlike Florida's Valencia oranges, which are raised for juice concentrate.

Dairy. Since the 1980s, California has led the nation in production of milk, butter, ice cream, and mozzarella cheese. California milk production grew from 5 percent nationally in 1950 to 20 percent in 2008, and accounts for 20 percent of the state's total agricultural receipts. Tulare County is the largest dairy producer in America, and it accounts for a majority of the state's 1.7 million cows. Previously, the dairy industry was located farther south in the Los Angeles metropolitan area towns of Cerritos (formerly Dairy Valley) and Chino. As Los Angeles expanded, the dairy land became more valuable and was sold for development. The dairies relocated to the less populated and less expensive Central Valley.

California surpassed Wisconsin in milk production in 1993 and in number of cows in 1998 (Chart 19.3). California was able to dominate the market by establishing large dairy herds. Whereas a Wisconsin herd averaged sixty cows, California herds grew from an average of ninety-eight cows in 1969 to over seven hundred in 2003. Concentration within the dairy industry has created fewer but larger farms. In the 1950s, six states produced 37 percent of the milk. In 2008, the top six states produced 57.8 percent of the milk.

California converts half of its fluid milk into producing one-sixth of the nation's cheese. About one-quarter of all mozzarella cheese is made in California, and the state produces more than 160 million pounds of its native *queso del pais*, Monterey Jack.

Agricultural Exports. Though 80 percent of California's crops are consumed domestically, California is the nation's leading exporter of food. In 2009, exported agricultural production was $12.4 billion. Almonds are the leading export crop, followed by rice, dairy, wine, table grapes, and cotton. The major export markets are Canada, the European Union, Japan, and China.

California agricultural exports account for 17 percent of all U.S. exports. However, international trade agreements, such as the World Trade Organization (WTO) and the North American Free Trade Agreement (NAFTA), have made California crops less profitable. The trade agreements have opened up trade with other countries, but they have harmed local production.

Specialty crops lack federal subsidies,[18] despite being almost 50 percent of the state's annual market value. This disadvantages specialty-crop farmers in comparison to the well-subsidized grain growers. The lack of subsidies allows other countries with reduced labor and land costs to gain market share in specialty crops. For example, government-supported Australian wine threatens the wine industry, and subsidized Chinese dehydrated garlic and onions threaten local growth.

Mineral Resources/Energy

Petroleum and Natural Gas   West Coast petroleum deposits in California are third in national oil and natural gas production. Leading producers are the Central Valley, Los Angeles Basin, and off Southern California's shore. In 1892, Edward Doheny drilled the first California wells in Los Angeles. Later, wells were drilled at the seeping La Brea Tar Pits. Four of the top ten oil production facilities in America are in California, including untapped offshore reserves.

California offshore oil production is expensive and requires drilling in deep areas beyond the continental shelf. Although California produces oil, it consumes more than it produces.

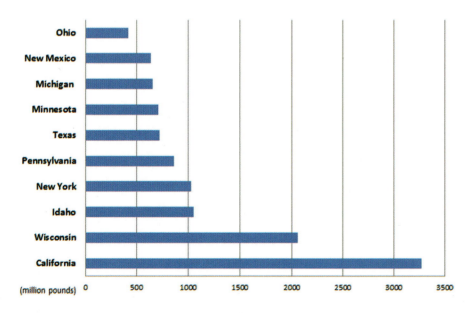

CHART 19.3. Milk Production, Top Ten States, 2010. California has been the number one producer of milk since 1993.

PHOTO 19.10. Long Beach Oil Rigs. Offshore oil production platforms can be seen from the coast on artificial islands with camouflaged wells. Also note the kite surfer in the foreground.

Controversies about increasing oil production, especially in the congested Los Angeles metropolitan area, focus on property values and the aesthetics of offshore drilling (Photo 19.10). Offshore oil leaks have caused concern and have resulted in increased regulations and drilling costs. Significant oil sands and shale in the basin may become important for future needs, as oil reserves decline and prices escalate.

California provides for 69 percent of its own electricity, but imported electricity depends on three sources: natural gas, hydropower, and coal (Chart 19.4). Hydropower comes from the Pacific Northwest, and 41 percent of gas is imported from Canada and the Rocky Mountains. Natural gas, California's first choice for residential heating, has become a subject of scrutiny since the energy crisis of 2001. Eighty-seven percent of California's natural gas production is from out-of-state facilities and delivered by the interstate natural gas pipeline.

Energy and population distribution continue to be unbalanced: Population multiplies in Southern California, but new power plants are in the north. The state has depended on Columbia River power as a standby, but this may be unavailable as the Northwest continues to gain population. Therefore, California has addressed its marginal energy status with novel environmental ideas.

From wind energy to solar panels, from ecological housing to eating local food, California continues to experiment with healthy energy and living standards. In 2009, California provided 11.6 percent of its electricity from renewable resources, with an additional 9.2 percent from hydro.

In February 2007, California announced plans to stop importing Intermontane coal-produced electricity and to achieve 20 percent renewable energy by 2020. This move could force Intermontane states to move toward cleaner fuels. Federal plans to build more coal-burning power plants may be

reviewed if other states can no longer sell their "dirty" power to their biggest potential customer, California. Additionally, California has instituted the California Solar Initiative, a financial incentive program that offers homeowners a tax rebate on top of a small federal tax credit. It is the most ambitious solar program in the nation.

Wind Energy   California has committed to wind energy production. The size and diversity of the topography gives California several large wind energy sites that have been utilized by more than thirteen thousand wind turbines, which made it the second-largest producer of wind power until it was surpassed by Iowa in 2009.[19] The sites generate about 2.6 percent of the state's power (2007).[20]

In 2000 and 2001, California experienced an energy crisis that resulted in blackouts and rapidly rising electricity costs, caused by energy traders manipulating the market; the state responded by investing in its energy future. By 2004, California led the nation in alternative energy use. However, the lack of government support, such as the fossil fuel industry receives, makes growth expensive and slow. Solar power becomes more popular as energy prices increase, but it receives relatively few tax incentives in relation to fossil fuels. Because of escalating fossil fuel energy costs and increased CO_2 levels, solar power and wind energy are becoming popular options for new homes and industry.

Formal Economy

The formal economy is the tax-paying economy of America, and it provides much of the tax base to run governmental services. California's formal economy has changed over time. Both Lockheed and Douglas aircraft industries were founded in California and were important defense industry employers in

Electricity Source, 2009

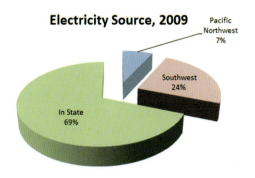

Natural Gas Source, 2008

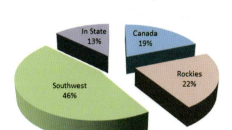

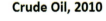

Electricity In-State Generation, 2009

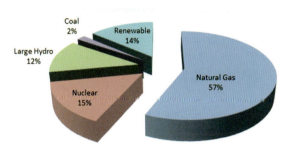

Crude Oil, 2010

CHART 19.4. Sources for California Energy

Source: California Energy Commission, Energy Almanac, at http://energyalmanac.ca.gov/overview/energy_sources.html

Southern California from the 1960s through 1970s; however, defense has shrunk to about 50 percent of its previous size, and in the process it eliminated many high-paying jobs. During the real estate boom of the early twenty-first century, construction grew at 6 percent annually, until the housing crash in 2008.

Informal Economy

Once the province of developing nations, the **informal economy** is expanding in the United States. About 28 percent of the Los Angeles and Bay Area economies runs outside of state-controlled economics. The informal economy is the result of economic desperation. It exploits undocumented workers, including small-scale vending, fruit/flower vendors, and sub-contracted unskilled labor, such as immigrant laborers who gather each morning on hundreds of corners or in parking lots seeking temporary employment. The informal economy also hires undocumented workers in several industries, including the apparel industry, landscaping, construction, and restaurants. Additionally, a growing segment of skilled workers unable to secure permanent positions are included in the informal economy.[21]

The immigrant informal economy includes low-skilled jobs that average $12,000 annually, paid in cash without taxes. Los Angeles alone loses more than $2 billion annually in tax revenue and payroll benefits because of the estimated seven hundred thousand non-taxpaying informal economy laborers.

In Los Angeles, the informal economy is visible everywhere. The workers are often Mexican or Central American Spanish-speaking immigrants with little education, who have no other way to earn a living. Informal economy wages are dishonest to laborers who are trapped in a system as the "working poor," and they are dishonest to tax-paying citizens.[22] The informal economy is present in all the western states, and it is increasingly present in the fast-growing southeastern states where low-paying jobs demand low-cost labor.

The informal economy, though, encompasses more than immigrant laborers. Escalating taxes and slimmer profits have many legitimate firms turning to under-the-table cash employees. High technology, hit hard by outsourcing, uses unemployed people for temporary work, money the "employees" are happy to receive in an economy of fewer "good" jobs.[23]

Several problems arise with the informal economy. Corporations can be heavily influenced by the short-term benefits of not paying workers' taxes. The informal economy brings the economy down in the long run, while short-term employees get trapped in the low-paying, temporary market and companies jeopardize long-term economic growth.

Manufacturing to Postindustrial

Although California was never a manufacturing center, moving from an industrial economy to a postindustrial economy has nevertheless cost California manufacturing jobs. Between

BOX 19.8 PORTS OF LOS ANGELES AND LONG BEACH

North America's western coastline lacks the East Coast's numerous indentations and harbors. Only three large natural harbors exist—San Diego, San Francisco Bay, and Puget Sound—and yet the busiest harbor in America and sixth largest in the world is the Los Angeles–Long Beach port (Map 19.5), which is also the world's largest artificial port. Los Angeles is the only major American city not built on a navigable waterway. The Los Angeles port at San Pedro was constructed twenty miles from the city center, after the annexation of a finger of land connecting to the port area.

A large harbor in Los Angeles was deemed unnecessary in the nineteenth century, because the Sierra Nevada Cordillera and the Intermontane isolated the West Coast from national population centers; rounding Cape Horn deterred access, until the opening of the Panama Canal in 1914 eased interocean access. However, the 1869 arrival of rail lines to the harbor opened up trade, and the San Pedro and Long Beach ports began to be dredged from tidal marshes and mudflats. The harbor was completed and officially opened in 1907, complementing the rapidly growing city of Los Angeles. Since that time, the port has continuously been updated to meet new shipping requirements, such as late-twentieth-century **containerization**, which no longer requires reloading from ship to truck. The combined ports handle two-thirds of the West Coast trade and act as an **entrepôt** (distribution center) for other states.

The American trade pattern has shifted during the late twentieth century, from one facing Europe to one facing Asia, and so the major ports are now on the West Coast. From 1970 to 2000, Asian imports increased from 8 percent to 40 percent of national trade. Trade with China has grown 34 percent annually since it entered the World Trade Organization (WTO) in 2002. Continued expansion has congested West Coast ports.

The increased imports from Asia to Los Angeles–Long Beach have resulted in further highway congestion and more pollution, and they are a large source of CO_2 emissions due to dependence on trucking. Local highways are now used around the clock, but trucking taxes and fees have not increased—which has resulted in residents subsidizing the wear and tear on infrastructure. If the port continues to grow, infrastructure expenses will require analysis and compensation. Pollution concerns extend across all boundaries of the Los Angeles–Long Beach port. Diesel fumes from congestion emit harmful pollutants to nearby residents and have become an environmental justice issue. The poor who live near warehouse areas are in more danger of industrial accidents because of daily exposure when trucks move goods from the port to warehouses.

The Los Angeles–Long Beach port requires expansion if it continues to be the number one American port, but the 2014 expansion of the Panama Canal may shift shipping away from the West Coast and toward East Coast ports. Transfers by truck and rail are more expensive than container shipping, and easy access to the East Coast may decrease shipping to the West Coast.

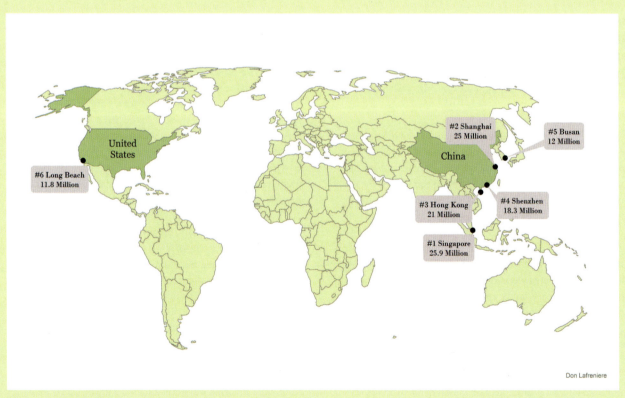

Don Lafreniere

MAP 19.5. The World's Largest Ports. The top five are in Asia. Los Angeles–Long Beach Harbor is the sixth-busiest port and the largest in the United States.

January 2000 and January 2009, California lost 471,000 or one-quarter of all manufacturing jobs.

Significant economic growth centers for the metropolitan area are the Los Angeles–Long Beach port and the informal economy. Having a good transportation network and infrastructure has always been important for trade competitiveness, yet California is outgrowing its infrastructure. In 2002, California's ports handled one-fifth of all U.S. import-export trade, and this has risen with the growth of the Pacific Rim economy. The ports require increased handling capacities, while decreasing the cost of labor to remain competitive. The ports augment their technology to decrease the need for labor. Port jobs have increased, but most are casual, fill-in work without benefits.

Foreign trade in California is significant nationally, accounting for 8 percent of the gross state product (GSP). Exported California products include agriculture, computers, electronics, machinery, transportation, and chemicals. In 2010, the top countries California exported to were Mexico (14.6 percent); Canada (11.3 percent); China (8.7 percent); Japan (8.5 percent); and South Korea (5.6 percent).[24]

Tourism

California remains the nation's number one travel destination. Tourism is a $75 billion industry, the state's third-largest employer, and the fifth-largest contributor to the gross state product (GSP). Growth in the travel industry continues, but it has had a negative impact on the environment and the quality of jobs.

California has long been a mecca for tourists. The state has several natural and human-made tourist destinations. The natural wonders include Yosemite, Death Valley, Big Sur, the many Sierra Nevada hiking and skiing areas, and expansive beaches (Photo 19.11). Many of these wonders are now crowded and restricted. Yosemite requires a reservation months to years in advance, and many beaches are contested grounds where wealthy residents no longer want the public on "their" beaches.

The most famous human-made attractions are Southern California's Disneyland, nearby Knott's Berry Farm, and the San Diego Zoo. In the Central Coast area, the Monterey Peninsula and its elite towns of Pebble Beach and Carmel are popular with the wealthy, while the Golden Gate Bridge, cable cars, and Chinatown beckon in San Francisco. Farther north is the wine country of Napa-Sonoma.

A Sustainable Future

California is utopia, if you do not mind crowds, traffic, and insanely priced housing (even after the housing crash). There was a time not that long ago when orange blossoms still perfumed the air, when the schools were good, the people solid, and a living could be earned with a high school education. Unless you are very wealthy, don't count on finding any of that in coastal California.

Population growth and quality of life can be mutually exclusive; the more one grows, the more the other declines. The

PHOTO 19.11. Yosemite Valley Aerial View (37.747°, −119.571°), looking down the deep, wide U-shaped valley created by glacial action. In the foreground on the left is El Capitan, and on the right midway in the valley is Half Dome.

popular beach, mountain, and desert areas are crowded, and the crowds further limit environmental health. The U.S. Census estimates that California in 2025 will have fifty million people. Architectural competitions garner ideas on how to house millions more in the Central Valley and still continue to grow California's agriculture, but is crowding in as many people as possible sustainable?

California withstood the passage of economic regimes—agriculture, manufacturing, postindustrial development, and stem cell research. But the recent outsourcing of jobs leaves many well-educated and talented high-tech workers out of the loop. Even when jobs are available, many employers no longer hire locals, but instead they search the global marketplace or pay local talent under the table as part of the informal economy.

Los Angeles is a beautiful place. The Mediterranean climate and vegetation have drawn people to the region for the past hundred years. But is this water-stressed semiarid metro area meant to house eighteen million people? Population problems will soon engulf all of America. As Los Angeles often leads the way in health, food, environment, and fashion trends, so it does also with urban dilemmas. Among the most trying issues for the everyday populace are pollution, education, housing, traffic, and living within a diverse and stressed population.[25]

California has a reputation for taking chances. After the millennium, California did not wait for the federal government to finally admit to climate change and its damage, but instead analyzed state pollution and acted to ensure a future as golden as the past. California vies for sustainability and takes the lead in sustainable projects, such as water recycling, green buildings, alternative energy use, and minimizing electricity consumption. However, the population problem, the numerous undocumented immigrants, and a dissipating middle class have yet to be dealt with.

During the new millennium, California has enacted legislation updating its appliance standards and building codes every three years as an important part of its sustainable credo. Oregon, Washington, and most states in the Atlantic Northeast have followed many of California's standards.

California accepted climate change as a problem long before other states or the federal government did, and it acted to reduce energy consumption and reduce fossil fuel dependence. Conservation has already been part of the state's goal. Since 1970, California electricity consumption has been flat, while U.S. consumption rose 50 percent. In September 2006, the state passed AB 32, which aims to reduce greenhouse gas emissions by 25 percent of 1990 levels by 2020.

Taking on the domestic auto industry and the federal government's reticence to recognize climate change, California passed the first state law, AB 1493 (twenty-one other states and Canada have since followed), to reduce automobile carbon dioxide emissions by 2016 (Map 19.6). California is a large market for automobiles, accounting for about 10 percent of the nation's sales, so the law threatened the auto industry. Eighteen states joined California's high standards for fuel efficiency and reduced carbon dioxide, but they were not backed by the EPA, the president, or Congress until 2009. But it may have been too late. By mid-2009, two of the big three domestic auto manufacturers had declared bankruptcy. While they have since reemerged, the message about fuel efficiency and reduced CO_2 is clear.

Additional measures passed in the state include energy-efficient options on new homes. All new homes now offer roofs capable of converting sunlight to electricity, and many lower costs by using a solar power option, which returns excess energy to the grid. The state has also long been a proponent of energy-efficient appliances.

The recession of 2008 hit California hard. A law passed in 2006 to curb carbon dioxide emissions may prove to be difficult to implement with budget shortfalls. The cost to curb emissions

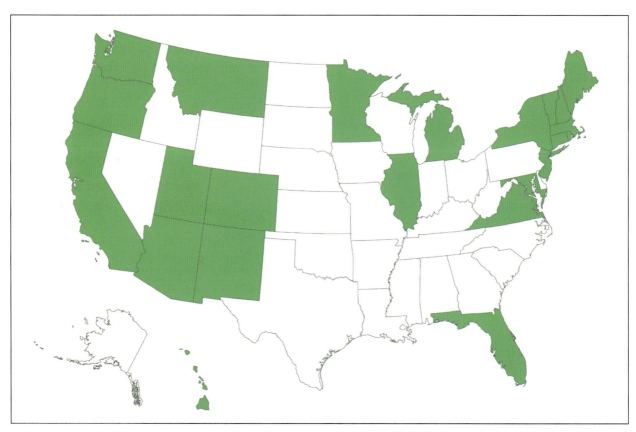

MAP 19.6. States with Greenhouse Gas Emissions Targets, 2011.

Source: Pew Center for Global Climate Change, Center for Climate and Energy Solutions, at http://www.c2es.org/what_s_being_done/in_the_states/emissionstargets_map.cfm

BOX 19.9 ENVIRONMENTAL INNOVATIONS

San Francisco [is] long the world's capital of greenwashing, the art of covering for anti-planet practice with Earth-friendly rhetoric. Our city is, indeed, environmentalism's New Jerusalem; it serves as headquarters to the Sierra Club, the Rainforest Action Network, and the Earth Island Institute, to name but a few locally officed lobbying and affinity groups of global reach. And some Bay Area environmental groups, the Sierra Club and Oakland-based Urban Ecology prominently among them, have promoted the idea of increased housing and other development inside cities as a way to prevent nature-consuming sprawl.*

These are some environmental ideas discussed in California since 2005:

- Environmentally friendly prefab housing: a portable house using lots of glass and sustainable materials. The house can be placed on a lot for $99,900. The biggest problem is the red tape required to set a house on a lot.
- Eating locally: eating from within your own "food shed." This addresses environmental issues: sustaining the local economy, supplying fossil fuels, and environmental deterioration. Eating food grown within one hundred miles of consumption is far below the national average of fifteen hundred miles that food now travels to reach the table.
- Green giants: sustainable high-rises. Builders are addressing resource depletion, energy consumption, biodiversity, and global warming within high-rise living areas. These buildings use simple orientation to take advantage of natural climatic effects. Examples are reducing insulation and air-conditioning with openings facing north and south, orienting windows to collect solar heat, breathing external walls that adjust to the climate, cross ventilation, and using landscaping to generate oxygen and cooling effects.
- Clean technologies: California has many small companies that are invested in alternative energy sources and food safety.
- Bucking the federal reticence to recognize global warming, Governor Schwarzenegger signed the nation's first bill capping greenhouse gas emissions in 2006. In February 2007 California joined with Arizona, New Mexico, Oregon, and Washington in an effort to reduce greenhouse gas emissions and address climate change. The Western Regional Climate Action Initiative will establish a cap-and-trade program and emissions registry.

* Matt Smith, "Environmental Cycle," San Francisco Weekly, June 8, 2005.

will be in the billions, which in a healthy economy would take some twenty years to amortize, but in a recession there is little room or will to spend money. The economic picture continued to look bleak in 2011.

Many people in California are known as "tree huggers"—people who choose a conservation lifestyle ethic and favor green vegetation and trees. The Tree People are an example of a Los Angeles group that supports a greener landscape by participating in planting restoration projects after fires. Tree plantings in the city absorb carbon dioxide and create oxygen, and they filter and collect water. Actions like these create more livable and sustainable cities.

Although other states sometimes feel energy initiatives are unprofitable, California seeks to enhance energy technology and build jobs based on being an incubator for clean-energy technologies, while reducing its energy impact. Now, California along with the rest of the United States needs to work to build the new Industrial Revolution based on its alternative energy resources and innovative ideas, incorporating energy-efficient cradle to cradle technology.

Questions for Discussion

1. If the trend of the past decades continues, will the divide between haves and have-nots continue?

2. Why might Southern California become effectively part of Mexico?

3. What are some of the social, political, and economic problems faced by multicultural California?

4. What is the direction of growth in California, and how might this play into the idea of two (or three?) Californias in the future?

5. How does the informal economy affect the state's economy?

6. Will California continue to be the number one producer of food? If not, where will the specialty crops come from? What are the advantages and disadvantages?

7. California has been at the leading edge of many cultural issues. Is California a harbinger of where the nation is headed in the long term in relation to diversity? Explain.

8. What impact have immigrants had on California's job market and on federal and state services?

9. What has California done to change energy production in the Intermontane? What effect will it have?

10. Explain the differences in water availability between Northern and Southern California.

11. Where is Silicon Valley located, and what factors led to its development?

Suggested Readings

Allen, James Paul, and Eugene Turner. *The Ethnic Quilt: Population Diversity in Southern California*. Northridge, Calif.: Center for Geographical Studies, 1997.

Brechin, Gray. *Imperial San Francisco: Urban Power, Earthly Ruin*. Berkeley: University of California Press, 2006.

Chinn, Thomas W., ed. *A History of the Chinese in California: A Syllabus*. San Francisco: Chinese Historical Society of America, 1969.

Conomos, T. John, ed. *San Francisco Bay: The Urbanized Estuary*. San Francisco: American Association for the Advancement of Science, 1979.

Davis, Mike. *City of Quartz: Excavating the Future in Los Angeles*. New York: Vintage Press, 1992.

———. *Ecology of Fear*. New York: Vintage Press, 1998.

Godfrey, Brian J. *Neighborhoods in Transition: The Making of San Francisco's Ethnic and Nonconformist Communities*. Berkeley: University of California Press, 1988.

Gumbrecht, Blake. *The Los Angeles River: Its Life, Death, and Possible Rebirth*. Baltimore: Johns Hopkins University Press, 2001.

Guyton, Bill. *Glaciers of California: Modern Glaciers, Ice Age Glaciers, the Origin of Yosemite Valley, and a Glacier Tour in the Sierra Nevada*. Berkeley: University of California Press, 1998.

Haddad, Brent. *Rivers of Gold: Designing Markets to Allocate Water in California*. Washington, D.C.: Island Press, 2000.

Hart, John Fraser. "Specialty Cropland in California." *Geographical Review* 93, no. 2 (2003).

Hornbeck, David. "The Patenting of California's Private Land Claims, 1851–1885." *Geographical Review* 69, no. 4 (October 1979): 434–48.

Hundley, Norris, Jr. *The Great Thirst: Californians and Water, 1770s–1990s*. Berkeley: University of California Press, 1992.

Ito, Kazuo. *Issei: A History of Japanese Immigrants in North America*. Trans. Shinichiro Nakamura and Jean S. Gerard. Seattle: Executive Committee for Publication of Issei, 1973.

Lopez-Garza, Marta, and David Diaz, eds. *Asian and Latino Immigrants in a Restructuring Economy: The Metamorphosis of Southern California*. Stanford, Calif.: Stanford University Press, 2001.

McWilliams, Carey. *Southern California Country: An Island on the Land*. New York: Duell, Sloan & Pearce, 1946.

Parsons, James J. "A Geographer Looks at the San Joaquin Valley." *Geographical Review* 76, no. 4 (October 1986): 371–89.

Pellow, David, and Lisa Park. *The Silicon Valley of Dreams: Environmental Injustice, Immigrant Workers, and the High-Tech Global Economy*. New York: New York University Press, 2002.

Peters, Gary L. *American Winescapes: The Cultural Landscapes of America's Wine Country*. Boulder, Colo.: Westview Press, 1997.

Reisner, Mark. *Cadillac Desert*. New York: Viking Penguin, 1986.

Savage, W. Sherman. *Blacks in the West*. Westport, Conn.: Greenwood Press, 1976.

Saxenian, A. L. *Regional Advantage: Culture and Competition in Silicon Valley and Route 128*. Cambridge, Mass.: Harvard University Press, 1994.

Webber, Herbert John. *History and Development of the Citrus Industry*. Revised by Walter Reuther and Harry W. Lawton. University of California, Division of Agricultural Sciences, 1967, at http:// lib.ucr.edu/agnic/webber/Vol1/Chapter1.htm.

Internet Sources

California Department of Food and Agriculture. California Agricultural Production Statistics, at http://www.cdfa.ca.gov/statistics/.

Nichols, Frederic H. "The San Francisco Bay and Delta: An Estuary Undergoing Change." USGS Science for a Changing World, at http://sfbay.wr.usgs.gov/general_factsheets/change.html.

Los Angeles Almanac. The Los Angeles Basin, at http://www.laalmanac .com/geography/ge08e.htm.

Center for Climate and Energy Solutions, at http://www.pewclimate .org/.

U.S. Geological Survey. Earthquake Hazards Program, at http:// earthquake.usgs.gov/.

Monterey Aquarium. Seafood Watch, at http://www.montereybay aquarium.org/cr/cr_seafoodwatch/issues/.

Kauai

1 Citizens of Moloka`i, still largely undeveloped, have fought a 200-home development.

6 Lāna`i, once the Pineapple Isle, is privately held, and there is talk of establishing wind farms and solar energy there.

Oahu

2 • 3
Honolulu

2 Honolulu, sometimes called the L.A. of the Pacific, is plagued with the same problems as other large cities.

Molokai
1

6

5

Maui

5 Lahaina, Maui, was the capital of the Hawaiian kingdom and then a whaling port.

3 Some Hawaiian natives, shut out of the land market, have taken to squatting.

Hawaii

Hilo •

4

4 Some shores of Hawai`i, the youngest and most volcanically active island, continue to build with lava from Kilauea.

0   25   50 Miles
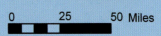

20
HAWAI`I
Aloha

Terms

abyss
atoll

closed ecosystem
Great Mahele
Hawai`i Land Reform Act
pali

poi
seamount
shield cluster

shield volcano
taro
vog

Places

The Big Island: Hawai`i

Honolulu
Kaho`olawe
Kaua`i

Lāna`i
Maui
Moloka`i

Ni`ihau
O`ahu

PHOTO 20.1. Deserted Shoreline, Moloka`i. The tranquility of the "friendly isle" is threatened with Honolulu-style development.

Introduction

Hawai`i is America's island paradise. Friendly and handsome Hawaiians share their year-round tropical weather, treetop fruit, world-famous hula, and laid-back culture (Photo 20.1). What more can one want? While this island lore is still the perception of many, the island paradise of Hawai`i has been transformed into kitschy tourism and a tragic dichotomy between homelessness and uber-wealth. There are few affordable housing options and a rising homeless rate amid multimillion-dollar houses. Even ramshackle shacks on the friendly and most remote public isle, Moloka`i, are worth millions. The dichotomy is reinforced by a reading of history; learning the story about the Native Hawaiian poverty and missionary-descendant oppression. Social injustice, housing inflation, island immigration, and environmental and water-related problems have resulted in an unsustainable environment.

Since the 1960s, sandy beaches, big waves, and the perfect Waikīkī vacation have been sold to the public. Hawaiian tourist classifications range between the ultimate one-week budget honeymoon getaways to visits to exclusive resorts on entire islands. But tourism is a latecomer to the Hawaiian economy. Hawai`i became a tourist mecca after the invention of the commercial jet airplane, and after successive economies (sandalwood, whaling, ranching, and farming) had run their course and left their waste debris. The island archipelago may be paradoxically loved and suffocated to death simultaneously.

Hawai`i has beckoned to westerners for centuries, first because of its isolated yet strategic location, then agriculturally, and finally as a tourist destination—all the while ignoring the rights of the native peoples. Keeping the islands pristine has proven impossible, but maintaining social and ecological integrity may be possible. Maintaining a **closed ecosystem**—one that recycles everything and wastes nothing—is an ideal goal on the isolated islands. Isolation should work to the island's advantage, but the ease of transportation and population growth has ended the isolation.

However, many Hawaiians are working toward maintaining the native habitats and species unique to the locale by safe-guarding water from pollution, developing renewable energy sources, and protecting land from thoughtless human encroachments. Keeping the island's environment healthy necessitates a holistic approach and requires an honest examination of how Western ideas impact indigenous cultures. While environment is important, many Native Hawaiians also pursue reestablishing their social ecology; they work to end the cultural imperialism imposed without their voice being heard.

Hawaiian environmental issues are a microcosm of the world situation. What is the carrying capacity of the islands? Only so many people can live on a limited land mass. Groups and individuals are beginning to invest in sustainable and renewable energy systems that address the environmental ills but still neglect the multiple societal ills on the islands. Although the islands are amongst the wealthiest in the world, they are also home to the working homeless and the disenfranchised Native Hawaiian population, who still fight for their own foothold on their island home.

Physical Geography

Stretched from the Aleutian Trench to the Big Island, 132 volcanically formed islands, reefs, atolls, and shoals compose the fifteen-hundred-mile Hawaiian archipelago. The eight populated islands, the state of "Hawai`i," are the largest and youngest of the islands. Together they stretch four hundred miles end to end from the Big Island to Ni`ihau, and they have a total area about the size of New Jersey. The major islands include the following (listed from largest to smallest):[1]

- Hawai`i (4,028 square miles)[2]
- Maui (727 square miles)
- O`ahu (597 square miles)
- Kaua`i (552 square miles)
- Moloka`i (260 square miles)
- Lāna`i (141 square miles)
- Ni`ihau (72 square miles)
- Kaho`olawe (45 square miles)

The Hawaiian Islands are located in the Pacific Ocean about twenty-one hundred miles southwest of the U.S. mainland and are the most remote islands in the world. The islands, ranging in latitude from 16°55'N to 23°N, are the only part of the United States south of the Tropic of Cancer. As part of the Hawaiian Ridge–Emperor Seamount, the islands extend in a wide arc between two eighteen-thousand-foot-deep Pacific **abysses** (the flat ocean floor found at the bottom of continental slopes). The still-growing chain was created over the past seventy million years.

The volcanic origins of the Hawaiian Islands are unusual because they are not at the edge of a tectonic plate where most volcanics are found; they lie beneath a stationary hot spot in the mantle below the Pacific Plate. Molten magma melts the plate above the hot spot. The volcanoes become inactive as the plate moves past the hot spot, and then the hot spot repeats the process, forming the next island. The older volcanoes on Kaua'i, for example, are extinct, cut off from the hot spot magma, while Big Island volcanoes are either still active (Kilauea) or inactive but not yet extinct.

Magma is lighter than the surrounding rock, so it rises through the mantle onto the seafloor and forms a basaltic **seamount**, which over geologic time rises through the mantle, the crust, and the ocean surface as a **shield volcano** island. The gentle-slope shield volcanoes are built by accretion of fluid lava flows. The complete cycle of volcano building and quiescence takes about six hundred thousand years—half the time rising from the ocean floor to sea level and half building the shield volcano.

The plate inches southeast, so the northwest islands are the oldest. The basaltic volcanic peaks are some of the largest and highest mountains in the world, when counting both the underwater and above–sea level masses.

The smaller landmasses of the island chain lie to the northwest. The twenty-six Northwestern or Leeward Islands, from Kure (twelve hundred miles northwest of Honolulu) to Kaula (twenty miles west-southwest of Ni'ihau), are either the ring-like coral reef **atolls** or the summits of submarine volcanoes. These small islands abound in endemic insects, plants, and coral reefs and are a wintering area for migratory birds. During the past fifty years, the Northwestern Island waters have lost species to overfishing and erosion. To prevent further ecosystem losses, in June 2006 the Northwestern Islands were declared a national monument and became the world's largest marine reserve. Commercial activities are banned throughout the marine reserve.

The Northwestern Islands are uninhabited, except for the minimally staffed crew from the U.S. Fish and Wildlife Service on Midway Atoll.[3] Prior to European contact, Hawaiians inhabited a few of these atolls for short periods of time, but generally the remote atolls and islands remained inviolate.

The youngest and most volcanically active island is the Big Island of Hawai`i, although fifteen miles east of the Big Island a seamount is building. The seamount is called Loihi; it is already over ten thousand feet high but still three thousand feet below the ocean's surface. If Loihi continues to erupt, it may reach sea level in ten to twenty thousand years.

Lava flows have defined the unique shape of each volcanic island. Islands with multiple volcanoes, such as Hawai`i and Maui, are called volcanic **shield clusters**.

The prehistoric Hawaiian Islands were a remote, tropical Eden with vegetation that varied according to the island's age. The forested islands teemed with more than eighty-seven hundred endemic flora and fauna species. The oldest inhabited island, Kaua'i, has been volcanically inactive in recorded history and has developed lush vegetation. The Big Island of Hawai`i, however, is bare where fresh lava has been deposited. The arrival of the Polynesians over the past fifteen hundred years brought new species to the islands, but the major challenge to island vegetation and animals has been since the jet age, when invasive species were imported to the detriment of crops and the extinction of native species. The numerous jet-age invasive species threaten the economy, environment, and lifestyle of the islands.

Water

The islands are a mix of dry and very wet topographies arranged according to their seaward orientation. In the mountainous island interiors, surface water erodes and cuts into the lava, shaping canyons. Kaua`i, the oldest island, has the largest canyon, Waimea, and the most erosion, while younger Hawai`i has the least erosion because the basalt is porous and rain infiltrates the rock. Infrequent flash floods where the rock is less porous can be a natural hazard that simultaneously enriches the biological diversity.

Offshore water is warm and clear. Coral reefs—partially responsible for the famous surf on Hawaiian beaches[4]—surround portions of the islands. Coral is home to more than five thousand species of fish, sea animals, and plants (Photo 20.2). Sewage discharge and septic systems threaten the reefs and disrupt the coastal nutrient balance. The water off the sparsely settled islands is healthy, but overfishing, pollution, invasive algae, runoff, and human contact threaten the heavily populated islands.

Water Issues

Hawai`i has regularly faced drought. While drought affected the agricultural economy in the past, today water shortages threaten the increasingly large population. In heavily populated O`ahu, freshwater has been capped or diverted from flowing into the

BOX 20.1 THE MAJOR HAWAIIAN ISLANDS

The individual islands from the north are: Kaua`i, Ni`ihau, O`ahu, Moloka`i, Lāna`i, Maui, Hawai`i, Kaho`olawe (Map 20.1).

Kaua`i (2010 pop. 66,921)

About 5.5 million years ago, a single shield volcano shaped the oldest of the eight islands, Kaua`i. The verdant "Garden Isle" is the oldest inhabited island, the most ecologically diverse and the most eroded. It has three major physical attractions: Waimea Canyon—"the Grand Canyon of the Pacific"—the Na Pali coastline, and Mount Waialeale, one of the wettest places on Earth (more than 450 inches of rainfall annually).

The island is a popular tourist attraction and had approximately 1.1 million visitors in 2005. But the impact of tourists has affected natural flora biodiversity on Kaua`i. Pristine areas still exist within the deep valleys of the island, such as Wainiha, now a private nature reserve, but even these are being threatened with invasive species. The island now has a number of restoration sites where alien and invasive vegetation is being replaced with native plants, such as the overharvested maile vine used in lei making.

Ni`ihau (2010 pop.170)

Ni`ihau is the "Forbidden Isle," a privately owned island eighteen miles southwest of Kaua`i. The Sinclair–Robinson family purchased the island from Kamehameha V in 1864 for $10,000 and remain the owners. Part of the original contract agreement was to preserve the Hawaiian language and culture. The island was a cattle and sheep ranch until 1999, when the ranch was shut down due to unprofitability. The closure of the ranch left the residents unemployed. They have since become subsistence farmers, fishers, and receive welfare. Most are Native Hawaiians and live a life that continues to preserve the native culture and language, and rejects most modern technology.

The island lies low on the horizon and does not catch the trade-wind rainfall, so it receives only about twelve inches of rain annually. The lack of rain often results in freshwater shortages, causing residents to occasionally evacuate for Kaua`i. While on Kaua`i, the Ni`ihau islanders have access to modern technology, but most choose to forgo it and return to Ni`ihau, even after the ranch was closed.

Until recently, only members of the owner's family, government officials, or invited guests have been allowed to visit the island. The owners have sought to maintain the culturally pristine and natural habitat, while at the same time finding economic viability. They have pursued, so far unsuccessfully, military contracts and have now allowed a select few to tour or hunt on the island. These tours respect the island residents' way of life by keeping them away from Western culture and tourism. Wild animals roam the island, such as an estimated six thousand feral pigs, which are a favorite hunting prize. The hunts are justified, since many of the pigs die during drought.

O`ahu (2010 pop. 953,207)

Two volcanoes, Waianae and Koolau, formed O`ahu. Lava created the Leilehua Plateau, the pineapple-growing agricultural region north of Honolulu. To the east of the plateau are the Waianae Mountains, which are part of the James Campbell Estate (leased to the Nature Conservancy) or part of the federally run military complex. To the west, the Koolau Mountains run the north-south extent of the island. Diamond Head to the south of Honolulu, visible from Waikīkī Beach, is an extinct volcano. The north shore of the island is called the surfing capital of the world, containing such famous beaches as Sunset, Waimea, and the Bonzai Pipeline. The big waves for surfing are due to winter storms and shallow reefs.

About 80 percent of the state's population resides in O`ahu. Honolulu, the largest urban and commercial area on all the islands, is complete with high rises, sprawl, and traffic. Its suburbs extend up the eastern side of the Koolau Mountain valleys to the northeast Ewa Plain and to Pearl Harbor, site of the Japanese attack on December 7, 1941, that brought the United States into World War II.

Moloka`i (See Maui County below; 2010 pop. 7,345)

Moloka`i is known as the "friendly isle," the most unspoiled and natural of the publicly held islands. Native Hawaiians constitute the majority of the population, and the Hawaiian language is evident in speech and signage. There are relatively few tourists. The island is dry on the leeward west end, and wet on the windward east end. The northern shore has the highest *pali* (cliffs) in the world, the "backside," dropping precipitously three thousand feet into the sea. The cliffs are the result of a tremendous landslide about 1.5 million years ago, after waves had undercut the shore for millions of years.

The Kalaupapa Peninsula (2010 pop. 90) and Leprosy

A prison fortified by nature.

—Robert Louis Stevenson

The sickness that is a crime.

—Nineteenth-century Hawaiian term for leprosy

In the middle of Moloka`i's northern shore, thousands of feet below steep cliffs, is the remote Kalaupapa Peninsula, which was once a leper colony. In 1865, a law was passed criminalizing leprosy. Fear of the deforming and contagious disease caused the extreme measure of isolating the afflicted. By 1866, anyone showing signs of what they took to be the disease—and many with psoriasis or acne were misdiagnosed—were banished from their homes, taken to the

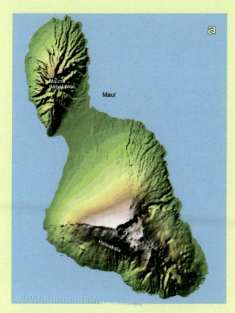

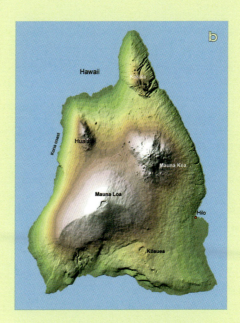

MAP 20.1. The Major Hawaiian Islands. (Maps not to scale.)

a. Maui is the second-largest island (727 square miles) and is composed of two volcanoes and a narrow isthmus. At one time, the four islands Lāna`i, Kaho`olawe, Moloka`i, and Maui were one island called Maui Nui.

b. The Big Island (4,028 square miles) is composed of five volcanoes. The most active is Kileaua, which has been continually active since 1993.

c. O`ahu is the third-largest island (597 square miles) and houses about 75 percent of the state's population, most of whom live in metro Honolulu. The North Shore is a world-famous surfing spot.

d. Kaua`i is the oldest of the islands and fourth largest (552 square miles). Ni`ihau is a privately held island inhabited by indigenous Hawaiians.

e. Moloka`i remains largely natural and inhabited by Hawaiian natives. Kalaupapa was the infamous leper colony.

(continued on next page)

BOX 20.1   continued

waters off the peninsula, dumped in the ocean, and left to swim to shore and to fend for themselves.

The peninsula was primitive at best, and the exiled led a wretched life until the arrival of Father Damien. No one can be on Moloka`i and not hear of the sacrifice of Father Damien. He arrived on Kalaupapa in 1873 and spent the rest of his life offering hope, help, and dignity to the exiles, before succumbing to the disease himself. More than eight thousand were banished to the peninsula in the century of quarantine, before antibiotics arrested leprosy (Hansen's disease) in the 1940s. Today a few of the exiles remain, now by choice, as it is often the only home they have ever known.

Maui (Maui County [includes Maui, Moloka`i, Lāna`i] 2010 population 154,834)

Maui is a remnant of a much bigger island that existed 1.2 million years ago. Maui Nui was perhaps 50 percent larger than the Big Island today. It was composed of Maui, Moloka`i, Lāna`i and Kaho`olawe, but over time global sea-level change and volcano subsidence has submerged the saddles between the islands.*

A narrow, low, fertile isthmus separates Maui's two volcanoes. On West Maui, Pu`u Kukui is considered extinct: The caldera is the present-day Iao Valley and has many incised valleys. East Maui has Hawai`i's third-largest shield volcano, Haleakala, which having last erupted in 1790 is still considered an active volcano. East Maui is less occupied than West Maui. The infamous and tortuous Hana-Piilani highway did not go completely around East Maui until the 1990s, and it is still partially gravel. West Maui is the more populated side and contains Lahaina, King Kamehameha's original island capital and an important whaling station. The first missionaries arrived at Lahaina.

The isthmus was an important producer of sugarcane, irrigated by an elaborate system originating in the wet, forested hillsides. Much of the remaining sugarcane grown on the islands is grown on thirty-seven thousand acres of the isthmus.

Lāna`i (2010 pop. 3,135)

Lāna`i is thirteen miles by eighteen miles—ninety-eight thousand acres—separated from Maui and Moloka`i by channels. Since 1917, the Dole pineapple plantation has run the Pineapple Island. It was a company island rather than a company town. Castle & Cooke—descendants of missionary families—purchased 98 percent of the island when the pineapple market migrated off island. Castle & Cooke tried to convert the island to tourism but ran out of money, and David Murdock purchased Castle & Cooke in 1985. He also built and owns the two luxury resorts on the island. The three thousand residents, mostly people who worked on the pineapple plantation, now staff the resorts. There is no "real" Hawai`i on Lāna`i, only a hideout for the uber-wealthy. Bill Gates rented the entire island for his wedding. Microsoft cofounder Paul Allen has the largest private residence on the island.

Hawai`i (2010 pop. 185,079)

Hawai`i, the Big Island, is the youngest—four hundred thousand years old—and largest island in the archipelago. It contains two-thirds of state land and is larger than all the other islands combined. Eruptions from Kilauea add an additional forty-two acres annually. The Big Island also has the most climatic regions—from desert at Ka`u rainforest near Hilo to the snowcapped peak of Mauna Kea.

Five volcanoes (in order of age, oldest first) Kohala, Mauna Kea, Hualalai, Mauna Loa, and Kilauea, shape the island. The oldest, Kohala, is extinct. Mauna Kea is a dormant volcano that last erupted forty-five hundred years ago. Measured from its underwater base instead of sea level, Mauna Kea is taller than Mount Everest (33,476 feet from its base, 13,796 from sea level, compared to Mount Everest's 29,035 feet). Super-powered telescopes mounted atop Mauna Kea take advantage of the lack of atmospheric pollution. The Mauna Kea Observatory is also used by the National Oceanic and Atmospheric Administration (NOAA) as the research facility that monitors CO_2 since the 1950s. Hualalai last erupted around 1800 and may erupt again in the next hundred years. Mauna Loa (13,679 feet) is the world's largest active volcano and covers half of the island, and Kilauea is the world's most active volcano, continuously erupting since 1983.

Agriculture and tourism dominate the Big Island's economy. The twenty-mile Kona Coast on the leeward side of the island has excellent soils and climate supporting the only American-grown coffee. The mountain slopes of Haualalai and Mauna Loa provide the soil, precipitation, protective cover, and **vog (v**olcano + sm**og),** volcanic smog formed by the mixture of sulfuric dioxide and other pollutants, necessary to make good coffee. The Parker Ranch—150,000 acres between Mauna Kea and Kohala—is one of America's largest cattle ranches and Hawai`i's largest privately held ranch. The ranch is run by a charitable trust since 1992.

Kaho`olawe (uninhabited)

A small extinct volcano forms this island. The island was used as a penal colony (1826–1853), for ranching (1858–1952), and for bombing practice. In 1976, a Native Hawaiian group occupied the island and protested for a return of the island to Hawaiian sovereignty. In 1981 the entire island was declared historic and placed on the National Register. In 1990, the bombing halted but unexploded ordnance hinders occupation.

Sheep and goats overgrazed the land during the ranching period. Today a native group protects environmental restoration and manages the island as a cultural reserve; eventually ownership will transfer to a sovereign Hawaiian nation. The U.S. Navy has cleared part of the island of surface ordnance and removed goats. Revegetation programs are in place. In November 2003, Kaho`olawe was officially transferred from the U.S. Navy to the state of Hawai`i.

---

* http://hvo.wr.usgs.gov/volcanowatch/2003/03_04_10.html.

PHOTO 20.2. Coral Reef off Moloka`i. Touching coral is a no-no while snorkeling, diving, or swimming in the ocean. Coral can be damaged or die because of trampling or oils from human bodies.

ocean, but this action has assaulted indigenous species ecosystems.

O`ahu

Access to freshwater has been an increased concern on O`ahu. The sugar crop consumed most of the water in the past, but today the major consumer is the growing population on the most populated island. Recent droughts have focused attention on the issue. Just north of Honolulu, water shortages threaten the island's fastest-growing region, the Ewa Plain. Groundwater once used for sugarcane fields is now being pumped at nonrenewable rates, and the region has turned to reverse osmosis desalination (desal) as an answer.

Desal water is more expensive than groundwater, but the increased cost of groundwater drilling has made desal a reasonable possibility. A disadvantage is the amount of energy required to convert the saltwater. Opponents to desalination believe that conserving water may be more cost effective before committing to the energy-intensive desalination process.

Desalination can currently provide about thirty thousand gallons daily (enough for about six hundred homes), but the goal is to provide forty million gallons, about one-quarter of daily water demand. Desalination is only being used by pilot projects testing several water resource alternatives to find the most cost-effective and energy-efficient method. The eleven million gallons of raw seawater required to produce five million gallons of desal water annually disrupts local ecosystems; this disruption has yet to be environmentally analyzed.

Maui

Maui faces water shortages in the near future because of urban population growth and competing agricultural claims. Because the water shortages and limited storage facilities are severe, Maui has been seeking help on water issues from sources outside Maui County.

One of the larger conflicts is between small traditional taro farmers and the much larger sugar and pineapple corporations. The starchy tuber **taro** is the traditional staple food, which few Hawaiians eat today due to the modern diet; however, the natives are more genetically disposed to taro, which has resulted in obesity. A few taro growers have been working to restore this significant element of the traditional Hawaiian diet, and therefore they are important on the island and for the native population. In 2003, Maui's Native Hawaiian taro farmers fought large corporate farmers and won continued water rights, although conserving water or efficient use remains problematic.

The major aquifer on Maui has reached 90 percent of its capacity; the county stopped issuing new permits, effectively ending new developments. Agriculture consumes 75 percent of the water, but escalating demands on water require more accountability of agricultural and urban water use. An additional issue with Maui water is the conversion of agricultural land to residential use. Former agricultural wells are now residential in use, but they are often contaminated with agricultural pesticides.

Climate

Hawai`i's tropical location is consistently warm throughout the year. The climate has little seasonality, but the trade winds and the mountainous topography have created a distinct rainfall pattern that determines the location of the Hawaiian tourism economy. Following the trade wind patterns, the windward (northeast) side of the islands receives plentiful rainfall, while the southwest leeward (protected from the wind and rain) side rainfall is scant. Tourist resorts are located on the dry leeward sides of the islands: for example, Honolulu and the Big Island's Kona Coast.

BOX 20.2 WASTE DISPOSAL AND GARBAGE

Hawai`i is filled with garbage. In the closed ecosystem, any waste created must remain on the islands in landfills or be dumped into the ocean. The ocean adds marine debris to the waste deposited on the islands.

Garbage in the Pacific rides the currents from the United States to Asia and back. One of the largest garbage collection areas is in the warm and cold water convergence zone northwest of the Hawaiian Islands. U.S. and Asian industries and populations dump waste into waterways that make their way to the ocean; ships cast trash overboard or lose containers filled with goods in storms. Trash is thrown "away" only to be caught in the gyre or turn up on the beaches of Hawai`i.

Land-based trash is also a problem. O`ahu, with a majority of the population and tourists, has two landfills. One is used for construction and demolition materials, the other for residential and commercial waste. They collect the 1.79 million tons of waste annually created on the island. Both landfills are all but full. Overfilled, there are times when there are spills.

In 2011, spills were blamed on "Mother Nature" and on worldwide climate change. At the University of Hawai`i, professor and state climatologist Pao-Shin Chu said that rainfall has become more intense since 1980, that the change in climate can become a public health concern, and to expect more in the future.*

Unintended Consequences

Waste disposal into Hawai`i's coastal waters has been noted since the 1970s. Pollution from urban and agricultural runoff is detrimental to coral reefs and accelerates eutrophication. Waste in building practices and the construction industry use of landfills has caused additional problems. While environmental management has been practiced, the unsustainable standard of life and tourism continues to exacerbate pollution.

The overwhelming majority of the trash on the beaches is plastics (60 to 80 percent), which do not biodegrade but rotate in the gyres until they settle on the beaches, sink, or are swallowed by marine organisms. The U.N. environmental program documenting the trash estimates there are perhaps forty-six thousand pieces of plastic litter in every square mile of ocean.† The plastics are resistant to biodegrading and instead break up into smaller and smaller pieces that can be mistaken by marine organisms as food. Additional damage from debris has been found on the Northwestern Hawaiian Islands, where nets caught on coral reefs damage the ecosystem.

Local and Ecoregional Impact

The growing population and consumption levels continue to escalate waste disposal problems. One out of every six days was posted as unsafe at Hawaiian beaches in 2005, with Honolulu closed fifty-two days because of unsafe sewage conditions. A massive sewage spill polluted Waikīkī Beach in March 2006, after forty-one days of heavy rains flooded a broken sewer line. The high bacteria levels closed Waikīkī Beach for two days. In January of 2011, all leeward beaches were closed twice. A massive garbage spill from the residential landfill (built next to the ocean) had overflowed due to heavy rains. Waste and medical debris were dumped into the ocean and then washed ashore. The landfill remained closed for weeks for repairs.

The garbage debris from the gyre litters several beaches on the islands. Kamilo Beach (*kamilo* means "twisting currents" in Hawaiian) is constantly exposed to the trade winds that blow debris onshore and has always been a beach where debris (it used to be logs) washed up. But today the beach on the Big Island's southern tip has earned Kamilo the title of the world's dirtiest beach, with debris piled up to a foot deep.

External Costs

A world-renowned resort area that closes its beaches has some public relations problems. What tourist wants to frolic in waste-lined beaches or lie on littered sand? The cost to the tourism industry can be monumental once people know the problems with waste disposal and the disregard for public health, especially with all the medical flotsam including fecal matter, vials of blood, and syringes.

Marine debris from trawlers has incurred costs to marine organisms and causing injury due to entanglements in nets that often result in death. The debris has prevented recovery for the endangered Hawaiian monk seal on the Northwestern Hawaiian Islands. Despite annual cleanups of the debris, the coral reefs on the remote islands were once again choked with castoff netting and fishing gear.‡

Solutions

Several nongovernment organizations (NGOs) have banded together to rid the coral reef ecosystems of derelict fishing gear along the Northwestern Hawaiian Islands. Marine debris on beaches has caused people to support the Beach Environmental Awareness Campaign Hawai`i (BEACH) that educates about marine debris and the waste in the eastern and western garbage patches in the Pacific. Several groups now encourage halting the use of plastic bags.

O`ahu has operated a waste-to-energy plant since 1990. The plant creates about 5 percent of island electricity that is distributed to residents and commerce. While the plant has reduced the solid waste created by the island, the plant is unable to convert all the waste sent to it, so at times there have been spills.

* Lucy Jokiel, "The Blame Game," *Honolulu Weekly*, February 2, 2011, at http://honoluluweekly.com/cover/2011/02/the-blame-game-3/.

† Greenpeace, "Plastic Debris in the World's Oceans," at http://www.unep.org/regionalseas/marinelitter/publications/docs/plastic_ocean_report.pdf.

‡ R. C. Boland and M. J. Donohue, "Marine Debris Accumulation in the Nearshore Marine Habitat of the Endangered Hawaiian Monk Seal, *Monachus schauinslandi*, 1999–2001" *Marine Pollution Bulletin* 46 (2003): 1385–94.

Average rainfall varies between the windward (four hundred inches in Kaua`i) and leeward (ten inches) sides, but it averages about twenty-five inches annually. The rainy season is between October and March. The warm air temperatures (85°F in summer, 78°F in winter) are influenced by 74°F to 80°F water year-round.

At the higher elevations atop volcanoes, temperatures average 40°F. Rainfall is scant above three thousand feet on the Big Island mountains and on Maui's Haleakala, but both can and occasionally do receive snow.

Historical Geography and Settlement

Hawai`i was one of the last places in the Pacific to be settled. While Polynesians settled the South Pacific two thousand years ago, remote Hawai`i was settled much later. Two major Polynesian migrations occurred, first from the Marquesas (approximately 400 CE) and later from Tahiti (900–1000 CE), but smaller migrations continued through the fifteenth century. Researchers have theorized about the migration patterns.

The path of Polynesian migration has puzzled researchers because it goes against prevailing winds. How did they do it? Researchers have hypothesized that during El Niño events (which may have been prolonged during the 750–1250 CE Little Climatic Optimum) there were prevailing westerlies, which would have facilitated navigation.[5] The Pacific migrations may also be part of a larger, world-scale pattern, similar to the tenth-century Viking navigation to Newfoundland. The pattern fits the climatic record—a period of warmth, which would end with the Little Ice Age, when further oversea migrations were halted as storms advanced with colder climates.

By the mid-sixteenth century, the Spanish made regular runs between the Philippines and Mexico but missed the Hawaiian Islands. Captain James Cook stumbled upon Kaua`i in 1778 and named the islands in honor of his patron, the Earl of Sandwich. The Sandwich Islands were renamed the Hawaiian Islands in 1847.

The islands were politically fragmented prior to the nineteenth century; each island was ruled by a different indigenous king until the unification reign of King Kamehameha I when Europeans reached the islands. Natives ruled the islands as a constitutional monarchy until 1893 when Queen Liliuokalani was deposed, although European arrival on the islands altered the importance of the royals.

Island life was transformed after the Europeans arrived, beginning with a scourge of sailor-spread venereal disease. Lacking immunity, many Hawaiians died. In the 1820s, the first missionaries arrived from New England. While the missionaries' moral code and religion conflicted with native beliefs, both the natives and the missionaries eventually compromised their positions. The natives accepted Christianity, and the missionary families often intermarried and therefore began acquiring land. Previously royals "owned" land, although it was shared and used by all. Europeans applied their ownership rules to the land, and the Hawaiians lost their previous rights to use land. Subsequent generations of the missionary families shifted their interests from religious conversion to socioeconomic conversion of the islands.

The missionary families' progeny became plantation owners, building economic empires that uprooted the natives, their culture, and their way of life. The reign of the last monarch, Queen Liliuokalani, sought to preserve and restore Hawaiian nationalism and sovereignty but threatened the nonnative sugar planters, who counted on the sugar crop and removal of tariffs to increase their profits.

Sugar was all the more lucrative for Hawai`i because it did not need refrigeration. Shipping the commodity to the United States was profitable and possible, but the tariffs to import the sugar into the United States were high. Tariffs were higher than the plantation owners' profits, and so the white plantation owners instituted the last of several policies to shift power from the Hawaiians to the whites; they imposed the Bayonet Constitution in 1887.[6]

In a bloodless coup, the planters overthrew the monarchy, despite opposition in the U.S. government. After the queen was deposed in 1893, the Republic of Hawai`i was established; it lasted until 1898, when the United States found it politically strategic to annex the islands as a coaling station for ships and the U.S. government claimed more than 1.8 million acres of Hawaiian land for military use. Hawai`i was annexed despite opposition from Native Hawaiians and became a U.S. territory in 1900. The plantation owners no longer had to pay tariffs.

In 1959, Hawai`i became the fiftieth state.

Native Hawaiians believe that the 1893 overthrow of the kingdom illegally expropriated their land and denied their rights. Native Hawaiians are not tribal and therefore have been denied Native rights. Today Native Hawaiians support a sovereignty movement that would give Native Hawaiians the same federal recognition as Native Americans. There are several sovereignty organizations that support a range of solutions, from restoring the monarchy to outright independence from outside rule (the United States). Included within the sovereignty movement are improved land rights for Native Hawaiians. The Hawaiian governor and senators recognize and promote Hawaiian sovereignty.

Cultural Perspectives

Kapu

Native Hawaiian laws prior to European contact revolved around *kapu*, a system of laws and regulations that separated the sacred from the common, the inferior classes from royalty, and men from women. *Kapu* acts were usually punished by death. Spatial segregation was common. Many *kapu* laws revolved around treatment of the chiefs, such as not having one's head higher, not gazing into a chief's eyes, not wearing the royal red or yellow colored feathers. Other *kapu* taboos involved food: Women were forbidden to eat bananas, coconuts, or pork.

Since the foreigners did not practice *kapu* and did not suffer its consequences, King Kamehameha I was obligated in 1819 to

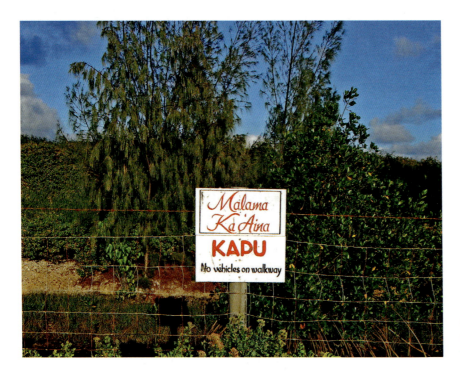

PHOTO 20.3. *Kapu*: "No Trespassing" Sign on Moloka`i. Malama Ka`Aina is translated as "Care for the Land."

end the *kapu* system. He did this by ceremonially eating the forbidden foods with women. The loss of the *kapu* taboos was instrumental in breaking the Hawaiian belief system and in their accepting Christianity.

Kapu, as used today on Hawai`i, often means "No trespassing," and it can be seen on signs forbidding entry into areas (Photo 20.3).

Hawaiian Diet

The traditional Hawaiian diet was based on seafood and local foods—coconut, bananas, breadfruit, taro, and yams—some of which were imported during the initial Hawaiian migrations. The staples of the diet were fish and starches, such as **poi** (made from taro). The diet was low in fat, making the Hawaiians genetically predisposed to store fat for times of scarcity, which may account for the disastrous effect of the current diet on the native population.[7]

The current sedentary Native Hawaiian lifestyle and foods differ from the traditional and are reflected in the native body. Today the Hawaiian native diet depends on fatty, processed foods rich in white flour and sugar, which are poorly adapted to the native lifestyle or genetic disposition to store fat. The highest prevalence of obesity, 61.3 percent, is among the Native Pacific Islanders.[8] Their lifespan is much shorter than that of the mainland population, due to high rates of diabetes, hypertension, stroke, and cardiovascular disease. For example, the prevalence of diabetes among the native population surpasses that of the rest of the U.S. population. Studies validate that Hawaiians eating a culturally appropriate traditional diet are healthier than when adopting a Western diet. The studies also reveal that Hawaiians today lack access to fresh produce and seafood, making a traditional diet difficult for natives to reclaim.[9] Crossover

foods, such as saimin, the Hawaiian version of Japanese ramen, have influenced the Hawaiian diet.

Saimin and Spam

Hawaiian fast food is saimin—a ramen soup with fish stock and garnishes, such as scrambled eggs, tofu, green onions, fish, and meat. Spam is the most popular saimin garnish in Hawai`i.

Spam is Hawai`i's comfort food, and Hawaiians eat about six million cans annually, which equates to six cans per person. Spam became a popular imported food among Hawaiians during World War II, before refrigeration was common (Spam has a long shelf life). Spam can be served with saimin, musubi—similar to a sushi roll—and with eggs and rice for breakfast. The nutritional content of Spam, high in saturated fat and sodium, accounts for some of the Hawaiian native weight gain and health problems.

Regional Life

Population

In 1960 just after statehood, the total population of the islands was 633,000, which more than doubled to 1,380,301 in 2010. The indigenous population declined after Europeans arrived, and subsequently many other ethnic groups have arrived.

The island population was approximately 300,000 in 1788. By 1830 the population of pure Hawaiians had dropped to 130,000 and declined to 57,000 by 1872 before growing again. Today there are perhaps 80,000 pure Native Hawaiians, although about 250,000 claim Hawaiian blood.

Hawai`i's population is one of the most diverse in the world. Diversity grew during the sugarcane era when there was a need for laborers, who were imported from China, Japan, the

Philippines, and Portugal. The largest ethnic group (2010) is Asians with about 38.6 percent, whites (*haole*) 24.7 percent, Native Hawaiian (*Kanaka Maoli*) 10 percent, and Hispanic 8.9 percent, while blacks are 1.6 percent of the total population (Table 20.1). The high degree of ethnic intermarriage is revealed in the almost one in four who identifies himself or herself as multiracial.[10]

Most Native Hawaiians have mixed blood. Those who identify as Hawaiian are the poorest, have the worst health statistics (mortality, suicide, and disease), high dropout rate, highest unemployment rate, and highest incarceration rate. Many are homeless and forced to "squat" on their expropriated land. A few have gained the right to reclaim land.

Land Ownership

Since the arrival of Europeans, Native Hawaiians, like American tribal indigenous, have lost control of their homelands. But unlike the Native Americans, the Hawaiians are not tribal and so have not been recognized as nations and or granted the rights of the tribal indigenous. This has led to a prolonged debate about Hawaiian native rights, sovereignty, and land ownership.

Hawaiian royalty controlled all land, but it was used by all in a sustainable system of communal tenure. Fee-simple land was unknown, but commoners cultivated "their" land, and assumed a collective "ownership" in which inhabitants shared their production. Natural boundaries divided the land into narrow strips that reached from the mountaintops to the beach (*ahupua`a*), and presented each farmer a variety of land types and a degree of self-sufficiency. Oceanside land offered fish. The shallows were converted into fishponds, and the bottomlands into taro patches; the uplands were used for dryland crops, and the mountainside for wooded products.

During the first half of the nineteenth century, a labor shortage developed for several reasons: Many natives died after contact with European diseases, the subsistent economy evolved into one of international trade, royalty sought the imported luxuries brought by Europeans, and many natives were leaving their land and migrating to the thriving cities of Lahaina and Honolulu. All of these shifts were borne on the back of the commoner, whose place in society worsened. Pressure built to modify land tenure from the native feudal-like practice to Western ownership. Gradually, foreigners gained access to the land, at first through grants from the king, but later through intermarriage and laws.

In 1848, the Western missionaries convinced the king to enact the **Great Mahele** (land reform) that redistributed land ownership. Although the Great Mahele was meant to keep land out of the hands of foreigners, it resulted in severing the rights to land for the Hawaiians. Land went from communal "ownership" by the king and chiefs to a Western commodity of private ownership. Although provisions were made for granting land to native commoners, few were able to prove claims. Westerners imposed their legal structure on land ownership and made it even more difficult for Hawaiians to gain land access. Although westerners comprised less than two thousand people during the second half of the nineteenth century, they acquired the vast majority of Hawaiian lands. By 1893, foreigners controlled 90 percent of the land.

By the time Hawai`i became a state, fewer than one hundred people owned half the land, and Native Hawaiians owned only 4 percent. The huge plantation estates of deceased *haole* (Caucasian) owners were kept intact through trusts that effectively froze land ownership. Trust land remained with the trusts either as plantations or leased residential lots.

Most plantations are now gone and converted to residential lots and resort communities. Many of these conversions occur in rural areas, where they ruin the nature of the native communities; regardless, the powerful estates and trusts have developed despite vigorous objections from local residents. Estates sell to politicians, who rezone the land from agricultural to resort (thereby increasing its value tremendously) and then flip the permitted land to developers for huge profits. During the beginning of the twenty-first century, several land deal corruption and injustice lawsuits have been filed.

TABLE 20.1. Hawai`i's Major Ethnic Group Populations, Percent Change, 2000–2010

	2000	2010	Percent increase
Asian	41.6	38.6	4.2
White (non-Hispanic)	22.9	24.7	14.4
Native Hawaiian	6.6	5.9	-10
Hispanic	7.2	8.9	37.8
Black	2.8	2.9	3.5
Two or more races	21.4	23.6	10.3

Source: U.S. Census, 2010, at http://factfinder2.census.gov/faces/tableservices/jsf/pages/productview.xhtml?src=bkmk

The major estates have tried to maintain title to their property, lease it out long term, and then renegotiate at much higher rates than the previous lease. Between 1950 and 1960, 80 percent of all residential land on O`ahu was leasehold. The leasehold practice slowed island development. There was little incentive to build, and land prices escalated well beyond mainland prices. Commercial development was stymied, because the estates would not sell the land and the costs of development were much higher than if the land was owned.

In 1967, the state legislature passed the **Hawai`i Land Reform Act**—allowing leasehold conversion to fee simple (full private ownership) based on market value. The reform act influenced the corporate development of Waikīkī. Corporations needed fee-simple ownership to amortize their high-rise investments. However, the act was unable to break the trusts on most residential land. Still the government and seventy-two private landowners owned 95 percent of all land (Map 20.2; Table 20.2). When long-term leases expired on suburban lots, the renegotiated leases escalated from $175 to $12,000–$18,000 annually for the land, excluding structures. Many longtime occupants who owned their houses could no longer afford the land rent and were forced to move.

Amended in 1975, the Land Reform Act stated that the breakup of the trusts attacked "certain perceived evils of concentrated property ownership." Thus ended the monopoly, because the large landowners were forced to convert the land to fee simple and sell to the inhabitants. The amendment allowed all residential lands to convert their leasehold, but courtroom battles still often decide land ownership conversion. Meanwhile, large developments of estate lands are still being pursued, often to the detriment of the native people, the land, and sustainable precepts.

Some current challenges are the development of five new resorts on the North Shore, and a slew of large resort bankruptcies since the 2007 recession. Other possible developments include the Ewa Plain near Pearl Harbor (O`ahu), and La`au Point on Moloka`i.

Homesteading

Native Hawaiians have lost control of their islands. Congress first addressed the native loss of land in the Hawaiian Homes Commission Act of 1920, commonly called the Homestead Act, which promised ninety-nine-year homestead land leases for $1 annually to natives who had at least 50 percent Hawaiian blood. The act conveyed second-class land while still protecting the sugar barons' acreage. There was little support for building homes on the homestead land or for selling the land to others. A few Hawaiians retained ownership of good farmland as a *kuleana* (rights received upon the Great Mahele land reform), but many were unable to retain their rights through the years. Hence, both rural and urban homestead land was seldom awarded to the more than two hundred thousand eligible Hawaiians.

By the 1960s, the home commission and its lands were transferred from federal hands to the state. By 1975, less than 15 percent of the 190,000 acres of land controlled by homestead laws was leased to Native Hawaiians, and since that time land has been released so slowly that lawsuits have been filed claiming breaches of trust.

Homesteaded land is both rural and urban, and the demand varies for the two. Rural homesteaded land is meant to be farmed traditionally, but few Hawaiians still farm, and the forty-acre parcels are second-class farmland in undesirable areas. Few of the families granted parcels actually farm; instead, they lease

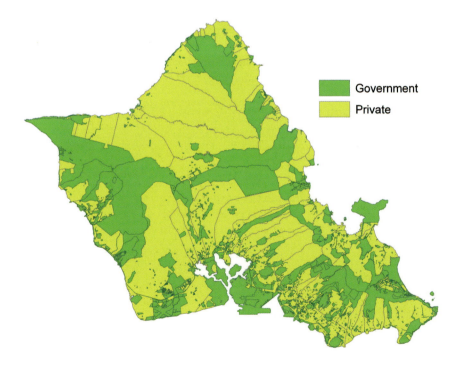

Government
Private

MAP 20.2. Ahupua`a Ownership of Land on O`ahu. Prior to European arrival, ownership was feudal in structure. It divided land in pie-shaped pieces from the tops of mountains to the sea. Many of the current landholdings still show the ahupua`a boundaries and divisions, but one-fifth of the land belongs to eight companies or estates, and the government remains a large landowner.

BOX 20.3   THE BIG FIVE

Land ownership was largely in the hands of the "Big Five" families, many descending from the missionary families: Castle & Cooke, Alexander & Baldwin, C. Brewer, Amfac, and Theo H. Davies and Co. As seen in Table 20.2, some of the Big Five are still major landowners. Each of the companies has evolved:

Castle & Cooke: Evolved from missionary families. Involved in sugar plantations and later shipping and Dole Food Company. Owned by David Murdock, Dole CEO.

Alexander & Baldwin: Missionary families involved in sugarcane plantations. Later involved in shipping and real estate. Still involved in sugar cultivation and shipping.

C. Brewer: Followed the evolution of Hawai`i's industry from sandalwood to whaling, to agriculture especially sugar. Dissolved company in 2006.

Amfac: Originally H. Hackfeld and Company. Was a dominant player in the sugar plantations with sixty thousand acres; now owns five thousand acres on Maui. Also founder of Liberty House Department Stores (now part of Macy's).

Theo H. Davies and Co.: Dry goods merchants who expanded into sugarcane in the 1850s. Company sold to Hong Kong–based conglomerate in 1973. Now owns Pizza Hut, Taco Bell, Mercedes, and Jaguar franchises in Hawai`i.

TABLE 20.2. Land Ownership Estates and Acreage, 2006

Landowner	2006
Federal government	500,318
Bishop Estate (Kamehameha Schools)	366,448
Parker Ranch	134,662
Castle & Cooke	126,084
Alexander & Baldwin	114,038
James Campbell Estate	54,907
Robinson Family	50,965
C. Brewer	19,837

Source: http://hawaii.gov/dbedt/info/economic/databook/2009-individual/06/060709.pdf

---

it to larger plantations for stipends. On the other hand, the demand for Homestead Act urban land has thousands of applicants waiting up to fifty years to gain access, although building on the land is still onerously difficult: No mortgages are allowed and infrastructure is slow to develop. For example, in 1986 Big Island homesteaders were granted land, but they still lacked running water in 1999. They relied on hauling water and rainwater catchment.[11]

The 50-percent blood requirement for the Homestead Act has bitterly divided the community. In 1999, a multiethnic group filed a lawsuit that challenged the Homestead Act on the basis of racial discrimination. The plaintiffs believe the homesteaded lands should benefit the entire population and not just Native Hawaiians. If won, it would shut out the Hawaiians who have been waiting for decades. The congressional Akaka bill has answered these lawsuits by giving Hawaiians the same protected status as Native Americans or Alaskan Natives.

Traditional and Sustainable City

Honolulu

(2010 pop. 337,256; MSA 953,207)

Honolulu has been the primary city of the islands since 1872. Honolulu became the Pacific's largest city because of the good harbor on a dry, leeward coast with access to freshwater. Eight of the ten largest cities are on the Isle of O`ahu; most are suburbs to Honolulu. Three-quarters of all Hawaiian residents live in Honolulu County. The largest city off of O`ahu is Hilo on the Big Island. Hilo is one-eighth the size of Honolulu, at 43,263.

Honolulu and Lahaina fought to be the dominant city during the nineteenth century. Lahaina was the capital and the center of whaling activity from 1840 to 1855, but by 1850 Honolulu replaced Lahaina as the capital

Honolulu sprawls across the low-lying land from Waikīkī to Pearl Harbor and the Ewa Plain and then up the mountain valleys, where master-planned residential communities have replaced fields of sugarcane, taro, bananas, or rice. Many residents now favor a sustainable local produce economy that will halt further development in favor of agricultural land.

But today much of the land has been converted to dense urban use (Photo 20.5)—the density exceeds sixty thousand per square mile in some parts of Honolulu—complete with urban problems, such as pollution and bumper-to-bumper traffic. Residents of sprawling bedroom towns spend three to four hours each day commuting to work in Honolulu. Gridlock is common.

Honolulu has been called the New York of the Pacific and shares urban features, such as skyscrapers, traffic, and a wealthy population. One in eight Honolulu households is worth more than $1 million, excluding their home. The city has the

BOX 20.4 MOLOKA`I RANCH AND LA`AU POINT: SHIFTING WINDS

Native Hawaiians occupy local communities throughout most of Moloka`i, and homestead ancient *ahupua`a* landholdings. One of these communities has been Muanaloa, where many Moloka`i Ranch workers live, along with the Moloka`i Ranch Lodge. The rest of the developments on the island are small condominium developments and lodges. The ranch, occupying the west end of the island, remains relatively undeveloped.

The ranch is the result of Kamehameha V granting 40 percent of Moloka`i in 1850 to Princess Bishop, married to Charles Bishop. Moloka`i Ranch was second only to Parker Ranch in size. Over the years, a succession of owners and lessors has controlled the ranch, raising cattle and growing pineapple. In the 1970s, about fourteen thousand acres were sold to developers for low-impact tourism and residential development; otherwise the ranch has remained intact. In 2001, the ranch was sold again, this time to Singapore-based BIL International, whose owner is eager to build luxury developments for wealthy Chinese.

In 2002, BIL purchased La`au Point and added it to the Moloka`i investment portfolio. The company then worked on a community-based master plan for the ranch. By mid-2006, the company announced plans to build two hundred luxury home sites on La`au Point at the southwestern end of the island. Immediately a resistance movement arose. The community-based plan initially included many community members, but many dropped out when they realized the plan's thrust and how it would destroy the island's way of life. Almost every home on the island, with the exception of those who work for the ranch, posted signs opposing the development (Photo 20.4).

Moloka`i is the "friendly island," the island least affected by development or tourism (7,345 tourists in 2010 compared to Maui's 2.2 million), and it is the only publicly held island where Native Hawaiians are the majority. The island residents are not wealthy. Their rights to land extend back sometimes to *ahupua`a*. They often live in small homes on the coast or have homesteaded in the interior. Unemployment has been a problem since the pineapple plantations closed in the 1980s, but the jobs promised by the La`au development would subject the residents to a servile role, which is not acceptable to islanders. The residents feel that an invasion of wealthy tourists would ruin their lifestyle, create a rift between haves and have-nots, desecrate sacred lands, and also threaten an already scarce water supply for the agricultural homesteaders.

The Moloka`i Ranch offered to donate twenty-five thousand acres to a Moloka`i Land Trust and Community Development Corporation in exchange for the La`au development. Residents

PHOTO 20.4. Opposition to La`au Development. Moloka`i residents were united in opposition to the development on Moloka`i Ranch. The island is the only publicly held island to remain "natural" and has a majority of Native Hawaiians, who saw the development as the end of their unique position on the islands.

felt that the trustees—all politically motivated and wealthy—would sell out the "trust" and they would lose all. The developers needed to rezone from agricultural to rural, granted by the state land-use commission. Unfortunately, land use in the state has been documented as corrupt. Moloka`i residents do not trust the system.

After years of community meetings, it became apparent that opposition to the La`au development was massive. In November 2007, Moloka`i Properties withdrew its proposed Environmental Impact Statement. A few months later, the Molokai Ranch was closed and 120 jobs lost. The 2010 unemployment rate in Moloka`i (15.9 percent) is more than twice the state rate (6.4 percent). The company then requested to raise water utility rates, which are controlled by the company. Residents are not pleased with the responses of the ranch. The land remains undeveloped in 2011.

In 2009, an offer was made by First Wind to purchase Moloka`i Ranch for a large wind farm that would provide renewable energy for both Moloka`i and O`ahu. The offer was rejected. First Wind and other companies continue to try to make a deal to lease the land for the wind farm, although opposition has built among islanders, who distrust agreements based on past experience.

PHOTO 20.5. Honolulu Skyline. Honolulu is the largest city in the islands, complete with high-rise canyons and monumental traffic problems.

tenth-highest number of millionaire families in the nation. Average homes prices doubled in Honolulu from $300,000 in 2000 to $595,000 in 2006, but they eased off to $557,000 in September 2011.[12]

In Honolulu, 10.5 percent of the population lives below the poverty level (2009), and several thousand are homeless. The homeless remain invisible to most tourists, removed from the tourist areas and parks, but a walk outside the tourist areas can reveal a seamier side to the city. Affordable housing is needed on the islands.

Waikīkī, Honolulu's main beach, receives the most tourism. The beach was a marshy wetland zone filled with rice paddies until hotels were able to own land and Waikīkī was drained and developed commercially. Today high rises block any view of the beach, except along narrow tourist access points. The once-beckoning Hawaiian paradise is gone, replaced by high-end hotels offering wireless Internet service and a simulacrum of traditional Hawaiian culture, from surfboard rides to hula shows and ukulele lessons (Photo 20.6).

Honolulu's continued growth has caused environmental and planning problems that need repair. A sustainable committee has been working to set limits for urban growth, keep open and green spaces, correct infrastructure deficiencies, and reduce automobile usage.[13] Honolulu has been recognized for some sustainable attributes, such as its air quality, local food, and agriculture, but a proposed and very expensive rapid transit line may not be the answer to congestion in the city.

Economy

After European contact, the island economy developed from 1800 to 1835 as a shipping stopover exporting fragrant sandalwood that was stripped from the forests until sandalwood was almost extinct. In the 1840s, Hawai`i was the headquarters for hundreds of whaling ships from New England that cruised the Pacific for two to four years at a time. By 1865, whales were becoming scarce and petroleum began replacing whale oil. But during the whaling era, Honolulu was established as the Pacific core city. *Haole* merchants controlled the land and set about consolidating the plantations that would become the next economy.

The agricultural domination of Hawai`i began in the pineapple and sugar plantations of the mid-nineteenth century, when the Big Five companies[14] gained control over the sugar industry. Pineapple and sugar agriculture were the state's leading economic activities from 1880 until statehood in 1959, a time when jet planes singlehandedly transformed the agricultural economy into the tourism economy. Tourism grew exponentially on the islands until it became the leading economic activity.

Primary Industry and Natural Resources

Agriculture

About one-tenth of island land is arable. But rich soil and a frost-free and ample rainfall environment enabled Hawai`i to grow tropical crops that are almost impossible to grow on the mainland. Agriculture, most importantly sugarcane and pineapples, was the leading Hawaiian economic sector until the 1960s.

Both sugarcane and pineapple production fell victim to high land and labor costs. Sugarcane all but disappeared as a crop in the 1970s, and in 2008 Del Monte pulled out of pineapple production. Dole and Maui pineapples are still producing, but pineapple is no longer among the top Hawaiian agricultural commodities.

In 2009, Hawaiian agriculture provided 0.2 percent of U.S. agricultural commodities and was ranked third in Hawaiian receipts. Hawai`i's top agricultural receipts are seeds, nursery/

PHOTO 20.6. Waikīkī Beach Looking toward Diamond Head. The beach, once a marshy zone filled with rice paddies, is a high-rise jungle with simulacra of traditional Hawaiian culture, such as staged surf rides.

greenhouse products, sugarcane, macadamia nuts, and cattle (Table 20.3).

Pineapple Pineapple flourishes in the red volcanic soil; it requires less water than sugar and therefore no irrigation.

The first European settlers found pineapple growing wild, but the variety grown today, Smooth Cayenne, was introduced in 1888. The pineapple industry grew under the direction of James Dole, cousin to Sanford Dole, president of the Republic of Hawai`i. After an initial investment on O`ahu, James purchased the island of Lāna`i in 1922 and established the largest pineapple plantation in the world, more than two hundred thousand acres. During the 1920s, Lāna`i produced up to

75 percent of the world's pineapples. But the Great Depression and cheaper Asian imports caused pineapple sales to decline, and the Dole family sold its holdings. By 2006, Hawai`i produced only 2 percent of the world's pineapples. Most pineapples are now grown in Thailand, the Philippines, Brazil, China, India, and Costa Rica.

Sugarcane In 1835, as the whaling industry waned, Europeans began sugarcane plantations. The cane requires abundant sunshine, water, and labor; however, ample water and labor were often unavailable. Both O`ahu and Maui improvised watering systems to grow the cane, and Chinese and Japanese laborers were imported to augment the native workforce.

TABLE 20.3. Top Five Agricultural Commodities, 2009

	Value of receipts $ (000)	Percent of state total farm receipts	Percent of U.S. value
Other seeds	180,000	31.0	18.1
Greenhouse/nursery	83,433	14.4	0.5
Cane for sugar	42,980	7.4	5.0
Macadamia nuts	29,400	5.1	100.0
Cattle and calves	28,945	5.0	0.1
All commodities	581,385		0.2

Source: http://www.ers.usda.gov/StateFacts/HI.htm

Cane was grown on all the islands, but Oʻahu took the lead in 1879, when James Campbell added artificial fertilizer and drilled for water on the dry plains of Ewa (near Pearl Harbor). Soon irrigated sugar was grown on the dry leeward sides of Maui and Kauaʻi.

At one time, the plantations employed up to one-sixth of the native population, but as so many had died of European diseases, the plantation owners looked to Asia for laborers.

Although sugar was grown in the 1840s, it became a lucrative crop during the Civil War when the Union was unable to access sugar from the southern states. The 1876 Treaty of Reciprocity with the United States removed tariffs for sugar planters and gave the United States military rights to Pearl Harbor. Rapid expansion of the industry followed, and westerners alienated most land for plantations. Sugar plantation profits were the underlying reason for the evolution of power from Hawaiians to the *haole* plantation owners.

Sugar production was highest from the end of World War II until the late 1980s. By 2003, sugar production had dropped from a 1970 high of 10.5 million tons to 2.0 million tons. As a comparison, the major sugar producer in the world in the twenty-first century, Brazil, produced 22.75 million tons in 2003. Only Kauaʻi and Maui still grow sugar (Table 20.4). Sugar refineries during the twentieth century transferred from on the plantation to the mainland in San Francisco Bay, California.

Sugar plantations were a boon to the economic wealth of the owners, but they destroyed the land. The sugar mills degraded forests, natural resources, and water. The mills also are a cause of air, water, and waste pollution. The fibrous stalk is used for biofuel and pulp and paper.[15]

Coffee In the 1880s, sugarcane replaced coffee as the primary Big Island crop, but small boutique coffee plantations have become popular investments in the twenty-first century. The distinct climate of the Kona coast of the Big Island is perfect for growing coffee. The coastal hills are the only region that receives more rain in summer than winter, and it is warmer and drier than other windward locations. The crop uses the local vog as a shade cover for coffee plants. Today, tiny independent coffee plantations are at the mercy of price fluctuations. There are about 650 small coffee farms that average three acres. A total of about thirty-five hundred acres produces about 3.8 million pounds annually. Today, coffee is mostly a tourist trade item centered on the small (two-by-twenty-mile) Kona district, along with a small plantation on Molokaʻi.

Taro Taro, the source for poi, arrived with the Polynesian migrations. But taro production and consumption almost halted during the plantation era. Recently, farmers returned to taro production in an effort to revive traditional and nutritious Hawaiian foods (Photo 20.7).

Fishing

Traditionally, fish has been the dominant Hawaiian protein. Ancient Hawaiians used the coral reefs to build fish ponds—an early method of fish farming—where juvenile fish grew to full size and provided year-round food. The fish fed the native population, but they were insufficient for large exports, although *haole*s developed an export economy.

Canneries complemented commercial fishing until the 1980s. After 1970 canneries closed, and the tuna market shifted from canned tuna to fresh fish. Complicating the fishery was

TABLE 20.4. Sugar Production in Hawaiʻi

	Total cane land acres (000)	Tons cane production (000)
1876	N/A	13
1898	N/A	225
1910	209	4,122
1930	243	7,857
1950	220	8,174
1970	238	10,457
1990	71	6,541
2003	48	2,030
2009	21.7	1,459

Source: Hawaiʻi Agriculture Research Center, at http://NASS.usda.gov

PHOTO 20.7. Taro Growing at Hanalei, Kaua`i. Taro has returned as a crop grown by native farmers on small plots of land. Taro is important within the traditional Hawaiian diet. The leaves are used to wrap meats and the root to make poi, the starch staple of the islands.

Photo: L. Czaban

confusion between the commercial fishery and the native fishery.

Natives are allowed traditional gathering and fishing rights, and many natives fish and sell a part of their catch to offset expenses or are obligated to share their catch with others. Living on islands, it would seem that Hawaiians should eat plenty of fish, but fish have become too expensive for many local residents. Fish have become the product of commercial deep-sea fishing expeditions rather than part of the Hawaiians' daily diet.

By the twenty-first century, overfishing along the major and northwestern islands has been a problem, and commercial enterprises are under increasing pressure to live within quotas, while management of fish stocks is failing. Commercial and tourist enterprises have limited access for the natives.

A belief that future wild fish stocks will be insufficient has led several companies to unsuccessfully attempt open-ocean cage fish farm mariculture (commercial cultivation of marine organisms in their natural habitats).[16]

Industry and Postindustrial

For many years, the defense budget ruled the Hawaiian economy, and the military was based in the strategic mid-Pacific location. Today, federal defense funding remains important but less than nondefense spending (civilian agencies, Social Security, Medicare, and federal retirement distributions). Overall military spending has accounted for about 10 percent of the state's gross state product (GSP) since the 1980s. The military presence has also declined from 33 percent in 1960 to 10 percent of the current total population (Table 20.5).

Corporate ownership on the island has grown since tourism has flourished. Most has been headquartered outside the islands. The outflow of money from the local to out-of-state enterprises has hurt the local economy.

Energy

Ninety-five percent of Hawai`i's energy is nonrenewable, including 86 percent fossil fuel and 6 percent coal.[17] Alternative sources account for 5 percent of the current energy source, including wind and solar farms (Maui, Hawai`i and O`ahu, and Lāna`i), waste-to-energy, and sugar-based biofuels. In 2004, lawmakers passed legislation to support alternative energy, with Maui endorsing and leading the program.

Six percent of Maui's energy comes from burning sugarcane residue and converting it to ethanol for auto and possibly

TABLE 20.5. Percentage of Gross State Product in Hawai`i for Three Major Economic Sectors

	Military/Defense	Sugar/Pineapples	Tourism
1958	40%[a]		4%
2005	11%	1%[b]	24%

[a] Military and sugar/pineapples together were 40% in 1958.
[b] Agriculture contributed 2.2% of total GSP.
Source: Hawaii State Info, at http://www.hawaiistateinfo.com/honolulu-county.php; http://www.ctahr.hawaii.edu/oc/freepubs/pdf/EI-4.pdf

home-heating use. In 2008 the military, which uses 15 percent of island energy, committed to become energy independent in 2015 by investing in solar panels and biofuel plants.

Additional renewable programs include a large wind farm in the west Maui mountains; they will produce enough energy to eliminate 240,000 barrels of oil annually. The 30 megawatts or 9 percent of Maui's electric needs will expand to 15 percent by 2015. The state plans to generate 20 percent renewable energy by 2020.

One of the unique ways to create energy in Hawai`i is to take advantage of its lack of a continental shelf. Researchers are studying a process called ocean thermal energy conversion (OTEC) as an alternative way to produce electricity. OTEC uses the difference in temperature of cold seawater and the warm surface to cool buildings. The technique was practiced in the 1970s during the Arab oil embargo, and the more recent increase in oil prices has drawn attention to the technology again.[18]

Tourism

Statehood, jet travel, and tourism all merged in 1959. Hawai`i's mid-ocean location was difficult for tourists to reach prior to commercial air travel. Even in 1959, the air trip to the islands from the mainland was eight and a half hours in a prop plane, but the Big Five plantation owners saw the future of tourism. Even as the ink dried on the state constitution, they were already planning new resorts to replace the agricultural plantations. In a few years, inexpensive and faster air travel shaped the middle-class, bigger-is-better tourist industry based on mass marketing.

As plantations were replaced with destination resorts, the Big Five also transformed from local *haole* owners to diversified global concerns, as did most of the businesses on the islands. Local sugar and pineapple plantations were replaced by global business, little of it owned by Hawaiian residents. Tourism became the raison d'être for the islands.

In 1950, only forty thousand tourists came to the islands. Tourism grew from the 1970s average of about 1.5 million visitors annually to 7.4 million in 2005, a welcome return after post-9/11's spare days, but then dropped somewhat again after the 2008 recession (6.5 million in 2009) (Photo 20.8).[19] The $10 billion tourist industry also provides construction and service jobs (32 percent of all jobs [2004]).

The dependence on tourism has led many companies to pursue high-price tourism over mass tourism. Catering to the uber-wealthy is not new; before jet planes only the wealthy could afford island travel. The wealthy population provides more profit than the slim margins of discount travel. When the Japanese economy was healthy in the 1970s and 1980s, the Japanese were an important element in the tourist economy. Their average spending was three times the average *haole* mainlander. Fewer Japanese came, but they spent more money. On the other hand, mass tourism focuses on economies of scale that rely on slim economic margins, leaving no room for ecological or social considerations.

A tourist economy alone is problematic. The islands' isolation from other landmasses, their reliance on imported food, and their dependence on tourism is unsustainable.

A Sustainable Future

As the globalized food system of the second half of the twentieth century affected the Hawaiian economy, the Big Five prepared by turning to tourism. It has proved successful and provided profit for globalized business concerns, but only for the short term. The total dependence on tourism and fossil fuels is a questionable formula in the twenty-first century. The islands, and especially Honolulu, face the same urban ills as the

PHOTO 20.8. Honolulu Tourism. The $10 billion tourism industry has little to do with the lure of the tropical paradise.

rest of the nation—drugs, high crime rates, lack of good water, a growing prison population, and failing educational systems—as well as their own special ills. Adapting sustainable standards on the islands can ameliorate a declining quality of life.

The importance of economic dependency and sustainability came to a head in 2000, when the Sierra Club filed a lawsuit against the state Tourism Authority because the board had implemented a marketing plan to bring more tourists to the islands but had failed to make an environmental assessment of tourism's negative impact. The Sierra Club lost the case in 2002, but the case highlights the islands' limited resource base and questions the number of tourists. No longer was bigger better. No longer could the old formulas work, but instead seeking sustainable methods may save these unique islands.[20]

In 2007, a state task force released the "Hawai`i 2050 Sustainability Task Force Report."[21] The report's objective was to incorporate everyday citizens in achieving sustainability by guiding the decision-making process. In the report, Hawaiian problems are highlighted:

- Population growth on limited land
- Rising cost of living
- Loss of traditional culture
- Environmental damage
- Energy dependency

A monumental island problem is the lack of room because of the growing population. Affordable housing and public infrastructure maintenance are only nominally addressed, and growth and congestion are seldom addressed for the good of all. Native Hawaiians especially have suffered from this injustice because of past unjust policies and actions.

The traditional Native Hawaiian lifestyle was sustainable and respected land, sea, and air, but most of this lifestyle has been lost. Plundered of land and culture, the Native Hawaiians are the islands' poorest ethnic group.

The denigration of the Native Hawaiians has left many natives poor, obese, and culturally deprived. Few Hawaiian places still maintain their cultural integrity, and many places are threatened. The closing of the ranches on both Ni`ihau and Moloka`i and plans to develop these properties may modify the islands' complexion and economy, perhaps to the further chagrin of the traditional Hawaiian culture. The loss will also be a death knell to peoples' perception of the Hawaiian paradise. Traditional culture and life still survive in isolated areas but require values that honor balance.

The multiethnic island mosaic has created divisiveness, including charges of racial discrimination, and native society is torn because of the dilution of pureblooded Hawaiians, which separate islanders based on access to homestead land. As the cost of land escalates on the island, partially because of large *haole* estates, and as the Chinese become a larger factor in the global economy, Native Hawaiians need to find justice in the law, the land, and their health. The indigenous population should be allowed to return to their traditional healthier diet, lifestyle, and have rights to their homelands.

Many Hawaiians believe that in the nineteenth century Native Hawaiian power was usurped. As a result, Native Hawaiian groups have formed activist organizations to claim sovereignty and to access land. The activist stance has had some small successes but has not returned them to their rightful place on the islands. Since the turn of the century, the homestead commission has adopted a master plan that accelerates native homestead settlement. The return to the land, often emulating the traditional *ahupua`a* system, has created islands of hope and has reinvigorated the sense of place for the indigenous population, but becoming a central tourism destination has disrupted any sense of balance.

Closed island ecosystems are an ideal for a place like isolated Hawai`i, but jet travel has ended the isolation. Modern transportation allows places like Hawai`i to be accessible to more people, but at the cost of dependence on tourism, one of Hawai`i's few economic growth potentials. Tourism provides almost one-third of all jobs in Hawai`i and more than one-quarter of the economy, but it is also a critical environmental issue. On the one hand, the islands seek to grow their tourist base, but on the other, tourism has caused and will continue to cause overcrowding, congestion, pollution, and water shortages.

Hawaiians require majority support to address some of Hawai`i's worst societal ills, its dependence on fossil fuels, and to continue the island lifestyle. A variety of alternative energy projects seek to break the dependence on fossil fuels.

The outside world has placed demands on Hawai`i that have shattered the delicate balance of economic viability, social justice, and environmental health. Maintaining the island paradise of the Aloha State requires supporting sustainability.

Questions for Discussion

1. When was Hawai`i settled and from where did the first inhabitants migrate?

2. Who were the first Americans to settle in Hawai`i and what were their interests? How did their interests change over time?

3. What role has sugar played in the evolution of Hawai`i?

4. How has the economy of Hawai`i changed since World War II? What were important factors in the change?

5. How can tourism be maintained at a sustainable cost to the environment?

6. What is the basis of claims for independence by Native Hawaiians? How does their status differ from that of Native Americans?

7. Should Native Hawaiians be treated like Native Americans and be given special status and opportunities? Why or why not?

8. How has land ownership affected the distribution of wealth and population on the islands?

9. What are the problems Hawai`i faces in achieving sustainability? How does tourism play into these problems?

Suggested Readings

Allen, Helena G. *The Betrayal of Liliuokalani, Last Queen of Hawai`i, 1838–1917*. Honolulu: Mutual Publishing, 1982.

Budnick, Rich. *Stolen Kingdom: An American Conspiracy*. Honolulu: Aloha Press, 1992.

Carlquist, Sherwin. *Hawai`i: A Natural History*. Lawai, Kaua`i, Hawai`i: National Tropical Botanical Garden, 1994.

Coffman, Tom. *Nation Within: The Story of America's Annexation of the Nation of Hawai`i*. Kaneohe, Hawai`i: Tom Coffman/Epicenter, 1998.

Cuddihy, Linda W., and Charles P. Stone. *Alteration of Native Hawaiian Vegetation: Effects of Humans, Their Activities and Introductions*. Honolulu: University of Hawai`i Cooperative National Park Resources Studies Unit, 1990.

Eyre, David L. *By Wind, by Wave: An Introduction to Hawai`i's Natural History*. Honolulu, Hawai`i: Bess Press, 2000.

Finney, Ben R. "Anomalous Westerlies, El Niño, and the Colonization of Polynesia." *American Anthropologist*, new series 87, no. 1 (March 1985): 9–26.

Fuchs, Lawrence H. *Hawai`i Pono: A Social History*. San Diego, Calif.: Harcourt Brace Jovanovich, 1984.

Haas, Michael, ed. *Multicultural Hawai`i: The Fabric of a Multiethnic Society*. New York: Garland, 1998.

Herman, R. D K. "The Aloha State: Place Names and the Anti-Conquest of Hawai`i." *Annals of the Association of American Geographers* 89, no. 1 (March 1999): 76–102.

Hulten, John J. "Land Reform in Hawai`i." *Land Economics* 42, no. 2 (May 1966): 235–40.

Jones, Stephen B. "Geography and Politics in the Hawaiian Islands." *Geographical Review* 28, no. 2 (April 1938): 193–213.

Ladefoged, Thegn N. "Spatial Similarities and Change in Hawaiian Architecture: The Expression of Ritual Offering and Kapu in Luakini Heiau, Residential Complexes, and Houses." *Asian Perspectives: Journal of Archaeology for Asia and the Pacific* 37, no. 1 (Spring 1998): 59–73.

Levy, Neil M. "Native Hawaiian Land Rights." *California Law Review* 63, no. 4 (July 1975): 848–85.

Mlot, Christine. "In Hawai`i, Taking Inventory of a Biological Hot Spot." *Science*, new series 269, no. 5222 (July 21, 1995): 322–23.

Morgan, Joseph. *Hawai`i: A Geography*. Boulder, Colo.: Westview Press, 1983.

Osorio, Jonathan Kay Kamakawiwo`ole. *Dismembering Lahui: A History of the Hawaiian Nation to 1887*. Honolulu: University of Hawai`i Press, 2002.

Pooley. Samuel G. "Hawai`i's Marine Fisheries: Some History, Long-Term Trends, and Recent Developments." *Marine Fisheries Review* 55, no. 2 (Spring 1993): 7–19.

Silva, Noenoe K. *Aloha Betrayed: Native Hawaiian Resistance to American Colonialism*. Durham, N.C.: Duke University Press, 2004.

Spickard, Paul, Joanne L. Rondilla, and Debbie Hippolite Wright, eds. *Pacific Diaspora: Island Peoples in the United States and across the Pacific*. Honolulu: University of Hawai`i Press, 2002.

Taylor, Frank J., David W. Eyre, and Earl M. Welty. *From Land and Sea: The Story of Castle and Cooke of Hawai`i*. San Francisco: Chronicle Books, San Francisco, 1976.

Tayman, John. *The Colony: The Harrowing True Story of the Exiles of Molokai*. New York: Scribner, 2006.

Trask, Haunani-Kay. *From a Native Daughter: Colonialism and Sovereignty in Hawai`i*. Monroe, Maine: Common Courage, 1993.

Wang, Chen-Yen, Lisa Abbott, Angela K. Goodbody, and Wai-Ting Hui. "Ideal Body Image and Health Status in Low-Income Pacific Islanders." *Journal of Cultural Diversity* 9, no. 1 (Spring 2002): 12–22.

Woodcock, D. W., ed. *Hawai`i: New Geographies*. Honolulu: Department of Geography, University of Hawai`i-Manoa, 1999.

Wooden, Wayne S. *Return to Paradise: Continuity and Change in Hawai`i*. Lanham, Md.: University Press of America, 1995.

Internet Sources

U.S. Geological Survey. "Vog: A Volcanic Hazard," May 29, 1996, at http://hvo.wr.usgs.gov/volcanowatch/1996/96_05_29.html.

U.S. Geological Survey. "Once a Big Island, Maui County Now Four Small Islands," April 10, 2003, at http://hvo.wr.usgs.gov/volcanowatch/2003/03_04_10.html.

Economic Research Service. State Fact Sheet: Hawai`i, at http://www.ers.usda.gov/StateFacts/HI.htm.

Notes

1. Regions and Ecoregions

1. Robert G. Bailey, *Ecoregion-Based Design for Sustainability* (New York: Springer, 2002).

2. The term *ecology* was coined in 1866 by Ernst Haeckel, who defined it as "the science of relations between the organism and the surrounding outer world." Fritof Capra, *The Web of Life* (New York: Doubleday, 1996).

3. Paul Hawken, *The Ecology of Commerce* (New York: HarperCollins, 1994).

4. While ecological theory has not been popular in American geography, I found solace in reading Clarence Glacken's *Traces on the Rhodian Shore* (Berkeley: University of California Press, 1967). "I am convinced that modern ecological theory, so important in our attitudes toward nature and man's interferences with it, owes its origin to the design argument: The wisdom of the creator is self-evident, everything in the creation is interrelated, no living thing is useless, and all are related one to the other" (423). Cited in James J. Parsons, "On 'Bioregionalism' and 'Watershed Consciousness,'" *Professional Geographer* 37, no. 1 (1985). In his article, Parsons quotes Peter Berg, one of the first bioregionalists, and defines bioregionalism as "a geographical province of marked ecological and often cultural unity, its subdivisions, at least ideally, often delimited by watersheds (water divides) of major streams." Parsons also discusses a "terrain of consciousness: a place and the ideas that have developed about how to live in that place." Bioregionalism has also been linked with the failed theory of environmental determinism that was popular prior to World War II. In many ways it is similar, but it does not propose that people return to indigenous lifeways and is no more "deterministic" than the current modern paradigm (certain ways are better than others). Bioregionalism or ecoregions does reject existing arbitrary political units and replace them with bioregions. Stephen Frenkel, "Old Theories in New Places? Environmental Determinism and Bioregionalism," *Professional Geographer* 46, no. 3 (1994): 291.

5. R. J. Johnston, "Fragmentation around a Defended Core: The Territoriality of Geography," *Geographical Journal* 164, no. 2 (July 1998): 138–47.

6. Global Footprint Network, at http://www.footprintnetwork.org/en/index.php/GFN/page/trends/us/.

7. Considerable debate in ecology has been rekindled since the advent of global warming and its impact on declines or changes in biodiversity.

> Although the tone of the debate has been regrettable, its magnitude signifies the emergence of a new paradigm, one in a series of debates associated with the dialectic that has structured ecological inquiry over two millennia of Western science. This dialectic concerns the tension between those who seek to explain nature by studying its parts and those who seek to explain nature by studying whole-system behavior. . . . An emerging paradigm, one that synthesizes community and ecosystem ecology while concentrating on functional rather than taxonomic diversity, promises to refocus attention on the broader significance of the earth's biota.

Shahid Naeem, "Ecosystem Consequences of Biodiversity Loss: The Evolution of a Paradigm," *Ecology* 83, no. 6 (June 2002): 1537–1552.

8. James Hansen et al., "Target Atmospheric CO_2: Where Should Humanity Aim?" *Open Atmospheric Science Journal* 2 (2008): 217–31.

9. For example, Louis Iverson and Anantha Prasad, "Potential Changes in Tree Species Richness and Forest Community Types following Climate Change," *Ecosystems* 4, no. 3 (April 2001): 186–99.

10. Jeffrey W. Johnson, "The Foul Side of 'Clean Coal,'" *Chemical & Engineering News* 87, no. 8 (February 23, 2009): 44–47.

11. An August 2010 report by the Environmental Integrity Project, Earthjustice, and the Sierra Club revealed inadequately monitored coal combustion waste. http://www.environmental-integrity.org/news_reports/08_26_10.php.

12. Nevin M. Fenneman, "The Circumference of Geography," *Annals of the Association of American Geographers* 9 (1919): 3–11. "No one has improved on the principle enunciated by Fenneman in the classic paper in which he defined the physiographic provinces of the United States: the best region is the one that permits the largest possible number of general statements before details and exceptions become necessary." John Fraser Hart, "The Highest Form of the Geographer's Art," *Annals of the Association of American Geographers* 72, no. 1 (March 1982): 1–29.

13. Regions can be defined as physical (e.g., based on landforms, precipitation), human (e.g., cultural, religious), and functional (arranged around a node, such as airplane routes).

14. Bailey, *Ecoregion-Based Design*.

15. Nevin M. Fenneman, "Physiographic Divisions of the United States," *Annals of the Association of American Geographers* 6 (1916): 19–98; "Physiographic Divisions of the United States," *Annals of the Association of American Geographers* 18, no. 4 (December 1928): 261–353.

16. "Description of the Ecoregions of the United States," at http://www.fs.fed.us/land/ecosysmgmt/index.html.

17. Agriculture and Agri-Food Canada, at http://sis.agr.gc.ca/cansis/nsdb/ecostrat/zones.gif; Nature Conservancy: Canada. Canada's Ecoregions, at http://science.natureconservancy.ca/initiatives/ecoregmap_w.php; Parks Canada, *Terrestrial Ecozones of Canada*, at http://www.pc.gc.ca/apprendre-learn/prof/itm2-crp-trc/htm/ecozone_e.asp.

18. The carto-conformity of the western states is explained in Mark Stein's *How the States Got Their Shapes* (New York: HarperCollins, 2008). Colorado is 7 degrees wide and 4 degrees high.

19. "The frontier is also an international meeting place as such, potentially a launching-pad for international cooperation to mutual benefit. . . . Little attention has been paid to the theoretical or practical existence of a frontier zone within which such boundary effects might be concentrated and which, in its turn, might serve as the basis for the organization of transnational contacts and cooperation." J. W. House, "The Frontier Zone: A Conceptual Problem for Policy Makers," *International Political Science Review / Revue internationale de science politique* 1, no. 4 (1980): 456–77.

20. Daphne A. Kenyon, "Theories of Interjuridsictional Competition," *New England Economic Review*, March–April 1997.

2. The Nonhuman World

1. Charles Wilkinson, *Messages from Frank's Landing* (Seattle: University of Washington Press, 2000).

2. "In 2007, the most recent year for which data are available, humanity used the equivalent of 1.5 planets to support its activities. Put another way, it now takes a year and six months for the Earth to absorb the CO_2 emissions and regenerate the renewable resources that people use in one year; we are currently using 50% more natural resources than the Earth can sustain." *2010 Living Planet Report*, at http://wwf.panda.org/about_our_earth/all_publications/living_planet_report/2010_lpr/.

3. Google Earth gives a good view of the continental shelf on all coasts.

4. See http://www.nature.org/initiatives/freshwater/.

5. "Septic System Checks Weighed," *The Olympian*, January 18, 2009; "Ingram Begins Work on Sewer System," *San Antonio News*, January 21, 2009; "Residents Deny Septics Pollute," *Malibu Times*, January 21, 2009.

6. Lewis M. Cowardin et al., *Classification of Wetlands and Deepwater Habitats of the United States*, Washington, D.C.: U.S. Fish and Wildlife Service, December 1979.

7. Earth System Research Laboratory, "Trends in Atmospheric Carbon Dioxide," at http://www.esrl.noaa.gov/gmd/ccgg/trends/.

8. B. W. Roberts et al., "Harnessing High-Altitude Wind Power," *IEEE Transactions on Energy Conversion* 22, no. 1 (March 2007).

9. Herman Shugart, Roger Sedjo, and Brent Sohngen, "Forests and Global Climate Change: Potential Impacts on United States Forest Resources," paper prepared for Pew Center on Global Climate Change, February 2003.

3. Sustainability

1. This quote is found on the Jefferson Memorial. It is a truncated version of the original in a letter to Samuel Kercheval, July 12, 1810.

2. U.S. water pollution: http://water.epa.gov/polwaste/nps/outreach/point1.cfm. Canadian water pollution: *Macleans*, October 17, 2005; April 30, 2009.

3. Helen Ingram, *Continuity and Change: Water Politics* (Albuquerque: University of New Mexico Press, 1990).

4. Herman Daly, "Five Policy Recommendations for a Sustainable Economy," in *Sustainable Planet*, ed. Julict B. Schor and Betsy Taylor (Boston: Beacon, 2003).

5. Statistics, Canada, at http://www.statcan.gc.ca/pub/16-002-x/2007001/tables/5008063-eng.htm.

6. McDonough, William, and Michael Braungart, *Cradle to Cradle: Remaking the Way We Make Things* (New York: North Point Press, 2002); Janine M. Benyus, *Biomimicry: Innovation Inspired by Nature* (New York: HarperCollins, 1997).

7. MIT News, at http://web.mit.edu/newsoffice/2008/oxygen-0731.html; http://web.mit.edu/newsoffice/2010/belcher-water-0412.html.

8. The Pax Group, at http://www.thepaxgroup.com/technology/index.html.

9. From the Bible (Genesis 21:33) through the Enlightenment, Christians have often perceived the Earth for our exclusive use. Lynn White Jr., "The Historical Roots of Our Ecologic Crisis," *Science* 155 (March 10, 1967): 1203–1207.

10. The recognized leader is Rachel Carson (*Silent Spring*), but others such as Aldo Leopold and John Muir are also early proponents of environmentalism.

11. George Lakoff and Mark Johnson, *Metaphors We Live By* (Chicago: University of Chicago Press, 1981).

12. American Council on Renewable Energy (ACORE) report released May 2, 2007.

13. "U.S. President George W. Bush said in a Danish TV interview aired Thursday that adhering to the Kyoto treaty on climate change would have 'wrecked' the U.S. economy." Associated Press, June 30, 2005.

14. Kathy Mulady, "Seattle Dreams of 'Green' Team." *Seattle Post-Intelligencer*, February 17, 2005.

15. UN Documents, "Our Common Future, From One Earth to One World," 1987, at www.un-documents.net/ocf-ov.htm#I.3.

16. United States Census, at www.census.gov/ipc/www/world.html.

17. Lester R. Brown, *Eco-Economy: Building an Economy for the Earth* (New York: Norton, 2001).

4. Population and Consumption

1. Commission on Population Growth and the American Future, "Perspective on Population," in *Population and the American Future*, chap. 1 (Washington, D.C.: Commission on Population Growth and the American Future, 27 March 1972).

2. Population Reference Bureau data sheet, 2010, at http://www.prb.org/pdf10/10wpds_eng.pdf.

3. World Bank, "GDP per Capita," at http://data.worldbank.org/indicator/NY.GDP.PCAP.CD.

4. Total fertility rates (TFR) from Population Reference Bureau, at http://www.prb.org.

5. Commission on Population Growth and the American Future, "Perspective on Population."

6. U.S. Bureau of Transportation Statistics, *Transportation Statistics Annual Report 1996*, (Washington, DC: U.S. Department of Transportation, 1996), 8; Daniel P. Moynihan, *Toward a National Urban Policy* (New York: Basic Books, 1970); Paul Ehrlich, *The Population Bomb* (New York: Ballantine, 1968); Commission on Population Growth and the American Future, "Perspective on Population."

7. Population doubling time is estimated by examining the rate of natural increase and immigration, which is calculated as the overall population growth rate. The world's overall growth rate is 1.14 percent annually, which calculates to a doubling time of 61 years. The rate of overall growth for the United States is 0.92 percent and for Canada, 0.9 percent, doubling times of 76 and 77 years respectively. Doubling times are not straight growth rates, but exponential. Any positive growth rate multiplies upon itself, like compound interest in a bank; it begins slowly but accelerates quickly.

8. Human Development Report 1998 Overview, United Nations Development Programme.

9. Re human influence: E. Sanderson et al., "The Human Footprint and the Last of the Wild," *BioScience* 52, no. 10 (2002): 891–904. Re direct impact: L. Hannah et al., "A Preliminary Inventory of Human Disturbance of World Ecosystems," *Ambio* 23, nos. 4–5 (1994): 246–50.

10. P. M. Vitousususek, et al., "Human Domination of Earth's Ecosystems," *Science* 277 (1997): 494–99.

11. Btu (British thermal unit) is a heat measurement. One Btu is the amount of heat required to raise the temperature of 1 pound of water 1°F.

12. In 1998, David Pimentel calculated the carrying capacity of North America (the United States and Canada) at two hundred million.

13. M. L. Munson and P. D. Sutton, "Births, Marriages, Divorces and Deaths: Provisional Data for 2005," National Vital Statistics Report 54, no. 20 (Hyattsville, Md.: National Center for Health Statistics, 2006).

14. The Group of Eight (G8) is an international forum of member states, which meet on occasion. The member states are arguably the most developed countries in the world and include the United States, Canada, France, Germany, Italy, Japan, Russia, and the United Kingdom. Rate of growth source: *CIA World Factbook*, January 2009. Canada 0.82%; United States 0.98%.

15. Perhaps 200,000 are illegal immigrants in Canada.

16. Jeffrey S. Passel, *Estimates of the Size and Characteristics of the Undocumented Population* (Washington, D.C.: Pew Research Center, 15 Dec. 2007).

17. "Recession Slows Population Rise across Sun Belt," *New York Times*, December 24, 2009, at http://www.nytimes.com/2009/12/24/us/24censusUS.html?_r=1&th&emc=th.

18. The Northeast region includes the states of Connecticut, Maine, Massachusetts, New Hampshire, New Jersey, New York, Pennsylvania, Rhode Island, and Vermont. The Midwest region includes the states of Illinois, Indiana, Iowa, Kansas, Michigan, Minnesota, Missouri, Nebraska, North Dakota, Ohio, South Dakota, and Wisconsin. The South region includes the states of Alabama, Arkansas, Delaware, Florida, Georgia, Kentucky, Louisiana, Maryland, Mississippi, North Carolina, Oklahoma, South Carolina, Tennessee, Texas, Virginia, West Virginia, and the District of Columbia, a state equivalent. The West region includes the states of Alaska, Arizona, California, Colorado, Hawai`i, Idaho, Montana, Nevada, New Mexico, Oregon, Utah, Washington, and Wyoming.

19. This number is not exact and is widely debated. Some place the arrival of indigenous people as late as twelve thousand years ago.

20. Aboriginal people in Canada include Inuit (Arctic region), Métis (mixed blood French and First Nation), and the First Nation tribal groups.

21. Some of the "growth" in those claiming Native American or First Nation ancestry is due to the more positive portrayal of indigenous people in the media, making it acceptable to belong to this group.

22. U.S. Census Bureau, "Population and Geographic Centers," at http://www.census.gov/population/censusdata/popctr.pdf.

23. Tjeerd H. van Andel, Eberhard Zangger, and Anne Demitrack, "Land Use and Soil Erosion in Prehistoric and Historical Greece," *Journal of Field Archaeology* 17, no. 4 (Winter 1990).

24. Elliot M. Abrams and David J. Rue, "The Causes and Consequences of Deforestation among the Prehistoric Maya." *Human Ecology* 16, no. 4 (1988).

25. E. O. Wilson, *The Diversity of Life* (New York: Norton, 1999).

26. John D. Rockefeller III, "Population and the American Future: Excerpts," *Studies in Family Planning* 3, no. 5 (May 1972): 77–78.

5. The Canadian Corridor

1. Speech, June 18, 1936, Canadian House of Commons. Full quotation is: "If some countries have too much history, we have too much geography."

2. The six cities are Toronto (1), Montreal (2), Ottawa-Gatineau (6), Quebec City (7), Hamilton (8), and Kitchener (10).

3. C. F. J. Whebell, "Corridors: A Theory of Urban Systems," *Annals of the Association of American Geographers* 59 (1969).

4. Maurice Yeates, *Main Street: Windsor to Quebec City* (Toronto: MacMillan of Canada, 1975).

5. Yeates, *Main Street*, 1975.

6. D. M. Ray, "Dimensions of Canadian Regionalism," Geographical Paper no. 49 (Ottawa: Department of Energy, Mines, and Resources, 1971).

7. L. S. Bourne and R. D. MacKinnon, eds., *Urban Systems Development in Central Canada: Selected Papers* (Toronto: University of Toronto Press, 1972).

8. Kari Lydersen, "Great Lakes' Lower Water Levels Propel a Cascade of Hardships," *Washington Post*, January 27, 2008; C. F. M. Lewis et al., "Dry Climate Disconnected the Laurentian Great Lakes," *EOS, Transactions, American Geophysical Union* 89, no. 52 (2008): 541–42.

9. Huguenot emigration resumed in 1654, but to Virginia, New Netherlands (founded by Peter Minuet, a Huguenot), or the West Indies.

10. Peter N. Moogk, "Reluctant Exiles: Emigrants from France in Canada before 1760," *William and Mary Quarterly*, 3rd series, 46, no. 3 (July 1989): 463–505.

11. Cole Harris, *The Reluctant Land: Society, Space, and Environment in Canada before Confederation* (Vancouver: University of British Columbia Press, 2008).

12. The Aboriginal peoples of Canada include the Indian, Inuit, and Métis peoples of Canada (Aboriginal Rights in the Constitution Act, 1982, Part II, part 35.2).

13. Micheline Labelle, "The Challenge of Diversity in Canada and Quebec," *Policy Options* (March–April 2005): 88–93.

14. "Economic Update: Quebec City Metropolitan Region," April 2011, at http://www.quebecinternational.ca/media/411694/economicupdate_april2011.pdf.

15. John Pucher and Ralph Buehler, "Sustainable Transport in Canadian Cities: Cycling Trends and Policies," *Berkeley Planning Journal* 19 (2006).

16. Sustainable Montreal, at http://www.sustainablemontreal.ca/category/economics/.

17. "Wastes: Non-Hazardous Waste—Municipal Solid Waste," at http://www.epa.gov/epawaste/nonhaz/municipal/index.htm.

18. Bruce Edward Walker, "Discarding False Notions: The Facts about Solid Waste Disposal in Michigan," *MichiganScience* 2, (January 31, 2007).

19. http://www1.agric.gov.ab.ca/$department/deptdocs.nsf/all/econ9631.

20. Tyler Hamilton, "Algae Prompt Reactor Shutdown," *Toronto Star*, August 10, 2007.

21. As of May 2009, British Columbia and Quebec have adopted cap and trade, with Manitoba and Ontario expected to follow shortly. This will include 75 percent of the Canadian population and exerts more pressure for a national policy.

22. http://www.oma.org/Media/news/pr080606a.asp.

23. http://www.freealberta.com/secession.html, www.youtube.com/watch?v=aBQvjNvCmng.

24. The Conference Board of Canada, at http://sso.conferenceboard.ca/HCP/Details/Environment.aspx#measure.

25. http://www.safecommunities.ca/images/Documents/Uploads/National%20Report%20Card%20Survey%20Final%20PDF1.pdf.

6. The North Atlantic Provinces and Northern New England

1. George Carroll Curtis, "The Fishing Banks off Our Atlantic Coast," *Bulletin of the American Geographical Society* 45, no. 6 (1913): 413–22.

2. A comparison of the whale's hump to the isolated mountain that is a monadnock. Herman Melville, *Moby Dick* (Charleston, S.C.: Nabu Press, 2010), 562.

3. S. Jewett, "The White Rose Road," *Country By-Ways* (Boston: Houghton Mifflin Press, 1881).

4. Sebastian Junger, *The Perfect Storm* (New York: Norton, 1997).

5. Human disturbances include overfishing, pollution, degradation of water quality, and anthropogenic climate change. Overfishing is the first disturbance and may often be a precondition for the other conditions. Additionally, overfishing may lead to susceptibility to disease in the remaining population at risk. Jeremy B. C. Jackson et al., "Historical Overfishing and the Recent Collapse of Coastal Ecosystems," *Science*, new series, 293, no. 5530 (July 27, 2001): 629–38.

6. V. Miller, "Aboriginal Micmac Population: A Review of the Evidence," *Ethnohistory* 23, no. 2 (1976).

7. Planning Decisions, Inc. Harpswell Comprehensive Planning Update Committee. Part II, 2004. Colin Woodard, *The Lobster Coast* (New York: Viking, 2004).

8. Newfoundland dictionary, at http://www.heritage.nf.ca/dictionary/.

9. Sharon Manson Singer, "Sailing Forward Together: Charting the Future for Newfoundland and Labrador," November 8, 2007, at http://www.cprn.org/documents/48997_EN.pdf.

10. Newfoundland GDP in 2007 was $57,348, compared to the Canadian average of $46,441. StatCan, *The Daily*, May 15, 2008.

11. Annie E. Casey Foundation, *Kids Count* (Executive Summary Opening Sentences, Fall 2004).

12. Corrie Fletcher-Naylor. "Green Is Good for Business," Summit, Ottawa, October 2006, 9:6; "Nova Scotia's Neo-Liberal Energy Policies," August 9, 2010, at http://halifax.mediacoop.ca/blog/macdonaldtomw/4407.

13. Robert Benzie and Rob Ferguson, "McGuinty Pressures Ottawa as Economy Stumbles," *Toronto Star*, May 1, 2008.

14. Edward A. Ackerman, "Depletion in New England Fisheries," *Economic Geography* 14, no. 3 (July 1938).

15. Forty-first Congress, Session III. Act of February 9, 1871.

16. Callum Roberts, *The Unnatural History of the Sea* (Washington, D.C.: Island Press, 2007).

17. Jeremy B. C. Jackson et al., "Historical Overfishing and the Recent Collapse of Coastal Ecosystems," *Science*, new series, 293, no. 5530 (July 27, 2001): 629–38.

18. Evelyn M. Dinsdale, "Spatial Patterns of Technological Change: The Lumber Industry of Northern New York," *Economic Geography* 41, no. 3 (1965): 252–74.

19. Rich Hewitt, "Fields of Dreams: Blueberry Land Increasingly Subject to Coastal Development Pressures," *Bangor Daily News*, June 11, 2005.

20. Nova Scotia House of Assembly: Exchange in Halifax, Nova Scotia, regarding Nova Scotia chicken, 2001.

21. http://www.atlantica.org/default.asp.

22. Nova Scotia Premier Rodney MacDonald.

23. Natalie Alcoba, "N.S. Aims to Be Greenest in the World by 2020," *National Post* (Canada), March 23, 2007.

7. Megalopolis

1. Jean Gottmann, "Megalopolis or the Urbanization of the Northeastern Seaboard," *Economic Geography* 33, no. 3 (July 1957): 189–200.

2. The Mannahatta Project, at http://themannahattaproject.org/home/.

3. Cynthia Barnett, *Mirage: Florida and the Vanishing Water of the Eastern U.S.* (Ann Arbor: University of Michigan Press, 2007).

4. National Wildlife Federation, 2008, at http://www.nwf.org/sealevelrise/pdfs/NWF_ChesapeakeReportFINAL.pdf.

5. http://www.usdoj.gov/opa/pr/2005/March/05_enrd_129.htm.

6. William Cronon, *Changes in the Land: Indians, Colonists, and the Ecology of New England* (New York: Hill & Wang, 1983).

7. Alexis de Tocqueville, *Democracy in America* (1839; Chicago: Regency Gateway, 2002), 24.

8. The combined statistical areas are the largest variant of metropolitan areas in the United States. They are several cities in close proximity and linked by commuting ties.

9. "Regional Planning and Sustainable Transportation in the Upper Connecticut River Valley," *Environmental Studies* 50 (Spring 2008), at http://www.dartmouth.edu/~envs/docs/ENVS%2050%2008S.

10. Intermodal shipping in standardized containers services ships, railroads, and trucks and revolutionized the shipping industry in the mid-twentieth century.

11. "Kill" is from the Dutch word *kille*, meaning a waterway or river channel.

12. "Greenworks Philadelphia," 2011 Progress Report, at http://www.phila.gov/green/PDFs/Greenworks_PrgrssRprt_2011.pdf.

13. Pennsylvania "Dutch" is a corruption of the German word *Deutsch*, which means "German." *Deutschland* is "Germany" in the German language.

14. Includes Washington, D.C.

15. Includes Baltimore.

16. http://money.cnn.com/magazines/fortune/fortune500/2008/states/NY.html.

17. Michael McDonough, "Newer York, New York," *Wired*, January 2000, at http://www.wired.com/wired/archive/8.01/futuretekture.html.

18. Comment at the "Making Green Building a Mainstream Practice" conference at the American Museum of Natural History, New York, February 2007.

8. Appalachia

1. National Park Service, "Great Smoky Mountains: Air Quality," at http://www.nps.gov/grsm/naturescience/air-quality.htm.

2. A good example of Appalachian English can be found on YouTube at http://www.youtube.com/watch?v=03iwAY4KlIU&feature=related.

3. The First Great Awakening (1730–1750) began in the United Kingdom and spread to the American colonies. It was a time of increased religious activity and Protestant conversions.

4. From Hugh Bartling and Don Ferris, Chattanooga: Is This Sustainable? at http://www.uky.edu/Classes/PS/776/Projects/chattanooga/chattnga.html.

5. Bartling and Ferris, "Chattanooga: Is This Sustainable?"; Kent E. Portney, *Taking Sustainable Cities Seriously* (Cambridge, Mass.: MIT Press, 2003).

6. Count of electric power industry power plants by sector, at http://www.eia.doe.gov/cneaf/electricity/epa/epat5p1.html.

7. Brian Bowling, "State Board Upholds Arch Coal Permit, Panel Also Back Plan for Reclamation," *Charleston (West Virginia) Daily Mail*, September 1, 2004.

8. An excellent movie on Appalachia and conserving energy is Kilowatt Ours, at http://www.kilowattours.org/.

9. The Future of Coal, Massachusetts Institute of Technology, at http://web.mit.edu/coal/.

10. Conventional sources of gas do not require large stimulation or special recovery processes. They recover economical volumes of gas (inexpensive). Unconventional gas reservoirs need massive stimulation and special recovery processes to be profitable. They are only profitable when gas prices are high. See http://www.srhces.org/Documents/Way_John_retired%20topo%20geo_powerpoint_PDF.pdf.

11. On water withdrawals for development of Marcellus Shale gas in Pennsylvania, see http://pubs.cas.psu.edu/freepubs/pdfs/ua460.pdf. Much of the information in this section is drawn from this report.

12. Ian Urbina, "Insiders Sound an Alarm amid a Natural Gas Rush," *New York Times*, June 25, 2011.

13. Berea College has made itself a source for sustainable Appalachian communities; see http://www.berea.edu/sens/sacresourceguide/default.asp.

14. An excellent and enjoyable read is Barbara Kingsolver's *Animal, Vegetable, Miracle* (New York: Harper, 2008).

15. Oliver's work in Huntington, West Virginia, can be seen on YouTube, at http://www.youtube.com/watch?v=t7eaHytpJWQ.

9. South Atlantic

1. Pat Conroy, *Prince of Tides* (Boston: Houghton Mifflin, 1986).

2. Dorothy Sterling, *The Trouble They Seen: Black People Tell the Story of Reconstruction* (Garden City, N.Y.: Doubleday, 1976; Eric Foner, *Nothing but Freedom: Emancipation and Its Legacy* (Baton Rouge: Louisiana State University, 1983); Eric Foner, *Reconstruction: America's Unfinished Revolution, 1863–1877* (New York: HarperCollins, 1988); Kenneth Stampp, *The Era of Reconstruction: 1865–1877* (New York: Knopf, 1965).

3. York County [South Carolina] Councilman Rick Lee, November 1, 2006.

4. Rebecca Sulock, "Leaders Urge against Water Transfer," *The (Rock Hill, S.C.) Herald*, November 2006; Bruce Henderson, "Water Fight May Go to D.C.: S.C. to Ask Supreme Court to Decide on N.C. Transfers from Catawba, Yadkin Basins," *Charlotte Observer*, March 29, 2007; Michael Gordon, "Carolinas Reach Deal on Catawba," *Charlotte Observer*, November 13, 2010.

5. Laura Moore, Jeffrey H. List, S. Jeffress Williams, and David Stolper, "Modeling Barrier Island Response to Sea-Level Rise in the Outer Banks, North Carolina," Proceedings of the Sixth International Symposium on Coastal Engineering and Science of Coastal Sediment Processes, May 13–17, 2007, New Orleans, at http://woodshole.er.usgs.gov/pubs/of2007-1278/html/future.html.

6. George Gershwin and DuBose Heyward, 1935.

7. Randall L. Hall, "Before NASCAR: The Corporate and Civic Promotion of Automobile Racing in the American South, 1903–1927," *Journal of Southern History* 68, no. 3 (August 2002).

8. Janisse Ray, *Ecology of a Cracker Childhood* (Minneapolis: Milkweed Editions, 1999).

9. James Webb, *Born Fighting: How the Scots-Irish Shaped America* (New York: Broadway Books, 2004).

10. John Fraser Hart and J. T. Morgan. "Spersopolis," *Southeastern Geographer* 35, no. 2 (1995): 103–17.

11. The fastest-growing states relatively (by percentage) were Nevada (35.1%), Arizona (24.6%), Utah (23.8%), Idaho (21.1%), Texas (20.6%), and North Carolina (18.5%). The fastest-growing state in population was Texas, adding 4.2 million.

12. Gavin Wright, *Old South, New South* (New York: Basic Books, 1986), 270.

13. http://www.frbatlanta.org/invoke.cfm?objectid=A6F99DCC-5056-9F12-121E318FFF684328&method=display_body.

14. Harry L. Watson. "Front Porch." *Southern Cultures* 12, no. 2 (Summer 2006): 1–5.

15. Annemarie Charlesworth and Stanton A. Glantz, "Smoking in the Movies Increases Adolescent Smoking: A Review," *Pediatrics* 116, no. 6 (December 2005): 1516.

16. *The Need to Improve Antimicrobial Use in Agriculture: Ecological and Human Health Consequences*, *Clinical Infectious Diseases*, supplement issue, June 1, 2002.

17. North Central Regional Center for Rural Development, "Bringing Home the Bacon? The Myth of the Role of Corporate Hog Farming in Rural Revitalization." Report to Kerr Center for Sustainable Agriculture (Poteau, OK: North Central Regional Center for Rural Development, 1999): 1–67; K. Thu and E. P. Durrenberger, eds., *Profits and Rural Communities* (Albany: State University of New York Press, 1998).

18. Ray, *Ecology of a Cracker Childhood*.

19. http://www.interfaceglobal.com/Sustainability/What-is-Sustainability-.aspx

10. Florida

1. Bonnie Kranzer, "Everglades Restoration: Interactions of Population and Environment," *Population and Environment* 24, no. 6 (July 2003): 455–84.

2. Jerry X. Mitrovica, Natalya Gomez, and Peter U. Clark, "The Sea-Level Fingerprint of West Antarctic Collapse," *Science*, February 6, 2009; Julie Harrington and Todd L. Walton, Jr., "Climate Change in Coastal Areas in Florida: Sea Level Rise Estimation and Economic Analysis to Year 2080," (Tallahassee: Florida State University, August 2008).

3. Michael Grunwald, *The Swamp: The Everglades, Florida, and the Politics of Paradise* (New York: Simon & Schuster, 2006).

4. Barbara Culliton, "Save the Beaches, Not the Buildings," *Nature* 357, June 18, 1992.

5. Charles W. Finkl and Roger H. Charlier, "Sustainability of Subtropical Coastal Zones in Southeastern Florida," *Journal of Coastal Research* 19, no. 4 (Autumn 2003): 934–43.

6. Cornelia Dean, *Against the Tide: The Battle for America's Beaches* (New York: Columbia University Press, 1999).

7. UNESCO Biosphere Reserves are 507 sites in 102 countries that are created to optimize conservation and sustainable development. They are not set aside as preserves to keep

humans out, but as experiments in maintaining unique ecology and landscapes with economic development.

8. Don Van Natta Jr. and Damien Cave, "Deal to Save Everglades May Help Sugar Firm," *New York Times*, March 7, 2010, at http://www.nytimes.com/2010/03/08/us/08everglades.html.

9. James W. Fourqurean and Michael B. Robblee, "Florida Bay: A History of Recent Ecological Changes," *Estuaries* 22, no. 2B (June 1999).

10. Thomas Cronin, "Increased Salinity in Florida Bay—Nature or Man?" Florida Bay Project Profile 142, 1998. at http://www.floridabay.org/pub/project_profiles/142increasedsalinity.shtml; J. W. Fourqurean and M. B. Robblee, "Florida Bay: A History of Recent Ecological Changes," *Estuaries* 22, no. 2B (1999): 345–57.

11. Carl Hiassen, "On the Beach, Waiting for Frances," *Bradenton (Florida) Herald*, at http://www.floridasunshinecoast.com/handbook.html.

12. Gary Landry, Florida Insurance Council, at www.flanews.com/?p=2332.

13. "Well-off Floridians have lobbied their state Legislature to pay lower rates. And, for the most part, they've managed to do so at the expense of many residents, including residents who are poorer than they are." Jim Lehrer, *NPR*, "Hurricane Funds in Financial Trouble," May 29, 2009.

14. Erin K. Lipp et al., "Preliminary Evidence for Human Fecal Contamination in Corals of the Florida Keys, USA," *Marine Pollution Bulletin* 44, no. 7 (July 2002).

15. Leon Kolankiewicz and Roy Beck, *Forsaking Fundamentals* (Washington, D.C.: The Center for Immigration Studies, 2001), quoted in Kranzer, "Everglades Restoration."

16. Information for this section from Kranzer, "Everglades Restoration," and Alice L. Clark and George H. Dalrymple, "$7.8 Billion for Everglades Restoration: Why Do Environmentalists Look So Worried?" *Population and Environment* 24, no. 6 (July 2003).

17. Theresa Bradley. "Residents Speak against Area's Unchecked Growth," *Miami Herald*, May 14, 2006, at http://www.miami.com/mld/miamiherald/news/local/states/florida/counties/miami-dade/cities_neighborhoods/pinecrest/14570575.htm.

18. "Governors' Smart Growth Initiatives," July 2001, at www.nemw.org/Gov_sgi.pdf.

19. http://www.1000friendsofflorida.org/PUBS/2060/A-Time-for-Leadership-Report-Final.pdf.

20. Robert P. Ingalls, "Lynching and Establishment Violence in Tampa, 1858–1935," *Journal of Southern History* 53, no. 4 (November 1987).

21. Kevin Archer, "The Limits to the Imagineered City: Sociospatial Polarization in Orlando," *Economic Geography* 73, no. 3 (July 1997): 322–36.

22. General Accounting Office, *Sugar Program: Supporting Sugar Prices Has Increased Users' Costs While Benefiting Producers,* June 2000, at http://www.gao.gov/archive/2000/rc00126.pdf.

23. W. Theodore Mealor Jr. and Merle C. Prunty. "Open-Range Ranching in Southern Florida," *Annals of the Association of American Geographers* 66, no. 3 (1976): 360–76.

24. Carl Hiaasen, "Folk Freak Out as Gator Panic Sweeps Florida," *Miami Herald*, May 21, 2006.

11. Gulf Coastal Plains and Mississippi Valley

1. William Faulkner, "The Bear," in *Go Down, Moses* (1940; New York: Vintage, 1990).

2. Eudora Welty, *Delta Wedding* (New York: Harcourt Brace, 1945).

3. James C. Cobb, *The Most Southern Place on Earth* (New York: Oxford University Press, 1992).

4. William W. Falk, *Rooted in Place: Family and Belonging in a Southern Black Community* (New Brunswick, N.J.: Rutgers University Press, 2004).

5. Ivor Ll. Van Heerden, "The Failure of the New Orleans Levee System Following Hurricane Katrina and the Pathway Forward," *Public Administration Review* 67, Special Issue on Administrative Failure in the Wake of Hurricane Katrina (December 2007): 24–35.

6. Peirce Lewis, *New Orleans: The Making of an Urban Landscape* (Charlottesville: University of Virginia Press, 2003).

7. Mark Twain, *Life on the Mississippi* (Boston: Osgood & Co., 1883).

8. "Browsing the Bosque," The Network News, at http://www.lternet.edu/news/article11.html.

9. Charles Ellet Jr., "Contributions to the physical geography of the United States. Part I: Of the physical geography of the Mississippi Valley, with Suggestions for the improvement of the navigation of the Ohio and other rivers," *Smithsonian Contributions to Knowledge* 323 (1851).

10. Edward Fontaine, "Contributions to the physical geography of the Mississippi River, and its delta," *Journal of the American Geographical Society of New York* 3 (1872).

11. http://biology.usgs.gov/s+t/SNT/noframe/ms137.htm.

12. James C. Knox, "Floodplain Sedimentation in the Upper Mississippi Valley: Natural versus Human Accelerated," *Geomorphology* 79, no. 3–4 (2006); Brooks Hanson, "Good Intensions Gone Awry," *Science* 294, October 12, 2001.

13. Peter Bartok, "Prebreakup Geology of the Gulf of Mexico–Caribbean: Its Relation to Triassic and Jurassic Rift Systems of the Region," *Tectonics* 12, no. 2 (1993): 441–59.

14. William J. Mitsch, John W. Day Jr., J. Wendell Gilliam, et al., "Reducing Nitrogen Loading to the Gulf of Mexico from the Mississippi River Basin: Strategies to Counter a Persistent Ecological Problem," *Bioscience* 51, no. 5 (May 2001).

15. http://www.lacoast.gov/news/press/1997-06-30.htm.

16. The French lost their American colonies except for two small islands off Newfoundland, St Pierre and Miquelon, which were kept to maintain the fishing rights off the Grand Banks.

17. Cobb, *The Most Southern Place on Earth*, 112.

18. John Egerton, *Southern Food: At Home, On the Road, in History*, Chapel Hill: University of North Carolina Press, 1987.

19. James Buckland, "Value of Birds to Man," *Smithsonian Report* (1913).

20. Megan Kate Nelson, "The Landscape of Disease: Swamps and Medical Discourse in the American Southeast, 1800–1880," *Mississippi Quarterly* 55, no. 4 (October 2002): 535–67.

21. Gerald M. Capers Jr., "Yellow Fever in Memphis in the 1870s," *Mississippi Valley Historical Review* 24 (March 1938): 483–502.

22. John Duffy, "Medical Practice in the Antebellum South," *Journal of Southern History* 25, no. 1 (February 1959): 53–72.

23. Duffy, "Medical Practice in the Antebellum South," 53–72.

24. Gerald McNeill, Southeastern Louisiana University, note, January 3, 2008.

25. Auburn University, *Bridging the Divide*, Auburn, Ala.: Auburn University, Office of the Vice President for University Outreach, 2004.

26. Peirce Lewis, *New Orleans*.

27. The New Orleans Index: State of Policy and Progress, April 2008.

28. Wendell Dufour, director of Department of Planning and Urban Studies at the University of New Orleans, quoted in Becky Bohrer, "Canal, Lower 9th among Areas Targeted for Rebirth," Associated Press, October 12, 2007.

29. http://www.ci.austin.tx.us/sustainable/.

30. John Fraser Hart, "Cropland Concentrations in the South," *Annals of the Association of American Geographers* 68, no. 4 (December 1978).

31. James C McKinley Jr. and Kristen Crawley, "Tough Season May Force Texas Oystermen to Fold," *New York Times*, December 2, 2009.

32. Barbara L. Allen, *Uneasy Alchemy: Citizens and Experts in Louisiana's Chemical Corridor Disputes* (Cambridge, Mass.: MIT Press, 2003).

33. Andy Meek, "Counties Adjust to Growth, Growth, and More Growth," *Daily News (Memphis)*, January 10, 2006.

12. The Ozarks

1. Robert Flanders, "Health and Healing in the Ozarks," *OzarksWatch* 8, no. 1 (1995).

2. Pennsylvanian period (320 million years ago) rock overlaps Mississippian period (360 million years ago) rock.

3. C. M. Woodruff Jr., "Regional Tectonic Features of the Inner Gulf Coast Basin and the Mississippi Embayment—Implication for Potential Low-Temperature Geothermal Resources," *Transactions—Gulf Coast Association of Geological Societies* 30 (1980).

4. Gale, R. W., T. W. May, C. E. Orazio, and M. J. McKee, *Determination of Polychlorinated Biphenyls, Selected Persistent Organochlorine Pesticides, and Polybrominated Flame Retardants in Fillets of Fishes from the 2006 Missouri Department of Conservation Monitoring Programs*, U.S. Geological Survey Open-File Report 2008–1028; H. Neill, M. Gutierrez, and T. Aley, "Influences of Agricultural Practices on Water Quality of Tumbling Creek Cave Stream in Taney County, Missouri," *Environmental Geology* 45, no. 4 (2004): 550–59.

5. "Computer Models Estimate Impact of Climate Change on Ozarks," *Missourian*, September 21, 2008, at http://www.columbiamissourian.com/stories/2008/09/21/computer-models-estimate-impact-climate-change-ozarks/.

6. E. Joan Wilson Miller, from Vance Randolph, *Sticks in the Knapsack and Other Ozark Folktales* (New York: Columbia University Press, 1958), 111.

7. St. Louis Five-Year Consolidate Plan Strategy, at stlouis.missouri.org/5yearstrategy/1999/ch2_conc.html.

8. http://water.usgs.gov/owq/AFO/proceedings/afo/OFR/OFR_00-204.pdf.

9. http://www.joplinglobe.com/editorial/local_story_146204023.html; http://www.ars.usda.gov/research/publications/Publications.htm?seq_no_115=210427; http://www.ars.usda.gov/research/publications/Publications.htm?seq_no_115=210427; http://www.dnr.mo.gov/pubs/WR47.pdf.

10. U.S. House, Committee on Agriculture, Subcommittee on Conservation, Credit, Energy, and Research, "Hearing to Review Renewable Fuels Standard Implementation and Agriculture Producer Eligibility," July 24, 2008, at http://www.gpo.gov/fdsys/pkg/CHRG-110hhrg51221/pdf/CHRG-110hhrg51221.pdf.

13. The Midwest

1. John Fraser Hart. *The Land That Feeds Us* (New York: Norton, 1993).

2. R. Douglas Hurt, "Midwestern Distinctiveness," in *The American Midwest: Essays on Regional History*, ed. Andrew R. L. Cayton and Susan E. Gray (Bloomington: Indiana University Press, 2001).

3. Andrew Cayton, "The Anti-region: Place and Identity," in *The American Midwest: Essays on Regional History*, ed. Andrew R. L. Cayton and Susan E. Gray (Bloomington: Indiana University Press, 2001).

4. David M. Nelson, Feng Sheng Hu; Eric C. Grimm, et al., "The Influence of Aridity and Fire on Holocene Prairie Communities in the Eastern Prairie Peninsula," *Ecology* 87, no. 10 (2006).

5. John Fraser Hart, "The Middle West," *Association of American Geographers* (1972). In a footnote, Dr. Hart famously stated: "[The Middle West is] a great climate for making a living, but it's no place to have to live, unless you consider making a living the principal purpose of living."

6. J. A. Austin and S. M. Colman, "Lake Superior Summer Water Temperatures Are Increasing More Rapidly Than Regional Air Temperatures: A Positive Ice-Albedo Feedback," *Geophysical Research Letters* 34, L06604, doi: 10.1029/2006GL029021, 2007.

7. T. Kevin O'Donnell and David L. Galat. "River Enhancement in the Upper Mississippi River Basin: Approaches Based on River Uses, Alternations, and Management Agencies," *Restoration Ecology* 15, no. 3 (2007).

8. www.agron.iastate.edu/courses/agron508/classes/503/lesson2/2.2.1.html; www.usgcrp.gov/usgcrp/Library/national assessment/overviewMidwest.htm.

9. "Tribal Revenues Up in '04," *Tulsa World*, June 15, 2005.

10. www.bea.gov/bea/newsrel/SPINewsRelease.htm.

11. City of Youngstown, at http://www.cityofyoungstownoh.org/about_youngstown/youngstown_2010/vision_files/vision.aspx; Recommendation to Shrinking Cities: Think Small, at http://www.suntimes.com/news/metro/4241979-418/recommendation-to-shrinking-cities-think-small.html.

12. "Chicago," Carl Sandburg, 1916.

13. Environment Commissioner Bill Abolt regarding Chicago Mayor Daley, 2001.

14. chibublib.org/cpl.html.

15. Larry Eugene Jones and Georg G. Iggers, *Crossing Boundaries: The Exclusion and Inclusion of Minorities in Germany and the United States* (New York: Berghahn Books, 2001).

16. www.michiganfuture.org/Reports/YoungTalentInTheGreatLakesFINAL.pdf.

17. http://www.ers.usda.gov/Briefing/FarmStructure/.

18. Paul M. Porter, Dave R. Huggins, Catherine A. Perillo, et al., "Organic and Other Management Strategies with Two- and Four-Year Crop Rotations in Minnesota," *Agronomy Journal* 95 (2003).

19. Changes in the Size and Location of U.S. Dairy Farms, at http://www.ers.usda.gov/publications/err47/err47b.pdf.

20. The Pew Charitable Trusts: Antibiotic Resistance and Food Animal Production: A Bibliography of Scientific Studies (1969–2010), at http://www.saveantibiotics.org/resources/Pew_ABR_Bibliography.pdf.

21. http://www.poultryegg.org/economic_data/.

22. Chicago Federal Reserve Bank, 2005.

23. Chris Christoff, "Your Electric Bill Is on Track to Go Higher," *Detroit Free Press*, April 18, 2008.

14. The Great Plains and Canadian Prairie

1. In Donald Worster, *Dust Bowl: The Southern Plains in the 1930s* (New York: Oxford University Press, 1979).

2. The Oklahoma-Kansas border was politically devised to accommodate the Missouri compromise and establish slave-free Plains states, all equally divided with three degrees latitude. Oklahoma's Panhandle was created because it was left over from Texas (a slave state) and the Kansas border had already been conceived, leaving the narrow strip as no-man's-land, which was eventually stapled onto the rest of Oklahoma upon statehood.

3. Manjula Guru and James Horne, "Ogallala Aquifer, 2000," at http://www.kerrcenter.com/publications/ogallala_aquifer.pdf; Mark Wallbridge, "The Ogallala: Cooperative Efforts to Preserve, Protect It," at http://www.ars.usda.gov/is/AR/archive/apr08/form0408.pdf.

4. The 100th meridian is used as a regional border according to precipitation patterns, although it varies between the 98th and 100th meridian.

5. D. E. Popper and F. J. Popper, "The Great Plains: From Dust to Dust," *Planning* 53, no. 6 (1987).

6. Norman J. Rosenberg, *A Biomass Future for the North American Great Plains*, Dordrecht, The Netherlands: Springer Press, 2010.

7. The one Spaniard who is thought to have passed through the Great Plains is Cabeza de Vaca in his epic journey. But it seems he veered south as he entered the territory.

8. Francis Parkman, *The Oregon Trail: Sketches of Prairie and Rocky-Mountain Life*, 4th ed. (1849; Boston: Little, Brown, 1872).

9. Edwin James, account of an expedition from Pittsburgh to the Rocky Mountains (London, 1823).

10. Paul Starrs, *Let the Cowboy Ride: Cattle Ranching in the American West* (Baltimore: Johns Hopkins University Press, 1998).

11. Quoted in Monique Roy-Sole, "Keeping the Métis Faith Alive," *Canadian Geographic* 115 (March–April 1995): 36–46.

12. The Palliser expedition from 1857 to 1860 believed the triangle that became the richest agricultural land in Canada to be "more or less arid desert," a wasteland. See also R. Douglas Francis and Chris Kitzan, eds., *The Prairie West as Promised Land* (Calgary, Alberta: University of Calgary Press, 2007).

13. http://www.eere.energy.gov/buildings/info/components/envelope/framing/strawbale.html.

14. Peter S. Morris, "Regional Ideas and the Montana-Alberta Borderlands," *Geographical Review* 89, no. 4 (October 1999).

15. http://geodepot.statcan.ca/Diss/Highlights/Page9/Page9d_e.cfm/.

16. Donald Worster, *Rivers of Empire* (New York: Pantheon, 1985).

17. 2002 U.S. Census, Table 2, Irrigated Farms by Acres Irrigated, Table 3, Land Use on Farms with Irrigation.

18. Mario Sophocleous, "Groundwater Recharge and Sustainability in the High Plains Aquifer in Kansas, USA," *Hydrogeology Journal* 13, no. 2 (May 2005).

19. The Ogallala is the largest portion of the total High Plains Aquifer. "There is no other aquifer in the United States pumped as intensely as the High Plains Aquifer. . . . For years many people thought the Aquifer was bottomless. Today we are being faced with the reality that the Aquifer supply is limited. There are some estimates that state that parts of the Aquifer could be completely dry in less than 25 years." Senator Sam Brownback, March 6, 2003, at http://brownback.senate.gov/pressapp/record.cfm?id=191072&&year=2003&.

20. Rezaul Mahmood, Kenneth G. Hubbard, and Christy Carlson, "Modification of Growing-Season Surface Temperature Records in the Northern Great Plains due to Land-use Transformation: Verification of Modeling Results and Implication for Global Climate Change," *International Journal of Climatology* 24 (2004): 311–27.

21. V. G. Allen, C. P. Brown, E. Segarra, et al. "In Search of Sustainable Agricultural Systems for the Llano Estacado of the U.S. Southern High Plains," *Agriculture, Ecosystems, and Environment* 124, nos. 1–2 (March 2008).

22. V. G. Allen, C.P. Brown, E. Segarra, et al. "In Search of Sustainable Agricultural Systems for the Llano Estacado of the U.S. Southern High Plains."

23. For more on the story of grass-fed versus corn-fed beef, read Michael Pollan, *Omnivore's Dilemma: A Natural History of Four Meals*, New York: Penguin Press, 2006.

24. G. M. Luciuk, M. A. Bonneau, D. M. Boyle, and E. Viberg, "Carbon Sequestration—Additional Environmental Benefits of Forages in the Prairie Farm Rehabilitation Administration Permanent Cover Program," 2007, at http://www4.agr .gc.ca/AAFC-AAC/display-afficher.do?id=1187979341393 &lang=eng.

25. R. M. Flores and L. R. Bader, "A Summary of Tertiary Coal Resources of the Raton Basin, Colorado and New Mexico," U.S. Geological Survey Professional Paper 1625-A, 1999.

26. Western Organization of Resource Councils, at http:// www.worc.org/.

27. According to 1990 electricity consumption; at http:// www.windpoweringamerica.gov/pdfs/factsheets/fs_nd.pdf.

28. Amanda Jacob, "Wind Power Market Shows No Signs of Slowing," *Reinforced Plastics* 49, no. 4 (April 2005): 24–29.

29. U.S. Department of Energy, "20% Wind Energy by 2030," July 2008, at http://www.20percentwind.org/report/Chapter4_ Transmission_and_Integration_into_the_US_Electric_System .pdf.

30. Kathleen Norris, *Dakota: A Spiritual Geography* (Boston: Houghton Mifflin, 1993).

15. The Rocky Mountains

1. Emily Faithfull, *Three Visits to America* (New York: Fowler & Wells, 1884).

2. Quoted in Patricia A. Stowkowski, *Riches and Regrets: Betting on Gambling in Two Colorado Mountain Towns* (Niwot: University Press of Colorado, 1996). These views have been challenged by New West historians, who critique traditional perspectives with revisionism.

3. C. M. Smith, R. Walker, B. Wilson, et al. "Whitebark Pine Decline and Restoration in the Northern Rocky Mountains," paper presented at Sixteenth International Conference, Society for Ecological Restoration, Victoria, Canada, August 24–26, 2004.

4. An excellent description of the changing social structure in the Bitterroots can be found in the opening chapter of Jared Diamond's *Collapse: How Societies Choose to Fail or Succeed* (New York: Viking, 2005).

5.http://www.dmns.org/main/en/Professionals/Press/ CurrentPressReleases/Press+Releases/Exhibitions/engineer ItInnovativeEngineering.htm.

6. Theo Stein, "West Slope Offers Plan to Ease Water Disputes," *Denver Post*, May 27, 2005.

7. http://wwa.colorado.edu/themes/changes_last_50_years .html; http://www.rockymountainclimate.org/.

8. Allan L. Carroll, Steve W. Taylor, Jacques Régnière, and Les Safranyik, "Effects of Climate Change on Range Expansion by the Mountain Pine Beetle in British Columbia," paper presented at Mountain Pine Beetle Symposium: Challenges and Solutions, Kelowna, British Columbia, October 30–31, 2003.

9. Quoted in the Shining Mountains Mapping Project, http:// conserveonline.org/library/crm_vol1_report_may2004.pdf.

10. George Frederick Ruxton, *Wildlife in the Rocky Mountains* (New York: Macmillan, 1916), at http://www.xmission. com/~drudy/mtman/html/ruxton.html.

11. D. Gates, "Chic Comes to Crested Butte," *Newsweek*, December 27, 1993.

12. Michael Naimark, "Aspen the Verb: Musings on Heritage and Virtuality," *Presence Journal*, vol. 15, no. 3 (June 2006), at http://www.naimark.net/writing/aspen.html.

13. Diamond, *Collapse*.

14. Patricia Nelson Limerick, "Of Forty-Nines, Oilmen, and the Dot-Com Boom," *New York Times*, May 7, 2000.

15. Average price according to Zillow.com, November 2010: $1.48 million.

16. National Public Radio (NPR), at http://www.kuow.org/ DefaultProgram.asp?ID=13827.

17. "British Columbia" (table), *2006 Community Profiles*, 2006 Census, Statistics Canada Catalogue No. 92-591-XWE. March 13, 2007.

18. Luis L. M. Aguiar, Patricia Tomic, and Ricardo Trumper, "Work Hard, Play Hard: Selling Kelowna, BC, as Year-Round Playground," *Canadian Geographer* 49, no. 2 (Summer 2005).

19. D. Neilsen, C. A. S. Smith, G. Frank, et al., "Impact of Climate Change on Crop Water Demand in the Okanagan Valley, B.C., Canada," *ISHS Acta Horticulturae* 638, Twenty-sixth International Horticultural Congress: Sustainability of Horticultural Systems in the 21st Century, at http://www.actahort.org/ books/638/638_36.htm

20. Johnnie Moore and S. N. Luoma, "Hazardous Wastes from Large-scale Metal Extraction: The Clark Fork Waste Complex, Montana," in *Proceedings of the 1990 Clark Fork River Symposium*, University of Montana, Missoula, Montana, April 20, 1990, 163–85, at http://www.umt.edu/clarkfork/Past_ Proceedings/1990_proceedings/moore/Moore.htm.

21. Most Canadian abandoned mines are in the north or in Ontario.

22. Colorado Dept. of Public Health, at http://www.cdphe .state.co.us/hm/clearcreek/index.htm#Site%20Summary,

23. "Canadian Rocky Mountains Ecoregional Assessment," May 2004, at http://conserveonline.org/.

16. Intermontane

1. Wallace Stegner, *Beyond the Hundredth Meridian* (New York: Penguin Books, 1992), 362.

2. Joel Garreau, *The Nine Nations of North America* (Boston: Houghton Mifflin, 1981); Katherine Morrissey, *Mental Territories: Environment and the Creation of the Inland Empire, 1870–1920* (New Haven, Conn.: Yale University Press, 1990).

3. Meinig, D. W. *The Great Columbia Plain* (Seattle: University of Washington Press, 1995), 3.

4. Stegner, *Beyond the Hundredth Meridian*, 119.

5. As of June 2010, Lake Powell storage is 15,539 thousand acre-feet (KAF) (64 percent of capacity). Lake Mead storage is 10,797 KAF (42 percent of capacity). Total system storage is 34,469 KAF (58 percent of capacity). Bureau of Reclamation, at http://www.usbr.gov/lc/region/g4000/hourly/rivops.html.

6. http://ucsdnews.ucsd.edu/newsrel/science/02-08 LakeMead.asp.

7. http://www.uswaternews.com/archives/arcsupply/ tarifac7.html.

8. "New Reservoir to Catch Colorado River Flowing Unused into Mexico," Associated Press, January 12, 2008.

9. Edward Abbey, *Desert Solitaire* (New York: Simon & Schuster, 1968).

10. Elizabeth K. Burns and Eric D. Kenney, "Building and Maintaining Urban Water Infrastructure: Phoenix, Arizona, from 1950 to 2003," *Yearbook of the Association of Pacific Coast Geographers* 67 (2005): 47–64.

11. "Groundwater Depletion," U.S. Geological Survey, at http://ga.water.usgs.gov/edu/gwdepletion.html.

12. htttp://www.portlandonline.com/water/index. cfm?a=behgie&c=ecica; http://geochange.er.usgs.gov/sw/ impacts/society/water_demand/; http://www.azwater.gov/dwr/ content/Publications/files/supplydemand.pdf.

13. http://indian.utah.gov/utah_tribes_today/dine.html.

14. http://www.nnwo.org/nnprofile.htm.

15. The empty quarter was one of the Nine Nations of North America in the book of the same name by Garreau in 1981. It included most of northern Canada, British Columbia, and Alberta, but also almost the entire Intermontane region. Joel Garreau, *The Nine Nations of North America* (Boston: Houghton Mifflin, 1981).

16. Paul Starrs, *Let the Cowboy Ride* (Baltimore: Johns Hopkins University Press, 1998).

17. http://www.sustainlane.com/us-city-rankings/.

18. Bob Golfen, "Valley 'Ministack' 4th worst U.S. bottleneck," *Arizona Republic*, February 19, 2004; 2003 Urban Mobility Study, Texas Transportation Institute.

19. Hal Rothman, *Neon Metropolis* (New York: Routledge, 2003).

20. Ken Ritter, "Las Vegas Area Land Prices Boom at BLM Auction," *Las Vegas Sun*, June 2, 2004.

21. Matt Canham, "Mormon Portion of Utah Population Steadily Shrinking," *Salt Lake Tribune*, July 24, 2005.

22. Abbey, *Desert Solitaire*.

23. S. W. Culman, S. T. DuPont, J. D. Glover, et al., "Long-Term Impacts of High-Input Annual Cropping and Unfertilized Perennial Grass Production on Soil Properties and Belowground Food Web in Kansas, USA." *Agriculture, Ecosystems & Environment* 137 (2010): 13–24.

24. "In fiscal year 2004, federal agencies spent a total of at least $144 million. The 10 federal agencies spent at least $135.9 million, with the Forest Service and BLM accounting for the majority. Other federal agencies have grazing related activities, such as pest control, and spent at least $8.4 million in fiscal year 2004. The 10 federal agencies' grazing fees generated about $21 million in fiscal year 2004—less than one-sixth of the expenditures to manage grazing. Of that amount, the agencies distributed about $5.7 million to states and counties in which grazing occurred, returned about $3.8 million to the Treasury, and deposited at least $11.7 million in separate Treasury accounts to help pay for agency programs, among other things." Government Accountability Office (GAO), *Livestock Grazing*, Report to Congressional Requesters, September 2005, at http://www.gao .gov/new.items/d05869.pdf.

25. GAO, *Livestock Grazing*.

26. Jim Robbins, "Where the Cattle Herds Roam, Ideally in Harmony with Their Neighbors," *New York Times*, July 11, 2006.

27. Judy Fahys, "Tailings Create a New Kind of Fallout," *Salt Lake Tribune*, August 24, 2005.

28. Arizona, Nevada, New Mexico, Utah, and Idaho. Washington and Oregon are included in Chapter 17.

29. *Utah Economic and Business Review* 64, nos. 1–2 (January–February 2004).

17. Pacific Northwest

1. T. E. Dawson, "Fog in the California Redwood Forest: Ecosystem Inputs and Use by Plants," *Oecologia* 117, no. 4 (1998).

2. Commission on Life Sciences, *Environmental Issues in Pacific Northwest Forest Management* (Washington, D.C.: National Academy Press, 2000).

3. Office of the Governor, Chris Gregoire, "Protecting and Restoring Puget Sound,"
December 15, 2005.

4. Quoted in Dorothee Schreiber, "Salmon Farming and Salmon People: Identity and Environment in the Leggatt Inquiry," *American Indian Culture and Research Journal* 27, no. 4 (2003): 79–103.

5. D. Bruce Johnson, "A Modern Potlatch? Privatizing British Columbia Salmon Fishing," *PERC Reports* 24, no. 2 (Summer 2006), at http://www.perc.org/articles/article805 .php.

6. 2008 U.S. city sustainability rankings, at http://www .sustainlane.com/us-city-rankings/overall-rankings; America's top greenest cities, at http://www.popsci.com/environment/ article/2008-02/americas-50-greenest-cities?page=1; U.S. and Canada Green City Index, at http://www.siemens.com/entry/cc/ en/greencityindex.htm.

7. Vancouver is tied at number 4 in "Top 50 Cities: Quality of Living Ranking," at http://www.mercer.com/quality oflivingpr#City_Ranking_Tables; "Global Livability Report: Vancouver Remains Top," *The Economist*, January 2011, at http://www.eiu.com/site_info.asp?info_name=The_ Global_Liveability_Report&page=noads&rf=0.

8. R. W. Galstar and W. T. Laprade, "Geology of Seattle, Washington, United States of America," *Bulletin of the Association of Engineering Geologists* 3 (1991): 235–302.

9. http://www.sustainableseattle.org/About; http://www .sightline.org/.

10. *City News Service*, November 5, 2004.

11. Sean Markey, John T. Pierce, Kelly Vodden, and Mark Roseland, *Second Growth: Community Economic Development in Rural British Columbia* (Vancouver: University of British Columbia Press, 2005).

12. Mary F. Willson, Scott M. Gende, and Brian H. Marston, "Fishes and the Forest," *Bioscience* 48, no. 6 (1998): 455–62.

13. Jeff Barnard, "Judge Continues Spring and Summer Spill to Help Salmon over Dams," Associated Press, December 29, 2005.

14. U.S. Fish and Wildlife Service, "Klamath River Fish Die-Off, September 2002: Report on Estimate of Mortality," Report number AFWO-01-03, at http://www.fws.gov/arcata/fisheries/reports/technical/Klamath_River_Dieoff_Mortality_Report_AFWO_01_03.pdf.

15. Nathan Mantua and Robert C. Francis, "Natural Climate Insurance for Pacific Northwest Salmon and Salmon Fisheries: Finding Our Way through the Entangled Bank," *American Fisheries Society Symposium* 43 (2004).

16. The Sightline Institute has published a Cascadia Scorecard measuring regional sustainability. In the latest version (July 2010), a sustainable region is estimated to be still forty-two years away, and this is one of the most sustainable regions in America and Canada; http://scorecard.sightline.org/.

18. Arctic Slope, Pacific Borderlands, and Boreal Forest

1. In Canada, Aboriginal peoples include Indian, Inuit, and Métis peoples of Canada. Constitution Act 1992, Subsection 35(2).

2. Most sources say that Alaska means "great land," but the translation may actually be more like "great big piece of land"—not as poetic, but perhaps more truthful when thought of in relation to the size of the Aleutian Islands.

3. M. L. Goulden, S. C. Wofsy, J. W. Harden, et al., "Sensitivity of Boreal Forest Carbon Balance to Soil Thaw," *Science*, January 9, 1998; Edward A. G. Schuur, James Bockheim, Josep G. Canadell, et al., "Vulnerability of Permafrost Carbon to Climate Change: Implications for the Global Carbon Cycle," *BioScience* 58, no. 8 (September 2008); Jeffrey Masek, "Stability of Boreal Forest Stands during Recent Climate Change: Evidence from Landsat Satellite Imagery," *Journal of Biogeography* 28 (2001): 967–76; Christy Ferguson, Elizabeth Nelson, and Geoff Sherman, "Turning up the Heat," Greenpeace, Canada, March 2008; G. Wendler, J. Conner, B. Moore, et al., "Climatology of Alaskan Wildfires with Special Emphasis on the Extreme Year of 2004," *Theoretical Applied Climatology*, 2010. The boreal forest may experience major shifts in its range as climate change continues to upset the ecological balance across the continent, but it has not yet shown a shift, perhaps due to a lag time, or perhaps because of competitive pressures from surrounding tundra and prairie regions. Logging in the boreal forest is, however, increasing the rate of global warming, as well as increasing wildfires and insect outbreaks. The area burned by forest fires has doubled between 1970 and 1990, which has increased

carbon dioxide content in the atmosphere. K. M. Walter, S. A. Zimov, J. P. Chanton, et al., "Methane Bubbling from Siberian Thaw Lakes as a Positive Feedback to Climate Warming," *Nature* 443, no. 7107, September 7, 2006.

4. Ian Stirling, Andrew E. Derocher, William A. Gough, and Karyn Rode. "Response to Dyck et al. (2007) on Polar Bears and Climate Change in Western Hudson Bay," *Ecological Complexity* 5, no. 3 (September 2008).

5. According to John Falkingham of the Canadian Ice Service, "Bottom-line, across the area of the Northwest Passage we can say that over the last 30 years, the amount of ice in the summer time has been decreasing by 4-6% per decade. And the minimum amount of ice over that period of time has been decreasing by about 8-9%/decade. So that we have observed a very significant decrease in Canadian Arctic ice." Canadian Arctic Resources Committee, "The Ice Evidence," *Northern Perspectives* 27, no. 2 (Spring 2002), 2; "Glaciers Surge When Ice Shelf Breaks Up," at http://www.gsfc.nasa.gov/topstory/2004/0913larsen.html.

6. "Canada has a choice when it comes to defending our sovereignty over the Arctic. We either use it or lose it. And make no mistake; this Government intends to use it. Because Canada's Arctic is central to our national identity as a northern nation. It is part of our history. And it represents the tremendous potential of our future." Prime Minister Stephen Harper, July 9, 2007, at http://www.pm.gc.ca/eng/media.asp?id=1742.

7. E. A. Hobbie, S. A. Macko, and H. H. Shugart, "Patterns in N Dynamics and N Isotopes during Primary Succession in Glacier Bay, Alaska," *Chemical Geology* 152 (1998): 3–11.

8. J. P. Schimel, R. G. Cates, and R. Ruess, "The Role of Balsam Poplar Secondary Chemicals in Controlling Soil Nutrient Dynamics through Succession in the Alaskan Taiga," *Biogeochemistry* 42 (1998): 221–34.

9. http://www.ic.gc.ca/epic/site/rei-ier.nsf/en/h_nz00010e.html.

10. Iliamna Lake—Fish First Project, at http://www.waurisa.org/conferences/2010/presentations/318_HarryRich_Iliamna_Lake.pdf.

11. E. M. Krümmel, R. W. Macdonald, L. E. Kimpe, et al., "Aquatic Ecology: Delivery of Pollutants by Spawning Salmon," *Nature*, September 18, 2003, 255–56.

12. In 2007, after a switch of federal government, the conservative prime minister of Canada, Steven Harper, announced that Canada would no longer support the Kyoto Protocol and instead join a coalition that endorsed voluntary reductions. Mayors in Canadian cities did as U.S. mayors and pledged to work toward the Kyoto goals.

13. Philip Ball, "Glaciers Are Flowing Faster," *Nature*, September 23, 2004, at http://www.nature.com/news/2004/040920/full/040920-13.html.

14. Charles Wohlforth, "Eskimos Bear Witness to Changing Climate in the Arctic," *Anchorage Daily News*, April 28, 2004, at http://forests.org/shared/reader/welcome.aspx?linkid=31270&keybold=climate%20AND%20%20deep%20AND%20%20freeze%20AND%20%20food.

15. U.S. General Accounting Office, "Alaska Native Villages," GAO-04-142, December 2003, at http://www.gao.gov/new.items/d04142.pdf.

16. U.S. General Accounting Office, "Alaska Native Villages."

17. http://www.ec.gc.ca/climate/home-e.html.

18. Thomas Maugh II, "Artifacts Upend Theory on First North Americans," *Los Angeles Times*, March 26, 2011, at http://www.latimes.com/news/science/la-sci-first-americans-20110326,0,7839145.story.

19. *Proceedings*, Fourteenth Inuit Studies Conference, August 11–15, 2004, University of Calgary, at http://pubs.aina.ucalgary.ca/aina/14thISCProceedings.pdf,

20. To read more about the Aleut experience upon Russian contact, see Douglas W. Veltre and Allen P. McCartney, "Russian Exploitation of Aleuts and Fur Seals: The Archaeology of Eighteenth- and Early-Nineteenth-Century Settlements in the Probilof Islands, Alaska," *Historical Archaeology* 36, no. 3 (2002).

21. The purchase of Alaska from the Russians was questioned by the various Native groups at the time, as they had occupied Alaska for millennia before the Russians. Why were they not paid the purchase price? (*The Works of Hubert Howe Bancroft*, vol. 33, 1730–1887 [San Francisco: A. C. Bancroft & Co., 1886], 609, cited in William Hensley, "What Rights to Land Have the Alaska Natives? The Primary Question." May 1966, at http://www.alaskool.org/projects/ancsa/WLH/WLH66_2.htm.) In addition, the Natives were exempted from laws governing mainland tribes.

22. Act of May 17, 1884, Sec. 8, 23 Stat. 26.

23. Skagway, at the base of the climb, grew into the largest town in Alaska—from two people in 1887 to twenty thousand in 1898.

24. www.cbc.ca/canada/north/story/2007/11/28/nu-fraser.html; www.nytimes.com/2006/06/18/world/americas/18canada.html?n=Top/Reference/Times%20Topics/Subjects/E/Eskimos.

25. CBC Digital Archives has an impressive background on the Berger Inquiry at http://archives.cbc.ca/politics/rights_freedoms/topics/295/.

26. MMBtu = Million British thermal units.

27. Legislative Assembly of Nunavut, March 18, 2005, 1969.

28. "Pollution and Human Health," in Arctic Monitoring and Assessment Program, *AMAP Assessment Report: Arctic Pollution Issues* (Oslo, Norway: AMAP, 1998), chap. 12.

29. Cold Climate Housing Research Center, at http://www.cchrc.org/anaktuvuk-pass-prototype-home.

30. "Subsistence productivity is substantial in most areas. . . . In the 1980s, 82 of the 98 sampled communities were harvesting wild resources at levels half or greater than the mean per capita use of meat, fish, and poultry in the United States." Robert J. Wolfe and Robert J. Walker, "Subsistence Economies in Alaska," *Arctic Anthropology* 24, no. 2 (1987). According to various estimates, a subsistence economy accounts for 30 to 80 percent of all production and income in many northern indigenous communities. Birger Poppel et al., *Survey of Living Conditions in the Arctic: Results* (Anchorage: Institute of Social and Economic Research, University of Alaska Anchorage, 2007).

31. Statistics Canada. Nunavut (table). 2006 Community Profiles. 2006 Census. Statistics Canada Catalogue no. 92-591-XWE. Ottawa. Released March 13, 2007, at http://www12.statcan.ca/english/census06/data/profiles/community/Index.cfm?Lang=E.

32. Sergei Wan, "Tlingit Women and Russian Orthodox Christianity," *Ethnohistory* (August 1996).

33. Wood Buffalo Municipal Census, 2010, at http://www.woodbuffalo.ab.ca/Assets/Corporate/Census+Reports/2010+Municipal+Census.pdf.

34. Fort McMurray—Alberta Labour Market Information, at http://www.woodbuffalo.net/AboutCostHouse.html.

35. http://king.collectionscanada.ca/EN/PageView.asp.

36. The Matanuska experiment is discussed in detail in James R. Shortridge, "The Collapse of Frontier Farming in Alaska," *Annals of the Association of American Geographers* 66, no. 4 (December 1976).

37. Sheldon Jackson, general agent for education in Alaska, submitting a request for federal funds to establish a reindeer-herding program in 1890.

38. "Senator Joseph I. Lieberman Holds a Hearing on U.S. Energy Security," July 24, 2008, at http://www.emediamillworks.com.

39. Doug Cardinal is a Deh Cho member and senior executive of Aboriginal Pipeline.Quoted in Robert Collier, "Fueling America: Canadian Oil Showdown," *San Francisco Chronicle*, May 23, 2005, at http://articles.sfgate.com/2005-05-23/news/17375313_1_oil-sands-pipeline-route-pipeline-right-of-way.

40. "Vale Voted World's Worst Corporation," January 27, 2012, at http://www.straightgoods.ca/2012/ViewArticle.cfm?Ref=104&Cookies=yes

41. The Wilderness Society, "Greater Than Zero: Toward the Total Economic Value of Alaska's National Forest Wildlands," at http://wilderness.org/content/greater-than-zero.

42. Ernest Gruening, *The Battle for Alaska Statehood* (Fairbanks: University of Alaska Press, 1967), 33

43. "Stevens Presents Fish Farm Permit Proposal to Congress," Associated Press, June 11, 2006.

44. J. A. Steigers, "Demonstrating the Use of Fish Oil as Fuel in a Large Stationary Diesel Engine," Alaska Energy Authority, at http://www.akenergyauthority.org/PDF%20files/FishOilv01.pdf.

45. Randall R. Reeves and Edward Mitchell, *Cetaceans of Canada* (Ottawa, Ontario: Communications Directorate, Department of Fisheries and Oceans, 1987); *Alaska Wildlife News*, November 2003, at http://www.wildlifenews.alaska.gov.

46. Fisheries and Oceans Canada, "Sustainable Development Strategy, 2001–2003," at http://www.dfo-mpo.gc.ca/sds-sdd/issues-enjeux-eng.htm.

47. http://www.ankn.uaf.edu/; http://www.cchrc.org/default.aspx.

48. Alaska Energy Authority, "Alaska Energy: A First Step toward Energy Independence," January 2009.

49. http://taiga.net/coop/index.html.

19. California

1. The deepest part of the basin is where the Rio Hondo and Los Angeles River meet in South Gate.

2. http://hetchhetchy.water.ca.gov/process/.

3. Alexander McAdie, *Climatology of California*, Washington, D.C.: U.S. Government Printing Office, 1903.

4. W. James Gauderman, Edward Avol, Frank Gilliland, et al., "The Effect of Air Pollution on Lung Development from 10 to 18 Years of Age," *New England Journal of Medicine* 351, no. 11 (September 9, 2004): 1057–1067.

5. American Lung Association, "State of the Air: 2009," at http://www.stateoftheair.org/2009/city-rankings/polluted-cities-ozone.html. Rankings shown are by ozone levels, although most also are in the top ten in short-term and year-round particulate pollution as well.

6. Daily earthquake records are kept and mapped at http://quake.usgs.gov/recenteqs/.

7. David Hornbeck, "The Patenting of California's Private Land Claims, 1851–1885," *Geographical Review* 69, no. 4 (October 1979): 434–48.

8. Joseph L. Love, "La Raza: Mexican Americans in Rebellion," *Society* 6, no. 4 (February 1969).

9. Richard Goldstein, in Barney Hoskyns, "The Meeting of the Twain: Monterey Pop and the Great California Divide," 2002, at http://www.criterion.com/asp/release.asp?id=168&eid=253&section=essay.

10. Average home values are from http://www.zillow.com and Real Estate News, at http://www.dqnews.com/Charts/Monthly-Charts/CA-City-Charts/ZIPCAR.aspx

11. Mike Davis, *City of Quartz: Excavating the Future in Los Angeles* (New York: Vintage Press, 1992).

12. For an excellent introduction to fortress living, see Davis, *City of Quartz*.

13. A. Alonso, at http://www.streetgangs.com/history/hist01.html.

14. Hans P. Johnson, "Movin' Out: Domestic Migration to and from California in the 1990s," Public Policy Institute of California, *California Counts: Population Trends and Profiles* 2, no. 1 (August 2000), at http://www.ppic.org/content/pubs/cacounts/CC_800HJCC.pdf; "Demographia: State Domestic Migration, 2000–2007," at http://www.demographia.com/db-statemigra2007.pdf.

15. Adam B. Ellick, "Recycling Rates Vary Widely among Cities," *New York Times*, July 29, 2008.

16. Jeff Swenerton, "The Greening of Oakland," *Oakland Magazine*, April 2007.

17. Kirsten Jerch, "Cooler on the Farm," *The Bulletin Online* 63, no. 6 (November 2007): 9, at http://thebulletin.metapress.com/content/f17w1wh90748m629/fulltext.pdf; Betsy Mason, "Cultivating a Defense against Global Warming," *ScienceNow* 227, no. 4 (February 27, 2007).

18. Farmers receive an irrigation-water "subsidy." Farms pay about one-tenth the urban price for water.

19. "Iowa, with 2,791 MW installed, surpassed California (2,517 MW) for the No. 2 position in wind power generating capacity." American Wind Energy Association, April 2009, at http://archive.awea.org/newsroom/releases/Annual_Industry_Rankings_2009_041309.html.

20. For up-to-date renewable energy figures, see U.S. Energy Information Administration, at http://www.eia.doe.gov/cneaf/solar.renewables/page/state_profiles/california.html.

21. Daniel Flaming, Brent Haydamack, and Pascale Joassart, "Hopeful Workers, Marginal Jobs: LA's Off-the Books Labor Force," (Los Angeles: Economic Roundtable, 2005).

22. George Avalos, "Shift in California's Business Climate Fosters Growth of Informal Labor," *Contra Costa Times*, June 20, 2005.

23. Avalos, "Shift in California's Business Climate Fosters Growth of Informal Labor."

24. U.S. Census, "State Exports for California," at http://www.census.gov/foreign-trade/statistics/state/data/ca.html.

25. The movie *Crash* is a good, though, fictional example of the stresses of living in the heavily multicultural city.

20. Hawai`i

1. All island names are approximations of the Hawaiian pronunciations, accented (except for Maui) by a single apostrophe called the *okina*, representing a glottal stop: Hawai`i, Kaho`olawe, Kaua`i, Lāna`i, Maui, Moloka`i, Ni`ihau, and O`ahu.

2. The island of Hawai`i is about twice the size of the combined area of the other seven islands and is known as the "Big Island," both for its size and to differentiate it from the archipelago.

3. The unincorporated Territory of Midway Island is the only atoll in the Hawaiian chain that is not a part of the state of Hawai`i. The U.S. Navy administers it.

4. Hawaiian surf is due to near-perfect conditions: coral reefs, strong tides and winds, and volcanic shore configurations.

5. Howard A. Bridgeman, "Could Climatic Change Have Had an Influence on the Polynesian Migrations?" *Palaeogeography, Palaeoclimatology, Palaeoecology* 41 (1983): 193–206; Ben R. Finney, "Anomalous Westerlies, El Niño, and the Colonization of Polynesia," *American Anthropologist*, new series, 87, no. 1 (March 1985): 9–26; Patrick Nunn, "The AD 1300 Event in the Pacific Basin," *Geographical Review* 97 (January 2007): 1–23.

6. Jonathan Kay Kamakawiwo`ole Osorio. *Dismembering Lahui: A History of the Hawaiian Nation to 1887* (Honolulu: University of Hawai`i Press, 2002); Noenoe K. Silva, *Aloha Betrayed: Native Hawaiian Resistance to American Colonialism* (Durham, N.C.: Duke University Press, 2004).

7. T. T. Shintani, C. K. Hughes, S. Beckham, and H. K. O'Connor. "Obesity and Cardiovascular Risk Intervention through the Ad Libitum Feeding of Traditional Hawaiian Diet," *American Journal of Clinical Nutrition* 53, no. 6 (June 1991): 1647S–1651S.

8. "In the Pacific, there is a relatively high level of sophistication about good nutritional practices, although people tend to continue to consume foods of lower nutritional value, but higher energy density. The consumption of high energy density foods results in the higher BMI. This consumption practice is based on cost and the lack of availability of traditional foods. When participants are placed on a traditional foods-diet, marked improvement in health status has been observed." D. M. K. Liu and A. Grandinetti, "Health Disparities in Hawai`i Part 2—Obesity," *Hawai`i Journal of Public Health* 2, no. 1 (September 2009): 34–35, at http://hawaii.gov/health/hjph/Volumes/Volume2.1.pdf.

9. T. T. Shintani et al., "Obesity and Cardiovascular Risk Intervention through the Ad Libitum Feeding of Traditional Hawaiian Diet"; T. T. Shintani, S. Beckham, A. C. Brown, and H. K. O'Connor, "The Hawai`i Diet," *Hawai`i Medical Journal* 60, no. 3 (March 2001): 69–73.

10. CensusScope: Multiracial Profile, at http://www.census-scope.org/us/s15/chart_multi.html.

11. "State Says Another Year before Water Comes to Puna Homestead," Associated Press, June 8, 1999.

12. "Honolulu Ranked as One of the Richest Cities," Associated Press, May 8, 2006; Hawai`i home prices and home values, at http://www.zillow.com/local-info/HI-home-value/r_18/ .

13. http://www.honolulu.gov/refs/roh/central/

14. The Big Five companies were Amfac, C. Brewer & Company, Theo Davies Company, Castle & Cooke, and Alexander & Baldwin.

15. Oliver Cheesman, *Environmental Impacts of Sugar Production* (New York: Oxford University Press, 2005).

16. "First Open-Ocean Aquaculture Farm in the USA, Files for Bankruptcy," November 3, 2010, at http://www.aquafeed.com/read-article.php?id=3614.

17. U.S. Energy Information Administration, at http://www.eia.gov/state/state-energy-profiles.cfm?sid=HI.

18. State of Hawai`i, Department of Business, Economic Development and Tourism, "Ocean Thermal Energy," at http://hawaii.gov/dbedt/info/energy/renewable/otec; "Hui revives plan to get electricity from water," July 10, 2011, at http://www.staradvertiser.com/business/businessnews/20110710_Hui_revives_plan_to_get_electricity_from_water.html.

19. www.hawaii.gov/dbedt/info/economic/data reports/qser/outlook-economy.

20. http://www.state.hi.us/jud/23080.htm.

21. http://www.hawaii2050.org/.

Glossary

Note: Numbers in brackets following the definitions indicate the chapter where the term appears.

Aboriginal: In Canada, a person identified with a North American Indian, Métis, or Inuit group. [18]

absolute growth: Numerical growth, versus relative growth, which is percentage growth. [4]

abyss: The flat ocean floor found at the bottom of continental slopes. [20]

acculturation: Modification in a culture by adopting outside cultural traits. [4]

acid mine drainage: Acidic water outflows from abandoned mines, contaminated with metals, that kill aquatic life. [8]

acid rain: Rain that has become more acidic than normal (below pH 5.0), as certain oxides present as airborne pollutants are absorbed by water droplets. [5]

agglomeration: A concentration of economic activities in an industrial sector in a geographic area. [13]

aging in place: Living in one's longtime home as one ages. Said of the farming population in the Midwest and Great Plains. [14]

agribusiness: Agriculture based on commercial principles and advanced technology. Also, huge commercial farms owned by large and often vertically integrated corporations. [14]

allophone: An immigrant whose mother tongue or home language is neither English nor French. This term is used this way in Quebec. [4]

alluvial fan: A fan-shaped deposit of sediment located at the base of a mountain. [16]

alpine glaciation: Glaciers that occupy U-shaped valleys on a mountain. Ice flows that are seemingly rivers of ice in mountainous areas. [2]

alternative lifestyle: A mode or style of conducting one's life that is considerably removed from the generally perceived norm. [19]

anadromous fish: Fish that migrate up rivers from the sea to breed in fresh water. Important in the Pacific Northwest with the salmon. [17]

anglophone: An English-speaking person, especially in a region where two or more languages are spoken. (See **francophone**.) [4]

antebellum: The period before a war; in the United States, before the Civil War. [11]

anthracite: Hard coal with high carbon content. Anthracite was mined in nineteenth-century Scranton, Pennsylvania, but little remains today. [8]

anthropocentric: Interpreting the world exclusively in terms of human values and experiences. Finding humans as the center of the universe, and basing all one's actions on furthering only human interests. [1]

Appalachian Regional Commission (ARC): Federal-state partnership formed in 1963 to increase jobs, improve infrastructure, and increase health care and education in Appalachia. [8]

aquifer: A permeable rock layer through which groundwater flows easily. [2]

archipelago: Any sea or broad sheet of water interspersed with many islands or with a group of islands. [18]

Army Corps of Engineers: Part of the U.S. Army responsible for engineering services, including planning and design of infrastructure such as bridges, levees, and construction of military facilities. [11]

arroyo (*Sp.* "dry creek"): A steep-sided gully or wash that fills with water after a heavy rain. Found in semiarid to arid areas. [16]

artesian spring: A spring that emits water from underground pressure. [10]

assimilation: The loss of all ethnic traits and complete blending into the host society. [4]

atoll: A low coral reef that surrounds an interior body of water called a lagoon. Atolls form around the fringes of sunken volcanoes. [20]

baby boom: The generation of people born after World War II (from 1945 until 1964). [4]

badlands: Lands eroded by wind and water into small gullies stripped of vegetation and soil. Areas having intricately dissected topography resulting from fluvial erosion and characterized by high drainage density and steep, mostly barren side slopes with narrow interfluvial ridges. [14]

bald: Bare mountaintop. Especially in the Ozarks and Appalachians. [12]

Bald Knobbers: Vigilantes in the Ozarks during 1883–1889. They retaliated against marauders in the area by killing them, but it got out of hand and many murders were committed. [12]

bank: A shoal; a shallow area that is an extension of the continental shelf before it drops abruptly down the continental slope to the ocean floor. Fish can be abundant on the banks. [6]

barrier island: A long, narrow, sandy island separated from the mainland by a shallow lagoon or wetland, which protects the mainland from the open ocean. A sand body that is essentially parallel to the shore, the crest of which is above normal high-water level. For example, the string of islands along the shore of North Carolina known as the Outer Banks. [9]

basalt: A dense, fine-grained, dark-gray igneous rock, which breaks through the crust of the earth and erupts on the surface before solidifying as lava. [2]

basement rock: The crust of the earth below sedimentary deposits, often of Precambrian age. [7]

basin: A low area of land, generally surrounded by mountains. [16]

Basque: People from the western Pyrenees who moved to the Intermontane and practiced their native sheep raising. [16]

batholith: A large body of igneous rock, usually granite, that has been exposed by erosion of the overlying rock. [15]

bayou: A small, sluggish stream that cuts through the low, swampy land of a delta. [11]

Beltway: A high-speed highway that encircles or skirts an urban area. For example, the highway surrounding Washington, D.C. [7]

Berger Inquiry: A 1974 plan to review the building of the Mackenzie Valley oil and gas pipeline. The inquiry determined that the Yukon was too susceptible to environmental damage, and suggested several sanctuaries for threatened species. The inquiry was among the first to recognize Native rights and economic needs. [18]

Bible Belt: Those sections of the United States, especially in the South and Midwest, where Protestant fundamentalism is widely practiced. [12]

bike station: A nonprofit organization that offers secure bicycle parking and amenities such as showers for cyclists. [13]

bioaccumulation: Accumulation of toxic substances in lower food chains, then consumed by higher levels and increasing the amount of toxins. For example, humans at the top of the food chain eat contaminated fish that have high levels of mercury, and intake is faster than the rate of excretion. [17]

biofuel: Fuel made from renewable sources, especially plant biomass and waste products. [3]

biome: A major regional biotic community consisting of plants, animals, and the prevailing climate. Terrestrial biomes include desert, grassland, tropical rainforest, deciduous and coniferous forests, and tundra. [2]

biomimicry: The process of emulating nature to design and produce products, systems, and buildings. [3]

bioregion (or ecoregion): A place defined by life-forms; a life-territory. An ecologically and geographically defined area that shares climate and geology, the main factors determining the distribution of plants and animals in the area. [1]

birthrate: Number of people born as a percentage of the total population in any given period of time. [4]

bituminous: Second-hardest coal after anthracite. It is primarily used for making coke for use in steel making, and for burning in power plants. Bituminous coal accounts for an overwhelming percentage of the coal presently mined. Most comes from the Appalachian mines. [8]

blackwater rivers: Dark-water rivers found in the southern United States. They flow through swamps and wetlands and are colored by the tannins from decaying vegetation. [9]

bog: A peat-accumulating wetland that has no significant inflows or outflows and supports acid-loving mosses, particularly sphagnum, and heaths that may develop into peat. Water comes mostly from precipitation. Some shrubs (heath family) and evergreens grow in bogs. Minnesota's peatland region in the north central part of the state has many examples of bogs. [2]

boll weevil: A beetle that feeds on and devastates cotton crops. An infestation of boll weevils in the 1920s ended cotton production in many southern states. [9]

boom and bust town: Town characterized by large jumps in population over a five- to ten-year construction period, after which the population settles to a lower level associated with the completed activities, such as mining or power plant operation. [15]

boreal forest (or taiga): High- to mid-latitude biome dominated by coniferous forest. Predominant vegetation of this biome is various species of spruce, fir, pine, and cedar. [2]

borough: An administrative unit of a city. In this book, borough is used in relation to New York City and the five boroughs (counties) that make up the city. [7]

bosque: Mesquite-cottonwood riparian forests found along the flood plains in Texas and the southwestern United States. Their presence is welcome in the semiarid to arid region. [11]

BosWash: That part of the east coast that is within the area of metropolitan Boston to Washington, D.C., megalopolis. [7]

break-in-bulk point: A place where goods are moved from one mode of transportation to another. Transfer point where goods change mode of transportation. For example, unloading goods from a ship and transferring to trucks. [5]

brewis: National food dish of Newfoundland made of hard bread (hard tack) and salt fish (cod). [6]

British North America Act (1867): Established the Dominion of Canada and gave the Canadian government the right to make their own laws. [5]

broiler chickens: Reared for meat rather than for eggs. The broiler industry began in the late 1950s, when strains were selectively bred for meat production. In 2001 in the United States, there were 8.4 billion broilers produced, with an average live weight of 5.06 pounds. [12]

brownfield: Any real property that has been contaminated by a hazardous substance, solid waste, or pollutant and is hampered for redevelopment because of cost and liability concerns. [13]

Bureau of Land Management (BLM): Agency of the U.S. Department of the Interior that oversees the management of public land, such as national forests. [14]

bush: Land remote from settlement. Said of Alaska outside of the Pacific borderland. [18]

butte: Isolated hill or mountain with steep sides, smaller than a mesa. [16]

cache: A specially designed container placed outside to store and keep food safe from animals. [18]

Cajun: A member of a group of people with an enduring cultural tradition, whose French Catholic ancestors established permanent communities in Louisiana and Maine after being expelled from Acadia in the late eighteenth century. [11]

caldera (*Sp.* "cauldron"): A basin-shaped volcanic depression, at least a mile in diameter. Formed when a large volume of magma is removed from beneath a volcano, resulting in the ground subsiding or collapsing into the emptied space. Such large depressions are typically formed by the subsidence of volcanoes. Crater Lake occupies the best-known caldera in the Cascades. [2]

caliche (or **hardpan**): Crust or layer of hard subsoil encrusted with calcium carbonate, occurring in arid or semiarid regions like the Great Plains in the United States. Term used in Oklahoma. [14]

Canadien: A Canadian of French descent. [5]

canebrake: Riverbottom in interior plateau and southern Appalachia overgrown with cane. Most has been cleared for agricultural use. [8]

canyon: A narrow, deep, steep-sided opening in the earth's surface with steep cliff walls, cut into the earth by running water; a gorge. In the United States, the most famous is the Grand Canyon, carved by the Colorado River over the past 60 million years and located mainly in northern Arizona. [16]

cap and trade: Emissions trading system to control greenhouse gas emissions, where total emissions are limited, or capped. [5]

cape: Land projecting out into a body of water. For example, Cape Cod, Cape Hatteras. [9]

capelin: Small fish that is very abundant on the coasts of Greenland, Iceland, Newfoundland, and Alaska. It is used as bait for cod. Similar to anchovies, smelt, or herring. [6]

carbon cycle: Carbon circulating through the biosphere, geosphere, atmosphere, and hydrosphere. Among the most complex of biogeochemical cycles. [2]

carbon sequestration: The long-term storage of carbon in soil (by incorporating it into biomass), underground, or in the ocean, thus reducing atmospheric levels of carbon dioxide. [2]

carbon sink: Removes carbon from the atmosphere. Using vegetation to store carbon dioxide in woods, roots, leaves, and starches, and to release oxygen. Fossil fuels are a carbon sink, but humans release these voluntarily. [2]

caribou: Seasonally migrating reindeer native to North America. Many Native communities are dependent on the caribou for their subsistence. [18]

Carolina bay: Oval-shaped depressions along the Atlantic coast. Vary from a few acres to square miles. Trend northwest to southeast and appear in groups. Vary between marsh and lake-like. Named for bay trees often found in the bays. [9]

carpetbagger: A Northerner who relocated to the South for financial or political advantage after the Civil War. [9]

carrying capacity: The number of people that an area can support given the quality of the natural environment and the level of technology of the population. [4]

center of population: Demographic term; calculated by finding the balance point for population, where an equal number live north-south-east-west of the given point. The center of population has steadily been moving southwest with each census. [4]

center pivot irrigation (CPI): A self-propelled irrigation method that uses sprinkler systems mounted on wheels. CPI irrigates a circular area and is more water efficient than older irrigation, but is dependent on fossil fuel to run the water pumps. [14]

chain migration: An individual or small group migration to foreign soil, influencing others, especially family and friends, to migrate with them in a channelized diffusion of movement. [11]

chaparral ecosystem: A Mediterranean natural plant community featuring the drought-hardy woody chaparral shrub. The ecosystem is subject to frequent intense wildfires. [19]

Chinese Exclusion Act (1882): Policy of prohibiting immigration of Chinese laborers to the United States. From the time of the U.S. acquisition of California in 1848, there had been a large influx of Chinese laborers to the Pacific coast. They were encouraged to immigrate because of the need for cheap labor and were employed largely in the building of transcontinental railroads. [19]

chinook (*Salishan language,* "snow eater"): A strong, dry, warm wind that blows from the Rocky Mountains onto the Great Plains, usually in winter and spring. Chinooks can result in temperature increases of 35°F to 40°F in fifteen minutes. [14]

Clean Water Act (CWA) (1972): The basic federal statute governing all aspects of water quality protection in the United States. [8]

clear-cut: A forest harvesting technique that cuts all trees in an area at one time. [17]

climate change: Changes in long-term trends in the average climate, such as changes in average temperatures. Most scientists today agree that we are in a period of climate change and that it is human induced. [2]

closed ecosystem: An ecosystem that does not rely on exchange of matter outside its system to exist. The waste products of one species are used by another, so there is no waste or pollution. Used to define Earth itself or smaller isolated units, such as Hawai`i. [20]

coalbed methane (CBM): Natural gas that lies trapped in coal seams at shallow depths. [14]

coastal plain: Low areas of the Earth that have been eroded nearly level or formed of flat-lying sediments. In the United States, located along the Atlantic Ocean and Gulf of Mexico. [9]

cod (or **codfish**): Any of various marine fishes of the family *Gadidae*, especially *Gadus morhua*, an important food fish of northern Atlantic waters, especially Newfoundland Grand Banks, until 1992 when the fishery was closed. [6]

colonia (*Sp.* "community"): A residential area in Texas along the border region that often lacks infrastructure such as potable water, sewers, or electricity. [11]

Colorado River Compact (1922): Agreement among the states in the Colorado River Basin, allocating the river waters between the states. [16]

Columbia Basin Project: A 1930s program to irrigate dryland-farming areas of the Columbia Basin. The centerpiece was Grand Coulee Dam. [16]

community-supported agriculture (CSA): A way for the public to create a relationship with a farm and receive a weekly basket of produce. [13]

concentrated animal feeding operations (CAFOs): A farm housing at least one thousand animal units. [9]

Confederation: (1) The union of the British North American colonies of New Brunswick, Nova Scotia, Quebec, and Ontario (Province of Canada), brought about July 1, 1867, under the name Dominion of Canada. (2) The federal union of all the Canadian provinces and territories, the most recent addition being Newfoundland in 1949. [5]

Conservation Reserve Program (CRP): A U.S. Department of Agriculture program that provides agricultural producers with annual rental payments and cost-share assistance for establishing protective cover on suitable farm property to protect and improve air, water, soil quality, and wildlife habitat. "Suitable property" is usually defined as being marginal for agricultural crops, and/or erodible. [14]

containerization: Standard-sized (20 ft. / 40 ft.), reusable receptacles that can accommodate smaller cartons or cases in a single shipment, designed for efficient handling of cargo. Containerization has become the dominant mode of shipping and trucking in the past thirty years. Shipping containers can be transferred to trucks without reloading, be simply placed on trucks, and moved to their next destination. [19]

continental climate: Inland areas have greater temperature extremes. Coastal regions have fewer extremes. Water holds warmth, while land loses warmth more quickly. [2]

continental divide: A drainage divide on a continent where each side of the divide drains into a different ocean or sea; specifically, the crest of the Rocky Mountains, which divides the rivers of North America into those that flow east and those that flow west. [15]

continental glaciation: An ice sheet covering a large part of a continent. [2]

continental shelf: The part of the sea floor that slopes gently down from the continents, the shallowest part of the ocean. [2]

continental slope: The connection between the continental shelf and the ocean bottom or abyss. The slope is usually marked by a steep drop-off. The slope is part of the continent and therefore marks the continental margin. [2]

contract farmer: A farmer who contracts with a vertically integrated conglomerate to grow or produce a crop or livestock to the company's specifications. The farmer owns the land and livestock buildings, but the company owns the crops or animals and provides all feed or nutrients. [9]

conurbation: An extensive urban area formed when two or more cities, originally separate, coalesce to form a continuous metropolitan region. The largest conurbation in the United States is the Boston–Washington, D.C., corridor. [4]

coquina: A soft limestone composed of fragments of shell and coral, found especially in Florida. Used as a vernacular building stone. [10]

cordillera: An extensive chain of mountains or mountain ranges, especially the principal mountain system of a continent, often referring to the system of mountain chains near the border of a continent. For example, the western cordillera within the United States includes the Rocky Mountains, Sierra Nevada, and the Cascade ranges. [15]

Corridor: The densely populated and industrialized areas of Ontario and Quebec, aka Inner Canada. [5]

cotton gin: Patented in 1784 by Eli Whitney; removed seeds from the blossoms. It sparked an explosion in Southern cotton production and fostered the associated expansion of racial slavery throughout the region. [9]

coulee: Large, abandoned meltwater channels. A gorge formed by glacial meltwaters or a stream that is now dry. A term primarily used in the northwestern United States. [16]

cove: Small, oval-shaped, smooth-floor valley in a woodland area. Used especially in the Appalachians. [8]

cracker: A poor white person who settled in the southern uplands. Often used in a disparaging way, but sometimes with pride, as in the excellent *Ecology of a Cracker Childhood* by Janisse Ray. [9]

cradle to cradle (C2C): A design framework that incorporates biomimicry and seeks to create efficient and waste-free production techniques; a circular path in which goods are built using nature's processes and nutrients are continually recirculated in the production cycle. [3]

cradle to grave (C2G): A design framework in which goods create waste and pollution; a linear path in which goods are produced and disposed of after a single use. [3]

craton: The continental core. The segment of the Earth's continents that have remained tectonically stable and relatively earthquake-free for a vast period of time. Composed of the continental shield and the surrounding continental platform. [2]

Creole: A language, culture, and group of people located in the New Orleans area. Creoles may be a mixture of Spanish, French, and African American blood. [11]

Crown Land: In Canada, areas that belong to the Crown, similar to government-owned lands in the United States. About 89 percent of all land in Canada is Crown Land, which is divided between federal and provincial. [5]

Crow Rate: A subsidy offered to the Canadian Pacific Railway by the Canadian government. It enabled the railroad to expand westward and thereby reduced the transportation costs for prairie farmers. [14]

cuesta: A ridge bounded by a gentle slope on one side and an escarpment on the other. [11]

cultural adaptation: Changing one's culture is response to a new environment. [1]

cultural hearth: A nuclear area within which an advanced and distinctive set of culture traits, ideas, and technologies develops and from which there is diffusion of those characteristics and the cultural landscape features they imply. The area from which the culture of a group diffused. Source areas from which radiated ideas and innovations that changed the world beyond. [5]

cultural preadaptation: Possessing adaptive traits prior to migration. Said of Ukrainian immigrants from the steppes who migrated to the plains and prairies. They were culturally preadapted to the harsh climate regimes and therefore able to survive. [6]

cutover: Area cleared of trees, especially those that bear valuable lumber. An area for forest regeneration. [17]

death rate: The ratio of total deaths to total population over a specified period of time. [4]

delta: A body of alluvium, nearly flat and fan-shaped (where the Greek letter delta Δ originates), at the mouth of a river where it enters a body of water. The alluvium is formed from deposited sediment carried by the body of water. Two major deltas in the United States are the Mississippi and Sacramento–San Joaquin deltas. [11]

demographic process: Changes in the size of a population through births, deaths, and migration. [4]

demographic transition: A model that describes population change over time. It describes how economic development and industrialization lead to low birth and death rates and thus low population growth. It is based on an interpretation (begun in 1929 by the American demographer Warren Thompson) of the observed changes, or transitions, in birth and death rates in industrialized societies over the past two hundred years or so. [4]

Dene: The Athabaskan-speaking peoples of northwest Canada and inland Alaska, considered as a group. [18]

desalination: Removing the salts from water to make it drinkable. [19]

dome mountain: Formed when tectonic forces lift the Earth's crust into a broad bulge or dome. The dome is raised above its surroundings, so erosion will occur, and as a result of erosion, peaks and valleys are formed. For example, the Black Hills in South Dakota. [2]

Dominion Lands Act: The Canadian homesteader act of 1872, meant to bring farmers onto the Canadian prairie. [14]

doubling time: The amount of time for a population to double, based on annual growth rate. [4]

downcycle: The process in which goods or waste materials are converted to products of lesser quality than the original source. [3]

drainage basin: The area of land drained by a river and its tributaries to a common outlet. [2]

drowned rivers: Ancient river mouths and valleys resulting from rising sea level over the past twelve thousand years. Found on the coastal plains of continents. [7]

dryland farming: Farming without irrigation, found in semiarid grassland areas. Dryland farming results in unpredictable crop and livestock production. Uses drought-tolerant crops. For example, the growing of sorghum in the Great Plains. [14]

Dust Bowl: The region in the south central United States that suffered ecological devastation from dust storms in the 1930s. The problem began during World War I, when farmers were encouraged to grow more wheat in areas previously used for grazing. When livestock returned, they pulverized the earth, and strong winds in the "dirty thirties" blew huge clouds that ruined crops and uprooted people. Creation of the Soil Conservation Service, which incorporated methods of erosion prevention, and the return of normal precipitation patterns ended the Dust Bowl by 1940. [14]

eco-industry: Companies providing goods and services for environmental protection. A more exacting definition: a cradle-to-cradle closed-loop industrial park linked to minimize its ecological footprint, in which the waste of one industry is the resource for another. [8]

ecological balance: A state of dynamic equilibrium within a community of organisms in which genetic, species, and ecosystem diversity remain relatively stable, subject to gradual changes through natural succession. [16]

ecological footprint: A measure of human demand on the Earth's ecosystems and natural resources. [3]

ecology: The scientific study of relations of living organisms with each other and their physical surroundings. [1]

ecoregion (or **bioregion**): A relatively large unit of land and water defined by the influences of shared climate and geology, the main factors determining the distribution of plants and animals in the area. [1]

ecosystem (or **ecological system**): An interconnected geographic area including all the living organisms (people, plants, animals, and microorganisms), their physical surroundings (such as soil, water, and air), and the natural cycles that sustain them. Ecosystems can be small scale (a small area in detail such as a single stand of aspen) or large scale (a large area such as an entire watershed including hundreds of forest stands across many different ownerships). [1]

ecotone: A transition zone between two ecosystems. [1]

embayment: A coastline recess forming a sediment-filled, low-lying basin or bay. The most prevalent U.S. embayment is the Mississippi Embayment, which reaches to Cairo, Illinois. [11]

entrepôt: A place where goods are stored or deposited and from which they are distributed. [19]

environmental justice: When poor communities are given equal protection from industrial and waste facilities. [11]

equalization payment: In Canada, a partial redistribution of wealth from the wealthier provinces to the less wealthy. In the past, Ontario was a wealthy province, but the lagging economy made Ontario in 2010 a "have-not" province, which received an equalization payment, while Newfoundland became for the first time a "have" province, which contributed to equalization. [5]

erosion: The wearing away of land by water, wind, waves, ice, and other agents. [2]

escarpment: A long cliff or steep slope separating two comparatively level or more gently sloping surfaces and resulting from erosion or faulting. [5]

estuary: A semi-enclosed coastal body of water where seawater and fresh water mix; a drowned river mouth. Estuaries and tidal creeks fluctuate and are nutrient-rich ecosystems. [11]

ethanol: A colorless volatile flammable liquid, C_2H_5OH, synthesized or obtained by fermentation of sugars and starches. In the United States, ethanol is created largely from corn; however, in Brazil sugar cane is the source of ethanol. [13]

eutrophication: Waters rich in organic nutrients in which algae proliferate. Leads to extinction of other organisms and possible ecosystem collapse. [11]

Exclusive Economic Zone (EEZ): A maritime zone beyond and adjacent to the territorial sea, the maximum being two hundred nautical miles from land. The coastal state has sovereign rights for the purpose of exploring, exploiting, conserving, and managing natural resources, both living and nonliving, of the seabed, subsoil, and the subjacent waters, and with regard to other activities, for the economic exploitation and exploration of the zone. The previous limit was twelve miles, but in the 1970s, most of the major fishing nations agreed to adopt a two-hundred-mile economic zone in order to preserve fish stocks, which even then were in serious decline. Fishing on the high seas was limited to a very few nations, primarily the former Soviet Union and Japan. Unfortunately, the two-hundred-mile limit has not had the desired effect; the Grand Banks were closed in 1992 and remain closed in 2011. [6]

Exodusters (exodus + dust as in Dust Bowl): Former slaves who fled the South for Kansas in 1879. They chose Kansas because it was the home of abolitionist John Brown, and the state was reputed to be progressive and tolerant. Several all-black towns, such as Nicodemus, still exist in the state. [14]

exotic stream: In the drier plateau section of the United States, a stream that carries water, something otherwise unknown—or exotic—into this arid environment. [16]

external costs (or **negative externalities**): Disadvantageous impacts paid for by the consumer for the actions of firms and individuals. For example, the environmental and social costs of the current economic system, where these external costs are passed on to the consumer. [1]

factory trawler (or freezer trawler): A type of ocean ship from which fish are caught, then processed, frozen, and stored on board. [6]

fall foliage season: Occurs in states famous for their flaming foliage during autumn. Now a part of an expanding tourist season, as people book hotels and travel tours to observe the changing leaves of fall. Websites abound telling when it is at its peak in areas throughout the United States. [6]

fall line: The line in the United States along which the coastal plain meets the harder rock piedmont. The drop from the rock to the sandy coastal plain is marked by waterfalls and rapids. [7]

family farm: Independently operated enterprise providing the main source of income for the family. Family farms once served as the social and economic foundation for rural communities. They provided both social capital and clientele for local businesses. Family farms declined steeply in the late twentieth century due to technologic change, low commodity prices, vertical integration, and globalization. [13]

fault: A feature of the Earth's crust created by the breaking and movement of rock layers below the surface. [2]

fault-block mountain: Mountain created either by the uplift or subsidence of land between faults. The land may be uplifted on one side and depressed on the other, resulting in a tilted fault block. For example, in the United States, the Sierra Nevada and the Basin and Range. [2]

feedback loop: A complex system interaction that occurs when a signal leaves one component (output) and returns to the original component (input) after passing through one or more other components in the system. The current climatic change is accelerating (positive or reinforcing feedback) because of feedback between carbon dioxide concentrations and methane production, and warming caused by reduced albedo in polar regions. An example of a balancing or negative feedback is a steady relationship between predator and prey without invasive species accounted for. [2]

fish farm: A commercial facility in which fish are raised for food. [17]

fish ladder: A series of shallow steps down which water is allowed to flow; designed to permit salmon to circumvent artificial barriers such as power dams as the salmon swim upstream to spawn. [17]

Five Civilized Tribes: Five Native nations in the southeastern United States (Cherokee, Chickasaw, Choctaw, Creek, and Seminole) considered civilized because of their advanced government and education. Regardless, when white settlers favored their native lands, they were relocated to Oklahoma territory. [13]

fjord: A long, narrow arm of the sea resulting from the drowning of a glaciated valley. [2]

flake: A frame or platform for drying fish or produce. Used in Newfoundland to dry cod. [6]

flash flood: A sudden local flood due to heavy rain, especially in desert areas. [16]

flatwoods: A pine forest wetland that is drier than a pocosin. Found along the southeastern coastal plain. [11]

folded mountain: The most common type of mountain. Created by tectonic plates pushing against each other, which creates intense pressure. Therefore, the only direction for these mountains to move is up. When two plates move away from each other, they create a rift valley in between them. Sometimes, if plates collide, one plate will force the other under itself and created a folded mountain. Folded mountains are mainly composed of limestone and shale. For example, the Appalachians in the United States. [2]

fortress living: Living isolated from others in a socioeconomically segregated, gated community. [19]

francophone: A French-speaking person, especially in a region where two or more languages are spoken. Very common term in Quebec. (See **anglophone**.) [4]

Frontier Thesis (or the Turner thesis): Famous thesis about settlement of the American West, delivered on July 12, 1893, at the annual meeting of the American Historical Association, by Frederick Jackson Turner. He first presented his thesis in the now famous paper "The Significance of the Frontier in American History." The Turner thesis was this: The settlement of the West by white people—"the existence of an area of free land, its continuous recession, and the advance of American settlement westward"—was the central story of American history. [14]

frost-freeze cycles: Swelling and shrinking of ground due to changes in temperature over the year. [14]

Gadsden Purchase (1853): A purchase from Mexico to settle a question as to the limits of the Mexican Cession of 1848. James Gadsden negotiated for the acquisition of 19 million acres of additional land and the settlement of the claims. The territory acquired lies in the states of Arizona and New Mexico and was purchased with the intent of building a southern transcontinental rail line through the Gila River tributary watershed. [16]

Geechee: An African American on the Sea Islands of Georgia who speaks Gullah. (See **Gullah**.) [9]

General Agreement on Tariffs and Trade (GATT) (1947): Trade agreement by the United Nations to facilitate international trade. Precursor to the World Trade Organization (WTO). [5]

genetically modified organism (GMO): An organism whose genetic material has been deliberately altered. [13]

geothermal spring: A spring heated by thermal vents in the Earth's crust. [12]

ghost town: A town that once flourished but is deserted today, usually because of depletion of a nearby resource such as gold or silver. [15]

glacial drift: Mass of rocks and finely ground material carried by a glacier, then deposited when the ice melted. [2]

glacial erratic: A rock transported by a glacier or glacial event that deviates from the size and composition of the surrounding landscape. [16]

glacier: A large mass of snow that accumulates and becomes granular and compact through settling and recrystallization. A thick mass of ice moving slowly across the Earth's surface. [2]

global warming: The increase in average Earth temperature, based on greenhouse gas emissions, and at least partially human induced. This term is now replaced by climate change because of irregular temperature fluctuations over the short term. Long-term indications now show an overall global warming. [2]

Golden Horseshoe: Densely populated and industrialized region of Ontario, centered on the west end of Lake Ontario. [5]

Gold Rush: The discovery of gold in California in 1848 (the "gold standard" for this term). However, there have been many gold rushes, mostly notably in the Klondike, the Yukon, and Alaska. [19]

grass banking: Mutually beneficial grazing management involving rotational grazing, in order to protect and restore grasslands. [16]

grassland: Land dominated by grasses, rather than trees or shrubs; prairie. [14]

Great Mahele: Land redistribution in Hawai`i in the 1830s that allowed commoners to hold private title to land. [20]

Great Migration: The movement of millions of African Americans from 1910 to 1970 from the South to the Northeast and Midwest. They were escaping Jim Crow racism and pursuing jobs in the manufacturing industries. [11]

greenhouse gas (GHG): Gases that contribute to the greenhouse effect by absorbing infrared radiation produced by solar warming of the Earth's surface. Major GHGs include carbon dioxide (CO_2), methane (CH_4), nitrous oxide (NO_2), and water vapor. Elevated levels of GHGs have been observed in the recent past and are related, at least in part, to human activities such as burning fossil fuels. [2]

Green Mountain Boys: Vermont's militia during the period of the Vermont Republic. Led by Ethan Allen, the group protected their land titles when given to New York. [6]

Green Revolution: In the 1960s, an effort to ostensibly end world hunger and feed a rapidly growing world population. The Rockefeller Foundation put one of their scientists, Norman Borlaug, to work on ways to increase the yield of food grains. [13]

groundwater: Fresh water found beneath the Earth's surface and beyond the root zone in tiny spaces between rock and soil. [2]

Gullah: A group of isolated African Americans brought over as slaves who were located on the Sea Islands off South Carolina. They developed their own form of English dialect, which has been disparaged. [9]

habitant (*Fr.*): An early inhabitant of French Canada, who worked the land as a renter for the seigneur. [5]

haboob: An intense dust storm, with winds up to thirty miles per hour, which often precedes summer monsoon rains in the Sonoran Desert. [16]

hammock: A hardwood- and evergreen-forested area rising slightly above a flat plain. Tropical hammocks are found in southern Florida. [10]

hatchery: A place where eggs (especially fish eggs) are hatched under artificial conditions. [17]

Hawai`i Land Reform Act (1967): A law that allowed lessees to buy fee interest in leased land formerly held by trusts. [20]

headwater stream: Smallest streams for river systems, often ephemeral. [8]

hillbilly: A term used disparagingly of a backwoods person, especially in the Ozarks or Appalachia. [12]

Hispanic: A U.S. citizen or resident of Latin American or Spanish descent. Though often used interchangeably in American English, *Hispanic* and *Latino* are not identical terms, and in certain contexts the choice between them can be significant. [19]

hogback: A sharp-crested ridge protruding from the surrounding area. [15]

holistic system: The process of how things influence one another within a whole. Looking at nature as an interconnected whole of interrelated ecosystems, which include humans as part of the biotic life community. [1]

homeless: Individuals who lack a fixed, regular, and adequate nighttime residence. [19]

Homestead Act (An Act to Secure Homesteads to Actual Settlers on the Public Domain): A law passed in 1862 to encourage settlers to move west to settle less desirable land. It became law on January 1, 1863, and allowed anyone to file for a quarter-section of free land (160 acres). The land was "proved up" and yours at the end of five years, if you had built a house on it, farmed a portion, and lived there. [14]

hot spot: An area where molten material from the Earth's interior rises through the crust. A volcanic center, 60 to 120 miles (100 to 200 km) across and persistent for at least a few tens of millions of years, that is thought to be the surface expression of a persistent rising plume of hot mantle material. [15]

hurricane: A severe tropical cyclone originating in the equatorial regions of the Atlantic Ocean, the Caribbean Sea, or eastern regions of the Pacific Ocean, traveling north, northwest, or northeast from its point of origin, and involving strong winds and heavy rains. [11]

Hutterites: Members of an Anabaptist sect originating in Moravia and now living communally in the prairies of Canada and the northwest United States. [14]

hydrocarbon: A mixture of hydrogen and carbon atoms in a variety of forms, which forms natural gas, oil, or coal in multiple levels of complexity and combinations. Burning hydrocarbons is the main source of electrical energy and heat. [11]

hypoxia (literally, "low oxygen"): Condition created when coastal waters or estuaries become polluted by nutrient overload, creating a lack of oxygen. The most direct result is fish kills, which lead to habitat loss and loss of ecological biodiversity. Hypoxia is evident throughout the coastal water of the United States, for example, Tampa Bay and the Chesapeake, but the largest zone is spring and summer in the Gulf of Mexico west of the mouth of the Mississippi River. [11]

ice age: A time of widespread glaciation. (See **Pleistocene**.) [2]

ice road: Canadian winter road made of frozen water over permafrost. Used to haul supplies to far northern areas. [18]

imagineer: A word formed by Disney, combining *imagine* and *engineering*. Imagineers were the creative force behind the building of the Disney theme parks. [10]

Indian Removal Act (1830): Legislation that forced Native Americans to relinquish their lands east of the Mississippi in exchange for land in Oklahoma, where they were forced to move. President Andrew Jackson pushed this act through, after years of divesting Native Americans of their land. [13]

industrial ecology: The network of all industrial processes as they may interact and live off each other, not only in the economic sense, but also in the sense of direct use of each other's material and energy wastes. [9]

informal economy: Economic activity that is neither taxed nor monitored by the government. Typical in developing economies but also prevalent in portions of the U.S. economy with substantial numbers of immigrants. [19]

Inner Canada: The densely populated and industrialized areas of Ontario and Quebec, aka The Corridor. [5]

Inuit: Native people of Arctic Alaska and Canada. Once called Eskimos ("eaters of raw flesh") by the nearby Algonquian tribes; this term is considered offensive. [18]

island arc: A chain of volcanic islands or mountains formed by plate tectonics, as an oceanic tectonic plate subducts under another tectonic plate along an oceanic trench. The Aleutian Islands are an island arc. [18]

isostatic rebound: The upward movement of the Earth's crust following isostatic depression (common after glaciation). [18]

James Bay and Northern Quebec Agreement (1975): Agreement with First Nations that cleared the way for the construction of the James Bay hydroelectric project in exchange for Cree hunting, fishing, and compensation. [18]

Jim Crow laws: Statutes enacted by Southern states and municipalities, beginning in the 1880s, that legalized segregation between blacks and whites. After years of legal suits, sit-ins, and boycotts, the Civil Rights Act of 1964, the Voting Rights Act of 1965, and the Fair Housing Act of 1968 finally ended the legal sanctions to Jim Crow. [11]

karst: A landscape characterized by the presence of caves, springs, sinkholes, and losing streams, created as groundwater dissolves soluble rock such as limestone or dolomite. [2]

kettle: A steep-sided, bowl-shaped depression commonly without surface drainage; usually formed by a large detached block of stagnant ice that had been partially or wholly buried in the drift. A depression formed as buried ice melted and overlying sediments collapsed. [13]

keystone species: A species that has a major influence on the structure of an ecosystem. When a keystone species is threatened, the entire ecosystem may collapse. Prairie dogs are a keystone species in the prairies. Animals depend on the prairie dogs as a food source or for their habitat. Salmon are a keystone species in coastal ecosystems. [17]

kudzu: A vine native to China and Japan but imported into the United States; originally planted for decoration, for forage, or as a ground cover to control erosion. It now grows wild in many parts of the southeastern United States. Known as "the plant that ate the South." [9]

Kyoto Protocol: An amendment to the international treaty on climate change, assigning mandatory targets for the reduction of greenhouse gas emissions to signatory nations. Canada and the European Union are included in the more than 140 member countries. The United States has not signed. [3]

lagoon: An excavated, diked, or walled structure or combination of structures designed for the treatment or storage of manure. In many states, lagoons must be designed and constructed in compliance with Natural Resources Conservation Service specifications. [9]

lahar: Landslide or mudflow of volcanic fragments down a volcano. Lahars have occurred in the Puget Sound area. [17]

lake effect: The effect of any lake, especially the Great Lakes, in modifying the weather in nearby areas. During the winter, lake effect causes heavy snowfall on the leeward side of the lake. During the growing season, lake effect extends the season, making it ideal for growing crops not usually associated with the area, such as on the east side of Lake Michigan or the east side of Lake Ontario, or between Lakes Ontario and Erie. [13]

Land Ordinance of 1785: Establishment of a system for surveying and subdividing public land outside the states, while raising money for the federal government after the Revolutionary War. Passed by the Congress of the Articles of Confederation, the statute provided for the surveying of blocks of land thirty-six square miles each, to be known as townships. Each township was to set aside one section for public education and schools, with each section containing 640 acres. [13]

land trust: Land sold to conservation groups to keep it preserved in its present use. Grazing land and farmland in danger of development are often preserved as land trusts. [15]

la raza (*Sp.*, "the race"): Refers to the Latino presence in the United States and working to protect and preserve the culture. Often used in the expression *Viva la raza* ("Long live the race"), most specifically the re-takeover of southwestern states. [19]

Latino: Refers more exclusively to persons or communities of Latin American origin. (See **Hispanic**.) [19]

Law of the Indies: Spanish guidelines set by the King of Spain to instruct colonists how to design newly settled towns. Part of the design was a layout with a central plaza. [15]

Leadership in Energy and Environmental Design (LEED): A green building rating system. [3]

levee: A ridge of earth along a river that hinders flooding. [11]

lichen: Organism consisting of a symbiotic joining of a species of fungi and a species of algae. [18]

life cycle assessment: Analysis of the environmental impacts of a good or service. Identifies the energy, material, and waste flows of a product. [3]

lignite: Low-grade coal. Brown coal. Lithified accumulations of organic debris. [8]

limestone: Sedimentary rock composed of carbonate minerals, especially calcium carbonate. Limestone is formed from deposition of shells, coral, and other marine organisms that accumulated on shallow sea floors. [12]

liquefaction: The transformation of soil from a solid state to a liquefied state due to pressure and stress. Said of soil in earthquake-prone areas with deep sediment and little surface bedrock. [19]

locks: A part of a waterway enclosed by gates, used to raise or lower boats from one water level to another. [5]

loess: Glacial material transported and deposited by wind, consisting primarily of silt-size particles. [13]

long lot: Land division system giving access to a transportation artery (river or road) for a maximum number of farms while still living in a linear neighborhood village. The early French government tried to transplant a vestigial form of feudalism, the seigneurial system, to its possessions in Canada. The long-lot system of land division associated with seigneuries remains vividly imprinted on the landscapes of North America that were settled by French-speaking people. Long lots can be found in many parts of Canada, where the French influence is strong, and near Detroit (for the same reason). [5]

losing stream: A surface stream that loses water to the subsurface through bedrock openings. Often found in karst topography or arid areas. [12]

Lower Canada: The southern, mainly French-speaking portion of Quebec from 1791 until 1841, when it was reunited with Upper Quebec to form the present-day province of Quebec. [5]

Loyalist: One who maintains loyalty to an established government, political party, or sovereign, especially during war or revolutionary change. Said of those who remained loyal to Britain during the American Revolution, many of whom moved to Canada. [5]

Mackenzie Valley Pipeline: Project in the Northwest Territories that calls for construction of a seven-hundred-mile pipeline and gas-gathering system for delivery to Alberta and the United States. Proposed in the 1970s, it was scrapped after the Berger Inquiry but resurrected in 2004. The pipeline will be the first to include Aborigines as major owners. [18]

Main Street: The Corridor of Canada in the densely populated St Lawrence Valley of Quebec and Great Lakes of Ontario. [5]

maitres chez nous (*Fr.*): "Masters of our own house." Rallying cry in Quebec during the Quiet Revolution, as the Québécois attempted to master their own economic destiny. [5]

Malthusian: Relating to the ideas of Thomas Malthus on population. His theory was that population tends to increase geometrically and therefore faster than the increase in subsistence, which increases arithmetically. He postulated that population must be checked by moral restraint or else disaster would inevitably result. (See **neo-Malthusian**.) [4]

managed use: Organized handling of forest property to provide optimum use. However, *optimum* can be defined by whoever is using the term, an environmentalist or a logger, for example. [17]

mangrove: A type of exposed-root tree or shrub that grows in tidal estuaries or salt marshes. [10]

Manifest Destiny: The nineteenth-century doctrine that the United States had the right and duty to expand throughout the North American continent. This view justified Jefferson's Louisiana Purchase from France, the claim to thousands of square miles in the heart of the continent that were inhabited solely by Indian nations. He was thus planting the American way of life on the continent. [16]

Mardi Gras (*Fr.*, "Fat Tuesday"): The last day before Lent, when many foods are given up for the season. Celebrated in many southern cities, especially New Orleans and other cities in Louisiana. [11]

marine climate: A climate strongly influenced by an oceanic environment, found on islands and the windward shores of continents. Characterized by small daily and yearly temperature ranges and high relative humidity. [17]

maritime influence: The movement onshore of prevailing westerly wind systems from the ocean, which moderates summer and winter temperature extremes. [6]

maroon: Escaped slave who hid out in the Dismal Swamp area of Albemarle and Chesapeake bays. [9]

marsh: A fresh, brackish, or saltwater wetland, vegetated mostly by herbaceous plants that grow up out of the water (emergent plants). Marshes are frequently or continually flooded and are often found at the edges of rivers, creeks, ponds, and lakes, in isolated depressions, and along the Atlantic, Pacific, and Gulf coasts. [2]

maximum sustainable yield: The largest average catch or yield that can continuously be taken from a stock under existing environmental conditions. [6]

meander: A curve or loop in a river. There is a relationship between the amount of meander and the gradient of a river; the less steep the more meander. But gradient is not the only variable in the amount of meanders in a river. [14]

Mediterranean climate: A climate characterized by moist, mild winters and hot, dry summers. [2]

Megalopolis: The region that contains the coastal area between Boston and Washington, D.C., so named by Jean Gottman in the 1950s. The most densely populated area in America, containing about 17 percent of the total population. [7]

melting pot: A place where immigrants of different cultures or races form an integrated society by assimilating socially. [11]

mesa (*Sp.*, "table"): An isolated, relatively flat-topped natural elevation, usually more extensive than a butte and less extensive than a plateau. [16]

Métis: A general term that refers to Canadians descended from North American Indians and Europeans; descendants of French explorers, fur traders, and settlers, and native North American peoples. [14]

Mexican Cession of 1848: Stemming from the Treaty of Guadalupe. The United States acquired a large tract of land, including what is now California, Nevada, Utah, most of Arizona, and parts of New Mexico, Colorado, and Wyoming. [16]

migration: Leaving one's native country to settle in another land. [4]

milkshed: A region producing milk for a specific community. Usually located near the community, due to the perishable nature of milk. [6]

Mining Law of 1872: Federal law in the United States that authorizes mining for minerals on publicly held land. [15]

mission: One of three settlement types used by the Spanish to settle California. The missions were built between 1769 and 1833, and they are some of the oldest buildings in California. The mission was the religious outpost, used to raise agricultural goods. (See also **presidio** and **pueblo**.) [19]

monadnock: An isolated hill or mountain of resistant rock rising above eroded lowlands. [6]

moonshine: Illegally distilled liquor, especially in Appalachia and the American South. Named because of the time of day the spirits were distilled and transported. [8]

moraine: A ridge of rocks, gravel, and sand deposited along the margins of a glacier or ice sheet. [2]

mountaintop removal (MTR): Strip-mining on steroids; removal of large portions of mountains to access coal layers beneath the overburden. Destroys communities, ecosystems, and causes flooding and loss of biodiversity. [8]

multiculturalism: A philosophy that recognizes a variety of cultural and ethnic backgrounds. [4]

muskeg: A large expanse of permafrost peatlands or bogs and fens filling in with vegetation, and sometimes containing stunted trees, especially black spruce. Peatlands are common to Canada, Alaska, and Siberia. Minnesota has the largest peatland areas in the lower forty-eight states, located in the north central part of the state. [18]

National Policy: Canadian economic program since 1879, based on protectionist high tariffs on manufactured goods and opposed to free trade. [5]

natural capital: Plants, animals, and minerals extracted as a means of production or provider of ecosystem services. It is the extension of environmental costs to economic costs. [3]

natural increase: Growth in population by births over deaths. The difference between the number of persons added due to births over a period of time, minus the number of persons who die. Expressed as increase or decrease per 1,000: ([births – deaths] / population) × 1,000. [4]

neo-Malthusian: One who believes in the ideas of Malthus, especially in relation to population control. Some neo-Malthusians are Paul and Anne Ehrlich, Garrett Hardin, and the Club of Rome think tank. [4]

New Homestead Act: Act being considered by Congress to repopulate the dying towns of the Great Plains. The bill focuses on small businesses and entrepreneurs, and it provides incentives such as free land, tax credits, and venture capital. [14]

New South: The abolition of slavery failed to provide African Americans with political or economic equality, and it took a long, concerted effort to end segregation. The New South has evolved into a manufacturing region, and high-rise buildings crowd the skylines of such cities as Atlanta and Little Rock. [9]

new urbanism: A return to traditional neighborhood design with walkable cities, deemphasizing cars and building community. Often with houses based on 1920–1930 designs. For example, Celebration, Florida. [10]

nonpoint source pollution: Pollution from diffuse sources; not from a single identifiable source. [3]

nonrenewable resource: A natural resource that cannot be renewed as quickly as it is consumed. Many minerals are non-renewable, but the resources most commonly referred to in this regard are fossil fuels. [3]

North American Free Trade Agreement (NAFTA): Formed in January 1994, between Canada, the United States, and Mexico. The world's largest free trade area, whose major objective is to eliminate trade barriers. [5]

North Atlantic Ocean Conveyor: A marine circular flow that is brought about by changes in seawater density. Increased salinity results in increased density, and water sinks. When water has decreased salinity, the density falls and can cause climatic changes. [6]

oil sands: Bituminous or tar sands that are a mixture of sand, water, and extremely heavy crude oil. Oil sands in Alberta, Canada, are among the world's largest. [18]

old growth: Mature ecosystem of forest with the associated plants and animals. [17]

open pit mine: A type of mine that uncovers ore by digging a large hole. The largest active open pit mine is the Bingham Canyon Mine near Salt Lake City. [16]

open-range ranching: A cattle- or sheep-ranching area characterized by a general absence of fences. [14]

orographic precipitation: Patterns that result when moist air encounters a topographic barrier and is forced to rise over it; for example, the increase in precipitation with elevation on the windward slopes of a mountain range and the rain shadow on the leeward side. The Front Range (leeward) of the Rocky Mountains is affected by orographic precipitation. [2]

Outer Canada: The part of Canada that is not in The Corridor or Inner Canada, therefore anything outside the St. Lawrence and Great Lakes basins. [5]

outport: Small seaside village in Newfoundland that lives off the fisheries. In 1949 there were approximately fourteen hundred of these villages, most with populations under two hundred. In 2005 there were about four hundred outports. [6]

overburden: Material covering a mineral seam or bed that must be removed before the mineral can be removed in strip mining or mountaintop removal. [8]

oxbow lake: A crescent-shaped lake lying alongside a winding river. Created over time as erosion and deposits of soil change the river's course, leaving the lake as a remnant of a meander. [11]

pali: Hawaiian word for steep hills or cliffs. [20]

panhandle: A narrow arm of land attached to a larger region or state. A classic example is the Oklahoma panhandle, which literally looks like a panhandle, versus the panhandle of Nebraska, which is far wider and not as obvious physically. [14]

park: A high-altitude, wide, grassy open valley in the Rocky Mountains, surrounded by wooded mountains. [15]

peat: Any wetland that accumulates partially decayed plant matter. The softest and most polluting coal. [8]

pedalfer: Soil rich in alumina and iron and deficient in carbonates, found in and characteristic of humid regions. [2]

pedocal: A soil of semiarid and arid regions that is rich in calcium carbonate and lime. [2]

Pennsylvania Dutch: A misnomer for Germans (*Deutsch*) who settled inland from Philadelphia. [7]

permafrost: A permanently frozen layer of soil. [18]

petroleum: Unprocessed oil after extraction; a complex mixture of hydrocarbons. [11]

phytoplankton: A microscopic plant that lives in the sea. It is at the bottom of the food chain. [6]

piedmont: An area of plains and low hills at or near the foot of a mountain region. In the United States, the Piedmont is a rolling plateau region inland from the coastal plain, east and south of the Appalachian Mountains. [9]

Pittsburgh Plus: A form of spatial price discrimination based on oligopolistic (monopoly) collusion. The mill price at one location determines the delivered price at all locations, regardless of the location of the plant from which delivery is actually made. (It was used in the marketing of steel in the United States, especially in the Birmingham-Chattanooga-Atlanta triangle.) [8]

plantation agriculture: The system of agricultural production begun with slaves working sugar plantations established in the Eastern Mediterranean by leaders of the Crusades in the twelfth century. In the 1540s, the Portuguese introduced sugar plantations and African slavery to Brazil. By the nineteenth century, plantation slavery had spread throughout the New World. Virtually all plantation societies shared certain characteristics: (1) they relied on forced labor, most often African slaves; (2) they were organized to export a single cash crop (sugar, tobacco, rice, indigo, cotton) to a distant, usually European, market; and (3) although they were organized as capitalist enterprises, their owners sought to control not only the labor of their workforce, but every aspect of their lives. By the time plantation agriculture reached North America in the seventeenth century, most English planters were fully aware of how essential African slave labor had been to every profitable plantation economy in the Caribbean and South American countries. [9]

platform: Sedimentary deposits covering basement rock. [2]

playa: A temporary, high-salinity lake that evaporate quickly and leaves behind an alkali flat or salt pan. [16]

Pleistocene: A period in geologic history (basically the last one million years) when ice sheets covered large sections of the Earth's land surface not now covered by glaciers. [2]

pocosin: A type of wetlands along the Atlantic coastal area. Pocosins are heavily vegetated with shrubs and pine. The transition from pocosins to a drier wetland is called the flatwoods. [2]

poi: Staple of the native Hawaiian diet, made from pounding and cooking taro root. [20]

point source pollution: Pollution from a single identifiable source of air, water, heat, light, or noise. For example, a pipe dumping chemicals into a river. [3]

polder: An area protected from incoming waters. Polders often imply an area at or below sea level surrounded by dikes to prevent the intrusion of river water and/or seawater. Usually there is an extensive drainage system to lower the water table within the polder. Excess water is pumped from the polder. Seen in North America in the Annapolis Valley of Nova Scotia settled by Acadians. [6]

polynucleated city: A metropolitan area with several city cores. A polynucleated city is usually dependent on fossil fuel transport, especially automobiles. [19]

population density: The number of individuals of a species per unit area. It is measured in persons per square mile (or kilometer or hectare), and can be obtained by dividing the number of persons by the land area measured. [4]

population pyramid: A bar chart that shows the age and sex distribution of members of a population. The age divisions are referred to as *cohorts* and may be in five- or ten-year increments, depending on the level of detail desired. By convention, females are always plotted to the right, males to the left. The units across the base may be either absolute numbers or percentage of the population. [4]

portage: Carrying boats and supplies overland between navigable waterways. [13]

postindustrial economy: An economy that gains its basic character from economic activities developed primarily after manufacturing grew to predominance. Most notable would be quaternary economic patterns. [4]

potlatch: A ceremonial feast of the natives of the northwest coast of North America, especially the Kwakiutl, entailing the public distribution of property. The host and his relatives lavishly distributed gifts to invited guests, who were expected to accept any gifts offered with the understanding that at a future time they were to reciprocate in kind. Property was destroyed by its owner in a show of wealth that the guests would later attempt to surpass. Potlatch was outlawed in 1884 due to the destruction of property and reinstated in 1951; by that time, the destruction of property was no longer practiced. [17]

prairie: A region of grassland and fertile soil. The French gave the name to the open space of the Midwest when they first saw it. [13]

Precambrian: The geologic time period preceding 600 million years ago. [2]

precipitation: The discharge of water, in a liquid or solid state, out of the atmosphere, generally onto a land or water surface. It is the common process by which atmospheric water becomes surface or subsurface water; it includes rainfall, snow, hail, and sleet, and is therefore a more general term than rainfall. [2]

presidio (*Sp.*): A military post. One of the three types of settlements in Spanish California. For example, the Presidio of Monterey. (See also **mission, pueblo**.) [19]

primary sector: That portion of a region's economy devoted to the extraction of basic materials (e.g., mining, lumbering, agriculture). [4]

prior appropriation: The commodification of water; when water rights are unconnected to land ownership and can be sold or mortgaged like other property. The first person to use a quantity of water from a water source for a beneficial use has the right to continue to use that quantity of water for that purpose. Subsequent users can use the remaining water for their own beneficial purposes provided that they do not impinge on the rights of previous users. [14]

privateer: A privately owned warship or captain authorized by a country's government. Sir Francis Drake was a privateer for Queen Elizabeth I of England. [6]

pueblo (*Sp.*, "town or village"): A type of Indian village constructed by some tribes in the southwestern United States. A large community dwelling, divided into many rooms, up to five stories high, and usually made of adobe. Pueblos were the original Spanish towns in California, including Los Angeles and San Jose. [19]

pulpwood: Timber ground up and reconstituted into paper, flake board, and other similar products. [11]

push and pull factors: A migration theory that suggests that circumstances at the place of origin (such as poverty and unemployment) repel or push people out of that place to other places that exert a positive attraction or pull (such as a high standard of living or job opportunities). [11]

quality of life: The level of enjoyment, comfort, and health in someone's life. Cities are often ranked as to their "quality of life," based on such factors as environment, income, crime, and traffic. [4]

quaternary sector: That portion of a region's economy devoted to informational and idea-generating activities (e.g., basic research, universities and colleges, and news media). [4]

Québécois nationalism: A "distinct society" maintaining French language and seeking independence from Canada as separatists. Formed after the Quiet Revolution. [5]

Quiet Revolution: Period of Quebec history (1950–1965) of social transformation from a backward, rural, religious (Roman Catholic), and agrarian society to one more modern, urban, industrial, and secular. This led to increased nationalism and even a vote (unsuccessful) on the separation of Quebec from Canada. [5]

"Rain follows the plow": Debunked nineteenth-century theory of climatology that human habitation, in particular agriculture, effected a permanent change in the climate of arid and semiarid regions, making these regions more humid. Popular past belief in the Great Plains. [14]

rain shadow: Reduction of precipitation commonly found on the leeward (downwind) side of a mountain. [2]

rancho: A large grazing farm where horses and cattle are raised; distinguished from *hacienda*, a cultivated farm or plantation. Found in pre-U.S. California. [19]

range war: Conflicts in the western United States between ranchers and farmers, or cattle ranchers and sheep ranchers, that often escalated to violence. In the twenty-first century, the range wars continue, but now are often between ranchers and environmentalist groups. [14]

rang system: Land division; French for range or row of farm lots (concession). Also, a road that runs beside or through a concession. In Quebec, the rows of farm lots were originally along water and, as the waterside filled up, were arranged back from the water in rows, as rang 2, rang 3, and so on. [5]

rate of growth: The percentage of population growth. For example, between 1990 and 2000 Nevada experienced a growth rate of 55 percent; it grew 55 percent from 1990 to 2000. [4]

Reciprocity Treaty of 1854: Agreement between the United States and Canada to reduce tariffs on goods. Also known as the Elgin-Marcy Treaty. Repealed in 1866. [5]

Reconstruction: The period (1865–1877) during which the states that had seceded to the Confederacy were controlled by the federal government before being readmitted to the Union. [9]

redneck: Disparaging term for poor whites who live in the South. A redneck has no need to impress and is seemingly at peace with the world, not a part of the rat race. [9]

reductionist: An approach to understanding the nature of complex things by reducing them to the interactions of their parts, or to simpler or more fundamental components. The belief that a complex system is nothing but the sum of its parts. [1]

redwater rivers: Rivers in the South that are colored due to the red-colored sediment load. [9]

region: A way to interpret Earth's surface. An area having characteristics that distinguish it from other areas. A territory of interest to people, for which one or more distinctive traits or a pattern are used as the basis for its identity. For example, the Midwestern region was largely one that was glaciated during the last ice age, remains flat, and contains many water features. Areas that are adjacent have a different landscape pattern because they were not glaciated or have other characteristics that differ from the Midwest. [1]

renewable resource: A natural resource such as sunlight, wind, tides, and geothermal heat, which are naturally replenished and therefore practically inexhaustible. [3]

replacement level: The mean number of births per woman necessary to assure the long-term replacement of a population for a given mortality level. [4]

resettlement: The period in Newfoundland when three hundred outports were moved or abandoned to larger outports. Lasted from approximately 1950 to 1972, during the premiership of Joey Smallwood. [6]

resource hinterland: A region outside the core that provides the core with resources. Typically not an affluent region in the twentieth century, but possibly more affluent as resource commodities grow rare in the twenty-first century. [6]

rift valley: A valley formed by the sinking of land between two faults. Evident in the Saint Lawrence lowlands, and in the Rio Grande rift valley extending from Mexico into Colorado. [5]

right-to-work state: States where employees can decide whether or not to join a union. There are twenty-two right-to-work states, mostly in the South and West. [9]

riparian rights: The rights of an owner of land bordering on a river, lake, bayou, or sea that relate to water use, ownership of the shore, right of ingress and egress, accretions, and so on. Riparian rights are allocated to all owners of water frontage land. Rooted in English common law and used in the eastern United States. [9]

Royal Proclamation of 1763: In Canada, determined Aboriginal title and allowed for self-governance of the indigenous population. [5]

rural: Outside of metropolitan urban areas. Redefined in 2003 in the United States as 75 percent of the land and 17 percent of the population. In Canada, 20 percent of the population are rural. [4]

salt dome: A vertical cylinder of salt. There are about five hundred underground salt domes in the Gulf Coast region, stretching from Mexico to the Florida panhandle. [11]

saw-grass: Tall, sharp-serrated grass found along the coastal area of eastern America. [10]

scabland: A flat region with exposed lava rock, a thin layer of soil, and sparse vegetation. Usually cut through with channels. Part of the eastern Washington landscape. [16]

seamount: An underwater mountain rising from the ocean floor and having a peaked or flat-topped summit below the surface of the sea. [20]

secondary sector: That portion of a region's economy devoted to the processing of basic materials extracted by the primary sector. [4]

Second Great Awakening: The early-nineteenth-century Christian religious revival that emphasized evangelism and lay ministers. The revival spread from the "burned-over district" of upstate New York, through the eastern half of the United States. [8]

seigneur (*Fr.*): A feudal lord who owned a large estate by grant from the king of France. Applicable in Quebec. [5]

seigneurie (*Fr.*): In the old French regime in Quebec, a tract of land granted by the Crown, usually as a reward for services rendered to the Crown or to a friend of the authorities. It was expected and usually a condition of the grant, that the seigneur would encourage settlement on the lands in his *seigneurie*. In general, the land was not sold but rather leased in perpetuity, and each settler had to pay an annual rent. When land was sold or transferred for a fee, it was the improvements on the land, the buildings, and so on that were sold, not the land itself. The feudal elements of this system quickly became irrelevant in the New World, where land was available in abundance for tenants who felt oppressed and wanted to move. The seigneurial system was abolished in Quebec in the mid-1850s, and the settlers (*habitants*) then had the opportunity to purchase the land outright. [5]

seismic line: A clearing made in dense boreal woods for geologic drilling and dynamiting. Interferes with wildlife migrations, habitat, and safety. [18]

selective cut: The practice of taking only certain trees that are deemed the most desirable for harvest, and leaving the rest. [17]

sharecropper: An agricultural tenant who pays for use of the land with a predetermined share of the crop rather than with a cash rent. [11]

shelter wood: Any regeneration cutting in a more or less regular and mature crop, designed to establish a new crop under the protection (overhead or side) of the old, or where the resultant crop will be more or less regular. [17]

shield: A broad area of very old rocks above sea level. Usually characterized by thin, poor soils and low population densities. [2]

shield cluster: Island composed of more than one shield volcano. For example, in the Hawaiian islands, Hawai`i and Maui. [20]

shield volcano: A gently sloping volcano in the shape of a flattened dome, built almost exclusively of lava flows. [20]

short sea shipping: Promoting the use of waterways to ease traffic congestion on national highways. Commercial waterborne transportation that does not transit an ocean. It is an alternative form of commercial transportation that utilizes inland and coastal waterways to move commercial freight from major domestic ports to its destination. [6]

shut-in: A river confined in a deep, narrow, water-sculpted gorge or channel. Common in the Ozarks. [12]

sinkhole (or sink): A rounded depression in the landscape, formed when an underground cavity collapses. Sinks may be a sheer vertical opening into a cave, or a shallow depression of many acres. [10]

site and situation: *Site* is the place where something is located; the internal factors in forming a city. Features of a place related to the immediate environment on which the place is located (e.g., terrain, soil, subsurface, geology, groundwater). *Situation* is the position of a place in relation to other places; external factors in forming a city. The two terms are standards in how and why cities have been located where they are. [1]

slough: A swamp or shallow lake in the northern or midwestern United States, or a slowly flowing, shallow swamp or marsh in the southeastern United States. [10]

smart growth: A set of policies governing transportation and planning of cities away from sprawl and favoring quality-of-life issues. Smart growth cities advocate compact land use, walkability, bicycle-friendliness, and mixed-used housing. [3]

smog: Mixture of particulate matter and chemical pollutants in the lower atmosphere, usually over urban areas. [19]

sod house: First houses built on the Great Plains in the nineteenth century, out of the only building material available: sod. [14]

specialty crop: Any agricultural crop except wheat, feed grains, oil seeds, cotton, rice, peanuts, and tobacco. Mostly orchard fruit and vegetable agriculture. [19]

sprawl: Unplanned and uncontrolled spreading of urban development on undeveloped land. [3]

spring: A natural discharge of water from a rock or soil to the surface. [12]

steppe: A vast semiarid, grass-covered plain, as found in southeast Europe, Siberia, and central North America. [14]

stratovolcano: A steep-sided, often symmetrical cone volcano composed of alternating layers of lava flows, ash, and pyroclastic material (from volcanic explosion or ejection), which tend to erupt explosively. Also known as a conical or composite volcano. For example, Mount St. Helens, Washington. [17]

strip cut: Logging of narrow strips of mature trees of a desirable species, leaving corridors of open spaces about 250 feet wide. These areas are used as seed sources for regrowth. Used in mixed hardwood forests. [17]

strip-mining (or **surface mining**): The type of mining in which soil and rock are stripped away by large machines to get at coal or other minerals buried just beneath the surface structures. [8]

subbituminous: Coal that is softer than bituminous and harder than lignite. Has a lower percentage of sulfur and therefore has become the favored coal since the Clean Air Act of 1970. Found predominately in the Powder River Basin. [8]

subduction: The process in which a tectonic plate collides with and dives under another tectonic plate. [2]

subregion: A portion of a larger region that shares its major characteristics but has a specific identity, which can be geographical, geological, cultural, or economic. A subregion of the Pacific Northwest is the glacially formed Puget trough, which is between the Coastal and Cascade mountains. [1]

subsidence: A sinking of Earth's crust due to underground excavations. Subsidence is prevalent along the Gulf Coast and in Florida. [11]

subsidy: Monetary assistance granted by a government to a person or group in support of an enterprise regarded as being in the public interest. The average farmer subsidy in the United States is $16,000, mainly in the form of tax reductions and low water prices. [14]

subsistence economy: A way of life prevalent in the North and in Alaska, sometimes used as synonymous with "living off the land." For Natives it is nothing less than a cultural, spiritual, and social way of life that relies on hunting, fishing, and gathering, as well as sharing of resources and dissemination of information across generational lines. Not a cash economy. [18]

suitcase farmer: A farmer who puts beef cattle to pasture for several months while pursuing leisure or other ventures, returning after several months to share in the profit. [14]

Sun Belt: The southern tier of the United States, focused on Florida, Texas, Arizona, and California, and extending as far north as Virginia. The term gained wide use in the 1970s, when the economic and political impact of the nation's overall shift in population to the South and West became conspicuous. [4]

Surface Mining Control and Reclamation Act (SMCRA) (1977): Act stating a need for balance between protection of the environment and agricultural productivity and the nation's need for coal as an essential source of energy. Provisions include the return of land to its original contour and condition; prime farmland cannot be mined unless it can be restored to an equivalent or higher level of yield. [8]

sustainability: Living on Earth while maintaining a balance of all natural ecosystems, including humans. Recognizing that resources are limited, so that they are sustained throughout time and for future generations. [1]

sustainable development: Development that meets the needs of the present without compromising the needs of future generations. [3]

sustainable geography: The study of human and physical landscapes that together create the ecological landscape, one that links the physical and human and is dynamically balanced to remain healthy and thriving over the long term. [1]

sustainable hazard mitigation: The viewing of disasters from a broad perspective and connecting the issues of disasters to other problems. The ability to tolerate and overcome damage, diminished productivity, and reduced quality of life from an extreme event without significant outside assistance. To be done sustainably, it must improve environmental quality, people's quality of life, and local resilience; it must enhance local economies and create community. [11]

sustainable yield: The amount of a naturally self-reproducing community, such as trees or fish, that can be harvested without diminishing the ability of the community to sustain itself. [11]

swamp: A wetland type, vegetated mostly by trees and shrubs; often associated with rivers, slow streams, or isolated depressions. [2]

syncretism: A form of cultural encounter in which the traditions entailed are fused into a novel emergent, whose meanings and symbolic expressions are in some respects different from either of the original singular traditions. [18]

taiga (or **boreal forest**): A moist, subarctic coniferous forest that begins where the tundra ends and is dominated by spruces and firs. [2]

tariff: A tax imposed by one country on imports from other countries. This could be to favor one's own goods. [5]

taro: A starchy tuber that was the staple plant for the native Hawaiian diet. Currently being resurrected as a crop to help improve the Hawaiian native diet. [20]

technopole: One form of enterprise zone, the mine and foundry of the informational economy. For example, Silicon Valley. [7]

Tennessee Valley Authority (TVA): A series of dams along the Tennessee River created to manage water resources in a region devastated by the Depression. Authorized in 1933, it was built to control floods, promote land conservation, and provide electrical service. [8]

territory: In Canada, an administrative division created and controlled by federal law. A territory therefore does not have the same rights and privileges as a province. [18]

tertiary sector: That portion of a region's economy devoted to service activities (e.g., transportation, retail and wholesale operations, insurance). [4]

thaw lake: A bog or marshy pond formed when permafrost melts. The ground beneath the lake remains frozen and prevents the water from draining away. [18]

thermal inversion: An inversion of the normal pattern of air being warmer near the surface of Earth. In thermal inversion, a mass of cold air is trapped below a mass of warmer air, creating the condition called smog. [19]

thermohaline circulation: Circulation in a large body of water caused by changes in water density brought about by variations in water temperature and salinity. Cold, salty water is heavier than warmer, less saline water and will sink into the deep ocean. [6]

tidal bore: A high wave (often dangerous) caused by tidal flow (as by colliding tidal currents or in a narrow estuary). Tidal bores form when an incoming tide rushes up a river, developing a steep forward slope due to resistance to the tide's advance by the river, which is flowing in the opposite direction. The river changes its direction of flow, flowing over the outgoing river water. [6]

tidewater: The area east of the fall line along the South Atlantic coast. In colonial America, the Tidewater was a region around Chesapeake Bay. [9]

tornado: A high-speed rotating column of air, usually occurring in the Great Plains or Midwest where warm and cold fronts meet. [14]

total fertility rate (TFR): The average number of children a woman will bear during her childbearing years. Developed countries have much lower TFRs than less developed countries, although TFRs are dropping in most less developed countries. [4]

township and range system: The system started by the U.S. government in the late 1780s, by which the land northwest of the Ohio River was divided into sections and offered to people who agreed to farm. [13]

trace: A path or trail made by animals and/or humans. [8]

tragedy of the commons: The exploitation of a common resource when competing parties share it, each pursuing their own interest. Term originated by Garrett Hardin, originally in relation to English common fields but now applied to many common areas, such as the ocean and fisheries. [6]

Trail of Tears: Forced march of Cherokee Nation and other tribes in the 1830s, from Georgia to Oklahoma territory. More than four thousand are estimated to have died on the march. [13]

transhumance: The seasonal movement of people and animals in search of pasture. Commonly, winters are spent in snow-free lowlands and summers in the cooler uplands. [15]

transit-oriented development (TOD): A mixed-use development designed to be easily accessed by public transportation. [3]

transmountain diversion: Moving water from an area that is not as needy to an area with high population growth that lacks sufficient water. [15]

Treaty of Guadalupe Hidalgo (1848): The treaty that ended the Mexican-American War and ceded to the United States California, Nevada, Utah, and parts of Colorado, Arizona, New Mexico, and Wyoming for $15 million. [19]

Treaty of Paris (1763): The treaty that ended the French and Indian War. England gained all French lands in North America, except two small islands off Newfoundland. Beginning of overseas British Empire. [5]

tree line: The latitude or the elevation on mountain slopes above which trees cannot grow. [15]

triangular trade: Trade between three ports, each receiving what it needs and sending what it produces in a closed loop. In the eighteenth- and nineteenth-century United States, the most famous was the shipment of tobacco and sugar to England, manufactured goods (textiles) to Africa, and slaves to America. [9]

triple bottom line: A calculation of financial, environmental, and social performance. Often referred to as "profits, planet, and people," which together form a more viable option toward sustainability goals than the conventional bottom line, which is profit alone. [3]

tundra: A treeless area between the icecap and the tree line of Arctic regions, having permanently frozen subsoil and supporting low-growing vegetation such as lichens, mosses, and stunted shrubs. [2]

unintended consequences: Outcomes that are not (or are not limited to) the results originally intended. Unintended consequences have been tied to the hubris humans have about their control of nature and its often undesirable consequences. [1]

Upper Canada: A historical region and province of British North America, roughly coextensive with southern Ontario, Canada. It was formed in 1791 and joined Lower Canada in 1841. [5]

urban: Characteristic of the city or city life. In the United States, an area is considered urban when it has more than twenty-five hundred people. In Canada, urban areas are those over one thousand people. [4]

urban village: A planning concept that features medium-density settlement, mixed uses, walkability, and a dependence on public transit. [13]

vernacular: Originally a linguistic term connoting the common speech of a people. It has been adopted by architectural historians to identify the common buildings of ordinary people that characterize a place or region. A vernacular cultural region is one recognized by the inhabitants. For example, Little Italy or a BBQ region in the South. [5]

vertical integration: The joining of companies engaged in different but related businesses. Often, a variety of businesses that create a product from raw material to final product. In the food industry, it is the control of multiple aspects of production, including animal production, processing, distribution, and marketing. In the pork industry, known as "birth to bacon." [9]

vertical zonation: Distribution of organisms, vegetation, and soils by altitude. [15]

vog: A portmanteau word of *volcanic* and *fog*. A form of volcanic smog on the big island of Hawai`i. The vog is a benefit for growing coffee on the Kona coast, but it also has respiratory health issues. [20]

volcanic mountain: Formed when molten rock, or magma deep within the Earth, erupts and piles up on the surface. Volcanic mountains are usually made of basalt and rhyolite. [2]

volcanic plug: Landforms created when lava hardens within the vent of an active volcano. Erosion may remove surrounding rock and produce distinctive landforms. For example, Devil's Tower in northwestern Wyoming. [14]

water gap: Deep valleys with water, such as rivers or streams, running through mountainous areas. The Appalachian region has many water and wind (dry) gaps. For example, Delaware Water Gap. [8]

watershed: A divide that separates neighboring drainage basins. In the United States, the term is used synonymously with drainage basin. [1]

water table: The level where ground is saturated with water. [14]

wetland: A transitional zone of waterlogged land that is usually between a dryland and water body. Wetlands include swamps, marshes, sloughs, bogs, and similar areas. They are important wildlife habitat and nurseries, as well as important filtration areas for water. [2]

White Paper on Indian Policy (1969): Canadian policy that abolished Native land claims in an attempt to assimilate Natives. [18]

Wilderness Act (1964): Act establishing the Wilderness Preservation System, in which land is to be preserved in its natural condition. The act began with 9 million acres of land in 54 different areas and grew to 95 million acres in 708 parcels by 1992. Most of the wilderness land is in the western states. Alaska has the most wilderness land: 57.6 million acres. [15]

wind gap: Notch in a mountain ridge, a dry water gap, where water once flowed. [8]

windmill: Traditionally used in dry areas of the United States to provide shallow groundwater for cattle and household use. [14]

wind turbine: Machine that converts wind energy into electricity. [3]

xerophytic: A plant adapted to living in an arid habitat; a desert plant. [2]

yeoman: Freeholder of lower status—conservative, family oriented, and holding communal values—who owned and worked his own farm. Thomas Jefferson idealized the independent yeoman farmer as the symbol of agrarian virtues for the United States. [9]

Index

Ellet, Charles, 259
El Niño, 389
embayment, 259
empty quarter, 423
energy, 50–54; economic sectors and, 55; and food production, 368; sources, 196; use of, 51
energy consumption: in Intermontane, 432; per capita, 71
energy production: in Appalachia, 183, 194–99; in California, 525–27, 531; in Canadian Corridor, 114–15; in Hawai`i, 552–53; in Intermontane, 433; in Megalopolis, 170; in Midwest, 334–35
entrepôt, 528
environmental justice, 256–57
Environmental Protection Agency, 8, 184, 195, 334
Environmental Report Card, 117
equalization payment, 114
equilibrium, 4
Ericsson, Leif, 130
Erie Canal, 294, 315, 321, 327
erosion, 20, 39, 86, 430
escarpment, 97
estuary(ies): in Florida, 238; in Gulf Coastal Plains, 257; in Megalopolis, 156
Esty, Daniel C., 153
ethanol, 52, 328, 368, 552
eutrophication, 262
Everglades, 234–38, 240–41, 244–45
Exclusive Economic Zone (EEZ), 140
Exodusters, 356–57
exotic streams, 413
external costs, 5; Aspenization and, 392–93; climate change and, 7; coal burning and, 334; dams and, 351; dredging and, 237; hog farming and, 227, 371; levees and, 313; Mississippi River control and, 262; rangelands and, 430; salmon hatcheries and, 461; San Francisco Bay and, 507; Tennessee River coal slurry spill and, 8; waste disposal and, 542

factory trawler, 139
Fairweather Range, 470
Faithfull, Emily, 382
fall foliage season, 145
fall line, 155, 206, 209
family farm, 316, 324–25, 364, 373
farms. See agriculture; rural populations
Faulkner, William, 256
fault, 28
fault-block mountains, 25
Fayetteville, Arkansas, 297
Federal Emergency Management Agency (FEMA), 212
Federal Mine Safety and Health Act, 195
feedback loop, 35–36
Fenneman, Nevin, 8–9

fens, 31
ferries, 454
Finger Lakes, 180, 194–95
fire, 42; in California, 510–11; Centralia, 191; and forests, 155, 159; sugarcane, 250
First Nations peoples, 80, 99–100, 357, 449–50
fish farm(s), 449, 462
fishing/fisheries: in Alaska and Arctic, 497–98; in California, 507–8; in Florida, 250; in Gulf Coastal Plains, 279; in Hawai`i, 551–52; in Megalopolis, 157–58, 169; in North Atlantic Provinces, 122–24, 128, 132, 139–40, 142; in Pacific Northwest, 446, 448–49, 459–62; in South Atlantic, 228
fish ladder, 460
Five Civilized Tribes, 315, 317
fjord, 32
Flagler, Henry, 241–42
flake, 139
Flanders, Robert, 293
flash flood, 413
flatwood, 257
Flemish Cap, 128
Flint, Timothy, 354
Flint Hills, 309
flooding, 197–98, 413; in Gulf Coastal Plains, 260–61, 276; in Midwest, 309, 313
Florida, 232–52; climate, 238–39; cultural perspectives, 241–43; historical geography and settlement, 241; physical geography, 234–36
Florida Bay, 238
flour mills, 325
FLQ. See Front de la Libération du Québec
fly ash, 7–8
folded mountains, 24–25
folk culture, in Appalachia, 186
Fontaine, Edward, 259
food: in Alaska and Arctic, 484; in Appalachia, 186–87; in Gulf Coastal Plains, 268; in Hawai`i, 544; meat availability, 225–26; in South Atlantic, 215–16; sustainable meat, 372
food processing, in Ozarks, 301
Ford, Henry, 321, 335
forests/forestry: boreal, 20, 38, 41–42, 468–69; ghost, 467; in Gulf Coastal Plains, 278; in Megalopolis, 155, 159; in Midwest, 332; in Pacific Northwest, 441–42, 456, 458; in Rocky Mountains, 384. See also logging
formal economy, 526–27
Fort Collins, Colorado, 398
Fort McMurray, 487, 489, 496–97
fortress living, 513–14
49th Parallel, 360
fossil fuels, 50–51

Four Corners, 420
fracking, 52, 198–99, 374–75
francophone, 78, 96, 103–4
Frank, Billy, 19
Fraser River, 445
freezer trawler, 139
Fremont, John C., 391
French and Indian Wars, 185, 241, 264, 316
French-Canadian culture, 104
freshwater, 25
Fresno, California, 521
Friedman, Thomas, 493
Frobisher, Martin, 489
Front de la Libération du Québec (FLQ), 105
Frontenac Axis, 97–98, 124
Frontier Thesis, 361
Front Range, 386–87, 394–95
frost-freeze cycles, 347
fruits, 328–30

Gadsden Purchase, 419
galena lead, 298
Galveston Bay, 259, 275
gangs, 514–15
Garlock Fault, 505
Garreau, Joel, 423, 440
gas: in Alaska and Arctic, 492; in Great Plains, 374; in Gulf Coastal Plains, 280–81; in North Atlantic Provinces, 141; in Pacific Northwest, 447; in Rocky Mountains, 401. See also natural gas
GDP (gross domestic product), 65
Geechee, 208, 214–15, 228
gender, 74
General Agreement on Tariffs and Trade (GATT), 111, 113
genetically modified organism (GMO), 324, 326, 367
geography, 3–4; Smith and, 391
geology, 20–22; landforms, 22–25
Georges Banks, 128
geothermal power, 52
geothermal spring(s), 290–91, 301
Gershwin, George, 214
GHG. See greenhouse gases
Ghost Dance, 356
ghost forest, 467
ghost town(s), 393–94, 396
ginseng, 399
glacial drift, 32
glacial erratic, 411
glaciation: eras of, 33; and Great Lakes, 311; and Great Plains, 350; maximum extent of, 34
glacier(s), 22, 29–33, 386–87, 468
Glacier Bay, 470
Glacier National Park, 383
global warming, 35
GMO. See genetically modified organism

About the Author

Chris Mayda is professor of geography and sustainability at Eastern Michigan University. She is lucky in that her passions, geography and sustainability, are what she practices in her career. Chris believes that fieldwork is an important part of research and therefore traveled to every state and province of the United States and Canada, documenting and photographing the subject matter as she wrote this book. She lives in Ypsilanti, Michigan. She can be reached at cmayda@emich.edu.